Cases and Materials on Criminal Law

'ege

Library
Tel: 208820

Cases and Materials on
Criminal Law

Fourth edition

Janet Dine

Professor of Law, University of Essex

James Gobert

Professor of Law, University of Essex

OXFORD

UNIVERSITY PRESS

Great Clarendon Street, Oxford OX2 6DP

Oxford University Press is a department of the University of Oxford.
It furthers the University's objective of excellence in research, scholarship,
and education by publishing worldwide in

Oxford New York

Auckland Bangkok Buenos Aires Cape Town Chennai
Dar es Salaam Delhi Hong Kong Istanbul Karachi Kolkata
Kuala Lumpur Madrid Melbourne Mexico City Mumbai Nairobi
São Paulo Shanghai Taipei Tokyo Toronto

Oxford is a registered trade mark of Oxford University Press
in the UK and in certain other countries

Published in the United States
by Oxford University Press Inc., New York

© J. Dine and J. Gobert, 2003

The moral rights of the authors have been asserted
Database right Oxford University Press (maker)

First edition 1993
Second edition 1998
Third edition 2000
Fourth edition 2003

British Library Cataloguing in Publication Data

Data available

Library of Congress Cataloging in Publication Data

Data available

ISBN 0–19–926070–2

7 9 10 8 6

Typeset by RefineCatch Limited, Bungay, Suffolk
Printed in Great Britain by
Ashford Colour Press Ltd,
Gosport, Hampshire.

OUTLINE CONTENTS

DETAILED CONTENTS

PREFACE

This fourth edition of *Cases and Materials on Criminal Law* is written during a period of significant political and legal change in the UK. Of the relevant changes, none is more likely to have a greater impact than the passage of the Human Rights Act 1998, which came into force on 2 October 2000. Not only does the Act open the door to procedural and substantive challenges in criminal trials, it requires English judges to analyse these challenges in light of decisions (not limited to those in which the UK was a party) of the European Court of Human Rights and with a critical scrutiny that gives far less deference to parliamentary sovereignty than was formerly the case. Close behind the European Convention on Human Rights in its impact on domestic UK law is the increasing number of decisions, treaties, directives and case law which emanate from the European Union. In addition, there is the to-be-expected new legislation from Parliament and cases of note from the judiciary. It all adds up to a period of significant ferment and transition within the UK criminal justice system.

Although the substantive materials contained in this volume have changed to reflect new and pending legislation, as well as cases decided since publication of the previous edition, our philosophical approach to the teaching of criminal law has not changed. As we explained in the preface to the first edition, our goal is both to impart substantive knowledge and to teach the skills needed to be a successful lawyer or judge.

Most of the criminal law (with a few notable exceptions) is contained in statutes. Ambiguities can arise both because of the inherent indeterminacy of language and because it is impossible for Parliament, in drafting criminal statutes, to envisage the myriad factual guises of future cases. The successful lawyer needs to be able to read a statute with a critical eye, break it into its component elements, and understand what each element requires in the way of proof.

In addition to statutory analysis skills, the successful lawyer needs to be able to identify the legal issues raised by a factual situation. This requires a careful sifting through the facts, a determination of which have legal significance, and an identification of the legal questions raised by these facts. It is only then that the legal analysis can start. For this reason we have tried to include as many of the facts of each case as possible, although space limitations have somewhat impaired our ability to do so. (Space limitations have also precluded exploration of the many fascinating questions of procedure and evidence which permeate the criminal law.)

The purpose of the Notes and Questions that are liberally sprinkled throughout the book is to raise issues and stimulate the student's thinking. Students should not accept uncritically judicial assumptions and assertions. Nor is judicial reasoning above criticism. Our aim in the Notes and Questions is to identify some of the questions that may have been inadequately answered or ignored altogether by the court in its decision. We also attempt to probe the future implications of various decisions. We do not, however, see the Notes and Questions as being exhaustive but rather designed to spur the student's own critical thinking about the case.

The book is divided into four Parts. Part I seeks to present fundamental principles of criminal liability and introduce the student to basic criminal law concepts. In Part II we move on to examine specific offences, primarily those against persons (murder, manslaughter, assault, battery, and rape) and property (theft, offences of deception, and related offences). In Part III we examine various doctrines and defences that allow defendants to escape from the net of criminal liability. A particular note should be taken of defences whose roots can be traced to the jurisprudence of the European Court of Human Rights and the European Court of Justice as these are becoming increasingly important. Lastly, in Part IV we examine how the law has been extended backwards in time to criminalise pre-crime actions and expanded outward in scope to ensnare parties to offences beyond the principal who actually commits the offence.

A word should be said about the first chapter, which might strike some as more appropriate to a course in philosophy or criminology. We believe that an appreciation of issues relating to criminalisation, human rights, grading of offences, and theories of punishment is critically important. At the heart of the criminal law are fundamental questions about the values of a society, and the balance which that society has struck between individual freedom and social control.

We wish to acknowledge, among others, the permissions received from Oxford University Press, Sweet & Maxwell, Butterworths, and the Incorporated Council for Law Reporting for England and Wales. We also wish to express our appreciation to the many readers of the previous editions who took the time to offer constructive comments. We have attempted to take account of these comments in the preparation of the present volume. We are indebted to the excellent research assistance of Annette Abanulo. We are also grateful to our colleagues, Fernne Brennan and Sabine Michalowski, for their contributions in analysing, respectively, racially aggravated crimes and necessity.

Janet Dine
James Gobert

February 2003

ACKNOWLEDGMENTS

The authors and publishers would like to thank the following for permission to reproduce copyright material:

Oxford University Press for extracts from N. Walker *Crime and Criminology* (1987); H. L. A. Hart *Law, Liberty and Morality*; and A. Ashworth *Principles of Criminal Law* (1991).

The Incorporated Council of Law Reporting for England and Wales for extracts from the following reports: King's/Queen's Bench Division, Appeal Cases and the *Weekly Law Reports*.

Extracts from *All England Law Reports* reproduced by permission of The Butterworth Division of Reed Elsevier (UK) Limited.

Kenneth Mason Publications for extracts from the *Road Traffic Reports*.

Sweet & Maxwell Ltd for extracts from the *Criminal Law Review* and *Criminal Appeal Reports*.

University of Pennsylvania Law Review for extracts from J. Andenaes 'The General Preventative Effects of Punishment' (1966).

The British Academy for extracts from the 1960 Maccabean Lecture by The Hon. Sir Patrick Devlin, 'The Enforcement of Morals', published in *Procceedings of the British Academy, Volume ILV* (1959).

TABLE OF CASES

(Bold face indicates extract material)

TABLE OF STATUTES

(Bold face indicates extract material)

TABLE OF SECONDARY LEGISLATION

(Bold face indicates extract material)

PART I

Foundational Principles

1

Crime, Punishment and Human Rights

SECTION 1: **Criminalisation**

A: The criminalisation decision

This chapter and the next are designed to introduce the student to the criminal law and what constitutes a crime. In this chapter we examine crime and punishment and the effect that human rights considerations have on the process. How does a crime come into being? Who makes the determination that conduct should be criminal, and who defines the crime? What limitations do the European Convention for the Protection of Human Rights and Fundamental Freedoms (ECHR) and the Human Rights Act 1998 portend for UK criminal law? What consequences follow from being convicted of a criminal offence?

There are three critical stages in the *criminalisation* process. In the first, a determination is made as to what should be made criminal. Criminal law constrains an individual's freedom of action; to do what is criminal invites a prosecution and, upon conviction, punishment. In the second or *grading* stage, offences are fitted within a general scheme of crimes that indicate their relative seriousness. This generally involves setting a punishment for violation of the law. The severity of the penalty that is attached to the crime indicates the seriousness that Parliament or the courts have attached to the offence. So, for example, because murder and manslaughter are deemed more serious offences than theft and criminal damage, a greater maximum sentence can be imposed for their commission. Lastly, the criminal law will be applied in individual cases, with the particular sanction in each case, should the defendant be convicted, determined by the particular facts and circumstances of the case.

In the United Kingdom, the responsibility for these decisions is shared by Parliament and the judiciary. Originally the courts were able to determine what was and was not a crime. The criminal offences established by the courts were known as common law crimes. While most of these common law crimes have since been replaced by statute, a few, most notably murder and manslaughter, retain their original common law definition. But common law decisions cannot be ignored even when the crime in question has been superseded by statute, for often the law that Parliament enacts will contain nondescript and undefined terms, such as *intent*, which draw their meaning from common law definitions. On the other hand, virtually any new criminal offence which is created today is the product of legislation. The courts retain some power to determine the parameters of that legislation because they are able to interpret its terms, and, by giving a term a broad or narrow interpretation, they in effect can give the criminal statute a broad or narrow reach.

Parliament not only establishes the offence, but gives it a ranking among existing offences by setting the maximum penalty that can be imposed for its violation. Usually a minimum sentence is not specified, although there are increasingly exceptions from this general rule (see, e.g., Crime (Sentences) Act 1997). The determination of the particular sentence in an individual case, on the other hand, is still left to the courts, the one notable exception from this practice occurring in respect to murder, where the court must impose a mandatory life sentence.

The tendency in most criminal law courses is to plunge directly into the substantive subject matter of the course, without ever examining how that behaviour which is classified as criminal came to occupy that status. And yet the most fundamental task in criminal law is to determine what conduct should be made criminal. From this decision all else flows.

Despite the critical nature of the criminalisation decision, relatively little attention has been paid to it. General criteria for determining what to criminalise are rarely set out formally. Often a criminal statute is precipitated by some widely publicised incident, and the statute is enacted with the aim of ensuring that in the future similar conduct will not escape penalty. Sometimes the criminal law is coopted to help solve social problems, such as drug addiction or prostitution. Too often, unfortunately, principle seems to play at best a secondary role. See Ashworth, 'Is the Criminal Law a Lost Cause' (2000) 116 LQR 225. Some offences – such as murder, rape and theft – all would agree are criminal (although the precise boundaries may be a matter of dispute), but what to add to this foundation is often controversial. What actually happens is that Parliament tends to add layer upon layer of crimes to the core. The reverse process of decriminalisation (the removal of existing offences from the rolls of the criminal law) is far more rare. The result may be, in the words of one commentator, a 'crisis of overcriminalisation.' See Kadish, 'The Crisis of Overcriminalization' (1958) 374 Annals 157.

NOTES AND QUESTIONS
1. Crime is often said to be on the increase, but what does this mean? To some extent an increase in crime merely reflects an increase in the number of criminal laws. In theory we could 'solve' the 'crime problem' by doing away with all criminal laws. But this is not suggested seriously (although Marxist philosophy did envisage an ultimate utopia in which criminal law would be unnecessary). Why not?
2. Is it better to err on the side of over- or under-inclusiveness when it comes to criminalisation? If too broad a spectrum of human behaviour is made illegal, will not the inevitable result be that many citizens will find themselves ensnared in the net of the criminal law, with the concomitant stigma of a criminal conviction? Is this desirable? Should there

be a general principle that criminal law should be a last rather than a first resort, to be employed only when all other means of addressing the social problem at issue have been exhausted?

3. Is there a practical solution to over-criminalisation, which is to have a large number of criminal offences on the books but to enforce relatively few of them? The statutory law would serve as a statement of the principles and values for which the society stands, and as a safety net to allow prosecutions in egregious cases. The decision not to prosecute would protect citizens who commit technical offences but who are not morally blameworthy. The prosecutor could be given discretion to proceed with formal charges only in those cases where the defendant's blameworthiness was manifest. What are the merits and demerits of such an approach?

If the criminalisation process is to become more rational and less haphazard, the challenge facing the law-maker is to develop general criteria and principles which can be employed in determining whether or not to make conduct criminal. Legislators are not averse to a principled approach. In response to a question from Lord Dholakia, Lord Williams of Mostyn, the then Minister of State at the Home Office, indicated that it was the Labour Government's policy that offences 'should be created only when absolutely necessary', and that:

In considering whether new offences should be created, factors taken into account include whether:

— the behaviour in question is sufficiently serious to warrant intervention by the criminal law;
— the mischief could be dealt with under existing legislation or by using other remedies;
— the proposed offence is enforceable in practice; – the proposed offence is tightly drawn and legally sound; and – the proposed penalty is commensurate with the seriousness of the offence.

The Government also takes into account the need to ensure, as far as practicable, that there is consistency across the sentencing framework.

(HL Deb, vol. 602, WA 57 (18 June, 1999) quoted in Ashworth, op. cit. at p. 229, who questions whether these criteria are followed in practice.)

Arguably, what is needed are general principles of inclusion and exclusion, i.e., principles which would advise the law-maker as to what should be made criminal (e.g., actions which cause or threaten physical harm to others should be made criminal) and principles that counsel against criminalisation (e.g. it is inadvisable to criminalise conduct which is approved of and engaged in by the vast majority of the citizenry). The following is an attempt by one noted criminologist to identify such principles:

N. Walker, *Crime and Criminology*
(1987)

i. *Objectives of the criminal law*
Is it possible to discuss the proper content of the criminal law in general terms? If the contents of criminal codes are examined with a sociological eye, no fewer than fourteen different objectives can be discerned:

(a) the protection of human persons (and to some extent animals also) against intentional violence, cruelty, or unwelcome sexual approaches;

(b) the protection of people against some forms of unintended harm (for example from traffic, poisons, infections, radiation);

(c) the protection of easily persuadable classes of people (that is, the young or the weak-minded) against the abuse of their persons or property (for example by sexual intercourse or hire-purchase);

(d) the prevention of acts which, even if the participants are adult and willing, are regarded as 'unnatural' (for example incest, sodomy, bestiality, drug 'trips');

(e) the prevention of acts which, though not included under any of the previous headings, are performed so publicly as to shock other people (for example public nakedness, obscene language, or heterosexual copulation between consenting adults);

(f) the discouragement of behaviour which might provoke disorder (such as insulting words at a public meeting);

(g) the protection of property against theft, fraud, or damage;

(h) the prevention of inconvenience (for example the obstruction of roads by vehicles);

(i) the collection of revenue (for example keeping a motor car or television set without a licence);

(j) the defence of the State (for example espionage or – in some countries – political criticism);

(k) the enforcement of compulsory benevolence (for example the offence of failing to send one's children to school);

(l) the protection of social institutions, such as marriage or religious worship (for example by prohibiting bigamy or blasphemy);

(m) the prevention of unreasonable discrimination (for example against ethnic groups, religions, the female sex);

(n) the enforcement of the processes regarded as essential to these other purposes (for example offences connected with arrest, assisting offenders to escape conviction, and testimony at trials).

ii. *Moral limits*

Now and again there have been attempts to formulate what might be called 'limiting principles', which declare that the criminal law should *not* be used for certain purposes, or in certain circumstances.

The oldest seems to be

(A) Prohibitions should not be included in the criminal law for the sole purpose of ensuring that breaches of them are visited with retributive punishment.

Some years later, Bentham's *An Introduction to the Principles of Morals and Legislation* (1789) stated three more limiting principles. The first was

(B) The criminal law should not be used to penalise behaviour which does no harm.

In his phraseology, punishment was groundless when, on the whole, there was no evil in the act. It is a principle to which everyone would give general assent, and would agree that it was the reason why we do not use the law to discourage bad manners or bad art. Nevertheless there would be many disagreements over other sorts of conduct. The idea of prohibiting bad art by law sounds ridiculous, but one of the things which town and country planning legislation tries to control is bad architecture, and anyone who flouts it can suffer heavy penalties.

Another of Bentham's principles was

(C) The criminal law should not be used to achieve a purpose which can be achieved as effectively at less cost in suffering.

. . . A better formulation of the principle would be

(CC) The criminal law should not be used where measures involving less suffering are as effective or almost as effective in reducing the frequency of the conduct in question.

Bentham's third principle was

(D) The criminal law should not be used if the harm done by the penalty is greater than the harm done by the offence.

For in such cases punishment would be 'unprofitable' when the felicific balance sheet was added up. The difficulty about this principle is that it requires us to weigh, let us say, the unhappiness caused by bad architecture against the unhappiness caused by a large fine. Since the two sorts of unhappiness are inflicted on different people we cannot simply leave it to individual choice, as we do when we ask someone whether he would rather be fined or pull his new house down. The difficulty of choosing between incommensurables is one of the weaknesses of Benthamism which have been exploited by its opponents.

(E) The criminal law should not be used for the purpose of compelling people to act in their own best interests.

Mill himself recognised that there should be exceptions to this rule. 'Despotism', he thought, 'is a legitimate mode of government in dealing with barbarians provided that the end be their improvement'; and he took much the same view of the upbringing of children. So far as children were concerned, therefore, he would not have said that his principle ruled out compulsory benevolence such as enforced attendance at school.

iii. *Pragmatic limits*

The principles which Beccaria, Bentham, and Mill formulated were moral prescriptions, which said that the penal system *ought* not to attempt this or that task. Other writers, however, were pursuing a more pragmatic line of thought and asking what the law could reasonably be expected to achieve. This is how Montesquieu approached the subject in *The Spirit of the Laws*. He recognised that prohibition by law can be carried further in some societies than in others, but thought that in any kind of society there were areas of conduct (which he called 'les moeurs et les manières') in which it was most unwise to use the law in the hope of effecting changes.

[T]his principle might read

(F) The criminal law should not include prohibitions which do not have strong public support.

The principle has its own weaknesses – such as the difficulty of measuring public opinion in a morally pluralistic society. . . . its justification is not self-evident, and it raises the question 'Why not?' . . .

iv. *A positive justification?*

The thoroughgoing pragmatist, however, is one who abandons the defensive approach. Instead of merely setting up warning notices in the form of limiting principles which try – not very practically – to indicate to legislators where they should stop, he asks why the onus of proof should not lie on those who want to extend the scope of the criminal law. They should, on this view, be required to show why it is desirable. Shifting the burden of proof in this way has obvious difficulties. The very diversity of functions to which I have already drawn attention makes any attempt to approach the problem in this way sound naïve. Nevertheless, if an institution is as costly – whether in terms of economic resources or of human happiness – as the penal system undoubtedly is, it seems more realistic to ask for positive justifications whenever it is to be used against a given sort of conduct. . . .

Something like a non-moralistic justification was offered by Sir Patrick (now Lord) Devlin, in his well-known lecture on *The Enforcement of Morals*, where he said

> The State must justify in some other way [than by reference to the moral law] the punish-
> ment which it imposes on wrongdoers and a function for the criminal law independent of
> morals must be found. This is not difficult to do. The smooth functioning of society and the
> preservation of order require that a number of activities should be regulated.

[T]he need to ensure 'the smooth functioning of society' must, after all, be the main justification for
the parts of the criminal code which are concerned with the protection of health, the collection of
revenue, and the defence of the realm – objectives (b), (i), and (j) in my list. Most, though probably
not all, of the other prohibitions can be regarded as necessary for 'the preservation of order', to the
extent at least that if they were not enforced on some occasions there would be disorder. Not all
thefts or damage would provoke public disturbances; some victims, for example, would be afraid to
retaliate. But some would not, and their methods of protecting themselves or avenging their losses
would lead to breaches of the peace. The same is true of intentional violence against the person or
unwelcome sexual advances. The prohibition of these can be justified because they are classes of
actions of which by no means all, but a substantial number, would provoke disorder.

Nevertheless, there are some prohibitions which it is not very plausible to justify in this way. The
obvious examples are in my group (d), which consists largely of sexual behaviour that has come to
be regarded as 'unnatural', and is prohibited by many criminal codes even if it takes place in private,
and between participants who are adult, sane, and under no coercion or inducement other than
their own desires. . . .

v. *Pragmatism versus morality*

One interesting feature distinguishes the pragmatist's approach which I have just been discussing
from the moralist's approach. Suppose that both are agreed in disapproving very strongly of some
type of conduct. For the pragmatist the question is simply whether on balance anything useful would
be achieved by invoking the criminal law against it. The moralist, however, seems to agonise in a
special way over this step. He may be willing to see all sorts of other steps taken to reduce the
frequency of the conduct – education, propaganda, restriction of opportunities – and yet may
consider it morally wrong to use the criminal law in the campaign.

It is hard to see, however, what it is that in the moralist's eyes distinguishes the criminal law. It may
of course be simply that he regards its penalties as excessively severe; but that is not an essential
feature of the criminal law. Would he still object if a fine were the maximum penalty for whatever
conduct is in question? He might still object that the criminal law seeks to *compel* whereas other
techniques of social control work by persuasion or indoctrination. This seems an undeniable distinction, which appeals to one's instinctive dislike of being ordered to do something, even if it is in one's
interests.

It raises two questions, however. Are all other techniques of social control less objectionable
morally than the compulsion of the criminal law? Is one-sided indoctrination – for example against
birth control or abortion – any better? The second question is whether a strong and sincere belief
in the harmfulness – or sinfulness – of the conduct does or does not create a duty to do what one
can to prevent it, short of doing even greater harm. Whether or not one takes sides on this issue,
it is clear that the moralist has a choice between three positions, two simple and one complex:

(a) he may hold sincere and well-defined views about the wrongness of conduct and yet think it
wrong to try to influence the behaviour of others by *any* means (a very rare position);

(b) he may on the other hand think it justifiable, even obligatory, to seek to influence the behaviour
of others by *any* means (a fairly rare position);

(c) he may take position (b) but with a difference, regarding *some* means as unacceptable (the
commonest position of the moralist).

Note that (c) involves ruling out certain *means*, not certain types of conduct. The difficulties for the
moralist of drawing distinctions between types of conduct which he may or must seek to eliminate

and those which he should not have already been shown to be insuperable, if not in theory, at least in practice. It is the techniques about which he has to worry. So far as the use of the criminal law is concerned, he has to decide whether, with all its crudities and undesirable side-effects, it is less acceptable than say, one-sided moral indoctrination.

NOTES AND QUESTIONS

1. Are there other objectives which might be added to Walker's list? Some that might be deleted? Other 'principles' which should bear on the decision to criminalise or decriminalise?

2. Having examined general criminalisation principles and criteria, it is valuable to attempt to apply these to specific examples. Examples often reveal weak spots in the principles and criteria, and contribute to the task of fine tuning. By going back and forth between specific examples and generalised criteria, one eventually will reach a state of 'reflective equilibrium', whereby both should be in balance, the criteria and principles yielding what seems to be the 'right' result in respect to the examples.

   Should the following conduct be made criminal?

   (a) failure to wear a seat belt while driving an automobile;
   (b) corporal punishment of children;
   (c) cruelty to animals;
   (d) industrial pollution;
   (e) abortion;
   (f) misleading advertising;
   (g) ticket touting (offering to sell a ticket to a theatrical or sporting event at a price above the face value of the ticket);
   (h) public drunkenness;
   (i) racially offensive speech.

B: The relationship between morality and the criminal law

Not all criminal offences involve immoral conduct (e.g., illegal parking), and not all immoral conduct is criminal (e.g., lying), but often the two overlap. One of the most controversial of criminalisation issues is whether Parliament may (should?) make illegal conduct which is immoral but not directly harmful to the participants or third parties. The topic gave rise to a famous debate between Lord Devlin, one of the most prominent and well-respected judges of his time, and Professor H.L.A. Hart, whom many would regard as the foremost British legal philosopher of the twentieth century. Consider their respective positions:

P. Devlin, *The Enforcement of Morals*
(1965)

. . . I have framed three interrogatories addressed to myself to answer:

1. Has society the right to pass judgement at all on matters of morals? Ought there, in other words, to be a public morality, or are morals always a matter for private judgement?

2. If society has the right to pass judgement, has it also the right to use the weapon of the law to enforce it?

3. If so, ought it to use that weapon in all cases or only in some; and if only in some, on what principles should it distinguish?

I shall begin with the first interrogatory and consider what is meant by the right of society to pass a moral judgement, that is, a judgement about what is good and what is evil. The fact that a majority of people may disapprove of a practice does not of itself make it a matter for society as a whole. Nine men out of ten may disapprove of what the tenth man is doing and still say that it is not their business. There is a case for a collective judgement (as distinct from a large number of individual opinions which sensible people may even refrain from pronouncing at all if it is upon somebody else's private affairs) only if society is affected. Without a collective judgement there can be no case at all for intervention. . . .

This view – that there is such a thing as public morality – can . . . be justified by *a priori* argument. What makes a society of any sort is a community of ideas, not only political ideas but also ideas about the way its members should behave and govern their lives; these latter ideas are its morals. Every society has a moral structure as well as a political one: or rather, since that might suggest two independent systems, I should say that the structure of every society is made up both of politics and morals. . . .

The institution of marriage is a good example for my purpose because it bridges the division, if there is one, between politics and morals. Marriage is part of the structure of our society and it is also the basis of a moral code which condemns fornication and adultery. The institution of marriage would be gravely threatened if individual judgements were permitted about the morality of adultery; on these points there must be a public morality. But public morality is not to be confined to those moral principles which support institutions such as marriage. People do not think of monogamy as something which has to be supported because our society has chosen to organise itself upon it; they think of it as something that is good in itself and offering a good way of life and that it is for that reason that our society has adopted it. I return to the statement that I have already made, that society means a community of ideas; without shared ideas on politics, morals, and ethics no society can exist. Each one of us has ideas about what is good and what is evil; they cannot be kept private from the society in which we live. If men and women try to create a society in which there is no fundamental agreement about good and evil they will fail; if, having based it on common agreement, the agreement goes, the society will disintegrate. For society is not something that is kept together physically; it is held by the invisible bonds of common thought. If the bonds were too far relaxed the members would drift apart. A common morality is part of the bondage. The bondage is part of the price of society; and mankind, which needs society, must pay its price.

. . . I believe that the answer to the first question determines the way in which the second should be approached and may indeed very nearly dictate the answer to the second question. If society has no right to make judgements on morals, the law must find some special justification for entering the field of morality: if homosexuality and prostitution are not in themselves wrong, then the onus is very clearly on the lawgiver who wants to frame a law against certain aspects of them to justify the exceptional treatment. But if society has the right to make a judgement and has it on the basis that a recognised morality is as necessary to society as, say, a recognised government, then society may use the law to preserve morality in the same way as it uses it to safeguard anything else that is essential to its existence. If therefore the first proposition is securely established with all its implications, society has a prima facie right to legislate against immorality as such.

. . . Society is entitled by means of its laws to protect itself from dangers, whether from within or without. Here again I think that the political parallel is legitimate. The law of treason is directed against aiding the king's enemies and against sedition from within. The justification for this is that established government is necessary for the existence of society and therefore its safety against violent overthrow must be secured. But an established morality is as necessary as good government to the welfare of society. Societies disintegrate from within more frequently than they are broken up by external pressures. There is disintegration when no common morality is observed and history shows that the loosening of moral bonds is often the first stage of disintegration, so that society is justified in taking the same steps to preserve its moral code as it does to preserve its government and other essential institutions. . . . There are no theoretical limits to the power of the State to legislate against treason and sedition, and likewise I think there can be no theoretical limits to legislation against immorality. . . .

. . . [T]his brings me to the third question – the individual has a *locus standi* too; he cannot be expected to surrender to the judgement of society the whole conduct of his life. It is the old and familiar question of striking a balance between the rights and interests of society and those of the individual. . . . While every decision which a court of law makes when it balances the public against the private interest is an *ad hoc* decision, the cases contain statements of principle to which the court should have regard when it reaches its decision. In the same way it is possible to make general statements of principle which it may be thought the legislature should bear in mind when it is considering the enactment of laws enforcing morals.

I believe that most people would agree upon the chief of these elastic principles. There must be toleration of the maximum individual freedom that is consistent with the integrity of society. . . . The principle appears to me to be peculiarly appropriate to all questions of morals. Nothing should be punished by the law that does not lie beyond the limits of tolerance. It is not nearly enough to say that a majority dislike a practice; there must be a real feeling of reprobation. Those who are dissatisfied with the present law on homosexuality often say that the opponents of reform are swayed simply by disgust. If that were so it would be wrong, but I do not think one can ignore disgust if it is deeply felt and not manufactured. Its presence is a good indication that the bounds of toleration are being reached. Not everything is to be tolerated. No society can do without intolerance, indignation, and disgust; they are the forces behind the moral law, and indeed it can be argued that if they or something like them are not present, the feelings of society cannot be weighty enough to deprive the individual of freedom of choice. . . .

. . . [M]atters of this sort are not determined by rational argument. Every moral judgement, unless it claims a divine source, is simply a feeling that no right-minded man could behave in any other way without admitting that he was doing wrong. It is the power of a common sense and not the power of reason that is behind the judgements of society. . . .

The limits of tolerance shift. This is supplementary to what I have been saying but of sufficient importance in itself to deserve statement as a separate principle which law-makers have to bear in mind. . . .

The last and the biggest thing to be remembered is that the law is concerned with the minimum and not with the maximum; there is much in the Sermon on the Mount that would be out of place in the Ten Commandments. We all recognise the gap between the moral law and the law of the land. No man is worth much who regulates his conduct with the sole object of escaping punishment, and every worthy society sets for its members standards which are above those of the law. We recognise the existence of such higher standards when we use expressions such as 'moral obligation' and 'morally bound'. The distinction was well put in the judgement of African elders in a family dispute: 'We have power to make you divide the crops, for this is our law, and we will see this is done. But we have not power to make you behave like an upright man.'

. . . The criminal law is not a statement of how people ought to behave; it is a statement of what will happen to them if they do not behave; good citizens are not expected to come within reach of it or to set their sights by it, and every enactment should be framed accordingly.

The arm of the law is an instrument to be used by society, and the decision about what particular cases it should be used in is essentially a practical one. . . .

The part that the jury plays in the enforcement of the criminal law, the fact that no grave offence against morals is punishable without their verdict, these are of great importance in relation to the statements of principle that I have been making. They turn what might otherwise be pure exhortation to the legislature into something like rules that the law-makers cannot safely ignore. The man in the jury box is not just an expression; he is an active reality. It will not in the long run work to make laws about morality that are not acceptable to him.

This then is how I believe my third interrogatory should be answered – not by the formulation of hard and fast rules, but by a judgement in each case taking into account the sort of factors I have been mentioning. The line that divides the criminal law from the moral is not determinable by the application of any clear-cut principle. It is like a line that divides land and sea, a coastline of irregularities and indentations. There are gaps and promontories, such as adultery and fornication, which the law has for centuries left substantially untouched. Adultery of the sort that breaks up marriage seems to me to be just as harmful to the social fabric as homosexuality or bigamy. The only ground for putting it outside the criminal law is that a law which made it a crime would be too difficult to enforce; it is too generally regarded as a human weakness not suitably punished by imprisonment. All that the law can do with fornication is to act against its worst manifestations; there is a general abhorrence of the commercialisation of vice, and that sentiment gives strength to the law against brothels and immoral earnings. There is no logic to be found in this. The boundary between the criminal law and the moral law is fixed by balancing in the case of each particular crime the pros and cons of legal enforcement in accordance with the sort of considerations I have been outlining. The fact that adultery, fornication, and lesbianism are untouched by the criminal law does not prove that homosexuality ought not to be touched. The error of jurisprudence in the Wolfenden Report is caused by the search for some single principle to explain the division between crime and sin. The Report finds it in the principle that the criminal law exists for the protection of individuals; on this principle fornication in private between consenting adults is outside the law and thus it becomes logically indefensible to bring homosexuality between consenting adults in private within it. But the true principle is that the law exists for the protection of society. It does not discharge its function by protecting the individual from injury, annoyance, corruption, and exploitation; the law must protect also the institutions and the community of ideas, political and moral, without which people cannot live together. Society cannot ignore the morality of the individual any more than it can his loyalty; it flourishes on both and without either it dies. . . .

I return now to the main thread of my argument and summarise it. Society cannot live without morals. Its morals are those standards of conduct which the reasonable man approves. A rational man, who is also a good man, may have other standards. If he has no standards at all he is not a good man and need not be further considered. If he has standards, they may be very different; he may, for example, not disapprove of homosexuality or abortion. In that case he will not share in the common morality; but that should not make him deny that it is a social necessity. A rebel may be rational in thinking that he is right but he is irrational if he thinks that society can leave him free to rebel.

A man who concedes that morality is necessary to society must support the use of those instruments without which morality cannot be maintained. The two instruments are those of teaching, which is doctrine, and of enforcement, which is the law. If morals could be taught simply on the basis that they are necessary to society, there would be no social need for religion; it could be left as a purely personal affair. But morality cannot be taught in that way. Loyalty is not taught in that way either. No society has yet solved the problem of how to teach morality without religion. So the law must base itself on Christian morals and to the limit of its ability enforce them, not simply because they are the morals of most of us, nor simply because they are the morals which are taught by the established Church – on these points the law recognises the right to dissent – but for the compelling reason that without the help of Christian teaching the law will fail.

H. L. A. Hart, *Law, Liberty, and Morality*
(1963)

Both in England and in America the criminal law still contains rules which can only be explained as attempts to enforce morality as such: to suppress practices condemned as immoral by positive morality though they involve nothing that would ordinarily be thought of as harm to other persons. . . .

I shall start with an example stressed by Lord Devlin. He points out that, subject to certain exceptions such as rape, the criminal law has never admitted the consent of the victim as a defence. It is not a defence to a charge of murder or a deliberate assault, and this is why euthanasia or mercy killing terminating a man's life at his own request is still murder. This is a rule of criminal law which many now would wish to retain, though they would also wish to object to the legal punishment of offences against positive morality which harm no one. Lord Devlin thinks that these attitudes are inconsistent, for he asserts of the rule under discussion, 'There is only one explanation,' and this is that 'there are certain standards of behaviour or moral principles which society requires to be observed'. . . .

But this argument is not really cogent, for Lord Devlin's statement that 'there is only one explanation' is simply not true. The rules excluding the victim's consent as a defence to charges of murder or assault may perfectly well be explained as a piece of paternalism, designed to protect individuals against themselves. . . . [P]aternalism – the protection of people against themselves – is a perfectly coherent policy. Indeed, it seems very strange in mid-twentieth century to insist upon this, for the wane of laissez faire since Mill's day is one of the commonplaces of social history, and instances of paternalism now abound in our law, criminal and civil. The supply of drugs or narcotics, even to adults, except under medical prescription is punishable by the criminal law, and it would seem very dogmatic to say of the law creating this offence that 'there is only one explanation,' namely, that the law was concerned not with the protection of the would-be purchasers against themselves, but only with the punishment of the seller for his immorality. If, as seems obvious, paternalism is a possible explanation of such laws, it is also possible in the case of the rule excluding the consent of the victim as a defence to a charge of assault. In neither case are we forced to conclude with Lord Devlin that the law's 'function' is 'to enforce a moral principle and nothing else'. . . .

According to the moderate thesis, a shared morality is the cement of society; without it there would be aggregates of individuals but no society. 'A recognised morality' is, in Lord Devlin's words, 'as necessary to society's existence as a recognised government,' and though a particular act of immorality may not harm or endanger or corrupt others nor, when done in private, either shock or give offence to others, this does not conclude the matter. For we must not view conduct in isolation from its effect on the moral code: if we remember this, we can see that one who is 'no menace to others' nonetheless may by his immoral conduct 'threaten one of the great moral principles on which society is based.' In this sense the breach of moral principle is an offence 'against society as a whole,' and society may use the law to preserve its morality as it uses it to safeguard anything else essential to its existence. This is why 'the suppression of vice is as much the law's business as the suppression of subversive activities'. . . .

Lord Devlin appears to defend the moderate thesis. I say 'appears' because, though he says that society has the right to enforce a morality as such on the ground that a shared morality is essential to society's existence, it is not at all clear that for him the statement that immorality jeopardises or weakens society is a statement of empirical fact. It seems sometimes to be an *a priori* assumption, and sometimes a necessary truth and a very odd one. The most important indication that this is so is that, apart from one vague reference to 'history' showing that 'the loosening of moral bonds is often the first stage of disintegration,' no evidence is produced to show that deviation from accepted sexual morality, even by adults in private, is something which, like treason, threatens the existence of society. No reputable historian has maintained this thesis, and there is indeed much evidence against it. As a proposition of fact it is entitled to no more respect than the Emperor Justinian's statement that homosexuality was the cause of earthquakes. Lord Devlin's belief in it, and his apparent indifference to the question of evidence, are at points traceable to an undiscussed assumption. This is that all morality – sexual morality together with the morality that forbids acts injurious to others such as killing, stealing, and dishonesty – forms a single seamless web, so that those who deviate from any part are likely or perhaps bound to deviate from the whole. It is of course clear (and one of the oldest insights of political theory) that society could not exist without a morality which mirrored and supplemented the law's proscription of conduct injurious to others. But there is again no evidence to support, and much to refute, the theory that those who deviate from conventional sexual morality are in other ways hostile to society.

There seems, however, to be central to Lord Devlin's thought something more interesting, though no more convincing, than the conception of social morality as a seamless web. For he appears to move from the acceptable proposition that *some* shared morality is essential to the existence of any society to the unacceptable proposition that a society is identical with its morality as that is at any given moment of its history, so that a change in its morality is tantamount to the destruction of a society. The former proposition might be even accepted as a necessary rather than an empirical truth depending on a quite plausible definition of society as a body of men who hold certain moral views in common. But the latter proposition is absurd. Taken strictly, it would prevent us saying that the morality of a given society had changed, and would compel us instead to say that one society had disappeared and another one taken its place. But it is only on this absurd criterion of what it is for the same society to continue to exist that it could be asserted without evidence that any deviation from a society's shared morality threatens its existence.

It is clear that only this tacit identification of a society with its shared morality supports Lord Devlin's denial that there could be such a thing as private immorality and his comparison of sexual immorality, even when it takes place 'in private,' with treason. No doubt it is true that if deviations from conventional sexual morality are tolerated by the law and come to be known, the conventional morality might change in a permissive direction, though this does not seem to be the case with homosexuality in those European countries where it is not punishable by law. But even if the conventional morality did so change, the society in question would not have been destroyed or 'subverted'. We should compare such a development not to the violent overthrow of government but to a peaceful constitutional change in its form, consistent not only with the preservation of a society but with its advance.

. . . A very great difference is apparent between inducing persons through fear of punishment to abstain from actions which are harmful to others, and inducing them to abstain from actions which deviate from accepted morality but harm no one. The value attached to the first is easy to understand; for the protection of human beings from murder or violence or others forms of injury remains a good whatever the motives are by which others are induced to abstain from these crimes. But where there is no harm to be prevented and no potential victim to be protected, as is often the case where conventional sexual morality is disregarded, it is difficult to understand the assertion that conformity, even if motivated merely by fear of the law's punishment, is a value worth pursuing, notwithstanding the misery and sacrifice of freedom which it involves . . . Lord Devlin assumes that the society to which his doctrine is to apply is marked by a considerable degree of moral solidarity, and is deeply disturbed by infringements of its moral code. Just as for Lord Devlin the morality to be enforced by law must be 'public', in the sense that it is generally shared and identifiable by the triple marks of 'intolerance, indignation, and disgust,' so for Stephen 'you cannot punish anything which public opinion as expressed in the common practice of society does not strenuously and unequivocally condemn . . . To be able to punish a moral majority must be overwhelming'.

It is possible that in mid-Victorian England these conditions were satisfied in relation to 'that considerable number of acts' which according to Stephen were treated as crimes merely because they were regarded as grossly immoral. Perhaps an 'overwhelming moral majority' then actually did harbour the healthy desire for revenge of which he speaks and which is to be gratified by the punishment of the guilty. But it would be sociologically naïve to assume that these conditions obtain in contemporary England at least as far as sexual morality is concerned. The fact that there is lip service to an official sexual morality should not lead us to neglect the possibility that in sexual, as in other matters, there may be a number of mutually tolerant moralities, and that even where there is some homogeneity of practice and belief, offenders may be viewed not with hatred or resentment but with amused contempt or pity.

In a sense, therefore, Stephen's doctrine, and much of Lord Devlin's, may seem to hover in the air above the *terra firma* of contemporary social reality; it may be a well-articulated construction, interesting because it reveals the outlook characteristic of the English judiciary but lacking application to contemporary society. . . .

NOTES AND QUESTIONS

1. The specific issue which triggered the Hart/Devlin debate was whether to decriminalise homosexual conduct between consenting adults, as was recommended in 1957 by the Wolfenden Committee Report on Homosexual Offences and Prostitution (Cmnd. 247) and implemented in the Sexual Offences Act 1967. The oft-quoted view of the Committee was that the function of the criminal law is to

   preserve public order and decency, . . . protect the citizen from what is offensive and injurious and . . . provide sufficient safeguards against exploitation or corruption of others, particularly those who are specially vulnerable because they are young, weak in body or inexperienced or in a state of special physical, official or economic dependence.

2. Is Hart correct when he asserts that there is no such thing as a moral consensus? Are moral judgments like tastes in food, there being no right or wrong but only personal preferences? If there is a popular morality, how can it be ascertained?

3. Should popular morality be enforced if it is based on stereotypes? Can (should?) the law distinguish between morality based on prejudice and morality based on virtue?

4. As a practical matter, is not the law powerless to enforce a prohibition against homosexual conduct? The crime typically occurs in private, the participants are unlikely to report their own criminal activity, and both police and prosecutors have more pressing business on their plate than to pursue homosexuals. Should these facts be relevant to the criminalisation decision? If the Government decides to prohibit an activity, does it thereby commit itself to those resources necessary to enforce that prohibition?

C: Human rights and the criminal law

States strive to strike a balance between the rights of the individual and society's interests in being protected from harmful and offensive behaviour. Following World War II, the Council of Europe promulgated the European Convention for the Protection of Human Rights and Fundamental Freedoms (often referred to as the Convention on Human Rights or, more simply, the ECHR). The UK played a key role in the drafting of the Convention and was the first country to ratify it (March 1951). The Convention sets out the basic rights to which all persons are entitled. It also created a European Commission (since abolished) and a European Court of Human Rights to enforce these rights.

While the UK ratified the European Convention early, it did not incorporate it into its domestic law, as did most other European States. The most significant ramification of the UK approach was that the rights set out in the Convention could not be enforced in a British court. A citizen was permitted to bring a case against the UK Government in Strasbourg (the home of the Commission and Court), but this was often an expensive and time-consuming process.

In 1997, the newly elected Labour government, fulfilling an election manifesto pledge, introduced a Human Rights Bill, the object of which was to incorporate the Convention into UK law. The Bill received strong support and was enacted as the Human Rights Act 1998. It came into force on 2 October 2000. The Act has the potential to have far-reaching effects on the scope of Parliament's authority to create crimes, as well as possibly altering the historic balance between the courts and Parliament. Although incorporation of the Convention into domestic law will affect all areas of the law, it is likely to have its greatest impact in the criminal arena.

Section 1 of the Act specifies the Articles and Protocols of the Convention which are to be incorporated into domestic law (see below for the specific provisions). Section 2 instructs courts and tribunals that they *must*, in determining issues which raise questions of rights under the Convention, take into account the relevant judgments, decisions, declarations and advisory opinions of the European Commission, the European Court of Human Rights and the Committee of Ministers of the Council of Europe. It should be noted that the UK need not have been a party to the relevant decision for its courts to have to take account of it. Section 3 provides that all primary and subordinate legislation must, as far as possible, be interpreted in a way that is compatible with the Convention, and s. 4 permits the courts to make a 'declaration of incompatibility' when the law in question fails to comply with the requirements of the Convention. The effect of a 'declaration of incompatibility' is not to invalidate primary legislation (the courts will, however, be able to strike down secondary legislation) but to alert Parliament of the need to amend the law so that it will be compatible. The White Paper accompanying the Bill confidently predicted that prompt Parliamentary action to redress any incompatibility would be forthcoming but to heighten the likelihood of this prediction coming true, the Act provides for a 'fast-track' procedure which allows a government Minister to take immediate steps to change the law with prompt subsequent submission of the Minister's order to Parliament for approval (s. 10). Judicial proceedings to enforce the Convention may be brought by any individual whose rights under the Convention have been or threaten to be violated by a public authority (s. 7) and reliance on Convention rights may be had in any legal proceeding.

Among the more important, from a criminal law perspective, of the Articles of the European Convention which have been incorporated into the Human Rights Act 1998 are the following:

Convention for the Protection of Human Rights and Fundamental Freedoms

Article 2

1. Everyone's right to life shall be protected by law. No one shall be deprived of his life intentionally save in the execution of a sentence of a court following his conviction of a crime for which this penalty is provided by law.

2. Deprivation of life shall not be regarded as inflicted in contravention of this Article when it results from the use of force which is no more than absolutely necessary:

(a) in defence of any person from unlawful violence;
(b) in order to effect a lawful arrest or to prevent the escape of a person lawfully detained;
(c) in action lawfully taken for the purpose of quelling a riot or insurrection.

Article 3

No one shall be subjected to torture or to inhuman or degrading treatment or punishment.

Article 4

. . .

Article 5

1. Everyone has the right to liberty and security of person. No one shall be deprived of his liberty save in the following cases and in accordance with a procedure prescribed by law:

(a) the lawful detention of a person after conviction by a competent court;
(b) the lawful arrest or detention of a person for non-compliance with the lawful order of a court or in order to secure the fulfilment of any obligation prescribed by law;
(c) the lawful arrest or detention of a person effected for the purpose of bringing him before the competent legal authority on reasonable suspicion of having committed an offence or when it is reasonably considered necessary to prevent his committing an offence or fleeing after having done so;
(d) the detention of a minor by lawful order for the purpose of educational supervision or his lawful detention for the purpose of bringing him before the competent legal authority;
(e) the lawful detention of persons for the prevention of the spreading of infectious diseases, of persons of unsound mind, alcoholics or drug addicts or vagrants;
(f) the lawful arrest or detention of a person to prevent his effecting an unauthorised entry into the country or of a person against whom action is being taken with a view to deportation or extradition.

2. Everyone who is arrested shall be informed promptly, in a language which he understands, of the reasons for his arrest and of any charge against him.

3. Everyone arrested or detained in accordance with the provisions of paragraph 1c of this Article shall be brought promptly before a judge or other officer authorised by law to exercise judicial power and shall be entitled to trial within a reasonable time or to release pending trial. Release may be conditioned by guarantees to appear for trial.

4. Everyone who is deprived of his liberty by arrest or detention shall be entitled to take proceedings by which the lawfulness of his detention shall be decided speedily by a court and his release ordered if the detention is not lawful.

5. Everyone who has been the victim of arrest or detention in contravention of the provisions of this Article shall have an enforceable right to compensation.

Article 6

1. In the determination of his civil rights and obligations or of any criminal charge against him, everyone is entitled to a fair and public hearing within a reasonable time by an independent and impartial tribunal established by law. Judgment shall be pronounced publicly but the press and public may be excluded from all or part of the trial in the interest of morals, public order or national security in a democratic society, where the interests of juveniles or the protection of the private life of the parties so require, or to the extent strictly necessary in the opinion of the court in special circumstances where publicity would prejudice the interests of justice.

2. Everyone charged with a criminal offence shall be presumed innocent until proved guilty according to law.

3. Everyone charged with a criminal offence has the following minimum rights:
   (a) to be informed promptly, in a language which he understands and in detail, of the nature and cause of the accusation against him;
   (b) to have adequate time and facilities for the preparation of his defence;
   (c) to defend himself in person or through legal assistance of his own choosing or, if he has not sufficient means to pay for legal assistance, to be given it free when the interests of justice so require;
   (d) to examine or have examined witnesses against him and to obtain the attendance and examination of witnesses on his behalf under the same conditions as witnesses against him;
   (e) to have the free assistance of an interpreter if he cannot understand or speak the language used in court.

Article 7

1. No one shall be held guilty of any criminal offence on account of any act or omission which did not constitute a criminal offence under national or international law at the time when it was committed. Nor shall a heavier penalty be imposed than the one that was applicable at the time the criminal offence was committed.

2. This Article shall not prejudice the trial and punishment of any person for any act or omission which, at the time when it was committed, was criminal according to the general principles of law recognised by civilised nations.

Article 8

1. Everyone has the right to respect for his private and family life, his home and his correspondence.

2. There shall be no interference by a public authority with the exercise of this right except such as is in accordance with the law and is necessary in a democratic society in the interests of national security, public safety or the economic well-being of the country, for the prevention of disorder or crime, for the protection of health or morals, or for the protection of the rights and freedoms of others.

Article 9

1. Everyone has the right to freedom of thought, conscience and religion; this right includes freedom to change his religion or belief and freedom, either alone or in community with others and in public or private, to manifest his religion or belief, in worship, teaching, practice and observance.

2. Freedom to manifest one's religion or beliefs shall be subject only to such limitations as are prescribed by law and are necessary in a democratic society in the interests of public safety, for the protection of public order, health or morals, or for the protection of the rights and freedoms of others.

Article 10

1. Everyone has the right to freedom of expression. This right shall include freedom to hold opinions and to receive and impart information and ideas without interference by public authority and. regardless of frontiers. This Article shall not prevent States from requiring the licensing of broadcasting, television or cinema enterprises.

2. The exercise of these freedoms, since it carries with it duties and responsibilities, may be subject to such formalities, conditions, restrictions or penalties as are prescribed by law and are necessary in a democratic society, in the interests of national security, territorial integrity or public safety, for the prevention of disorder or crime, for the protection of health or morals, for the protection of the reputation or rights of others, for preventing the disclosure of information received in confidence, or for maintaining the authority and impartiality of the judiciary.

Article 11

1. Everyone has the right to freedom of peaceful assembly and to freedom of association with others, including the right to form and to join trade unions for the protection of his interests.

2. No restrictions shall be placed on the exercise of these rights other than such as are prescribed by law and are necessary in a democratic society in the interests of national security or public safety, for the prevention of disorder or crime, for the protection of health or morals or for the protection of the rights and freedoms of others. This Article shall not prevent the imposition of lawful restrictions on the exercise of these rights by members of the armed forces, of the police or of the administration of the State.

. . .

Article 14

The enjoyment of the rights and freedoms set forth in this Convention shall be secured without discrimination on any ground such as sex, race, colour, language, religion, political or other opinion, national or social origin, association with a national minority, property, birth or other status.

R (on the application of Pretty) v *Director of Public Prosecutions*
[2002] 1 All ER 1 House of Lords

LORD BINGHAM OF CORNHILL: . . . My Lords, no one of ordinary sensitivity could be unmoved by the frightening ordeal which faces Mrs Dianne Pretty, the appellant. She suffers from motor neurone disease, a progressive degenerative illness from which she has no hope of recovery. She has only a short time to live and faces the prospect of a humiliating and distressing death. She is mentally alert and would like to be able to take steps to bring her life to a peaceful end at a time of her choosing. But her physical incapacity is now such that she can no longer, without help, take her own life. With the support of her family, she wishes to enlist the help of her husband to that end. He himself is willing to give such help, but only if he can be sure that he will not be prosecuted under s 2(1) of the Suicide Act 1961 for aiding and abetting her suicide. Asked to undertake that he would not under s 2(4) of that Act consent to the prosecution of Mr Pretty under s 2(1) if Mr Pretty were to assist his wife to commit suicide, the Director of Public Prosecutions (the Director) has refused to give such an undertaking. On Mrs Pretty's application for judicial review of that refusal, the Queen's Bench Divisional Court ([2001] EWHC Admin 788, [2001] All ER (D) 251 (Oct)) upheld the Director's decision and refused relief. Mrs Pretty claims that she has a right to her husband's assistance in committing suicide and that s 2 of the 1961 Act, if it prohibits his helping and prevents the Director undertaking not to prosecute if he does; is incompatible with the European Convention for the Protection of Human Rights and Fundamental Freedoms (Rome, 4 November 1950; TS 71 (1953): Cmd 8969) (as set out in Sch 1 to the Human Rights Act 1998). It is on the convention, brought into force in this country by the 1998 Act, that Mrs Pretty's claim to relief depends. It is accepted by her counsel on her behalf that under the common law of England she could not have hoped to succeed.

. . .

Article 2 of the convention

[3] Article 2 of the convention provides:

'Right to life

1. Everyone's right to life shall be protected by law. No one shall be deprived of his life intentionally save in the execution of a sentence of a court following his conviction of a crime for which this penalty is provided by law.

2. Deprivation of life shall not be regarded as inflicted in contravention of this Article when it results from the use of force which is no more than absolutely necessary: (a) in defence of any person from unlawful violence; (b) in order to effect a lawful arrest or to prevent the escape of a person lawfully detained; (c) in action lawfully taken for the purpose of quelling a riot or insurrection.'

The article is to be read in conjunction with arts 1 and 2 of the Sixth Protocol, which are among the convention rights protected by the 1998 Act (see s 1(1)(c)) and which abolished the death penalty in time of peace.

[4] On behalf of Mrs Pretty it is submitted that art 2 of the convention protects not life itself but the right to life. The purpose of the article is to protect individuals from third parties (the state and public authorities). But the article recognises that it is for the individual to choose whether or not to live and so protects the individual's right to self-determination in relation to issues of life and death. Thus a person may refuse life-saving or life-prolonging medical treatment, and may lawfully choose to commit suicide. The article acknowledges that right of the individual. While most people want to live, some want to die, and the article protects both rights. The right to die is not the antithesis of the right to life but the corollary of it, and the state has a positive obligation to protect both.

[5] The Secretary of State has advanced a number of unanswerable objections to this argument which were rightly upheld by the Divisional Court. The starting point must be the language of the article. The thrust of this is to reflect the sanctity which, particularly in Western eyes, attaches to life. The article protects the right to life and prevents the deliberate taking of life save in very narrowly defined circumstances. An article with that effect cannot be interpreted as conferring a right to die or to enlist the aid of another in bringing about one's own death. In his argument for Mrs Pretty, Mr Havers QC was at pains to limit his argument to assisted suicide, accepting that the right claimed could not extend to cover an intentional consensual killing (usually described in this context as 'voluntary euthanasia', but regarded in English law as murder). The right claimed would be sufficient to cover Mrs Pretty's case and counsel's unwillingness to go further is understandable. But there is in logic no justification for drawing a line at this point. If art 2 does confer a right to self-determination in relation to life and death, and if a person were so gravely disabled as to be unable to perform any act whatever to cause his or her own death, it would necessarily follow in logic that such a person would have a right to be killed at the hands of a third party without giving any help to the third party and the state would be in breach of the convention if it were to interfere with the exercise of that right. No such right can possibly be derived from an article having the object already defined.

[6] It is true that some of the guaranteed convention rights have been interpreted as conferring rights not to do that which is the antithesis of what there is an express right to do. Article 11, for example, confers a right not to join an association (*Young v UK* (1981) 4 EHRR 38), art 9 embraces a right to freedom from any compulsion to express thoughts or change an opinion or divulge convictions (Clayton and Tomlinson *The Law of Human Rights* (2000) p 974 (para 14.49)) and I would for my part be inclined to infer that art 12 confers a right not to marry (but see Clayton and Tomlinson p 913 (para 13.76)). It cannot, however, be suggested (to take some obvious examples) that arts 3, 4, 5 and

6 confer an implied right to do or experience the opposite of that which the articles guarantee. Whatever the benefits which, in the view of many, attach to voluntary euthanasia, suicide, physician-assisted suicide and suicide assisted without the intervention of a physician, these are not benefits which derive protection from an article framed to protect the sanctity of life.

. . .

Article 3 of the convention

[10] Article 3 of the convention provides:

> 'Prohibition of torture
> No one shall be subjected to torture or to inhuman or degrading treatment or punishment.'

This is one of the articles from which a member state may not derogate even in time of war or other public emergency threatening the life of the nation (see art 15). I shall for convenience use the expression 'proscribed treatment' to mean 'inhuman or degrading treatment' as that expression is used in the convention.

[11] In brief summary the argument for Mrs Pretty proceeded by these steps. (1) Member states have an absolute and unqualified obligation not to inflict the proscribed treatment and also to take positive action to prevent the subjection of individuals to such treatment (see *A v UK* (1998) 5 BHRC 137, *Z v UK* [2001] 2 FCR 246 at 265 (para 73)). (2) Suffering attributable to the progression of a disease may amount to such treatment if the state can prevent or ameliorate such suffering and does not do so (see *D v UK* (1997) 2 BHRC 273 at 283–285 (paras 46–54)). (3) In denying Mrs Pretty the opportunity to bring her suffering to an end the United Kingdom (by the Director) will subject her to the proscribed treatment. The state can spare Mrs Pretty the suffering which she will otherwise endure since, if the Director undertakes not to give his consent to prosecution, Mr Pretty will assist his wife to commit suicide and so she will be spared much suffering. (4) Since, as the Divisional Court held, it is open to the United Kingdom under the convention to refrain from prohibiting assisted suicide, the Director can give the undertaking sought without breaking the United Kingdom's obligations under the convention. (5) If the Director may not give the undertaking, s 2 of the 1961 Act is incompatible with the convention.

. . .

[13] Article 3 enshrines one of the fundamental values of democratic societies and its prohibition of the proscribed treatment is absolute (*D v UK* (1997) 2 BHRC 273 at 283 (para 47)). Article 3 is, as I think, complementary to art 2. As art 2 requires states to respect and safeguard the lives of individuals within their jurisdiction, so art 3 obliges them to respect the physical and human integrity of such individuals. There is in my opinion nothing in art 3 which bears on an individual's right to live or to choose not to live. That is not its sphere of application: indeed, as is clear from *X v Germany*, a state may on occasion be justified in inflicting treatment which would otherwise be in breach of art 3 in order to serve the ends of art 2. Moreover, the absolute and unqualified prohibition on a member state inflicting the proscribed treatment requires that 'treatment' should not be given an unrestricted or extravagant meaning. It cannot, in my opinion, be plausibly suggested that the Director or any other agent of the United Kingdom is inflicting the proscribed treatment on Mrs Pretty, whose suffering derives from her cruel disease.

. . .

Article 8 of the convention

[16] Article 8 of the convention provides:

> 'Right to respect for private and family life
> 1. Everyone has the right to respect for his private and family life, his home and his correspondence.

2. There shall be no interference by a public authority with the exercise of this right except such as is in accordance with the law and is necessary in a democratic society in the interests of national security, public safety or the economic well-being of the country, for the prevention of disorder or crime, for the protection of health or morals, or for the protection of the rights and freedoms of others.'

[17] Counsel for Mrs Pretty submitted that this article conferred a right to self-determination (see *X v Netherlands* (1985) 8 EHRR 235, *Rodriguez v A-G of Canada* [1994] 2 LRC 136, *Re A (children) (conjoined twins: surgical separation)* [2000] 4 All ER 961, [2001] Fam 147). This right embraces a right to choose when and how to die so that suffering and indignity can be avoided. Section 2(1) of the 1961 Act interferes with this right of self-determination: it is therefore for the United Kingdom to show that the interference meets the convention tests of legality, necessity, responsiveness to pressing social need and proportionality (see *R v A (No 2)* [2001] UKHL 25, [2001] 3 All ER 1, [2001] 2 WLR 1546, *Johansen v Norway* (1996) 23 EHRR 33, *R (P) v Secretary of State for the Home Dept, R (Q) v Secretary of State for the Home Dept* [2001] EWCA Civ 1151, [2001] 1 WLR 2002). Where the interference is with an intimate part of an individual's private life, there must be particularly serious reasons to justify the interference (*Smith v UK* (2000) 29 EHRR 493 at 530 (para 89)). The court must in this case rule whether it could be other than disproportionate for the Director to refuse to give the undertaking sought and, in the case of the Secretary of State, whether the interference with Mrs Pretty's right to self-determination is proportionate to whatever legitimate aim the prohibition on assisted suicide pursues. Counsel placed particular reliance on certain features of Mrs Pretty's case: her mental competence, the frightening prospect which faces her, her willingness to commit suicide if she were able, the imminence of death, the absence of harm to anyone else, the absence of far-reaching implications if her application were granted. Counsel suggested that the blanket prohibition in s 2(1), applied without taking account of particular cases, is wholly disproportionate, and the materials relied on do not justify it. Reference was made to *R v UK* (1983) 33 DR 270 and *Sanles v Spain* [2001] EHRLR 348.

[18] The Secretary of State questioned whether Mrs Pretty's rights under art 8 were engaged at all, and gave a negative answer. He submitted that the right to private life under art 8 relates to the manner in which a person conducts his life, not the manner in which he departs from it. Any attempt to base a right to die on art 8 founders on exactly the same objection as the attempt based on art 2, namely, that the alleged right would extinguish the very benefit on which it is supposedly based. Article 8 protects the physical, moral and psychological integrity of the individual, including rights over the individual's own body, but there is nothing to suggest that it confers a right to decide when or how to die.

. . .

[26] I would for my part accept the Secretary of State's submission that Mrs Pretty's rights under art 8 are not engaged at all. If, however, that conclusion is wrong, and the prohibition of assisted suicide in s 2 of the 1961 Act infringes her convention right under art 8, it is necessary to consider whether the infringement is shown by the Secretary of State to be justifiable under the terms of art 8(2). In considering that question I would adopt the test advocated by counsel for Mrs Pretty, which is clearly laid down in the authorities cited.

[27] Since suicide ceased to be a crime in 1961, the question whether assisted suicide also should be decriminalised has been reviewed on more than one occasion. The Criminal Law Revision Committee in its fourteenth report *Offences against the Person* (Cmnd 7844 (1980)) reported some divergence of opinion among its distinguished legal membership, and recognised a distinction between assisting a person who had formed a settled intention to kill himself and the more heinous case where one person persuaded another to commit suicide, but a majority was of the clear opinion that aiding and abetting suicide should remain an offence (pp 60–61 (para 135)).

[28] Following the decision in *Bland*'s case a much more broadly-constituted House of Lords Select Committee on Medical Ethics received extensive evidence and reported. The committee in its report (HL Paper (1993–94) 21–b drew a distinction between assisted suicide and physician-assisted suicide (p 11 (para 26)) but its conclusion was unambiguous (p 54 (para 262)):

> 'As far as assisted suicide is concerned, we see no reason to recommend any change in the law. We identify no circumstances in which assisted suicide should be permitted, nor do we see any reason to distinguish between the act of a doctor or of any other person in this connection.'

. . .

Article 9 of the convention

[31] It is unnecessary to recite the terms of art 9 of the convention, to which very little argument was addressed. It is an article which protects freedom of thought, conscience and religion and the manifestation of religion or belief in worship, teaching, practice or observance. One may accept that Mrs Pretty has a sincere belief in the virtue of assisted suicide. She is free to hold and express that belief. But her belief cannot found a requirement that her husband should be absolved from the consequences of conduct which, although it would be consistent with her belief, is proscribed by the criminal law. And if she were able to establish an infringement of her right, the justification shown by the state in relation to art 8 would still defeat it.

Article 14 of the convention

[32] Article 14 of the convention provides:

> 'Prohibition of discrimination
> The enjoyment of the rights and freedoms set forth in this Convention shall be secured without discrimination on any ground such as sex, race, colour, language, religion, political or other opinion, national or social origin, association with a national minority, property, birth or other status.'

Mrs Pretty claims that s 2(1) of the 1961 Act discriminates against those who, like herself, cannot because of incapacity take their own lives without assistance. She relies on the judgment of the European Court of Human Rights in *Thlimmenes v Greece* (2000) 9 BHRC 12 at 22 where the court said:

> '44. The court has so far considered that the right under art 14 not to be discriminated against in the enjoyment of the rights guaranteed under the convention is violated when states treat differently persons in analogous situations without providing an objective and reasonable justification . . . However, the court considers that this is not the only facet of the prohibition of discrimination in art 14. The right not to be discriminated against in the enjoyment of the rights guaranteed under the convention is also violated when states without an objective and reasonable justification fail to treat differently persons whose situations are significantly different.'

[33] The European Court of Human Rights has repeatedly held that art 14 is not autonomous but has effect only in relation to convention rights. As it was put in *Van Raalte v Netherlands* (1997) 24 EHRR 503 at 516–517:

> '33. As the Court has consistently held, Article 14 of the Convention complements the other substantive provisions of the Convention and the Protocols. It has no independent existence since it has effect solely in relation to "the enjoyment of the rights and freedoms" safeguarded by those provisions. Although the application of Article 14 does not presuppose a breach of those provisions—and to this extent it is autonomous—there can be no room for its application unless the facts at issue fall within the ambit of one or more of the latter.'

See also *Botta v Italy* (1998) 4 BHRC 81 at 90 (para 39).

[34] If, as I have concluded, none of the articles on which Mrs Pretty relies gives her the right which she has claimed, it follows that art 14 would not avail her even if she could establish that the operation of s 2(1) is discriminatory. A claim under this article must fail on this ground.

NOTES AND QUESTIONS
1. The ultimate effect of the Human Rights Act 1998 will depend on how 'activist' the courts are prepared to be in interpreting and implementing its provisions. Except in respect of the UK's obligations arising from its membership of the European Union (where Community law takes precedence in the case of a conflict), British courts have tended to give great deference to 'Parliamentary sovereignty' (the principle that the courts may not question laws properly enacted by Parliament). The justification for this doctrine is that members of Parliament (or, more accurately, members of the House of Commons) derive their authority from a democratic mandate, while the courts do not. Under the 1998 Act, the courts will not have the power to strike down legislation although they can make a declaration of incompatibility. This obviously represents a compromise. It remains to be seen the extent to which the judges will be prepared to make a 'declaration of incompatibility'. The potential for legislative – judicial conflicts may lead to caution on both sides: Parliament in enacting legislation (indeed, in the future the Government will have to make a statement that any proposed Bill is compatible with the Convention); and the judiciary in making a declaration of incompatibility.
2. In addition to giving the courts greater powers, the 1998 Act may lead to their taking a more distinctly 'European' approach to decision-making. UK courts have tended to give great weight to precedent (the practice of adhering to past judicial decisions which have addressed the same or similar issues). The European Court of Human Rights, on the other hand, regards the Convention as a 'living instrument' and is therefore not averse to departing from past decisions when changing social conditions and attitudes support doing so.
3. When cases involving a State's law are considered by the European Court of Human Rights, the Court is prepared to allow the State a 'margin of appreciation'. Why? Should this 'margin of appreciation' also be extended when a UK court considers a domestic statute pursuant to the Human Rights Act 1998? What is the difference? What is the purpose of allowing a 'margin of appreciation' in the first place?

D: The relationship between European and domestic law

The government and Parliament enjoy what is a largely unfettered discretion to decide what conduct should be made criminal and what conduct should be left unregulated. However, in shaping its criminal law and criminal justice system, the UK has to take account of its European Community obligations. This may work either positively or negatively. In some instances the UK is precluded from criminalising certain conduct because to do so would infringe on a European recognised right. In other instances, the UK is required to criminalise certain conduct in order to give effect to a European mandate.

If the law of a member State of the European Union (EU) is in conflict with EU law, it is not valid. In *Costa v ENEL* (case 6/64) [1964] ECR 585, the European Court of Justice stated:

By contrast with ordinary national treaties, [the Treaty founding the European Community] has created its own legal systems which, on the entry into force of the Treaty, became an integral part of the legal systems of the Member States and which their courts are bound to apply.

By creating a Community of unlimited duration, having its own institutions, its own personality, its own legal capacity . . . the Member States have limited their sovereign rights, albeit within limited fields, and have thus created a body of law which binds their nationals and themselves.

Note that this case was decided before the UK joined the Community on 1 January 1973. The European Communities Act 1972 is the UK Act which implemented the decision to join the Community and the supremacy of EC law is accepted in s. 9(2) of that Act. It is thus open to a defendant charged with an offence under UK law to challenge the validity of the law creating the offence. This is the case whether or not the creation of the UK offence pre-dated the relevant European law (*Marleasing SA* v *La Commercial Internacional de Alimentacion SA* (case C-106/89) [1990] ECR 1–4135).

The method of challenging the validity of the law is by persuading the UK court that a relevant EU rule is involved and that it is in conflict with the UK law creating the offence. If there is any doubt about this the UK court should refer the case to the European Court of Justice (ECJ) for its interpretation. The reference will take place under Article 236 of the EC Treaty. The ECJ will consider the referred question and return the case to the member state court which will then give judgment, taking note of the guidance issued by the ECJ.

In cases involving European law it is necessary to take account of the purposive interpretation of the Treaty adopted by the ECJ. A literal interpretation of the text is not a proper approach.

R v *Henn and Darby (case 34/79)*
[1979] ECR 3795, European Court of Justice

. . .

I – FACTS AND PROCEDURE

1. The national legislation applicable
Section 42 of the Customs Consolidation Act, 1876, prohibits the importation into the United Kingdom of 'indecent or obscene' articles, and provides that articles imported contrary to the prohibition shall be forfeited and may be destroyed or otherwise disposed of as the Commissioners of Customs may direct. The seventh schedule to the Customs and Excise Act, 1952, provides a procedure for testing the liability of goods to forfeiture under section 42 either in the High Court of Justice or in a court of summary jurisdiction.

. . .

Section 304 of the Customs and Excise Act, 1952, makes it a criminal offence for any person to be in any way knowingly concerned in the fraudulent evasion or attempted evasion of the prohibition on importation. Infringement is made punishable by the imposition of a financial penalty of three times the value of the goods involved or £100, whichever is the greater, and/or imprisonment for a term not exceeding two years.

Donald Henn met the lorry on the road from Felixstowe to Ipswich. He was seen to collect the boxes and put them into his car. He was followed to London where on 15 October he was arrested and the boxes and contents seized by officers of customs under section 42 of the Customs Consolidation Act, 1876, on the ground that their importation was prohibited. The appellant John Frederick Ernest Darby was arrested the same day in London where he was waiting to make arrangements with Henn to collect and distribute the films and magazines.

At the material time both appellants were concerned in distributing by post in England articles of the kind which had been seized. They advertised the films and magazines in brochures sent by post from an accommodation address in Holland and then supplied any orders received from an unknown source in the United Kingdom. The brochures were sent out by them unsolicited.

Examination of the films and magazines imported on 14 October showed that they had originated in Denmark, Germany and Sweden.

On 17 May 1977 at Ipswich Crown Court the appellants were indicted, *inter alia*, with being knowingly concerned in the fraudulent evasion of the prohibition of the importation of indecent or obscene articles contrary to section 42 of the Customs Consolidation Act, 1876, and section 304 of the Customs and Excise Act, 1952.

Both the films (which were of a size ordinarily used in domestic projectors) and the magazines depict detailed and explicit sexual activities, including aberrant sexual behaviour. The films include a number of scenes of violence and two of the magazines contain only photographs of naked girls between about five and fourteen years old engaging in or having engaged in sexual activity with an adult man. Five of the magazines contain advertisements inviting readers to apply to a 'Model Contact', and one magazine advertises for models for another magazine which depicts acts of buggery. All the films and magazines included in the charge were made by a firm called 'Color Climax' and originated in Denmark.

The films and magazines depict the commission of acts which are contrary to the criminal law of the United Kingdom in a variety of ways.

At the outset of the trial application was made to the trial judge by counsel acting for both appellants to quash the count which is the subject of this reference on the grounds that since the accession of the United Kingdom to the European Communities by reason of section 2(1) and Schedule I part 1 paragraph 2 of the European Communities Act, 1972, Article 30 (now Article 28) of the EEC Treaty operated so as to invalidate section 42 of the Customs Consolidation Act, 1876, in so far as it related to goods coming from a Member State and defined by Article 9 of the Treaty. This application was rejected. The appellants pleaded 'Not Guilty' to the charge. The application was renewed at the end of the case for the prosecution. It was again rejected.

Both appellants were convicted. On 15 July they were sentenced: Henn to eighteen months' imprisonment, Darby to two years' imprisonment. They were further ordered to pay a financial penalty.

Both appellants appealed against their convictions. The appeals were heard by the Court of Appeal (Criminal Division) on 4 to 7 July 1978. The court refused to refer any questions to the Court of Justice under Article 177 of the Treaty and dismissed the appeals. The court certified in accordance with section 33 of the Criminal Appeal Act, 1968, that a point of law, of general public importance was involved in the appeals, namely:

> Whether section 42 of the Customs Consolidation Act, 1876, is effective to prevent the importation of pornographic articles from Holland notwithstanding Articles 30 and 36 of the European Economic Community Treaty.

JUDGMENT OF THE COURT

. . .

Under the terms of Article 36 (now Article 30) of the Treaty the provisions relating to the free movement of goods within the Community are not to preclude prohibitions on imports which are justified *inter alia* 'on grounds of public morality'. In principle, it is for each Member State to determine in accordance with its own scale of values and in the form selected by it the requirements of public morality in its territory. In any event, it cannot be disputed that the statutory provisions applied by the United Kingdom in regard to the importation of articles having an indecent or obscene character come within the powers reserved to the Member States by the first sentence of Article 36.

Each Member State is entitled to impose prohibitions on imports justified on grounds of public morality for the whole of its territory, as defined in Article 227 (now Art 229) of the Treaty, whatever the structure of its constitution may be and however the powers of legislating in regard to the subject in question may be distributed. The fact that certain differences exist between the laws enforced in the different constituent parts of a Member State does not thereby prevent that State from applying a unitary concept in regard to prohibitions on imports imposed, on grounds of public morality, on trade with other Member States.

. . . According to the second sentence of Article 36 the restrictions on imports referred to in the first sentence may not 'constitute a means of arbitrary discrimination or a disguised restriction on trade between Member States'.

In order to answer the questions which have been referred to the Court it is appropriate to have regard to the function of this provision, which is designed to prevent restrictions on trade based on the grounds mentioned in the first sentence of Article 36 from being diverted from their proper purpose and used in such a way as either to create discrimination in respect of goods originating in other Member States or indirectly to protect certain national products. That is not the purport of a prohibition, such as that in force in the United Kingdom, on the importation of articles which are of an indecent or obscene character. Whatever may be the differences between the laws on this subject in force in the different constituent parts of the United Kingdom, and notwithstanding the fact that they contain certain exceptions of limited scope, these laws, taken as a whole, have as their purpose the prohibition, or at least, the restraining, of the manufacture and marketing of publications or articles of an indecent or obscene character. In these circumstances it is permissible to conclude, on a comprehensive view, that there is no lawful trade in such goods in the United Kingdom. A prohibition on imports which may in certain respects be more strict than some of the laws applied within the United Kingdom cannot therefore be regarded as amounting to a measure designed to give indirect protection to some national product or aimed at creating arbitrary discrimination between goods of this type depending on whether they are produced within the national territory or another Member State.

The answer to the fourth question must therefore be that if a prohibition on the importation of goods is justifiable on grounds of public morality and if it is imposed with that purpose the enforcement of that prohibition cannot, in the absence within the Member State concerned of a lawful trade in the same goods, constitute a means of arbitrary discrimination or a disguised restriction on trade contrary to Article 36.

THE COURT, in answer to the questions referred to it by the House of Lords by order of 22 February 1979, hereby rules:

1. A law of a Member State prohibiting any importation of pornographic articles into that State constitutes a quantitative restriction on imports within the meaning of Article 30 of the Treaty.

2. The first sentence of Article 36 upon its true construction means that a Member State may, in principle, lawfully impose prohibitions on the importation from any other Member State of articles which are of an indecent or obscene character as understood by its domestic laws and that such prohibitions may lawfully be applied to the whole of its national territory even if, in regard to the field in question, variations exist between the laws in force in the different constituent parts of the Member State concerned.

3. If a prohibition on the importation of goods is justifiable on grounds of public morality and if it is imposed with that purpose the enforcement of that prohibition cannot, in the absence within the Member State concerned of a lawful trade in the same goods, constitute a means of arbitrary discrimination or a disguised restriction on trade contrary to Article 36.

E: What provisions of EU law may be relevant?

All of them! Treaty Articles, Regulations and Directives all may nullify or modify member state criminal provisions. In view of the purposive interpretations adopted by the ECJ, considerable expertise in EU law is required in order to understand the potentially far-reaching effect of some European provisions.

(i) *Treaty Articles*
See *R* v *Henn and Darby* (above) and consider the following decision:

R v *Robert Tymen (case 269/80)*
[1981] CMLR 493, European Court of Justice

Decision
By order of 14 November 1980, which was received at the Court on 5 December 1980, the Court of Appeal, Criminal Division, London, referred to the Court for a preliminary ruling under Article 177 (now Art 234) of the EEC Treaty five questions as to the interpretation of Article 102 of the Act of 22 January 1972 concerning Conditions of Accession and the Adjustments to the Treaties and certain other provisions of Community law in relation to a United Kingdom measure concerning fisheries.

These questions were raised in the context of criminal proceedings against the master of a French trawler, Mr Tymen, for the infringement of the Fishing Nets (North-East Atlantic) (Variation) Order 1979 (SI 1979 No 744). That order, which entered into force on 1 July 1979 and which amended the Fishing Nets (North-East Atlantic) Order 1977 (SI 1977 No 440), prohibits in a specified zone of the Atlantic and Arctic Oceans and the seas adjacent to those oceans the presence on board fishing boats of nets having a mesh-size less than certain prescribed minimum sizes.

In the case in point Mr Tymen was found guilty by Cardiff Crown Court of offences contrary to the above-mentioned orders, having been found in possession on 16 October 1979 on board his ship within the United Kingdom fishing zone of nets having an average mesh-size less than the minimum permitted mesh-size. He appealed against that judgment to the Court of Appeal, Criminal Division.

. . .

First question
The first question inquires whether the Member States still retained power after 31 December 1978 to adopt conservation measures of the kind contained in the United Kingdom order in question.

As the Court has already held in its above-mentioned judgment of 5 May 1981, the power to adopt, as part of the common fisheries policy, measures relating to the conservation of the resources of the sea has belonged fully and definitively to the Communities since the expiration on 1 January 1979 of the transitional period laid down by Article 102 of the Act of Accession so that after that date the Member States are no longer entitled to exercise any power of their own in this matter and may henceforth only act as trustees of the common interest, in the absence of appropriate action on the part of the Council.

Second question

The second question inquires in substance whether individuals may be prosecuted under a measure which is found to be contrary to Community law.

The same question has already formed the subject-matter of the judgment 16 February 1978 (*Schonenberg* (case 88/77) [1978] ECR 473). In that judgment, which, like the present case, concerned a breach of national fishery provisions, the Court found that where criminal proceedings were brought by virtue of a national measure which is held to be contrary to Community law a conviction in those proceedings is also incompatible with that law.

The reply to the second question must accordingly be that where criminal proceedings are brought by virtue of a national measure which is held to be contrary to Community law a conviction in those proceedings is also incompatible with that law.

(ii) *Penalties and the proportionality rule*

As we have seen, some offences are in direct conflict with EU rules. On other occasions it is both the offence and relevant sanctions that can fall foul of EU rules. Sanctions must comply with EU *proportionality*, i.e. they must not be more severe than is necessary for the object of the rule to be achieved.

R v Stanislaus Pieck (case 157/79)

[1980] 3 CMLR 220, European Court of Justice

Mr Pieck is a Dutch national. As may be seen from his passport he first entered the United Kingdom on 3 August 1973 and subsequently has resided there on several occasions. His passport was renewed at the Netherlands Consulate in London on 12 April 1976; on that occasion his address on the passport was changed from 'Wellington, New Zealand' to 'Cardiff, G.B.'. Since entering the United Kingdom on 3 December 1977, Mr Pieck has been and is still employed as a printer at an undertaking known as 'Graphics Prints' at Taffs Well near Cardiff.

Mr Pieck left the United Kingdom on 22 July 1978 and returned one week later, on 29 July. On each occasion on which he entered the United Kingdom the immigration authorities entered on his passport the date and place of entry together with the words 'given leave to enter the United Kingdom for six months' in compliance with Rule 51 of the Statement of Immigration Rules for Control on Entry (EEC and other Non-Commonwealth Nationals) (HP 81), adopted by the Home Secretary in pursuance of section 3(2) of the Immigration Act 1971.

Rule 51 reads:

> When an EEC national is given leave to enter, no condition is to be imposed restricting his employment or occupation in the United Kingdom. Admission should normally be for a period of six months, except in the case of a returning resident or the holder of a valid residence permit.

The six months' leave of entry into the United Kingdom granted to Mr Pieck on 29 July 1978 expired on 21 January 1979. In March 1979 Mr Pieck voluntarily went to the South Wales Constabulary, explained that he had overstayed his leave and asked for advice. He was advised to send his passport to the Home Office together with an application for a further stay. Mr Pieck did nothing. On 3 May 1979 he was required by a police officer to produce his passport. He replied: 'I was going to send it off but I forgot.' On that date Mr Pieck was charged with an offence contrary to the Immigration Act 1971, section 24(1)(b)(i), which reads:

> (24)(1): A person who is not a patrial shall be guilty of an offence punishable on summary conviction with a fine of not more than £200 or with imprisonment for not more than six months or with both, in any of the following cases . . .

(b) if, having only a limited leave to enter or remain in the United Kingdom he knowingly . . .

    (i)   remains beyond the time limited by the leave.

The charge against Mr Pieck reads as follows:

For that you being a person who is not patrial and only having a limited leave to remain in the United Kingdom knowingly remained in the United Kingdom beyond 29 January 1979, the time limited by the leave.

At the same time a notice was served on Mr Pieck in pursuance of section 6(2) of the Immigration Act 1971 to the effect that if he was convicted of the above offence the court would have power to recommend his deportation under section 3(6) of the Immigration Act 1971.

On 12 July 1979 Mr Pieck appeared before the Pontypridd Magistrates' Court and, whilst not contesting the evidence adduced by the prosecution, pleaded not guilty to the charge. He relied on Article 48(3)(b) and (c) of the EEC Treaty and the provisions of Directive 68/360 to show that the initial grant of six months' leave to enter the United Kingdom and the requirement to extend it were incompatible with Community law.

By order of 5 September 1979 the Magistrates' Court asked the Court of Justice to give a preliminary ruling on the three following questions:

1. What is the meaning of 'entry visa or equivalent document' in Article 3(2) of Council Directive 68/360/EEC of 15 October 1968?

2. Upon entry into a member-State by a EEC national, is the granting by that member-State of an initial leave to remain for a period limited to six months consistent with the rights secured to such a national by Articles 7 and 48 of the Treaty establishing the EEC and the provisions of Council Directives 64/221/EEC of 25 February 1964 and 68/360/EEC of 15 October 1968?

3. (Only applicable if the answer to Question 2 is affirmative) Where such a national is given a six months' limited leave to remain in a member-State and being employed as a worker but having failed to apply for a resident's permit he overstays that leave, can such a breach of law be punished in that member-State by measures which include imprisonment and/or a recommendation for deportation?

THE COURT RULED THAT:

1. Article 3(2) of Council Directive 68/360 of 15 October 1958 prohibiting member-States from demanding an entry visa or equivalent requirement from Community workers moving within the Community must be interpreted meaning as that the phrase 'entry visa or equivalent requirement' covers any formality for the purpose of granting leave to enter the territory of a member-State which is coupled with a passport or identity card check at the frontier, whatever may be the place or time at which that leave is granted and in whatever form it may be granted.

2.(a) The issue of a special residence document provided for in Article 4 of Council Directive 68/360 of 15 October 1968 has only a declaratory effect and for aliens to whom Article 48 of the Treaty or parallel provisions give rights, it cannot be assimilated to a residence permit such as is prescribed for aliens in general, in connection with the issue of which the national authorities have a discretion.

(b) A member-State may not require from a person enjoying the protection of Community law that he should possess a general residence permit instead of the document provided for in Article 4(2) of Directive 68/360 in conjunction with the Annex thereto.

3. The failure on the part of a national of a member-State of the Community, to whom the rules on freedom of movement for workers apply, to obtain the special residence permit prescribed in Article 4 of Directive 68/360 may not be punished by a recommendation for deportation or by measures which go as far as imprisonment.

(i) *European law as a brake on national law*

European law guarantees various rights, including, most notably, the free movement of persons, goods, services and capital. These rights take priority over any national legislation purporting to restrict them (see *Costa* v *ENEL* [1964] ECR 585 above). In case of conflict, national legislation must yield to the European right, as the following case illustrates:

Aldo Bordessa and Others

(cases C-358/93 and C-416/93), [1995] ECR I-361, European Court of Justice

Those questions were raised in two sets of criminal proceedings. On 10 November 1992 Aldo Bordessa (Case C-358/93), an Italian national residing in Italy, arrived at the customs post of La Junquera, Gerona (Spain) travelling towards France. When his car was inspected, banknotes worth approximately PTA 50 million were discovered in it, concealed in different places. Since Mr Bordessa did not possess the authorization required under Spanish law for the export of such a sum, he was arrested and the money confiscated. On 19 November 1992, Mari Mellado and Barbero Maestre (Case C-416/93), a married couple of Spanish nationality residing in Spain, crossed the frontier at the same customs post. In the course of an inspection carried out inside France, the French authorities subsequently discovered banknotes worth a total of PTA 38 million in their car. Since no application had been made to the Spanish authorities for authorisation to export that amount, criminal proceedings were initiated before the Spanish courts.

Under Article 4(1) of Royal Decree 1816 of 20 December 1991 on economic transactions with other countries, the export of such items as coins, banknotes and bank cheques payable to the bearer, made out in pesetas or in foreign currencies, is subject to a prior declaration when the amount is in excess of PTA 1 million per person and per journey and subject to prior administrative authorisation when the amount is in excess of PTA 5 million per person and per journey.

That decree was amended by Royal Decree 42 of 15 January 1993 which, according to the national court, constitutes no more than a technical improvement.

The national court considers that it is necessary to determine the validity and effect of that provision in the light of Community law before making a finding on a criminal offence under Law No. 40 of 10 December 1979 on the regulations governing exchange control, as amended by Organic Law No. 10 of 16 August 1983. Accordingly it stayed proceedings and submitted the following questions to the Court for a preliminary ruling:

(1) Does Article 30 [now Art 28] of the EEC Treaty preclude rules of a Member State which require a person leaving national territory bearing coins, banknotes or bearer cheques to make a prior declaration if the amount is in excess of PTA 1 million and to obtain prior administrative authorisation if the amount exceeds PTA 5 million, where non-compliance with those requirements entails criminal penalties which may include detention?

(2) Does Article 59 [now Art 49] of the EEC Treaty preclude rules such as those described in Question 1?

(3) Are rules such as those described in the previous questions compatible with Articles 1 and 4 of Directive 88/361/EEC?

(4) If Question 3 is answered in the negative, do the rules in Article 1 in conjunction with Article 4 of Directive 88/361/EEC meet the necessary conditions in order for them to be relied on as against the Spanish State before national courts and to render inapplicable national rules which conflict with them?

By order of the President of 13 June 1994 the two cases were joined, in accordance with Article 43 of the Rules of Procedure, for the purposes of the oral procedure and the final judgment.

. . .

By its third question, the national court is essentially asking whether Articles 1 and 4 of the Directive preclude national legislation from making the export of coins, banknotes or bearer cheques conditional on a prior declaration or authorisation.

It should first be noted that the Directive brought about the full liberalization of capital movements, for which purpose Article 1 required Member States to abolish restrictions on movements of capital taking place between persons resident in Member States.

Under the first paragraph of Article 4 of the Directive, Member States may 'take all requisite measures to prevent infringements of their laws and regulations, *inter alia* in the field of taxation and prudential supervision of financial institutions, or to lay down procedures for the declaration of capital movements for purposes of administrative or statistical information'.

The effectiveness of tax controls and the fight against illegal activities, such as tax evasion, money laundering, drug trafficking and terrorism, have been invoked as aims justifying the rules at issue.

It must therefore be examined whether Member States, in pursuing those aims, are taking measures which fall under the first paragraph of Article 4 of the Directive and consequently concern interests which those States are entitled to protect.

The first paragraph of Article 4 of the Directive expressly refers to the requisite measures to prevent infringements of the laws and regulations of Member States, *'inter alia'* in the field of taxation and the prudential supervision of financial institutions. It follows that other measures are also permitted in so far as they are designed to prevent illegal activities of comparable seriousness, such as money laundering, drug trafficking or terrorism.

That interpretation is confirmed moreover by the insertion in the Treaty establishing the European Community of Article 73d, paragraph (1)(b) of which essentially reproduces the first paragraph of Article 4 of the Directive but also provides that Member States have the right to take measures which are justified on grounds of public policy or public security.

It is in the light of those considerations that it should be determined whether the requirement laid down by the authorities of a Member State of a prior declaration or authorization for the transfer of coins, banknotes or bearer cheques is to be regarded as a requisite measure within the meaning of the first paragraph of Article 4 of the Directive.

As the Advocate General pointed out at point 17 of his Opinion, authorisation has the effect of suspending currency exports and makes them conditional in each case upon the consent of the administrative authorities, which must be sought by means of a special application.

A requirement of that nature would cause the exercise of the free movement of capital to be subject to the discretion of the administrative authorities and thus be such as to render that freedom illusory (see *Luisi and Carbone* v *Ministero del Tesoro* (cases 286/82 and 26/83) [1984] ECR 377, paragraph 34). It might have the effect of impeding capital movements carried out in accordance with Community law, contrary to the second paragraph of Article 4 of the Directive.

However, the Spanish Government defended the need for prior authorisation, claiming that it was only by virtue of such a system that non-compliance could be classified as criminal and hence criminal penalties imposed. Failure to meet that requirement could also lead to confiscation of the capital sums involved in the crime.

That view must, however, be rejected.

The Spanish Government has failed to provide sufficient proof that it is impossible to attach criminal penalties to the failure to make a prior declaration.

Consequently, it should be stated in reply to the third question that Articles 1 and 4 of the Directive preclude the export of coins, banknotes or bearer cheques being made conditional on prior authorisation but do not by contrast preclude transactions of that nature being made conditional on a prior declaration.

By its fourth question, the national court is asking whether the provisions of Article 1 in conjunction with Article 4 of the Directive have direct effect.

The requirement under Article 1 of the Directive for Member States to abolish all restrictions on movements of capital is precise and unconditional and does not require a specific implementing measure.

Application of the proviso in Article 4 of the Directive is amenable to review by the courts, and hence the fact that a Member State may avail itself of that possibility does not prevent Article 1 of the Directive, which enshrines the principle of the free movement of capital, from conferring rights on individuals which they may rely on before the courts and which the national courts must uphold.

Consequently, the reply to the national court's fourth question should be that Article 1 in conjunction with Article 4 of the Directive may be relied on before national courts and render inapplicable national rules which conflict with those provisions.

NOTE
1. For an example of a case where a State national law was found to infringe the free movement of persons, see *Royer* (case 48/75) [1976] ECR 497.

(ii) *National laws required to implement European legislation*

The preceding text examined instances where European law served as a brake on the development of national law. The converse can also occur. Sometimes European initiatives will require states to add to its body of criminal law. Examples include the European Directive on Insider Dealing (89/529/EEC) and the European Directive on the Prevention of Money Laundering (91/308/EEC). Both of these Directives require member states to enact legislation into their domestic law to achieve the objectives of the Directive. The precise form that the legislation will take is left for each member state to decide for itself.

NOTES AND QUESTIONS
1. The Money Laundering Directive was 'transposed' into UK law through the Criminal Justice Act 1993, s. 93A and following sections (money laundering and other offences) and by the issuance of the Money Laundering Regulations 1993 (SI 1993 No. 1933) (Banks and Banking Financial Services). The Criminal Justice Act 1993, Part V, transposes the offence of insider dealing into UK law.

(iii) *The relationship between the jurisprudence of the European Court of Justice and the European Court of Human Rights*

We have seen that claims of human rights violations can be raised in the European Court of Human Rights and, under the Human Rights Act 1998, in UK courts as well. The European Court of Justice also is prepared to intervene to protect human rights:

Elliniki Radiophonia Tileorassi AE v *Dimotiki Etairia Pliroforissis and Sotirios Kouvelas*
Case C-260/89 [1991] ECR I-2925, European Court of Justice

. . . With regard to Article 10 of the European Convention on Human Rights, referred to in the ninth and tenth questions, it must first be pointed out that, as the Court has consistently held, fundamental rights form an integral part of the general principles of law, the observance of which it ensures. For that purpose the Court draws inspiration from the constitutional traditions common to the Member States and from the guidelines supplied by international treaties for the protection of human rights on which the Member States have collaborated or of which they are signatories (see, in particular the judgment in *Nold* v *Commission* (case C-4/73) [1974] ECR 491, paragraph 13). The European Convention on Human Rights has special significance in that respect (see in particular *Johnston* v *Chief Constable of the Royal Ulster Constabulary* (case C-222/84) [1986] ECR 1651, paragraph 18). It follows that, as the Court held in its judgment in *Wachauf* v *Federal Republic of Germany* (case C-5/88) [1989] ECR 2609, paragraph 19, the Community cannot accept measures which are incompatible with observance of the human rights thus recognised and guaranteed.

As the Court has held (see the judgment in *Cinéthéque* v *Fédration Nationale des Cinémas Français* (cases C-60 and C-61/84) [1985] ECR 2605, paragraph 25, and the judgment in *Demirel* v *Stadt Schwäbisch Gmund* (case C-12/86) [1987] ECR 3719, paragraph 28), it has no power to examine the compatibility with the European Convention on Human Rights of national rules which do not fall within the scope of Community law. On the other hand, where such rules do fall within the scope of Community law, and reference is made to the Court for a preliminary ruling, it must provide all the criteria of interpretation needed by the national court to determine whether those rules are compatible with the fundamental rights the observance of which the Court ensures and which derive in particular from the European Convention on Human Rights.

In particular, where a Member State relies on the combined provisions of Articles 56 and 66 in order to justify rules which are likely to obstruct the exercise of the freedom to provide services, such justification, provided for by Community law, must be interpreted in the light of the general principles of law and in particular of fundamental rights. Thus the national rules in question can fall under the exceptions provided for by the combined provisions of Articles 56 and 66 (now Articles 46 and 53) only if they are compatible with the fundamental rights the observance of which is ensured by the Court.

It follows that in such a case it is for the national court, and if necessary, the Court of Justice to appraise the application of those provisions having regard to all the rules of Community law, including freedom of expression, as embodied in Article 10 of the European Convention on Human Rights, as a general principle of law the observance of which is ensured by the Court.

The reply to the national court must therefore be that the limitations imposed on the power of the Member States to apply the provisions referred to in Articles 66 and 56 of the Treaty on grounds of public policy, public security and public health must be appraised in the light of the general principle of freedom of expression embodied in Article 10 of the European Convention on Human Rights.

NOTES AND QUESTIONS
1. What is the relationship between the European Court of Justice and the European Court of Human Rights on issues of human rights law? To which Court should a litigant present a human rights claim?
2. The European Court of Justice is a 'supreme court' in the sense that its decisions cannot be appealed to a higher court and it is not bound by the decisions of any other court, including the European Court of Human Rights. That said, the European Court of Justice will respect and give great deference to the decisions of the European Court of Human Rights. The potential for conflicting decisions arises where a human rights claim is raised in the first instance in the European Court of Justice. Perhaps to avoid the potential for conflict the European Court of Justice speaks in terms of 'fundamental rights', which may or may not be as broad or broader than the rights found in the European Convention on Human Rights. It also speaks in terms of rights which are part of 'Community law', which brings the issues squarely within its expertise and jurisdiction.

3. Whether a rights violation is declared by either Court might seem to make little difference as a practical matter but this is not so. Under the European Communities Act 1972, EC law overrides all conflicting national legislation. Not so in the case of the decisions of the European Court of Human Rights. The latter might find that a State law is contrary to the provisions of the European Convention on Human Rights and award damages, but it cannot invalidate the national legislation. Even under the Human Rights Act 1998, the most that a court can do is make a declaration that a law is 'incompatible' with the Convention. Parliament is expected to rectify the incompatibility, but it is not obliged to do so.

SECTION 2:   **The grading of offences**

Once the decision to criminalise has been made, there is a still a grading issue to be considered. Not all crimes engender the same degree of concern, or cause the same amount of harm. Few would disagree that murder and rape are more serious offences than criminal damage and tax evasion. All may need to be made criminal, but the same penalty should not be attached to each. The penalty that is attached reflects the grading of the offence by Parliament.

There are issues of both absolute ranking (which is the most serious crime, the second most serious, etc.) and relative ranking (*how much* more serious is one crime than another).

A. Ashworth, *Principles of Criminal Law*
2nd ed. (1995)

. . . In essence, then, we may distinguish five stages in the calculation of offence-seriousness that von Hirsch and Jareborg [A. von Hirsch and N. Jareborg 'Gauging Criminal Harms: A Living Standard Analysis' [1991] OJLS 1] propose:

1. the interests violated by the offence are identified;

2. the effect on a typical victim's living standard is quantified on the scale ranging from offences that merely affect significant enhancement to those that affect subsistence;

3. the culpability of the offender is taken into account;

4. the level of seriousness may be reduced to reflect the remoteness of the offence from the actual harm; and

5. transfer this assessment on to a scale that in some way quantifies the degree of seriousness.

It would be possible to devise an elaborate 100-point scale for this, but von Hirsch and Jareborg say that this would give the impression of a 'misleading sense of precision', and their preference is for a scale with five broad bands. This both allows further adjustment within each band and signifies that it remains a rather approximate enterprise.

Inexact it may be, but the enterprise is essential. Judgments of relative seriousness are made frequently in all walks of life – not just by legislators when deciding whether to criminalize and what maximum penalty to assign to an offence, but also by judges and magistrates when sentencing, and also by lay people in commenting on whether the official response is proportionate. The value of the von Hirsch-Jareborg approach is that it identifies the stages of thought through which it is desirable to pass when making these judgments. In practice many of the judgments are made impressionistically, often on the basis of traditional assumptions about the ranking of offences. The von Hirsch-Jareborg approach urges one to dig deeper, and to look more closely at the interests affected. However, their approach is confined to harms with individual victims. It awaits development to deal with the myriad other forms of conduct that modern systems of criminal law tend to criminalize. . . . We must enquire . . . not only whether the behaviour is serious enough to be made into a criminal offence, but also, if it is an offence, how serious it is when compared with other crimes.

It is not difficult to see some toeholds for the assessment of relative seriousness. There is a widely held view that, in general, offences of violence are more serious than property offences. Thus Lord Lane CJ, assessing the relative seriousness of frauds on the social security system, remarked that 'it must be remembered that they are non-violent nonsexual and non-frightening crimes'. However, the very breadth of modern systems of criminal law means that this point is no more than a toehold. It is not difficult to think of circumstances in which an offence against property (say, stealing £1 million) might be thought more serious than a particular offence of violence (such as one person pushing another while queuing). Thus it is necessary to press the enquiry further by examining those values or interests which are protected by the offence, and those elements which distinguished it from other similar offences. This task soon reveals a bewildering number of separate factors. When passing sentence, the courts have to range the different crimes along a single scale of relative gravity (represented by imprisonment, fines, and other non-custodial sentences). Is it possible to range the various offences along a single scale of social seriousness?

There are some who would argue that, academically interesting though this enquiry might be, it is quite unnecessary in practice, because most people in most countries agree on the relative gravity of harms. Research by the criminologists Sellin and Wolfgang purported to find considerable agreement in ranking criminal offences, whether amongst people from different countries or from different social groups in one country. However, the questions asked in this research were relatively unsophisticated for the purpose of the criminal law, and its findings cannot sustain the argument that it is unnecessary to think further about the grading of crimes as more or less serious. . . .

NOTES AND QUESTIONS
1. Issues of both inter-crime and intra-crime grading can arise. Intra-crime grading relates to offences which address a related subject matter, while inter-crime grading involves unrelated and dissimilar offences.
2. Consider the following inter-crime grading problem. Rank the following offences on 'most serious' to 'least serious' scale, identifying the reasons for each ranking.
   • aggressive begging
   • assault
   • assault with a deadly weapon
   • burglary
   • reckless driving
   • murder
   • rape
   • theft
   • vagrancy
   When you have completed the exercise, you might find it instructive to compare your rankings with those of other students.
3. Now let us look at a problem of intra-crime grading. In the following statutes Parliament has attempted to draw distinctions between a number of vehicular-related offences:

Road Traffic Act 1991

1. Causing death by dangerous driving
A person who causes the death of another person by driving a mechanically propelled vehicle dangerously on a road or other public place is guilty of an offence.

2. Dangerous driving
A person who drives a mechanically propelled vehicle dangerously on a road or other public place is guilty of an offence.

3. Careless, and inconsiderate, driving
If a person drives a mechanically propelled vehicle on a road or other public place without due care and attention, or without reasonable consideration for other persons using the road or place, he is guilty of an offence.

3A. Causing death by careless driving when under influence of drink or drugs
(1) If a person causes the death of another person by driving a mechanically propelled vehicle on a road or other public place without due care and attention, or without reasonable consideration for other persons using the road or place, and—

(a) he is, at the time when he is driving, unfit to drive through drink or drugs, or

(b) he has consumed so much alcohol that the proportion of it in his breath, blood or urine at that time exceeds the prescribed limit, or

(c) he is, within 18 hours after that time, required to provide a specimen in pursuance of section 7 of this Act, but without reasonable excuse fails to provide it, he is guilty of an offence.

22A. Causing danger to road-users
(1) A person is guilty of an offence if he intentionally and without lawful authority or reasonable cause—

(a) causes anything to be on or over a road, or

(b) interferes with a motor vehicle, trailer or cycle, or

(c) interferes (directly or indirectly) with traffic equipment, in such circumstances that it would be obvious to a reasonable person that to do so would be dangerous.

28. Dangerous cycling
(1) A person who rides a cycle on a road dangerously is guilty of an offence.

Aggravated Vehicle Taking Act 1992

12A. Aggravated vehicle-taking
(1) Subject to subsection (3) below, a person is guilty of aggravated taking of a vehicle if—

(a) he commits an offence under section 12(1) above (in this section referred to as a 'basic offence') in relation to a mechanically propelled vehicle; and

(b) it is proved that, at any time after the vehicle was unlawfully taken (whether by him or another) and before it was recovered, the vehicle was driven, or injury or damage was caused, in one or more of the circumstances set out in paragraphs (a) to (d) of subsection (2) below.

(2) The circumstances referred to in subsection (1)(b) above are—

(a) that the vehicle was driven dangerously on a road or other public place;

(b) that, owing to the driving of the vehicle, an accident occurred by which injury was caused to any person;

(c) that, owing to the driving of the vehicle, an accident occurred by which damage was caused to any property, other than the vehicle;

(d) that damage was caused to the vehicle.

NOTES AND QUESTIONS

1. What penalties would you attach to each of these offences? You might be interested in comparing your answers to those of Parliament. The penalties under the Road Traffic Act 1991 can be found in the schedules attached to the statute. The penalty for violation of the Aggravated Vehicle Taking Act 1992 is contained in s. 4 of the statute.

2. One apparent critical difference which often serves for attaching greater penalties to one crime rather than another which involves similar conduct, is that one offence results in death while the other does not. Thus causing death by dangerous driving attracts a greater penalty than dangerous driving. But is the difference between the two offences simply a matter of chance, one of the drivers being unlucky enough to have a child dart into the road while engaged in his act of dangerous driving? In cases such as this, should the penalties for the offence be based on the risk of death that has been created rather than on whether a death actually occurs? See generally J. Gobert, 'The Fortuity of Consequences' (1993) 4 Criminal Law Forum 1; J.C. Smith, 'The Element of Chance in Criminal Liability' [1971] Crim LR 63.

3. For a discussion of racially aggravated offences, see p. 307 etc.

SECTION 3: **Punishment**

One critical effect of having been convicted of a criminal offence is that sanctions may be imposed on the offender in the name of the state. But what purpose is sought to be achieved through this punishment? Four answers are most commonly given:

A: Retribution

Retribution is the oldest of the rationales for punishment, tracing its roots to the Bible:

Leviticus 24:17–22, The New English Bible

When one man strikes another and kills him, he shall be put to death. Whoever strikes a beast and kills it shall make restitution, life for life. When one man injures and disfigures his fellow-countryman, it shall be done to him as he has done; fracture for fracture, eye for eye, tooth for tooth; the injury and disfigurement that he has inflicted upon another shall in turn be inflicted upon him.

Retribution is often assimilated to revenge, but a public rather than a private revenge. Sir James Stephen put it this way: 'The sentence of the law is to the moral sentiment of the public in relation to any offence what a seal is to wax' (Stephen, *A History of the Criminal Law in England*, II (1883), p. 81). Indeed, one of the arguments for a retributive theory of punishment is that it forestalls the need for private revenge. Implicit in retribution is the condemnation or denunciation of both the offender and the offending behaviour. Retribution, however, is not in kind – society does not rape rapists or steal from thieves (although in some countries the death penalty is exacted for murder). Instead, the law attempts to convert the offence into a common currency, and to impose a sentence which is proportional to the harm caused. In this regard it might be observed that retribution, with its emphasis on proportional punishment, provides a basis for the grading of offences.

Retribution as a justification for punishment has been criticised as backwards-looking and vindictive. As retribution has fallen into disfavour, however, there has been a rise in interest in the concept of 'just deserts'. Both retribution and 'just deserts' theory boil down to the idea that criminals are punished because they deserve to be. Society is right to denounce criminals and to punish them for their crimes.

B: Restraint

Restraint theory has a more pragmatic focus. Offenders need to be separated from the rest of society in order to protect ordinary citizens from their committing other offences. The implicit premise is that, if not incarcerated, offenders will continue in their criminal ways. Whether this is true as an empirical proposition is not entirely clear. Even if true, the question arises for how long the offender should be confined. A plausible answer is until he or she is no longer a threat to society. This answer is troublesome, however, for it can lead to lengthy imprisonment for some who commit minor offences but who are likely to do so again (e.g., shoplifters) and minimal imprisonment for some who commit serious offences but who are unlikely to do so ever again (e.g., a bank robber who is rendered paraplegic as a consequence of a shoot-out with police).

C: Rehabilitation

The other side of the restraint coin is rehabilitation. If a dangerous offender needs to be isolated until no longer dangerous, it behoves the state to rehabilitate offenders so that they can be released. This makes sense both from the altruistic perspective of helping the offender and from the pragmatic perspective of not burdening the state with the costs of maintaining an offender in prison any longer than is necessary. But being in favour of rehabilitation is one thing and knowing how to rehabilitate criminals is quite another. Innumerable rehabilitation pro-grammes have been essayed over the years with marginal success and unpredictable results. It may well be that our hopes for rehabilitation exceed our knowledge of why people commit crimes. Despite what seemed at one time to be promising advances in the fields of psychology and sociology, we still find the scientific control of criminal behaviour to be beyond our capability.

D: Deterrence

Whereas restraint and rehabilitation theory focus on the individual offender, general deterrence is concerned with other would-be offenders. The idea is to make an example of the actual offenders so that others will learn from their experience and not be tempted into criminal activity. In like vein, the offenders themselves should also be deterred from future criminal activities as a result of the punishment. Society will be protected if deterrence works as envisaged. Whether or not it in fact does is difficult to prove, for success can only be measured by the incidence of those who do not commit crimes. And how is one to measure this negative? Moreover, the process by which deterrence works, assuming it does, is not at all clear. Consider the views of the respected criminologist Johannes Andenaes:

Johannes Andenaes, '*The General Preventive Effects of Punishment*'
(1966) 114 *University of Pennsylvania Law Review* 949

In continental theories of criminal law, a basic distinction is made between the effects of punishment on the man being punished – individual prevention or special prevention – and the effects of punishment upon the members of society in general – general prevention. The characteristics of special prevention are termed 'deterrence,' 'reformation' and 'incapacitation,' and these terms have meanings similar to their meanings in the English speaking world. General prevention, on the other hand, may be described as the *restraining influences emanating from the criminal law and the legal machinery*.

By means of the criminal law, and by means of specific applications of this law, 'messages' are sent to members of a society. The criminal law lists those actions which are liable to prosecution, and it specifies the penalties involved. The decisions of the courts and actions by the police and prison officials transmit knowledge about the law, underlining the fact that criminal laws are not mere empty threats, and providing detailed information as to what kind of penalty might be expected for violations of specific laws. To the extent that these stimuli restrain citizens from socially undesired actions which they might otherwise have committed, a general preventive effect is secured.

. . . While the effects of special prevention depend upon how the law is implemented in each individual case, general prevention occurs as a result of an interplay between the provisions of the law and its enforcement in specific cases. In former times, emphasis was often placed on the physical exhibition of punishment as a deterrent influence, for example, by performing executions in public. Today it is customary to emphasize the *threat* of punishment as such. From this point of view the significance of the individual sentence and the execution of it lies in the support that these actions give to the law. . . .

The effect of the criminal law and its enforcement may be *mere deterrence*. Because of the hazards involved, a person who contemplates a punishable offense might not act. But it is not correct to regard general prevention and deterrence as one and the same thing. The concept of general prevention also includes the *moral* or *sociopedagogical* influence of punishment. The 'messages' sent by law and the legal processes contain factual information about what would be risked by disobedience, but they also contain proclamations specifying that it is *wrong* to disobey. . . .

The moral influence of the criminal law may take various forms. It seems to be quite generally accepted among the members of society that the law should be obeyed even though one is dissatisfied with it and wants it changed. If this is true, we may conclude that the law as an institution itself to some extent creates conformity. But more important than this formal respect for the law is respect for the values which the law seeks to protect. It may be said that from law and the legal machinery there emanates a flow of propaganda which favors such respect. Punishment is a means of expressing social disapproval. In this way the criminal law and its enforcement supplement and enhance the moral influence acquired through education and other non-legal processes. Stated negatively, the penalty neutralizes the demoralizing consequences that arise when people witness crimes being perpetrated.

Deterrence and moral influence may both operate on the conscious level. The potential criminal may deliberate about the hazards involved, or he may be influenced by a conscious desire to behave lawfully. However, with fear or moral influence as an intermediate link, it is possible to create unconscious inhibitions against crime, and perhaps to establish a condition of habitual lawfulness. In this case, illegal actions will not present themselves consciously as real alternatives to conformity, even in situations where the potential criminal would run no risk whatsoever of being caught.

General preventive effects do not occur only among those who have been informed about penal provisions and their applications. Through a process of learning and social imitation, norms and taboos may be transmitted to persons who have no idea about their origins – in much the way that innovations in Parisian fashions appear in the clothing of country girls who have never heard of Dior or Lanvin.

There is an interesting interplay between moral reprobation and legal implementation. At least three conditions combine to prevent an individual from perpetrating a punishable act he is tempted to perform: his moral inhibitions, his fear of the censure of his associates and his fear of punishment. The latter two elements are interwoven in many ways. A law violation may become known to the criminal's family, friends and neighbors even if there is no arrest or prosecution. However, it is frequently the process of arrest, prosecution and trial which brings the affair into the open and exposes the criminal to the censure of his associates. If the criminal can be sure that there will be no police action, he can generally rest assured that there will be no social reprobation. The legal machinery, therefore, is in itself the most effective means of mobilizing that kind of social control which emanates from community condemnation.

NOTES AND QUESTIONS

1. The theories of punishment which have been discussed are not mutually exclusive. Imprisoning an offender may serve both retributive and deterrent functions, while at the same time restraining the offender for the duration of the sentence. While in prison, rehabilitative services may be provided.
2. To what extent under each theory will punishment fit (a) the crime, (b) the criminal?
3. Consider the task of a Parliament which has decided to make careless driving a criminal offence. What penalties should be imposed if the goal is (a) restraint, (b) rehabilitation, (c) deterrence, (d) retribution?
4. To what extent are the various theories based on different theories of human nature? Which of the theories is premised on an assumption of 'free will'? What would be the implications if one were to accept a determinist philosophy that events are predetermined by forces beyond the control of individuals?
5. Some persons, such as children and the mentally ill, may not be deterrable. Does it logically follow that the criminal law is useless in such cases? What of criminals who assume that they will never be caught (is it not the exceptional and masochistic criminal who proceeds on the opposite assumption)? For these individuals, is not the potential penalty little more than a matter of academic interest?

6. A philosophy of punishment often is implicit in legislation. Consider the following statute (the substance of which has now been repealed by the Powers of Criminal Courts (Sentencing) Act 2000):

Criminal Justice Act 1991

1. Restrictions on imposing custodial sentences

(1) This section applies where a person is convicted of an offence punishable with a custodial sentence other than one fixed by law.

(2) Subject to subsection (3) below, the court shall not pass a custodial sentence on the offender unless it is of the opinion—

    (a) that the offence, or the combination of the offence and one other offence associated with it, was so serious that only such a sentence can be justified for the offence; or

    (b) where the offence is a violent or sexual offence, that only such a sentence would be adequate to protect the public from serious harm from him.

(3) Nothing in subsection (2) above shall prevent the court from passing a custodial sentence on the offender if he refuses to give his consent to a community sentence which is proposed by the court and requires that consent.

(4) Where a court passes a custodial sentence, it shall be its duty—

    (a) in a case not falling within subsection (3) above, to state in open court that it is of the opinion that either or both of paragraphs (a) and (b) of subsection (2) above apply and why it is of that opinion; and

    (b) in any case, to explain to the offender in open court and in ordinary language why it is passing a custodial sentence on him.

(5) A magistrates' court shall cause a reason stated by it under subsection (4) above to be specified in the warrant of commitment and to be entered in the register.

2. Length of custodial sentences

(1) This section applies where a court passes a custodial sentence other than one fixed by law.

(2) The custodial sentence shall be—

    (a) for such term (not exceeding the permitted maximum) as in the opinion of the court is commensurate with the seriousness of the offence, or the combination of the offence and other offences associated with it; or

    (b) where the offence is a violent or sexual offence, for such longer term (not exceeding that maximum) as in the opinion of the court is necessary to protect the public from serious harm from the offender.

(3) Where the court passes a custodial sentence for a term longer than is commensurate with the seriousness of the offence, or the combination of the offence and other offences associated with it, the court shall—

    (a) state in open court that it is of the opinion that subsection (2)(b) above applies and why it is of that opinion; and

    (b) explain to the offender in open court and in ordinary language why the sentence is for such a term.

(4) A custodial sentence for an indeterminate period shall be regarded for the purposes of subsections (2) and (3) above as a custodial sentence for a term longer than any actual term.

29. Effect of previous convictions etc.

(1) An offence shall not be regarded as more serious for the purposes of any provision of

this Part by reason of any previous convictions of the offender or any failure of his to respond to previous sentences.

(2) Where any aggravating factors of an offence are disclosed by the circumstances of other offences committed by the offender, nothing in this Part shall prevent the court from taking those factors into account for the purpose of forming an opinion as to the seriousness of the offence.

NOTES AND QUESTIONS
1. What theory of punishment underlies ss. 1(2)(a) and 2(2)(a) of the 1991 Act? Sections 1(2)(b) and 2(2)(b)? Section 29?
2. The White Paper preceding the Act (*Crime, Justice, and Protecting the Public* (Cmd. 965, 1990)) had this to say about deterrence:

> [M]uch crime is committed on impulse, given the opportunity presented by an open window or unlocked door, and it is committed by offenders who live from moment to moment; their crimes are as impulsive as the rest of their feckless, sad or pathetic lives. It is unrealistic to construct sentencing arrangements on the assumption that most offenders will weigh up the possibilities in advance and base their conduct on rational calculation. Often they do not.

Compare the Criminal Justice Act 1991 with the Crime (Sentences) Act 1997 (the substance of which has now been repealed by the Powers of Criminal Courts (Sentencing) Act 2000):

Crime (Sentences) Act 1997

2. Mandatory life sentence for second serious offence
(1) This section applies where–
   (a) a person is convicted of a serious offence committed after the commencement of this section; and
   (b) at the time when that offence was committed, he was 18 or over and had been convicted in any part of the United Kingdom of another serious offence.
(2) The court shall impose a life sentence, that is to say—
   (a) where the person is 21 or over, a sentence of imprisonment for life;
   (b) where he is under 21, a sentence of custody for life under section 8(2) of the Criminal Justice Act 1982 ('the 1982 Act'),
unless the court is of the opinion that there are exceptional circumstances relating to either of the offences or to the offender which justify its not doing so.
(3) Where the court does not impose a life sentence, it shall state in open court that it is of that opinion and what the exceptional circumstances are.
(4) An offence the sentence for which is imposed under subsection (2) above shall not be regarded as an offence the sentence for which is fixed by law.
(5) An offence committed in England and Wales is a serious offence for the purposes of this section if it is any of the following, namely—
   (a) an attempt to commit murder, a conspiracy to commit murder or an incitement to murder;
   (b) an offence under section 4 of the offences Against the Person Act 1861 (soliciting murder);
   (c) manslaughter;
   (d) an offence under section 18 of the Offences Against the Person Act 1861 (wounding, or causing grievous bodily harm, with intent);
   (e) rape or an attempt to commit rape;

    (f) an offence under section 5 of the Sexual Offences Act 1956 (intercourse with a girl under 13);

    (g) an offence under section 16 (possession of a firearm with intent to injure), section 17 (use of a firearm to resist arrest) or section 18 (carrying a firearm with criminal intent) of the Firearms Act 1968; and

    (h) robbery where, at some time during the commission of the offences, the offender had in his possession a firearm or imitation firearm within the meaning of that Act.

3. Minimum of seven years for third class A drug trafficking offence

(1) This section applies where—

    (a) a person is convicted of a class A drug trafficking offence committed after the commencement of this section;

    (b) at the time when that offence was committed, he was 18 or over and had been convicted in any part of the United Kingdom of two other class A drug trafficking offences; and

    (c) one of those other offences was committed after he had been convicted of the other.

(2) The court shall impose a custodial sentence for a term of at least seven years except where the court is of the opinion that there are specific circumstances which—

    (a) relate to any of the offences or to the offender; and

    (b) would make the prescribed custodial sentence unjust in circumstances.

(3) Where the court does not impose such a sentence, it shall state in open court that it is of that opinion and what the specific circumstances are.

4. Minimum of three years for third domestic burglary

(1) This section applies where—

    (a) a person is convicted of a domestic burglary committed after the commencement of this section;

    (b) at the time when that burglary was committed, he was 18 or over and had been convicted in England and Wales of two other domestic burglaries; and

    (c) one of those other burglaries was committed after he had been convicted of the other, and both of them were committed after the commencement of this section.

(2) The court shall impose a custodial sentence for a term of at least three years except where the court is of the opinion that there are specific circumstances which—

    (a) relate to any of the offences or to the offender; and

    (b) would make the prescribed custodial sentence unjust in all the circumstances.

(3) Where the court does not impose such a sentence, it shall state in open court that it is of that opinion and what the specific circumstances are.

NOTES AND QUESTIONS

1. What theories of punishment underlie the Crime (Sentences) Act 1997? Are these the same theories which underlie the 1991 Act? Philosophies of punishment sometimes seem to change like fashions in clothes.

2. While general deterrence theory may seem to suggest that harsh punishments are likely to lead to a decrease in crime, sometimes they can have the opposite effect. Consider the offender who commits a non-homicide crime that might lead to life imprisonment under the 1997 Act. The offender might rationally decide to reduce the likelihood of a conviction by murdering any witnesses. In the offender's view, little may be lost, for the penalty for murder is also life imprisonment.

3. In addition to being implicit in legislation, a philosophy of punishment may be seen in judicial thinking, most typically when a court is called upon to review a sentence.

R v Sargeant

(1974) 60 Cr App R 74, Court of Appeal

LAWTON LJ: On May 20, 1974, at the Central Criminal Court, the appellant pleaded guilty to a charge of affray at the end of the prosecution's case. On May 24, 1974, he was sentenced by His Honour Judge Argyle to two years' imprisonment. He now appeals against that sentence.

During the evening of October 26, 1973, the appellant was on duty at a discotheque at Crown Hill at Croydon, together with three other doormen. Their job in colloquial language was to act as 'bouncers.' The appellant had no criminal record. The other bouncers had. One of them had a bad criminal record. There was another man on the staff of this discotheque who was taking part in what the prosecution alleged was the affray. He too had a bad criminal record.

. . . [The] appellant has had no previous convictions. He is 26 years of age, and a skilled green-keeper in the golfing world. He started acting as an assistant green-keeper in his adolescence. He has acquired a good deal of expertise. He has had jobs as green-keeper with a number of distinguished and well-known golf clubs. The tragedy of his case is that the very day on which he appeared at the Central Criminal Court he should have been starting work as head green-keeper with one of the best known golf clubs in the south of England. His conviction has inevitably meant that that job is no longer available to him, and it also means that there is a strong possibility that no golf club will ever employ him again. By his stupidity on this occasion he has deprived himself of a career in the golfing world, and all because he lost his temper when trouble started. The very fact that he has lost his career is of course a severe penalty for him.

The problem for this Court is whether the sentence was wrong in principle. It is necessary for this Court to analyse the facts of this case. We have come to the conclusion that, if the trial judge did analyse them, he analysed them incorrectly. What really was the case against this appellant? His job was to help to keep order. He was inexperienced in that job. It is clear from his record that he is inclined to be headstrong. I say that, because despite his skill as a green-keeper, he has had some difficulty in keeping jobs, because he cannot always see eye to eye with golf clubs' secretaries. He had had something to drink whilst he was on duty that night, though there was nothing to suggest that he had had too much to drink. If he had followed the instructions of his employers, he would not have had anything to drink. He was faced with a situation in which a young man had been misbehaving. He took the view, wrongly with hindsight, that the best way of dealing with the potential difficulties which that young man might cause, if he resumed misbehaving, was to use some force on him. He used no weapon. What he did do was to butt the young man, which can be very painful for the victim. If he had thought for a moment, he would have appreciated the nature and extent of the chain of events which he was starting. It is almost certain that he did not think. Young men who act in this kind of physical way seldom do think of which the consequences are going to be. The evidence establishes that very soon after he did what he did he was put out of action and took no further part in the appalling violence which followed.

What ought the proper penalty to be? We have thought it necessary not only to analyse the facts, but to apply to those facts the classical principles of sentencing. Those classical principles are summed up in four words: retribution, deterrence, prevention and rehabilitation. Any judge who comes to sentence ought always to have those four classical principles in mind and to apply them to the facts of the case to see which of them has the greatest importance in the case with which he is dealing.

I will start with retribution. The Old Testament concept of an eye for an eye and tooth for tooth no longer plays any part in our criminal law. There is, however, another aspect of retribution which is frequently overlooked; it is that society, through the courts, must show its abhorrence of particular types of crime, and the only way in which the courts can show this is by the sentences they pass. The courts do not have to reflect public opinion. On the other hand courts must not disregard it. Perhaps the main duty of the court is to lead public opinion. Anyone who surveys the criminal scene at the present time must be alive to the appalling problem of violence. Society, we are satisfied, expects the courts to deal with violence. The weapons which the courts have at their disposal for doing so are few. We are satisfied that in most cases fines are not sufficient punishment for senseless violence. The time has come, in the opinion of this Court, when those who indulge in the kind of violence with which we are concerned in this case must expect custodial sentences.

But we are also satisfied that, although society expects the courts to impose punishment for violence which really hurts, it does not expect the courts to go on hurting for a long time, which is what this sentence is likely to do. We agree with the trial judge that the kind of violence which occurred in this case called for a custodial sentence. This young man has had a custodial sentence. Despite his good character, despite the excellent background from which he comes, very deservedly he has had the humiliation of hearing prison gates closing behind him. We take the view that for men of good character the very fact that prison gates have closed is the main punishment. It does not necessarily follow that they should remain closed for a long time.

I turn now to the element of deterrence, because it seems to us the trial judge probably passed this sentence as a deterrent one. There are two aspects of deterrence: deterrence of the offender and deterrence of likely offenders. Experience has shown over the years that deterrence of the offender is not a very useful approach, because those who have their wits about them usually find the closing of prison gates an experience which they do not want again. If they do not learn that lesson, there is likely to be a high degree of recidivism anyway. So far as deterrence of others is concerned, it is the experience of the courts that deterrent sentences are of little value in respect of offences which are committed on the spur of the moment, either in hot blood or in drink or both. Deterrent sentences may very well be of considerable value where crime is premeditated. Burglars, robbers and users of firearms and weapons may very well be put off by deterrent sentences. We think it unlikely that deterrence would be of any value in this case.

We come now to the element of prevention. Unfortunately it is one of the facts of life that there are some offenders for whom neither deterrence nor rehabilitation works. They will go on committing crimes as long as they are able to do so. In those cases the only protection which the public has is that such persons should be locked up for a long period. This case does not call for a preventive sentence.

Finally, there is the principle of rehabilitation. Some 20 to 25 years ago there was a view abroad, held by many people in executive authority, that short sentences were of little value, because there was not enough time to give in prison the benefit of training. That view is no longer held as firmly as it was. This young man does not want prison training. It is not going to do him any good. It is his memory of the clanging of prison gates which is likely to keep him from crime in the future.

In the light of that analysis of the classical principles to be applied in sentencing, what is the result on the facts of this case? The answer is that this sentence is much too long. It was submitted that a suspended sentence should have been passed. For the reasons I have already given, we do not agree. But we are satisfied, having regard to the facts of this case and the social inquiry and prison reports which the Court has been given that we can deal with this case by substituting for the sentence which was passed such a sentence as will enable him to be discharged today. To that extent the appeal is allowed.

NOTES AND QUESTIONS

1. Is the matter of the appropriate theory (theories) of punishment for the legislature or the judiciary to decide? Is it appropriate for courts in individual cases to go against the philosophy of punishment embodied in legislation?

2. The court in *Sargeant* states its view that 'for men of good character the very fact that the prison gates have closed is the main punishment'. Would sentencing based on 'character'

(whatever the court means by this term) be discriminatory, in violation of Article 14 of the European Convention on Human Rights?

E: The limits of permissible punishments

Increasingly, punishments authorised by statute are being challenged as violative of the Human Rights Act 1998.

[2001] 4 All ER 934, Queen's Bench Division, Divisional Court and Court of Appeal (Criminal Division)

KENNEDY LJ: [1] Each of these claimants seeks judicial review of a decision to impose a mandatory sentence of life imprisonment following their separate convictions for murder. They contend that s 1 of the Murder (Abolition of Death Penalty) Act 1965 is incompatible with arts 3 and 5 of the European Convention for the Protection of Human Rights and Fundamental Freedoms (Rome, 4 November 1950; TS 71 (1953); Cmd 8969) (as set out in Sch 1 to the Human Rights Act 1998). Section 1(1) of the 1965 Act so far as material provides that 'a person convicted of murder shall . . . be sentenced to imprisonment for life'. Article 3 of the convention reads: 'No one shall be subjected to torture or to inhuman or degrading treatment or punishment.'

[2] Article 5 so far as material reads:

'1. Everyone has the right to liberty and security of person. No one shall be deprived of his liberty save in the following cases and in accordance with a procedure prescribed by law:
(a) the lawful detention of a person after conviction by a competent court . . .'

[3] Permission to apply for judicial review was granted by Scott Baker J on 23 January 2001 when he also ordered that this court sit both as a Divisional Court and as the Court of Appeal (Criminal Division), which we have done.

. . .

The basic submission

[9] Mr Fitzgerald's basic submission is that now that all mandatory life sentences are recognised to fall into two parts, namely first a penal element to meet the requirements of retribution and general deterrence (fixed by the Home Secretary after considering the views of the trial judge and the Lord Chief Justice) and, secondly, a subsequent period of detention justified on preventive grounds, life sentences should not be imposed where at the time of sentencing there is no foreseeable risk of the defendant being a danger to the public after he or she has served the penal element of the sentence. Referring to the convention, Mr Fitzgerald argues that the mandatory life sentence has no clear penological objective. It violates art 5 because it is arbitrary, and art 3 because it is disproportionate. Before we turn to look at these submissions in more detail we must say something about the jurisdiction of this court.

. . .

General approach

[19] Mr Fitzgerald submits that under art 5 of the convention the basic principle is that no one should be deprived of their liberty in an arbitrary fashion, and that if a life sentence is imposed where there is no objective justification for that sentence then the sentence is both arbitrary and disproportionate. Under art 3 a sentence which is manifestly disproportionate can be an 'inhuman and degrading' punishment.

[20] For the defendant Mr Pannick's response is that these issues have been addressed by the European Court of Human Rights in *V v UK, T v UK* (1999) 30 EHRR 121, where the appellants had

been sentenced to be detained during Her Majesty's pleasure. That too is a sentence which is automatically imposed where a defendant of the prescribed age is convicted of murder. It is imposed irrespective of the circumstances of the offence and of the offender. Some offenders may present no risk of future offending, and may have committed an offence less grave than other offences which do not require a mandatory indeterminate sentence from which the offender will only be released after serving a tariff period, when it is considered that he may safely be released, and on the basis that thereafter he will be at risk of recall for the rest of his life. In other words, Mr Pannick submits, for present purposes the cases of *T* and *V* are indistinguishable on their facts, and this court is required by s 2(1) of the 1998 Act to take into account the decisions of the European Court. Mr Fitzgerald submits that in *V v UK*, *T v UK* there was an important distinction, in that the two boys could not be regarded as presenting no danger if released at the end of their tariff period, and that is something which we must examine more closely in due course.

[21] Mr Pannick goes on to submit that there was a very good reason why the European Court decided *V v UK*, *T v UK* as it did – namely because an indeterminate sentence (whether it be mandatory life imprisonment or detention during Her Majesty's pleasure) allows for and involves in practice an individualised assessment of tariff, risk and recall, so that it is neither degrading nor arbitrary. It may be that an assessment should not be made by the executive, but that is not something for consideration in this case.

. . .

[23] Mr Pannick further submits that there are three principles established under the convention to which we must have regard. First, the relevant provisions of the convention require a balance between the interests of the applicant and those of the community. In *Soering v UK* (1989) 11 EHRR 439 a West German national was seeking to avoid extradition to Virginia to face a charge of capital murder, and in its judgment the court said (at 468 (para 89)).

> '. . . inherent in the whole of the Convention is a search for a fair balance between the demands of the general interest of the community and the requirements of the protection of the individual's fundamental rights.'

[24] Secondly, the European Court in its approach to the convention does not concentrate on formal procedures, but looks at the realities. In *Van Droogenbroeck v Belgium* (1982) 4 EHRR 443, a case concerned with detention of a recidivist, the court said (at 456 (para 38)) 'one must look beyond the appearances and the language used and concentrate on the realities of the situation'. Here, Mr Pannick submits, the claimants are putting too much weight on the language used when a judge sentences a defendant to life imprisonment, and not concentrating on the realities of the situation.

[25] Thirdly, Mr Pannick reminds us that in *Brown v Stott (Procurator Fiscal, Dunfermline)* [2001] 2 All ER 97 at 114, [2001] 2 WLR 817 at 834 Lord Bingham of Cornhill said:

> 'Judicial recognition and assertion of the human rights defined in the convention is not a substitute for the processes of democratic government but a complement to them. While a national court does not accord the margin of appreciation recognised by the European Court as a supra-national court, it will give weight to the decisions of a representative legislature and a democratic government within the discretionary area of judgment accorded to those bodies.'

Other members of the Privy Council made observations to the same effect. That, he submits, is of particular relevance to a controversial issue of policy which has been the subject of repeated consideration by Parliament. In his reply Mr Fitzgerald reminded us of an additional principle, that decisions of the European Court and Commission are made on their particular facts rather than reviewing national law in abstracto (see *Håkansson and Sturesson v Sweden* (1990) 13 EHRR 1 at 11 (para 46)). Decisions need to be read with that in mind.

Previous litigation

[26] Mr Pannick submits that this case is the latest in a series of cases in England and in Strasbourg which have challenged various aspects of the requirement that a life sentence be imposed after a conviction for murder. Each challenge has failed because on each occasion the courts have said that Parliament is entitled to maintain its statutory requirement.

Article 3

[34] In *Costello-Roberts v UK* (1993) 19 EHRR 112, a case about corporal punishment in a school, the European Court stated (at 133 (para 30)):

'. . . in order for punishment to be "degrading" and in breach of Article 3, the humiliation or debasement involved must attain a particular level of severity and must in any event be other than that usual element of humiliation inherent in any punishment. Indeed Article 3, by expressly prohibiting "inhuman" and "degrading" punishment, implies that there is a distinction between such punishment and punishment more generally. The assessment of this minimal level of severity depends on all the circumstances of the case. Factors such as the nature and context of the punishment, the manner and method of its execution, its duration, its physical and mental effects and, in some instances, the sex, age and state of health of the victim must all be taken into account.'

[35] In *V v UK, T v UK* (1999) 30 EHRR 121 the European Court considered whether that article could be invoked in relation to the sentence of detention during Her Majesty's pleasure passed on the two boys. It recorded the Commission's acceptance of the case for the government, saying (at 182 (para 95)):

'[The Commission] referred to [*Hussain v UK* (1996) 22 EHRR 1] where the Court held that the sentence of detention during Her Majesty's pleasure was primarily preventative, attracting the guarantees of Article 5(4). It could not, therefore, be said that the applicant had forfeited his liberty for life or that his detention gave rise to a violation of Article 3.'

[36] Mr Fitzgerald submits that the reference to *Hussain's* case is significant because in that case, which also concerned a sentence of detention during Her Majesty's pleasure, the court had said (at 24 (para 53)):

'. . . an indeterminate term of detention for a convicted young person, which may be as long as that person's life, can only be justified by considerations based on the need to protect the public.'

[37] The same point was repeated by the court in *V v UK, T v UK* (1999) 30 EHRR 121 at 183 (para 96). Thus the context, submits Mr Fitzgerald, is an indeterminate sentence for which the only justification is preventive.

[38] In *V v UK, T v UK* the court expressed its conclusion in relation to art 3, saying (at 183 (para 98)):

'The Court recalls that States have a duty under the Convention to take measures for the protection of the public from violent crime. It does not consider that the punitive element inherent in the tariff approach itself gives rise to a breach of Article 3, or that the Convention prohibits States from subjecting a child or young person convicted of a serious crime to an indeterminate sentence allowing for the offenders continued detention or recall to detention following release where necessary for the protection of the public.'

[39] As Mr Pannick points out, there is nothing there to suggest that the sentence will only be legitimate if at the time of sentencing it is envisaged that the offender will present an ongoing risk. Indeed para 99 (at 183) begins:

'The applicant has not yet reached the stage in his sentence where he is able to have the continued lawfulness of his detention reviewed with regard to the question of dangerousness . . .'

[40] That would tend to suggest that so far as the European Court was concerned any assessment of dangerousness that may or may not have been made at the time of sentence was of no significance. Overall, the court's conclusions are expressed in terms that indicate no objection under art 3 to a mandatory indeterminate sentence for murder.

[41] The only other decision to which we need refer in relation to art 3 is the decision on admissibility of the European Commission in *Bromfield v UK* (1 July 1998, unreported). There the applicant, aged 20, had been sentenced to custody for life after being convicted of murder. Dealing with his complaint in relation to art 3, para 2 of the decision states:

'The Commission recalls that there is no incompatibility with the convention in the imposition of a life sentence as a security or retributive measure in a particular case or in a decision to keep a recidivist or habitual offender at the disposal of the government (*Weeks v UK* (1987) 10 EHRR 293). While in the cases concerning detention during Her Majesty's pleasure, the court commented that a sentence pursuant to which young persons forfeited their liberty for the rest of their lives might raise issues under art 3 of the convention (see eg *Hussain v UK* (1996) 22 EHRR 1), the Commission considers that these remarks apply to sentences of life imprisonment imposed on children under the age of 18 to whom special considerations apply. It does not find that the imposition of a mandatory sentence of life imprisonment in respect of the offence of murder committed by young adults between the ages of 18 and 21 discloses treatment or punishment prohibited by art 3 of the convention.'

[42] In our judgment the weight of the jurisprudence is overwhelming. Whatever one may think about the desirability of a change of policy, it cannot be accepted that a mandatory sentence of life imprisonment for murder is incompatible with art 3. In reality, as Mr Pannick points out, the sentence is an indeterminate one – rarely will there be imprisonment for life. In other cases the penal element having been decided upon at a earlier stage, when that element has been served the Secretary of State may, if recommended to do so by the Parole Board, after consultation with the Lord Chief Justice and the trial judge if available, release the prisoner on licence (see s 29 of the Crime (Sentences) Act 1997). In practice the Secretary of State does refer cases to the Parole Board for consideration, and if a prisoner has been released on licence and is recalled he will have the opportunity to have his recall considered by the Parole Board (see s 31 of the 1997 Act). That is all part of what is involved in the mandatory life sentence, and in reality such a sentence, which includes the policy applied in relation to it, cannot be labelled inhuman or degrading. There is sufficient individualised consideration of the offender's case within the context of the sentence. Thus it is open to Parliament, acting within its discretionary area of judgment, to retain the sentence without violating art 3.

Article 5

[43] We turn now to the complaint in relation to art 5. Mr Fitzgerald submits that to have an indeterminate sentence for all murders is arbitrary. In some cases a lesser determinate sentence would suffice because culpability and the needs of retribution and deterrence can be evaluated at the end of the trial, and there is no discernible risk to warrant an indeterminate sentence. Furthermore, as such a sentence is at least in theory the most severe sentence available to an English judge it should not be imposed as a matter of course for murders where the gravity of the offence is less than the gravity of other crimes. It is arbitrary to impose a sentence that can neither be justified on preventive grounds nor justified on the basis of retributive proportionality.

. . .

[47] In so far as Mr Fitzgerald submits that where there is not a discernible risk of re-offending it is wrong to impose an indeterminate sentence, Mr Pannick responds by saying that such a submission falls outside the scope of art 5. In *Weeks v UK* (1987) 10 EHRR 293, a case concerned with the lawfulness of detention after recall, the European Court said (at 312 (para 50)) that 'it is not for the Court, within the context of Article 5, to review the appropriateness of the original sentence'. Even if that be wrong, Mr Pannick submits, and we accept, that a sentence cannot be arbitrary for an adult when an equivalent sentence has been found not to be so in the case of a young offender, and when in each case the application of the sentence is individualised, and everyone knows that it will be individualised from the moment it is imposed. Although, as Mr Fitzgerald pointed out, decisions of the European Court are related to their own particular facts, the process of reasoning displayed by the European Court is of assistance, as illustrated by both counsel during the course of this case. The reasoning in the decided cases tells strongly against the claimant's case on art 5.

. . .

Conclusion

[51] The arguments put forward by Mr Fitzgerald are persuasive in favour of a change of policy, and may carry weight in a political debate, but in our judgment, as the law now stands, they do not enable this court to allow these appeals against sentence on the basis that the mandatory sentences imposed were incompatible with the convention. We therefore dismiss these appeals.

Appeals dismissed. Court certifying that a point of law of general public importance was involved in its decision, namely 'Whether s 1(1) of the Murder (Abolition of Death Penalty) Act 1965 is incompatible with arts 3 and/or 5 of the European Convention on Human Rights'.

Matthew Barry, James Offen

[2001] 1 Cr App R 24, Court of Appeal . . .

LORD WOOLF CJ: This judgment relates to five appeals. In each case where leave is required to appeal against sentence, we give leave. The five appeals all involve section 2 of the Crime (Sentences) Act 1997 'the 1997 Act'. (This is now section 109 Powers of the Criminal Courts (Sentencing) Act 2000. In this judgment we will refer to section 2 in the 1997 Act.) The application of section 2 has already given rise to a number of decisions by this Court. They illustrate the problems which can arise in practice in applying statutory provisions which require the courts to impose an automatic life sentence on certain offenders.

The policy of Parliament for establishing the automatic life sentences emerges clearly from the then Government's White Paper, *Protecting the Public, the Government's Strategy on Crime in England and Wales* (1996). In Cm 3190, paragraph 10.11 the White Paper states:

> 'Too often in the past, those who had shown a propensity to commit serious, violent or sex offences have served their sentences and been released only to offend again. In many such cases the danger of releasing the offender has been plain for all to see – but nothing could be done, because once the offender has completed the sentence imposed, he or she has to be released. Too often, victims have paid the price when the offender has repeated the same offences. The Government is determined that the public should receive proper protection from persistent violent or sex offenders. That means requiring the courts to impose an automatic indeterminate sentence, and releasing the offender if and only if it is safe to do so.'

In *Buckland* [2000] 1 Cr.App.R.471; [2000] 1 W.L.R. 1262 Lord Bingham of Cornhill C.J. described the rationale of section 2 in these terms, at pages 478 and 1268:

'The section is founded on an assumption that those who have been convicted of two qualifying serious offences present such a serious and continuing danger to the safety of the public that they should be liable to indefinite incarceration and, if released should be liable indefinitely to recall to prison. In any case where, on all the evidence, it appears that such a danger does or may exist, it is hard to see how the court can consider itself justified in not imposing the statutory penalty, even if exceptional circumstances are found to exist. But if exceptional circumstances are found, and the evidence suggests that an offender does not present a serious and continuing danger to the safety of the public, the court may be justified in imposing a lesser penalty.'

The reason why we have heard these appeals together is because in each case it is contended that either the interpretation of section 2 of the 1997 Act is affected by section 3 of the Human Rights Act 1998 ('the 1998 Act'), or that section 2 is incompatible with a Convention right so that the appellants are entitled to a declaration of incompatibility. The impact of the 1998 Act on the interpretation of legislation arises under section 3 of the Act, which provides:

'3.—(1) So far as it is possible to do so, primary legislation and subordinate legislation must be read and given effect in a way which is compatible with the Convention rights.'

The legislation
5. Section 2 of the 1997 Act, so far as relevant, is in the following terms:

'(1) This section applies where—

(a) a person is convicted of a serious offence committed after the commencement of this section; and

(b) at the time when that offence was committed, he was 18 or over and had been convicted in any part of the United Kingdom of another serious offence.

(2) The court shall impose a life sentence, that is to say—

(a) where the person is 21 or over, a sentence of imprisonment for life;

(b) where he is under 21, a sentence of custody for life under section (2) of the Criminal Justice Act 1982 ("the 1982 Act"),

unless the court is of the opinion that there are *exceptional circumstances relating to either of the offences or to the offender which justify its not doing so*. [Emphasis added.]

(3) Where the court does not impose a life sentence, it shall state in open court that it is of that opinion and what the exceptional circumstances are.

(4) An offence the sentence for which is imposed under sub-section (2) above shall not be regarded as an offence the sentence for which is fixed by law.

(5) An offence committed in England and Wales is a serious offence for the purposes of this section if it is any of the following, namely—

(a) an attempt to commit murder, a conspiracy to commit murder or an incitement to murder;

(b) an offence under section 4 of the Offences against the Person Act 1861 (soliciting murder);

(c) manslaughter;

(d) an offence under section 18 of the Offences against the Person Act 1861 (wounding, or causing grievous bodily harm, with intent);

(e) rape or an attempt to commit rape;

(f) an offence under section 5 of the Sexual Offences Act 1956 (intercourse with a girl under 13);

(g) an offence under section 16 (possession of a firearm with intent to injure), section 17 (use of a firearm to resist arrest) or section 18 (carrying a firearm with criminal intent) of the Firearms Act 1968; and

(h) robbery where, at some time during the commission of the offence, the offender had in his possession a firearm or imitation firearm within the meaning of that Act.'

The following features of the section will be noted:

(i) It refers to two offences having been committed by the offender.

(ii) It is only the second offence (the 'trigger offence') which has to have been committed after the commencement of the section. The earlier offence may have been committed at any time.

(iii) When the second offence is committed the offender is required to be over 18, but there is no age requirement in relation to the first offence.

(iv) The proviso of 'exceptional circumstances' applies to both offences. The 'exceptional circumstances' can relate either to the offences or to the offender but what constitutes exceptional circumstances is not otherwise defined by the section.

(v) All offences identified as serious offences are offences for which life imprisonment could be imposed quite apart from section 2.

. . .

The Human Rights Act 1998

The appellants contend that as previously applied, section 2 of the 1997 Act is incompatible with Articles 3, 5, 7 and 8 of the Convention.

Article 7

As the argument as to Article 7 is discrete, it is convenient to start with that Article. It is Article 7.1 which is relevant. It provides:

> 'No one shall be held guilty of any criminal offence on account of any actual omission which did not constitute a criminal offence under national or international law at the time it was committed. Nor shall a heavier penalty be imposed than one that was applicable at the time the criminal offence was committed.'

. . .

Mr Fitzgerald advances the argument, which is adopted by all appellants, that there is a contravention. He submits that the argument has two aspects. Both involve changing the consequences of a conviction of the first serious offence after the date of the offence and after the sentence for which it was imposed. It is submitted that after a punishment for the first serious offence had been imposed, the subsequent coming into force of section 2 increased the penalty for the initial offence since the offender then became liable, if he committed a further serious offence, to be automatically sentenced to life imprisonment. It is also submitted that section 2 itself increased the penalty for the first serious offence since on conviction of the second serious offence a life sentence would be imposed, in reality, in respect of both offences.

Mr Fitzgerald's argument was well illustrated by the practice in Association Football of sending off a player who is shown two yellow cards. If the rule which brings this about was to be imposed after one yellow card had been shown this would give greater significance to the first yellow card than was the case when it was shown. It could adversely affect a player, since if a player knew he would be sent off if he had two yellow cards, he would make greater efforts to avoid being shown even the first yellow card.

This attractive argument depends upon treating the life sentence as being imposed at least in part for both offences. This is not, however, the manner in which, in our judgment, section 2 works. Section 2 imposes the penalty of the automatic life sentence for the second offence alone. The imposition of the automatic life sentence is, however, subject to certain conditions. Those are that the offender was 18 or over and that he had been previously convicted of another serious offence. The language of section 2(1) makes this clear. The sentence is not being imposed in relation to the earlier offence.

Articles 3 and 5

The relevant provisions of Article 3 and Article 5 are as follows:

'Article 3: Prohibition of torture

No one shall be subjected to torture or to inhuman or degrading treatment or punishment.'

'Article 5: Right to Liberty and Security

1. Everyone has the right to liberty and security of person. No one shall be deprived of his liberty save in the following cases and in accordance with a procedure prescribed by law:

(a) the lawful detention of a person after conviction by a competent court.

. . .

4. Everyone who is deprived of his liberty by arrest or detention shall be entitled to take proceedings by which the lawfulness of his detention shall be decided speedily by a court and his release ordered if the detention is not lawful.'

In approaching these articles, it is important to recognise that the 1998 Act is a constitutional instrument introducing into domestic law the relevant articles of the Convention. The consequence of section 3 is that legislation which affects human rights is required to be construed in a manner which conforms with the Convention wherever this is possible.

. . .

The problem arises because of the restrictive approach which has so far been adopted to the interpretation of exceptional circumstances in section 2. If exceptional circumstances are construed in a manner which accords with the policy of Parliament in passing section 2, the problem disappears.

Section 2 establishes a norm. The norm is that those who commit two serious offences are a danger or risk to the public. If in fact, taking into account all the circumstances relating to a particular offender, he does not create an unacceptable risk to the public, he is an exception to this norm. If the offences are of a different kind, or if there is a long period which elapses between the offences during which the offender has not committed other offences, that may be a very relevant indicator as to the degree of risk to the public that he constitutes. Construing section 2 in accordance with the duty imposed upon us by section 3 of the 1998 Act, and taking into account the rationale of the section as identified by Lord Bingham gives content to exceptional circumstances. In our judgment, section 2 will not contravene Convention rights if courts apply the section so that it does not result in offenders being sentenced to life imprisonment when they do not constitute a significant risk to the public. Whether there is significant risk will depend on the evidence which is before the court. If the offender is a significant risk, the court can impose a life sentence under section 2 without contravening the Convention. Either there will be no exceptional circumstances, or despite the exceptional circumstances the facts will justify imposing a life sentence.

Under section 2 it will be part of the responsibility of judges to assess the risk to the public that offenders constitute. In many cases the degree of risk that an offender constitutes will be established by his record, with or without the assistance of assessments made in reports which are available to the court. If a court needs further assistance, they can call for it. The courts have traditionally had to make a similar assessment when deciding whether a discretionary life sentence should be imposed. There should be no undue difficulty in making a similar assessment when considering whether the court is required to impose an automatic life sentence, although the task will not be straightforward, because of the lack of information as to the first serious offence which will sometimes exist because of the passage of time.

This does not mean that we are approaching the passing of an automatic life sentence as though it is no different from the imposition of a discretionary life sentence. Notwithstanding the interpretation resulting from the application of section 3(1) of the 1998 Act suggested, section 2 will still give effect to the intention of Parliament. It will do so, however, in a more just, less arbitrary and more proportionate manner. Section 2 will still mean that a judge is obliged to pass a life sentence in accordance with its terms unless, in all the circumstances, the offender poses no significant risk to the public. There is no such obligation in cases where section 2 does not apply. In addition, if the judge decides not to impose a life sentence under section 2, he will have to give reasons as required by section 2(3). Furthermore, the issue of dangerousness will have to be addressed in every case and a decision made as to whether or not to impose a life sentence.

The objective of the legislature will be achieved, because it will be mandatory to impose a life sentence in situations where the offender constitutes a significant risk to the public. Section 2 therefore provides a good example of how the 1998 Act can have a beneficial effect on the administration of justice, without defeating the policy which Parliament was seeking to implement.

In view of our conclusions as to the impact of Articles 3 and 5, it is not necessary to consider Article 8.

Tyrer v *United Kingdom*
(1978) 2 EHRR 1, European Court of Human Rights

Mr Anthony M. Tyrer, a citizen of the United Kingdom born on 21 September 1956, is resident in Castletown, Isle of Man. On 7 March 1972, being then aged 15 and of previous good character, he pleaded guilty before the local juvenile court to unlawful assault occasioning actual bodily harm to a senior pupil at his school. The assault, committed by the applicant in company with three other boys, was apparently motivated by the fact that the victim had reported the boys for taking beer into the school, as a result of which they had been caned. The applicant was sentenced on the same day to three strokes of the birch in accordance with the relevant legislation. . . .

The applicant claimed before the Commission that the facts of his case constituted a breach of Article 3 of the Convention which provides:

> No one shall be subjected to torture or to inhuman or degrading treatment or punishment.

He alleged that there had been torture or inhuman or degrading treatment or punishment, or any combination thereof. . . .

The Court shares the Commission's view that Mr Tyrer's punishment did not amount to 'torture' within the meaning of Article 3. The Court does not consider that the facts of this particular case reveal that the applicant underwent suffering of the level inherent in this notion as it was interpreted and applied by the Court in its judgment of 18 January 1978 (*Ireland* v *The United Kingdom*, Series A no. 25, pp. 66–67 and 68, paras 167 and 174).

That judgment also contains various indications concerning the notions of 'inhuman treatment' and 'degrading treatment' but it deliberately left aside the notions of 'inhuman punishment' and 'degrading punishment' which alone are relevant in the present case. Those indications accordingly cannot, as such, serve here. Nevertheless, it remains true that the suffering occasioned must attain a particular level before a punishment can be classified as 'inhuman' within the meaning of Article 3. Here again, the Court does not consider on the facts of the case that that level was attained and it therefore concurs with the Commission that the penalty imposed on Mr Tyrer was not 'inhuman punishment' within the meaning of Article 3. Accordingly, the only question for decision is whether he was subjected to a 'degrading punishment' contrary to that Article.

[T]he prohibition contained in Article 3 of the Convention is absolute: no provision is made for exceptions and, under Article 15(2) there can be no derogation from Article 3. It would be absurd to hold that judicial punishment generally, by reason of its usual and perhaps almost inevitable element of humiliation, is 'degrading' within the meaning of Article 3. Some further criterion must be read into the text. Indeed, Article 3, by expressly prohibiting 'inhuman' and 'degrading' punishment, implies that there is a distinction between such punishment and punishment in general.

In the Court's view, in order for a punishment to be 'degrading' and in breach of Article 3, the humiliation or debasement involved must attain a particular level and must in any event be other than that usual element of humiliation referred to in the preceding subparagraph. The assessment is, in the nature of things, relative: it depends on all the circumstances of the case and, in particular, on the nature and context of the punishment itself and the manner and method of its execution.

. . .

[A] punishment does not lose its degrading character just because it is believed to be, or actually is, an effective deterrent or aid to crime control. Above all, as the Court must emphasise, it is never permissible to have recourse to punishments which are contrary to Article 3, whatever their deterrent effect may be.

The Court must also recall that the Convention is a living instrument which, as the Commission rightly stressed, must be interpreted in the light of present-day conditions. In the case now before it the Court cannot but be influenced by the developments and commonly accepted standards in the penal policy of the member States of the Council of Europe in this field. Indeed, the Attorney-General for the Isle of Man mentioned that, for many years, the provisions of Manx legislation concerning judicial corporal punishment had been under review.

As regards the manner and method of execution of the birching inflicted on Mr Tyrer, the Attorney-General for the Isle of Man drew particular attention to the fact that the punishment was carried out in private and without publication of the name of the offender.

Publicity may be a relevant factor in assessing whether a punishment is 'degrading' within the meaning of Article 3, but the Court does not consider that absence of publicity will necessarily prevent a given punishment from falling into that category: it may well suffice that the victim is humiliated in his own eyes, even if not in the eyes of others.

The very nature of judicial corporal punishment is that it involves one human being inflicting physical violence on another human being. Furthermore, it is institutionalised violence, that is in the present case violence permitted by the law, ordered by the judicial authorities of the State and carried out by the police authorities of the State. Thus, although the applicant did not suffer any severe or long-lasting physical effects, his punishment – whereby he was treated as an object in the power of the authorities – constituted an assault on precisely that which it is one of the main purposes of Article 3 to protect, namely a person's dignity and physical integrity. Neither can it be excluded that the punishment may have had adverse psychological effects.

In the present case, the Court does not consider it relevant that the sentence of judicial corporal punishment was imposed on the applicant for an offence of violence. Neither does it consider it relevant that, for Mr Tyrer, birching was an alternative to a period of detention: the fact that one penalty may be preferable to, or have less adverse effects or be less serious than, another penalty does not of itself mean that the first penalty is not 'degrading' within the meaning of Article 3.

Accordingly, viewing these circumstances as a whole the Court finds that the applicant was Subjected to a punishment in which the element of humiliation attained the level inherent in the notion of 'degrading punishment'. The indignity of having the punishment administered over the bare posterior aggravated to some extent the degrading character of the applicant's punishment but it was not the only or determining factor.

The Court therefore concludes that the judicial corporal punishment inflicted on the applicant amounted to degrading punishment within the meaning of Article 3 of the Convention.

NOTES AND QUESTIONS

1. Was the 'degrading' nature of the punishment in *Tyrer* aggravated or diminished by the fact that the defendant was a juvenile? Is all corporal punishment to be condemned under Article 3?
2. In *Soering* v *United Kingdom* (1989) 11 EHRR 439, the European Court of Human Rights had to consider the extradition of a German national to the US State of Virginia, which intended to

put him on trial for murder. Had he been convicted, he was potentially subject to the death penalty. The European Court, while 'declining' to find the death penalty *per se* violative of Article 3, was of the opinion that the extended period on death-row which US prisoners often had to endure before their execution could amount to torture or inhuman or degrading treatment in violation of Article 3. See also the decision of the European Commission in *Altum* v *Germany* (1983) 36 DR 209.

2

Deconstructing a Crime

In this chapter we shift our attention from theoretical questions of criminalisation and punishment to the more practical question of how one identifies a crime and what are its component parts. Identifying the elements of a crime is particularly important, for it is the responsibility of the Crown to establish each and every element by proof beyond a reasonable doubt (see *Woolmington* v *DPP* [1935] AC 462); for a defendant to secure an acquittal, he needs only to create a reasonable doubt about one – not all – of the elements. The first step in achieving either goal lies in identifying the elements of the offence. Two ways of analysing a crime are presented in this chapter. The first is a conceptual model, which does not focus on any particular crime but instead seeks to identify the generic components of a crime and understand how they fit together. The second approach involves looking at each crime on an individualistic basis and attempting to break it down into its elements. This requires attention not only to the words of the statute but also to how they have been construed by the courts. The two approaches are not mutually exclusive, as we shall see, and the conscientious student and lawyer will use the two in tandem.

SECTION 1: **What is a crime?**

How can one tell whether or not a statute creates a 'crime'? This is important to know for it will determine not only the potential consequences of failing to abide by the law, but also the procedures which will be followed if a legal trial ensues. Indeed, the latter point was given central prominence by Glanville Williams in his definition of a crime as an act capable of being followed by criminal proceedings (Williams, 'The Definition of Crime' [1955] *Current Legal Problems* 107). The problem with this definition is that it puts the cart before the horse. As the jurisprudence of the European Court of Human Rights (whose decisions must be taken into account by domestic UK courts under the Human Rights Act 1998) reveals, often it is crucial to determine whether an offence or charge is criminal in order to determine what procedures apply. In making this determination, a court is not bound by the characterisation placed on the proceeding by Parliament:

Benham v *United Kingdom*
(1996) 22 EHRR 293, European Court of Human Rights

I. Circumstances of the case

On 1 April 1990 Mr Benham became liable to pay a community charge of £325. Since he did not pay it, on 21 August 1990 the Poole Magistrates' Court ordered the issue of a liability order, entitling Poole Borough Council ('the charging authority') to commence enforcement proceedings against him.

Mr Benham did not pay the amount owed, and bailiffs visited his parents' house (where he was living), but were told that he had no goods of any value there or elsewhere which could be seized by them and sold in order to pay the debt.

Under Regulation 41 of the Community Charge (Administration and Enforcement) Regulations 1989 if a person is found to have insufficient goods on which to levy outstanding community charge the charging authority may apply to a magistrates' court for an order committing him to prison. On such an application being made, the court must inquire in the presence of the debtor as to his present means and also whether his failure to pay which led to the liability order being made was due to wilful refusal or culpable neglect.

The charging authority applied for such an order, and on 25 March 1991 Mr Benham appeared at the Poole Magistrates' Court for the inquiry required by the Regulations.

He was not assisted or represented by a lawyer, although he was eligible for 'Green Form' legal advice and assistance before the hearing, and the magistrates could have made an order for Assistance by Way of Representation ('ABWOR') if they had thought it necessary.

The magistrates found that Mr Benham, who had 9 '0' level General Certificates of Secondary Education, had started a Government Employment Training Scheme in September 1989, but had left it in March 1990 and had not worked since. He had applied for income support, but had been turned down because it is not payable to those who are voluntarily unemployed, and he had no personal assets or income.

On the basis of this evidence, the magistrates concluded that his failure to pay the community charge was due to his culpable neglect, 'as he clearly had the potential to earn money to discharge his obligation to pay'. Accordingly, they decided that he ought to be sent to prison for thirty days unless he paid what was owing.

Mr Benham was taken to Dorchester prison on the same day.

. . .

The applicant, with whom the Commission agreed, argued that the proceedings before the magistrates involved the determination of a criminal charge for the purposes of Article 6(3)(c). He referred to the facts that what was in issue was not a dispute between individuals but rather liability to pay a tax to a public authority, and that the proceedings had many 'criminal' features, such as the safeguards available to defendants aged under 21, the severity of the applicable penalty and the requirement of a finding of culpability before a term of imprisonment could be imposed. Furthermore, it was by no means clear that the proceedings were classified as civil rather than criminal under the domestic law.

The Government argued that Article 6(3)(c) did not apply because the proceedings before the magistrates were civil rather than criminal in nature, as was borne out by the weight of the English case-law. The purpose of the detention was to coerce the applicant into paying the tax owed, rather than to punish him for not having paid it.

The case-law of the Court establishes that there are three criteria to be taken into account when deciding whether a person was 'charged with a criminal offence' for the purposes of Article 6. These are the classification of the proceedings under national law, the nature of the proceedings and the nature and degree of severity of the penalty.

As to the first of these criteria, the Court agrees with the Government that the weight of the domestic authority indicates that, under English law, the proceedings in question are regarded as civil rather than criminal in nature. However, this factor is of relative weight and serves only as a starting-point.

The second criterion, the nature of the proceedings, carries more weight. In this connection, the Court notes that the law concerning liability to pay the community charge and the procedure upon non-payment was of general application to all citizens, and that the proceedings in question were brought by a public authority under statutory powers of enforcement. In addition, the proceedings had some punitive elements. For example, the magistrates could only exercise their power of committal to prison on a finding of wilful refusal to pay or of culpable neglect.

Finally, it is to be recalled that the applicant faced a relatively severe maximum penalty of three months' imprisonment and was in fact ordered to be detained for thirty days.

Having regard to these factors, the Court concludes that Mr Benham was 'charged with a criminal offence' for the purposes of Article 6(1) and (3). Accordingly, these two paragraphs of Article 6 are applicable. . . .

Campbell and Fell v United Kingdom
(1984) 7 EHRR 165, European Court of Human Rights

The applicants, both convicted prisoners, were injured during a disturbance in prison and were afterwards charged with contravening prison disciplinary regulations. They were convicted by the Board of Visitors of the prison and sentenced to substantial loss of remission of their sentences. They were denied legal representation at the hearing, which was held in private and which gave its decision in private. They were also denied access to legal advice in respect of their injuries until their complaints had been investigated internally, in compliance with the Home Office's 'prior ventilation' rule for prisoners' complaints. When access to a solicitor was eventually permitted consultations had to take place in the presence of a prison officer.

Mr Campbell alleged that he had been convicted by the Board of Visitors of disciplinary charges amounting in substance to 'criminal' charges, without having been afforded a hearing complying with the requirements of Article 6 of the Convention, which provides certain guarantees 'in the determination of . . . civil rights and obligations or of any criminal charge'.

A. The applicability of Article 6

1. The existence of a 'criminal charge'
The Commission came to the conclusion that the adjudication by the Board of Visitors in Mr Campbell's case did involve the determination of 'criminal charges' and that Article 6 was therefore applicable.

As their principal submission, the Government contested this view.

The Court was confronted with a similar issue in the case of *Engle and others* (1979) (1 EHRR 647), which was cited in argument by those appearing before it in the present proceedings. In its judgment of 8 June 1976 in that case, the Court, after drawing attention to the 'autonomy' of the notion of 'criminal charge' as conceived of under Article 6, set forth the following principles which it re-affirmed in its *Öztürk* judgment of 21 February 1984 (6 EHRR 409).

(a) The Convention is not opposed to the Contracting States creating or maintaining a distinction between criminal law and disciplinary law and drawing the dividing line, but it does not follow that the classification thus made is decisive for the purposes of the Convention.

(b) If the Contracting States were able at their discretion, by classifying an offence as disciplinary instead of criminal, to exclude the operation of the fundamental clauses of Articles 6 and 7, the application of these provisions would be subordinated to their sovereign will. A latitude extending thus far might lead to results incompatible with the object and purpose of the Convention.

The Court was careful in the *Engel and others* judgment to state that, as regards the dividing line between the 'criminal' and the 'disciplinary', it was confining its attention to the sphere with which the case was concerned, namely military service. It is well aware that in the prison context there are practical reasons and reasons of policy for establishing a special disciplinary regime, for example security considerations and the interests of public order, the need to deal with misconduct by inmates as expeditiously as possible, the availability of tailor-made sanctions which may not be at the disposal of the ordinary courts and the desire of the prison authorities to retain ultimate responsibility for discipline within their establishments.

However, the guarantee of a fair hearing, which is the aim of Article 6, is one of the fundamental principles of any democratic society, within the meaning of the Convention. As the *Golder* judgment shows, justice cannot stop at the prison gate and there is, in appropriate cases, no warrant for depriving inmates of the safeguards of Article 6.

It follows that the principles set forth in the *Engel and others* judgment are also relevant, *mutatis mutandis*, in a custodial setting and that the reasons mentioned above cannot override the necessity of maintaining, there too, a dividing line between the 'criminal' and the 'disciplinary' that is consistent with the object and purpose of Article 6. It therefore has to be determined whether the proceedings against Mr Campbell have to be regarded as coming within the 'criminal' sphere for Convention purposes. To this end, the Court considers it right to apply, making due allowance for the different context, the criteria stated in that judgment.

The first matter to be ascertained is whether or not the text defining the offences in issue belongs, according to the domestic legal system, to criminal law, disciplinary law or both concurrently.

It is clear that, in English law, the offences with which Mr Campbell was charged belong to disciplinary law: Rule 47 states that conduct of this kind on the part of a prisoner shall be 'an offence against discipline' and the Rules go on to provide how it shall be dealt with under the special prison disciplinary regime. Confirmation that domestic law regards Board of Visitors' adjudications as falling outside the criminal sphere is to be found in the Court of Appeal's decision in the *St Germain* case [1978] 2 All ER 198 that they are not a 'criminal cause or matter'. Lord Justice Shaw there expressed the view that such an adjudication was essentially a domestic disciplinary proceeding, which did not purport to deal with misconduct in its relation to the public law or the public interest and was designed and pursued with the limited objective of maintaining order within the confines of the prison. Indeed, the Court notes that it is for this precise purpose, amongst others, that the Home Secretary is empowered by s. 47(1) of the Prison Act 1952 to make rules. Nevertheless, the Court also notes that certain parallels between Board of Visitors' proceedings and criminal proceedings were drawn in the *McConkey* and the *Tarrant* cases.

In any event, the indications so afforded by the national law have only a relative value; the very nature of the offence is a factor of greater import.

In this respect, it has to be borne in mind that misconduct by a prisoner may take different forms; certain acts are clearly no more than a question of internal discipline, whereas others cannot be seen in the same light. Firstly, some matters may be more serious than others; in fact, the Rules grade offences, classifying those committed by Mr Campbell as 'especially grave'. Secondly, the illegality of some acts may not turn on the fact that they were committed in prison: certain conduct which constitutes an offence under the Rules may also amount to an offence under the criminal law. Thus, doing gross personal violence to a prison officer may correspond to the crime of 'assault occasioning actual bodily harm' and, although mutiny and incitement to mutiny are not as such offences under the general criminal law, the underlying facts may found a criminal charge of conspiracy. It also has to be remembered that, theoretically at least, there is nothing to prevent conduct of this kind being the subject of both criminal and disciplinary proceedings.

The Court considers that these factors, whilst not of themselves sufficient to lead to the conclusion that the offences with which the applicant was charged have to be regarded as 'criminal' for Convention purposes, do give them a certain colouring which does not entirely coincide with that of a purely disciplinary matter.

It is therefore necessary to turn to the last criterion stated in the above mentioned *Engel and others* judgment and in the above mentioned *Öztürk* judgment, namely the nature and degree of severity of the penalty that Mr Campbell risked incurring. The maximum penalties which could have been imposed on him included forfeiture of all of the remission of sentence available to him at the time of the Board's award (slightly less than three years), forfeiture of certain privileges for an unlimited time and, for each offence, exclusion from associated work, stoppage of earnings and cellular confinement for a maximum of 56 days; he was in fact awarded a total of 570 days' loss of remission and subjected to the other penalties mentioned for a total of 91 days.

There was considerable discussion, both in the *St Germain* case and before the Convention institutions, as to the nature of remission of sentence and its forfeiture. Under English law, remission is a discretionary measure. It is regarded by the English courts as being technically a privilege rather than a right, but the Court of Appeal did observe in the *St Germain* case that 'although in form remission of sentence may have been the grant of a privilege, loss of remission was in fact a punishment or deprivation affecting the rights of the subject'.

The Court, for its part, does not find that the distinction between privilege and right is of great assistance to it for the present purposes; what is more important is that the practice of granting remission – whereby a prisoner will be set free on the estimated date for release given to him at the outset of his sentence, unless remission has been forfeited in disciplinary proceedings – creates in him a legitimate expectation that he will recover his liberty before the end of his term of imprisonment. Forfeiture of remission thus has the effect of causing the detention to continue beyond the period corresponding to that expectation.

. . .

In its abovementioned *Engel and others* judgment, the Court stated that deprivation of liberty liable to be imposed as a punishment was, in general, a penalty that belonged to the 'criminal' sphere. It is true that in the present case the legal basis for the detention remained, even after the Board's award, the original sentence of imprisonment and that nothing was added thereto. However, the Court is of the opinion that the forfeiture of remission which Mr Campbell risked incurring and the forfeiture actually awarded involved such serious consequences as regards the length of his detention that these penalties have to be regarded, for Convention purposes, as 'criminal'. By causing detention to continue for substantially longer than would otherwise have been the case, the sanction came close to, even if it did not technically constitute, deprivation of liberty and the object and purpose of the Convention require that the imposition of a measure of such gravity should be accompanied by the guarantees of Article 6. This conclusion is not altered by the fact that a considerable number of days of remission were subsequently restored to the applicant.

Taking into account, therefore, both the 'especially grave' character of the offences with which Mr Campbell was charged and the nature and severity of the penalty that he risked incurring – and did in fact incur – the Court finds that Article 6 is applicable to the Board of Visitors' adjudication in his case. It is accordingly not necessary to consider the sanctions, other than forfeiture of remission, which could have been or were imposed on him.

NOTES AND QUESTIONS

1. Recall that as a result of the Human Rights Act 1998, the decisions of the European Court of Human Rights must be followed in UK courts, even though the UK was not a party to the original litigation. Consider a decision such as *Schmautzer v Austria* (1995) 21 EHRR 511, in which the European Court ruled that the Austrian offence of failing to wear a seat belt, characterised as administrative under Austria law, but subject to a fine and imprisonment if the fine was not paid, was criminal in nature. This decision could affect all UK road traffic laws.

2. The most common effect of a finding that an action is criminal in nature is that the fair trial provisions of Article 6 of the Convention must be observed. At a minimum, a criminal

defendant will be entitled to a presumption of innocence, prompt notice of the charges, adequate time and facilities for the preparation of a defence, legal assistance and the right to an interpreter if needed, the right to compel the attendance of witnesses and to cross-examine witnesses, and the right to be tried by an independent and impartial tribunal at a public hearing held within a reasonable time of the offence. Included in the right to legal assistance is the right to a free lawyer if required by the defendant's financial circumstances and the interests of justice. Satisfying the right to a free lawyer can be economically burdensome to a State. How might Parliament structure an offence to avoid this burden, assuming that the government so wished? Will such 'structuring' be acceptable if a defendant's human rights are affected?

What, as a practical matter, is at stake? What are the differences between a civil suit and criminal prosecution? Bearing in mind that the same fact situation can give rise to either criminal liability, civil liability or both, let us examine the differences that typically will follow depending on whether a criminal or civil action is brought.

Example

An absent-minded professor, while driving his automobile out of the university parking lot, hits a student. The student suffers serious injuries. There is, however, some question whether either the student or the professor was paying close attention to what the other was doing.

	Civil	Criminal
Initiator of suit	student	DPP, CPS
Victim	student	State
Title of case	Student v Professor	R v Professor
Fault standard	negligence	recklessness
Damage	harm to claimant	harm to State
Burden of proof	balance of probabilities	beyond reasonable doubt
Procedures	no jury; differing rules of evidence	jury possibility in serious cases
Remedies/sanctions	damages	fine/imprisonment/community service
Goal	compensate victim	punish offender

(i) *Generally*

Civil law is concerned with private rights; criminal law is concerned with public wrongs. Civil law is also primarily concerned with compensating the injured victim; criminal law is concerned with condemning and punishing the guilty offender. Both may aim to redress past harms and shape future behaviour.

(ii) *Who decides to bring the action?*

In civil cases, it is for the victim to decide whether or not to bring suit. No State authority can force the victim to do so. In our example, a decision by Student to curry favour with Professor by not suing, might be crass but nonetheless legally permissible. In criminal law, on the other hand, the decision to proceed is made by the state in its various guises. The police will decide whether to arrest or caution the offender, or to take no action. The prosecutor (Director of Public Prosecutions or Crown Prosecution Service) will determine whether formal charges will be brought. Technically, the desires of the victim are irrelevant, although often they will be taken into account.

(iii) *Title of case*

A criminal case is brought in the name of the Crown (*R* v *Defendant*), while a civil case is brought in the name of the injured party (*Claimant* v *Defendant*). The title of the case illustrates an important theoretical point about who is considered to be the aggrieved party. In both of our suits, the person physically injured is Student, but the titular victim in a criminal case is the state. Because the victim in the civil suit is the claimant, his negligence may be a relevant legal consideration. But in the criminal case the victim is the State; the contributory negligence of the person injured is irrelevant (although where the victim is largely at fault, the defendant may be able to argue that the victim's negligence was the cause of the injury).

(iv) *Fault*

Criminal law is concerned with moral fault and blameworthiness. Civil law is more concerned with victim compensation. One consequence is that the legal system makes it easier for a civil claimant to recover than it does for the Crown to obtain a criminal conviction. In our example, Student will succeed in his civil suit if he can establish that Professor was negligent. To secure a conviction in criminal court, the Crown will have to establish more than mere negligence, probably recklessness or intention.

(v) *Damage*

The goal of civil law is to provide compensation to an injured victim; in our example, Student. If Student had not been injured, either physically or psychologically, there would be little point in a civil suit. In criminal law, however, it is not necessary that any person be injured. In our example Professor could be prosecuted for dangerous or careless driving even if he was fortunate enough to avoid hitting anybody. If he had intentionally tried to run down Student but failed, he could be charged with attempted murder.

(vi) *Burden of proof*

Another manifestation of the greater rigour demanded in criminal law is the higher burden of proof placed on the Crown. In order to secure a criminal conviction, the prosecution must establish its case by proof beyond a reasonable doubt. In order to prevail in his civil case, Student would need only to establish his case on a balance of probabilities. Thus if a court or jury were to conclude that a defendant had probably committed the wrongful act alleged, but still had some reasonable doubts, it could return a verdict for a claimant in the civil case but would have to acquit in the criminal prosecution. Before imposing the stigma and sanctions (including possible imprisonment) of a criminal conviction, society wants to be sure that it is doing the right thing.

(vii) *Difference in procedures*

Beside the burden of proof, procedures are generally stricter in criminal cases than in civil cases. Again, the concern with the consequences of getting it wrong inclines the law to err on the side of caution in criminal cases. Rules of evidence differ, with the rules in criminal trials on the whole being more stringent. Furthermore, the defendant facing a serious criminal charge has the right to a jury trial. Jury trials are permitted in only a small category of civil cases, and as a practical matter are very rare. Lastly, the right of the State to appeal against a jury acquittal in a criminal case is severely restricted; not so the right of a civil claimant to appeal.

(viii) *Remedies and sanctions*

One of the key features which distinguishes criminal from civil law is the penalty attached to a verdict against the defendant. The criminal defendant can sometimes be sent to jail. In a civil case the worst that can happen to the defendant is to be required to pay money damages. The defendant's liberty is not in jeopardy. The amount of damages in a particular case is determined by the extent of the harm to the victim; this is not necessarily the most critical variable in determining the length of sentence imposed on the convicted criminal defendant. Note that while one of the primary goals of both systems is to deter future would-be wrongdoers, civil damages may not be a sufficient deterrent to wealthy defendants. In these cases criminal sanctions may have greater effect. Conversely, for many crimes the penalty is a relatively minor fine, but civil damages can be very expensive. In cases where corporate fault has resulted in, for example, an aeroplane crash, the civil penalty may be far in excess of the criminal fine. The two sets of remedies, in any event, are not mutually exclusive. In our example Professor can be made to pay damages in civil court and be sent to prison as a result of the criminal trial.

SECTION 2: The sources of the criminal law

Originally criminal law was the primary responsibility of the judiciary. The courts laid down general principles of criminal liability, established the elements of specific crimes, and determined what defences to a criminal charge should be permitted. This so-called common law was not contained in any code or statute book but had to be distilled from the opinions of the judges.

Over the years, the responsibility for determining what to make criminal and for defining crimes has shifted from the judiciary to the legislature. There are many reasons for and advantages to this shift. Unlike a court, Parliament is not limited by the facts of a particular case and can consider the global dimensions of a problem. Courts are also restricted to the evidence presented by the lawyers in the case, while Parliament can hold hearings, receive opinions of expert authorities and commission studies. Parliamentary debates may clarify the issues, and any resulting law represents a consensus judgment. The trial judge is more of a solitary figure, deciding cases with little input from others. Appellate courts will usually not consist of more than a panel of five. Finally, members of Parliament are democratically accountable for their decisions – they must periodically face the electorate, which can vote them out of office if dissatisfied with their performance. Judges are appointed rather than elected, and are not directly accountable to the public.

Today the common law of crimes has been largely, but not completely, displaced by statute. *But*:

(a) Some crimes, such as murder and manslaughter, have never been defined in statute. One needs to look at common law decisions to determine the elements of these crimes. Likewise, many defences to crime have never been reduced to statute and retain their common law definition.

(b) Often Parliament will use a term in a statute without defining it formally. There is no statutory definition of even such basic criminal law terms as 'intention' or 'recklessness'. There may, however, be a well settled meaning of the term in the law. It may be Parliament's intent to preserve that meaning, in which case judicial decisions will need to be consulted in order to determine that meaning. In the case of terms that are not given specific definition by Parliament, judges may resort to common law cases for guidance or may utilise techniques of interpretation embodied in common law decisions.

(c) Common law crimes may still be in force:

Shaw v *Director of Public Prosecutions*
[1962] AC 220, House of Lords

The appellant published a booklet, the Ladies' Directory, of some 28 pages, most of which were taken up with the names and addresses of prostitutes; the matter published left no doubt that the advertisers could be got in touch with at the telephone numbers given and were offering their services for sexual intercourse and, in some cases, for the practice of sexual perversions. The appellant's avowed purpose in publication was to assist prostitutes to ply their trade when, as a result of the Street Offences Act 1959, they were no longer able to solicit in the street. The prostitutes paid for the advertisements and the appellant derived a profit from the publication. The appellant pleaded not guilty to an indictment charging him with (1) conspiracy to corrupt public morals in that he conspired with the advertisers and other persons by means of the Ladies' Directory and the advertisements to debauch and corrupt the morals of youth and other subjects of the Queen; (2) living on the earnings of prostitution contrary to s. 30 of the Sexual Offences Act 1956; and (3) publishing an obscene article contrary to s. 2 of the Obscene Publications Act 1959.

At the trial evidence was given by prostitutes that they had paid for the advertisements out of their earnings, that the advertisements were good at bringing clients in, and as to the ages of the persons resorting to them and the meaning of abbreviations and expressions in the advertisements; they also gave evidence of the practices in which they indulged and there was evidence by the police as to objects found at their addresses. The summing-up gave no direction to the jury as to the relevance of the appellant's honesty of purpose. The jury convicted the appellant. He appealed, on the ground, *inter alia*, that there was no such offence at common law as the conspiracy alleged.

VISCOUNT SIMONDS: My Lords, . . . the first count in the indictment is 'Conspiracy to corrupt public morals,' and the particulars of offence will have sufficiently appeared. I am concerned only to assert what was vigorously denied by counsel for the appellant, that such an offence is known to the common law, and that it was open to the jury to find on the facts of this case that the appellant was guilty of such an offence. I must say categorically that, if it were not so, Her Majesty's courts would strangely have failed in their duty as servants and guardians of the common law. Need I say, my Lords, that I am no advocate of the right of the judges to create new criminal offences? I will repeat well-known words:

> Amongst many other points of happiness and freedom which your Majesty's subjects have enjoyed there is none which they have accounted more dear and precious than this, to be guided and governed by certain rules of law which giveth both to the head and members that which of right belongeth to them and not by any arbitrary or uncertain form of government.

These words are as true today as they were in the seventeenth century and command the allegiance of us all. But I am at a loss to understand how it can be said either that the law does not recognise a conspiracy to corrupt public morals or that, though there may not be an exact precedent for such a conspiracy as this case reveals, it does not fall fairly within the general words by which it is described. . . . The fallacy in the argument that was addressed to us lay in the attempt to exclude from the scope of general words acts well calculated to corrupt public morals just because they had not been committed or had not been brought to the notice of the court before. It is not thus that the common law has developed. We are perhaps more accustomed to hear this matter discussed upon the question whether such and such a transaction is contrary to public policy. At once the controversy arises. On the one hand it is said that it is not possible in the twentieth century for the court to create a new head of public policy, on the other it is said that this is but a new example of a well-established head. In the sphere of criminal law I entertain no doubt that there remains in the courts of law a residual power to enforce the supreme and fundamental purpose of the law, to conserve not only the safety and order but also the moral welfare of the State and that it is their duty to guard it against attacks which may be the more insidious because they are novel and unprepared for. . . .

NOTE

After *Shaw* the question remained whether courts were limited to discovering existing common law crimes, or whether they could create new common law crimes. The issue was addressed in *Knuller* v *Director of Public Prosecutions* [1973] AC 435, where the House of Lords purported to limit the judiciary's power to create new common law crimes. One might question whether it really matters, however, given the breadth of many common law crimes. Take, for instance, the common law crime of outraging public decency:

R v *Gibson and Another*
[1991] 1 All ER 439, Court of Appeal

The first defendant exhibited at an exhibition in a commercial art gallery run by the second defendant a model's head to which were attached earrings made out of freeze-dried human foetuses. The exhibit was entitled 'Human Earrings'. The gallery was open to, and was visited by, members of the public. The defendants were charged with, and convicted of, outraging public decency contrary to common law.

LORD LANE CJ: The article in question was one of 41 items which had been selected for display out of a much larger number by Sylveire. It was exhibit number 9, and was described in the catalogue as 'Human Earrings'.

Although it was not suggested that Sylveire had taken active steps to publicise this particular exhibit, there was no doubt that the more people who attended the gallery, the better pleased Sylveire would be, and the greater would be the likelihood of selling exhibits.

Now by leave of this court these two men appeal against their convictions.

. . .

The first ground is that the prosecution were precluded from proceeding on count 1, on which the appellants were eventually convicted, by s. 2(4) of the Obscene Publications Act 1959. That subsection reads as follows:

> A person publishing an article shall not be proceeded against for an offence at common law consisting of the publication of any matter contained or embodied in the article where it is of the essence of the offence that the matter is obscene.

The first question to decide then is whether there is an offence at common law of outraging public decency. The answer to that question is to be found in the speech of Lord Simon of Glaisdale in the well-known case of *Knuller (Publishing Printing and Promotions) Ltd* v *DPP* [1972] 2 All ER 898 at 935:

> Fourthly, my noble and learned friend, Lord Morris of Borth-y-Gest, in [*Shaw* v *DPP*] [1961] 2 All ER 446 at 467, where, though there was no count of conspiracy to outrage public decency, most of the cases were reviewed, said: 'The cases afford examples of the conduct of individuals which has been punished because it outraged public decency . . .' And my noble and learned friend, Lord Reid, though dissenting on the main issue, said ([1961] 2 All ER 446 at 460): 'I think that they [the authorities] establish that it is an indictable offence to say or do or exhibit anything in public which outrages public decency, whether or not it also tends to corrupt and deprave those who see or hear it.'

. . . Mr Worsley points out, and points out correctly, that the object of the common law offence is to protect the public from suffering feelings of outrage by such exhibition. Thus, if a defendant intentionally does an act which in fact outrages public decency, the public will suffer outrage whatever the defendant's state of mind may be. If the defendant's state of mind is a critical factor, then, he submits, a man could escape liability by the very baseness of his own standards.

. . . The authorities on the question of exhibition outraging public decency are few and far between. One of the very few which it has been possible to trace is *R* v *Crumden* (1809) 2 Camp 89. That was a case where a gentleman was bathing in the nude at Brighton. It is a brief report, and M'Donald CB said (2 Camp 89 at 90):

> I can entertain no doubt that the defendant, by exposing his naked person on the occasion alluded to, was guilty of a misdemeanour. The law will not tolerate such an exhibition. Whatever his intention might be, the necessary tendency of his conduct was to outrage decency, and to corrupt the public morals. Nor is it any justification that bathing at this spot might a few years ago be innocent. For any thing that I know, a man might a few years ago have harmlessly danced naked in the fields beyond Montague house; but it will scarcely be said by the learned counsel for the defendant, that any one might now do so with impunity in Russell Square. Whatever place becomes the habitation of civilized men, there the laws of decency must be enforced. The defendant was found guilty; and when he was brought up for judgment, the Court of KB expressed a clear opinion, that the offence imputed to him was a misdemeanour, and that he had been properly convicted.

The result, in our judgment, seems to be this. First of all the requirements with regard to *mens rea* should be the same in this offence as they are in the cognate offence of obscene libel. That is borne out by what Lord Scarman said in *R v Lemon* [1979] 1 All ER 898. If that is so, then the decision of the House of Lords in *R v Lemon*, albeit by a majority, indicates that the submissions of the prosecution in this case are to be preferred to those of the appellants'.

One turns then to examine in a little more detail the speeches of their Lordships in that case. They are most conveniently summarised by Lord Russell of Killowen, where he said, in his usual trenchant and felicitous language ([1979] 1 All ER 898 at 921):

> So I return to the question of intent. The authorities embrace an abundance of apparently contradictory or ambivalent comments. There is no authority in your Lordships' House on the point. The question is open for decision. I do not, with all respect to the speech of my noble and learned friend, Lord Diplock, consider that the question is whether this is an offence of strict liability. It is necessary that the editor or publisher should be aware of that which he publishes. Indeed that was the function of Lord Campbell's Act (Libel Act 1843), which assumed the law to be that an intention in the accused to blaspheme was not an ingredient of the offence, since it removed by statute a vicarious liability for an act of publication done by another without authority. Why then should this House, faced with a deliberate publication of that which a jury with every justification has held to be a blasphemous libel, consider that it should be for the prosecution to prove, presumably beyond reasonable doubt, that the accused recognised and intended it to be such or regarded it as immaterial whether it was? I see no ground for that. It does not to my mind make sense: and I consider that sense should retain a function in our criminal law. The reason why the law considers that the publication of a blasphemous libel is an offence is that the law considers that such publication should not take place. And if it takes place, and the publication is deliberate, I see no justification for holding that there is no offence when the publisher is incapable for some reason particular to himself of agreeing with a jury on the true nature of the publication.

Moreover, *R v Lemon*, as will have been clear from the passages which we have cited, was an allegation of an outrage on the public on a religious basis rather than a general basis, which is the case in the instant appeal. But outrage it certainly was, and the same considerations in logic should apply to this case as applied to the religious outrage in *R v Lemon*. That is the submission to us this morning of Mr Worsley, and we find that a cogent argument.

The result is this. Those passages, and the argument of Mr Worsley to which I have just made reference, lead us to the conclusion that, where the charge is one of outraging public decency, there is no requirement that the prosecution should prove an intention to outrage or such recklessness as is submitted by Mr Robertson. If the publication takes place, and if it is deliberate, there is, in the words of Lord Russell – no justification for holding that there is no offence when the publisher is incapable for some reason particular to himself of agreeing with the jury on the true nature of the publication.

. . .

NOTES AND QUESTIONS

1. It is said that hard cases make bad law. Do *Shaw* and *Gibson* illustrate the point? Do common law crimes simply provide judges (who have been characterised as middle-aged, middle-class, and middle-minded) with a way to punish conduct of which they personally disapprove?

2. Some would argue that common law crimes serve as a safety net in which to catch those individuals who violate society's norms but not its statutory criminal law. Which functions of punishment are served by having this residual catch-all category of crime? Which are not?

3. For the citizenry to obey the state's criminal law, they must first know what it is the law forbids. Do common law crimes, contained in a number of judicial decisions as opposed to a single statute, provide 'fair notice' to ordinary people? More specifically, do common law

crimes contravene Article 7 of the European Convention on Human Rights, which provides that no one shall be convicted of a criminal offence which was not an offence at the time of its commission? That issue, amongst others, was considered in the following case:

Gay News Ltd and Lemon v *United Kingdom*
(1982) 5 EHRR 123, European Court of Human Rights

The applicants, who are respectively the publisher and the responsible editor of a journal for homosexuals, were found guilty of the common law offence of blasphemous libel in connection with the publication of a certain poem. They complain that this conviction amounted to an unjustified interference with their freedom of expression as guaranteed by Article 10 of the Convention. They further claim that the publication of the poem amounted to an exercise of their right to freedom of thought and religion within the meaning of Article 9 of the Convention, and that the interference with this right was likewise unjustified. Apart from the argument that the restriction imposed on them was not necessary in a democratic society for any of the legitimate purposes enumerated in the above two Convention Articles, the applicants submit in particular that their conviction was based on legal principles which had not existed, or at least had not been defined with sufficient clarity, at the time of the commission of the offence. In this respect they claim that the restriction was not 'prescribed by law' as required under paragraph (2) of Articles 9 and 10, and they allege in addition a violation of Article 7 of the Convention. The applicants finally complain that they have been discriminated against, contrary to Article 14 of the Convention, in the exercise of their freedom under Articles 9 and 10 of the Convention.

. . .

In the present case, the parties are first of all in disagreement as to whether the criminal offence of blasphemous libel was defined with sufficient certainty in the common law principles which were applied by the courts. The existence of the offence, i.e. the fact that it has not fallen in *desuetudo*, is apparently no longer challenged even by the applicants themselves. But they contend that essential elements of the offence, in particular the principle of strict liability (i.e. the necessity to prove only the intent to publish but not the intent to blaspheme), had not been laid down in pre-existing rules of law hut were developed by the courts only in the course of the proceedings in their own case. In this connection it is alleged that even the majority of the House of Lords itself recognised the lawmaking function of its decision when it took up this particular issue. The Government, on the other hand, denies that the courts, including the House of Lords, created new law in this case when they applied a standard of strict liability. They merely clarified the existing law and in doing so based themselves on established case law without departing from the views expressed in recent leading textbooks.

The Commission first observes that not only written statutes. but also rules of common or other customary law may provide a sufficient legal basis both for restrictions of fundamental rights subject to exception clauses such as the one contained in Article 10(2) of the Convention, and for the criminal convictions envisaged in Article 7 of the Convention. The problem in the present case therefore does not reside in the fact that the offence of blasphemous libel was not a statutory, but a common law offence.

The crucial point is rather one of the certainty of the law, and the functions of the courts in clarifying or developing vague legal provisions or concepts. This problem was also considered in the *Sunday Times* case both by the Commission and the Court (see European Court of Human Rights A30 (1979)). In paragraph 49 of its judgment, the Court said the following:

> In the Court's opinion, the following are two of the requirements that flow from the expression 'prescribed by law'. Firstly, the law must be adequately accessible: the citizen must be able to have an indication that is adequate in the circumstances of the legal rules applicable to a given case. Secondly, a norm cannot be regarded as a 'law' unless it is formulated with sufficient precision to enable the citizen to regulate his conduct: he must

be able – if need be with appropriate advice – to foresee, to a degree that is reasonable in the circumstances, the consequences which a given action may entail. Those consequences need not be foreseeable with absolute certainty: experience shows this to be unattainable. Again, whilst certainty is highly desirable, it may bring in its train excessive rigidity and the law must be able to keep pace with changing circumstances. Accordingly, many laws are inevitably couched in terms which, to a greater or lesser extent, are vague and whose interpretation and application are questions of practice.

These considerations are of a general nature, but the Commission has also dealt with the more particular question of extensive interpretation of criminal law, and its relevance under Article 7(1) of the Convention. One case was in fact declared admissible because the Commission considered that the extensive interpretation of a certain statutory provision, applied for the first time by the courts after the commission of the acts of which the applicant was accused, could raise an issue under this provision. In another case brought against the Federal Republic of Germany the Commission rejected a similar complaint on the ground that the application of a specific article of the Penal Code to certain facts had not gone beyond the limits of a reasonable interpretation of the provision in question. It stated that Article 7(1) of the Convention forbids the retrospective application of the criminal law to the detriment of the accused and stipulates in a general way the principle of the legality of criminal offences and penalties (*nullum crimen, nulla poena sine lege*). What is, among other things, prohibited is the application of the penal law *in malam partem* in relation to facts which the text of the law cannot reasonably extend to. A similar test had already been applied in an earlier case.

The Commission considers that the same principles also apply to the interpretation and application of the common law. While this branch of the law presents certain particularities for the very reason that it is by definition law developed by the courts, it is nevertheless subject to the rule that the law-making function of the courts must remain within reasonable limits. In particular in the area of the criminal law it is excluded, by virtue of Article 7(1) of the Convention, that any acts not previously punishable should be held by the courts to entail criminal liability, or that existing offences should be extended to cover facts which previously clearly did not constitute a criminal offence. This implies that constituent elements of an offence such as, e.g. the particular form of culpability required for its completion may not be essentially changed, at least not to the detriment of the accused, by the case law of the courts. On the other hand it is not objectionable that the existing elements of the offence are clarified and adapted to new circumstances which can reasonably be brought under the original concept of the offence.

The Commission notes that the Law Commission has criticised the state of the law of blasphemous libel in particular with regard to its lacking clarity, but it nevertheless considers that the courts in the present case in fact did not go beyond the limits of a reasonable interpretation of the existing law. The House of Lords in particular was aware of the limits of its law-making functions in the area of the criminal law which had been circumscribed in the practice statement of 1966 and put into operation in the case of *Knuller v DPP* [1973] AC 435. The courts of all degrees confirmed the continued existence of the offence of blasphemous libel. There was only one point which was not clear, namely the particular requirements as to the *mens rea* of a person who commits this offence. This question was answered in the same way by each of the courts. Despite the admission by the Court of Appeal and the majority of the House of Lords that a point of principle was involved in the determination of this question which required clarification, it is equally clear that the application of a test of strict liability and the exclusion of evidence as to the publisher's and editor's intention to blaspheme did not amount to the creation of new law in the sense that earlier case law clearly denying such strict liability and admitting evidence as to the blasphemous intentions was overruled. By stating that the *mens rea* in this offence did only relate to the intention to publish, the courts therefore did not overstep the limits of what can still be regarded as an acceptable clarification of the law. The Commission further considers that the law was also accessible to the applicants and that its interpretation in this way was reasonably foreseeable for them with the assistance of appropriate legal advice. In conclusion therefore the Commission finds that there is no appearance of a violation of Article 7(1) of the Convention in this case, and the applicants' complaint in this respect must accordingly be rejected as being manifestly ill-founded within the meaning of Article 27(2) of the Convention. From that it follows that the requirement under Article 10(2) of the Convention that any restriction on the freedom of expression must be 'prescribed by law' has also been complied with.

NOTES AND QUESTIONS

1. In most of Europe there are neither common law crimes nor statutes but written codes. Unlike statutes, which are adopted piecemeal over time, a code constitutes a comprehensive and integrated expression of the whole of a country's criminal law. Greater consistency in terminology can be achieved than in statutes passed by different Parliaments at different times. Often the code will go beyond a simple listing of crimes and defences to include a statement of general criminal law principles. Examples and commentary may also be included. The Law Commission has proposed a draft criminal code for the UK. Its provisions will on occasion be referred to in this book, not because they are the current law (to date Parliament has not enacted the code into law), but because they represent the well thought out views of those who have given the matter serious consideration. The Hon. Mrs Justice Arden has argued that the passage of the Human Rights Act 1998 strengthens the case for a criminal code (Arden, 'Criminal Law at the Cross-roads: The Impact of Human Rights from the Law Commission's Perspective and the Need for a Code' [1999] Crim LR 439). Why?

2. To say that the common law has largely been replaced by statute is not to say that judges no longer have a role in the development of the law. It remains the judge's responsibility:
   (a) to interpret the meaning of the terms of the statute;
   (b) to determine what conduct falls within the ambit of the statute and what defences may be raised by way of excuse, justification, or mitigation;
   (c) to provide guidance to juries, and, in the case of appellate courts, to trial judges; and
   (d) to determine the appropriate sentence, within limits set by Parliament, for those convicted of violating the statute.

SECTION 3: Identifying the elements of a crime

A: A conceptual model

It is possible to look at a crime as consisting of a number of building blocks. These building blocks draw our attention not only to the common elements of the typical offence, but also to how the elements relate to one another. In addition, they provide a benchmark against which any crime might be critically evaluated, and thereby further our understanding of the nature of the criminal law. That said, there is no legal requirement that each of the elements must be present in every offence, and the fact that an element may be omitted from the definition of a particular crime does not serve to invalidate the relevant statute.

The elements themselves can be schematically subdivided. There are two formal preconditions to a crime – the existence of a law that makes conduct criminal and the attachment of a potential sanction to a violation of that law. In order to be subject to the criminal law, an individual must also be deemed to have the legal capacity to commit a crime. The courts recognise certain categories of individuals, such as children and the insane, as not having this capacity and exempt them from the law.

In terms of the crime itself, there are two core elements – *actus reus* and *mens rea*. The former refers to the conduct element of the crime and the latter to the mental element. The relationship that needs to exist between *actus reus* and *mens rea* is, somewhat inaccurately because it seems to imply simultaneity, described as one of 'concurrence'. Offences that are defined in terms of a result (murder and manslaughter, for example, require that a person be killed) envisage a certain relationship between *actus reus* and result, which is referred to, again somewhat inaccurately, as 'causation'. Lastly, there are circumstances that justify or excuse what would otherwise be a crime.

(i) *Preconditions to criminal liability*
(a) *Law*. The existence of a law forbidding the conduct in question is an absolute prerequisite to the imposition of criminal liability (*nullum crimen sine lege*). One cannot be prosecuted for an offence that was not in existence at the time it was committed. See Article 7 of the European Convention on Human Rights. The law need not necessarily be written in a statute book, as we saw in the case of common law crimes, but it must exist. Those subject to the law have a right to know what it proscribes, in order that they may conform their conduct to the law's requirements.

(b) *Punishment*. A second prerequisite is that the law in question must prescribe punishment for its violation. Without prescribed punishment the law is not a criminal law. The punishment is inflicted in the name of the state for the violation of its law, and exists separate and independent of whether the defendant is required to pay damages in a civil suit and of any disgrace that the defendant might suffer as a result of the attendant publicity.

(ii) *Capacity*
The working assumption of the criminal law is that human beings are autonomous individuals with free will and the ability to choose between good and evil. Although biological, psychological, social and economic forces may impinge on the exercise of free will, the law generally chooses to ignore these factors in assessing a defendant's criminality (considerations such as these are more likely to be taken into account at the sentencing stage). Nonetheless, there are instances where the courts are prepared to recognise that certain individuals may not have the requisite capacity to choose between legal and illegal conduct. Young children, for example, often do not understand the wrongfulness of their mischief. Individuals who suffer from mental illness likewise may be incapable of appreciating when they are doing something wrong. Such persons may not be morally responsible for their actions, and the law, recognising this incapacity, does not seek to hold them criminally responsible. The rationale behind this allowance, however, does

not apply to individuals who are responsible for their own lack of capacity, such as by becoming voluntarily intoxicated and thereafter committing an offence that they would not have committed had they been sober, and the law takes a less indulgent view in these circumstances.

The incapacity of the mentally ill and children is a mental incapacity – they lack the ability to understand the nature of their actions. Sometimes, however, individuals have the requisite understanding but are unable to prevent themselves from committing the criminal action. When a defendant acts involuntarily against his will, and there is no fault on the defendant's part in being unable to control his conduct, the law again is prepared to make an exception from a general rule of liability. Such individuals are permitted a defence of automatism. Technically this defence turns on the involuntary nature of the defendant's acts, but in recent times the courts have drawn a distinction between insane and non-insane automatism, thereby confusing issues of mental incapacity and physical incapacity. Both automatism and insanity, as well as incapacity based on age, will be examined in Chapter 5.

(iii) Actus reus *and* mens rea

Actus reus and *mens rea* are the two most critical components of a crime. *Actus reus* refers to the conduct component, and *mens rea* to the mental component. At common law it was said that '*Actus non facit reum nisi mens sit rea*', which literally means that an act is not wrongful unless accompanied by a wrongful state of mind. However, the maxim has typically been construed to mean that before criminal liability can attach, at least for serious offences, the Crown must prove both *actus reus* and *mens rea*.

(a) *Actus reus*. While literally translated as a wrongful act, the term *actus reus* may actually encompass three distinct dimensions. There is first the conduct which one must engage in before one can be held criminally liable, although it is also important to note that in some instances a failure to act or omission may satisfy the requirement of *actus reus*. The second dimension arises in respect of a crime defined in terms of a specified result (murder requires the killing of a human being, and criminal damage the destruction of or damage to property) and embodies the relationship between the defendant's act and the result. If no person has died, the defendant cannot be convicted of murder; and if no property has been damaged, there is no crime of criminal damage. The final dimension to *actus reus* consists of the attendant circumstances that lend colour to what might otherwise appear to be a neutral act. The attendant circumstance that converts sexual relations with an adult woman into rape is the absence of consent on the part of the woman, and that which converts an ordinary marriage into bigamy is the fact that the defendant is already married to another at the time. Thus *actus reus*, like *mens rea*, although on the one hand a seemingly out-moded Latin term of art, conveys a commonly understood (at least among the legal community) constellation of ideas and concepts that facilitate analysis. *Actus reus*, along with causation, will be examined in Chapter 3.

(b) *Mens rea*. Just as one cannot be punished for bad thoughts alone, one generally cannot be punished for acts which are not accompanied by a guilty mind. The term *mens rea* refers to the wrongful state of mind required to be proven by the prosecutor in order to secure a conviction. Usually the type of *mens rea* which will suffice for a conviction will be specified by statute or case law. In some instances the prosecutor will have to prove that the defendant acted intentionally; in others only that the defendant acted recklessly; and in still others simply that the defendant acted negligently or carelessly. A sliding scale of mental fault exists which varies depending on the crime charged. At the far end of this scale can be found statutes which do away with *mens rea* altogether and impose strict liability. *Mens rea*, along with concurrence, will be examined in Chapter 4.

(iv) *Critical relationships*

(a) *Concurrence*. Concurrence refers to the temporal relationship between *mens rea* and *actus reus*. Usually they will coincide at the point of the *actus reus*, but in crimes of intention it may be a more accurate description of the relationship to say that the *mens rea* was the precipitating factor in the defendant's decision to commit the crime.

(b) *Causation*. Crimes are defined in terms of the occurrence of a particular result, of which murder is the clearest example. The defendant's acts must be the cause of that result. As we will see, problems arise when the results are other than those intended or occur in a way other than intended.

(v) *Justifications and excuses*

If the Crown has established each and every element of the crime charged by proof beyond a reasonable doubt, it would seem to follow that the defendant will be convicted. However, this is not necessarily so. Sometimes the defendant is prepared to concede that he has violated the law, but argues that he was justified in doing so or should be excused despite having done so. The courts have recognise a limited number of *general defences* that will in effect negate the defendant's liability.

Conceptually, these *general defences* can be divided into justifications and excuses, although the practical effect is the same – they both lead to a verdict of not guilty. To say that the defendant's conduct was justified is to say that the defendant was right to have acted as he did. Acting in self-defence or to prevent a crime are examples of justifications. In contrast, criminal conduct which is excusable is still wrong, but the law is prepared to relieve the defendant of the normal consequences of a conviction. A defendant who claims that he committed a crime under duress, for instance, is seeking to be excused.

While both justifications and excuses result in the defendant's not being subjected to penal sanction, there are some technical differences that emanate from the fact that the defendant is raising one or the other. For example, some cases suggest that a defendant charged with aiding and abetting cannot be convicted if the principal's conduct is found to have been justified but conviction is possible if the conduct is only excusable. Interestingly, it is not the defendant's burden to prove a justification or excuse, but rather the Crown's obligation to negate the claim by proof beyond reasonable doubt. The defendant does have the burden, however, of introducing evidence to support his claim.

The topic of justifications and excuses will be examined in Chapter 13.

B: An element-by-element approach

The conceptual model of a criminal offence is extremely useful in indicating the criminological basis of legal liability and how the key features of a crime fit together. However, the model holds the danger of leading astray anybody who takes it too literally. Some crimes, for example, impose strict liability, and any attempt to identify the *mens rea* of the crime would be impossible; there is no *mens rea*. Similarly, issues of causation arise only in respect of crimes which are defined in terms of a particular result. Where the offence consists of simply an act, such as driving a motor vehicle in excess of the speed limit, any effort to identify a causation relationship would be doomed to failure.

The conceptual model can also be frustrating, for it fails to accord with the way that criminal laws are written in practice. No statute declares that the *actus reus* of an offence is X and the *mens rea* is Y. Statutes are drafted in ordinary English and not Latin. Nor do statutes generally speak in terms of concurrence or causation; these are relationships which are implicit within the law. In many statutes, moreover, there may be multiple mental and conduct elements which have more complex interrelationships than the simple statement of the conceptual model might suggest.

The conceptual model, because of its abstract nature, can be misleading in another sense. *Actus reus* and *mens rea* do not exist in a vacuum, as the model might seem to intimate. They come to life only within the context of a specific criminal offence. Each crime has its own *actus reus* and its own *mens rea*, and, although the terminology of *actus reus* and *mens rea* may remain constant, their specific content will differ from statute to statute. One must examine each crime on an individual basis in order to determine its particular *actus reus* and *mens rea*. Thus one needs to dissect a statute in the same way as a student of English might identify the subject, verb, object, etc. of a sentence. In criminal law it is necessary to identify each element of the crime. In a criminal case a prosecutor will go through this exercise in order to ensure that no element is overlooked (as noted previously, the Crown must prove each and every element of the offence beyond a reasonable doubt or its case fails); and a defence lawyer will go through the same exercise in order to hold the prosecution to its legal burden of proof. It is helpful at this stage of your career to get into the habit of identifying the elements of a crime and determining how each of the elements is satisfied in a particular case.

It may be useful to illustrate both the conceptual and element-by-element approaches to understanding a crime in respect of a specific statute. Consider s. 1 of the Criminal Damage Act 1971:

Criminal Damage Act 1971

1. Destroying or damaging property

(1) A person who without lawful excuse destroys or damages any property belonging to another intending to destroy or damage any such property or being reckless as to whether any such property would be destroyed or damaged shall be guilty of an offence.

If one were to dissect this provision, element by element, six distinct elements would emerge. In respect of each, one might also perceive a number of issues which may require clarification before the element can be fully understood. We have attempted, for purposes of illustration, to flag the relevant elements and some (but by no means all) of the possible issues:

(a) *'A person'*. It might not be readily apparent when 'personhood' might become an issue. Consider, however, the case of a company charged with criminal damage for polluting a river. Is the company a person?

(b) *'without lawful excuse'*. This provision raises the question of what constitutes a 'lawful excuse'. Part of the answer is provided in a separate section of the statute (see s. 5).

(c) *'destroys or damages'*. Note that the Crown can succeed by proving either that the defendant has destroyed or has damaged property. But how much must one alter the state of property before it can be said to be sufficiently damaged to come within the criminal law? One might also wonder why the two terms are used and whether it is possible to destroy property without damaging it.

(d) *'property'*. What constitutes 'property'? Are both personal and real property included? Can one destroy or damage intangible property? Are there some things that within normal parlance we may refer to as property but which are not considered such for the purposes of the law (an issue which will be explored in Chapter 8 on Theft)?

(e) *'belonging to another'*. Note that a defendant cannot be convicted for destroying or damaging his or her own property. But what if the defendant has possession of the property pursuant to a rental agreement, or has simply been left in charge of property?

(f) *'intending to destroy or damage . . . property or being reckless as to whether any such property would be destroyed or damaged'*. Note again that the Crown has alternative methods of establishing its case. It can prove that the defendant acted either intentionally *or* recklessly. The question of what constitutes 'recklessness' has been one that has proved extremely problematic and controversial. The leading case of *R v Caldwell* [1982] AC 341 will be examined in Chapter 4 which examines the mental elements of a crime.

If one were to take a conceptual approach to this same provision, one might be led to the following conclusions:

(a) The preconditions of law and punishment are established. Section 1 establishes the offence and a subsequent section (s. 4) establishes the maximum penalty following a conviction.

(b) The law says nothing about capacity other than its reference to 'person'. But this would be misleading if it were taken to imply, for example, that a child – who undoubtedly is a person – can be convicted of criminal damage. No judge would have any doubt that a child of, say, eight cannot be prosecuted under the statute. Criminal statutes tend not to indicate that children, the mentally ill, and those who act in a state of automatism are not subject to its provisions, for the repetition of such a provision in every statute would become tedious. On the other hand, this omission illustrates how looking at a statute in terms of its expressed elements might cause one to overlook critical issues.

(c) The *actus reus* of the offence is destroying or damaging property belonging to another.

(d) The crime is defined in terms of a result – damaging or destroying property. This automatically raises the question of whether the defendant's conduct caused the result. Again this is 'hidden' issue in that there is no reference to causation on the face of the statute.

(e) The *mens rea of* the offence is '*intending* to destroy or damage . . . property or *being reckless* as to whether any such property would be destroyed or damaged'.

(f) The statute, rather oddly, specifies that the defendant's conduct must be 'without lawful excuse'. This is otiose because a 'lawful excuse' would in any event excuse what would otherwise be a crime. Moreover, even more oddly in light of this reference to excuses, the Act is silent on justifications. Yet, criminal damage can clearly be justifiable, as, for example, when the victim of an attack breaks a chair over the head of the attacker.

Thus it can be seen that one can effectively use either the conceptual approach or an element-by-element approach to analysing a statute, but using the two together allows one to see issues that might be overlooked if either approach were to be used by itself.

C: Statutory interpretation

As can be seen in the Criminal Damage Act 1971, often terms in a criminal statute may be ambiguous or susceptible to more than one meaning. Under the terms of that Act, who is a person, what constitutes property, how much damage must be done to property before it is sufficiently damaged to constitute a violation of the law, does recklessness require that the defendant had a conscious appreciation of the risk to property that he created, etc., etc.

The task of interpreting the terms of a statute is left to the courts. But where does a court look for answers? Sometimes an answer is supplied by Parliament in the same statute. In respect to the Criminal Damage Act 1971, for example, the term 'property' is defined in a separate section of the Act (see s. 10) and similarly Parliament has provided a partial answer to what it means by 'without lawful excuse' (see s. 5).

Sometimes the answer to the interpretive question can be found in another statute. So, for instance, to find an answer to whether the term 'person' in the Criminal Damage Act 1971 includes a company, one can look at:

Interpretation Act 1889

2.—(1) In the construction of every enactment relating to an offence punishable on indictment or on summary conviction whether contained in an Act passed before or after the commencement of this Act, the expression 'person' shall, unless the contrary intention appears, include a body corporate.

Criminal Justice Act 1925

33.—(1) Where a corporation is charged, whether alone or jointly with some other person, with an indictable offence, the examining justices may, if they are of opinion that the evidence offered on the part of the prosecution is sufficient to put the accused corporation upon trial, make an order empowering the prosecutor to present . . . at assizes or quarter sessions, as the case may be, a bill in respect of the offence named in the order, and for the purpose of any enactments referring to committal for trial (including this Act) any such order shall be deemed to be a committal for trial:

When there is no legislative answer to the question of interpretation, the court may look to judicial precedents that have addressed the issue under consideration. Of course this begs the question, for one must then ask on what basis those earlier courts reached their decision. When the issue of interpretation is one of first impression, how does a court go about resolving it? There are many helpful rules of construction and many excellent books have been written about them. It is a topic deserving of a course in itself, and it will be possible here only to draw the student's attention to some of its more salient features.

Issues of statutory interpretation can arise simply because language has an indeterminate quality to it. A word may have multiple dictionary definitions, a common meaning, and technical meanings depending on its usage within a particular trade or profession. Indeterminacy of language is, moreover, a two-edged sword. On the one hand, such language broadens the sweep of the statute and helps to ensure that wrongdoers do not escape a conviction because of a narrow reading of the statute, but, on the other hand, can lead to situations where conduct which Parliament may not have intended to be made criminal falls within the literal wording of the statute.

NOTES AND QUESTIONS
1. If the words of a statute are susceptible to more than one interpretation, should a court choose the interpretation that benefits the defendant or the Crown? In *Sweet* v *Parsley* [1970] AC 132 Lord Reid wrote that 'it is a universal principle that if a penal provision is reasonably capable of two interpretations, that interpretation which is most favourable to the accused must be adopted'. As you read the various cases in this book, you might note the extent to which this principle is observed in practice.

2. In tackling issues of statutory interpretation, some judges will read a statute fairly literally, giving the words of the statute their ordinary meaning, while others will give the statute a purposive reading, attempting to interpret the statute in light of the evil which Parliament designed it to address. Which of these approaches a court takes will determine the scope of criminal liability. Consider the following statute:

Protection from Harassment Act 1997

1. Prohibition of harassment
(1) A person must not pursue a course of conduct—
   (a) which amounts to harassment of another, and
   (b) which he knows or ought to know amounts to harassment of the other.

(2) For the purposes of this section, the person whose course of conduct is in question ought to know that it amounts to harassment of another if a reasonable person in possession of the same information would think the course of conduct amounted to harassment of the other.

(3) Subsection (1) does not apply to a course of conduct if the person who pursued it shows—
   (a) that it was pursued for the purpose of preventing or detecting crime,
   (b) that it was pursued under any enactment or rule of law or to comply with any condition or requirement imposed by any person under any enactment, or
   (c) that in the particular circumstances the pursuit of the course of conduct was reasonable.

2. Offence of harassment
(1) A person who pursues a course of conduct in breach of section 1 is guilty of an offence.

(2) A person guilty of an offence under this section is liable on summary conviction to imprisonment for a term not exceeding six months, or a fine not exceeding level 5 on the standard scale, or both.

4. Putting people in fear of violence
(1) A person whose course of conduct causes another to fear, on at least two occasions, that violence will be used against him is guilty of an offence if he knows or ought to know that his course of conduct will cause the other so to fear on each of those occasions.

(2) For the purposes of this section, the person whose course of conduct is in question ought to know that it will cause another to fear that violence will be used against him on any occasion if a reasonable person in possession of the same information would think the course of conduct would cause the other so to fear on that occasion.

(3) It is a defence for a person charged with an offence under this section to show that—
   (a) his course of conduct was pursued for the purpose of preventing or detecting crime,
   (b) his course of conduct was pursued under any enactment or rule of law or to comply with any condition or requirement imposed by any person under any enactment, or
   (c) the pursuit of his course of conduct was reasonable for the protection of himself or another or for the protection of his or another's property.

(4) A person guilty of an offence under this section is liable—
   (a) on conviction on indictment, to imprisonment for a term not exceeding five years, or a fine, or both, or
   (b) on summary conviction, to imprisonment for a term not exceeding six months, or a fine not exceeding the statutory maximum, or both.

NOTES AND QUESTIONS

1. Both the social and legislative history of the Act make it quite clear that it was designed to address the then much publicised problem of 'stalking'. Yet the Act itself uses neither the word 'stalking' nor any of its variants.

2. In the employment context, harassment has more far-reaching connotations, often referring to sexual harassment. Is this now a crime under the Act?

3. Shortly after the Act came into force, the following case was reported in the newspapers (see *The Times*, 31 December 1997):

   > A businessman was charged with harassment after he had tried to stop his neighbour's pigeons from coming on to his property by singing 'Come Fly with Me' at the top of his lungs, throwing a ball about and installing a one-eyed plastic owl as a sort of scarecrow.

   Although the Crown Prosecution Service decided not to pursue the case, it is interesting to speculate whether the conduct falls within the statute if given a literal interpretation. A purposive interpretation?

   Historically, the doctrine of Parliamentary sovereignty has required courts to defer to the will of Parliament as expressed in its statutory enactments. A court cannot substitute its views for those of Parliament as to the scope of the statute or whether the conduct in question should be criminal. Difficulties often arise, however, in determining Parliament's will. Members of Parliament do not speak with one voice, and, even if they did, their purpose may not be clear. Until recently, judges were not permitted to consult Parliamentary debates to determine the objective of the statute (see *Davis* v *Johnson* [1979] AC 264). This position was relaxed in *Pepper* v *Hart* [1992] 3 WLR 1032, where the House of Lords stated that a court could refer to Hansard if a statute was ambiguous or obscure, or when a particular interpretation might lead to absurdity, as long as the reference was to a statement of a Minister or the promoter of the Bill. The courts are not required to do so, however, if they do not believe it would be helpful. See *R* v *Gomez* [1992] 3 WLR 1067.

4. The Human Rights Act 1998 requires courts to construe legislation consistently with the European Convention on Human Rights, at least as far as it is possible to do so. As a result, any ambiguity in a statute will have to be resolved in a way that renders the statute compatible with Convention rights. This may not yield the same interpretation of the statute that would have been given had a literal approach been taken or even an approach in which Parliament's intent or purpose was the operative guide.

3

The Conduct Component of Crime:
Actus Reus

SECTION 1: **Introduction**

A common law maxim held that *actus non facit reum nisi mens sit rea*. The maxim served to draw attention to the two most critical elements of a crime: *actus reus* and *mens rea*. Literally it meant that an act was not wrongful unless accompanied by a wrongful state of mind. It was generally interpreted, however, to require the prosecutor to prove both a wrongful act *and* a wrongful state of mind on the part of the accused. As it related to *actus reus*, the maxim was correct in this sense: as a general proposition, one cannot be convicted for mere criminal thoughts; one must normally do something towards bringing those thoughts to fruition. This approach to criminal liability is justified by three primary considerations:

(a) the difficulty in proving what a person is thinking;

(b) the difficulty in distinguishing between those with a genuine criminal purpose and those who are simply engaged in idle fantasy; and

(c) perhaps most importantly, to exclude from criminal liability those whose adventures do not extend beyond the thought stage. In terms of punishment, such individuals are neither dangerous nor in need of restraint or rehabilitation. They cause no harm and do not pose a threat to the public.

To the extent that the maxim seems to imply that in regard to every crime the offender must have committed a personal positive act, it is incorrect. Some crimes are defined in such a way that the failure to act constitutes the *actus reus* of the offence; in others an omission to act when there is a legal duty to act is treated as the equivalent of a positive act. Further, in some offences the *actus reus* is a state of affairs, with no requirement of an 'act' as such on the part of the accused. There are, for example, crimes in which the *actus reus* is possession of an illegal or dangerous item. Lastly, there are situations in which it is not necessary for the offender to have acted personally: the act of another will satisfy the requirement of *actus reus*.

The student should be advised that *actus reus* is an artificial construct which has no significance in and of itself. It provides a shorthand way of referring to that part of the crime concerned with the conduct prohibited by the law and conveys to others involved in legal matters a number of conceptual features which form the basis for legal analysis. The value of this approach is not without its critics, however.

R v *Miller*
[1983] 1 All ER 978, House of Lords

LORD DIPLOCK: . . . My Lords, it would I think be conducive to clarity of analysis of the ingredients of a crime that is created by statute, as are the great majority of criminal offences today, if we were to avoid bad Latin and instead to think and speak . . . about the conduct of the accused and his state of mind at the time of that conduct, instead of speaking of *actus reus* and *mens rea*.

Whether or not Lord Diplock is correct, he draws our attention to two important points. First, a coherent criminal law code could easily be constructed without using the terms *actus reus* or *mens rea*; and indeed, Parliament does not use these terms in its criminal law codifications. Neither did the Law Commission in its Draft Criminal Code Bill (1989), preferring 'fault' to *mens rea* and 'act' to *actus reus*. Secondly, the concepts of *actus reus* and *mens rea* are intended to aid analysis. If they have the opposite effect, then there is little point in stubbornly pursuing the search for them as such. It is sufficient to be clear about the elements of the crime as spelled out in the relevant statute.

To the extent that it remains useful to speak of an *actus reus*, and courts and commentators alike do continue to use the term, it is best understood to refer to the prohibited conduct component, as opposed to the mental component, of the crime. As commonly used in practice, the term may also encompass the results of the defendant's conduct and/or the attendant circumstances which convert what might otherwise be an innocent or neutral act into one that is criminal. While it may be no crime to fire a gun in a deserted area, it is attempted murder if the gun is aimed at another human being; and if the bullet finds its human target, the defendant may be guilty of either murder of manslaughter.

Some respected theorists, such as Glanville Williams, have suggested that *actus reus* should be conceived of as including the absence of excuse or justification. It may promote clarity of analysis, however, to discuss excuse and justification in the context of defences rather than as part of *actus reus*. This is the usual approach adopted and that taken in this book (see Chapter 10).

. . .

A somewhat different merger of elements may, on the other hand, be warranted. Literally translated, *actus reus* seems to refer to a physical act. There is, however, a mental component to most physical acts, in that they are the product of the will, and the courts have long accepted that a defendant whose acts are not the product of the defendant's will has not committed an *actus reus*. While if starting afresh one might include this so-called requirement of voluntariness within the rubric of *mens rea*, the judicial tradition is to view it as part of the *actus reus*.

Actus reus and *mens rea* are linked in another way. Many acts are ambiguous, and *mens rea* can help determine whether the act is wrongful (*reus*). In *R v Court* [1988] 2 All ER 221, for example, a defendant who smacked a 12-year-old girl on her buttocks was charged with indecent assault. To determine whether the assault was indecent, the court looked at the defendant's state of mind. See also *R v Marcus* [1981] 2 All ER 833 (whether sleeping pills are a 'noxious thing' within the meaning of a statute depends in part on the intent with which they are administered).

Conversely, a defendant's acts can assist the jury in determining whether the defendant had the *mens rea* required for a crime. If an accused has shot her victim in the heart from close range, the jury may infer an intent to kill. This, however, must be understood only as a *logical inference* for a jury to draw; it is not a conclusion that they can be required to reach as we will see in the next chapter.

SECTION 2:　Liability for failure to act

A:　Crimes defined in terms of a failure to act

Some statutory offences are defined in terms of a failure to act.

Road Traffic Act 1988

6.　Breath tests
　(1) Where a constable in uniform has reasonable cause to suspect—
　　(a) that a person driving or attempting to drive or in charge of a motor vehicle on a road or other public place has alcohol in his body or has committed a traffic offence whilst the vehicle was in motion, or
　　(b) that a person has been driving or attempting to drive or been in charge of a motor vehicle on a road or other public place with alcohol in his body and that that person still has alcohol in his body, or
　　(c) that a person has been driving or attempting to drive or been in charge of a motor vehicle on a road or other public place and has committed a traffic offence whilst the vehicle was in motion,
he may, subject to section 9 of this Act, require him to provide a specimen of breath for a breath test.
　(4) A person who, without reasonable excuse, fails to provide a specimen of breath when required to do so in pursuance of this section is guilty of an offence.

Prevention of Terrorism (Temporary Provisions) Act 1989

18. Information about acts of terrorism
　(1) A person is guilty of an offence if he has information which he knows or believes might be of material assistance—
　　(a) in preventing the commission by any other person of an act of terrorism connected with the affairs of Northern Ireland; or
　　(b) in securing the apprehension, prosecution or conviction of any other person for an offence involving the commission, preparation or instigation of such an act, and

fails without reasonable excuse to disclose that information as soon as reasonably practicable—

    (i)   in England and Wales, to a constable;

    (ii) in Scotland, to a constable or the procurator fiscal; or

    (iii) in Northern Ireland, to a constable or a member of Her Majesty's Forces.

(2) A person guilty of an offence under this section is liable—

    (a) on conviction on indictment, to imprisonment for a term not exceeding five years or a fine or both;

    (b) on summary conviction, to imprisonment for a term not exceeding six months or a fine not exceeding the statutory maximum or both.

Although most of the crimes in which a failure to act will satisfy the *actus reus* requirement are creations of Parliament, the issue may arise in respect to common law crimes.

R v Mavji

[1987] 2 All ER 758, Court of Appeal

MICHAEL DAVIES J: . . . [I]t was alleged by the prosecution that . . . the appellant was trading in gold on a large scale at prices which would have inevitably produced a loss but for the fact that the appellant pocketed value added tax moneys which he charged but for which he did not account. The appellant was a director of a company called Princeve Ltd which traded from a shop with workshop and flat attached in North Wembley. . . .

'Cheating' is, as counsel for the appellant correctly submitted, a common law offence. As such, it was abolished by s. 32(1)(a) of the Theft Act 1968 'except as regards offences relating to the public revenue'. Punishment for cheating the revenue at common law remains at large . . . To establish cheating, so it was submitted, there must be an actual deceit, a positive act such as a false representation and not merely an omission such as a failure to make a value added tax return, even if the purpose of the omission is to avoid the payment of value added tax lawfully due. No such deceit or misrepresentation or other positive act was alleged in this indictment or in the prosecution's evidence or argument at the trials.

. . . In our judgment, 'cheating the revenue' can take place without any positive act of deceit or, to adopt and respectfully indorse the words of Drake J when ruling on this matter in the appellant's first trial:

> The common law offence of cheating does not necessarily require a false representation, either by words or conduct. Cheating can include any form of fraudulent conduct which results in diverting money from the revenue and in depriving the revenue of money to which it is entitled.

The appellant was in circumstances in which he had a statutory duty to make value added tax returns and to pay over to the Crown the value added tax due. He dishonestly failed to do either. Accordingly, he was guilty of cheating HM The Queen and the public revenue. No further act or omission required to be alleged or proved.

Appeal dismissed.

R v Dytham

[1979] 3 All ER 641, Court of Appeal

LORD WIDGERY CJ: The appellant was a police constable in Lancashire. On 17th March 1977 at about one o'clock in the morning he was on duty in uniform and was standing by a hot dog stall in Duke Street, St Helens. A Mr Wincke was inside the stall and a Mr Sothern was by it. Some thirty yards away was the entrance to Cindy's Club. A man named Stubbs was ejected from the club by a bouncer. A fight ensued in which a number of men joined. There arose cries and screams and other indications of great violence. Mr Stubbs became the object of a murderous assault. He was beaten and kicked to death in the gutter outside the club. All this was audible and visible to the three men at the hot dog stall. At no stage did the appellant make any move to intervene or any attempt to quell the disturbance or to stop the attack on the victim. When the hubbub had died down he adjusted his helmet and drove away. . . .

His conduct was brought to the notice of the police authority. As a result he appeared on 10th October 1978 in the Crown Court at Liverpool to answer an indictment which was in these terms:

> . . . the charge against you is one of misconduct of an officer of justice, in that you . . . misconducted yourself whilst acting as an officer of justice in that you being present and a witness to a criminal offence namely a violent assault upon one . . . Stubbs by three others deliberately failed to carry out your duty as a police constable by wilfully omitting to take any steps to preserve the Queen's Peace or to protect the person of the said . . . Stubbs or to arrest or otherwise bring to justice [his] assailants.

[After conceding that a police constable was a public officer and that there did exist at common law an offence of misconduct in office, counsel for the appellant argued] that not every failure to discharge a duty which devolved on a person as the holder of a public office gave rise to the common law offence of misconduct in that office. As counsel for the appellant put it, non-feasance was not enough. There must be a malfeasance or at least a misfeasance involving an element of corruption. In support of this contention a number of cases were cited from 18th and 19th century reports. It is the fact that in nearly all of them the misconduct asserted involved some corrupt taint; but this appears to have been an accident of circumstance and not a necessary incident of the offence. . . .

In the present case it was not suggested that the appellant could not have summoned or sought assistance to help the victim or to arrest his assailants. The charge as framed left this answer open to him. Not surprisingly he did not seek to avail himself of it, for the facts spoke strongly against any such answer. The allegation made was not of mere non-feasance but of deliberate failure and wilful neglect. This involves an element of culpability which is not restricted to corruption or dishonesty but which must be of such a degree that the misconduct impugned is calculated to injure the public interest so as to call for condemnation and punishment. Whether such a situation is revealed by the evidence is a matter that a jury has to decide . . .

. . . The appeal is dismissed. . . .

NOTES AND QUESTIONS

1. The court in *Dytham* distinguishes between failing to do what one ought to do (nonfeasance) and deliberate and wilful neglect (often referred to as misfeasance; see also *R v Pittwood*, below). Is this distinction a meaningful one in practice, or simply a way of characterising those cases where the accused's inaction has deviated so far from what would generally deemed to be acceptable that a court has no compunctions about imposing criminal liability?
2. To anticipate an issue which will be addressed later in this chapter, is there a problem in saying that in crimes such as Dytham's, the defendant's inaction, rather than the assailant's actions, caused the victim's death? If Dytham had not been present, the victim would still have died. Perhaps it was for this reason that Dytham was charged with misconduct in office rather than with manslaughter, which would have required proof that Dytham's inaction caused the victim's death.
3. Is there a difference in *moral* culpability between the infliction of harm and the failure to prevent harm; between one whose inaction causes death and one whose actions cause death? If so, should this difference be reflected in the criminal law?

B: Crimes of commission by omission

In the preceding section we saw instances where the failure to act was itself criminal. These cases pose little problem other than semantic – is the absence of an act an act? The problem is created by the tradition of using the term *actus reus* to include inaction. Once it is recognised that the illegality is itself the failure to act, the problem disappears.

A somewhat different situation occurs where the definition of the crime appears to require affirmative conduct leading to a particular result, but the defendant is tried for a failure to act that would have prevented that result. The issue has arisen most often in cases of homicide, where the victim would have lived if the defendant had taken appropriate action. When should such a failure warrant criminal liability?

There is in the UK no general legal, as opposed to moral, duty to help others. There is, for example, no legal obligation to shout a warning to a blind man about to walk off a cliff or to summon aid when he in fact falls over the cliff. Whether such duties should be imposed by law is an issue for Parliament. In many European countries there is a statutory duty to help a person in peril if the actor can do so without personal risk or risk to others. For example, Article 63(2) of the French Penal Code provides:

Any person who voluntarily fails to render assistance to a person in peril, which he or she could have given either personally or by calling for help, without personal danger or danger to others, is guilty of an offence and may be punished by imprisonment from three months to five years or by a fine of 360 francs to 20,000 francs or both.

NOTES AND QUESTIONS
What are the arguments for and against a general duty to help others in distress? Should a duty to help others be deemed part of the obligation of citizenship? See generally E.J. Weinrib, 'The Case for a Duty to Rescue' (1980) *Yale LJ* 247.

In some instances one may be under a legal, not simply a moral, duty to help another. The situations where liability can arise tend to be divided into distinct categories.

(i) *Duties created by contract or office*
A professional swimmer who happens to be standing by the pool in which a child is drowning has no legal duty to rescue the child. But is the same true for the lifeguard employed to watch the children in the pool? The lifeguard is under a contractual duty to prevent harms of precisely this type. The lifeguard who sits idly by while a child drowns is in breach of contract, but is he also criminally liable for the child's death?

R v Pittwood
(1902) 19 TLR 37, Taunton Assizes

Philip Pittwood was charged with the manslaughter. It appeared that the prisoner occupied a hut as a gate-keeper on the Somerset and Dorset Railway near

Glastonbury. His duties were to keep the gate shut whenever a train was passing along the line, which was a single line, and not many trains used to pass during the day. His hours of duty were from 7 in the morning till 7 p.m. On 18 July, at about 2.45 in the afternoon, White was in a hay cart crossing the line with several others, when a train came up and hit the cart, White being struck and killed. Another man was also seriously injured, while the three remaining men by jumping out of the cart saved their lives.

MR JUSTICE WRIGHT: without calling upon the prosecution, gave judgment. He said he was clearly of opinion that in this case there was gross and criminal negligence, as the man was paid to keep the gate shut and protect the public. In his opinion: – (1) There might be cases of misfeasance and cases of mere non-feasance. Here it was quite clear there was evidence of misfeasance as the prisoner directly contributed to the accident. (2) A man might incur criminal liability from a duty arising out of contract.

NOTES AND QUESTIONS
1. Compare *Pittwood* with *Dytham*, above. Dytham was convicted of misconduct in office; Pittwood of manslaughter. Is it more appropriate to charge defendants such as Pittwood and Dytham with crimes based on their failure to act, without regard to the consequences of their inaction, or crimes reflecting the resulting harm? Often the harm is a result of chance. If no person had been crossing the railroad tracks, or if the conductor of the train had been able to bring it to a timely stop, there would have been no death.
2. Pittwood's liability would seem to turn on the fact that there was a clause in his contract that could be made the basis for imposing liability. Yet the contract was between Pittwood and his employer, and the contractual duty was owed to the employer, not to members of the general public. Is it possible (desirable) to find an implied contractual duty to the public in regard to all occupations where the failure to perform competently can give rise to injury? Consider the situation of prison officials or warders in an institution for the criminally insane. Should they be held criminally responsible if, due to their incompetence, one of their charges were to escape and commit murder? Reconsider *Dytham*.

(ii) *Duties arising from the voluntary assumption of care*
Similar and yet distinguishable from cases of duties arising out of the obligation of office (e.g., *Dytham*) and duties arising out of the obligation of contract (e.g., *Pittwood*) are cases where a duty of care has been voluntarily undertaken. In these cases the person has undertaken a duty but, unlike in the other two categories, there is no legal consideration for the undertaking. Can there nonetheless be criminal liability?

R v Instan
[1893] 1 QB 450, Queen's Bench Division

DAY J: Kate Instan . . . who is between thirty and forty years of age and unmarried, had no occupation and no means of her own of living. She was a niece of the deceased.

At the time of the committal of the alleged offence, and for some time previous thereto, she had been living with and had been maintained by the deceased. Deceased was a woman of some seventy-three years of age, and until a few weeks before her death was healthy and able to take care of herself. . . .

The deceased shortly before her death suffered from gangrene in the leg, which rendered her during the last ten days of her life quite unable to attend to herself or to move about or to do anything to procure assistance. No one but the prisoner had previous to the death any knowledge of the condition in which her aunt thus was. The prisoner continued to live in the house at the cost of the deceased, and took in the food supplied by the tradespeople; but does not appear to have given any to the deceased, and she certainly did not give or procure any medical or nursing attendance to or for her, or give notice to any neighbour of her condition or wants, although she had abundant opportunity and occasion to do so.

The body of the deceased was on August 2, while the prisoner was still living in the house, found much decomposed, partially dressed in her day clothes, and lying partly on the ground and partly prone upon the bed. The death probably occurred from four to seven days before August 3, the date of the post-mortem examination of the body. The cause of death was exhaustion caused by the gangrene, but substantially accelerated by neglect, want of food, of nursing, and of medical attendance during several days previous to the death. . . .

LORD COLERIDGE CJ: We are all of opinion that this conviction must be affirmed. It would not be correct to say that every moral obligation involves a legal duty; but every legal duty is founded on a moral obligation. A legal common law duty is nothing else than the enforcing by law of that which is a moral obligation without legal enforcement. There can be no question in this case that it was the clear duty of the prisoner to impart to the deceased so much as was necessary to sustain life of the food which she from time to time took in, and which was paid for by the deceased's own money for the purpose of the maintenance of herself and the prisoner; it was only through the instrumentality of the prisoner that the deceased could get the food. There was, therefore, a common law duty imposed upon the prisoner which she did not discharge.

Nor can there be any question that the failure of the prisoner to discharge her legal duty at least accelerated the death of the deceased, if it did not actually cause it. There is no case directly in point; but it would be a slur upon and a discredit to the administration of justice in this country if there were any doubt as to the legal principle, or as to the present case being within it. The prisoner was under a moral obligation to the deceased from which arose a legal duty towards her; that legal duty the prisoner has wilfully and deliberately left unperformed, with the consequence that there has been an acceleration of the death of the deceased owing to the non-performance of that legal duty. It is unnecessary to say more than that upon the evidence this conviction was most properly arrived at.

Is the decision in the following case a logical extension of *Instan*?

R v Stone; R v Dobinson
[1977] 2 All ER 341, Court of Appeal

GEOFFREY LANE LJ: . . . In 1972, at 75 Broadwater, Bolton-on-Dearne in Yorkshire, there lived three people. Stone, an ex-miner now aged 67, widowed for ten years, who is partially deaf, almost totally blind and has no appreciable sense of smell; Gwendoline Dobinson, now aged 43, who had been his housekeeper and mistress for some eight years, and Stone's son called Cyril, aged 34, who is mentally subnormal. Stone is of low average intelligence. Dobinson is described as ineffectual and somewhat inadequate.

. . . Stone had a younger sister called Fanny, about 61 at the date of her death. She had been living with another sister called Rosy. For some reason, probably because Rosy could not tolerate her any longer, she had decided to leave. She came to live at no. 75, where she occupied a small front room. She was in receipt of a pension of £11.60 per week and gave her brother £1.50 towards the rent. She was eccentric in many ways. She was morbidly and unnecessarily anxious about putting on weight and so denied herself proper meals. She would take to her room for days. She would often stay in her room all day until the two appellants went to the public house in the evening, when she would creep down and make herself a meal.

In early spring 1975 the police called at the house. Fanny had been found wandering about in the street by herself without apparently knowing where she was. This caused the appellants to try and find Fanny's doctor. They tried to trace him through Rosy, but having walked a very considerable distance in their search they failed. . . . Fanny herself refused to tell them the doctor's name. She thought she would be 'put away' if she did. Nothing more was done to enlist outside professional aid.

In the light of what happened subsequently there can be no doubt that Fanny's condition over the succeeding weeks and months must have deteriorated rapidly. By July 1975 she was, it seems, unable or unwilling to leave her bed . . .

. . . It seems that some efforts were made to get a local doctor, but the neighbour who volunteered to do the telephoning (the appellants being incapable of managing the instrument themselves) was unsuccessful.

On 2nd August 1975 Fanny was found by Dobinson to be dead in her bed. . . .

[The] contention was advanced by counsel . . . that the evidence which the judge had suggested to the jury might support the assumption of a duty by the appellants did not, when examined, succeed in doing so. He suggested that the situation here was unlike any reported case. Fanny came to this house as a lodger. Largely, if not entirely due to her own eccentricity and failure to look after herself or feed herself properly, she became increasingly infirm and immobile and eventually unable to look after herself. Is it to be said, asks counsel for the appellants rhetorically, that by the mere fact of becoming infirm and helpless in these circumstances, she casts a duty on her brother and Mrs Dobinson to take steps to have her looked after or taken to hospital? The suggestion is that, heartless though it may seem, this is one of those situations where the appellants were entitled to do nothing; where no duty was cast on them to help, any more than it is cast on a man to rescue a stranger from drowning, however easy such a rescue might be.

This court rejects that proposition. Whether Fanny was a lodger or not she was a blood relation of the appellant Stone; she was occupying a room in his house; Mrs Dobinson had undertaken the duty of trying to wash her, of taking such food to her as she required. There was ample evidence that each appellant was aware of the poor condition she was in by mid-July. It was not disputed that no effort was made to summon an ambulance or the social services or the police despite the entreaties of Mrs Wilson and Mrs West. A social worker used to visit Cyril. No word was spoken to him. All these were matters which the jury were entitled to take into account when considering whether the necessary assumption of a duty to care for Fanny had been proved.

This was *not* a situation analagous to the drowning stranger. They *did* make efforts to care. They tried to get a doctor; they tried to discover the previous doctor. Mrs Dobinson helped with the washing and the provision of food. All these matters were put before the jury in terms which we find it impossible to fault. The jury were entitled to find that the duty had been assumed. They were entitled to conclude that once Fanny became helplessly infirm, as she had by 19th July, the appellants were, in the circumstances, obliged either to summon help or else to care for Fanny themselves. . . .

The duty which a defendant has undertaken is a duty of caring for the health and welfare of the infirm person. What the Crown has to prove is a breach of that duty in such circumstances that the jury feel convinced that the defendant's conduct can properly be described as reckless. That is to say a reckless disregard of danger to the health and welfare of the infirm person. Mere inadvertence is not enough. The defendant must be proved to have been indifferent to an obvious risk of injury to health, or actually to have foreseen the risk but to have determined nevertheless to run it.

The direction given by the judge was wholly in accord with these principles. If any criticism is to be made it would be that the direction was unduly favourable to the defence. The appeals against conviction therefore fail.

Appeals against conviction dismissed.

NOTES AND QUESTIONS
1. Both Stone and Dobinson left something to be desired in terms of competence – Stone was described as deaf, blind, and of low intelligence; his mistress Dobinson as ineffectual and inadequate. Was it fair to impose a duty on them to care for Fanny when they could barely care for themselves? The Court of Appeal did not seem at all troubled by their general inadequacy, let alone their inability to cope with the extraordinary situation in which they found themselves, one which would have taxed persons of far greater competence.
2. What was the legal basis for imposing a duty on Stone and Dobinson? Of what relevance was:
   (a) The fact that Fanny was a blood relation? (In the case, Stone, the victim's brother, initially received almost twice the sentence of Dobinson, who was not a blood relative. The sentence, however, was modified on appeal because of Stone's handicapped condition.)
   (b) The fact that Fanny paid £1.50 per week towards the rent? Did this create a contractual obligation? Are landlords generally responsible for the welfare of their tenants?
   (c) The fact that Stone and Dobinson had taken Fanny into their home and provided her with shelter? From a legal point of view, would they have been better advised to have been more cold-hearted and turned Fanny away at the door? What if she had refused to leave?
   (d) The fact that if Stone and Dobinson had not undertaken the care of Fanny, some social agency might have discovered her plight and provided the necessary care? Indeed, a social worker regularly visited Stone and Dobinson because of their disabled child, yet they failed to take advantage of the opportunity to alert the social worker of Fanny's condition. In a sense, Stone and Dobinson isolated Fanny and prevented her from receiving help from others.
   (e) The fact that at the end Fanny was totally helpless. See *R v Smith* [1979] Crim LR 251.
3. What of the responsibility of Fanny, an adult, to help herself? She refused to cooperate in the search for a doctor and also refused to eat properly. Did Stone and Dobinson have an obligation to force feed her?
4. If Stone and Dobinson – ordinary individuals – can incur a duty to care for a third party, what is the responsibility of professional carers, such as nurses and doctors (who may also be under a contractual duty and ethical duty to provide care for their patients)? And can that duty ever come to an end? In the next case the House of Lords grappled with these issues in tragic circumstances.

Airedale NHS Trust v *Bland*
[1993] 1 All ER 821, House of Lords

LORD KEITH OF KINKEL: My Lords, as a result of injuries sustained in the Hillsborough disaster, Anthony Bland has for over three years been in the condition known as persistent vegetative state (PVS). It is unnecessary to go into all the details about the manifestations of this state, which are fully set out in the judgments of the courts below. It is sufficient to say that it arises from the destruction, through prolonged deprivation of oxygen, of the cerebral cortex, which has resolved into a watery mass. The cortex is that part of the brain which is the seat of cognitive function and sensory capacity. Anthony Bland cannot see, hear or feel anything. He cannot communicate in any way. The consciousness which is the essential feature of individual personality has departed for ever. On the other hand the brain stem, which controls the reflexive functions of the body, in particular heartbeat, breathing and digestion, continues to operate. In the eyes of the medical world and of the law a person is not clinically dead so long as the brain stem retains its function. In order to maintain Anthony Bland in his present condition, feeding and hydration are achieved artificially by means of a nasogastric tube and excretionary functions are regulated by a catheter and by enemas. The catheter from time to time gives rise to infections which have to be dealt with by appropriate medical treatment. The undisputed consensus of eminent medical opinion is that there is no prospect whatever that Anthony Bland will ever make any recovery from his present condition, but that there is every likelihood that he will maintain his present state of existence for many years to come, provided that the medical care which he is now receiving is continued.

In that state of affairs the medical men in charge of Anthony Bland's case formed the view, which was supported by his parents, that no useful purpose was to be served by continuing that medical care and that it was appropriate to stop the artificial feeding and other measures aimed at prolonging his existence. Since, however, there were doubts as to whether this course might not constitute a criminal offence, the responsible hospital authority, the Airedale NHS Trust, sought in the High Court of Justice declarations designed to resolve these doubts. In the result declarations on the lines asked for were granted by judgment of Sir Stephen Brown P on 19 November 1992. That judgment was affirmed by the Court of Appeal (Sir Thomas Bingham MR, Butler-Sloss and Hoffmann LJJ) on 9 December 1992. The declarations are in these terms:

> . . . that despite the inability of [the defendant] to consent thereto the Plaintiffs and the responsible attending physicians: (1) may lawfully discontinue all life-sustaining treatment and medical support measures designed to keep [the defendant] alive in his existing persistent vegetative state including the termination of ventilation nutrition and hydration by artificial means; and (2) may lawfully discontinue and thereafter need not furnish medical treatment to [the defendant] except for the sole purpose of enabling [him] to end his life and die peacefully with the greatest dignity and the least of pain suffering and distress . . .

Anthony Bland, by the Official Solicitor as his guardian ad litem, now appeals, with leave given in the Court of Appeal, to your Lordships' House. At the hearing of the appeal your Lordships were assisted by submissions made by Mr Anthony Lester QC as amicus curiae instructed by the Treasury Solicitor.

The broad issue raised by the appeal is stated by the parties to be: 'In what circumstances, if ever, can those having a duty to feed an invalid lawfully stop doing so?' The immediate issue, however, is whether in the particular circumstances of Anthony Bland's case those in charge of it would be acting lawfully if they discontinued the particular measures, including feeding by nasogastric tube, which are now being used to maintain Anthony Bland in his existing condition.

. . .

Where one individual has assumed responsibility for the care of another who cannot look after himself or herself, whether as a medical practitioner or otherwise, that responsibility cannot lawfully be shed unless arrangements are made for the responsibility to be taken over by someone else. Thus a person having charge of a baby who fails to feed it, so that it dies, will be guilty at least of manslaughter. The same is true of one having charge of an adult who is frail and cannot look after herself: see *R v Stone* [1977] 2 All ER 341, [1977] QB 354. It was argued for the guardian ad litem, by analogy with that case, that here the doctors in charge of Anthony Bland had a continuing duty to feed him by means of the nasogastric tube and that if they failed to carry out that duty they were guilty of manslaughter, if not murder. This was coupled with the argument that feeding by means of the nasogastric tube was not medical treatment at all, but simply feeding indistinguishable from feeding by normal means. As regards this latter argument, I am of opinion that regard should be had to the whole regime, including the artificial feeding, which at present keeps Anthony Bland alive. That regime amounts to medical treatment and care, and it is incorrect to direct attention exclusively to the fact that nourishment is being provided. In any event, the administration of nourishment by the means adopted involves the application of a medical technique. But it is, of course, true that in general it would not be lawful for a medical practitioner who assumed responsibility for the care of an unconscious patient simply to give up treatment in circumstances where continuance of it would confer some benefit on the patient. On the other hand a medical practitioner is under no duty to continue to treat such a patient where a large body of informed and responsible medical opinion is to the effect that no benefit at all would be conferred by continuance. Existence in a vegetative state with no prospect of recovery is by that opinion regarded as not being a benefit, and that, if not unarguably correct, at least forms a proper basis for the decision to discontinue treatment and care: see *Bolam v Friern Hospital Management Committee* [1957] 2 All ER 118, [1957] 1 WLR 582.

Given that existence in the persistent vegetative state is not a benefit to the patient, it remains to consider whether the principle of the sanctity of life, which it is the concern of the state, and the judiciary as one of the arms of the state, to maintain, requires this House to hold that the judgment of the Court of Appeal was incorrect. In my opinion it does not. The principle is not an absolute one. It does not compel a medical practitioner on pain of criminal sanctions to treat a patient, who will die if he does not, contrary to the express wishes of the patient. It does not authorise forcible feeding of prisoners on hunger strike. It does not compel the temporary keeping alive of patients who are terminally ill where to do so would merely prolong their suffering. On the other hand it forbids the taking of active measures to cut short the life of a terminally ill patient. In my judgment it does no violence to the principle to hold that it is lawful to cease to give medical treatment and care to a PVS patient who has been in that state for over three years, considering that to do so involves invasive manipulation of the patient's body to which he has not consented and which confers no benefit upon him.

LORD GOFF OF CHIEVELEY: . . . I start with the simple fact that, in law, Anthony is still alive. It is true that his condition is such that it can be described as a living death; but he is nevertheless still alive. This is because, as a result of developments in modern medical technology, doctors no longer associate death exclusively with breathing and heart beat, and it has come to be accepted that death occurs when the brain, and in particular the brain stem, has been destroyed (see Professor Ian Kennedy's paper entitled 'Switching off life support machines: the legal implications' reprinted in *Treat Me Right, Essays in Medical Law and Ethics* (1988) esp at 351–352 and the material there cited). There has been no dispute on this point in the present case, and it is unnecessary for me to consider it further. The evidence is that Anthony's brain stem is still alive and functioning and it follows that, in the present state of medical science, he is still alive and should be so regarded as a matter of law.

It is on this basis that I turn to the applicable principles of law. Here, the fundamental principle is the principle of the sanctity of human life – a principle long recognised not only in our own society but also in most, if not all, civilised societies throughout the modern world, as is indeed evidenced by its recognition both in art 2 of the European Convention on Human Rights (Convention for the Protection of Human Rights and Fundamental Freedoms (Rome, 4 November 1950; TS 71 (1953); Cmd 8969)) and in art 6 of the International Covenant on Civil and Political Rights (New York, 19 December 1966; TS 6 (1977); Cmnd 6702).

But this principle, fundamental though it is, is not absolute. Indeed there are circumstances in which it is lawful to take another man's life, for example by a lawful act of self-defence, or (in the days when capital punishment was acceptable in our society) by lawful execution. We are not however concerned with cases such as these. We are concerned with circumstances in which it may be lawful to withhold from a patient medical treatment or care by means of which his life may be prolonged. But here too there is no absolute rule that the patient's life must be prolonged by such treatment or care, if available, regardless of the circumstances.

First, it is established that the principle of self-determination requires that respect must be given to the wishes of the patient, so that, if an adult patient of sound mind refuses, however unreasonably, to consent to treatment or care by which his life would or might be prolonged, the doctors responsible for his care must give effect to his wishes, even though they do not consider it to be in his best interests to do so (see *Schloendorff* v *Society of New York Hospital* (1914) 211 NY 125 at 129–130 per Cardozo J, *S* v *S*, *W* v *Official Solicitor* [1970] 3 All ER 107 at 111, [1972] AC 24 at 43 per Lord Reid and *Sidaway* v *Bethlem Royal Hospital Governors* [1985] 1 All ER 643 at 649, [1985] AC 871 at 882 per Lord Scarman). To this extent, the principle of the sanctity of human life must yield to the principle of self-determination (see p 851 ante, per Hoffmann LJ), and, for present purposes perhaps more important, the doctor's duty to act in the best interests of his patient must likewise be qualified. On this basis, it has been held that a patient of sound mind may, if properly informed, require that life support should be discontinued: see *Nancy B* v *Hôtel-Dieu de Québec* (1992) 86 DLR (4th) 385. Moreover the same principle applies where the patient's refusal to give his consent has been expressed at an earlier date, before he became unconscious or otherwise incapable of communicating it; though in such circumstances especial care may be necessary to ensure that the prior refusal of consent is still properly to be regarded as applicable in the circumstances which have subsequently occurred (see e.g. *Re T (adult: refusal of medical treatment), Re* [1992] 4 All ER 649, [1992] 3 WLR 782). I wish to add that, in cases of this kind, there is no question of the patient having committed suicide, nor therefore of the doctor having aided or abetted him in doing so. It is simply that the patient has, as he is entitled to do, declined to consent to treatment which might or would have the effect of prolonging his life, and the doctor has, in accordance with his duty, complied with his patient's wishes.

But in many cases not only may the patient be in no condition to be able to say whether or not he consents to the relevant treatment or care, but also he may have given no prior indication of his wishes with regard to it. In the case of a child who is a ward of court, the court itself will decide whether medical treatment should be provided in the child's best interests, taking into account medical opinion. But the court cannot give its consent on behalf of an adult patient who is incapable of himself deciding whether or not to consent to treatment. I am of the opinion that there is nevertheless no absolute obligation upon the doctor who has the patient in his care to prolong his life, regardless of the circumstances. . . .

I must however stress, at this point, that the law draws a crucial distinction between cases in which a doctor decides not to provide, or to continue to provide, for his patient treatment or care which could or might prolong his life and those in which he decides, for example by administering a lethal drug, actively to bring his patient's life to an end. As I have already indicated, the former may be lawful, either because the doctor is giving effect to his patient's wishes by withholding the treatment or care, or even in certain circumstances in which (on principles which I shall describe) the patient is incapacitated from stating whether or not he gives his consent. But it is not lawful for a doctor to administer a drug to his patient to bring about his death, even though that course is prompted by a humanitarian desire to end his suffering, however great that suffering may be.

. . .

At the heart of this distinction lies a theoretical question. Why is it that the doctor who gives his patient a lethal injection which kills him commits an unlawful act and indeed is guilty of murder, whereas a doctor who, by discontinuing life support, allows his patient to die may not act unlawfully and will not do so if he commits no breach of duty to his patient? Professor Glanville Williams has suggested (see *Textbook of Criminal Law* (2nd edn, 1983) p 282) that the reason is that what the doctor does when he switches off a life support machine 'is in substance not an act but an omission to struggle' and that 'the omission is not a breach of duty by the doctor, because he is not obliged to continue in a hopeless case'.

I agree that the doctor's conduct in discontinuing life support can properly be categorised as an omission. It is true that it may be difficult to describe what the doctor actually does as an omission, for example where he takes some positive step to bring the life support to an end. But discontinuation of life support is, for present purposes, no different from not initiating life support in the first place. In each case, the doctor is simply allowing his patient to die in the sense that he is desisting from taking a step which might, in certain circumstances, prevent his patient from dying as a result of his pre-existing condition; and as a matter of general principle an omission such as this will not be unlawful unless it constitutes a breach of duty to the patient. I also agree that the doctor's conduct is to be differentiated from that of, for example, an interloper who maliciously switches off a life support machine because, although the interloper may perform exactly the same act as the doctor who discontinues life support, his doing so constitutes interference with the life-prolonging treatment then being administered by the doctor. Accordingly, whereas the doctor, in discontinuing life support, is simply allowing his patient to die of his pre-existing condition, the interloper is actively intervening to stop the doctor from prolonging the patient's life, and such conduct cannot possibly be categorised as an omission.

The distinction appears, therefore, to be useful in the present context in that it can be invoked to explain how discontinuance of life support can be differentiated from ending a patient's life by a lethal injection. But in the end the reason for that difference is that, whereas the law considers that discontinuance of life support may be consistent with the doctor's duty to care for his patient, it does not, for reasons of policy, consider that it forms any part of his duty to give his patient a lethal injection to put him out of his agony.

. . .

It is of course the development of modern medical technology, and in particular the development of life support systems, which has rendered cases such as the present so much more relevant than in the past. Even so, where, for example, a patient is brought into hospital in such a condition that, without the benefit of a life support system, he will not continue to live, the decision has to be made whether or not to give him that benefit, if available. That decision can only be made in the best interests of the patient. No doubt, his best interests will ordinarily require that he should be placed on a life support system as soon as necessary, if only to make an accurate assessment of his condition and a prognosis for the future. But, if he neither recovers sufficiently to be taken off it nor dies, the question will ultimately arise whether he should be kept on it indefinitely. As I see it, that question (assuming the continued availability of the system) can only be answered by reference to the best interests of the patient himself having regard to established medical practice. Indeed, if the justification for treating a patient who lacks the capacity to consent lies in the fact that the treatment is provided in his best interests, it must follow that the treatment may, and indeed ultimately should, be discontinued where it is no longer in his best interests to provide it. The question which lies at the heart of the present case is, as I see it, whether on that principle the doctors responsible for the treatment and care of Anthony Bland can justifiably discontinue the process of artificial feeding upon which the prolongation of his life depends.

It is crucial for the understanding of this question that the question itself should be correctly formulated. The question is not whether the doctor should take a course which will kill his patient, or even take a course which has the effect of accelerating his death. The question is whether the doctor should or should not continue to provide his patient with medical treatment or care which, if continued, will prolong his patient's life. The question is sometimes put in striking or emotional terms, which can be misleading. For example, in the case of a life support system, it is sometimes asked: should a doctor be entitled to switch it off, or to pull the plug? And then it is asked: can it be in the best interests of the patient that a doctor should be able to switch the life support system off, when this will inevitably result in the patient's death? Such an approach has rightly been criticised as misleading, for example by Professor Ian Kennedy (in his paper in *Treat Me Right, Essays in Medical Law and Ethics* (1988)), and by Thomas J in *Auckland Area Health Board* v *A-G* [1993] 1 NZLR 235 at 247. This is because the question is not whether it is in the best interests of the patient that he should die. The question is whether it is in the best interests of the patient that his life should be prolonged by the continuance of this form of medical treatment or care.

The correct formulation of the question is of particular importance in a case such as the present, where the patient is totally unconscious and where there is no hope whatsoever of any amelioration of his condition. In circumstances such as these, it may be difficult to say that it is in his best interests that the treatment should be ended. But, if the question is asked, as in my opinion it should be, whether it is in his best interests that treatment which has the effect of artificially prolonging his life should be continued, that question can sensibly be answered to the effect that it is not in his best interests to do so.

NOTES AND QUESTIONS

1. Consider in this context the care of Re A (Conjoined Twins: Medical Treatment) [2001] 1 FLR 1 for facts and holding see pp. 473 where the duty to provide care for one conjoined twin conflicted with the duty not to kill the other.

BROOKE LJ said:

13. The meaning of the word 'kills'

I turn now to the world 'kills' in the definition of murder. In the Tony Bland case (*Airedale NHS Trust v Bland* [1993] AC 789) the House of Lords was much exercised with the question whether the cessation of medical treatment and care to a patient who had been in a persistent vegetative state for three years constituted an intentional killing of that patient for the purposes of the law of murder. Lord Goff identified what he described as a crucial distinction in these terms at p 865:

> 'I must however stress, at this point, that the law draws a crucial distinction between cases in which a doctor decides not to provide, or to continue to provide, for his patient treatment or care which could or might prolong his life, and those in which he decides, for example by administering a lethal drug, actively to bring his patient's life to an end. As I have already indicated, the former may be lawful, either because the doctor is giving effect to his patient's wishes by withholding the treatment or care or even in certain circumstances in which (on principles which I shall describe) the patient is incapacitated from stating whether or not he gives his consent. But it is not lawful for a doctor to administer a drug to his patient to bring about his death, even though that course is prompted by a humanitarian desire to end his suffering, however great that suffering may be: see Reg v Cox (unreported), 18 September 1992. So to act is to cross the Rubicon which runs between on the one hand the care of the living patient and on the other hand euthanasia – actively causing his death to avoid or to end his suffering. Euthanasia is not lawful at common law.'

In the Tony Bland case the House of Lords was satisfied that the cessation of life-prolonging treatment or care could not be categorised as a positive act for the purposes of the law of murder, and since on the facts of that case the doctors owed no duty to the patient to prolong his life (since that course, the House of Lords held, would not be in their patient's best interests), they could not be found guilty of a culpable omission to act, either.

It was this distinction between acts and omissions which the judge had in mind when he held that it would be lawful to perform the proposed operation. He explained his thinking in the long passage which Ward LJ has recited fully in his judgment. He believed, in short, that the proposed operation was not unlawful because it did not represented a positive act but merely the withdrawal of Mary's blood supply.

On the hearing of the appeal only Mr Whitfield QC sought to persuade us to uphold the judge's approach. I am satisfied that the judge's approach was wrong. The proposed operation would involve a number of invasions of Mary's body, in the process of identifying which organ belonged to which child, before the positive step was taken of clamping the aorta and bringing about Mary's death. These acts would bear no resemblance to the discontinuance of artificial feeding sanctioned by the House of Lords in the Tony Bland case. They would be positive acts, and they would directly cause Mary's death.

NOTE

The issues raised by *Re A* are explained in depth in Michalowski, 'Sanctity of life – are some lives more sacred than others?' [2002] 22 Legal Studies 377.

(iii) *Duties arising from a close familial relationship*

We said previously that an experienced swimmer would not be criminally liable for failing to rescue a drowning child in a pool, but that a lifeguard under a contractual duty to safeguard the welfare of those in the pool would be liable. What of the parents of the child? Are they under a legal duty to save their drowning child?

R v *Gibbins and Proctor*
(1919) 13 Cr App R 134, Court of Criminal Appeal

DARLING J: The two appellants were indicted and tried together for the wilful murder of Nelly Gibbins, the daughter of Gibbins. The facts were that Gibbins's wife had left him, and he was living in adultery with Proctor. There were several children, one of whom was the child of Proctor, in the house. He earned good wages, which he brought home and gave to Proctor to maintain the house and those in it. There is no evidence that there was not enough to keep them all in health. And all were looked after except one, namely Nelly, who was starved to death. Her organs were healthy, and there was no reason why she should have died if she had been supplied with food.

. . .

. . . It is sufficient to refer to *Bubb and Hook* [(1850) 4 Cox CC 457], where Williams J said:

> It remains for me to explain to what extent she is responsible. If the omission or neglect to perform the duty was malicious, then the indictment would be supported, and the crime of murder would be made out against the prisoner; but if the omission or neglect were simply culpable, but not arising from a malicious motive on the part of the prisoner, then, though it would be your duty to find her guilty, it should be of manslaughter only. And here it becomes necessary to explain what is meant by the expression malicious, which is thus used. If the omission to provide necessary food or raiment was accompanied with an intention to cause the death of the child, or to cause some serious bodily injury to it, then it would be malicious in the sense imputed by this indictment, and in a case of this kind it is difficult, if not impossible, to understand how a person who contemplated doing serious bodily injury to the child by the deprivation of food, could have meditated anything else than causing its death.

The word used is 'contemplated,' but what has to be proved is an intention to do grievous bodily injury. In our opinion the judge left the question correctly to the jury, and there is no ground for interfering with the convictions for those reasons.

It has been said that there ought not to have been a finding of guilty of murder against Gibbins. The Court agrees that the evidence was less against Gibbins than Proctor, Gibbins gave her money, and as far as we can see it was sufficient to provide for the wants of themselves and all the children. But he lived in the house and the child was his own, a little girl of seven, and he grossly neglected the child. . . .

The case of Proctor is plainer. She had charge of the child. She was under no obligation to do so or to live with Gibbins, but she did so, and receiving money, as it is admitted she did, for the purpose of supplying food, her duty was to see that the child was properly fed and looked after, and to see that she had medical attention if necessary. We agree with what Lord Coleridge CJ said in *Instan* [1893] 1 QB 450. 'There is no case directly in point, but it would be a slur upon, and a discredit to the administration of, justice in this country if there were any doubt as to the legal principle, or as to the present case being within it. The prisoner was under a moral obligation to the deceased from which arose a legal duty towards her; that legal duty the prisoner has wilfully and deliberately left unperformed, with the consequence that there has been an acceleration of the death of the deceased owing to the non-performance of that legal duty.' Here Proctor took upon herself the moral obligation of looking after the children; she was *de facto*, though not *de jure*, the wife of Gibbins and had excluded the child's own mother. She neglected the child undoubtedly, and the evidence shews that as a result the child died. So a verdict of manslaughter at least was inevitable.

Appeals dismissed.

QUESTIONS

Is the rationale for imposing criminal liability on Gibbons (the father) and Proctor (his unmarried partner) the same? Does the court treat Proctor as if she was Gibbons's wife and the victim's mother, when the fact is that she was not? Compare the following case, decided over half a century later.

R v Lowe

[1973] 1 QB 702, Court of Appeal

On 20 July 1972, at Nottingham Crown Court (May J), the defendant, Robert Lowe, was charged jointly with Patricia Marshall, with whom he was living, on two counts in an indictment. The first count charged him with manslaughter, in that between 4 October 1971, and 5 November 1971, he unlawfully caused the death of Amanda Marshall. The second count charged him with cruelty to a child, contrary to s. 1(1) of the Children and Young Persons Act 1933, in that he, being a person who had attained the age of 16 years and who had the custody, charge or care of Amanda Marshall, a child under the age of 16 years, wilfully neglected Amanda Marshall in a manner likely to cause her unnecessary suffering or injury to health. The defendant submitted that he had done all that he could have been expected to do and that it was possible that the child's critical condition had arisen only in the last few days prior to 5 November 1971, when he assumed that Patricia Marshall had taken the child to the doctor. By their verdict the jury exonerated the defendant of gross negligence or recklessness but found him guilty of wilful neglect.

PHILLIMORE LJ: . . . In the present case the jury negatived recklessness. How then can mere neglect, albeit wilful, amount to manslaughter? This court feels that there is something inherently unattractive in a theory of constructive manslaughter. It seems strange that an omission which is wilful solely in the sense that it is not inadvertent and the consequences of which are not in fact foreseen by the person who is neglectful should, if death results, automatically give rise to an indeterminate sentence instead of the maximum of two years which would otherwise be the limit imposed.

We think that there is a clear distinction between an act of omission and an act of commission likely to cause harm. Whatever may be the position with regard to the latter it does not follow that the same is true of the former. In other words, if I strike a child in a manner likely to cause harm it is right that, if the child dies, I may be charged with manslaughter. If, however, I omit to do something with the result that it suffers injury to health which results in its death, we think that a charge of manslaughter should not be an inevitable consequence, even if the omission is deliberate.

NOTES AND QUESTIONS

1. Which decision – that in *Lowe* or that in *Gibbons and Proctor* – contains the more persuasive reasoning? Which is likely to promote the welfare of young children?
2. Where a legal duty is imposed as a result of contract or voluntary agreement, the scope and extent of the duty are determined by the terms of the contract or agreement. Where a legal duty arises as a result of a relationship, however, no such terms exist. Are there logical limits on the scope and extent of the duty?
3. In the drowning child situation, would a parent who could not swim be liable for failing to jump into the water to attempt to save his or her child? A parent who was a weak swimmer?
4. What if the parents are unaware of the plight of their child – that the child has jumped into the neighbour's swimming pool? Is there a duty to be aware of what is happening to one's child? In this context one must carefully distinguish between unawareness of a legal duty, which is generally not a defence (ignorance of the law will not excuse), and unawareness of facts which give rise to a legal duty, which may be a defence.
5. Is there a geographical limitation on liability? Is a parent responsible for his or her child when the child is visiting a friend? When the child is living with one's ex-spouse in another country? Does the duty extend only to members of one's household?
6. If a parent has a duty to his or her child, does an adult child have a duty to his or her parents? Do spouses have duties to one another? See *R v Smith* [1979] Crim LR 251. Do siblings? Reconsider *Stone and Dobinson*, above.

(iv) *Duties arising by virtue of the creation of danger*

Consider the person whose actions or inactions are responsible for creating a peril. By virtue of those actions or inactions, does a legal duty arise which did not previously exist?

R v Miller

[1983] 1 All ER 978, House of Lords

LORD DIPLOCK: My Lords, the facts which give rise to this appeal are sufficiently narrated in the written statement made to the police by the appellant Miller. That statement, subject to two minor orthographical corrections, reads:

> Last night I went out for a few drinks and at closing time I went back to the house where I have been kipping for a couple of weeks. I went upstairs into the back bedroom where I've been sleeping. I lay on my mattress and lit a cigarette. I must have fell to sleep because I woke up to find the mattress on fire. I just got up and went into the next room and went back to sleep. Then the next thing I remember was the police and fire people arriving. I hadn't got anything to put the fire out with so I just left it.

He was charged on indictment with the offence of 'arson contrary to section 1(1) and (3) of the Criminal Damage Act, 1971'. . . .

Since arson is a result-crime the period may be considerable, and during it the conduct of the accused that is causative of the result may consist not only of his doing physical acts which cause the fire to start or spread but also of his failing to take measures that lie within his power to counteract the danger that he has himself created. And if his conduct, active or passive, varies in the course of the period, so may his state of mind at the time of each piece of conduct. If, at the time of any particular piece of conduct by the accused that is causative of the result, the state of mind that actuates his conduct falls within the description of one or other of the states of mind that are made a necessary ingredient of the offence of arson by s. 1(1) of the Criminal Damage Act 1971 (i.e. intending to damage property belonging to another or being reckless whether such property would be damaged), I know of no principle of English criminal law that would prevent his being guilty of the offence created by that subsection. Likewise I see no rational ground for excluding from conduct capable of giving rise to criminal liability conduct which consists of failing to take measures that lie within one's power to counteract a danger that one has oneself created, if at the time of such conduct one's state of mind is such as constitutes a necessary ingredient of the offence. I venture to think that the habit of lawyers to talk of 'actus reus', suggestive as it is of action rather than inaction, is responsible for any erroneous notion that failure to act cannot give rise to criminal liability in English law.

No one has been bold enough to suggest that if, in the instant case, the accused had been aware at the time that he dropped the cigarette that it would probably set fire to his mattress and yet had taken no steps to extinguish it he would not have been guilty of the offence of arson, since he would have damaged property of another being reckless whether any such property would be damaged.

I cannot see any good reason why, so far as liability under criminal law is concerned, it should matter at what point of time before the resultant damage is complete a person becomes aware that he has done a physical act which, whether or not he appreciated that it would at the time when he did it, does in fact create a risk that property of another will be damaged, provided that, at the moment of awareness, it lies within his power to take steps, either himself or by calling for the assistance of the fire brigade if this be necessary, to prevent or minimise the damage to the property at risk.

. . .

My Lords, in the instant case the prosecution did not rely on the state of mind of the accused as being reckless during that part of his conduct that consisted of his lighting and smoking a cigarette while lying on his mattress and falling asleep without extinguishing it. So the jury were not invited to make any finding as to this. What the prosecution did rely on as being reckless was his state of mind during that part of his conduct after he awoke to find that he had set his mattress on fire and that it was smouldering, but did not then take any steps either to try to extinguish it himself or to send for the fire brigade, but simply went into the other room to resume his slumbers, leaving the fire from the already smouldering mattress to spread and to damage that part of the house in which the mattress was.

The recorder, in his lucid summing up to the jury (they took 22 minutes only to reach their verdict), told them that the accused, having by his own act started a fire in the mattress which, when he became aware of its existence, presented an obvious risk of damaging the house, became under a duty to take some action to put it out. The Court of Appeal upheld the conviction, but its ratio decidendi appears to be somewhat different from that of the recorder. As I understand the judgment, in effect it treats the whole course of conduct of the accused, from the moment at which he fell asleep and dropped the cigarette onto the mattress until the time the damage to the house by fire was complete, as a continuous act of the accused, and holds that it is sufficient to constitute the statutory offence of arson if at any stage in that course of conduct the state of mind of the accused, when he fails to try to prevent or minimise the damage which will result from his initial act, although it lies within his power to do so, is that of being reckless whether property belonging to another would be damaged.

My Lords, these alternative ways of analysing the legal theory that justifies a decision which has received nothing but commendation for its accord with common sense and justice have, since the publication of the judgment of the Court of Appeal in the instant case, provoked academic controversy. Each theory has distinguished support. Professor J C Smith espouses the 'duty theory' (see [1982] Crim LR 526 at 528); Professor Glanville Williams who, after the decision of the Divisional Court in *Fagan v Metropolitan Police Comr* [1968] 3 All ER 442, [1969] 1 QB 439 appears to have been attracted by the duty theory, now prefers that of the continuous act (see [1982] Crim LR 773). When applied to cases where a person has unknowingly done an act which sets in train events that, when he becomes aware of them, present an obvious risk that property belonging to another will be damaged, both theories lead to an identical result and, since what your Lordships are concerned with is to give guidance to trial judges in their task of summing up to juries, I would for this purpose adopt the duty theory as being the easier to explain to a jury; though I would commend the use of the word 'responsibility', rather than 'duty' which is more appropriate to civil than to criminal law since it suggests an obligation owed to another person, i.e. the person to whom the endangered property belongs, whereas a criminal statute defines combinations of conduct and state of mind which render a person liable to punishment by the state itself.

While, in the general run of cases of destruction or damage to property belonging to another by fire (or other means) where the prosecution relies on the recklessness of the accused, the direction recommended by this House in *R v Caldwell* [1982] AC 341 is appropriate, in the exceptional case (which is most likely to be one of arson and of which the instant appeal affords a striking example), where the accused is initially unaware that he has done an act that in fact sets in train events which, by the time the accused becomes aware of them, would make it obvious to anyone who troubled to give his mind to them that they present a risk that property belonging to another would be damaged, a suitable direction to the jury would be that the accused is guilty of the offence under s. 1(1) of the 1971 Act if, when he does become aware that the events in question have happened as a result of his own act, he does not try to prevent or reduce the risk of damage by his own efforts or if necessary by sending for help from the fire brigade and the reason why he does not is either because he has not given any thought to the possibility of there being any such risk or because having recognised that there was some risk involved he has decided not to try to prevent or reduce it.

Appeal dismissed. Certified question answered in the affirmative.

NOTES AND QUESTIONS
1. What was Miller's *actus reus* – the setting of the fire, or the failure to take steps to extinguish it after he became aware of it? The problem with finding the *actus reus* in the former is that at that time Miller did not have the mental state required by the statute; indeed, at that time he was asleep. There may have been an *actus reus* but there was no *mens rea*. After awakening and discovering the fire, however, Miller took no steps to cause it to be extinguished. Now there was a *mens rea* (recklessness) but no act. The problem is one of 'concurrence' – the requirement that the *actus reus* and the *mens rea* concur, or, stated perhaps more accurately, that the *actus reus* be the product of the *mens rea*. Lord Diplock resolved the problem by finding that Miller's failure to act when he had a duty to do so constituted the *actus reus*. An alternative approach would have been to regard the entire series of events as one transaction, with the concurrence element satisfied if there was the requisite *mens rea* at any time during the course of the transaction. See, e.g., *Attorney-General's Reference (No. 4 of 1980)* [1981] 1 WLR 705; *Fagan v Metropolitan Police Commissioner* [1968] 3 All ER 442; *R v Thabo Meli* [1954] 1 WLR 228. Issues of concurrence will be discussed in greater depth in Chapter 4.

2. What if the fire had been accidentally set by a visiting friend who had since departed? Would Miller still be liable for failing to take steps to extinguish it? If so, on what basis could a duty to act be said to arise?

(v) *Duties arising by virtue of a duty to control*

In some instances persons who have the power to control other persons or animals can be held criminally responsible for harm caused by those other entities. An owner of a dangerous animal, for example, may be liable if the animal escapes and attacks another. Sometimes this duty is imposed by statute:

Dangerous Dogs Act 1991

3. Keeping dogs under proper control

(1) If a dog is dangerously out of control in a public place—

    (a) the owner; and

    (b) if different, the person for the time being in charge of the dog, is guilty of an offence, or, if the dog while so out of control injures any person, an aggravated offence, under this subsection.

. . .

(3) If the owner or, if different, the person for the time being in charge of a dog allows it to enter a place which is not a public place but where it is not permitted to be and while it is there—

    (a) it injures any person; or

    (b) there are grounds for reasonable apprehension that it will do so, he is guilty of an offence, or, if the dog injures any person, an aggravated offence, under this subsection.

Where one's power to control relates to another person, liability may also be imposed. Often the crime charged will be one of aiding and abetting, the *actus reus* consisting of the failure to prevent or discourage the other's actions.

Du Cros v *Lambourne*
[1907] 1 KB 40, King's Bench Division

LORD ALVERSTONE CJ: . . . We have to consider the facts found in this case. The case states that the appellant must have known that the speed of the car was dangerous; that if Miss Godwin was driving, she was doing so with the consent and approval of the appellant, who was in control of the car, and that he could, and ought to, have prevented her from driving at this excessive and dangerous speed, but that he allowed her to do so and did not interfere in any way. I will not attempt to lay down any general rule or principle, but having regard to these findings of fact, it is, in my opinion, impossible to say that there was in this case no evidence of aiding and abetting on the part of the appellant. . . .

DARLING J: I am of the same opinion. I think that there was ample evidence on which the appellant could be convicted of aiding and abetting Miss Godwin in driving the car at a speed dangerous to the public. The appellant was the owner of the car and in control of it, and he was therefore the person to say who should drive it. The case finds that he *allowed* (I emphasise that) Miss Godwin to do so; that he knew that the speed was dangerous, and that he could and ought to have prevented it. Now, does it affect the validity of the conviction that the appellant was not charged with aiding and abetting but with having driven the car himself? I do not think that it does. . . .

Appeal dismissed.

C: Vicarious liability

Similar to cases involving a duty to control are those in which there is the authority to supervise the actions of others. Does one then become liable for the criminal acts of those others? In such cases there has been an *actus reus* committed, but not by the accused. The cases generally arise in the employment context, and the defendant's liability is said to be 'vicarious'. Such liability has long been recognised in tort law, where the concern is to provide compensation for the injured party. However, in criminal law vicarious liability is more controversial. Where it does occur, it is often the product of statute.

Licensing Act 1964

59. Prohibition of sale, etc. of intoxicating liquor outside permitted hours
   (1) Subject to the provisions of this Act, no person shall, except during the permitted hours—
       (a) himself or by his servant or agent sell or supply to any person in licensed premises or in premises in respect of which a club is registered any intoxicating liquor, whether to be consumed on or off the premises;
   . . .

QUESTIONS

1. .What considerations might prompt Parliament to enact a statute imposing vicarious liability? What are the pros and cons of such liability?

2. A publican instructs her employees that under no circumstances is any of them to sell liquor to customers outside permitted hours. The publican maintains a constant supervision of the employees. One day, however, the publican falls seriously ill, and remains at home so as not to infect her customers. On that day her employee sells liquor during a time when such sales are prohibited. Is the publican liable under s. 59(1) above? See *Lindsay* v *Vickers Ltd* [1978] Crim LR 55; *Anderton* v *Rodgers and Others* [1981] Crim LR 404.

3. What if the publican's employee, unbeknownst to her, sells stolen radios to customers in the pub? Assume that the employee is guilty of handling stolen goods. Would the publican also be vicariously liable? Is this situation different from the previous hypothetical? How so?

NOTE
In some situations vicarious liability is contemplated by Parliament and the statute in question is clear. In others, the statute does not on its face impose vicarious liability. If vicarious liability is to be imposed, it will be as a result of the court's interpretation of the statutory language.

Mousell Brothers Ltd v *London and North-Western Railway Company*
[1917] 2 KB 836, King's Bench Division

VISCOUNT READING CJ: In this case Foss, whose duty it was as manager to fill up or direct the filling up of the consignment notes from his principals, the appellants, to the respondents, wrongly described the goods with intent to avoid the payment of the rate payable in respect of the right classification of the goods. The question of law is whether the appellants, a limited liability company, can be convicted for this offence. It was not suggested that the directors of the appellant company were themselves parties to this false description. But it is suggested that they can be made criminally responsible for the act of their servant entrusted with the performance of this class of acts, and therefore acting within the scope of his employment. The magistrate convicted the appellants and stated a case for this Court. . . .

The first thing to consider is the language of the statute. Section 98 imposes upon every person being the owner or having the care of goods the obligation to give an exact account in writing of the number or quantity of goods liable to each of the tolls. Then by s. 99: 'If any such owner or other such person fail to give such account, or to produce his way-bill or bill of lading to such . . . servant of the company demanding the same' – then comes these important words – 'or if he give a false account . . . with intent to avoid the payment of any tolls payable in respect thereof, he shall for every such offence forfeit to the company a sum not exceeding ten pounds for every ton of goods, . . . and such penalty shall be in addition to the toll to which such goods may be liable.' By s. 2 of the Interpretation Act 1899, it is provided that 'In the construction of every enactment relating to an offence punishable on indictment or on summary conviction, whether contained in an Act passed before or after the commencement of this Act, the expression "person" shall, unless the contrary intention appears, include a body corporate.' In order to determine whether or not the contrary intention does appear, we must consider the broad question under what circumstances can a principal be made criminally responsible for the act of his servant. And then the narrower question, does this section, which imposes the penalty upon the owner, make the principal liable for the act of his servant done within the scope of his employment, but without the knowledge or the instructions of the principal?

The true principle of law is laid down in the case of *Pearks, Gunston & Tee* v *Ward* [1902] 2 KB 1. The passage to which I particularly wish to refer is in the judgment of Channell J:

> By the general principles of the criminal law, if a matter is made a criminal offence, it is essential that there should be something in the nature of mens rea, and, therefore, in ordinary cases a corporation cannot be guilty of a criminal offence, nor can a master be liable criminally for an offence committed by his servant. But there are exceptions to this rule in the case of quasi-criminal offences, as they may be termed, that is to say, where certain acts are forbidden by law under a penalty, possibly even under a personal penalty, such as imprisonment, at any rate in default of payment of a fine.

. . .

Prima facie, then, a master is not to be made criminally responsible for the acts of his servant to which the master is not a party. But it may be the intention of the Legislature, in order to guard against the happening of the forbidden thing, to impose a liability upon a principal even though he does not know of, and is not party to, the forbidden act done by his servant. Many statutes are passed with this object. Acts done by the servant of the licensed holder of licensed premises render the licensed holder in some instances liable, even though the act was done by his servant without the knowledge of the master. Under the Food and Drugs Acts there are again instances well known in these Courts where the master is made responsible, even though he knows nothing of the act done by his servant, and he may be fined or rendered amenable to the penalty enjoined by the law. In those cases the Legislature absolutely forbids the act and makes the principal liable without a mens rea.

. . .

Coming now to the present case, in my view the Legislature must be taken to have known that the forbidden acts were of a kind which, even in the year 1845, would in most cases be done by servants; and yet the penalty is imposed upon 'every person being the owner or having the care of any carriage or goods passing or being upon the railway.' It may be that the words 'person having the care of any carriage or goods,' etc., are wide enough to cover a person who occupied the position of Foss. I am by no means convinced of it. I am inclined to think they mean the bailee who is entrusted with the goods for carriage and who is not the owner. They would clearly not include a servant merely entrusted with the duty of filling up a consignment note. But the forbidden acts are such as would be performed by a servant. The object of the statute was, in my opinion, to forbid the giving of a false description of goods carried by the railway and so protect the railway company from being cheated into carrying goods at less than the due rate. I think, looking at the language and the purpose of this Act, that the Legislature intended to fix responsibility for this quasi-criminal act upon the principal if the forbidden acts were done by his servant within the scope of his employment. If that is the true view, there is nothing to distinguish a limited company from any other principal, and the defendants are properly made liable for the acts of Foss. The magistrate was right and this appeal fails.

ATKIN J: I agree, but I should like to add a few words in view of the argument of Mr Atkinson. I think that the authorities cited by my Lord make it plain that while prima facie a principal is not to be made criminally responsible for the acts of his servants, yet the Legislature may prohibit an act or enforce a duty in such words as to make the prohibition or the duty absolute; in which case the principal is liable if the act is in fact done by his servants. To ascertain whether a particular Act of Parliament has that effect or not regard must be had to the object of the statute, the words used, the nature of the duty laid down, the person upon whom it is imposed, the person by whom it would in ordinary circumstances be performed, and the person upon whom the penalty is imposed. . . .

NOTES

1. Vicarious liability is not limited to the employer–employee context. See, e.g., *Quality Dairies (York) Ltd* v *Pedley* [1952] 1 KB 275 (liability for acts of sub-contractor); *Linnet* v *Metropolitan Police Commissioner* [1946] 1 All ER 380 (liability for acts of co-licensee); *Clode* v *Barnes* [1974] 1 All ER 1166 (liability for acts of partner); *Anderton* v *Rodgers* [1981] Crim LR 404 (committee members of club liable for illegal sales of barman).

2. Crimes imposing vicarious liability need to be distinguished from those imposing strict liability (to be discussed in the next chapter). In regard to the latter, Parliament has dispensed with the need for the Crown to prove *mens rea*; in regard to the former, it is the requirement of a personal *actus reus* which has been dispensed with. Often crimes which impose strict liability are construed to allow vicarious liability as well. This coupling is not mere coincidence. *Mens rea* cannot as easily be attributed to another as *actus reus*, so if strict liability could not be imposed, there would be no vicarious liability where such was intended by Parliament. The courts have been willing to impute *mens rea* to an employer who has delegated responsibility to an employee. See *Allen* v *Whitehead* [1930] 1 KB 211; *Vane* v *Yiannopoullos* [1965] AC 486.

D: Status offences

Occasionally one's status constitutes the *actus reus* of a crime. As in cases of a failure to act, the defendant has not performed any act. In the failure to act cases, however, the defendant has omitted to do something which he or she should have done. In status offences, it is often not clear what, if anything, the defendant could have done to avoid prosecution.

R v *Larsonneur*

(1933) 149 LT 542, Court of Criminal Appeal

The appellant who was a French subject, landed in the United Kingdom on the 14 March 1933 with a French passport, which was endorsed with conditions prohibiting her employment in the United Kingdom. On the 22 March 1933 these conditions were varied by a condition requiring her to leave the United Kingdom on that date. She went . . . to the Irish Free State, and an order for her deportation therefrom was subsequently made by the executive of that country. On the 20 April she was brought to Holyhead in the custody of the Irish Free State police, who there handed her over to the police of the United Kingdom, and she was kept in custody until her trial. She was convicted of a charge that she 'being an alien to whom leave to land in the United Kingdom had been refused was found in the United Kingdom' contrary to arts 1(3) and 18(1)(b) of the Aliens Order 1920, as amended.

LORD HEWART C J: . . . The fact is, as the evidence shows, that the appellant is an alien. She has a French passport, which bears this statement under the date the 14th March 1933, 'Leave to land granted at Folkestone this day on condition that the holder does not enter any employment, paid or unpaid, while in the United Kingdom,' but on the 22nd March that condition was varied and one finds these words: 'The condition attached to the grant of leave to land is hereby varied so as to require departure from the United Kingdom not later than the 22nd March 1933.' Then follows the signature of an Under-Secretary of State. In fact, the appellant went to the Irish Free State and afterwards, in circumstances which are perfectly immaterial, so far as this appeal is concerned, came back to Holyhead. She was at Holyhead on the 21st April 1933, a day after the day limited by the condition on her passport.

In these circumstances, it seems to be quite clear that art. 1(4) of the Aliens Order 1920 (as varied by the Orders of the 12th March 1923 and the 11th Aug. 1931) applies. The article is in the following terms:

> An immigration officer, in accordance with general or special directions of the Secretary of State, may, by general order or notice or otherwise, attach such conditions as he may think fit to the grant of leave to land, and the Secretary of State may at any time vary such conditions in such manner as he thinks fit, and the alien shall comply with the conditions so attached or varied. An alien who fails to comply with any conditions so attached or varied, and an alien who is found in the United Kingdom at any time after the expiration of the period limited by any such condition, shall for the purposes of this Order be deemed to be an alien to whom leave to land has been refused.

The appellant was, therefore, on the 21st April 1933, in the position in which she would have been if she had been prohibited from landing by the Secretary of State and, that being so, there is no reason to interfere with the finding of the jury. She was found here and was, therefore, deemed to be in the class of persons whose landing had been prohibited by the Secretary of State, by reason of the fact that she had violated the condition on her passport. The appeal, therefore, is dismissed and the recommendation for deportation remains.

Appeal dismissed.

NOTES AND QUESTIONS

1. Lord Hewart CJ, says that the circumstances by which Madame Larsonneur found herself in England were 'perfectly immaterial'. Is not the fact that she was returned involuntarily by the police entitled to no weight? See generally D.J. Lanham, 'Larsonneur Revisited' [1976] Crim LR 276. In *Winzar* v *Chief Constable of Kent* (1983) *The Times*, 28 March 1983, the defendant was brought to a hospital in a state of intoxication. He was subsequently removed by the police to a public highway, where he was arrested and charged with being found drunk in the highway. His conviction was affirmed on appeal.

2. A contrary result to *Winzar* was reached in an American case, *Martin* v *State* (1944) 31 Ala App 334, 17 So 2d 427, where the court said that 'an accusation of drunkenness in a designated public place cannot be established by proof that the accused, while in an intoxicated condition, was involuntarily and forcibly carried to that place by the arresting officer'.

3. As advocated in Chapter 2, it often is critical to determine the precise elements of the crime. Part of the reason for the result in *Larsonneur* lay in how the offence was defined – 'being found' in England. The *actus reus* was physical presence in a particular place.

The potentially harsh results which can flow from status offences which, as in *Larsonneur*, also purport to impose strict liability, can sometimes be avoided by resourceful statutory interpretation:

Lim Chin Aik v *R*
[1963] 1 All ER 223, Judicial Committee of the Privy Council

LORD EVERSHED: The appellant Lim Chin Aik (who appears to have been known by several other names but to whom their Lordships will hereafter refer as 'the appellant') has appealed to the Board by special leave from the dismissal on Feb. 24, 1960, by the High Court of Singapore of his appeal against conviction by a magistrate on Aug. 27, 1959, for an offence under s. 6 of the Immigration Ordinance, (1), of the State of Singapore (as later amended) and the sentence then imposed of a fine of $1,250 or three months' imprisonment. The relevant facts fall within a small compass but the point involved in the appeal is one, their Lordships think, of no little importance.

. . . This charge was in the following terms:

. . . you . . . having entered Singapore from the Federation of Malaya in May, 1959, did remain therein whilst prohibited by an order made by the minister under s. 9 prohibiting you from entering Singapore and have thereby contravened s. 6(2) of the Immigration Ordinance, an offence under s. 6(3) punishable under s. 57 thereof.

It is not in dispute that . . . the Minister of Labour and Welfare did make, on May 28, 1959, an order prohibiting the appellant from entering Singapore.

At the trial (which as already stated took place on Aug. 17, 1959) it was proved by the Deputy Assistant Controller of Immigration that the minister's order was received by him on the day on which it was made; but there was no evidence of what was done with the order thereafter and no evidence of any step having been taken by way of publication or otherwise so as to bring the order to the attention of the appellant – or indeed of anyone else. The appellant at his trial did not personally give any evidence at all.

It follows from the foregoing recital of facts that there was at the trial no evidence at all from which it could be properly inferred that the order had in fact come to the notice or attention of the appellant. It was therefore said on the appellant's behalf before the magistrate that, since there was no evidence of guilty intent on his part and that since such a guilty intent on general principles must be an ingredient of any criminal offence, it therefore followed that no offence had been proved against the appellant under the ordinance. This plea was rejected by the magistrate who, basing himself on the terms of the relevant section of the ordinance, held that there was in this case no need for any evidence of *mens rea*. The appellant then appealed to the High Court of Singapore but that court dismissed his appeal without stating any reasons for the dismissal. . . .

Where the subject-matter of the statute is the regulation for the public welfare of a particular activity – statutes regulating the sale of food and drink are to be found among the earliest examples – it can be and frequently has been inferred that the legislature intended that such activities should be carried out under conditions of strict liability. The presumption is that the statute or statutory instrument can be effectively enforced only if those in charge of the relevant activities are made responsible for seeing that they are complied with. When such a presumption is to be inferred, it displaces the ordinary presumption of *mens rea*. . . .

But it is not enough in their Lordships' opinion merely to label the statute as one dealing with a grave social evil and from that to infer that strict liability was intended. It is pertinent also to inquire whether putting the defendant under strict liability will assist in the enforcement of the regulations. That means that there must be something he can do, directly or indirectly, by supervision or inspection, by improvement of his business methods or by exhorting those whom he may be expected to influence or control, which will promote the observance of the regulations. Unless this is so, there is no reason in penalising him, and it cannot be inferred that the legislature imposed strict liability merely in order to find a luckless victim. . . .

. . . Counsel for the respondent was unable to point to anything that the appellant could possibly have done so as to ensure that he complied with the regulations. It was not, for example, suggested that it would be practicable for him to make continuous inquiry to see whether an order had been made against him. Clearly one of the objects of the ordinance is the expulsion of prohibited persons from Singapore, but there is nothing that a man can do about it if, before the commission of the offence, there is no practical or sensible way in which he can ascertain whether he is a prohibited person or not.

Counsel for the respondent, therefore, relied chiefly on the text of the ordinance and their Lordships return, accordingly, to the language of the two material sections. It is to be observed that the Board is here concerned with one who is said (within the terms of s. 6(3)) to have 'contravened' the subsection by 'remaining' in Singapore (after having entered) when he had been 'prohibited' from entering by an 'order' made by the ministry containing such prohibition. It seems to their Lordships that, where a man is said to have contravened an order or an order of prohibition, the common sense of the language presumes that he was aware of the order before he can be said to have contravened it. Their Lordships realise that this statement is something of an oversimplification when applied to the present case: for the 'contravention' alleged is of the unlawful act, prescribed by sub-s. (2) of the section, of remaining in Singapore after the date of the order of prohibition. None the less it is their Lordships' view that, applying the test of ordinary sense to the language used, the notion of contravention here alleged is more consistent with the assumption that the person charged had knowledge of the order than the converse. But such a conclusion is in their Lordships' view much reinforced by the use of the word 'remains' in its context. It is to be observed that if the respondent is right a man could lawfully enter Singapore and could thereafter lawfully remain in Singapore until the moment when an order of prohibition against his entering was made; that then, instanter, his purely passive conduct in remaining – that is, the mere continuance, quite unchanged, of his previous behaviour, hitherto perfectly lawful – would become criminal. These considerations bring their Lordships clearly to the conclusion that the sense of the language here in question requires for the commission of a crime thereunder *mens rea* as a constituent of such crime; or at least that there is nothing in the language used which suffices to exclude the ordinary presumption. Their Lordships do not forget the emphasis placed by counsel for the respondent on the fact that the word 'knowingly' or the phrases 'without reasonable cause' or 'without reasonable excuse' are found in various sections of the ordinance (as amended) but find no place in the section now under consideration – see for example s. 16(4), s. 18(4), s. 19(2), s. 29, s. 31(2), s. 41(2) and s. 56(d) and (e) of the ordinance. In their Lordships' view the absence of such a word or phrase in the relevant section is not sufficient in the present case to prevail against the conclusion which the language as a whole suggests. In the first place, it is to be noted that to have inserted such words as 'knowingly' or 'without lawful excuse' in the relevant part of s. 6(3) of the Immigration Ordinance would in any case not have been sensible. Further, in all the various instances where the word or phrase is used in the other sections of the ordinance before-mentioned the use is with reference to the doing of some specific act or the failure to do some specific act as distinct from the more passive continuance of behaviour theretofore perfectly lawful. . . .

NOTES AND QUESTIONS
1. In which case, *Larsonneur* or *Lim Chin Aik*, was the court more faithful to the legislature's intent? Note that, unlike Mrs Larsonneur, Lim Chin Aik could, at least in theory, have avoided violating the law if he had known of its existence.
2. Crimes of 'possession' can also be interpreted to require 'knowing' possession. See, e.g., *Lockyer* v *Gibb* [1967] 2 QB 243. Problems can be avoided if more care is taken in drafting the statute in the first place. In *Warner* v *Metropolitan Police Commissioner* [1969] 2 AC 256 Lord Pearce suggested:

> It would, I think, be an improvement of a difficult position if Parliament were to enact that when a person has ownership or physical possession of drugs he shall be guilty unless he proves on a balance of probabilities that he was unaware of their nature or had reasonable excuse for their possession.

SECTION 3: **Causation**

Some crimes are defined such that the offence consists of wrongful conduct accompanied by a wrongful state of mind. No harmful result need occur. Examples include perjury (neither the judge nor the jury need believe the perjurer's lies) and dangerous driving (no accident need result from defendant's driving). Other crimes, however, have as a requirement that a certain result occur. Examples include homicide, where a human being must be killed, and arson, where there must be some damage to property. In crimes defined in terms of results, the prosecution must prove beyond a reasonable doubt that the defendant's acts caused the harmful result.

The term 'causation' is an unfortunate one. The criminal law is not really concerned with causation at all but with whether it is fair and just to hold a particular defendant responsible for a particular result. Sometimes the answer to this question is 'yes' because the defendant caused the result. But sometimes the answer is 'yes' although we cannot really say in any strictly logical sense that the defendant caused the result.

The issue most commonly arises in homicide. A person has set out to cause death, and the intended victim has died. The issue may at first blush seem straightforward but often it is complicated by intervening events. For example, X shoots Y. An ambulance is summoned and Y is rushed to a hospital. On the way to the hospital, the ambulance is struck by a car which is being recklessly driven by Z. All in the ambulance, including Y, are killed. Who caused Y's death – X, but for whose assault

Y would not have been in the ambulance, or Z? Or what if the ambulance arrives safely at the hospital, but an incompetent doctor botches a simple operation which would have saved Y's life? Who caused Y's death – X or the doctor? Or what if the operation is successful, but Y subsequently contracts pneumonia due to a combination of his weakened condition and his own failure to take adequate care of himself? Or what if the hospital is struck by lightning and Y dies in the ensuing blaze?

The question of causation becomes even more complex when the *actus reus* is an omission. Say that a lifeguard fails to rescue a child in waters which are under the lifeguard's control. We have already noted that the lifeguard is under a legal, and not just a moral, duty to save the child. But in what sense can it be said that the lifeguard caused the child's death? Let us examine this hypothetical more closely, for it points out several features of causation:

(a) The coroner's report will read 'death by drowning'. The doctor who performs an autopsy will not be able to say whose acts caused that death. The point is that medical cause should not be confused with legal cause. Medical cause is concerned with *what* caused the death; legal cause is concerned with *who* caused the death.

(b) There are often multiple causes of a result. One cause of the child's death was the child's inability to swim. Another was the lifeguard's failure to rescue the child. If others were present who could have saved the child, must they too be considered as part of the cause of the child's death? The death may further be traced back to the parent's decision to send the child to the pool unaccompanied, knowing that the child was a poor swimmer. Which of these multiple contributors to the child's death should be held legally responsible? Or should they all?

(c) To hold a defendant criminally liable for a death one must at a minimum be able to say that 'but for' that person's action or inaction, the death would not have resulted. However, 'but for' or *sine qua non* causation, while *necessary* to justify criminal liability, is not *sufficient* to justify criminal liability. There may be, as we have just seen, an infinite number of 'but for' causes – but for the lifeguard's inaction, the child would not have drowned; but for the parents' decision to send the child to the pool, the child would be alive; but for an earlier decision not to provide the child with swimming lessons, the child would have been capable of staying afloat; but for the parents' decision to conceive the child, etc., etc. Obviously a line must be drawn somewhere, and equally obviously most of the 'but for' causes will be legally irrelevant. *Sine qua non* or 'but for' causation is a *necessary but not a sufficient condition* of criminal liability. It would be improper to convict somebody of a result crime if we cannot say that but for that person's actions the result would have occurred; but the fact that we can say that but for defendant's actions the result would not have occurred is not enough to justify a conviction.

The cause beyond 'but for' cause that is necessary for criminal liability is sometimes called legal or proximate cause. The term 'legal', however, seems tautologous, and the term 'proximate' is positively misleading. If A sends a letter bomb through the post to B, the fact that it does not arrive until two months later will not break the chain of causation. Nor will the postman who delivers the letter be liable, even though his acts are most proximate to the victim's death. The real issue is one of imputability or attribution – is it fair and just to attribute the bad result to a particular defendant's act or failure to act, as the case may be? Recognition that this is the real issue in one sense advances our enquiry and in one sense does not. It advances our enquiry in that it directs our attention to questions other than the narrow one of simply whether the defendant's acts caused the result in question. It does not, however, tell us when it would be fair and just to attribute the bad result to the defendant. The student should be aware that a statement that a defendant caused a harmful result is often a shorthand way of stating a conclusion rather than providing an explanation.

There are therefore two questions which must be answered in the affirmative before a defendant can be said to have caused a harmful result:

(a) But for the defendant's action or inaction, would the harmful result have occurred?

(b) Should the defendant's action be deemed the legal cause of the harmful result?

A thoughtful and probing work on the subject is H.L.A. Hart and Tony Honore, *Causation in the Law* (2nd edn) (1985).

A: 'But for' causation

'But for' or *sine qua non* cause (sometimes also referred to as cause in fact) is, as we have said, a necessary but not sufficient condition of liability. Consider, for example, the case of theft by deception, where it must be shown that it was the defendant's deception which caused the victim to part with his property.

R v Hensler

[1861–73] All ER Rep Ext 1806, Crown Cases Reserved

The attempt to obtain money by false pretences was made by the writing and sending of a letter to John Hutton, Esq., M.P., for Northallerton.

This letter dated 23 October 1869, is as follows:—

Southampton, 23 October, 1869.

Honered Sir, – I humbly hope you will pardon the liberty a poor ship-wrecked widow, the native of Northallerton, as taking, in thus addressing you, I beg to state I was proceeding to Sydney, New South Wales, with my husband and four children, thinking of bettering my condition, but fortune proved unkind, and cast me with my poor orphans ashore in France, and my husband to the boundless deep.

Sir, I have no friends at Northallerton to appeal to, as they all emigrated some years ago, and sir,

it is useless me returning home as the workhouse would be my doom, all I want is a outfit, my passage being secured, and to effect that purpose the British Consul at Boulogne as most kindly granted me the enclosed certificate to appeal to the humane and benevolent, one of my children is lying in a dying state owing to the injuries it received at the time of the melancholy catastrophe. Sir, if your late much respected father was living, he would know me, and knowing your family's humane and tender feelings to the truly unfortunate, humbly do I trust you will be so kind as to take my distressed case into your kind consideration, and sir, you will have the prayers of a poor shipwrecked widow and orphans when far away on the ocean. Sir, I have part towards accomplishing my wishes. I will not take up your time with a further detail of my distresses, but will not forget to acknowledge your kindness when I reach my destination. – I am, Honered Sir, your humble and obedient servant,
ELLEN HOLMES

P.S., – Honered sir, I am waiting your kind and benevolent answer by return of post, as I cannot appeal to any person without my certificate. Sir, please to address to 'ELLEN HOLMES, 12 Simbol Street, Southampton.'

This letter was addressed for, 'John Hutton, Esq., M.P., Sowler Hill, Northallerton, Yorks.'

With it was enclosed a certificate purporting to be a confirmation of the facts contained in this letter, and to be signed by the English Consul at Boulogne.

Mr Hutton in answer to this letter sent a post office order for 5s., he also received two other letters dated 30 October, which are as follows:

12 Simbol Street, Southampton.
30 October, 1869.
Honered Sir, – The poor shipwrecked family of the name of Ellen Holmes, that enclosed the British Consuls certificate to your honour and did not receive it back, being in a most destitute state not having sufficient to obtain a outfit and, Sir, I cannot make application without my certificate humbly do I trust you will be so kind as to return it, and your kind answer, as it is useless me returning home to Northallerton, to which place I am a native, one of my children is lying very ill owing to the injuries it received at the time of the melancholy catastrophe. I am, honered sir, your humble and obedient servant,

ELLEN HOLMES.

12, Simbol Street, Southampton, Hants.
Southampton, 30 October, 1869.

Honered Sir, – Thinking you had mislaid my certificate, I wrote to you this morning, since which time I received your letter together with my certificate and a post office order for 5s., and with heartfelt gratitude I return my sincere thanks, and, sir, you will have the prayers of the widow and orphans when far away on the ocean. I am honered sir, your humble and obedient servant,

ELLEN HOLMES.

To J. Hutton, Esq., M.P.

Both these letters were addressed, 'John Hutton, Esq., M.P., Sowler Hill, Northallerton, Yorks.'

Mr Hutton on his examination, stated that he knew that the statements contained in the letter of 23 October were untrue.

The counsel for the prisoner objected, on the authority of *R v Mills* (1857) 26 LJ MC 79, that inasmuch as Mr Hutton knew the falsehood of the pretences made in the letter of 23 October, the prisoner could not be convicted for attempting to obtain money from Mr Hutton by false pretences.

. . .

NOTES AND QUESTIONS

1. If counsel's assertions were correct, i.e., the victim knew that the defendant was not telling the truth, then it could not be said that her deceptions were the cause of his parting with his money. Perhaps for this reason the defendant was convicted of an attempt to obtain money by false pretences. Would the result have been the same if the victim suspected, but did not know, that the defendant was lying?
2. In a case of a homicide, if it can be shown that the defendant's acts were not the cause of the death, then the defendant cannot be convicted of murder, even where he had the intent to kill. See *R v White* [1910] 2 KB 124. He can, on the other hand, be guilty of attempted murder. It is only the result crime which is affected by the failure of proof of causation.

Even if a result would not have occurred but for a defendant's acts, it is appropriate to ask to what extent the defendant's acts contributed to the result. An old Latin maxim holds that *de minimis non curat lex* (the law does not care about trifles). The critical question then is, how much must a defendant's acts have contributed to the harmful result before the law will take notice? Compare the following cases:

R v Cato and Others
[1976] 1 All ER 260, Court of Appeal

LORD WIDGERY CJ: . . . The victim was a young man called Anthony Farmer. The events leading up to his death occurred on 25th July 1974. On that day Cato and Farmer had been in each other's company for most of the day. The evidence suggests certain intervals when they were apart, but by and large they seem to have been together all that day, and they spent much of the day with Morris and Dudley as well. All four of them at that time were living at a house called 34 Russell Street, and on 25th July their activities brought them to the Crown public house where they were until closing time, and after closing time they went back to 34 Russell Street.

There were others living in the house. They went to bed, and the four (that is to say, Cato, Morris, Dudley and the deceased Farmer) remained downstairs for a time. The moment came when Farmer produced a bag of white powder and some syringes and invited the others to have a 'fix' with him; and so they did. The white powder was put in its bag on the mantelpiece, the syringes were distributed amongst the four who were to participate, and the procedure which they adopted (which may or may not be a common one) was to pair off so that each could do the actual act of injection into the other half of his pair. Following this procedure Morris and Dudley paired off together and so did Cato and Farmer (the deceased). All four had a number of injections following this procedure, but the time came when Dudley and Morris went to bed, leaving Cato and Farmer downstairs in the sitting room. Cato and Farmer continued to give each other these injections from time to time right through the night.

. . . The method, as I have already indicated, was that each would take his own syringe. He would fill it to his own taste with whatever mixture of powder and water he thought proper. He would then give his syringe to the other half of his pair – in this case Farmer would give his syringe to Cato – and the other half of the pair would conduct the actual act of injection. It is important to notice that the strength of the mixture to be used was entirely dictated by the person who was to receive it because he prepared his own syringe; but it is also to be noticed that the actual act of injection was done by the other half of the pair, which of course has a very important influence on this case when one comes to causation.

. . . The first question was: was there sufficient evidence on which the jury could conclude, as they must have concluded, that adequate causation was present?

When one looks at the evidence it is important to realise that no other cause of Farmer's death was supplied. Dr Robinson thought that there might have been another drug, and she said at one stage it might have been cocaine, but there was never any cocaine found in the body. The only cause of death actually supplied by the evidence was morphine. No natural disease was present and no other drug was identified. Furthermore, the symptoms of the external appearance of the body, and the nature of the final terminal cause, were consistent with poison by the administration of heroin in the way which was described.

Further, when the people who lived in the house were giving their evidence about the death of Farmer, it was, as the judge pointed out, quite clear that they thought there was no doubt about what the cause had been. It may be of course that young people living in those circumstances know a great deal about the symptoms of heroin poisoning; I know not.

The judge said:

> Members of the jury, it seems to me that that evidence about the condition of Cato when he was senseless on the floor and was put to bed, what he looked like and so forth is quite material in regard to the cause of Tony Farmer's death because Cato and he had both been dosing themselves with the same sort of thing, in the same sort of way, in the same sort of number of times, and that is clear evidence in this particular case. The opinions of the people in the house is of course not medical opinion but everybody there seemed to draw the conclusion that probably the heroin injections had caused both of them to be in the condition they were in.

That is an important and proper conclusion, if the jury thought fit to adopt it, because the fact that Cato very nearly suffered the same fate as Farmer, and showed the same kind of symptoms following the same kind of injections, is a pointer to indicate that the cause of Farmer's condition was the heroin which he had taken; and, furthermore, the jury were entitled, if they thought fit, to be influenced by the fact that the non-medical evidence from the residents was of the kind which the judge related.

Of course behind this whole question of the sufficiency of evidence of causation is the fact that it was not necessary for the prosecution to prove that the heroin was the only cause. As a matter of law, it was sufficient if the prosecution could establish that it was *a* cause, provided it was a cause outside the de minimis range, and effectively bearing on the acceleration of the moment of the victim's death.

When one has that in mind it is, we think, really possible to say that if the jury had been directed to look for heroin as a cause, not de minimis but a cause of substance, and they came back with a verdict of not guilty, the verdict could really be described as a perverse one. The whole background of the evidence was the other way and there certainly was ample evidence, given a proper direction, on which a charge of manslaughter could be supported.

But what about the proper direction? It will be noted that in none of the versions which I have quoted of the judge's direction on this point, nor in any of those which I have not quoted which appear in the summing-up, is there any reference to it being necessary for the cause to be a substantial one. It is said in clear terms in one of the six questions that the jury can consider whether the administration of the heroin was a cause or contributed to or accelerated the death, and in precise terms the word 'contributed' is not qualified to show that a substantial contribution is required.

Counsel for Cato, whose eagle eye misses nothing, sees here, and seeks to exploit here, what is a misdirection on the part of the trial judge. In other words, taking the judge's words literally, it would be possible for the jury to bring in a verdict of guilty of manslaughter even though the contribution was not of substance.

Before pursuing that, it is worth reminding oneself that some of the more recent dicta in the textbooks about this point do not support as strongly as was once the case the theory that the contribution must be substantial.

In Smith and Hogan there is this rather interesting extract:

It is commonly said by judges and writers that, while the accused's act need not be the sole cause of the death, it must be a substantial cause. This appears to mean only that a minute contribution to the cause of death will not entail responsibility. It may therefore be misleading to direct a jury that D is not liable unless his conduct was a 'substantial' cause. Killing is merely an acceleration of death and factors which produce a very trivial acceleration will be ignored.

Whether that be so or not, and we do not propose to give that passage the court's blessing today at all events, if one looks at the circumstances of the present case with any real sense of reality, we think there can be no doubt that when the judge was talking about contribution the jury knew perfectly well that he was talking about something more than the mere de minimis contribution. We have given this point particular care in our consideration of the case because it worried us to some extent originally, but we do feel in the end, having looked at all the circumstances, that there could not have been any question in this case of the jury making the mistake of thinking that the contribution would suffice if it were de minimis. Therefore in our judgment there is no substance in the attack of counsel for Cato on the basis of causation, whether it be an attack on the available evidence or on the trial judge's treatment of that evidence.

R v Armstrong

[1989] Crim LR 149 St Albans Crown Court

OWEN J: The defendant, a drug addict, supplied to C, who had already consumed a potentially lethal quantity of alcohol, heroin and the means by which to mix and inject the heroin. There was no evidence that D had injected the heroin into C. The case proceeded upon the assumption that C injected himself. Shortly after injecting himself, C died.

D was charged *inter alia* with manslaughter. At the trial the Crown called a pathologist and a toxicologist: the former opined that death was caused primarily by the deceased's alcohol intake and said that it was 'possible' that heroin had been a contributory cause; the latter initially expressed a different view but deferred to the pathologist's opinion.

It was submitted at the close of the Crown's case (1) that there was no or insufficient evidence that heroin had been a substantial cause of death, alternatively (2) that if heroin did cause death, C injecting himself was a *novus actus interveniens* breaking the chain of causation flowing from D's acts. *Held*, upholding the submissions, (1) that if the experts could not be sure that heroin caused C's death, the jury could not be and (2) that the alternative submission was well-founded. Regard was held to *Cato* 62 Cr App R 41 and *Dalby* 74 Cr App R 348: the facts proved were closest to *Dalby*.

NOTES AND QUESTIONS

1. Is the *Cato* court concerned with who caused death or with what caused death? What is the test that it uses to determine whether the defendant caused the victim's death? Why does the court in *Armstrong* reach a different result?

2. Armstrong supplied the heroin which proved fatal to the victim. In *Cato* the heroin appears to have been supplied by the victim and, in any event, the victim mixed the fatal dose. Are these facts relevant? If so, should they not have led to the opposite result in the two cases?

3. Of what relevance is the identity of the person who injects the heroin? In *Armstrong* the court seems prepared to hold that the victim's injection of himself would preclude the defendant's conviction. However, in *R v Kennedy* [1999] Crim LR 65, the defendant supplied the drugs and the victim voluntarily administered the drug to himself. Kennedy was found guilty of manslaughter, apparently on the grounds that he was still present when the victim administered the injection and could therefore be guilty of aiding and abetting the self-injection. Is the fortuity of who administers the fatal injection a satisfactory basis for distinguishing *Armstrong* from *Cato*? And can *Kennedy* be reconciled with *Armstrong*?

4. Note that under the test used by the courts, it is possible that a defendant can be held to have caused a death even though the defendant was not the primary causer of death. Why should not a result be attributed to the person who can be said to be most responsible for bringing it about?

5. It is inappropriate for a judge to attempt to quantify the degree to which the defendant's conduct contributed to the harmful result. In *Hennigan* [1971] 3 All ER 133, it was held to be error for the trial court to instruct the jury that the defendant could not be held liable if he was less than one-fifth to blame for the result.

Draft Criminal Code Bill 1989

17.—(1) Subject to subsections (2) and (3), a person causes a result which is an element of an offence when—

(a) he does an act which makes a more than negligible contribution to its occurrence; or

(b) he omits to do an act which might prevent its occurrence and which he is under a duty to do according to the law relating to the offence.

(2) A person does not cause a result where, after he does such an act or makes such an omission, an act or event occurs—

(a) which is the immediate and sufficient cause of the result,

(b) which he did not foresee, and

(c) which could not in the circumstances reasonably have been foreseen.

(3) A person who procures, assists or encourages another to cause a result that is an element of an offence does not himself cause that result so as to be guilty of the offence as a principal except when—

(a) section 26(1)(c) applies; or

(b) the offence itself consists in the procuring, assisting or encouraging another to cause the result.

NOTES AND QUESTIONS

1. Does the proposed section impose a more or less demanding standard than that reflected in judicial decisions? Are the different formulations likely, as a practical matter, to make any difference to a jury?

2. The commentary to the Bill states that a substantial or significant contribution is envisaged. Is this a more demanding standard than that contained in the actual language of the Bill? Some courts in fact use the term 'substantial' in their instructions, although this may be more favourable to a defendant than the letter of the law requires.

The fact that a victim was near death will not affect the defendant's liability if the defendant's acts hastened the death. All homicide is but a hastening of the inevitable. Thus a mercy killing may still constitute murder or manslaughter. The legal position was set out by Devlin J in the trial of Dr Adams for murder:

Henry Palmer, 'Dr Adams' Trial for Murder'
[1957] Crim LR 365

Devlin J, summing-up to the jury, said murder was an act or series of acts, done by the prisoner, which were intended to kill, and did in fact kill. It did not matter whether Mrs Morrell's death was inevitable and that her days were numbered. If her life were cut short by weeks or months it was just as much murder as if it was cut short by years. There had been a good deal of discussion as to the circumstances in which doctors might be justified in administering drugs which would shorten life. Cases of severe pain were suggested and also cases of helpless misery. The law knew of no special defence in this category, but that did not mean that a doctor who was aiding the sick and dying had to calculate in minutes or even hours, perhaps not in days or weeks, the effect on a patient's life of the medicines which he would administer. If the first purpose of medicine – the restoration of health – could no longer be achieved, there was still much for the doctor to do, and he was entitled to do all that was proper and necessary to relieve pain and suffering even if the measures he took might incidentally shorten life by hours or perhaps even longer. The doctor who decided whether or not to administer the drug could not do his job if he were thinking in terms of hours or months of life. The defence in the present case was that the treatment given by Dr Adams was designed to promote comfort, and if it was the right and proper treatment, the fact that it shortened life did not convict him of murder.

NOTE

Raising similar issues to the *Adams* case is that of Dr Cox reported in (1992) 12 BMLR 38. See generally Price, 'Euthanasia, pain relief and double effect' 17 *Legal Studies* 323 and J C Smith, 'A Comment on Moor's Case' [2000] Crim LR 41. The relevant themes will be returned to in Chapter 5 on Homicide. Consider also *Re A (Conjoined Twins: Medical Treatment)* [2001] 1 FLR 1; for facts and holding see p. 473.

B: Legal or proximate cause

Once the Crown has established 'but for' cause, the issue becomes whether the defendant's acts were the legal or proximate cause of the result. The real question is whether it is fair and just to impute or attribute the resulting harm to the defendant's conduct. The answer to this question to a large extent turns on the defendant's moral culpability. The most difficult cases involve intervening acts by the victim or a third party.

(i) *Intervening acts of the victim*

We can start with the general proposition that the contributory negligence of the victim will usually not relieve a defendant of criminal liability. For example, Anthony, not paying attention to whether there is any traffic, stumbles into the middle of the street, where he is fatally struck by a car driven by Debra. If Debra is driving dangerously, she will be liable for causing death by dangerous driving (see *Swindall and Osborn* (1846) 2 Car & Kir 230). However, there is authority to the effect that if the injuries could not have been avoided even if Debra were driving safely, she would not be liable for the harm caused (see *R v Dalloway* (1847) 2 Cox CC 273).

A different type of negligence case involves the victim of a serious but not fatal wound. If the victim is negligent in treating the wound, such that it becomes infected and the victim dies, is the person who inflicted the wound liable for the death?

R v Holland
(1841) 2 Mood & R 351, King's Bench

It appeared by the evidence that the deceased had been waylaid and assaulted by the prisoner, and that, amongst other wounds, he was severely cut across one of his fingers by an iron instrument.

On being brought to the infirmary, the surgeon urged him to submit to the amputation of the finger, telling him, unless it were amputated, he considered that his life would be in great hazard. The deceased refused to allow the finger to be amputated. It was thereupon dressed by the surgeon, and the deceased attended at the infirmary from day to day to have his wounds dressed; at the end of a fortnight, however, lock-jaw came on, induced by the wound on the finger; the finger was then amputated, but too late, and the lockjaw ultimately caused death. The surgeon deposed, that if the finger had been amputated in the first instance, he thought it most probable that the life of the deceased would have been preserved.

For the prisoner, it was contended that the cause of death was not the wound inflicted by the prisoner, but the obstinate refusal of the deceased to submit to proper surgical treatment, by which the fatal result would, according to the evidence, have been prevented.

Maule J, however, was clearly of opinion that this was no defence, and told the jury that if the prisoner wilfully, and without any justifiable cause, inflicted the wound on the party, which wound was ultimately the cause of death, the prisoner was guilty of murder; that for this purpose it made no difference whether the wound was in its own nature instantly mortal, or whether it became the cause of death by reason of the deceased not having adopted the best mode of treatment; the real question is, whether in the end the wound inflicted by the prisoner was the cause of death?

Guilty.

R v Dear
[1996] Crim LR 595, Court of Appeal

The appellant appealed against his conviction of murder. The prosecution case was that, following allegations by the appellant's 12-year-old daughter that the deceased had sexually interfered with her, the appellant had slashed the deceased repeatedly with a Stanley knife, and that he had died two days later as a result of the wounds inflicted. The appellant's case was that he had been provoked, but that in any event the chain of causation had been broken between his actions and the death because the deceased had committed suicide either by reopening his wounds or, the wounds having reopened themselves, by failing to take steps to staunch the consequent blood flow. It was argued on the appeal that the suicide of the deceased would have been a *novus actus interveniens* and that the judge had misdirected the jury on the issue of causation.

Held, dismissing the appeal, that the real question in the case was, as the judge had correctly directed the jury, whether the injuries inflicted by the appellant were an operating and significant cause of the death. That had been enunciated as the correct approach in *R v Smith* [1959] 2 QB 35; *R v Blaue* [1975] 1 WLR 1411; *R v Malcherek* [1981] 1 WLR 690; *R v Cheshire* (1991) 93 Cr App R 251, and Smith & Hogan's *Criminal Law* (7th ed.). It would not be helpful to juries if the law required them to decide causation in a case such as the present by embarking on an analysis of whether a victim had treated himself with mere negligence or gross neglect, the latter breaking but the former not breaking the chain of causation between the defendant's wrongful act and the victim's death. It would be a retrograde step if the niceties of apportionment of fault and causation in the civil law, and the roles which the concepts of *novus actus interveniens* and foreseeability did or should play in causation, were to invade the criminal law. In the present case the cause of the deceased's death was bleeding from the artery which the defendant had severed. Whether or not the resumption or continuation of that bleeding was deliberately caused by the deceased, the jury were entitled to find that the appellant's conduct made an operative and significant contribution to the death.

QUESTIONS

1. What is the justification for treating differently two similarly situated defendants, each of whom stabs his victim, where one victim takes proper care of himself and recovers while the other does not and dies?

2. Assume that the victim in *Dear*, not two days but two years later, overcome by feelings of guilt, hanged himself. Would the defendant still have been responsible? What if, instead of feelings of guilt, the main factor behind the victim's suicide was the pain that was caused by the wounds inflicted by Dear? Is the foreseeability of the suicide a relevant factor?

3. What if, rather than negligently treating the wounds, the victim refuses all treatment?

R v *Blaue*
[1975] 1 WLR 1411, Court of Appeal

LAWTON LJ: . . . The victim was aged 18. She was a Jehovah's Witness. She professed the tenets of that sect and lived her life by them. During the late afternoon of May 3, 1974, the defendant came into her house and asked her for sexual intercourse. She refused. He then attacked her with a knife inflicting four serious wounds. One pierced her lung. The defendant ran away. She staggered out into the road. She collapsed outside a neighbour's house. An ambulance took her to hospital, where she arrived at about 7.30 p.m. Soon after she was admitted to the intensive care ward. At about 8.30 p.m. she was examined by the surgical registrar who quickly decided that serious injury had been caused which would require surgery. As she had lost a lot of blood, before there could be an operation there would have to be a blood transfusion. As soon as the girl appreciated that the surgeon was thinking of organising a blood transfusion for her, she said that she should not be given one and that she would not have one. To have one, she said, would be contrary to her religious beliefs as a Jehovah's Witness. She was told that if she did not have a blood transfusion she would die. She said that she did not care if she did die. She was asked to acknowledge in writing that she had refused to have a blood transfusion under any circumstances. She did so. The prosecution admitted at the trial that had she had a blood transfusion when advised to have one she would not have died. She did so at 12.45 a.m. the next day. The evidence called by the prosecution proved that at all relevant times she was conscious and decided as she did deliberately, and knowing what the consequences of her decision would be. In his final speech to the jury, Mr Herrod for the prosecution accepted that her refusal to have a blood transfusion was *a* cause of her death. . . .

As was pointed out to Mr Comyn in the course of argument, two cases, each raising the same issue of reasonableness because of religious beliefs, could produce different verdicts depending on where the cases were tried. A jury drawn from Preston, sometimes said to be the most Catholic town in England, might have different views about martyrdom to one drawn from the inner suburbs of London. Mr Comyn accepted that this might be so: it was, he said, inherent in trial by jury. It is not inherent in the common law as expounded by Sir Matthew Hale and Maule J. It has long been the policy of the law that those who use violence on other people must take their victims as they find them. This in our judgment means the whole man, not just the physical man. It does not lie in the mouth of the assailant to say that his victim's religious beliefs which inhibited him from accepting certain kinds of treatment were unreasonable. The question for decision is what caused her death. The answer is the stab wound. The fact that the victim refused to stop this end coming about did not break the causal connection between the act and death.

If a victim's personal representatives claim compensation for his death the concept of foreseeability can operate in favour of the wrong-doer in the assessment of such compensation:

the wrongdoer is entitled to expect his victim to mitigate his damage by accepting treatment of a normal kind: see *Steele v R. George & Co. (1937) Ltd* [1942] AC 497. As Mr Herrod pointed out, the criminal law is concerned with the maintenance of law and order and the protection of the public generally. A policy of the common law applicable to the settlement of tortious liability between subjects may not be, and in our judgment is not, appropriate for the criminal law.

The issue of the cause of death in a trial for either murder or manslaughter is one of fact for the jury to decide. But if, as in this case, there is no conflict of evidence and all the jury has to do is to apply the law to the admitted facts, the judge is entitled to tell the jury what the result of that application will be. In this case the judge would have been entitled to have told the jury that the defendant's stab wound was an operative cause of death. The appeal fails.

Does there come a point where the victim's response to an assailant's attack is so absurd as to break the chain of causation?

R v Roberts
(1971) 56 Cr App Rep 95, Court of Appeal

The girl's story was that on the evening of May 1 she went to a base camp for troops in Lancashire, being at that time engaged to be married to an American serviceman who had gone to Vietnam. She was friendly with many of the people at that base, and from there she went on to a party where she met the appellant, for the first time. She left that party at about 3 a.m., having agreed to travel with the appellant in his car to what he said was another party in Warrington. After they had driven out of Warrington in the direction of Liverpool, she asked the appellant where the party was, and he said that they were going to Runcorn. They took a curious route to Runcorn, and eventually, she said, they stopped on what seemed like a big cinder-track. The time by then was apparently about 4 a.m. Then, she said, 'He just jumped on me. He put his hands up my clothes and tried to take my tights off. I started to fight him off, but the door of the car was locked and I could not find the catch. Suddenly he grabbed me and then he drove off and I started to cry and asked him to take me home. He told me to take my clothes off and, if I did not take my clothes off, he would let me walk home, so I asked him to let me do that. He said, if he did, he would beat me up before he let me go. He said that he had done this before and had got away with it and he started to pull my coat off. He was using foul language.' And then she said that she told him, 'I am not like this,' and he said something like, 'You are all like that.' Then he drove on. 'Again,' said the girl, 'he tried to get my coat off, so I got hold of my handbag and I jumped out of the car. When I opened the door he said something and revved the car up and I jumped out. . . .'

STEPHENSON LJ: We have been helpfully referred to a number of reported cases, some well over a century old, of women jumping out of windows, or jumping or throwing themselves into a river, as a consequence of threats of violence or actual violence. The most recent case is the case of *R v Lewis* [1970] Crim LR 647. An earlier case is that of *R v Beech* (1912) 7 Cr App R 197, which was a case of a woman jumping out of a window and injuring herself, and of a man who had friendly relations with her, whom she knew and might have had reason to be afraid of, being prosecuted for inflicting grievous bodily harm upon her, contrary to section 20 of the Offences against the Person Act. In that case the Court of Criminal Appeal (at p. 200) approved the direction given by the trial judge in these terms: 'Will you say whether the conduct of the prisoner amounted to a threat of causing injury to this young woman, was the act of jumping the natural consequence of the conduct of the prisoner, and was the grievous bodily harm the result of the conduct of the prisoner?' That, said the Court, was a proper direction as far as the law went, and they were satisfied that there was evidence before the jury of the prisoner causing actual bodily harm to the woman. 'No-one could say,' said Darling J when giving the judgment of the Court, 'that if she jumped from the window it was not a natural consequence of the prisoner's conduct. It was a very likely thing for a woman to do as the result of the threats of a man who was conducting himself as this man indisputably was.'

This Court thinks that that correctly states the law, and that Mr Carus was wrong in submitting to this Court that the jury must be sure that a defendant, who is charged either with inflicting grievous bodily harm or assault occasioning actual bodily harm, must foresee the actions of the victim which result in the grievous bodily harm, or the actual bodily harm. That, in the view of this Court, is not the test. The test is: Was it the natural result of what the alleged assailant said and did, in the sense that it was something that could reasonably have been foreseen as the consequence of what he was saying or doing? As it was put in one of the old cases, it had got to be shown to be his act, and if of course the victim does something so 'daft,' in the words of the appellant in this case, or so unexpected, not that this particular assailant did not actually foresee it but that no reasonable man could be expected to foresee it, then it is only in a very remote and unreal sense a consequence of his assault, it is really occasioned by a voluntary act on the part of the victim which could not reasonably be foreseen and which breaks the chain of causation between the assault and the harm or injury.

QUESTIONS

1. Were the victim's actions in *Roberts* reasonable, or rash and precipitous? When the court speaks of an action being reasonably foreseeable, is it saying that a reasonable person in Roberts's position would have judged that his passenger was, under the circumstances, likely to jump from the moving vehicle, or that this was simply a possibility? Or is the court rather saying that in retrospect the victim's actions were not unreasonable?

2. Would the result in *Roberts* have been the same if the victim had jumped from the car because Roberts had threatened to kiss her? Would it matter whether the victim had warned Roberts that she would jump out of the car if he tried to kiss her?

3. What of the jilted lover who threatens suicide if his beloved will not marry him? If she declines and he carries through with his threat, can she be said to have been the legal cause of her lover's death?

Are the actions of the victim in the following case more or less reasonable than those of the victim in *Roberts*? More or less foreseeable?

R v *Williams and another*
[1992] 2 All ER 182, Court of Appeal

STUART-SMITH LJ. On 21 November 1990 in the Crown Court at Bristol the appellants were convicted of manslaughter (count 1) and robbery (count 2) (Williams by a majority of 10 to 1 on each count).

A co-accused Siraz Ahmed Bobat was acquitted on both counts.

The appellants appeal against conviction with the leave of the single judge.

The facts were these. On 15 June 1989 the deceased, John Shephard, was hitchhiking to a free festival at Glastonbury. He was picked up in a car driven by Williams; Davis and the co-accused Bobat were passengers. After some five miles, while the car was travelling at about 30 mph, the deceased jumped from the car, and died from head injuries caused by falling onto the road.

The key issue in the case was whether anything had happened in the car, and, if so, what, to cause him to jump.

The prosecution case was that this was a planned robbery of the hitch-hiker, conceived before the deceased got into the car and involving all three occupants, and that the deceased met his death trying to escape.

The deceased, John Shephard, was 28. He smoked cannabis quite often. At the post-mortem cannabinoids were found in his blood, consistent with his having smoked one or two joints. The psychiatric evidence was that the cannabis would not have caused him to act in an irrational manner.

A Mr Brickell was driving behind the car (a Toyota) in which the deceased had been given a lift. He noticed that the car was drifting across the road and narrowly missed an oncoming lorry but he saw nothing untoward going on inside the car. Suddenly the rear nearside door opened, someone looked out and then jumped from the car into the path of Mr Brickell's car. At the same time an object went up in the air, almost certainly the deceased's wallet. The door closed and the car sped away.

The car was followed by a motor cyclist who eventually formed the view that the occupants had realised that he was following them and became apprehensive. He stopped at a motor cycle shop and the car pulled up outside. The occupants of the car went into the shop. Their manner was threatening. Williams and Davis did most of the talking. He said that they had picked up a crazy hitch-hiker who had jumped out of the car and they did not want trouble with the police (although there was also evidence that one of them said, 'Call the police'). They gave the impression that they were concerned that the shop manager had written down their car registration number and the owner of the shop tore up the piece of paper on which it was written.

The next day Williams took the Toyota to a garage and was advised to scrap it as the steering was so dangerous. Later the same day Williams and another man swapped it for a Renault and moved, amongst other things, a wooden stick about three feet long from one car to the other.

There was expert evidence that the car's steering was in a very dangerous condition so that it would be difficult to control but that the car doors functioned properly. A knife was found in the Renault.

Williams told his girlfriend, Vanessa Carty, on the evening of the incident that he had picked up a hitch-hiker. He said something about the hitch-hiker giving him £5 to be taken to the festival and that Davis made a rush on the hitch-hiker, who had jumped out of the car. (She said that she saw a knife with Williams that evening but it was not the knife found later in the Renault.)

None of the three defendants gave evidence, but each was interviewed by the police.

In his interviews with the police Williams reiterated that he had not done anything to cause the deceased to jump from the car. He had asked for money for petrol in return for taking the deceased all the way to Glastonbury and had been given £5 after rejecting an offer of £2 and some cannabis. The appellant Davis had, as far as he could tell, tried to take money from the deceased's wallet. There had been no prior agreement to rob. After the incident he had been terrified, which was why he had driven on. The stick belonged to Davis. The knife found in the Renault was his, but he gave conflicting accounts of where it had been in the Toyota.

Bobat was the front-seat passenger. He too denied being involved in any plan or attempt to rob the deceased, and blamed Davis. His account was substantially the same as that of Williams.

Davis had sat in the rear offside seat. He blamed Williams for what happened. He admitted that the stick was his but denied using it. He said that the knife belonged to Williams and had been on the dashboard in the Toyota but no one used it to threaten the deceased. In answer to the question,

'Did you make any threats?' He said, 'I made one threat, but that was not a big, big threat. I told him to give me £2 so we could give him a life, so he did.'

. . .

It is plain that in fatal cases there are two requirements. The first, as in non-fatal cases, relates to the deceased's conduct, which would be something that a reasonable and responsible man in the assailant's shoes would have foreseen. The second, which applies only in fatal cases, relates to the quality of the unlawful act, which must be such that all sober and reasonable people would inevitably recognise must subject the other person to some harm resulting therefrom, albeit not serious harm.

The harm must be physical harm. Where the unlawful act is a battery, there is no difficulty with the second ingredient. Where however the unlawful act, is merely a threat unaccompanied and not preceded by any actual violence, the position may be more difficult. In the case of a life-threatening assault, such as pointing a gun or knife at the victim, all sober and reasonable people may well anticipate some physical injury through shock to the victim, as for example in *R v Dawson* (1985) 81 Cr App R 150, where the victim died of a heart attack following a robbery in which two of the appellants had been masked, armed with a replica gun and pickaxe handles. But the nature of the threat is of importance in considering both the foreseeability of harm to the victim from the threat and the question whether the deceased's conduct was proportionate to the threat, that is to say that it was within the ambit of reasonableness and not so daft as to make it his own voluntary act which amounted to a novus actus interveniens and consequently broke the chain of causation. It should of course be borne in mind that a victim may in the agony of the moment do the wrong thing.

In this case there was an almost total lack of evidence as to the nature of the threat. The prosecution invited the jury to infer the gravity of the threat from the action of the deceased. The judge put it this way:

'. . . what he was frightened of was robbery, that this was going to be taken from him by force, and the measure of the force can be taken from his reaction to it. The prosecution suggest that if he is prepared to get out of a moving car, then it was a very serious threat involving him in the risk of, as he saw it, serious injury.'

In our judgment that was a wholly impermissible argument and was simply a case of the prosecution pulling itself up by its own bootstraps.

Moreover in a case of robbery the threat of force is made to persuade the victim to hand over money: if the money is handed over actual violence may not eventuate. The jury should consider two questions: first, whether it was reasonably foreseeable that some harm, albeit not serious harm, was likely to result from the threat itself; and, secondly, whether the deceased's reaction in jumping from the moving car was within the range of responses which might be expected from a victim placed in the situation which he was. The jury should bear in mind any particular characteristic of the victim and the fact that in the agony of the moment he may act without thought and deliberation.

. . .

In our judgment the failure of the judge to give any direction on causation was a misdirection and the conviction on this count must be quashed. This, of course, is an additional ground for quashing the conviction for manslaughter in the case of Williams.

NOTES AND QUESTIONS

1. Is the test of causation objective or subjective? See also *R v. Marjoram* [2000] Crim L. Rev. 372.
2. Are the personal characteristics of the victim relevant? Should they be? See J.C. Smith 'The element of chance in criminal liability' [1971] Crim LR 63.

Consider the case where an assailant's non-fatal attack causes the victim to be in a certain place at a certain time where the victim meets an untimely end.

R v Corbett

[1996] Crim LR 594, Court of Appeal

The appellant was convicted of the manslaughter of B. B was a mentally handicapped man of 26 who suffered from time to time with mental illness and had problems with high alcohol consumption. The appellant and B had been drinking all day. At about 9.30 in the evening the appellant had an argument with B and started to hit and head-butt him. B ran away, and fell into the gutter where he was struck by a passing car and killed. In the course of his summing up the judge gave a direction on manslaughter and told the jury that they had to consider whether what B had done was within the foreseeable range, the judge referred to the fact that B had been immensely drunk and asked the jury to decide whether what B had done was something that might be expected as a reaction of somebody in that state. On appeal counsel for the appellant contended that the judge should have told the jury that the Crown had to prove the death occurred as *the* natural consequence of what the defendant had done and that if there had been scope for any other consequence the Crown would not have discharged the burden of proof on them.

Held, dismissing the appeal, the judgment in *Roberts* (1971) 56 Cr App R 95 at 102 undermined the submission made by counsel for the appellant because it clearly envisaged a foreseeable range of consequences and held that it would only be a daft reaction on the part of a victim which would be beyond that range and which would thus break the chain of causation. Here the judge had emphasised to the jury that the victim's reaction had to be in the foreseeable range.

(ii) *Intervening acts of third parties*

As a general proposition, one is legally responsible only for one's own acts. If Smith invites Jones to a party at her house and Jones is assaulted and robbed en route, Smith is not legally liable, even if she was well aware that she lived in a high crime area where an assault was foreseeable. The fact that Smith's act of inviting Jones to her house provided the setting for the robbery is mere coincidence. On the other hand, clearly Smith would be liable if the robber acted on her directions, she having set up Jones for the robbery. In this case the intervening acts of the third party were an integral part of Smith's criminal plan.

Between the case of the innocent act which sets the stage for the commission of a crime and the not-so-innocent act which is part and parcel of the criminal scheme, lie the more troublesome cases where the initial act is wrongful but a subsequent act neither intended nor foreseen by the original actor causes fatal results. If the cause of death is clearly foreseeable, such as the victim who is left unconscious by the ocean's edge and is drowned when the tide comes in, the defendant will be held liable. When the act is less clearly foreseeable, however, the courts have experienced difficulties. The situation most often arises in cases of medical malpractice. For example, Frank inflicts a non-fatal wound on Guy. Guy is rushed to the hospital, where a doctor botches an operation that would have saved his life. Is it Frank's wound or the doctor's negligence, or both, which has caused Guy's death?

(Frank would still be liable, of course, for assault, but the question is whether he is liable for manslaughter.)

These cases have proved troublesome both in theory and practice. In part the problem is that, perhaps more clearly than in other causation cases, the actions of several individuals have contributed to the resulting death, yet the Crown has chosen to single out one (usually the most morally culpable of the actors) for prosecution. The confusion is in no way lessened by the invocation of the Latin phrase *novus actus interveniens* to describe the case where the second act prevents the defendant's conviction. Compare the following cases:

R v Jordan
(1956) 40 Cr App R 152, Court of Criminal Appeal

HALLETT J: The facts of the case, so far as I need refer to them, are as follows. The appellant, together with three other men, all serving airmen of the United States Forces, were charged with the murder of a man named Beaumont as the result of a disturbance which arose in a café at Hull. Beaumont was stabbed with a knife. There was no evidence that any one of the other three men used a knife on Beaumont or was acting in concert with the man who did use the knife, and accordingly Byrne J, who tried the case, directed the acquittal of those three men. With regard to the appellant it was ultimately conceded by Mr Veale, who appeared for him in the court below and in this court, that he did use the knife and stab Beaumont. Beaumont was admitted to hospital very promptly and the wound was stitched up, but none the less he died not many days after. In those circumstances the appellant was tried for murder. Various defences were raised, accident, self-defence, provocation and stabbing in the course of a quarrel. On all of those defences the direction of the learned judge is not in any way challenged and the jury rejected them.

. . . The further evidence is said to show that death was not, to use the words of Byrne J, 'consequent upon the wound inflicted.' On the contrary, both the doctors called are of opinion that, from the medical point of view, it cannot be described as caused by the wound at all. Whether from the legal point of view it could be described as caused by the wound is a more doubtful question. . . . First, as to the requirements allowing fresh evidence to be called; in the present case it seems clear to us that the fresh evidence was not in any true sense available at the trial. It did not occur to the prosecution, the defence, the judge, or the jury that there could be any doubt but that the stab caused death. The trial proceeded upon that basis. In those circumstances we thought it right to take the view that this was a case where the evidence sought to be given had not been in any true sense available at the trial. . . .

As to the second requisite, namely, that the evidence proposed to be tendered is such that, if the jury had heard that evidence, they might very likely, and indeed probably would, have come to a different verdict, we feel that, if the jury had heard two doctors of the standing of Dr Keith Simpson and Mr Blackburn give evidence that in their judgment death was not due to the stab wound but to something else, the jury might certainly have hesitated very long before saying that they were satisfied that death was due to the stab wound. The jury, of course, would not be bound by medical opinion, but flying in the face of it, particularly in a capital case, is a thing any jury would hesitate to do. . . . There were two things other than the wound which were stated by these two medical witnesses to have brought about death. The stab wound had penetrated the intestine in two places, but it was mainly healed at the time of death. With a view to preventing infection it was thought right to administer an antibiotic, terramycin.

It was agreed by the two additional witnesses that that was the proper course to take, and a proper dose was administered. Some people, however, are intolerant to terramycin, and Beaumont was one of those people. After the initial doses he developed diarrhoea, which was only properly attributable, in the opinion of those doctors, to the fact that the patient was intolerant to terramycin. Thereupon the administration of terramycin was stopped, but unfortunately the very next day the resumption of such administration was ordered by another doctor and it was recommenced the following day. The two doctors both take the same view about it. Dr Simpson said that to introduce a poisonous substance after the intolerance of the patient was shown was palpably wrong. Mr Blackburn agreed.

Other steps were taken which were also regarded by the doctors as wrong – namely, the intravenous introduction of wholly abnormal quantities of liquid far exceeding the output. As a result the lungs became waterlogged and pulmonary oedema was discovered. Mr Blackburn said that he was not surprised to see that condition after the introduction of so much liquid, and that pulmonary oedema leads to broncho-pneumonia as an inevitable sequel, and it was from broncho-pneumonia that Beaumont died.

We are disposed to accept it as the law that death resulting from any normal treatment employed to deal with a felonious injury may be regarded as caused by the felonious injury, but we do not think it necessary to examine the cases in detail or to formulate for the assistance of those who have to deal with such matters in the future the correct test which ought to be laid down with regard to what is necessary to be proved in order to establish causal connection between the death and the felonious injury. It is sufficient to point out here that this was not normal treatment. Not only one feature, but two separate and independent features, of treatment were, in the opinion of the doctors, palpably wrong and these produced the symptoms discovered at the post-mortem examination which were the direct and immediate cause of death, namely, the pneumonia resulting from the condition of oedema which was found.

The question then is whether it can be said that, if that evidence had been before the jury, it ought not to have, and in all probability would not have, affected their decision. We recognise that the learned judge, if this matter had been before him, would have had to direct the jury correctly on how far such supervening matters could be regarded as interrupting the chain of causation; but we feel that in the end it would have been a question of fact for the jury depending on what evidence they accepted as correct and the view they took on that evidence. We feel no uncertainty at all that, whatever direction had been given to the jury and however correct it had been, the jury would have felt precluded from saying that they were satisfied that death was caused by the stab wound.

For these reasons we come to the conclusion that the appeal must be allowed and the conviction set aside.

R v Smith

[1959] 2 QB 35, Courts-Martial Appeal Court

LORD PARKER CJ: . . . The deceased man in fact received two bayonet wounds, one in the arm and one in the back. The one in the back, unknown to anybody, had pierced the lung and caused haemorrhage. There followed a series of unfortunate occurrences. A fellow-member of his company tried to carry him to the medical reception station. On the way he tripped over a wire and dropped the deceased man. He picked him up again, went a little farther, and fell apparently a second time, causing the deceased man to be dropped onto the ground. Thereafter he did not try a third time but went for help, and ultimately the deceased man was brought into the reception station. There, the medical officer, Captain Millward, and his orderly were trying to cope with a number of other cases, two serious stabbings and some minor injuries, and it is clear that they did not appreciate the seriousness of the deceased man's condition or exactly what had happened. A transfusion of saline solution was attempted and failed. When his breathing seemed impaired he was given oxygen and artificial respiration was applied, and in fact he died after he had been in the station about an hour, which was about two hours after the original stabbing. It is now known that having regard to the injuries which the man had in fact suffered, his lung being pierced, the treatment that he was given was thoroughly bad and might well have affected his chances of recovery. There was evidence that there is a tendency for a wound of this sort to heal and for the haemorrhage to stop. No doubt his being dropped on the ground and having artificial respiration applied would halt or at any rate impede the chances of healing. Further, there were no facilities whatsoever for blood transfusion, which would have been the best possible treatment. There was evidence that if he had received immediate and different treatment, he might not have died. Indeed, had facilities for blood transfusion been available and been administered, Dr Camps, who gave evidence for the defence, said that his chances of recovery were as high as 75 per cent.

In these circumstances Mr Bowen urges that not only was a careful summing-up required but that a correct direction to the court would have been that they must be satisfied that the death of Private Creed was a natural consequence and the sole consequence of the wound sustained by him and flowed directly from it. If there was, says Mr Bowen, any other cause, whether resulting from negligence or not, if, as he contends here, something happened which impeded the chance of the deceased recovering, then the death did not result from the wound. The court is quite unable to accept that contention. It seems to the court that if at the time of death the original wound is still an operating cause and a substantial cause, then the death can properly be said to be the result of the wound, albeit that some other cause of death is also operating. Only if it can be said that the original wounding is merely the setting in which another cause operates can it be said that the death does not result from the wound. Putting it in another way, only if the second cause is so overwhelming as to make the original wound merely part of the history can it be said that the death does not flow from the wound.

. . .

In the present case it is true that the judge-advocate did not in his summing-up go into the refinements of causation. Indeed, in the opinion of this court he was probably wise to refrain from doing so. He did leave the broad question to the court whether they were satisfied that the wound had caused the death in the sense that the death flowed from the wound, albeit that the treatment he received was in the light of after-knowledge a bad thing. In the opinion of this court that was on the facts of the case a perfectly adequate summing-up on causation; I say 'on the facts of the case' because, in the opinion of the court, they can only lead to one conclusion: a man is stabbed in the back, his lung is pierced and haemorrhage results; two hours later he dies of haemorrhage from that wound; in the interval there is no time for a careful examination, and the treatment given turns out in the light of subsequent knowledge to have been inappropriate and, indeed, harmful. In those circumstances no reasonable jury or court could, properly directed, in our view possibly come to any other conclusion than that the death resulted from the original wound. Accordingly, the court dismisses this appeal.

R v Cheshire

[1991] 3 All ER 670, Court of Appeal

In the course of an argument in a fish and chip shop the appellant shot the deceased in the leg and stomach seriously wounding him. The deceased was taken to hospital where he was operated on and placed in intensive care. While in hospital he developed respiratory problems and a tracheotomy tube was placed in his windpipe to assist his breathing. The tube remained in place for four weeks. The deceased suffered further chest infections and other complications and complained of difficulty in breathing. More than two months after the shooting, while still in hospital, the deceased died of cardio-respiratory arrest because his windpipe had become obstructed due to narrowing where the tracheotomy had been performed, such a condition being a rare but not unknown complication arising out of a tracheotomy. The appellant was charged with murder. At his trial evidence for the defence was given by a consultant surgeon that the deceased's leg and stomach wounds no longer threatened his life at the time of his death and that his death was caused by the negligent failure of the medical staff at the hospital to diagnose and treat the deceased's respiratory condition. The trial judge directed the jury that the appellant was responsible for the deceased's death even if the treatment given by the hospital medical staff was incompetent and negligent and it was only if they had been reckless in their treatment of the deceased that he was entitled to be acquitted. The appellant was convicted. He appealed.

BELDAM LJ: . . . [W]hat we think does emerge from . . . the . . . cases is that when the victim of a criminal attack is treated for wounds or injuries by doctors or other medical staff attempting to repair the harm done, it will only be in the most extraordinary and unusual case that such treatment can be said to be so independent of the acts of the accused that it could be regarded in law as the cause of the victim's death to the exclusion of the accused's acts.

Where the law requires proof of the relationship between an act and its consequences as an element of responsibility, a simple and sufficient explanation of the basis of such relationship has proved notoriously elusive.

In a case in which the jury have to consider whether negligence in the treatment of injuries inflicted by the accused was the cause of death we think it is sufficient for the judge to tell the jury that they must be satisfied that the Crown have proved that the acts of the accused caused the death of the deceased, adding that the accused's acts need not be the sole cause or even the main cause of his death, it being sufficient that his acts contributed significantly to that result. Even though negligence in the treatment of the victim was the immediate cause of his death, the jury should not regard it as excluding the responsibility of the accused unless the negligent treatment was so independent of his acts, and in itself so potent in causing death, that they regard the contribution made by his acts as insignificant.

It is not the function of the jury to evaluate competing causes or to choose which is dominant provided they are satisfied that the accused's acts can fairly be said to have made a significant contribution to the victim's death. We think the word 'significant' conveys the necessary substance of a contribution made to the death which is more than negligible.

In the present case the passage in the summing up complained of has to be set in the context of the remainder of the direction given by the judge on the issue of causation. He directed the jury that they had to decide whether the two bullets fired into the deceased on 10 December caused his death on 15 February following. Or, he said, put in another way, did the injuries caused cease to operate as a cause of death because something else intervened? He told them that the prosecution did not have to prove that the bullets were the only cause of death but they had to prove that they were one operative and substantial cause of death. He was thus following the words used in *R v Smith*.

The judge then gave several examples for the jury to consider before reverting to a paraphrase of the alternative formulation used by Lord Parker CJ in *R v Smith*. Finally, he reminded the jury of the evidence which they had heard on this issue. We would remark that on several occasions during this evidence the jury had passed notes to the judge asking for clarification of expressions used by the medical witnesses, which showed that they were following closely the factual issues they had to consider. If the passage to which exception has been taken had not been included, no possible criticism could have been levelled at the summing up. Although for reasons we have stated we think that the judge erred when he invited the jury to consider the degree of fault in the medical treatment rather than its consequences, we consider that no miscarriage of justice has actually occurred. Even if more experienced doctors than those who attended the deceased would have recognised the rare complication in time to have prevented the deceased's death, that complication was a direct consequence of the appellant's acts, which remained a significant cause of his death. We cannot conceive that, on the evidence given, any jury would have found otherwise.

According, we dismiss the appeal.

Gavin Thomas Mellor v R
[1996] 2 Cr App R 245, Court of Appeal

SCHIEMANN LJ: Gavin Thomas Mellor appeals by leave of the single judge against his conviction on February 22, 1995 in the Crown Court at Chester before Curtis J of murder. The deceased was 71 years old and was attacked by some hooligans at 11.15 p.m. on January 15, 1994. He was taken to hospital suffering from bruising to the eyes, a damaged nose and complaining of chest pain and a pain in his right shoulder. He died in hospital two days later. The defence of Mr Mellor who gave evidence was twofold:

. . .

The substantial cause of Mr Sims' death was not the beating which he had received from the hooligan who attacked him but rather the actions and inactions of the hospital.

The immediate cause of death was broncho-pneumonia which, upon the evidence, was brought on directly by the injuries inflicted by the appellant. Those injuries were certainly the cause of death. Probably if the appellant had been administered sufficient oxygen in time, the broncho-pneumonia would not have been fatal, and therefore the failure to administer sufficient oxygen could be regarded as a cause of death. It was asserted on behalf of the appellant, and supported by expert evidence, that the failure to administer sufficient oxygen in time amounted to negligence or incompetence in the care of Mr Sims in hospital.

The question for the trial judge was how he should frame his direction to the jury in these circumstances. The question was debated with counsel before leading counsel's final speeches and the case of *Cheshire* (1991) 93 Cr App R 251, [1992] 1 WLR 844, was considered.

In homicide cases, where the victim of the alleged crime does not die immediately, supervening events will occur which are likely to have some causative effect leading to the victim's death; for example, a delay in the arrival of the ambulance, a delay in resuscitation, the victim's individual response to medical or surgical treatment, and the quality of medical, surgical and nursing care. Sometimes such an event may be the result of negligence or mistake or bad luck. It is a question of fact and degree in each case for the jury to decide, having regard to the gravity of the supervening event, however caused, whether the injuries inflicted by the defendant were a significant cause of death.

The onus on the Crown is to make the jury sure that the injuries inflicted by the defendant were a significant cause of death. However, the Crown have no onus of establishing that any supervening event was not a significant cause of death or that there was no medical negligence in the deceased's treatment.

If the issue of medical negligence is raised, the jury must have regard to the evidence adduced on the issue. If they conclude that there was or may have been medical negligence, they must have regard to that conclusion when answering the all-important question; 'has the Crown proved that the injuries inflicted by the defendant were *a* significant cause of death?' In appropriate cases the jury can be told that there may be a number of significant causes leading to a victim's death. So as long as the Crown proves that the injuries inflicted by the defendant were at least a significant, if not the only, cause of death that will be sufficient to prove the nexus between injury and death.

. . .

What the Crown had to prove in the present case was that the injuries inflicted by the appellant significantly contributed to Mr Sims' death. There was no onus whatever on the Crown to negative medical negligence. Equally, there was no onus on the appellant to establish medical negligence. However, if negligence was established it was a factor to be taken into account by the jury in deciding whether the Crown had established that, notwithstanding this negligence, the injuries inflicted by the appellant had significantly contributed to Mr Sims' death. In the event of a jury being sure that medical negligence has been negatived by the Crown as a significant contributory cause of death, the medical negligence factor would be out of the equation.

In our judgment, it is undesirable in most cases for juries to be asked to embark upon the question of whether medical negligence as a significant contributory cause of death has been negatived because it diverts the jury from the relevant question, namely, has the accused's act contributed significantly to the victim's death?

. . .

An appropriate, but we do not suggest the only appropriate, form of words on the particular facts of this case would have been:

> You must acquit the defendant of murder unless the Crown has made you sure that the injuries that he inflicted contributed significantly to Mr Sims' death. Provided you are sure of that, it matters not whether incompetence or mistake in treatment at the hospital may have also contributed significantly to the death.

In our judgment, if the medical/causation issue had been put in this way there could only have been one answer. The evidence was overwhelming that having regard to the extent and nature of the injuries inflicted upon the 71-year-old Mr Sims those injuries significantly contributed to his death less than two days later.

NOTES AND QUESTIONS

1. Is there a common principle that runs through the preceding cases?
2. Assume that in *Mellor* the jurors concluded that the actions of the doctors contributed significantly to the death. Who then should they convict?
3. Why should a defendant's criminal liability turn on the competence of the doctor who treats the victim, given that the defendant has no control over the doctor's performance? Would it make more sense to ask whether the victim was on the way to recovery at the time of the medical intervention, or would have survived but for the medical intervention? Is it in fact fatuous to try to determine whether it was defendant's wound or the medical intervention which was the cause of death, since the latter would not have been necessary except for the former, and since the victim would have died anyway if there had been no available medical assistance (a fact beyond the defendant's control). Should the risk of medical incompetence simply be something that a defendant has to absorb, just as the defendant must take the victim as he finds him?
4. In *R v Malcherek and Steel* [1981] 2 All ER 422, the doctors were alleged to have switched off life support machines prematurely, thereby causing the victim's death. At the time there was a legitimate medical debate as to when a person should be deemed to have died. The court held that the fact that the doctors in the case had adopted a definition of death with which other doctors might disagree would not break the chain of causation. Whatever might be said about the doctors' treatment, the wound inflicted by the accused was one of the operative causes of death. Stepping back from a strict legal perspective, courts may well be reluctant to expose doctors, trying to do their best in an often difficult situation, to either criminal liability or the civil liability which might follow if any legal responsibility were to be attributed to their actions.

Doctors are under a legal duty to save lives. Sometimes others, under a similar duty, find themselves in a position where they must endanger life in order to protect life. See *Re A (Conjoined Twins: Medical Treatment)* [2001] 1 FLR 1 (for facts and holding, see p. 473).

Conflicting duties can also arise in a non-medical context:

R v Pagett

(1983) 76 Cr App R 279, Court of Appeal

> The defendant, who was armed with a shotgun, used his pregnant girlfriend (Ms Kinchen) as a shield to prevent his arrest by armed police. He fired at the police, who returned his shots. One of the bullets fired by the police killed the girlfriend.

ROBERT GOFF LJ: . . . [I]t was pressed upon us by Lord Gifford that there either was, or should be, a . . . rule of English law, whereby, as a matter of policy, no man should be convicted of homicide (or, we imagine, any crime of violence to another person) unless he himself, or another person acting in concert with him, fired the shot (or, we imagine, struck the blow) which was the immediate cause of the victim's death (or injury).

No English authority was cited to us in support of any such proposition, and we know of none. So far as we are aware, there is no such rule in English law; and, in the absence of any doctrine of constructive malice, we can see no basis in principle for any such rule in English law. Lord Gifford urged upon us that, in a case where the accused did not, for example, fire the shot which was the immediate cause of the victim's death, he will inevitably have committed some lesser crime, and that it would be sufficient that he should be convicted of that lesser crime. So, on the facts of the present case, it would be enough that the appellant was convicted of the crime of attempted murder of the two police officers, D.S. Sartain and D.C. Richards. We see no force in this submission. In point of fact, it is not difficult to imagine circumstances in which it would manifestly be inadequate for the accused merely to be convicted of a lesser offence; for example, a man besieged by armed terrorists in a house might attempt to make his escape by forcing some other person to act as a shield, knowing full well that that person would in all probability be shot, and possibly killed, in consequence. For that man merely to be convicted of an assault would, if the person he used as a shield were to be shot and killed, surely be inadequate in the circumstances; we can see no reason why he should not be convicted at least of manslaughter. But in any event there is, so far as we can discern, no basis of legal principle for Lord Gifford's submission. We are therefore unable to accept it.

In our judgment, the question whether an accused person can be held guilty of homicide, either murder or manslaughter, of a victim the immediate cause of whose death is the act of another person must be determined on the ordinary principles of causation, uninhibited by any such rule of policy as that for which Lord Gifford has contended. We therefore reject the second ground of appeal.

We turn to the first ground of appeal, which is that the learned judge erred in directing the jury that it was for him to decide *as a matter of law* whether by his unlawful and deliberate acts the appellant caused or was a cause of Gail Kinchen's death. . . .

In cases of homicide, it is rarely necessary to give the jury any direction on causation as such. Of course, a necessary ingredient of the crimes of murder and manslaughter is that the accused has by his act caused the victim's death. But how the victim came by his death is usually not in dispute. What is in dispute is more likely to be some other matter: for example, the identity of the person who committed the act which indisputably caused the victim's death; or whether the accused had the necessary intent; or whether the accused acted in self-defence, or was provoked. Even where it is necessary to direct the jury's minds to the question of causation, it is usually enough to direct them simply that in law the accused's act need not be the sole cause, or even the main cause, of the victim's death, it being enough that his act contributed significantly to that result. It is right to observe in passing, however, that even this simple direction is a direction of law relating to causation, on the basis of which the jury are bound to act in concluding whether the prosecution has established, as a matter of fact, that the accused's act did in this sense cause the victim's death. Occasionally, however, a specific issue of causation may arise. One such case is where, although an act of the accused constitutes a *causa sine qua non* of (or necessary condition for) the death of the victim, nevertheless the intervention of a third person may be regarded as the sole cause of the victim's death, thereby relieving the accused of criminal responsibility. Such intervention, if it has such an effect, has often been described by lawyers as a *novus actus interveniens*. We are aware that this time-honoured Latin term has been the subject of criticism. We are also aware that attempts have been made to translate it into English; though no simple translation has proved satisfactory, really because the Latin term has become a term of art which conveys to lawyers the crucial feature that there has not merely been an intervening act of another person, but that that act was so independent of the act of the accused that it should be regarded in law as the cause of the victim's death, to the exclusion of the act of the accused. At the risk of scholarly criticism, we shall for the purposes of this judgment continue to use the Latin term.

Now the whole subject of causation in the law has been the subject of a well-known and most distinguished treatise by Professors Hart and Honoré, *Causation in the Law*. Passages from this book were cited to the learned judge, and were plainly relied upon by him; we, too, wish to express our indebtedness to it. It would be quite wrong for us to consider in this judgment the wider issues discussed in that work. But, for present purposes, the passage which is of most immediate relevance is to be found in Chapter XII, in which the learned authors consider the circumstances in which the intervention of a third person, not acting in concert with the accused, may have the effect of relieving the accused of criminal responsibility. The criterion which they suggest should be applied in such circumstances is whether the intervention is voluntary i.e. whether it is 'free, deliberate and informed.' We resist the temptation of expressing the judicial opinion whether we find ourselves in complete agreement with that definition; though we certainly consider it to be broadly correct and supported by authority. Among the examples which the authors give of non-voluntary conduct, which is not effective to relieve the accused of responsibility, are two which are germane to the present case, *viz*, a reasonable act performed for the purpose of self-preservation, and an act done in performance of a legal duty.

There can, we consider, be no doubt that a reasonable act performed for the purpose of self-preservation, being of course itself an act caused by the accused's own act, does not operate as a *novus actus interveniens*. . . . if a reasonable act of self-defence against the act of the accused causes the death of a third party, we can see no reason in principle why the act of self-defence, being an involuntary act caused by the act of the accused, should relieve the accused from criminal responsibility for the death of the third party. Of course, it does not necessarily follow that the accused will be guilty of the murder, or even of the manslaughter, of the third party; though in the majority of cases he is likely to be guilty at least of manslaughter. Whether he is guilty of murder or manslaughter will depend upon the question whether all the ingredients of the relevant offence have been proved; in particular, on a charge of murder, it will be necessary that the accused had the necessary intent. . . .

No English authority was cited to us, nor we think to the learned judge, in support of the proposition that an act done in the execution of a legal duty, again of course being an act itself caused by the act of the accused, does not operate as a *novus actus interveniens*. . . . We agree with the learned judge that the proposition is sound in law, because as a matter of principle such an act cannot be regarded as a voluntary act independent of the wrongful act of the accused. A parallel may be drawn with the so-called 'rescue' cases in the law of negligence, where a wrongdoer may be held liable in negligence to a third party who suffers injury in going to the rescue of a person who has been put in danger by the defendant's negligent act. Where, for example, a police officer in the execution of his duty acts to prevent a crime, or to apprehend a person suspected of a crime, the case is surely *a fortiori*. Of course, it is inherent in the requirement that the police officer, or other person, must be acting in the execution of his duty that his act should be reasonable in all the circumstances: see section 3 of the Criminal Law Act 1967. Furthermore, once again we are only considering the issue of causation. If intervention by a third party in the execution of a legal duty, caused by the act of the accused, results in the death of the victim, the question whether the accused is guilty of the murder or manslaughter of the victim must depend on whether the necessary ingredients of the relevant offence have been proved against the accused, including in particular, in the case of murder, whether the accused had the necessary intent.

The principles which we have stated are principles of law. This is plain from, for example, the case of *Pitts* (1842) C & M 284, to which we have already referred. It follows that where, in any particular case, there is an issue concerned with what we have for convenience called *novus actus interveniens*, it will be appropriate for the judge to direct the jury in accordance with these principles. It does not however follow that it is accurate to state broadly that causation is a question of law. On the contrary, generally speaking causation is a question of fact for the jury. . . . But that does not mean that there are no principles of law relating to causation, so that no directions on law are ever to be given to a jury on the question of causation. On the contrary, we have already pointed out one familiar direction which is given on causation, which is that the accused's act need not be the sole, or even the main, cause of the victim's death for his act to be held to have caused the death. . . . [I]n cases where there is an issue whether the act of the victim or of a third party constituted a *novus actus interveniens*, breaking the causal connection between the act of the accused and the death of the victim, it would be appropriate for the judge to direct the jury, of course in the most simple terms, in accordance with the legal principles which they have to apply. It would then fall to the jury to decide the relevant factual issues which, identified with reference to those legal principles, will lead to the conclusion whether or not the prosecution have established the guilt of the accused of the crime of which he is charged.

. . .

There is however one further aspect of the present case to which we must advert. On the evidence, Gail Kinchen was not just an innocent bystander killed by a shot fired from the gun of a police officer who, acting in reasonable self-defence, fired his gun in response to a lethal attack by the appellant: though on those facts alone it would, in our opinion, have been open to the jury to convict the appellant of murder or manslaughter. But if, as the jury must have found to have occurred in the present case, the appellant used Gail Kinchen by force and against her will as a shield to protect him from any shots fired by the police, the effect is that he committed not one but two unlawful acts, both of which were dangerous – the act of firing at the police, and the act of holding Gail Kinchen as a shield in front of him when the police might well fire shots in his direction in self-defence. Either act could in our judgment, if on the principles we have stated it was held to cause the death of Gail Kinchen, constitute the *actus reus* of the manslaughter or, if the necessary intent were established, murder of Gail Kinchen by the appellant, even though the shot was fired not by the appellant but by a police officer.

QUESTIONS

1. On what basis can it be said that Pagett's acts killed the victim when the fatal shots were fired by the police? What was Pagett's *actus reus*? His *mens rea*? It is understandable that the courts would not, given the circumstances, want to hold the police liable, but does it necessarily follow that Pagett should have been held liable?

2. Was the result foreseeable? Does it matter?

3. Would Pagett have been liable if a third party had been killed as a result of an errant shot by the police? Would this be a stronger or weaker case for liability?

4. Did the decision turn on the fact that the shots fired by the police were justifiable? If the judge had ruled at the trial that the police should have held their fire and were wrong not to do so, would (should) it have made any difference to Pagett's liability? Could it not be argued that the police acted irresponsibly in exposing the hostage to the risk of harm?

5. In April 1993, in Waco, Texas, a religious sect known as the Branch Davidians set their compound on fire rather than submit to arrest by federal officers. The latter had laid siege to the compound for 51 days following the killing of several of their number in the initial attempt to arrest the Branch Davidians for firearms violations. Eighty-six members of the cult were killed in the blaze. Did the FBI 'cause' the deaths?

C: Reflections on causation

Cases which raise causation issues are, as we have seen, problematic. Fortunately for the courts, they arise infrequently. When they do, however, they expose a certain fortuity inherent in the criminal law – two offenders who do the same act with the same *mens rea* may wind up with quite different punishments because of the results that their actions produce. Fair enough, one might say – offenders should have to bear the risk of the consequences of their evil acts – but is it really fair to treat as a murderer the defendant whose victim neglects his wound with the result that gangrene sets in with fatal effect, while the defendant whose victim takes proper care of himself is convicted only of assault? Is it fair that whether a defendant receives a mandatory life sentence turns on whether, unbeknownst to the defendant, the victim is a religious zealot who refuses all medical treatment, preferring to place her faith in God? Granted that if convicted of attempted murder, the defendant may receive the same life sentence as a murderer, but this does not automatically follow as it does after a conviction for murder. In practice the attempted murderer is likely to receive a significantly lesser sentence. In some instances focusing on results allows an offender to receive less in the way of punishment than one would have predicted if one had looked at the situation as of the time the defendant committed the *actus reus*; while in other instances it leads to an offender facing charges far more serious than would have been predicted as of the same time.

Faced with the sometimes almost random results of legal principles of causation, and understandably reluctant to allow malefactors to escape their just deserts because of the intervening acts of a victim, a third party or simply fate, courts stretch legal principle to reach equitable results. They are not content with simply finding a defendant liable for the way he has behaved, but strive to hold him liable for all the results which follow from his actions. To a large extent this desire to hold a defendant liable for the full effects of his conduct is traceable to the retributive philosophy that a defendant's punishment should be in proportion to the harm which the defendant's acts have produced.

The problem in part is that the perspective of a criminal trial is always backwards-looking. The jurors know what results have occurred, and they ask themselves whether such results were foreseeable. The fact that they have occurred skews the enquiry, while casting the defendant's character in a more sinister light than it might otherwise have appeared had the results of the defendant's conduct been more benign. The proper focal point, it could be argued, is the time of the defendant's acts: What results were foreseeable as of that moment? But once we accept this proposition, a short further step seems logical. That would be to make actual results irrelevant. If the defendant's acts could have produced the harmful results, it should not matter, from a point of view of moral blameworthiness, whether they in fact did. Crimes should be defined in terms of *actus reus*, *mens rea* and the results that a type of conduct *threatens* to produce, as opposed to the results the conduct in fact produces, which may be completely fortuitous. A defendant should be punished not for the harm that he or she actually causes, but for the harm that he or she sets out to cause or recklessly risks causing, at least in the absence of excuse or justification. In this connection, consider the merits of the following proposed statute (NZ):

Endangering

130. Endangering with intent to cause serious bodily harm
(1) Every person is liable to imprisonment for 14 years who—
- (a) Does any act, or omits without lawful excuse to perform or observe any legal duty, with intent to cause serious bodily harm to any other person; or
- (b) With reckless disregard for the safety of others, does any act or omits without lawful excuse to perform or observe any legal duty, knowing that the act or omission is likely to cause serious bodily harm to any other person.

(2) This section applies whether or not the act or omission results in death or bodily harm to any other person.
. . .

132. Endangering with intent to injure, etc.
(1) Every person is liable to imprisonment for five years who—
- (a) Does any act, or omits without lawful excuse to perform or observe any legal duty, with intent to injure any other person; or
- (b) With reckless disregard for the safety of others, or heedlessly, does any act or omits without lawful excuse to perform or observe any legal duty, the act or omission being likely to cause injury to any other person or to endanger the safety or health of any other person.

(2) Every person is liable to imprisonment for two years who negligently does any or omits without lawful excuse to perform or observe any legal duty, the act or omission being likely to cause injury.

NOTES AND QUESTIONS

1. Does the proposed legislation go too far? Should negligent endangerment be criminal? What constitutes heedlessness?
2. Late to catch her train, Maria dashes down the street. Rounding the corner, she collides with Greg, who is knocked over and injured. Has Maria violated the New Zealand statute? Should such conduct be criminal?
3. The issues raised by the fortuity of consequences have been well explored in the legal literature. See, e.g., A. Ashworth, 'Criminal attempts and the role of resulting harm under the Code and in the common law' 19 Rutgers LJ 725 (1988); A. Ashworth, 'Belief, Intent, and Criminal Liability' in J. Eekelar and J. Bell (eds) *Oxford Essays in Jurisprudence* 1 (1987); J. Gobert, 'The Fortuity of Consequence' (1993) 4 Crim Law Forum 1; J.C. Smith, 'The element of chance in criminal liability' [1971] Crim LR 63.

4

···

The Mental Component of Crime: *Mens Rea*

SECTION 1: **Introduction**

Mens rea is the generic term which refers to the mental element of a crime. It is misleading, however, to talk of *mens rea* in the abstract. In regard to any specific crime, the statutory or common law definition of the crime must be consulted in order to determine the *mens rea* of the crime in question. In addition, many crimes have more than one mental element, and different types of *mens rea* may be applicable to different elements of the crime.

Mens rea is more elusive than *actus reus*. An act is observable, and provable through objective evidence. Witnesses can and will testify to what a defendant did. They cannot testify as accurately to what the defendant was thinking. State of mind often can only be inferred from actions. If X stands immediately in front of Y with a loaded gun and shoots Y, a jury might infer that X intended to kill Y. But what if X testifies that she was aiming at an area to the left of Y, or was only intending to scare Y? Or what if X says that she did not know that the gun was loaded, or that she thought Y was a dummy (cardboard) or that she thought that Y was about to shoot her and fired in self-defence? Implausible, perhaps; but how does one know for sure? Unless a defendant confesses (and sometimes not even then: there are many documented cases of false confessions, for reasons ranging from improper police pressure to guilt on the part of the confessor for some unrelated incident), there will always remain doubt about what was going on in the defendant's mind at the time of the offence.

Notwithstanding the problems relating to proof, *mens rea* is perhaps the most critical concept in criminal law. Mental state will often be the determining factor as to whether one who causes another's death will receive a life sentence, a term of years in prison short of life, or no legal sanction whatsoever. For example, driving through the High Street Zachary hits a child who subsequently dies from the injuries: if Zachary intended to kill the child, he is guilty of murder; if he was driving recklessly, he is guilty of manslaughter or causing death by dangerous driving; and if the child jumped in front of his car and the accident was unavoidable, he is guilty of no crime. The same act, the same result, but entirely different legal consequences because of Zachary's state of mind.

A: Motive

Before examining specific cases, there are several preliminary points worth making.

The first relates to motive – the reason why the defendant acted as he did. Generally speaking, the law is not concerned with motive. A praiseworthy motive will not alter what would otherwise be a crime, and a blameworthy motive will not justify the conviction of a defendant who lacks *mens rea*. For example, if Marshall robs Barclay's Bank, it does not matter, for legal purposes, whether Marshall planned to give the money to charity or to spend it on himself.

The reason motive is said to be irrelevant is not only that motive is so difficult to prove (so is intent), nor that it is so easy to fabricate (of course I was going to give the proceeds from the bank robbery to charity), but that we do not want to get into the messy business of evaluating individual motives and saying whether or not they justify criminal conduct. What if our bank robber wanted to give the money to the Labour Party? The leader of the Labour Party might find this an honourable motive, but would jurors who belonged to the Conservative or Liberal Democrat Parties?

While motive is not relevant to guilt, it may be relevant at other stages of the criminal process. First, it may affect the decision to bring formal charges. Prosecutors often have considerable discretion in this matter, both so that the Crown's limited resources are not wasted in frivolous actions, and so that defendants who are not truly blameworthy are not subjected to the emotional trauma and legal expense of a criminal prosecution, despite a technical violation of the law. The defendant's motive may have some bearing at this point. Secondly, at trial the prosecution may want to introduce evidence of motive, although it is not required to do so, because it supports the state's contention that the defendant was the one who committed the crime (the fact that the defendant was the sole beneficiary under the terms of the will of the wealthy victim provides a motive for the killing; if nobody else had a motive, it makes it more likely that the defendant was the murderer). Motive may also influence a jury's uncontrollable discretion to acquit – either the absence of motive may lead them to conclude that the defendant did not commit the crime; or an honourable motive, as in the case of a mercy killing, may lead them to acquit despite the belief that the defendant was technically guilty. Lastly, a judge may take motive into account in sentencing (except in cases of murder).

To say that motive is legally irrelevant may also be a bit misleading. Motive may have legal significance in some instances. If Beatrice's motive in striking Elvin is to prevent him from attacking her, that motive will lead to a viable claim of self-defence. Similarly, if Beatrice's motive for driving the car of the bank robbers was that they had kidnapped her children and were threatening to kill them if she did not cooperate, that motive may lead to a successful defence of duress. Whether it is semantically correct to use motive in the context of defences is debatable, but clearly we are talking about the reasons why the defendant acted as he or she did.

B: Subjective and objective *mens rea*

A distinction that is worth bearing in mind is that between subjective and objective states of mind. Subjective states of mind are concerned with what a defendant was actually thinking; objective states of mind refer to what a reasonable person in the position of the defendant would have been thinking. Where *mens rea* is objective, a defendant's fault consists of failing to appreciate a risk that would have been appreciated by a reasonable person. Crimes which involve subjective fault require that the prosecution prove that the defendant actually had the state of mind required for the crime. Crimes that involve objective fault do not require that the prosecution prove that the defendant actually had a particular state of mind but only that the defendant failed to meet a certain standard of conduct, usually determined by what would have been expected of a reasonable person. For example, if Edward drives his car on the High Street at a pedestrian, intending to run him over, his subjective state of mind is to kill the pedestrian. But when Edward is not paying sufficient attention to what he is doing, his subjective state of mind is not to run anybody over, although a reasonable person would have seen that there was a clear risk that this might occur. As a general proposition (although it is not always true), persons who commit crimes with subjective *mens rea* are considered to be more morally blameworthy, and therefore deserving of greater punishment, than persons whose *mens rea* is objective.

To determine whether a statute requires proof of objective or subjective *mens rea* one needs to look at the statute, the words it uses, and how those words have been interpreted by the courts. Listed below are examples of words which are generally held to connote subjective or objective fault.

Subjective Fault	*Objective Fault*
purposely	
recklessly	recklessly
knowingly	negligently
intentionally	carelessly
wilfully	
deliberately	
with intent to . . .	without due care and attention

The observant reader will have noticed that 'recklessly' appears in both columns. The courts have recognised both a subjective and an objective strain of this type of *mens rea*.

In addition to objective and subjective *mens rea*, sometimes statutes appear to contain no *mens rea*. The statute defines the crime only in terms of the *actus reus* without any express reference to mental state, imposing what is commonly referred to as strict liability. This category of strict liability crimes is obviously an exception to the Latin maxim *actus non facit reum mens sit rea*. Problems arise, however, because Parliament does not always say what it means, or so the courts believe. Thus statutes which contain no mental element on their face may be interpreted by a court so as to require proof of some sort of *mens rea*, as we shall see later.

In creating a new offence, Parliament can draft the statute to require proof of either subjective or objective *mens rea*, or can make the offence one of strict liability. Which path it chooses will be reflected in the wording of the statute. Say, for instance, Parliament decides to make the handling of stolen goods a crime. It can make an element of the offence 'knowing the goods to be stolen', thus requiring subjective *mens rea* in the form of proof that the defendant actually knew the goods were stolen. Or it can write the statute in terms of 'having reason to know' the goods are stolen, thus requiring only objective *mens rea* and proof that a reasonable person would have realised that the goods were stolen. Or it can make the crime into one of strict liability, mentioning nothing about knowing or having reason to know the goods are stolen, but simply making criminal the handling of goods that are in fact stolen. Now a court might nonetheless read into such a statute a *mens rea* element but if Parliament really wanted to, it could expressly declare that proof that a defendant knew or had reason to know that the goods were stolen is not required for conviction.

Whenever you analyse the *mens rea* of a statute, you should ask yourself whether the statute requires it to be subjective or objective, or whether the statute imposes no requirement of proof of *mens rea*. If *mens rea* is an element of a crime and the prosecution do not prove it, or the defence raise a reasonable doubt about that element in the jury's mind, the defendant cannot be convicted, even though he may have committed the *actus reus* of the crime and even brought about the proscribed consequences.

While courts will often draw a sharp distinction in theory between objective and subjective states of mind, in practice the distinction is often blurred. The reason is this: The question of whether the defendant possessed the subjective *mens rea* required for a particular crime is a question of fact for the jury. Suppose that after pumping six bullets into her victim's heart from close range, a defendant claims that she did not intend to kill but simply intended to frighten the victim. The jury is likely to decide that the defendant's denial is not credible. Why? – because it makes no sense to them. If they were in the defendant's shoes they would have realised that the bullets would kill the victim. They would have realised it because they are reasonable persons, and any reasonable person would have so realised. By projecting on to the defendant the thought process which they themselves would have gone through the jurors reason that the defendant in all probability lied, and in fact had the requisite subjective intent to kill. As a result of an objective exercise in logical reasoning the jurors will have *inferred* a subjective state of mind on the part of the defendant.

C: *Mens rea* in respect of what?

Often a crime will contain more than one *mens rea* element. Different elements of a crime may have attached to them different *mens rea* requirements. In rape, for example, the Crown must prove that the accused had the intent to have sexual intercourse with the victim, but need only prove that he was reckless in respect to whether the victim was consenting. Thus it is always important to ask what it is that the *mens rea* element or elements refer to:

Mens rea can refer to:

(a) acts (but where the act is not the product of the defendant's will the practice of the courts is to speak of an involuntary *actus reus* rather than a lack of *mens rea*);
(b) circumstances (as, in theft, the defendant's knowledge that the property he is taking belongs to another);
(c) results (as, in homicide, the death of the victim).

Criminal Damage Act 1971

1. Destroying or damaging property

(1) A person who without lawful excuse destroys or damages any property belonging to another intending to destroy or damage any such property or being reckless as to whether any such property would be destroyed or damaged shall be guilty of an offence.

(2) A person who without lawful excuse destroys or damages any property, whether belonging to himself or another—

(a) intending to destroy or damage any property or being reckless as to whether any property would be destroyed or damaged; and
(b) intending by the destruction or damage to endanger the life of another or being reckless as to whether the life of another would be thereby endangered;

shall be guilty of an offence.

(3) An offence committed under this section by destroying or damaging property by fire shall be charged as arson.

NOTES AND QUESTIONS
1. What are the *mens rea* elements of s. 1(2)? To what does each of the elements refer? Which of the *mens rea* elements are subjective and which are objective?
2. Note in s. 1(2) the conjunction 'and' between paras (a) and (b). The appropriate *mens rea* elements in each part must be proved. Where the conjunction instead is '*or*' (as it is in s.1(1) and in each of the paragraphs of s. 1(2)), the prosecution can satisfy their burden by proof of either *mens rea*.
3. Sometimes a *mens rea* may be implicit rather than explicit, although litigants may have to await a judicial interpretation to this effect. Is part of the *mens rea* of criminal damage in s. 1(1) a requirement that the defendant must *know* or have reason to know that the property which is damaged 'belongs to another'? The issue might arise where defendant claimed that he thought that it was his own property that he was destroying.

D: Proof of *mens rea*

We noted previously the difficulty of establishing what is going on in a defendant's mind at the time of the crime. How does the Crown prove *mens rea*?

R v Steane

[1947] KB 997, Court of Criminal Appeal

The appellant, a British subject, entered the service of the German broadcasting system, and on several occasions broadcast through that system. The evidence called by the prosecution was that of one witness who proved that the appellant did, in fact, so broadcast and said that he had seen a telegram, in the appellant's possession, signed Emmie Goering, which stated that he could expect to be released and be home very shortly. The principal evidence against him was a statement taken from him by an officer of the British Intelligence Service in October, 1945, purporting to give an account of his activities in the German broadcasting service, concluding with the words: 'I have read this statement over and to the best of my knowledge and belief it is all true, and must request it to be used in conjunction with my written report dated July 5, 1945 to the American C.I.C. in Augsburg.' This earlier report was not produced in evidence. Before the war, the appellant was employed in Germany as a film actor and was so engaged when the war broke out. His wife and two sons were living in Germany. On the outbreak of war the appellant was at once arrested, but his wife and two sons remained in Oberammergau.

The only other evidence was that of the appellant. He said that on his arrest he was questioned and that the interview ended with the order: 'Say Heil Hitler, you dirty swine.' He refused and was thereupon knocked down losing several teeth, and he was interned on September 11, 1939. Just before Christmas of that year he was sent for by Goebbels, who asked him to broadcast. He refused. He was thereupon warned that he was in an enemy country and that they had methods of making people do things. A week later an official named von Bockman saw him and dropped hints as to German methods of persuasion. A professor named Kossuth also warned him that these people could be dangerous to those who gave trouble. In consequence he submitted to a voice test, trying to perform as badly as he could. The next day he was ordered to read news three times a day, and did so until April, 1940. In that month he refused to do any more broadcasting. Two Gestapo men called on him. They said: 'If you don't obey, your wife and children will be put in a concentration camp.' In May three Gestapo men saw him and he was badly beaten up, one ear being partly torn off. He agreed to work for his old employers, helping to produce films. There was no evidence that the films he helped to produce were or could be of any assistance to the Germans or at all harmful to this country. He swore that he was in continual fear for his wife and children. He asserted, and said he had asserted, in his report of July 5, 1945, that he never had the slightest idea or intention of assisting the enemy, and that what he did was done to save his wife and children and that what he did could not have assisted the enemy except in a very technical sense. There was no record of the actual broadcasts made by the appellant.

LORD GODDARD: . . . In the opinion of the court, there was undoubtedly evidence from which a jury could infer that the acts done by the appellant were acts likely to assist the enemy.

The far more difficult question that arises, however, is in connexion with the direction to the jury with regard to whether these acts were done with the intention of assisting the enemy. The case as opened, and indeed, as put by the learned judge appears to this court to be this: A man is taken to intend the natural consequences of his acts; if, therefore, he does an act which is likely to assist the enemy, it must be assumed that he did it with the intention of assisting the enemy. Now, the first thing which the court would observe is that, where the essence of an offence or a necessary constituent of an offence is a particular intent, that intent must be proved by the Crown just as much as any other fact necessary to constitute the offence.

The wording of the regulation itself shows that it is not enough merely to charge a prisoner with doing an act likely to assist the enemy; he must do it with the particular intent specified in the regulation. While no doubt the motive of a man's act and his intention in doing the act are, in law, different things, it is, none the less, true that in many offences a specific intention is a necessary ingredient and the jury have to be satisfied that a particular act was done with that specific intent, although the natural consequences of the act might, if nothing else were proved, be said to show the intent for which it was done. . . .

. . . No doubt, if the prosecution prove an act the natural consequence of which would be a certain result and no evidence or explanation is given, then a jury may, on a proper direction, find that the prisoner is guilty of doing the act with the intent alleged, but if on the totality of the evidence there is room for more than one view as to the intent of the prisoner, the jury should be directed that it is for the prosecution to prove the intent to the jury's satisfaction, and if, on a review of the whole evidence, they either think that the intent did not exist or they are left in doubt as to the intent, the prisoner is entitled to be acquitted. . . .

Now, another matter which is of considerable importance in the case, but does not seem to have been brought directly to the attention of the jury, is that very different considerations may apply where the accused at the time he did the acts is in subjection to an enemy power and where he is not. British soldiers who were set to work on the Burma road or, if invasion had unhappily taken place, British subjects who might have been set to work by the enemy digging trenches would undoubtedly be doing acts likely to assist the enemy. It would be unnecessary surely in their cases to consider, any of the niceties of the law relating to duress, because no jury would find that merely by doing this work they were intending to assist the enemy. In our opinion it is impossible to say that where an act was done by a person in subjection to the power of others, especially if that other be a brutal enemy, an inference that he intended the natural consequences of his act must be drawn merely from the fact that he did it. The guilty intent cannot be presumed and must be proved. The proper direction to the jury in this case would have been that it was for the prosecution to prove the criminal intent, and that while the jury would be entitled to presume that intent if they thought that the act was done as the result of the free uncontrolled action of the accused, they would not be entitled to presume it, if the circumstances showed that the act was done in subjection to the power of the enemy, or was as consistent with an innocent intent as with a criminal intent, for example, the innocent intent of a desire to save his wife and children from a concentration camp. They should only convict if satisfied by the evidence that the act complained of was in fact done to assist the enemy, and if there was doubt about the matter, the prisoner was entitled to be acquitted.

NOTES AND QUESTIONS

1. What was Steane's intent? His motive? Does the court confuse the two?
2. Given its logical force, why does the court reject the position that a defendant should be held to have intended the natural and probable consequences of his acts?
3. If the *mens rea* refers to acts which Steane knows will help the enemy, he may well be guilty but if it refers to acts which Steane should know will help the enemy, he is undoubtedly guilty. The actual statutory language was *'with intent to assist the enemy'*. Did Steane have this intent?

4. What if Steane did his broadcasts in order to establish his reputation as an announcer but without any thought as to whether his acts would help the enemy? Would the court's decision have been the same? In such a case, as in the original, there may be no intent to assist the cause of the enemy, but might not a jury have less sympathy for Steane? If *Steane* had been analysed in terms of whether he had a valid defence of duress (he committed the crime in order to avoid the greater evil of death to his family), as perhaps it should have been, there would have been a sound basis for distinguishing the original case from our example.

5. Alan Norrie in 'After Woollin' [1999] Crim LR 532 argues that where good motives are involved (as in *Steane*), a moral threshold should have to be passed before an outcome seen as virtually certain can be regarded as intended. Is this a better explanation of *Steane*? See also A. Simester and S. Shute, 'Letter to the Editor' [2000] Crim LR 204.

6. Review in respect to the motive/intent context the medical cases, pp. 126–131, where doctors hastened death. Consider particularly in this regard *Re A (Conjoined Twins – Medical Treatment)* [2001] 1 FLR 1 (for facts and holding see p. 473).

Subsequent to *Steane* the issue of proof of intent was addressed by Parliament.

Criminal Justice Act 1967

8. A court or jury, in determining whether a person has committed an offence—
   (a) shall not be bound in law to infer that he intended or foresaw a result of his actions by reason only of its being a natural and probable consequence of those actions; but
   (b) shall decide whether he did intend or foresee that result by reference to all the evidence, drawing such inferences from the evidence as appear proper in the circumstances.

SECTION 2:   Varieties of *mens rea*

It is difficult to generalise about *mens rea*, for there are so many different states of mind that can be seen in the law. The following list, which contains the most common varieties of *mens rea*, is by no means exclusive:

— intention
— knowledge
— recklessness (subjective)
— recklessness (objective)
— gross negligence
— negligence
— strict liability

In the sections which follow, an attempt will be made to analyse each of these states of mind.

A: Intention

(i) *Foresight of consequences*
What does it mean to say that a defendant acted intentionally? The paradigmatic situation is where the defendant brings about the very result which it was the

defendant's purpose to bring about. More troublesome has been the situation where results are virtually certain to follow from the defendant's acts and which the defendant knew (or should have known?) would follow from his acts as a virtual certainty. Is it fair to say under the latter circumstances that the defendant intended the consequences? This was one of the issues raised by *Steane* (above): If Steane knew that his acts would help the enemy, can it be said that he intended to help the enemy?

In an incident that attracted international condemnation, a bomb was placed on Pan Am flight 103 in Germany. The bomb exploded over Scotland, killing the passengers and crew. Assume that the bomber was intending only to make a political statement but 'knew' that the aircraft would blow up in mid-air, in all probability killing everybody aboard. Assume further that the bomber could not have cared one way or the other if there were survivors, or, alternatively, hoped that no deaths would result. Did the bomber 'intend' the resulting deaths?

Perhaps the more important point for criminalisation purposes is: Should it matter? If not, then Parliament could draft the statute accordingly. A murder statute, for example, could be written so that the mental element was either intending to cause death or engaging in conduct which the actor is aware is virtually certain to cause death. This is in fact the approach taken by the drafters of the Model Penal Code in America. In England, however, murder retains its common law definition, which requires proof of malice aforethought, which the courts define as either an intent to kill or an intent to inflict grievous bodily harm (GBH). This definition has forced the courts to wrestle with the question of whether engaging in acts 'knowing' that death or GBH is virtually certain to follow amounts to an intent to kill.

R v Moloney
[1985] 1 AC 905, House of Lords

LORD BRIDGE OF HARWICH: . . . [T]he appellant was interviewed by the acting detective chief superintendent, Superintendent Cole, and Detective Sergeant Fletcher. Sergeant Fletcher made a full written record of this interview which the appellant in due course signed as correct. It is in the course of this record that one reads the appellant's full account of the tragic events at his family home on the morning of 22 November. He has, in all essentials, adhered to that account ever since. The material part of the statement reads as follows:

> It started with a dinner party which was thrown for my grandparents' fortieth wedding anniversary. Towards the end, we all had a lot to drink and our guests had left and I told me Dad I wanted to leave the army. He disagreed with me and started to outline his reasons for disagreeing with me. It was obviously set for being a long discussion so my mother, my sister and grandparents went to bed. We had a couple more drinks while the discussion went on and I was very drunk, and I suspect he was as well. At this point I have to become vague because the conversation came round to personal prowess and in particular with a shotgun. Me Dad claimed that he could not only outshoot me but outload me, outdraw me, i.e. he was faster than me, and claimed even with a crippled left arm he was still faster than me. I disagreed with him and said: 'Don't be silly' or words to that effect. In fact we were swearing at each other at this time. So he said: 'We'll prove it. Go and get two of the

shotguns.' He has four, I have one. So I went upstairs and got my shotgun and I got his shotgun. I gave him his shotgun and he told me to get two cartridges out of a box in the cupboard. I gave him one and took the other myself. He opened his gun and started to remove his snap caps. I opened my gun and removed two empty cartridges which I use as snap caps as I don't have any. I inserted the cartridge in the right hand barrel, closed the gun, took off the safety catch and pulled the trigger of the left hand barrel, and told him he'd lost. By this time I don't think he'd even cleared his barrel of the snap caps. He looked at me and said: 'I didn't think you'd got the guts, but if you have pull the trigger.' I didn't aim the gun. I just pulled the trigger and he was dead. I then went and called the police and told the operator I had just murdered my father, and that's the story.

. . .

The golden rule should be that, when directing a jury on the mental element necessary in a crime of specific intent, the judge should avoid any elaboration or paraphrase of what is meant by intent, and leave it to the jury's good sense to decide whether the accused acted with the necessary intent, unless the judge is convinced that, on the facts and having regard to the way the case has been presented to the jury in evidence and argument, some further explanation or elaboration is strictly necessary to avoid misunderstanding. In trials for murder or wounding with intent, I find it very difficult to visualise a case where any such explanation or elaboration could be required, if the offence consisted of a direct attack on the victim with a weapon, except possibly the case where the accused shot at A and killed B, which any first year law student could explain to a jury in the simplest of terms. Even where the death results indirectly from the act of the accused, I believe the cases that will call for a direction by reference to foresight of consequences will be of extremely rare occurrence.

I do not, of course mean to question the necessity, which frequently arises, to explain to a jury that intention is something quite distinct from motive or desire. But this can normally be quite simply explained by reference to the case before the court or, if necessary, by some homely example. A man who, at London Airport, boards a plane which he knows to be bound for Manchester, clearly intends to travel to Manchester, even though Manchester is the last place he wants to be and his motive for boarding the plane is simply to escape pursuit. The possibility that the plane may have engine trouble and be diverted to Luton does not affect the matter. By boarding the Manchester plane, the man conclusively demonstrates his intention to go there, because it is a moral certainty that that is where he will arrive.

In the rare cases in which it is necessary to direct a jury by reference to foresight of consequences, I do not believe it is necessary for the judge to do more than invite the jury to consider two questions. First, was death or really serious injury in a murder case (or whatever relevant consequence must be proved to have been intended in any other case) a natural consequence of the defendant's voluntary act? Secondly, did the defendant foresee that consequence as being a natural consequence of his act? The jury should then be told that if they answer yes to both questions it is a proper inference for them to draw that he intended that consequence.

QUESTIONS

1. The trial judge in *Moloney* had instructed the jury that it could convict if it concluded that the accused had foreseen the consequences, even though he did not desire them. In what respect, according to the House of Lords, was this instruction incorrect?

2. Of what relevance, according to Lord Bridge, is foresight of consequences? What, according to Lord Bridge, should a jury be told:

(a) in the ordinary case?

(b) in a case requiring instruction regarding foresight of consequence?

Lord Bridge's proposed guidelines for instructing the jury in the rare cases involving foresight of consequences were reconsidered by the House of Lords one year later.

R v *Hancock and Shankland*

[1986] 1 AC 455, House of Lords

LORD SCARMAN: . . . On 16 May 1985 at the Crown Court, Cardiff, Reginald Dean Hancock and Russell Shankland were convicted of the murder of Mr Wilkie. In the dark hours of the early morning of 30 November 1984 Mr David Wilkie was driving his taxi along the Heads of the Valley Road. As he approached the bridge over the road at Rhymney he was killed when two lumps of concrete hit the car. The two lumps, a block and a post, had been dropped from the bridge as he approached it.

Mr Wilkie's passenger was a miner going to work. Mr Hancock and Mr Shankland were miners on strike, and strongly objected to Mr Wilkie's passenger going to work. That morning they had collected the block and the post from nearby, had brought them to the bridge under which the Heads of the Valley Road runs through a cutting, and had placed them on the parapet on the side facing towards the Rhymney roundabout. They then awaited the arrival of a convoy escorting the miner on his way to work. The convoy approached the bridge at about 5.15 a.m.: it consisted of a police motor-cycle, a police Land Rover, the taxi driven by Mr Wilkie, and a police Sherpa van. The convoy was travelling from the Rhymney roundabout towards the bridge in the nearside lane of the carriageway. Estimates of its speed varied: it was put somewhere between 30 and 40 mph. As the convoy neared the bridge, the concrete block struck the taxi's windscreen. The post struck the carriageway some 4ft. 8in. from the nearside verge. Before, however, the post subsided on the ground, it was hit by the taxi. The taxi skidded out of control, coming to rest on the embankment. Mr Wilkie died from the injuries he received in the wrecking of the taxi by the two lumps of concrete.

The case for the prosecution was that the two concrete objects were either thrown from the bridge or pushed over its parapet in the path of the taxi at a time when the taxi could not avoid being struck by one or both of them. And, as the trial judge told the jury, the prosecution case could be compressed into one question and answer, the question being 'what else could a person who pushed or threw such objects have intended but to cause really serious bodily harm to the occupants of the car?' The answer in the prosecution's submission was that a person acting in that way could in the circumstances have intended nothing less.

The defence was simple enough: that the two men intended to block the road, to stop the miner going to work, but not to kill or to do serious bodily harm to anyone.

. . .

. . . The issue was ultimately one of intention. Did they (or either of them) intend to kill or to cause anyone serious bodily harm?

The case called for a careful direction by judge to jury as to the state of mind required by law to be proved to their satisfaction before they could return a verdict of murder. The jury would also want his help in weighing up the evidence. The judge's direction as to the intention required by law was impeccable. He said:

> If the prosecution has made you satisfied so as to be sure that Dean Hancock and Russell Shankland agreed that they would, in concert, push or throw missiles from the bridge, each having the intention either to kill or to cause really serious injury, then you will find each of them guilty of murder as the block was thrown or pushed by Dean Hancock in pursuance of the agreement.

When he came to help them on the facts, he offered guidance along the *Moloney* lines:

You may think that critical to the resolution of this case is the question of intent. In determining whether a person intended to kill or to cause really serious injury, you must have regard to all of the evidence which has been put before you, and draw from it such inferences as to you seem proper and appropriate. You may or may not, for the purpose of considering what inferences to draw, find it helpful to ask: Was death or serious injury a natural consequence of what was done? Did a defendant foresee that consequence as a natural consequence? That is a possible question which you may care to ask yourselves. If you find yourselves not satisfied so as to be sure that there was an intent to kill or to cause really serious injury, then it is open to you to return a verdict of not guilty of murder, but guilty of manslaughter.

The question for the House is, therefore, whether the *Moloney* guidelines are sound. In *Moloney's* case the ratio decidendi was that the judge never properly put to the jury the defence, namely that the accused was unaware that the gun was pointing at his stepfather. The House, however, held it necessary in view of the history of confusion in this branch of the law to attempt to clarify the law relating to the establishment of the mental element necessary to constitute the crime of murder and to lay down guidelines for assisting juries to determine in what circumstances it is proper to infer intent from foresight. The House certainly clarified the law. First, the House cleared away the confusions which had obscured the law during the last 25 years laying down authoritatively that the mental element in murder is a specific intent, the intent to kill or to inflict serious bodily harm. Nothing less suffices: and the jury must be sure that the intent existed when the act was done which resulted in death before they can return a verdict of murder.

Secondly, the House made it absolutely clear that foresight of consequences is no more than evidence of the existence of the intent; it must be considered, and its weight assessed, together with all the evidence in the case.

. . .

Thirdly, the House emphasised that the probability of the result of an act is an important matter for the jury to consider and can be critical in their determining whether the result was intended.

These three propositions were made abundantly clear by Lord Bridge of Harwich.

. . .

It is only when Lord Bridge of Harwich turned to the task of formulating guidelines that difficulty arises. It is said by the Court of Appeal that the guidelines by omitting any express reference to probability are ambiguous and may well lead a jury to a wrong conclusion. The omission was deliberate. Lord Bridge omitted the adjective 'probable' from the time-honoured formula 'foresight of the natural and probable consequences of his acts' because he thought that 'if a consequence is natural, it is really otiose to speak of it as also being probable' [1985] AC 905, 929B. But is it?

Lord Bridge of Harwich did not deny the importance of probability. He put it thus, at p. 925:

> But looking on their facts at the decided cases where a crime of specific intent was under consideration, including *R v Hyam* [1975] AC 55 itself, they suggest to me that the probability of the consequence taken to have been foreseen must be little short of overwhelming before it will suffice to establish the necessary intent.

In his discussion of the relationship between foresight and intention, Lord Bridge of Harwich reviewed the case law since the passing of the Homicide Act 1957 and concluded, at p. 928:

> foresight of the consequences, as an element bearing on the issue of intention in murder, or indeed any other crime of specific intent, belongs, not to the substantive law, but to the law of evidence.

. . .

Yet he omitted any reference in his guidelines to probability. He did so because he included probability in the meaning which he attributed to 'natural.' My Lords, I very much doubt whether a jury without further explanation would think that 'probable' added nothing to 'natural.' I agree with the Court of Appeal that the probability of a consequence is a factor of sufficient importance to be drawn specifically to the attention of the jury and to be explained. In a murder case where it is necessary to direct a jury on the issue of intent by reference to foresight of consequences the probability of death or serious injury resulting from the act done may be critically important. Its importance will depend on the degree of probability: if the likelihood that death or serious injury will result is high, the probability of that result may, as Lord Bridge of Harwich noted and the Lord Chief Justice emphasised, be seen as overwhelming evidence of the existence of the intent to kill or injure. Failure to explain the relevance of probability may, therefore, mislead a jury into thinking that it is of little or no importance and into concentrating exclusively on the causal link between the act and its consequence. In framing his guidelines Lord Bridge of Harwich [1985] AC 1905, 929G, emphasised that he did not believe it necessary to do more than to invite the jury to consider his two questions. Neither question makes any reference (beyond the use of the word 'natural') to probability. I am not surprised that when in this case the judge faithfully followed this guidance the jury found themselves perplexed and unsure. In my judgment, therefore, the *Moloney* guidelines as they stand are unsafe and misleading. They require a reference to probability. They also require an explanation that the greater the probability of a consequence the more likely it is that the consequence was foreseen and that if that consequence was foreseen the greater the probability is that that consequence was also intended. But juries also require to be reminded that the decision is theirs to be reached upon a consideration of all the evidence.

Accordingly, I accept the view of the Court of Appeal that the *Moloney* guidelines are defective. I am, however, not persuaded that guidelines of general application, albeit within a limited class of case, are wise or desirable. . . .

. . . It is better, I suggest, notwithstanding my respect for the comprehensive formulation of the Court of Appeal's guidelines, that the trial judge should follow the traditional course of a summing up. He must explain the nature of the offence charged, give directions as to the law applicable to the particular facts of the case, explain the incidence and burden of proof, put both sides' cases making especially sure that the defence is put; he should offer help in understanding and weighing up all the evidence and should make certain that the jury understand that whereas the law is for him the facts are for them to decide. Guidelines, if given, are not to be treated as rules of law but as a guide indicating the sort of approach the jury may properly adopt to the evidence when coming to their decision on the facts.

In a case where foresight of a consequence is part of the evidence supporting a prosecution submission that the accused intended the consequence, the judge, if he thinks some general observations would help the jury, could well, having in mind section 8 of the Criminal Justice Act 1967, emphasise that the probability, however high, of a consequence is only a factor, though it may in some cases be a very significant factor, to be considered with all the other evidence in determining whether the accused intended to bring it about. The distinction between the offence and the evidence relied on to prove it is vital. Lord Bridge's speech in *Moloney* made the distinction crystal clear: it would be a disservice to the law to allow his guidelines to mislead a jury into overlooking it.

For these reasons I would hold that the *Moloney* guidelines are defective and should not be used as they stand without further explanation. The laying down of guidelines for use in directing juries in cases of complexity is a function which can be usefully exercised by the Court of Appeal. But it should be done sparingly, and limited to cases of real difficulty. If it is done, the guidelines should avoid generalisation so far as is possible and encourage the jury to exercise their common sense in reaching what is their decision on the facts. Guidelines are not rules of law: judges should not think that they must use them. A judge's duty is to direct the jury in law and to help them upon the particular facts of the case.

QUESTIONS

1. What was the defendants' intent? Their motive?

2. Lord Scarman found the *Moloney* guidelines deficient. How so? Are his suggestions any more helpful? In the final analysis, does not Lord Scarman simply
   dump into the laps of the jurors an issue which their Lordships had been unable
   to resolve, hoping that the jury would do a better job of it in practice than they
   had been able to do in theory?

3. What, according to Lord Scarman, is the proper relationship between
   probability, foresight, and intention?

The Court of Appeal has subsequently attempted to provide further clarification:

R v Nedrick
[1986] 3 All ER 1, Court of Appeal

LORD LANE CJ: . . . The case for the Crown was that the appellant had a grudge against a woman
called Viola Foreshaw, as a result of which, after threats that he would 'burn her out', he went to her
house in the early hours of 15 July 1984, poured paraffin through the letter box and onto the front
door and set it alight. He gave no warning. The house was burnt down and one of Viola Foreshaw's
children, a boy aged 12 called Lloyd, died of asphyxiation and burns.

After a number of interviews during which he denied any responsibility, the appellant eventually
confessed to the police that he had started the fire in the manner described, adding, 'I didn't want
anyone to die, I am not a murderer; please tell the judge; God knows I am not a murderer.' When
asked why he did it, he replied. 'Just to wake her up and frighten her.'

We have endeavoured to crystallise the effect of their Lordships' speeches in R v Moloney
and R v Hancock in a way which we hope may be helpful to judges who have to handle this type
of case.

It may be advisable first of all to explain to the jury that a man may intend to a certain result
whilst at the same time not desiring it to come about. In R v Moloney [1985] 1 All ER 1025 at 1037,
[1985] AC 905 at 926 Lord Bridge gave an illustration of the distinction:

> A man who, at London Airport, boards a plane which he knows to be bound for
> Manchester, clearly intends to travel to Manchester, even though Manchester is the last
> place he wants to be and his motive for boarding the plane is simply to escape pursuit.

The man who knowingly boards the Manchester aircraft wants to go there in the sense that
boarding it is a voluntary act. His desire to leave London predominates over his desire not to go to
Manchester. When he decides to board the aircraft, if not before, he forms the intention to travel
to Manchester.

In R v Hancock the House decided that the R v Moloney guidelines require a reference to
probability. Lord Scarman said ([1986] 1 All ER 641 at 651, [1986] AC 455 at 473):

> They also require an explanation that the greater the probability of a consequence the
> more likely it is that the consequence was foreseen and that if that consequence was
> foreseen the greater the probability is that that consequence was also intended.

When determining whether the defendant had the necessary intent, it may therefore be helpful
for a jury to ask themselves two questions. (1) How probable was the consequence which resulted
from the defendant's voluntary act? (2) Did he foresee that consequence?

If he did not appreciate that death or serious harm was likely to result from his act, he cannot have
intended to bring it about. If he did, but thought that the risk to which he was exposing the person
killed was only slight, then it may be easy for the jury to conclude that he did not intend to bring

about that result. On the other hand, if the jury are satisfied that at the material time the defendant recognised that death or serious harm would be virtually certain (barring some unforeseen intervention) to result from his voluntary act, then that is a fact from which they may find it easy to infer that he intended to kill or do serious bodily harm, even though he may not have had any desire to achieve that result.

As Lord Bridge said in *R v Moloney* [1985] 1 All ER 1025 at 1036, [1985] AC 905 at 925:

> . . . the probability of the consequence taken to have been foreseen must be little short of overwhelming before it will suffice to establish the necessary intent.

Later he uses the expression 'moral certainty' (see [1985] 1 All ER 1025 at 1037, [1985] AC 905 at 926) and says, 'will lead to a certain consequence unless something unexpected supervenes to prevent it' (see [1985] 1 All ER 1025 at 1039, [1985] AC 905 at 929).

Where the charge is murder and in the rare cases where the simple direction is not enough, the jury should be directed that they are not entitled to infer the necessary intention unless they feel sure that death or serious bodily harm was a virtual certainty (barring some unforeseen intervention) as a result of the defendant's actions and that the defendant appreciated that such was the case.

Where a man realises that it is for all practical purposes inevitable that his actions will result in death or serious harm, the inference may be irresistible that he intended that result, however little he may have desired or wished it to happen. The decision is one for the jury to be reached on a consideration of all the evidence.

R v *Woollin*

[1998] 3 WLR 382, House of Lords

> [The defendant threw his 3-month-old son four or five feet across a room in the direction of his pram, causing him to suffer a fractured skull, from which he died.]

LORD STEYN: The Court of Appeal certified the following questions as of general importance:

> 1. In murder, where there is no direct evidence that the purpose of a defendant was to kill or to inflict serious injury on the victim, is it necessary to direct the jury that they may only infer an intent to do serious injury if they are satisfied (a) that serious bodily harm was a virtually certain consequence of the defendant's voluntary act and (b) that the defendant appreciated that fact? 2. If the answer to question 1 is 'Yes,' is such a direction necessary in all cases or is it only necessary in cases where the sole evidence of the defendant's intention is to be found in his actions and their consequence to the victim?

On appeal to your Lordships' House the terrain of the debate covered the correctness in law of the direction recommended by Lord Lane CJ in *Nedrick* and, if that direction is sound, whether it should be used only in the limited category of cases envisaged by the Court of Appeal. And counsel for the appellant renewed his submission that by directing the jury in terms of substantial risk the judge illegitimately widened the mental element of murder.

. . .

The Crown did not argue that as a matter of policy foresight of a virtual certainty is too narrow a test in murder. Subject to minor qualifications, the decision in *Nedrick* was widely welcomed by distinguished academic writers: see Professor J.C. Smith QC's commentary on *Nedrick* [1986] Crim LR 742, 743–744; Glanville Williams, 'The *Mens Rea* for Murder: Leave it Alone' (1989) 105 LQR 387; J.R. Spencer, 'Murder in the Dark: A Glimmer of Light?' [1986] CLJ 366–367; Ashworth, *Principles of Criminal Law*, 2nd ed. (1995), p. 172. It is also of interest that it is very similar to the threshold of being aware 'that it *will* occur in the ordinary course of events' in the Law Commission's draft Criminal Code (see Criminal Law: Legislating the Criminal Code: Offences against the Person and General Principles, Law Com. No. 218 (1993) (Cm. 2370), Appendix A (Draft Criminal Law Bill with Explanatory Notes), pp. 90–91): compare also Professor J.C. Smith QC, 'A Note on "Intention"' [1990] Crim LR 85, 86. Moreover, over a period of 12 years since *Nedrick* the test of foresight of virtual certainty has apparently caused no practical difficulties. It is simple and clear. It is true that it may exclude a conviction of murder in the often cited terrorist example where a member of the bomb disposal team is killed. In such a case it may realistically be said that the terrorist did not foresee the killing of a member of the bomb disposal team as a virtual certainty. That may be a consequence of not framing the principle in terms of risk-taking. Such cases ought to cause no substantial difficulty since immediately below murder there is available a verdict of manslaughter which may attract in the discretion of the court a life sentence. In any event, as Lord Lane CJ eloquently argued in a debate in the House of Lords, to frame a principle for particular difficulties regarding terrorism 'would produce corresponding injustices which would be very hard to eradicate:' Hansard (H.L. Debates), 6 November 1989. col. 480. I am satisfied that the *Nedrick* test, which was squarely based on the decision of the House in *Moloney*, is pitched at the right level of foresight.

The status of Nedrick
In my view Lord Lane CJ's judgment in *Nedrick* provided valuable assistance to trial judges. The model direction is by now a tried-and-tested formula. Trial judges ought to continue to use it. On matters of detail I have three observations, which can best be understood if I set out again the relevant part of Lord Lane's judgment. It was:

(A) When determining whether the defendant had the necessary intent, it may therefore be helpful for a jury to ask themselves two questions. (1) How probable was the consequence which resulted from the defendant's voluntary act? (2) Did he foresee that consequence? If he did not appreciate that death or serious harm was likely to result from his act, he cannot have intended to bring it about. If he did, but thought that the risk to which he was exposing the person killed was only slight, then it may be easy for the jury to conclude that he did not intend to bring about that result. On the other hand, if the jury are satisfied that at the material time the defendant recognised that death or serious harm would be virtually certain (barring some unforeseen intervention) to result from his voluntary act, then that is a fact from which they may find it easy to infer that he intended to kill or do serious bodily harm, even though he may not have had any desire to achieve that result . . .
(B) Where the charge is murder and in the rare cases where the simple direction is not enough, the jury should be directed that they are not entitled to infer the necessary intention, unless they feel sure that death or serious bodily harm was a virtual certainty (barring some unforeseen intervention) as a result of the defendant's actions and that the defendant appreciated that such was the case.
(C) Where a man realises that it is for all practical purposes inevitable that his actions will result in death or serious harm, the inference may be irresistible that he intended that result, however little he may have desired or wished it to happen. The decision is one for the jury to be reached upon a consideration of all the evidence. (Lettering added.)

First, I am persuaded by the speech of my noble and learned friend, Lord Hope of Craighead, that it is unlikely, if ever, to be helpful to direct the jury in terms of the two questions set out in (A). I agree that these questions may detract from the clarity of the critical direction in (B). Secondly, in their writings previously cited Glanville Williams, Professor Smith and Andrew Ashworth observed that the use of the words 'to infer' in (B) may detract from the clarity of the model direction. I agree. I would substitute the words 'to find'. Thirdly, the first sentence of (C) does not form part of the model direction. But it would always be right for the judge to say, as Lord Lane CJ put it, that the decision is for the jury upon a consideration of all the evidence in the case.

The certified questions
Given my conclusions the certified questions fall away.

LORD HOPE OF CRAIGHEAD: My Lords, I have had the advantage of reading in draft the speech which has been prepared by my noble and learned friend, Lord Steyn. I agree with it, and I wish to add only these brief comments.

I attach great importance to the search for a direction which is both clear and simple. It should be expressed in as few words as possible. That is essential if it is to be intelligible. A jury cannot be expected to absorb and apply a direction which attempts to deal with every situation which might conceivably arise. I think that the *Nedrick* direction, which is (B) in Lord Steyn's analysis, fulfils this requirement admirably. But the substitution of the word 'find' for 'infer' is an improvement, in the interests of clarity, and I also would make this change to it. However I regard the questions in (A), which are derived from Lord Scarman's speech in *R v Hancock* [1986] AC 455, 473, as detracting from the clarity of the critical direction. I would prefer to say therefore that it is unlikely, if ever, to be helpful to tell the jury that they should ask themselves these questions. I think that it would be better to give them the critical direction, and then to tell them that the decision was theirs upon a consideration of all the evidence.

As for the terrorist example. I think that Lord Mustill's observations in *Attorney-General's Reference (No. 3 of 1994)* [1998] AC 245, 261 are also relevant. In that passage he gave as an example of 'indiscriminate malice', which belongs to the category of deliberate murder where the defendant consciously intended to kill the victim, the example of the terrorist who hides a bomb in an aircraft. As he explained, the intention is aimed at the class of potential victims of which the actual victim forms part, even although the identity of the ultimate victim is not yet fixed at the start when the intent is combined with the *actus reus* which ultimately causes the explosion. The answer to the question whether those who attempt to dispose of the bomb are within that class will depend on the circumstances. All that needs to be said is that it may not be necessary in every such case to rely on the alternative verdict of manslaughter.

Appeal allowed.
Conviction of murder quashed.
Conviction of manslaughter substituted.

NOTES AND QUESTIONS
1. If the defendant foresees death or serious injury as a virtual certainty Lord Steyn believes the jury are 'entitled to find' intention. Alan Norrie in 'After *Woollin*' [1999] Crim LR 532 points out that the problem is not with the 'find' rather than 'infer' formulation but with the word 'entitled'. He argues:

    The use of the word 'entitled' ... suggests that the jury may so identify intention, but, alternatively may not do so. 'Entitled' is permissive rather than obligatory so that the formulation 'involves some ambiguity with the hint of the existence of some ineffable, undefinable, notice of intent, locked in the breast of the jurors' (quote from Lord Goff, 'The Mental Element in the Crime of Murder' (1988) 104 LQR 30).

    Should the jury be given this discretion?
2. Is there a category of 'indiscriminate malice'? See the discussion of transferred malice below and Alan Norrie [1999] Crim LR 532.
3. When a defendant acts with the intent to achieve a particular result (A), which cannot be brought about without causing a secondary result (B), the defendant is often said to have intended result B as well as result A. The intent to cause B is often referred to as an 'oblique'

intent. See G. Williams, 'Oblique Intention' [1987] CLJ 417. In *Re A (Conjoined Twins: Medical Treatment)* [2001] 1 FLR 1 and (for facts and holding see p. 473), in order to save the life of one conjoined twin, it was necessary to perform an operation that would inevitably cause the death of the other twin. In these circumstances can it be said that the doctor had an intent to kill?

4. In addition to 'oblique' intent, the courts have at times distinguished between so-called 'basic' and 'specific' intent. Again it is not clear whether the distinction is helpful for analytic purposes, but, as it is most commonly drawn in respect of crimes committed while the defendant is intoxicated, the issue will be deferred to the discussion of that topic. See Chapter 13.

5. The general subject matter of intent has produced a rich literature. See, e.g., Lord Goff, 'The mental element in the crime of murder' (1988) 104 LQR 30, A. Norrie, 'Oblique intention and legal politics' [1989] Crim LR 793; R. Duff, 'The politics of intention: a response to Norrie' [1990] Crim LR 637; J.C. Smith, 'A note on intention' [1990] Crim LR 85.

(ii) *Transferred intent*

Must *mens rea* be directed towards a specific goal, or, in cases of homicide, a particular person? Suppose that X shoots at Y, intending to kill him. His aim is off, and the bullet hits Z with fatal results. Alternatively, Y moves at the critical moment and the bullet hits Z, who is directly behind him, again with fatal results. Is X, who had no intent to kill Z, guilty of Z's murder?

R v *Saunders and Archer*
(1573) 2 Plowden 473

John Saunders had a wife whom he intended to kill, in order that he might marry another woman with whom he was in love, and he opened his design to the said Alexander Archer, and desired his assistance and advice in the execution of it, who advised him to put an end to her life by poison. With this intent the said Archer bought the poison, viz. arsenick and roseacre, and delivered it to the said John Saunders to give it to his wife, who accordingly gave it to her, being sick, in a roasted apple, and she eat a small part of it, and gave the rest to the said Eleanor Saunders, an infant, about three years of age, who was the daughter of her and the said John Saunders her husband. And the said John Saunders seeing it, blamed his wife for it, and said that apples were not good for such infants; to which his wife replied that they were better for such infants than for herself: and the daughter eat the poisoned apple, and the said John Saunders, her father, saw her eat it, and did not offer to take it from her lest he should be suspected, and afterwards the wife recovered, and the daughter died of the said poison.

And whether or no this was murder in John Saunders, the father, was somewhat doubted, for he had no intent to poison his daughter, nor had he any malice against her, but on the contrary he had a great affection for her, and he did not give her the poison, but his wife ignorantly gave it her, and although he might have taken it from the daughter, and so have preserved her life, yet the not taking it from her did not make it felony, for it was all one whether he had been present or absent, as to this point, inasmuch as he had no malice against the daughter, nor any inclination to do her any harm. But at last the said justices, upon consideration of the matter, and with the assent of Saunders, Chief Baron, who had the examination of the said John Saunders before, and who had signified his opinion to the said justices (as he afterwards said to me) were of opinion that the said offence was murder in the said John Saunders. And the reason thereof (as the said justices and the Chief Baron told me) was, because the said John Saunders gave the poison with an intent to kill a person, and in the giving of it he intended that death should follow. And when death followed from his act, although it happened in another person than her whose death he directly meditated, yet it shall be murder in him, for he was the original cause of the death, and if such death should not be punished in him, it would go unpunished; for here the wife, who gave the poisoned apple to her daughter, cannot be guilty of any offence, because she was ignorant of any poison contained in it, and she innocently gave it to the infant by way of necessary food, and therefore it is reasonable to adjudge her innocent in this case, and to charge the death of the infant, by which the Queen has lost a subject, upon him who was the cause of it, and who intended death in the act which occasioned the death here. (a) But if a man prepares poison, and lays it in several parts of his house, with an intent to kill rats and such sort of vermin, and a person comes and eats it, and dies of it, this is not felony in him who prepared and laid it there, because he had no intent to kill any reasonable creature. (b) But when he lays the poison with an intent to kill some reasonable creature, and another reasonable creature, whom he does not intend to kill, is poisoned by it, such death shall not be dispunishable, but he who prepared the poison shall be punished for it, because his intent was evil. And therefore it is every man's business to foresee what wrong or mischief may happen from that which he does with an ill intention, and it shall be no excuse for him to say that he intended to kill another, and not the person killed. (c) For if a man of malice prepense shoots an arrow at another with an intent to kill him, and a person to whom he bore no malice is killed by it, this shall be murder in him, for when he shot the arrow he intended to kill, and inasmuch as he directed his instrument of death at one, and thereby has killed another, it shall be the same offence in him as if he had killed the person he aimed at, for the end of the act shall be construed by the beginning of it, and the last part shall taste of the first, and as the beginning of the act had malice prepense in it, and consequently imported murder, so the end of the act, viz. the killing of another, shall be in the same degree, and therefore it shall be murder, and not homicide only. (d) For if one lies in wait in a certain place to kill a person, and another comes by the place, and he who lies in wait kills him out of mistake, thinking that he is the very person whom he waited for, this offence is murder in him, and not homicide only, for the killing was founded upon malice prepense. So in the principal case, when John Saunders of malice prepense gave to his wife the instrument of death, viz. the poisoned apple, and this upon a subsequent accident killed his daughter, whom he had no intention to kill, this is the same offence in him as if his act had met with the intended effect, and his intention in doing the act was to commit murder, wherefore the event of it shall be murder. And so the justices declared their opinion, to the jurors, whereupon they found both the prisoners guilty, and John Saunders had his judgment, and was hanged.

NOTES AND QUESTIONS

1. Why charge Saunders with a crime that he did not intend to commit (murder of the child) rather than the crime that he did intend to commit (attempt to murder his wife)? Would it have made more sense to say that Saunders acted recklessly in ignoring the known risk of death to the child, and to charge him with a crime (manslaughter) whose *mens rea* was recklessness?

2. The doctrine of transferred malice was subjected to close scrutiny by Lord Mustill in *Attorney-General's Reference (No. 3 of 1994)*:

Attorney-General's Reference (No. 3 of 1994)
[1997] 3 All ER 936, House of Lords

LORD MUSTILL: . . . As will appear, the events which founder the appeal were never conclusively proved at the trial, but are assumed to have been as follows. At the time in question a young woman M was pregnant, with between 22 and 24 weeks of gestation. According to the present state of medical knowledge if her baby had been born after 22 weeks it would not have had any significant prospect of survival. Two further weeks would have increased the chance to about 10 per cent. The pregnancy was, however, proceeding normally, and the risk that it would fail to continue to full term and be followed by an uneventful birth was very small indeed. Sadly, however, the natural father B quarrelled with M and stabbed her in the face, back and abdomen with a long-bladed kitchen knife in circumstances raising a prima facie inference that he intended to do her grievous bodily harm. M was admitted to hospital for surgical treatment and was later discharged in an apparently satisfactory state, still carrying the baby. Unfortunately, some 17 days after the incident M went into premature labour. The baby, named S, was born alive. The birth was still grossly premature, although by that time the chance that the baby would survive had increased to 50 per cent. Thereafter S lived for 121 days, when she succumbed to broncho-pulmonary dysplasia from the effects of premature birth. After her birth it was discovered that one of the knife cuts had penetrated her lower abdomen. The wound needed surgical repair, but it is agreed that this 'made no provable contribution to her death'.

The case for the Crown at the trial of B was that the wounding of M by B had set in train the events which caused the premature birth of S and hence her failure to achieve the normal prospect of survival which she would have had if the pregnancy had proceeded to full term. In this sense, therefore, we must assume that the wounding of M, at a time when S was a barely viable foetus, was the reason why she later died when she did.

. . . The point of law referred was as follows:

> 1.1 Subject to the proof by the prosecution of the requisite intent in either case: whether the crimes of murder or manslaughter can be committed where unlawful injury is deliberately inflicted:
>
> (i)   to a child in utero
> (ii) to a mother carrying a child in utero
>
> where the child is subsequently born alive, enjoys an existence independent of the mother, thereafter dies and the injuries inflicted while in utero either caused or made a substantial contribution to the death.

> 1.2 Whether the fact that the death of the child is caused solely as a consequence of injury to the mother rather than as a consequence of direct injury to the foetus can negative any liability for murder or manslaughter in the circumstances set out in question 1.1.

> . . .

I turn to the second rule, of 'transferred malice.' For present purposes this is more important and more difficult. Again, one must look at its origins to see whether they provide a theme which can be applied today. Three of them are familiar. Taking Lord Coke's example of the glancing arrow we have seen how one explanation of the poacher's responsibility founded on the notion of risk. The person who committed a crime took the chance that the outcome would be worse than he expected. Amongst many sources one can find the idea in *Russell on Crime*, 4th ed. (1845), p. 739:

> If an action, unlawful in itself, be done deliberately, and with the intention of mischief or great bodily harm to particular individuals, or of mischief indiscriminately, fall where it may, and death ensue or beside the original intention of the party, it will be murder.

In a later edition (1855: p. 759) this was exemplified by cases of particular malice to one individual failing by mistake upon another. In support are cited *R v Saunders* (1573) 2 Plowd 473 (a poisoned apple intended for the mother but given to the child) and *Gore 9* Co Rep 81 (medicine poisoned by the wife to kill her husband and consumed by the apothecary to prove his innocence); also 1 Hawkins P.C., c. 31, 545 and 1 Hale 436. As already suggested, this doctrine does survive in some small degree today, but as the foundation of a modem doctrine of transferred malice broad enough to encompass the present case it seems to me quite unsupportable.

Secondly, there is the reversed burden of proof whereby the causing of death is prima facie murder, unless it falls within one of the extenuating categories recognised by the institutional writers. Again, this concept is long out-of-date. Nobody could seriously think of using it to make new law.

Third, there was the idea of 'general malice', of an evil disposition existing in the general and manifesting itself in the particular, uniting the aim of the offender and the result which his deeds actually produced. According to this theory, there was no need to 'transfer' the wrongful intent from the intended to the actual victim; for since the offender was (in the words of *Blackstone*, supra, pp. 198–200) 'an enemy to all mankind in general', the actual victim was the direct object of the offender's enmity. Plainly, this will no longer do, for the last vestiges of the idea disappeared with the abolition of the murder/felony doctrine.

. . . [H]arking back to a concept of general malice, which amounts to no more than this, that a wrongful act displays a malevolence which can be attached to any adverse consequence, has long been out of date. And to speak of a particular malice which is 'transferred' simply disguises the problem by idiomatic language. The defendant's malice is directed at one objective, and when after the event the court treats it as directed at another object it is not recognising a 'transfer' but creating a new malice which never existed before. As Dr Glanville Williams pointed out (*Criminal Law*, the General Part 2nd Ed. (1961), p. 184) the doctrine is 'rather an arbitrary exception to general principles.' Like many of its kind this is useful enough to yield rough justice, in particular cases, and it can sensibly be retained notwithstanding its lack of any sound intellectual basis. But it is another matter to build a new rule upon it.

I pause to distinguish the case of indiscriminate malice from those already discussed, although even now it is sometimes confused with them. The terrorist who hides a bomb in an aircraft provides an example. This is not a case of 'general malice' where under the old law any wrongful act sufficed to prove the evil disposition which was taken to supply the necessary intent for homicide. Nor is it transferred malice, for there is no need of a transfer. The intention is already aimed directly at the class of potential victims of which the actual victim forms part. The intent and the actus reus completed by the explosion are joined from the start, even though the identity of the ultimate victim is not yet fixed. So also with the shots fired indiscriminately into a crowd. No ancient fictions are needed to make these cases of murder.

My Lords, the purpose of this enquiry has been to see whether the existing rules are based on principles sound enough to justify their extension to a case where the defendant acts without an intent to injure either the foetus or the child which it will become. In my opinion they are not. To give an affirmative answer requires a double 'transfer' of intent: first from the mother to the foetus and then from the foetus to the child as yet unborn. Then one would have to deploy the fiction (or at least the doctrine) which converts an intention to commit serious harm into the mens rea of murder. For me, this is too much. If one could find any logic in the rules I would follow it from one fiction to another, but whatever grounds there may once have been ave long since disappeared. I am willing to follow old laws until they are overturned, but not to make a new law on a basis for which there is no principle.

Moreover, even on a narrower approach the argument breaks down. The effect of transferred malice, as I understand it, is that the intended victim and the actual victim are treated as if they were one, so that what was intended to happen to the first person (but did not happen) is added to what actually did happen to the second person (but was not intended to happen), with the result that what was intended and what happened are married to make a notionally intended and actually consummated crime. The cases are treated as if the actual victim had been the intended victim from the start. To make any sense of this process there must, as it seems to me, be some compatibility between the original intention and the actual occurrence, and this is, indeed, what one finds in the cases. There is no such compatibility here. The defendant intended to commit and did commit an immediate crime of violence to the mother. He committed no relevant violence to the foetus, which was not a person, either at the time or in the future, and intended no harm to the foetus or to the human person which it would become. If fictions are useful, as they can be, they are only damaged by straining them beyond their limits. I would not overstrain the idea of transferred malice by trying to make it fit the present case.

Accordingly, I would . . . hold that on the presumed facts the judge was right to direct an acquittal on the count of murder.

NOTES AND QUESTIONS

1. In *Saunders and Archer* and in *Attorney-General's Reference (No. 3 of 1994)* the crime charged was of the same type (homicide) as was intended. All that changed was the victim. In such circumstances the courts have had little difficulty concluding that an accused who has the intent to kill, who acts pursuant to that intent and whose acts result in death, is liable for that death. The identity of the victim is not relevant for legal purposes. An even clearer example would occur where P, intending to kill Q, mistook T for Q and killed T. P would still be liable for murder. These are cases of what we might call intra-crime transferred intent. More troublesome analytically are cases of inter-crime transferred intent (see *Pembliton*, below).

2. See also the discussion of indiscriminate malice in *Woollin* (above). Is a terrorist guilty of the murder of a bomb disposal operative who manages, fatally, to set off the bomb he is attempting to dismantle?

R v Pembliton

[1874–80] All ER 1163, Court for Consideration of Crown Cases Reserved

At the quarter sessions of the peace held at Wolverhampton on Jan. 8, 1874, Henry Pembliton was indicted for that he 'unlawfully and maliciously did commit damage, injury, and spoil upon a window in the house of Henry Kirkham,' contrary to s. 51 of the Malicious Damage Act 1861.

On the night of Dec. 6, 1873, the prisoner was drinking with others at a public house called 'The Grand Turk' kept by the prosecutor. At about eleven o'clock p.m. the whole party were turned out of the house for being disorderly, and they then began to fight in the street and near the prosecutor's window, where a crowd of from 40 to 50 persons collected. The prisoner, after fighting some time with persons in the crowd, separated himself from them, and removed to the other side of the street, where he picked up a large stone, and threw it at the persons he had been fighting with. The stone passed over the heads of those persons, and struck a large plate glass window in the prosecutor's house, and broke it, thereby doing damage to the extent of £7 12s. 9d. The jury, after hearing evidence on both sides, found that the prisoner threw the stone which broke the window, but that he threw it at the people he had been fighting with, intending to strike one or more of them with it, but not intending to break the window. They returned a verdict of 'guilty.' The recorder respited the sentence, and admitted the prisoner to bail, and prayed the judgment of the Court for Crown Cases Reserved, whether, on the facts stated, and the finding of the jury, the prisoner was rightly convicted or not.

LORD COLERIDGE CJ: I am of opinion that this conviction must be quashed. [His Lordship stated the facts, and continued:] The question is whether, under an indictment for unlawfully and maliciously committing an injury to the window in the house of the prosecutor, the proof of these facts alone coupled with the finding of the jury will do. I think that is not enough. The indictment is framed under the Malicious Damage Act 1861, s. 51, which relates to malicious injuries to property, and the section enacts that whosoever shall unlawfully and maliciously commit any damage, etc., to or upon any real or personal property whatsoever either of a public or a private nature shall be guilty of a misdemeanour. Section 58 also deserves attention. That enacts:

> Every punishment and forfeiture by this Act imposed on any person maliciously com-
> mitting any offence, whether the same be punishable upon indictment or upon summary
> conviction, shall equally apply and be enforced, whether the offence shall be committed
> from malice conceived against the owner of the property in respect of which it shall be
> committed, or otherwise.

It seems to me that, in both these sections, what was intended to be provided against by the Act is the wilfully doing an unlawful act, and that that act must be wilfully and intentionally done on the part of the person doing it to render him liable to be convicted. Without saying that, on these facts, if the jury had found that the prisoner had been guilty of throwing the stone recklessly, knowing that there was a window near which it might probably hit. I should have been disposed to interfere with the conviction, yet, as they have found that he threw the stone at the people he had been fighting with intending to strike them and not intending to break the window, I think that the conviction must be quashed. I do not intend to throw any doubt on the cases which have been cited and which show what is sufficient to constitute malice in the case of murder. They rest on the principles of the common law, and have no application to a statutory offence.

Conviction quashed.

NOTES AND QUESTIONS
1. In principle, what is the problem with mixing and matching the *actus reus* of one crime with the *mens rea* of another, particularly when the defendant might otherwise escape liability for both crimes? At a minimum, why not permit inter-crime transferred intent when the crime actually committed is less serious than the crime intended?
2. Usually there is little difficulty in holding an accused such as Pembliton criminally liable. Either the accused can be charged with an attempt to commit the crime intended, or, alternatively, he can be charged with a crime of recklessness if that would be appropriate. Under modern law, Pembliton could have been charged with criminal damage, since his arguably reckless acts caused the damage and recklessness is, as we have seen, a sufficient *mens rea* for criminal damage.

B: Knowledge

We have seen that where a result is virtually certain to follow, 'knowingly' can become tantamount to 'intentionally'. Does the term have meaning in other contexts?

Roper v *Taylor's Central Garage (Exeter) Ltd*
[1951] 2 TLR 284, King's Bench Division

DEVLIN J.: . . . All that the word 'knowingly' does is to say expressly what is normally implied, and if the presumption that the statute requires *mens rea* is not rebutted I find difficulty in seeing how it can be said that the omission of the word 'knowingly' has, as a matter of construction the effect of shifting the burden of proof from the prosecution to the defence . . . it seems to me to be very important, in cases of this sort, that the prosecution, where the burden lies on the prosecution, should explain to lay justices, who are not necessarily very skilled in the handling of evidence and in the drawing of distinctions which the law requires to be drawn, exactly what sort of knowledge the prosecution desires to be found. There are, I think, three degrees of knowledge which it may be relevant to consider in cases of this kind. The first is actual knowledge, which the justices may find because they infer it from the nature of the act done, for no man can prove the state of another man's mind; and they may find it even if the defendant gives evidence to the contrary. They may say, 'We do not believe him; we think that that was his state of mind.' They may feel that the evidence falls short of that, and if they do they have then to consider what might be described as knowledge of the second degree; whether the defendant was, as it has been called, shutting his eyes to an obvious means of knowledge. Various expressions have been used to describe that state of mind. I do not think it necessary to look further, certainly not in cases of this type, than the phrase which Lord Hewart, CJ, used in a case under this section, *Evans* v *Dell* ((1937) 53 *The Times* LR 310), where he said (at p. 313): ' . . . the respondent deliberately refrained from making inquiries the results of which he might not care to have.' . . .

The third kind of knowledge is what is generally known in the law as constructive knowledge: it is what is encompassed by the words 'ought to have known' in the phrase 'knew or ought to have known.' It does not mean actual knowledge at all; it means that the defendant had in effect the means of knowledge. When, therefore, the case of the prosecution is that the defendant fails to make what they think were reasonable inquiries it is, I think, incumbent on them to make it plain which of the two things they are saying. There is a vast distinction between a state of mind which consists of deliberately refraining from making inquiries, the result of which the person does not care to have, and a state of mind which is merely neglecting to make such inquiries as a reasonable and prudent person would make. If that distinction is kept well in mind I think that justices will have less difficulty than this case appears to show they have had in determining what is the true position. The case of shutting the eyes is actual knowledge in the eyes of the law; the case of merely neglecting to make inquiries is not knowledge at all – it comes within the legal conception of constructive knowledge, a conception which, generally speaking, has no place in the criminal law.

NOTES AND QUESTIONS

1. What does it mean to 'know' something? If an individual believes that a particular result is 70 per cent likely to follow from her acts, does she 'know' that the result will follow? What if the result is 90 per cent likely? Must she be 100 per cent certain? Is there such a thing as 100 per cent certainty?

2. Is Devlin J correct in stating that 'knowingly' only says expressly what is implied? If so, why would Parliament include 'knowingly' as part of the definition of the crime?

3. Does 'knowingly' imply a subjective or objective standard? If a reasonable person, albeit not the defendant, 'knows' what results will occur as a result of particular acts, should the defendant be deemed to have this knowledge?

4. Devlin J's second category of knowledge is sometimes referred to as 'wilful blindness'. It occurs where the reason why a defendant does not have the requisite knowledge of consequences is because he chooses to turn a blind eye to them. Is it appropriate to equate wilful blindness and knowledge?

5 Why does Devlin J say that, generally speaking 'constructive knowledge' has no place in the criminal law?

'Knowingly' often is used in connection with the existence of circumstances, and knowledge thereof.

R v *Taaffe*
[1984] AC 539, House of Lords

On his arraignment on a charge of having been knowingly concerned in the fraudulent evasion of the prohibition on the importation of cannabis resin, contrary to section 170(2) of the Customs and Excise Management Act 1979 and the Misuse of Drugs Act 1971, the defendant pleaded not guilty. No evidence having been called, the recorder was asked to rule on the question whether the defendant's version of events, if accepted by the jury, would entitle him to be acquitted. That version was: (a) the defendant had been enlisted by a third party in Holland to import a substance from that country into England in fraudulent evasion of the prohibition on its importation and had so imported it; (b) that substance had in fact been cannabis, importation of which was prohibited by the Act of 1971; (c) the defendant had mistakenly believed the substance to be currency; (d) currency was not subject to any such prohibition; (e) the defendant had believed that it was. The recorder ruled that he would be obliged, even on the defendant's version of events, to direct the jury to convict. Thereupon, the defendant pleaded guilty and was sentenced. The Court of Appeal (Criminal Division) allowed his appeal against conviction.

LORD SCARMAN: . . . Lord Lane CJ construed the subsection under which the respondent was charged as creating not an offence of absolute liability but an offence of which an essential ingredient is a guilty mind. To be 'knowingly concerned' meant, in his judgment, knowledge not only of the existence of a smuggling operation but also that the substance being smuggled into the country was one the importation of which was prohibited by statute. The respondent thought he was concerned in a smuggling operation but believed that the substance was currency. The importation of currency is not subject to any prohibition. Lord Lane CJ concluded, at p. 631:

> [The respondent] is to be judged against the facts that he believed them to be. Had this indeed been currency and not cannabis, no offence would have been committed.

Lord Lane CJ went on to ask this question:

> Does it make any difference that the [respondent] thought wrongly that by clandestinely importing currency he was committing an offence?

The Crown submitted that it does. The court rejected the submission: the respondent's mistake of law could not convert the importation of currency into a criminal offence: and importing currency is what it had to be assumed that the respondent believed he was doing.

My Lords, I find the reasoning of the Lord Chief Justice compelling. I agree with his construction of section 170(2) of the Act of 1979: and the principle that a man must be judged upon the facts as he believes them to be is an accepted principle of the criminal law when the state of a man's mind and his knowledge are ingredients of the offence with which he is charged.

NOTES AND QUESTIONS

1. The Draft Criminal Code Bill 1989 provides as follows:

Draft Criminal Code Bill 1989

18. For the purposes of this Act and of any offence other than a pre-Code offence as defined in section 6 (to which section 2(3) applies) a person acts—
    (a) 'Knowingly' with respect to a circumstance not only when he is aware that it exists or will exist, but also when he avoids taking steps that might confirm his belief that it exists or will exist;

    . . .

Does the Draft Bill adopt a subjective or an objective test of 'knowingly'?

2. In *R v Leeson* [2000] Cr App R 233, the Court of Appeal held that it was irrelevant that the defendant did not know the drug in his possession was cocaine but believed it to be amphetamine since the drug belonged to the same category of prohibited drugs. See also *R v McNamara* (1988) 87 Cr App R 246.

In addition to actual knowledge there are offences which impose liability where a reasonable person would have the necessary knowledge.

Protection from Harassment Act 1997

1. Prohibition of harassment

(1) A person must not pursue a course of conduct—

(a) which amounts to harassment of another, and

(b) which he knows or ought to know amounts to harassment of the other.

(2) For the purposes of this section, the person whose course of conduct is in question ought to know that it amounts to harassment of another if a reasonable person in possession of the same information would think the course of conduct amounted to harassment of the other.

(3) Subsection (1) does not apply to a course of conduct if the person who pursued it shows—

(a) that it was pursued for the purpose of preventing or detecting crime,

(b) that it was pursued under any enactment or rule of law or to comply with any condition or requirement imposed by any person under any enactment, or

(c) that in the particular circumstances the pursuit of the course of conduct was reasonable.

. . .

4. Putting people in fear of violence

(1) A person whose course of conduct causes another to fear, on at least two occasions, that violence will be used against him is guilty of an offence if he knows or ought to know that his course of conduct will cause the other so to fear on each of those occasions.

(2) For the purposes of this section, the person whose course of conduct is in question ought to know that it will cause another to fear that violence will be used against him on any occasion if a reasonable person in possession of the same information would think the course of conduct would cause the other so to fear on that occasion.

(3) It is a defence for a person charged with an offence under this section to show that—

(a) his course of conduct was pursued for the purpose of preventing or detecting crime,

(b) his course of conduct was pursued under any enactment or rule of law or to comply with any condition or requirement imposed by any person under any enactment, or

(c) the pursuit of his course of conduct was reasonable for the protection of himself or another or for the protection of his or another's property.

(4) A person guilty of an offence under this section is liable—

(a) on conviction on indictment, to imprisonment for a term not exceeding five years, or a fine, or both, or

(b) on summary conviction, to imprisonment for a term not exceeding six months, or a fine not exceeding the statutory maximum, or both.

(5) If on the trial on indictment of a person charged with an offence under this section the jury find him not guilty of the offence charged, they may find him guilty of an offence under section 2.

(6) The Crown Court has the same powers and duties in relation to a person who is by virtue of subsection (5) convicted before it of an offence under section 2 as a magistrates' court would have on convicting him of the offence.

QUESTION

Does the concept of constructive knowledge make any sense? Either a person knows something or he does not. To speak in terms of what a reasonable person would know is to convert a subjective standard into one that is objective.

C: Recklessness, gross negligence and negligence

When the law refers to intent in relation to results, it is concerned with results which it was the actor's purpose to bring about. When it speaks in terms of knowledge, it is concerned with results that the actor knows will come about. When the reference is to recklessness, on the other hand, the courts are concerned not with results which the actor wishes to bring about or knows will come about, but rather with results in regard to which the actor is ambivalent or ignorant. The actor's fault lies in not taking into account or failing sufficiently to take into account the relevant risks.

Recklessness may exist in respect of:

(a) acts;

(b) circumstances; or

(c) consequences.

A driver who fails to observe the speedometer of the car as it creeps over 100 mph may be reckless in respect of the act of driving; if he ignores the pedestrians crossing the road, he may be reckless as to the consequences of his speeding. If a would-be seducer pays insufficient attention to whether his companion's protests to his sexual advances are perfunctory or real, he is reckless as to circumstances.

The subjective-objective distinction discussed previously is extremely relevant also in the context of recklessness. Subjective recklessness refers to a risk that the actor appreciated might be brought about by his conduct, but to which he was indifferent. The reckless driver who proceeds at 100 mph may well be aware that his driving may result in his being unable to stop if a pedestrian should step into the roadway, but he proceeds in conscious disregard of that risk. Objective recklessness, in contrast, refers to risks that the actor was not aware of but which a reasonable person would have been aware of – the possibility that by driving 100 mph he was creating risks to pedestrians may not have occurred to our driver, but would have occurred to a reasonable person. The critical difference between objective and subjective recklessness is this: in subjective recklessness the actor is aware of the risk that is created; in objective recklessness he is not, but a reasonable person would be. Neither the subjectively nor objectively reckless actor desires the harmful result to occur.

At common law, most crimes required proof of subjective intent. Today, for many crimes, proof of recklessness will be an alternative basis for the imposition of criminal sanctions. Often new statutory crimes (or codifications of common law crimes by Parliament) allow for proof of either intent or recklessness (see, e.g., the Criminal Damage Act 1971). Unfortunately the term 'recklessness' is not always defined. When this occurs, the courts must determine whether subjective or objective recklessness will suffice.

(i) *Subjective recklessness*
That subjective recklessness should satisfy the mental element of a crime whose *mens rea* is recklessness is uncontroversial. The leading case is *R* v *Cunningham*.

R v *Cunningham*
[1957] 2 QB 396, Court of Criminal Appeal

BYRNE J: . . . The facts were that the appellant was engaged to be married and his prospective mother-in-law was the tenant of a house, No. 7A, Bakes Street, Bradford, which was unoccupied, but which was to be occupied by the appellant after his marriage. Mrs Wade and her husband, an elderly couple, lived in the house next door. At one time the two houses had been one, but when the building was converted into two houses a wall had been erected to divide the cellars of the two houses, and that wall was composed of rubble loosely cemented.

On the evening of January 17, 1957, the appellant went to the cellar of No. 7A, Bakes Street, wrenched the gas meter from the gas pipes and stole it, together with its contents, and in a second indictment he was charged with the larceny of the gas meter and its contents. To that indictment he pleaded guilty and was sentenced to six months' imprisonment. In respect of that matter he does not appeal.

The facts were not really in dispute, and in a statement to a police officer the appellant said: 'All right, I will tell you. I was short of money, I had been off work for three days, I got eight shillings from the gas meter. I tore it off the wall and threw it away.' Although there was a stop tap within two feet of the meter the appellant did not turn off the gas, with the result that a very considerable volume of gas escaped, some of which seeped through the wall of the cellar and partially asphyxiated Mrs Wade, who was asleep in her bedroom next door, with the result that her life was endangered.

. . .

The act of the appellant was clearly unlawful and therefore the real question for the jury was whether it was also malicious within the meaning of section 23 of the Offences against the Person Act, 1861.

Before this court Mr Brodie has taken three points, all dependent upon the construction of that section. Section 23 provides: 'Whosoever shall unlawfully and maliciously administer to or cause to be administered to or taken by any other person any poison or other destructive or noxious thing, so as thereby to endanger the life of such person, or so as thereby to inflict upon such person any grievous bodily harm, shall be guilty of felony . . .'

Mr Brodie argued, first, that *mens rea* of some kind is necessary. Secondly, that the nature of the mens rea required is that the appellant must intend to do the particular kind of harm that was done, or, alternatively, that he must foresee that that harm may occur yet nevertheless continue recklessly to do the act. . . .

. . . [W]e have . . . considered, . . ., the following principle which was propounded by the late Professor C. S. Kenny in the first edition of his Outlines of Criminal Law published in 1902 and repeated at p. 186 of the 16th edition edited by Mr J. W. Cecil Turner and published in 1952:

> In any statutory definition of a crime, malice must be taken not in the old vague sense of wickedness in general but as requiring either (1) An actual intention to do the particular kind of harm that in fact was done; or (2) recklessness as to whether such harm should occur or not (i.e., the accused has foreseen that the particular kind of harm might be done and yet has gone on to take the risk of it). It is neither limited to nor does it indeed require any ill will towards the person injured.

The same principle is repeated by Mr Turner in his 10th edition of Russell on Crime at p. 1592.

We think that this is an accurate statement of the law. It derives some support from the judgments of Lord Coleridge CJ and Blackburn J in *Pembliton's* case [1874–80] All ER 1163. In our opinion the word 'maliciously' in a statutory crime postulates foresight of consequence.

NOTES AND QUESTIONS

1. The trial judge had instructed the jury that maliciously could be equated with wickedly, and this was clearly an error. The Court of Appeal did not have to go any further to decide the case, but nonetheless chose to seize the occasion to explain what it deemed to constitute recklessness. How did it define this term?

2. Which of the following facts would the prosecution have had to have established in order to prove that Cunningham was reckless?

   (a) that he knew that coal gas could cause asphyxiation;
   (b) that he foresaw that coal gas would escape as a result of his removal of the meter;
   (c) that he knew that coal gas would remain in its lethal form after being exposed to air;
   (d) that he foresaw that the coal gas could and would seep through the wall connecting the basements of two houses;
   (e) that he foresaw that the coal gas could and would seriously harm the occupant of the house next door;
   (f) that a reasonable person would have foreseen or known all of the above.

How would the Crown go about satisfying a jury of each of the above elements that needed to be proved?

(ii) *Objective recklessness*

The possibility that a defendant might lie about his lack of awareness of a risk (and in so doing fool the jury) may have been part of the impetus behind the search for a more objective standard of recklessness. The leading case is *Caldwell*.

R v *Caldwell*

[1982] AC 341 House of Lords

> By section 1 of the Criminal Damage Act 1971:
>
> (1) A person who . . . destroys or damages any property belonging to another intending to destroy or damage any such property or being reckless as to whether any such property would be destroyed or damaged shall be guilty of an offence. (2) A person who . . . destroys or damages any property . . . (a) intending to destroy or damage any property or being reckless as to whether

any property would be destroyed or damaged; and (b) intending by the destruction or damage to endanger the life of another or being reckless as to whether the life of another would be thereby endangered; shall be guilty of an offence. . . .

The defendant set fire by night to a residential hotel where he had been employed and against the proprietor of which he bore a grudge. According to his evidence he was so drunk at the time that it did not occur to him that there might be people there whose lives might be endangered. He pleaded guilty to a charge under section 1(1) of the Act of 1971 but not guilty to a charge under section 1(2) of intending to damage property intending to endanger life or being reckless as to whether life was endangered.

LORD DIPLOCK: . . . My Lords, the restricted meaning that the Court of Appeal in *R* v *Cunningham* had placed upon the adverb 'maliciously' in the Malicious Damage Act 1861 in cases where the prosecution did not rely upon an actual intention of the accused to cause the damage that was in fact done, called for a meticulous analysis by the jury of the thoughts that passed through the mind of the accused at or before the time he did the act that caused the damage, in order to see on which side of a narrow dividing line they fell. If it had crossed his mind that there was a risk that someone's property might be damaged but, because his mind was affected by rage or excitement or confused by drink, he did not appreciate the seriousness of the risk or trusted that good luck would prevent its happening, this state of mind would amount to malice in the restricted meaning placed upon that term by the Court of Appeal; whereas if, for any of these reasons, he did not even trouble to give his mind to the question whether there was any risk of damaging the property, this state of mind would not suffice to make him guilty of an offence under the Malicious Damage Act 1861.

Neither state of mind seems to me to be less blameworthy than the other; but if the difference between the two constituted the distinction between what does and what does not in legal theory amount to a guilty state of mind for the purposes of a statutory offence of damage to property, it would not be a practicable distinction for use in a trial by jury. The only person who knows what the accused's mental processes were is the accused himself – and probably not even he can recall them accurately when the rage or excitement under which he acted has passed, or he has sobered up if he were under the influence of drink at the relevant time. If the accused gives evidence that because of his rage, excitement or drunkenness the risk of particular harmful consequences of his acts simply did not occur to him, a jury would find it hard to be satisfied beyond reasonable doubt that his true mental process was not that, but was the slightly different mental process required if one applies the restricted meaning of 'being reckless as to whether' something would happen, adopted by the Court of Appeal in *R* v *Cunningham*.

My Lords, I can see no reason why Parliament when it decided to revise the law as to offences of damage to property should go out of its way to perpetuate fine and impracticable distinctions such as these, between one mental state and another. One would think that the sooner they were got rid of, the better.

. . . 'Reckless' as used in the new statutory definition of the mens rea of these offences is an ordinary English word. It had not by 1971 become a term of legal art with some more limited esoteric meaning than that which it bore in ordinary speech – a meaning which surely includes not only deciding to ignore a risk of harmful consequences resulting from one's acts that one has recognised as existing, but also failing to give any thought to whether or not there is any such risk in circumstances where, if any thought were given to the matter, it would be obvious that there was.

In my opinion, a person charged with an offence under section 1(1) of the Criminal Damage Act

1971 is 'reckless as to whether any such property would be destroyed or damaged' if (1) he does an act which in fact creates an obvious risk that property will be destroyed or damaged and (2) when he does the act he either has not given any thought to the possibility of there being any such risk or has recognised that there was some risk involved and has nonetheless gone on to do it. That would be a proper direction to the jury; cases in the Court of Appeal which held otherwise should be regarded as overruled.

Where the charge is under section 1(2) the question of the state of mind of the accused must be approached in stages, corresponding to paragraphs (a) and (b). The jury must be satisfied that what the accused did amounted to an offence under section 1(1), either because he actually intended to destroy or damage the property or because he was reckless (in the sense that I have described) as to whether it might be destroyed or damaged. Only if they are so satisfied must the jury go on to consider whether the accused also either actually intended that the destruction or damage of the property should endanger someone's life or was reckless (in a similar sense) as to whether a human life might be endangered.

. . .

So, in the instant case, the fact that the respondent was unaware of the risk of endangering lives of residents in the hotel owing to his self-induced intoxication, would be no defence if that risk would have been obvious to him had he been sober.

NOTES AND QUESTIONS

1. In what respect does the test of recklessness adopted in *Caldwell* differ from that of *Cunningham*?

2. Lord Diplock observes that there is little difference in terms of blameworthiness between the defendant who ignores a risk of which he is conscious and the defendant who gives no thought to the potential risk. Do you agree?

3. Lord Diplock also observes that the distinction between the defendant who ignores a risk of which he is conscious and the defendant who gives no thought to the potential risk is not a practicable one. Why?

4. Lord Diplock notes that *Cunningham* was based on an interpretation of the term 'maliciously', which has been replaced by the term 'recklessly' in the Criminal Damage Act 1971 which was at issue in *Caldwell*. Of what significance is this fact given the equating of maliciousness with recklessness by the court in *Cunningham*? Has Lord Diplock in effect adopted a definition of recklessness which equates recklessness with negligence?

In *Caldwell* and its companion decision *R v Lawrence* [1982] AC 510, Lord Diplock expanded recklessness beyond the defendant who is aware of the risk to the defendant who, had he stopped to consider the risk, would have been aware of it. But what if the defendant did stop to think and concluded incorrectly that there was no risk? At one point in *Caldwell* Lord Diplock spoke of circumstances where, if any thought were given to the matter, it would be obvious that there was a risk. This seemed to suggest a risk that would be obvious to a reasonable person, and that the defendant who stopped to think but arrived at the wrong conclusion would be deemed reckless. But in *Lawrence* Lord Diplock clouded the issue by referring to the doer of the act not giving any thought to the risk, and throughout both opinions his concern seemed more with those who cannot be bothered to think than with those who stop to think but come to the wrong conclusions. Is there, as some commentators have maintained, a lacuna in the law? Consider the following two cases:

Chief Constable of Avon and Somerset Constabulary v *Shimmen*
(1986) 84 Cr App R 7, Queen's Bench Division

TAYLOR J: . . . The charge against the defendant was that on February 15, 1985, in the City of Bristol, without lawful excuse, he destroyed property belonging to Maskreys Ltd, namely a plate glass window of the value of £495, intending to destroy such property or being reckless as to whether such property would be destroyed, contrary to section 1(1) of the Criminal Damage Act 1971. The justices found the following facts, inter alia.

The defendant had, on the relevant evening, been in the company of four friends. They had been in a public-house and later they went to a club. During the evening, the defendant consumed a quantity of alcohol. He and his four friends left the club together and made their way along the road to a position outside Maskrey's shop. There the defendant and one of his friends, David Woodhouse were laughing, joking, and larking around. Woodhouse pushed the defendant who then started flailing his arms and legs, contriving not to make any contact with Mr Woodhouse. Mr Woodhouse issued a warning to the defendant that he might one day hurt someone. The defendant assured Woodhouse that he had everything under control and, to prove it, he made as if to strike the window with his foot. His foot, however, did make contact with the window and broke it. The defendant was the holder of a green-belt and yellow-belt in the Korean art of self-defence. He was a skilled and experienced practitioner of that art.

It was conceded that he had no intent to break the window. But the prosecutor's contention was that his act amounted to recklessness and that he ought to be convicted on that ground. The defendant contended that by reason of the skill which he had, he had satisfied himself that the window would not break and that he was, in those circumstances, not reckless. The court was, as one would expect, referred to the leading authorities on the nature of recklessness. They are two decisions of the House of Lords. The first is *R* v *Caldwell* (1981) 73 Cr App R 13; [1982] AC 341. The second is *R* v *Lawrence* (1981) 73 Cr App R 1; [1982] AC 510. The defendant relied particularly on a passage in the speech of Lord Diplock in *R* v *Lawrence* at p. 11 and p. 527 respectively. The passage reads as follows:

> If satisfied that an obvious and serious risk was created by the manner of the defendant's driving, the jury are entitled to infer that he was in one or other of the states of mind required to constitute the offence and will probably do so; but regard must be given to any explanation he gives as to his state of mind which may displace the inference.

Relying upon that passage, it was suggested that the explanation which had been given by the defendant in this case, that he had taken what he considered to be the necessary steps to avoid any risk of damage, entitled him to be acquitted. The two states of mind which were referred to by Lord Diplock were those which he himself described in the earlier case of *Caldwell* . . .

> In my opinion, a person charged with an offence under section 1(1) of the Criminal Damage Act 1971 is 'reckless as to whether any such property would be destroyed or damaged' if (1) he does an act which in fact creates an obvious risk that property will be destroyed or damaged and (2) when he does the act he either has not given any thought to the possibility of there being any such risk or has recognised that there was some risk involved and has nonetheless gone on to do it.

The two decisions in *R* v *Caldwell* (*supra*) and *R* v *Lawrence* (*supra*) have been followed by a considerable volume of academic writing. It was conceded on behalf of the prosecutor here that a number of the writers have expressed the view that between the two possible states of mind constituting recklessness as defined in *R* v *Caldwell*, there exists or could exist a lacuna, that is a state of mind which fell into neither of the two alternative categories posed by Lord Diplock. The way in which the matter is put is perhaps most helpfully, in the circumstances of this case, illustrated by an article 'Reckless Damage and Reckless Driving: Living with Caldwell and Lawrence' in the Criminal

Law Review of 1981 at p. 743 by Professor Griew. At p. 748, he cited two hypothetical cases under the heading 'The conscientious but inefficient actor.' The Professor said:

> The following cases are outside the terms of the model direction in *Caldwell*. (a) M does give thought to whether there is a risk of damage to another's property attending his proposed act. He mistakenly concludes that there is no risk; or he perceives only a risk such as would in the circumstances be treated as negligible by the ordinary prudent individual. He missed the obvious and substantial risk. (b) N's case is a more likely one. He is indeed aware of the kind of risk that will attend his act if he does not take adequate precautions. He takes precautions that are intended and expected to eliminate the risk (or to reduce it to negligible proportions). But the precautions are plainly, though not plainly to him, inadequate for this purpose. These appear not to be cases of recklessness. Evidence of conscientiousness displaces what would otherwise be an available inference of recklessness, (to use the language of Lord Diplock in *Lawrence*, . . . The position of the person doing his best is further considered in the special context of reckless driving . . .')

He then went on to refer to *R* v *Lawrence* (*supra*).

Those two examples which were given by Professor Griew seem to me not to be 'on all fours.' In the first example, it may well be arguable that the lacuna exists because it is not a case where M failed to give any consideration to the possibility of a risk. It is a case where he did give consideration to the possibility of the risk and concluded, albeit mistakenly, that there was no risk. In terms, therefore, of Lord Diplock's definition, he has not recognised that there was some risk involved. He therefore is outside the second possible state of mind referred to in *R* v *Caldwell* (*supra*).

A different situation, however, seems to me to apply in the case of N posed by Professor Griew. He was aware of the kind of risk which would attend his act if he did not take adequate precautions. He seeks to rely upon the fact that he did take precautions which were intended, and by him expected, to eliminate the risk. He was wrong, but the fact that he was conscientious to the degree of trying to minimise the risk does not mean that he falls outside the second limb of Lord Diplock's test. Lord Diplock's second limb is simply whether or not he has recognised that there was some risk. It seems clear to me that in the case of N, as posed by Professor Griew, N certainly did recognise that there was some risk and went on to do the act.

In my judgment, therefore, the second example given by Professor Griew does not constitute any lacuna in the definition given by Lord Diplock. Applying those examples to the present case, it seems to me that on the findings of the justices and more particularly, as I shall indicate in a moment, on the evidence which they exhibited to their case, this defendant did recognise the risk. It was not a case of his considering the possibility and coming to the conclusion that there was no risk. What he said to the justices in cross-examination should be quoted. He said: 'I thought I might break the window but then I thought I will not break the window . . . I thought to myself, the window is not going to break.' A little later on he said: 'I weighed up the odds and thought I had eliminated as much risk as possible by missing by two inches instead of two millimetres.'

The specific finding of the justices, at para. 5(c) of the case, was as follows: '. . . the defendant perceived there could be a risk of damage but after considering such risk concluded that no damage would result.' It seems to me that what this case amounts to is as follows; that this defendant did perceive, which is the same as Lord Diplock's word 'recognise' that there could be a risk, but by aiming off rather more than he normally would in this sort of display, he thought he had minimised it and therefore no damage would result. In my judgment, that is far from saying that he falls outside the state of mind described by Lord Diplock in these terms, '. . . has recognised that there was some risk involved and has nonetheless gone on to do it.'

In my judgment, therefore, whatever may be the situation in a hypothetical case such as that of M as detailed by Professor Griew, which may need to be considered on another occasion, so far as this case is concerned, the justices were wrong in coming to the conclusion that this was not recklessness by reason of what the defendant had put forward. I should say that I have considerable sympathy with the justices when there is so much academic discussion of this particular test and where, as I have indicated, some of that discussion does not seem to result in accurate conclusions. However that may be, I, for my part, would allow this appeal and send the case back to the justices and require them to convict.

R v Crossman
[1986] RTR 49, Court of Appeal

LORD LANE CJ: . . . The facts of the case are not in dispute and they are these. At about 1.30 p.m. on 26 September 1984 the appellant was driving a large articulated lorry with a tractor unit and a trailer unit. The circumstances in which he was driving it were these. He had collected the trailer unit from the compound of Caterpillar Tractors in Birtley. The trailer unit had been loaded with a very large and weighty piece of machinery called a welding positioner. It seems that that piece of machinery weighed between 3 and 5 tons. There were other extensive pieces of metal on the back of the lorry together with the welding positioner making the load which was to be transported.

Mr Richardson was the loader and, according to him, and for purposes of argument it can be taken as correct, it is the driver's responsibility to secure the load. Mr Richardson told the appellant that in his, Mr Richardson's, view this load was unsafe and that it should be chained down and sheeted before the lorry was taken on to the road. The appellant disregarded that advice. In his view, he said, it was 'as safe as houses', and in any event he was just going round the corner in order to chain the load down at the depot. There was evidence of two other employees of the firm who were likewise of the view that this load was unsafe.

So, without the load having been chained down or sheeted, the lorry was driven by the appellant on to the public road and along a highway called Station Lane. As the vehicle went over some depression or pot-hole in the road the welding positioner, which in any event was top heavy quite apart from being not secure, fell off on to the near side footpath, and unhappily on to a pedestrian, Mrs Fenton, who was killed almost instantly. The lorry then continued on for 40 yards and the appellant drove on without ascertaining what had happened, but that does not form part of this case.

At the close of the prosecution case, a summary of which I have just given, counsel for the appellant submitted that the appellant had been charged with the wrong offence, and that there was no evidence capable of justifying the jury in coming to the conclusion that there had been what amounted to reckless driving. . . .

. . . Mr Gatland on behalf of the appellant suggests that where something in the nature of a load falls off a lorry and kills someone, the driver of the lorry cannot properly be charged with or convicted of causing death by reckless driving. His suggestion is that 'reckless driving' must be something to do with the handling or control of the vehicle itself. If a person is driving along the road gingerly and with great care, as no doubt the appellant was, the mere fact that something falls off that lorry cannot be the basis of a charge of reckless driving, even though the driver may have known that the load was unsafe, or likely to fall off, and nevertheless determined to run the risk that it might.

. . . Counsel for the appellant submits in effect that there is a distinction between deciding to drive recklessly and recklessly deciding to drive. The latter does not come within the mischief of the Act, he contends. What has to be considered, in his submission, is the actual care and control of the vehicle and, if no criticism can be made of the way the vehicle was driven, steered or braked, or if no criticism can be made of the constituent parts of the vehicle, what may happen to the load being carried on the vehicle is not relevant to the offence.

We respectfully disagree with those contentions.

The jury could, and no doubt would, have found that the appellant foresaw the high degree of risk that the load would fall off and if it did might injure someone, but nevertheless decided to run that risk. He caused that risk, or put it into operation by driving the vehicle on to the road. He was driving with the knowledge that by doing so, however slowly, however gingerly, however carefully he drove, he was putting other road users at risk of serious injury or death. This seems to us to fall quite clearly as a matter of simple wording under the expression 'reckless driving', driving with the knowledge that by moving the vehicle along the road at all, he was running the serious risk of injuring someone. That, in our view, was reckless driving and in consequence we are of the view that the judge was correct in the conclusion which he reached. Accordingly this appeal must be dismissed.

NOTES AND QUESTIONS

1. Do *Shimmen* and *Crossman* confirm or refute the lacuna thesis? In what way could it be said that the defendants were reckless? See also *R v Merrick* [1996] 1 Cr App R 130.

2. An alternative way of approaching *Shimmen* would have been to say that where the risk created is high and the social utility of the conduct in question low, a defendant will be judged to have acted unreasonably in taking the risk. From this perspective the critical question becomes not whether a reasonable person would have foreseen the risk, but whether a reasonable person would have taken the risk.

3. In which of the following situations would a defendant be held to have acted recklessly, assuming the proscribed harm resulted? Which type of recklessness (subjective or objective) is involved?

   (a) defendant thinks about the risk, recognises its seriousness, but decides to proceed in disregard of it;

   (b) defendant thinks about the risk but incorrectly and unreasonably concludes that it is negligible or non-existent;

   (c) defendant thinks about the risk, recognises its seriousness, but takes inadequate precautions to avoid the risk;

   (d) defendant fails to think about a risk that a reasonable person would have recognised as serious;

   (e) defendant fails to consider a risk that the reasonable person would have thought about but would have concluded was not serious.

It may make sense to hold criminally liable a defendant who is aware of a danger and disregards it. That defendant consciously chooses to risk causing harm. It may also make sense to hold criminally liable a defendant who is indifferent to a danger that he should have appreciated, but which he did not because, as in *Caldwell*, he drank himself to a point where he was unable to think critically about the risk. That defendant consciously chooses to put himself in a state where he is unable to exercise rational choice. It may even make sense to hold criminally liable a defendant who is shown to be a reasonable person and who is indifferent to an obvious risk that a reasonable person would have appreciated. Indeed, in this situation it may well be that the court does not really believe the defendant's denial but is unwilling to run the risk of a jury being taken in by perjurious testimony. In any event, in all these cases the defendant is in some respect morally blameworthy. But what of the defendant who is incapable, through no fault of his own, of appreciating the risk in the first place?

Elliott v C
[1983] 1 WLR 939, Queen's Bench Division

ROBERT GOFF LJ: . . . I start of course with the facts of the case, which have been set out with clarity by the justices. For present purposes, the salient features are these. (1) The defendant,

14-year-old schoolgirl, set fire to a shed by pouring white spirit onto a carpet on the floor of the shed and throwing two lighted matches onto the spirit, the second of which ignited it. (2) While she realised that the contents of the bottle which contained the white spirit were possibly inflammable, she had not handled it before and had not appreciated how explosively it would burn and immediately become out of control, thereby destroying both the shed and its contents. (3) She gave no thought at the time when she started the fire to the possibility of there being a risk that the shed and its contents would be destroyed. (4) This risk would not have been obvious to her or have been appreciated by her if she had given thought to the matter. I add that these conclusions were reached by the justices, having regard to the age and understanding of the defendant, her lack of experience of dealing with inflammable spirit, and the fact that she must have been tired and exhausted at the time.

I turn next to the crime with which she was charged, viz. that she without lawful excuse destroyed by fire the shed and contents, intending to destroy such property or being reckless as to whether such property would be destroyed, contrary to section 1(1) of the Criminal Damage Act 1971. The case advanced against her was not that she intended to destroy the property, but that she was reckless as to whether the property would be destroyed.

Plainly, she did destroy the shed and its contents by fire; plainly, too, she did so without lawful excuse. But was she reckless as to whether the shed and its contents would be destroyed? Here I turn, as Glidewell J, has done, to authority; and in the decision of the House of Lords in *R* v *Caldwell* [1982] AC 341, I find an authority, binding upon this court, which was concerned with the interpretation of the word 'recklessness' as used in the very subsection under which the defendant was charged. In that case, although the House was divided, the ratio decidendi of the decision of the House is to be found in the speech of Lord Diplock, with which both Lord Keith and Lord Roskill agreed. Lord Diplock analysed the word 'reckless' as used in this subsection, and his analysis culminated in the conclusion, expressed, at p. 354:

> In my opinion, a person charged with an offence under section 1(1) of the Criminal Damage Act 1971 is 'reckless as to whether any such property would be destroyed or damaged' if (1) he does an act which in fact creates an obvious risk that property will be destroyed or damaged and (2) when he does the act he either has not given any thought to the possibility of there being any such risk or has recognised that there was some risk involved and has nonetheless gone on to do it. That would be a proper direction to the jury; cases in the Court of Appeal which held otherwise should be regarded as overruled.

Now, if that test is applied literally in the present case, the conclusion appears inevitable that, on the facts found by the justices, the defendant was reckless whether the shed and contents would be destroyed; because first she did an act which carried an obvious risk that the property would be destroyed, and second she had not given any thought to the possibility of there being such risk.

Yet, if I next pause (as I have done, in accordance with what I consider to be my proper function) and ask myself the question – would I, having regard only to the ordinary meaning of the word, consider this girl to have been, on the facts found, *reckless* whether the shed and contents would be destroyed, my answer would, I confess, be in the negative. This is not a case where there was a deliberate disregard of a known risk of damage or injury of a certain type or degree; nor is it a case where there was mindless indifference to a risk of such damage or injury, as is expressed in common speech in the context of motoring offences (though not, I think, of arson) as 'blazing on regardless'; nor is it even a case where failure to give thought to the possibility of the risk was due to some blameworthy cause, such as intoxication. This is a case where it appears that the only basis upon which the accused might be held to have been reckless would be if the appropriate test to be applied was purely objective – a test which might in some circumstances be thought justifiable in relation to certain conduct (e.g. reckless driving), particularly where the word 'reckless' is used simply to characterise the relevant conduct. But such a test does not appear at first sight to be appropriate to a crime such as that under consideration in the present case, especially as recklessness in that crime has to be related to a particular consequence. I therefore next ask myself the question whether I can, consistently with the doctrine of precedent, sensibly interpreted, legitimately construe or qualify the principle stated by Lord Diplock in *R v Caldwell* [1982] AC 341 so as to accommodate what I conceive to be the appropriate result on the facts of the present case, bearing in mind that those facts are very different from the facts under consideration by the House of Lords in *R v Caldwell*, where the defendant had set fire to a hotel when in a state of intoxication.

Here again, it would be unrealistic if I were to disguise the fact that I am well aware that the statement of principle by Lord Diplock in *R v Caldwell* has been the subject of comment, much of it critical, in articles written by jurists; and that I have studied certain of these articles with interest. I find it striking that the justices, in reaching their conclusion in the present case, have done so (no doubt in response to an argument advanced on the defendant's behalf) by imposing upon Lord Diplock's statement of principle a qualification similar to one considered by Professor Glanville Williams in his article 'Recklessness Redefined' in (1981) 40 CLJ 252, 270–271. This is that a defendant should only be regarded as having acted recklessly by virtue of his failure to give any thought to an obvious risk that property would be destroyed or damaged where such risk would have been obvious *to him* if he had given any thought to the matter. However, having studied Lord Diplock's speech, I do not think it would be consistent with his reasoning to impose any such qualification. . . .

NOTES AND QUESTIONS

1. What purpose is served by holding Elliott liable? Is she deserving of punishment? Will her punishment serve to deter others of her age and experience? What type of rehabilitation can be offered to her? On the other hand, does she constitute a dange to society? How so?

2. The Draft Criminal Code Bill 1989 defines recklessness in the following terms:

Draft Criminal Code 1989

18. For the purposes of this Act and of any offence other than a pre-Code offence as defined in section 6 (to which section 2(3) applies) a person acts—
> . . .
> (c) 'recklessly' with respect to—
> (i)   a circumstance when he is aware of a risk that it exists or will exist;
> (ii) a result when he is aware of a risk that it will occur; and it is, in the circumstances known to him, unreasonable to take the risk;
> . . .

What would have been the decision in **Elliott** v **C** if this standard had been in effect?

One possible way to avoid the result in *Elliott* while remaining true to the test of *Caldwell* would be to imbue the reasonable person with the characteristics of the accused. As we shall see later, this is an approach which has appealed to the judges in the context of manslaughter. It represents a half-way house between a pure subjective and a pure objective standard. The possibility of imbuing the reasonable person with relevant characteristics of the accused was considered by the Court of Appeal in the next case:

R v *Stephen Malcolm R*
(1984) 79 Cr App R 334, Court of Appeal

> The appellant, when aged 15, committed a series of burglaries, other youths being involved in two of them. A few days after the last burglary, after receiving an anonymous telephone call, police went to a ground floor flat occupied by a mother and daughter and found the appellant there and the other youths and the stolen property. Four days later, at 11.30 p.m., when the mother was in the sitting room and the daughter in her bedroom, they heard three loud bangs and the daughter saw sheets of flame at her bedroom window, caused by three separate fires coming from three milk bottles. She ran screaming from her room. The police found blackened areas on the wall in the close proximity of the daughter's bedroom. They went straight to the appellant's house. It smelt of petrol and a pair of gloves soaked in petrol belonging to the appellant were found there. The next day when seen by the police the appellant said that he and one of the aforesaid youths had formed the opinion that the daughter had 'grassed' upon them, giving information leading to their arrests for the burglaries. They made and used the petrol bombs, intending, he said, not to injure the girl but only to frighten her. He did not realise that if the petrol bomb had gone through her window it might have killed her.

ACKNER LJ: . . . When the matter came on for trial the appellant admitted the facts which were the basis of count 6, which did not charge with intent to endanger human life, but he pleaded not guilty to count 5 on the ground that he did not have the requisite intent and had not acted recklessly. That question – 'had he acted recklessly?' – was the real issue. Mr Timms at the beginning of the trial sought a ruling from the trial judge as to the direction which the learned judge would give on the subject of recklessness. He submitted that when considering recklessness, the jury could only convict the appellant if he did an act which created a risk to life obvious to someone of his age and with such of his characteristics as would affect his appreciation of the risk. He should not in law be capable of being convicted if the act created a risk which was obvious to an ordinary prudent person of mature years and understanding, but was not obvious to him at his age and with his characteristics. The learned judge ruled against that submission and accordingly, Mr Timms, with characteristic good sense, advised his client to alter his plea. The appellant then pleaded guilty and was sentenced as we have indicated.

The point of law which is raised before us is the point which Mr Timms took before Judge Abdela. It is said that the learned judge erred in law in deciding that the test of recklessness as to whether life was endangered was as follows: A person is guilty of the offence if (i) he does an act which in fact creates a risk to the ordinary prudent man, i.e. one of mature years and understanding, that life will be endangered; (ii) he did the act not having given thought to the possibility of such a risk; or (iii) recognising that there was some risk, he nonetheless continued the act.

The learned judge, it is urged, was wrong in law because he failed to apply the law in relation to what constitutes the 'ordinary prudent man' and failed adequately to consider *Director of Public Prosecutions* v *Camplin* (1978) 67 Cr App R 14; [1978] AC 705. He should have found that the ordinary prudent man is synonymous with the reasonable man and therefore the jury should have had regard to the particular situation of the appellant, namely his age, and any other characteristics which would affect his appreciation of the risk.

. . . Mr Timms sought to induce us to adopt a *via media*. He said he accepted it would be wrong to ask the question whether the defendant himself was aware of the risk, but it would be right to inquire whether a person of the age of the defendant and with his characteristics which might be relevant to his ability to foresee the risk, would have appreciated it. He drew our attention in particular to the submission made by the prosecution before the justices in *Elliott's* case (1983) 77 Cr App R 103; [1983] 1 WLR 939 (see p. 110 and p. 940 respectively) 'that in relation to the defendant aged 14 years, the proper approach was whether such risk would have been obvious to a normal 14 year old child.' Therefore he said he was not seeking to relate the test to the particular defendant, but merely, so to speak, to a class of which he is a member. This, he says, provides him with the same logical basis of approach to the reasonable man or the reasonably prudent person as *DPP* v *Camplin* (*supra*) had suggested. We do not think that that *via media* was for one moment in the mind of Lord Diplock. The opportunity so to ingraft this important modification on the principle which he had enunciated had arisen in the subsequent cases and would have been just the sort of point (if it was a valid one) which we would have expected the House of Lords to have desired to have dealt with, thus clearing up the position, when they had the opportunity to do so when considering whether or not to give leave in *Elliott's* case (*supra*). If they had desired to say, for instance, that the age of the defendant was a factor to which particular regard must be had in applying the test, then *Elliott* was just the sort of case to do that, excising, if appropriate, any reference to any other ephemeral characteristics such as exhaustion from which the girl was said to be suffering. But they did not take that opportunity. We do not think that we should seek by this subtlety to avoid applying principles which we also have difficulty in accepting. We respectfully share the regrets voiced by Robert Goff LJ that in essence 'recklessness' has now been construed synonymously with 'carelessness.'

QUESTIONS

1. Janet hands Gerry, who is blind, a loaded pistol, telling him that it is unloaded. He pulls the trigger to experience the sensation, and an innocent bystander is killed. Should Gerry's blindness be taken into account in determining whether he acted recklessly? If your answer is 'Yes', on what basis would you distinguish *Stephen Malcolm R*?

2. Consider the case where it is shown that the defendant possesses more knowledge than the ordinary person. A chemistry professor knows that agents X and Y when left together for more than an hour will cause an explosion. She leaves her laboratory at night, forgetting that she has mixed X and Y in a beaker. The laboratory explodes. Has our professor acted recklessly if an ordinary person would not have appreciated the danger?

3. Consider the converse case. The chemistry professor knows that the mixing of agents C and D is extremely unlikely to cause an explosion. The ordinary person, however, seeing the smoke and hearing the crackling noises when the chemicals are mixed, might reasonably believe that an explosion was imminent. If in fact a fluke explosion occurs, would the chemistry professor be liable?

(iii) *Gross negligence*

To what offences does *Caldwell* apply? The courts have answered this question on a case by case basis. The logic of *Caldwell* would seem to suggest that the decision should apply wherever recklessness, or some variant thereof, is required to be proved. But the courts have not disturbed precedents where recklessness has been defined in terms of subjective fault. Thus where 'maliciously' constitutes the *mens rea* the courts have adhered to the subjective standard of *Cunningham*. See, e.g., *W (a minor)* v *Dolbey* [1983] Crim LR 691. In other contexts as well the courts have opted for the *Cunningham* standard. See, e.g., *Large* v *Mainprize* [1989] Crim LR 213 (recklessly furnishing false information relating to a fish catch).

At one time the trend appeared to favour extension of *Caldwell* into any area where it might possibly apply. In *R* v *Seymour* [1983] 2 All ER 1058, *Caldwell* was applied in a case of motor manslaughter. *Seymour* was reconsidered in *R* v *Adomako* (below). Rather than yet again redefining recklessness, however, their Lordships opted for a standard of gross negligence.

R v *Adomako*
[1994] 3 All ER 79, House of Lords

LORD MACKAY OF CLASHFERN LC: . . . The conviction arose out of the conduct of an eye operation carried out at the Mayday Hospital, Croydon on 4 January 1987. The appellant was, during the latter part of that operation, the anaesthetist in charge of the patient.

The operation was carried out by two surgeons supported by a team of five nurses and a theatre sister. Anaesthesia commenced at about 9.45 am. The patient was paralysed by injection of a drug and an endotracheal tube was inserted to enable the patient to breathe by mechanical means. At the start of the operation the anaesthetist was Dr Said, a registrar. An operating department assistant was also present to help him. At about 10.30 am there was a changeover of anaesthetists. The appellant was called to attend and take Dr Said's place following which both Dr Said and his assistant departed to deal with another operation elsewhere in the hospital. Another assistant was called to attend but did not arrive until later.

At approximately 11.05 am a disconnection occurred at the endotracheal tube connection. The supply of oxygen to the patient ceased and this led to cardiac arrest at 11.14 am. During this period the appellant failed to notice or remedy the disconnection.

. . .

The jury convicted the appellant of manslaughter by a majority of 11 to 1. The Court of Appeal, Criminal Division dismissed the appellant's appeal against conviction but certified that a point of law of general public importance was involved in the decision to dismiss the appeal, namely:

> In cases of manslaughter by criminal negligence not involving driving but involving a breach of duty is it a sufficient direction to the jury to adopt the gross negligence test set out by the Court of Appeal in the present case following *R* v *Bateman* (1925) 19 Cr App R 8 and *Andrews* v *DPP* [1937] 2 All ER 552, [1937] AC 576 without reference to the test of recklessness as defined in *R* v *Lawrence* [1981] 1 All ER 974, [1982] AC 510 or as adapted to the circumstances of the case?

In opening his very cogent argument for the appellant before your Lordships, counsel submitted that the law in this area should have the characteristics of clarity, certainty, intellectual coherence and general applicability and acceptability. For these reasons he said the law applying to involuntary manslaughter generally should involve a universal test and that test should be the test already applied in this House to motor manslaughter. He criticised the concept of gross negligence which was the basis of the judgment of the Court of Appeal submitting that its formulation involved circularity, the jury being told in effect to convict of a crime if they thought a crime had been committed and that accordingly using gross negligence as the conceptual basis for the crime of involuntary manslaughter was unsatisfactory and the court should apply the law laid down in

R v *Seymour* [1983] 2 All ER 1058, [1983] 2 AC 493 generally to all cases of involuntary manslaughter or at least use this as the basis for providing general applicability and acceptability.

Like the Court of Appeal your Lordships were treated to a considerable review of authority. I begin with *R* v *Bateman* (1925) 19 Cr App R 8 and the opinion of Lord Hewart CJ, where he said (at 10–12):

> In expounding the law to juries on the trial of indictments for manslaughter by negligence, judges have often referred to the distinction between civil and criminal liability for death by negligence. The law of criminal liability for negligence is conveniently explained in that way. If A. has caused the death of B. by alleged negligence, then, in order to establish civil liability, the plaintiff must prove (in addition to pecuniary loss caused by the death) that A. owed a duty to B. to take care, that that duty was not discharged, and that the default caused the death of B. To convict A. of manslaughter, the prosecution must prove the three things above mentioned and must satisfy the jury, in addition, that A.'s negligence amounted to a crime. In the civil action, if it is proved that A. fell short of the standard of reasonable care required by law, it matters not how far he fell short of that standard. The extent of his liability depends not on the degree of negligence, but on the amount of damage done. In a criminal Court, on the contrary, the amount and degree of negligence are the determining question. There must be *mens rea* . . . In explaining to juries the test which they should apply to determine whether the negligence, in the particular case, amounted or did not amount to a crime, judges have used many epithets, such as 'culpable,' 'criminal,' 'gross,' 'wicked,' 'clear,' 'complete.' But, whatever epithet be used and whether an epithet be used or not, in order to establish criminal liability the facts must be such that, in the opinion of the jury, the negligence of the accused went beyond a mere matter of compensation between subjects and showed such disregard for the life and safety of others as to amount to a crime against the State and conduct deserving punishment.

After dealing with a number of authorities Lord Hewart CJ went on (at 12–13):

> The law as laid down in these cases may be thus summarised: If a person holds himself out as possessing special skill and knowledge and he is consulted, as possessing such skill and knowledge, by or on behalf of a patient, he owes a duty to the patient to use due caution in undertaking the treatment. If he accepts the responsibility and undertakes the treatment and the patient submits to his direction and treatment accordingly, he owes a duty to the patient to use diligence, care, knowledge, skill and caution in administering the treatment. No contractual relation is necessary, nor is it necessary that the service be rendered for reward. It is for the judge to direct the jury what standard to apply and for the jury to say whether that standard has been reached. The jury should not exact the highest, or a very high, standard, nor should they be content with a very low standard. The law requires a fair and reasonable standard of care and competence . . . be reached in all the matters above mentioned. . . .

Next I turn to *Andrews* v *DPP* [1937] 2 All ER 552, [1937] AC 576 which was a case of manslaughter through the dangerous driving of a motor car. In a speech with which all the other members of this House who sat agreed, Lord Atkin said ([1937] 2 All ER 552 at 554–555, [1937] AC 576 at 581–582):

> . . . of all crimes manslaughter appears to afford most difficulties of definition, for it concerns homicide in so many and so varying conditions. From the early days, when any homicide involved penalty, the law has gradually evolved 'through successive differentiations and integrations' until it recognises murder on the one hand, based mainly, though not exclusively, on an intention to kill, and manslaughter on the other hand, based mainly, though not exclusively, on the absence of intention to kill, but with the presence of an element of 'unlawfulness' which is the elusive factor. In the present case it is necessary

to consider manslaughter only from the point of view of an unintentional killing caused by negligence, i.e., the omission of a duty to take care. I do not propose to discuss the development of this branch of the subject as treated in the successive treatises of Coke, Hale, Foster and East, and in the judgments of the courts to be found either in directions to juries by individual judges, or in the more considered pronouncements of the body of judges which preceded the formal Court of Crown Cases Reserved. Expressions will be found which indicate that to cause death by any lack of due care will amount to manslaughter; but, as manners softened and the law became more humane, a narrower criterion appeared. After all, manslaughter is a felony, and was capital, and men shrank from attaching the serious consequences of a conviction for felony to results produced by mere inadvertence. The stricter view became apparent in prosecutions of medical men, or men who professed medical or surgical skill, for manslaughter by reason of negligence. As an instance I will cite *R* v *Williamson* ((1807) 3 C & P 635, 172 ER 579) where a man who practised as an accoucheur, owing to a mistake in his observation of the actual symptoms, inflicted on a patient terrible injuries from which she died. Lord Ellenborough said: 'To substantiate that charge [of manslaughter] the prisoner must have been guilty of criminal misconduct, arising either from the grossest ignorance or the most criminal inattention.' The word 'criminal' in any attempt to define a crime is perhaps not the most helpful, but it is plain that Lord Ellenborough meant to indicate to the jury a high degree of negligence. So at a much later date in *R* v *Bateman* (1925) 19 Cr App R 8) a charge of manslaughter was made against a qualified medical practitioner in similar circumstances to those of *Williamson's* case.

Lord Atkin then refers to the judgment of Lord Hewart CJ from which I have already quoted and goes on ([1937] 2 All ER 552 at 556, [1937] AC 576 at 583):

Here, again, I think, with respect, the expressions used are not, indeed they probably were not intended to be, a precise definition of the crime. I do not myself find the connotations of *mens rea* helpful in distinguishing between degrees of negligence, nor do the ideas of crime and punishment in themselves carry a jury much further in deciding whether, in a particular case, the degree of negligence shown is a crime, and deserves punishment. But the substance of the judgment is most valuable, and, in my opinion, is correct. In practice, it has generally been adopted by judges in charging juries in all cases of manslaughter by negligence, whether in driving vehicles or otherwise. The principle to be observed is that cases of manslaughter in driving motor cars are but instances of a general rule applicable to all charges of homicide by negligence. Simple lack of care such as will constitute civil liability is not enough. For purposes of the criminal law there are degrees of negligence, and a very high degree of negligence is required to be proved before the felony is established. Probably of all the epithets that can be applied 'reckless' most nearly covers the case. It is difficult to visualise a case of death caused by 'reckless' driving, in the connotation of that term in ordinary speech, which would not justify a conviction for manslaughter, but it is probably not all-embracing, for 'reckless' suggests an indifference to risk, whereas the accused may have appreciated the risk, and intended to avoid it, and yet shown in the means adopted to avoid the risk, such a high degree of negligence as would justify a conviction. If the principle of *Bateman's* case ((1925) 19 Cr App R 8) is observed, it will appear that the law of manslaughter has not changed by the introduction of motor vehicles on the road. Death caused by their negligent driving, though unhappily much more frequent, is to be treated in law as death caused by any other form of negligence, and juries should be directed accordingly.

In my opinion the law as stated in these two authorities is satisfactory as providing a proper basis for describing the crime of involuntary manslaughter. Since the decision in *Andrews* v *DPP* [1937]

2 All ER 552, [1937] AC 576 was a decision of your Lordships' House, it remains the most authoritative statement of the present law which I have been able to find and although its relationship to *R v Seymour* [1983] 2 All ER 1058, [1983] 2 AC 493 is a matter to which I shall have to return, it is a decision which has not been departed from. On this basis in my opinion the ordinary principles of the law of negligence apply to ascertain whether or not the defendant has been in breach of a duty of care towards the victim who has died. If such breach of duty is established the next question is whether that breach of duty caused the death of the victim. If so, the jury must go on to consider whether that breach of duty should be characterised as gross negligence and therefore as a crime. This will depend on the seriousness of the breach of duty committed by the defendant in all the circumstances in which the defendant was placed when it occurred. The jury will have to consider whether the extent to which the defendant's conduct departed from the proper standard of care incumbent upon him, involving as it must have done a risk of death to the patient, was such that it should be judged criminal.

. . .

My Lords in my view the law as stated in *R v Seymour* [1983] 2 All ER 1058, [1983] 2 AC 493 should no longer apply since the underlying statutory provisions on which it rested have now been repealed by the Road Traffic Act 1991. It may be that cases of involuntary motor manslaughter will as a result become rare but I consider it unsatisfactory that there should be any exception to the generality of the statement which I have made, since such exception, in my view, gives rise to unnecessary complexity. . . .

In my opinion it is quite unnecessary in the context of gross negligence to give the detailed directions with regard to the meaning of the word 'reckless' associated with *R v Lawrence* [1981] 1 All ER 974, [1982] AC 510. The decision of the Court of Appeal, Criminal Division in the other cases with which they were concerned at the same time as they heard the appeal in this case indicates that the circumstances in which involuntary manslaughter has to be considered may make the somewhat elaborate and rather rigid directions inappropriate. I entirely agree with the view that the circumstances to which a charge of involuntary manslaughter may apply are so various that it is unwise to attempt to categorise or detail specimen directions. For my part I would not wish to go beyond the description of the basis in law which I have already given.

NOTES AND QUESTIONS

1. What is the difference between gross negligence and recklessness? Which is the better defined concept? In *Adomako* it was argued that the court's definition of gross negligence provided juries with little in the way of guidance. Lord MacKay responded:

   It is true that to a certain extent this involves an element of circularity, but in this branch of the law I do not believe that is fatal to its being correct as a test of how far conduct must depart from accepted standards to be characterised as criminal. This is necessarily a question of degree and an attempt to specify that degree more closely is I think likely to achieve only a spurious precision. The essence of the matter, which is supremely a jury question, is whether, having regard to the risk of death involved, the conduct of the defendant was so bad in all the circumstances as to amount in their judgment to a criminal act or omission.

   Is this a satisfactory answer?

2. Is it appropriate to characterise gross negligence as a *mens rea*? In *Attorney-General's Reference (No. 2 of 1999)* [2000] QB 796 (for facts and holding, see p. 259), the Court of Appeal Stated that 'evidence of . . . state of mind is not a pre-requisite to a conviction for manslaughter by gross negligence'. The court added, however, that 'there may be cases where the defendant's state of mind is relevant to the jury's consideration when assessing the grossness and criminality of his conduct'.

(iv) *Negligence*

Less culpable than gross negligence (though how much so may be unclear) is ordinary negligence. One of the problems with *Caldwell* recklessness is that it seems to eliminate the traditional distinction between recklessness and ordinary negligence. Nonetheless, there continue to be crimes of negligence, such as driving without due care and attention (see Road Traffic Act 1991, s. 2).

One possible distinction may lie in the nature of the risk, 'recklessness' referring to risks that are obvious and serious (*Lawrence*) and 'negligence' to risks that are of a lesser order; or perhaps the difference lies in the degree of departure from the standard of a reasonable person, recklessness requiring a greater departure from this standard. In support of the latter distinction, the Road Traffic Act 1991 defines driving dangerously as driving that falls *far below* what would be expected of a competent and careful driver (see Road Traffic Act 1991, s. 2A(1)(a)); there is a lesser form of culpability which consists of careless and inconsiderate driving. A further possibility is that negligence fills in the so-called lacuna in *Caldwell*, where the defendant considered the risk but incorrectly concluded that it was negligible or non-existent.

Negligence is measured by an objective standard, the failure to measure up to what the reasonable person would have done under the circumstances. It is a standard that does not vary with the individual qualities of the defendant.

McCrone v *Riding*
[1938] 1 All ER 157, King's Bench Division

> The respondent was charged with driving a private motor vehicle without due care and attention contrary to the Road Traffic Act 1930, s. 12. The justices dismissed the charge, on the ground that the respondent 'was exercising all the skill and attention to be expected from a person with his short experience'.

LORD HEWART LCJ: . . . That standard is an objective standard, impersonal and universal, fixed in relation to the safety of other users of the highway. It is in no way related to the degree of proficiency or degree of experience attained by the individual driver. I think that it is made quite plain that the justices held the notion that two standards could be entertained, because they say in their findings ultimately that they were of opinion that, 'had the respondent been an ordinary driver, we would have convicted him on the information.' They add, however:

> Though he failed to display such skill as would be expected from an ordinary driver under the circumstances and drove into the said pedestrian, such failure being due to his inexperience and lack of skill did not constitute such want of care and attention [as amounted to an offence].

I think, therefore, that the proper course is that the appeal should be allowed, and that the case should go back to the justices with the direction that regard must be had to the words of this statute 'without due care and attention,' and that it is wrong to assume that the word 'skill' is synonymous with the word 'care,' and that it is wrong to assume that there can be one standard for an ordinary driver and another standard for somebody else. . . .

QUESTION

The court in *McCrone* does not ask whether the defendant exercised the due care and caution that it would be reasonable to expect from a learner driver. Why is this not relevant? What purposes are served by applying an objective standard to all?

D: Strict liability

The final group of crimes which needs to be examined consists of those which, at least on their face, appear to have no *mens rea*. These are referred to as offences of strict or (less accurately) absolute liability. Looks can be deceiving, however. While the crimes in question may appear on their face to have no *mens rea* requirement, courts have been known to interpret the statute in a way which introduces a *mens rea* requirement.

(i) *Common law crimes*
Strict liability offences are generally the product of statute, but there have been some common law offences that have been construed to impose strict liability. The clear implication of the common law maxim *'actus non facit reum nisi mens sit rea'* is that *mens rea* is required for all crimes. The law, however, was never this stringent, and the most that could be said is that crimes without *mens rea* were the exception (with libel and public nuisance being the most prominent examples).

Curiously, in recent years, there seems to have been a revival of prosecutions for common law crimes, in regard to which the courts have found no *mens rea* requirement.

R v Lemon, R v Gay News Ltd
[1979] 1 All ER 898, House of Lords

LORD DIPLOCK (dissenting): My Lords, the appellants are the editor and publishers of a news-paper called Gay News. As its name suggests its readership consists mainly of homosexuals though it is on sale to the general public at some bookstalls. In an issue of Gay News published in June 1976 there appeared a poem by a Professor James Kirkup entitled 'The Love that Dares to Speak its Name' and accompanied by a drawing illustrating its subject-matter. The poem purports to describe in explicit detail acts of sodomy and fellatio with the body of Christ immediately after His death and to ascribe to Him during His lifetime promiscuous homosexual practices with the Apostles and with other men.

The issue in this appeal is not whether the words and drawing are blasphemous. The jury, though only by a majority of ten to two, have found them to be so. As expressed in the charge against them they 'vilify Christ in His life and His crucifixion', and do so in terms that are likely to arouse a sense of outrage among those who believe in or respect the Christian faith and are not homosexuals and probably among many of them that are. The only question in this appeal is whether in 1976 the mental element or mens rea in the common law offence of blasphemy is satisfied by proof only of an intention to publish material which in the opinion of the jury is likely to shock and arouse resentment among believing Christians or whether the prosecution must go further and prove that the accused in publishing the material in fact intended to produce that effect on believers, or (what comes to the same thing in criminal law) although aware of the likelihood that such effect might be produced, did not care whether it was or not, so long as the publication achieved some other purpose that constituted his motive for publishing it. Wherever I speak hereafter of 'intention' I use the expression as a term of art in that extended sense. . . .

My Lords, if your Lordships were to hold that Lord Coleridge CJ and those judges who preceded and followed him in directing juries that the accused's intention to shock and arouse resentment among believing Christians was a necessary element in the offence of blasphemous libel were wrong in doing so, this would effectively exclude that particular offence from the benefit of Parliament's general substitution of the subjective for the objective test in applying the presumption that a man intends the natural consequences of his acts; and blasphemous libel would revert to the exceptional category of crimes of strict liability from which, on what is, to say the least, a plausible analysis of the contemporaneous authorities, it appeared to have escaped nearly a century ago. This would, in my view, be a retrograde step which could not be justified by any considerations of public policy.

The usual justification for creating by statute a criminal offence of strict liability, in which the prosecution need not prove mens rea as to one of the elements of the actus reus, is the threat that the actus reus of the offence poses to public health, public safety, public morals or public order. The very fact that there have been no prosecutions for blasphemous libel for more than fifty years is sufficient to dispose of any suggestion that in modern times a judicial decision to include this common law offence in this exceptional class of offences of strict liability could be justified on grounds of public morals or public order. . . .

VISCOUNT DILHORNE: In the light of the authorities to which I have referred and for the reasons I have stated, I am unable to reach the conclusion that the ingredients of the offence of publishing a blasphemous libel have changed since 1792. Indeed, it would, I think, be surprising if they had. If it be accepted, as I think it must, that that which it is sought to prevent is the publication of blasphemous libels, the harm is done by their intentional publication, whether or not the publisher intended to blaspheme. To hold that it must be proved that he had that intent appears to me to be going some way to making the accused judge in his own cause. If Mr Lemon had testified that he did not regard the poem and drawing as blasphemous, that he had no intention to blaspheme, and it might be, that his intention was to promote the love and affection of some homosexuals for Our Lord, the jury properly directed would surely have been told that unless satisfied beyond reasonable doubt that he intended to blaspheme they should acquit, no matter how blasphemous they thought the publication. Whether or not they would have done so on such evidence is a matter of speculation on which views may differ.

The question we have to decide is a pure question of law and my conclusions thereon do not, I hope, evince any distrust of juries. The question here is what is the proper direction to give to them, not how they might act on such a direction; and distrust, which I do not have, of the way a jury might act, does not enter into it.

My Lords, for the reasons I have stated in my opinion the question certified should be answered in the affirmative. Guilt of the offence of publishing a blasphemous libel does not depend on the accused having an intent to blaspheme but on proof that the publication was intentional (or, in the case of a bookseller, negligent (Lord Campbell's Libel Act 1843)) and that the matter published was blasphemous.

I would dismiss these appeals.

Appeals dismissed.

NOTE

The decision of the European Court of Human Rights in this case ((1982) 5 EHRR 123) is considered on p. 71.

(ii) *Statutory offences*

Most crimes which impose strict liability are the product of statute. Some statutes are quite clear in this regard:

Contempt of Court Act 1981

1. The strict liability rule

In this Act 'the strict liability rule' means the rule of law whereby conduct may be treated as a contempt of court as tending to interfere with the course of justice in particular legal proceedings regardless of intent to do so.

2. Limitation of scope of strict liability

(1) The strict liability rule applies only in relation to publications, and for this purpose 'publication' includes any speech, writing, broadcast or other communication in whatever form, which is addressed to the public at large or any section of the public.

(2) The strict liability rule applies only to a publication which creates a substantial risk that the course of justice in the proceedings in question will be seriously impeded or prejudiced.

(3) The strict liability rule applies to a publication only if the proceedings in question are active within the meaning of this section at the time of the publication.

Most of the time, however, Parliament is not as clear as to whether its aim is to impose strict liability. The question which then confronts the courts is whether to read a *mens rea* requirement into a statute when none appears on its face.

The judicial decisions are not distinguished by their consistency. In some cases the judicial analysis begins and ends with the words of the statute; but in others the courts take a less literal and more functional approach, looking at the purpose to be served by the statute. It is also not uncommon to find courts proclaiming that they are merely implementing Parliamentary intent, but until quite recently the courts would not allow themselves to look at Parliamentary debates, White Papers or other official reports to determine Parliamentary intent.

As well as the general conflict between a literal and a functional approach to statutory interpretation, one can identify conflicts relating to specific interpretative guides. The evil to be eradicated is often cited as a factor in imposing strict liability, with the implication that the greater the evil, the more likely the statute will be found to impose strict liability. This rationale was used to justify strict liability for offences involving drugs (see *Yeandel* v *Fisher* [1966] 1 QB 440). But in other cases the courts reason that because strict liability offences are not true crimes and carry little stigma, it is not necessary to put the Crown to the inconvenience and expense of proving *mens rea*. In construing a statute to require *mens rea*, the courts may point to the fact that there was nothing more that the defendant could have done to avoid liability; but when they want liability to be strict they say that such considerations are irrelevant. Sometimes the courts will compare the wording of a specific provision of a statute with other parts of the same statute or comparable statutes; but at other times they will simply brush aside any striking change of expression as being entitled to no weight.

If a statute contains words expressive of a *mens rea* element – such as 'intention-ally', 'recklessly', or 'knowingly' – the courts will not construe the statute to be one of strict liability. To do so would be in clear contradiction of Parliamentary intent. Sometimes, however, whether a verb or adverb carries connotations of *mens rea* is not all that clear.

Cotterill v Penn
[1936] 1 KB 53, King's Bench Division

LORD HEWART CJ: This is a case stated by justices for the county of Worcester arising out of an information preferred by the appellant against the respondent under the Larceny Act 1861, s. 23, for unlawfully and wilfully killing a pigeon in such circumstances as did not amount to larceny at common law. . . .

Section 23 of the Larceny Act 1861, which is a compendious section, provides that: 'Whosoever shall unlawfully and wilfully kill, wound, or take any house dove or pigeon under such circumstances as shall not amount to larceny at common law, shall, on conviction,' pay a penalty.

One contention on behalf of the respondent was that to sustain a charge under the section it is necessary to prove that the pigeon was killed or taken with felonious intent. In my opinion, although the section says 'unlawfully and wilfully,' it does not require the element of *mens rea* beyond the point that the facts must show an intention on the part of the person accused to do the act forbidden, which was here that of shooting. It seems to me to be immaterial that the bird which the respondent shot was of a different kind from that which he thought that he was shooting. If the section had used the word 'maliciously,' the state of mind of the person charged would have been relevant. But using the terms 'unlawfully and wilfully' the section seems to me only to mean that the person accused intended to shoot and that the shooting was without a lawful excuse.

Another contention for the respondent was that he was entitled to kill the pigeon if he thought that it was a wood pigeon which might damage his crops, and the justices, adopting that contention, were of opinion that he was not liable, inasmuch as he shot the pigeon honestly believing it to be a wood pigeon about to feed off his crops. He shot the pigeon not because it was actually damaging his crops, but because he thought that it might or would do so – an event which was purely hypothetical. It seems to me to be an undue straining of the authorities to say that an apprehension of danger which may or may not turn out to be real is a lawful excuse. If such an extension of the principle were to be permitted one wonders where the process would end.

NOTES AND QUESTIONS
Cotterill's belief that the bird in question was a wild pigeon was held to be irrelevant. The approach is similar to that which we saw in *Lemon*. What the court has done is to limit the *mens rea* so that it applies only to the *actus reus* and not to the critical circumstances of the offence. But in that sense does *mens rea* add anything to the requirement of a voluntary *actus reus*, which the Crown is already under a duty to prove?

While courts will not abrogate a *mens rea* element where Parliament has clearly included one, the converse is not true. The courts may read in a mental element although the wording of the statute contains none on its face. But when will (should) they do so? The leading modern case is *Sweet* v *Parsley*:

Sweet v Parsley
[1970] AC 132, House of Lords

By section 5 of the Dangerous Drugs Act, 1965:

If a person – (a) being the occupier of any premises, permits those premises to be used for the purpose of smoking . . . cannabis resin . . . or (b) is concerned in the management of any premises used for any such purpose as aforesaid; he shall be guilty of an offence against this Act.

The appellant, the sub-tenant of a farmhouse, let out several rooms to tenants who shared the use of the kitchen. She herself retained and occupied a bedroom. Later she gave up living there, though she came occasionally to collect letters and rent. On June 11, 1967, quantities of drugs, including cannabis resin, were found in the farmhouse and the appellant was charged with being concerned in the management of premises used for the purpose of smoking cannabis resin, contrary to section 5(b) of this Act. The appellant conceded that the premises had been so used. The prosecutor conceded that she did not know this. She was convicted of the offence.

LORD REID: . . . My Lords, a Divisional Court dismissed her appeal, holding that she had been concerned in the management of those premises. The reasons given for holding that she was managing the property were that she was in a position to choose her tenants: that she could put them under as long or as short a tenancy as she desired: and that she could make it a term of any letting that smoking of cannabis was not to take place. All these reasons would apply to every occupier who lets out parts of his house or takes in lodgers or paying guests. But this was held to be an absolute offence, following the earlier decision in *Yeandel* v *Fisher* [1966] 1 QB 440.

How has it come about that the Divisional Court has felt bound to reach such an obviously unjust result? It has in effect held that it was carrying out the will of Parliament because Parliament has chosen to make this an absolute offence. And, of course, if Parliament has so chosen the courts must carry out its will, and they cannot be blamed for any unjust consequences. But has Parliament so chosen?

. . .

Our first duty is to consider the words of the Act: if they show a clear intention to create an absolute offence that is an end of the matter. But such cases are very rare. Sometimes the words of the section which creates a particular offence make it clear that *mens rea* is required in one form or another. Such cases are quite frequent. But in a very large number of cases there is no clear indication either way. In such cases there has for centuries been a presumption that Parliament did not intend to make criminals of persons who were in no way blameworthy in what they did. That means that whenever a section is silent as to *mens rea* there is a presumption that, in order to give effect to the will of Parliament, we must read in words appropriate to require *mens rea*.

. . .

It is also firmly established that the fact that other sections of the Act expressly require *mens rea*, for example because they contain the word 'knowingly,' is not in itself sufficient to justify a decision that a section which is silent as to *mens rea* creates an absolute offence. In the absence of a clear indication in the Act that an offence is intended to be an absolute offence, it is necessary to go outside the Act and examine all relevant circumstances in order to establish that this must have been the intention of Parliament. I say 'must have been' because it is a universal principle that if a penal provision is reasonably capable of two interpretations, that interpretation which is most favourable to the accused must be adopted.

What, then, are the circumstances which it is proper to take into account? In the well known case of *Sherras* v *De Rutzen* [1895] 1 QB 918 Wright J only mentioned the subject matter with which the Act deals. But he was there dealing with something which was one of a class of acts which 'are not criminal in any real sense, but are acts which in the public interest are prohibited under a penalty'

(p. 922). It does not in the least follow that when one is dealing with a truly criminal act it is sufficient merely to have regard to the subject matter of the enactment. One must put oneself in the position of a legislator. It has long been the practice to recognise absolute offences in this class of quasi-criminal acts, and one can safely assume that, when Parliament is passing new legislation dealing with this class of offences, its silence as to *mens rea* means that the old practice is to apply. But when one comes to acts of a truly criminal character, it appears to me that there are at least two other factors which any reasonable legislator would have in mind. In the first place a stigma still attaches to any person convicted of a truly criminal offence, and the more serious or more disgraceful the offence the greater the stigma. So he would have to consider whether, in a case of this gravity, the public interest really requires that an innocent person should be prevented from proving his innocence in order that fewer guilty men may escape. And equally important is the fact that fortunately the Press in this country are vigilant to expose injustice and every manifestly unjust conviction made known to the public tends to injure the body politic by undermining public confidence in the justice of the law and of its administration. But I regret to observe that, in some recent cases where serious offences have been held to be absolute offences, the court has taken into account no more than the wording of the Act and the character and seriousness of the mischief which constitutes the offence.

The choice would be much more difficult if there were no other way open than either *mens rea* in the full sense or an absolute offence; for there are many kinds of case where putting on the prosecutor the full burden of proving *mens rea* creates great difficulties and may lead to many unjust acquittals. But there are at least two other possibilities. Parliament has not infrequently transferred the onus as regards *mens rea* to the accused, so that, once the necessary facts are proved, he must convince the jury that on balance of probabilities he is innocent of any criminal intention. I find it a little surprising that more use has not been made of this method: but one of the bad effects of the decision of this House in *Woolmington* v *Director of Public Prosecutions* [1935] AC 462 may have been to discourage its use. The other method would be in effect to substitute in appropriate classes of cases gross negligence for *mens rea* in the full sense as the mental element necessary to constitute the crime. It would often be much easier to infer that Parliament must have meant that gross negligence should be the necessary mental element than to infer that Parliament intended to create an absolute offence. A variant of this would be to accept the view of Cave J in *R* v *Tolson* (1889) 23 QBD 168, 181. This appears to have been done in Australia where authority appears to support what Dixon J said in *Proudman* v *Dayman* (1941) 67 CLR 536, 540:

> As a general rule an honest and reasonable belief in a state of facts which, if they existed, would make the defendant's act innocent affords an excuse for doing what would otherwise be an offence.

It may be that none of these methods is wholly satisfactory but at least the public scandal of convicting on a serious charge persons who are in no way blameworthy would be avoided.

If this section means what the Divisional Court have held that it means, then hundreds of thousands of people who sublet part of their premises or take in lodgers or are concerned in the management of residential premises or institutions are daily incurring a risk of being convicted of a serious offence in circumstances where they are in no way to blame. For the greatest vigilance cannot prevent tenants, lodgers or inmates or guests whom they bring in from smoking cannabis cigarettes in their own rooms. It was suggested in argument that this appellant brought this conviction on herself because it is found as a fact that when the police searched the premises there were people there of the 'beatnik fraternity.' But surely it would be going a very long way to say that persons managing premises of any kind ought to safeguard themselves by refusing accommodation to all who are of slovenly or exotic appearance, or who bring in guests of that kind. And unfortunately drug taking is by no means confined to those of unusual appearance.

NOTES AND QUESTIONS

1. Lord Reid says that if a statute contains no *mens rea* on its face, the presumption should be that proof of *mens rea* is intended. Why should a court engage in this presumption rather than the opposite one – that Parliament meant what it said and did not intend to require the Crown to be put to the proof of *mens rea*? Is not the latter presumption more logical? Is not the absence of words of *mens rea* themselves a *clear indication*, in Lord Reid's words, of the intent to omit *mens rea*?

2. If a court is to presume *mens rea* when a statute is silent, what *mens rea* should it presume – intent, knowledge of circumstances, recklessness, negligence? Since the statute is silent, how is the court to choose? Interestingly, the House of Lords in *Sweet* was not prepared to adopt a negligence standard, deeming the choice to lie between no *mens rea* or some form of traditional *mens rea*. Is the court's reasoning on this point persuasive?

3. The reluctance of the court to adopt a negligence standard makes even less sense when placed against the assertions of several of their Lordships that Ms Sweet had taken appropriate steps to inform herself of the true state of affairs, and that it would be unfair to punish her when there had been no showing that she had been anything but diligent. Is this not in effect saying that she was not negligent? Had it been proved that she had been negligent, on the other hand, in, say, turning a blind eye to the strange and sweet-smelling aroma which was emanating from the farmhouse and which was making her giddy, would their Lordships have strained so to avoid holding her liable?

4. Lord Reid draws a distinction between truly criminal acts and those which are illegal only because the public welfare so demands. Is this distinction a viable one? How does a court determine whether an offence falls into the true crime or the public welfare category? Into which camp did Ms Sweet's offence fall?

5. Taking a functional approach to the issue of strict liability, what purposes would be served by imposing strict liability? Would there be counterbalancing undesirable effects in a case like Sweet's?

6. In *Sweet* several of their Lordships suggested a middle position between traditional *mens rea* and strict liability, which would be to allow the Crown to establish its case without proof of *mens rea*, but to permit the defendant to have a defence of due diligence or reasonable care. What are the relative merits of such an approach? Note that, unlike in the case of offences, most defences are created by the courts. Their Lordships, had they wanted, could have created a defence of due diligence without infringing on Parliamentary sovereignty. Such a defence of due diligence was adopted by the Canadian Supreme Court in *R v City of Sault Ste Marie* (1978) 85 DLR (3d) 161. Furthermore, some statutes, such as the Trade Descriptions Act 1968, s. 24(1), the Weights and Measures Act 1985, s. 34, and the Food Safety Act 1991, s. 21, incorporate a due diligence defence.

Sweet was not followed in all subsequent cases:

Pharmaceutical Society of Great Britain v *Storkwain*
[1986] 2 All ER 635, House of Lords

LORD GOFF OF CHIEVELEY: My Lords, this appeal is concerned with a question of construction of s. 58 of the Medicines Act 1968. Section 58(2)(a) of that Act provides as follows:

Subject to the following provisions of this section – (a) no person shall sell by retail, or supply in circumstances corresponding to retail sale, a medicinal product of a description, or falling within a class, specified in an order under this section except in accordance with a prescription given by an appropriate practitioner . . .

By s. 67(2) of the 1968 Act it is provided that any person who contravenes, inter alia, s. 58 shall be guilty of an offence. The question which has arisen for decision in the present case is whether, in accordance with the well-recognised presumption, there are to be read into s. 58(2)(a) words appropriate to require mens rea, on the principle stated in *R* v *Tolson* (1889) 23 QBD 168, [1886–90] All ER Rep 26 and *Sweet* v *Parsley* [1969] 1 All ER 347, [1970] AC 132.

The matter has arisen in the following way. On 2 February 1984 informations were preferred by the respondents, the Pharmaceutical Society of Great Britain, against the appellants, Storkwain Ltd, alleging that the appellants had on 14 December 1982 . . . unlawfully sold by retail, to a person purporting to be Linda Largey, 200 Physeptone tablets and 50 Ritalin tablets, and further that they unlawfully sold by retail, to a person purporting to be Thomas J. Paterson, 50 ampoules of Physeptone and 30 Valium tablets. All these medicines are substances controlled under art. 3(1)(b) of the Medicines (Prescription Only) Order 1980, SI 1980/1921; and the informations alleged in each case that the sale was not in accordance with a prescription issued by an appropriate practitioner, contrary to ss. 58(2) and 67(2) of the 1968 Act. Before the magistrate, the evidence (which was all agreed) was to the effect that the medicines were supplied under documents which purported to be prescriptions signed by a doctor, Dr Irani, of Queensdale Road, London, but that subsequent inquiries revealed that the prescriptions were both forgeries. It was submitted on behalf of the appellants that the presumption of mens rea applied to the prohibition in s. 58(2)(a) of the 1968 Act and that, the medicines having been supplied by the appellants on the basis of prescriptions which they believed in good faith and on reasonable grounds to be valid prescriptions, the informations should be dismissed. The magistrate accepted that submission and accordingly dismissed the informations: but he stated a case for the opinion of the High Court, the question for the opinion of the court being whether or not mens rea was required in the case of a prosecution under ss. 58(2) and 67(2) of the 1968 Act. On 2 May 1985 a Divisional Court (Farquharson and Tudor Price JJ) ([1985] 3 All ER 4 answered the question in the negative, and accordingly allowed the appeal of the respondents and directed that the case should be remitted to the magistrate with a direction to convict. The Divisional Court certified the following point of law as being of general public importance:

> Whether the prosecution have to prove mens rea where an information is laid under Section 58(2)(a) of the Medicines Act 1968 where the allegation is that the supply of 'prescription only' drugs was made by the [defendant] in accordance with a forged prescription and without fault on [his] part.

From that decision, the appellants now appeal with leave of your Lordships' House, the Divisional Court having refused leave.

For the appellants, counsel submitted that there must, in accordance with the well-recognised presumption, be read into s. 58(2)(a) words appropriate to require mens rea in accordance with *R* v *Tolson* (1889) 23 QBD 168, [1886–90] All ER Rep 26; in other words, to adopt the language of Lord Diplock in *Sweet* v *Parsley* [1969] 1 All ER 347 at 361, [1970] AC 132 at 163, the subsection must be read subject to the implication that a necessary element in the prohibition (and hence in the offence created by the subsection together with s. 67(2) of the 1968 Act) is the absence of belief, held honestly and on reasonable grounds, in the existence of facts which, if true, would make the act innocent. He further submitted, with reference to the speech of Lord Reid in *Sweet* v *Parsley* [1969] 1 All ER 347 at 350, [1970] AC 132 at 149, that the offence created by ss. 58(2a) and 67(2) of the 1968 Act was not to be classified as merely an offence of a quasi-criminal character in which the presumption of mens rea might more readily be rebutted, because in his submission the offence was one which would result in a stigma attaching to a person who was convicted of it, especially as Parliament had regarded it as sufficiently serious to provide that it should be triable on indictment, and that the maximum penalty should be two years' imprisonment. He also submitted that, if Parliament had considered that a pharmacist who dispensed under a forged prescription in good faith and without fault should be convicted of the offence, it would surely have made express provision to that effect: and that the imposition of so strict a liability could not be justified on the basis that it would tend towards greater efficiency on the part of pharmacists in detecting forged prescriptions. Finally, he referred your Lordships to the Misuse of Drugs Act 1971. Under s. 4(1) and (3) of that Act it is an offence to supply a controlled drug to another: but it is provided in s. 28 that subject to an immaterial exception) it shall be a defence for the accused to prove that he neither knew of nor suspected nor had reason to suspect the existence of some fact alleged by the prosecution which it is necessary for the prosecution to prove if he is to be convicted of the offence charged. Counsel for the appellants submitted that it would be anomalous if such a defence were available in the case of the more serious offence of supplying a controlled drug to another, but that the presumption of mens rea should be held inapplicable in the case of the offence created by ss. 58(2)(a) and 67(2) of the 1968 Act.

I am unable to accept counsel's submission, for the simple reason that it is, in my opinion, clear from the 1968 Act that Parliament must have intended that the presumption of mens rea should be inapplicable to s. 58(2)(a). First of all, it appears from the 1968 Act that, where Parliament wished to recognise that mens rea should be an ingredient of an offence created by the Act, it has expressly so provided. Thus, taking first of all offences created under provisions of Pt II of the 1968 Act, express requirements of mens rea are to be found both in s. 45(2) and in s. 46(1), (2) and (3) of the Act. More particularly, in relation to offences created by Pt III and Pts V and VI of the 1968 Act, s. 121 makes detailed provision for a requirement of mens rea in respect of certain specified sections of the act, including ss. 63 to 65 (which are contained in Pt III), but significantly not s. 58, nor indeed ss. 52 and 53. I have already set out the full text of s. 121 and need not repeat it. It is very difficult to avoid the conclusion that, by omitting s. 58 from those sections to which s. 121 is expressly made applicable, Parliament intended that there should be no implication of a requirement of mens rea in s. 58(2)(a). This view is fortified by sub-ss. (4) and (5) of s. 58 itself. Subsection (4)(a) provides that any order made by the appropriate ministers for the purposes of s. 58 may provide that s. 58(2)(a) or (b), or both, shall have effect subject to such exemptions as may be specified in the order. From this subsection alone it follows that the ministers, if they think it right, can provide for exemption where there is no mens rea on the part of the accused. Subsection (5) provides that any exemption conferred by an order in accordance with sub-s. (4)(a) may be conferred subject to such conditions or limitations as may be specified in the order. From this it follows that, if the ministers, acting under sub-s. (4), were to confer an exemption relating to sales where the vendor lacked the requisite mens rea, they may nevertheless circumscribe their exemption with conditions and limitations which render the exemption far narrower than the implication for which counsel for the appellants contends should be read into the statute itself. I find this to be very difficult to reconcile with the proposed implication.

It comes as no surprise to me, therefore, to discover that the relevant order in force at that time, the Medicines (Prescriptions Only) Order 1980, is drawn entirely in conformity with the construction of the statute which I favour. It is unnecessary, in the present case, to consider whether the relevant articles of the order may be taken into account in construing s. 58 of the 1968 Act; it is enough, for present purposes, that I am able to draw support from the fact that the ministers, in making the order, plainly did not read s. 58 as subject to the implication proposed by counsel for the appellants. . . .

NOTES AND QUESTIONS

1. There is an aspect of *Storkwain* worth noting. When a statute is aimed at those in a particular trade, business or profession, there is a greater willingness to construe a regulatory provision to require strict liability. Those in the trade can be presumed to have made a conscious choice to enter it. If they do not like the idea of strict liability, they can earn their living in some other way. Those who choose to continue in the trade, business or profession are expected to

be aware of and fully conversant with the statutes which affect them, and how those statutes are interpreted by the courts. That said, what can pharmacists do, as a practical matter, to avoid a criminal prosecution? What advice would you give to your pharmacist client? Note also the maximum sentence in *Storkwain* (two years). Did this make the imposition of criminal liability more or less likely?

2. Under the Draft Criminal Code Bill 1989, *mens rea* is presumed and strict liability can be imposed only if Parliament expressly or impliedly so provides. See Commentary on Draft Criminal Code Bill, Clause 20. Many would have preferred it if the drafters had stopped after 'expressly'.

3. What policies support the imposition of strict liability? Are these policy considerations counter-balanced by the risk that morally blameless individuals may be subjected to criminal prosecution and conviction?

4. In recent years, however, the 'subjectivist' approach to criminal offences has gained ground. See *B v DPP* [2000] 2 WLR 452 (for facts and holding, see p. 338) and *R v K* [2001] 3 All ER 899 (for facts and holding, see p. 327):

SECTION 3: **Relationship between *actus reus* and *mens rea*: concurrence**

The coincidence of *actus reus* and *mens rea* will not necessarily lead to criminal liability. There is the additional requirement that there be a concurrence between the *actus reus* and *mens rea*. What this means is that the two must be related in a particular way. It is not simply enough that a disgruntled spouse is speeding home, thinking about killing her husband, when he suddenly leaps in front of her car, bent on committing suicide. The speeding may be the cause of the resulting death, and the wife's mind may have been full of homicidal thoughts at the critical moment, but all that is a matter of coincidence. What the law requires is that the evil thoughts be the activating cause of the evil deeds. This is what the courts have in mind when they refer to concurrence. The problem cases involve situations where the defendant's *mens rea* occurs after the *actus reus* is completed, and cases where the defendant's *mens rea* is claimed to have been abandoned before the *actus reus* was complete.

If a defendant has *mens rea*, but never takes any steps to actuate that *mens rea*, there is no crime – evil thoughts by themselves do not a criminal make. Conversely, once the crime is complete, a subsequent change of heart is irrelevant. Courts are no doubt suspicious when a putative criminal who has been apprehended says, 'Well, the fact is that I had already changed my mind'.

R v Jakeman
(1982) 76 Cr App R 223, Court of Appeal

The applicant travelled by air to Accra in Ghana. She took with her two suitcases. There she booked a return flight to Rome two days later and a day after that a further flight from there to London. When she checked in at Accra for the return flight with her two suitcases, she booked them through to London. They contained 21.44 kilogrammes of cannabis, a controlled drug pursuant to section 2(1) of, and Part II of Schedule 2 to, the Misuse of Drugs Act 1971, and the importation of which to the United Kingdom was prohibited by section 3(1) of that Act. The flight to Rome was cancelled and the next day the passengers, including the applicant, were flown to Paris, where she took a flight to Rome, leaving her luggage in Paris, and then on to London. The customs officials in Paris assumed that the applicant's luggage there had been mis-routed and sent it on to London where customs officers on examination found the aforesaid amount of cannabis. They interviewed the applicant who eventually admitted that the two suitcases were hers and that she knew they contained cannabis. She was charged with being knowingly concerned in the fraudulent evasion of a prohibition in relation to goods contrary to section 170(2) of the Customs and Excise Management Act 1979, 'goods' in that subsection under paragraphs 1 and 3 of Schedule 1 to that Act including cannabis. At her trial she contended that she had been persuaded by two unknown men to take the drugs to London for £500; but that upon leaving Accra she had decided to have nothing further to do with the fraudulent enterprise and so had not collected the suitcases in Paris and had torn up her baggage tags. Her counsel then asked the trial judge whether in his view the intention to abandon her part in the importation, if accepted by the jury, provided a defence. The judge indicated that he thought that it did not and that he would so direct the jury. The applicant thereupon changed her plea to one of guilty. On an application for leave to appeal against conviction on the ground that the judge's ruling was wrong it was argued that for the offence under section 170(2) the participation of the applicant and her *mens rea* must continue throughout the offence, i.e. until the aircraft touched down at London Airport.

WOOD J: . . . We will deal first with the application for leave to appeal against conviction. Mr Mansfield first submits that the learned judge was wrong in the ruling which he gave. He submits that for the offence under section 170(2) of the 1979 Act, the participation of the applicant and her *mens rea* must continue throughout the offence – in this case at least until the wheels of the aircraft touched down at Heathrow Airport.

. . .

In developing his submission on the first ground of appeal, Mr Mansfield relied upon the applicant's assertion that she had changed her mind immediately on leaving Accra and on the facts that she did not collect her suitcases in Paris, that she tore up the baggage tags on arrival at Heathrow and that she did not seek to claim her suitcases. He submitted that whether one referred to 'withdrawal' or 'abandonment' or 'lack of *mens rea*' as the necessary ingredient of the defence, assistance was to be obtained from such cases as *R v Croft* (1944) 29 Cr App R 169 and *R v Becerra and Cooper* (1975) 62 Cr App R 212. These cases are concerned with accomplices and secondary parties to crime, not to the principal offender, and in the view of this court are not of assistance to test the submission which is made. It is our view that the correct approach is to analyse the offence itself, but before turning to consider the wording of the section as a whole, it is valuable to look at decided cases and to see what assistance can be derived from them.

The following propositions are supported by decisions of this court. First, that the importation takes place when the aircraft bringing the goods lands at an airport in this country, see *R v Smith*

(Donald) (1973) 57 Cr App R 737, 748. Secondly, acts done abroad in order to further the fraudulent evasion of a restriction on importation into this country are punishable under this section, see *R* v *Wall (Geoffrey)* (1974) 59 Cr App R 58, 61.

For guilt to be established the importation must, of course, result as a consequence, if only in part, of the activity of the accused. If, for example, in the present case the applicant had taken her two suitcases off the carousel at Charles de Gaulle airport in Paris, removed all the luggage tags, placed the suitcases in a left luggage compartment and thrown the key of that compartment into the Seine, and then subsequently, in a general emergency, all left luggage compartments had been opened, a well-known English travel label had been found on her suitcase and those suitcases had been sent to the Travel Agents' agency, care of Customs and Excise at Heathrow, then that undoubted importation would not be the relevant one for the purposes of a charge against the applicant.

We have already set out the wording of the relevant section and where the allegation concerns cannabis, the offence is, to be knowingly concerned in the fraudulent evasion (or attempt at evasion) of the prohibition on the importation of cannabis. Put more shortly, it is to be knowingly concerned in the fraudulent importation (or attempt at importation) of cannabis.

Although the importation takes place at one precise moment – when the aircraft lands – a person who is concerned in the importation may play his part before or after that moment. Commonly, the person responsible for despatching the prohibited drugs to England acts fraudulently and so does the person who removes them from the airport at which they have arrived. Each is guilty. *Wall (supra)* is an example of the former and *R* v *Green* (1975) 62 Cr App R 74 of the latter.

There is no doubt, that, putting aside the question of duress, as we have done, the applicant had a guilty mind when at Accra she booked her luggage to London. By that act, she brought about the importation through the instrumentation of innocent agents. In this way, she caused the airline to label it to London, and the labels were responsible for the authorities in Paris sending it on to London.

What is suggested is that she should not be convicted unless her guilty state of mind subsisted at the time of importation. We see no reason to construe the Act in this way. If a guilty mind at the time of importation is an essential, the man recruited to collect the package which has already arrived and which he knows contains prohibited drugs commits no offence. What matters is the state of mind at the time the relevant acts are done, i.e. at the time the defendant is concerned in bringing about the importation. This accords with the general principles of common law. To stab a victim in a rage with the necessary intent for murder or manslaughter leads to criminal responsibility for the resulting death regardless of any repentance between the act of stabbing and the time of death, which may be hours or days later. This is so even if, within seconds of the stabbing, the criminal comes to his senses and does everything possible to assist his victim. Only the victim's survival will save him from conviction for murder or manslaughter.

The applicant alleged that she repented as soon as she boarded the aircraft; that she deliberately failed to claim her luggage in Paris, that she tore up the baggage tags attached to her ticket and so on, but none of this could have saved her from being held criminally responsible for the importation which she had brought about by deliberate actions committed with guilty intent. Thus, the learned judge was right in the ruling he made.

Appeal dismissed.

The more troublesome cases, at least intellectually, involve the defendant who commits a series of acts: the original acts are done with intent to bring about a result but are ineffectual; the subsequent acts are not done with any criminal intent but bring about the originally desired result:

Thabo Meli and Others v R
[1954] 1 WLR 228, Privy Council

LORD REID: The four appellants in this case were convicted of murder after a trial before Sir Walter Harragin, judge of the High Court of Basutoland, in March, 1953. The appeal which has been heard by this Board dealt with two matters: first, whether the conclusions of the learned judge on questions of fact were warranted: and, secondly, whether, on a point of law, the accused are entitled to have the verdict quashed.

On the first matter, there really is no ground for criticising the learned judge's treatment of the facts. It is established by evidence, which was believed and which is apparently credible, that there was a preconceived plot on the part of the four accused to bring the deceased man to a hut and there to kill him, and then to fake an accident, so that the accused should escape the penalty for their act. The deceased man was brought to the hut. He was there treated to beer and was at least partially intoxicated; and he was then struck over the head in accordance with the plan of the accused. Witnesses say that while the deceased was seated and bending forward he was struck a heavy blow on the back of the head with a piece of iron like the instrument produced at the trial. But a post-mortem examination showed that his skull had not been fractured and medical evidence was to the effect that a blow such as the witnesses described would have produced more severe injuries than those found at the post-mortem examination. There is at least doubt whether the weapon which was produced as being like the weapon which was used could have produced the injuries that were found, but it may be that this weapon is not exactly similar to the one which was used, or it may be that the blow was a glancing blow and produced less severe injuries than those which one might expect. In any event, the man was unconscious after receiving the blow, but he was not then dead. There is no evidence that the accused then believed that he was dead, but their Lordships are prepared to assume from their subsequent conduct that they did so believe; and it is only on that assumption that any statable case can be made for this appeal. The accused took out the body, rolled it over a low krantz or cliff, and dressed up the scene to make it look like an accident. Obviously, they believed at that time that the man was dead, but it appears from the medical evidence that the injuries which he received in the hut were not sufficient to cause the death and that the final cause of his death was exposure when he was left unconscious at the foot of the krantz.

The point of law which was raised in this case can be simply stated. It is said that two acts were done: – first, the attack in the hut; and, secondly, the placing of the body outside afterwards – and that they were separate acts. It is said that, while the first act was accompanied by *mens rea*, it was not the cause of death; but that the second act, while it was the cause of death, was not accompanied by *mens rea*; and on that ground, it is said that the accused are not guilty of murder, though they may have been guilty of culpable homicide. It is said that the *mens rea* necessary to establish murder is an intention to kill, and that there could be no intention to kill when the accused thought that the man was already dead, so their original intention to kill had ceased before they did the act which caused the man's death. It appears to their Lordships impossible to divide up what was really one series of acts in this way. There is no doubt that the accused set out to do all these acts in order to achieve their plan, and as parts of their plan; and it is much too refined a ground of judgment to say that, because they were under a misapprehension at one stage and thought that their guilty purpose had been achieved before, in fact, it was achieved, therefore they are to escape the penalties of the law. Their Lordships do not think that this is a matter which is susceptible of elaboration. There appears to be no case, either in South Africa or England, or for that matter elsewhere, which resembles the present. Their Lordships can find no difference relevant to the present case between the law of South Africa and the law of England; and they are of opinion that by both laws there can be no separation such as that for which the accused contend. Their crime is not reduced from murder to a lesser crime merely because the accused were under some misapprehension for a time during the completion of their criminal plot.

Their Lordships must, therefore, humbly advise Her Majesty that this appeal should be dismissed.

NOTE

Glanville Williams suggests that an alternative way of dealing with cases such as *Thabo Meli* is to hold that if the first act would have constituted manslaughter if the victim died, death which occurs during a subsequent attempt to dispose of the body should not affect liability. Another approach is presented in the following case:

Attorney-General's Reference (No. 4 of 1980)
[1981] 1 WLR 705, Court of Appeal

ACKNER LJ: This is a reference to the court by the Attorney-General of a point of law seeking the opinion of the court pursuant to s. 36 of the Criminal Justice Act 1972. It raises yet again the problem of the supposed corpse, and the facts, which I take from the terms of the reference itself, are inevitably macabre.

The deceased was the fiancée of the accused and for some months before her death they had lived together in a maisonette consisting of two floors of a house connected by two short flights of carpeted wooden stairs. The deceased was employed locally and was last seen at work on 17th January 1979 at about 5 p.m. Thereafter no one, other than the accused, ever saw her alive again.

The deceased met her death on 18th January 1979, although this fact was not known until over three weeks later when the defendant so informed a friend. His account, the first of a number, was that in the course of an argument on the evening of 17th January he had slapped her on the face causing her to fall downstairs and bang her head. He said that he had then put her to bed but discovered next morning that she was dead. He then took her body to his home town and buried her.

On the following day, 14th February, he gave his second account, telling the same friend that after the deceased had 'fallen downstairs' he had dragged her upstairs by a piece of rope tied round her neck. He subsequently cut up her body with a saw before burying it. The next day, on the advice of his friend, the accused went to see a superior and gave an account similar to the one he had given his friend.

We now come to the statements which he made to the police. On 27th February, having consulted solicitors, the accused was interviewed by the police at his solicitors' office. He began by giving the police substantially the same account that he had given to his friend and his superior but added that instead of burying the deceased he had 'dumped' the various parts of her body on a tip. At the police station later that day he amplified his statement by saying that the incident when the deceased 'fell downstairs' occurred at about 7 p.m. on 17th January and that it was the following day, when he found her motionless, that he pulled her upstairs by a rope around her neck and then cut up her body in the bathroom. On the following day after much questioning by the police he changed his account stating that everything had happened on Thursday, 18th January at about 7 a.m. This is what he then said happened. (i) He and the deceased had an argument on the landing in the course of which each slapped the other; he seized the deceased and shook her hard; she dug her nails into him and he pushed her away instinctively, causing her to fall backwards over the handrail, down the stairs head first onto the floor. (ii) He went downstairs immediately to find her motionless and on a very cursory examination discovered no pulse, and no sign of breath but frothy blood coming from her mouth. (iii) Almost immediately thereafter he dragged her upstairs by a rope tied around her neck, placed her in the bath and cut her neck with a penknife to let out her blood, having already decided to cut up her body and dispose of the pieces.

He agreed that his previous account was untrue and he made a detailed voluntary statement along the lines set out in (i), (ii) and (iii) above describing how subsequently he had cut up and disposed of her body.

Subsequently the police discovered evidence which corroborated the accused's account of how, where and when he had cut up the body. They also found the saw he had used and the shopkeeper who sold it to him. However, the body of the deceased was never found, only some minute fragments of bone, which were discovered in the maisonette. There was thus no expert evidence as to the cause of death. The deceased died either as a result of being pushed and thus caused to fall backwards over the handrail and backwards down the stairs head first onto the floor, or by being strangled with the rope, or having her throat cut. The Crown conceded that it was not possible for them to prove whether the deceased died as the result of the 'fall' downstairs or from what the accused did to the deceased thereafter.

The indictment charged the accused with (i) manslaughter, (ii) obstructing the coroner in the execution of his duty, and (iii) preventing the burial of a corpse.

The accused pleaded guilty to the third count, the Crown offered no evidence on the second and the trial proceeded on the count of manslaughter.

At the close of the Crown's case counsel for the accused stated that he proposed to submit that on the facts proved there was no case of manslaughter capable of going to the jury. It is not easy to follow from the transcript the exact basis of his submissions, but what he appears to have been contending was that (a) it was not possible for the jury to be sure what caused the deceased's death and (b) whether the death was caused as a result of her 'fall' down the stairs or from what the accused subsequently did, believing her to be dead, in neither event was there a prima facie case of manslaughter.

The judge, although expressing his reluctance to accept that the accused could be in a better position as a result of his dismembering the body of the deceased, appeared to have been very concerned at what he described as 'an insuperable problem of sentencing', were the accused to be convicted of manslaughter. He expressed the view that the real criminality of the accused's behaviour was in disposing of the body, a view which this court is unable to accept. These views appear to have influenced his decision, which was to withdraw the case from the jury and to direct an acquittal on the ground that the Crown had failed to prove the cause of the death of the deceased.

On the above facts this reference raises a single and simple question, *viz*, if an accused kills another by one or other of two or more different acts each of which, if it caused the death, is a sufficient act to establish manslaughter, is it necessary in order to found a conviction to prove which act caused the death? The answer to that question is No, it is is not necessary to found a conviction to prove which act caused the death. No authority is required to justify this answer, which is clear beyond argument, as was indeed immediately conceded by counsel on behalf of the accused.

What went wrong in this case was that counsel made jury points to the judge and not submissions of law. He was in effect contending that the jury should not convict of manslaughter if the death had resulted from the 'fall', because the push which had projected the deceased over the handrail was a reflex and not a voluntary action, as a result of her digging her nails into him. If, however, the deceased was still alive when he cut her throat, since he then genuinely believed her to be dead, having discovered neither pulse nor sign of breath, but frothy blood coming from her mouth, he could not be guilty of manslaughter because he had not behaved with gross criminal negligence. What counsel and the judge unfortunately overlooked was that there was material available to the jury which would have entitled them to have convicted the accused of manslaughter, whichever of the two sets of acts caused her death. It being common ground that the deceased was killed by an act done to her by the accused and it being conceded that the jury could not be satisfied which was the act which caused the death, they should have been directed in due course in the summing up, to ask themselves the following questions: (i) 'Are we satisfied beyond reasonable doubt that the deceased's "fall" downstairs was the result of an intentional act by the accused which was unlawful and dangerous?' If the answer was No, then they would acquit. If the answer was Yes, then they would need to ask themselves a second question, namely: (ii) 'Are we satisfied beyond reasonable doubt that the act of cutting the girl's throat was an act of gross criminal negligence?' If the answer to that question was No, then they would acquit, but if the answer was Yes, then the verdict would be guilty of manslaughter. The jury would thus have been satisfied that, whichever act had killed the deceased, each was a sufficient act to establish the offence of manslaughter.

QUESTIONS

1. According to the Court of Appeal, what would the jury need to have found to justify a conviction? Is the Court's position still unduly favourable to the defendant?

2. Reconsider *Thabo Meli*. Would it have been preferable for the court in *Attorney-General's Reference (No. 4 of 1980)* to have adopted an approach that did not divide up the defendant's acts into discrete incidents? Is *Thabo Meli* nonetheless distinguishable in that the defendants were acting pursuant to a plan?

R v Le Brun
[1991] 4 All ER 673, Court of Appeal

LORD LANE CJ. On 31 March 1990 in the Crown Court at Plymouth before Hutchison J and a jury the appellant, John Le Brun, was convicted on a majority verdict of manslaughter. He was found not guilty of murder, with which he had originally been charged. He was sentenced to four years' imprisonment. He now appeals against conviction by leave of the single judge.

The facts giving rise to the charge were these. In September 1989 the appellant, who was then serving in the Royal Navy, was living at an address in Plymouth with his wife, who was the victim in the present case. They went out for the evening to some friends, the Cartwrights, on 23 September 1989. They left the house of the friends in the early hours at about 2 am. They did not have very far to go to their own home. They had been drinking. They were both described as merry, but neither, it was said, was drunk.

It was only two or three minutes' walk to get to their own home. But during that short journey it is quite plain that a heated argument developed between the two of them. To come to the end of the story, after a short interval, which was really only sufficient for the friends whose house they had visited to have tidied up the house, taken the dog for a walk and prepared for bed, the appellant returned to the Cartwrights, banged on the door and shouted, 'It's Joannie . . . she's collapsed. There's blood everywhere. Get an ambulance.'

In fact the wife (as I shall call her now) was lying near the top of some steps leading from the pathway to their home. She had sustained two wounds to the back of her head: a fracture to the back of the skull and a severe injury to her chin, which had produced what might be described as a star-shaped wound. That wound had broken the jaw and caused bleeding into the joints on each side. She had sustained also a bruise on the outer edge of the lip on the left, a fracture to both wings of the hyoid bone at the top of the neck. As can be seen from the photographs, there was a good deal of blood at the scene and – a matter of some importance – some hair which had plainly been pulled by the roots out of her scalp was lying at the scene.

The cause of death was bruising to the brain, which in its turn had been caused by the fracture to the back of the skull.

. . .

The main thrust of [defendant's] argument is to be found in ground 3 of the notice of appeal, which I will now read:

'The learned judge erred in law in directing the jury that they could convict the appellant of murder or manslaughter (depending on the intention with which he had previously assaulted the victim) if they were sure that, having committed the assault with no serious injury resulting, the appellant had accidentally dropped the victim causing her death whilst either: (a) attempting to move her to her home against her wishes, including any wishes she may have expressed prior to the previous assault, and/or (b) attempting to dispose of her body or otherwise cover up the previous assault.'

Problems of causation and remoteness of damage are never easy of solution. We have had helpful arguments from both counsel on this point, the point in the present case being, to put it in summary before coming to deal with it in more detail, that the intention of the appellant to harm his wife one way or another may have been separated by a period of time from the act which in fact caused the death, namely the fact of her falling to the ground and fracturing her skull. That second incident may have taken place without any guilty mind on the part of the appellant.

. . .

The question can be perhaps framed in this way. There was here an initial unlawful blow to the chin delivered by the appellant. That, again on what must have been the jury's finding, was not delivered with the intention of doing really serious harm to the wife. The guilty intent accompanying that blow was sufficient to have rendered the appellant guilty of manslaughter, but not murder, had it caused death. But it did not cause death. What caused death was the later impact when the wife's head hit the pavement. At the moment of impact the appellant's intention was to remove her, probably unconscious, body to avoid detection. To that extent the impact may have been pro tanto accidental. May the earlier guilty intent be joined with the later non-guilty blow which caused death to produce in the conglomerate a proper verdict of manslaughter?

. . .

It will be observed that the present case is different from the facts of those two cases *[Thabo Meli* and *R. v. Moore and Dern* [1975] Crim L. R. 229] in that death here was not the result of a preconceived plan which went wrong, as was the case in those two decisions which we have cited. Here the death, again assuming the jury's finding to be such as it must have been, was the result of an initial unlawful blow, not intended to cause serious harm, in its turn causing the appellant to take steps possibly to evade the consequences of his unlawful act. During the taking of those steps he commits the actus reus but without the mens rea necessary for murder or manslaughter. Therefore the mens rea is contained in the initial unlawful assault, but the actus reus is the eventual dropping of the head on the ground.

Normally the actus reus and the means rea coincide in point of time. What is the situation when they do not? Is it permissible, as the Crown contends here, to combine them to produce a conviction for manslaughter?

The answer is perhaps to be found in the next case to which we were referred, and that was *R v Church* [1965] 2 All ER 72, [1966] 1 QB 59. In that case the defendant was charged with the murder of a woman whose body was found in a river. The cause of death was drowning. The defendant had it seemed attacked the woman and rendered her semi-conscious. He thought she was dead and in his panic he threw her into the river. He was acquitted of murder but convicted of manslaughter. Edmund Davies J, giving the judgment of the court, said ([1965] 2 All ER 72 at 76, [1966] 1 QB 59 at 70):

'. . . the conclusion of this court is that an unlawful act causing the death of another cannot, simply because it is an unlawful act, render a manslaughter verdict inevitable. For such a verdict inexorably to follow, the unlawful act must be such as all sober and reasonable people would inevitably recognise must subject the other person to, at least, the risk of some harm resulting therefrom, albeit not serious harm . . . In the light of *Thabo Meli* v. *R.* ([1954]) 1 All ER 373, [1954] 1 WLR 228), it is conceded on behalf of the appellant that, on the murder charge, the trial judge was perfectly entitled to direct the jury, as he did: "Unless you find that something happened in the course of this evening between the infliction of the injuries and the decision to throw the body into the water, you may undoubtedly treat the whole course of conduct of the [appellant] as one." For some reason, however, which is not clear to this court, counsel for the appellant denies that such an approach is possible when one is considering a charge of manslaughter. We fail to see why. We adopt as sound DR. GLANVILLE WILLIAMS' view in [*Criminal Law: The General Part* (2nd edn, 1961) p 174] that, "If a killing by the first act would have be manslaughter, a later destruction of the supposed corpse should also be manslaughter." Had Mrs. Nott [the victim] died of her initial injuries, a manslaughter verdict might quite conceivably have been returned on the basis that the appellant inflicted them under the influence of provocation or that the jury were not convinced that they were inflicted with murderous intent. All that was lacking in the direction given in this was that, when the judge turned to consider manslaughter, he did not again tell the jury that they were entitled (if they thought fit) to regard the conduct of the appellant in relation to Mrs. Nott as constituting throughout a series of acts which culminated in her death, and that, if that was how they regarded the appellant's behaviour, it mattered not whether he believed her to be alive or dead when he threw her in the river.'

It seems to us that where the unlawful application of force and the eventual act causing death are parts of the same sequence of events, the same transaction, the fact that there is an appreciable interval of time between the two does not serve to exonerate the defendant from liability. That is certainly so where the appellant's subsequent actions which caused death, after the initial unlawful blow, are designed to conceal his commission of the original unlawful assault.

It would be possible to express the problem as one of causation. The original unlawful blow to the chin was a causa sine qua non of the later actus reus. It was the opening event in a series which was to culminate in death: the first link in the chain of causation, to use another metaphor. It cannot be said that the actions of the appellant in dragging the victim away with the intention of evading liability broke the chain which linked the initial blow with the death.

In short, in circumstances such as the present, which is the only concern of this court, the act which causes death and the necessary mental state to constitute manslaughter need not coincide in point of time.

Appeal dismissed

NOTES AND QUESTIONS
1. Reconsider *R v Miller* (p. 100). Might liability in the preceding three cases have been based on the failure to assist a victim in peril, where the defendant was the creator of the peril?
2. Should *Le Brun* be considered as a case of concurrence of causation? Would it matter?

PART II

Substantive Offences

5

Homicide

SECTION 1: **Introduction: Homicide**

Homicide for the purposes of the criminal law consists of an *unlawful* killing of a human being. Particular problems are encountered with the limits of this offence because all human beings eventually die. What does it mean to say that a defendant 'caused' what is an inevitable event? Properly defined, 'killing' in the context of homicide refers to any acceleration of the time of death.

The unjustified killing of another human being has traditionally been regarded as the most serious offence known to the law. For this reason the most severe sentences authorised by the law are reserved for this crime. Because murder and manslaughter were and are severely punished, the borderline between a killing which falls into these categories and other justifiable or excusable killings has been the subject of numerous closely reasoned decisions.

Save for constructive manslaughter, the offences of murder and manslaughter have a common *actus reus* which is the unlawful killing of another human being. The following discussion of the *actus reus* of murder will therefore be equally pertinent when the offence of manslaughter is under consideration.

SECTION 2: **Murder**

It is interesting to note that murder is a common law offence. There is no statutory definition of the crime. The usual starting place for consideration of the elements of murder is the definition put forward by Coke:

Murder is when a man of sound memory, and of the age of discretion, unlawfully killeth within any county of the realm any reasonable creature *in rerum natura* under the king's peace, with malice aforethought, either expressed by the party or implied by law, so as the party wounded, or hurt etc. die of the wound or hurt, etc. within a year and a day after the same. (3 Inst 47) [the year and a day requirement has now been abolished]

At common law the sentence for murder was death, the extreme example of retributive theory in practice. The death penalty has now been abolished, but the judge is constrained to impose a mandatory sentence of life imprisonment. (This does not mean that the prisoner will necessarily remain in prison for life; he may be released on licence by the Home Secretary on the advice of the Parole Board and Lord Chief Justice.) However, he will remain subject to supervision for the whole of his natural life. The mandatory life sentence leaves no room for consideration by the sentencing judge of mitigating circumstances. As a consequence, there have been created several 'defences' which will reduce murder to manslaughter. The most important of these defences are diminished responsibility and provocation. Although the maximum penalty for manslaughter is also life imprisonment, a judge has the discretion to impose a lesser sentence – anything from life imprisonment to absolute discharge may be the result.

A: The killer and the victim

The term 'man' in Coke's definition is not to be taken literally. Any person may be guilty of murder, provided that he or she satisfies the general principles of criminal responsibility.

Any human being can be the victim of murder. The two problems that can be encountered relate to when life begins for the purposes of being a victim and when life ends such that one can no longer be a victim. The courts have taken a very conservative view of the commencement of life:

R v Poulton
(1832) 5 C & P 329, Central Criminal Court

> The prisoner was indicted for wilful murder. The indictment stated, in substance, that the prisoner, on a certain day, was delivered of a female bastard child, which was born alive; and that she afterwards, to wit, on the same day, a certain string of no value, around the neck of the said female bastard child, did bind, tie, and fasten, and by such binding, etc., the said child feloniously and wilfully, of her malice aforethought, did choke and strangle, etc.

LITTLEDALE J: . . . With respect to the birth, the being born must mean that the whole body is brought into the world; and it is not sufficient that the child respires in the progress of the birth. Whether the child was born alive or not depends mainly upon the evidence of the medical men. None of them say that the child was born alive; they only say that it had breathed: and if there is all this uncertainty among these medical men, perhaps you would think it too much for you to say that you are satisfied that the child was born alive.

R v Brain
(1834) 6 C & P 350, Oxford Assizes

> The prisoner was indicted for the murder of her male bastard child. It appeared that the prisoner had been delivered of a child at Sandford Ferry; and that the body of the child was afterwards found in the water, about fifteen feet from the lock gate, near the ferry-house; but it was proved by two surgeons, Mr Box and Mr Hester, that the child had never breathed.

PARK J: A child must be actually wholly in the world in a living state to be the subject of a charge of murder; but if it has been wholly born, and is alive, it is not essential that it should have breathed at the time it was killed; as many children are born alive, and yet do not breathe for some time after their birth. But you must be satisfied that the child was wholly born into the world at the time it was killed, or you ought not to find the prisoner guilty of murder. This is not only my opinion, but the law was so laid down in a case as strong as this, by a very learned Judge (Mr Justice Littledale) at the Old Bailey. (His Lordship read the case of *R* v *Poulton*.)

Verdict – Not guilty of murder, but guilty of concealment.

NOTE

The child must be born alive in order for it to be a victim of homicide but the act which caused the death can take place before the birth:

Attorney-General's Reference (No. 3 of 1994)
[1997] 3 All ER 936

For the facts, see p. 157.

NOTES AND QUESTIONS
1. The point at which a human entity is capable of being killed is an issue with both legal and moral dimensions. Some people believe that human life begins at conception, and that therefore abortion is murder. English law clearly does not accept this view, although in appropriate circumstances both abortion and the destruction of a child capable of being born alive can be criminal.
2. When the initial assault is directed at the mother and, as a result the child is born prematurely and as a result of the premature birth dies, is the defendant guilty of homicide? Or is it necessary that the fatal blow be directed at the foetus?
3. The killing of an infant under 12 months old by its mother may constitute the crime of infanticide rather than murder (Infanticide Act 1938) if the mother establishes that her mind was disturbed by virtue of her not having fully recovered from the effect of giving birth or by reason of lactation consequent on the birth. The medical underpinnings of this crime (breast feeding adversely affects the mother's mental state) are no longer regarded as valid. If so, are there other justifications for preserving the offence? Should it be extended to fathers (given that its aim is to allow a distraught parent who has killed a baby to be prosecuted for a less serious crime than murder)?

Re A (Conjoined Twins: Medical Treatment)
[2001] 1 FLR 1

For the facts see p. 473.

LORD JUSTICE BROOKE:
12. Is Mary a reasonable creature?
For the reasons given by Ward LJ and Robert Walker LJ, with which I agree, I am satisfied that Mary's life is a human life that falls to be protected by the law of murder. Although she has for all practical purposes a useless brain, a useless heart and useless lungs, she is alive, and it would in my judgment be an act of murder if someone deliberately acted so as to extinguish that life unless a justification or excuse could be shown which English law is willing to recognise.

In recent editions of Archbold, including the 2000 Edition, the editors have suggested that the word 'reasonable' in Coke's definition (which they wrongly ascribe to Lord Hale in para 19.1) related to the appearance rather than the mental capacity of the victim and was apt to exclude 'monstrous births'. Spurred on by this suggestion, and because the present case broke so much novel ground, we explored with counsel some of the thinking of seventeenth century English philosophers in an effort to ascertain what Coke may have meant when he used the expression 'any reasonable creature' as part of his definition. We had in mind their absorbing interest in the nature of 'strange and deformed births' and 'monstrous births' (see Thomas Hobbes, Elements of Law, II. 10.8, and John Locke, An Essay Concerning Human Understanding, III.III.17, III.VI.15 and 26 and III.XI.20).

In Attorney-General's Reference (No. 3 of 1994) [1998] AC 245 Lord Mustill referred at p 254F to another statement in Coke's Institutes, not mentioned in that passage in Archbold, where after referring to prenatal injuries which lead to the delivery of a dead child, Coke writes (Co Inst Pt III, Ch. 7, p 50):

'if the childe be born alive, and dieth of the potion, battery, or other cause, this is murder; for in law it is accounted a reasonable creature, in rerum natura, when it is born alive'.

In these circumstances I have no hesitation in accepting the submission by Miss Davies QC (whose assistance, as the friend of the court, was of the greatest value), which was in these terms:

'In "The Sanctity of Life and the Criminal Law" (1958), Professor Glanville Williams stated at p 31:

"There is, indeed some kind of legal argument that a 'monster' is not protected even under the existing law. This argument depends upon the very old legal writers, because the matter has not been considered in any modern work or in any court judgment."

After discussing the meaning of the word 'monster' (which might originally have connoted animal paternity) he states at pp 33–34:

"Locked (Siamese) twins present a special case, though they are treated in medical works as a species of monster. Here the recent medical practice is to attempt a severance, notwithstanding the risks involved. Either the twins are successfully unlocked, or they die" (emphasis added).

It is implicit in this analysis that the author is of the view that "Siamese" twins are capable of being murdered and the amicus curiae supports this view.

Advances in medical treatment of deformed neonates suggest that the criminal law's protection should be as wide as possible and a conclusion that a creature in being was not reasonable would be confined only to the most extreme cases, of which this is not an example. Whatever might have been thought of as "monstrous" by Bracton, Coke, Blackstone, Locke and Hobbes, different considerations would clearly apply today. This proposition might be tested in this way: suppose an intruder broke into the hospital and stabbed twin M causing her death. Clearly it could not be said that his actions would be outside the ambit of the law of homicide.'

Problems have also been encountered with identifying when life ends. For example, consider the case of a victim of a serious assault who is placed on a life support system. Such systems are capable of supporting breathing and heart function after a patient has no functioning of the central nervous system and is so-called 'brain dead'. Is it open to the perpetrator of the assault to argue that the doctors who turn off the life support system of a victim deemed to be 'brain dead' are the cause of the victim's death?

R v Malcherek and Steel
[1981] 1 WLR 690, Court of Appeal

LORD LANE CJ: . . . This is not the occasion for any decision as to what constitutes death. Modern techniques have undoubtedly resulted in the blurring of many of the conventional and traditional concepts of death. A person's heart can now be removed altogether without death supervening;

machines can keep the blood circulating through the vessels of the body until a new heart can be implanted in the patient, and even though a person is no longer able to breathe spontaneously a ventilating machine can, so to speak, do his breathing for him, as is demonstrated in the two cases before us. There is, it seems, a body of opinion in the medical profession that there is only one true test of death and that is the irreversible death of the brain stem, which controls the basic functions of the body such as breathing. When that occurs it is said the body has died, even though by mechanical means the lungs are being caused to operate and some circulation of blood is taking place.

Airedale NHS Trust v *Bland*
[1993] 1 All ER 821, House of Lords

For facts and holding, see p. 92.

R (on the application of Pretty) v *Director of Public Prosecutions*
[2002] 1 All ER 1, House of Lords

For facts and holding, see p. 19.

LORD BINGHAM OF CORNHILL: . . . Mrs Pretty bases her case on the convention. But it is worthy of note that her argument is inconsistent with two principles deeply embedded in English law. The first is a distinction between the taking of one's own life by one's own act and the taking of life through the intervention or with the help of a third party. The former has been permissible since suicide ceased to be a crime in 1961. The latter has continued to be proscribed. The distinction was very clearly expressed by Hoffmann LJ in *Airedale NHS Trust v Bland* [1993] 1 All ER 821 at 855, [1993] AC 789 at 831:

> 'No one in this case is suggesting that Anthony Bland should be given a lethal injection. But there is concern about ceasing to supply food as against, for example, ceasing to treat an infection with antibiotics. Is there any real distinction? In order to come to terms with our intuitive feelings about whether there is a distinction, I must start by considering why most of us would be appalled if he was given a lethal injection. It is, I think, connected with our view that the sanctity of life entails its inviolability by an outsider. Subject to exceptions like self-defence, human life is inviolate even if the person in question has consented to its violation. That is why although suicide is not a crime, assisting someone to commit suicide is. It follows that, even if we think Anthony Bland would have consented, we would not be entitled to end his life by a lethal injection.'

The second distinction is between the cessation of life-saving or life-prolonging treatment on the one hand and the taking of action lacking medical, therapeutic or palliative justification but intended solely to terminate life on the other. This distinction provided the rationale of the decisions in *Bland*'s case. It was very succinctly expressed in the Court of Appeal in *Re J (a minor) (wardship: medical treatment)* [1990] 3 All ER 930, [1991] Fam 33, in which Lord Donaldson of Lymington MR said:

> 'What doctors and the court have to decide is whether, in the best interests of the child patient, a particular decision as to medical treatment should be taken which *as a side effect* will render death more or less likely. This is not a matter of semantics. It is fundamental. At the other end of the age spectrum, the use of drugs to reduce pain will often be fully justified, notwithstanding that this will hasten the moment of death. What can never be justified is the use of drugs or surgical procedures with the primary purpose of doing so' (See [1990] 3 All ER 930 at 938, [1991] Fam 33 at 46.)

Similar observations were made by Balcombe and Taylor LJJ ([1990] 3 All ER 930 at 941–942, 943, [1991] Fam 33 at 51, 53 respectively). While these distinctions are in no way binding on the European Court of Human Rights there is nothing to suggest that they are inconsistent with the jurisprudence which has grown up around the convention. It is not enough for Mrs Pretty to show that the United Kingdom would not be acting inconsistently with the convention if it were to permit assisted suicide; she must go further and establish that the United Kingdom is in breach of the convention by falling to permit it or would be in breach of the convention if it did not permit it. Such a contention is in my opinion untenable, as the Divisional Court rightly held.

NOTE

Since 1976, the medical profession has accepted the brain death test for determining when a patient is dead. Is this the correct standard for the law to adopt? You might recall in this regard that in other areas of the law, such as in respect of the legal definition of insanity, legal doctrine does not necessarily accord with medical doctrine.

B: Causation

(i) *Death within a year and a day*

In the case of both murder and manslaughter the common law rule was that death must occur within a year and a day of the infliction of injury. The original rationale for this rule lay in the difficulty in proving a causal connection between old injuries and a subsequent death. This rationale became increasingly tenuous with scientific advances and the rule has now been abolished by statute (Law Reform (Year and a Day Rule) Act 1996). Prosecutions brought more than three years after the relevant act was committed, or where the defendant has already been convicted of an offence in connection with the death, require the consent of the Attorney-General (s. 2).

(ii) *Contributing causes*

The problems involved in determining causation were examined in Chapter 3. As was seen then, causation does not turn solely on a test that asks whether 'but for' the defendant's conduct the victim would be dead. The 'reductio ad absurdem' of the pure 'but for' test could lead to the prosecution of the killer's parents. If they had never met and had sexual intercourse the killer would not exist, so, 'but for' their acts, the killing could not have taken place. In the context of homicide the courts ask whether the defendant's acts were the legal or proximate cause, often expressed in the cases as the 'substantial and operating' cause, of the death. In the following cases we can see how this rule operates when the defendant's act is combined with other factors to cause the death of the victim. Troublesome are the cases where death would not have occurred except for the negligence or deliberate acts of others (including the victim) and where the act of the defendant was so insubstantial as to be negligible (where, for example, a person is bleeding rapidly to death because of a cut throat and the defendant accelerates the death by adding a pin prick). Another difficult case is where there is a cause of death which occurs after the defendant's acts – when should it displace the defendant's acts so as to relieve him of liability? Reconsider *R* v *Le Brun* p. 198.

NOTES AND QUESTIONS

1. Where there are alternative factual versions of how a homicide was committed, involving different acts occurring at different times, the jurors must agree as to which version they base

their conviction. If they cannot agree, they cannot convict, even though they believe that under either version, the defendant is responsible for the death. See *R v Boreman* [2000] 1 All ER 307. Why should this be so? Reconsider Atty.-Gen's Reference (No 4 of 1980) [1981] 1 WLR 705, discussed p. 196.

(a) *Acts of the victim.* The victim's contribution to his own death is generally deemed to be irrelevant.

R v Benge
(1865) 4 F & F 504, Maidstone Crown Court

The prosecution arose out of a fatal railway accident, which occurred on the South Eastern Railway at a place called Staplehurst, where there was a bridge, about two miles in the direction towards London from a station called Headcorn. . . .

Piggott, B, said, that assuming culpable negligence on the part of the prisoner which materially contributed to the accident, it would not be material that others also by their negligence contributed to cause it. Therefore he must leave it to the jury whether there was negligence of the prisoner which had been the substantial cause of the accident. In summing up the case to the jury, he said, their verdict must depend upon whether the death was mainly caused by the culpable negligence of the prisoner. Was the accident mainly caused by the taking up of the rails at a time when an express train was about to arrive, was that the act of the prisoner, and was it owing to culpable negligence on his part? His counsel had urged that it was not so, because the flagman and engine-driver had been guilty of negligence, which had contributed to cause the catastrophe; but they, in their turn, might make the same excuse, and so, if it was valid, no one could be criminally responsible at all. This would be an absurd and unreasonable conclusion, and showed that the contention of the prisoner's counsel could not be sound. Such was not the right view of the law – that of the negligence of several persons at different times and places contributed to cause an accident, any one of them could set up that his was not the sole cause of it. It was enough against any one of them that his negligence was the substantial cause of it. Now, here the primary cause was certainly the taking up of the rails at a time when the train was about to arrive, and when it would be impossible to replace them in time to avoid the accident. And this the prisoner admitted was owing to his own mistake. Was that mistake culpable negligence, and did it mainly or substantially cause the accident? The book was clearly and plainly printed, and must have been read carelessly to admit of such a mistake. Was it not the duty of the prisoner who knew the fearful consequences of a mistake to take reasonable care to be correct? And had he taken such care? Then as to its being the main cause of the accident, it was true that the company had provided other precautions to avoid any impending catastrophe, and that these were not observed upon this occasion; but was it not owing to the prisoner's culpable negligence that the accident was impending, and, if so, did his negligence the less cause it, because if other persons had not been negligent it might possibly have been avoided?

Verdict – Guilty.

R v Swindall and Osborne
(1846) 2 Car & Kir 230, Nisi Prius

Manslaughter. – The prisoners were indicted for the manslaughter of one James Durose. The second count of the indictment charged the prisoners with inciting each other to drive their carts and horses at a furious and dangerous rate along a public road, and with driving their carts and horses over the deceased at such furious and dangerous rate, and thereby killing him.

. . .

Pollock, CB (in summing up). – The prisoners are charged with contributing to the death of the deceased, by their negligence and improper conduct, and, if they did so, it matters not whether he was deaf, or drunk, or negligent, or in part contributed to his own death . . .

NOTE

As we have seen in Chapter 3, courts generally take the view that one must take one's victim as one finds him. Normally the rule applies to physical frailties such as the haemophilia or eggshell skull of the victim but the rule can be more far-reaching.

R v Blaue

[1975] 3 All ER 446, Court of Appeal

For facts and holding, see p. 120.

NOTES AND QUESTIONS

1. For what proposition does *Blaue* stand? That one must take one's victim as one finds her, even if she is not a reasonable person? That the victim, a Jehovah's Witness, was not unreasonable in her refusal to accept a blood transfusion, even though it would cost her her life? That whether or not the victim's refusal was unreasonable, it did not 'break the chain of causation' so that the death would no longer be attributable to the acts of the defendant? That the contributory acts of a victim are not (or rarely) relevant to issues of causation? That events intervening between the defendant's act and the victim's death must be of earth-shattering significance before they will remove the defendant's responsibility?
2. The rule that the actions of the victim do not break the chain of causation extends to two other situations:
   (a) where the cause of the death is pressure exerted by threats; and
   (b) where the victim is frightened into taking his own life.

R v Hayward

(1908) 21 Cox CC 692, Maidstone Autumn Assizes

It appeared from the evidence of neighbours that on the night in question the prisoner came home before his wife. He was in a condition of violent excitement, and was overheard to express a determination of 'giving his wife something' when she came in. When the woman did come home there were at once sounds of an altercation, and shortly afterwards the woman was seen by several witnesses to rush from the house into the road closely pursued by the prisoner, who was at the same time using violent threats towards her. She was then seen to fall into the roadway, and lying there she was kicked on the left forearm by the prisoner. When picked up she was found to be dead.

The medical evidence showed that the bruise on her arm, due to the kick, could not have been the cause of death. The post-mortem examination showed that the deceased, whose organs were otherwise in a perfectly healthy condition, was suffering from a persistent thymus gland, two inches wide and weighing one and three-quarter ounces, lying at the base of the heart. Such a state of affairs was proved to be quite abnormal at the deceased's age – 22. The cause of death was given as cardiac inhibition, and the medical evidence was to the effect that in a person the subject of persistent thymus gland, such as the deceased, any combination of physical exertion and fright or strong emotion might occasion death in such a fashion.

. . .

Ridley, J, in summing up, directed the jury that if they believed the witnesses there was a sufficient chain of evidence to support a conviction of manslaughter. He pointed out that no proof of actual physical violence was necessary, but that death from fright alone, caused by an illegal act, such as threats of violence, would be sufficient. The abnormal state of the deceased's health did not affect the question whether the prisoner knew or did not know of it if it were proved to the satisfaction of the jury that the death was accelerated by the prisoner's illegal act.

The prisoner was convicted and sentenced to three months' imprisonment with hard labour.

R v Halliday
(1889) 61 LT 701, Court of Appeal

LORD COLERIDGE CJ: . . . Here the woman came by her mischief by getting out of the window – I use a vague word on purpose – and in her fall broke her leg. Now that might have been caused by an act which was done accidentally or deliberately, in which case the prisoner would not have been guilty. It appears from the case, however, that the prisoner had threatened his wife more than once, and that on this occasion he came home drunk, and used words which amounted to a threat against her life saying, 'I'll make you so that you can't go to bed;' that she rushing to the window got half out of the window when she was restrained by her daughter. The prisoner threatened the daughter, who let go, and her mother fell. It is suggested to me by my learned brother that, supposing the prisoner had struck his daughter's arm without hurting her but sufficiently to cause her to let go and she had let her mother fall, could anyone doubt but that that would be the same thing as if he had pushed her out himself? If a man creates in another man's mind an immediate sense of danger which causes such person to try to escape, and in so doing he injures himself, the person who creates such a state of mind is responsible for the injuries which result. I think that in this case there was abundant evidence that there was a sense of immediate danger in the mind of the woman caused by the acts of the prisoner, and that her injuries resulted from what such sense of danger caused her to do. I am therefore of opinion that the prisoner was rightly convicted, and that this conviction must be affirmed.

A defendant who has the *mens rea* for murder or manslaughter but does not cause death cannot be liable for the substantive crime (although there could be liability for attempted murder).

R v White
[1910] 2 KB 124, Court of Criminal Appeal

BRAY J: In this case the appellant was indicted for the murder of his mother and was convicted of an attempt to murder her and sentenced to penal servitude for life. He appeals from this conviction on several grounds, which we will deal with one by one. First it is said that there was no reasonable evidence on which he could be convicted, or, as it is put in s. 4 of the Criminal Appeal Act, that the verdict cannot be supported having regard to the evidence.

The evidence put shortly was this. On January 9 last the mother was found dead in a sitting posture on a sofa in a sitting-room in her house. There was a round table standing two feet from the sofa, on the further side of which was a wine glass three parts filled with a liquid made up of a drink called nectar and, as was afterwards shewn, containing two grains of cyanide of potassium. There were also on the table a nectar bottle, two lumps of sugar, and a spoon. There was no evidence to shew that she had taken any of this liquid, and the result of the post-mortem examination and of the analysis of the contents of the stomach and of the contents of the wine glass was to shew that she had not died from poisoning by cyanide of potassium, but that death was most probably caused by syncope or heart failure, due to fright or some other external cause.

Appeal dismissed.

R v Dalloway

(1847) 2 Cox CC 273, Stafford Crown Court

The prisoner was indicted for the manslaughter of one Henry Clarke, by reason of his negligence as driver of a cart.

It appeared that the prisoner was standing up in a spring-cart, and having the conduct of it along a public thoroughfare. The cart was drawn by one horse. The reins were not in the hands of the prisoner, but loose on the horse's back. While the cart was so proceeding down the slope of a hill, the horse trotting at the time, the deceased child, who was about three years of age, ran across the road before the horse, at the distance of a few yards, and one of the wheels of the cart knocking it down and passing over it, caused its death. It did not appear that the prisoner saw the child in the road before the accident.

Erle, J, in summing up to the jury, directed them that a party neglecting ordinary caution, and, by reason of that neglect, causing the death of another, is guilty of manslaughter; that if the prisoner had reins, and by using the reins could have saved the child, he was guilty of manslaughter; but that if they thought he could not have saved the child by pulling the reins, or otherwise by their assistance, they must acquit him.

The jury acquitted the prisoner.

QUESTIONS

1. In *White*, was the death caused by the victim's heart attack or by the defendant's action? What if it could be shown that the victim realised that the glass contained poison and, distraught that her child would contemplate killing her, suffered a fatal heart attack?

2. Dalloway clearly caused the death of the child. Why, then, did he escape criminal liability?

(b) *Acts of third parties*. The action or inaction of third parties is often claimed to be the cause of death, rather than the acts of the defendant. The medical cases were examined in Chapter 3, as was *R v Pagett*, involving the death of a 'human shield'. These cases should be reviewed in light of the above material on murder/manslaughter.

Where the death occurs in the manner intended, the unwitting intervention of a third party is generally deemed to be irrelevant.

R v Michael

(1840) 9 C & P 356, Central Criminal Court

It appeared that the deceased was a child between nine and ten months old, and that the prisoner was its mother, and was a single woman living in service as wet nurse at Mrs Kelly's, in Hunter Street, Brunswick Square. The child was taken care of by a woman named Stevens, living at Paddington, who received five shillings a week from the prisoner for its support. A few days before its death the prisoner told Mrs Stevens that she had an old frock for the child, and a bottle of medicine, which she gave her, telling her it would do the baby's bowels good. Mrs Stevens said the baby was very well, and did not want medicine; but the prisoner said it had done her mistress's baby good, and it would do her baby good, and desired Mrs Stevens to give it one tea-spoonful every night. Mrs Stevens did not open the bottle, or give the child any of its contents, but put the bottle on the mantel-piece, where it remained till Tuesday, the 31st of March, on which day, about half-past four in the afternoon, Mrs Stevens went out, leaving the prisoner's child playing on the floor with her children, one of whom, about five years of age, during the absence for about ten minutes of his elder sister, gave the prisoner's child about half the contents of the bottle, which made it extremely ill, and in the course of a few hours it died. The bottle was found to contain laudanum.

Alderson B, in his summing up, told the jury, that if the prisoner delivered the laudanum to Sarah Stevens with the intention that she should administer it to the child, and thereby produce its death, and the quantity so directed to be administered was sufficient to cause death, and while the prisoner's original intention continued, the laudanum was administered by an unconscious agent, the death of the child, under such circumstances, would sustain the charge of murder against the prisoner. His Lordship added, that if the tea-spoonful of laudanum was sufficient to produce death, the administration by the little boy of a much larger quantity would make no difference.

The jury found the prisoner guilty. . . .

At a subsequent Session, Mr Baron Alderson, in passing sentence upon the prisoner, said, that the Judges were of opinion that the administering of the poison by the child of Mrs Stevens, was, under the circumstances of the case, as much, in point of law, an administering by the prisoner as if the prisoner had actually administered it with her own hand. They therefore held that she was rightly convicted.

C: Jurisdiction

The normal territorial jurisdiction of the English courts has been extended for the offences of murder and manslaughter:

(a) A killing by a British citizen can found a conviction for murder or manslaughter whether the killing takes place in England or Wales or abroad (i.e. outside the normal territorial limits of the court's jurisdiction) (Offences Against the Person Act 1861, s. 9 and British Nationality Act 1948, s. 3). The defendant may also be subject to the jurisdiction of the courts in the territory where the killing takes place. However, while the government has proposed a crime of 'corporate killing', under which a company may be criminally liable where a management failure causes a death (see p. 265), it does not propose to hold a British company liable for a death occurring in another country and caused by one of the company's subsidiaries. Is this position reconcilable with killings committed abroad by individuals? See Gobert (2002) 'Corporate Killings at Home and Abroad – Refelections on the Government's Proposals' 118 LQR 72.

(b) Murder or manslaughter committed on a British ship or aircraft is triable in England or Wales whether the killing is committed by a British citizen or not.

(c) Murder *of* a British citizen committed abroad is *not* triable in England or Wales merely because of the nationality of the victim.

Where the crime is committed outside the jurisdiction of the courts of the United Kingdom and the offender is arrested where the crime is committed, it will be necessary to extradite the defendant if he or she is to stand trial in the United Kingdom. Although most countries will allow extradition for murder or manslaughter, it is not automatic. If the courts of the foreign jurisdiction conclude that the defendant will not receive a fair trial in the United Kingdom, they may refuse to order extradition. The relevance of the European Convention on Human Rights in this context is examined in *Soering* v *United Kingdom* (1989) 11 EHRR 439, where a German national sought to block the UK from extraditing him to the United States.

D: *Mens rea*

Under Coke's definition of murder (see p. 203 above), the prosecution must establish *malice aforethought*. The meaning of this concept must be gleaned from judicial pronouncements in decided cases as there is no statutory definition of the term. The courts have now settled that malice aforethought means an intention to kill any person or an intention to cause grievous bodily harm to any person. The meaning of intention was examined in Chapter 4 in *Moloney, Hancock and Shankland, Nedrick* and *Woollin*. These cases should be reviewed at this point.

NOTES AND QUESTIONS
1. In most cases the presence of an intention to kill will be clear. The probability of death or serious injury resulting from the actions of the defendant are not relevant where the defendant desires the death (see *Michael*, above).
2. Where the intention to kill or cause serious harm is not so clear the courts have held that the defendant's foresight of death or serious harm as a consequence of his actions is evidence of his intention to cause those consequences. The less likely he believes such an outcome to be, the weaker the inference of an intent to kill.
3. The alternative *mens rea* which will justify a conviction for murder is an intent to cause 'grievous bodily harm'. This is the 'implied malice' referred to in Coke's definition. See *Cunningham* [1982] AC 566. In *Director of Public Prosecutions* v *Smith* [1961] AC 290, 'grievous bodily harm' was explained as 'really serious harm'. Whether this clarification adds much to our understanding of the concept is debatable. The basic policy question presented is whether one who does not have the intent to kill should be subject to a conviction for murder. What is the justification for convicting in these circumstances? What are the arguments against? It should be recalled that in order to convict a defendant for attempted murder, the Crown must prove an intent to kill; an intent to commit grievous bodily harm is not sufficient.
4. For a discussion by one of the current Law Lords of some of the issues involved in *mens rea* in murder, see Goff, 'The mental element in the crime of murder' (1988) 104 LQR 30.
5. Both the Draft Criminal Code (Law Com. No. 177) and the Report of the Select Committee of the House of Lords on Murder and Life Imprisonment (HL Paper 78–1, 1989) suggested that this aspect of *mens rea* should be changed to 'intending to cause serious personal harm and being aware that he may cause death'. Would such a change make a difference as a matter of theory? As a matter of practice?
6. If there is an intent to cause serious harm, is it merely luck whether the victim lives or dies?

SECTION 3: Manslaughter

There are two categories of manslaughter, voluntary and involuntary. A killing which would otherwise be murder may be reduced to *voluntary manslaughter* if the jury consider that the defendant is entitled to rely on one of three statutory defences specific to murder. *Involuntary manslaughter* consists of all other killings which do not amount to murder, but for which a defendant is criminally liable. Unlike for murder, there is no mandatory sentence of life imprisonment for manslaughter.

A: Voluntary manslaughter

The Homicide Act 1957 establishes three murder-specific defences which will reduce murder to manslaughter. These are provocation, diminished responsibility, and suicide pact. The general defences discussed in Chapter 10 are also available to a defendant charged with murder, but if they succeed the defendant will be acquitted. In contrast, a successful defence of provocation, diminished responsibility or suicide pact will not lead to an acquittal, but only to a reduction in charge from murder to manslaughter.

(i) *Diminished responsibility*
The defence of diminished responsibility was established in the Homicide Act 1957, s. 2:

Homicide Act 1957

2.—(1) Where a person kills or is a party to the killing of another, he shall not be convicted of murder if he was suffering from such abnormality of mind (whether arising from a condition of arrested or retarded development or any inherent causes or induced by disease or injury) as substantially impaired his mental responsibility for his acts and omissions in doing or being a party to the killing.

(2) On a charge of murder, it shall be for the defence to prove that the person charged is by virtue of this section not liable to be convicted of murder.

(3) A person who but for this section would be liable, whether as principal or as accessory, to be convicted of murder shall be liable instead to be convicted of manslaughter.

(4) The fact that one party to a killing is by virtue of this section not liable to be convicted of murder shall not affect the question whether the killing amounted to murder in the case of any other party to it.

The burden of proving the defence rests on the defendant. The standard of proof required is a balance of probabilities (*Dunbar* [1958] 1 QB 1). Unlike in the case of insanity, the issue of diminished responsibility may not be raised by the prosecution; and, indeed, the judge cannot instruct the jury on the issue without the defendant's consent. See *Campbell* (1986) 84 Cr App R 255. The defence must be supported by medical or other scientific evidence.

R v Dix
(1982) 74 Cr App R 306, Court of Appeal

SHAW LJ: . . [Counsel] pointed out that there have been cases in which medical evidence was tendered by both defence and prosecution supporting a plea of diminished responsibility, but the jury rejected that evidence and convicted of murder. The history and circumstances of the offence were treated by the jury as having greater significance than the scientific evidence. If, so Mr Hamilton contended, a jury was entitled to act in that way and to convict of murder, why are they not entitled to come to a conclusion, one way or the other, as to diminished responsibility when there is no medical evidence at all?

The logic of this argument might be stronger if there was no onus on the defence to prove diminished responsibility. Having regard to that onus the argument must fail. In any case, it is inseparable from the proposition that the part of section 2(1) in parenthesis is descriptive of all forms of abnormality of the mind so that no proof is required that an accused's asserted abnormality of mind falls within the categories described within the brackets. Mr Hamilton's argument to this effect was cogent and almost persuasive but the judgment of the Court of Criminal Appeal in *Byrne* (1960) 44 Cr App R 246; [1960] 2 QB 396 is conclusive against his proposition. Giving the judgment of the Court, Lord Parker CJ said at p. 252 and p. 402 respectively: 'It is against that background of the existing law that section 2(1) of the Homicide Act 1957 falls to be construed. To satisfy the requirements of the subsection the accused must show: (a) that he was suffering from an abnormality of mind; and (b) that such abnormality of mind (i) arose from a condition of arrested or retarded development of mind or any inherent causes or was induced by disease or injury; and (ii) was such as substantially impaired his mental responsibility for his acts in doing or being a party to the killing.'

This analysis of the subsection has not been doubted or criticised. Notwithstanding Mr Hamilton's attractive argument, this Court sees no reason to qualify it in any way whatsoever. What emerges from Lord Parker's statement is that scientific evidence of a medical kind is essential to establish what is referred to in (b)(i) and (b)(ii). Thus while the subsection does not in terms require that medical evidence be adduced in support of a defence of diminished responsibility, it makes it a practical necessity if that defence is to begin to run at all. In the result, Griffith J's ruling was in substance a correct one. The appeal accordingly fails and is dismissed.

NOTES AND QUESTIONS

1. Why should the law require medical or other scientific evidence? Why should not the testimony of ordinary persons who observed the defendant at the time of the killing suffice?

2. One problem is that a medical examination may not occur until after arrest, which may be some time after the killing. The examining doctor must make an informed guess at the defendant's mental state at a previous point in time based on this later examination. A further complicating factor is that the killing itself may have had an effect on the defendant's mental state. Guilt about the killing may have exacerbated the defendant's condition, or conversely, the killing may have relieved the mental stress which gave rise to the urge to kill. In either case the doctor will not see the same person that he or she would have seen had the examination taken place prior to the killing.

Three major problems have been encountered in the use of the defence of diminished responsibility. The first is the definition of *abnormality of mind*; the second the relationship between the abnormality and the defendant's responsibility for the killing; and the third the relationship between diminished responsibility and other defences.

(a) *Abnormality of mind.* What constitutes 'abnormality of mind'? The leading case interpreting this phrase is *Byrne*.

R v Byrne

[1960] 2 QB 396, Court of Criminal Appeal

LORD PARKER CJ: . . . The appellant was convicted of murder before Stable J at Birmingham Assizes and sentenced to imprisonment for life. The victim was a young woman whom he strangled in the YWCA hostel, and after her death he committed horrifying mutilations upon her dead body. The facts as to the killing were not disputed, and were admitted in a long statement made by the accused. The only defence was that in killing his victim the accused was suffering from diminished responsibility as defined by section 2 of the Homicide Act, 1957, and was, accordingly, guilty not of murder but of manslaughter.

Three medical witnesses were called by the defence, the senior medical officer at Birmingham Prison and two specialists in psychological medicine. Their uncontradicted evidence was that the accused was a sexual psychopath, that he suffered from abnormality of mind, as indeed was abundantly clear from the other evidence in the case, and that such abnormality of mind arose from a condition of arrested or retarded development of mind or inherent causes. The nature of the abnormality of mind of a sexual psychopath, according to the medical evidence, is that he suffers from violent perverted sexual desires which he finds it difficult or impossible to control. Save when under the influence of his perverted sexual desires he may be normal. All three doctors were of opinion that the killing was done under the influence of his perverted sexual desires, and although all three were of opinion that he was not insane in the technical sense of insanity laid down in the M'Naughten Rules it was their view that his sexual psychopathy could properly be described as partial insanity.

. . .

'Abnormality of mind,' which has to be contrasted with the time-honoured expression in the M'Naughten Rules 'defect of reason,' means a state of mind so different from that of ordinary human beings that the reasonable man would term it abnormal. It appears to us to be wide enough to cover the mind's activities in all its aspects, not only the perception of physical acts and matters, and the ability to form a rational judgment as to whether an act is right or wrong, but also the ability to exercise will power to control physical acts in accordance with that rational judgment. The expression 'mental responsibility for his acts' points to a consideration of the extent to which the accused's mind is answerable for his physical acts which must include a consideration of the extent of his ability to exercise will power to control his physical acts.

Whether the accused was at the time of the killing suffering from any 'abnormality of mind' in the broad sense which we have indicated above is a question for the jury. On this question medical evidence is no doubt of importance, but the jury are entitled to take into consideration all the evidence, including the acts or statements of the accused and his demeanour. They are not bound to accept the medical evidence if there is other material before them which, in their good judgment, conflicts with it and outweighs it.

The aetiology of the abnormality of mind (namely, whether it arose from a condition of arrested or retarded development of mind or any inherent causes, or was induced by disease or injury) does, however, seem to be a matter to be determined on expert evidence.

Assuming that the jury are satisfied on the balance of probabilities that the accused was suffering from 'abnormality of mind' from one of the causes specified in the parenthesis of the subsection, the crucial question nevertheless arises: was the abnormality such as substantially impaired his mental responsibility for his acts in doing or being a party to the killing? This is a question of degree and essentially one for the jury. Medical evidence is, of course, relevant, but the question involves a decision not merely as to whether there was some impairment of the mental responsibility of the accused for his acts but whether such impairment can properly be called 'substantial,' a matter upon which juries may quite legitimately differ from doctors.

Furthermore, in a case where the abnormality of mind is one which affects the accused's self-control the step between 'he did not resist his impulse' and 'he could not resist his impulse' is, as the evidence in this case shows, one which is incapable of scientific proof. A fortiori there is no scientific measurement of the degree of difficulty which an abnormal person finds in controlling his impulses. These problem which in the present state of medical knowledge are scientifically insoluble, the jury can only approach in a broad, common-sense way. This court has repeatedly approved directions to the jury which have followed directions given in Scots cases where the doctrine of diminished responsibility forms part of the common law. We need not repeat them. They indicate that such abnormality as 'substantially impairs his mental responsibility' involves a mental state which in popular language (not that of the M'Naughten Rules) a jury would regard as amounting to partial insanity or being on the border-line of insanity.

NOTES AND QUESTIONS
1. Is the test of the *Byrne* court – that an abnormality of mind is 'a state of mind so different from that of ordinary human beings that the reasonable man would term it abnormal' – at all helpful? How could more in the way of guidance be provided to the jury?
2. Does the source of the abnormality of mind matter? A bracketed clause after the phrase 'abnormality of mind' in s. 2(1) states '(whether arising from a condition of arrested or retarded development of mind or any inherent causes or induced by disease or injury)'. What does this mean? Is a lay jury likely to understand? This leads to the question of whether and when a jury should be allowed to reject the medical testimony of abnormality of mind. Would it make more sense to allow this specific issue to be decided by a panel of medical experts? See generally R. Macay, 'The Abnormality of Mind Factor in Diminished Responsibiality' [1999] Crim LR 117.
3. The test of partial insanity referred to in *Byrne* should be approached with caution; it is not appropriate in all cases. See *R v Seers* (1984) 79 Cr App R 261.

(b) *Impaired responsibility for the killing.* Mere proof of abnormality of mind is not enough to establish the defence. The abnormality of mind must *substantially impair* the defendant's mental responsibility for his acts and omissions in doing or being a party to the killing. The problem with this formula is that it confuses two concepts: that of reduced capacity to control one's actions and that of moral culpability. The jury is asked to decide whether an abnormality has reduced the defendant's control over his actions and omissions and whether, as a consequence, his moral responsibility for the killing is reduced. Because of this difficulty and difficulties defining 'abnormality of mind' the defence has attracted much criticism. See, e.g., Griew, E., 'The future of diminished responsibility' [1988] Crim LR 75.

Rather than risk a lengthy and expensive prosecution for murder in which the defendant is likely to raise the defence of diminished responsibility, the Crown is often inclined to accept a plea of guilty to manslaughter.

NOTES AND QUESTIONS
1. The Butler Committee, examining the defence of diminished responsibility, found evidence that there was a tendency for the legal and medical professions to stretch the terms of s. 2 out of motives of humanity (see Cmnd 6244, 1975, para. 19.5).
2. As a practical matter, defendants charged with murder have historically been reluctant to raise a defence of insanity, as an acquittal on the grounds of insanity led to automatic committal to a mental institution for an indefinite period, potentially for life. It was partly in recognition of this fact that the defence of diminished responsibility was created. The Criminal Procedure (Insanity and Unfitness to Plead) Act 1991 (discussed in Chapter 9) does

away with automatic commitment. In the light of this development, is there any point in retaining the defence of diminished responsibility? To what extent do the two defences overlap?

(c) *Relationship with other defences.* In addition to any overlap between diminished responsibility and insanity (see above), the question often arises as to the relationship between diminished responsibility and other defences. What happens when there are multiple causes of the defendant's abnormal behaviour, one of which is outside those listed in the Homicide Act 1957, s. 2? The most common example is intoxication. This would seem to be excluded by the words in brackets in that section '(whether arising from a condition of arrested or retarded development of mind or any inherent causes or induced by disease or injury)'. However, alcoholism may give rise to an admissible abnormality if proof of brain damage is forthcoming.

In circumstances where the defendant is suffering from two causes of abnormality, one within the section and the other not, the usual approach adopted by the courts is to ask the jury to ignore the cause of abnormality outside the section and to try to assess the effects of the admissible abnormality. Clearly this is a difficult, if not near impossible, task.

R v Atkinson
[1985] Crim LR 314, Court of Appeal

The appellant, aged 18, together with other youths stole spirits which they drank and later burgled a house occupied by a 77 year old woman, who disturbed them and shouted for help. The appellant threatened to kill her if she did not stop shouting, punched her in the back of the head and then beat her including stamping on her face and she died of a fractured skull. In February 1984 he was tried on a charge of murder. He did not give evidence and a defence of diminished responsibility was advanced. Medical evidence was that he had grossly arrested or retarded development of mind and that alcohol had played a part in the events. The jury were directed to pose themselves the questions, first, whether they thought it more probable than not at the time of the killing his responsibility was substantially impaired by the fact that he was suffering from arrested or retarded development; and, if they thought that drink had something to do with it, secondly, whether that was the substantial cause, the root cause, of his inability to control himself at the time of the killing. He was convicted of murder. He appealed on the ground of misdirection on diminished responsibility.

Held, dismissing the appeal, that at the trial in February the trial judge had, so to speak, to anticipate what the Court of Appeal would say in *R v Gittens* [1984] QB 698. *Gittens* was reported and commented on by Professor J. C. Smith at [1984] Crim LR 553–554, where he stated that the two questions for the jury, in logical sequence, would seem to be: 'Have the defence satisfied you on the balance of probabilities – that if the defendant had not taken drink – (i) he would have killed as he in fact did? And (ii) he would have been under diminished responsibility when he did so?' The Court would like respectfully and gratefully to agree with Professor Smith's analysis, which put the matter clearly and in a way which could be understood by all. In the direction to the jury the judge was, in effect, posing the questions posed by Professor Smith in his commentary, although the other way round. The question for the jury was: if the appellant had not taken drink would he have killed as in fact did? The jury were entitled to answer the question as they had. The direction of the authorities was to be drawn to the medical reports, which were ordered to be appended to the transcript.

NOTES AND QUESTIONS

1. The Criminal Law Revision Committee in its 'Fourteenth Report: Offences Against the Person' (Cmnd 7844) recommended a revision of the defence of diminished responsibility. The Law Commission in its Draft Criminal Code Bill 1989 largely adopted the suggested revisions. Clause 56 of the Draft Code provides:

56.—(1) A person who, but for this section, would be guilty of murder is not guilty of murder if, at the time of his act, he is suffering from such mental abnormality as is a substantial enough reason to reduce his offence to manslaughter.

(2) In this section 'mental abnormality' means mental illness, arrested or incomplete development of mind, psychopathic disorder, and any other disorder or disability of mind, except intoxication.

(3) Where a person suffering from mental abnormality is also intoxicated, this section applies only where it would apply if he were not intoxicated.

The proposed formulation has the advantage of:

(a) requiring the defendant only to raise evidence of diminished responsibility rather than prove it on a balance of probabilities as at present;

(b) providing a clearer definition of the states of mind covered, using terms more readily understood by the medical profession;

(c) disentangling the medical issue as to whether the defendant is suffering from abnormality (which will remain a matter for medical testimony) and the moral issue of the effect of that abnormality on the defendant's moral responsibility. The latter is a matter clearly put within the jury's domain by cl. 56(1).

There are, unfortunately, no moves at present to implement the proposed reform.

2. To a large extent the defence of diminished responsibility owes its existence to the fact that the mandatory sentence for murder is life imprisonment. If the defence did not exist, a judge in sentencing could not take into account extenuating cirumstances such as the defendant's mental state at the time of the crime. Would the Butler Committee's suggestion of abolition of the mandatory life sentence be an acceptable alternative solution to the problems encountered in this area?

3. *Atkinson* was approved in *R v Egan* [1993] Crim LR 131. The question remains, however, whether juries can realistically be expected to disentangle different causes of abnormality.

(ii) *Provocation*

Provocation was a defence at common law, but was modified by the Homicide Act 1957, s. 3:

Homicide Act 1957

3. Where on a charge of murder there is evidence on which the jury can find that the person charged was provoked (whether by things done or by things said or by both together) to lose his self-control, the question whether the provocation was enough to make a reasonable man do as he did shall be left to be determined by the jury; and in determining that question the jury shall take into account everything both done and said according to the effect which, in their opinion, it would have on a reasonable man.

Like diminished responsibility, the defence of provocation is *only* a partial defence and *only* a defence to a charge of murder. Provocation is not a defence to lesser crimes, even attempted murder. However, provoked killings have long been thought to be qualitatively different and less reprehensible than other killings. The effect of successfully pleading provocation is to reduce one's crime from murder to manslaughter. Unlike in diminished responsibility, the defendant needs only introduce some evidence of provocation to force the prosecution to prove beyond reasonable doubt that the defendant was not provoked.

R v Cascoe
[1970] 2 All ER 833, Court of Appeal

SALMON LJ: . . . At about 5.00 am on 19th January 1969 a party was still going on at a dance hall somewhere in north London. At that late or early hour a man called 'Manny' Francis, with three or four other guests, arrived at the party. The appellant had been there for some time. Very shortly after Mr Francis arrived, there was a good deal of evidence that the appellant shot Mr Francis. He was seen with a smoking pistol in his hand. The evidence showed conclusively that he shot Mr Francis no fewer than seven times and that as a result Mr Francis died.

According to the case for the prosecution, the appellant had come to that dance hall armed with the pistol. Evidence had been called of persons who had seen him with the pistol prior to 19th January 1969. The appellant, however, when he gave evidence, said that it was entirely untrue to say that he had ever possessed that pistol or any other. His case was that shortly after he arrived at the dance hall he saw Mr Francis, whom he had known for some two years and with whom he was on very bad terms owing to an association which the appellant had previously formed with Mr Francis's stepdaughter. Indeed, on one occasion Mr Francis had attacked him with a knife. According to the appellant, Mr Francis came up to him, put his hand in his pocket as if to produce a pistol and then half drew a pistol from his pocket. The appellant, who said that he was a karate expert, acted very promptly. He administered what is called a karate chop just above Mr Francis's right wrist which caused him to drop the pistol on the floor. The appellant then picked up the pistol. As he did so, so he said, he saw four or five of Mr Francis's cronies advancing towards him. According to the appellant, he knew that they were all violent men and carried knives, whereupon in order to defend himself and to dissuade Mr Francis's cronies from attacking him with their knives, he fired at Mr Francis and hit him with all seven shots. There was no suggestion by the appellant that he fired at Mr Francis other than with the intention of hitting him.

The defence that was run at the trial was based on three grounds: first of all, that the appellant was suffering from diminished responsibility; secondly, that he was acting in self-defence; thirdly, that if the actions which he took exceeded what could reasonably be done by way of self-defence, the jury would be entitled to find the appellant guilty of manslaughter.

. . .

I now turn to the only real point made on behalf of the appellant on this appeal, and it concerns provocation. It should be noted that this was never run by the defence at the trial. Nevertheless, it is quite plain that although the defence is not run at the trial, the judge, if he considers that there is evidence on which a jury might reasonably, and I repeat the word 'might', find provocation, has a duty to leave that issue to the jury. The learned recorder clearly thought that there was some evidence on which a jury might reasonably find provocation which would reduce the appellant's crime from murder to manslaughter.

The complaint that is made of the recorder's direction on provocation is as follows. Counsel for the appellant says that when the recorder came to deal with provocation, he explained the law in relation to provocation with complete accuracy except in one important respect. He failed to tell the jury, as he had done when he dealt with self-defence, that from beginning to end the onus lay on the Crown, that it was not for the appellant to prove provocation, but that if, at the end of the day, the jury were left in any reasonable doubt by the evidence whether the appellant had been provoked, then they should acquit him of murder and find him guilty of manslaughter.

. . .

It seems to this court that the evidence of provocation was extremely tenuous. On the other hand, we consider it impossible to say that there was no evidence of provocation. All matters of fact were for the jury to decide.

. . . It seems to this court that a jury might have come to the conclusion that acts done by Mr Francis in those circumstances so frightened and angered the appellant that he lost all control of himself and took up the gun, and in a passion fired it at Mr Francis. We are far from saying that it is probable that the jury would have taken that view. All that we conclude is that there was evidence on which they could have taken that view. If they could have taken that view, then the question whether the provocation was enough to make a reasonable man do as the appellant did had to be left to be determined by the jury. It was left, and no one in all the circumstances here can criticise the learned recorder for leaving that question to the jury. Having left it to the jury, it was essential that they should have been given a correct direction on where the burden of proof lay so far as provocation was concerned.

. . . Whether the issue is raised at the trial or not, if there is evidence which might lead the jury to find provocation, then it is the duty of the court to leave that issue to the jury. The evidence in this case was very thin indeed. The very experienced recorder, however, considered that there was some evidence or he would not have left that issue to the jury. We cannot disagree with him in the view which he took on that point. It follows from what has been said that since there was the oversight in the summing-up to which reference has been made, the appeal must be allowed and a verdict of manslaughter substituted for the verdict of murder.

NOTES AND QUESTIONS

1. Note that defendants who raise the issue of provocation are not saying that they did not have an intent to kill or cause grievous bodily harm. Rather they are saying that they did so in a situation where they were provoked to the point that they lost self-control.
2. Why should not the burden of persuading the jury of the defence of provocation be on the defendant, as it is with diminished responsibility?
3. Cascoe underlines the fact that the issue of provocation must be left to the jury even when the defence does not put forward evidence of provocation as such. For affirmation of this in a case involving joint enterprise, see *R v Marks* [1998] Crim LR 676. This situation may arise when the main plank of the defence is self-defence rather than provocation:

R v Johnson
[1989] 1 WLR 740, Court of Appeal

WATKINS LJ: . . . The deceased died during the night of 18/19 May 1987 in a night club in Sheffield when the appellant stabbed him in the chest with a knife. The blade of the knife, 3.8 inches long, penetrated the chest to the heart. The wound, there was but one, travelled from the deceased's left to right parallel with the ground. There were no defensive wounds on the deceased.

During the evening both the appellant and the deceased had been drinking at the night club. The appellant was carrying a knife. It was a flick or 'swish' knife. The deceased was unarmed. A tense atmosphere developed in the club when the appellant started to behave in an unpleasant way. Threats of violence were made by him to a female friend of the deceased and then to the deceased himself. This woman and the deceased became extremely annoyed. A struggle developed between the two men during the course of which the stabbing occurred.

. . .

It was accepted before us by counsel for the Crown that the evidence before the jury included the following. Before the stabbing incident the appellant had been taunted by a woman who called him a 'white nigger'. Apparently, although a white man himself, he affected at times a West Indian accent. He reacted to that abuse. It upset him. It made him angry. There were high words between him and others, the deceased included. Seemingly to leave the club or that part of it, the appellant walked away towards the exit. The deceased however followed him and poured beer over him. The deceased then removed his jacket. The appellant did not. The deceased by placing his arm across the appellant's chest or throat seized hold of the appellant and pinned him against a wall. While he was thus pinned against the wall the woman, who had described him as a 'white nigger,' attacked him by punching his head and pulling his hair. There were shouts from some of the others present that the deceased should drop the glass which he held in his hand. He did so. Until this moment the appellant had not retaliated. But his attitude to being held captive suddenly changed. He somehow bent down and produced the knife and lunged at the deceased with it. He lunged again, so it was said, but failed to make contact. He was restrained by one of his friends. His explanation for his conduct was, as has been stated, a fear of being 'glassed'. He did not, as has also been stated, claim that he had lost his self-control.

Nevertheless, if the jury rejected, as they did, his account that he was acting in self-defence they might, in our judgement, very well have inferred from all that evidence that there had indeed been a sudden loss of self-control.

That evidence may not have been powerfully suggestive of provocation. But it was, in our view, rather more than tenuous. It is easily conceivable, we think, that the jury, if directed on the issue, would have come to the conclusion that the appellant was so provoked as to reduce murder to manslaughter. Therefore, subject only to the question of self-induced provocation referred to by the judge, in our judgment this defence should have been left to the jury.

. . . In view of the express wording of section 3, as interpreted in *R* v *Camplin* [1978] AC 705 which was decided after *Edwards* v *The Queen* [1973] AC 648, we find it impossible to accept that the mere fact that a defendant caused a reaction in others, which in turn led him to lose his self-control, should result in the issue of provocation being kept outside a jury's consideration. Section 3 clearly provides that the question is whether things done or said or both provoked the defendant to lose his self-control. If there is any evidence that it may have done, the issue must be left to the jury. The jury would then have to consider all the circumstances of the incident, including all the relevant behaviour of the defendant, in deciding (a) whether he was in fact provoked and (b) whether the provocation was enough to make a reasonable man do what the defendant did.

Accordingly, whether or not there were elements in the appellant's conduct which justified the conclusion that he had started the trouble and induced others, including the deceased, to react in the way they did, we are firmly of the view that the defence of provocation should have been left to the jury.

Since it is not possible for us to infer from their verdict that the jury inevitably would have concluded that provocation as well as self-defence had been disproved the verdict of murder will be set aside. A conviction for manslaughter on the basis of provocation will be substituted.

The defence of provocation contains a subjective and an objective component. To succeed the defendant must produce some evidence that:

(a) he was provoked to lose his self-control; and

(b) the provocation was enough to make a reasonable man lose self-control and do as the defendant did.

The subjective element should not be overlooked. If a reasonable man would have been driven wild with rage by the provoking act, but the defendant was not in fact provoked, the defence will not succeed. Why should this be so?

The objective element presents the jury with a conundrum. Section 3 speaks in terms of the provocation being 'enough to make a reasonable man do as he [the defendant] did'. But arguably, reasonable men do not kill; and if reasonable men do kill, why should the defendant be punished for doing only what other reasonable men would do in his place? Yet the fact remains that provocation is not a complete defence. On this issue Consider Lord Hoffman's judgment in *R* v *Smith* (below). Does Lord Hoffman manage to avoid this difficulty?

What is clear is that s. 3 modified the common law by laying greater emphasis on the role of the jury. Prior to passage of the section it was possible for a judge to withdraw the defence from jury consideration if the judge formed the opinion that there was no evidence that a reasonable man would have been provoked in the circumstances. This led to some curious case law on the reactions of the reasonable man (see, e.g., *Mancini* v *Director of Public Prosecutions* [1942] AC 1). Section 3 specifically provides that where there is evidence that the defendant himself was provoked, the question as to the reaction of the reasonable man must be left to the jury.

(a) *What constitutes provocation?* Prior to passage of the Homicide Act 1957, the judges developed narrow and fairly rigid categories of provocation. The Act opted in favour of a more flexible approach. Section 3 refers to provocation by 'things done or by things said or by both together'. Any words or action *may* thus constitute provocation, even a lawful act by an innocent party. In *Doughty* (1986) 83 Cr App R 319, the alleged provocation was the crying and restlessness of the defendant's 17-day-old baby. The defendant gave evidence that this behaviour had caused him to lose his self-control and kill the child. The judge refused to leave the issue of provocation to the jury. The Court of Appeal quashed the resultant conviction for murder on the grounds that the issue should have been left to the jury.

However, there must be evidence of provoking words or acts and not simply evidence that the defendant was provoked.

R v *Acott*
[1997] 1 All ER 706, House of Lords

LORD STEYN: . . . The trial took place in June 1995 before the Recorder of London. The prosecution case was as follows. In 1993 he appellant lived with his mother. He was 48 years old and his mother was 78 years of age. At 9.15 pm on 17 February 1993 the appellant, in a state of agitation, telephoned for an ambulance. He said that his mother had been injured as the result of a fall. The ambulance men met the appellant in his mother's bungalow and found the deceased dead on the floor of the hallway. An examination showed that the deceased had sustained multiple injuries, particularly in the area of the head, face and neck.

The appellant was of good character. He was a mild man. He worked until 1991 when he gave up his job and moved to Rainham to live with his mother. The appellant tried to obtain another job but he was unsuccessful. After exhausting his savings he became financially dependent on his mother. He found his dependence on his mother somewhat irksome. But in his interviews and at the trial he repeatedly said he was very fond of his mother. There was other evidence to the same effect. In accordance with a recent will of his mother he was her sole beneficiary.

When questioned by the police, and at the trial, the appellant consistently denied that he was responsible for his mother's death. He said his mother had come to his bedroom to say 'goodnight' and almost immediately afterwards he heard her fall. He said he tried to help her but she fell again. He tried to pick her up and she again fell heavily. He tried to resuscitate her, he thumped her chest and slapped her face in an effort to bring her round. He said her injuries had been caused by her falls and his unskilled efforts to resuscitate her.

Three pathologists testified: two pathologists, with varying degrees of emphasis, said that the deceased died as a result of a sustained attack, and a third pathologist testifying on behalf of the defence said the injuries were explicable on the basis of the defendant's account.

The appellant's case at the trial was therefore that he had not attacked his mother and that he was entitled to a complete acquittal. Counsel in their speeches and the recorder in his summing up treated it as a case involving a single issue. The recorder directed the jury that 'This is murder or nothing'. The jury rejected the appellant's explanation and, having been given the directions required by law in regard to burden and standard of proof, the jury convicted the appellant of murder by a majority verdict.

The evidence said to justify a direction on provocation

It is now possible to summarise the materials relied on by the appellant in support of the argument before the Court of Appeal, which was repeated before your Lordships' House, that the judge ought to have left provocation as an issue to the jury. First, counsel for the appellant pointed out correctly that leading counsel for the Crown had repeatedly put to the appellant in cross-examination that he had lost his self-control and attacked his mother. Counsel for the Crown cross-examined on the basis that the appellant had been angered by his mother treating him like a little boy and berating him. Counsel for the appellant submitted that the Crown had made provocation an issue and that accordingly the judge should have summed up on provocation. Instead, counsel for the appellant said, the judge reminded the jury of these passages in the evidence but failed to leave the issue of provocation to the jury.

Counsel for the appellant further argued that the extent of the injuries to the deceased was testimony to a frenzied attack which was prima facie indicative of a loss of self-control. Moreover, counsel argued that this inference was reinforced by the cumulative effect of the following factors: the appellant was unemployed; he was in the humiliating position of having to ask his mother for money; the evidence was that she sometimes treated him like a little boy; she was given to black moods; and apparently sometimes she drank excessively.

. . .

The proposition that the Crown made provocation an issue

Counsel for the appellant argued that the Crown made provocation an issue by putting to him in cross-examination that he attacked his mother as a result of a loss of self-control caused by momentary anger at the way in which his mother treated him. The appellant throughout denied these suggestions, and he insisted that his relationship with his mother was good and that she had done nothing to anger him. The cross-examination produced no evidence of provoking conduct or of a loss of self-control. In deciding what issues must be left to the jury a judge must be guided by the state of the evidence. Suggestions in cross-examination cannot by themselves raise an issue of provocation where the evidence, on the most favourable view for the defendant, reveals no issue. It follows that I would reject this way of putting the appellant's case.

The relevant evidence

The disposal of the appeal therefore depends on the state of the evidence. Like Rougier J I am willing to infer from the injuries of the deceased that there was a reasonable possibility that the appellant lost his self-control and attacked his mother in anger. But by itself that is not enough. The question is whether there is any evidence of specific provoking conduct. As the issues became refined during the helpful oral submissions of both counsel, it became clear that counsel for the appellant was submitting in this part of his argument that from the fact of loss of self-control and the evidence that the appellant was sometimes treated by his mother as a little boy it is a rational inference that the appellant's loss of self-control might have followed upon a specific provoking element albeit perhaps of a trivial and 'last straw' variety. Subject to his earlier argument already discussed, counsel for the appellant accepted that if such an inference is not justified, the appeal must fail. In my judgment that concession was rightly made. It is a short point not of law but of logic and common sense. The recorder plainly took the view that the evidence did not justify an inference of a specific provoking event. In my view the evidence was insufficient to support the suggested inference. It was not a reasonable possibility arising on the evidence: it was mere speculation. In these circumstances the appeal must fail on the facts.

. . . Section 3 is only applicable 'if there is evidence . . . that the person charged was provoked (whether by things done or things said or by both together) to lose his self-control'. A loss of self-control caused by fear, panic, sheer bad temper or circumstances (e.g. a slow down of traffic due to snow) would not be enough. There must be some evidence tending to show that the killing might have been an uncontrolled reaction to provoking conduct rather than an act of revenge. . . .

. . . It follows that there can only be an issue of provocation to be considered by the jury if the judge considers that there is some evidence of a specific act or words of provocation resulting in a loss of self-control. It does not matter from what source that evidence emerges or whether it is relied on at trial by the defendant or not. If there is such evidence, the judge must leave the issue to the jury. If there is no such evidence, but merely the speculative possibility that there had been an act of provocation, it is wrong for the judge to direct the jury to consider provocation. In such a case there is simply no triable issue of provocation. . . .

It is now clear that any person's (and not just the victim's) actions or words may constitute provocation. It is therefore incorrect for a judge to instruct the jury to consider only the victim's behaviour.

The conviction was quashed. The case was remitted to the Court of Appeal in the Bahamas to determine if a retrial should take place.

R v Davies

[1975] 1 QB 691, Court of Appeal

LORD WIDGERY CJ: . . . The defendant killed his wife by shooting her in the presence of her lover. The only issue in the court below was whether the charge should have been reduced to manslaughter on account of provocation. The contention of the defendant is that in directing the jury as to provocation the judge excluded provocation from any source other than from the victim, that is to say, other than the wife. The question is whether that exclusion was justified or not.

. . . [I]t seems quite clear to us that we should construe section 3 as providing a new test, and on that test that we should give the wide words of section 3 their ordinary wide meaning. Thus we come to the conclusion that whatever the position at common law, the situation since 1957 has been that acts or words otherwise to be treated as provocative for present purposes are not excluded from such consideration merely because they emanate from someone other than the victim.

NOTES AND QUESTIONS
1. Note that in *Acott* the court did not decide that the defence of provocation had succeeded, merely that there was sufficient evidence to leave the defence to the jury.
2. While 'any person's' acts or behaviour may constitute provocation, what of natural events? Marion returns home to find her house has been struck by lightning and has burned to the ground. In her rage at this development she throws her child to the ground with fatal results. Has there been provocation that the law will recognise? Should the law recognise this type of provocation?
3. What if in the preceding example the house had been destroyed by a terrorist bomb? Again an out-of-control Marion throws her child to the ground with fatal results. Will her defence of provocation succeed, or is there (should there be) a requirement that the *actus reus* be directed at the provoker?

(b) *The objective prong.*

Director of Public Prosecutions v Camplin
[1978] AC 705, House of Lords

LORD DIPLOCK: My Lords, for the purpose of answering the question of law upon which this appeal will turn only a brief account is needed of the facts that have given rise to it. The respondent, Camplin, who was 15 years of age, killed a middle-aged Pakistani, Mohammed Lal Khan, by splitting his skull with a chapati pan, a heavy kitchen utensil like a rimless frying pan. At the time, the two of them were alone together in Khan's flat. At Camplin's trial for murder before Boreham J his only defence was that of provocation so as to reduce the offence to manslaughter. According to the story that he told in the witness box but which differed materially from that which he had told to the police, Khan had buggered him in spite of his resistance and had then laughed at him. Whereupon Camplin had lost his self-control and attacked Khan fatally with the chapati pan.

In his address to the jury on the defence of provocation Mr Baker, who was counsel for Camplin, had suggested to them that when they addressed their minds to the question whether the provocation relied on was enough to make a reasonable man do as Camplin had done, what they ought to consider was not the reaction of a reasonable adult but the reaction of a reasonable boy of Camplin's age. The judge thought that this was wrong in law. So in his summing up he took pains to instruct the jury that they must consider whether:

... the provocation was sufficient to make a reasonable man in like circumstances act as the defendant did. Not a reasonable boy, as Mr Baker would have it, or a reasonable lad; it is an objective test – a reasonable man.

The jury found Camplin guilty of murder. On appeal the Court of Appeal (Criminal Division) allowed the appeal and substituted a conviction for manslaughter upon the ground that the passage I have cited from the summing up was a misdirection. The court held that

... the proper direction to the jury is to invite the jury to consider whether the provocation was enough to have made a reasonable person of the same age as the defendant in the same circumstances do as he did.

The point of law of general public importance involved in the case has been certified as being:

Whether on the prosecution for murder of a boy of 15, where the issue of provocation arises, the jury should be directed to consider the question under section 3 of the Homicide Act 1957 whether the provocation was enough to make a reasonable man do as he did by reference to a 'reasonable adult' or by reference to a 'reasonable boy of 15.'

... [F]or the purposes of the law of provocation the 'reasonable man' has never been confined to the adult male. It means an ordinary person of either sex, not exceptionally excitable or pugnacious, but possessed of such powers of self-control as everyone is entitled to expect that his fellow citizens will exercise in society as it is today. . . . now that the law has been changed so as to permit of words being treated as provocation even though unaccompanied by any other acts, the gravity of verbal provocation may well depend upon the particular characteristics or circumstances of the person to whom a taunt or insult is addressed. To taunt a person because of his race, his physical infirmities or some shameful incident in his past may well be considered by the jury to be more offensive to the person addressed, however equable his temperament, if the facts on which the taunt is founded are true than it would be if they were not. It would stultify much of the mitigation of the previous harshness of the common law in ruling out verbal provocation as capable of reducing murder to manslaughter if the jury could not take into consideration all those factors which in their opinion would affect the gravity of taunts or insults when applied to the person whom they are addressed.

. . .

That he was only 15 years of age at the time of the killing is the relevant characteristic of the accused in the instant case. It is a characteristic which may have its effects on temperament as well as physique. If the jury think that the same power of self-control is not to be expected in an ordinary, average or normal boy of 15 as in an older person, are they to treat the lesser powers of self-control possessed by an ordinary, average or normal boy of 15 as the standard of self-control with which the conduct of the accused is to be compared?

. . .

In my opinion a proper direction to a jury on the question left to their exclusive determination by section 3 of the Act of 1957 would be on the following lines. The judge should state what the question is using the very terms of the section. He should then explain to them that the reasonable man referred to in the question is a person having the power of self-control to be expected of an ordinary person of the sex and age of the accused, but in other respects sharing such of the accused's characteristics as they think would affect the gravity of the provocation to him; and that the question is not merely whether such a person would in like circumstances be provoked to lose his self-control but also whether he would react to the provocation as the accused did.

I accordingly agree with the Court of Appeal that the judge ought not to have instructed the jury to pay no account to the age of the accused even though they themselves might be of opinion that the degree of self-control to be expected in a boy of that age was less than in an adult. So to direct them was to impose a fetter on the right and duty of the jury which the Act accords to them to act upon their own opinion on the matter.

I would dismiss this appeal.

The characteristic to be attributed to the reasonable man must be relevant to the provocation; taunting a one-armed man about his lack of a sense of humour would not be regarded as provoking behaviour. As the reasonable man is deemed to be sober, the defendant's voluntary intoxication will also be ignored. What remains unclear is the extent to which any mental characteristics are to be attributed to the person envisaged by the objective test.

R v Smith (Morgan)

[2000] 3 WLR 654, House of Lords

LORD HOFFMANN: My Lords,

1. *The facts*

On a November evening in 1996 Morgan Smith received a visit from his old friend James McCullagh. They were both alcoholics and spent the evening in drinking and recrimination. Smith had grievances against McCullagh, some of which went back many years. The most recent was his belief that McCullagh had stolen the tools of his trade as a carpenter and sold them to buy drink. McCullagh's repeated denials only inflamed Smith further. A friend arrived to find the row in full swing. While the friend was using the lavatory, Smith took up a kitchen knife and stabbed McCullagh several times. One of the blows was fatal.

Smith was indicted on a charge of murder before Judge Coombe and a jury. His defences were, first, that he did not intend to kill or cause grievous bodily harm; secondly, that he was suffering from diminished responsibility and thirdly that he was acting under provocation. The jury rejected all three defences and convicted Smith of murder. It is accepted that no criticism can be made of the judge's summing-up on the first two defences. The question is whether he gave the jury the correct directions on the law of provocation.

. . .

The question which came before the House in *Reg*. v *Camplin* [1978] AC 705 was whether by implication [section 3 of the Homicide Act 1957] had also changed a third common law doctrine. This was the rule in *Bedder* [1954] 1 WLR 1119 which required the 'reasonable person' to be devoid of any particular characteristics. The accused was a youth of 15 who claimed that he had been provoked to kill an older man by sexual abuse and taunting. The judge had directed the jury that they should consider what effect the provocation would have had upon a reasonable person of full age. The House decided that since provocation by words was frequently directed at some characteristic of the accused, such as his past behaviour, disabilities or race, the change in the law which allowed such taunts or insults to constitute provocation would be ineffectual if the accused had to be assumed to lack such a characteristic. It was therefore decided that, at least for the purpose of considering the gravity of the provocation, the reasonable man should normally be assumed to share the relevant characteristics of the accused. Whether the decision went further and allowed the jury to take into account characteristics of the accused which affected his powers of self-control is the chief question in this appeal and, in order to answer it, I shall have to analyse the case later in more detail. It can however be said that *Camplin* [1978] AC 705 allowed at least one such character-istic to be taken into account, namely, the youth of the accused. The actual decision was that the jury should have been told to consider what the effect of the provocation would have been upon a person with the powers of self-control of a reasonable boy of 15 and not those of a grown-up.

The extent to which matters affecting the power of self-control should be taken into account divided the Judicial Committee of the Privy Council in *Luc Thiet Thuan* v *The Queen* [1997] AC 131. The majority, in an opinion given by Lord Goff of Chieveley, decided that in principle the actual characteristics of the accused were relevant only to the gravity of the provocation. The only charac-teristics of the accused which could be attributed to the reasonable person for the purpose of expressing a standard of self-control were his or her age and sex. There had been evidence that the accused suffered from brain damage which made it difficult for him to control his impulses in response to minor provocation. But this was held irrelevant to the question of whether the objective element in the defence had been satisfied. The majority said that the English cases after *Camplin* (to some of which I shall later refer) which had held that the jury should be directed that they could take such matters into account, had been wrongly decided. Lord Steyn, in a minority opinion, said that the later cases were not inconsistent with *Camplin*, constituted a logical extension of its reasoning and were in accordance with justice and common sense.

3. *The trial, summing-up and appeal*
In the present case there was psychiatric evidence on both sides. It dealt mainly with the question of whether Smith was suffering from diminished responsibility but the expert witnesses also con-sidered his susceptibility to react to provocation. A psychiatrist called by the defence, who had seen Smith in prison less than a fortnight after the offence, said that he was suffering from an abnormality of the mind, namely depression, which could reduce his 'threshold for erupting with violence.' Another said that he was suffering from clinical depression which made him 'more disinhibited', i.e. less able to control his reactions.

The judge . . . told the jury that if they considered that the accused might have been suffering from a depressive illness, they should decide whether a man suffering from such illness, but with a reasonable man's powers of self-control, might have responded to McCullagh's behaviour by stabbing him to death. The fact that the depressive illness may have reduced Smith's own powers of self-control was 'neither here nor there' and should not be taken into account.

In *Reg.* v *Campbell* [1997] 1 Cr App R 199 the Court of Appeal considered the majority opinion in *Luc Thiet Thuan* v *The Queen* [1997] AC 131 and held that, unless your Lordships' House decided otherwise, it would continue to follow its earlier decisions and the minority opinion of Lord Steyn. In the Court of Appeal in the present case Potts J gave a careful judgment explaining why he considered that those decisions were correct. The court therefore allowed the appeal and substituted a verdict of manslaughter. But in view of the state of the authorities it gave leave to appeal and certified the following point of law of general public importance:

> Are characteristics other than age and sex, attributable to a reasonable man, for the purpose of section 3 of the Homicide Act 1957, relevant not only to the gravity of the provocation to him but also to the standard of self-control to be expected?

4. *The historical background*

My Lords, it is impossible to read even a selection of the extensive modern literature on provocation without coming to the conclusion that the concept has serious logical and moral flaws. But your Lordships must take the law as it stands. Whatever your decision in this case, the result is not likely to be wholly satisfactory. The doctrine of provocation has always been described as a concession to human frailty and the law illustrates Kant's dictum that, from the crooked timber of humanity, nothing completely straight can be made. Nevertheless, I shall suggest to your Lordships that this appeal offers an opportunity, within the constraints imposed by history and by Parliament, to make some serviceable improvements.

The researches of Dr Horder (*Provocation and Responsibility*, (1992)) show that although the doctrine has much earlier roots, it emerged in recognisably modern form in the late 17th and early 18th centuries. It comes from a world of Restoration gallantry in which gentlemen habitually carried lethal weapons, acted in accordance with a code of honour which required insult to be personally avenged by instant angry retaliation and in which the mandatory penalty for premeditated murder was death. To show anger 'in hot blood' for a proper reason by an appropriate response was not merely permissible but the badge of a man of honour. The human frailty to which the defence of provocation made allowance was the possibility that the man of honour might overreact and kill when a lesser retaliation would have been appropriate. Provided that he did not grossly overreact in the extent or manner of his retaliation, the offence would be manslaughter and execution avoided.

. . .

6. *The construction of section 3*

As I have already said, the issue in *Camplin* [1978] AC 705 was whether, in addition to the two express changes in the law made by the statute concerning the provinces of judge and jury and the status of words as provocation, there was by necessary implication a change in the concept of the reasonable man as formulated in *Bedder* [1954] 1 WLR 1119. I shall in due course analyse the answer which the House gave to that question. But before doing so, I shall consider what seems to me, apart from authority, to have been the effect of the Act.

My Lords, if one reads the debates touching upon this subject in your Lordships House during the passage of the bill, there can be no doubt that Lord Kilmuir, the Lord Chancellor, was of opinion that the clause made no change in the concept of the reasonable man. That merely shows how unhelpful such debates often are as a guide to construction. Lord Kilmuir had not thought through the consequences of the changes made by the section in the way in which the House had to do in *Camplin*. If one approaches the question of construction in the orthodox way, namely by considering the language of the section against the background of the common law of provocation, one has to conclude that the concept of the reasonable man as a touchstone of the objective element could not have been intended to stay the same.

The reasons are to be found in both the other changes expressly made by the section. The first, namely the admission of words as a legitimate source of provocation, I have already mentioned. It was this reason which received the main emphasis in *Camplin*. But the other change, in the respective roles of judge and jury, was equally important. The Royal Commission, it will be remembered, said (at para. 134) that a change in the law was unnecessary because juries, some-times in the face of the judge's directions on the law, returned verdicts of manslaughter in cases in which justice appeared to require a concession to human frailty. That is to say, juries arrived at verdicts in favour of the accused which were contrary to law. The traditional way in which judges attempt to deflect the jury from a perverse verdict of this kind is to withdraw the issue. But section 3 was intended to deprive the judge of even this method of control. The jury was to be sovereign and have the power in theory as well as in practice to decide whether the objective element was satisfied.

I do not think it possible to attribute to Parliament, in making this change, any intention other than to legitimate the relaxation of the old law in those cases in which justice appeared to require it and to allow the jury in good conscience to arrive at a verdict which previously would have been perverse. In other words, the jury was given a normative as well as a fact-finding function. They were to determine not merely whether the behaviour of the accused complied with some legal standard but could determine for themselves what the standard in the particular case should be. In this way they could, as the Royal Commission said, 'give weight to factors personal to the prisoner' in cases in which it appeared unjust not to do so.

It follows, in my opinion, that it would not be consistent with section 3 for the judge to tell the jury as a matter of law that they should ignore any factor or characteristic of the accused in deciding whether the objective element of provocation had been satisfied. That would be to trespass upon their province. In a case in which the jury might consider that only by virtue of that characteristic was the act in question sufficiently provocative, the effect of such a direction would be to withdraw the issue of provocation altogether and this would be contrary to the terms of section 3.

If, therefore, the purpose of section 3 was to legitimate the normative role of the jury and free their consciences from the burden of having to give a perverse verdict in order to do justice, it must have had a corresponding effect upon the nature of the directions they were to be given by the judge. It is inconceivable that he was intended to instruct them according to the letter of the old law, in the expectation or even the hope that in an appropriate case his directions would be ignored. It meant, as I have said, that he could no longer tell them that they were obliged as a matter of law to exclude 'factors personal to the prisoner' from their consideration. But that did not mean that he was required to leave the jury at large and without any assistance in the exercise of their normative role. He could tell the jury that the doctrine of provocation included the principle of objectivity and that they should have regard to that principle in deciding whether the act in question was sufficiently provocative to be acceptable as a partial excuse.

. . .

7. *DPP v Camplin [1978] AC 705*

The Court of Appeal in *Camplin* held that section 3 had made no change in the concept of the reasonable man and that it was still bound by *Bedder* [1954] 1 WLR 1119. But it distinguished that case on the ground that impotence was an abnormal characteristic, whereas nothing could be more normal than to be a boy of 15. As Bridge LJ said, ([1978] 1 QB, 261):

> youth, and the immaturity which naturally accompanies youth, are not deviations from the norm; they are norms through which we must all of us have passed before attaining adulthood and maturity.

The jury ought therefore to have been directed to consider whether the provocation was enough to make a reasonable person of the same age as the defendant behave as he did.

In the House of Lords Lord Diplock, with whom Lords Fraser of Tullybelton and Lord Scarman agreed, gave the leading judgment. Lord Diplock drew attention to the express changes which section 3 made to the nature of a provocative act and to the role of judge and jury. He noted (at [1978] AC 705, 716) that the 'reasonable man' had been preserved by the Act but said that it 'falls to be applied now in the context of a law of provocation that is significantly different from what it was before the Act was passed.' He pointed out, at p. 717, that:

> now that the law has been changed so as to permit of words being treated as provocation . . . the gravity of verbal provocation may well depend upon the particular characteristics or circumstances of the person to whom a taunt or insult is addressed.

It would stultify this change in the law if the jury could not take into account 'all those factors which in their opinion would affect the gravity of taunts or insults when applied to the person to whom they are addressed.'

So far, the reasoning is concerned solely with the relevance of the characteristics or circumstances of the accused to the gravity of the provocation. But the actual facts in *Camplin* were not primarily concerned with a characteristic with affected the gravity of the provocation. It is true that the gravity of the alleged taunts and sexual abuse may have been affected by the accused's consciousness of his physical and intellectual inferiority in relation to the deceased. But the main case for the defence was that a 15-year-old boy could not be expected to have the same powers of self-control as an adult. Lord Diplock acknowledged at pp. 717 – 718, that:

> in strict logic there is a transition between treating age as a characteristic that may be taken into account in assessing the gravity of the provocation addressed to the accused and treating it as a characteristic to be taken into account in determining what is the degree of self-control to be expected of the ordinary person with whom the accused's conduct is to be compared. But to require old heads upon young shoulders is inconsistent with the law's compassion to human infirmity to which Sir Michael Foster ascribed the doctrine of provocation more than two centuries ago. The distinction as to the purposes for which it is legitimate to take the age of the accused into account involves considerations of too great nicety to warrant a place in deciding a matter of opinion, which is no longer one to be decided by a judge trained in logical reasoning but is to be decided by a jury drawing on their experience of how ordinary human beings behave in real life.

This is a most important passage and I invite your Lordships' attention to the following points:

(1) Lord Diplock says that youth may be taken into account because the principle of compassion to human infirmity, as a jury drawing on their experience may apply it, requires one to do so. He does not say that the same principle of compassion is incapable of applying to any other characteristics which a jury might on similar grounds think should be taken into account. It would have been easy for him to have said that youth was for this purpose unique.

(2) Lord Diplock expressly rejects the distinction between the effect of age on the gravity of the provocation and on the power of self-control on the grounds that it is 'of too great nicety' for application by a jury. Again, there is nothing to suggest that this comment is not equally true of other characteristics. Since *Camplin*, there is a great deal of material which demonstrates that Lord Diplock's scepticism about whether the distinction could be made to work in practice was well founded.

(3) If age were to be the only case in which a particular characteristic could be taken into account as relevant to the expected power of self-control, it would be necessary to explain why it should be so singled out. The High Court of Australia, in *Stingel v The Queen* (1990) 171 CLR 312, 330, said that

it was because age is a normal characteristic: 'the process of development from childhood to maturity is something which, being common to us all, is an aspect of ordinariness.' This explanation was embraced by Lord Goff of Chieveley in *Luc Thiet Thuan* v *The Queen* [1997] AC 131, 140. It had, as I have said, been relied upon in *Camplin* by the Court of Appeal to distinguish *Bedder*. But the distinction between normal and abnormal characteristics was expressly rejected by Lord Diplock. He said (at p. 718) that:

> The reasoning in *Bedder* would, I think, permit of this distinction between normal and abnormal characteristics, which may affect the powers of self-control of the accused; but for reasons that I have already mentioned the proposition stated in *Bedder* requires qualification as a consequence of the changes in the law effected by the Act of 1957. To try to salve what can remain of it without conflict with the Act could in my view only lead to unnecessary and unsatisfactory complexity in a question which has now become a question for the jury alone.

My Lords, the important passage which I have cited from Lord Diplock's speech provides in my view no support for the theory, widely advanced in the literature, that he was making a clear distinction between characteristics relevant to the gravity of the provocation and characteristics relevant to the power of self-control, with age (and possibly sex) as arbitrary exceptions which could be taken into account for the latter purpose. This interpretation depends principally upon what Lord Diplock described as 'a proper direction to the jury' which he gave at the end of his speech at p. 718:

> The judge should state what the question is using the very terms of the section. He should then explain to them that the reasonable man referred to in the question is a person having the power of self-control to be expected of an ordinary person of the sex and age of the accused, but in other respects sharing such of the accused's characteristics as they think would affect the gravity of the provocation to him; and that the question is not merely whether such a person would in like circumstances be provoked to lose his self-control but also whether he would react to the provocation as the accused did.

The references to age and sex have been taken to mean that in all cases these are the only matters which should be mentioned as relevant to the question of self-control. It seems to me clear, however, that Lord Diplock was framing a suitable direction for a case like *Camplin* [1978] AC 705 and not a one-size-fits-all direction for every case of provocation. A jury would be puzzled about why they were being asked to pay particular attention to the age and sex of the defendant if he was an ordinary adult. A number of writers and judges have thought that Lord Diplock was wrong to include the sex of the accused (see for example, *Stingel* v *The Queen* (1990) 171 CLR 312, 331) and if the direction had been intended to be of general application, I would agree. But in my view Lord Diplock was only drawing attention to the fact that the hormonal development of male adolescents is different from that of females.

Finally, my Lords, I draw attention to the concluding sentence of Lord Diplock's speech, in which he summed up why he thought it would be wrong to direct the jury that they were not entitled to take into account the youth of the accused. It was because:

> So to direct them was to impose a fetter on the right and duty of the jury which the Act accords to them to act upon their own opinion on the matter.

This, in my view, goes to the heart of the matter and is in accordance with the analysis of the effect of section 3 which I have made earlier in my speech. The jury is entitled to act upon its own opinion of whether the objective element of provocation has been satisfied and the judge is not entitled to tell them that for this purpose the law requires them to exclude from consideration any of the circumstances or characteristics of the accused.

8. *The gravity of provocation/self-control distinction*

Although *DPP* v *Camplin* [1978] AC 705 does not in my opinion provide authoritative support for the distinction between gravity of provocation and powers of self-control, it has been adopted in Australia (*Stingel* v *The Queen* (1990) 171 CLR 312); New Zealand (*Reg*. v *Campbell* [1997] 1 NZLR 16 and *Reg*. v *Rongonui* (Court of Appeal, 13 April 2000, unreported)); Canada (*Reg*. v *Hill* [1986] 1 SCR 313) and by the Privy Council for Hong Kong (*Luc Thiet Thuan* v *The Queen* [1997] AC 131). It also has a good deal of academic support: see in particular Professor Ashworth's influential article 'The Doctrine of Provocation' [1976] CLJ 292–320, Jeremy Horder, 'Between Provocation and Diminished Responsibility' (1999) 2 KCLJ 143–166 and Professor MJ Allen, 'Provocation's Reasonable Man: A Plea for Self-Control' [2000] Journal of Criminal Law 216–244. It must therefore be considered on its own merits.

The theoretical basis for the distinction is that provocation is a defence for people who are, as Professor Ashworth put it, 'in a broad sense mentally normal': see [1976] CLJ at p. 312. If they claim that they had abnormal characteristics which reduced their powers of self-control, they should plead diminished responsibility. There is a clear philosophical distinction between a claim that an act was at least partially excused as normal behaviour in response to external circumstances and a claim that the actor had mental characteristics which prevented him from behaving normally: see Sir Peter Strawson, *Freedom and Resentment*, in *Free Will* (Watson, ed. 1982) at pp. 64–67.

The difficulty about the practical application of this distinction in the law of provocation is that in many cases the two forms of claim are inextricably muddled up with each other. A good example is the recent New Zealand case of *Reg*. v *Rongonui* (Court of Appeal, 13 April 2000, unreported). The accused was a woman with a history of violence against her, suffering from post-traumatic stress disorder. The alleged provocation was that a neighbour she was visiting to ask for help in babysitting her children had produced a knife – not in a threatening way, but sufficient to make her lose control of herself, seize the knife and stab the neighbour to death. The Court of Appeal agreed that it was very difficult in such a case to distinguish between the gravity of the provocation (the accused's previous experience of violence making the mere production of a knife a graver provocation than it would be to someone who had led a more sheltered life) and the accused's capacity for self-control which had been affected by the psychological stress of the violence she had suffered. Tipping J., giving one of the majority judgments which held that the New Zealand statute on provocation (section 169 of the Crimes Act 1961) mandated the application of the distinction, said that it required 'mental gymnastics.' Thomas J, who thought that the statute did not have to be construed so rigidly, said that most trial judges had seen:

> the glazed look in the jurors' eyes as, immediately after instructing them that it is open to them to have regard to the accused's alleged characteristic in assessing the gravity of the provocation, they are then advised that they must revert to the test of the ordinary person and disregard that characteristic when determining the sufficiency of the accused's loss of self-control.

Professor Stanley Yeo, in his recent book *Unrestrained Killings and the Law* (1998) at p. 61 points out that the reason why jurors find the distinction so difficult is that it:

> bears no conceivable relationship with the underlying rationales of the defence of provocation. . . . The defence has been variously regarded as premised upon the contributory fault of the victim and, alternatively, upon the fact that the accused was not fully in control of his or her behaviour when the homicide was committed. Neither of these premises requires the distinction to be made between characteristics of the accused affecting the gravity of the provocation from those concerned with the power of self-control.

Besides these practical difficulties in explaining the distinction to the jury, I think it is wrong to assume that there is a neat dichotomy between the 'ordinary person' contemplated by the law of provocation and the 'abnormal person' contemplated by the law of diminished responsibility. The

Act of 1957 made a miscellany of changes of the law of homicide which can hardly be described as amounting to a coherent and interlocking scheme. Diminished responsibility as defined in section 2 ('such abnormality of mind . . . as substantially impaired his mental responsibility for his acts and omissions . . .') is a general defence which can apply whatever the circumstances of the killing and was introduced because of what was regarded as the undue strictness of the defence of insanity. Provocation is a defence which depends upon the circumstances of the killing and section 3 was introduced, as I have suggested, to legitimate the consideration by juries of 'factors personal to the prisoner.' If one asks whether Parliament contemplated that there might be an overlap between these two defences, I think that the realistic answer is that no one gave the matter a thought. But the possibility of overlap seems to me to follow inevitably from consigning the whole of the objective element in provocation to the jury. If the jury cannot be told that the law requires characteristics which could found a defence of diminished responsibility to be ignored in relation to the defence of provocation, there is no point in claiming that the defences are mutually exclusive.

There are in practice bound to be cases in which the accused will not be suffering from 'abnormality of mind' within the meaning of section 2 ('a state of mind so different from that of ordinary human beings that the reasonable man would term it abnormal': *Reg.* v *Byrne* [1960] 2 QB 396, 403) but will nevertheless have mental characteristics (temporary or permanent) which the jury might think should be taken into account for the purposes of the provocation defence. The boundary between the normal and abnormal is very often a matter of opinion. Some people are entirely normal in most respects and behave unusually in others. There are people (such as battered wives) who would reject any suggestion that they were 'different from ordinary human beings' but have undergone experiences which, without any fault or defect of character on their part, have affected their powers of self-control. In such cases the law now recognises that the emotions which may cause loss of self-control are not confined to anger but may include fear and despair. Professor Ashworth, who argued in 1976 that diminished responsibility and provocation were logically mutually exclusive, was cautious enough to say ('The Doctrine of Provocation' [1976] CLJ 292, 314) that it was 'difficult to shed all one's misgivings about whether the law actually operates in this way.' I think not only that this scepticism was justified but also that section 3 prevents the judges from trying to force cases into logical dichotomies.

There is however one really serious argument in favour of the distinction between characteristics affecting the gravity of the provocation and characteristics affecting the power of self-control. This is the claim that, despite all its difficulties of application, it is the only way to hold the line against complete erosion of the objective element in provocation. The purpose of the objective element in provocation is to mark the distinction between (partially) excusable and inexcusable loss of self-control. As Lord Diplock said in *DPP* v *Camplin* [1978] AC 705, 717, the conduct of the accused should be measured against 'such powers of self-control as everyone is entitled to expect that his fellow citizens will exercise in society as it is today.' If there is no limit to the characteristics which can be taken into account, the fact that the accused lost self-control will show that he is a person liable in such circumstances to lose his self-control. The objective element will have disappeared completely.

My Lords, I share the concern that this should not happen. For the protection of the public, the law should continue to insist that people must exercise self-control. A person who flies into a murderous rage when he is crossed, thwarted or disappointed in the vicissitudes of life should not be able to rely upon his anti-social propensity as even a partial excuse for killing. In *Stingel* v *The Queen* (1990) 171 CLR 312, for example, the accused was obsessively infatuated with a woman who had terminated their relationship. He became a stalker, following her about. She obtained a court order restraining him from approaching her. One evening after a party he found the woman in a car with another man. According to his own account, they were having sex. He went back to his own car, fetched a butcher's knife and came back and killed the man. His evidence conformed to the standard narrative which the legal requirement of 'loss of control' imposes on such defences:

I was all worked up and feeling funny. It was like I was in a rage, almost to the stage where I felt dazed. It was like I really didn't know what happened until the knife went into him.

The High Court of Australia held that the judge was right to withdraw the issue of provocation from the jury on the ground that such conduct could not raise even a reasonable doubt as to whether the objective element in the defence had been satisfied. I respectfully agree. Male possessiveness and jealousy should not today be an acceptable reason for loss of self-control leading to homicide, whether inflicted upon the woman herself or her new lover. In Australia the judge was able to give effect to this policy by withdrawing issue from the jury. But section 3 prevents an English judge from doing so. So, it is suggested, a direction that characteristics such as jealousy and obsession should be ignored in relation to the objective element is the best way to ensure that people like Stingel cannot rely upon the defence.

9. The English cases

The first important English case after *DPP* v *Camplin* [1978] AC 705 was the judgment of Lord Lane CJ in *Reg.* v *Newell* (1980) 71 Cr App R 331. He interpreted section 3 as meaning that the jury can be directed to take into account personal characteristics of the accused in relation to both the gravity of the provocation and the degree of self-control which could reasonably have been expected. It is true, as Lord Goff of Chieveley pointed out in *Luc Thiet Thuan* v *The Queen* [1997] AC 131, 141–144, the Lord Chief Justice adopted the construction which had been given to a somewhat different statute in New Zealand. He approved a passage in *Reg.* v *McGregor* [1962] NZLR 1069 in which North J had said:

> The offender must be presumed to possess in general the power of self-control of the ordinary man, save in so far as his power of self-control is weakened because of some particular characteristic possessed by him.

But the course of the law in New Zealand has been a rather tangled story, as the judgments in *Reg.* v *Rongonui* (Court of Appeal, 13 April 2000) reveal. I have already said enough to explain why I think that the construction of section 3 adopted by the Court of Appeal was in this respect correct, independently of any support which might be obtained from New Zealand. It is therefore inappropriate for me to undertake any analysis of the New Zealand cases or comment upon the construction which the courts have given to their statute. Nor can any direct assistance be obtained from Australia and Canada, where the objective standard remains a matter of law for the judge.

The construction adopted in *Newell* 71 Cr App R 331 was followed by Lord Taylor of Gosforth CJ in *Reg.* v *Ahluwalia* [1992] 4 All ER 889, a case of a battered wife. He said that characteristics relating to the 'mental state or personality of an individual' such as the fact that a battered wife was suffering from post-traumatic stress disorder, could be taken into account. It is true that he recorded counsel for the appellant as having described this as a characteristic which the jury 'might think might affect the gravity of the provocation'. The same comment may be made about Lord Taylor's later judgment in *Reg.* v *Dryden* [1995] 4 All ER 987. In that case the accused was convicted of murder after he had shot and killed a planning officer who was engaged in demolishing his bungalow pursuant to an enforcement notice. There was psychiatric evidence that the accused had developed an obsession about his planning problems. The Court of Appeal said that the obsessiveness and eccentricity of the defendant should have been left to the jury as 'mental characteristics' which they should take into account. In neither case, however, did Lord Taylor suggest that the jury should have been directed to have regard to these characteristics only insofar as they might have affected the gravity of the provocation and not insofar as they may have affected the accused's power of self-control. No doubt this omission was for the very good reason that, on the facts of both cases, no jury would have understood what such a distinction meant.

Finally, in *Reg*. v *Campbell* [1997] 1 C App R 199 Lord Bingham of Cornhill CJ affirmed the principle of the earlier decisions, which he said represented 'a judicial response, born of everyday experience in criminal trials up and down the country, as to what fairness seems to require'.

My Lords, in the face of these views of three successive Lord Chief Justices, I would be most reluctant to advise your Lordships to turn back such a strong current of authority unless it was clearly inconsistent with the statute. But I do not think it is. On the contrary, it seems to me to reflect a realistic appreciation of what the statute has done.

10. *Guiding the jury*

My Lords, I think that some of the concern about the recent trend of authority in the English Court of Appeal has been due to the assumption that unless the judge can direct the jury that certain characteristics of the accused are legally irrelevant to the objective element in the defence, the jury may receive the impression that the law actually requires them to take such matters into account. The effect would be to encourage juries to find provocation on inappropriate grounds. Obviously, my Lords, there is always the risk that a jury may do so. That is the risk which Parliament took when it gave the jury an unfettered right to give effect to its own opinion on the objective element. But it considered that risk less likely to cause injustice than to confine the jury within the rules of law which had been developed about the notional characteristics of the reasonable man. In any case, I think that much can be done to reduce that risk if judges guide juries on this issue in a way which fully takes into account the difference which section 3 has made to their respective roles.

. . .

The effect of section 3 is that once the judge has ruled that there is evidence upon which the jury can find that something caused the accused to lose self-control (compare *Reg*. v *Acott* [1997] 1 WLR 306), he cannot tell the jury that the act in question was incapable of amounting to provocation. But that no longer involves any decision by the judge that it would be rational so to decide. For example, in *Reg*. v *Doughty* [1986] Cr App R 319 the Court of Appeal held that the judge had been wrong to direct the jury that the crying of 17 day old baby, which had caused its father to kill it by covering its head with cushions and kneeling on them, could not constitute a provocative act. Section 3 said that the jury were entitled to take into account 'everything both done and said'. I respectfully think that this construction of the Act was correct. But that does not mean that the judge should tell the jury that the crying of the baby was, in the traditional language, capable of amounting to provocation. This would give the jury the impression that the judge thought it would be rational and in accordance with principle to hold that the crying of the baby constituted an acceptable partial excuse for killing it. The point about section 3 is that it no longer matters whether the judge thinks so or not. He should therefore be able simply to tell the jury that the question of whether such behaviour fell below the standard which should reasonably have been expected of the accused was entirely a matter for them. He should not be obliged to let the jury imagine that the law now regards anything whatever which caused loss of self-control (whether an external event or a personal characteristic of the accused) as necessarily being an acceptable reason for loss of self-control.

11. *The reasonable man*

The main obstacle to directing the jury in a way which does not give such a false impression is the highly artificial way in which courts and writers have attempted to marry two discordant ideas: first, the old formula that the provocation must have been such as to cause a 'reasonable man' to act in the same way as the accused and, secondly, the rule in section 3 that no circumstances or characteristics should be excluded from the consideration of the jury. They have done so by telling the jury that certain characteristics are to be 'attributed' to the reasonable man. By such a combination, they have produced monsters like the reasonable obsessive, the reasonable depressive alcoholic and even (with all respect to the explanations of Lord Goff of Chieveley in *Reg*. v *Morhall* [1996] 1 AC 90, 98) the reasonable glue sniffer. Nor does it elucidate matters to substitute 'ordinary' for 'reasonable'. Quite apart from the question of whether the jury can understand what such concepts mean, it is bound to suggest to them that obsession, alcoholism and so forth are not merely matters which they are entitled in law to take into account but that, being 'attributed' to the reasonable man, they are qualities for which allowances must be made.

So, for example, in *Reg*. v *Humphreys* [1995] 4 All ER 1008 there was a good deal of discussion as to whether 'attention seeking' and 'immaturity' were 'eligible characteristics' in the sense that they were to be attributed to (in that case) the reasonable woman. The Court of Appeal decided that they were. Similarly in *Reg*. v *Dryden* [1995] 4 All ER 987, which I have already mentioned, the question was framed as being whether the obsessiveness and eccentricity of the defendant were 'mental characteristics' which the jury should attribute to the reasonable man. Professor MJ Allen, in the article to which I have referred in [2000] Journal of Criminal Law 216, 239, says with some force that this decision, 'endorsing obsession as a characteristic to attribute to the reasonable man should sound an alarm bell for all sexual partners'. If Dryden's obsession could be attributed to 'the reasonable man', why not Stingel's?

My Lords, the concept of the 'reasonable man' has never been more than a way of explaining the law to a jury; an anthropomorphic image to convey to them, with a suitable degree of vividness, the legal principle that even under provocation, people must conform to an objective standard of behaviour which society is entitled to expect: see Lord Diplock in *Camplin* [1978] AC 705, 714. In referring to 'the reasonable man' section 3 invokes that standard. But I do not think that it was intended to require judges always to use that particular image, even in cases in which its use is more likely to confuse than illuminate. When Keating J in *Reg*. v *Welsh* (1869) 11 Cox CC, 336, 339 borrowed the *mot juste* which Baron Alderson had used in *Blyth* v *Birmingham Waterworks* (1856) 11 Exch 781, 784 to define negligence, he did not imagine that he was changing the law. He merely thought he had hit upon a felicitous way of explaining it. Whether he was right is perhaps questionable. Even before the Act of 1957, there had been expressions of doubt about the extent to which it really was a helpful way to explain the notion of objectivity in the particular context of provocation. The jury may have some difficulty with the notion that the 'reasonable man' will, even under severe provocation, kill someone else. But, my Lords, whatever the force of the earlier criticisms, the value of the image has been hopelessly compromised by the Act of 1957. This may not have been foreseen, just as many did not foresee the effect which the Act would have upon the concept of the reasonable man and the abandonment in *Camplin* [1978] AC 705 of the law laid down in *Mancini* [1941] AC 1 and *Bedder* [1954] 1 WLR 1119. But it seems to me now, since *Camplin*, impossible to avoid giving the jury a misleading, not to say unintelligible, account of the law when particular characteristics, sometimes highly unusual and even repulsive, are welded onto the concept of the reasonable man. I do not find it surprising that nine judges who gave written evidence to the House of Lords *Select Committee on Murder and Life Imprisonment* (HL Paper 78-III Session 1988–89) said that the reasonable man test was 'logically unworkable, or [rendered] the defence almost ineffective if it were strictly applied by juries'.

My Lords, I do emphasise that what has been rendered unworkable is not the principle of objectivity which (subject to the changes noted in *Camplin*) section 3 was plainly intended to preserve, but a particular way of explaining it. I am not suggesting that your Lordships should in any way depart from the legal principle embodied in section 3 but only that the principle should be expounded in clear language rather than by the use of an opaque formula.

In my opinion, therefore, judges should not be required to describe the objective element in the provocation defence by reference to a reasonable man, with or without attribution of personal characteristics. They may instead find it more helpful to explain in simple language the principles of the doctrine of provocation. First, it requires that the accused should have killed while he had lost self-control and that something should have caused him to lose self-control. For better or for worse, section 3 left this part of the law untouched. Secondly, the fact that something caused him to lose self-control is not enough. The law expects people to exercise control over their emotions. A tendency to violent rages or childish tantrums is a defect in character rather than an excuse. The jury must think that the circumstances were such as to make the loss of self-control sufficiently *excusable* to reduce the gravity of the offence from murder to manslaughter. This is entirely a question for the jury. In deciding what should count as a sufficient excuse, they have to apply what they consider to be appropriate standards of behaviour; on the one hand making allowance for human nature and the power of the emotions but, on the other hand, not allowing someone to rely upon his own violent disposition. In applying these standards of behaviour, the jury represent the community and decide, as Lord Diplock said in *Camplin* ([1978] AC 717), what degree of self-control 'everyone is entitled to expect that his fellow citizens will exercise in society as it is today.' The maintenance of such standards is important. As Viscount Simon L.C. said more than 50 years ago in *Holmes* v *DPP* [1946] AC 588, 601, 'as society advances, it ought to call for a higher measure of self-control'.

The general principle is that the same standards of behaviour are expected of everyone, regardless of their individual psychological make-up. In most cases, nothing more will need to be said. But the jury should in an appropriate case be told, in whatever language will best convey the distinction, that this is a principle and not a rigid rule. It may sometimes have to yield to a more important principle, which is to do justice in the particular case. So the jury may think that there was some characteristic of the accused, whether temporary or permanent, which affected the degree of control which society could reasonably have expected of *him* and which it would be unjust not to take into account. If the jury take this view, they are at liberty to give effect to it.

My Lords, I do not wish to lay down any prescriptive formula for the way in which the matter is explained to the jury. I am sure that if judges are freed from the necessity of invoking the formula of the reasonable man equipped with an array of unreasonable 'eligible characteristics', they will be able to explain the principles in simple terms. Provided that the judge makes it clear that the question is in the end one for the jury and that he is not seeking to 'impose a fetter on the right and duty of the jury which the Act accords to them', the guidance which he gives must be a matter for his judgment on the facts of the case.

12. *The burden of proof*
The burden is upon the prosecution to disprove provocation. This means that the prosecution must satisfy the jury that a version of the facts in which the accused was provoked could not reasonably be true. But the decision as to whether, having regard to the objective principle, those facts should count as sufficient provocation to reduce the offence to manslaughter has nothing to do with the burden of proof. The jury either think it does or they do not. It is irrelevant that they may think that a different jury could have taken a different view.

13. *Conclusion*
In my opinion the judge should not have directed the jury as a matter of law that the effect of Smith's depression on his powers of self-control was 'neither here nor there'. They should have been told that whether they took it into account in relation to the question of whether the behaviour of the accused had measured up to the standard of self-control which ought reasonably to have been expected of him was a matter for them to decide. For the above reasons and those given by my noble and learned friends Lord Slynn of Hadley and Lord Clyde, I would dismiss the appeal.

NOTES AND QUESTIONS
1. Is Lord Hoffmann's opinion consistent with the wording of s. 3 of the Homicide Act 1957? What is left of the concept of the reference to the 'reasonable man' in the statute after the decision in *Smith (Morgan)*? Is Lord Hoffmann's treatment of the 'reasonable man' consistent with that of the House of Lords in *Camplin*?

2. If a defendant can show that, because of a genetic defect, he is more prone to lose self-control than would a reasonable man, should this be a factor that should be considered by a jury? If not, why not? What does Lord Hoffmann have to say on this point? Is his analysis persuasive? Would it make a difference if his self-control was weak because of brain damage suffered in a car crash?
3. Lord Hoffmann discusses the guidance that should be given to the jury. Are his suggestions likely to prove helpful to the jury?
4. Does the Homicide Act 1957 need to be re-drafted to be consistent with *Smith (Morgan)*? Would it be helpful or unhelpful simply to state that a murder could be reduced to manslaughter if the jurors concluded that the defendant was provoked and lost self-control, and that the circumstances, while not making the killing excusable, reduced the moral fault of the defendant?

(d) *Self-induced provocation.* In *Edwards* [1973] AC 648, the Privy Council stated that ordinarily a blackmailer could not rely on the predictable hostile reaction to his blackmail attempt as constituting provocation sufficient to reduce murder to manslaughter. This position was subsequently disapproved.

R v Johnson
[1989] 1 WLR 740, Court of Appeal

For the facts of this case, see p. 222.

WATKINS LJ: . . . That evidence may not have been powerfully suggestive of provocation. But it was, in our view, rather more than tenuous. It is easily conceivable, we think, that the jury, if directed on the issue, would have come to the conclusion that the appellant was so provoked as to reduce murder to manslaughter. Therefore, subject only to the question of self-induced provocation referred to by the judge, in our judgment this defence should have been left to the jury.

There was undoubtedly evidence to suggest that, if the appellant had lost his self-control, it was his own behaviour which caused others to react towards him in the way we have described.

We were referred to the decision of the Privy Council in *Edwards* v *The Queen* [1973] AC 648. In that case the trial judge had directed the jury, at p. 658:

> In my view the defence of provocation cannot be of any avail to the accused in this case . . . it ill befits the accused in this case, having gone there with the deliberate purpose of blackmailing this man – you may well think it ill befits him to say out of his own mouth that he was provoked by any attack. In my view the defence of provocation is not one which you need consider in this case.

The full court in Hong Kong held that this direction was erroneous. The Privy Council agreed with the full court. On the particular facts of the case Lord Pearson, giving the judgment of the Board, said, at p. 658:

> On principle it seems reasonable to say that – (1) a blackmailer cannot rely on the predictable results of his own blackmailing conduct as constituting provocation . . . and the predictable results may include a considerable degree of hostile reaction by the person sought to be blackmailed . . . (2) but if the hostile reaction by the person sought to be blackmailed goes to extreme lengths it might constitute sufficient provocation even for the blackmailer; (3) there would in many cases be a question of degree to be decided by the jury.

Those words cannot, we think, be understood to mean, as was suggested to us, that provocation which is 'self-induced' ceases to be provocation for the purposes of section 3.

The relevant statutory provision being considered by the Privy Council was in similar terms to section 3. In view of the express wording of section 3, as interpreted in *R v Camplin* [1978] AC 705 which was decided after *Edwards* v *The Queen* [1973] AC 648, we find it impossible to accept that the mere fact that a defendant caused a reaction in others, which in turn led him to lose his self-control, should result in the issue of provocation being kept outside a jury's consideration. Section 3 clearly provides that the question is whether things done or said or both provoked the defendant to lose his self-control. If there is any evidence that it may have done, the issue must be left to the jury. The jury would then have to consider all the circumstances of the incident, including all the relevant behaviour of the defendant, in deciding (a) whether he was in fact provoked and (b) whether the provocation was enough to make a reasonable man do what the defendant did.

Accordingly, whether or not there were elements in the appellant's conduct which justified the conclusion that he had started the trouble and induced others, including the deceased, to react in the way they did, we are firmly of the view that the defence of provocation should have been left to the jury.

Since it is not possible for us to infer from their verdict that the jury inevitably would have concluded that provocation as well as self-defence had been disproved the verdict of murder will be set aside. A conviction for manslaughter on the basis of provocation will be substituted.

(iii) *Suicide pact*

Homicide Act 1957

4.—(1) It shall be manslaughter, and shall not be murder, for a person acting in pursuance of a suicide pact between him and another to kill the other or be a party to the other killing himself or being killed by a third person.

(2) Where it is shown that a person charged with the murder of another killed the other or was a party to his killing himself or being killed, it shall be for the defence to prove that the person charged was acting in pursuance of a suicide pact between him and the other.

(3) For the purposes of this section 'suicide pact' means a common agreement between two or more persons having for its object the death of all of them, whether or not each is to take his own life, but nothing done by a person who enters into a suicide pact shall be treated as done by him in pursuance of the pact unless it is done while he has the settled intention of dying in pursuance of the pact.

NOTES AND QUESTIONS
1. The burden of proving the defence to the balance of probabilities standard is on the defendant.
2. At common law suicide was a crime. Although the individual who was successful could obviously not be tried, his estate was forfeited to the Crown. Today, suicide is no longer a crime. Should the killing of a partner in the course of a suicide pact therefore also cease to attract criminal sanctions? Is the issue of consent to one's own death a relevant consideration here? If so, should euthanasia (or mercy killing) be decriminalised?

B: Involuntary manslaughter

This category of homicide includes all killings which are regarded as criminally unlawful but where the defendant does not have the *mens rea* of murder. The term 'involuntary manslaughter' is, however, a misnomer, for the killings involved are not involuntary as that term has traditionally been used in the context of *actus reus*. It is used only to distinguish this class of homicide from murder and voluntary manslaughter. In struggling to define the boundaries of involuntary manslaughter the courts have encountered considerable difficulties and the resulting muddle is not a credit to English jurisprudence. There are at least two categories, but some killings could fit into both, and there may also be some less clearly defined categories. The two categories are:

(a) constructive manslaughter;
(b) gross negligence manslaughter.

(i) *Constructive manslaughter*

It is manslaughter when the defendant performs an unlawful and dangerous act likely to cause physical harm and death results. This is an offence which is 'built upon' another, i.e. the death is an incidental result of the unlawful act. For that reason there has been some confusion as to whether the usual causation rules apply. The issue has appeared in the case law as a question as to whether the defendant's act must be 'aimed or directed' at the victim (see extracts below).

(a) An *unlawful act*. Taken literally, the term 'unlawful act' would include a tort, and, indeed, that was the position at early common law. It is now settled that more is required for purposes of convicting a defendant of manslaughter. Not even all criminal offences may qualify as unlawful acts.

Andrews v *Director of Public Prosecutions*
[1937] AC 576, House of Lords

LORD ATKIN: . . . There is an obvious difference in the law of manslaughter between doing an unlawful act and doing a lawful act with a degree of carelessness which the Legislature makes criminal. If it were otherwise a man who killed another while driving without due care and attention would ex necessitate commit manslaughter. . . .

NOTES AND QUESTIONS
1. Is Lord Atkin's distinction a helpful one? Are there degrees of carelessness such that a defend-ant might act *so* carelessly that his act will be deemed unlawful? In such a case, the category of constructive manslaughter may become redundant as the actor will be guilty of gross negligence manslaughter (see below).
2. An act is not 'unlawful' if it is justifiable, as it might be if the defendant struck a fatal blow to the victim in self-defence.
3. Whether the defendant has committed an unlawful act is a jury question and the court may not decide the issue on its own authority. See *R* v *Jennings* [1990] Crim LR 588.

Both the *mens rea* and the *actus reus* of the unlawful act must be proved:

R v *Lamb*
[1967] 2 QB 981, Court of Appeal

SACHS LJ: . . . The defendant, Terence Walter Lamb, aged 25, had become possessed of a Smith & Wesson revolver. It was a revolver in the literal old-fashioned sense, having a five-chambered cylinder which rotated clockwise each time the trigger was pulled. The defendant, in jest, with no intention to do any harm pointed the revolver at the deceased, his best friend, when it had two bullets in the chambers, but neither bullet was in the chamber opposite the barrel. His friend was similarly treating the incident as a joke. The defendant then pulled the trigger and thus killed his friend, still having no intention to fire the revolver. The reason why the pulling of the trigger produced that fatal result was that its pulling rotated the cylinder and so placed a bullet opposite the barrel so that it was struck by the striking pin or hammer.

The defendant's defence was that, as neither bullet was opposite the barrel, he thought they were in such chambers that the striking pin could not hit them; that he was unaware that the pulling of the trigger would bring one bullet into the firing position opposite the barrel; and that the killing was thus an accident. There was not only no dispute that that was what he in fact thought, but the mistake he made was one which three experts agreed was natural for somebody who was not aware of the way the revolver mechanism worked. . . . The trial judge took the view that the pointing of the revolver and the pulling of the trigger was something which could of itself be unlawful even if there was no attempt to alarm or intent to injure. . . .

[Prosecution counsel] had at all times put forward the correct view that for the act to be unlawful it must constitute at least what he then termed 'a technical assault.' In this court moreover he rightly conceded that there was no evidence to go to the jury of any assault of any kind. Nor did he feel able to submit that the acts of the defendant were on any other ground unlawful in the criminal sense of that word. Indeed no such submission could in law be made: if, for instance, the pulling of the trigger had had no effect because the striking mechanism or the ammunition had been defective no offence would have been committed by the defendant.

Another way of putting it is that *mens rea*, being now an essential ingredient in manslaughter . . . that could not in the present case be established in relation to the first ground except by proving that element of intent without which there can be no assault.

Appeal allowed.

NOTES AND QUESTIONS

Is the decision in *Lamb* based on the fact that the victim was not put in fear (a requirement of the crime of assault), or the fact that there was no assault because the defendant lacked the *mens rea* of the crime?

In *Director of Public Prosecutions* v *Newbury* [1976] 2 All ER 365, the House of Lords indicated that it was sufficient that the defendants, who had pushed a paving stone from a railway bridge on to a passing train, killing a guard, had 'basic intent'. This was defined as an 'intention to do the acts which constitute the crime'. As we have noted previously, this adds little to the requirement of a voluntary *actus reus*.

(b) A *dangerous* act. Not all unlawful acts support a conviction for manslaughter. The act must also pose a danger of harm.

R v *Church*
[1965] 2 All ER 72, Court of Criminal Appeal

EDMUND DAVIES J: . . . The facts may be shortly stated. On Sunday, May 31, 1964, the dead body of Mrs Nott was found in the River Ouse within a few yards of the appellant's van which stood near the bank. The corpse bore the marks of grave injuries. The face had been battered, the hyoid bone had been broken and there had been some degree of manual strangulation. These injuries were likely to have caused unconsciousness and eventually death, but they were inflicted a half-hour or an hour before death supervened and did not in fact cause it. According to the medical evidence, her injuries were inflicted not long before Mrs Nott was thrown into the river, but she was alive when that was done, she continued to breathe for an appreciable time afterwards, and the eventual cause of death was drowning. When the appellant was first interviewed about the matter he lied, but ultimately signed a statement admitting complicity in the death. He then said that he had taken Mrs Nott to his van for sexual purposes, that he was unable to satisfy her and she then reproached him and slapped his face; that they then had a fight during which he knocked her out and thereafter she only moaned. The statement continued:

> 'I was shaking her to wake her for about half-an-hour, but she didn't wake up, so I panicked and dragged her out of the van and put her in the river.'

He repeated this account at his trial and then said for the first time, 'I thought she was dead'.

. . .

(c) *An unlawful act causing death*. Two passages in the summing up are here material. They are these: (i)–

> If, by an unlawful act of violence done deliberately to the person of another, that other is killed, the killing is manslaughter even though the accused never intended either death or grievous bodily harm to result. If [the deceased] was alive, as she was, when he threw her in the river, what he did was a deliberate act of throwing a living body into the river. That is an unlawful killing and it does not matter whether he believed she was dead, or not, and that is my direction to you.

and (ii)–

> I would suggest to you, though, of course, it is for you to approach your task as you think fit, that a convenient way of approaching it would be to say: What do we think about this defence that he honestly believed the [deceased] to be dead? If you think that it is true, why then, as I have told you, your proper verdict would be one of manslaughter, not murder.

Such a direction is not lacking in authority . . . Nevertheless, in the judgment of this court [that] was a misdirection. It amounted to telling the jury that, whenever any unlawful act is committed in relation to a human being which resulted in death there must be, at least, a conviction for manslaughter. This might at one time have been regarded as good law. It appears to this court, however, that the passage of years has achieved a transformation in this branch of the law and, even in relation to manslaughter, a degree of mens rea has become recognised as essential. To define it is a difficult task, and in *Andrews v Director of Public Prosecutions* [1937] AC 576 Lord Atkin spoke of 'the element of "unlawfulness" which is the elusive factor'. Stressing that we are here leaving entirely out of account those ingredients of homicide which might justify a verdict of manslaughter on the grounds of (a) criminal negligence, or (b) provocation or (c) diminished responsibility, the conclusion of this court is that an unlawful act causing the death of another cannot, simply because it is an unlawful act, render a manslaughter verdict inevitable. For such a verdict inexorably to follow, the unlawful act must be such as all sober and reasonable people would inevitably recognise must subject the other person to, at least, the risk of some harm resulting therefrom, albeit not serious harm. See, for example, *R v Franklin* (1883) 15 Cox CC 163, *R v Senior* [1899] 1 QB 283.

If such be the test, as we adjudge it to be, then it follows that, in our view, it was a misdirection to tell the jury simpliciter that it mattered nothing for manslaughter whether or not the appellant believed Mrs Nott to be dead when he threw her into the river. . . .

NOTES AND QUESTIONS

1. According to the court, the unlawful act has to be such that 'all sober and reasonable people would inevitably recognise [it as an act which] must subject the other person to, at least, the risk of some harm resulting therefrom, albeit not serious harm'. This test was affirmed by Lord Hope of Craighead in *Attorney-General's Reference (No. 3 of 1994)*, who said: 'Dangerousness in this context is not a high standard. All it requires is that it was an act which was likely to injure another person.' The test is an objective one; actual foresight by the defendant of

danger to others is not required; what is critical is the perception of the reasonable man. If so, why did the court deem it a misdirection for the trial judge to have told the jury that the defendant's belief as to whether the victim was dead at the time that he threw her into the river mattered nothing?

2. What if it could be shown that the defendant was not a reasonable man; that, for example, he was mentally retarded? Is it just to hold a defendant to the standard of the reasonable man if the defendant is incapable through no fault of his own of achieving such a standard? Similar issues were raised by *Elliot* v *C (A minor)* [1983] 1 WLR 939, discussed in Chapter 4.

The harm which the reasonable person must be able to foresee is physical harm, but shock which produces physical injury will suffice if the other elements of the offence are present.

R v Dawson

(1985) 81 Cr App R 150, Court of Appeal

After midnight one night two masked men, one carrying a pickaxe handle and another armed with a replica gun, while a third kept watch, demanded money from a 60-year-old petrol filling station attendant who, unknown to them, suffered from heart disease. The attendant pressed the alarm button and the three men fled. Shortly after the police arrived, the attendant collapsed and died from a heart attack.

WATKINS LJ: . . . It has, in our experience, been generally understood that the harm referred to in the second element of the offence of manslaughter, namely, the unlawful act, must be one that all sober and reasonable people would realise was likely to cause some, albeit not serious, harm, means physical harm. . . .

However, there seems to us to be no sensible reason why shock produced by fright should not come within the definition of harm in this context. From time to time one hears the expression 'frightened to death' without thinking that the possibility of such event occurring would be an affront to reason or medical knowledge. Shock can produce devastating and lasting effects, for instance upon the nervous system. That is surely harm, i.e. injury to the person. Why not harm in this context?

. . . [The judge] directed the jury that a definition of harm was 'emotional disturbance which is detrimental produced by terror'. He had, as we have seen from a transcript of discussion between him and counsel, intended to direct the jury that a definition of harm for present purposes was emotional *and* physical disturbance produced by terror. We think it was unfortunate that the judge, probably through inadvertence, used the disjunctive 'or.' As it was, the jury were left with a choice. Which they chose and acted upon we cannot tell. If they acted upon the basis that emotional disturbance was enough to constitute harm then, in our judgment, they would have done so upon a misdirection. Emotional disturbance does not occur to us as sensibly descriptive of injury or harm to the person through the operation of shock produced by terror or fright; morever, we do not think the word 'deterimental' assists to clarify whatever the expression 'emotional disturbance' is meant to convey. The further phrase used, namely, 'some such disturbance which would be bad for him' is likewise not helpful.

In his endeavours to give the jury appropriate guidance upon the meaning of harm within the facts of this case the judge was sailing uncharted seas. We have every sympathy with him. Unfortunately we think that what he said, other than the use of the phrase 'physical disturbance which is detrimental' (this was, we think, by itself, though easier to understand, inadequate) could have led the jury to contemplate merely a disturbance of the emotions as harm sufficient for the purpose of the second element when clearly, in our view, it is not.

In our judgment, a proper direction would have been that the requisite harm is caused if the unlawful act so shocks the victim to cause him physical injury.

NOTES AND QUESTIONS

1. The reasonable person is taken to know facts known to the defendant or which would be evident to the reasonable bystander. Watkins LJ continued:

> We look finally at the direction, 'That is to say all reasonable people who knew the facts that you know.' What the jury knew included, of course, the undisputed fact that the deceased had a very bad heart which at any moment could have ceased to function. It may be the judge did not intend that this fact should be included in the phrase 'the facts that you know.' If that was so, it is regrettable that he did not make it clear. By saying as he did, it is argued 'including the fact that the gun was a replica' and so on, the jury must have taken him to be telling them that all facts known to them, including the heart condition, should be taken into account in performing what is undoubtedly an objective test. We think there was a grave danger of that.
>
> This test can only be undertaken upon the basis of the knowledge gained by a sober and reasonable man as though he were present at the scene of and watched the unlawful act being performed and who knows that, as in the present case, an unloaded replica gun was in use, but that the victim may have thought it was a loaded gun in working order. In other words, he has the same knowledge as the man attempting to rob and no more. It was never suggested that any of these appellants knew that their victim had a bad heart. They knew nothing about him.
>
> A jury must be informed by the judge when trying the offence of manslaughter what facts they may and those which they may not use for the purpose of performing the test in the second element of this offence. . . .

2. Is there tension between the decision in *Dawson* and the general rule of causation that maintains that one must take one's victim as one finds her?

3. In *R v Watson* [1989] 2 All ER 865, the Court of Appeal indicated that the jury could take into account facts acquired by a defendant during the course of the crime. In *Watson* the defendants, two burglars, discovered that the resident of the house which they were burgling was an old and frail lady. An hour and a half after the crime she died of a heart attack. The Court of Appeal held that the defendants should be credited with knowledge of the victim's condition, even though they became aware of it only after the break-in.

(c) An *unlawful and dangerous act.* Should the requirement of an *act* be taken literally? A strange (and probably unjustified) distinction between acts and omissions in this context was made in *Lowe*.

R v Lowe

[1973] 1 QB 702, Court of Appeal

The defendant, who was of low average intelligence, knew that his infant child was sick but did not call a doctor. The child died from dehydration and gross emaciation. The defendant was indicted on counts of manslaughter of the child and of wilfully neglecting it so as to cause unnecessary suffering or injury to health, contrary to s. 1(1) of the Children and Young Persons Act 1933. The jury, in convicting the defendant on both counts, negatived reckless behaviour by him as being the cause of death and emphasised that the conviction of manslaughter was solely due to the direction of the judge that a finding of manslaughter must follow a conviction of wilful neglect if that neglect was the cause of death.

PHILLIMORE LJ: . . . Now in the present case the jury negatived recklessness. How then can mere neglect, albeit wilful, amount to manslaughter? This court feels that there is something inherently unattractive in a theory of constructive manslaughter. It seems strange that an omission which is wilful solely in the sense that it is not inadvertent and the consequences of which are not in fact foreseen by the person who is neglectful should, if death results, automatically give rise to an indeterminate sentence instead of the maximum of two years which would otherwise be the limit imposed.

We think that there is a clear distinction between an act of omission and an act of commission likely to cause harm. Whatever may be the position with regard to the latter it does not follow that the same is true of the former. In other words, if I strike a child in a manner likely to cause harm it is right that, if the child dies, I may be charged with manslaughter. If, however, I omit to do something with the result that it suffers injury to health which results in its death, we think that a charge of manslaughter should not be an inevitable consequence, even if the omission is deliberate.

Appeal against conviction of manslaughter allowed.

NOTE

The reference to a 'deliberate' omission in *Lowe* might best be understood in relation to the particular facts of the case. It is clear that the defendant neglected the child 'deliberately' in the sense that he decided not to call the doctor. However, the defendant was not aware of the probable consequences of his failure. It is therefore likely that the problems which commentators have with regard to the concept of 'deliberate' neglect are unfounded as the word was used in a rather curious fashion in the case. If that is so, however, what is the purpose of drawing a distinction between omissions and actions?

(d) *The effect of intoxication.* Where intoxication would not prevent a conviction of the defendant for the alleged unlawful act, it follows that he may be convicted of manslaughter if death results.

R v Lipman
[1970] 1 QB 152, Court of Appeal

WIDGERY LJ: . . . Both the defendant and the victim were addicted to drugs, and on the evening of September 16, 1967, both took a quantity of a drug known as LSD. Early on the morning of September 18, the defendant, who is a United States citizen, hurriedly booked out of his hotel and left the country. On the following day, September 19, the victim's landlord found her dead in her room. She had suffered two blows on the head causing haemorrhage of the brain, but she had died of asphyxia as a result of some eight inches of sheet having been crammed into her mouth.

The defendant was returned to this country by extradition proceedings, and at the trial he gave evidence of having gone with the victim to her room and there experienced what he described as an LSD 'trip'. He explained how he had the illusion of descending to the centre of the earth and being attacked by snakes, with which he had fought. It was not seriously disputed that he had killed the victim in the course of this experience, but he said he had no knowledge of what he was doing and no intention to harm her. He was charged with murder, but the jury evidently accepted that he lacked the necessary intention to kill or to do grievous bodily harm.

. . .

It was pointed out in this court that [in *R v Lamb* [1967] 2 QB 981] no unlawful act on the part of the prisoner had been proved in the absence of the necessary intent to constitute an assault. But this is intention of a different kind. Even if intent has to be proved to constitute the unlawful act, no specific further intent is required to turn that act into manslaughter. Manslaughter remains a most difficult offence to define because it arises in so many different ways and, as the mental element (if any) required to establish it varies so widely, any general reference to mens rea is apt to mislead.

We can dispose of the present application by reiterating that when the killing results from an unlawful act of the prisoner no specific intent has to be proved to convict of manslaughter, and self-induced intoxication is accordingly no defence. Since in the present case the acts complained of were obviously likely to cause harm to the victim (and did, in fact, kill her) no acquittal was possible and the verdict of manslaughter, at the least, was inevitable.

If and so far as this matter raises a point of law on which the defendant was entitled to appeal without leave, such appeal is dismissed.

NOTES AND QUESTIONS
1. What was the unlawful act in Lipman? What was the *mens rea* of that crime? How is this case distinguishable from *Lamb*? See also *O'Driscoll* (1977) 65 Cr App R 50.
2. Another case in which the unlawful act doctrine may have been stretched is *Cato* [1976] All ER 260. The Court of Appeal upheld a manslaughter verdict where the defendant had injected the victim with heroin, fatally as it transpired, supplied by the victim for that purpose. The defendant had also been convicted of administering a noxious thing with intent to endanger life contrary to s. 23 of the Offences Against the Person Act 1861. The Court of Appeal stated that even if they had not upheld the conviction for the s. 23 offence, they still would have confirmed the conviction for manslaughter. It is difficult to see what would have constituted the unlawful act in those circumstances, however, as the injection would not have been in violation of the Misuse of Drugs Act 1971.

(e) *Causation – must the act be directed at the victim?*. Because constructive manslaughter requires proof of the *mens rea* and *actus reus* of the 'unlawful act', it might be thought that if death follows from the unlawful act, however tenuous the causal link, then the offence would be made out. However, the courts were reluctant to abandon all the principles of causation. The position now is that if death follows from an unlawful and dangerous act aimed at anyone, manslaughter has been committed.

Attorney-General's Reference (No. 3 of 1994)
[1997] 3 All ER 936, House of Lords

For facts and holding, see p. 157.

LORD HOPE OF CRAIGHEAD: . . . [I]t is enough that the original unlawful and dangerous act, to which the required mental state is related, and the eventual death of the victim are both part of the same sequence of events.

Nor is it necessary, in order to constitute manslaughter, that the death resulted from an unlawful and dangerous act which was done with the intention to cause the victim to sustain harm. This is because it is clear from the authorities that, although the accused must be proved to have intended to do what he did, it is not necessary to prove that he knew that his act was unlawful or dangerous. So it must follow that it is unnecessary to prove that he knew that his act was likely to injure the person who died as a result of it. All that need be proved is that he intentionally did what he did, that the death was caused by it and that, applying an objective test, all sober and reasonable people would recognise the risk that some harm would result. The case of *R v Mitchell* [1983] QB 741 is a good example of this point. During an altercation in a queue at a busy post office the appellant hit a man who fell against an old lady, causing her to fall to the ground. Her leg was broken, with the result that she died later as a result of a pulmonary embolism. The Court of Appeal held that he was rightly convicted of manslaughter, although he had aimed no blow at the lady and had had no other physical contact with her. . . .

In *R* v *Dalby* [1982] 1 WLR 425, 428H Waller LJ said that, in all the cases of manslaughter by an unlawful and dangerous act, the researches of counsel had failed to find any case where the act which led to the death of the victim was not a direct act. In that case the appellant had supplied to the deceased a number of tablets of a class A controlled drug. A substantial cause of his death was the intravenous consumption of the drug with which he had injected himself on receipt of it from the appellant. The appellant's conviction of manslaughter was quashed on the ground that, where a charge of manslaughter was based on an unlawful and dangerous act, the act must be directed at the victim and likely to cause immediate injury, however slight. In the judgment of the court, the unlawful act of supplying drugs was not an act directed to the person of the deceased, and the supply did not cause any direct injury to him. Waller LJ summarised the effect of the cases to which the court was referred in this way at p. 429C:

> The kind of harm envisaged in all the reported cases of involuntary manslaughter was physical injury of some kind as an immediate and inevitable result of the unlawful act, e.g. a blow on the chin which knocks the victim against a wall causing a fractured skull and death, or threatening with a loaded gun which accidentally fires, or dropping a large stone on a train (*Director of Public Prosecutions* v *Newbury* [1977] AC 500) or threatening another with an open razor and stumbling with death resulting: *R* v *Larkin*, 29 Cr App R 18.

But none of the examples which were discussed in *R* v *Dalby*, which raised a different issue in view of the nature of the unlawful act of supplying the controlled drug, was concerned with the problem which arises here. In each of the cases which were cited as examples of an unlawful and dangerous act causing death which was held to be manslaughter the act was directed at the person who died as a result of it. In *R* v *Church* [1966] 1 QB 59 the victim was a woman whom the appellant believed to be already dead when, after knocking her semi-conscious, he threw her into a river when she was still alive. In *Director of Public Prosecutions* v *Newbury* [1977] AC 500 the victim was a train guard who was sitting next to the driver in the front cab when the appellants pushed a paving stone over the parapet of a bridge in the path of the oncoming train. It is important to notice that it was not suggested in that case that it was an essential element, in finding the appellants guilty of manslaughter, that their act was directed at the train guard in particular. It was enough that their act was dangerous because it was likely to injure some person on the train. This can be seen from the words used by the trial judge, Watkins J, who said at p. 502D:

> If that is your conclusion you then proceed to consider whether the next ingredient, as it is called, of this offence of manslaughter has been established. It is this: that the unlawful act was such as all sober and reasonable people would be bound to realise must expose someone such as the guard on this train or, . . . the driver on this train to, at least, the risk of some harm although not serious.

Lord Salmon, in rejecting the argument that the trial judge should have told the jury that they should acquit unless they were satisfied that the appellants had foreseen that they might cause harm to someone by pushing the paving stone off the parapet into the path of the train, said at p. 506G that his direction was completely in accordance with established law. He went on to add this, at p. 506H:

> In *R* v *Larkin* (1942) 29 Cr App R 18, Humphreys J said, at p. 23:
>
> > 'Where the act which a person is engaged in performing is unlawful, then if at the same time it is a dangerous act, that is, an act which is likely to injure another person, and quite inadvertently the doer of the act causes the death of that other person by that act, then he is guilty of manslaughter.'

I agree entirely with Lawton LJ that that is an admirably clear statement of the law which has been applied many times. It makes it plain (a) that an accused is guilty of manslaughter if it is proved that he intentionally did an act which was unlawful and dangerous and that that act inadvertently caused death and (b) that it is unnecessary to prove that the accused knew that the act was unlawful or dangerous.

Although the passage which Lord Salmon quoted from what was said by Humphreys J might be taken as suggesting that the accused's act must have been directed against the other person who dies as a result of it, the circumstances of that case and Lord Salmon's own statement of the law both show that this is not an essential element of the offence. The only questions which need to be addressed are (1) whether the act was done intentionally, (2) whether it was unlawful, (3) whether it was also dangerous because it was likely to cause harm to somebody and (4) whether that unlawful and dangerous act caused the death.

I think, then, that the position can be summarised in this way. The intention which must be discovered is an intention to do an act which is unlawful and dangerous. In this case the act which had to be shown to be an unlawful and dangerous act was the stabbing of the child's mother. There can be no doubt that all sober and reasonable people would regard that act, within the appropriate meaning of this term, as dangerous. It is plain that it was unlawful as it was done with the intention of causing her injury. As the defendant intended to commit that act, all the ingredients necessary for *mens rea* in regard to the crime of manslaughter were established, irrespective of who was the ultimate victim of it. The fact that the child whom the mother was carrying at the time was born alive and then died as a result of the stabbing is all that was needed for the offence of manslaughter when *actus reus*, for that crime was completed by the child's death. The question, once all the other elements are satisfied, is simply one of causation. The defendant must accept all the consequences of his act, so long as the jury are satisfied that he did what he did intentionally, that what he did was unlawful and that, applying the correct test, it was also dangerous. The death of the child was unintentional, but the nature and quality of the act which caused it was such that it was criminal and therefore punishable. In my opinion that is sufficient for the offence of manslaughter. There is no need to look to the doctrine of transferred malice for a solution to the problem raised by this case so far as manslaughter is concerned.

NOTES AND QUESTIONS

1. Is the whole idea of constructive manslaughter misconceived? What justifies convicting a defendant of a homicide offence when the defendant did not intend to kill and was not even reckless as to endangering life? Often the death is due to a fortuity. Would it not make more sense to convict the defendant of the underlying crime, taking into account where appropriate at sentencing the fact that a death resulted? See J. Gobert 'The Fortuity of Consequences' [1993] 4 Crim Law Forum 1.
2. What does Lord Hope of Craighead mean when he says that *Dalby* 'raised a different issue in view of the nature of the unlawful act of supplying the controlled drug'?

(ii) *Gross negligence manslaughter*

The classic definition of this category of manslaughter is to be found in *Bateman*:

R v *Bateman*

(1925) 19 Cr App R 8, Court of Criminal Appeal

LORD HEWART LCJ: . . . In explaining to juries the test which they should apply to determine whether the negligence, in the particular case, amounted or did not amount to a crime, judges have used many epithets, such as 'culpable,' 'criminal,' 'gross,' 'wicked,' 'clear,' 'complete.' But, whatever epithet be used and whether an epithet be used or not, in order to establish criminal liability the facts must be such that, in the opinion of the jury, the negligence of the accused went beyond a mere matter of compensation between subjects and showed such disregard for the life and safety of others as to amount to a crime against the State and conduct deserving punishment.

R v Adomako
[1995] 1 AC 171, House of Lords

LORD MACKAY OF CLASHFERN LC: . . . The conviction arose out of the conduct of an eye operation carried out at the Mayday Hospital, Croydon on 4 January 1987. The appellant was, during the latter part of that operation, the anaesthetist in charge of the patient.

The operation was carried out by two surgeons supported by a team of five nurses and a theatre sister. Anaesthesia commenced at about 9.45 a.m. The patient was paralysed by injection of a drug and an endotracheal tube was inserted to enable the patient to breathe by mechanical means. At the start of the operation the anaesthetist was Dr Said, a registrar. An operating department assistant was also present to help him. At about 10.30 a.m. there was a changeover of anaesthetists. The appellant was called to attend and take Dr Said's place following which both Dr Said and his assistant departed to deal with another operation elsewhere in the hospital. Another assistant was called to attend but did not arrive until later.

At approximately 11.05 a.m. a disconnection occurred at the endotracheal tube connection. The supply of oxygen to the patient ceased and this led to cardiac arrest at 11.14 a.m. During this period the appellant failed to notice or remedy the disconnection.

The appellant first became aware that something was amiss when an alarm sounded on the Dinamap machine, which monitors the patient's blood pressure. From the evidence it appears that some 4½ minutes would have elapsed between the disconnection and the sounding of this alarm. When this alarm sounded the appellant responded in various ways by checking the equipment and by administering atropine to raise the patient's pulse. But at no stage before the cardiac arrest did he check the integrity of the endotracheal tube connection. The disconnection itself was not discovered until after resuscitation measures had been commenced.

For the prosecution it was alleged that the appellant was guilty of gross negligence in failing to notice or respond appropriately to obvious signs that a disconnection had occurred and that the patient had ceased to breathe. In particular the prosecution alleged that the appellant had failed to notice at various stages during the period after disconnection and before the arrest either occurred or became inevitable that the patient's chest was not moving, the dials on the mechanical ventilating machine were not operating, the disconnection in the endotracheal tube, that the alarm on the ventilator was not switched on and that the patient was becoming progressively blue. Further the prosecution alleged that the appellant had noticed but failed to understand the correct significance of the fact that during this period the patient's pulse had dropped and the patient's blood pressure had dropped.

. . .

The jury convicted the appellant of manslaughter by a majority of 11 to 1. The Court of Appeal (Criminal Division) dismissed the appellant's appeal against conviction but certified that a point of law of general public importance was involved in the decision to dismiss the appeal, namely:

> in cases of manslaughter by criminal negligence not involving driving but involving a breach of duty is it a sufficient direction to the jury to adopt the gross negligence test set out by the Court of Appeal in the present case following Rex v Bateman (1925) 19 Cr App R 8 and Andrews v Director of Public Prosecutions [1937] AC 576, without reference to the test of recklessness as defined in Reg v Lawrence (Stephen) [1982] AC 510 or as adapted to the circumstances of the case?

. . .

The decision of the Court of Appeal is reported sub nom. *R v Prentice* [1994] QB 302 along with a number of other cases involving similar questions of law. The Court of Appeal held that except in cases of motor manslaughter the ingredients which had to be proved to establish an offence of involuntary manslaughter by breach of duty were the existence of the duty, a breach of the duty which had caused death and the jury considered to justify a criminal conviction; the jury might properly find gross negligence on proof of indifference to an obvious risk of injury to health or of actual foresight of the risk coupled either with a determination nevertheless to run it or with an intention to avoid it but involving such a high degree of negligence in the attempted avoidance as the jury considered justified conviction or of inattention or failure to advert to a serious risk going beyond mere inadvertence in respect of an obvious and important matter which the defendant's duty demanded he should address; and that, in the circumstances, the appeals of the two junior doctors and the electrician would be allowed and the appeal of the anaesthetist, namely Dr Adomako, would be dismissed. The reason that the Court of Appeal excepted the cases of motor manslaughter and their formulation of the law was the decision of this House in *R v Seymour (Edward)* [1983] 2 AC 493 in which it was held that where manslaughter was charged and the circumstances were that the victim was killed as a result of the reckless driving of the defendant on a public highway, the trial judge should give the jury the direction which had been suggested in *R v Lawrence (Stephen)* [1982] AC 510 but that it was appropriate also to point out that in order to constitute the offence of manslaughter the risk of death being caused by the manner of the defendant's driving must be very high.

. . . in my opinion the ordinary principles of the law of negligence apply to ascertain whether or not the defendant has been in breach of a duty of care towards the victim who has died. If such breach of duty is established the next question is whether that breach of duty caused the death of the victim. If so, the jury must go on to consider whether that breach of duty should be characterised as gross negligence and therefore as a crime. This will depend on the serious-ness of the breach of duty committed by the defendant in all the circumstances in which the defendant was placed when it occurred. The jury will have to consider whether the extent to which the defendant's conduct departed from the proper standard of care incumbent upon him, involving as it must have done a risk of death to the patient, was such that it should be judged criminal.

It is true that to a certain extent this involves an element of circularity, but in this branch of the law I do not believe that is fatal to its being correct as a test of how far conduct must depart from accepted standards to be characterised as criminal. This is necessarily a question of degree and an attempt to specify that degree more closely is I think likely to achieve only a spurious precision. The essence of the matter which is supremely a jury question is whether having regard to the risk of death involved, the conduct of the defendant was so bad in all the circumstances as to amount in their judgment to a criminal act or omission.

My Lords, the view which I have stated of the correct basis in law for the crime of involuntary manslaughter accords I consider with the criteria stated by counsel although I have not reached the degree of precision in definition which he required, but in my opinion it has been reached so far as practicable and with a result which leaves the matter properly stated for a jury's determination.

My Lords, in my view the law as stated in *R v Seymour* [1983] 2 AC 493 should no longer apply since the underlying statutory provisions on which it rested have now been repealed by the Road Traffic Act 1991. It may be that cases of involuntary motor manslaughter will as a result become rare but I consider it unsatisfactory that there should be any exception to the generality of the statement which I have made, since such exception, in my view, gives rise to unnecessary complexity. For example in *Kong Cheuk Kwan v The Queen* (1985) 82 Cr App R 18 it would give rise to unnecessary differences between the law applicable to those navigating vessels and the lookouts on the vessels.

I consider it perfectly appropriate that the word 'reckless' should be used in cases of involuntary manslaughter, but as Lord Atkin put it 'in the ordinary connotation of that word.' Examples in which this was done, to my mind, with complete accuracy are *R* v *Stone* [1977] QB 354 and *R* v *West London Coroner, Ex parte Gray* [1988] QB 467.

In my opinion it is quite unnecessary in the context of gross negligence to give the detailed directions with regard to the meaning of the word 'reckless' associated with *R* v *Lawrence* [1982] AC 510. The decision of the Court of Appeal (Criminal Division) in the other cases with which they were concerned at the same time as they heard the appeal in this case indicates that the circumstances in which involuntary manslaughter has to be considered may make the somewhat elaborate and rather rigid directions inappropriate. I entirely agree with the view that the circumstances to which a charge of involuntary manslaughter may apply are so various that it is unwise to attempt to categorise or detail specimen directions. For my part I would not wish to go beyond the description of the basis in law which I have already given.

For these reasons I am of the opinion that this appeal should be dismissed and that the certified question should be answered by saying:

> In cases of manslaughter by criminal negligence involving a breach of duty, it is a sufficient direction to the jury to adopt the gross negligence test set out by the Court of Appeal in the present case following *R* v *Bateman*, 19 Cr App R 8 and *Andrews* v *Director of Public Prosecutions* [1937] AC 576 and that it is not necessary to refer to the definition of recklessness in *R* v *Lawrence* [1982] AC 510, although it is perfectly open to the trial judge to use the word 'reckless' in its ordinary meaning as part of his exposition of the law if he deems it appropriate in the circumstances of the particular case.

NOTES AND QUESTIONS

1. At one time the courts recognised a separate category of reckless manslaughter which incorporated the *Caldwell* objective approach to recklessness (see, e.g., *R* v *Seymour* [1983] 2 AC 493). It is unclear whether the crime of reckless manslaughter survives the decision in *Adomako*, but if it does, it would now seem to require a subjective awareness of the risk (so-called *Cunningham* recklessness) in order for the defendant to be convicted.

2. In *Adomako*, Lord Mackay did not elaborate when a defendant was under a duty, implying that the tort standard of duty applied. In *R* v *Khan* [1998] Crim LR 830, the Court of Appeal held that it was the judge's responsibility to rule whether the facts of the case were capable of giving rise to a duty. The Court implied that to extend a duty to summon medical assistance to a drug dealer who supplied heroin to a person who subsequently died would enlarge the class of persons to whom a duty was owed. Why should this be so, given that the drug dealer is responsible for the victim's peril? Further confusion was caused by the Court of Appeal's ruling in *R* v *Singh (Gurphal)* [1999] Crim LR 582 where the Court of Appeal accepted that the existence of the duty of care was a matter of law on which the judge was entitled to give a conclusive ruling.

3. In *R* v *Singh (Gurphal)* [1999] Crim LR 582 the Court of Appeal ruled that the 'circumstances must be such that a reasonably prudent person would have foreseen a serious and obvious risk not merely of injury or even of serious injury but of death'. Is this too high a standard?

4. What is the *mens rea* of gross negligence manslaughter under *Adomako*? In *Attorney-General's Reference (No. 2 of 1999)* [2000] QB 796 (for facts and holding, see p. 259), the Court of Appeal stated that 'evidence of . . . state of mind is not a pre-requisite to conviction for manslaughter by gross negligence'. The court added, however, that 'there may be cases where the defendant's state of mind is relevant to the jury's consideration when assessing the grossness and criminality of his conduct'.

SECTION 4: **Reform of the law**

The law of homicide seems almost a quaint oddity in modern times. In an era where the definitions of virtually all crimes can be found in statute, it is anomalous that one must search ancient tomes to find the definition of the most serious crime known to the law (murder). Other doctrines in both the law of murder and manslaughter also cry out for clarification. This task of providing guidance was undertaken by the Criminal Law Revision Committee in its Fourteenth Report. The fruits of its efforts are reflected in the Draft Criminal Code Bill 1989:

Draft Criminal Code Bill 1989

53. For the purposes of this Chapter—
   (a) 'another' means a person who has been born and has an existence independent of his mother and, unless the context otherwise requires, 'death' and 'personal harm' mean the death of, or personal harm to, such a person;
   (b) a person does not cause death unless the death occurs within a year after the day on which any act causing it was done by that person or on which any fatal injury resulting from such an act was sustained, or (where the fatal injury was done to an unborn child) within a year after the day on which he was born and had an independent existence.

Homicide

54.—(1) A person is guilty of murder if he causes the death of another—
   (a) intending to cause death; or
   (b) intending to cause serious personal harm and being aware that he may cause death,
unless section 56, 58, 59, 62 or 64 applies.

(2) A person convicted of murder shall be sentenced to life imprisonment, except that, where he appears to the court to have been under the age of eighteen years at the time the offence was committed, he shall be sentenced to detention in such place and for such period and subject to such conditions as to release as the Secretary of State may determine.

55. A person is guilty of manslaughter if—
   (a) he is not guilty of murder by reason only of the fact that a defence provided by section 56 (diminished responsibility), 58 (provocation) or 59 (use of excessive force) applies; or
   (b) he is not guilty of murder by reason only of the fact that, because of voluntary intoxication, he is not aware that death may be caused or believes that an exempting circumstance exists; or
   (c) he causes the death of another—
      (i) intending to cause serious personal harm; or
      (ii) being reckless whether death or serious personal harm will be caused.

56.—(1) A person who, but for this section, would be guilty of murder is not guilty of murder if, at the time of his act, he is suffering from such mental abnormality as is a substantial enough reason to reduce his offence to manslaughter.

(2) In this section 'mental abnormality' means mental illness, arrested or incomplete development of mind, psychopathic disorder, and any other disorder or disability of mind, except intoxication.

(3) Where a person suffering from mental abnormality is also intoxicated, this section applies only where it would apply if he were not intoxicated.

57.—(1) Whether evidence is evidence of mental abnormality is a question of law.

(2) Where on a charge of murder or attempted murder the defendant has given or adduced evidence of mental disorder, severe mental handicap or automatism, the prosecution may adduce evidence of mental abnormality; but the court may give directions as to the stage of the proceedings at which it may do so.

(3) Where a person is charged with murder (or attempted murder) the prosecution may, with his consent, adduce evidence of mental abnormality at the committal proceedings, whereupon the magistrates' court may commit him for trial for manslaughter (or attempted manslaughter).

(4) Where the defendant has been committed for trial for murder (or attempted murder) the prosecution may, with the consent of the defendant, serve notice in accordance with Rules of Court of evidence of mental abnormality and indict him for manslaughter (or attempted manslaughter).

58. A person who, but for this section, would be guilty of murder is not guilty of murder if—

    (a) he acts when provoked (whether by things done or by things said or by both and whether by the deceased person or by another) to lose his self-control; and

    (b) the provocation is, in all the circumstances (including any of his personal characteristics that affect its gravity), sufficient ground for the loss of self-control.

59. A person who, but for this section, would be guilty of murder is not guilty of murder if, at the time of his act, he believes the use of the force which causes death to be necessary and reasonable to effect a purpose referred to in section 44 (use of force in public or private defence), but the force exceeds that which is necessary and reasonable in the circumstances which exist or (where there is a difference) in those which he believes to exist.

60. A person is guilty of murder or manslaughter (where section 54 or 55 applies) if—

    (a) he causes a fatal injury to another to occur within the ordinary limits of criminal jurisdiction, whether his act is done within or outside and whether the death occurs within or outside those limits;

    (b) he causes the death of another anywhere in the world by an act done within the ordinary limits of criminal jurisdiction; or

    (c) being a British citizen, he causes the death of another anywhere in the world by an act done anywhere in the world.

61. A person who attempts to cause the death of another, where section 56, 58 or 59 would apply if death were caused, is not guilty of attempted murder but is guilty of attempted manslaughter.

62.—(1) A person who, but for this section, would be guilty of murder is not guilty of murder but is guilty of suicide pact killing if his act is done in pursuance of a suicide pact between himself and the person killed.

(2) 'Suicide pact' means an agreement between two or more persons having for its object the death of all of them, whether or not each is to take his own life, but nothing done by a person who enters into a suicide pact shall be treated as done by him in pursuance of the pact unless it is done while he has the settled intention of dying in pursuance of the pact.

(3) A person acting in pursuance of a suicide pact between himself and another is not guilty of attempted murder but is guilty of attempted suicide pact killing if he attempts to cause the death of the other.

63. A person is guilty of an offence if he procures, assists or encourages suicide or attempted suicide committed by another.

NOTES AND QUESTIONS
1. In what ways would the Draft Criminal Code change the existing law?
2. A more radical reform would be to do away with murder and manslaughter, crimes which turn on result, and substitute for them crimes of endangering life. Should a defendant who commits an assault be guilty of a homicide offence punishable by life imprisonment if the victim happens to die, but only be guilty of what may be a summary offence punishable by a maximum of six months' imprisonment if the victim is fortunate enough to live? Consider in this regard the proposed (but yet to be enacted) New Zealand endangering statute, extracted in Chapter 3. Many of the issues raised by the proposals are explored in the final section of that chapter.
3. In May 2000, the government published a consultation paper on reforming the law of involuntary manslaughter. Drawing on a 1996 Law Commission Report (No. 239) on the same topic, the government proposed the creation of two separate offences of unintentional killing – 'reckless killing' and 'killing by gross carelessness'.

   A person would commit reckless killing if:
   (a) his or her conduct caused the death of another;
   (b) he or she was aware that his or her conduct would cause death or serious injury; and
   (c) it was unreasonable for him or her to take that risk having regard to the circumstances as he or she knew or believed them to be.

   A person would commit killing by gross carelessness if:
   (a) his or her conduct caused the death of another;
   (b) a risk that his or her conduct would cause death or serious injury would be obvious to a reasonable person in his or her position;
   (c) he or she was capable of appreciating that risk at the material time (but did not in fact do so); and either
   (d) his or her conduct fell far below what could reasonably be expected in the circumstances; or
   (e) he or she intended by his or her conduct to cause some injury, or was aware of, and unreasonably took, the risk that it might do so, *and* the conduct causing (or intended to cause) the injury constituted an offence.

   What are the differences between the proposed offences of 'reckless killing' and 'killing by gross carelessness'? What are the differences between the proposed offences and the present law?

   In the consultation paper, the government also indicated that there might be a need for an additional homicide offence covering the situation where a person, by his or her conduct, caused the death of another, intended to or was reckless as to whether some injury was caused, and the conduct causing, or intended to cause, the injury constituted an offence. In its 1996 Report, the Law Commission had opposed the creation of such an offence because it would introduce too much of a 'lottery effect' into the law of homicide.

SECTION 5: **Corporate manslaughter**

Many deaths occur in the workplace. Even where attributable to the company's arguable negligence, the company is typically charged with a violation of the Health and Safety at Work etc. Act 1974. See, e.g. *R v British Steel Ltd* [1995] ICR 586. Part of the reluctance to charge the company with manslaughter has been lack of a coherent theory whereby a company, a fictitious entity, can be held to have committed this crime. Whether a company could be guilty of manslaughter remained an unanswered question as recently as 1990. The capsizing of the Herald of Free Enterprise outside of Zeebrugge, however, caused much public outcry and gave rise to a prosecution for manslaughter against the ship's parent company, P&O. The Sheen Committee, which was appointed to investigate the disaster, had concluded that the company was 'infected with sloppiness' from top to bottom.

P&O European Ferries (Dover) Ltd
(1991) 93 Cr App R 72, Central Criminal Court

TURNER J: . . . The main thrust of the argument for the company in support of the submission that the four counts of manslaughter in this indictment should be quashed was not merely that English law does not recognise the offence of corporate manslaughter but that, as a matter of positive English Law, manslaughter can only be committed when one natural person kills another natural person. Hence it was no accident that there is no record of any corporation or non-natural person having been successfully prosecuted for manslaughter in any English Court. It was, however, accepted that there is no conceptual difficulty in attributing a criminal state of mind to a corporation. The broad argument advanced on behalf of the prosecution was that, there being no all embracing statutory definition of murder or manslaughter, there is, in principle, no reason why a corporation, or other non-natural person, cannot be found guilty of most offences in the criminal calendar. The exceptions to such a broad proposition could be found either in the form of punishment, which would be inappropriate for a corporation, or in the very personal nature of individual crimes or categories of crime such as offences under the Sexual Offences Act, bigamy and, arguably, perjury. It was further argued that the definitions of homicide to be found in the works of such as *Coke, Hale, Blackstone* and *Stephen* and which were strongly relied upon by the company, were and were not intended to be exclusive, but reflected the historical fact that, at the dates when these definitions originated, the concept of criminal liability of a corporation, just as their very existence, was not within the contemplation of the courts or the writers of the legal treatises referred to. Before the days when corporate crime was in contemplation, it can be a matter of no surprise to find that the definition of homicide did not include the possibility of a corporation committing such a crime. As recently as 1701 Sir John Holt, CJ is reported as having said: 'A corporation is not indictable but the particular members of it are.' Reported in 12 Mod 559. History does not, however, relate what was the subject matter of the litigation which provoked the above *dictum*.

The prosecution advanced an alternative argument to the effect that, if it were necessary that the death be, in fact, caused by a human being, then given the modern doctrine of 'identification,' as to which see below, if the perpetrator of the act who was a human being which caused death could be treated as the embodiment of the corporation, then to that extent the test would be satisfied. It is obvious however, that this alternative argument detracts from the force of the main argument.

Since the nineteenth century there has been a huge increase in the numbers and activities of corporations whether nationalised, municipal or commercial, which enter the private lives of all or most of 'men and subjects' in a diversity of ways. A clear case can be made for imputing to such corporations social duties including the duty not to offend all relevant parts of the criminal law. By tracing the history of the cases decided by the English Courts over the period of the last 150 years, it can be seen how first tentatively and, finally confidently the Courts have been able to ascribe to corporations a 'mind' which is generally one of the essential ingredients of common law and statutory offences. Indeed, it can be seen that in many Acts of Parliament the same concept has been embraced. The parliamentary approach is, perhaps, exemplified by section 18 of the Theft Act, 1968 which provides for directors and managers of a limited company to be rendered liable to conviction if an offence under section 15, 16 or 17 of the Act is proved to have been committed – and I quote: 'with the consent, connivance of any director, manager, secretary . . . purporting to act in such capacity, then such director, manager or secretary shall be guilty of the offence.' Once a state of mind could be effectively attributed to a corporation, all that remained was to determine the means by which that state of mind could be ascertained and imputed to a non-natural person. That done, the obstacle to the acceptance of general criminal liability of a corporation was overcome. *Cessante ratione legis, cessat ipsa lex.* As some of the decisions in other common law countries indicate, there is nothing essentially incongruous in the notion that a corporation should be guilty of an offence of unlawful killing. I find unpersuasive the argument of the company that the old definitions of homicide positively exclude the liability of a non-natural person to conviction of an offence of manslaughter. Any crime, in order to be justiciable must have been committed by or through the agency of a human being. Consequently, the inclusion in the definition of the expression 'human being' as the author of the killing was either tautologous or, as I think more probable, intended to differentiate those cases of death in which a human being played no direct part and which would have led to forfeiture of the inanimate, or if animate non-human object which caused the death (*deodand*) from those in which the cause of death was initiated by human activity albeit the instrument of death was inanimate or if animate non-human. I am confident that the expression 'human being' in the definition of homicide was not intended to have the effect of words of limitation as might have been the case had it been found in some Act of Parliament or legal deed. It is not for me to attempt to set the limits of corporate liability for criminal offences in English Law. Examples of other crimes which may or may not be committed by corporations will, no doubt, be decided on a case by case basis in conformity with the manner in which the common law has adapted itself in the past. Suffice it that where a corporation, through the controlling mind of one of its agents, does an act which fulfils the prerequisites of the crime of manslaughter, it is properly indictable for the crime of manslaughter.

In arriving at this decision, which may be thought by some to have increased the scope of English criminal law, but which I believe merely reflects the extent of developments which have already occurred, I have borne fully in mind the warning shot put across my bows by Mr Kentridge when he referred me to the passage in *Withers* v *Director of Public Prosecutions* (1974) 60 Cr App R 85, [1975] AC 842, in the course of which Lord Simon of Glaisdale, p. 95 and at p. 863, had said: 'The first principle is that it is not open to the courts nowadays either to create new offences or so to widen existing offences as to make punishable conduct of a type hitherto not subject to punishment (*Newland* (1953) 37 Cr App R 154, 153, [1954] 1 QB 158, 167; *Shaw* v *Director of Public Prosecutions* (1961) 45 Cr App R 113, 157, [1962] AC 220, 267; *R* v *Knuller (Publishing, Printing and Promotions) Limited* (1972) 56 Cr App R 633, [1973] AC 435).'

As it seemed to me, however, the decision that manslaughter is an offence which may be committed by corporations involves neither the widening of any existing offence nor the making punishable conduct of a type hitherto not subject to punishment. Counsel for the Crown, in his admirable reply, reminded me of the second of Lord Simon's principles in *Withers* case which is that 'the courts cannot refuse to apply a legal rule deducible from an authoritative decision to circumstances analogous to those inherent in such decision.' In support of which Lord Simon referred to *Mirehouse* v *Rennell* (1833) 1 Cl & F 527. 546, which was approved in *Shaw* v *Director of Public Prosecutions* and *Knuller*, already referred to. My decision in the present case is, I believe, in accord with the second rather than the first of these principles.

NOTES AND QUESTIONS

1. The charges against P&O were dismissed after Turner, J. ruled that P&O's directors had not been reckless in failing to appreciate the risks of an open bow sailing. Under the 'identification' test of a company's criminal liability, a company can only be convicted of a crime committed by a person 'identified' with the company (usually a director, executive

officer or senior manager). Thus, as the directors were not guilty of reckless manslaughter, the company also could not be convicted of that crime.

2. At the trial of P&O, executives of other companies testified that they too did not appreciate the risks associated with open bow sailings. It was in part on the basis of this evidence that Turner, J. ruled as he did. Does the judge's ruling render it in the industry's interest to remain ignorant of the risks of their business operation? If so, is this ignorance in the public's interest?
3. At the time of the decision, the prevailing test of involuntary manslaughter was that of recklessness. Thereafter, the House of Lords in *Adomako* indicated that the proper test was that of 'gross negligence'. Would this have made a difference?

Attorney-General's Reference (No. 2 of 1999)
[2000] QB 796, Court of Appeal

15 February. ROSE L.J. handed down the following opinion of the court. The court's opinion is sought in relation to two questions referred by the Attorney-General under section 36 of the Criminal Justice Act 1972. (1) Can a defendant be properly convicted of manslaughter by gross negligence in the absence of evidence as to that defendant's state of mind? (2) Can a non-human defendant be convicted of the crime of manslaughter by gross negligence in the absence of evidence establishing the guilt of an identified human individual for the same crime?

The questions arise from a ruling given by Scott Baker J. at the Central Criminal Court on 30 June 1999. At the outset of the trial of the defendant train operating company, on an indictment containing seven counts of manslaughter, he ruled that it is a condition precedent to a conviction for manslaughter by gross negligence for a guilty mind to be proved and that where a non-human defendant is prosecuted it may only be convicted via the guilt of a human being with whom it may be identified. It is submitted for the Attorney-General that the judge was wrong in both respects.

The prosecution arose from the disastrous collision which occurred at Southall at 1.15 p.m. on 19 September 1997. The 10.32 a.m. high speed train ('H.S.T.') from Swansea to London Paddington, with approximately 180 passengers and staff on board, operated by the defendant and travelling on the up main line, collided with a freight train crossing from the down relief line to Southall Yard. Seven passengers died. 151 people were injured. Millions of pounds' worth of damage was done.

The H.S.T. had a driver of considerable experience but no second competent person with him. The power car was fitted with two safety devices independent of the driver. Each was designed to prevent a signal being passed at danger. One system was the Automatic Warning System ('A.W.S.') which had been in common use in the United Kingdom since the 1950s. It had been deliberately switched off. The other system was Automatic Train Protection ('A.T.P.') which the defendant was piloting for Railtrack and was the only United Kingdom operator using it. It had been switched off. The driver knew that neither A.W.S. nor A.T.P. were operating.

The movement of the train was correctly signalled, i.e. the signals on the up main line affecting the H.S.T. prior to the junction were set successively at green, double yellow, single yellow and red. The H.S.T. driver remembered passing through the green signal but next recalled seeing the red signal. He braked as hard as he could, but, as he was travelling at an average of 116 m.p.h. over the 3,600 metres immediately preceding the accident, it was too late.

The case for the prosecution was that the cause of the collision was, first, the driver's failure to see or heed the double yellow and single yellow signals warning of impending red and, secondly, the defendant's manner of operating the H.S.T. The case against the defendant was that it owed a duty to take reasonable care for the safety of its passengers, of which it was in grossly negligent breach. Three signals were passed because the A.W.S. and A.T.P. were switched off and there was only one man in the cab. The defendant should not have permitted such a train to operate in such circumstances.

. . .

As a result of *Reg. v. Adomako*, Mr. Lissack submitted, gross negligence manslaughter can be proved without the need to enquire into the state of the defendant's mind. This proposition is supported by a passage in *Smith & Hogan on Criminal Law*, 7th ed. (1992), at pp. 90 and 91, which culminates in contrasting crimes requiring mens rea with crimes of negligence. The *Adomako* test was derived from *Rex v. Bateman* (1925) 19 Cr.App.R. 8, which was an objective test: see the Law Commission's Consultation Paper on Involuntary Manslaughter (1994) (Law Com. No. 135), p. 43, para. 3.32.

For the defendant, Mr. Caplan, in relation to question 1, submitted that there is a difference between whether mens rea must be proved and whether it may be relevant. He accepted that it need not be proved for gross negligence. But, he said, it may be relevant because the *Adomako* test requires the jury, when deciding if the breach is criminal, to consider it in all the circumstances. Furthermore, in *Reg. v. Adomako* [1995] 1 A.C. 171, 187, Lord Mackay L.C. went on to say that it was perfectly appropriate to use the word 'reckless' in cases of involuntary manslaughter, in its ordinary connotation as in *Reg. v. Stone* [1977] Q.B. 354. In *Stone's* case Geoffrey Lane L.J. said that, where a defendant had undertaken a duty of care for the health and welfare of an infirm person, the prosecution had to prove, at p. 363:

> 'a reckless disregard of danger to the health and welfare of the infirm person. Mere inadvertence is not enough. The defendant must be proved to have been indifferent to an obvious risk of injury to health, or actually to have foreseen the risk but to have determined nevertheless to run it.'

On this question, we accept the submissions of both Mr. Lissack and Mr. Caplan. They lead to the conclusion that question I must be answered 'Yes.' Although there may be cases where the defendant's state of mind is relevant to the jury's consideration when assessing the grossness and criminality of his conduct, evidence of his state of mind is not a prerequisite to a conviction for manslaughter by gross negligence. The *Adomako* test is objective, but a defendant who is reckless as defined in *Reg. v. Stone* [1977] Q.B. 354 may well be the more readily found to be grossly negligent to a criminal degree.

As to question 2, Mr. Lissack accepted that policy considerations arise. Large companies should be as susceptible to prosecution for manslaughter as one-man companies. Where the ingredients of a common law offence are identical to those of a statutory offence there is no justification for drawing a distinction as to liability between the two and the public interest requires the more emphatic denunciation of a company inherent in a conviction for manslaughter. He submitted that the ingredients of the offence of gross negligence manslaughter are the same in relation to a body corporate as to a human being, namely grossly negligent breach of a duty to a deceased causative of his death. It is, he submitted, unnecessary and inappropriate to enquire whether there is an employee in the company who is guilty of the offence of manslaughter who can properly be said to have been acting as the embodiment of the company. The criminal law of negligence follows the civil law of negligence as applied to corporations: the only difference is that, to be criminal, the negligence must be gross. Of the three theories of corporate criminal liability, namely vicarious liability, identification and personal liability, it is personal liability which should here apply. In the present case, it would have been open to the jury to convict if they were satisfied that the deaths occurred by reason of a gross breach by the defendant of its personal duty to have a safe system of train operation in place. The identification theory, attributing to the company the mind and will of senior directors and managers, was developed in order to avoid injustice: it would bring the law into disrepute if every act and state of mind of an individual employee was attributed to a company which was entirely blameless.

. . .

Before turning to Mr. Lissack's submission in relation to personal liability it is convenient first to refer to the speech of Lord Hoffmann in *Meridian Global Funds Management Asia Ltd. v. Securities Commission* [1995] 2 A.C. 500, on which Mr. Lissack relied as the linchpin of this part of his argument. It was a case in which the chief investment officer and senior portfolio manager of an investment management company, with the company's authority but unknown to the board of directors and managing director, used funds managed by the company to acquire shares, but failed to comply with a statutory obligation to give notice of the acquisition to the Securities Commission. The trial judge held that the knowledge of the officer and manager should be attributed to the company, and the Court of Appeal of New Zealand upheld the decision on the basis that the officer was the directing mind and will of the company. The Privy Council dismissed an appeal. Lord Hoffmann, giving the judgment of the Privy Council, said, at p. 506, that the company's primary rules of attribution were generally found in its constitution or implied by company law. But, in an exceptional case, where the application of those principles would defeat the intended application of a particular provision to companies, it was necessary to devise a special rule of attribution. Lord Hoffmann said, at p. 507:

> 'For example, a rule may be stated in language primarily applicable to a natural person and require some act or state of mind on the part of that person "himself", as opposed to his servants or agents. This is generally true of the rules of the criminal law, which ordinarily impose liability only for the actus reus and mens rea of the defendant himself. How is such a rule to be applied to a company? One possibility is that the court may come to the conclusion that the rule was not intended to apply to companies at all; for example, a law which created an offence for which the only penalty was community service. Another possibility is that the court might interpret the law as meaning that it could apply to a company only on the basis of its primary rules of attribution, i.e. if the act giving rise to liability was specifically authorised by a resolution of the board or a unanimous agreement of the shareholders. But there will be many cases in which neither of these solutions is satisfactory; in which the court considers that the law was intended to apply to companies and that, although it excludes ordinary vicarious liability, insistence on the primary rules of attribution would in practice defeat that intention. In such a case, the court must fashion a special rule of attribution for the particular substantive rule. This is always a matter of interpretation: given that it was intended to apply to a company, how was it intended to apply? Whose act (or knowledge, or state of mind) was *for this purpose* intended to count as the act etc. of the company? One finds the answer to this question by applying the usual canons of interpretation, taking into account the language of the rule (if it is a statute) and its content and policy.'

Lord Hoffmann then referred to *Tesco Supermarkets Ltd. v. Nattrass* [1972] A.C. 153 and *In re Supply of Ready Mixed Concrete (No. 2)* [1995] 1 A.C. 456, Viscount Haldane's speech in *Lennard's Carrying Co. Ltd. v. Asiatic Petroleum Co. Ltd.* [1915] A.C. 705 and Denning L.J.'s judgment in *H. L. Bolton (Engineering) Co. Ltd. v. T. J. Graham & Sons Ltd.* [1957] 1 Q.B. 159. Having referred to the concept of directing mind and will, he went on to say [1995] 2 A.C. 500, 511:

> 'It will often be the most appropriate description of the person designated by the relevant attribution rule, but it might be better to acknowledge that not every such rule has to be forced into the same formula. Once it is appreciated that the question is one of construction rather than metaphysics, the answer in this case seems to their Lordships to be as straightforward as it did to Heron J. The policy of section 20 of the Securities Amendment Act 1988 is to compel, in fast-moving markets, the immediate disclosure of the identity of persons who become substantial security holders in public issuers . . . what rule should be implied as to the person whose knowledge for this purpose is to count as the knowledge of the company? Surely the person who, with the authority of the company, acquired the

relevant interest. Otherwise the policy of the Act would be defeated . . . the company knows that it has become a substantial security holder when that is known to the person who had authority to do the deal. It is then obliged to give notice.'

Lord Hoffmann went on to comment that it was not necessary in that case to inquire whether the chief investment officer could be described as the 'directing mind and will' of the company. He said, at p. 511:

'It is a question of construction in each case as to whether the particular rule requires that the knowledge that an act has been done, or the state of mind with which it was done, should be attributed to the company.'

Mr. Lissack's submission that personal liability on the part of the company is capable of arising in the present case was based on a number of authorities in addition to *Meridian Global Funds Management Asia Ltd. v. Securities Commission* [1995] 2 A.C. 500. In *Reg. v. British Steel Plc.* [1995] 1 W.L.R. 1356 the defendant was prosecuted, as was the present defendant, for a breach of sections 3(1) and 33(1)(a) of the Health and Safety at Work etc. Act 1974. A worker was killed because of the collapse of a steel platform during a repositioning operation which a competent supervisor would have recognised was inherently dangerous. The defence was that the workmen had disobeyed instructions and, even if the supervisor was at fault, the company at the level of its directing mind had taken reasonable care. An appeal against conviction was dismissed by the Court of Appeal, Criminal Division. The judgment was given by Steyn L.J., who said, at pp. 1362–1363:

'counsel for British Steel Plc. concedes that it is not easy to fit the idea of corporate criminal liability only for acts of the "directing mind" of the company into the language of section 3(1). We would go further. If it be accepted that Parliament considered it necessary for the protection of public health and safety to impose, subject to the defence of reasonable practicability, absolute criminal liability, it would drive a juggernaut through the legislative scheme if corporate employers could avoid criminal liability where the potentially harmful event is committed by someone who is not the directing mind of the company . . . That would emasculate the legislation.'

. . .

Mr. Lissack submitted that, in accordance with the speech of Lord Hoffmann in *Meridian Global Funds Management Asia Ltd. v. Securities Commission* [1995] 2 A.C. 500, the choice of the appropriate theory depends on the ingredients of the offence itself; and the requirements of both retribution and deterrence point to corporate liability where death is caused through the company's gross negligence. He relied on a passage in Steyn L.J.'s judgment in the *Reg. v. British Steel Plc.* [1995] 1 W.L.R. 1356, 1364 where there is reference to the promotion of 'a culture of guarding against the risks to health and safety by virtue of hazardous industrial operations.'

Mr. Lissack advanced two subsidiary submissions. First, if, contrary to his primary submission, a corporation cannot be convicted unless an employee embodying the company can be identified as guilty of manslaughter, the presence of such an employee can be inferred: he relied on a passage in the speech of Lord Hoffmann in *Meridian Global Funds Management Asia Ltd. v. Securities Commission* [1995] 2 A.C. 500. 510 which seems to us to afford no support whatever for this submission. We reject it. Secondly, he suggested that aggregation has a role to play, i.e. where a series of venial management failures is aggregated and cumulatively amounts to gross negligence, a company may be convicted. There is a tentatively-expressed passage in *Smith & Hogan's Criminal Law*, 9th ed. (1999), at p. 186, based on an analogy with civil negligence, which supports this suggestion. But there is no supporting and clear contrary judicial authority: see *Reg. v. Coroner for East Kent. Ex parte Spooner* (1987) 88 Cr.App.R. 10, 16–17, *per* Bingham L.J.:

'A case against a personal defendant cannot be fortified by evidence against another defendant. The case against a corporation can only be made by evidence properly addressed to showing guilt on the part of the corporation as such.'

The Law Commission, in their report on Legislating the Criminal Code: Involuntary Manslaughter (1996) (Law Com. No. 237), p. 96, para. 7.33, are against introducing the concept of aggregation. We reject the suggestion that aggregation has any proper role to play.

For the defendant, Mr. Caplan submitted, in relation to question 2, that *Reg. v. Adomako* [1995] 1 A.C. 171 was not concerned with corporate liability. It is necessarily implicit in the Law Commission's recommendation, in Law Com. No. 237, that Parliament should enact a new offence of corporate killing, that the doctrine of identification still continues to apply to gross negligence manslaughter since *Adomako's* case. *Tesco Supermarkets Ltd. v. Nattrass* [1972] A.C. 153 is still authoritative (see *Seaboard Offshore Ltd. v. Secretary of State for Transport* [1994] 1 W.L.R. 541) and it is impossible to find a company guilty unless its alter ego is identified. None of the authorities since *Tesco Supermarkets Ltd. v. Nattrass* relied on by Mr. Lissack supports the demise of the doctrine of identification: all are concerned with statutory construction of different substantive offences and the appropriate rule of attribution was decided having regard to the legislative intent, namely whether Parliament intended companies to be liable. There is a sound reason for a special rule of attribution in relation to statutory offences rather than common law offences, namely there is, subject to a defence of reasonable practicability, an absolute duty imposed by the statutes. The authorities on statutory offences do not bear on the common law principle in relation to manslaughter. Lord Hoffmann's speech in *Meridian Global Funds Management Asia Ltd. v. Securities Commission* [1995] 2 A.C. 500 is a restatement, not an abandonment, of existing principles: see, for example, Lord Diplock in *Tesco Supermarkets Ltd. v. Nattrass* [1972] A.C. 153, 200:

> 'there may be criminal statues which upon their true construction ascribe to a corporation criminal responsibility for the acts of servants and agents who would be excluded by the test that I have stated . . .'

(viz. those exercising the powers of the company under its articles of association.) The Law Commission's proposals were made after *Meridian Global Funds Management Asia Ltd. v. Securities Commission* [1995] 2 A.C. 500 and *Reg. v. British Steel Plc.* [1995] 1 W.L.R. 1356. Identification is necessary in relation to the actus reus, i.e. whose acts or omissions are to be attributed to the company and the *Adomako* case's objective test in relation to gross negligence in no way affects this. Furthermore, the civil negligence rule of liability for the acts of servants or agents has no place in the criminal law – which is why the identification principle was developed. That principle is still the rule of attribution in criminal law whether or not mens rea needs to be proved.

. . .

There is, as it seems to us, no sound basis for suggesting that, by their recent decisions, the courts have started a process of moving from identification to personal liability as a basis for corporate liability for manslaughter. In *Reg. v. Adomako* [1995] 1 A.C. 171 the House of Lords were, as it seems to us, seeking to escape from the unnecessarily complex accretions in relation to recklessness arising from *Reg. v. Lawrence (Stephen)* [1982] A.C. 510 and *Reg. v. Caldwell* [1982] A.C. 341. To do so, they simplified the ingredients of gross negligence manslaughter by restating them in line with *Rex. v. Bateman* (1925) 19 Cr.App.R. 8. But corporate liability was not mentioned anywhere in the submissions of counsel or their Lordship's speeches. In any event, the identification principle is in our judgment just as relevant to the actus reus as to mens rea. In *Tesco Supermarkets Ltd. v. Nattrass* [1972] A.C. 153, 173 Lord Reid said:

> 'the judge must direct the jury that if they find certain facts proved then as a matter of law they must find that the criminal act of the officer, servant or agent including his state of mind, intention, knowledge or belief is the act of the company.'

In *Reg. v. Coroner for East Kent, Ex parte Spooner*, 88 Cr.App.R. 10. 16 Bingham L.J. said:

'for a company to be criminally liable for manslaughter . . . it is required that the mens rea and the actus reus of manslaughter should be established . . . against those who were to be identified as the embodiment of the company itself.'

In *Reg. v. P. & O. European Ferries (Dover) Ltd.* (1990) 93 Cr.App.R. 72. 84 Turner J., in his classic analysis of the relevant principles, said that:

'where a corporation, through the controlling mind of one of its agents, does an act which fulfils the prerequisites of the crime of manslaughter, it is properly indictable for the crime of manslaughter.'

In our judgment, unless an identified individual's conduct, characterisable as gross criminal negligence, can be attributed to the company, the company is not, in the present state of the common law, liable for manslaughter. Civil negligence rules, e.g. as enunciated in *Wilsons & Clyde Coal Co. Ltd. v. English* [1938] A.C. 57, are not apt to confer criminal liability on a company.

None of the authorities relied on by Mr. Lissack as pointing to personal liability for manslaughter by a company supports that contention. In each, the decision was dependent on the purposive construction that the particular statute imposed, subject to a defence of reasonable practicability, liability on a company for conducting its undertaking in a manner exposing employees or the public to health and safety risk. In each case there was an identified employee whose conduct was held to be that of the company. In each case it was held that the concept of directing mind and will had no application when construing the statute. But it was not suggested or implied that the concept of identification is dead or moribund in relation to common law offences. Indeed, if that were so, it might have been expected that Lord Hoffmann, in *Reg. v. Associated Octel Ltd.* [1996] 1 W.L.R. 1543, would have referred to the ill health of the doctrine in the light of his own speech, less than a year before, in *Meridian Global Funds Management Asia Ltd. v. Securities Commission* [1995] 2 A.C. 500. He made no such reference, nor was the *Meridian* case cited in *Reg. v. Associated Octel Ltd.* It therefore seems safe to conclude that Lord Hoffmann (and, similarly, the members of the Court of Appeal (Criminal Division), in *Reg. v. British Steel Plc.* [1995] 1 W.L.R. 1356 and in *Reg. v. Gateway Foodmarkets Ltd.* [1997] I.C.R. 382) did not think that the common law principles as to the need for identification have changed. Indeed, Lord Hoffmann's speech in *Meridian Global Funds Management Asia Ltd. v. Securities Commission* [1995] 2 A.C. 500, in fashioning an additional special rule of attribution geared to the purpose of the statute, proceeded on the basis that the primary 'directing mind and will' rule still applies although it is not determinative in all cases. In other words, he was not departing from the identification theory but reaffirming its existence.

This approach is entirely consonant with the Law Commission's analysis of the present state of the law and the terms of their proposals for reform in their report on Legislating the Criminal Code: Involuntary Manslaughter (Law Com. No. 237). In this report, both the House of Lords's decision in *Reg. v. Adomako* [1995] 1 A.C. 171 and the Privy Council's decision in *Meridian Global Funds Management Asia Ltd. v. Securities Commission* [1995] 2 A.C. 500, were discussed. In the light of their analysis, the Law Commission concluded (Law Com. No. 237, at para. 6.27 and following and para. 7.5) that, in the present state of the law, a corporation's liability for manslaughter is based solely on the principle of identification and they drafted a Bill to confer liability based on management failure not involving the principle of identification: see clause 4 of the draft Bill annexed to their report. If Mr. Lissack's submissions are correct there is no need for such a Bill and, as Scott Baker J. put it, the Law Commission have missed the point. We agree with the judge that the Law Commission have not missed the point and Mr. Lissack's submissions are not correct: the identification principle remains the only basis in common law for corporate liability for gross negligence manslaughter.

We should add that, if we entertained doubt on the matter, being mindful of the observations of Lord Lowry in *C. (A Minor) v. Director of Public Prosecutions* [1996] A.C. 1. 28, we would not think it appropriate for this court to propel the law in the direction which Mr. Lissack seeks. That, in our judgment, taking into account the policy considerations to which Mr. Lissack referred, is a matter for Parliament, not the courts. For almost four years, the Law Commission's draft Bill has been to hand as a useful starting point for that purpose.

It follows that, in our opinion, the answer to question 2 is 'No.'

Opinions accordingly.

NOTES AND QUESTIONS
1. The 'identification' test of corporate criminal liability has been heavily criticised, not only because of the difficulties of determining who can be 'identified' with a company, but also because a company can seemingly avoid criminal liability by insulating its officers and directors from knowledge of wrongdoing perpetrated by lower-echelon employees. See generally D. Bergman, *The Case for Corporate* Responsibility (2000); J. Gobert & M. Punch, *Rethinking Corporate Crime* (2003); C. Wells, *Corporations and Criminal Responsibility* (2d Ed. 2000)
2. The end of the opinion in *Attorney-General's Reference*, the Court of Appeal suggested it was the responsibility of Parliament, and not that of the courts, to reform the law of corporate manslaughter. Given that the law of murder and manslaughter were common law creations (that is, the law was fashioned by the judges), is it not the court's responsibility to 'clean up its own house'?

In any event, the government in 2002 issued a consultation paper proposing a crime of 'corporate killing' based on a proposal of The Law Commission made some four years previously. Under the government's proposal;

(1) A corporation is guilty of corporate killing if—

(a) a management failure by the corporation is the cause or one of the causes of a person's death; and

(b) that failure constitutes conduct falling far below what can reasonably be expected of the corporation in the circumstances.

(2) For the purposes of subsection (1) above—

(a) there is a management failure by a corporation if the way in which its activities are managed or organised fails to ensure the health and safety of persons employed in or affected by those activities; and

(b) such a failure may be regarded as a cause of a person's death notwithstanding that the immediate cause is the act or omission of an individual.

NOTES AND QUESTIONS
1. In one of the few departures from The Law Commission's recommendations, the government would extend the offence of corporate killing to all 'undertakings', a term which has also been used in the Health and Safety at Work etc. Act 1974). The effect would be to significantly broaden the scope of potential liability.
2. What constitutes a 'management failure' under the proposed offence? Is it a failure of persons who qualify as management? The Law Commission rejected this interpretation, indicating that the term was to refer to the management of the company's business, and not to the acts or omissions of persons who could be characterised as managers.

3. When can it be said that a management failure has fallen 'far below what can reasonably be expected of the corporation in the circumstances'? Like the test of 'gross negligence', culpability seems to be a matter of degree. But against what benchmark is the corporate defendant's failure to be judged—that of a 'reasonable company' (an analogy to the 'reasonable person')? What constitutes a 'reasonable company'?

4. Note the test of causation in 3.(2)(b). How does it differ from conceptions of causation discussed previously (see Chapter 3, Section 3)?

5. The government's proposed corporate killing offence is analysed in Sullivan 'Corporate Killing – Some Government Proposals' [2001] Crim LR 31; and in Gobert 'Corporate Killings at Home and Abroad – Reflections on The Government's Proposals' (2002) 118 LQR 72.

6

Non-fatal Offences Against the Person

SECTION 1: **Introduction**

This chapter deals with attacks on the personal integrity of a victim. The criminal law in this area is very muddled. The basic offences, of common law origin, have been replaced by a number of statutory offences. In *DPP v Little* [1992] 1 All ER 299 the Divisional Court stated that assault and battery have been statutory crimes since 1861. The statute (Offences Against the Person Act 1861) itself dates from the mid-nineteenth century and contains many anachronisms. It covers several aggravated offences which require proof of a common law assault as a prerequisite to conviction of a more serious, aggravated offence under the statute.

It would require a separate book to examine all the offences contained in the 1861 Act, and many of them are rarely charged. However, a student would be well advised to look at the whole statute in order to acquire the flavour of the legislation. In this chapter the common law offences and the main aggravated assaults.

Anyone studying the topic of assault needs to be sensitive to the value judgments which have to be made; for instance, the age at which people may consent to various activities or the purposes for which consent may be given. The answer to such questions may vary as society's attitudes change over time.

SECTION 2: **Assault**

Confusion is often caused by the court's use of the term 'assault' to cover two distinct offences:

(a) assault; and

(b) battery.

This is perhaps because typically a defendant commits both offences at the same time. However, the two offences are not identical and each will be examined separately. It should be noted that this, as well as many of the other common law distinctions, will lose its importance if the Government's 1998 proposals for reform (set out later in the chapter) are enacted into law.

An assault (or 'common assault', as it is sometimes called) is committed when the accused intentionally or recklessly causes the victim to apprehend the application of immediate and unlawful physical force to his or her person. The essence of the offence is the inducing of fear and no touching is necessary.

A: *Actus reus*

The victim must anticipate the immediate unlawful application of force to his or her person. No force need actually be applied (if it is, the defendant is guilty of battery). The victim has only to be in fear of a battery which 'need not necessarily be hostile, rude or aggressive' according to Lord Lane in *Faulkner* v *Talbot* [1981] 3 All ER 468, at p. 471.

It should be noted that the force which must be apprehended is *unlawful* force. If there is evidence that the victim consented or that the force was in any other way lawful (see defences, below) it will be for the prosecution to establish beyond reasonable doubt that the force was unlawful. If the victim did not apprehend the application of force no offence is committed, even if the victim was tragically wrong, as in *R* v *Lamb* [1967] 2 QB 981 (for facts and holding see p. 242):

The victim must apprehend the *immediate* application of force:

Smith v Chief Superintendent of Woking Police Station
(1983) 76 Cr App R 234, Divisional Court

KERR LJ: . . . The justices found the following facts. On the evening of September 8, 1982, the defendant entered the grounds of Milford House and looked through the windows of Miss Mooney's bed-sitting room, and that the grounds form part of an enclosed garden. Then they found that Miss Mooney saw the defendant through the windows and recognised him and, 'she was absolutely terrified, to the extent that she was very nervous and jumpy for a few days afterwards.' Finally, they found that the defendant intended to frighten the person in that room.

In view of the question of law I must also refer shortly to the evidence on the basis of which the justices convicted. The incident happened at about 11 p.m., when Miss Mooney was in her room wearing a pink, knee-length nightie. There was a bay window and a side window. The curtains were drawn but they left a gap. She saw the defendant peering in and stated that he was right up against the window. She said: 'I instantly recognised him. I was very scared, very shocked. He was there about three or four seconds. I walked backwards and could no longer see him. I turned and he was at the other window, again right against the glass. I just stood and stared at him, didn't know what to do. He was just standing there, didn't seem he was going to go away. I jumped across the bed towards the window and screamed. I was terrified, absolutely terrified. He must have seen me look at him. He moved away when I went across the bed. I looked at him for about 20 seconds at the side window. . . .'

. . .

Ultimately, as it seems to me, the only point taken by Mr Denny which requires some consideration is whether there was a sufficient apprehension, within the definition which I have read, of immediate and unlawful violence. He takes the point that there is no finding here that what Miss Mooney was terrified of was some violence, and indeed some violence which can be described as immediate. However, as it seems to me, Mr Greenbourne is right when he submits, really in the form of a question: 'What else, other than some form of immediate violence, could Miss Mooney have been terrified about?'

When one is in a state of terror one is very often unable to analyse precisely what one is frightened of as likely to happen next. When I say that, I am speaking of a situation such as the present, where the person who causes one to be terrified is immediately adjacent, albeit on the other side of a window. Mr Denny relied on a sentence in Smith and Hogan's *Criminal Law* (4th ed.), p. 351, where an illustration is given as follows: 'There can be no assault if it is obvious to P' – the complainant – 'that D' – the defendant – 'is unable to carry out his threat, as where D shakes his fist at P who is safely locked inside his car.' That may be so, but those are not the facts of the present case.

In the present case the defendant intended to frighten Miss Mooney and Miss Mooney was frightened. As it seems to me, there is no need for a finding that what she was frightened of, which she probably could not analyse at that moment, was some innominate terror of some potential violence. It was clearly a situation where the basis of the fear which was instilled in her was that she did not know what the defendant was going to do next, but that, whatever he might be going to do next, and sufficiently immediately for the purposes of the offence, was something of a violent nature. In effect, as it seems to me, it was wholly open to the justices to infer that her state of mind was not only that of terror, which they did find, but terror of some immediate violence. In those circumstances, it seems to me that they were perfectly entitled to convict the defendant who had gone there, as they found, with the intention of frightening her and causing her to fear some act of immediate violence, and therefore with the intention of committing an assault upon her. Accordingly, I would dismiss this appeal.

The requirement that the threat must be immediate was addressed in *R* v *Constanza* and *R* v *Ireland, R* v *Burstow*. These cases also raise the issue whether silence and, by implication, words can form the basis of a charge of assault, and whether harm includes psychological harm.

R v *Constanza*
[1997] Crim LR 576, Court of Appeal

The appellant was convicted of occasioning actual bodily harm. The victim was a female ex-colleague. Between October 1993 and June 1995 he followed her home from work, made numerous silent telephone calls, sent over 800 letters, repeatedly drove past her home, visited against her expressed wish, and on three occasions wrote offensive words on her front door. In June of 1995 the victim received two further letters which she interpreted as clear threats. She believed that he had 'flipped' and that he might do something to her at any time. On July 27, 1995 she was diagnosed as suffering from clinical depression and anxiety. It was the doctor's view that the appellant's actions had caused this harm.

The defence conceded that the appellant's behaviour had occasioned actual bodily harm but submitted that what the appellant had done could not amount in law to an assault and that the judge should have allowed a submission of no case to answer.

Held, dismissing the appeal, the issue before the Court was whether it was enough if the Crown have proved a fear of violence at some time not excluding the immediate future. In the Court's view it was. It was an important factor that the appellant lived near the victim and she thought that something could happen at any time. The judge was entitled to leave to the jury the question whether or not she had a fear of immediate violence, and the jury were entitled to find that she did. The Court rejected the defence submission that a person cannot have a fear of immediate violence unless they can see the potential perpetrator. It rejected a further submission that an assault could not be committed by words alone without a physical action. The indictment made it clear that the assault relied on was that constituted by the last letter. The Court certified a point of general public importance but refused leave to appeal to the House of Lords.

R v *Ireland, R* v *Burstow*
[1997] 3 WLR 534, House of Lords

LORD STEYN: My Lords, it is easy to understand the terrifying effect of a campaign of telephone calls at night by a silent caller to a woman living on her own. It would be natural for the victim to regard the calls as menacing. What may heighten her fear is that she will not know what the caller may do next. The spectre of the caller arriving at her doorstep bent on inflicting personal violence on her may come to dominate her thinking. After all, as a matter of common sense, what else would she be terrified about? The victim may suffer psychiatric illness such as anxiety neurosis or acute depression. Harassment of women by repeated silent telephone calls, accompanied on occasions by heavy breathing, is apparently a significant social problem. That the criminal law should be able to deal with this problem, and so far as is practicable, afford effective protection to victims is self-evident.

From the point of view, however, of the general policy of our law towards the imposition of criminal responsibility, three specific features of the problem must be faced squarely. First, the medium used by the caller is the telephone: arguably it differs qualitatively from a face to face offer of violence to a sufficient extent to make a difference. Secondly, ex hypothesi the caller remains silent: arguably a caller may avoid the reach of the criminal law by remaining silent however menacing the context may be. Thirdly, it is arguable that the criminal law does not take into account 'mere' psychiatric illnesses.

The two appeals before the House
There are two appeals before the House. In *R* v *Ireland* appellant was convicted on his plea of guilty of three offences of assault occasioning actual bodily harm, contrary to section 47 of the Act of 1861. The judgment of the Court of Appeal dismissing his appeal is reported [1997] QB 114. The case against Ireland was that during a period of three months in 1994 covered by the indictment he harassed three women by making repeated telephone calls to them during which he remained silent. Sometimes, he resorted to heavy breathing. The calls were mostly made at night. The case against him, which was accepted by the judge and the Court of Appeal, was that he caused his victim to suffer psychiatric illness. Ireland had a substantial record of making offensive telephone calls to women. The judge sentenced him to a total of three years' imprisonment.

Before the Court of Appeal there were two principal issues. The first was whether psychiatric illness may amount to bodily harm within the meaning of section 47 of the Act of 1861. Relying on a decision of the Court of Appeal in *R* v *Chan-Fook* [1994] 1 WLR 689 the Court of Appeal in *Ireland's* case concluded that psychiatric injury may amount to bodily harm under section 47 of the Act of 1861. The second issue was whether Ireland's conduct was capable of amounting to an assault. In giving the judgment of the court in Ireland's case Swinton Thomas LJ said at p. 119:

> It has been recognised for many centuries that putting a person in fear may amount to an assault. The early cases predate the invention of the telephone. We must apply the law to conditions as they are in the 20th century.

The court concluded that repeated telephone calls of a menacing nature may cause victims to apprehend immediate and unlawful violence. Given these conclusions of law, and Ireland's guilty plea, the Court of Appeal dismissed the appeal. The Court of Appeal certified the following question as being of general public importance, namely 'As to whether the making of a series of silent telephone calls can amount in law to an assault'. But it will also be necessary to consider the question whether psychiatric illness may in law amount to bodily harm under section 47 of the Act of 1861. Those are the issues of law before the House in the appeal of *R* v *Ireland*.

In *R* v *Burstow* the appellant was indicted on one count of unlawfully and maliciously inflicting grievous bodily harm, contrary to section 20 of the Act of 1861. The facts are fully set out in the reported judgment of the Court of Appeal [1997] 1 Cr App R 144. I can therefore describe the facts shortly. Burstow had a social relationship with a woman. She broke it off. He could not accept her decision. He proceeded to harass her in various ways over a lengthy period. His conduct led to several convictions and periods of imprisonment. During an eight-month period in 1995 covered by the indictment he continued his campaign of harassment. He made some silent telephone calls to her. He also made abusive calls to her. He distributed offensive cards in the street where she lived. He was frequently, and unnecessarily, at her home and place of work. He surreptitiously took photographs of the victim and her family. He sent her a note which was intended to be menacing, and was so understood. The victim was badly affected by this campaign of harassment. It preyed on her mind. She was fearful of personal violence. A consultant psychiatrist stated that she was suffering from a severe depressive illness. In the Crown Court counsel asked for a ruling whether an offence of unlawfully and maliciously inflicting grievous bodily harm contrary to section 20 may be committed where no physical violence has been applied directly or indirectly to the body of the victim. The judge answered this question in the affirmative. Burstow thereupon changed his plea to guilty. The judge sentenced him to three years' imprisonment. Burstow applied for leave to appeal against conviction. The Court of Appeal heard full oral argument on the application, and granted the application for leave to appeal but dismissed the appeal. Two questions of law were canvassed before the Court of Appeal. First, there was the question whether psychiatric injury may amount to bodily harm under section 20. The Court of Appeal regarded itself as bound by the affirmative decision in *R* v *Chan-Fook* [1994] 1 WLR 689. The second issue was whether in the absence of physical violence applied directly or indirectly to the body of the victim an offence under section 20 may be committed. The Court of Appeal concluded that this question must be answered in the affirmative. The concluding observations of Lord Bingham of Cornhill CJ were, at p. 149:

> It is not straining language to speak of one person inflicting psychiatric injury on another. It would in our judgment be an affront to common sense to distinguish between section 18 and section 20 in the way contended for by the applicant. It would also, we think, introduce extreme and undesirable artificiality into what should be a very practical area of the law if we were to hold that, although grievous bodily harm includes psychiatric injury, no offence against section 20 is committed unless such psychiatric injury is the result of physical violence applied directly or indirectly to the body of the victim. The decision in *Chan-Fook* is in our view fatal to the applicant's submission.

In the result the Court of Appeal dismissed the appeal against conviction. The court certified the following point as of general importance, namely:

> Whether an offence of inflicting grievous bodily harm under section 20 of the offences against the Person Act 1861 can be committed where no physical violence is applied directly or indirectly to the body of the victim.

It will be noted that in neither appeal is there an issue on *mens rea*: the appeals focus on questions of law regarding the *actus reus*.

The common question: Can psychiatric illness amount to bodily harm?
It will now be convenient to consider the question which is common to the two appeals, namely, whether psychiatric illness is capable of amounting to bodily harm in terms of sections 18, 20 and 47 of the Act of 1861. The answer must be the same for the three sections.

The only abiding thing about the processes of the human mind, and the causes of its disorders and disturbances, is that there will never be a complete explanation. Psychiatry is and will always remain an imperfectly understood branch of medical science. This idea is explained by Vallar's psychiatrist in Iris Murdoch's *The Message to the Planet*:

> Our knowledge of the soul, if I may use that unclinical but essential word, encounters certain seemingly impassable limits, set there perhaps by the gods, if I may refer to them, in order to preserve their privacy, and beyond which it may be not only futile but lethal to attempt to pass and though it is our duty to seek for knowledge, it is also incumbent on us to realise when it is denied us, and not to prefer a fake solution to no solution at all.

But there has been progress since 1861. And courts of law can only act on the best scientific understanding of the day. Some elementary distinctions can be made. The appeals under consideration do not involve structural injuries to the brain such as might require the intervention of a neurologist. One is also not considering either psychotic illness or personality disorders. The victims in the two appeals suffered from no such conditions. As a result of the behaviour of the appellants they did not develop psychotic or psychoneurotic conditions. The case was that they developed mental disturbances of a lesser order, namely neurotic disorders. For present purposes the relevant forms of neurosis are anxiety disorders and depressive disorders. Neuroses must be distinguished from simple states of fear, or problems in coping with everyday life. Where the line is to be drawn must be a matter of psychiatric judgment. But for present purposes it is important to note that modern psychiatry treats neuroses as recognisable psychiatric illnesses: see 'Liability for Psychiatric Injury', Law Commission Consultation paper No. 137 (1995) Part III (The Medical Background); *Mullany and Hanford, Tort Liability for Psychiatric Damages* (1993), discussion on 'The Medical Perspective', at pp. 24–42, and particularly at p. 30, footnote 88. Moreover, it is essential to bear in mind that neurotic illnesses affect the central nervous system of the body, because emotions such as fear and anxiety are brain functions.

The civil law has for a long time taken account of the fact that there is no rigid distinction between body and mind. In *Bourhill* v *Young* [1943] AC 92, 103 Lord Macmillan said:

> The crude view that the law should take cognisance only of physical injury resulting from actual impact has been discarded, and it is now well recognised that an action will lie for injury by shock sustained through the medium of the eye or the ear without direct contact. The distinction between mental shock and bodily injury was never a scientific one.

This idea underlies the subsequent decisions of the House of Lords regarding post-traumatic stress disorder in *McLoughlin* v *O'Brian* [1983] 1 AC 410, 418, *per* Lord Wilberforce; and *Page* v *Smith* [1996] AC 155, 181A–D, *per* Lord Browne-Wilkinson. So far as such cases are concerned with the precise boundaries of tort liability they are not relevant. But so far as those decisions are based on the principle that the claimant must be able to prove that he suffered a recognisable psychiatric illness or condition they are by analogy relevant. The decisions of the House of Lords on post-traumatic stress disorder hold that where the line is to be drawn is a matter for expert psychiatric evidence. By analogy those decisions suggest a possible principled approach to the question whether psychiatric injury may amount to bodily harm in terms of the Act of 1861.

The criminal law has been slow to follow this path. But in *R* v *Chan-Fook* [1994] 1 WLR 689 the Court of Appeal squarely addressed the question whether psychiatric injury may amount to bodily harm under section 47 of the Act of 1861. The issue arose in a case where the defendant had aggressively questioned and locked in a suspected thief. There was a dispute as to whether the defendant had physically assaulted the victim. But the prosecution also alleged that even if the victim had suffered no physical injury, he had been reduced to a mental state which amounted to actual bodily harm under section 47. No psychiatric evidence was given. The judge directed the jury that an assault which caused an hysterical and nervous condition was an assault occasioning actual bodily harm. The defendant was convicted. Upon appeal the conviction was quashed on the ground of misdirections in the summing up and the absence of psychiatric evidence to support the prosecution's alternative case. The interest of the decision lies in the reasoning on psychiatric injury in the context of section 47. In a detailed and careful judgment given on behalf of the court Hobhouse LJ said, at p. 695:

> The first question on the present appeal is whether the inclusion of the word 'bodily' in the phrase 'actual bodily harm' limits harm to harm to the skin, flesh and bones of the victim. . . . The body of the victim includes all parts of his body, including his organs, his nervous system and his brain. Bodily injury therefore may include injury to any of those parts of his body responsible for his mental and at faculties.

In concluding that 'actual bodily harm' is capable of including psychiatric injury Hobhouse LJ emphasised, at p. 696:

> it does not include mere emotions such as fear or distress nor panic nor does it include, as such, states of mind that are not themselves evidence of some identifiable clinical condition.

He observed that in the absence of psychiatric evidence a question whether or not an assault occasioned psychiatric injury should not be left to the jury.

The Court of Appeal, as differently constituted in *R* v *Ireland* and *R* v *Burstow*, was bound by the decision in *R* v *Chan-Fook*. The House is not so bound. Counsel for the appellants in both appeals submitted that bodily harm in Victorian legislation cannot include psychiatric injury. For this reason they argued that *R* v *Chan-Fook* was wrongly decided. They relied on the following observation of Lord Bingham of Cornhill CJ in *R* v *Burstow* [1997] 1 Cr App R 144 148–149:

> Were the question free from authority we should entertain some doubt whether the Victorian draftsman of the 1861 Act intended to embrace psychiatric injury within the expressions 'grievous bodily harm' and 'actual bodily harm'.

Nevertheless, Lord Bingham CJ observed that it is now accepted that in the relevant context the distinction between physical and mental injury is no means clear cut. He welcomed the ruling in *R* v *Chan-Fook* at p. 149B. I respectfully agree. But I would go further and point out that, although out of considerations of piety we frequently refer to the actual intention of the draftsman, the correct approach is simply to consider whether the words of the Act of 1861 considered in the light of contemporary knowledge cover a recognisable psychiatric injury. It is undoubtedly true that there are statutes where the correct approach is to construe the legislation 'as if one were interpreting it the day after it was passed': *The Longford* (1889) 14 PD 34. Thus in *The Longford* the word 'action' in a statute was held not to be apt to cover an Admiralty action in rem since when it was passed the Admiralty Court 'was not one of His Majesty's Courts of Law': see pp. 37, 38. Bearing in mind that statutes are usually intended to operate for many years it would be most inconvenient if courts could never rely in difficult cases on the current meaning of statutes. Recognising the problem Lord Thring, the great Victorian draftsman of the second half of the last century, exhorted draftsmen to draft so that 'An Act of Parliament should be deemed to be 'always speaking': *Practical Legislation* (1902), p. 83; see also Cross, *Statutory Interpretation*, 3rd ed. (1995), p. 51; Pearce and Geddes, *Statutory Interpretation in Australia*, 4th ed. (1996), pp. 90–93. In cases where the problem arises it is a matter of interpretation whether a court must search for the historical or original meaning of a statute or whether it is free to apply the current meaning of the statute to present day conditions. Statutes dealing with a particular grievance or problem may sometimes require to be historically interpreted. But the drafting technique of Lord Thring and his successors have brought about the situation that statutes will generally be found to be of the 'always speaking' variety: see *Royal College of Nursing of the United Kingdom* v *Department of Health and Social Security* [1981] AC 800 for an example of an 'always speaking' construction in the House of Lords.

The proposition that the Victorian legislator when enacting sections 18, 20 and 47 of the Act 1861, would not have had in mind psychiatric illness is no doubt correct. Psychiatry was in its infancy in 1861. But the subjective intention of the draftsman is immaterial. The only relevant inquiry is as to the sense of the words in the context in which they are used. Moreover the Act of 1861 is a statute of the 'always speaking' type: the statute must be interpreted in the light of the best current scientific appreciation of the link between the body and psychiatric injury.

For these reasons I would, therefore, reject the challenge to the correctness of *R* v *Chan-Fook* [1994] 1 WLR 689. In my view the ruling in that case was based on principled and cogent reasoning and it marked a sound and essential clarification of the law. I would hold that 'bodily harm' in sections 18, 20 and 47 must be interpreted so as to include recognisable psychiatric illness.

. . .

For the reasons I have given I would answer the certified question in *R* v *Burstow* in the affirmative.

R v *Ireland: was there an assault?*

It is now necessary to consider whether the making of silent telephone calls causing psychiatric injury is capable of constituting an assault under section 47. The Court of Appeal, as constituted in *R* v *Ireland* case, answered that question in the affirmative. There has been substantial academic criticism of the conclusion and reasoning in *R* v *Ireland*; see *Archbold News*, Issue 6, 12 July 1996; *Archbold's Criminal Pleading, Evidence & Practice*, Supplement No. 4 (1996), pp. 345–347; *Smith and Hogan, Criminal Law*, 8th ed. (1996), 413; 'Assault by Telephone' by Jonathan Herring [1997] CLJ 11; 'Assault' [1997] Crim LR 434, 435–436. Counsel's arguments, broadly speaking, challenged the decision in *R* v *Ireland* on very similar lines. Having carefully considered the literature and counsel's arguments, I have come to the conclusion that the appeal ought to be dismissed.

The starting point must be that an assault is an ingredient of the offence under section 47. It is necessary to consider the two forms which an assault may take. The first is battery, which involves the unlawful application of force by the defendant upon the victim. Usually, section 47 is used to prosecute in cases of this kind. The second form of assault is an act causing the victim to apprehend an imminent application of force upon her: see *Fagan* v *Metropolitan Police Commissioner* [1969] 1 QB 439, 444D–E.

One point can be disposed of, quite briefly. The Court of Appeal was not asked to consider whether silent telephone calls resulting in psychiatric injury is capable of constituting a battery. But encouraged by some academic comment it was raised before your Lordships' House. Counsel for Ireland was most economical in his argument on the point. I will to match his economy of words. In my view it is not feasible to enlarge the generally accepted legal meaning of what is a battery to include the circumstances of a silent caller who causes psychiatric injury.

It is to assault in the form of an act causing the victim to fear an immediate application of force to her that I must turn. Counsel argued that as a matter of law an assault can never be committed by words alone and therefore it cannot be committed by silence. The premise depends on the slenderest authority, namely, an observation by Holroyd J to a jury that 'no words or singing are equivalent to an assault': *R* v *Meade and Belt* (1823) 1 Lew 184. The proposition that a gesture may amount to an assault, but that words can never suffice, is unrealistic and indefensible. A thing said is also a thing done. There is no reason why something said should be incapable of causing an apprehension of immediate personal violence, e.g. a man accosting a woman in a dark alley saying, 'Come with me or I will stab you'. I would, therefore, reject the proposition that an assault can never be committed by words.

That brings me to the critical question whether a silent caller may be guilty of an assault. The answer to this question seems to me to be 'Yes depending on the facts.'

It involves questions of fact within the province of the jury. After all, there is no reason why a telephone caller who says to a woman in a menacing way 'I will be at your door in a minute or two' may not be guilty of an assault if he causes his victim to apprehend immediate personal violence. Take now the case of the silent caller. He intends by his silence to cause fear and he is so understood.

The victim is assailed by uncertainty about his intentions. Fear may dominate her emotions, and it may be the fear that the caller's arrival at her door may be imminent. She may fear the *possibility* of immediate personal violence. As a matter of law the caller may be guilty of an assault: whether he is or not will depend on the circumstance and in particular on the impact of the caller's potentially menacing call or calls on the victim. Such a prosecution case under section 47 may be fit to leave to the jury. And a trial judge may, depending on the circumstances, put a common sense consideration before jury, namely what, if not the possibility of imminent personal violence, was the victim terrified about? I conclude that an assault may be committed in the particular factual circumstances which I have envisaged. For this reason I reject the submission that as a matter of law a silent telephone caller cannot ever be guilty of an offence under section 47. In these circumstances no useful purpose would be served by answering the vague certified question in *R v Ireland*.

Having concluded that the legal arguments advanced on behalf of Ireland on section 47 must fail, I nevertheless accept that the concept of an assault involving immediate personal violence as an ingredient of the section 47 offence is a considerable complicating factor in bringing prosecutions under it in respect of silent telephone callers and stalkers. That the least serious of the ladder of offences is difficult to apply in such cases is unfortunate. At the hearing of the appeal of *R v Ireland* attention was drawn to the Bill which is annexed to Law Commission report, 'Legislating the Criminal Code: Offences Against the Person and General Principles,' (Law Com. No. 218) (1993) (Cm. 2370). Clause 4 of that Bill is intended to replace section 47. Clause 4 provides that 'A person is guilty of an offence if he intentionally or recklessly causes injury to another'. This simple and readily comprehensible provision would eliminate the problems inherent in section 47. In expressing this view I do not, however, wish to comment on the appropriateness of the definition of 'injury' in clause 18 of the Bill, and in particular the provision that 'injury' means 'impairment of a person's mental health'.

The disposal of the appeals
The legal arguments advanced on behalf of Burstow have failed. The appeal must be dismissed.

The legal arguments advanced on behalf of Ireland have also failed. But counsel for the appellant submitted that the appeal should be allowed because on an examination of the statements there was no prima facie case against him. I reject this submission. The prosecution case was never fully deployed because Ireland pleaded guilty. The fact of his plea demonstrated his *mens rea*. It was said, however, that the ingredient of psychiatric injury was not established on the statements. It is true that the statement from the psychiatrist is vague. But I would not accept that read in context it was insufficient to allow the case to go before a jury. It would be an exceptional course, in the face of an unequivocal and deliberate plea of guilty, to entertain an appeal directed exclusively to the sufficiency of evidence. Such a course is not warranted in the present case. I would therefore dismiss the appeal of Ireland.

NOTES AND QUESTIONS
1. Do *Ireland* and *Constanza* eliminate the immediacy requirement altogether? The Court of Appeal in *Ireland* referred to *Smith* v *Chief Superintendent of Woking Police Station* (above) on this point. Are the two cases in fact distinguishable?
2. The psychological symptoms experienced by the victims in *Ireland* and *Constanza* developed gradually over time. This being so, at what point did the actions of the defendants become an assault?
3. The type of behaviour (stalking) involved in these cases is now dealt with by the Protection from Harassment Act 1997. If the facts of the cases were to arise again, the prosecution would presumably be brought under this statute. Thus, the precedential effect of the two decisions may be limited and the door remains open for the restoration of an immediacy requirement in other cases of assault.
4. Were the House of Lords interpreting the Victorian legislation or inventing a new offence?

While words may constitute an assault, they may also serve to remove a victim's fear of immediate harm.

Turberville v *Savage*
(1669) 1 Mod Rep 3, King's Bench Division

Action of *assault*, *battery*, and *wounding*. The evidence to prove a provocation was, that the plaintiff put his hand upon his sword and said, '*If it were not assize-time, I would not take such language from you.*' – The question was, If that were an assault? – The Court agreed that it was not; for the declaration of the plaintiff was, that he would not assault him, the Judges being in town; and *the intention* as well as *the act* makes an assault. Therefore if one strike another upon the hand, or arm, or breast in discourse, it is no assault, there being no *intention* to assault; but if one, intending to assault, strike *at* another and miss him, this is an assault: so if he hold up his hand against another in a threatening manner and say nothing, it is an assault. – In the principal case the plaintiff had judgment.

Can a failure to act, or an omission, constitute an assault?

Fagan v *Metropolitan Police Commissioner*
[1969] 1 QB 439, Queen's Bench Division

JAMES J: . . . On August 31, 1967, the appellant was reversing a motor car in Fortunegate Road, London, N.W.10, when Police Constable Morris directed him to drive the car forwards to the kerbside and standing in front of the car pointed out a suitable place in which to park. At first the appellant stopped the car too far from the kerb for the officer's liking. Morris asked him to park closer and indicated a precise spot. The appellant drove forward towards him and stopped it with the offside wheel on Morris's left foot. 'Get off, you are on my foot,' said the officer. 'Fuck you, you can wait,' said the appellant. The engine of the car stopped running. Morris repeated several times 'Get off my foot.' The appellant said reluctantly 'Okay man, okay,' and then slowly turned on the ignition of the vehicle and reversed it off the officer's foot. The appellant had either turned the ignition off to stop the engine or turned it off after the engine had stopped running.

. . . An assault is any act which intentionally – or possibly recklessly – causes another person to apprehend immediate and unlawful personal violence. Although 'assault' is an independent crime and is to be treated as such, for practical purposes today 'assault' is generally synonymous with the term 'battery' and is a term used to mean the actual intended use of unlawful force to another person without his consent. On the facts of the present case the 'assault' alleged involved a 'battery'. Where an assault involves a battery, it matters not, in our judgement, whether the battery is inflicted directly by the body of the offender or through the medium of some weapon or instrument controlled by the action of the offender. An assault may be committed by the laying of a hand upon another, and the action does not cease to be an assault if it is a stick held in the hand and not the hand itself which is laid on the person of the victim. So for our part we see no difference in principle between the action of stepping on to a person's toe and maintaining that position and the action of driving a car on to a person's foot and sitting in the car whilst its position on the foot is maintained . . .

To constitute the offence of assault some intentional act must have been performed: a mere omission to act cannot amount to an assault. . . .

Appeal dismissed.

NOTES AND QUESTIONS
1. James J in his opinion in *Fagan* v *MPC* stated that 'a *mere* omission to act cannot amount to an assault'. Does the thrust of the opinion contradict this observation?

2. Fagan v *MPC* was decided prior to *R* v *Miller* (for facts and holding, see p. 100) and the court's reasoning was based on the series of events constituting a single transaction. *Miller* would now provide an alternative rationale for reaching the same result.

3. In *Director of Public Prosecutions* v *K* [1990] 1 All ER 331, a 15-year-old schoolboy took a test tube of sulphuric acid to the boys' toilet. Panicking at the sound of footsteps, he deposited the acid in an electric hand drier. He intended subsequently to remove the acid, but before he had the opportunity to do so, another student used the drier. The acid squirted on the student's face, causing scarring. The Queen's Bench Division held that the defendant was guilty of occasioning bodily harm. What was the *actus reus* of the offence?

B: *Mens rea*

The *mens rea* of assault was rendered uncertain by a number of incompatible judicial opinions over the past decade. In *R* v *Savage* and *Director of Public Prosecutions* v *Parmenter* the House of Lords had to choose between conflicting decisions of the Court of Appeal.

R v *Savage, Director of Public Prosecutions* v *Parmenter*
[1991] 3 WLR 914, House of Lords

LORD ACKNER: My Lords, these two appeals have been heard together, because they each raise the issue of the mental element which the prosecution have to establish in relation to offences under two sections of the Offences against the Person Act 1861, viz. section 20, unlawfully and maliciously wounding or inflicting grievous bodily harm and section 47, assault occasioning actual bodily harm.

It will be observed that some of the certified questions in *Parmenter* overlap with those in *Savage*.
My Lords, I will now seek to deal with the issues raised by these appeals seriatim.
. . .

2. *Can a verdict of assault occasioning actual bodily harm be returned upon proof of an assault together with proof of the fact that actual bodily harm was occasioned by the assault, or must the prosecution also prove that the defendant intended to cause some actual bodily harm or was reckless as to whether such harm would be caused?*
Your Lordships are concerned with the mental element of a particular kind of assault, an assault 'occasioning actual bodily harm'. It is common ground that the mental element of assault is an intention to cause the victim to apprehend immediate and unlawful violence or recklessness whether such apprehension be caused: see *R* v *Venna* [1976] QB 421. It is of course common ground that Mrs Savage committed an assault upon Miss Beal when she threw the contents of her glass of beer over her. It is also common ground that however the glass came to be broken and Miss Beal's wrist thereby cut, it was, on the finding of the jury, Mrs Savage's handling of the glass which caused Miss Beal 'actual bodily harm.' Was the offence thus established or is there a further mental state that has to be established in relation to the bodily harm element of the offence? Clearly the section, by its terms, expressly imposes no such a requirement. Does it do so by necessary implication? It neither uses the word 'intentionally' or 'maliciously'. The words 'occasioning actual bodily harm' are descriptive of the word 'assault', by reference to a particular kind of consequence.

In neither *Savage*, nor *Spratt*, nor in *Parmenter* was the court's attention invited to the decision of the Court of Appeal in *R* v *Roberts* (1971) 56 Cr App R 95. [In that case the Court of Appeal used the following test:]

Was it [the action of the victim which resulted in actual bodily harm] the natural result of what the alleged assailant said and did, in the sense that it was something that could reasonably have been foreseen as the consequence of what he was saying or doing? As it was put in one of the old cases, it had got to be shown to be his act, and if of course the victim does something so 'daft', in the words of the appellant in this case, or so unexpected, not that this particular assailant did not actually foresee it but that no reasonable man could be expected to foresee it, then it is only in a very remote and unreal sense a consequence of his assault, it is really occasioned by a voluntary act on the part of the victim which could not reasonably be foreseen and which breaks the chain of causation between the assault and the harm or injury.

Accordingly no fault was found in the following direction of the chairman to the jury, at p. 103:

if you accept the evidence of the girl in preference to that of the man, that means that there was an assault occasioning actual bodily harm, that means that she did jump out as a direct result of what he was threatening her with, and what he was doing to her, holding her coat, telling her he had beaten up girls who had refused his advances, and that means that through his acts he was in law and in fact responsible for the injuries which were caused to her by her decision, if it can be called that, to get away from his violence, his threats, by jumping out of the car.

Thus once the assault was established, the only remaining question was whether the victim's conduct was the natural consequence of that assault. The words 'occasioning' raised solely a question of causation, an objective question which does not involve inquiring into the accused's state of mind. . . . The decision in *Roberts'* case, 56 Cr App R 95 was correct. The verdict of assault occasioning actual bodily harm may be returned upon proof of an assault together with proof of the fact that actual bodily harm was occasioned by the assault. The prosecution are not obliged to prove that the defendant intended to cause some actual bodily harm or was reckless as to whether such harm would be caused.

3. *In order to establish an offence under section 20 of the Act, must the prosecution prove that the defendant actually foresaw that his act would cause harm, or is it sufficient to prove that he ought so to have foreseen?*

. . . [I]n order to establish an offence under section 20 the prosecution must prove either the defendant intended or that he actually foresaw that his act would cause harm.

4. *In order to establish an offence under section 20 is it sufficient to prove that the defendant intended or foresaw the risk of some physical harm or must he intend or foresee either wounding or grievous bodily harm?*

. . . Professor Glanville Williams and . . . Professor J. C. Smith in their text books and in articles [and] commentaries . . . argue that a person should not be criminally liable for consequences of his conduct unless he foresaw a consequence falling into the same legal category as that set out in the indictment.

Such a general principle runs contrary to the decision in *Roberts'* case, 56 Cr App R 95 which I have already stated to be, in my opinion, correct. The contention is apparently based on the proposition that as the actus reus of a section 20 offence is the wounding or the infliction of grievous bodily harm, the mens rea must consist of foreseeing such wounding or grievous bodily harm. But there is no such hard and fast principle. To take but two examples, the actus reus of murder is the killing of the victim, but foresight of grievous bodily harm is sufficient and indeed, such bodily harm, need not be such as to be dangerous to life. Again, in the case of manslaughter, death is frequently the unforeseen consequence of the violence used.

The argument that as section 20 and section 47 have both the same penalty, this somehow supports the proposition that the foreseen consequences must coincide with the harm actually done, overlooks the oft repeated statement that this is the irrational result of this piece-meal legislation.

If section 20 was to be limited to cases where the accused does not desire but does foresee wounding or grievous bodily harm, it would have a very limited scope. The mens rea in a section 20 crime is comprised in the word 'maliciously'. As was pointed out by Lord Lane CJ, giving the judgment of the Court of Appeal in R v Sullivan on 27 October 1980 (unreported save in [1981] Crim LR 46) the 'particular kind of harm' in the citation from Professor Kenny was directed to 'harm to the person' as opposed to 'harm to property.' Thus it was not concerned with the degree of the harm foreseen. It is accordingly in my judgment wrong to look upon the decision in Mowatt [1968] 1 QB 421 as being in any way inconsistent with the decision in Cunningham [1957] 2 QB 396.

My Lords, I am satisfied that the decision in Mowatt was correct and that it is quite unnecessary that the accused should either have intended or have foreseen that his unlawful act might cause physical harm of the gravity described in section 20, i.e. a wound or serious physical injury. It is enough that he should have foreseen that some physical harm to some person, albeit of a minor character, might result.

NOTES AND QUESTIONS
1. In requiring that the defendant actually foresee that his act would cause harm, the House of Lords apparently adopts the Cunningham (subjective) approach to recklessness, rejecting the Caldwell (objective) approach which would have required proof only that a reasonable person would have foreseen the risk. But in requiring that the defendant should have to see only *some* harm, rather than the type of harm which occurred, does the court undermine its subjective test? One issue in the case was whether a defendant could be convicted of inflicting *grievous* bodily harm if he foresaw only *some* harm.
2. Note that the *mens rea* of assault will be clarified if the Government's proposals for reform are enacted (see below).

SECTION 3: **Battery**

A: *Actus reus*

The *actus reus* of battery is the application of unlawful physical force against the person of the victim. An assault is not necessary – there need be no apprehension of an attack by the victim. Thus, if the victim is struck from behind, unaware of the presence of her assailant, that will be a battery, although it will not have been preceded by an assault.

(i) *When is an application of force unlawful?*
The problems of analysis are compounded by the fact that a battery may consist of anything from a slight touching to a severe beating. Is it possible for the law to recognise the types of distinctions that ordinary people make in their everyday lives?

Collins v *Wilcock*

[1984] 3 All ER 374, Queen's Bench Division

ROBERT GOFF LJ: There is before the court an appeal by way of a case stated by a metropolitan stipendiary magistrate sitting at Marylebone, under which the appellant, Alexis Collins, appeals against her conviction on 20 January 1983, of assaulting the respondent, Tracey Wilcock, a constable of the Metropolitan Police Force, in the execution of her duty at Craven Road, London W2, on 22 July 1982, contrary to s. 51(1) of the Police Act 1964. The magistrate found the following facts. (a) On 22 July 1982 the respondent and Police Sgt Benjamen were on duty in a police vehicle and saw two women walking along the street; one of the two was a known prostitute, the other was the appellant. (b) The officers observed the two women, both of whom appeared to them to be soliciting men in the street. (c) The officers, without alighting from their vehicle, asked the two women to get into the police car so that they could have a word with them. One woman got into the car, the appellant refused to do so. (d) The officers repeated their request to the appellant, who again refused and walked away, followed by the police car which then pulled up alongside her. She again walked away. (e) The respondent got out of the car and followed the appellant on foot, asking her why she didn't want to talk to the police, and also for her name and address. The appellant again started to walk away. The respondent told her that she had not finished talking to her and the appellant replied, 'Fuck off', and started to walk away yet again. (f) The respondent took hold of the appellant by the left arm to restrain her and the appellant shouted, 'Just fuck off, Copper' and scratched the respondent's right forearm with her fingernails. (g) The appellant was then arrested for assaulting a police officer in the execution of her duty.

Before the magistrate, the contentions of the parties were as follows. For the appellant, it was contended that the respondent was not acting in the execution of her duty at the time when the assault (if any) took place, having gone beyond the scope of her duty in detaining the appellant in circumstances short of arresting her. It was contended by the respondent, on the other hand, that there was on the evidence good ground for her to make inquiries and administer a caution under the Street Offences Act 1959, and that she was therefore acting in the execution of her duty at the time when the assault took place.

. . . [W]e think it right to consider whether, on the facts found in the case, the magistrate could properly hold that the respondent was acting in the execution of her duty. In order to consider this question, it is desirable that we should expose the underlying principles.

The law draws a distinction, in terms more easily understood by philologists than by ordinary citizens, between an assault and a battery. An assault is an act which causes another person to apprehend the infliction of immediate, unlawful, force on his person; a battery is the actual infliction of unlawful force on another person. Both assault and battery are forms of trespass to the person.

. . .

We are here concerned primarily with battery. The fundamental principle, plain and incontestable, is that every person's body is inviolate. It has long been established that any touching of another person, however slight, may amount to a battery. So Holt CJ held in 1704 that 'the least touching of another in anger is a battery': see *Cole* v *Turner* (1704) 6 Mod Rep 149, 90 ER 958. The breadth of the principle reflects the fundamental nature of the interest so protected; as Blackstone wrote in his Commentaries, 'the law cannot draw the line between different degrees of violence, and therefore totally prohibits the first and lowest stage of it; every man's person being sacred, and no other having a right to meddle with it, in any the slightest manner' (see 3 Bl Com 120). The effect is that everybody is protected not only against physical injury but against any form of physical molestation.

But so widely drawn a principle must inevitably be subject to exceptions. For example, children may be subjected to reasonable punishment; people may be subjected to the lawful exercise of the power of arrest; and reasonable force may be used in self-defence or for the prevention of crime. But, apart from these special instances where the control or constraint is lawful, a broader exception has been created to allow for the exigencies of everyday life. Generally speaking, consent is a defence to battery; and most of the physical contacts of ordinary life are not actionable because they are impliedly consented to by all who move in society and so expose themselves to the risk of bodily contact. So nobody can complain of the jostling which is inevitable from his presence in, for example, a supermarket, an underground station or a busy street; nor can a person who attends a party complain if his hand is seized in friendship, or even if his back is (within reason) slapped (see *Tuberville* v *Savage* (1669) 1 Mod Rep 3, 86 ER 684). Although such cases are regarded as examples of implied consent, it is more common nowadays to treat them as falling within a general exception embracing all physical contact which is generally acceptable in the ordinary conduct of daily life. We observe that, although in the past it has sometimes been stated that a battery is only committed where the action is 'angry, or revengeful, or rude, or insolent' (see 1 Hawk PC c. 62, s. 2), we think that nowadays it is more realistic, and indeed more accurate, to state the broad underlying principle, subject to the broad exception.

Among such forms of conduct, long held to be acceptable, is touching a person for the purpose of engaging his attention, though of course using no greater degree of physical contact than is reasonably necessary in the circumstances for that purpose. So, for example, it was held by the Court of Common Pleas in 1807 that a touch by a constable's staff on the shoulder of a man who had climbed on a gentleman's railing to gain a better view of a mad ox, the touch being only to engage the man's attention, did not amount to a battery (see *Wiffin* v *Kincard* (1807) 2 Bos & PNR 471, 127 ER 713; for another example, see *Coward* v *Baddeley* (1859) 4 H & N 478, 157 ER 927). But a distinction is drawn between a touch to draw a man's attention, which is generally acceptable, and a physical restraint, which is not. So we find Parke B observing in *Rawlings* v *Till* (1837) 3 M & W 28 at 29, 150 ER 1042, with reference to *Wiffin* v *Kincard*, that 'There the touch was merely to engage a man's attention, not to put a restraint on his person.' Furthermore, persistent touching to gain attention in the face of obvious disregard may transcend the norms of acceptable behaviour, and so be outside the exception. We do not say that more than one touch is never permitted; for example, the lost or distressed may surely be permitted a second touch, or possibly even more, on a reluctant or impervious sleeve or shoulder, as may a person who is acting reasonably in the exercise of a duty. In each case, the test must be whether the physical contact so persisted in has in the circumstances gone beyond generally acceptable standards of conduct; and the answer to that question will depend on the facts of the particular case.

The distinction drawn by Parke B in *Rawlings* v *Till* is of importance in the case of police officers. Of course, a police officer may subject another to restraint when he lawfully exercises his power of arrest; and he has other statutory powers, for example, his power to stop, search and detain persons under s. 66 of the Metropolitan Police Act 1839, with which we are not concerned. But, putting such cases aside, police officers have for present purposes no greater rights than ordinary citizens. It follows that, subject to such cases, physical contact by a police officer with another person may be unlawful as a battery, just as it might be if he was an ordinary member of the public. But a police officer has his rights as a citizen, as well as his duties as a policeman. A police officer may wish to engage a man's attention, for example if he wishes to question him. If he lays his hand on the man's sleeve or taps his shoulder for that purpose, he commits no wrong. He may even do so more than once; for he is under a duty to prevent and investigate crime, and so his seeking further, in the exercise of that duty, to engage a man's attention in order to speak to him may in the circumstances be regarded as acceptable (see *Donnelly* v *Jackman* [1970] 1 All ER 987, [1970] 1 WLR 562). But if, taking into account the nature of his duty, his use of physical contact in the face of non-co-operation persists beyond generally acceptable standards of conduct, his action will become unlawful; and if a police officer restrains a man, for example by gripping his arm or his shoulder, then his action will also be unlawful, unless he is lawfully exercising his power of arrest. A police officer has no power to require a man to answer him, though he has the advantage of authority, enhanced as it is by the uniform which the state provides and requires him to wear, in seeking a response to his inquiry. What is not permitted, however, is the unlawful use of force or the unlawful threat (actual or implicit) to use force; and, excepting the lawful exercise of his power of arrest, the lawfulness of a police officer's conduct is judged by the same criteria as are applied to the conduct of any ordinary citizen of this country.

. . . The fact is that the respondent took hold of the appellant by the left arm to restrain her. In so acting, she was not proceeding to arrest the appellant; and since her action went beyond the generally acceptable conduct of touching a person to engage his or her attention, it must follow, in our judgement, that her action constituted a battery on the appellant, and was therefore unlawful. It follows that the appellant's appeal must be allowed, and her conviction quashed.

NOTES AND QUESTIONS

1. What should the officer have done? Was she required to permit the defendant to walk away?
2. The court creates an exception for 'all' physical contact which is generally acceptable in the ordinary conduct of daily life. Who decides? Is this (should this be) a question of law or fact? If in a given community it is customary to punch a friend in the ribs as a greeting, would this be a battery elsewhere?

(ii) *Must the touching be hostile?*

Wilson v Pringle
[1986] 2 All ER 440, Court of Appeal

The plaintiff and the defendant were two schoolboys involved in an incident in a school corridor as the result of which the plaintiff fell and suffered injuries. The plaintiff issued a writ claiming damages and alleging that the defendant had committed a trespass to the person of the plaintiff. In his defence the defendant admitted that he had indulged in horseplay with the plaintiff.

CROOM-JOHNSON LJ: . . . Nevertheless, it still remains to indicate what is to be proved by a plaintiff who brings an action for battery. Robert Goff LJ's judgment [in *Collins* v *Wilcock* [1984] 3 All ER 374] is illustrative of the considerations which underlie such an action, but it is not practicable to define a battery as 'physical contact which is not generally acceptable in the ordinary conduct of daily life'.

In our view, the authorities lead one to the conclusion that in a battery there must be an intentional touching or contact in one form or another of the plaintiff by the defendant. That touching must be proved to be a hostile touching. That still leaves unanswered the question, when is a touching to be called hostile? Hostility cannot be equated with ill-will or malevolence. It cannot be governed by the obvious intention shown in acts like punching, stabbing or shooting. It cannot be solely governed by an expressed intention, although that may be strong evidence. But the element of hostility, in the sense in which it is now to be considered, must be a question of fact for the tribunal of fact. It may be imported from the circumstances. Take the example of the police officer in *Collins* v *Wilcock*. She touched the woman deliberately, but without an intention to do more than restrain her temporarily. Nevertheless, she was acting unlawfully and in that way was acting with hostility. She was acting contrary to the woman's legal right not to be physically restrained. . . .

NOTES AND QUESTIONS

1. Is 'hostility' as defined in *Wilson* v *Pringle* a helpful concept? What does it add to the notion of unlawfulness as defined in *Collins* v *Wilcock*?

2. Can an action be hostile but not unlawful? Unlawful but not hostile?
3. In *F* v *West Berkshire Health Authority* [1989] 2 All ER 545, at pp. 563–64, Lord Goff doubted the correctness of a requirement that the touching be hostile.
4. It is generally assumed that a battery requires a positive action on the part of the defendant (see *Innes* v *Wylie* (1844) 1 Car & Kir 257), although it may be seen that an accidental application of force followed by a refusal to desist may be a battery (see *Fagan* v *MPC* above). The court held that there was a continuing act, not a mere omission. Further, the above), Parker LJ stated (at pp. 333–34) that he had no doubt that if the defendant in the case had placed acid in a hand drier, which ejected onto the next user, an assault or battery would have been committed.
5. In this context consider also *R* v *Wilson* [1996] 3 WLR 125, discussed below, p. 294.

Can the force be applied indirectly?

Haystead v *Chief Constable of Derbyshire*
[2000] 3 All ER 890, Queen's Bench Division

Appeal by way of case stated against the appellant's conviction of an offence of assault upon a child.

. . .

11.(ii) Did the facts disclose a battery properly so called? It is to this question that the appeal is directed. It is accepted that the meaning of battery is correctly given in the current edition of *Archbold's Criminal Pleading, Evidence and Practice* (2000 edn), para 19-166a: '. . . an act by which a person intentionally or recklessly applies unlawful force to the complainant . . .'

12. The crucial question is, what is meant by the application of force in the context of the offence of battery?

13. The case stated makes it plain that the magistrates heard only exiguous argument on this issue. This is what they said in conclusion:

> 'To be guilty of a reckless battery it was necessary to establish in this case that unlawful force was applied by the appellant to the child and that the appellant saw that possibility. The appellant's use of force on this occasion was unlawful. He punched Angela Wright twice and in such a way that the child fell from her hands and was injured. It is plain to us that the application of the force to Miss Wright is indistinguishable from the application of force to the child. The fact that the unlawful force caused the child to fall is in our view the same as applying the force directly to the person of the child. The situation was entirely foreseeable. The force applied to Miss Wright was the same force which caused the child to fall, and it was unlawful force. If the appellant had swung a punch at the child and missed it is likely that no "assault" would have taken place because the child would not have apprehended immediate violence. If he had swung a punch at Miss Wright and missed but hit the child he would have been guilty of a reckless assault by beating. There is no suggestion that the child jumped – he fell as a direct consequence of the application of force to person that was holding him. Accordingly, to suggest that by swinging a punch at Miss Wright, connecting and directly causing the child to fall thereby suffering an injury, no offence is committed in respect of the child, we believe to be absurd. The single act of unlawful violence by the appellant was a battery to both Angela Wright and the child.'

14. The question for this court is put in this way:

'The question for the opinion of the High Court is whether on the facts found in this case the defendant could be said to have assaulted the child Matthew Wright by beating.'

15. I should add, perhaps it is plain already, that in putting forward the question in that way the magistrates were not, as I understand it, proposing that this court should examine their finding as to recklessness. I have already said there is no challenge to that. The case is concerned entirely with the proper meaning of 'battery' within the context here of a common assault by beating.

16. The appellant's submission is summarised by Mr Head in para 9 of his skeleton argument:

'It is submitted that a direct application of force requires the assailant to have had direct physical contact with the complainant either through his body eg a punch or through a medium controlled by his actions eg a weapon.'

. . .

32. Here the movement of Miss Wright whereby she lost hold of the child was entirely and immediately the result of the appellant's action in punching her. There is no difference in logic or good sense between the facts of this case and one where the defendant might have used a weapon to fell the child to the floor, save only that this is a case of reckless and not intentional battery.

33. In a case such as the present, it seems to me plain that it is right that the offence of assault by beating should be available for the criminal condemnation of the defendant's conduct.

34. Mr King for the respondent prosecutor put in a short skeleton argument submitting that on the facts this was a case of transferred malice. With respect to him, I greatly doubt whether that is the case; but I would uphold this conviction and dismiss the appeal on the grounds I have set out. If my Lord were to agree, then any question of transferred malice does not arise.

35. I would answer the question posed by the magistrates in the affirmative.

SILBER J. I agree.

Appeal dismissed. Permission to appeal to the House of Lords refused, but court certifying that a point of law of general public importance was involved in its decision, namely whether the actus reus of the offence of battery required that there be direct physical contact between defendant and complainant (whether by the body or by a medium controlled by the defendant such as a weapon).

R v Martin
(1881) 8 QBD 54, Divisional Court

Shortly before the conclusion of a performance at a theatre, M, with the intention and with the result of causing terror in the minds of persons leaving the theatre, put out the gaslights on a staircase which a large number of such persons had to descend in order to leave the theatre, and he also, with the intention and with the result of obstructing the exit, placed an iron bar across a doorway through which they had in leaving to pass.

Upon the lights being thus extinguished a panic seized a large portion of the audience, and they rushed in fright down the staircase forcing those in front against the iron bar. By reason of the pressure and struggling of the crowd thus created on the staircase, several of the audience were thrown down or otherwise severely injured, and amongst them A and B.

On proof of these facts the jury convicted M of unlawfully and maliciously inflicting grievous bodily harm upon A and B:—

Held, by the Court (Lord Coleridge, CJ, Field, Hawkins, Stephen, and Cave, JJ), that M was rightly convicted.

B: *Mens rea*

The *mens rea* of battery is an intention to apply unlawful force, or subjective reck-lessness as to whether such force will be applied (see *R v Savage* and *DPP v Parmenter*, above).

SECTION 4: **Defences to assault and battery**

A: In general

The defences which may defeat a charge of assault and/or battery are also relevant to the more serious (aggravated) assaults discussed later in this chapter. This is because some of the latter require proof of an assault or battery before a conviction for the more serious offence can be made out.

Any of the general defences discussed in Chapter 10 may be relevant, although self-defence is the most commonly pleaded. It must be noted that provocation is not a defence to either assault or battery; it is a defence only in the sense that it will reduce a charge of murder to manslaughter. Provocation may be relevant to reduce the sentence of the court following a conviction, but it will not prevent the defendant from being convicted in the first place.

B: Consent

A defence which often arises in cases of assault and battery and which may prevent conviction is that of consent. We have already examined that aspect of consent which operates to prevent a conviction for battery when a touching is 'generally acceptable in the ordinary conduct of daily life' (*Collins v Wilcock*, above). Ordinary citizens are deemed to have given an implied consent to such touching. More delicate issues arise when a decision has to be taken as to what conduct can be the subject of consent. Is it permissible, for example, for two people to batter each other in a contest which carries a high risk of brain damage and some risk of immediate death? The law so far has permitted this in the context of boxing. There are many intractable issues in this area, not least the meaning of consent itself and the age and/or mental capacity which is necessary before a 'real' consent can be given. Further, where the behaviour carries a hidden risk (such as a risk of AIDS), can a true consent be given if the victim is unaware of the hidden risk?

The issues raised may be broken down into the following questions, although they overlap to a degree:

(a) What limits will the State place on the ability of a victim to consent to conduct which would be criminal in the absence of consent?

(b) When will the State imply or impose consent on a victim?

(c) What constitutes valid consent?

(i) *State limitations on effective consent*

Consent is not a defence to a charge of murder or manslaughter. This is the case even if a victim begs to be killed because he or she is in intolerable pain.

Further down the 'harm' table, the courts seek to balance the benefit that the behaviour may bring, either to the public or to the individual, against the degree of harm that is inflicted upon the victim. Thus, even quite serious injury may be consented to where the perception of a useful outcome is high. This is the case in consent to surgery. Conversely, where the harm inflicted is slight but there is no benefit, the courts are less willing to recognise consent as a defence. As a general proposition, the more serious the harm inflicted, the less likely consent is to be effective, even where the behaviour takes place in private and the only persons directly affected are the participants. The factors to consider are:

(a) the possible benefits to individuals or to the public;

(b) the degree of harm inflicted on the victim;

(c) the extent to which the law is prepared to interfere with private behaviour.

The delicate balancing required will often result in decisions which are controversial.

R v Brown

[1993] 2 All ER 75, House of Lords

> The appellants, a group of sado-masochistics, willingly and enthusiastically participated in the commission of acts of violence against each other for the sexual pleasure it engendered in the giving and receiving of pain. They pleaded guilty on arraignment to counts charging various offences under ss. 20 and 47 of the Offences against the Person Act 1861, relating to the infliction of wounds or actual bodily harm on genital and other areas of the body of the consenting victim. On a ruling by the trial judge that, in the particular circumstances, the prosecution did not have to prove lack of consent by the victim, the appellants were re-arraigned, pleaded guilty, some to offences under s. 20 and all to offences under s. 47 and they were convicted. They appealed against conviction on the ground that the judge had erred in his rulings, in that the willing and enthusiastic consent of the victim to the acts on him prevented the prosecution from proving an essential element of the offence, whether charged under s. 20 or s. 47.

LORD TEMPLEMAN: . . . In some circumstances violence is not punishable under the criminal law. When no actual bodily harm is caused, the consent of the person affected precludes him from complaining. There can be no conviction for the summary offence of common assault if the victim has consented to the assault. Even when violence is intentionally inflicted and results in actual bodily harm, wounding or serious bodily harm the acused is entitled to be acquitted if the injury was a foreseeable incident of a lawful activity in which the person injured was participating. Surgery involves intentional violence resulting in actual or sometimes serious bodily harm but surgery is a lawful activity. Other activities carried on with consent by or on behalf of the injured person have been accepted as lawful notwithstanding that they involve actual bodily harm or may cause serious bodily harm. Ritual circumcision, tattooing, ear-piercing and violent sports including boxing are lawful activities.

In earlier days some other forms of violence were lawful and when they ceased to be lawful they were tolerated until well into the 19th century. Duelling and fighting were at first lawful and then tolerated provided the protagonists were voluntary participants. But where the results of these activities was the maiming of one of the participants, the defence of consent never availed the aggressor; see *Hawkins' Pleas of the Crown*, 8th ed. (1824), vol. 1, ch. 15. A maim was bodily harm whereby a man was deprived of the use of any member of his body which he needed to use in order to fight but a bodily injury was not a maim merely because it was a disfigurement. The act of maim was unlawful because the King was deprived of the services of an able-bodied citizen for the defence of the realm. Violence which maimed was unlawful despite consent to the activity which produced the maiming. In these days there is no difference between maiming on the one hand and wounding or causing grievous bodily harm on the other hand except with regard to sentence.

When duelling became unlawful, juries remained unwilling to convict but the judges insisted that persons guilty of causing death or bodily injury should be convicted despite the consent of the victim.

Similarly, in the old days, fighting was lawful provided the protagonists consented because it was thought that fighting inculcated bravery and skill and physical fitness. The brutality of knuckle fighting however caused the courts to declare that such fights were unlawful even if the protagonists consented. Rightly or wrongly the courts accepted that boxing is a lawful activity.

. . .

The question whether the defence of consent should be extended to the consequences of sado-masochistic encounters can only be decided by consideration of policy and public interest. Parliament can call on the advice of doctors, psychiatrists, criminologists, sociologists and other experts and can also sound and take into account public opinion. But the question must at this stage be decided by this House in its judicial capacity in order to determine whether the convictions of the appellants should be upheld or quashed.

Counsel for some of the appellants argued that the defence of consent should be extended to the offence of occasioning actual bodily harm under section 47 of the Act of 1861 but should not be available to charges of serious wounding and the infliction of serious bodily harm under section 20. I do not consider that this solution is practicable. Sado-masochistic participants have no way of foretelling the degree of bodily harm which will result from their encounters. The differences between actual bodily harm and serious bodily harm cannot be satisfactorily applied by a jury in order to determine acquittal or conviction.

Counsel for the appellants argued that consent should provide a defence to charges under both section 20 and section 47 because, it was said, every person has a right to deal with his body as he pleases. I do not consider that this slogan provides a sufficient guide to the policy decision which must now be made. It is an offence for a person to abuse his own body and mind by taking drugs. Although the law is often broken, the criminal law restrains a practice which is regarded as dangerous and injurious to individuals and which if allowed and extended is harmful to society generally. In any event the appellants in this case did not mutilate their own bodies. They inflicted bodily harm on willing victims. Suicide is no longer an offence but a person who assists another to commit suicide is guilty of murder or manslaughter.

The assertion was made on behalf of the appellants that the sexual appetites of sadists and masochists can only be satisfied by the infliction of bodily harm and that the law should not punish the consensual achievement of sexual satisfaction. There was no evidence to support the assertion that sado-masochist activities are essential to the happiness of the appellants or any other participants but the argument would be acceptable if sado-masochism were only concerned with sex, as the appellants contend. In my opinion sado-masochism is not only concerned with sex. Sado-masochism is also concerned with violence. The evidence discloses that the practices of the appellants were unpredictably dangerous and degrading to body and mind and were developed with increasing barbarity and taught to persons whose consents were dubious or worthless.

A sadist draws pleasure from inflicting or watching cruelty. A masochist derives pleasure from his own pain or humiliation. The appellants are middle-aged men. The victims were youths some of whom were introduced to sado-masochism before they attained the age of 21. In his judgment in the Court of Appeal, Lord Lane CJ said that two members of the group of which the appellants formed part, namely one Cadman and the appellant Laskey:

> were responsible in part for the corruption of a youth K . . . It is some comfort at least to be told, as we were, that K has now it seems settled into a normal heterosexual relationship. Cadman had befriended K when the boy was 15 years old. He met him in a cafeteria and, so he says, found out that the boy was interested in homosexual activities. He introduced and encouraged K in 'bondage affairs'. He was interested in viewing and recording on videotape K and other teenage boys in homosexual scenes . . . One cannot overlook the danger that the gravity of the assaults and injuries in this type of case may escalate to even more unacceptable heights.

The evidence disclosed that drink and drugs were employed to obtain consent and increase enthusiasm. The victim was usually manacled so that the sadist could enjoy the thrill of power and the victim could enjoy the thrill of helplessness. The victim had no control over the harm which the sadist, also stimulated by drink and drugs might inflict. In one case a victim was branded twice on the thigh and there was some doubt as to whether he consented to or protested against the second branding. The dangers involved in administering violence must have been appreciated by the appellants because, so it was said by their counsel, each victim was given a code word which he could pronounce when excessive harm or pain was caused. The efficiency of this precaution, when taken, depends on the circumstances and on the personalities involved. No one can feel the pain of another. The charges against the appellants were based on genital torture and violence to the buttocks, anus, penis, testicles and nipples. The victims were degraded and humiliated, sometimes beaten, sometimes wounded with instruments and sometimes branded. Bloodletting and the smearing of human blood produced excitement. There were obvious dangers of serious personal injury and blood infection. Prosecuting counsel informed the trial judge against the protests of defence counsel, that although the appellants had not contracted Aids, two members of the group had died from Aids and one other had contracted an H.I.V. infection although not necessarily from the practices of the group. Some activities involved excrement. The assertion that the instruments employed by the sadists were clean and sterilised could not have removed the danger of infection, and the assertion that care was taken demonstrates the possibility of infection. Cruelty to human beings was on occasions supplemented by cruelty to animals in the form of bestiality. It is fortunate that there were no permanent injuries to a victim though no one knows the extent of harm inflicted in other cases. It is not surprising that a victim does not complain to the police when the complaint would involve him in giving details of acts in which he participated. Doctors of course are subject to a code of confidentiality.

In principle there is a difference between violence which is incidental and violence which is inflicted for the indulgence of cruelty. The violence of sado-masochistic encounters involves the indulgence of cruelty by sadists and the degradation of victims. Such violence is injurious to the participants and unpredictably dangerous. I am not prepared to invent a defence of consent for sado-masochistic enounters which breed and glorify cruelty and result in offences under sections 47 and 20 of the Act of 1861.

Society is entitled and bound to protect itself against a cult of violence. Pleasure derived from the infliction of pain is an evil thing. Cruelty is uncivilised. I would answer the certified question in the negative and dismiss the appeals of the appellants against conviction.

Lord Mustill (dissenting) . . .

I: THE DECIDED CASES

Throughout the argument of the appeal I was attracted by an analysis on the following lines. First, one would construct a continuous spectrum of the infliction of bodily harm, with killing at one end and a trifling touch at the other. Next, with the help of reported cases one would identify the point on this spectrum at which consent ordinarily ceases to be an answer to a prosecution for inflicting harm. This could be called 'the critical level'. It would soon become plain however that this analysis is too simple and that there are certain types of special situation to which the general rule does not apply. Thus, for example, surgical treatment which requires a degree of bodily invasion well on the upper side of the critical level will nevertheless be legitimate if performed in accordance with good medical practice and with the consent of the patient. Conversely, there will be cases in which even a moderate degree of harm cannot be legitimated by consent. Accordingly, the next stage in the analysis will be to identify those situations which have been identified as special by the decided cases, and to examine them to see whether the instant case either falls within one of them or is sufficiently close for an analogy to be valid. If the answer is negative, then the court will have to decide whether simply to apply the general law simply by deciding whether the bodily harm in the case under review is above or below the critical level, or to break new ground by recognising a new special situation to which the general law does not apply.

For all the intellectual neatness of this method I must recognise that it will not do, for it imposes on the reported cases and on the diversities of human life an order which they do not possess. Thus, when one comes to map out the spectrum of ordinary consensual physical harm, to which the special situations form exceptions, it is found that the task is almost impossible, since people do not ordinarily consent to the infliction of harm. In effect, either all or almost all the instances of the consensual infliction of violence are special. They have been in the past, and will continue to be in the future, the subject of special treatment by the law.

There are other objections to a general theory of consent and violence. Thus, for example, it is too simple to speak only of consent, for it comes in various sorts. Of these, four spring immediately to mind. First, there is an express agreement to the infliction of the injury which was in the event inflicted. Next, there is express agreement to the infliction of some harm, but not to that harm which in the event was actually caused. These two categories are matched by two more, in which the recipient expressly consents not to the infliction of harm, but to engagement in an activity which creates a risk of harm; again, either the harm which actually results, or to something less. These examples do not exhaust the categories, for corresponding with each are situations of frequent occurrence in practice where the consent is not express but implied. These numerous categories are not the fruit of academic over-elaboration, but are a reflection of real life. Yet they are scarcely touched on in the cases, which just do not bear the weight of any general theory of violence and consent.

4. 'Contact' sports

Some sports, such as the various codes of football, have deliberate bodily contact as an essential element. They lie at a mid-point between fighting, where the participant knows that his opponent will try to harm him, and the milder sports where there is at most an acknowledgement that someone may be accidentally hurt. In the contact sports each player knows and by taking part agrees that an opponent may from time to time inflict upon his body (for example by a rugby tackle) what would otherwise be a painful battery. By taking part he also assumes the risk that the deliberate contact may have unintended effects, conceivably of sufficient severity to amount to grievous bodily harm. But he does not agree that this more serious kind of injury may be inflicted deliberately. This simple analysis conceals a number of difficult problems, which are discussed in a series of Canadian decisions, culminating in *R v Ciccarelli* (1989) 54 CCC (3d) 121, on the subject of ice hockey, a sport in which an ethos of physical contact is deeply entrenched. The courts appear to have started with the proposition that some level of violence is lawful if the recipient agrees to it, and have dealt with the question of excessive violence by enquiring whether the recipient could really have tacitly accepted a risk of violence at the level which actually occurred. These decisions do not help us in the present appeal, where the consent of the recipients was express, and where it is known that they gladly agreed, not simply to some degree of harm but to everything that was done. What we need to know is whether, notwithstanding the recipient's implied consent, there comes a point at which it is too severe for the law to tolerate. Whilst common sense suggests that this must be so, and that the law will not license brutality under the name of sport, one of the very few reported indications of the point at which tolerable harm becomes intolerable violence is in the direction to the jury given by Bramwell LJ in *R v Bradshaw* (1878) 14 Cox CC 83 that the act (in this case a charge at football) would be unlawful if intended to cause 'serious hurt'. This accords with my own instinct, but I must recognise that a direction at nisi prius, even by a great judge, cannot be given the same weight as a judgment on appeal, consequent upon full argument and reflection. The same comment may be made about *R v Moore* (1898) 14 TLR 229.

5. Surgery

Many of the acts done by surgeons would be very serious crimes if done by anyone else, and yet the surgeons incur no liability. Actual consent, or the substitute for consent deemed by the law to exist where an emergency creates a need for action, is an essential element in this immunity; but it cannot be a direct explanation for it, since much of the bodily invasion involved in surgery lies well above any point at which consent could even arguably be regarded as furnishing a defence. Why is this so? The answer must in my opinion be that proper medical treatment, for which actual or deemed consent is a prerequisite, is in a category of its own.

6. Lawful correction

It is probably still the position at common law, as distinct from statute, that a parent or someone to whom the parent has delegated authority may inflict physical hurt on his or her child, provided that it does not go too far and is for the purpose of correction and not the gratification of passion or rage: see *R v Conner* (1836) 7 C & P 438; *R v Cheeseman* (1836) 7 C & P 455; *R v Hopley* (1860) 2 F & F 202; *R v Griffin* (1869) 11 Cox CC 402. These cases have nothing to do with consent, and are useful only as another demonstration that specially exempt situations can exist and that they can involve an upper limit of tolerable harm.

. . . I ask myself, not whether as a result of the decision in this appeal, activities such as those of the appellants should *cease* to be criminal, but rather whether the Act of 1861 (a statute which I venture to repeat once again was clearly intended to penalise conduct of a quite different nature) should in this new situation be interpreted so as to *make* it criminal. Why should this step be taken? Leaving aside repugnance and moral objection, both of which are entirely natural but neither of which are in my opinion grounds upon which the court could properly create a new crime, I can visualise only the following reasons. (1) Some of the practices obviously created a risk of genito-urinary infection, and others of septicaemia. These might indeed have been grave in former times, but the risk of serious harm must surely have been greatly reduced by modern medical science.

(2) The possibility that matters might get out of hand, with grave results. It has been acknow-ledged throughout the present proceedings that the appellants' activities were performed as a

pre-arranged ritual, which at the same time enhanced their excitement and minimised the risk that the infliction of injury would go too far. Of course things might go wrong and really serious injury or death might ensue. If this happened, those responsible would be punished according to the ordinary law, in the same way as those who kill or injure in the course of more ordinary sexual activities are regularly punished. But to penalise the appellants' conduct even if the extreme consequences do not ensue, just because they might have done so would require an assessment of the degree of risk, and the balancing of this risk against the interests of individual freedom. Such a balancing is in my opinion for Parliament, not the courts; and even if your Lordships' House were to embark upon it the attempt must in my opinion fail at the outset for there is no evidence at all of the seriousness of the hazards to which sado-masochistic conduct of this kind gives rise. this is not surprising, since the impressive argument of Mr Purnell for the respondents did not seek to persuade your Lordships' to bring the matter within the Act of 1861 on the ground of special risks, but rather to establish that the appellants are liable *under the general law* because the level of harm exceeded the critical level marking off criminal from non-criminal consensual violence which he invited your Lordships to endorse.

(3) I would give the same answer to the suggestion that these activities involved a risk of accelerating the spread of auto-immune deficiency syndrome, and that they should be brought within the Act of 1861 in the interests of public health. The consequence would be strange, since what is currently the principal cause for the transmission of this scourge, namely consenting buggery between males, is now legal. Nevertheless, I would have been compelled to give this proposition the most anxious consideration if there had been any evidence to support it. But there is none, since the case for the respondent was advanced on an entirely different ground.

(4) There remains an argument to which I have given much greater weight. As the evidence in the present case has shown, there is a risk that strangers (and especially young strangers) may be drawn into these activities at an early age and will then become established in them for life. This is indeed a disturbing prospect, but I have come to the conclusion that it is not a sufficient ground for declaring these activities to be criminal under the Act of 1861. The element of the corruption of youth is already catered for by the existing legislation; and if there is a gap in it which needs to be filled the remedy surely lies in the hands of Parliament, not in the application of a statute which is aimed at other forms of wrongdoing. As regards proselytisation for adult sado-masochism the argument appears to me circular. For if the activity is not itself so much against the public interest that it ought to be declared criminal under the Act of 1861 then the risk that others will be induced to join in cannot be a ground for making it criminal.

Leaving aside the logic of this answer, which seems to me impregnable, plain humanity demands that a court addressing the criminality of conduct such as that of the present should recognise and respond to the profound dismay which all members of the community share about the apparent increase of cruel and senseless crimes against the defenceless. Whilst doing so I must repeat for the last time that in the answer which I propose I do not advocate the decriminalisation of conduct which has hitherto been a crime; nor do I rebut a submission that a new crime should be created, penalising this conduct, for Mr Purnell has rightly not invited the House to take this course. The only question is whether these consensual private acts are offences against the existing law of violence. To this question I return a negative response.

Appeal dismissed.

The defendants proceeded to take their claims to the European Court of Human rights:

Laskey, Jaggard and Brown v United Kingdom
(1997) 24 EHRR 39, European Court of Human Rights

Alleged violation of Article 8 of the Convention
The applicants contended that their prosecution and convictions for assault and wounding in the course of consensual sado-masochistic activities between adults was in breach of Article 8 of the Convention which provides:

> 1. Everyone has the right to respect for his private and family life, his home and correspondence.
> 2. There shall he no interference by a public authority with the exercise of this right except such as is in accordance with the law and is necessary in a democratic society in the interests of national security, public safety or the economic well-being of the country, for the prevention of disorder or crime, for the protection of health or morals, or for the protection of the rights and freedoms of others.

It was common ground among those appearing before the Court that the criminal proceedings against the applicants which resulted in their conviction constituted an 'interference by a public authority' with the applicants' right to respect for their private life. It was similarly undisputed that the interference had been 'in accordance with the law'. Furthermore, the Commission and the applicants accepted the Government's assertion that the interference pursued the legitimate aim of the 'protection of health or morals', within the meaning of the second paragraph of Article 8.

The Court observes that not every sexual activity carried out behind closed doors necessarily falls within the scope of Article 8. In the present case, the applicants were involved in consensual sado-masochistic activities for purposes of sexual gratification. There can be no doubt that sexual orientation and activity concern an intimate aspect of private life. However, a considerable number of people were involved in the activities in question which included, *inter alia*, the recruitment of new 'Members', the provision of several specially-equipped 'chambers', and the shooting of many video-tapes which were distributed among the 'Members'. It may thus be open to question whether the sexual activities of the applicants fell entirely within the notion of 'private life' in the particular circumstances of the case.

However, since this point has not been disputed by those appearing before it, the Court sees no reason to examine it of its own motion in the present case. Assuming, therefore, that the prosecution and conviction of the applicants amounted to an interference with their private life, the question arises whether such an interference was 'necessary in a democratic society' within the meaning of the second paragraph of Article 8.

'Necessary in a democratic society'
The applicants maintained that the interference at issue could not be regarded as 'necessary in a democratic society'. This submission was contested by the Government and by a majority of the Commission.

In support of their submission, the applicants alleged that all those involved in the sado-masochistic encounters were willing adult participants; that participation in the acts complained of was carefully restricted and controlled and was limited to persons with like-minded sado-masochistic proclivities; that the acts were not witnessed by the public at large and that there was no danger or likelihood that they would ever be so witnessed: that no serious or permanent injury had been sustained, no infection had been caused to the wounds, and that no medical treatment had been required. Furthermore, no complaint was ever made to the police – who learnt about the applicants' activities by chance. . . .

The applicants submitted that their case should be viewed as one involving matters of sexual expression, rather than violence. With due regard to this consideration, the line beyond which consent is no defence to physical injury should only be drawn at the level of intentional or reckless causing of serious disabling injury.

For the Government. the State was entitled to punish acts of violence, such as those for which the applicants were convicted, that could not be considered of a trifling or transient nature, irrespective of the consent of the victim. In fact, in the present case, some of these acts could well be compared to 'genital torture' and a Contracting State could not be said to have an obligation to tolerate acts of torture because they are committed in the context of a consenting sexual relationship. The State was moreover entitled to prohibit activities because of their potential danger.

The Government further contended that the criminal law should seek to deter certain forms of behaviour on public health grounds but also for broader moral reasons. In this respect, acts of torture – such as those at issue in the present case – may be banned also on the ground that they undermine the respect which human beings should confer upon each other. In any event, the whole issue of the role of consent in the criminal law is of great complexity and the contracting States should enjoy a wide margin of appreciation to consider all the public policy options.

The Commission noted that the injuries that were or could be caused by the applicants' activities were of a significant nature and degree, and that the conduct in question was, on any view, of an extreme character. The State authorities therefore acted within their margin of appreciation in order to protect its citizens from real risk of serious physical harm or injury.

According to the Court's established case law, the notion of necessity implies that the interference corresponds to a pressing social need and, in particular, that it is proportionate to the legitimate aim pursued; in determining whether an interference is 'necessary in a democratic society', the Court will take into account that a margin of appreciation is left to the national authorities, whose decision remains subject to review by the Court for conformity with the requirements of the Convention.

The scope of this margin of appreciation is not identical in each case but will vary according to the context. Relevant factors include the nature of the Convention right in issue, its importance for the individual and the nature of the activities concerned.

The Court considers that one of the roles which the State is unquestionably entitled to undertake is to seek to regulate, through the operation of the criminal law, activities which involve the infliction of physical harm. This is so whether the activities in question occur in the course of sexual conduct or otherwise.

The determination of the level of harm that should be tolerated by the law in situations where the victim consents is in the first instance a matter for the State concerned since what is at stake is related, on the one hand, to the public health considerations and to the general deterrent effect of the criminal law, and, on the other, to the personal autonomy of the individual.

The applicants have contended that, in the circumstances of the case, the behaviour in question formed part of private morality which is not the State's business to regulate. In their submission the matters for which they were prosecuted and convicted concerned only private sexual behaviour.

The Court is not persuaded by this submission. It is evident from the facts established by the national courts that the applicants' sado-masochistic activities involved a significant degree of injury or wounding which could not be characterised as trifling or transient. This, in itself, suffices to distinguish the present case from those applications which have previously been examined by the Court concerning consensual homosexual behaviour in private between adults where no such feature was present.

Nor does the Court accept the applicants' submission that no prosecution should have been brought against them since their injuries were not severe and since no medical treatment had been required.

In deciding whether or not to prosecute, the State authorities were entitled to have regard not only to the actual seriousness of the harm caused – which as noted above was considered to be significant – but also as stated by Lord Jauncey of Tullichettle, to the potential for harm inherent in the acts in question. In this respect it is recalled that the activities were considered by Lord Templeman to be 'unpredictably dangerous'.

The applicants have further submitted that they were singled out partly because of the authorities' bias against homosexuals. They referred to the recent judgment in the *Wilson* case, where, in their view, similar behaviour in the context of a heterosexual couple was not considered to deserve criminal punishment.

The Court finds no evidence in support of the applicants' allegations in either the conduct of the proceedings against them or the judgment of the House of Lords. In this respect it recalls the remark of the trial judge when passing sentence that 'the unlawful conduct now before the court would be dealt with equally in the prosecution of heterosexuals or bisexuals if carried out by them'.

Moreover, it is clear from the judgment of the House of Lords that the opinions of the majority were based on the extreme nature of the practices involved and not the sexual proclivities of the applicants.

R v Wilson

[1996] 3 WLR 125, Court of Appeal

At his wife's instigation the appellant branded his initials on her buttocks with a hot knife. He was charged with assault occasioning actual bodily harm contrary to section 47 of the Offences against the Person Act 1861. At the close of the prosecution case, on a submission of no case to answer, the judge ruled that despite the wife's consent he was bound by authority to direct the jury to convict. In the light of that ruling the appellant was not called to give evidence and defence counsel did not make any submissions to the jury. The appellant was convicted. On appeal against conviction:

RUSSELL LJ: . . . We are abundantly satisfied that there is no factual comparison to be made between the instant case and the facts of either *R v Donovan* [1934] 2 KB 498 or *R v Brown* [1994] 1 AC 212: Mrs Wilson not only consented to that which the appellant did, she instigated it. There was no aggressive intent on the part of the appellant. On the contrary, far from wishing to cause injury to his wife, the appellant's desire was to assist her in what she regarded as the acquisition of a desirable piece of personal adornment, perhaps in this day and age no less understandable than the piercing of nostrils or even tongues for the purposes of inserting decorative jewellery.

In our judgment *R v Brown* is not authority for the proposition that consent is no defence to a charge under section 47 of the Act of 1861, in all circumstances where actual bodily harm is deliberately inflicted. It is to be observed that the question certified for their Lordships in *R v Brown* related only to a 'sado-masochistic encounter.' . . .

Does public policy or the public interest demand that the appellant's activity should be visited by the sanctions of the criminal law? The majority in *R v Brown* clearly took the view that such considerations were relevant. If that is so, then we are firmly of the opinion that it is not in the public interest that activities such as the appellant's in this appeal should amount to criminal behaviour. Consensual activity between husband and wife, in the privacy of the matrimonial home, is not, in our judgment, normally a proper matter for criminal investigation, let alone criminal prosecution. Accordingly we take the view that the judge failed to have full regard to the facts of this case and misdirected himself in saying that *R v Donovan* [1934] 2 KB 498 and *R v Brown* [1994] 1 AC 212 constrained him to rule that consent was no defence.

In this field, in our judgment, the law should develop upon a case basis rather than upon general propositions to which, in the changing times in which we live, exceptions may arise from time to time not expressly covered by authority.

We shall allow the appeal and quash the conviction. . . .

NOTES AND QUESTIONS

1. In his commentary on *Wilson*, Prof J.C. Smith states ([1996] Crim LR 573):

> It is not at all surprising that the trial judge reluctantly took the view that he was bound by *Brown* to direct the jury to convict. Thus Lord Jauncey, one of the majority in *Brown* stated ([1993] 2 All ER 75 at 90):
>
>> In my view the line properly falls to be drawn between assault at common law and the offence of assault occasioning actual bodily harm created by section 47 of the 1861 Act, with the result that consent of the victim is no answer to anyone charged with the latter offence or with a contravention of the section 20 unless the circumstances fall within one of the well-known exceptions such as organised sporting contests and games, parental chastisement or reasonable surgery.

Who was to know that marital bottom-branding was to be added to the list of exceptions? What reasons can be discerned in the present judgment for the distinction?

(i) Mrs W did not only consent to the branding but 'instigated' it. Would the House in *Brown* have taken a different view of a particular activity if it had been shown to have been instigated by the 'victim'? It seems highly unlikely. It was said, for example (p. 83), that the victim was usually manacled so that he 'could enjoy the thrill of helplessness.' He wanted to be manacled. (ii) There was in the present case 'no aggressive intent.' But the goings-on in *Brown* could hardly have been more friendly. Everyone was having a jolly good time. (iii) W had no wish to cause injury to his wife. If the branding had been done without consent, the court would not have had the slightest hesitation in describing it as 'injury;' and W intended to cause it. (iv) This was consensual activity between husband and wife in the privacy of the matrimonial home. It can hardly be supposed, in these days, that the decision is limited to marital activity. 'Partners' and adult girl or boy friends could hardly be treated differently. But group branding sessions might fall foul of the next point. (v) *Brown* was a case involving 'sadomasochism of the grossest kind.' This is perhaps the substantial reason. W, unlike the defendants in *Brown*, apparently derived no sexual satisfaction from what he did, any more than a surgeon or professional tattooist. It was not essentially different from the lawful practice of tattooing. This seems to be the only basis on which *Donovan* (the court says '[Donovan's] act had about it an aggressive element') can realistically be distinguished. What if the Wilsons had admitted that the operation gave them a thrill?

The approach of the majority in *Brown* was to ask, does public policy require us to create a new defence to sections 47 and 20, so as to exempt these revolting sadomasochists? The answer, inevitably, was no. The approach of the present court was to ask, does the public interest require that this activity be condemned as criminal? It is not surprising that the answer to that question too should be in the negative. This is more in tune with the approach of the minority in *Brown*; and it is submitted that it is to be preferred. The decision leaves the law in an uncertain state; and it is noteworthy that the court thought that the law should be left to develop on a case by case basis. Contrast the effort made by the Law Commission to introduce principle into the law – with a second, large, Consultation Paper (No. 139).

2. Why should competent, rational adults free from duress or coercion be prevented from consenting to activities which give them pleasure, particularly if those activities are conducted in private? In *R v Emmett (Stephen Ray), The Times*, 15 October 1999, the Court of Appeal followed *Brown* rather than *Wilson* and held that the risk of non-temporary or

permanent injury out-weighed consent to sado-masochistic practices. It will be recalled that in *Dudgeon* v *United Kingdom* (1981) 4 EHRR 149, the European Court of Human Rights had held that Northern Ireland laws which criminalised homosexual activities between consenting adults committed in private infringed the right to respect for private life contained in Article 8 of the European Convention on Human Rights. In what sense is *Brown* distinguishable?

3. Does the court in *Brown* assume an unduly paternalistic role? Does the State and/or the judiciary have an obligation to enforce the prevailing moral values of the community? How does one determine what those values are?

4. Is there a *qualitative* distinction between permitting a person to consent to his own death and permitting a person to consent to lesser harms? Is the concern in the former that unscrupulous individuals may be able to talk gullible victims into consenting to their death? With the victim dead, the task of proving or disproving consent is likely to be extremely difficult. Or is the critical factor that death is qualitatively different from all other forms of harm?

5. How does *Brown* differ from a permitted boxing match? Does the difference have anything to do with consent? Even in the context of professional and amateur sport, the possibility of a prosecution for battery has been recognised where the force exceeds the legitimate parameters of the rules of the game. See, e.g., *Lloyd* [1989] Crim LR 513.

6. May a person consent to cosmetic surgery? Whom does it benefit? Why does Lord Mustill reject a distinction based on the seriousness of the harm caused and then place surgery in a category of its own because of the degree of harm caused?

7. Note that the Government's proposals for reform (see below) do not address the issue of consent. However, the issue generally is under review by the Law Commission, which has issued a Consultation Paper on the subject (Law Commission Consultation Paper No. 139).

(ii) *When will the State imply or impose consent?*

We have already seen in *Collins* v *Wilcock* that the law implies consent to physical contact which is generally acceptable in the ordinary conduct of daily life. Similarly, the courts will not allow the absence of formal consent by an unconscious patient to convert a beneficial medical procedure into a battery. Thus, if a paramedic comes upon an unconscious victim of a car accident and gives a blood transfusion it will not amount to a battery, even though the recipient is a Jehovah's Witness who would have refused such treatment on religious grounds had she been conscious. Medical treatment of a person incapable of consent because of mental incapacity will also not amount to assault or battery (*In re F (Mental Patient: Sterilisation)* [1990] 2 AC 1). In the case of an emergency, a doctor should do no more than is reasonably required in the best interests of the patient. Where the incapacity is more permanent, treatment is justified 'if it is carried out in order either to save their lives, or to ensure improvement or prevent deterioration in their physical or mental health'. Parents too are allowed to use reasonable force for the purpose of corporal punishment, although whether it is strictly accurate to say that the child 'consents' to such force is questionable.

(iii) *What constitutes valid consent?*

If a victim is unable to comprehend the nature of the act to which he or she apparently consented, the consent will be invalid.

Burrell v *Harmer*

[1965] 3 All ER 684, Divisional Court

The defendant tattooed devices on the arms of two boys aged respectively 12 and 13. The marks subsequently became inflamed and he was charged with, and convicted of, causing the boys actual bodily harm.

Held, dismissing his appeal, that if a child of the age of understanding was unable to appreciate the nature of an act, apparent consent to it was no consent at all.

NOTES AND QUESTIONS

1. Is the court's position that the boys did not appreciate what it meant to be tattooed; or that even if they did know, they were not legally capable of giving consent? Would the result have been different if the boys had been 15? 18? Tattooing of minors below the age of 16 is now illegal under the Tattooing of Minors Act 1969.
2. Note that the court's ruling may lead to the conviction of a defendant who had not only an honest but also a reasonable belief in the consent of the victim. This appears to be in direct contravention of *Director of Public Prosecutions* v *Morgan* [1976] AC 182 and the similar decision in *R* v *Kimber* [1983] 1 WLR 1118, where it was held by the Court of Appeal that an honest belief in the consent of a mentally retarded woman would have been sufficient to negative a charge of indecent assault. Both *Morgan* and *Kimber* are examined in Chapter 13.
3. In the case of a very young child, absence of consent will be implied from the child's age. See, e.g. *R* v *Howard* [1965] 3 All ER 684 (child of six unable to comprehend sexual intercourse and so unable to consent). In other cases the jury must decide whether there was a valid consent:

R v *D*

[1984] 1 AC 778, House of Lords

LORD BRANDON OF OAKBROOK: . . . I must now deal with two matters to which I said that I would return later. One of those matters is whether the doctrine laid down by the Irish Supreme Court in *Edge's* case [1943] IR 115 that the person the absence of whose consent is an essential ingredient of the common law offence of kidnapping is that of the child if it has reached an age of discretion fixed by law, but that of its father or other guardian if it has not, applies also under English law.

In my opinion, to accept that doctrine as applicable under English law would not be consistent with the formulation of the third ingredient of the common law offence of kidnapping which I made earlier on the basis of the wide body of authority to which your Lordships were referred. That third ingredient, as I formulated it earlier, consists of the absence of consent on the part of the person taken or carried away. I see no good reason why, in relation to the kidnapping of a child, it should not in all cases be the absence of the child's consent which is material, whatever its age may be. In the case of a very young child, it would not have the understanding or the intelligence to give its consent, so that absence of consent would be a necessary inference from its age. In the case of an older child, however, it must, I think be a question of fact for a jury whether the child concerned has sufficient understanding and intelligence to give its consent; if, but only if, the jury considers that a child has these qualities, it must then go on to consider whether it has been proved that the child did not give its consent. While the matter will always be for the jury alone to decide, I should not expect a jury to find at all frequently that a child under 14 had sufficient understanding and intelligence to give its consent.

An apparent consent which is the product of a threat will not be valid. What then of consent induced by fraud?

R v Tabassum

[2000] Crim LR 686, Court of Appeal

Three women, all of whom knew the defendant, made complaints of indecent assault against him. The first took a computer course on which he was a lecturer. He told her that he had worked at Christies, a well-known cancer hospital is Manchester, and was a breast cancer specialist. She thought that he was a doctor. He said that he was doing a study on breast cancer, and she agreed to take part. There was a meeting at which she filled in a questionnaire and signed a consent form, then she removed her bra at his request and he showed her how to examine her breasts. A little later, after asking her some questions, he asked her to take off her top again, but she declined and asked him to leave, which he did. Her evidence was that he showed no sign of sexual excitement, but she would not have allowed him to touch her if she had known that he had no relevant qualifications.

The second complainant said that the defendant came to her house, and told her he was doing a survey on breast cancer. He seemed very knowledgeable and she agreed to take part. He returned at a later date. She filled in the questionnaire and the consent form and he examined her breasts. She would not have allowed him to do so if she had known that he had no relevant qualifications, which he had led her to believe he had. The third complainant also knew the defendant through his lectures. She filled in the form and he visited her at her home by appointment. He checked her blood pressure, pulse and heart. She asked him if he was a doctor, and he said he was not but had done a lot of work for Christies cancer hospital. She refused to let him examine her breasts, though he put his stethoscope under her bra.

She would not have let him touch her if she had known that he did not work at Christies hospital, where she thought he had been training.

At the trial evidence was adduced that the defendant had worked for several years as a hospital representative, who called on doctors to tell them about drugs. He had received training on drugs and diseases.

In evidence, the defendant said that he had no convictions, and had postgraduate degrees in science and business administration. In his work as a hospital representative he had gained knowledge about breast cancer and seen the need for a database. He had prepared a leaflet to guide women in examining their breasts. The complainants had given their consent to what he did. He agreed that he had no medical qualifications but felt entitled to say that he had medical training. He accepted that he had not been trained to examine for breast cancer. At the time of his arrest he had not started his database, because he did not have enough details.

The defendant was convicted of three offences of indecent assault and appealed against his conviction. Counsel submitted that: (1) consent could be negatived only where the victim was deceived or mistaken about the identity of the perpetrator of the act, or where the nature and quality of the act was different from that for which consent was given. Consent was not negatived merely because the victim would not have consented if she had known all the facts. (2) The judge failed to direct the jury to the reasonableness of the defendant's belief in the complainants' consent.

Held, dismissing the appeal, that (1) the victims had consented to the nature of the defendant's acts, but not their quality, since they believed he was medically qualified or had trained at Christies, and that the touching was for a medical purpose; and that, accordingly, there was no true consent. (2) The only issues were consent and whether the defendant may have believed that the complainants were consenting. On these issues the judge's directions were entirely adequate.

Bolduc and Bird v R

(1967) 63 DLR (2d) 82, Supreme Court of Canada

A physician, about to conduct a vaginal examination and, if necessary, perform a medical procedure in the area to be examined, falsely introduced a lay friend of his to the patient as a medical intern and asked if the friend, who, in fact, was present for his own gratification, might observe the examination.

The patient consented to the friend's presence and the physician proceeded with the examination during which he touched the patient's private parts and inserted an instrument therein for the purposes of the examination while the friend looked on but at no time touched the patient. Both the physician and his friend were convicted of indecent assault on the patient and their conviction was affirmed by the Court of Appeal but on their further appeal from conviction, *held*, Spence, J, dissenting, the appeals should be allowed and the convictions quashed.

Per Hall, J, Cartwright, Fauteux and Ritchie, JJ, concurring: It cannot be said that the fraud practised on the patient vitiated her consent to what the physician was supposed to do and to what, in fact, he did do and, accordingly, the consent of the patient was not obtained by false and fraudulent representations as to the nature and quality of the act. The fraud related rather to the friend's identity as a medical intern and his presence, having regard for the fact that he did not touch the patient, was not an assault.

Per Spence, J, dissenting: Under s. 230 of the *Criminal Code*, the application of force, however slight, is an assault when it is 'without the consent of another person or with consent, where it is obtained by fraud.' The patient's consent to the touching of her person by the physician was a consent to such touching in the presence of a doctor and not a mere layman. The indecent assault upon her was not, then, the act to which she consented and, hence, even without recourse to the provisions of s. 141(2), the accused physician's conduct amounted to the offence of indecent assault to which the co-accused was a party by virtue of the provisions of s. 21 of the *Code*.

NOTES AND QUESTIONS
1. What is the rationale of these decisions? Is it at all relevant whether the woman would have consented to the examination if she had known the true state of affairs? See also *R v Richardson* [1998] 3 WLR 1292, in which it was held that a dentist who had been suspended from her profession was not guilty of assault merely because she was no longer qualified to carry out dental procedures. Her patients had consented to dental treatment and were not deceived about her identity, only about her continuing qualification to practice.
2. What if a doctor indicates that he intends only to perform a vaginal examination. The patient consents and the doctor proceeds (in a highly unprofessional manner) to engage in conduct which in law would amount to an indecent assault. Would consent be a defence to the ensuing charge? How does this case differ from *Bolduc and Bird*? See *R v Williams* [1980] Crim LR 589.
3. In *R v Clarence* (1888) 22 QBD 23, the defendant had intercourse with the victim, who was not aware that he had a venereal disease. It was held that his concealment of his condition was *not* a sufficient fraud as to the nature and quality of the act so as to prevent the victim's consent from being a valid consent. Would the same result be reached today if the concealed condition were AIDS? See the proposals for reform of the law set out later in this chapter.

C: Limits on defences

Some defences traditionally permitted under the common law may be in conflict with the rights guaranteed by the European Convention on Human Rights:

A v *United Kingdom*
(1999) 27 EHRR 611, European Court of Human Rights

On 5 February 1993 the applicant was examined by a consultant paediatrician, who found the following marks on his body, *inter alia*: (1) a fresh red linear bruise on the back of the right thigh, consistent with a blow from a garden cane, probably within the preceding twenty-four hours; (2) a double linear bruise on the back of the left calf, consistent with two separate blows given some time before the first injury; (3) two lines on the back of the left thigh, probably caused by two blows inflicted one or two days previously; (4) three linear bruises on the right bottom, consistent with three blows, possibly given at different times and up to one week old; (5) a fading linear bruise, probably several days old.

The paediatrician considered that the bruising was consistent with the use of a garden cane applied with considerable force on more than one occasion.

The stepfather was charged with assault occasioning actual bodily harm and tried in February 1994. It was not disputed by the defence that the stepfather had caned the boy on a number of occasions, but it was argued that this had been necessary and reasonable since A was a difficult boy who did not respond to parental or school discipline.

In summing up, the judge advised the jury on the law as follows:

> . . . What is it the prosecution must prove? If a man deliberately and unjustifiably hits another and causes some bodily injury, bruising or swelling will do, he is guilty of actual bodily harm. What does 'unjustifiably' mean in the context of this case? It is a perfectly good defence that the alleged assault was merely the correcting of a child by its parent, in this case the stepfather, provided that the correction be moderate in the manner, the instrument and the quantity of it. Or, put another way, reasonable. It is not for the defendant to prove it was lawful correction. It is for the prosecution to prove it was not.
>
> This case is not about whether you should punish a very difficult boy. It is about whether what was done here was reasonable or not and you must judge that . . .

The jury found by a majority verdict that the applicant's stepfather was not guilty of assault occasioning actual bodily harm.

In criminal proceedings for the assault of a child, the burden of proof is on the prosecution to satisfy the jury, beyond a reasonable doubt, *inter alia* that the assault did not constitute lawful punishment.

Parents or other persons *in loco parentis* are protected by the law if they administer punishment which is moderate and reasonable in the circumstances. The concept of 'reasonableness' permits the courts to apply standards prevailing in contemporary society with regard to the physical punishment of children.

Corporal punishment of a child by a teacher cannot be justified if the punishment is inhuman or degrading. In determining whether punishment is inhuman or degrading, regard is to be had to 'all the circumstances of the case, including the reason for giving it, how soon after the event it is given, its nature, the manner and circumstances in which it is given, the persons involved and its mental and physical effects' (section 47(1)(a) and (b) of the Education (No. 2) Act 1986, as amended by section 293 of the Education Act 1993).

The Court recalls that ill-treatment must attain a minimum level of severity if it is to fall within the scope of Article 3. The assessment of this minimum is relative: it depends on all the circumstances of the case, such as the nature and context of the treatment, its duration, its physical and mental effects and, in some instances, the sex, age and state of health of the victim (see the *Costello-Roberts* v *The United Kingdom*, 25 March 1993, Series A No. 247-C, p. 59, H 30).

The Court recalls that the applicant, who was then nine years old, was found by the consultant paediatrician who examined him to have been beaten with a garden cane which had been applied with considerable force on more than one occasion.

The Court considers that treatment of this kind reaches the level of severity prohibited by Article 3.

It remains to be determined whether the State should be held responsible, under Article 3, for the beating of the applicant by his stepfather.

The Court considers that the obligation on the High Contracting Parties under Article 1 of the Convention to secure to everyone within their jurisdiction the rights and freedoms defined in the Convention, taken together with Article 3, requires States to take measures designed to ensure that individuals within their jurisdiction are not subjected to torture or inhuman or degrading treatment or punishment, including such ill-treatment administered by private individuals (see, *mutatis mutandis, HLR* v *France*, 29 April 1997, *Reports* 1997-III, p. 758, n 40). Children and other vulnerable individuals, in particular, are entitled to State protection in the form of effective deterrence, against such serious breaches of personal integrity.

The Court recalls that under English law it is a defence to a charge of assault on a child that the treatment in question amounted to 'reasonable chastisement'. The burden of proof is on the prosecution to establish beyond reasonable doubt that the assault went beyond the limits of lawful punishment. In the present case, despite the fact that the applicant had been subjected to treatment of sufficient severity to fall within the scope of Article 3, the jury acquitted his stepfather, who had administered the treatment.

In the Court's view, the law did not provide adequate protection to the applicant against treatment or punishment contrary to Article 3. Indeed, the Government have accepted that this law currently fails to provide adequate protection to children and should be amended.

In the circumstances of the present case, the failure to provide adequate protection constitutes a violation of Article 3 of the Convention. . . .

NOTES AND QUESTIONS
1. Is the disciplining of a child by a parent a matter of 'private life' protected by Article 8 of the European Convention? Even if not, is it a matter in which the State should not, as a matter of policy, become involved?
2. Opinion polls in the UK show general public support for a parent's right to 'smack' a child. Does the European Court's decision preclude 'smacking'? In *Costello-Roberts* v *United Kingdom* (1993) 19 EHRR 112, the Court held that there had not been a violation of Article 3 where a school master had 'whacked' a seven-year-old boy three times on his clothed buttocks with a slipper for repeated violations of school rules. Note, however, that the European Convention is a 'living instrument' whose content may change with changing times. In several European countries, child 'smacking' is illegal.
3. Note that in *A* and *Costello-Roberts* it is the UK's failure to protect its citizens from Article 3 violations which is at issue, not the criminal liability of the perpetrator of the assaults.

SECTION 5: Aggravated assaults

The Offences Against the Person Act 1861 and other statutes contain many offences which are regarded as more serious than assault and battery because of aggravating factors. The most commonly charged are examined here. In most of these offences the *actus reus* and *mens rea* of assault or battery must be proved as well as the aggravating factor.

A: Assault occasioning actual bodily harm

Offences Against the Person Act 1861

47. Whosoever shall be convicted upon an indictment of any assault occasioning actual bodily harm shall be liable . . . to be kept in penal servitude . . .; and whosoever shall be convicted upon an indictment for a common assault shall be liable, at the discretion of the court, to be imprisoned for any term not exceeding one year, with or without hard labour.

'Actual bodily harm' was defined in the following case:

R v Miller

[1954] 2 QB 282, Queen's Bench Division

LYNSKEY J: . . . The point has been taken that there is no evidence of bodily harm. The bodily harm alleged is said to be the result of the prisoner's actions, and that is, if the jury accept the evidence, that he threw the wife down three times. There is evidence that afterwards she was in a hysterical and nervous condition, but it is said by counsel that that is not actual bodily harm. Actual bodily harm, according to Archbold, 32nd ed., p. 959, includes 'any hurt or injury calculated to interfere with the health or comfort of the prosecutor.' There was a time when shock was not regarded as bodily hurt, but the day has gone by when that could be said. It seems to me now that if a person is caused hurt or injury resulting, not in any physical injury, but in an injury to her state of mind for the time being, that is within the definition of actual bodily harm, and on that point I would leave the case to the jury.

NOTES
1. In *R v Ireland* [1997] 3 WLR 534 and *R v Constanza* [1997] Crim LR 576, it was accepted that telephone calls causing significant psychological symptoms were capable of constituting assault occasioning actual bodily harm. However, where psychological rather than physical injury is the harm alleged, expert testimony may be required. See *R v Chan-Fook* [1994] 1 WLR 689.
2. There was some doubt as to the *mens rea* for this offence, in particular the extent to which the defendant must foresee the degree of harm which would result. This controversy has now been settled by the opinion of the House of Lords in *R v Savage* and *DPP v Parmenter* [1991] 3 WLR 914, discussed at p. 277.

QUESTION

Naomi hits Jacob intentionally, not foreseeing any actual bodily harm, but he (reasonably foreseeably) trips, falls and fractures his skull. Is Naomi guilty of a s. 47 offence? What would be the position if Jacob died?

B: Wounding and inflicting grievous bodily harm

Offences Against the Person Act 1861

18. Whosoever shall unlawfully and maliciously by any means whatsoever wound or cause any grievous bodily harm to any person, or shoot at any person, or, by drawing a trigger or in any other manner attempt to discharge any kind of loaded arms at any person, with intent, in any of the cases aforesaid, to maim, disfigure, or disable any person, or with intent to resist or prevent the lawful apprehension or detainer of any person, shall be guilty of felony, and being convicted thereof shall be liable . . . to be kept in penal servitude for life . . .

20. Whosoever shall unlawfully and maliciously wound or inflict any grievous bodily harm upon any other person, either with or without any weapon or instrument, shall be guilty of a misdemeanour, and being convicted thereof shall be liable . . . to be kept in penal servitude . . .

(i) *Actus reus*

The *actus reus* of a s. 20 offence is an unlawful wounding *or* the unlawful infliction of grievous bodily harm. In contrast, a s. 18 offence requires proof of an unlawful wounding or the causing of grievous bodily harm. The courts had in the past drawn a distinction between infliction and causing, but this distinction was rejected in *R v Burstow* [1997] 1 Cr App R 144. There is also a difference in the *mens rea* requirements for the two sections. This is also explored below.

The reasons for treating wounding and infliction of GBH as equivalent are historical, since when the Act was passed even a small breaking of the skin was liable to lead to infection and death.

A wound is a breaking of the skin:

Moriarty v Brooks
(1834) 6 C & P 684, Court of Appeal

LORD LYNDHURST CB: The definition of a wound in criminal cases is an injury to the person, by which the skin is broken. If the skin is broken, and there was a bleeding, that is a wound.

His Lordship (in summing up) said – If the violence which occurred took place in an endeavour by the defendant to turn the plaintiff out of the house, the third plea is proved. However, this plea does not profess to justify any wounding; therefore, if there was a wound, the plaintiff is entitled to recover for that. It is proved that the plaintiff was cut under the eye, and that it bled; and I am of opinion that that is a wound. . . .

R v McLoughlin
(1838) 8 C & P 635, Central Criminal Court

A surgeon, named Hore, was called as a witness, and said, – 'About eleven o'clock on the night of the 14th of July, I was called on to attend the prosecutor; I examined his head and found an abrasion of the skin, with blood issuing from it; he had received a violent blow on the left temple, there was great tumefaction; I could not ascertain at the time whether the bone was fractured; he lost the sight of his left eye, and it rendered him deaf on the left ear; he had great difficulty of speech; he could scarcely answer questions put to him, not being able to articulate; and on moving the bandage off his head, he shortly became insensible; I have seen the fragments of the bottle; it was such a wound as might have been inflicted with a bottle; I have attended him ever since, frequently twice a-day; I considered him in a dangerous state for several weeks; he is not yet recovered.' On his cross-examination, *inter alia*, he said – 'The skin was broken on the left temple, that would not be visible now, nor the cicatrix, from its having healed; I never said the skin was not broken; I have said it was a sort of injury which a medical man would hardly consider a wound, but it was in the eye of the law a wound; there were signs of it visible four days after.'

COLERIDGE J: . . . It is essential for you to be quite clear that a wound was inflicted. I am inclined to understand, and my learned brothers are of the same opinion, that, if it is necessary to constitute a wound, that the skin should be broken, it must be the whole skin, and it is not sufficient to shew a separation of the cuticle only. You will, therefore, have to say on the first three counts, whether there was a wounding in the sense in which I have stated it, viz. was there a wound – a separation of the whole skin? If you think there was not, you will find the prisoner not guilty upon these counts. Then, as to the fourth count, which charges an intent to murder, you will, perhaps, think, that under all the circumstances of this case, there is not sufficient evidence of that malice aforethought which is necessary to constitute such an intent. But you may on either of the counts find the prisoner guilty of an assault.

C (a minor) v Eisenhower
[1984] 1 QB 331, Queen's Bench Division

The defendant, aged 15, was involved in an incident in which C was hit by an air gun pellet near his eye. The defendant was charged with unlawfully and maliciously wounding C, contrary to section 20 of the Offences against the Person Act 1861. The justices held that the abnormal presence of red blood cells in the fluid of the eye, indicating at least the rupture of one or more internal blood vessels, was sufficient to constitute a wound for the purposes of section 20.

On appeal by the defendant:—

Held, allowing the appeal, that on the authorities, the word 'wound' meant a break in the continuity of the whole skin; that, accordingly, the rupture of internal blood vessels was not sufficient to constitute a wound for the purposes of section 20 of the Act of 1861; and that, therefore, the defendant had not committed an offence under the section . . .

NOTE
'Grievous bodily harm' was rather unhelpfully redefined as 'really serious harm' in *Director of Public Prosecutions* v *Smith* [1961] AC 290.

(ii) 'Inflict' and 'wound'
In respect of *actus reus*, what are the differences between the aggravated offences? The precise differences have been the subject of some confusion in the case law, but basically:

(a) s. 47 requires an assault or a battery;

(b) s. 20 requires *infliction* of GBH or a '*wounding*';

(c) s. 18 requires the *causing* of GBH.

In a series of cases it was held that 'inflict' and 'wound' required proof of an assault. See *R* v *Taylor* (1869) LR 1 CCR 194, *R* v *Clarence* (1888) 22 QBD 23. However, in a poorly reasoned judgment in *R* v *Wilson* [1984] AC 242, the House of Lords held that the word 'inflict' did not necessarily imply an assault. This ruling was considered and better explained in *R* v *Ireland, R* v *Burstow*.

R v Ireland, R v Burstow
[1997] 3 WLR 534, House of Lords

For facts and findings, see p. 270.

LORD HOPE OF CRAIGHEAD: . . .
R v *Burstow: 'inflict'*
In this case the appellant changed his plea to guilty after a ruling by the trial judge that the offence of unlawfully and maliciously inflicting grievous bodily harm contrary to section 20 of the Act of 1861 may be committed where no physical violence has been applied directly or indirectly to the body of the victim. Counsel for the appellant accepted that if *R* v *Chan-Fook* [1994] 1 WLR 689 was correctly decided, with the result that 'actual bodily harm' in section 47 is capable of including

psychiatric injury, the victim in this case had suffered grievous bodily harm within the meaning of section 20. But he submitted that no offence against section 20 had been committed in this case because, although the appellant might be said to have 'caused' the victim to sustain grievous bodily harm, he had not 'inflicted' that harm on her because he had not used any personal violence against her.

Counsel based his submission on the decision in *R* v *Clarence* 22 QBD 23. In that case it was held that some form of direct personal violence was required for a conviction under section 20. The use of the word 'inflict' in the section was said to imply that some form of battery was involved in the assault. The conviction was quashed because although the venereal infection from which the victim was suffering was the result of direct physical contact, there had been no violence used and thus there was no element of battery. It seems to me however that there are three reasons for regarding that case as an uncertain guide to the question which arises where the bodily harm which has resulted from the defendant's conduct consists of psychiatric injury.

The first is that the judges in *R* v *Clarence* were concerned with a case of physical, not psychiatric, injury. They did not have to consider the problem which arises where the grievous bodily harm is of a kind which may result without any form of physical contact. The second is that the intercourse had taken place with consent, as the defendant's wife was ignorant of his venereal disease. So there was no question in that case of an assault having been committed, if there was no element of violence or battery. Also, as Lord Roskill pointed out in *R* v *Wilson (Clarence)* [1984] AC 242, 260c the judgments of the judges who formed the majority are not wholly consistent with each other. This casts some doubt on the weight which should be attached to the judgment when the facts are entirely different, as they are in the present case.

In *R* v *Wilson*, Lord Roskill referred, at pp. 259E–260B, with approval to the judgment of the Supreme Court of Victoria in *R* v *Salisbury* [1976] VR 452, in which the following passage appears, at p. 461:

> although the word 'inflicts' . . . does not have as wide a meaning as the word 'causes' . . . the word 'inflicts' does have a wider meaning than it would have if it were construed so that inflicting grievous bodily harm always involved assaulting the victim.

Lord Roskill said [1984] AC 242, 260H that he was content to accept, as was the full court in *R* v *Salisbury*, that there can be an infliction of grievous bodily harm contrary to section 20 without an assault being committed. But these observations do not wholly resolve the issue which arises in this case, in the context of grievous bodily harm which consists only of psychiatric injury.

The question is whether there is any difference in meaning, in this context, between the word 'cause' and the word 'inflict'. The fact that the word 'caused' is used in section 18, whereas the word used in section 20 is 'inflict', might be taken at first sight to indicate that there is a difference. But for all practical purposes there is, in my opinion, no difference between these two words. In *R* v *Mandair* [1995] 1 AC 208, 215B Lord Mackay of Clashfern LC said that the word 'cause' is wider or at least not narrower than the word 'inflict'. I respectfully agree with that observation. But I would add that there is this difference, that the word 'inflict' implies that the consequence of the act is something which the victim is likely to find unpleasant or harmful. The relationship between cause and effect, when the word 'cause' is used, is neutral. It may embrace pleasure as well as pain. The relationship when the word 'inflict' is used is more precise, because it invariably implies detriment to the victim of some kind.

In the context of a criminal act therefore the words 'cause' and 'inflict' may be taken to be interchangeable. As the Supreme Court of Victoria held in *R* v *Salisbury* [1976] VR 452, it is not a necessary ingredient of the word 'inflict' that whatever causes the harm must be applied directly to the victim. It may be applied indirectly, so long as the result is that the harm is caused by what has been done. In my opinion it is entirely consistent with the ordinary use of the word 'inflict' in the English language to say that the appellant's actions 'inflicted' the psychiatric harm from which the victim has admittedly suffered in this case. The issues which remain are issues of fact and, as the appellant pled guilty to the offence, I would dismiss his appeal.

The House of Lords in *Wilson* and *Burstow* did not deal with whether 'wound' implied an assault, but in *R v Savage* [1991] 3 WLR 418, Glidewell LJ was of the opinion that wounding did require an assault. This question was dealt with on appeal to the House of Lords in *R v Savage* and *DPP v Parmenter*:

R v Savage, Director of Public Prosecutions v Parmenter
[1991] 3 WLR 914, House of Lords

For Facts and holding, see p. 277

LORD ACKNER: . . . 1. *Is a verdict of guilty of assault occasioning actual bodily harm a permissible alternative verdict on a count alleging unlawful wounding contrary to section 20 of the Act?*

. . . The allegation of inflicting grievous bodily harm or for that matter wounding, as was observed by Glidewell LJ, giving the judgment of the court in the *Savage* case [1991] 3 WLR 418, 421, inevitably imports or includes an allegation of assault, unless there are some quite extraordinary facts.

The critical question remained – do the allegations in a section 20 charge 'include either expressly or by implication' allegations of assault occasioning actual bodily harm. As to this, Lord Roskill concluded [1984] AC 247, 261:

> If 'inflicting' can, as the cases show, include 'inflicting by assault', then even though such a charge may not necessarily do so, I do not for myself see why on a fair reading of section 6(3) these allegations do not at least impliedly *include* 'inflicting by assault.' That is sufficient for present purposes though I also regard it as also a possible view that those former allegations *expressly* include the other allegations.

I respectfully agree with this reasoning and accordingly reject the submission that *R v Wilson* was wrongly decided. I would therefore answer the first of the certified questions in the *Savage* case in the affirmative. A verdict of guilty of assault occasioning actual bodily harm is a permissible alternative verdict on a count alleging unlawful wounding contrary to section 20 of the Offences against the Persons Act 1861.

(iii) *Mens rea*
The wounding or infliction of GBH must be done 'maliciously'. Must the defendant actually foresee the possibility of harm, and, if so, what degree of harm must be foreseen?

R v Mowatt
[1968] 1 QB 421, Court of Appeal

DIPLOCK LJ: . . . In the offence under section 20, and in the alternative verdict which may be given on a charge under section 18, for neither of which is any specific intent required, the word 'maliciously' does import upon the part of the person who unlawfully inflicts the wound or other grievous bodily harm an awareness that his act may have the consequence of causing some physical harm to some other person. That is what is meant by 'the particular kind of harm' in the citation from Professor Kenny. It is quite unnecessary that the accused should have foreseen that his unlawful act might cause physical harm of the gravity described in the section, i.e., a wound or serious physical injury. It is enough that he should have foreseen that some physical harm to some person, albeit of a minor character, might result.

What of an intention merely to frighten the victim?

R v *Sullivan*
[1981] Crim LR 46, Court of Appeal

The victim's evidence was that the appellant and a companion were undoubtedly drunk and, while the victim was in a street only eight feet wide with a narrow pavement, the appellant drove his car through the street at 25 to 30 miles per hour, mounted the pavement and injured the victim. The appellant, who had made a written statement to the police denying that he was the driver, did not give evidence and, in an unsworn statement from the dock, said that he could add nothing to the written statement he had given to the police. The sole defence was that the appellant was not driving, but during counsel's closing speech for the defence he suggested that all that the appellant had been intending to do was to frighten the victim and no more and that was insufficient mens rea.

Held . . . [M]ere intention to frighten without more was insufficient; the person charged must be proved to have been aware that probable consequences of his voluntary act would be to cause some injury to the victim, but not necessarily grievous bodily harm.

C: Wounding or causing grievous bodily harm with intent

Offences Against the Person Act 1861

18. Whosoever shall unlawfully and maliciously by any means whatsoever wound or cause any grievous bodily harm to any person, or shoot at any person, or, by drawing a trigger or in any other manner attempt to discharge any kind of loaded arms at any person, with intent, in any of the cases aforesaid, to maim, disfigure, or disable any person, or to do some other grievous bodily harm to any person, or with intent to resist or prevent the lawful apprehension or detainer of any person, shall be guilty of felony, and being convicted thereof shall be liable . . . to be kept in penal servitude for life . . .

NOTE AND QUESTIONS
The offence in question requires proof of one of the ulterior intentions specified, i.e. an intent to wound, an intent to do GBH, or an intent to prevent lawful apprehension or detention of any person. It is necessary that intention as to the relevant consequence be proved. Recklessness is not enough. Why should this be so?

D: Racially aggravated crimes

The Crime and Disorder Act 1998 came into force on September 30 1998, making provision for the imposition of greater sentences for existing crimes where they have been 'racially motivated'. This was followed by the Anti-terrorism, Crime and Security Act 2001 which added the possibility of longer sentences for crimes motivated by religious hostility. The crimes affected are assault, including ss 47 and 20 Offences Against the Person Act 1861, Criminal Damage, Public Order Offences such as causing fear of violence (s 4 Public Offences Act 1986 and s 5 Causing harassment, alarm or distress) and ss 2 and 4 of the Prevention of Harassment Act 1998, Harassment and Putting people in fear of violence).

The definitions of the offences remain the same, the only change is the maximum permissible penalty. The crucial provisions are: s 28 of the Crime and Disorder Act 1998 (as amended by the Anti-Terrorism, Crime and Security Act 2001). The penalty is raised if:

at the time of committing the offence, or immediately before or after having done so, the offender demonstrates towards the victim of the offence hostility based on the victim's membership (or presumed membership) of a racial or religious group, or the offence is motivated (wholly or partly) by racial or religious hostility towards members of a racial or religious group based on their membership of that group. [section 28]

When is an offence 'racially motivated'?

Director of Public Prosecutions v *Pal*
[2000] Crim LR 756, Divisional Court

E, a man in his 60s of Asian appearance was a caretaker at a community centre. In accordance with his duties, he asked four youths, two white and two of Asian appearance, to leave the premises. Three of the youths left, but the respondent, one of the two Asians, remained. He assaulted E and called him a 'white man's arse licker' and a 'brown Englishman'. E did not retaliate, he again asked the respondent to leave which he then did. The respondent was charged with an offence of racially aggravated common assault contrary to section 29(1)(c) and (3) of the Crime and Disorder Act 1998. The justices concluded that the phrases used by the respondent were not motivated by any racial hostility in accordance with section 28(1) of the 1998 Act, but that he had used those particular phrases because he was aggrieved at being asked to leave the premises rather than intentionally engaging in racial hostility. They accordingly acquitted the respondent. The prosecution appealed by way of case stated.

Held, dismissing the appeal, an offence of racially aggravated common assault might be made out if, for example, one white man were to assault another white man and to make a grossly offensive remark, such as 'nigger lover' to that man upon seeing his victim rejoin a group of black friends, but that was not what had occurred in the present case. It would always be necessary for the prosecution to prove the demonstration of racial hostility, but the use of racially abusive insults would ordinarily be found sufficient for that purpose. Moreover, section 28(1) would have application to a street argument when insults were thrown without thought being given to whether the same were racially abusive. In the present case, but for E being an Asian, the respondent would not have used the words he had used as they would have had no meaning, however, that *sine qua non* was not a sufficient basis for concluding that the respondent's hostility towards E was in any material sense based on the E's membership of the Asian race. What he was demonstrating was not hostility towards Asians, but hostility towards E's conduct that night. It followed that the justices were correct to be satisfied that the use of the phrases 'white man's arse licker' and 'brown Englishman' which accompanied the assault did not make the offence racially aggravated within the meaning of section 28.

NOTES AND QUESTIONS

1. The motive behind passing these provisions was to provide for greater punishment for crimes which have racial motivation. However, commentators have pointed out that There is a danger that people charged with aggravated offences will tender pleas to the lesser [charge], and equally there is a danger that the CPS or prosecuting counsel will be tempted to accept such pleas'. See Brennan 'Racially Motivated Crime: the Response of the Criminal Justice System' [1999] Crim LR 17. Further, there is a difficulty with the reduction in sentence usually applied where there is a plea of guilty. Is this to be cancelled out by the finding of racial aggravation?

2. In his commentary on *Pal* Professor Sir John Smith states:

> It is a very great pity that our already over-complex law of offences against the person should have been further complicated by these elaborate provisions. If it was necessary to do anything at all, surely a Practice Direction requiring courts and judges to give full weight to racially aggravating features of offences would have been enough. Maxima were high enough already.
>
> *Law reform.* It is deplorable that the Government is able to find time for ill-considered, 'politically correct', legislation of this kind when the very fully considered proposals for the much-needed reform of the law of non-fatal offences against the person gather still more dust. What has become of the Home Office Consultation Document of February 1998? Mr Straw personally expressed his 'delight' in writing the foreword, for the paper – 'Not just because it sets out the Government's proposals for reforming outmoded and unclear Victorian legislation, but because it demonstrates this Government's commitment to modernising and improving the law.' We were asked for our comments by May 15, 1998. All that has happened is that the law which was acknowledged to be 'archaic and unclear and . . . now in urgent need of reform' has been further complicated by the new racially aggravated versions of that archaic legislation. Please, Mr Straw, revive your delight (and ours) by introducing a Bill.

3. Brennan (note 1) argues that the issues of racial or religious motivation and racial or religious group membership have been confused in the legislation as the hostility must be based on the victim's membership of a particular racial or religious group. Could a group of racists be victims under the CDA of those who want racists out of their community?

4. Should victims of crimes be treated as individuals or as belonging to victimised groups? See further Brennan 'Punishing Islamophobic Hostility: are any lessons to be learned from Racially Hostile Crimes? (2002) Journal of Civil Liberties

SECTION 6: **Reform of the law**

The law of non-fatal offences has been heavily criticised. It is not just that it is archaic, but, more importantly, that it lacks coherence, uses confusing terminology, and fails to provide useful guidance both to citizens who are expected to obey it and to courts who are required to implement it. The Criminal Law Revision Commission proposed its overhaul, and the Law Commission subsequently produced a draft statute which was incorporated into its Draft Criminal Code Bill 1989. That draft in turn formed the basis for a proposed Bill that was brought forth by the Labour Government in 1998 but which was never enacted. The Bill consisted of 28 clauses, the most significant of which are set out below:

Violence: Reforming Offences against the Person: Draft Bill

1.—(1) A person is guilty of an offence if he intentionally causes serious injury to another.

(2) A person is guilty of an offence if he omits to do an act which he has a duty to do at common law, the omission results in serious injury to another, and he intends the omission to have that result.

2.—(1) A person is guilty of an offence if he recklessly causes serious injury to another.

3.—(1) A person is guilty of an offence if he intentionally or recklessly causes injury to another.

4.—(1) A person is guilty of an offence if—
   (a) he intentionally or recklessly applies force to or causes an impact on the body of another, or
   (b) he intentionally or recklessly causes the other to believe that any such force or impact is imminent.

(2) No such offence is committed if the force or impact, not being intended or likely to cause injury, is in the circumstances such as is generally acceptable in the ordinary conduct of daily life and the defendant does not know or believe that it is in fact unacceptable to the other person.

. . .

6.—(1) A person is guilty of an offence under this section if he causes serious injury to another intending to resist, prevent or terminate the lawful arrest or detention of himself or a third person.

(2) The question whether the defendant believes the arrest or detention is lawful must be determined according to the circumstances as he believes them to be.

7.—(1) A person is guilty of an offence if he assaults another intending to resist, prevent or terminate the lawful arrest or detention of himself or a third person.

(2) The question whether the defendant believes the arrest or detention is lawful must be determined according to the circumstances as he believes them to be.

8.—(1) A person is guilty of an offence if he acts as mentioned in subsection (2) and—
   (a) he intends to cause serious injury, or
   (b) he is reckless whether serious injury is caused.

(2) A person acts as mentioned in this subsection if he—
   (a) causes an explosive substance to explode,
   (b) places a dangerous substance in any place,
   (c) delivers or sends a dangerous substance to a person,
   (d) throws a dangerous substance at or near a person, or
   (e) applies a dangerous substance to a person.

. . .

10.—(1) A person is guilty of an offence if he makes to another a threat to cause the death of, or serious injury to, that other or a third person, intending that other to believe that it will be carried out.

. . .

12.—(1) A person is guilty of an offence if he intentionally inflicts severe pain or suffering on another and he does the act—
   (a) in the performance or purported performance of his official duties as a public official, or
   (b) at the instigation or with the consent or acquiescence of a public official who is performing or purporting to perform his official duties.

(2) A person is guilty of an offence if—
   (a) he omits to do an act which he has a duty to do at common law,
   (b) he makes the omission as mentioned in subsection (1)(a) or (b),
   (c) the omission results in the infliction of severe pain, or suffering on another, and
   (d) he intends the omission to have that result.

(3) The following are immaterial—
   (a) the nationality of the persons concerned,
   (b) whether anything occurs in the United Kingdom or elsewhere,
   (c) whether the pain or suffering is physical or mental.

. . .

Meaning of fault terms and of injury

14.—(1) A person acts intentionally with respect to a result if—

(a) it is his purpose to cause it, or

(b) although it is not his purpose to cause it, he knows that it would occur in the ordinary course of events if he were to succeed in his purpose of causing some other result.

(2) A person acts recklessly with respect to a result if he is aware of a risk that it will occur and it is unreasonable to take that risk having regard to the circumstances as he knows or believes them to be.

(3) A person intends an omission to have a result if—

(a) it is his purpose that the result will occur, or

(b) although it is not his purpose that the result will occur, he knows that it would occur in the ordinary course of events if he were to succeed in his purpose that some other result will occur.

(4) A person is reckless whether an omission will have a result if he is aware of a risk that the result will occur and it is unreasonable to take that risk having regard to the circumstances as he knows or believes them to be.

(5) Related expressions must be construed accordingly.

(6) This section has effect for the purposes of this Act.

15.—(1) In this Act 'injury' means—

(a) physical injury, or

(b) mental injury.

Matters affecting liability

16.—(1) Where it is an offence under this Act to be at fault in causing a result by an act and a person lacks the fault required when he does an act that may cause or does cause the result, he nevertheless commits the offence if—

(a) being aware that he has done the act and that the result may occur or (as the case may be) has occurred and may continue, and

(b) with the fault required, he fails to take reasonable steps to prevent the result occurring or continuing and it does occur or continue.

(2) Where it is an offence under this Act to be at fault in causing a result by an omission and a person lacks the fault required when he makes an omission that may cause or does cause the result, he nevertheless commits the offence if—

(a) being aware that he has made the omission and that the result may occur or (as the case may be) has occurred and may continue, and

(b) with the fault required, he fails to take reasonable steps to prevent the result occurring or continuing and it does occur or continue.

(3) For the purposes of this section fault is intention or recklessness, and references to a person being at fault must be construed accordingly.

(4) Common law rules relating to matters provided for in this section do not apply to offences under this Act.

17.—(1) This section applies in determining whether a person is guilty of an offence under this Act.

(2) A person's intention, or awareness of a risk, that his act will cause a result in relation to a person capable of being the victim of the offence must be treated as an intention or (as the case may be) awareness of a risk that his act will cause that result in relation to any other person affected by his act.

(3) A person's intention, or awareness of a risk, that his omission will have a result in relation to a person capable of being the victim of the offence must be treated as an intention or

(as the case may be) awareness of a risk that his omission will have that result in relation to any other person affected as a result of his omission.

(4) Common law rules relating to matters provided for in this section do not apply to offences under this Act.

. . .

19.—(1) For the purposes of this Act a person who was voluntarily intoxicated at any material time must be treated—

(a) as having been aware of any risk of which he would have been aware had he not been intoxicated, and

(b) as having known or believed in any circumstances which he would have known or believed in had he not been intoxicated.

(2) Whether a person is voluntarily intoxicated for this purpose must be determined in accordance with the following provisions.

(3) A person is voluntarily intoxicated if—

(a) he takes an intoxicant otherwise than properly for a medicinal purpose,

(b) he is aware that it is or may be an intoxicant, and

(c) he takes it in such a quantity as impairs his awareness or understanding.

(4) An intoxicant, although taken for a medicinal purpose, is not properly so taken if–

(a) the intoxicant is not taken on medical advice, and the taker is aware that the taking may result in his doing an act or making an omission capable of constituting an offence of the kind in question, or

(b) the intoxicant is taken on medical advice, but the taker fails then or afterwards to comply with any condition forming part of the advice and he is aware that the failure may result in his doing an act or making an omission capable of constituting an offence of the kind in question.

(5) Intoxication must be presumed to have been voluntary unless there is adduced such evidence as might lead the court or jury to conclude that there is a reasonable possibility that the intoxication was involuntary.

(6) An intoxicant is any alcohol, drug or other thing which, when taken into the body, may impair the awareness or understanding of the person taking it.

(7) A person must be treated as taking an intoxicant if he permits it to be administered to him.

NOTES AND QUESTIONS

1. Compare the proposed new law with that contained in the Offences Against the Person Act 1861. What are the major differences?

2. Notice that the proposed Act not only sets out the various substantive of offences, but also defines such fault terms as 'intentional' and 'reckless'. In what way do these definitions differ from those developed by the courts (discussed in Chapter 4)? Should these definitions be adopted across the board?

3. Notice also that the proposed Act addresses the question of when liability should be based on an omission. In what way does it differ from the existing law developed by the courts (discussed in Chapter 3)? Should the proposed approach be adopted across the board?

4. In some instances acts of physical and mental violence, including acts of rape, may be so extreme as to constitute torture and cause a state to be in violation of Article 3 of the European Convention on Human Rights. See, e.g., *Aydin* v *Turkey* (1997) 25 EHRR 251.

7

Sexual Offences

There are a great number of sexual offences, the most important of which – rape, procuring intercourse, and indecent assault – will now be examined. This is also an area under discussion for reform at the time of the writing of this book [February 2003] so vigilance will be needed to discover if any new law has come into force.

A: Rape

Rape is defined by s. 1(1) of the Sexual Offences Act 1956 (SOA 1956) as substituted by the Criminal Justice and Public Order Act 1994. The maximum punishment is life imprisonment:

Sexual Offences Act 1956 (as amended)

1.—(1) It is an offence for a man to rape a woman or another man.
(2) A man commits rape if—
  (a) he has sexual intercourse with a person (whether vaginal or anal) who at the time of the intercourse does not consent to it; and
  (b) at the time he knows that the person does not consent to the intercourse or is reckless as to whether that person consents to it.
(3) A man also commits rape if he induces a married woman to have sexual intercourse with him by impersonating her husband.

The 1994 Act was prompted by a number of considerations. The word 'unlawful' was removed from the definition of rape because it had in the past been interpreted to mean intercourse outside marriage. Marriage was held to imply consent to intercourse. This interpretation was rejected by the House of Lords in R v R [1991] 1 AC 599, leaving the word 'unlawful' with no apparent meaning. Second, the reform recognised anal rape of both males and females. Both were previously outside the definition of rape.

(i) *Actus reus*
This consists of two elements:

  (a) sexual intercourse;
  (b) absence of consent.

(a) *Sexual intercourse.* Sexual intercourse is defined in s. 44, SOA 1956:

Sexual Offences Act 1956

44. Where, on the trial of any offence under this Act, it is necessary to prove sexual intercourse (whether natural or unnatural), it shall not be necessary to prove the completion of the intercourse by the emission of seed, but the intercourse shall be deemed complete upon proof of penetration only.

Slight penetration is sufficient:

R v Hughes
(1841) 9 C & P 752, Court of Appeal

. . . The prisoner was charged with having feloniously ravished Mary Ann Wesley.

The facts of the case were very clearly proved by the prosecutrix, a girl between eleven and twelve years old, and by a woman who detected the prisoner committing the offence; but with respect to the penetration a surgeon was called, who deposed to the appearances in and about the child's private parts, and stated his belief that penetration had taken place, but that the hymen, which in the prosecutrix was placed at the usual distance from the opening, had not been ruptured.

Allen, for the prisoner, submitted, that as the hymen was entire there could not have been sufficient penetration of the person of the prosecutrix to constitute the capital offence of rape.

Coleridge, J, summed up the case to the jury, and desired them to find whether there had been penetration, and whether it had or had not proceeded to the rupture of the hymen.

Verdict – Guilty; the jury finding that there had been penetration, but that the penetration had not proceeded to the rupture of the hymen.

Intercourse continues until terminated by withdrawal:

R v Kaitamaki
[1985] AC 147, Privy Council

LORD SCARMAN: In the early hours of 19 November 1978 the appellant broke and entered a dwelling house. The Crown's case was that he then twice raped a young woman who was an occupier of the premises. There was no dispute that intercourse had taken place on the two occasions. The defence was that the woman consented (or that the appellant honestly believed that she was consenting).

But when the appellant came to give evidence, his case as to the second occasion was that after he had penetrated the woman for the second time he became aware that she was not consenting; he admitted, however, that he did not desist from intercourse. In summing up this part of the case the trial judge said to the jury:

> I tell you, as a matter of law . . . that if, having realised she is not willing, he continues with the act of intercourse, it then becomes rape . . .

It is said that this direction was wrong in law. The appellant's counsel submits that by the criminal law of New Zealand if a man penetrates a woman with her consent he cannot become guilty of rape by continuing the intercourse after a stage when he realises that she is no longer consenting.

The submission raises a question as to the true construction of sections 127 and 128 of the Crimes Act 1961. Section 127 defines sexual intercourse and is in these terms:

> For the purposes of this Part of this Act, sexual intercourse is complete upon penetration; and there shall be no presumption of law that any person is by reason of his age incapable of such intercourse.

Section 128 defines rape and, so far as is material, is in these terms: '(1) Rape is the act of a male person having sexual intercourse with a woman or girl – (a) Without her consent; . . .'

Counsel for the appellant took one point only; but he submitted that it was all he needed. He relied on the definition in section 127 to establish the proposition that rape is penetration without consent: once penetration is complete the act of rape is concluded. Intercourse, if it continues, is not rape, because for the purposes of the Act it is complete upon penetration.

The Court of Appeal by a majority rejected the submission, expressing the opinion that the purpose of section 127 was to remove any doubts as to the minimum conduct needed to prove the fact of sexual intercourse. 'Complete' is used in the statutory definition in the sense of having come into existence, but not in the sense of being at an end. Sexual intercourse is a continuing act which only ends with withdrawal. And the offence of rape is defined in section 128 as that of 'having' intercourse without consent.

Their Lordships agree with the majority decision of the Court of Appeal, and with the reasons which they gave for rejecting the appellant's submission and for construing the two sections in the way in which they did. As Lord Brightman observed in the course of argument before the Board section 127 says 'complete,' not 'completed.' . . .

R v *Cooper and Schaub*
[1994] Crim LR 531, Court of Appeal

C and S were convicted of rape. They had met the complainant, 21, in a public house and later she had gone with them to a nightclub. At the end of the evening, C and S offered to take her home. She got into the back of the car and fell asleep. She awoke to find S in the back with her. S proceeded to have sexual intercourse with her whilst C put his penis in her mouth. The two then changed places and C had sexual intercourse with her whilst S put his penis in her mouth. It was alleged by the prosecution that the complainant had not consented to any of the sexual activity. The defence case was that she had consented throughout.

Held: Penetration is a continuing act. Where a man continues to penetrate a woman after she has withdrawn consent, then the other elements being present he commits rape. The judge was right, therefore, in his direction.

The appeal did not, however, end there. The possibility of the complainant having given her consent and then changed her mind was never canvassed before the jury. The judge should therefore have told the jury to ignore that possibility completely and concentrate on the question of whether or not the complainant was consenting from the outset. In the event, it was not possible to know on what basis the jury convicted C and S, or if some jurors did so on one basis and others on another. The jury were not properly directed on this issue and, accordingly, the convictions were unsafe.

NOTES AND QUESTIONS
1. Is penetration, as the court asserts, really a continuing act? If a woman consents to sexual intercourse, but then objects midway through the intercourse because it is painful, is the man then guilty of rape? Must he be afforded a reasonable opportunity to withdraw?
2. The presumption that boys under the age of 14 were incapable of sexual intercourse so that they could not be convicted of rape was abolished by the Sexual Offences Act 1993, s. 1. A boy under the age of 10 cannot be convicted of rape even if there is conclusive proof that non-consensual sexual intercourse has occurred. Conversely, consensual sexual intercourse between two 10-year-olds can lead to the criminal prosecution of the male partner (but not the female; see *R* v *Tyrell* [1894] 1 QB 710). Fortunately, but perhaps not surprisingly, few prosecutions have been brought in cases involving youthful 'experimentation'.

(b) *Age of consent.* A girl over the age of 16 is legally capable of consenting to sexual relations. In the case of male homosexual relationships the age is 18. Does this disparity of treatment violate a 16-year-old male's human rights?

Sutherland v *United Kingdom*
[1998] EHRLR 117, European Commission of Human Rights

. . . Complaints declared admissible
31. The Commission has declared admissible the applicant's complaints that the fixing of the minimum age for lawful homosexual activities at 18, rather than 16, is in violation of his right to respect for his private life, and is discriminatory.

. . .

32. Accordingly, the issue to be determined is whether there has been a violation of Article 8 alone or taken in conjunction with Article 14 of the Convention by reason of the prohibition of consensual homosexual acts between males over the age of 16 but under the age of 18 years.

. . .

33. Article 8 of the Convention provides so far as is material, as follows:

1. Everyone has the right to respect for his private . . . life . . .

2. There shall be no interference by a public authority with the exercise of this right except such as is in accordance with the law and is necessary in a democratic society . . . for the protection of health or morals, or for the protection of the rights and freedoms of others.

. . . [T]he Commission considers that the maintenance in force of the impugned legislation constituted an interference with the applicant's right to respect for his private life (which includes his sexual life) within the meaning of Article 8 para. 1 of the Convention. Even though the applicant has not in the event been prosecuted or threatened with prosecution, the very existence of the legislation directly affected his private life: either he respected the law and refrained from engaging in any prohibited sexual acts prior to the age of 18 or he committed such acts and thereby became liable to criminal prosecution. The Commission further finds no reason to doubt the general truth of the applicant's allegations as to the distress he felt in having to choose between engaging in a sexual relationship with a like-orientated person of around the same age and breaking the law.

38. The Commission recalls that the compatibility with Article 8 of the Convention of the setting of a minimum age below which male homosexual acts are prohibited has been considered in the case-law of the Court and of the Commission. It is well established by that case-law that there is a legitimate necessity in a democratic society for some restrictions over homosexual conduct, notably in order to provide safeguards against the exploitation and corruption of those who are specially vulnerable by reason of their youth . . .

Article 14 of the Convention provides as follows:

The enjoyment of the rights and freedoms set forth in this Convention shall be secured without discrimination on any ground such as sex, race, colour, language, religion, political or other opinion, national or social origin, association with a national minority, property, birth or other status.

. . . In the United Kingdom, prior to 3 November 1994, the minimum age for consensual male homosexual relations was 21 and, since that date, the minimum age has been 18. The age of consent for consensual heterosexual and lesbian relations has at all material times been 16. There were and are therefore at least two differences which are at issue: the difference in treatment of homosexual and heterosexual relationships, and the difference in treatment between male homo-sexual and lesbian relationships. The parties submissions as to discrimination have concentrated principally on the difference of treatment between homosexuals and heterosexuals, and in the following discussion, the Commission will do likewise.

. . .

52. The Commission notes that it is not contested that the applicant, as a young man of 17 years of age who wished to enter into and maintain sexual relations with a male friend of the same age, was in a 'relevantly similar situation' to a young man of the same age who wished to enter into and maintain sexual relations with a female friend of the same age.

53. The Commission must accordingly next determine whether the difference in treatment of these categories pursued a legitimate aim.

54. The Commission accepts, as does the applicant, that the aim of protecting morals and the rights of others is legitimate. The Commission also accepts that legal measures which prescribe age limits for particular types of sexual behaviour are, in principle, a legitimate way of pursuing that aim. Whether, in the specific case, the aim of protection of morals can be sufficient to justify differing ages is a matter which the Commission will consider in connection with the proportionality of the means and the aim.

55. The third question for the Commission is whether there was a reasonable relationship of proportionality between the means employed and the aim sought to be realised, and it is in this connection that the Commission must bear in mind the margin of appreciation which the respondent enjoys in assessing whether and to what extent differences justify a different treatment.

56. The Government argue that it is well-established that Contracting States enjoy a very broad margin of appreciation concerning the assessment of the measures appropriate in relation to matters associated with questions of morality. It is true that, in the context of measures designed to protect the moral interests and welfare of the society, the Court has held that State authorities are in principle in a better position than the international judge to give an opinion on the exact content of those requirements. It is true too that, as noted above, the Court, in the context of Article 8 of the Convention, has acknowledged the legitimate necessity in a democratic society for some degree of control over homosexual conduct 'notably in order to provide safeguards against the exploitation of those who are specially vulnerable by reason, for example, of their youth' . . . On the other hand, the Court has underlined that in areas involving intimate aspects of private life, there must exist particularly serious reasons before interferences on the part of public authorities can be legitimate for the purposes of Article 8 para. 2 . . . Moreover, in matters concerning alleged discrimination on grounds of sex, very weighty reasons would have to be put forward before the Convention organs could regard a difference of treatment based exclusively on the ground of sex as compatible with the Convention (see Eur. Court HR, *Karlheinz Schmidt* v *Germany* judgment of 18 July 1994, Series A no. 291-B, p. 32, para. 24).

57. The Commission is of the opinion that, regardless of whether the difference in treatment of heterosexuals and homosexuals is based on 'sex' or 'other status', given that it impinges on a most intimate aspect of affected individuals' private lives, the margin of appreciation must be relatively narrow.

58. The Government draw attention to the consistent series of decisions by the Commission recognising that the criterion of social protection justifies not only the imposition of restrictions on male homosexual activity but the setting of a higher minimum age than in the case of hetero-sexuals. In particular, in *X* v *The United Kingdom* (No. 7212/75 . . .) the Commission found that an objective and reasonable justification existed for the different ages of consent, there being a realistic basis for the Government's opinion that, given the controversial and sensitive nature of the question involved, young men in the 18–21 bracket who were involved in homosexual relationships would

be subject to substantial social pressures which could be harmful to their psychological development . . .

60. The Commission . . . considers it opportune to reconsider its earlier case-law in the light of . . . modern developments and, more especially, in the light of the weight of current medical opinion that to reduce the age of consent to 16 might have positively beneficial effects on the sexual health of young homosexual men without any corresponding harmful consequences.

61. In contending that there remains a reasonable and objective justification for maintaining different ages of consent for homosexual males and for heterosexuals, the Government place considerable reliance on the fact that the issue was recently and fully debated by a democratically elected Parliament which, on a free vote, decided to reduce the minimum age of consent to homosexual acts to 18 but rejected a proposal to assimilate the age of consent to that for heterosexuals.

62. The Commission agrees with the Government that some weight should be attached to the fact that the issue has been recently considered by the legislature and that the reduction of the minimum age to 16 was rejected. Nevertheless, this factor cannot of itself be decisive. Of more importance is the sufficiency of the reasons advanced to justify maintaining a different age of consent.

63. Two such principal arguments emerge from the speeches in Parliament and are adopted and repeated in the Government's submissions. In the first place it is argued that certain young men between the ages of 16 and 18 do not have a settled sexual orientation and that the aim of the law is to protect such vulnerable young men from activities which will result in considerable social pressures and isolation which their lack of maturity might cause them later to repent: it is claimed that the possibility of criminal sanctions against persons aged 16 or 17 is likely to have a deterrent effect and give the individual time to make up his mind. Secondly, it is argued that society is entitled to indicate its disapproval of homosexual conduct and its preference that children follow a heterosexual way of life.

64. The Commission does not consider that either argument offers a reasonable and objective justification for maintaining a different age of consent for homosexual and heterosexual acts or that maintaining such a differential age is proportionate to any legitimate aim served thereby. As to the former argument, as was conceded in the Parliamentary debates, current medical opinion is to the effect that sexual orientation is fixed in both sexes by the age of 16 and that men aged 16–21 are not in need of special protection because of the risk of their being 'recruited' into homosexuality. Moreover, as noted by the BMA, the risk posed by predatory older men would appear to be as serious whether the victim is a man or woman and does not justify a differential age of consent. Even if, as claimed in the Parliamentary debate, there may be certain young men for whom homosexual experience after the age of 16 will have influential and potentially disturbing effects and who may require protection, the Commission is unable to accept that it is a proportionate response to the need for protection to expose to criminal sanctions not only the older man who engages in homosexual acts with a person under the age of 18 but the young man himself who is claimed to be in need of such protection.

65. As to the second ground relied on – society's claimed entitlement to indicate disapproval of homosexual conduct and its preference for a heterosexual lifestyle – the Commission cannot accept that this could in any event constitute an objective or reasonable justification for inequality of treatment under the criminal law. As the Court observed in its *Dudgeon* judgment in the context of Article 8 of the Convention:

> 'Decriminalisation' does not imply approval, and a fear that some sectors of the population might draw misguided conclusions in this respect from reform of the legislation does not afford a good ground for maintaining it in force with all its unjustifiable features.

. . .

66. Consequently, the Commission finds that no objective and reasonable justification exists for the maintenance of a higher minimum age of consent to male homosexual, than to heterosexual, acts and that the application discloses discriminatory treatment in the exercise of the applicant's right to respect for private life under Article 8 of the Convention.

CONCLUSION

67. The Commission concludes, by fourteen votes to four, that in the present case there has been a violation of Article 8 of the Convention, taken in conjunction with Article 14 of the Convention.

NOTE

Following the decision in *Sutherland*, the age of consent was reduced to 16 for males, bringing it in line with that for females, in s.1 Sexual Offences (Amendment) Act 2000.

(c) *The meaning of consent.*

Positive dissent need not be proved:

R v Olugboja

[1982] QB 320, Court of Appeal

The defendant and the co-accused L met the complainant and K, at a discotheque and offered to take them home but, instead of taking them home, the defendant drove them to L's bungalow. They refused to go in and began walking away. The defendant went into the bungalow but L followed the girls and raped the complainant in the car. The three returned to the bungalow where L dragged K into a bedroom. The defendant then told the complainant that he was going to have intercourse with her. She told him what had happened in the car and asked him to leave her alone. He told her to take off her trousers. She did and he had intercourse with her. The defendant, who admitted having sexual intercourse with the complainant, was charged with rape. The judge directed the jury that, although the complainant had neither screamed nor struggled and she had submitted to sexual intercourse without the defendant using force or making any threats of violence, they had to consider whether the complainant had consented to sexual intercourse. The defendant was convicted. On appeal:

DUNN LJ: The question of law raised by this appeal is whether to constitute the offence of rape it is necessary for the consent of the victim of sexual intercourse to be vitiated by force, the fear of force, or fraud; or whether it is sufficient to prove that in fact the victim did not consent.

. . .

The judge dealt with the question of consent in his summing-up in a number of passages. He said:

> The question of consent is a question of fact for you to decide, approaching it in a commonsense way. You are concerned. are you not, with the field of human sexual behaviour and in particular in this case, teenage sexual behaviour? You have to consider it in a commonsense way applying your own experience or knowledge of human nature and your knowledge of the ways of the world. . . . Sometimes a woman gives in and submits out of fear, or constraint, or duress.

These directions were quite general in relation to both girls. In relation to Jayne the judge said:

> You will consider her evidence very carefully and decide whether or not there were any constraints operating on her will, so that you are satisfied that in taking her trousers down, and letting him have sexual intercourse with her, she was not, in fact, consenting to it.

Later, the judge said:

> Members of the jury, you are concerned with what was the reason? Was it circumstances in which she was consenting, or was it circumstances in which there was constraint operating on her mind, fear or constraint, so that in doing that she was doing it without her consent.

Finally, the judge said:

> Let me remind you finally that the defence point out that it is not a case where the girl was struggling or screaming. Unless what was said about intercourse and then going home contained any implied threat in it, no threats were uttered; certainly no threats of force or violence, or anything of that sort. The defence say this girl removed her own trousers and that was in itself an open invitation to sex. That of course depends on why and in what circumstances she removed her trousers. Was it because she was consenting, or was it because she was giving in out of fear or constraint, so that she was removing her own trousers without consent? It is a matter for you to decide.

The defendant was convicted of rape by a majority of 11–1 and sentenced to 30 months' imprisonment.

Mrs Trewella, in a series of very able submissions, said that these statements by the judge constituted a misdirection. She submitted that the statutory definition of rape introduced by the 1976 amendment into section 1 of the Sexual Offences Act 1956 was declaratory only, and had not changed the common law whereby the type of threat that vitiates consent is limited to threats of violence either to the victim or, as in duress, to some close or near relative. She relied in support of that submission on a number of cases going back to the middle of the last century: *R v Hallett* (1841) 9 C & P 748; *R v Day* (1841) 9 C & P 722; *R v Wright* (1866) 4 F & F 967; *R v Mayers* (1872) 12 Cox CC 311 and by analogy, *Latter v Braddell* (1880) 50 LJCP 166, where a domestic servant whose mistress had insisted that she be examined for pregnancy by a doctor was held to have no cause of action in assault because, although she was tearful and did not wish to be examined, no force or violence or threat had been used to persuade her to undergo the examination.

Mrs Trewella also relied on two more recent cases. *R v Howard* [1966] 1 WLR 13 and *R v Lang* (1975) 62 Cr App R 50, where it was held that sexual intercourse after submission induced by force or the threat of force was the classic example of rape. She also relied on a case, *R v Kirby* (unreported), December 19, 1961, decided by Winn J reported in 'The Times' as a news item, on December 19 and 20, 1961, where the judge appears to have withdrawn from the jury a case where a police constable was charged with rape on the basis that he had threatened the victim that he would report her for an offence unless she had sexual intercourse with him, which she did. Mrs Trewella submitted that in that case there was certainly a constraint on the will of the victim but she did not submit by reason of force or the threat of force.

Mrs Trewella accepted that submission by the victim did not necessarily involve consent, but the submission must be induced because of fear of violence: see *R v Day*, 9 C & P 722. She submitted that moral or economic pressure or even blackmail causing a woman to submit to sexual intercourse could never be enough to found a charge of rape. Otherwise she said the film producer who induced an actress to have sexual intercourse by telling her she would not get a part in his new film if she did not, or the man who induced a woman to have sexual intercourse by telling her that if she did not he would tell her fiancé that she had been a prostitute, would be guilty of rape.

. . .

Mrs Trewella submitted finally that to say, as the judge did, that any constraint upon Jayne's will could negative consent constituted a misdirection. The word 'constraint' includes moral as well as physical pressure and moral pressure is not enough. Even to tell a girl that she would not be taken home until she had sexual intercourse, in the absence of any threat of violence expressed or implied, would not vitiate her consent.

. . . in so far as the *actus reus* is concerned the question now is simply: 'At the time of the sexual intercourse did the woman consent to it? It is not necessary for the prosecution to prove that what might otherwise appear to have been consent was in reality merely submission induced by force, fear or fraud, although one or more of these factors will no doubt be present in the majority of cases of rape.

. . . Although 'consent' is [a] common word it covers a wide range of states of mind in the context of intercourse between a man and a woman, ranging from actual desire on the one hand to reluctant acquiescence on the other. We do not think that the issue of consent should be left to a jury without some further direction. What this should be will depend on the circumstances of each case. The jury will have been reminded of the burden and standard of proof required to establish each ingredient, including lack of consent, of the offence. They should be directed that consent, or the absence of it, is to be given its ordinary meaning and if need be, by way of example, that there is a difference between consent and submission; every consent involves a submission, but it by no means follows that a mere submission involves consent: *per* Coleridge J in *R* v *Day*, 9 C & P 722, 724. In the majority of cases, where the allegation is that the intercourse was had by force or the fear of force, such a direction coupled with specific references to, and comments on, the evidence relevant to the absence of real consent will clearly suffice. In the less common type of case where intercourse takes place after threats not involving violence or the fear of it, as in the examples given by Mrs Trewella to which we have referred earlier in this judgment, we think that an appropriate direction to a jury will have to be fuller. They should be directed to concentrate on the state of mind of the victim immediately before the act of sexual intercourse, having regard to all the relevant circumstances; and in particular, the events leading up to the act and her reaction to them showing their impact on her mind. Apparent acquiescence after penetration does not necessarily involve consent, which must have occurred before the act takes place. In addition to the general direction about consent which we have outlined, the jury will probably be helped in such cases by being reminded that in this context consent does comprehend the wide spectrum of states of mind to which we earlier referred, and that the dividing line in such circumstances between real consent on the one hand and mere submission on the other may not be easy to draw. Where it is to be drawn in a given case is for the jury to decide, applying their combined good sense, experience and knowledge of human nature and modern behaviour to all the relevant facts of that case.

Looked at in this way we find no misdirection by the judge in this case. We think it would have been better not to use the word 'constraint' in explaining the offence, but whenever he used it the judge linked it with the word 'fear,' so that in the context the word seems to us to be unexceptional.

R v *Larter and Castleton*
[1995] Crim LR 75, Court of Appeal

The appellants appealed against their conviction of rape of a 14-year-old girl. The girl was said to be asleep during the alleged offence and she gave evidence that she remembered nothing of what had happened. For the appellants it was submitted, *inter alia*, that the judge should have given an express direction as in *R* v *Howard* (1965) 50 Cr App R 56, that the prosecution had to prove either that the complainant physically resisted or, if she did not, that her understanding and knowledge were such that she was not in a position to decide whether to consent or resist.

Held, dismissing the appeals, the law is now governed by the Sexual Offences (Amendment) Act 1976. The essential element in the definition of rape is the absence of consent. Any attempt to introduce a different legal criterion was both mistaken and contrary to the law – *R* v *Olugboja* (1981) 73 Cr App R 344. It was surprising that *Archbold* still referred to cases which did not take that into account. The jury should be directed that consent, or the absence of it, is to be given its ordinary meaning, and, if need be by way of example, that there is a difference between consent and submission; every consent involves a submission but it did not follow that a mere submission involves consent. The judge gave a proper, adequate and full direction on the law of rape, on the presence or absence of the consent and full directions on the element of *mens rea*.

R v McAllister

[1997] Crim LR 233, Court of Appeal

D was convicted of indecently assaulting his wife, from whom he was separated. He came to her house and a variety of sexual acts but not sexual intercourse took place, including oral sex and certain practices which the complainant found very painful. D's defence was that she consented throughout, but he did not give evidence. The jury asked the judge to define the difference between consent and submission. It was submitted that the judge failed to direct the jury that reluctant acquiescence amounted to consent (*Olugboja* [1982] 1 QB 320, 331).

Held, dismissing the appeal, the judge had been persuaded by counsel for D not to give the jury the dictionary definitions of consent and submit, though the definitions (recited by the court) would have made more vivid the choice the jury had to make. Parliament had left it to the jury to decide whether there was or may have been consent in relation to sexual acts between adults. It was clear that a wife had the right to say 'no' and the jury's experience and sense should lead them to the right decision on whether there was consent or not (*Zafar*, June 18, 1993; *Day* (1841) 9 C & P 722, 724 considered). The judge directed the jury fully on 'consent' and 'submission' and did not have to spell out the possibility of reluctant acquiescence.

R v Malone

[1998] 2 Cr App R 447, Court of Appeal

ROCH LJ: . . . The judge then went on to say:

> She says she did not consent.
>
> She does not claim to have physically resisted nor to have verbally protested. She says the drink had disabled her from doing either. The kick she gave, and on each version of these events, his and hers, she did kick him, but she says the kick was a reflex action to the pain caused by the penetration of his penis and you may wish to consider, having regard to your assessment of her condition, whether consenting to an act of sexual intercourse was consistent with it. She has told you she did not consent.
>
> For the prosecution to have proved this second ingredient you must be sure that the act of sexual intercourse occurred without C's consent. Submitting to an act of sexual intercourse, because through drink she was unable physically to resist though she wished to, is not consent. If she submits to intercourse because of the drink she cannot physically resist that, of course, is not consent. No right thinking person would say that in those circumstances she was genuinely consenting to what occurred. What occurred in those circumstances, not wishing to have intercourse but being physically unable to do anything about it, if intercourse occurred in those circumstances it would plainly, as a matter of common sense, be against her will. It would be without her consent.
>
> Drink, of course, has different effects upon different people. It makes people do things they otherwise would not do. If you come to the conclusion that in drink she did consent to sexual intercourse then, of course, the prosecution would fail to clear this hurdle. Do not be confused about state of mind and being physically unable to do anything about it. Consent is essentially a state of mind. She tells you she did not wish to have sexual intercourse, that she did not consent to it, and she was unable to do anything about it because of the drink. She was unable to physically resist him.
>
> If you come to the conclusion that the drink resulted in her doing something she otherwise would not have done and that is give her consent, then, of course, that is a sufficient

consent. The prosecution would fail on this second ingredient. Equally, if you come to the conclusion that in drink she may have given her consent to having intercourse with him then again the prosecution would fail. You have to be sure [that] what occurred when his penis penetrated her vagina occurred without her consent. If you are sure that there was an act of sexual intercourse but that you decide she consented to it or that she may have consented to it – not guilty.

No doubt in order to obtain a conviction there will have to be some evidence of lack of consent to go before the jury. But what that evidence will be will depend on the particular circumstances of the case that the jury is trying. The evidence may be of widely differing kinds as a few illustrations will show. It may be the complainant's simple assertion 'I did not consent to sexual intercourse with the defendant'. It may be evidence of threats uttered by the defendant It may be evidence of the use of physical force by the defendant. It may be evidence that the complainant was by reason of drink or drugs incapable of giving consent or incapable of being aware of what was occurring. It may be evidence that by reason of age or lack of understanding due to mental handicap the complainant did not give consent. The jury may accept that the complainant was asleep when sexual intercourse occurred or that she was tricked into giving her consent in the belief that the defendant was her husband or partner. We do not for a moment suggest that these examples exhaust the possible factual situations which may arise. They suffice to demonstrate that it is not the law that the prosecution in order to obtain a conviction for rape [has] to show that the complainant was either incapable of saying no or putting up some physical resistance or did say no or put up some physical resistance.

Mr Williams for the respondents was quite correct to underline the importance of distinguishing between the correct definition of the *actus reus* of rape and the evidence on which the prosecution relies to establish the existence of that *actus reus*.

NOTES AND QUESTIONS
1. Should promises of benefit be considered differently from threats of detriment? John offers to buy Mary a diamond ring if she will have sex with him. If she agrees, is her consent voluntary? What if John says that he will not continue to go out with Mary if she does not have sex with him? Is the line between detriment and benefit all that clear?
2. Is the *propriety* of the pressure applied the key feature? Is the focus on the sexual autonomy of the particular complainant the right one, or should some objective standard be formulated? Would objectivity be possible?
3. Note that apparent consent will be vitiated where the complainant is not in a position to assess the circumstances due to youth (*R v Howard* [1965] 3 All ER 684), mental deficiency (*R v Barratt* (1873) LR 2 CCR 81), intoxication (*R v Lang* (1975) 62 Cr App R 50) or fraud as to the nature of the act (*R v Flattery* (1877) 2 QBD 410). In the case of fraud the defendant could not claim that he believed the consent was valid. In all the other circumstances above it would be open to the defendant to argue that he made an honest mistake as to the validity of the consent (see *mens rea*, below).
4. Section 1(3), SOA 1956, as enacted by the Criminal Justice and Public Order Act 1994, declares that a rape has been committed by a man 'if he induces a married woman to have sexual intercourse with him by impersonating her husband'. This section came into force after the decision in *R v Elbekkay* [1995] Crim LR 163 where the Court of Appeal held that *any* impersonation would vitiate consent. It is not clear whether the specific reference in s. 1(3) implicitly overrules this decision. Why enact such a specific reference to one situation and ignore other possible impersonations? Allen, *Textbook on Criminal Law*, 5th ed (1999), p. 343 asks what would be the situation now if a defendant impersonated the victim's long-time homosexual lover.

(ii) *Mens rea*

The defendant must intend to have sexual intercourse. Rape is a crime of basic intent so that intoxication is no defence. The defendant must be subjectively reckless as to whether the victim consents.

It was held in *DPP* v *Morgan* [1976] AC 182 that an honest belief in consent is sufficient.

Director of Public Prosecutions v *Morgan*
[1976] AC 182, House of Lords

LORD HAILSHAM OF ST MARYLEBONE: . . . The appellant Morgan and his three co-defendants, who were all members of the RAF, spent the evening of August 15, 1973, in one another's company. The appellant Morgan was significantly older than the other three, and considerably senior to them in rank. He was, as I have said, married to the alleged victim, but not, it seems at the time habitually sleeping in the same bed. At this time, Mrs Morgan occupied a single bed in the same room as her younger son aged about 11 years, and by the time the appellants arrived at Morgan's house, Mrs Morgan was already in bed and asleep, until she was awoken by their presence.

According to the version of the facts which she gave in evidence, and which was evidently accepted by the jury, she was aroused from her sleep, frog-marched into another room where there was a double bed, held by each of her limbs, arms and legs apart, by the four appellants, while each of the three young appellants in turn had intercourse with her in the presence of the others, during which time the other two committed various lewd acts upon various parts of her body. When each had finished and had left the room, the appellant Morgan completed the series of incidents by having intercourse with her himself.

According to Mrs Morgan she consented to none of this and made her opposition to what was being done very plain indeed. In her evidence to the court, she said that her husband was the first to seize her and pull her out of bed. She then 'yelled' to the little boy who was sleeping with her to call the police, and later, when the elder boy came out on the landing, she called to him also to get the police, and 'screamed.' Her assailants, however, covered her face and pinched her nose, until she begged them to let her breathe. She was held, wrists and feet, 'dragged' to the neighbouring room, put on the bed where the various incidents occurred. At this stage she was overcome by fear of 'being hit.' There was never a time when her body was free from being held. When it was all over she grabbed her coat, ran out of the house, drove straight to the hospital and immediately complained to the staff of having been raped. This last fact was fully borne out by evidence from the hospital.

In their evidence in court, the appellants made various damaging admissions which certainly amounted to some corroboration of all this. They admitted that some degree of struggle took place in the bedroom, that Mrs Morgan made some noise which was forcibly suppressed, and that she was carried out forcibly into the other bedroom, and that her arms and legs were separately held. In addition to this, Mrs Morgan's evidence was far more fully corroborated by a number of statements (each, of course, admissible only against the maker) which virtually repeated Mrs Morgan's own story but in far greater and more lurid detail. Of course, the appellants repudiated their statements in the witness box, saying that the words were put into their mouths by the police, even though at least one was written out in the hands of the makers of the statement. I think it likely to the extent of moral certainly that the jury accepted that these statements were made as alleged and contained the truth. But I need not rest my opinion upon this, since the undeniable fact is that the jury accepted, after an impeccable summing up and adequate corroboration, that Mrs Morgan was telling the truth in her evidence. I mention all these details simply to show, that if, as I think plain, the jury accepted Mrs Morgan's statement *in substance* there was no possibility whatever of any of the appellants holding any belief whatever, reasonable or otherwise, in their victim's consent to what was being done.

The primary 'defence' was consent. I use the word 'defence' in inverted commas, because, of course, in establishing the crime of rape, the prosecution must exclude consent in order to establish the essential ingredients of the crime. There is no burden at the outset on the accused to raise the issue. Nevertheless, at the close of the prosecution case the accused had a formidable case to answer, and they answered by going into the witness box and swearing to facts which, if accepted, would have meant, not merely that they reasonably believed that Mrs Morgan had consented, but that, after she entered the bedroom where the acts of intercourse took place, she not merely consented but took an active and enthusiastic part in a sexual orgy which might have excited unfavourable comment in the court of Caligula or Nero.

All four defendants explained in the witness box that they had spent the evening together in Wolverhampton, and by the time of the alleged offences had had a good deal to drink. Their original intention had been to find some women in the town, but when this failed, Morgan made the surprising suggestion to the others that they should all return to his home and have sexual intercourse with his wife. According to the three younger appellants (but not according to Morgan who described this part of their story as 'lying') Morgan told them that they must not be surprised if his wife struggled a bit, since she was 'kinky' and this was the only way in which she could get 'turned on.' However this may be, it is clear that Morgan did invite his three companions home in order that they might have sexual intercourse with his wife, and, no doubt, he may well have led them in one way or another to believe that she would consent to their doing so. This however, would only be matter predisposing them to believe that Mrs Morgan consented, and would not in any way establish that, at the time, they believed she did consent whilst they were having intercourse.

. . .

Once one has accepted, what seems to me abundantly clear, that the prohibited act in rape is non-consensual sexual intercourse, and that the guilty state of mind is an intention to commit it, it seems to me to follow as a matter of inexorable logic that there is no room either for a 'defence' of honest belief or mistake, or of a defence of honest and reasonable belief or mistake. Either the prosecution proves that the accused had the requisite intent, or it does not. In the former case it succeeds, and in the latter it fails. Since honest belief clearly negatives intent, the reasonableness or otherwise of that belief can only be evidence for or against the view that the belief and therefore the intent was actually held, and it matters not whether, to quote Bridge J in the passage cited above, 'the definition of a crime includes no specific element beyond the prohibited act.' If the mental element be primarily an intention and not a state of belief comes within his second proposition and not his third. Any other view as for insertion of the word 'reasonable' can only have the effect of saying that a man intends something which he does not.

The decision in *Morgan* caused considerable controversy and Parliament enacted The Sexual Offices (Amendment) Act 1976 as a result:

Sexual Offences (Amendment) Act 1976

1.—(2) It is hereby declared that, if at a trial for a rape offence the jury has to consider whether a man believed that a woman or man was consenting to sexual intercourse, the presence or absence of reasonable grounds for such a belief is a matter to which the jury is to have regard, in conjunction with any other relevant matters in considering whether he so believed.

Both honest mistake and the issue of recklessness were addressed in the following case:

R v Satnam and Kewal

[1983] 78 Cr App R 149, Court of Appeal

The appellants were both indicted, *inter alia*, with the rape of a 13 year old girl and of aiding and abetting the other to commit such rape. Their defence in each case was that the girl consented, for there was no dispute that sexual intercourse had in fact taken place. In summing-up to the jury the judge, in turning to the element of recklessness, referred to a risk 'obvious to an ordinary observer' that the girl was not consenting but gave no further direction as to the necessary elements to be proved in the crime of reckless rape. The appellants were convicted and appealed on the grounds (1) that the judge should have directed the jury that a genuine though mistaken belief that the girl was consenting offered a defence to a charge of reckless rape; and (2) that the judge erred in referring to an 'ordinary observer' in his direction as to recklessness, and that he should have directed the jury that it was necessary to prove that each appellant was actually aware of the possibility that the girl was not consenting before they could find him guilty.

BRISTOW J: . . . The question of law is whether, in directing the jury as to the state of mind of the appellants in 'reckless' rape, the judge should have left to the jury the question whether they genuinely though mistakenly believed that the victim was consenting to sexual intercourse; and whether the judge was right to direct them that it was sufficient, in order to prove recklessness, if it was obvious to an ordinary observer that she was not consenting. On November 4, 1983, we allowed the appeals and quashed the convictions. We now give our reasons.

. . .

A practical definition of recklessness in sexual offences was given in *Kimber* (1983) 77 Cr App R 225; [1983] 1 WLR 1118, where the Court was concerned with how far an honest belief in consent constituted a defence to a charge of indecent assault. The defendant said in evidence: 'I was not really interested in Betty's' (the victim's) 'feelings at all.' Lawton LJ said at p. 230 and p. 1123 of the respective reports: 'We have already set out in this judgment the admissions which he is alleged to have made to the police and relevant parts of his own evidence. In our judgment a reasonable jury would inevitably have decided that he had no honest belief that Betty was consenting. His own evidence showed that his attitude to her was one of indifference to her feelings and wishes. This state of mind is aptly described in the colloquial expression, "couldn't care less." In law this is recklessness.'

In summing-up a case of rape which involves the issue of consent, the judge should, in dealing with the state of mind of the defendant, first of all direct the jury that before they could convict of rape the Crown had to prove either that the defendant knew the woman did not want to have sexual intercourse, or was reckless as to whether she wanted to or not. If they were sure he knew she did not want to they should find him guilty of rape knowing there to be no consent. If they were not sure about that, then they would find him not guilty of such rape and should go on to consider reckless rape. If they thought he might genuinely have believed that she did want to, even though he was mistaken in his belief, they would find him not guilty. In considering whether his belief was genuine, they should take into account all the relevant circumstances (which could at that point be summarised) and ask themselves whether, in the light of those circumstances, he had reasonable grounds for such a belief. If, after considering those circumstances, they were sure he had no genuine belief that she wanted to, they would find him guilty. If they came to the conclusion that he could not care less whether she wanted to or not, but pressed on regardless, then he would have been reckless and could not have believed that she wanted to, and they would find him guilty of reckless rape.

NOTES AND QUESTIONS
1. How could a defendant who had not considered the victim's state of mind have an honest belief in her consent? Is the court duplicating the tests unnecessarily?
2. In *Aydin* v *Turkey* (1997) 25 EHRR 251, the European Court of Human Rights indicated that rape by State police could in some instances constitute 'torture' prohibited by Article 3 of the European Convention on Human Rights.

B: Unlawful sexual intercourse with girls under 16

Section 5 of the SOA 1956 provides that it is an offence punishable with life imprisonment to have unlawful sexual intercourse with a girl under the age of 13. Section 6 makes it an offence to have unlawful sexual intercourse with a girl under 16, the maximum penalty being two years' imprisonment. The 'unlawful' provision is thought to provide a defence to a man having intercourse with an under-age girl whom he has lawfully married in another jurisdiction. Further, s. 5(2) provides that if the defendant has married the victim and the marriage is invalid due to the girl's age, but the defendant 'believes her to be his wife and has reasonable cause for the belief', he will not be guilty of an offence. The defendant must prove on a balance of probabilities that he comes within this defence.

Although it is a criminal offence to have sexual intercourse with a girl under the age of 16 (who is legally incapable of giving consent), s. 5(3) provides an exception where the defendant is under 24 years of age, has not previously been charged with a s. 6 offence or an attempt to commit it, and believes the victim to be 16 or over and has reasonable cause for that belief. In *R* v *Prince* (1875) LR 2 CCR 154, it was held that no *mens rea* is required in respect of the girl's age but this decision was reconsidered in:

R v *K*
[2001] 3 All ER 897, House of Lords

LORD BINGHAM OF CORNHILL. [1] My Lords, the appellant K was indicted on a single count of indecent assault committed against a girl C who at the time was aged 14, contrary to s 14(1) of the Sexual Offences Act 1956. His defence was to be that the sexual activity between him and C was consensual, that she had told him she was 16 and that he had had no reason to disbelieve her. He is a man of good character, aged 26 at the date of the offence charged against him. Before the trial a preliminary issue was raised on behalf of K: whether, to establish K's guilt under the section, the prosecution had to prove that at the time of the incident K did not honestly believe that C was 16 or over. Argument on this issue was heard by Judge Thorpe at the Crown Court at Chichester. He ruled, in favour of K, that the prosecution did have to prove an absence of genuine belief on the part of the accused that the victim was aged 16 or over. In so ruling the judge relied on the recent decision of the House of Lords in *B (a minor)* v *DPP* [2000] 1 All ER 833, [2000] 2 AC 428. The prosecution appealed against that ruling under s 35 of the Criminal Procedure and Investigations Act 1996. The Court of Appeal (Criminal Division) (Roch LJ, Rougier and Gray JJ) allowed the appeal and held that such absence of genuine belief did not have to be proved (see *CPS* v *K* (2000) Times, 7 November). The court certified the following point of law of general public importance:

'(a) Is a defendant entitled to be acquitted of the offence of indecent assault on a complainant under the age of 16 years, contrary to s 14(1) of the 1956 Act, if he may hold an honest belief that the complainant in question was aged 16 years or over? (b) If yes, must the belief be held on reasonable grounds?'

Leave to appeal was refused by the Court of Appeal but granted by the House.

[2] Section 14 of the 1956 Act is in these terms:

'(1) It is an offence, subject to the exception mentioned in subsection (3) of this section, for a person to make an indecent assault on a woman.

(2) A girl under the age of sixteen cannot in law give any consent which would prevent an act being an assault for the purposes of this section.

. . .

s 2 of the 1922 Act, provided:

'Reasonable cause to believe that a girl was of or above the age of sixteen years shall not be a defence to a charge under sections five or six of the Criminal Law Amendment Act, 1885 . . . Provided that in the case of a man of twenty-three years of age or under the presence of reasonable cause to believe that the girl was over the age of sixteen years shall be a valid defence on the first occasion on which he is charged with an offence under this section.'

Thus was introduced what came to be known as the statutory or young man's defence. The slipshod drafting of the section is evident from its closing words since s 2 created no offence with which any defendant could ever be charged. But the section gave rise to a much more fundamental anomaly. If a defendant was charged under s 5(1) with the very serious offence of having unlawful carnal knowledge of a girl aged between 13 and 16, the statutory defence was potentially open to a man of 23 or under charged for the first time. If, however, the man was charged with the lesser offence of indecently assaulting a child or young person under the age of 16 (an offence inevitably committed if he had intercourse with her), there was no express provision enabling the defendant to rely on an honest belief that the child or young person was over the age of 16.

[15] Since the 1956 Act was a consolidation Act, there was no opportunity to correct this apparent absurdity. Section 5 of this Act again made it a felony to have unlawful sexual intercourse with a girl under the age of 13. Section 6 as enacted again made it an offence, subject to the exceptions in the section, for a man to have unlawful sexual intercourse with a girl not under the age of 13 but under the age of 16. One of the exceptions, in sub-s(2), corresponded to the invalid marriage exception in s 14(3). The second exception, in sub-s(3), reproduced the statutory or young man's defence. Thus the anomaly highlighted by the cases cited above was perpetuated. Asked to suggest any reason why it could rationally have been intended to provide the statutory defence where full intercourse took place and no defence based on belief as to the child's age when intercourse was charged as indecent assault, leading counsel for the Crown in the present appeal was unable to assist, as his predecessor in *R v Forde* [1923] 2 KB 400, [1923] All ER Rep 477 had been in 1923.

[16] Even before enactment of the 1956 Act, a lacuna in the existing legislation had come to light. In both *Fairclough v Whipp* [1951] 2 All ER 834 and *DPP v Rogers* [1953] 2 All ER 644, [1953] 1 WLR 1017 there had been objectionable acts of indecency, in the first case involving an adult man and a child of nine, in the second a father and his eleven year-old daughter. But in neither case had there been an assault since the child had, at the adult's invitation, touched him, albeit indecently. Following a report of the Criminal Law Revision Committee in 1959 (*First Report* (*Indecency with Children*) (Cmnd 835)). Parliament enacted the Indecency with Children Act 1960 which in s 1(1) provided:

'Any person who commits an act of gross indecency with or towards a child under the age of fourteen, or who incites a child under that age to such an act with him or another, shall be liable on conviction on indictment to imprisonment for a term not exceeding two years . . .'

In B (a minor) v DPP [2000] 1 All ER 833, [2000] 2 AC 428 the issue was whether, under that section, it was necessary for the prosecution to prove the absence of a genuine belief on the part of the defendant that the child was over the specified age of 14. The House (Lord Irvine of Lairg LC, Lord Mackay of Clashfern, Lord Nicholls, Lord Steyn and Lord Hutton) unanimously held that it was.

[17] In reaching this conclusion the House relied on—

'the established common law presumption that a mental element, traditionally labelled mens rea, is an essential ingredient unless Parliament has indicated a contrary intention either expressly or by necessary implication. The common law presumes that, unless Parliament indicated otherwise, the appropriate mental element is an unexpressed ingredient of every statutory offence.' (See [2000] 1 All ER 833 at 836, [2000] 2 AC 428 at 460 per Lord Nicholls.)

Lord Steyn, quoting from Professor Sir Rupert Cross, referred ([2000] 1 All ER 833 at 845, [2000] 2 AC 428 at 470) to the presumption that mens rea is required in the case of all statutory crimes, a presumption operating as a constitutional principle and not easily displaced by a statutory text. Crucial to the conclusion of the House was the now classic statement of principle in the speech of Lord Reid in Sweet v Parsley [1969] 1 All ER 347 at 349–351, [1970] AC 132 at 148–150. The speech is too well known to require extensive citation; brief extracts will suffice:

'. . . there has for centuries been a presumption that Parliament did not intend to make criminals of persons who were in no way blameworthy in what they did. That means that, whenever a section is silent as to mens rea, there is a presumption that, in order to give effect to the will of Parliament, we must read in words appropriate to require mens rea . . . it is firmly established by a host of authorities that mens rea is an essential ingredient of every offence unless some reason can be found for holding that that is not necessary.' (See [1969] 1 All ER 347 at 349, 350, [1970] AC 132 at 148, 149.)

. .

[18] The rule that a person under the age of 16 could not in law consent to what would otherwise be an indecent assault led to the description of an offence under ss 14(1) or 15(1) against a victim under the age of 16 as an absolute offence or an offence of strict liability. These descriptions were a misnomer. There always had to be such deliberation in the conduct of the defendant as would be necessary to prove an assault. But the need for mens rea in a fuller sense was made clear by the Court of Appeal (Criminal Division) (Lawton LJ, Michael Davies and Sheldon JJ) in R v Kimber [1983] 3 All ER 316, [1983] 1 WLR 1118. In that case the charge was one of indecent assault contrary to s 14(1) of the 1956 Act and the victim was an adult. The recorder directed the jury that the sole issue for their consideration was whether the victim had given her real and genuine consent, adding that it did not matter whether the defendant believed or thought she was consenting. This was held to be a misdirection:

. . .

[19] In B (a minor) v DPP [2000] 1 All ER 833, [2000] 2 AC 428 the House considered s 1(1) of the 1960 Act in the light of the presumption that guilty knowledge is an essential ingredient of a statutory offence unless it is shown to be excluded by express words or necessary implication. It found no express words and no necessary implication having that effect. It was accordingly necessary for the prosecution to prove the absence of a genuine belief on the part of the defendant, whether reasonable or not, that the victim had been 14 or over. The House was invited in that case to treat the Acts of 1956 and 1960 as part of a single code (see [2000] 2 AC 428 at 457, 473), and that approach seems to me to be plainly correct. It is at once obvious that if an absence of genuine belief as to the age of an underage victim must be proved against a defendant under s 1 of the 1960 Act but not against a defendant under s 14 of the 1956 Act, another glaring anomaly would be

introduced into this legislation. But that conclusion does not relieve the House of the need to carry out, in relation to s 14, the task that it carried out in relation to s 1.

[20] Neither in s 14 nor elsewhere in the 1956 Act is there any express exclusion of the need to prove an absence of genuine belief on the part of a defendant as to the age of an underage victim. Had it been intended to exclude that element of mens rea it could very conveniently have been so provided in or following sub-s (2).

. . .

[23] I would accordingly give an affirmative answer to the first certified question. It is common ground that a negative answer should be given to the second question. In giving those answers I would make the following concluding points: (1) Nothing in this opinion has any bearing on a case in which the victim does not in fact consent. While s 14(2) provides that a girl under the age of 16 cannot in law give any consent which would prevent an act being an assault, she may in fact (although not in law) consent. If it is shown that she did not consent, and that the defendant did not genuinely believe that she consented, any belief by the defendant concerning her age is irrelevant, since her age is relevant only to her capacity to consent. (2) While a defendant's belief need not be reasonable provided it is honest and genuine, the reasonableness or unreasonableness of the belief is by no means irrelevant. The more unreasonable the belief, the less likely it is to be accepted as genuine (see *R v Gladstone Williams* [1987] 3 All ER 411 at 415.) (3) Although properly applied to s 1 of the 1960 Act and s 14 of the 1956 Act, the presumption cannot be applied to ss 5 and 6 of the 1956 Act. Those sections as a pair derive directly from corresponding sections in the 1861 Act, as demonstrated above. The statutory or young man's defence was introduced into what is now s 6. Its omission from what is now s 5 is plainly deliberate. A genuine belief that a child three years under the age of consent was over that age would in any event defy credulity. Section 6(3) of the 1956 Act plainly defines the state of knowledge which will exonerate a defendant accused under that section, and this express provision necessarily excludes the more general presumption. (4) Nothing in this opinion should be taken to minimise the potential seriousness of the offence of indecent assault. While some instances of the offence may be relatively minor, others may be scarcely less serious than rape itself. This is reflected in the maximum penalty, now increased to ten years' imprisonment, and the mandatory requirement that those convicted be subject to the notification requirements of the Sex Offenders Act 1997.

Appeal allowed

NOTES AND QUESTIONS
1. Note that the victim cannot be guilty of aiding and abetting the offence as the statute is there for her protection (see *R v Tyrell* [1894] 1 QB 710). This is so even if the girl was the initiator of the offence.
2. The Sexual Offences (Amendment) Act 2000 makes it an offence for a person aged 18 or over to engage in sexual activity with a person under that age if the offender is in a 'position of trust' with respect to the victim. The creation of the offence was opposed by teacher representatives, who argued that it would criminalise even non-exploitative relationships with persons able to give consent, and would also expose teachers to malicious false accusations. Was this new legislation needed? Is it desirable?

C: Indecent assault

By ss. 14 and 15, SOA 1956 indecent assaults on a woman or man are offences punishable by a maximum of 10 years' imprisonment. Section 14(3) provides a defence to a man who believes on reasonable grounds that an under-age girl is his wife. Strangely there is no equivalent defence for a woman. A person under the age of 16 is incapable of consent, otherwise consent provides a defence to these charges. Consent has the same meaning as in rape. Where harm amounting to at least actual bodily harm was intended or foreseen, the consent will not be effective. Similarly, consent is not relevant if the action is objectively 'likely' to cause injury which is more than 'transient or trifling' understood in a modern context.

(i) *Consent*

R v Boyea
[1992] Crim LR 574, Court of Appeal

B was convicted of indecent assault, which had taken the form of his hand being inserted into the complainant's vagina and being twisted causing injuries which were consistent with force. On appeal the main ground was that the judge had directed the jury that the question of whether the complainant consented was not relevant if they were satisfied that B's actions were likely or intended to cause bodily harm. It was submitted that the question whether an act would be likely to cause bodily harm was equivalent to asking 'did the defendant do the act intending to cause bodily harm or recklessly?' If that was correct, the jury should have been directed that the test of recklessness for this purpose was subjective, that was to say they should have been directed to ask themselves: 'did this defendant know, or should it have been obvious to him, that if he did the act, bodily harm might result?'

Held, dismissing the appeal. The judge's directions were based on *Donovan* [1934] 2 KB 498. The question whether recklessness was an ingredient in the offence of assault occasioning actual bodily harm was considered in *Savage* [1991] 3 WLR 914, and it was held that a verdict on that charge could be returned upon proof of an assault together with proof of the fact that actual bodily harm was occasioned by the assault. The Crown was not obliged to prove that the defendant intended to cause some actual bodily harm or was reckless as to whether such harm would be caused. Applying the logic of this decision to the principle of *Donovan* the question whether the act of the defendant was 'likely or intended to do bodily harm' to the complainant was to be answered giving the word 'likely' its ordinary meaning, that was to say objectively. The question was not equivalent to asking 'did the defendant inflict the harm recklessly?' In *Att.-Gen. Ref. (No. 6 of 1980)* [1981] QB 715, it was held, in relation to a fist fight in the street, that consent was no defence because it was not in the public interest for people to cause each other actual bodily harm for no good reason. The central proposition in *Donovan* was consistent with *Att-Gen. Ref.*, which proposition could be expressed as follows: an assault intended or which was likely to cause bodily harm, accompanied by indecency, was an offence irrespective of consent, provided that the injury was not 'transient or trifling.' The judge so summed-up, read as a whole, referring to that test, and making specific reference to the phrase 'transient or trifling.' There was no misdirection.

However, the court must take account of the fact that social attitudes have changed, particularly in the held of sexual relations between adults. As a generality, the level of vigour in sexual congress which was generally acceptable, and therefore the voluntarily accepted risk of incurring some injury was probably higher now than it was in 1934. It followed that the phrase 'transient or trifling' must be understood in the light of condition, in 1992 rather than those of nearly 60 years ago. But with that qualification, there was no doubt that the extent of the violence inflicted on the complainant went far beyond the risk of minor injury to which, if she did consent, her consent would have been a defence. Moreover, it was inconceivable that she would have consented to the injuries which were in fact inflicted on her. If therefore it had been concluded that the judge had misdirected the jury in following, without qualification, the decision in *Donovan* which was binding on him, it would have been considered right to apply the proviso because even in those circumstances no injustice would have been caused.

R v *Simon Slingsby*
[1995] Crim LR 571, Crown Court

> After meeting the deceased, V, at a club on April 29, 1994, S had sexual inter-course with her and buggered her, all with her consent. Subsequently, also with her consent he penetrated her vagina and her rectum with his hand. V suffered cuts caused by a signet ring on S's hand. V did not realise for some time that her injuries were potentially very serious. Eventually she was admitted to hospital but died of septicaemia resulting from the cuts.

JUDGE, J: . . . Mr Goldring had submitted that if any significant injury was a likely consequence of vigorous, but consensual sexual activity, and injury resulted, that would amount to an assault. He accepted that the act of inserting fingers or hand into the vagina, or the rectum for the purposes of sexual stimulation, if consensual, would not amount to an assault, or to any other crime. He focused, however, on the injuries which were sustained and argued that as the deceased could not have consented to the injuries themselves, their occurrence made the defendant's actions unlawful.

The difficulty with this submission was that the sexual activity to which both the deceased and the defendant agreed did not involve deliberate infliction of injury or harm and but for the coincidental fact that the defendant happened to be wearing a signet ring, no injury at all would have been caused or could have been contemplated. The question of consent to injury did not, in fact, arise because neither anticipated or considered it. At the time, all they were considering was this vigorous sexual activity.

Therefore, the reality was that the deceased sustained her unfortunate injuries, not when she or the defendants were consenting to injury, but as an accidental consequence of the sexual activity which was taking place with her consent. It would, in Judge J's judgment, be contrary to principle to treat as criminal activity that which would not otherwise amount to assault merely because in the course of the activity an injury occurred. Although not cited, nor analysed in the argument, Judge J added that he believed that this conclusion was supported by the decision in *R v Clarence* (1888) 22 QBD 23, a decision which so far as he was aware had never been doubted.

In his judgment, therefore, the authorities cited by Mr Goldring had no application to the present case. This case did not come within the area of sexual activity which notwithstanding the consent of the parties is prohibited by the criminal law. Accordingly, notwithstanding the desperate and tragic consequence of what happened, he should hold that this count of manslaughter cannot be sustained on the basis of the agreed facts.

The Crown offered no evidence and the judge entered a verdict of not guilty.

NOTES AND QUESTIONS
The type of manslaughter referred to in *Slingsby* requires an *unlawful* and dangerous act. The court accepted that because no injury was intended or foreseen and the victim consented to the acts, there was no unlawful act. How does this fit with the decision in *Boyea* where the Court of Appeal clearly held that an act which causes injury which is neither intended nor foreseen by the defendant is nevertheless an assault because injury does in fact occur? Can *Boyea* be distinguished on the grounds that in that case injury was objectively likely to be caused? If so why was that test not considered relevant in *Slingsby*?

Difficult issues concerning consent will arise where the 'victim' is suffering from mental incapacity;

R v *Kimber*
[1983] 1 WLR 1118, Court of Appeal

LAWTON LJ: . . . The victim was a female patient in a mental hospital. Her mental disorder had been diagnosed as schizophrenia. She was aged 56. We will refer to her as 'Betty'. Although she was not a defective within the meaning of sections 7 and 45 of the Sexual Offences Act 1956, as amended by section 127 of the Mental Health Act 1959, she was suffering from a severe degree of mental disorder. She had been a patient in the mental hospital since 1957. Her movements and appearance were odd: she made strange movements with her face and mouth. She tended to give one word answers to questions. She was usually quiet and withdrawn but could become manic and aggressive without provocation. Most days she had to be helped to eat and dress. It must have been obvious to anyone of sound mind meeting her that she was suffering from a severe degree of mental disorder. She had never been known to take any erotic interest in men or to respond to sexual stimuli. The hospital doctor in charge of her said that it was highly unlikely that she would be capable of giving comprehending consent to sexual advances, but she might argree without understanding the full implications of what she was agreeing to. Her condition was such that the prosecution did not call her as a witness.

On August 1, 1981, she was walking by herself in the hospital gardens near the cricket ground when she was approached by the appellant. He had come to the hospital to visit a relative who was a patient. A ward sister said in evidence that she saw the appellant talking to Betty. He had his hands cupped. There were coins in them and he went through the motions of counting them out. The appellant then nodded in the direction of a lane and walked down it. Betty followed a pace or so behind. Ten minutes later the ward sister saw her again. She was naked from the waist down, her dress having been rolled up to her waist. She was screaming loudly and was so distressed that she had to be given a tranquilliser injection and put to bed. Her knickers were found later in the lane. A hospital porter who had been alerted by the ward sister that something untoward might have happened saw the appellant in the grounds. He stopped him and asked him if he had been near the cricket ground with the woman. He said he had not. This he admitted at his trial was a lie. Later the same day he was interviewed by the police. At first he denied that he had been involved in any incident. Later, according to the police witnesses, he admitted trying to have sexual intercourse with Betty but said he had not succeeded. He told them that she had followed him and 'chucked' her knickers on the ground and that he had interfered with her in a way which clearly amounted to an indecent assault if it had been done without her consent. He admitted to them that he knew she was a patient. He was asked whether she had said anything. He replied: 'No, she did not. She just started mumbling. I couldn't understand that. She was mumbling all the time really stupid.' Then came these questions and answers:

> (Q) You accept that this woman was mentally subnormal? (A) Well I should think so, the way she was mumbling and that. (Q) Did you ask her to have intercourse with you? (A) No, I did not. (Q) Why? (A) Silly thing to do isn't it – ask a woman for intercourse.

The offence of indecent assault is now statutory: see section 14 of the Sexual Offences Act 1956. The prosecution had to prove that the appellant made an indecent assault on Betty. As there are no words in the section to indicate that Parliament intended to exclude mens rea as an element in this offence, it follows that the prosecution had to prove that the appellant intended to commit it. This could not be done without first proving that the appellant intended to assault Betty. In this context assault clearly includes battery. An assault is an act by which the defendant intentionally or recklessly causes the complainant to apprehend immediate, or to sustain, unlawful personal violence: see *R* v

Venna [1976] QB 421, 428–429. In this case the appellant by his own admissions did intentionally lay his hands on Betty. That would not, however, have been enough to prove the charge. There had to be evidence that the appellant had intended to do what he did unlawfully. When there is a charge of indecent assault on a woman, the unlawfulness can be proved, as was sought to be done in *R v Donovan* [1934] 2 KB 498, by evidence that the defendant intended to cause bodily harm. In most cases, however, the prosecution tries to prove that the complainant did not consent to what was done. The burden of proving lack of consent rests upon the prosecution: see *R v May* [1912] 3 KB 572, 575, *per* Lord Alverstone CJ. The consequence is that the prosecution has to prove that the defendant intended to lay hands on his victim without her consent. If he did not intend to do this, he is entitled to be found not guilty; and if he did not so intend because . . . he believed she was consenting, the prosecution will have failed to prove the charge. It is the defendant's belief, not the grounds on which it was based, which goes to negative the intent.

In analysing the issue in this way we have followed what was said by the majority in *R v Morgan* [1976] AC 182: see Lord Hailsham of St Marylebone at p. 214F–H and Lord Fraser of Tullybelton at p. 237E–G. If, as we adjudge, the prohibited act in indecent assault is the use of personal violence to a woman without her consent, then the guilty state of mind is the intent to do it without her consent. Then, as in rape at common law, the inexorable logic, to which Lord Hailsham referred in *R v Morgan*, takes over and there is no room either for a 'defence' of honest belief or mistake, or of a 'defence' of honest and reasonable belief or mistake: [1976] AC 182, 214F–H.

(ii) *Actus reus*

The issue of consent is also relevant to the *actus reus* of the crime since there must be either an assault or a battery (*R v Leeson* (1968) 52 Cr App R 185). An invitation by a defendant to a victim asking the victim to touch him cannot amount to an assault unless accompanied by force or the threat of force.

Fairclough v *Whipp*

[1951] 2 All ER 834, King's Bench Division

While making water on the bank of a river, the respondent, with his person exposed, said to a girl of nine who was passing, 'Touch it,' and she did so.

Held: an invitation to someone to touch the invitor could not amount to an assault on the invitee, and, therefore, there had been no assault, and, consequently, no indecent assault on the girl by the respondent.

NOTE

This case would be decided under the Indecency with Children Act 1960. See below and *B* v *DPP* p. 338.

(iii) *What constitutes indecency?*

R v *Court*

[1989] AC 28, House of Lords

The appellant, an assistant in a shop, struck a 12-year-old girl visitor some 12 times, for no apparent reason as she thought, outside her shorts on her buttocks. In response to a question by the police as to why the appellant had done so he said 'I don't know – buttock fetish.' He was tried on a count charging indecent assault contrary to section 14(1) of the Sexual Offences Act 1956. He pleaded guilty to assault, denied that it was indecent and submitted that his statement about 'buttock fetish' should be excluded as being a secret uncommunicated motive and could not make indecent an assault not overtly indecent. The trial judge refused to exclude the statement, the appellant did not give evidence and he was convicted. The Court of Appeal (Criminal Division) dismissed the appellant's appeal against conviction.

LORD ACKNER: . . . It need not necessarily be hostile or rude or aggressive, as some of the cases seem to indicate. But the 'assault' relied upon need not involve any physical contact but may consist merely of conduct which causes the victim to apprehend immediate and unlawful personal violence. In the case law on the offence of indecent assault, both categories of assault feature.

The judge in assisting the jury in his summing up as to the meaning of an *indecent* assault adopted, inter alia, a definition used by Professor Glanville Williams, *Textbook of Criminal Law*, 2nd ed. (1983), p. 231: ' "indecent" may be defined as "overtly sexual." ' This is a convenient shorthand expression, since most, but not necessarily all, indecent assaults will be clearly of a sexual nature although they, as in this case, may have only sexual undertones. A simpler way of putting the matter to the jury is to ask them to decide whether 'right-minded persons would consider the conduct indecent or not.' It is for the jury to decide whether what occurred was so offensive to contemporary standards of modesty and privacy as to be indecent.

It also was common ground before your Lordships, as it was in the Court of Appeal, that if the circumstances of the assault are *incapable* of being regarded as indecent, then the undisclosed intention of the accused could not make the assault an indecent one. The validity of this proposition is well illustrated by *R* v *George* [1956] Crim LR 52. The basis of the prosecution's case was that the defendant on a number of occasions removed a shoe from a girl's foot and that he did so, as indeed he admitted, because it gave him a kind of perverted sexual gratification. Counsel for the prosecution submitted that an assault was indecent if it was committed to gratify an indecent motive in the mind of a defendant, even though there was no overt circumstances of indecency. Streatfeild J ruled that an assault became indecent only if it was accompanied by circumstances of indecency towards the person alleged to have been assaulted, and that none of the assaults (the removal or attempted removal of the shoes) could possibly amount to an indecent assault.

Again it was common ground that if, as in this case, the assault involved touching the victim, it was not necessary to prove that she was aware of the circumstances of indecency or apprehended indecency. An indecent assault can clearly be committed by the touching of someone who is asleep or unconscious.

As to the facts of this case, it is important to bear in mind that at the trial, not only did the appellant admit that he was guilty of an assault, but on his behalf his counsel expressly conceded that what had happened *was capable* of amounting to an indecent assault. That concession was repeated in the Court of Appeal and accepted by the court as being a correct concession. Sensibly no attempt was made before your Lordships to withdraw this concession, for the sound reason that the explanation of this unprovoked assault would reveal that the assault was an indecent one, as indeed the girl's father suspected and, as the jury so decided.

The assault which the prosecution seek to establish may be of a kind which is inherently indecent. The defendant removes against her will, a woman's clothing. Such a case, to my mind, raises no problem. Those very facts, *devoid of any explanation*, would give rise to the irresistible inference that the defendant intended to assault his victim in a manner which right-minded persons would clearly think was indecent. Whether he did so for his own personal sexual gratification or because, being a misogynist or for some other reason, he wished to embarrass or humiliate his victim, seems to me to be irrelevant. He has failed, ex-hypothesi, to show any lawful justification for his indecent conduct. This of course, was not such a case. The conduct of the appellant in assaulting the girl by spanking her was only *capable* of being an indecent assault. To decide whether or not right-minded persons might think that assault was indecent, the following factors were clearly relevant – the relationship of the defendant to his victim – were they relatives, friends or virtually complete strangers? How had the defendant come to embark on this conduct and *why* was he behaving in this way? Aided by such material, a jury would be helped to determine the quality of the act, the true nature of the assault and to answer the vital question – were they sure that the defendant not only intended to commit an assault upon the girl, but an assault which was indecent – was such an inference irresistible? For the defendant to be liable to be convicted of the offence of indecent assault, where the circumstances of the alleged offence can be given an innocent as well as an indecent interpretation, without the prosecution being obliged to establish that the defendant intended to commit both an assault and an indecent one, seems to me quite unacceptable and not what Parliament intended.

(iv) *Mens rea*

This has two elements:

(a) the necessary *mens rea* for assault or battery;

(b) intention to commit an indecent assault.

With regard to the latter, it is unclear exactly what role the defendant's motive plays. (See *R* v *Court*, above.)

R v Pratt
[1984] Crim LR 41, Crown Court

The defendant was charged on an indictment containing two counts of indecent assault. Two 13-year-old boys were night fishing at a lonely quay on the coast. They were each dressed in several layers of clothing. Shortly after midnight the defendant appeared wearing a stocking mask. The defendant threatened the boys by pretending he had a gun. By threatening the boys the defendant forced them to undress almost completely so as to reveal their private parts. As each boy undressed the other was forced to shine a torch on him. The defendant did not touch either boy and stood five yards away. The defendant gave evidence that his sole motive in causing the boys to reveal their private parts was to search for cannabis he thought the boys had taken from him the previous afternoon. Counsel addressed the Assistant Recorder as to whether the defendant's evidence if believed could provide a defence to the charges. Counsel for the prosecution referred the Assistant Recorder to: *Kosmos Publications* v *DPP* [1975] Crim LR 345; *Straker* [1965] Crim LR 239; *George* [1956] Crim LR 52; *DPP* v *Kilbourne* [1972] 3 All ER 551; *DPP* v *Rogers* [1953] 2 All ER 644; *R* v *Leeson* (1968) 52 Cr App R 185; *R* v *Sutton* [1977] 3 All ER 476; *Beal* v *Kelley* [1951] 2 All ER 763; and Glanville Williams' *Textbook of Criminal Law* (1st ed., 1978). He submitted it was only necessary for the prosecution to prove a common assault and having proved a common assault for there to be circumstances of indecency. If this was so it was not necessary for defendant's state of mind to be considered further. The prosecution need only prove intention or recklessness as to the common assault and the jury could then find if there were circumstances of indecency accompanying the assault. The jury were not required to consider any intention as to indecency. Counsel for the defendant submitted an indecent motive or intention was a necessary element of the offence. The Assistant Recorder held that it was necessary for the prosecution to prove an indecent intention.

R v Sargeant
[1997] Crim LR 50, Court of Appeal

The appellant was charged with indecent assault on a male contrary to section 15(1) of the Sexual Offences Act 1956. The complainant, aged 16, gave evidence that the appellant had grabbed him while he was on his way home after a disco and forced him to masturbate into a condom. The boy said he was terrified of the appellant. Although the appellant had plainly assaulted the boy when he grabbed him, he had not touched him in a sexual manner. At the close of the prosecution case counsel for the appellant submitted that there was no case to answer, on the basis that, in order for there to be an indecent assault in law where there was no actual indecent touching of the complainant by the defendant, the threat must be one of indecent touching. The judge rejected that submission, and the appellant appealed against his conviction on the ground, *inter alia*, that he was wrong to do so.

Held, dismissing the appeal, that Lord Ackner had said in *R v Court* [1989] AC 28 that on a charge of indecent assault the prosecution must prove (1) that the accused intentionally assaulted the victim; (2) that the assault or the circumstances accompanying it were capable of being considered by right-minded persons as indecent, and (3) that the accused intended to commit such an assault as is referred to in (2). It seemed to the court that to compel somebody to masturbate in a public place was an indecent act and there was, accordingly, in the circumstances of the present case a coincidence of the ingredients required to establish indecent assault.

QUESTION

Why are the defendant's motives relevant in these offences when considerable effort has gone into attempts to exclude motive from the law's understanding of *mens rea* in relation to other offences?

(v) *Indecency with children*

Because of the absence of an offence where a defendant invites the victim to touch him the Indecency with Children Act 1960 provides as follows:

Indecency with Children Act 1960

1.   Indecent conduct towards young child

(1) Any person who commits an act of gross indecency with or towards a child under the age of fourteen, or who incites a child under that age to such an act with him or another, shall be liable on conviction on indictment to imprisonment for a term not exceeding two years, or on summary conviction to imprisonment for a term not exceeding six months, to a fine not exceeding the prescribed sum, or to both.

R v Speck
[1977] 2 All ER 859, Court of Appeal

LORD WIDGERY CJ: . . . In this case counsel for the Crown proceeded to open the matter, and it became clear at once that the essence of the case was simply this. The appellant had been sitting down in a chair. A small girl of the age of eight, who was with other girls, came up to him and put her hand on his penis outside his trousers as he sat in the chair. She had left her hand there for a period variously estimated, but probably of the order of five minutes. By reason of the pressure of her hand the appellant had an erection. He said that he did absolutely nothing to encourage the child. He did not move. He stayed there placid, and indeed in a statement which he made to the police he puts this in very clear terms:

> Minnie put her hand on my flies. They were done up. I left her hand there because I submitted to what was happening. I had an erection. She asked me what it was. I passed it off by saying it was something in my pocket. I did not ejaculate or 'come' any where near it.

I understand that Minnie has said that I touched her on her private parts over her pants but I honestly didn't. I admit I did wrong by not taking her hand away.

Getting to the essential features of this problem, and accepting that for present purposes there was inactivity on the part of the appellant at all material times, we think that such inactivity can nevertheless amount to an invitation to the child to undertake the act. If a fair view of the facts be that the appellant has in any sense invited the child to do what she did, then the mere fact that the appellant himself remained inactive is no defence to it.

The point was powerfully put in the course of argument by counsel for the Crown when he said 'Suppose a man has done this on a number of occasions with a child, and suppose on a later occasion the child comes into the room. The man is sitting there and the child, hoping to get a reward (which was given in the instant case) proceeds to go and fondle the man's private parts. Is it going to be an answer for him to lie back and say 'No, I am not moving; I am not active; I am not committing an offence'? If the circumstances justified the view that his conduct amounted to an invitation to the child that she was to continue the act, then it is clear that that is sufficient activity to justify a conviction.

Appeal dismissed.

NOTES AND QUESTIONS

1. Was the conduct in *Speck* an instance of omission to act, or was the Court imposing a positive duty on the defendant to prevent the child's actions?
2. Note the age of 14 in s. 1(1) of the 1960 Act. It is not clear why 14 and not 16 was chosen.
3. The *mens rea* required under this statute was considered at length by the House of Lords in the following case:

B v DPP

[2000] 2 WLR 452, House of Lords

The defendant, aged 15, was convicted of inciting a girl under the age of 14 to commit an act of gross indecency with him. It was accepted that he honestly believed that the girl was over the age of 14.

LORD NICHOLLS OF BIRKENHEAD: My Lords, an indecent assault on a woman is a criminal offence. So is an indecent assault on a man. Neither a boy nor a girl under the age of 16 can, in law, give any consent which would prevent an act being an assault. These offences have existed for many years. Currently they are to be found in sections 14 and 15 of the Sexual Offences Act 1956. They have their origins in sections 52 and 62 of the Offences against the Person Act 1861 (24 & 25 Vict. c. 100).

In the early 1950s a lacuna in this legislation became apparent. A man was charged with indecent assault on a girl aged nine. At the man's invitation the girl had committed an indecent act on the man. The Court of Criminal Appeal held that an invitation to another person to touch the invitor could not amount to an assault on the invitee. As the man had done nothing to the girl which, if done against her will, would have amounted to an assault on her, the man's conduct did not constitute an indecent assault on the girl. That was *Fairclough v Whipp* [1951] 2 All ER 834. Two years later the same point arose and was similarly decided regarding a girl aged 11: see *Director of Public Prosecutions v Rogers* [1953] 1 WLR 1017. Following a report of the Criminal Law Revision Committee in August 1959 (First Report on Indecency with Children (Cmnd. 835)), Parliament enacted the Indecency with Children Act 1960. Section 1(1) of this Act makes it a criminal offence to commit an act of gross indecency with or towards a child under the age of 14, or to incite a child under that age to such an act. The question raised by the appeal concerns the mental element in this offence so far as the age ingredient is concerned.

The answer to this question depends upon the proper interpretation of the section. There are, broadly, three possibilities. The first possible answer is that it matters not whether the accused honestly believed that the person with whom he was dealing was over 14. So far as the age element is concerned, the offence created by section 1 of the Act of 1960 is one of strict liability. The second possible answer is that a necessary element of this offence is the absence of a belief, held honestly and on reasonable grounds by the accused, that the person with whom he was dealing was over 14. The third possibility is that the existence or not of reasonable grounds for an honest belief is irrelevant. The necessary mental element is simply the absence of an honest belief by the accused that the other person was over 14.

The common law presumption

As habitually happens with statutory offences, when enacting this offence Parliament defined the prohibited conduct solely in terms of the proscribed physical acts. Section 1(1) says nothing about the mental element. In particular, the section says nothing about what shall be the position if the person who commits or incites the act of gross indecency honestly but mistakenly believed that the child was 14 or over.

In these circumstances the starting-point for a court is the established common law presumption that a mental element, traditionally labelled *mens rea*, is an essential ingredient unless Parliament has indicated a contrary intention either expressly or by necessary implication. The common law presumes that, unless Parliament indicated otherwise, the appropriate mental element is an unexpressed ingredient of every statutory offence. On this I need do no more than refer to Lord Reid's magisterial statement in the leading case of *Sweet* v *Parsley* [1970] AC 132, 148–149:

> there has for centuries been a presumption that Parliament did not intend to make criminals of persons who were in no way blameworthy in what they did. That means that whenever a section is silent as to *mens rea* there is a presumption that, in order to give effect to the will of Parliament, we must read in words appropriate to require *mens rea* . . . it is firmly established by a host of authorities that *mens rea* is an essential ingredient of every offence unless some reason can be found for holding that that is not necessary.

. . .

The construction of section 1 of the Act of 1960

In section 1(1) of the Act of 1960 Parliament has not expressly negatived the need for a mental element in respect of the age element of the offence. The question, therefore, is whether, although not expressly negatived, the need for a mental element is negatived by necessary implication. 'Necessary implication' connotes an implication which is compellingly clear. Such an implication may be found in the language used, the nature of the offence, the mischief sought to be prevented and any other circumstances which may assist in determining what intention is properly to be attributed to Parliament when creating the offence.

I venture to think that, leaving aside the statutory context of section 1, there is no great difficulty in this case. The section created an entirely new criminal offence, in simple unadorned language. The offence so created is a serious offence. The more serious the offence, the greater is the weight to be attached to the presumption, because the more severe is the punishment and the graver the stigma which accompanies a conviction. Under section 1 conviction originally attracted a punishment of up to two years imprisonment. This has since been increased to a maximum of 10 years' imprisonment. The notification requirements under Part 1 of the Sex Offenders Act 1997 now apply, no matter what the age of the offender: see Schedule 1, paragraph 1(1)(b). Further, in addition to being a serious offence, the offence is drawn broadly ('an act of gross indecency'). It can embrace conduct ranging from predatory approaches by a much older paedophile to consensual sexual experimentation between precocious teenagers of whom the offender may be the younger of the two. The conduct may be depraved by any acceptable standard, or it may be relatively innocuous behaviour in private between two young people. These factors reinforce, rather than negative, the application of the presumption in this case.

The purpose of the section is, of course, to protect children. An age ingredient was therefore an essential ingredient of the offence. This factor in itself does not assist greatly. Without more, this does not lead to the conclusion that liability was intended to be strict so far as the age element is concerned, so that the offence is committed irrespective of the alleged offender's belief about the age of the 'victim' and irrespective of how the offender came to hold this belief.

Nor can I attach much weight to a fear that it may be difficult sometimes for the prosecution to prove that the defendant knew the child was under fourteen or was recklessly indifferent about the child's age. A well known passage from a judgment of that great jurist, Sir Owen Dixon, in *Thomas* v *The King* (1937) 59 CLR 279, 309, bears repetition:

> The truth appears to be that a reluctance on the part of courts has repeatedly appeared to allow a prisoner to avail himself of a defence depending simply on his own state of knowledge and belief. The reluctance is due in great measure, if not entirely, to a mistrust of the tribunal of fact – the jury. Through a feeling that, if the law allows such a defence to be submitted to the jury, prisoners may too readily escape by deposing to conditions of mind and describing sources of information, matters upon which their evidence cannot be adequately tested and contradicted, judges have been misled into a failure steadily to adhere to principle. It is not difficult to understand such tendencies, but a lack of confidence in the ability of a tribunal correctly to estimate evidence of states of mind and the like can never be sufficient ground for excluding from inquiry the most fundamental element in a rational and humane criminal code.

Similarly, it is far from clear that strict liability regarding the age ingredient of the offence would further the purpose of section 1 more effectively than would be the case if a mental element were read into this ingredient. There is no general agreement that strict liability is necessary to the enforcement of the law protecting children in sexual matters. For instance, the draft criminal code Bill prepared by the Law Commission in 1989 (Criminal Law, A Criminal Code for England and Wales (Law Com. No. 177)) proposed a compromise solution. Clauses 114 and 115 of the Bill provided for committing or inciting acts of gross indecency with children aged under 13 or under 16. Belief that the child is over 16 would be a defence in each case: see vol 1, Report and Draft Criminal Code Bill, p. 81.

Is there here a compellingly clear implication that Parliament should be taken to have intended that the ordinary common law requirement of a mental element should be excluded in respect of the age ingredient of this new offence? Thus far, having regard especially to the breadth of the offence and the gravity of the stigma and penal consequences which a conviction brings, I see no sufficient ground for so concluding.

Indeed, the Crown's argument before your Lordships did not place much reliance on any of the matters just mentioned. The thrust of the Crown's argument lay in a different direction: the statutory context. This is understandable, because the statutory background is undoubtedly the Crown's strongest point. The Crown submitted that the law in this field has been regarded as settled for well over 100 years, ever since the decision in *R v Prince* (1875) LR 2 CCR 154. That well known case concerned the unlawful abduction of a girl under the age of 16. The defendant honestly believed she was over 16, and he had reasonable grounds for believing this. No fewer than 15 judges held that this provided no defence. Subsequently, in *R v Maughan* (1934) 24 Cr App R 130 the Court of Criminal Appeal (Lord Hewart CJ, Avory and Roche JJ) held that a reasonable and honest belief that a girl was over 16 could never be a defence to a charge of indecent assault. The court held that this point had been decided in *R v Forde* [1923] 2 KB 400. The court also observed that in any event the answer was to be found in *Prince's* case. Building on this foundation Mr Scrivener submitted that the Act of 1956 was not intended to change this established law, and that section 1 of the Act of 1960 was to be read with the Act of 1956. The preamble to the Act of 1960 stated that its purpose was to make 'further' provision for the punishment of indecent conduct towards young people. In this field, where Parliament intended belief as to age to be a defence, this was stated expressly: see, for instance, the 'young man's defence' in section 6(3) of the Act of 1956.

This is a formidable argument, but I cannot accept it. I leave on one side Mr O'Connor's sustained criticisms of the reasoning in *Prince's* case and *Maughan's* case. Where the Crown's argument breaks down is that the motley collection of offences, of diverse origins, gathered into the Act of 1956 displays no satisfactorily clear or coherent pattern. If the interpretation of section 1 of the Act of 1960 is to be gleaned from the contents of another statute, that other statute must give compelling guidance. The, Act of 1956 as a whole falls short of this standard. So do the two sections, sections 14 and 15, which were the genesis of section 1 of the Act of 1960.

Accordingly, I cannot find, either in the statutory context or otherwise, any indication of sufficient cogency to displace the application of the common law presumption. In my view the necessary mental element regarding the age ingredient in section 1 of the Act of 1960 is the absence of a genuine belief by the accused that the victim was 14 years of age or above. The burden of proof of this rests upon the prosecution in the usual way. If Parliament considers that the position should be otherwise regarding this serious social problem, Parliament must itself confront the difficulties and express its will in clear terms. I would allow this appeal.

I add a final observation. As just mentioned, in reaching my conclusion I have left on one side the criticisms made of *Prince's* case and *Maughan's* case. Those cases concerned different offences and different statutory provisions. The correctness of the decisions in those cases does not call for decision on the present appeal. But, without expressing a view on the correctness of the actual decisions in those cases, I must observe that some of the reasoning in *Prince's* case is at variance with the common law presumption regarding *mens rea* as discussed above. To that extent, the reasoning must be regarded as unsound. For instance, Bramwell B, at p. 174, seems to have regarded the common law presumption as ousted because the act forbidden was 'wrong in itself'. Denman J, at p. 178, appears to have considered it was 'reasonably clear' that the Act of 1861 was an Act of strict liability so far as the age element was concerned. On its face this is a lesser standard than necessary implication. And in the majority judgment, Blackburn J reached his conclusion by inference from the intention Parliament must have had when enacting two other, ineptly drawn, sections of the Act. But clumsy parliamentary drafting is an insecure basis for finding a necessary implication elsewhere, even in the same statute. *Prince's* case, and later decisions based on it, must now be read in the light of this decision of your Lordships' House on the nature and weight of the common law presumption.

NOTE

1. The House of Lords decision in *B* is critically examined in Horder 'How culpability can, and cannot, be denied in Under-age Sex Crimes' [2001] Crim LR 15, who questions its 'subjectivist' approach.

8

Property Offences

SECTION 1: Introduction

The law of theft expresses society's view of the extent to which property rights ought to be protected. Although Parliament has decided to bring these matters within the scope of the criminal law, most of the matters we shall discuss in this chapter and those immediately following may also give rise to a civil action by the victim. A number of factors prompt the criminalisation of interference with property interests. One is the view (which may or may not be accurate) that making theft subject to criminal penalties is a more powerful deterrent than civil remedies because the villain may not have the means of repaying money or restoring goods taken. Leaving a victim to a civil suit may also not convey the full depths of society's antipathy to the offence.

The laws promoting the security of property in this country take little account of disparities in wealth. The concentration on protection of the status quo as far as wealth is concerned reveals an inherent tension when such laws are applied in a capitalist society. It is extremely difficult to draw the line between acceptable, thrusting entrepreneurial activity which is normally regarded as useful to society and immoral greed which should be subject to criminal sanctions. In some of the instances we will discuss you may feel that the courts have drawn the line in the wrong place.

When the Theft Act 1968 was drafted, the aim was to use simple terminology so far as was possible. Because the protection of property must to some extent depend on complicated rules concerning ownership of property, the rules are not always as simple as the legislators would have wished. Problems have arisen because the statutes, as well as the courts, have imported into the criminal law civil law concepts relating to property while interpreting them differently. This problem of 'same terms, different meaning' is not unique to the law of theft but it seems to be more pronounced here than elsewhere.

In some instances, too, the courts have created their own difficulties, or have had such difficulties thrust upon them by prosecutors choosing to charge the defendant with the wrong offence. *DPP* v *Gomez* [1993] AC 442, discussed later in this chapter, provides a graphic example of a case where arguably such mischarging occurred (the defendant was charged with theft rather than obtaining property by deception). The House of Lords, reluctant to allow the defendant to escape his just deserts, stretched the meaning of 'appropriation' in order to uphold a conviction. This stretching may well have resulted in a distortion of the overall scheme intended by the legislators. The Court of Appeal has called for urgent reform as the law has become over-complicated (*R v Hallam and Blackburn* [1995] Crim LR 323).

The Theft Act 1968 can be usefully approached by thinking in terms of three 'tiers'. At the first tier is the definition of the crime. The definition of 'theft' is set out in s. 1 of the 1968 Act. From this definition one can extract the basic elements of the crime. At the second tier, also to be found in the statute, is either a qualification or a more detailed description of one of the elements to be found in the definition section. Thus, for example, s. 3 of the Act defines 'appropriation' and identifies whether there is an appropriation in certain areas that had previously proved troublesome, and s. 5 discusses what it means for property to 'belong to another'. Despite the guidance provided in the statute, cases will arise that require the courts to interpret and apply specific provisions of the statute. The third tier consists of the judgments of the courts interpreting and applying the statutory provisions.

Theft Act 1968

1.—(1) A person is guilty of theft if he dishonestly appropriates property belonging to another with the intention of permanently depriving the other of it; and 'thief' and 'steal' shall be construed accordingly.

Section 1 can be broken down into the following elements:

(a) an appropriation,

(b) of property,

(c) which belongs to another;

(d) dishonestly, and

(e) with an intent permanently to deprive the person to whom the property belongs of that property.

SECTION 2: *Actus reus*

The first three of the above elements – (a) an appropriation (b) of property (c) which belongs to another – collectively comprise the *actus reus* of theft. These elements are themselves explained by other sections of the Theft Act 1968 and the case law.

A: Appropriation

What is an appropriation? As will be seen, it may range from an outright taking of property to a relatively trivial interference with property. Indeed, it may occur without any physical contact with the property on the part of the defendant. Section 3 of the Theft Act 1968 defines appropriation as 'any assumption . . . of the rights of an owner'. The section then addresses specific problem areas.

In s. 3 and the cases raising the issue of appropriation, one can identify six areas which have proved particularly troublesome:

(a) Where the defendant is innocently in possession of the goods at the outset, but then forms a dishonest intent.

(b) Where the defendant assumes the rights of an owner without being in possession of the goods.

(c) Where the defendant's acts are consented to by the owner, especially if the owner's consent is obtained by deception.

(d) Where not all the rights of the owner are assumed by the defendant.

(e) Where title to the goods passes immediately before or at the time of the appropriation.

(f) Where the defendant was a bona fide purchaser of the property but subsequently discovers that he has no title to the goods.

(i) *Original possession without stealing*

Theft Act 1968

3.—(1) Any assumption by a person of the rights of an owner amounts to an appropriation, and this includes, where he has come by the property (innocently or not) without stealing it, any later assumption of a right to it by keeping or dealing with it as an owner.

NOTES AND QUESTIONS

1. An example of where a later assumption of goods innocently obtained can constitute an appropriation is provided by *Pilgram* v *Rice-Smith* [1977] 1 WLR 671. The defendant was a shop assistant who supplied her friend with cold meat at a reduced price. She was dishonest in respect of the transaction. The Court of Appeal found it perfectly proper to convict the shop assistant of theft. The whole of the corned beef and bacon had been stolen by her despite the fact that when the defendant was behaving honestly she was innocently in possession of all the articles at her counter.

2. In *R* v *Atakpu and Abrahams* [1994] QB 69, the defendants hired cars in Germany and Belgium using false driving licences and passports, with the objective of selling the cars in England. The Court of Appeal ruled that the cars had been fraudulently obtained out of the jurisdiction. At the point they were obtained there was an appropriation. As the defendants had as a result already stolen the cars (although they could not be convicted for theft in England), the continued use of the cars in England could not amount to a further theft, according to the Court. But why not? The Court seems to have been swayed by the fact that the dishonest

obtaining occurred abroad, but that feature of the case does not resolve the question whether a crime was committed in England. Is this a case where the prosecution simply charged the wrong offence? Were the defendants guilty of handling stolen goods (Theft Act 1968 s. 22)?

(ii) *Assumption of the rights of an owner while not in possession of the goods*

R v *Pitham and Hehl*

(1976) 65 Cr App R 45, Court of Appeal

One M, who knew an acquaintance X was in prison, decided to take advantage of X's incarceration to steal his furniture and sell it. M offered the furniture to the appellants for sale and they both went individually to X's house to look at the furniture and agreed to buy it, paying M a sum which they knew to be considerably under the true value. M and the appellants were later seen to enter X's house after arriving there in a furniture van. M was arrested, but the appellants escaped, but both were later interviewed by the police. They insisted that 'they had not screwed the place'. All three were charged on counts of burglary, the appellants additionally each on an individual count of handling stolen goods. M was convicted on two counts of burglary and the appellants only on the individual handling counts.

R v *Gallasso*

[1993] Crim LR 459, Court of Appeal

G, a nurse, was a house leader of a home for severely mentally handicapped adults and was (*inter alia*) in charge of the patients' finances. Each of the patients had a trust account at a building society into which various benefits were paid; G was the sole signatory and drew out money to pay for patients' day-to-day needs. A very severely handicapped patient, J, had accrued benefits which G paid into his trust account. Later a further cheque for £4,000 arrived for J; G opened a second account for him (count 1) and later transferred £3,000 from the second to the first account. She then withdrew the remaining £1,000 which she paid into her own account (count 2). A few months later she paid another cheque, for £1,800, into a new cash card account for J at the same branch as the first account (count 3). The judge rejected a submission of no case to answer on count 3 (and count 1) made on the basis that the cheques were properly paid in by G, J being unable to pay them in himself, and that there was no evidence of appropriation on G's part. G was convicted of two counts of theft: count 2 – the payment of £1,000 into her own account – and count 3 – the payment of the cheque for £1,800 into the new account for J. (The jury acquitted her of count 1: theft of the cheque for £4,000, count 2 being an alternative.) She appealed against conviction on count 3 only – the theft of the cheque for £1,800 – submitting that the judge wrongly rejected the submission of no case to answer.

Held, allowing the appeal and quashing the conviction on count 3, it was now clear that a taking of property with the owner's consent could amount to appropriation. . . . The Crown had based its argument on G dealing in the cheque in a way which was not to J's advantage, and that there was no need for the second account to have been opened, except to assist G to make unauthorised withdrawals. However, the court accepted G's argument that a dishonest motive or a breach of employers' rules (which was in any case not proved) could not turn into an appropriation something which was not; and it was significant that the jury had acquitted G on count 1 which alleged theft of a cheque paid into a different account in J's name. Paying the cheque into J's account could not be regarded as appropriation since it was evidence of G affirming J's rights rather than assuming them for herself.

NOTES AND QUESTIONS
1. Would the decision in *Pitham and Hehl* have been the same if the purchasers had offered to buy the goods before the defendants had offered to sell them? Did M steal *all* the contents of the house, or only those items which he eventually sold?
2. The appellants in *Pitham and Hehl* argued that they could not be convicted of handling stolen goods because they were 'in the course of stealing' the goods. This would have exempted them from liability under s. 22 of the Theft Act 1968 (handling), but the exemption applies only to the 'first thief'. The court concluded that M was the first thief and had appropriated the contents of the house when he took the appellants to X's house and showed them the furniture, inviting them to buy what they wanted. The appellants were therefore rightly convicted of handling as M had committed the 'first theft'. In the light of *Gallasso*, is *Pitham and Hehl* still good law, or does appropriation require an actual taking?
3. If Kevin offers to sell Tower Bridge to an unsuspecting American tourist, has he stolen it? How is an intention permanently to deprive established in such a case?

(iii) *Is it an appropriation where the defendant's acts are consented to by the owner?*
Whether or not an appropriation takes place in these circumstances has been a matter of considerable controversy. The issue has been settled for the time being by the House of Lords:

DPP v *Gomez*
[1993] AC 442, House of Lords

LORD KEITH OF KINKEL: . . . The facts of this case are that the defendant, Edwin Gomez, was employed as an assistant manager at a shop trading by retail in electrical goods. In September 1987 he was asked by an acquaintance called Jit Ballay to supply goods from the shop and to accept payment by two stolen building society cheques, one for £7,950 and the other for £9,250, which were undated and bore no payee's name. The defendant agreed, and prepared a list of goods to the value of £7,950 which he submitted to the manager, Mr Gilberd, saying that it represented a genuine order by one Johal and asking him to authorise the supply of the goods in return for a building society cheque in that sum. Mr Gilberd instructed the defendant to confirm with the bank that the cheque was acceptable, and the defendant later told him that he had done so and that such a cheque was 'as good as cash'. Mr Gilberd agreed to the transaction, the defendant paid the cheque into the bank, and a few days later Ballay took possession of the goods, the defendant helping him to load them into his vehicle. Shortly afterwards a further consignment of goods to the value of £9,250 was ordered and supplied in similar fashion (apart from one item valued at £1,002.99 which was not delivered), against the second stolen building society cheque. Mr Gilberd agreed to this transaction without further inquiry. Later the two cheques were returned by the bank marked 'Orders not to pay. Stolen cheque.'

The defendant, Ballay and another employee of the shop, named Rai, were arrested and later tried on an indictment the fourth and fifth counts in which charged all three with theft contrary to section 1(1) of the Theft Act 1968 in respect of the two transactions. After evidence had been led for the prosecution counsel for the defendant submitted that there was no case to answer on the theft charges because the manager of the shop had authorised the transactions, so that there had been no appropriation within the meaning of section 1(1) of the Act. . . .

In my opinion Lord Roskill was undoubtedly right when he said in [*Morris* [1983] QB 587] that the assumption by the defendant of any of the rights of an owner could amount to an appropriation within the meaning of section 3(1), and that the removal of an article from the shelf and the changing of the price label on it constituted the assumption of one of the rights of the owner and hence an appropriation within the meaning of the subsection. But there are observations in the passage which, with the greatest possible respect to my noble and learned friend Lord Roskill, I must regard as unnecessary for the decision of the case and as being incorrect. In the first place, it seems to me that the switching of price labels on the article is in itself an assumption of one of the rights of the owner, whether or not it is accompanied by some other act such as removing the article from the shelf and placing it in a basket or trolley. No one but the owner has the right to remove a price label from an article or to place a price label upon it. If anyone else does so, he does an act, as Lord Roskill puts it, by way of adverse interference with or usurpation of that right. This is no less so in the case of the practical joker figured by Lord Roskill than in the case of one who makes the switch with dishonest intent. The practical joker, of course, is not guilty of theft because he has not acted dishonestly and does not intend to deprive the owner permanently of the article. So the label switching in itself constitutes an appropriation and so to have held would have been sufficient for the dismissal of both appeals. On the facts of the two cases it was unnecessary to decide whether, as argued by Mr Jeffreys, the mere taking of the article from the shelf and putting it in a trolley or other receptacle amounted to the assumption of one of the rights of the owner, and hence an appropriation. There was much to be said in favour of the view that it did, in respect that doing so gave the shopper control of the article and the capacity to exclude any other shopper from taking it. However, Lord Roskill expressed the opinion, at p. 332, that it did not, on the ground that the concept of appropriation in the context of section 3(1)

> involves not an act expressly or impliedly authorised by the owner but an act by way of adverse interference with or usurpation of those rights.

While it is correct to say that appropriation for purposes of section 3(1) includes the latter sort of act, it does not necessarily follow that no other act can amount to an appropriation and in particular that no act expressly or impliedly authorised by the owner can in any circumstances do so. Indeed, *R v Lawrence* [1972] AC 626 is a clear decision to the contrary since it laid down unequivocally that an act may be an appropriation notwithstanding that it is done with the consent of the owner. It does not appear to me that any sensible distinction can be made in this context between consent and authorisation.

. . . *Lawrence* makes it clear that consent to or authorisation by the owner of the taking by the rogue is irrelevant. The taking amounted to an appropriation within the meaning of secton 1(1) of the Act of 1968. *Lawrence* also makes it clear that it is no less irrelevant that what happened may also have constituted the offence of obtaining property by deception under section 15(1) of the Act.

In my opinion it serves no useful purpose at the present time to seek to construe the relevant provisions of the Theft Act by reference to the report which preceded it, namely the Eighth Report of the Criminal Law Revision Committee on Theft and Related Offences (1966) (Cmnd. 2977). The decision in *Lawrence* was a clear decision of this House upon the construction of the word 'appropriate' in section 1(1) of the Act, which had stood for 12 years when doubt was thrown upon it by obiter dicta in *Morris. Lawrence* must be regarded as authoritative and correct, and there is no question of it now being right to depart from it.

. . .

LORD LOWRY (dissenting): . . . The certified question in this appeal is:

> When theft is alleged and that which is alleged to be stolen passes to the defendant with the consent of the owner, but that consent has been obtained by a false representation, has, (a) an appropriation within the meaning of section 1(1) of the Theft Act 1968 taken place, or, (b) must such a passing of property necessarily involve an element of adverse interference with or usurpation of some right of the owner?

I can say now that I would answer (a) 'No', and (b) 'No, because such a passing of property does not involve an appropriation.'

. . .

To be guilty of theft the offender, as I shall call him, must act dishonestly and must have the intention of permanently depriving the owner of property. Section 1(3) shows that in order to interpret the word 'appropriates' (and thereby to define theft), sections 1 to 6 must be read together. The ordinary and natural meaning of 'appropriate' is to take for oneself, or to treat as one's own, property which belongs to someone else. The primary dictionary meaning is 'take possession of, take to oneself, especially without authority,' and that is in my opinion the meaning which the word bears in section 1(1). The act of appropriating property is a one-sided act, done without the consent or authority of the owner. And, if the owner consents to transfer property to the offender or to a third party, the offender does not appropriate the property, even if the owner's consent has been obtained by fraud.

. . . I turn, for such guidance as it may afford, to the Eighth Report of the Criminal Law Revision Committee on Theft and Related Offences.

While the report may not completely resolve the question for your Lordships, it provides in the first place a very useful summary of the state of the law in 1966. It also discusses in some detail the shortcomings of the law in regard to theft and kindred offences, as they appeared to the committee, and it proposes remedies. A reading of the Act of 1968, which was based on the draft Bill annexed to the report, leads me to the conclusion that, when using the very words of the draft, Parliament intended to implement the committee's thinking. Of course, if the words of the Act clearly achieve a different result from that which seemed to be intended by the committee, it is the words which must prevail and strained constructions must not be adopted in order to give effect to the report.

. . .

The committee's proposed remedies for the defects of the law as they found it appear clearly from the foregoing paragraphs. 'Fraudulent conversion' is accepted as the starting point for the new and comprehensive definition of theft and 'dishonest appropriation' is chosen as a synonym. Both expressions embody the notion of an adverse unilateral act done to the prejudice of the owner and without his authority; indeed, fraudulent conversion can have no other meaning. . . .

Before going on to consider the cases and some of the observations which the academic writers have made on section 1, I should like to say something more about section 15. According to the Crown's argument, this provision seems to be unnecessary and must have been included in the Act (and presumably also in the draft Bill) as a mere matter of convenience. A possible alternative theory is that the committee, the responsible government department and the parliamentary draftsmen all thought that section 15 (clause 12) was needed, which turns out to be a mistaken view when section 1 is properly understood. I call this an alternative theory because it seems obvious to me that the committee *did* think that clause 12 was necessary – and I am not simply referring to the definition of 'deception'. The Crown say that section 15 merely describes a particular type of theft and that all stealing by means of deception can be prosecuted under section 1 just as well as under section 15. I would point out that section 15 covers what were formerly two offences, obtaining by false pretences (where the ownership of the property is transferred by the deceived victim) and theft (or larceny) by a trick (where the possession of the property passes, but not the ownership). In the former case, according to the interpretation which I prefer, the offender does not *appropriate* the property, because the ownership (in colloquial terms, the property) is transferred with the owner's consent, albeit obtained by deception. In the latter case the offender does appropriate the property because, although the owner has handed over *possession* by consent (which was obtained by deception), he has not transferred the property (that is, the ownership) and the offender, intending to deprive the owner permanently of his property, appropriates it, not by taking possession, but by the unilateral act, adverse to the owner, of treating as his own and taking to himself property of which he was merely given *possession*. Thus, the kind of obtaining by deception which amounts to larceny by a trick and involves appropriation *could* be successfully prosecuted under section 1, but the old false pretences type of obtaining by deception could not. Of course, unless the facts were absolutely clear, it would be foolish to prosecute under section 1 an offence of obtaining by deception, since something which at first looked like larceny by a trick might turn out to have involved a transfer of the ownership, in which case only section 15 would meet the prosecution's needs, if I am right. Some theft cases can be prosecuted under section 15, but it is fallacious, having regard to what I perceive as the true meaning of appropriation, to say that *all* cases of obtaining by deception can be prosecuted under section 1.

. . .

My Lords, I think I have in passing taken account of most of the points made in the pro-*Lawrence* academic contributions to the debate. I feel no qualms about taking sides against these contributions, nearly all of which seem to me to disregard the Criminal Law Revision Committee Report and to neglect to analyse the meaning in its context of the word 'appropriate.' Morever, they choose to disregard the ordinary law governing the transfer of title, calling it the civil law, as if to contrast it with the criminal law and thus render it surplus to requirements. At least, Bingham LJ refused to fall in with this idea, saying in *Dobson* v *General Accident Fire and Life Assurance Corporation Plc* [1990] 1 QB 274, 289:

> But whether, in the ordinary case to which section 5 of the Theft Act 1968 does not apply, goods are to be regarded as belonging to another is a question to which the criminal law offers no answer and which can only be answered by reference to civil law principles.

Accordingly, it is both proper and rational to rely on such cases as *Phillips* v *Brooks Ltd* [1919] 2 KB 243 and *Lewis* v *Averay* [1972] 1 QB 198, 207G.

. . .

In my opinion, any attempt to reconcile the statements of principle in *Lawrence* and *Morris* is a complete waste of time. And certainly reconciliation cannot be achieved by the unattractive solution of varying the meaning of 'appropriation' in different provisions of the Act of 1968. It is clear that, whether they succeeded or not, both the Criminal Law Revision Committee and the draftsman must have intended to give the word one meaning, which would be the same in the Act as in the committee's report.

To simplify the law, where possible, is a worthy objective but, my Lords, I maintain that the law, as envisaged in the report, is simple enough: there is no problem (and there would have been none in *Lawrence*, *Morris* and the present case) if one prosecutes under section 15 all offences involving obtaining by deception and prosecutes theft in general under section 1. In that way some thefts will come under section 15, but no 'false pretences' will come under section 1.

. . .

LORD BROWNE-WILKINSON: . . . For myself, . . . I regard the word 'appropriation' in isolation as being an objective description of the act done irrespective of the mental state of either the owner or the accused. It is impossible to reconcile the decision in *Lawrence* (that the question of consent is irrelevant in considering whether there has been an appropriation) with the views expressed in *Morris*, which latter views in my judgment were incorrect.

It is suggested that this conclusion renders section 15 of the Act of 1968 otiose since a person who, by deception, persuades the owner to consent to part with his property will necessarily be guilty of theft within section 1. This may be so though I venture to doubt it. Take for example a man who obtains land by deception. Save as otherwise expressly provided, the definitions in sections 4 and 5 of the Act apply only for the purposes of interpreting section 1 of the Act: see section 1(3). Section 34(1) applies subsection (1) of section 4 and subsection (1) of section 5 generally for the purposes of the Act. Accordingly the other subsections of section 4 and section 5 do not apply to section 15. Suppose that a fraudster has persuaded a victim to part with his house: the fraudster is not guilty of theft of the land since section 4(2) provides that you cannot steal land. The charge could only be laid under section 15 which contains no provisions excluding land from the definition of property. Therefore, although there is a substantial overlap between section 1 and section 15, section 15 is not otiose.

NOTES AND QUESTIONS
1. Should their Lordships have paid greater attention to the Eighth Report of the Criminal Law Revision Committee? Lord Keith suggested that no useful purpose would have been served, but is he correct? Does not Lord Keith's dismissal of the Report fly in the face of the principles of statutory interpretation?
2. After *Gomez*, is there any distinction between obtaining property by deception under s. 15 of the Theft Act 1968 and s. 1 theft? Is this what Parliament intended? Might *DPP v Gomez* be limited to cases of fraud, deception or false representation? While this view is consistent with the facts of *DPP v Gomez*, does it accord with the language and spirit of the decision? What would be the implication for cases where the consent was not induced by fraud or other artifice?
3. In his commentary on *Gomez*, Professor Smith writes ([1993] Crim LR, p. 306):

    > Anyone doing anything whatever to property belonging to another, with or without the authority or consent of the owner, appropriates it: and, if he does so dishonestly and with intent, by that act or any subsequent act, permanently to deprive, he commits theft.

    Is Professor Smith correct? If he is, is *Gallasso* (above) correctly decided? A.T.H. Smith, in *Property Offences*, para. 5–56, states that *Gallasso* is 'simply wrong'. At what point in time must the property belong to another? (See discussion of 'belonging to another', below.)
4. As a result of *Gomez*, 'appropriation' should no longer be viewed as a pejorative but rather as a neutral term. One effect of neutering 'appropriation' is to shift the focus even more than may ordinarily be the case onto the *mens rea* elements of the crime in order to determine a defendant's culpability.

Consider the following cases:

R v Hinks

[2001] 2 AC 241, House of Lords

LORD STEYN: In 1996 the appellant was 38 years old. She was the mother of a young son. She was friendly with a 53-year-old man, John Dolphin. He was a man of limited intelligence. The appellant described herself as the main carer for John Dolphin. It is not in dispute that in the period April to November 1996 Mr Dolphin withdrew sums totalling around £60,000 from his building society account and that these sums were deposited in the appellant's account. During the summer of that year Mr Dolphin made withdrawals of the maximum permissible sum of £300 almost every day. Towards the end of this period Mr Dolphin had lost most of his savings and moneys inherited from his father. In 1997 the appellant was charged with six counts of theft, five counts covering moneys withdrawn and one count a television set transferred by Mr Dolphin to the appellant. In November 1997 the appellant stood trial on these counts in the Wolverhampton Crown Court before Judge Warner and a jury. It was the prosecution case that the appellant had influenced and coerced Mr Dolphin to withdraw the moneys from his building society account, which were then deposited in her account. A substantial volume of evidence was led during the trial which lasted five days. A police analyst produced documents summarising the flow of funds from Mr Dolphin's account to that of the appellant. Building society employees testified about the daily visits by the appellant and Mr Dolphin to effect withdrawals. The thrust of their evidence was that the appellant did most of the talking and would interrupt Mr Dolphin if he tried to say something. Dr Fuller, a consultant psychiatrist, assessed Mr Dolphin's IQ as in the range between 70 to 80 (the average being 90 to 110). He said that Mr Dolphin was able to live a normal if undemanding life. Mr Dolphin had worked as a packer in a dairy for some 30 years. Dr Fuller described him as naive and trusting and having no idea of the value of his assets or the ability to calculate their value. Dr Fuller accepted that Mr Dolphin would be capable of making a gift and understood the concept of ownership. He thought that Mr Dolphin was capable of making the decision to divest himself of money, but that it was unlikely that he could make the decision alone. Two police officers testified that after cautioning the appellant she denied 'having any money' from Mr Dolphin except for a single cheque which she said represented a loan. In a nutshell the prosecution case was that the appellant had taken Mr Dolphin for as much as she could get.

. . .

Counsel for the appellant submitted in the first place that the law as expounded in *Gomez* and *Lawrence* must be qualified to say that there can be no appropriation unless the other party (the owner) retains some proprietary interest, or the right to resume or recover some proprietary interest, in the property. Alternatively, counsel argued that 'appropriates' should be interpreted as if the word 'unlawfully' preceded it. Counsel said that the effect of the decisions in Lawrence and Gomez is to reduce the *actus reus* of theft to 'vanishing point' (see Smith & Hogan, Criminal Law, 9th ed (1999), p 505). He argued that the result is to bring the criminal law 'into conflict' with the civil law. Moreover, he argued that the decisions in *Lawrence* and *Gomez* may produce absurd and grotesque results. He argued that the mental requirements of dishonesty and intention of permanently depriving the owner of property are insufficient to filter out some cases of conduct which should not sensibly be regarded as theft. He did not suggest that the appellant's dishonest and repellent conduct came within such a category. Instead he deployed four examples for this purpose, namely:

(1) S makes a handsome gift to D because he believes that D has obtained a First. D has not and knows that S is acting under that misapprehension. He makes the gift. There is here a motivational mistake which, it is submitted, does not avoid the transaction. (Glanville Williams, Textbook of Criminal Law, 1st ed (1978), p 788.)

(2) P sees D's painting and, thinking he is getting a bargain, offers £100,000 for it. D realises that P thinks the painting is a Constable, but knows that it was painted by his sister and is worth no more than £100. He accepts P's offer. D has made an enforceable contract and is entitled to recover and retain the purchase price. (Smith & Hogan, Criminal Law, pp 507, 508.)

(3) A buys a roadside garage business from B, abutting on a public thoroughfare; unknown to A but known to B, it has already been decided to construct a bypass road which will divert substantially the whole of the traffic from passing A's garage. There is an enforceable contract and A is entitled to recover and retain the purchase price. The same would be true if B knew that A was unaware of the intended plan to construct a bypass road. (Compare Lord Atkin in *Bell v Lever Brothers Ltd* [1932] AC 161, 224.)

(4) An employee agrees to retire before the end of his contract of employment, receiving a sure of money by way of compensation from his employer. Unknown to the employer, the employee has committed serious breaches of contract which would have enabled the employer to dismiss him without compensation. Assuming that the employee's failure to reveal his defaults does not affect the validity of the contract, so that the employee is entitled to sue for the promised compensation, is the employee liable to be arrested for the theft the moment he receives the money? (Glanville Williams, 'Theft and Voidable Title' [1981] Crim LR 666, 672.)

My Lords, at first glance these are rather telling examples. They may conceivably have justified a more restricted meaning of section 3(1) than prevailed in *Lawrence* [1972] AC 626 and Gomez [1993] AC 442. The House ruled otherwise and I am quite unpersuaded that the House overlooked the consequences of its decision. On the facts set out in the examples a jury could possibly find that the acceptance of the transfer took place in the belief that the transferee had the right in law to deprive the other of it within the meaning of section 2(1)(a) of the Act. Moreover, in such cases a prosecution is hardly likely and if mounted, is likely to founder on the basis that the jury will not be persuaded that there was dishonesty in the required sense. And one must retain a sense of perspective. At the extremity of the application of legal rules there are sometimes results which may seem strange. A matter of judgment is then involved. The rule may have to be recast. Sir John Smith has eloquently argued that the rule in question ought to be recast. I am unpersuaded. If the law is restated by adopting a narrower definition of appropriation, the outcome is likely to place beyond the reach of the criminal law dishonest persons who should be found guilty of theft. The suggested revisions would unwarrantably restrict the scope of the law of theft and complicate the fair and effective prosecution of theft. In my view the law as settled in Lawrence and Gomez does not demand the suggested revision. Those decisions can be applied by judges and juries in a way which, absent human error, does not result in injustice.

Counsel for the appellant further pointed out that the law as stated in *Lawrence* [1972] AC 626 and *Gomez* [1993] AC 442 creates a tension between the civil and the criminal law. In other words, conduct which is not wrongful in ii civil law sense may constitute the crime of theft. Undoubtedly, this is so. The question whether the civil claim to title by a convicted thief, who committed no civil wrong, may be defeated by the principle that nobody may benefit from his own civil or criminal wrong does not arise for decision. Nevertheless there is a more general point, namely that the interaction between criminal law and civil law can cause problems: compare J Beatson and AP Simester, 'Stealing One's Own Property' (1999) 115 LQR 372. The purposes of the civil law and the criminal law are somewhat different. In theory the two systems should be in perfect harmony. In a practical world there will sometimes be some disharmony between the two systems. In any event, it would be wrong to assume on a priori grounds that the criminal law rather than the civil law is defective. Given the jury's conclusions, one is entitled to observe that the appellant's conduct should constitute theft, the only available charge. The tension between the civil and the criminal law is therefore not in my view a factor which justifies a departure from the law as stated in *Lawrence* and *Gomez*. Moreover, these decisions of the House have a marked beneficial consequence. While in some contexts of the law of theft a judge cannot avoid explaining civil law concepts to a jury (eg in respect of section 2(1)(a)), the decisions of the House of Lords eliminate the need for such explanations in respect of appropriation. That is a great advantage in an overly complex corner of the law.

Appeal Dismissed

(iv) Do all rights of the owner need to be assumed?

Ownership confers many rights; for example, one can sell one's own property, give it away, move it, destroy it, etc. In *Morris*, the House of Lords held that it was not necessary to appropriate *all* of the rights of an owner to be guilty of theft; an appropriation of *any* of them would be sufficient.

R v *Morris*
[1983] 3 WLR 697, House of Lords

LORD ROSKILL: Mr Denison submitted that the phrase in section 3(1) 'any assumption by a person of *the rights*' (my emphasis) 'of an owner amounts to an appropriation' must mean any assumption of '*all* the rights of an owner.' Since neither respondent had at the time of the removal of the goods from the shelves and of the label switching assumed *all* the rights of the owner, there was no appropriation and therefore no theft. Mr Jeffreys for the prosecution, on the other hand, contended that *the rights* in this context only meant *any* of the rights. An owner of goods has many rights – they have been described as 'a bundle or package of rights.' Mr Jeffreys contended that on a fair reading of the subsection it cannot have been the intention that every one of an owner's rights had to be assumed by the alleged thief before an appropriation was proved and that essential ingredient of the offence of theft established.

My Lords, if one reads the words 'the rights' at the opening of section 3(1) literally and in isolation from the rest of the section, Mr Denison's submission undoubtedly has force. But the later words 'any later assumption of a right' in subsection (1) and the words in subsection (2) 'no later assumption by him of rights' seem to me to militate strongly against the correctness of the submission. Moreover the provisions of section 2(1)(a) also seem to point in the same direction. It follows therefore that it is enough for the prosecution if they have proved in these cases the assumption by the respondents of *any* of the rights of the owner of the goods in question, that is to say, the supermarket concerned. . . .

NOTES AND QUESTIONS
1. Is *Morris* consistent with the words of the statute? When read together with *Gomez*, does it virtually eliminate the need for the Crown to prove wrongful conduct by the defendant or harm to the victim?
2. Should the courts distinguish between those rights of an owner that go to the essence of the nature of property (such as the right to sell the property) and those which are of less importance? In *Morris*, Lord Roskill opined that the practical joker who switched labels on supermarket products did not commit an appropriation, but Lord Keith in *DPP v Gomez*, while not disagreeing with the basic proposition that the assumption of *any* of the rights of an owner could amount to an appropriation, thought that the label-switcher would commit an appropriation. But so too would the ordinary shopper who puts goods in her trolley. The crucial point to bear in mind is that the latter is not guilty of theft because she has not acted dishonestly. One should never confuse one of the elements of a crime with the entire crime.

(v) *Must the property belong to another at the time of the appropriation?*
The usual concurrence rule requires that the *actus reus* and *mens rea* should coincide. This rule seems to require that the property should belong to another at the time of the appropriation. Indeed the House of Lords has so stated:

Lawrence v *Metropolitan Police Commissioner*
[1972] AC 626, House of Lords

LORD DONOVAN: . . . I now turn to the third element 'property belonging to another.' Mr Back QC, for the appellant, contended that if Mr Occhi consented to the appellant taking the £6, he consented to the property in the money passing from him to the appellant and that the appellant had not, therefore, appropriated property belonging to another. He argued that the old distinction between the offence of false pretences and larceny had been preserved. I am unable to agree with this. The new offence of obtaining property by deception created by section 15(1) of the Theft Act also contains the words 'belonging to another.' 'A person who by any deception dishonestly obtains property belonging to another, with the intention of permanently depriving the other of it' commits that offence. 'Belonging to another' in section 1(1) and in section 15(1) in my view signifies no more than that, at the time of the appropriation or the obtaining, the property belonged to another, with the words 'belonging to another' having the extended meaning given by section 5. The short answer to this contention on behalf of the appellant is that the money in the wallet which he appropriated belonged to another, to Mr Occhi.

NOTE
Both *Lawrence* and *Gomez* were cases where the defendant obtained property by trickery. In terms of contract law, the ownership of the property would pass to the defendant but the con-

tract would be voidable for fraud. The contract would be valid unless the victim subsequently took steps to avoid the sale. Seen in this light, it might seem that the defendants in *Lawrence* and *Gomez* appropriated their own property. It is precisely because of this conundrum that the Criminal Law Revision Committee recommended an offence of obtaining property by deception.

NOTES AND QUESTIONS
1. If the appropriation and the fact that the property must belong to another need no longer occur at the same point in time, is the same true for the dishonesty and the appropriation? Consider again Professor Smith's comment on *Gomez* (above, p. 350) and see *R v Coady* [1996] Crim LR 578 and the commentary following the case.
2. Carol obtains a ring from a jeweller's shop by giving the shop a forged note. John, the manager of the shop, discovers the forgery but decides to do nothing because he feels his reputation will suffer if it is known that he has been tricked. Is Carol, who now owns the ring, guilty of theft?
3. The Theft Act 1978, s. 3 created the offence of making off without payment.

(vi) *The bona fide purchaser*

The problem of the bona fide purchaser is specifically dealt with by s. 3(2) of the Theft Act 1968:

Theft Act 1968

3.—(2) Where property or a right or interest in property is or purports to be transferred for value to a person acting in good faith, no later assumption by him of rights which he believed himself to be acquiring shall, by reason of any defect in the transferor's title, amount to theft of the property.

NOTE

The effect of this section is that a person who pays for stolen goods is not guilty of theft if he or she was not aware of the stolen character of the goods at the time of purchase. Nor does the purchaser become a thief if he or she subsequently discovers that the goods were stolen. (Whether or not he or she can keep the goods if sued by the original owner is an altogether different question and is a matter for the civil law.) However, having discovered the true state of affairs, if the purchaser later re-sells the goods, claiming to have good title, he or she will be guilty of obtaining property by deception under the Theft Act 1968, s. 15.

B: Property

Section 4 of the 1968 Act excludes real property (land and rights to do with land) from the definition of property for the purposes of s. 1 of the Act unless the exceptions set out in the section are satisfied. Section 4 also makes clear that wild flowers are not property within s. 1 unless the defendant has a commercial purpose when picking them. Similarly, wild animals are not property unless another person has or is about to get possession.

Theft Act 1968

4.—(1) 'Property' includes money and all other property, real or personal, including things in action and other intangible property.

NOTES
1. 'Money' refers only to current coins and banknotes.
2. 'Real property' includes land and houses.
3. 'Personal property' includes all moveable things which can be owned.
4. 'Things in action' are rights of action which are protected by law but cannot be seen. Examples are copyrights, trade marks and contractual rights. The last includes the right to sue the bank which arises between a customer and his bank when a current bank account is in credit. But in *R* v *Preddy* [1996] AC 815, the House of Lords held that no property belonging to another had been obtained where payments by cheque or electronic transfer were induced by deception. This is because the civil action represented by the cheque or transfer did not pass from payer to payee. What happened was that a different right to sue arose as a result of the transfer and this 'thing in action' belonged to the person to whom the money was paid (in this case the defendants). So, if £10,000 is to be transferred, the situation before the transfer is that X (the payer) has a 'thing in action' worth £10,000. After the transaction transfer this 'thing in action' is reduced to nil. The payee before the transfer has no 'thing in action'; and afterwards he has a 'thing in action' worth £10,000 but there is *no* legal connection between the extinguishing of the payer's right of action and the birth of the payee's new right of action. Following this decision an amendment was made to the Theft Acts to catch such dishonestly induced transfers (see p. 382).
5. 'Other intangible property' includes patents which, by the Patents Act 1977, s. 30, are not things in action but are personal property. Information is not included:

Oxford v *Moss*
[1979] Crim LR 119, Queen's Bench Division

In 1976, M was an engineering student at Liverpool University. He acquired the proof of an examination paper for a Civil Engineering examination at the University: An information was preferred against him by O, alleging that he stole certain intangible property, i.e. confidential information, being property of the Senate of the University. It was agreed that he never intended to permanently deprive the owner of the piece of paper on which the questions were printed.

Held, by the stipendiary at Liverpool: on the facts of the case, confidential information is not a form of intangible property as opposed to property in the paper itself, and that confidence consisted in the right to control the publication of the proof paper and was a right over property other than a form of intangible property. The owner had not been permanently deprived of any intangible property. The charge was dismissed.

On appeal by the prosecutor, as to whether confidential information can amount to property within the meaning of section 4 of the Theft Act 1968.

Held: there was no property in the information capable of being the subject of a charge of theft, i.e. it was not intangible property within the meaning of section 4.

NOTES AND QUESTIONS
1. The court in *Oxford* v *Moss* was faced with a question to which the statute provided no clear answer. In certain circumstances confidential information is treated by the civil law as the property of a company (see *Island Export Finance* v *Umunna* [1986] BCLC 460 and *Industrial Developments* v *Cooley* [1972] 2 All ER 162). Further, the Patents Act 1977 treats an invention

for which no patent has been granted or applied for as intangible property. Allen, in his *Textbook of Criminal Law*, 5th ed (1999) p. 356, argues that this latter situation is analogous to that in *Oxford* v *Moss*.

2. It has also been argued that confidential information cannot be appropriated. (Griew, *The Theft Acts 1968 and 1978*, 6th ed.). Is this right? If not, what acts constitute the appropriation? See generally, R. Hammond, 'Theft of information' (1984) 100 LQR 252.

3. Export quotas were held by the Privy Council to be intangible property in *Attorney-General of Hong Kong* v *Nai-Keung* (1987) 86 Cr App R 174. In what way do they differ from the information in *Oxford* v *Moss*?

Electricity is also not included in the definition of property. The Theft Act 1968, s. 13 creates a specific offence to cover misuse of electricity.

A human corpse is also outside the definition of property for the purposes of s. 1:

R v Sharpe
(1857) Dears & B 160, Court of Criminal Appeal

The indictment in the first count charged that the defendant a certain burial ground belonging to a certain meeting house of a congregation of Protestants, dissenting from the Church of England, unlawfully and wilfully did break and enter; a certain grave there, in which the body of one Louisa Sharpe had before then been interred, with force and arms unlawfully, wilfully, and indecently did dig open, and the said body of the said Louisa Sharpe out of the same grave unlawfully, wilfully, and indecently did take and carry away.

ERLE J: We are of opinion that the conviction ought to be affirmed. The defendant was wrongfully in the burial ground, and wrongfully opened the grave, and took out several corpses, and carried away one. We say he did this wrongfully, that is to say, by trespass; for the licence which he obtained to enter and open, from the person who had the care of the place, was not given or intended for the purpose to which he applied it, and was, as to that purpose, no licence at all. Neither does our law recognise the right of any one child to the corpse of its parent as claimed by the defendant. Our law recognises no property in a corpse, and the protection of the grave at common law, as contradistinguished from ecclesiastical protection to consecrated ground, depends upon this form of indictment; and there is no authority for saying that relationship will justify the taking a corpse away from the grave where it has been buried.

NOTES AND QUESTIONS
1. In *R* v *Kelly, The Times*, 4 April 1998, (News Report) a sculptor was found guilty of theft by a jury for stealing a corpse. Rivlin J ruled that a corpse or parts thereof could be owned if subjected to some form of skill as in embalming or dissection. Would this case (now on appeal) reverse the result in *Sharpe*?
2. That fluids taken from a living body can be stolen was confirmed in *Rothery*:

R v Rothery
[1976] RTR 550, Court of Appeal

By s. 9(3) of the Road Traffic Act 1972, 'A person who, without reasonable excuse, fails to supply a specimen for a laboratory test in pursuance of a requirement imposed under this section shall be guilty of an offence.'

A motorist who has complied with the provisions of ss. 8 and 9 of the Road Traffic Act 1972 and provides a specimen of blood when requested to do so by a constable at a police station and later steals the police part specimen, though guilty of the theft, is not guilty of the statutory offence under s. 9(3) of the Act of 1972, for the theft was a subsequent and distinct event from the provision of the specimen.

(i) *Real property*

Theft Act 1968

4.—(2) A person cannot steal land, or things forming part of land and severed from it by him or by his directions, except in the following cases, that is to say—

(a) when he is a trustee or personal representative, or is authorised by power of attorney, or as liquidator of a company, or otherwise, to sell or dispose of land belonging to another, and he appropriates the land or anything forming part of it by dealing with it in breach of the confidence reposed in him; or

(b) when he is not in possession of the land and he appropriates anything forming part of the land by severing it or causing it to be severed, or after it has been severed; or

(c) when, being in possession of the land under a tenancy, he appropriates the whole or part of any fixture or structure let to be used with the land.

For purposes of this subsection 'land' does not include incorporeal hereditaments; 'tenancy' means a tenancy for years or any less period and includes an agreement for such a tenancy, but a person who after the end of a tenancy remains in possession under the tenancy, and 'let' shall be construed accordingly.

QUESTION

A distinction is made between property which is 'on' the land and property which 'forms part of the land'. The latter can be stolen only in the circumstances specified in s. 4(a), (b) and (c). What is the purpose of this distinction? Does the following case, interpreting a similar provision in the Larceny Act 1916, supply an answer?

Billing v *Pill*

[1954] 1 QB 70, Queen's Bench Division

An army hut, which was constructed in seven sections, rested on a concrete foundation, the floor of the hut being secured to the foundation by bolts let into the concrete. The hut was one of a number erected by the War Office during the war on land used as a gun emplacement. In 1946 the army vacated the huts, and in 1947 the local authority was instructed to demolish them. In 1951 the appellant, without lawful authority, dismantled the hut in question, removed it from the site and re-erected it on his own land. He was convicted by justices of stealing the hut. . . .

LORD GODDARD CJ: Can anybody doubt that the hut in question was erected for a temporary purpose? It can be removed without doing any damage to the freehold at all. It rests upon a concrete bed which is let into the land. I should say that there is no question but that the concrete bed has become part of the land, but the hut which stands upon it has not become part of the land merely because some bolts have been put through the floor of the hut to stabilise or steady it. It was erected merely for a temporary purpose so that the Army personnel who were going to the site for a presumed temporary purpose, to man a gun emplacement during the war, would have somewhere to sleep.

In my opinion, it would be quite wrong to hold that this hut was attached to or formed part of the realty. It was not so attached any more than if one takes a garden seat out into one's garden and, because the seat may be in an exposed position and liable to be blown over, one drives a spike through it to hold it to the ground. In one sense that is an attachment, but it is not an attachment sufficient to make it part of the realty. It is simply a spike put in to hold the chattel firm. In my opinion, this hut was a chattel, remained a chattel and is capable of larceny. . . .

NOTES AND QUESTIONS
1. The more difficult a 'thing' is to remove from the ground, the more likely it is that it will be regarded as 'land' or a 'thing forming part of the land'. Should the 'difficulty of removal' take into account the tools possessed by the would-be thief?
2. What would be the position of a telegraph pole? A coffin which had been buried?

Section 4 sets out the only three instances in which 'land' or 'things forming part of land' can be stolen. The following is a summary of the effects of that section:

(a) If the defendant is in a position of trust then, according to s. 4(2)(a), he can steal land (or things forming part of it) to which his position of trust relates.

(b) When the defendant is not in possession of land he can steal anything forming part of the land (but not the land itself) (s. 4(2)(b)).

(c) When the defendant is in possession of the land under a tenancy he can steal a fixture or structure (e.g. a bath or a greenhouse – if a greenhouse is a structure – it is not a fixture: *Dean* v *Andrews and another, The Times,* 25 May 1985).

None of the subsections specifically covers a person who has permission to be on the land but who has no lease. It is not clear whether such a person would be considered to be 'in possession' of the land. If he were, the curious situation would be that he would be in a better position than a person in possession of land under a tenancy.

Incorporeal hereditaments can be stolen. Examples would be rights of way and rent charges. These could be stolen by conveying the benefit of the right dishonestly. The occasions on which this type of theft will occur will be very rare.

'Tenancy' includes a statutory tenancy. A statutory tenancy arises most frequently when an ordinary lease comes to an end and yet the tenant remains in possession and continues to pay rent to the landlord.

(ii) *Mushrooms, flowers, etc.*

Theft Act 1968

4.—(3) A person who picks mushrooms growing wild on any land, or who picks flowers, fruit or foliage from a plant growing wild on any land, does not (although not in possession of the land) steal what he picks, unless he does it for reward or for sale or other commercial purpose.

For purposes of this subsection 'mushroom' includes any fungus, and 'plant' includes any shrub or tree.

NOTES AND QUESTIONS
1. What is the borderline between s. 4(2) and s. 4(3)? What is the difference between 'severance' of a plant growing wild and 'picking' part of that plant? If Jill cuts off a branch of an oak tree with a chain saw, is that picking or severance?
2. Taking a whole plant will probably be theft (if the *mens rea* is present). This will be the case because there was severance of a 'thing forming part of land' (s. 4(2)), and because the defendant's action could not be described as 'picking from' a plant within s. 4(3).
3. It will be theft if all other elements of s. 1 theft are present and the picking is done 'for sale or other commercial purpose'. When must the commercial purpose be formed? If Dora picks blackberries growing wild and later decides to make jam to sell at the local church bazaar, will this be theft?

(iii) *Wild creatures*

Theft Act 1968

4.—(4) Wild creatures, tamed or untamed, shall be regarded as property; but a person cannot steal a wild creature not tamed nor ordinarily kept in captivity, or the carcase of any such creature, unless either it has been reduced into possession by or on behalf of another person and possession of it has not since been lost or abandoned, or another person is in course of reducing it into possession.

NOTE
'Wild' refers to the way of life of the creature rather than its disposition:

R v *Howlett*
[1968] Crim LR 222, Court of Appeal

H was convicted of stealing, in 1965, mussels from a mussel bed on the foreshore. The foreshore was alleged to belong to S who had granted to L the exclusive right of taking shellfish from it. L had tended the bed in order to try to preserve and improve it but it remained subject to the action of the sea. H appealed on the grounds, *inter alia*, that the mussels were not capable of being stolen since they adhered to the realty, alternatively they were animals *ferae naturae* and not capable of being stolen until reduced into possession.

Held, allowing the appeal, it was not necessary to decide the first question because there was not sufficient evidence that the mussels had been reduced into possession. The most that could be said to have been done was that the bed was tended with a view to improving the growth and edible qualities of the mussels until they were removed from the bed. The mere act of raking over an existing natural bed, and occasionally moving some mussels from a place where they were growing too thickly to a place where they were growing too thinly, and where they would again come to rest and adhere to the soil, did not amount to the reduction into possession of the mussels, particularly since in 1966 the majority of the mussels had disappeared as the result of the action of the sea.

NOTES AND QUESTIONS
1. Although *Howlett* was a decision under the Larceny Act 1916, there seems to be no reason why the position should be any different under the 1968 Act. Thus a wild creature can only be stolen if:

(a) it is tamed or ordinarily kept in captivity;

(b) it is in the course of being reduced into another's possession or has been reduced into and remains in another's possession.

2. Land and wild creatures not reduced into possession are outside the law of theft under s. 1 but can theoretically be obtained by deception under s. 15 of the Theft Act 1968. Following *Gomez*, this is one of the few areas where the two offences do not overlap.

3. If Emma shot a pheasant and her gun dog is on its way to fetch it, can it be stolen from her? At what point in time has it been reduced into possession?

C: Belonging to another

Section 5 of the 1968 Act expands the scope of theft to protect not only those who own property, but also those who possess or control property. For the purposes of the Theft Act 1968, property 'belongs to another' when that other person has ownership, or possession or control. Section 5(3) extends the concept of property to cover the situation where, although ownership of the property has passed to the defendant, the defendant is under an obligation to deal with that property in a particular way. Section 5(4) also extends the notion of property belonging to another to the situation where the defendant has received the relevant item only because of a mistake made by another person. Where the defendant is under an obligation to return the property, the law regards ownership as being retained by the person making the mistake.

Theft Act 1968

5.—(1) Property shall be regarded as belonging to any person having possession or control of it, or having in it any proprietary right or interest (not being an equitable interest arising only from an agreement to transfer or grant an interest).

NOTES AND QUESTIONS

Equitable interests arising from an agreement to transfer or grant an interest will arise in at least two situations. Where there is a contract to sell land or to sell shares, the transaction is in two stages. The conclusion of an agreement to sell gives the buyer a right to have the sale completed. This right is the equitable right referred to in s. 5(1). It is excluded from the rights protected by the Theft Act 1968. Why should this be so? Should the criminal law, for the sake of consistency if nothing else, incorporate the rules of the civil law?

Several issues arise under the provision of the statute:

(i) *What is a proprietary right or interest?*

Subject to the implications of *Gomez* (above), the property appropriated must belong to another at the time of appropriation. The term 'belong to another' is not restricted to the owner of the property, but includes those in rightful possession or control of the property.

An owner of land owns the things on the land if he intends to exclude trespassers from the land.

R v Woodman
[1974] QB 754, Court of Appeal

The defendant was charged with the theft of scrap metal remnants from a disused factory site. The occupier of the site had no knowledge of the existence of the scrap, although a barbed-wire fence had been erected around the site to exclude trespassers. The defendant submitted that there was no case to answer on the ground that the scrap did not belong to another within the meaning of s. 5(1) of the Theft Act 1968. The recorder allowed the case to go to the jury on the question whether the occupier was in control of the scrap, and the defendant was convicted.

On appeal against conviction:—

Held, dismissing the appeal, that a person in control of a site, by excluding others from it, was prima facie also in control of articles on that site within the meaning of s. 5(1) of the Theft Act 1968, it being immaterial that he was unconcious [sic] of their existence; and accordingly the case had been rightly allowed to go to the jury.

Per curiam. If articles of serious criminal consequence, such as explosives or drugs, were placed within the barbed-wire fence by some third person in circumstances in which the occupier had no means of knowledge, it might produce a different result from that which arose under the general presumption. . . .

NOTES AND QUESTIONS
1. Why does the court say that the victim's awareness of the existence of the items taken is irrelevant? Abandoned property belongs to nobody and cannot be the subject of theft. Was the property taken in *Woodman* abandoned?
2. The courts have held that property is not abandoned if it is put in a dustbin for the council to collect. See *Williams* v *Phillips* (1957) 41 Cr App R 5. Only if the owner becomes indifferent as to the fate of the property is it deemed to be abandoned.
3. Why did the court adopt one test for the objects in *Woodman* and suggest the possibility of another test for objects of 'serious consequence'? What should the test be in the latter case?

Property can 'belong' to more than one person. In the case of a partnership each partner has an interest in the partnership property and can steal it from the other partners:

R v Bonner
[1970] 1 WLR 838, Court of Appeal

EDMUND DAVIES LJ: The facts which gave rise to this complicated trial were that on May 16, 1969, Bonner and the other three appellants called at the house of a Mr Webb. Putting it quite neutrally for the moment, Bonner and Webb were business associates. The defence was, in fact, that they were partners and, therefore, co-owners of all the property with which the trial was concerned. Having called with a van at Webb's house in the afternoon at a time when Webb was out, they broke the lock of a garage and splintered the door and, having gained access that way, they loaded some metal from inside the garage on to the van and Anthony Town and Michael Town claimed that they were moving it for Bonner, who they thought had a right to do what he had asked them to do. Bonner's defence was that he honestly thought he had a right to take the lead as it was partnership property owned by himself and Webb, and, in any event, he did not intend to deprive Webb of it permanently.

Webb's case at first was that there was no partnership at all, and then that it was not what he called 'a true partnership'. During his evidence he specifically denied that he had ever applied for registration in the Business Names Register of himself and Bonner as partners. But this court has been furnished with a document, which unhappily was not before the lower court. It is a certified copy of an application made on March 8, 1966, for registration by a firm, and the business name is 'J. Webb, Excavation & Demolition Co.,' the partners are described as 'Joseph Webb' and 'George Andrew Bonner,' and it was signed by each of them.

I said a little earlier that the object of the Theft Act, 1968, was to get rid of the subtleties and, indeed, in many cases the absurd anomalies of the pre-existing law. The view of this court is that in relation to partnership property the provisions in the Theft Act, 1968, have the following result: provided there is the basic ingredient of dishonesty, provided there be no question of there being a claim of right made in good faith, provided there be an intent permanently to deprive, one partner can commit theft of partnership property just as much as one person can commit the theft of the property of another to whom he is a complete stranger.

Early though these days are, this matter has not gone without comment by learned writers. Professor Smith in his valuable work on the Theft Act, 1968, expresses his own view quite clearly in paragraph 80 under the heading 'Co-owners and partners' in this way:

> D and P are co-owners of a car. D sells the car without P's consent. Since P has a proprietary right in the car, it belongs to him under s. 5(1). The position is precisely the same where a partner appropriates the partnership property.

In the joint work of Professor Smith and Professor Hogan, the matter is thus dealt with (*Smith and Hogan's 'Criminal Law'*, 2nd ed. (1969), p. 361):

> . . . D and P . . . may . . . be joint owners of property. Obviously, there is no reason in principle why D should not be treated as a thief if he dishonestly appropriate's P's share, and he is so treated under the Theft Act.

We thus have no doubt that there may be an 'appropriation' by a partner within the meaning of the Act, and that in a proper case there is nothing in law to prevent his being convicted of the theft of partnership property.

(ii) *Theft of the defendant's own property by the defendant*

This may occur where another person has a right to possess or control the property which the owner violates. A typical case might involve a lease or bailment. Gerald rents his car to Neil for a week. Mid-week he finds himself in desperate need of an automobile and, using his spare key to the car, takes it without asking Neil's permission. Gerald in fact is guilty of stealing his own car. The situation where a second individual has an interest in an owner's property such that the owner can commit theft of his own property can arise in other situations as well:

R v *Turner (No. 2)*
[1971] 1 WLR 901, Court of Appeal

> The defendant took the car of which he was the registered owner to a garage to have it repaired. Those repairs having been practically completed, the car was left in the road outside the garage. The defendant called at the garage and told the proprietor that he would return the following day, pay him and take the car: instead, he took the car away several hours later without paying for the repairs.
>
> He was charged on indictment with theft of the car contrary to s. 1 of the Theft Act 1968. The defendant submitted that the car did not 'belong' to the proprietor

within the meaning of s. 5(1) of the Theft Act 1968 and that the appropriation was not dishonest within the meaning of s. 2(1)(a) of the Act.

LORD PARKER CJ: This court is quite satisfied that there is no ground whatever for qualifying the words 'possession or control' in any way. It is sufficient if it is found that the person from whom the property is taken, or to use the words of the Act, appropriated, was at the time in fact in possession or control. At the trial there was a long argument as to whether that possession or control must be lawful, it being said that by reason of the fact that this car was subject to a hire purchase agreement, Mr Brown could never even as against the defendant obtain lawful possession or control. As I have said, this court is quite satisfied that the judge was quite correct in telling the jury they need not bother about lien, and that they need not bother about hire purchase agreements. The only question was whether Mr Brown was in fact in possession or control.

NOTES AND QUESTIONS

1. In *Turner* the garage almost certainly had a better right to possession of the car than the owner at the time it was taken by him. This is because the garage would have had a repairer's lien on the car – a right to keep the car until the bill was paid. However, the judge told the jury that they were not concerned with liens and the Court of Appeal upheld this direction. What if the bill for repairs was greater than originally agreed by the parties, the owner had paid the amount originally agreed and then taken the car – would this be theft?
2. Suppose a book is stolen from Mary, who later finds it among the possessions of the thief. If Mary believes it is against the law to take the book back, is she guilty of theft if she takes it?
3. Can a mother steal property belonging to her son of three months? Thirteen years? Can a wife steal her husband's property? (See the Theft Act 1968, s. 30.)

(iii) *Where the defendant gets ownership by fraud*

The House of Lords in *Gomez* established that where property is obtained with the consent of the owner but that consent is induced by fraud, the defendant can be convicted of theft. The implications of the case have been examined previously (see above p. 346).

(iv) *To whom does trust property belong?*

Theft Act 1968

5.—(1) Property shall be regarded as belonging to any person having possession or control of it, or having in it any proprietary right or interest (not being an equitable interest arising only from an agreement to transfer or grant an interest).

There is doubt about the ambit of this section in relation to 'constructive trusts'. An ordinary trust is set up when persons are appointed as trustees to look after property on behalf of others. Both the trustees and the beneficiaries have interests in the property that are defined by law. A constructive trust occurs when a court believes that the imposition of a trust-like framework will do justice in particular circumstances. The court will impose such a trust where, for example, a company director joins with others in the misuse of company property (*Selangor United Rubber Estates Ltd* v *Cradock (No. 3)* [1968] 1 WLR 1555. In *Attorney-General's Reference (No. 1 of 1985)* [1986] QB 491, the court excluded interests arising under constructive trusts from the ambit of the Theft Act. However, the seemingly opposite conclusion was reached in *Shadrokh-Cigari*, a decision which also has implications for the interpretation of s. 5(4) (see below).

R v Shadrokh-Cigari
[1988] Crim LR 465, Court of Appeal

The appellant was convicted of four counts of theft. He acted as guardian to his nephew whose father in Iran arranged for money to be paid to the child's bank account from the USA. Through an error by the United States bank $286,000 was credited to the account instead of $286. At the appellant's suggestion the child signed an authority for the issue of four banker's drafts drawn in favour of the appellant for sums of £51,300, £64,000, £53,000 and £29,000. The appellant paid two into his own bank account and used the others to open other accounts to his name. By the time of his arrest some three weeks later only £21,000 remained. He appealed against conviction on the ground that the judge should have directed the jury that they had to be satisfied that the drafts belonged to the Bank and that had he done so the jury would have been bound to have concluded that the drafts did not belong to the bank but were the property of the appellant and so there was no question of him appropriating property belonging to another.

Held, dismissing the appeal, the submission erred in assuming that the entire proprietary interest in the drafts existed and vested in the appellant leaving the bank with no rights at all. The mistake of the United States bank totally undermined the basic assumption upon which the English bank issued the drafts, namely that the funds which had been received could properly be dealt with as directed by the account holder. As between the English bank and the appellant, the transaction fell fairly and squarely within the principles of the law relating to the mistake – *Kelly* v *Solari* [1941] 9 M & W 547. The mistake must be fundamental or basic, one in respect of the underlying assumption of the contract or transaction – *Norwich Union* v *Price* [1934] AC 455. That was so here. If the mistake must be one of fact rather than law, that condition was satisfied in the present case. Thus the appellant was under an obligation to make restoration of the instruments on the basis that the English bank retained an equitable proprietary interest in the drafts as a result of the mistake. The fact that the choses in action created by the drafts could not be owned by the bank, since they were debts due from the bank was irrelevant. The bank created the drafts and before delivery they owned them, although as promissory notes they were inchoate and incomplete. Upon delivery under the mistake, the bank retained an equitable interest in those instruments. Such an equitable interest amounted to property within s. 5(1) of the Theft Act 1968. That conclusion was not only supported by s. 5(4) of the 1968 Act, but could be reached by another route through the application of that subsection. Even if it could not be said that the property belonged to another in the sense of that other having proprietary rights over the property itself, nevertheless (other things being equal) the property was to be regarded for the purposes of theft as belonging to that other even if the person getting it was only under an obligation to restore the proceeds of the property or its value as opposed to the property itself. The appellant was obliged to restore the proceeds or value of the instruments.

NOTES AND QUESTIONS
1. In *Shadrokh-Cigari* the court held that an equitable proprietary interest arising from the imposition of a constructive trust *did* amount to property within s. 5(1). As we shall see, where there is an obligation to make restoration of property obtained because of a mistake, s. 5(4) creates fictional ownership in the original owner for the purpose of the statute. In the light of s. 5(4), why was it necessary for the court to decide on an extended meaning of s. 5(1)?
2. In the light of *Gomez*, is an extended definition of either s. 5(1) or s. 5(4) necessary at all?

Theft Act 1968

5.—(2) Where property is subject to a trust, the persons to whom it belongs shall be regarded as including any person having a right to enforce the trust, and an intention to defeat the trust shall be regarded accordingly as an intention to deprive of the property any person having that right.

Any beneficiary of a trust has a right to enforce the trust. A charitable trust, which may or may ot have particular individuals as beneficiaries, is enforceable by the Attorney-General so that property which is the subject to such a trust would be regarded as belonging to him. Any non-charitable trust without human beneficiaries would be regarded as belonging to the person entitled to the residue. This subsection makes it impossible for anyone dishonestly taking trust funds to argue that the funds belonged to no one.

(v) *When does an obligation arise to retain and deal with another's property?*

Theft Act 1968

5.—(3) Where a person receives property from or on account of another, and is under an obligation to the other to retain and deal with that property or its proceeds in a particular way, the property or proceeds shall be regarded (as against him) as belonging to the other.

When does an obligation envisaged by the section arise, and to what property does it attach?

R v Hall
[1973] 1 QB 126, Court of Appeal

The defendant, who carried on the business of a travel agent, received money as deposits and payments for air trips to America. No flights were provided for the defendant's clients and no money was refunded. He was charged with seven counts of theft, contrary to s. 1 of the Theft Act 1968. The defendant claimed that the money received had become his property which he had applied in the conduct of the firm's business and that he had not been guilty of theft merely because the firm had failed and no money remained. He was convicted.

The defendant appealed on the ground, *inter alia*, that the moneys belonged to him and not to his clients as he was under no obligation, under s. 5(3) of the Theft Act 1968, to retain and deal with the money or its proceedings in a particular way.

EDMUND DAVIES LJ: Point (1) turns on the application of s. 5(3) of the Theft Act 1968, which provides that:

Where a person receives property from or on account of another, and is under an obligation to the other to retain and deal with that property or its proceeds in a particular way, the property or proceeds shall be regarded (as against him) as belonging to the other.

Mr Jolly submitted that in the circumstances arising in [previous] cases there arose no such 'obligation' upon the defendant. He referred us to a passage in the eighth report the Criminal Law Revision Committee (1966) (Cmnd. 2977), at p. 127, which reads:

> Subsection (3) provides for the special case where property is transferred to a person to retain and deal with for a particular person and he misapplies it or its proceeds. An example would be the treasurer of a holiday fund. The person in question is in law the owner of the property; but the subsection treats the property, as against him, as belonging to the persons to whom he owes the duty to retain and deal with the property as agreed. He will therefore be guilty of stealing from them if he misapplies the property or its proceeds.

Mr Jolly submitted that the example there given is, for all practical purposes, identical with the actual facts in *R v Pulham* (unreported) June 15, 1971, where, incidentally, s. 5(3) was not discussed, the convictions there being quashed, as we have already indicated, owing to the lack of a proper direction as to the accused's state of mind at the time he appropriated. But he submits that the position of a treasurer of a solitary fund is quite different from that of a person like the defendant, who was in general, and genuine, business as a travel agent, and to whom people pay money in order to achieve a certain object – in the present cases, to obtain charter flights to America. It is true, he concedes, that thereby the travel agent undertakes a contractual obligation in relation to arranging flights and at the proper time paying the air line and any other expenses. Indeed, the defendant throughout acknowledged that this was so, though contending that in some of the seven cases it was the other party who was in breach. But what Mr Jolly resists is that in such circumstances the travel agent 'is under an obligation' to the client 'to retain and deal with . . . in a particular way' sums paid to him in such circumstances.

What cannot of itself be decisive of the matter is the fact that the defendant paid the money into the firm's general trading account. As Widgery J said in *R v Yule* [1964] 1 QB 5, decided under s. 20(1)(iv) of the Larceny Act 1916, at p. 10:

> The fact that a particular sum is paid into a particular banking account . . . does not affect the right of persons interested in that sum or any duty of the solicitor either towards his client or towards third parties with regard to disposal of that sum.

Nevertheless, when a client goes to a firm carrying on the business of travel agents and pays them money, he expects that in return he will, in due course, receive the tickets and other documents necessary for him to accomplish the trip for which he is paying, and the firm are 'under an obligation' to perform their part to fulfil his expectation and are liable to pay him damages if they do not. But, in our judgment, what was not here established was that these clients expected them 'to retain and deal with that property or its proceeds in a particular way,' and that an 'obligation' to do this was undertaken by the defendant.

We must make clear, however, that each case turns on its own facts. Cases could, we suppose, conceivably arise where by some special arrangement (preferably evidenced by documents), the client could impose upon the travel agent an 'obligation' falling within s. 5(3). But no such special arrangement was made in any of the seven cases here being considered. It is true that in some of them documents were signed by the parties; thus, in respect of the counts 1 and 3 incidents there was a clause to the effect that the 'People to People' organisation did not guarantee to refund deposits if withdrawals were made later than a certain date; and in respect of counts 6, 7 and 8 the defendant wrote promising 'a full refund' after the flights paid for failed to materialise. But neither in those nor in the remaining two cases (in relation to which there was no documentary evidence of any kind) was there, in our judgment, such a special arrangement as would give rise to an 'obligation' within s. 5(3).

It follows from this that, despite what on any view must be condemned as scandalous conduct by the defendant, in our judgment upon this ground alone this appeal must be allowed and the conviction quashed.

R v Hayes

(1977) 64 Cr App Rep 82, Court of Appeal

The appellant started trading with another man as estate agents. He received money from clients as deposits on account of sales or purchase of houses. He was charged, *inter alia*, on 11 counts alleging theft contrary to s. 1 of the Theft Act 1968. In summing-up the judge, *inter alia*, failed to invite the jury to consider whether there was an obligation on the appellant to deal with the clients' money within s. 5(3) of the Act of 1968; nor did he direct them that there was an obligation on the prosecution to prove that at the time when the misappropriation took place there was already an intention to be dishonest. The appellant was convicted, *inter alia*, of theft.

. . .

THE LORD CHIEF JUSTICE: The case really revolved around s. 5(3) because, as will be understood from the brief extracts I have already given of the facts, the real issue which arose between the prosecution and the defence was whether the appellant was appropriating and therefore stealing property of another which would amount to an offence under the Theft Act 1968, or whether the true position was that he was apparently appropriating or stealing money which had become his because it had become his property according to this argument when the payment was made.

The circumstances which gave rise to count 1 form a useful illustration of the working of those principles. In the transaction on October 23, 1970 the appellant through Blake gave a receipt to a Mr Newman for £300, which was described as being a deposit and part-payment of a dwelling house at Sheppart Street, Stoke, the purchase price being £600. That money was paid over in cash. It was not paid into the bank, the bank at that time having only a credit balance of £13 in it. It was entered in a book kept by the appellant which was intended to disclose cash in hand, and it was entered in that book at a time in October 1970 when, according to the book, there was cash in hand to the tune of £6,480. The prosecution sought, not without some success, to show that this record of cash in hand was itself bogus and that the money referred to as being in hand never was in hand. But conclusions of that sort were not necessarily obtained on the directions which were given to the jury in this case, and I cite those facts merely to disclose the oddities of the transaction upon which count 1 is based, the other counts being based on similar oddities.

It is important, we think, to compare the situation in *Hall* [1973] 1 QB 126 with the situation in our present case. In *Hall* (*supra*) the argument on the one side was that the ticket agent receiving the money for the tickets was obliged to use that money in a particular way and to go and buy tickets with it. On the other side it was argued that he was not bound to use the particular money in a particular way. All that happened on his receiving the money was that he incurred a civil responsibility to carry out his side of the bargain. Edmund Davies LJ is taking the point there that in the absence of some special term in the contract the second view is the right one.

Convictions quashed.

NOTE

In *R v Klineberg and Marsden* [1999] Crim LR 417 the Court of Appeal held that s. 5(3) would be effective in a situation where purchasers of timeshares had paid money on the basis that it would be held by a stakeholding trust company until the apartments were ready to be occupied. Only £233 of the £500,000 paid by the intending purchasers was transmitted to the trust company. The money was deemed to 'belong to the purchasers' because of s. 5(3).

Davidge v *Bunnett*

[1984] Crim LR 297, Queen's Bench Division

In July 1982 D shared a flat with two other young women, C and McF. In September 1982 they were joined by H. There was an oral agreement to share the costs of gas, electricity and telephone. The gas account was in C's name. In October 1982 C received a gas bill for £159.75. D, C and McF each agreed to pay £50, and H the balance of £9.75. D did not have a bank account. The others all did, and gave D cheques in the appropriate sums, made payable to P, D's employer. They thought that D would either encash the cheques with P, add her own £50 and pay the gas bill, or that P would write out a cheque for the Gas Board on receipt of funds totalling £159.75. They did not expect D to apply any actual banknotes received from P to the discharge of the bill. On November 18, 1982, £59.75 was paid to the Gas Board. The balance of £100 was carried over to the next account in December. In January 1983 C received a final demand. C asked D to look into the matter, to which D agreed. D then left the flat without giving notice or leaving a forwarding address. C and McF later discovered that their cheques for £50 had been cashed on November 1, 1982. When interviewed by the police, D admitted 'I spent the £100 on Christmas presents but intended to pay it back.' The magistrates convicted D of theft, finding that D was under a legal obligation to apply the proceeds of C and McF's cheques to the payment of the gas bill. They also found that the proceeds of the cheques were property belonging to another within the meaning of the Theft Act 1968, and that there was evidence of an appropriation of two sums of £50, notwithstanding the payment of £59.75.

Held, dismissing the appeal, that the position was simple. D was under an obligation to use the cheques or their proceeds in whatever way she saw fit to long as they were applied *pro tanto* to the discharge of the gas bill. This could have been achieved by one cheque from her employer, or a banker's draft, or her own cheque had so opened her own bank account, or by endorsing the other cheques. Hence the magistrates' finding that she was not obliged to use the actual banknotes. Using the proceeds of the cheques on presents amounted to a very negation of her obligation to discharge the bill. She was under an obligation to deal with the proceeds in a particular way. As against D, the proceeds of the cheques were property belonging to another within s. 5(3) of the Act.

R v *Wain*

[1995] 2 Cr App R 660, Court of Appeal

McCOWAN LJ: On January 9, 1992 in the Crown Court at York, before His Honour Judge Herrod QC, the appellant was convicted of theft and sentenced to six months' imprisonment. He appeals against that conviction, as of right, the trial judge having granted a certificate of fitness for appeal on the day of the conviction. The judge also granted the appellant bail on the same date.

It was the case for the Crown that the appellant had stolen £2,833.25 which he had helped to raise for charity over a nine month period in 1990/1991. The Yorkshire Television Company is the guiding hand behind a trust called 'The Telethon Trust'. This raises monies for various charities and distributes them amongst those it considers most deserving. The monies are raised by way of a bi-annual appeal, during which various people organise events and onlookers make donations to charity, which are collected by the organiser. The matter is well-publicised and selected events are screened on Yorkshire Television.

Each organiser running an event is required to complete a registration form and return it to the television company. Once the form is returned Telethon Trust, according to their usual practice, send out a whole package of documents which provide help in organising events, a recommendation that the money be paid into a separate bank account and information on where to obtain collecting boxes, balloons and such like. In this case the appellant said that he had never received such a package from Telethon Trust, but nonetheless he did in fact open a separate bank account in the name of the Scarborough Telethon Appeal.

The appellant organised a number of successful events on Whit Monday 1990, including two discotheques. The amount raised was £2,833.25. He was invited along to Yorkshire Television Headquarters where he presented a dummy cheque to a television celebrity. The monies remained in the bank account that he had opened until September 5, 1990.

In the meantime, the Deputy Chief Executive of Yorkshire Television contacted him requesting the monies which he had raised for Telethon. The appellant told him that the monies were still outstanding, and some of them, at any rate, had not yet been paid.

On September 5 one of the company representatives, Miss Wills, visited the appellant with a view to collecting the money on the spot. The appellant, on this occasion, had a different story. He told her that he was unable to hand over a cheque without some second signatory. He did, however, get authority from Miss Wills to transfer the money into his own account, which he did that day. That meant he was able to, and did, hand over to her a cheque drawn on his own business account. That seemed all right, but in fact the cheque was not honoured due to insufficient funds in his account.

He continued to make excuses on a number of occasions thereafter, even stating that he had broken his arms and was unable to sign cheques. He sent four cheques in all, none of which were honoured. In a period of about six days, following the transfer of the money into his own account, the appellant withdrew about £640 in cash (something which, the prosecution pointed out, he had never done before). He must have known, they said, that that cash was coming from the monies he had paid in, monies which belonged to The Telethon Trust.

The appellant was eventually arrested on February 21, 1991 and charged with the theft of the sum of £2,833.25. . . .

It seems to us that the approach of the court in *Lethbridge* [1987] Crim LR 59 was a very narrow one based, apparently, on the finding by the justices that there was no requirement of the charity that the appellant hand over the same notes and coins. Neither was there in the present case. But what the Divisional Court does not appear to have considered in that case was the trust aspect. It was either not argued or the court felt, for some reason, that it could not be considered because of that finding of the justices. We are, unable to agree with them about that. In our judgment, the criticisms of that case by Professor Smith are fully justified.

As we have already indicated, we feel that in deciding, as they did in the *Lethbridge* case, the Divisional Court was not following the decision in *Davidge* v *Bunnett*. In our judgment, those decisions conflict and we prefer the decision in *Davidge* v *Bunnett*. There the obligation on the defendant was 'to keep in existence a fund sufficient to pay the bill'. So also in the *Lethbridge* case, and so also in the present case.

Leaving aside all authorities, it seems to us that by virtue of section 5(3), the appellant was plainly under an obligation to retain, if not the actual notes and coins, at least their proceeds, that is to say the money credited in the bank account which he opened for the trust with the actual property. When he took the money credited to that account and moved it over to his own bank account, it was still the proceeds of the notes and coins donated which he proceeded to use for his own purposes, thereby appropriating them. There remained the question of dishonesty which Judge Herrod properly left to the jury.

We would add this. Whether a person in the position of the appellant is a trustee is to be judged on an objective basis. It is an obligation imposed on him by law. It is not essential that he should have realised that he was a trustee, but of course the question remains as to whether he was acting honestly or dishonestly in using the money for his own purposes. That is a matter of fact for the jury.

. . .

QUESTIONS

1. Do the above cases turn on the obligation of the holder of the funds or the expectations of those whose moneys comprise the funds? Must the obligation attach to particular property?

2. Will s. 5(3) be of use only where the relationship between the victim and the defendant is contractual? See *R* v *Hallam and Blackburn* [1995] Crim LR 323. In civil law a defendant's liability will turn on the obligations of a person in a fiduciary position. At what point does a matter of family trust become a legal obligation? See *Attorney-General for Hong Kong* v *Reid* [1994] 1 AC 324. Should the criminal law embrace a similar approach?

3. Will the obligation in s. 5(3) arise only when a contractual relationship obliges the defendant to keep in existence a fund sufficient to fulfil the purpose for which the money was given within a reasonable time?

4. Carla is given money by Abdul, her uncle. He tells her that the money is to pay for pet food for his dog. As she leaves to go shopping, the window cleaner arrives, demanding payment, so she uses the money to pay him. Has Carla committed theft? Would it make a difference if the window cleaner was Carla's lover and the money was later used to buy Carla a present?

Must the 'obligation' be legally enforceable?

R v *Mainwaring*
(1982) 74 Cr App R 99, Court of Appeal

LAWTON LJ: The prosecution case was that when Mainwaring and Madders received money from prospective purchasers they did so knowing that it was in part payment of villas purchased from Frenchmen or Spaniards, that they were under an obligation to hand that money over to the developers in France or Spain, as the case might be, and that it would have been, and in fact was, dishonest of them to appropriate the money there and then for their own purposes.

. . .

Clearly there was some confusion in the mind of the learned judge about the operation of s. 5(3) of the Theft Act 1968.

We think that it may help judges if we make this comment about that section of the Act. Whether or not an obligation arises is a matter of law, because an obligation must be a legal obligation. But a legal obligation arises only in certain circumstances, and in many cases the circumstances cannot be known until the facts have been established. It is for the jury, not the judge, to establish the facts, if they are in dispute.

What, in our judgment, a judge ought to do is this: if the facts relied upon by the prosecution are in dispute he should direct the jury to make their findings on the facts, and then say to them: 'If you find the facts to be such-and-such, then I direct you as a matter of law that a legal obligation arose to which s. 5(3) applies.'

R v *Meech*
[1974] QB 549, Court of Appeal

ROSKILL LJ: . . . A man named McCord had obtained a cheque for £1,450 from a hire-purchase finance company by means of a forged instrument. The cheque itself was a perfectly valid document. McCord, who was an undischarged bankrupt, feared that were he to cash this cheque himself his crime would be more likely to be discovered than if he persuaded a friend to cash it for him. McCord, therefore, asked Meech (to whom McCord owed £40) to cash the cheque for him and Meech agreed so to do. At the time he agreed so to do Meech was wholly unaware of the dishonest means whereby McCord had become possessed of the cheque. Meech paid the cheque into his own account at a branch of Lloyds Bank Ltd. at High Wycombe on September 11, 1972. The bank was seemingly unwilling to allow him to cash the cheque until it had been cleared. On September 13, 1972, Meech drew his own cheque for £1,410 on his own account at that branch and that cheque was duly cashed by the bank on that day. The difference between the two sums was represented by McCord's £40 debt to Meech. By the time this cheque was cashed, the original cheque had been cleared. Between the paying in of the original cheque on September 11 and the obtaining of the cash on September 13, Meech became aware that McCord had acquired the original cheque dishonestly.

We were told by counsel that Meech, following legal argument at the end of the evidence, was allowed by the judge to be re-called. Meech then told the jury that not only did he find out about McCord's dishonesty but that he then honestly believed that if he cashed the cheque he would commit an offence. In view of the direction given by the judge to which we refer later, we think it clear that the jury must be taken to have rejected this story of honest belief on Meech's part.

Before the cheque was cashed but after Meech discovered its dishonest origin, Meech agreed with Parslow and Jolliffe that after the cheque was cashed Meech would take the money to a prearranged destination. The two other men were to join him there. A fake robbery, with Meech as the victim, was to be staged and indeed was staged, the purpose clearly being to provide some explanation to McCord of Meech's inability to hand over the money to McCord.

This was done; Parslow and Jolliffe between them removed the money after leaving Meech as the apparent victim. The bogus robbery was reported to the police, who being less credulous than the three men imagined McCord might be, investigated the matter and soon became convinced that the robbery story was bogus, as indeed it was soon shown to be. It is clear that Meech was influenced by the thought that even if the bogus nature of the robbery were suspected by McCord, McCord would never dare to go to the police and complain for that would involve revealing his own dishonesty.

Counsel for all the defendants relied strongly on the series of recent decisions that 'obligation' means 'legal obligation'. The judge so directed the jury. In giving this direction he no doubt had in mind the successive decisions of this court in *R v Hall* [1973] QB 126; *R v Gilks* [1972] 1 WLR 1341 and *R v Pearce* (unreported), November 21, 1972 (both the court and counsel were supplied with copies of the judgment). Reliance was also placed on paragraph 76 of Professor Smith's *The Law of Theft*, 2nd ed. (1972) – a passage written just before the decisions referred to. Since the judge so directed the jury, we do not find it necessary further to consider those decisions beyond observing that the facts of those cases were vastly different from those of the present case.

Starting from this premise – that 'obligation' means 'legal obligation' – it was argued that even at the time when Meech was ignorant of the dishonest origin of the cheque, as he was at the time when he agreed to cash the cheque and hand the proceeds less the £40 to McCord, McCord could never have enforced that obligation because McCord had acquired the cheque illegally. In our view this submission is unsound in principle. The question has to be looked at from Meech's point of view, not McCord's.

Meech plainly assumed an 'obligation' to McCord which, on the facts then known to him, he remained obliged to fulfil and, on the facts as found, he must be taken at that time honestly to have intended to fulfil. The fact that on the true facts if known McCord might not and indeed would not subsequently have been permitted to enforce that obligation in a civil court does not prevent that 'obligation' on Meech having arisen. The argument confuses the creation of the obligation with the subsequent discharge of that obligation either by performance or otherwise. That the obligation might have become impossible of performance by Meech or of enforcement by McCord on grounds of illegality or for reasons of public policy is irrelevant. The opening words of s. 5(3) clearly look to the time of the creation of or the acceptance of the obligation by the bailee and not to the time of performance by him of the obligation so created and accepted by him.

NOTES AND QUESTIONS

1. Lord Roskill's judgment in *Meech* looks not at whether the obligation was legally enforceable, but at whether the defendant believed the obligation to be enforceable. In fact no legally enforceable obligation ever arose between Meech and McCord. It seems strange that if the defendant believes such an obligation to exist, this should cause s. 5(3) to operate. The subsection refers to a situation where the defendant *is* 'under an obligation', not where he believes himself to be so.

   A possible way out of the difficulty would be to hold that a legal obligation did arise but it was not such a one as could be enforced by the dishonest McCord. This raises the whole question of whether there is such a thing as an 'unenforceable obligation'. Such a thing would, of course, be quite useless to its owner.

2. Whether s. 5(3) operates where no legally enforceable obligation has in fact arisen but the defendant believes himself to be under such an obligation must remain doubtful. Where the section does operate, ownership of the property concerned, by a fiction, remains with the person who has given the property to the defendant. The property therefore 'belongs to another' within the definition of theft in s. 1 of the 1968 Act. In view of the discussion of *Gomez* (above), is s. 5(3) necessary?

3. In deciding *Meech*, was the court unduly influenced by the evident dishonesty of the defendants?

(vi) *When does an obligation arise to restore property got by another's mistake?*

Theft Act 1968

5.—(4) Where a person gets property by another's mistake, and is under an obligation to make restoration (in whole or in part) of the property or its proceeds or of the value thereof, then to the extent of that obligation the property or proceeds shall be regarded (as against him) as belonging to the person entitled to restoration, and an intention not to make restoration shall be regarded accordingly as an intention to deprive that person of the property or proceeds.

Attorney-General's Reference (No. 1 of 1983)
[1985] QB 182, Court of Appeal

LORD LANE CJ: This is a reference under s. 36 of the Criminal Justice Act 1972 by the Attorney-General. It arises by virtue of the following facts. The respondent is a woman police officer and she received her pay from the Receiver of the Metropolitan Police. Owing to an error in the receiver's department she was credited, in a way which will have to be described in more detail in a moment, with the sum of £74.74 for wages and overtime in respect of a day when she was not at work at all. That amount, together with other sums which were properly due to her, was paid into her bank by direct debit by the receiver's bank. She knew nothing of the error until later, though it was not proved precisely when. There was some evidence before the jury that she had decided to say nothing about this unsolicited windfall which had come her way, and had decided to take no action about it after she discovered the error. No demand for payment of the sum was made by the Receiver of the Metropolitan Police or anyone else.

. . .

First of all, what is the legal position with regard to the payment of money by one bank to another for the credit of a customer's account? The position was described in clear language by Lord Goddard CJ in *R* v *Davenport* [1954] 1 WLR 569. He said [1954] 1 All ER 602, 603:

although we talk about people having money in a bank, the only person who has money in a bank is a banker. If I pay money into my bank, either by paying cash or a cheque, that money at once becomes the money of the banker. The relationship between banker and customer is that of debtor and creditor. He does not hold my money as an agent or trustee. The leading case of *Foley v Hill* (1848) 2 HL Cas 28 exploded that idea. When the banker is paying out, whether in cash over the counter or whether by crediting the bank account of somebody else, he is paying out of his own money, not my money, but he is debiting me in my account with him. I have a chose in action, that is to say, I have a right to expect that the banker will honour my cheque, but he does it out of his own money.

From that exposition of the true relationship between bank and client, it follows that what the respondent in the present case got was simply the debt due to her from her own bank. That is so unless her account was overdrawn or overdrawn beyond any overdraft limit, in which case she did not even get that right to money. That point is made in a decision of this court in *R v Kohn* (1979) 69 Cr App R 395. There was no evidence in the present case as to whether the respondent's bank balance was in credit, overdrawn or anything about overdraft limits imposed by the manager of the bank. It was assumed on all hands that the account was in credit.

That brings us to the question of the basic definition of theft, which is to be found in s. 1(1) of the Theft Act 1968, which provides: 'A person is guilty of theft if he dishonestly appropriates property belonging to another with the intention of permanently depriving the other of it; and "thief" and "steal" shall be construed accordingly.'

The property in the present case was the debt owed by the bank to the respondent and in order to show that that can be property one turns to s. 4(1) of the Act of 1968 which reads: 'Property includes money and all other property, real or personal, including things in action and other intangible property.' The debt here was a thing in action, therefore the property was capable of being stolen.

It will be apparent that, at first blush, that debt did not belong to anyone except the respondent herself. She was the only person who had the right to go to her bank and demand the handing over of that £74.74. Had there been no statutory provision which altered that particular situation that would have been the end of the case, but if one turns to s. 5(4) of the Act, one finds these words:

> Where a person gets property by another's mistake, and is under an obligation to make restoration (in whole or in part) of the property or its proceeds or of the value thereof, then to the extent of that obligation the property or proceeds shall be regarded (as against him) as belonging to the person entitled to restoration, and an intention not to make restoration shall be regarded accordingly as an intention to deprive that person of the property or proceeds.

In order to determine the effect of that subsection upon this case one has to take it piece by piece to see what the result is read against the circumstances of this particular prosecution. First of all: 'Did the respondent get property?' The word 'get' is about as wide a word as could possibly have been adopted by the draftsman of the Act. The answer is 'Yes,' the respondent in this case did get her chose in action, that is, her right to sue the bank for the debt which they owed her – money which they held in their hands to which she was entitled by virtue of the contract between bank and customer.

Secondly: 'Did she get it by another's mistake?' The answer to that is plainly: 'Yes.' The Receiver of the Metropolitan Police made the mistake of thinking she was entitled to £74.74 when she was not entitled to that at all.

'Was she under an obligation to make restoration of either the property or its proceeds or its value?' We take each of those in turn. 'Was she under an obligation to make restoration of the property?' – the chose in action. The answer to that is 'No.' It was something which could not be restored in the ordinary meaning of the word. 'Was she under an obligation to make restoration of its proceeds?' The answer to that is 'No.' There were no proceeds of the chose in action to restore. 'Was she under an obligation to make restoration of the value thereof?' – the value of the chose in action. The answer to that seems to us to be 'Yes.'

As a result of the provisions of s. 5(4) the debt of £74.74 due from the respondent's bank to the respondent notionally belonged to the Receiver of the Metropolitan Police; therefore the prosecution, up to this point, have succeeded in proving – remarkable though it may seem – that the 'property' in this case belonged to another within the meaning of s. 1 in the Theft Act 1968 from the moment when the respondent became aware that this mistake had been made and that her account had been credited with the £74.74 and she consequently became obliged to restore the value. Furthermore, by the final words of s. 5(4), once the prosecution succeed in proving that the respondent intended not to make restoration, that is notionally to be regarded as an intention to deprive the receiver of that property which notionally belongs to him.

. . .

Before parting with the case we would like to say that it should often be possible to resolve this type of situation without resorting to the criminal law. We do, however, accept that there may be occasions – of which this may have been one – where a prosecution is necessary. We do not feel it possible to answer the question posed to us in any more specific form than the form in which this opinion has been delivered and that is our answer to the question posed to us.

R v Davis

(1988) 88 Cr App R 347, Court of Appeal

The appellant was convicted of six counts of theft. The counts charged theft of specified amounts of money belonging to the London Borough of Richmond. The appellant was eligible for housing benefit from the local authority. By mistake the authority's computer generated duplicate issues of a number of payments, sending the appellant two cheques. When he ceased to be eligible for the benefit only one of the computer entries was deleted and the remaining entry continued to generate cheques. The appellant admitted to police that he had 'cashed' the cheques he had received. The evidence before the jury was that he had either endorsed the cheque over to a shopkeeper in return for cash or had endorsed it to his landlord for accommodation etc. He denied receiving some cheques and was acquitted of counts relating to those cheques. The appellant appealed against conviction.

Held, allowing the appeal in part and quashing two of the convictions, there was not sufficient evidence in relation to the cheques endorsed to the landlord that the appellant had received cash in exchange for the cheques. As to the remaining counts, the language of the first part of s. 5(4) of the Theft Act 1968 was framed to cater for the ordinary tangible article and to recognise that by the time the defendant comes to commit his dishonest appropriation, the article may be in one of three conditions: it may still exist, so that it can and should be returned: it may have been exchanged for money or goods, in which case the defendant may be under an obligation to account for the fruits of the exchange, at least if they are traceable; and it may have ceased to exist altogether or to have gone out of reach of recovery, in which event the defendant may be obliged to 'restore' the value. In those cases where the defendant is indeed under a duty to 'make restoration' the second part of the subsection will put him in peril of conviction for stealing the article or its proceeds, although not its value, since there is no reference to value in this part of the subsection. The deceptively plain words of s. 5(4) give rise to problems, e.g. when is the defendant obliged to 'make restoration'; where the property received by the defendant by mistake is exchanged for something else? The Court did not need to answer those questions in the circumstances of the present case. It was plain that if an article is sold for cash, the sum represents the 'proceeds' of the article; there is no reason why this should be any the less so where the transaction involves not simply the piece of paper but also the rights which it conveys. On the assumption that the appellant was paid cash for the cheque, the offences were made out subject to the proof of dishonesty.

QUESTIONS

1. In *Davis*, could the same result have been reached by the application of the reasoning used in *Shadrokh-Cigari* (above)? In the light of the latter case and/or *Gomez*, is s. 5(4) necessary?

2. In the *Attorney-General's Reference* (above), the court stated that such situations might be resolved without resort to the criminal law. Why? Do you agree?

3. If a student receives an overpayment in her grant cheque, tells the relevant authorities of the overpayment and they do nothing, may she spend the money? Will she be guilty of theft if she does so? How does the situation change if the student fails to inform the authorities of the overpayment?

NOTE

In *R v Gilks* [1972] 3 All ER 280, the court held that s. 5(4) was concerned with legal obligations and not those of a purely social or moral nature.

(vii) *Who owns the property of a vacant corporation sole?*

For the sake of completeness the provisions of s. 5(5) should be noted:

Theft Act 1968

5.—(5) Property of a corporation sole shall be regarded as belonging to the corporation notwithstanding a vacancy in the corporation.

SECTION 3: *Mens rea*

Theft Act 1968

1.—(1) A person is guilty of theft if he dishonestly appropriates property belonging to another with the intention of permanently depriving the other of it: and 'thief' and 'steal' shall be construed accordingly.

The two elements in the *mens rea* of theft are:

(a) Dishonesty.

(b) Intent permanently to deprive.

A: Dishonesty

Dishonesty is probably the key concept in theft. Its central importance has been increased with the watering-down in *Gomez* of the requirement of an appropriation. Yet what constitutes dishonesty remains clouded.

(i) *The application of s. 2*
The Theft Act 1968, s. 2, while not providing a test of dishonesty, identifies three situations where a defendant will not be deemed to have acted dishonestly.

Theft Act 1968

2.—(1) A person's appropriation of property belonging to another is not to be regarded as dishonest—

(a) if he appropriates property in the belief that he has in law the right to deprive the other of it, on behalf of himself or of a third person; or

(b) if he appropriates the property in the belief that he would have the other's consent if the other knew of the appropriation and the circumstances of it; or

(c) (except where the property came to him as trustee or personal representative) if he appropriates the property in the belief that the person to whom the property belongs cannot be discovered by taking reasonable steps.

In addition, s. 2 identifies a situation where a willingness to pay for property may not be inconsistent with a conviction for theft.

(2) A person's appropriation of property belonging to another may be dishonest notwithstanding that he is willing to pay for the property.

NOTES AND QUESTIONS

1. The belief referred to in all three situations identified in s. 2(1) is an honest belief, i.e. one actually held by the defendant. There is no requirement that the belief should be reasonable (*R* v *Kell* [1985] Crim LR 239, *R* v *Holden* [1991] Crim LR 478). Why should it not have to be reasonable? Of course, if a defendant's belief is unreasonable a jury may not credit the claim that it was honestly held.

2. Notice that under s. 2(2) a willingness to pay for the items taken will not prevent a finding that the defendant acted dishonestly.

(ii) *The test of dishonesty*
In most cases the dishonesty of the defendant will be obvious if the facts alleged by the prosecution are proved. Normally, therefore, the jury need not be directed as to the legal meaning of 'dishonesty' (see *R* v *Squire* [1990] Crim LR 341). Where there is some doubt, the jury must be directed in accordance with the model direction set out in *Ghosh* (below). This case achieves a reconciliation between two conflicting lines of authority. One of these advocated a subjective test of dishonesty (i.e. did the defendant believe that he had been acting dishonestly?) (see, e.g. *R* v *Gilks* [1972] 3 All ER 280). The other line of authority put forward a wholly objective test (i.e. would a reasonable person, as embodied by the jury, consider such behaviour dishonest?) (see, e.g., *R* v *Greenstein* [1976] 1 All ER 1).

R v *Ghosh*
[1982] 1 QB 1053, Court of Appeal

LORD LANE CJ: . . . Is 'dishonesty' in s. 1 of the Theft Act 1968 intended to characterise a course of conduct? Or is it intended to describe a state of mind? If the former, then we can well understand that it could be established independently of the knowledge or belief of the accused. But if, as we think, it is the latter, then the knowledge and belief of the accused are at the root of the problem.

Take for example a man who comes from a country where public transport is free. On his first day here he travels on a bus. He gets off without paying. He never had an intention of paying. His mind is clearly honest; but his conduct, judged objectively by what he has done, is dishonest. It seems to us that in using the word 'dishonestly' in the Theft Act 1968, Parliament cannot have intended to catch dishonest conduct in that sense, that is to say conduct to which no moral obloquy could possibly attach. This is sufficiently established by the partial definition in section 2 of the Theft Act itself. All the matters covered by section 2(1) relate to the belief of the accused. Section 2(2) relates to his willingness to pay. A man's belief and his willingness to pay are things which can only be established subjectively. It is difficult to see how a partially subjective definition can be made to work in harness with the test which in all other respects is wholly objective.

If we are right that dishonesty is something in the mind of the accused (what Professor Glanville Williams calls 'a special mental state'), then if the mind of the accused is honest, it cannot be deemed dishonest merely because members of the jury would have regarded it as dishonest to embark on that course of conduct.

So we would reject the simple uncomplicated approach that the test is purely objective, however attractive from the practical point of view that solution may be.

There remains the objection that to adopt a subjective test is to abandon all standards but that of the accused himself, and to bring about a state of affairs in which 'Robin Hood would be no robber': R v *Greenstein* [1975] 1 WLR 1353. This objection misunderstands the nature of the subjective test. It is no defence for a man to say 'I knew that what I was doing is generally regarded as dishonest; but I do not regard it as dishonest myself. Therefore I am not guilty.' What he is however entitled to say is 'I did not know that anybody would regard what I was doing as dishonest.' He may not be believed: just as he may not be believed if he sets up 'a claim of right' under section 2(1) of the Theft Act 1968, or asserts that he believed in the truth of a misrepresentation under section 15 of the Act of 1968. But if he *is* believed, or raises a real doubt about the matter, the jury cannot be sure that he was dishonest.

In determining whether the prosecution has proved that the defendant was acting dishonestly, a jury must first of all decide whether according to the ordinary standards of reasonable and honest people what was done was dishonest. If it was not dishonest by those standards, that is the end of the matter and the prosecution fails.

If it was dishonest by those standards, then the jury must consider whether the defendant himself must have realised that what he was doing was by those standards dishonest. In most cases, where the actions are obviously dishonest by ordinary standards, there will be no doubt about it. It will be obvious that the defendant himself knew that he was acting dishonestly. It is dishonest for a defendant to act in a way which he knows ordinary people consider to be dishonest, even if he asserts or genuinely believes that he is morally justified in acting as he did. For example, Robin Hood or those ardent anti-vivisectionists who remove animals from vivisection laboratories are acting dishonestly, even though they may consider themselves to be morally justified in doing what they do, because they know that ordinary people would consider these actions to be dishonest.

NOTES AND QUESTIONS

1. Does the decision in *Ghosh* reflect the frustration involved in fashioning a definition of dishonesty? J. C. Smith, *Law of Theft* (6th ed.) suggests that the test of dishonesty should be 'knowing that the appropriation will or may be detrimental to the interests of the owner in a significantly practical way'. Is this a more useful test?
2. Consider the case of a man who takes a loaf of bread to feed his starving child, believing no one would begrudge him it? Or a woman stranded on a cross-Channel ferry who breaks into a

canteen to take biscuits for her sister who is about to go into a diabetic coma because of lack of sugar. Does the subjective element in *Ghosh* import a defence of necessity?

3. The problem with the *Ghosh* test, it has been argued, is that it leaves each jury free to apply their own moral and social views of what is dishonest. As these will vary from jury to jury, inconsistent verdicts in similar cases appear virtually inevitable. See Griew, 'Dishonesty: The Objections to *Feely* and *Ghosh*' [1985] Crim LR 341.

4. The *Ghosh* test may prove particularly troublesome in the context of business crime, where the standards of the marketplace and the standards of ordinary people may well clash, most ordinary people not being conversant with what is acceptable in the world of businesses. Should this matter?

5. The second part of the *Ghosh* test would appear to allow a defence to those whose sense of the community's standard of dishonesty is markedly distorted. Can this be squared with the general proposition that ignorance of the law is no excuse?

6. In *R v Hinks* [2000] 1 Cr App R 1 the Court of Appeal made it clear that receiving a valid gift would amount to an appropriation and would be theft if the recipient was dishonest. Does this difference between the civil law and the criminal law make sense?

B: Intent permanently to deprive

The intention of the defendant must be to deprive the victim of the whole of his interest. If this is a limited interest, then, so long as an intention to deprive him of all of that interest can be shown, the requisite intent will be present. There is no requirement that the victim actually be physically deprived of any item.

Three main issues arise in determining when there is an intent permanently to deprive:

(a) Is there an intent permanently to deprive if the defendant intends to return the goods?

(b) In what circumstances can an intended borrowing amount to an intention permanently to deprive?

(c) Can a 'conditional intention' be sufficient *mens rea*?

(i) *Intention to return goods*
An intention to return money taken is not inconsistent with an intent permanently to deprive. The courts have reached this seemingly strange result by ruling that a defendant has to have the intent to return the identical coins and not their equivalent value (*R v Velumyl* [1989] Crim LR 299). Less troublesome are cases where the defendant may not be in a position to return the goods taken. This is specifically covered in the statute.

Theft Act 1968

6.—(2) Without prejudice to the generality of subsection (1) above, where a person, having possession or control (lawfully or not) of property belonging to another, parts with the property under a condition as to its return which he may not be able to perform, this (if done for purposes of his own and without the other's authority) amounts to treating the property as his own to dispose of regardless of the other's rights.

Section 6(2) was specifically designed to cover the case where the defendant pawns another's property without authority. The condition 'which he may not be able to perform' in those circumstances is the condition imposed by the pawnbroker that the property will not be returned unless repayment of the loan with interest is first forthcoming. However, the subsection is not confined to pawning situations and there may well be other cases falling within its ambit.

(ii) *When can an intended borrowing amount to an intention permanently to deprive?*

Theft Act 1968

6.—(1) A person appropriating property belonging to another without meaning the other permanently to lose the thing itself is nevertheless to be regarded as having the intention of permanently depriving the other of it if his intention is to treat the thing as his own to dispose of regardless of the other's rights; and a borrowing or lending of it may amount to so treating it if, but only if, the borrowing or lending is for a period and in circumstances making it equivalent to an outright taking or disposal.

Section 6(1) covers situations in which the defendant takes property intending to sell it back to the owner or to return it only upon payment of a ransom. There may be no permanent deprivation but the defendant treats the property as his own to dispose of. In *R v Fernandes* [1996] 1 Cr App R 175, the Court of Appeal stated: 'We consider that section 6 may apply to a person in possession or control of another's property who, dishonestly and for his own purpose, deals with that property in such a manner as he is risking its loss.'

Some confusion about the meaning of 'dispose of' in s. 6 has arisen, however:

R v Marshall
[1998] 2 Cr App R 282, Court of Appeal

MANTELL LJ: As part of an operation by London Underground Limited at Victoria Station the appellants were observed and videoed obtaining used travel tickets from passengers leaving the underground and selling them at a reduced rate to persons intending to travel. The tickets, which had been issued by London Underground Limited remained valid in the sense that their usefulness had not been exhausted. Thereby London Underground Limited was deprived of revenue which it might have expected to receive from those persons who had bought the tickets.

A number of submissions were made to the learned judge. The first was that the travel tickets were not the property of London Underground Limited within the meaning of section 1 of the Theft Act 1968. The judge rejected the submission ruling that although the tickets had passed into the possession and control of the customers, London Underground Limited retained a proprietary right or interest in the tickets which were to be regarded therefore as the property of London Underground Limited pursuant to section 5(1) of the Act. As a secondary reason for rejecting the submission he referred to the express term on the reverse of each ticket to the effect that it remained throughout the property of LRT, of which of London Underground Limited is a part.

A second submission was made that in the circumstances there had been no appropriation so as to bring the case within the basic definition of theft. In rejecting the submission the judge referred to section 3(1) which reads:

> Any assumption by a person of the rights of an owner amounts to an appropriation, and this includes, where he has come by the property (innocently or not) without stealing it any later assumption of a right to it by keeping or dealing with it as owner.

and to the decision of the House of Lords in *R* v *Morris* (1983) 77 Cr App R 309 in which it was held that it was not necessary to demonstrate an assumption by the accused of all the owners' rights, simply to show the assumption of some of the rights of the owner of the goods in question. The learned judge considered that the use of the ticket to the detriment of London Underground Limited was inconsistent with London Underground Limited's rights and consequently that the actions of the appellants amounted to an appropriation in law.

Thirdly, and lastly, it was submitted that on the agreed facts there was no evidence of an intention to permanently deprive. That submission also was rejected, the learned judge taking the view that the provisions of section 6(1) of the Theft Act covered the position. It will be necessary to refer to the terms of the subsection later in this judgment.

. . .

In our judgment and following *Fernandes* the subsection is not to be given the restricted interpretation for which the appellants contend.

The principal submission put forward on behalf of the appellants is that the issuing of the ticket is analogous to the drawing of a cheque in that in each instance a *chose in action* is created which in the first case belongs to the customer and in the second to the payee. So by parity of reasoning with that advanced by Lord Goff in *R* v *Preddy and Others* [1996] 2 Cr App R 524, the property acquired belonged to the customer and not London Underground Limited and there can have been no intention on the part of the appellant to deprive London Underground Limited of the ticket which would in due course be returned to the possession of London Underground Limited. Attractive though the submission appears at first blush we do not think that it can possibly be correct.

'A " *chose in action*" is a known legal expression used to describe all personal rights of property which can only be claimed or enforced by action, and not by taking physical possession.' (See *Talkington* v *Magee* (1902) 2 KB 427, *per* Channell J at p. 430.) On the issuing of an underground ticket a contract is created between London Underground Limited and the purchaser. Under that contract each party has rights and obligations. Theoretically those rights are enforceable by action. Therefore, it is arguable, we suppose, that by the transaction each party has acquired a *chose in action*. On the side of the purchaser it is represented by a right to use the ticket to the extent which it allows travel on the underground system. On the side of London Underground Limited it encompasses the right to insist that the ticket is used by no one other than the purchaser. It is that right which is disregarded when the ticket is acquired by the appellant and sold on. But here the charges were in relation to the tickets and travel cards themselves and a ticket form or travel card and, dare we say, a cheque form is not a *chose in action*. The fact that the ticket form or travel card may find its way back into the possession of London Underground Limited, albeit with its usefulness or 'virtue' exhausted, is nothing to the point. Section 6(1) prevails for the reasons we have given.

The appellants by their pleas having acknowledged that they were acting dishonestly it seems to us that there is no reason to consider the convictions unsafe and these appeals must be dismissed.

Appeals dismissed.

In *R* v *Cahill* [1993] Crim LR 141, the Court of Appeal approved the meaning given by the *Shorter Oxford Dictionary*: 'Dispose of – to deal with definitively: to get of;

to get done with; finish. To make over by way of sale or bargain, sell.' But consider the following case:

DPP v *Lavender*
[1994] Crim LR 297, Queen's Bench Division

An information was preferred against the respondent that he had stolen two doors. Justices dismissed the information but stated a case for the opinion of the High Court.

The respondent had taken the doors from a council property undergoing repair, and had used them to replace damaged doors at another council property of which his girlfriend was the tenant. He argued that he had not had the intention permanently to deprive the council of the doors.

Section 6(1) of the Theft Act 1968 provides that a person is to be regarded as having the intention to permanently deprive another of property if his intention is to treat the property as his own to dispose of regardless of the other's rights, and that borrowing property may amount to such an intention if for a period and in circumstances making it equivalent to an outright taking or disposal.

The question posed for the High Court was whether, on a proper construction of section 6(1), theft was made out.

Held, allowing the appeal and remitting the case to the justices to convict, the respondent had stolen the doors.

In *Lloyd and others* [1985] 2 All ER 661 the Court of Appeal had said that mere borrowing was never enough to constitute the necessary guilty mind, unless the intention was to return the thing in such a changed state that all its goodness or virtue was gone. It was difficult to describe the taking of the doors as borrowing but, even if it was, the doors would not change their character. The second limb of section 6(1) did not apply.

In regard to the first limb, the justices had applied a dictionary definition to the words 'to dispose of' and had decided they meant to get rid of, or to sell. That was too narrow a definition. A disposal could include disposal to the owner of the property (as contemplated in *Lloyd*) and could include dealing with the property (*Chan Man-Sin* v *A-G for Hong Kong* [1988] 1 All ER 1). The proper question was whether the respondent intended to treat the doors as his own, regardless of the council's rights. The answer was yes, the respondent had dealt with the doors regardless of the council's rights not to have them removed, and in so doing had manifested an intention to treat the doors as his own.

. . .

NOTES AND QUESTIONS
1. In view of the different interpretations of s. 6, consider whether it would cover the taking of a season ticket which has almost expired. Jane has a season ticket to watch Sheffield Wednesday football club. The ticket is valid for 13 matches. David takes the season ticket after Jane has been to three matches and returns it in time for her to attend the last match. Has David stolen the ticket?
2. In 'Current Topic; Stealing Tickets' [1998] Crim LR 723, John Smith argues that *Marshall* is rightly decided but that the Court of Appeal should have recognised that *Preddy* is wrongly decided. See Consideration of *R* v *Preddy* at p. 355 above.
3. Could the law be simplified by eliminating the requirement of proof of an intent permanently to deprive someone of his property? Why should not unauthorised borrowing constitute theft, even if there is not an intent permanently to deprive? See G. Williams, 'Temporary appropriation should be theft' [1981] Crim LR 129. The all too prevalent problem of joyriding (where there is usually no intent to deprive the owner of her car) is specifically

addressed in the Theft Act 1968, s. 12, and, more recently, the Aggravated Vehicle Taking Act 1992. Another possible approach would be to enact a crime of unlawful temporary deprivation of property belonging to another.

(iii) *Can a 'conditional intention' be sufficient* mens rea?

This problem arises where the defendant only intends permanently to keep anything which he finds to be valuable after he has examined the property. In *Easom* [1971] 2 QB 315, where the defendant examined the contents of a handbag and decided nothing was worth taking such an intention was held not to be sufficient for theft. Whether the defendant is guilty of attempted theft used to turn on the way in which the indictment was framed. According to the court in *Re Attorney-General's References (Nos 1 & 2 of 1979)* [1980] QB 180, the defendant in *Easom* could have been convicted if he had been charged with 'attempting to steal some or all of the contents of the handbag'. The problem has now been solved by the Criminal Attempts Act 1981 (impossibility no defence). See Chapter 11.

SECTION 4: **Robbery**

Theft Act 1968

8.—(1) A person is guilty of robbery if he steals, and immediately before or at the time of doing so, and in order to do so, he uses force on any person or puts or seeks to put any person in fear of being then and there subjected to force.

(2) A person guilty of robbery, or of an assault with intent to rob, shall on conviction on indictment be liable to imprisonment for life.

A: Theft

Robbery is essentially an aggravated form of stealing. It follows that if a defendant is not guilty of theft he cannot be guilty of robbery.

R v *Robinson*
[1977] Crim LR 173, Court of Appeal

R ran a clothing club. He was charged (with others) with robbing and assaulting I, who, with his wife, was a contributor to the club. I's wife owed £7. It was the prosecution case that R and two others had approached him in the street late at night, R brandishing a knife, and that a fight ensued during the course of which a £5 note fell from I's pocket. R had snatched the note and asked if I had any more money as he was still owed £2. R's defence to robbery, reduced by the jury to theft, was that I gave him the money and he had received it willingly as repayment of the debt and that it was not dishonestly appropriated. R appealed on the ground of misdirection to the jury that an honest belief by the defendant that he was entitled in law to get his money in a particular way was necessary before he could avail himself of the defence under s. 2(1)(a) of the Theft Act 1968.

Held, allowing the appeal, that the law as laid down in *Skivington* [1968] 1 QB 166 had not been altered by s. 2(1)(a) of the Theft Act 1968, and that it was unnecessary for a defendant to show that he had an honest belief not only that he was entitled to take the money but also that he was entitled to take it in the way that he did.

Corcoran v Anderton
[1980] Crim LR 385, Queen's Bench Division

Two youths, the defendant and his co-accused, saw a woman in the street, and agreed together to steal her handbag. The co-accused hit her in the back and tugged at her bag to release it, while the defendant participated. She released her bag, screamed, and fell to the ground. The two youths ran away empty-handed, and the woman recovered her bag, neither youth having had sole control of the bag at any time. The defendant was later convicted of robbery under s. 8 of the Theft Act 1968; which provided that a person was guilty of robbery if he stole, using force.

The defendant appealed against conviction on the ground that neither he nor the co-accused had sole control of the boy at any time.

Held, dismissing the appeal, that an appropriation took place at the moment when the youths, acting with an intention to deprive the woman of the bag, snatched it from her grasp so that she no longer had physical control of it. In doing so each accused was trying to exclude the woman from her exclusive claim to the bag, and was trying to treat the bag as his. Such an action was an unlawful assumption of the rights of the owner and accordingly the defendant was properly convicted by the justices.

QUESTIONS

1. Robinson was not guilty of robbery because no theft could be proved. Could he have been found guilty of blackmail?

2. Reconsider the approach to appropriation adopted by the House of Lords in *Gomez*. Would it have simplified or complicated the analysis in *Corocan* v *Anderton*?

B: Force or threat of force

Section 8 is satisfied only if the defendant is found to have used 'force on any person' or to have sought 'to put any person in fear of being then and there subjected to force'. What amounts to force is a matter for the jury.

R v Dawson
[1976] Crim LR 692, Court of Appeal

D was convicted of robbery. He and two others approached a man in the street and two of them stood either side of him and the third behind him. One of them nudged the man so that he lost his balance and whilst he was thus unbalanced another stole his wallet. It was submitted that what D and his accomplices did could not amount to the use of force, relying on cases prior to the Theft Act 1968.

Held, dismissing the appeal, what counted now was the words of the Act, the object of which was to get rid of the old technicalities. The choice of the word force was not without interest because the Larceny Act 1916 used violence. Whether there was any difference between the words was not relevant to the case. Force was a word in ordinary use which juries understood. The judge left it to the jury to decide whether jostling to an extent which caused a person to have difficulty in keeping his balance amounted to the use of force. In deference to the submissions he said that the force must be substantial. It was not necessary to consider whether he was right to apply an adjective to the word of the Act. It was a matter for the jury and it could not be said that they were wrong. It had also been canvassed whether the force had been used for distracting the victim's attention or for overcoming resistance. That sort of refinement might have been relevant under the old law: the sole question under the new was whether force had been used in order to steal.

Must the force be used to overcome resistance to the theft, or is force used to gain possession of an article enough?

R v Clouden
[1987] Crim LR 56, Court of Appeal

The appellant was seen to follow a woman who was carrying a shopping basket in her left hand. He approached her from behind and wrenched the basket down and out of her grasp with both hands and ran off with it. He was charged in two counts with robbery and theft respectively and convicted on the first count of robbery. He appealed on the grounds (i) that there was insufficient evidence of resistance to the snatching of the bag to constitute force on the person under s. 8 of the Theft Act 1968; and (ii) that the learned judge's direction to the jury on the requirement of force on the person was inadequate and confused.

Held, dismissing the appeal, the old cases distinguished between force on the actual person and force on the property which in fact causes force on the person but, following *Dawson and James* (1976) 64 Cr App R 170, the court should direct attention to the words of the statute without referring to the old authorities. The old distinctions have gone. Whether the defendant used force on any person in order to steal is an issue that should be left to the jury. The judge's direction to the jury was adequate. He told the jury quite clearly at the outset what the statutory definition was, though thereafter he merely used the word 'force' and did not use the expression 'on the person'.

NOTE AND QUESTIONS
The Criminal Law Revision Committee which was responsible for drafting the Theft Act 1968 said (Cmnd 2977, para. 65) that they 'would not regard mere snatching of property, such as a handbag, from an unresisting owner as using force for the purpose of the definition'. Does *Clouden* reflect this opinion? Which view more accurately reflects the wording of the statute?

C: Before or at the time of the theft

When must the force or threat of force occur? It seems that (as with burglary) an appropriation can be a continuing act for the purposes of robbery:

R v Hale
(1978) 68 Cr App R 415, Court of Appeal

The appellant was charged with robbery. The prosecution case was that he and one M, both wearing stocking masks, had forced their way into the house of a Mrs C who had answered the door to their knock. The appellant had then put his hand over Mrs C's mouth to stop her screaming while M went upstairs and returned carrying a jewellery box and had asked Mrs C 'where the rest was.' A neighbour who had heard Mrs C's scream had then rung up to ask if she was all right. Under threats from the appellant and M she replied that she was. They again asked Mrs C where she kept her money and before leaving the house tied her up and threatened what would happen to her young boy if she informed the police within five minutes of their leaving.

The trial judge read the definition of robbery in s. 8 of the Theft Act 1968 to the jury and the meaning of 'steal' in s. 1 of that Act. He directed them that the question they had to decide was whether they felt sure that the appellant by use of force or putting Mrs C in fear got hold of her property without her consent and without believing that he had her consent and intending to appropriate that property to himself without giving it back to her afterwards. The jury convicted. On appeal that the jury had been misdirected in that the judge's direction could indicate to the jury that if an accused used force in order to effect his escape with the stolen goods that would be sufficient to constitute robbery and that on the facts of the present case it was submitted that the theft was completed as soon as the jewellery box was seized.

EVELEIGH LJ: . . . In so far as the facts of the present case are concerned, counsel submitted that the theft was completed when the jewellery box was first seized and any force thereafter could not have been 'immediately before or at the time of stealing' and certainly not 'in order to steal.' The essence of the submission was that the theft was completed as soon as the jewellery box was seized.

Section 8 of the Theft Act 1968 begins: 'A person is guilty of robbery if he steals . . .' He steals when he acts in accordance with the basic definition of theft in s. 1 of the Theft Act; that is to say when he dishonestly appropriates property belonging to another with the intention of permanently depriving the other of it. It thus becomes necessary to consider what is 'appropriation' or, according to s. 3, 'any assumption by a person of the rights of an owner.' An assumption of the rights of an owner describes the conduct of a person towards a particular article. It is conduct which usurps the rights of the owner. To say that the conduct is over and done with as soon as he lays hands upon the property, or when he first manifests an intention to deal with it as his, is contrary to common-sense and to the natural meaning of words. A thief who steals a motor car first opens the door. It is to be said that the act of starting up the motor is no more a part of the theft?

In the present case there can be little doubt that if the appellant had been interrupted after the seizure of the jewellery box the jury would have been entitled to find that the appellant and his accomplice were assuming the rights of an owner at the time when the jewellery box was seized. However, the act of appropriation does not suddenly cease. It is a continuous act and it is a matter for the jury to decide whether or not the act of appropriation has finished. Moreover, it is quite clear that the intention to deprive the owner permanently, which accompanied the assumption of the owner's rights was a continuing one at all material times. This Court therefore rejects the contention that the theft had ceased by the time the lady was tied up. As a matter of common-sense the appellant was in the course of committing theft; he was stealing.

There remains the question whether there was robbery. Quite clearly the jury were at liberty to find the appellant guilty of robbery relying upon the force used when he put his hand over Mrs Carrett's mouth to restrain her from calling for help. We also think that they were also entitled to rely upon the act of tying her up provided they were satisfied (and it is difficult to see how they could not be satisfied) that the force so used was to enable them to steal. If they were still engaged in the act of stealing the force was clearly used to enable them to continue to assume the rights of the owner and permanently to deprive Mrs Carrett of her box, which is what they began to do when they first seized it.

D: In order to steal

The force must be used 'in order to steal':

R v *Shendley*
[1970] Crim LR 49, Court of Appeal

S was convicted of robbery, contrary to s. 8 of the Theft Act 1968. The complainant said that S attacked him, took some of his property and forced him to sign receipts purporting to show that S had brought the property from him. S said that he had purchased the property. The judge directed the jury: 'robbery is stealing property in the presence of the owner . . . the allegation is that immediately before taking the property, or at the time of taking it, or immediately after, force was used towards [the complainant] to put him in fear . . . if you came to the conclusion that the violence was unconnected with the stealing but you were satisfied there was a stealing it does not mean that is an acquittal because it would be open to you to find [him] guilty of robbery, that is, robbery without violence.'

Held: the directions were wrong. The judge must have had in mind s. 23 of the Larceny Act 1916 and overlooked the fact that the definition of robbery in the Theft Act is different. There is no such thing as robbery without violence. What the judge no doubt intended to say was that if the jury were satisfied that S stole the property but not satisfied that he used violence for the purpose of stealing they should find him not guilty of robbery but guilty of theft (the court substituted a conviction for theft).

QUESTIONS

1. George rapes Vera. He runs off taking her handbag. Has he committed robbery as well as rape?

2. John and David were involved in a heated argument. John lost his temper and hit David who was knocked unconscious. John took David's wallet from him and ran off. Is John a robber?

SECTION 5: **Offences of deception**

The Theft Acts contain a number of offences which prohibit a defendant from obtaining various advantages by deception. They are:

  (a) Obtaining property (Theft Act 1968, s. 15);

  (b) Obtaining a pecuniary advantage (Theft Act 1968, s. 16);

  (c) Procuring the execution of a valuable security (Theft Act 1968, s. 20(2));

  (d) Obtaining services (Theft Act, 1978, s. 1);

  (e) Securing the remission of a liability (Theft Act 1978, s. 2(1)(a));

  (f) Inducing a creditor to wait for or to forgo payment (Theft Act 1978, s. 2(1)(b));

  (g) Obtaining an exemption from or an abatement of liability (Theft Act 1978, s. 2(1)(c));

  (h) Dishonestly obtaining a money transfer by deception (Theft Act 1968, s. 15(a)).

Each of the various deception offences has its own statutory nuances, which have led to extensive judicial analysis and sometimes legislative amendment. We do not propose to delve into the offences separately for to do so would consume a disproportionate amount of space in this text. However, we would note the common elements which characterise this area of the law:

(a) There must be a causal link between the deception and the prohibited result.

   (i) The deception must be operative.

   (ii) Where cheque or credit cards are involved the deception will be presumed to be operative in certain circumstances.

   (iii) A human mind must be deceived.

   (iv) The deception must not be too remote from the prohibited result.

(b) There must be a deception, that is, an untrue 'statement'.

   (i) The statement must actually be false.

   (ii) The defendant must be deliberate or reckless as to the falsity of the statement.

   (iii) The statement must be by words or conduct (including implied statements).

(c) The defendant must be dishonest.

SECTION 6: **Burglary**

Burglary has always been regarded as a serious crime, because it involves not only a threat to property but also a threat to the privacy of one's own home. It was this factor which differentiated the offence from simple theft. Over time, however, the offence expanded beyond application to a dwelling place to encompass any building, and the criminal activity linked to the invasion of the building was no longer limited to theft. The modern incarnation of the offence is found in the Theft Act 1968, s. 9. The section creates two quite distinct offences.

Theft Act 1968

9.—(1) A person is guilty of burglary if—

   (a) he enters any building or part of a building as a trespasser and with intent to commit any such offence as is mentioned in subsection (2) below; or

   (b) having entered any building or part of a building as a trespasser he steals or attempts to steal anything in the building or that part of it or inflicts or attempts to inflict on any person therein any grievous bodily harm.

(2) The offences referred to in subsection (1)(a) above are offences of stealing anything in the building or part of a building in question, of inflicting on any person therein any grievous

bodily harm or raping any woman therein, and of doing unlawful damage to the building or anything therein.

(3) A person guilty of burglary shall on conviction on indictment be liable to imprisonment for a term not exceeding—

      (a) where the offence was committed in respect of a building or part of a building which is a dwelling, fourteen years;

      (b) in any other case ten years.

(4) References in subsections (1) and (2) above to a building, and the reference in subsection (3) above to a building which is a dwelling, shall also apply to an inhabited vehicle or vessel, and shall apply to any such vehicle or vessel at times when the person having a habitation in it is not there as well as at times when he is.

A: *Actus reus*

Both parts of s. 9(1) require proof that the defendant entered as a trespasser. If the requisite intent is present, a s. 9(1)(a) offence is committed at the moment of entry, whereas a s. 9(1)(b) offence is committed at the time that the ulterior offence is complete.

The *actus reus* of burglary presents a number of questions:

    (a) What constitutes sufficient entry?

    (b) When is a defendant trespassing?

    (c) How are 'building' and 'part of a building' defined?

    (d) For s. 9(1)(b) only, when can the ulterior offence be considered to have been committed?

(i) *Entry*

Many of the problems encountered in proving burglary were discussed in the following case:

R v Collins
[1972] 2 All ER 1105, Court of Appeal

EDMUND DAVIES LJ: . . . This is about as extraordinary a case as my brethren and I have ever heard either on the Bench or while at the Bar. Stephen William George Collins was convicted on 29th October 1971 at Essex Assizes of burglary with intent to commit rape and he was sentenced to 21 months' imprisonment. He is a 19 year old youth, and he appeals against that conviction by the certificate of the trial judge. The terms in which that certificate is expressed reveals that the judge was clearly troubled about the case and the conviction.

Let me relate the facts. Were they put into a novel or portrayed on the stage, they would be regarded as being so improbable as to be unworthy of serious consideration and as verging at times on farce. At about two o'clock in the early morning of Saturday, 24th July 1971, a young lady of 18 went to bed at her mother's home in Colchester. She had spent the evening with her boyfriend. She had taken a certain amount of drink, and it may be that this fact affords some explanation of her inability to answer satisfactorily certain crucial questions put to her. She has the habit of sleeping without wearing night apparel in a bed which is very near the lattice-type window of her room. At one stage of her evidence she seemed to be saying that the bed was close up against the window which, in accordance with her practice, was wide open. In the photographs which we have before us, however, there appears to be a gap of some sort between the two, but the bed was clearly quite near the window. At about 3.30 or 4.00 a.m. she awoke and she then saw in the moonlight a vague form crouched in the open window. She was unable to remember, and this is important, whether the form was on the outside of the window sill or on the part of the sill which was inside the room, and for reasons which will later become clear, that seemingly narrow point is of crucial importance. The young lady then realised several things: first of all that the form in the window was that of a male; secondly that he was a naked male; and thirdly that he was a naked male with an erect penis. She also saw in the moonlight that his hair was blond. She thereupon leapt to the conclusion that her boyfriend, with whom for some time she had been on terms of regular and frequent sexual intimacy, was paying her an ardent nocturnal visit. She promptly sat up in bed, and the man descended from the sill and joined her in bed and they had full sexual intercourse. But there was something about him which made her think that things were not as they usually were between her and her boyfriend. The length of his hair, his voice as they had exchanged what was described as 'love talk', and other features led her to the conclusion that somehow there was something different. So she turned on the bed-side light, saw that her companion was not her boyfriend and slapped the face of the intruder, who was none other than the appellant. He said to her, 'give me a good time tonight', and got hold of her arm, but she bit him and told him to go. She then went into the bathroom and he promptly vanished.

The complainant said that she would not have agreed to intercourse if she had known that the person entering her room was not her boyfriend. But there was no suggestion of any force having been used on her, and the intercourse which took place was undoubtedly effected with no resistance on her part.

The appellant was seen by the police at about 10.30 a.m. later that same morning. According to the police, the conversation which took place then elicited these points: He was very lustful the previous night. He had taken a lot of drink, and we may here note that drink (which to him is a very real problem) had brought this young man into trouble several times before, but never for an offence of this kind. He went on to say that he knew the complainant because he had worked around her house. On this occasion, desiring sexual intercourse – and according to the police evidence he had added that he was determined to have a girl, by force if necessary, although that part of the police evidence he challenged – he went on to say that he walked around the house, saw a light in an upstairs bedroom, and he knew that this was the girl's bedroom. He found a step ladder, leaned it against the wall and climbed up and looked into the bedroom. What he could see inside through the wide open window was a girl who was naked and asleep. So he descended the ladder and stripped off all his clothes, with the exception of his socks, because apparently he took the view that if the girl's mother entered the bedroom it would be easier to effect a rapid escape if he had his socks on than if he was in his bare feet. That is a matter about which we are not called on to express any view, and would in any event find ourselves unable to express one. Having undressed, he then climbed the ladder and pulled himself up on to the window sill. His version of the matter is that he was pulling himself in when she awoke. She then got up and knelt on the bed, she put her arms around his neck and body, and she seemed to pull him into the bed. He went on:

> . . . I was rather dazed, because I didn't think she would want to know me. We kissed and cuddled for about ten or fifteen minutes and then I had it away with her but found it hard because I had had so much to drink.

The police officer said to the appellant:

> It appears that it was your intention to have intercourse with this girl by force if neces-sary and it was only pure coincidence that this girl was under the impression that you were her boyfriend and apparently that is why she consented to allowing you to have sexual intercourse with her.

It was alleged that he then said:

Yes, I feel awful about this. It is the worst day of my life, but I know it could have been worse.

Thereupon the officer said to him – and the appellant challenges this – 'What do you mean, you know it could have been worse?' to which he is alleged to have replied:

Well, my trouble is drink and I got very frustrated. As I've told you I only wanted to have it away with a girl and I'm only glad I haven't really hurt her.

Then he made a statement under caution, in the course of which he said:

When I stripped off and got up the ladder I made my mind up that I was going to try and have it away with this girl. I feel terrible about this now, but I had too much to drink. I am sorry for what I have done.

In the course of his testimony, the appellant said that he would not have gone into the room if the girl had not knelt on the bed and beckoned him into the room. He said that if she had objected immediately to his being there or to his having intercourse he would not have persisted. While he was keen on having sexual intercourse that night, it was only if he could find someone who was willing. He strongly denied having told the police that he would, if necessary, have pushed over some girl for the purpose of having intercourse.

There was a submission of no case to answer on the ground that the evidence did not support the charge, particularly that ingredient of it which had reference to entry into the house 'as a trespasser'. But the submission was overruled, and as we have already related, he gave evidence.

Now, one feature of the case which remained at the conclusion of the evidence in great obscurity is where exactly the appellant was at the moment when according to him, the girl manifested that she was welcoming him. Was he kneeling on the sill outside the window or was he already inside the room, having climbed through the window frame, and kneeling on the inner sill? It was a crucial matter, for there were certainly three ingredients that it was incumbent on the Crown to establish. Under s. 9 of the Theft Act 1968, which renders a person guilty of burglary if he enters any building or part of a building as a trespasser and with the intention of committing rape, the entry of the appellant into the building must first be proved. Well, there is no doubt about that, for it is common ground that he did enter this girl's bedroom. Secondly, it must be proved that he entered as a trespasser. We will develop that point a little later. Thirdly it must be proved that he entered as a trespasser with intent at the time of entry to commit rape therein.

. . . Unless the jury were entirely satisfied that the appellant made an effective and substantial entry into the bedroom without the complainant doing or saying anything to cause him to believe that she was consenting to his entering it, he ought not to be convicted of the offence charged. The point is a narrow one, as narrow maybe as the window sill which is crucial to this case. But this is a criminal charge of gravity and, even though one may suspect that his *intention* was to commit the offence charged, unless the facts show with clarity that he in fact committed it he ought not to remain convicted.

NOTES AND QUESTIONS
1. The court speaks of an 'effective entry'. What is the difference between that and an ordinary entry? What if only part of Collins's body had entered into the room? Whether there has been an effective entry is a question of fact for the jury.
2. What of instruments used to effect entry? Say that Matthew inserts a crowbar under a window for the purpose of prising it open. Has he effected an entry? At common law the courts distinguished between instruments used to effect the criminal purpose (e.g., a hook to remove items) and those used to gain access. Only the former satisfied the 'entry' requirement.
3. Permission to enter premises may be either express or implied. There is, for example, implied permission to enter a public building.

The problem of the effectiveness of the entry has continued to trouble the courts. In particular, it is not clear whether the entry should have to be sufficiently effective to enable the defendant to be in a position to achieve his ulterior purpose. Since the intent to effect the ulterior purpose is all that is required under s. 9(1)(a), it would seem irrelevant that the entry should be sufficient to carry it out. However, this leaves in doubt the utility of the 'effective' criterion in *R v Collins*.

R v Ryan
[1996] Crim LR 320, Court of Appeal

At about 2.30 a.m. one morning an elderly householder found the defendant stuck in a downstairs window of his house. The defendant had his head and right arm inside the window and was trapped by the window itself which rested on his neck. The rest of his body remained outside the window. He was convicted of burglary. He appealed on the ground that, as a matter of law, his action was not capable of constituting an entry within the meaning of section 9 of the Theft Act 1968 since he could not have stolen anything from within the building because he was stuck firmly by his neck in the window.

Held, dismissing the appeal, that it was clear from *Brown* [1985] Crim LR 212 that for the purposes of section 9 of the 1968 Act a person could enter a building even if only part of his body was actually within the premises and it was totally irrelevant whether he was or was not capable of stealing anything because he was trapped halfway through the window.

(ii) *Trespass*
In *Collins* the Court of Appeal made it clear that not all the technicalities of the tort of trespass will be used to define the concept of trespass as an ingredient of the offence of burglary. Three issues are raised by the decision:

(a) Does the defendant need to know he is trespassing?

(b) Is it trespass when the defendant is invited into premises but, unknown to the person issuing the invitation, he has a secret unlawful intent?

(c) Will the doctrine of *trespass ab initio* apply?

(a) *Does the defendant need to know that he is trespassing? What are the limits of an invitation?*

R v Collins
[1972] 2 All ER 1105, Court of Appeal

For the facts, see p. 388.

EDMUND DAVIES LJ: . . . The second ingredient of the offence – the entry must be as a trespasser – is one which has not, to the best of our knowledge, been previously canvassed in the courts. Views as to its ambit have naturally been canvassed by the textbook writers, and it is perhaps not wholly irrelevant to recall that those who were advising the Home Secretary before the Theft Bill was presented to Parliament had it in mind to get rid of some of the frequently absurd technical rules which had been built up in relation to the old requirement in burglary of a 'breaking and entering'. The cases are legion as to what this did or did not amount to, and happily it is not now necessary for us to consider them. But it was in order to get rid of those technical rules that a new test was introduced, namely that the entry must be as a 'trespasser'.

. . . In the judgment of this court, there cannot be a conviction for entering premises 'as a trespasser' within the meaning of s. 9 of the Theft Act 1968 unless the person entering does so knowing that he is a trespasser and nevertheless deliberately enters, or, at the very least, is reckless whether or not he is entering the premises of another without the other party's consent.

R v Smith and Jones
[1976] 3 All ER 54, Court of Appeal

JAMES LJ: . . . Christopher Smith's father, Alfred Smith, lived at 72 Chapel Lane, Farnborough. He was in the course of negotiating a move from the house to other premises. At the material time, in May 1975, in that house were two television sets; one owned by Mr Alfred Smith, the other owned by another person but lawfully in possession of Mr Alfred Smith. Christopher Smith lived with his own family at Aberfield. The appellant Jones lived in the opposite direction from Chapel Lane, Farnborough to Aberfield, namely in Lakeside Road, Ashvale.

In the early hours of 10 May, 1975, a police officer in Ashvale saw a motor car with the two appellants inside and a television set protruding from the boot of the car. Having regard to that which he saw and the time of the morning he followed the car which turned into a side road where eventually it was stopped by a gate being in its way. The officer called for further officers to attend and when another officer went to the car he saw the appellant Jones sitting on the back seat with a second television set behind him. In the front of the car was Smith. They were told that the police believed that the television sets were stolen and that they were being arrested. Smith responded with the questions: 'Are they bent?' and Jones made the observation: 'You cannot arrest me for just having a ride in a car.'

At the trial both of the appellants gave evidence. It was the case for Smith that he had permission from his father to go into the house of his father. With that permission was a general licence to go there at any time he wanted to. It was the case for Jones at the trial that, contrary to what he had said to the police, he had gone into the house, he had gone purely as a passenger with Smith and gone in in the belief, honestly held, that Smith had permission to take the television sets from his father and that in taking them Smith was not stealing them or acting in any dishonest way. He himself, in so far as he was concerned with the matter, was not acting in any dishonest way.

Mr Rose argues that a person who had a general permission to enter premises of another person cannot be a trespasser. His submission is as short and as simple as that. Related to this case he says that a son to whom a father thas given permission generally to enter the father's house cannot be a trespasser if he enters it even though he had decided in his mind before making the entry to commit a criminal offence of theft against the father once he had got into the house and had entered the house solely for the purpose of committing that theft. It is a bold submission. Mr Rose frankly accepts that there has been no decision of the Court since this statute was passed which governs particularly this point. He has reminded us of the decision in *Byrne* v *Kinematograph Renters Society Ltd* [1958] 2 All ER 579, which he prays in aid of his argument. In that case persons had entered a cinema by producing tickets not for the purpose of seeing the show, but for an ulterior purpose. It was held in the action, which sought to show that they entered as trespassers pursuant to a conspiracy to trespass, that in fact they were not trespassers. The important words in the judgment of Harman J at p. 593D are 'They did nothing that they were not invited to do, . . .' That provides a distinction between that case and what we consider the position to be in this case.

Mr Rose has also referred us to one of the trickery cases, a case of *R* v *Boyle* (1954) 38 Cr App R 111, and in particular the passage on pp. 112–113, 295 of the respective reports. He accepts that the trickery cases can be distinguished from such a case as the present because in the trickery cases it can be said that that which would otherwise have been consent to enter was negatived by the fact that consents was obtained by a trick. We do not gain any help in the particular case from that decision.

We are also referred to *R v Collins* (1972) 56 Cr App R 554 and in particular to the long passage of Edmund Davies LJ, as he then was, commencing at pp. 559 and 104 of the respective reports where the learned Lord Justice commenced the consideration of what is involved by the words ' . . . the entry must be "as a trespasser".' At p. 561 and pp. 104–105 – again it is unnecessary to cite the long passage in full, suffice it to say that this Court on that occasion expressly approved the view expressed in Professor Smith's book on the *Law of Theft* (1968) (1st ed.) para. 462, and also the view of Professor Griew in his book on the *Theft Act* (1968) (1st ed.) para. 4–05 upon this aspect of what is involved in being a trespasser.

In our view the passage there referred to is consonant with the passage in the well known case of *Hillen and Pettigrew v I.C.I. (Alkali) Ltd* [1936] AC 65 where, in the speech of Lord Atkin these words appear at p. 69:

> My Lords, in my opinion this duty to an invitee only extends so long as and so far as the invitee is making what can reasonably be contemplated as an ordinary and reasonable use of the premises by the invitee for the purpose for which he has been invited. He is not invited to use any part of the premises for purposes which he knows are wrongfully dangerous and constitute an improper use. As Scrutton LJ has pointedly said [in *The Calgarth* [1926] P 93 at p. 110] 'When you invite a person into your house to use the staircase you do not invite him to slide down the banisters'.

That case of course was a civil case in which it was sought to make the defendant liable for a tort.

The decision in *Collins* (*supra*) in this Court, a decision upon the criminal law, added to the concept of trespass as a civil wrong only the mental element of *mens rea*, which is essential to the criminal offence. Taking the law as expressed in *Hillen and Pettigrew v I.C.I. Ltd* (*supra*) and in the case of *Collins* (*supra*) it is our view that a person is a trespasser for the purpose of section 9(1)(b) of the Theft Act 1968, if he enters premises of another knowing that he is entering in excess of the permission that has been given to him, or being reckless as to whether he is entering in excess of the permission that has been given to him to enter, providing the facts are known to the accused which enable him to realise that he is acting in excess of the permission given or that he is acting recklessly as to whether he exceeds that permission, then that is sufficient for the jury to decide that he is in fact a trespasser.

In this particular case it was a matter for the jury to consider whether, on all the facts, it was shown by the prosecution that the appellants entered with the knowledge that entry was being effected against the consent or in excess of the consent that had been given by Mr Smith senior to his son Christopher. The jury were, by their verdict satisfied of that. . . .

NOTES AND QUESTIONS

1. Do *Collins* and *Smith and Jones* take the same approach to what constitutes a trespass? If not, are the positions reconcilable?

2. Is it trespass when the defendant is invited into premises but, unknown to the person issuing the invitation, he has a secret unlawful intent? Does the rationale of *Smith and Jones* convert all instances of shoplifting into burglary?

3. We noted previously instances where prosecutors created problems for the courts by charging theft in cases where property was in fact obtained by deception. In *Smith and Jones*, it would arguably have made more sense to charge the defendants with theft, a crime they clearly committed, rather than forcing the courts to strain the boundaries of burglary. Part of the justification for the higher maximum penalty for burglary as compared to theft is the concern to protect the residents of a dwelling from uninvited intruders. Was this the case in *Smith and Jones*?

4. If Collins knew that the parents of the girl would not have approved of his presence, did he know he was trespassing? Can a lodger invite guests into a house to a party contrary to the wishes of a landlord? What if the guests stay for a week?

(b) *Will the doctrine of* trespass ab initio *apply?*

The doctrine of *trespass ab initio* holds that even if one is on premises lawfully as an invitee, one can become a trespasser by exceeding the limits of the invitation.

R v *Collins*
[1972] 2 All ER 1105, Court of Appeal

For the facts, see p. 388.

EDMUND DAVIES LJ: . . . Some question arose whether or not the appellant can be regarded as a trespasser *ab initio*. But we are entirely in agreement with the view expressed in *Archbold* that the common law doctrine of *trespass ab initio* has no application to burglary under the Theft Act 1968. One further matter that was canvassed ought perhaps to be mentioned. The point was raised that, the complainant not being the tenant or occupier of the dwelling-house and her mother being apparently in occupation, this girl herself could not in any event have extended an effective invitation to enter, so that even if she had expressly and with full knowledge of all material facts invited the appellant in, he would nevertheless be a trespasser. Whatever be the position in the law of tort, to regard such a proposition as acceptable in the criminal law would be unthinkable.

NOTES AND QUESTIONS

Why should the doctrine of *trespass ab initio* apply in the context of criminal law? Does it not in effect convert all thieves into burglars?

Part of the need for the doctrine is obviated by the language in s. 9(1) referring to 'building or part of a building.' See the discussion below.

(iii) *Building/part of a building*

The maximum sentence for the offence of burglary varies depending on the type of building entered. Section 26 of the Criminal Justice Act 1991 introduced a two-tier system, substituting new s. 9(3) and (4) into the Theft Act 1968. If the building is a 'dwelling' the maximum penalty is 14 years' imprisonment; if it is any other building the maximum penalty is 10 years' imprisonment.

The Act speaks in terms of a 'building' or 'part of a building'. 'Part of a building' includes any part into which the defendant has no authority to go. There need be no physical barrier between the 'part' into which the defendant is invited and the 'part' in which he is trespassing:

R v *Walkington*
(1979) 68 Cr App Rep 427, Court of Appeal

At 5.40 pm one evening the appellant entered a department store at a time when the assistants were 'cashing-up' their tills, the store closing at 6 pm. A store detective and two colleagues noticed that the appellant only appeared to be interested in the tills in the menswear department; but he was seen to ascend an escalator to the first floor to the dress display part where there was an unattached till in the centre of a three-sided counter, the till being left partially open and, unknown to the appellant but appreciated by the staff, empty. That drawer was located at least four yards inside the private area of the store restricted to the sales staff. The appellant moved into the opening of that counter, looked around him, and bent down and opened the drawer of the partially open till. After looking inside it, he slammed it shut and left the store when he was detained for questioning and later charged with burglary contrary to s. 9(1)(a) and (2) of the Theft Act 1968. The particulars of the offence alleged that he had entered the store in question as a trespasser with intent to steal therein. At the end of the prosecution case the appellant submitted that he had no case to answer in that there had been no trespass. The trial judge overruled that submission and directed that jury to consider first, so far as the store was concerned, whether the area where the half-opened till was situated was a prohibited area; secondly, if so, did the appellant realise when he crossed the limit that that area was prohibited; thirdly, at the time when he crossed that limit, the first two questions being decided against the appellant, did he have the intention to steal? The jury convicted. On appeal it was contended that the judge had erred in refusing to withdraw the case from the jury in that it was wrong to divide the store artificially and the appellant could not be said to have trespassed behind the counter . . .

GEOFFREY LANE LJ (approving the judge's summing-up which he quoted):

> . . . The first question really arising out of this, which you have to consider is the use of the words 'part of a building'. The case for the prosecution is that the defendant formed an intent to steal while within this Debenhams, but before he entered the cash desk area, so that the prosecution are alleging that when he entered that area he was entering part of a building. Now, it is for you to decide whether on this section of the Theft Act that area was part of a building. Now, if you take the case of an ordinary shop, at the ordinary shop, which comprises a room with one part of it separated off by a counter, you might find little difficulty in deciding that the part of the room behind the counter was a separate part of the building from the shop area, and one which the public were not allowed to enter unless invited to do so. On the other hand, if you have the case of a large store, such as Debenhams, and there is a till placed on a table situated in the middle of the shop area, you might find it difficult, or even impossible, to say that any particular area, definable area, round that table was a separate part of the building. So that in approaching the problem you are entitled, of course, to use your own experience. You have been round shops, so you know the sort of layout you find in shops, so you may find it helpful to ask yourselves whether a shopper coming into a store and seeing the area with which you are concerned in this case would realise that that is an area to which the public were not entitled to go, and separate from the rest of the shopping area where they were entitled to go. It is a matter for you to decide. It is for you to decide whether that is the case. Coming back to the question of the definition of trespass, that is to say, of entering any part of a building as a trespasser, you now have to consider the next part of the definition, that is to say, 'with intent to steal.' Now in order to convict under this part of the section, section 9 of the Theft Act, the intent to steal must have been formed before the defendant entered that part of the area which was a separate part of the building. . . .

When considering the definition of 'building', the extended definition in s. 9(4) should be noted:

Theft Act 1968

9.—(4) References in subsection (1) and (2) above to a building, and the reference in subsection (3) above to a building which is a dwelling, shall also apply to an inhabited vehicle or vessel, and shall apply to any such vehicle or vessel at times when the person having a habitation in it is not there as well as at times when he is.

NOTES AND QUESTIONS
1. When is a vehicle or vessel 'inhabited'? Is a caravan 'inhabited' during the week if it is kept ready to be used, but only used, at weekends? What about a yacht, fitted out but not yet launched?
2. While s. 9(1)(a) requires only an intent to commit an offence within the building, s. 9(1)(b) requires that the defendant steal or attempt to steal something that is in the building, or inflict or attempt to inflict grievous bodily harm on a person in the building. Thus in construing the statute one must refer back to the substantive law of theft and that of attempt. However, for the purposes of s. 9(1)(b) the infliction of grievous bodily harm on any person need not amount to an offence under ss. 18 or 20 of the Offences Against the Person Act 1861. See *R v Jenkins* [1983] Crim LR 386. *Jenkins* was reversed by the House of Lords ([1983] 3 All ER 448) on other grounds. The House of Lords decision does not affect the Court of Appeal ruling that the infliction of grievous bodily harm for purposes of s. 9(1)(b) need not amount to an offence.
3. Nigel enters Buckingham Palace to see how the Queen lives. He wanders around undetected for several hours before being discovered and apprehended by security guards. Has he committed any offence? If he had picked up a vase intending to smash it on the pavement outside, would he have committed burglary? When would the burglary have taken place?

B: *Mens rea*

There are different *mens rea* which may have to be proved, depending on which part of the statute is charged:

(a) An intention to commit one of the ulterior offences is required for a s. 9(1)(a) burglary.

(b) For a s. 9(1)(b) burglary, the *mens rea* of the ulterior offence must be proved.

Recall also that in respect to both s. 9(1)(a) and s. 9(1)(b), the defendant must know that he is entering as a trespasser.

The s. 9(1)(a) *mens rea* must be present at the time of entering the building; the s. 9(1)(b) *mens rea* need not be present at the time of entry, only at the time of the commission of the ulterior offence.

The ulterior offences relevant to s. 9(1)(a) are contained in s. 9(2):

Theft Act 1968

9.—(2) The offences referred to in subsection (1)(a) above are offences of stealing anything in the building or part of a building in question, of inflicting on any person therein any grievous bodily harm or raping any woman therein, and of doing unlawful damage to the building or anything therein.

The ulterior offences relevant to s. 9(1)(b) are contained in the subsection itself. They are stealing or attempting to steal anything in the building or that part of it, or inflicting or attempting to inflict on any person therein any grievous bodily harm.

What if the defendant's intention is conditional?

Attorney-General's References (Nos 1 & 2 of 1979)
[1980] QB 180, Court of Appeal

In the first reference a grocer who lived above his shop heard the backdoor open and close late one night and intercepted the defendant who was ascending the stairs. The police were called and arrested the defendant. They asked him why he had entered the house and he replied 'To rob £2,000' and on being asked why he thought there was £2,000 there he said 'I don't know, I was just going to take something.' The indictment before the Crown Court averred that he had entered the grocer's premises as a trespasser 'with intent to steal therein'. The trial judge withdrew the case from the jury at the close of the prosecution case and directed an acquittal. The Attorney-General referred to the court for opinion the question whether a man who had entered a house as a trespasser with the intention of stealing money therein was entitled to be acquitted of an offence against s. 9(1)(a) of the Theft Act 1968 on the ground that his intention to steal was conditional upon his finding money in the house.

In the second reference a householder heard a sound at the French windows at the rear of her house. She called the police who went to the rear of the house and found the defendant holding and turning the handle of the French windows and inserting a long thin stick between the door and the doorframe. Later at the police station the defendant made a written statement in which he said 'I wasn't going to do any damage in the house, only see if there was anything lying around.' The indictment averred that the defendant had attempted to enter the dwelling house concerned 'with intent to steal therein'. At the close of the prosecution case the judge directed the jury to return a verdict of not guilty upon the ground that the evidence did not disclose a present intention to steal but merely a conditional intention. The Attorney-General referred to the court for opinion the question whether a man who was atempting to enter a house as a trespasser with the intention of stealing anything of value which he might find therein was entitled to be acquitted of the offence of attempted burglary on the ground that at the time of the attempt his intention was insufficient to amount to 'the intention of stealing anything' necessary for conviction under s. 9 of the Theft Act 1968.

On the hearing of both references:—

Held: (1) that, under s. 9(1)(a) of the Theft Act 1968, the offence of burglary was committed if a person entered a building as a trespasser with an intention to steal; that, where a person was charged with burglary, it was no defence to show that he did not intend to steal any specific objects, and, accordingly, the fact that the intention to steal was conditional on finding money in the house did not entitle a person to be acquitted on a charge of entering premises as a trespasser with intent to steal therein; and that the question asked in the first reference was to be answered in the negative.

NOTES AND QUESTIONS
1. The issue of conditional intent is in a sense a red herring for the defendant can be convicted of a crime of attempted burglary, where impossibility will not be a defence. This observation suggests a more fundamental question about burglary: Why is there a need for the offence at all? Why is it not sufficient to charge the defendant with either the ulterior offence commit-

ted, or, where the ulterior offence is not completed, an attempt to commit the ulterior offence?

2. As burglary under s. 9(1)(a) is a type of inchoate crime, in that it could have the effect of frustrating the ultimate offence that the offender contemplates when entering as a trespasser, is it too far for removed to have a crime of attempted burglary?

SECTION 7: **Criminal damage**

Like theft offences, the law of criminal damage seeks to protect property interests; but whereas theft protects the owner from having his property appropriated, the present offence protects against damage to or destruction of property. The controlling statute is the Criminal Damage Act 1971. There are also aggravated forms of the offence.

In almost all the circumstances envisaged by the statute, the victim will also have a right to seek compensation in the civil courts (although, of course, the defendant may not have sufficient funds to pay). In many circumstances the loss may also be covered by insurance.

QUESTIONS

What are the arguments for and against using the criminal law to protect property from damage? Are they the same as for protecting property from theft?

A: Damaging or destroying property belonging to another

The basic offence is set out in s. 1 of the Criminal Damage Act 1971:

Criminal Damage Act 1971

1.—(1) A person who without lawful excuse destroys or damages any property belonging to another intending to destroy or damage any such property or being reckless as to whether any such property would be destroyed or damaged shall be guilty of an offence.
. . .

(8) An offence committed under this section by destroying or damaging property by fire shall be charged as arson.

The maximum punishment for a violation of s. 1(1) following a trial on indictment is 10 years' imprisonment (s. 4(2)). Where the offence is committed by fire it will be charged as arson and the maximum sentence is then life imprisonment (s. 1(3) and s. 4(1)).

(i) *Actus reus*
Three main problems arise:

(a) What is damage?

(b) What is property?

(c) When can property be regarded as belonging to another?

(a) *Damage.* Whether property is damaged is a question of fact. What constitutes damage is not defined in the Act, but it appears to involve a reduction in the value or usefulness of the property.

Cox v Riley
(1986) 83 Cr App R 54, Queen's Bench Division

STEPHEN BROWN LJ: This is an appeal by way of case stated from the decision of the justices for the petty sessional division of Tamworth in the county of Stafford on April 1, 1985. On that day the defendant was charged on 'an information which alleged that on July 30, 1984 at Tamworth without lawful excuse he damaged the plastic circuit card of a G.S.C. computerised saw to the value of £620, belonging to High-Tech Profiles Ltd., intending to damage such property or being reckless as to whether such property would be damaged, contrary to section 1(1) of the Criminal Damage Act, 1971.

The justices in the case state that they found the following facts: (i) the defendant was employed by Hi-Tech Profiles Limited to work on a computerised saw owned by that company; (ii) that the computerised saw relied for its operation on a printed circuit card being inserted into it, containing programs which enabled the saw to be operated so that it could cut window frame profiles of different designs; (iii) that the printed circuit card was of no use to the company unless it contained programs which enabled it to cause the saw to operate as (ii) above; (iv) that on July 30, 1984 the defendant blanked the computerised saw of all its 16 programs thereby erasing the said programs from the printed circuit card by operating the program cancellation facility, contained within the computerised saw, once for each individual program removed; (v) that the defendant's action rendered the computerised saw inoperable, save for limited manual operation, which would cause production to be slowed dramatically.

The damage alleged was the removing of the program and really, it seems to me, the only possible argument which Mr Orme could put forward is that there was no damage within the meaning of the Act.

The question of damage has been considered by the Court of Appeal, Criminal Division, on November 29, 1984 in the unreported case of *Henderson & Battley*. The Court was presided over by Lawton CJ and he was sitting with Cantley J and Sir John Thompson. Cantley J gave the judgment of the Court.

In that case the facts were different, but it is relevant on the meaning of damage. In that case the charge was one of damaging a development land site, intending to damage that property or being reckless as to whether it would be damaged. The facts concerned a development site in the Isle of Dogs which had been cleared for development. It was flat except for a pile of crushed concrete which was kept there intentionally so that it could be used eventually in the laying of temporary roads whilst the development was carried on.

On the occasion in question 30 lorry loads of soil and rubble and mud were tipped on to the site. The appellants in that case, pretending to act with authority, had been operating the site, as Cantley J said, impudently as a public tip and charging their customers for the rubbish which was tipped. There was a submission before the trial judge which was repeated before the Court of Appeal that what they had done could not be said to have damaged the land, bearing in mind that this was a site cleared for building development. The argument was that the land was not damaged because the land beneath the piles of rubbish which had been tipped upon it was in the same condition as it was before the rubbish was tipped upon it. It was argued that there must be a distinction between the cost of putting something right and actual damage.

Cantley J said in the course of his judgment at p. 3B of the transcript:

> There is of course such a distinction, but if as here there is evidence that the owner of the land reasonably found it necessary to spend about £2,000 to remove the results of the appellants' operations it is not irrelevant to the question of whether this land, as a building site, was damaged. Ultimately whether damage was done to this land was a question of fact and degree for the jury. Damage can be of various kinds. In the *Concise Oxford Dictionary* 'damage' is defined as 'injury impairing value or usefulness'. That is a definition which would fit in very well with doing something to a cleared building site which at any rate for the time being impairs its usefulness as such. In addition, as it necessitates work and the expenditure of a large sum of money to restore it to its former state, it reduces its present value as a building site. This land was a perfectly good building site which did not need £2,000 spending on it in order to sell or use it as such until the appellants began their operations.

Cantley J continued:

> It was held as long ago as 1865 in the case of *Fisher* (LR 1 CCR 7) that an obstruction temporarily rendering a machine useless for the purpose for which it was intended to be used can be damage. In that case the facts were briefly these. A disgruntled employee who had been employed to operate an agricultural steam-engine had parted from his employer and it had seemed to him to be a good idea to put the steam-engine out of action. He screwed it up fairly tightly and he put a piece of stick up the water feed, and did other things of that kind. It is not necessary to enumerate them all: it is sufficient if I say that it took two hours, but no more, and no materials, to restore the machine to proper working order.

Some 'ancestor' of counsel in that case said Cantley J

> argued that in all the cases decided on the statute charging his client with malicious damage a certain portion of the machinery had been removed, and some absolute damage had been done to prevent the machine from working, and that there must be some 'lesion', as he put it, to the machine. Pigott B said there was damage because labour was required to reinstate the machine; not money, be it noted, but just two hours labour. Delivering a very short judgment of the Court for Crown Cases Reserved Pollock CB said: 'We are all of opinion that the conviction is good. It is like the case of spiking a gun, where there is no actual damage done to the gun, although it is rendered useless.'

It seems to me that the principle as explained by Cantley J applies in full measure to the present case. Undoubtedly, as in the old case of *Fisher (supra)*, the defendant in this instance for some reason, perhaps a grudge, wished to put out of action, albeit temporarily, the computerised saw, and he was able to do that by operating the computer blanking mechanism in order to erase from the printed circuit card the relevant programs. That made it necessary for time and labour and money to be expended in order to replace the relevant programs on the printed circuit card.

NOTES AND QUESTIONS

1. The misconduct at issue in *Cox* v *Riley* would now be covered by the Computer Misuse Act 1990 rather than the Criminal Damage Act. Section 3(6) of the 1990 Act provides that a modification of the contents of a computer 'shall not be regarded as damaging any computer or computer storage medium unless its effect on that computer or computer storage medium impairs its physical condition'.

2. The defendants in *Cox* v *Riley* would now be guilty of the offence of unauthorised modification of computer material contrary to s. 3 of the 1990 Act. Could they also be charged with criminal damage? On what basis should a Crown prosecutor determine which offence to charge?

Is there a *'de minimis'* principle (*de minimis non curat lex*) in respect of damage? Compare the following two cases:

R v *A*
[1978] Crim LR 689, Kent Crown Court

A was convicted by the Brentford Juvenile Court of an offence of criminal damage and remitted to Folkestone Juvenile Court for sentence. He appealed against conviction. He was one of a number of football supporters who were being escorted to an 'away' football ground 'crocodile fashion' by several police officers. The evidence given for the prosecution was that a police constable walking beside the 'crocodile' saw the appellant spit once at the back of a uniformed police sergeant. The police constable saw spittle land upon the sergeant's raincoat which was already covered with similar spittle, and arrested A. The sergeant continued on duty unaware of what had happened. When later informed of the state of his raincoat, he attempted to remove the spittle with a paper tissue, so as to present a less embarrassing spectacle.

On his return to the police station, the sergeant heard of the arrest of the appellant for the offence of criminal damage to his coat and so no further attempts were made to clean the raincoat. At the hearing, the raincoat was produced and a faint mark could be seen upon it, in the general vicinity of where the constable said he saw the spittle land. The prosecution contended that the raincoat required dry-cleaning, and must, therefore, have been 'damaged'.

It was contended on behalf of A that there was no case to answer because the prosecution had failed to prove any damage. The court was referred to a definition of 'damage' as 'rendering imperfect or inoperative.'

Held, allowing the appeal, that when interpreting the word 'damage,' the court must consider the use of an ordinary English word. Spitting at a garment could be an act capable of causing damage. However, one must consider the specific garment which has been allegedly damaged. If someone spat upon a satin wedding dress, for example, any attempt to remove the spittle might in itself leave a mark or stain. The court would find no difficulty in saying that an article had been rendered 'imperfect' if, after a reasonable attempt at cleaning it, a stain remained. An article might also have been rendered 'inoperative' if, as a result of what happened, it had been taken to dry cleaners.

However, in the present case, no attempt had been made, even with soap and water, to clean the raincoat, which was a service raincoat designed to resist the elements. Consequently, there was no likelihood that if wiped with a damp cloth, the first obvious remedy, there would be any trace or mark remaining on the raincoat requiring further cleaning. Furthermore, the raincoat was not rendered 'inoperative' at the time; if it was 'inoperative,' it was solely on account of being kept as an exhibit.

Thus, in the view of the court, nothing occurred which could properly be described as damage. An offence of assault might well have been appropriate but this was not a point which the court had to decide.

Hardman and Others v *The Chief Constable of Avon and Somerset Constabulary*
[1986] Crim LR 330, Bristol Crown Court

The appellants were convicted by the Justices of causing criminal damage to a pavement. They appealed.

They were members of the Campaign for Nuclear Disarmament. On 6 August, 1985 (which was the fortieth anniversary of the Hiroshima bombing) they painted human silhouettes on an asphalt pavement to represent vaporised human remains. The 'paint' was a fat free unstable whitewash, which was soluble in water. It was specially mixed in the expectation that rainwater would wash away the markings. The evidence suggested that this was correct and that rainwater and pedestrian traffic would *eventually* eradicate the markings. However, the Local Authority had acted before this happened and a 'Graffiti Squad' was employed to clean the pavement using high pressure water jets. It was contended by the appellants that following *'A' (a Juvenile)* v *The Queen* (1978) Crim LR 689 there was no 'damage' within the meaning of s. 1 of the Criminal Damage Act 1971.

Held: Notwithstanding the fact that the markings could be washed away there had nonetheless been damage, which had caused expense and inconvenience to the Local Authority. An unduly narrow definition of damage was not appropriate. The approach of Walters J in *Samuels* v *Stubbs*, 4 SASR 200 was approved when he said at p. 203:

> It seems to me that it is difficult to lay down any very general and, at the same time, precise and absolute rule as to what constitutes 'damage'. One must be guided in a great degree by the circumstances of each case, the nature of the article, and the mode in which it is affected or treated. Moreover, the meaning of the word 'damage' must as I have already said, be controlled by its context. The word may be used in the sense of 'mischief done to property.' . . .

NOTES AND QUESTIONS

1. Are *Hardman* and *R* v *A* reconcilable? How much damage must be done to give rise to a charge of criminal damage? Is it critical whether the damage requires the expenditure of money to repair?
2. Damage to a machine can be caused by dismantling it, even if the individual components are not themselves damaged. However, if damage by dismantling is alleged it must be charged as damage to the machine and not to the individual parts. In *Morphitis* v *Salmon* [1990] Crim LR 48, the defendant dismantled a barrier across the road. He was charged with damage to the bar component of the barrier and acquitted. If he had been charged with damage to the barrier as a whole he could have been convicted. The court also made the point that a scratch on the bar of the barrier would not have constituted sufficient damage for a conviction as it could not have impaired its value or usefulness as scaffolding components get scratched in the normal course of events.
3. Would a charge of battery have been successful in *R* v *A*?
4. The s. 1(1) offence speaks in terms of either damage to or destruction of property. Is the reference to destruction of property otiose? Can one destroy property without damaging it? Does the destruction of another's property constitute theft?
5. In *R (On the application of Abbott)* v *Colchester Magistrates Court* [2001] Crim LR 564 the court experienced difficulty in estimating the value of a crop of genetically modified maize which the defendants had damaged in an environmental protest. The defendants were subsequently tried by jury and acquitted, having pleaded that they were defending nearby organic crops from damage by the spread of pollen from the GM crops. Is this case consistent with Hardman? *R* v *A*?

(b) *Property.*

Criminal Damage Act 1971

10.—(1) In this Act 'property' means property of a tangible nature, whether real or personal, including money and—

(a) including wild creatures which have been tamed or are ordinarily kept in captivity, and any other wild creatures or their carcases if, but only if, they have been reduced into possession which has not been lost or abandoned or are in the course of being reduced into possession; but

(b) not including mushrooms growing wild on any land or flowers, fruit or foliage of a plant growing wild on any land.

For the purposes of this subsection 'mushrooms' includes any fungus and 'plant' includes any shrub or tree.

QUESTION

What are the differences between this definition of property and that contained in s. 4 of the Theft Act 1968? Why are the definitions different?

(c) *Belonging to another.*

Criminal Damage Act 1971

10.—(2) Property shall be treated for the purposes of this act as belonging to any person—
(a) having the custody or control of it;
(b) having in it any proprietary right or interest (not being an equitable interest arising only from an agreement to transfer or grant an interest); or
(c) having a charge on it.

(3) Where property is subject to a trust, the persons to whom it belongs shall be so treated as including any person having a right to enforce the trust.

(4) Property of a corporation sole shall be so treated as belonging to the corporation notwithstanding a vacancy in the corporation.

QUESTIONS

1. The Theft Act 1968 s. 5 uses the concepts of 'possession or control'. Is the Criminal Damage Act's term 'custody or control' clearer? See *Warner* v *MPC* [1969] 2 AC 256.

2. Is it possible to be guilty of criminal damage to property which you own? If you lend your property to another and then destroy it, have you committed criminal damage? If you destroy your own property in order to collect the insurance money, have you committed criminal damage? Any other criminal offence?

(ii) *Mens rea*
The defendant must intend or be reckless in respect of causing the damage. The requisite intent is lacking if the defendant believes the property is his own. This latter requirement overlaps to some extent with the statutory defence set out in s. 5(2). See *R* v *Smith (David)* [1974] 1 QB 354, below p. 455.

NOTES AND QUESTIONS

1. Recklessness in this context means *Caldwell* recklessness (see Chapter 4). Indeed, *Caldwell* involved an interpretation of the Criminal Damage Act. What this means is that the defend-

ant is guilty if his or her acts create an obvious risk of damage to property and (i) he or she recognises that there is some risk but nevertheless goes on to take it; or (ii) gives no thought to the possibility of there being such a risk. The defendant is reckless even if incapable of recognising the risk because of an incapacity (see *Elliott* v *C* [1983] 2 All ER 1005, discussed in Chapter 5). The defendant can also be convicted even if the risk of damage foreseen is slight and the defendant takes what he or she sees as adequate precautions to avoid the risk (see *Shimmen* (1986) 84 Cr App R 7).

2. What purposes are served by taking an objective approach to recklessness? Are they out-weighed by the danger of convicting individuals whose only fault is that they are not as intelligent as the ordinary person and, as a result, do not perceive a risk to property that an ordinary person would have appreciated?

(iii) *'Without lawful excuse'*

The Criminal Damage Act 1971, s. 1(1) contains the phrase 'without lawful excuse'. This phrase is defined in s. 5:

Criminal Damage Act 1971

5. 'Without lawful excuse'

(1) This section applies to any offence under section 1(1) above and any offence under section 2 or 3 above other than one involving a threat by the person charged to destroy or damage property in a way which he knows is likely to endanger the life of another or involving an intent by the person charged to use or cause or permit the use of something in his custody or under his control so to destroy or damage property.

(2) A person charged with an offence to which this section applies shall whether or not he would be treated for the purposes of this Act as having a lawful excuse apart from this subsection, be treated for those purposes as having a lawful excuse—

(a) if at the time of the act or acts alleged to constitute the offence he believed that the person or persons whom he believed to be entitled to consent to the destruction of or damage to the property in question had so consented, or would have so con-sented to it if he or they had known of the destruction or damage and its circum-stances; or

(b) if he destroyed or damaged or threatened to destroy or damage the property in ques-tion or, in the cause of a charge of an offence under section 3 above, intended to use or cause or permit the use of something to destroy or damage it, in order to protect property belonging to himself or another or a right or interest in property which was or which he believed to be vested in himself or another, and at the time of the act or acts alleged to constitute the offence he believed—

(i) that the property, right or interest was in immediate need of protection; and

(ii) that the means of protection adopted or proposed to be adopted were or would be reasonable having regard to all the circumstances.

(3) For the purposes of this section it is immaterial whether a belief is justified or not if it is honestly held.

(4) For the purposes of subsection (2) above a right or interest in property includes any right or privilege in or over land, whether created by grant, licence or otherwise.

(5) This section shall not be construed as casting doubt on any defence recognised by law as a defence to criminal charges.

NOTES AND QUESTIONS

1. What if the defendant makes a mistake about the ownership of property because she is drunk? See *Jaggard* v *Dickinson* [1980] 3 All ER 716 (for Facts and holding, see p. 450).
2. Voluntary intoxication is not usually a defence to a charge where the *mens rea* is *Caldwell* recklessness. Indeed, Caldwell was drunk at the time he committed his crime. Why should it afford a defence under s. 5(2)? Is *Jaggard* v *Dickinson* consistent with *DPP* v *Majewski* (for Facts and holding, see p. 456)?

If the belief in permission to damage the property is honest, the reason for the action is not relevant, even if fraud is involved.

R v *Denton*

[1982] 1 All ER 65, Court of Appeal

LORD LANE CJ: . . . The facts of the case were somewhat unusual. There is no dispute that on 3 January 1980 the defendant set light to some machinery in the cotton mill. The machinery was very badly damaged, and as a result of that conflagration damage was also done, to a much lesser degree it is true, to the building itself. The total damage to stock and building was said to be some £40,000.

On Monday, 17 March 1980 the defendant presented himself at the police station and told the police that he had in fact started that fire. He described how he had done it, and he then made a statement under caution, in which he gave his reason for having started the fire: that it was for the benefit of the business, because the business was in difficulties, and, although he was going to get no direct benefit from it himself, he thought he would be doing a good turn to the financial status of the company if he were to set light to the premises and goods as he did. Hence the charge against him.

When it came to the trial he gave evidence that his employer, to whom we will refer to as 'T' for obvious reasons, had asked him to put the machines out of action and he had agreed to set light to it. The reason given to him by the employer for that request was because the company was in difficulties; the way that T put it was: 'There is nothing like a good fire for improving the financial circumstances of a business.'

. . . The fact that somebody may have had a dishonest intent which in the end he was going to carry out, namely to claim from the insurance company, cannot turn what was not originally a crime into a crime. There is no unlawfulness under the 1971 Act in burning a house. It does not become unlawful because there may be an inchoate attempt to commit fraud contained in it; that is to say it does not become a crime under the 1971 Act, whatever may be the situation outside of the Act.

Consequently it is apparent to us that the judge, in his ruling in this respect, was wrong. Indeed it seems to us, if it is necessary to go as far as this, that it was probably unnecessary for the defendant to invoke s. 5 of the 1971 Act at all, because he probably had a lawful excuse without it, in that T was lawfully entitled to burn the premises down. The defendant believed it. He believed that he was acting under the directions of T and that on its own, it seems to us, may well have provided him with a lawful excuse without having resort to s. 5.

NOTES AND QUESTIONS

1. Note that God is not a person capable of giving consent to damage property (*Blake* v *DPP* [1993] Crim LR 587).
2. In *Chamberlain* v *Lindon* [1998] 1 WLR 1252 the defendant demolished a wall which had been built by his neighbour and which he believed was obstructing his right of way. The Court (Queen's Bench Division) held that the defendant had a lawful excuse within s. 5(2)(b) in that he honestly believed that he had to destroy the wall in order to protect a right or interest in property that was in immediate need of protection and that the means adopted were reasonable in all the circumstances.

3. Of what offence, if any, could Denton be convicted? His employer?
4. Is there an inconsistency in the 'subjective' approach taken in *Denton* and the 'objective' approach taken in respect to *mens rea* (see *Caldwell*, Chapter 3)?
5. Under s. 5(2) the question of whether or not a particular act was done in order to protect property is answered by applying an objective test. See *R* v *Hunt* (1978) 66 Cr App R 105; *R* v *Hill* [1989] Crim LR 136; *Blake* v *DPP*, above; *Johnson* v *DPP* [1994] Crim LR 673. Is this inconsistent with *Denton*?

B: Destroying or damaging property with intent to endanger life

Criminal Damage Act 1971

1.—(2) A person who without lawful excuse destroys or damages any property, whether belonging to himself or another—

(a) intending to destroy or damage any property or being reckless as to whether any property would be destroyed or damaged; and

(b) intending by the destruction or damage to endanger the life of another or being reckless as to whether the life of another would be thereby endangered;

shall be guilty of an offence.

(3) An offence committed under this section by destroying or damaging property by fire shall be charged as arson.

The maximum punishment for this aggravated offence is life imprisonment (s. 4(1)). In many cases the defendant may also be subject to a charge of attempted murder. However, while the criminal damage offence requires proof of damage to property, it is wider than attempted murder because it is sufficient that the defendant is reckless as to whether life is endangered. Attempted murder will require proof of an attempt to kill.

(i) *Actus reus*

The terms 'damage', 'destroy' and 'property' are defined as for s. 1(1), above. However, here there is no need to prove that the property belonged to another. Why this difference? Is it because the gist of the offence is against persons rather than against property?

(ii) *Mens rea*

The defendant must:

(a) intend or be reckless as to damaging or destroying property; and

(b) intend or be reckless that by that damage will endanger life.

R v *Steer*
[1987] 2 All ER 833, House of Lords

The defendant went to the house of his former business partner, against whom he had a grudge, and fired several shots at the house with an automatic rifle. No injuries were caused to the partner or his wife inside the house and there was no suggestions that any of the shots had been aimed at either of them. The defendant was charged with and convicted of, *inter alia*, damaging property being reckless whether the life of another would be endangered thereby, contrary to s. 1(2) of the Criminal Damage Act 1971. He appealed, contending that s. 1(2) only applied if property was damaged and the damage in turn caused danger to life, whereas any danger to the defendant's partner and his wife had been directly caused by the bullets fired by the defendant and not by the damaged property. The Crown contended that 'intending by the destruction or damage' in s. 1(2)(b) referred to the act which caused the destruction of or damage to property was the cause of the danger to life. The Court of Appeal allowed the defendant's appeal and quashed the conviction, holding that a person could only be convicted under s. 1(2) of recklessly endangering the life of another by damaging or destroying property if it was proved that the danger to life resulted from the destruction of or damage to property. The Crown appealed to the House of Lords.

Held: For a person to be guilty of the offence under s. 1(2) of the 1971 Act of destroying or damaging any property with intent to endanger the life of another by the destruction or damage or being reckless whether the life of another would be thereby endangered the prosecution had to prove that the danger to life resulted from the destruction of or damage to the property and it was not sufficient for the prosecution to prove that the danger to life resulted from the act which caused the destruction or damage. It followed therefore that the defendant was not guilty of the offence charged and the appeal would accordingly be dismissed . . .

The fact that lives are not endangered is not relevant if the requisite intention can be proved:

R v *Dudley*
[1989] Crim LR 57, Court of Appeal

D who had a grievance against the J family, consumed drink and drugs, went to their house and, using an accelerant, threw a fire bomb at the house, causing a high sheet of flame outside the glass door. The fire was extinguished by the J family and only trivial damage was caused. He was charged with arson under s. 1(1) and (2) of the Criminal Damage Act 1971; he pleaded guilty to simple arson and a trial proceeded on the counts laid under s. 1(2). At the close of the prosecution case D's counsel submitted that there was no case to answer because the jury could not properly find that the actual damage caused was intended to endanger life or was likely to do so, and he relied on R v *Steer* [1988] AC 111. The trial judge rejected the submission and D thereupon changed his plea to guilty to the count of arson being reckless as whether life would be endangered. He appealed against conviction, submitting that the judge's ruling was wrong in law.

Held, the appeal would be dismissed. The words 'destruction or damage' in s. 1(2)(b) of the Act (endangering life) referred back to destruction or damage intended, or as to which there was recklessness, in s. 1(2)(a) (damaging property). The words did not refer to the destruction or damage actually caused . . .

R v *Sangha*
[1988] 2 All ER 385, Court of Appeal

During a visit to squatters who occupied a council-owned flat the appellant set fire to a mattress. Later that afternoon the appellant returned to the flat and set fire to two armchairs in it, with the result that the premises were burnt out. The appellant was charged with, *inter alia*, arson in that he damaged the flat by fire, being reckless whether the life of another would be thereby endangered, contrary to s. 1(2)(b) of the Criminal Damage Act 1971. At the time the fire was started there was no one in the flat and because of its construction there was no danger of the fire spreading to adjoining properties. At his trial the appellant submitted that there was no case to answer because if when starting the fire he had known that no one was in the flat or if in fact there was no one there his act could not be said to have created a risk of danger to the life of another and he could not have been reckless whether life was endangered. The judge rejected that submission and the appellant was convicted. He appealed to the Court of Appeal.

TUCKER J: . . . In our judgment, when consideration is given whether an act of setting fire to something creates an obvious and serious risk of damaging property and thereby endangering the life of another, the test to be applied is this: is it proved that an ordinary prudent bystander would have perceived an obvious risk that property would be damaged and that life would thereby be endangered? The ordinary prudent bystander is not deemed to be invested with expert knowledge relating to the construction of the property, nor to have the benefit of hindsight. The time at which his perception is material is the time when the fire is started.

Section 1(2) of the 1971 Act uses the word 'would' in the context of recklessness whether property would be destroyed or damaged, and whether the life of another would be thereby endangered. We interpret this word 'would' as going to the expectations of the normal prudent bystander.

Applying this test to the facts of the case before us, it is clear that in setting fire to these armchairs as the jury found the appellant did, he created a risk which was obvious and serious that property would be damaged and that the life of another would thereby be endangered. The fact that there were special features here which prevented that risk from materialising is irrelevant.

NOTES AND QUESTIONS

1. How satisfactory is the 'ordinary prudent bystander' test? What if the defendant has less knowledge than the ordinary prudent bystander? More knowledge?
2. Without lawful excuse does not have the same meaning in s. 1(2) as in s. 1(1). Section 5 specifically states that it does not apply to s. 1(2). Lawful excuse in the context of s. 1(2) is therefore confined to situations where the defendant acts in self-defence, defence of another, or in prevention of crime, or to apprehend an offender.

PART III

Exculpatory Conditions and Defences

9

The Principle of Capacity

The twin assumptions upon which the criminal law rests are that human beings have the capacity to choose between good and evil and the capacity to control their actions. At the same time the law is prepared to recognise that there are instances when these assumptions are less likely to be correct. There are certain classes of individuals – children and the mentally ill are the most common examples – who are not able to appreciate the social consequences of their acts. Although they may not also understand the legality of their acts, there are many non-law trained individuals who also lack legal understanding. Yet, as we shall see later and as most of the public are already aware, ignorance of the law is generally not an excuse. What differentiates children and the mentally ill from others who may not know the requirements of the law is that they lack the capacity to appreciate, in a deeper sense, when their actions are seriously wrong.

The incapacity of the mentally ill is a *mental* incapacity. That of children is the product of a lack of maturity and intellectual development. In both instances, the criminal law is prepared to accept that offenders are unable to appreciate the significance of their actions. There is also a class of persons who understand when they are committing a criminal offence, but are unable to stop themselves from doing so. The courts sometimes refer to these individuals as automatons and characterise their defence as one of automatism. What these persons really lack is the capacity to control their actions. Stated in these terms, it is apparent that automatism is linked to the concept of *actus reus*, and the requirement of a voluntary act. However, since the source of the incapacity may be mental, the courts have sometimes confused automatism with insanity, and have distinguished between insane and non-insane automatism.

This chapter examines capacity, in both its mental and physical guises.

SECTION 1: Age (infancy)

As indicated above, the courts proceed on the assumption that those subject to the criminal law are able to understand its commands and to distinguish between what is permitted and what is forbidden. If an individual chooses to do what is forbidden, it is appropriate to punish that person for his or her acts. The assumption, however, is called into question when the actor is a child. It is generally accepted that children below a certain age may not truly understand the social significance of their acts, and the law is prepared to make allowance. As children grow older and mature, their understanding also increases. Flexibility in the law is needed to accommodate the fact that different children mature at a different pace; but fixed points are also desirable, lest every trial involving a non-adult degenerate into a psychological inquiry of the individual child's state of maturation. The law has developed with these two themes in mind. A distinction was originally drawn between children under 10, children between 10 and 14, and children above 14. The special treatment of 10–14 year olds has been abolished.

A: Children under 10

There is an irrebuttable presumption that a child under the age of 10 at the time of the alleged offence lacks the capacity to commit the offence (Children and Young Persons Act 1933, s. 50). In these circumstances no crime has been committed by the child.

Walters v *Lunt*
[1951] 2 All ER 645, King's Bench Division

LORD GODDARD CJ: This is a Case stated by justices for the city of Lincoln, before whom the respondents, a husband and wife, were charged under the Larceny Act 1916, s. 33(1), that

> . . . they between Aug. 1 and 31, 1950, at the city of Lincoln, jointly feloniously did receive from Richard Norman Lunt (aged seven years) a child's tricycle of the value of £2, the property of Walter Cole, which had theretofore been feloniously stolen, knowing the same to have been so stolen.

There was a similar charge in respect of a child's fairy cycle alleged to have been received by them on Mar. 11, 1951, from Richard Norman Lunt, aged seven years, and we infer from the Case that Richard Norman Lunt is the child of the respondents. The justices refused to convict on the ground that, as the child was under eight years of age, under the Children and Young Persons Act 1933, s. 50, he was incapable of stealing and could not be convicted of the felonious act of larceny, and, therefore, the respondents could not be convicted, under s. 33(1) of the Act of 1916, of receiving stolen property because the property taken by the child was not property 'stolen or obtained . . . under circumstances which amount to felony or misdemeanour.'

   . . . In the case now before us the child could not have been found guilty of larceny because he was under eight years of age, and, unless he is eight years old, he is not considered in law capable of forming the intention necessary to support a charge of larceny. Therefore, the justices came to a perfectly proper decision in point of law on the charge of receiving.

NOTES AND QUESTIONS
1. While no crime may have been committed by the child who executes the *actus reus*, others may be guilty of committing the offence through use of the child as an innocent agent. Were the parents in *Walters* v *Lunt* guilty of theft? See also in this regard, *DPP* v *K and B* [1997] 1 Cr App R 36.
2. Until fairly recently, boys under the age of 14 were conclusively presumed to be incapable of

sexual intercourse and thus could not be convicted of rape, even in cases where there was incontrovertible evidence that sexual intercourse had taken place. See, e.g., *R v Groombridge* (1835) C&P 582. This outdated and irrational presumption was abolished in the Sexual Offences Act 1993, s. 1.

3. All references to age are to chronological age and not mental age. But which does it make more sense to treat as an adult – a nine-year-old with the mental age and maturity of a 15-year-old, or a 15-year-old with the mental age and maturity of a nine-year-old?

B: Children between 10 and 14

Historically, there was a common law presumption – known as *doli incapax* – that a child between ten and fourteen was incapable of committing a criminal offence. This presumption, however, could be rebutted by proof that the child knew that the conduct in question was 'seriously wrong'. The presumption came into being at a time when defendants found guilty of many crimes were routinely hanged. With the virtual abolition of capital punishment, many questioned the continuing role of the presumption and it was finally abolished in s. 34 of the Crime and Disorder Act 1998.

NOTES

1. The House of Lords in *C (a minor) vDPP* [1996] 1 AC 1, a pre-Act case, had observed that:

   > The distinction between the treatment and the punishment of child 'offenders' has popular and political overtones, a fact which shows that we have been discussing not so much a legal as a social problem, with a dash of politics thrown in, and emphasises that it should be within the exclusive remit of Parliament. There is need to study other systems, including that which holds sway in Scotland, a task for which the courts are not equipped. Whatever change is made, it should come only after collating and considering the evidence and after taking account of the effect which a change would have on the whole law relating to children's anti-social behaviour. This is a classic case for parliamentary investigation, deliberation and legislation.

2. One of the difficulties with the presumption of *doli incapax* related to the type and quantum of evidence needed to rebut it. See, e.g., *R v Runeckles* (1984) 79 Cr App R 255; *R v DPP* [1992] Crim LR 334. The United Nations Convention on the Rights of the Child, to which the UK is a signatory, requires states to establish a minimum age below which a child shall be presumed not to have the capacity to commit a crime. The difficult problem, of course, lies in determining what the appropriate age should be. Different countries have set different minimum ages, but at 10 the age set in England is lower than that of any other European country except Ireland (7) and Scotland (8).

Having the age of responsibility begin at ten has been challenged before the European Court of Human Rights as being contrary to Article 3 (prohibition of torture or inhuman or degrading treatment).

T v United Kingdom (appl. no. 24724/94)
1999, European Court of Human Rights

1. The offence
The applicant was born in August 1982.
On 12 February 1993, when he was ten years old, he and another ten-year-old boy, 'V', had played truant from school and abducted a two-year-old boy from a shopping precinct, taken him on a

journey of over two miles and then battered him to death and left him on a railway line to be run over [the victim in the case was Jamie Bulger].
. . .

The Court has considered first whether the attribution to the applicant of criminal responsibility in respect of acts committed when he was ten years old could, in itself, give rise to a violation of Article 3. In doing so, it has regard to the principle, well established in its case-law that, since the Convention is a living instrument, it is legitimate when deciding whether a certain measure is acceptable under one of its provisions to take account of the standards prevailing amongst the member States of the Council of Europe . . .

In this connection, the Court observes that, at the present time there is not yet a commonly accepted minimum age for the imposition of criminal responsibility in Europe. While most of the Contracting States have adopted an age-limit which is higher than that in force in England and Wales, other States, such as Cyprus, Ireland, Liechtenstein and Switzerland, attribute criminal responsibility from a younger age. Moreover, no clear tendency can be ascertained from examination of the relevant international texts and instruments. Rule 4 of the Beijing Rules which, although not legally binding, might provide some indication of the existence of an international consensus, does not specify the age at which criminal responsibility should be fixed but merely invites States not to fix it too low, and Article 40(3)(a) of the UN Convention requires States Parties to establish a minimum age below which children shall be presumed not to have the capacity to infringe the criminal law, but contains no provision as to what that age should be.

The Court does not consider that there is at this stage any clear common standard amongst the member States of the Council of Europe as to the minimum age of criminal responsibility. Even if England and Wales is among the few European jurisdictions to retain a low age of criminal responsibility, the age of ten cannot be said to be so young as to differ disproportionately from the age-limit followed by other European States. The Court concludes that the attribution of criminal responsibility to the applicant does not in itself give rise to a breach of Article 3 of the Convention.
. . .

NOTES AND QUESTIONS

1. Although the European Court of Human Rights rejected the argument that setting the age of criminal responsibility at ten was contrary to Article 3 of the Convention, it did find a violation of Article 6 (the right to a fair trial). The Court stated that a public trial in an adult court was inappropriate for children so young because it impeded their ability to participate effectively. Does this aspect of the Court's judgment signify the end of trials of young offenders in adult courts?

2. What arguments support the case for treating child murderers differently than other murderers? In what ways should the law be altered, if at all – in its substantive content – in the applicable trial procedures, in the penalty imposed following a conviction (an adult convicted of murder is subject to a mandatory life sentence)?

3. Another issue in *T* involved the fact that the Home Secretary had set the 'tariff' (the minimum sentence to be served) for the defendants. The Court ruled that the Home Secretary was not the 'independent and impartial tribunal' envisaged by Article 6(1) of the Convention. Furthermore, the tariff effectively precluded the periodic review by a judicial body to which the defendants were entitled under Article 5(4) of the Convention. It should be noted, however, that these aspects of the Court's decision apply only to defendants under the age of 18 (who are held in confinement 'at Her Majesty's pleasure').

SECTION 2: **Insanity**

While the number of cases in which an insanity defence is raised is statistically low, the defence raises some of the most profound issues in criminal law. Why should the insane offender be excused from criminal liability? He has caused harm to society; often, as in the case of a killer, quite grave harm. He is also a danger to society, and, if let loose, may well reoffend. He is clearly in need of restraint and rehabilitation.

There are several considerations which are said to justify the defence. First, it is felt that an insane offender is not morally blameworthy. Offenders who, through no fault of their own, lack the capacity to know what they are doing or that it is wrong do not have the rational autonomy which the law envisages, and should not be held responsible for their breaches of the law any more than should a child. There is the additional point that there is little purpose served in imposing criminal punishment for deterrent purposes, as those who are truly insane are unlikely to understand the commands of the law (indeed, this is implicit in the definition of insanity), or be deterred by criminal sanctions.

Insanity is a defence to all crimes, including those which impose strict liability. The legal test of insanity was enunciated in *M'Naghten's Case*:

M'Naghten's Case
(1843) 10 Cl & F 200, House of Lords

The prisoner had been indicted for that he, on the 20th day of January 1843, at the parish of Saint Martin in the Fields, in the county of Middlesex, and within the jurisdiction of the Central Criminal Court, in and upon one Edward Drummond, feloniously, wilfully, and of his malice aforethought, did make an assault; and that the said Daniel M'Naghten, a certain pistol of the value of 20s., loaded and charged with gunpowder and a leaden bullet (which pistol he in his right hand had and held), to, against and upon the said Edward Drummond, feloniously, wilfully, and of his malice aforethought, did shoot and discharge; and that the said Daniel M'Naghten, with the leaden bullet aforesaid, out of the pistol aforesaid, by force of the gunpowder, etc., the said Edward Drummond, in and upon the back of him the said Edward Drummond, feloniously, etc. did strike, penetrate and wound, giving to the said Edward Drummond, in and upon the back of the said Edward Drummond, one mortal wound, etc., of which mortal wound the said E. Drummond languished until the 25th of April and then died; and that by the means aforesaid, he the prisoner did kill and murder the said Edward Drummond. The prisoner pleaded Not guilty.

Evidence having been given of the fact of the shooting of Mr Drummond, and of his death in consequence thereof, witnesses were called on the part of the prisoner, to prove that he was not, at the time of committing the act, in a sound state of mind. The medical evidence was in substance this: That persons of otherwise sound mind, might be affected by morbid delusions: that the prisoner was in that condition: that a person so labouring under a morbid delusion, might have a moral perception of right and wrong, but that in the case of the prisoner it was a delusion which carried him away beyond the power of his own control, and left him no such perception; and that he was not capable of exercising any control over acts which had connexion with his delusion: that it was of the nature of the disease with which the prisoner was affected, to go on gradually until it had reached a climax, when it burst forth with irresistible intensity: that a man might go on for years quietly, though at the same time under its influence, but would all at once break out into the most extravagant and violent paroxysms.

. . .

Verdict, Not guilty, on the ground of insanity. This verdict, and the question of the nature and extent of the unsoundness of mind which would excuse the commission of a felony of this sort, having been made the subject of debate in the House of Lords (the 6th and 13th March 1843; see Hansard's Debates, vol. 67, pp. 288, 714), it was determined to take the opinion of the Judges on the law governing such cases.

LORD CHIEF JUSTICE TINDAL: . . . The first question proposed by your Lordships is this: 'What is the law respecting alleged crimes committed by persons afflicted with insane delusion in respect of one or more particular subjects or persons: as, for instance, where at the time of the commission of the alleged crime the accused knew he was acting contrary to law, but did the act complained of with a view, under the influence of insane delusion, of redressing or revenging some supposed grievance or injury, or of producing some supposed public benefit?'

In answer to which question, assuming that your Lordships' inquiries are confined to those persons who labour under such partial delusions only, and are not in other respects insane, we are of opinion that, notwithstanding the party accused did the act complained of with a view, under the influence of insane delusion, of redressing or revenging some supposed grievance or injury, or of producing some public benefit, he is nevertheless punishable according to the nature of the crime committed, if he knew at the time of committing such crime that he was acting contrary to law; by which expression we understand your Lordships to mean the law of the land.

Your Lordships are pleased to inquire of us, secondly, 'What are the proper questions to be submitted to the jury, where a person alleged to be afflicted with insane delusion respecting one or more particular subjects or persons, is charged with the commission of a crime (murder, for example), and insanity is set up as a defence?' And, thirdly, 'In what terms ought the question to be left to the jury as to the prisoner's state of mind at the time when the act was committed?' And as these two questions appear to us to be more conveniently answered together, we have to submit our opinion to be that the jurors ought to be told in all cases that every man is to be presumed to be sane, and to possess a sufficient degree of reason to be responsible for his crimes, until the contrary be proved to their satisfaction: and that to establish a defence on the ground of insanity, it must be clearly proved that, at the time of the committing of the act, the party accused was labouring under such a defect of reason from disease of the mind, as not to know the nature and quality of the act he was doing; or if he did know it, that he did not know he was doing what was wrong. The mode of putting the latter part of the question to the jury on these occasions has generally been, whether the accused at the time of doing the act knew the difference between right and wrong: which mode, though rarely, if ever leading to any mistake with the jury, is not, as we conceive, so accurate when put generally and in the abstract, as when put with reference to the party's knowledge of right and wrong in respect to the very act with which he is charged. If the question were to be put as to the knowledge of the accused solely and exclusively with reference to the law of the land, it might tend to confound the jury, by inducing them to believe that an actual knowledge of the law of the land was essential in order to lead to a conviction; whereas the law is administered upon the principle that every one must be taken conclusively to know it, without proof that he does know it. If the accused was conscious that the act was one which he ought not to do, and if that act was at the same time contrary to the law of the land, he is punishable; and the usual course therefore has been to leave the question to the jury, whether the party accused had a sufficient degree of reason to know that he was doing an act that was wrong: and this course we think is correct, accompanied with such observations and explanations as the circumstances of each particular case may require.

The fourth question which your Lordships have proposed to us is this: – 'If a person under an insane delusion as to existing facts, commits an offence in consequence thereof, is he thereby excused?' To which question the answer must of course depend on the nature of the delusion: but, making the same assumption as we did before, namely, that he labours under such partial delusion only, and is not in other respects insane, we think he must be considered in the same situation as to responsibility as if the facts with respect to which the delusion exists were real. For example, if under the influence of his delusion he supposes another man to be in the act of attempting to take away his life, and he kills that man, as he supposes, in self-defence, he would be exempt from punishment. If his delusion was that the deceased had inflicted a serious injury to his character and fortune, and he killed him in revenge for such supposed injury, he would be liable to punishment.

NOTES AND QUESTIONS

1. A defendant is presumed to be sane. How does one go about rebutting this presumption? Under s. 1(1) of the Criminal Procedure (Insanity and Unfitness to Plead) Act 1991, a defendant may not be acquitted by reason of insanity except on the evidence of at least two registered medical practitioners, one of whom is a specialist approved by the Home Secretary.

2. The insanity defence is concerned with the defendant's state of mind at the time of commission of the crime, not at the time of trial. One can be sane immediately prior to one's criminal act and immediately afterwards, but if insane at the time of the act the defence is available.

3. The court in *M'Naghten* said that the defence must be clearly proved – but by whom and by what standard? The rule is that the defence must be proved by the defendant on a balance of probabilities rather than by the more typical criminal law standard of proof beyond a reasonable doubt. Nonetheless, the allocation to the defendant of this burden of persuasion reverses the prevailing practice in regard to most other defences. What is the justification for this departure from standard practice?

4. Note the difficulty facing a jury. The law is concerned with the defendant's mental state at the time of the crime; but a psychiatric examination of the defendant will probably not be conducted until after arrest. This may be some time after the crime was committed. The jury will have to attempt to reconstruct what the defendant's state of mind was at the time of the crime, based on an after-the-fact psychiatric examination. Nor can the jurors rely on their observations of the defendant at trial, for the defendant's mental state at the time of the trial also may not be the same as at the time of the crime.

5. In the normal case where the jury decide that the defendant has a defence to the crime charged, they return a verdict of 'not guilty'. If the jury find that the defendant was insane, on the other hand, they return a verdict of 'not guilty by reason of insanity'. Why this departure from standard practice?

The *M'Naghten* test requires proof '*that . . . the . . . accused was labouring under such a defect of reason, from disease of the mind*'. The defect must be more than stupidity, absent-mindedness or confusion. See *Clarke* [1972] 1 All ER 219. Rather, there must be a total deprivation of the power to reason brought on by a disease of the mind. But what is meant by 'disease of the mind'?

R v Sullivan

[1984] 1 AC 156, House of Lords

LORD DIPLOCK: My Lords, the appellant, Mr Sullivan, a man of blameless reputation, has the misfortune to have been a lifelong sufferer from epilepsy. There was a period when he was subject to major seizures known as grand mal; but, as a result of treatment which he was receiving as an out-patient of the Maudsley Hospital from 1976 onwards, these major seizures had, by the use of drugs, been reduced by 1979 to seizures of less severity known as petit mal, or psychomotor epilepsy, though they continued to occur at a frequency of one or two per week.

One such seizure occurred on May 8, 1981, when Mr Sullivan, then aged 51, was visiting a neighbour, Mrs Killick, an old lady aged 86 for whom he was accustomed to perform regular acts of kindness. He was chatting there to a fellow visitor and friend of his, a Mr Payne aged 80, when the epileptic fit came on. It appears likely from the expert medical evidence about the way in which epileptics behave at the various stages of a petit mal seizure that Mr Payne got up from the chair to help Mr Sullivan. The only evidence of an eyewitness was that of Mrs Killick, who did not see what had happened before she saw Mr Payne lying on the floor and Mr Sullivan kicking him about the head and body, in consequence of which Mr Payne suffered injuries severe enough to require hospital treatment.

As a result of this occurrence Mr Sullivan was indicted upon two counts: the first was of causing grievous bodily harm with intent contrary to section 18 of the Offences against the Person Act 1861; the second of causing grievous bodily harm contrary to section 20 of that Act. At his trial, which took place at the Central Criminal Court before Judge Lymbery and a jury, Mr Sullivan pleaded not guilty to both counts. Mrs Killick's evidence that he had kicked Mr Payne violently about the head and body was undisputed and Mr Sullivan himself gave evidence of his history of epilepsy and his absence of all recollection of what had occurred at Mrs Killick's flat between the time that he was chatting peacefully to Mr Payne there and his returning to the flat from somewhere else to find that Mr Payne was injured and that an ambulance had been sent for. The prosecution accepted his evidence as true. . . .

The evidence as to the pathology of a seizure due to psychomotor epilepsy can be sufficiently stated for the purposes of this appeal by saying that after the first stage, the prodram, which precedes the fit itself, there is a second stage, the ictus, lasting a few seconds, during which there are electrical discharges into the temporal lobes of the brain of the sufferer. The effect of these discharges is to cause him in the post-ictal stage to make movements which he is not conscious that he is making, including, and this was a characteristic of previous seizures which Mr Sullivan had suffered, automatic movements of resistance to anyone trying to come to his aid. These movements of resistance might, though in practice they very rarely would, involve violence.

. . ., [I]t is submitted the medical evidence in the instant case shows that psychomotor epilepsy is not a disease of the mind, whereas in *Bratty* [1963] AC 386 it was accepted by all the doctors that it was. The only evidential basis for this submission is that Dr Fenwick said that in medical terms to constitute a 'disease of the mind' or 'mental illness,' which he appeared to regard as interchangeable descriptions, a disorder of brain functions (which undoubtedly occurs during a seizure in psycho-motor epilepsy) must be prolonged for a period of time usually more than a day; while Dr Taylor would have it that the disorder must continue for a minimum of a month to qualify for the description 'a disease of the mind.'

The nomenclature adopted by the medical profession may change from time to time; Bratty was tried in 1961. But the meaning of the expression 'disease of the mind' as the cause of 'a defect of reason' remains unchanged for the purposes of the application of the M'Naghten Rules. I agree with what was said by Devlin J in *R v Kemp* [1957] 1 QB 399, 407, that 'mind' in the M'Naghten Rules is used in the ordinary sense of the mental faculties of reason, memory and understanding. If the effect of a disease is to impair these faculties so severely as to have either of the consequences referred to in the latter part of the rules, it matters not whether the aetiology of the impairment is organic, as in epilepsy, or functional, or whether the impairment itself is permanent or is transient and intermittent, provided that it subsisted at the time of commission of the act. The purpose of the legislation relating to the defence of insanity, ever since its origin in 1800, has been to protect society against recurrence of the dangerous conduct. The duration of a temporary suspension of the mental faculties of reason, memory and understanding, particularly if, as in Mr Sullivan's case, it is recurrent, cannot on any rational ground be relevant to the application by the courts of the M'Naghten Rules, though it may be relevant to the course adopted by the Secretary of State, to whom the responsibility for how the defendant is to be dealt with passes after the return of the special verdict of 'not guilty by reason of insanity.'

R v *Hennessy*
[1989] 1 WLR 287, Court of Appeal

LORD LANE CJ: . . . On Thursday, 28 May 1987, two police constables, Barnes and Grace, were on duty in St Leonards-on-Sea on the Sussex coast, among other things looking for a Ford Granada car which had been stolen. They found the car. It was unattended. They kept it under watch. As they watched they saw the appellant get into the car, switch on the headlights and ignition, start the car and drive off. The appellant at the wheel of the car correctly stopped the car at a set of traffic lights which were showing red against him. Pc Grace then went over to the car as it was stationary, removed the ignition keys from the ignition-lock, but not before the appellant had tried to drive the motor car away and escape from the attention of the policeman. The appellant was put in the police car. On the way to the police station an informal conversation about motor vehicles took place between the appellant and the police officers, in particular about the respective merits of the new Rover motor car and the Ford Sierra. Indeed, the appellant appeared to Pc Barnes not only to be fully in possession of his faculties but to be quite cheerful and intelligent. Indeed he went so far as to say to the police officer that if he had only got the car, which he was in the process of removing, onto the open road, he would have given the policemen a real run for their money.

However after having been at the police station for a time, the appellant was at a later stage escorted by Pc Barnes to hospital. He seemed to be normal when he left the cell block at the police station, but when he arrived at the hospital he appeared to be dazed and confused. He complained to the sister in the casualty ward that he had failed to take his insulin and indeed had had no insulin since the previous Monday when he should have had regular self-injected doses. He was given insulin, with which he injected himself, and the hospital discharged him and he was taken back to the police station.

The appellant gave evidence to the effect that he had been a diabetic for about ten years. He needed, in order to stabilise his metabolism, two insulin injections on a daily basis, morning and afternoon. The amount required would depend on factors such as stress and eating habits. He was on a strict carbohydrate diet. At the time of the offence he said he had been having marital and employment problems. His wife had submitted a divorce petition some time shortly before, and he was very upset. He had not been eating and he had not been taking his insulin. He remembered very few details of the day. He could recall being handcuffed and taken to the chargeroom at the police station. He remembered being given insulin at the hospital and injecting himself and he remembers feeling better when he got back to the police station afterwards. He said he did not recall taking the car.

When cross-examined he agreed that he had understood proceedings at the police station and what had gone on there. Indeed he had given the name and address of his solicitor. That was a considerable time before he had had his insulin at the hospital.

His general practitioner, Dr Higginson, was called to give evidence. He spoke as to the appellant's medical condition. He described in broad outlines the effect of diabetes: it is a deficiency in the system of the production of hormones which should balance the sugar metabolism. The lacking hormone is of course insulin. In the absence of the hormone the blood sugar rises and that results in hyperglycaemia. If the patient does not take his insulin and does not stick to the proper diet, then hyperglycaemia will supervene. If unchecked, the liver will become affected and the increasingly high level of sugar makes the patient drowsy and he will ultimately go into a coma.

If on the other hand the balance tips the other way, if too much insulin is taken, then the blood sugar will fall and hypoglycaemia, that is to say too little sugar in the blood, will supervene.

According to the hospital notes, on the evening in question the appellant's blood sugar had been high at 22 plus millimolecules per litre, the normal being 8 or 9. According to Dr Higginson one would expect to see some physical manifestation of hyperglycaemia at that level. So the doctor was saying in short that eventually hyperglycaemia can result in drowsiness, loss of consciousness and coma, greater or less unresponsiveness to stimuli according to the degree of hyperglycaemia present. He added, I will read a passage from his evidence in a moment, that anxiety or depression can increase the blood sugar level, a person's ability and awareness of what is going on could be impaired if there were 'associated symptoms and he had other conditions and worries at the same time . . .'

. . .

The importance of the [M'Naghten] rules in the present context, namely the context of automatism, is this. If the defendant did not know the nature and quality of his act because of something which *did not* amount to defect of reason from disease of the mind then he will probably be entitled to be acquitted on the basis that the necessary criminal intent which the prosecution has to prove is not proved. But, if, on the other hand, his failure to realise the nature and quality of his act was due to a defect of reason from disease of the mind, then in the eyes of the law he is suffering from insanity, albeit M'Naghten insanity.

. . .

The question in many cases, and this is one such case, is whether the function of the mind was disturbed on the one hand by disease or on the other hand by some external factor. . . .

The point was neatly raised in *R v Quick, R v Paddison* [1973] 3 All ER 347, [1973] QB 910. also referred to us by counsel for the appellant, in which Lawton LJ reviewed the authorities. It might perhaps help if I read a short passage from the headnote ([1973] QB 910):

> The defendants, Q and P, nurses at a mental hospital, were jointly and severally charged with assaulting a patient occasioning actual bodily harm. Both pleaded not guilty. Q, a diabetic, relied on the defence of automatism. He gave evidence that he had taken insulin as prescribed on the morning of the assault, had drunk a quantity of spirits and eaten little food thereafter and had no recollection of the assault. He called medical evidence to the effect that his condition at the material time was consistent with that of hypoglycaemia. The judge ruled that that evidence could only support a defence of insanity, not automatism. Q then pleaded guilty and P was convicted of aiding and abetting Q by encouragement. The defendants appealed against conviction.

I turn to the passage in the judgment where Lawton LJ said ([1973] 3 All ER 347 at 356, [1973] QB 910 at 922 – 923):

> A malfunctioning of the mind of transitory effect caused by the application to the body of some external factor such as violence, drugs, including anaesthetics, alcohol and hypnotic influences cannot fairly be said to be due to disease. Such malfunctioning, unlike that caused by a defect of reason from disease of the mind, will not always relieve an accused from criminal responsibility . . . Inthis case Quick's alleged mental condition, if it ever

existed, was not caused by his diabetes but by his use of the insulin prescribed by his doctor. Such malfunctioning of his mind as there was, was caused by an external factor and not by a bodily disorder in the nature of a disease which disturbed the working of his mind. It follows in our judgment that Quick was entitled to have his defence of automatism left to the jury and that Bridge J's ruling as to the effect of the medical evidence called by him was wrong.

Thus in *R v Quick* the fact that his condition was, or may have been, due to the injections of insulin meant that the malfunction was due to an external factor and not to the disease. The drug it was that caused the hypoglycaemia, the low blood sugar. As suggested in another passage of the judgment of Lawton LJ, hyperglycaemia, high blood sugar, caused by an inherent defect and not corrected by insulin is a disease, and if, as the defendant was asserting here, it does cause a malfunction of the mind, then the case may fall within the M'Naghten rules.

The burden of the argument of counsel for the appellant to us is this. It is that the appellant's depression and marital troubles were a sufficiently potent external factor in his condition to override, so to speak, the effect of the diabetic shortage of insulin on him. . . .

In our judgment, stress, anxiety and depression can no doubt be the result of the operation of external factors, but they are not, it seems to us, in themselves separately or together external factors of the kind capable in law of causing or contributing to a state of automatism. . . .

R v T
[1990] Crim LR 256, Snaresbrook Crown Court

T, a young French woman aged 23 and two others (R and B) were arrested and charged with robbery (two cases) and T was further charged with ABH. The Crown alleged a joint enterprise by all three to rob two females whilst armed with a Stanley knife (not recovered) and a pen knife, of their handbags, as the two victims were returning to a car late at night. When first seen, T was leaning on the victims' car and said 'I'm ill, I'm ill.' The three accused then surrounded one of the girls and there was a scuffle. Her bag opened and the contents spilled out, whereupon the two victims ran away. A few minutes later, they met another young woman, dressed in a dark coloured jogging suit, who offered to accompany them to the local police station. En route to the car, T saw the two victims and (allegedly) misidentified the third person as a male. T then followed the three women to the motor vehicle and she was followed by R and B. Near the car, the contents of the first victim's handbag were recovered and she got behind the wheel of the car. The second victim sat in the rear nearside passenger seat and the third woman was standing by the open front nearside passenger's door when they were approached by the three defendants. R went to the driver's side and held a Stanley-type knife to the face of the first victim and demanded her bag, which he was given. T approached the open passenger's door where the third woman was standing. When asked what she was doing and why, T stabbed the third woman in the stomach causing a small puncture wound (no medical treatment required other than a dressing). T then pushed past the third woman, leant into the car and demanded the second victim's handbag, which was given to her. All three defendants remained in the vicinity for about one minute. The third woman realised she had been stabbed and started to scream, whereupon the three defendants decamped. The three victims drove away and pointed out T, R and B to a police officer whereupon R and B decamped. R was seen to discard a pen knife in a rubbish bin and discard the first victim's handbag, both of which were recovered. After a short chase R was arrested and brought back to where the victims were, and the officer also detained T who was standing at the side of the road. On being arrested, T was described as being passive and indifferent to what was happening. During a subsequent interview, T could only recollect some of the events. B was arrested the following day and all three were charged. Seven days later, T was examined by a doctor at H.M. Prison Holloway when it was found that her hymen was ruptured and was bleeding, and that there were injuries posterior to the hymen. T complained that she had been raped three days prior to her arrest but had not told anyone about it. T was later examined on a number of occasions by a psychiatrist who diagnosed that after the rape she was suffering from Post Traumatic Stress Disorder and at the time of the offence she had entered a Dissociative State and the offences had been committed during a psychogenic fugue and she was not acting with a conscious mind or will.

The Defence submitted that the 'defence' of 'non-insane automatism' was open to T on the grounds that the categories of non-insane automatism are not limited to a blow causing concussion, an injection of insulin or anaesthetic or sleep walking (*per* Lord Diplock in *R v Sullivan* [1983] 3 WLR 123); that rape is the application of an 'external force' (*per* Lawton LJ in *R v Quick* [1973] 3 WLR 26 at p. 35); that the rape was such an extraordinary external event that might be presumed to affect the average normal person and it contained features of novelty of accident (*per* Lord Lane CJ in *R v Hennessy* [1989] 1 WLR 287 at p. 294 and Martin J in *R v Rabey*, 79 Dominion Law Reports 435 (Ontario Court of Appeal); that a proper foundation had been laid for leaving the defence to the jury (*per* Lord Denning in *Bratty v Att.-Gen. for Northern Ireland* [1963] AC 368 at p. 413. The Crown argued that the evidence showed the Defendant had some recollection of what happened. Further that the opening of the blade of the pen knife required a controlled and positive action by the Defendant, therefore this was a case where there was 'partial control' (*per Broom v Perkins* (1987) 85, Cr App R 321 and *Issit* [1977] RTR 211) and the only 'defence' open to the defendant was 'insane automatism' under the M'Naghton [*sic*] Rules.

Held, that there had been no previous case in which an incident of rape had been held to be 'an external factor' causing a malfunctioning of the mind within the definition laid down in *Quick*; that, if what the Defendant says about the rape is true, such an incident could have an appalling effect on any young woman, however well balanced normally, and that could satisfy the requirement; that a condition of Post Traumatic Stress involving a normal person in an act of violence is not itself a disease of the mind, even if there is a delay before a period of dissociation manifests itself; that if the medical evidence is correct this case is distinguishable from *Broom* and *Issit* where there was only a partial loss of control whereas in this case T was acting as though in a 'dream'; that the categories of automatism are not closed and that, on the evidence before the court, a proper foundation had been laid for the matter to go before the jury.

NOTES AND QUESTIONS

1. In *Sullivan* and *Hennessy*, do the courts treat a physical illness as if it were a mental illness? Does the court in *R v T* treat a mental illness as if it were a physical illness? What motivates the courts in these matters?

2. In *Bratty v Attorney-General for Northern Ireland* [1963] AC 386, Lord Denning stated: 'It seems to me that any mental disorder which has manifested itself in violence and is prone to recur is a disease of the mind.' This does not purport to be a medical opinion. Does Lord Denning's *dictum* accord with the internal-external distinction of later cases?

3. Is the likelihood of future violence by a defendant a proper basis on which to determine criminality? Is it inevitably a matter of conjecture?

4. One might question whether the requirement of a 'disease of the mind' is really necessary. If a defendant does not know the nature and quality of her act or that it is wrong, and this is due to a defect of reason, why should it matter that the defect of reason is the product of a disease of the mind? In light of the reasons behind the insanity defence, does the source make any difference?

The defendant who is suffering from a defect of reason from a disease of the mind can come within the *M'Naghten* rules in either of two ways:

(a) the defendant can show that she did not know the nature and quality of the act she was doing; or

(b) the defendant can show that she did not know that what she was doing was wrong.

But is the word 'wrong' used in a legal or moral sense?

R v Windle
[1952] 2 QB 826, Court of Criminal Appeal

The appellant, Francis Wilfred Windle, was convicted before Devlin J at Birmingham Assizes of the murder of his wife, and sentenced to death. He was a man, 40 years of age, of little resolution and weak character, and was married to a woman 18 years his senior. His married life was very unhappy; his wife was always speaking of committing suicide and the doctors who gave evidence at the trial were of opinion, from the history of the case, that she was certifiably insane. The appellant frequently discussed his home life with his workmates, until, as one of them said, they were sick and tired of hearing about it. Eventually a workmate said to the appellant, 'Give her a dozen aspirins,' and on the following day the appellant gave his wife 100 tablets. He sent for a doctor and told him that he had given his wife so many aspirins. She was taken to hospital, where she died. The appellant informed the police that he had given his wife 100 aspirins, and added: 'I suppose they will hang me for this?' At his trial a defence of insanity was put forward. A doctor was called for him who said that the appellant was suffering from a form of communicated insanity known as *folie à deux*. It was said that if a person was in constant attendance on another of unsound mind, in some way the insanity might be communicated to the attendant, so that, for a time at any rate, the attendant might develop a defect of reason or of mind. Rebutting medical evidence was allowed to be called for the prosecution, and the doctors called on either side expressed the opinion that the appellant, when administering the fatal dose of aspirin to his wife, knew that he was doing an act which the law forbade.

LORD GODDARD CJ: . . . The argument before us has really been on what is the meaning of the word 'wrong.' In this particular case, the only evidence given on the issue of insanity was that of the doctor called by the appellant and of the prison doctor who was allowed to be called by the prosecution to rebut, if indeed it was necessary, any evidence which had been given. It was probably right that the prison doctor should be called as he had had the appellant under constant observation. Both the doctors gave their evidence in a way that commended itself to the judge, and both, without hesitation, expressed the view that the appellant knew, when administering this poison, for such it was, to his wife, that he was doing an act which the law forbade. I need not put it higher than that.

It may well be that, in the misery in which he had been living, with this nagging and tiresome wife who constantly expressed the desire to commit suicide, he thought that she would be better out of this world than in it. He may have thought that it would be a kindly act to release her from what she was suffering from – or thought she was suffering from – but that the law does not permit. In the present case there was some exceedingly vague evidence that the appellant was suffering from a defect of reason. In the opinion of his own doctor, there was a defect of reason which he attributed to communicated insanity. In my opinion, if the only question in this case had been whether the appellant was suffering from a disease of the mind, I should say that that was a question which must have been left to the jury. That, however, is not the question.

. . . A man may be suffering from a defect of reason, but if he knows that what he is doing is 'wrong,' and by 'wrong' is meant contrary to law, he is responsible. Mr Shawcross, in the course of his very careful argument, suggested that the word 'wrong,' as it was used in the M'Naghten rules, did not mean contrary to law but had some kind of qualified meaning, such as morally wrong, and that if a person was in such a state of mind through a defect of reason that, although he knew that what he was doing was wrong in law, he thought that it was beneficial or kind or praiseworthy, that would excuse him.

Courts of law can only distinguish between that which is in accordance with law and that which is contrary to law. . . .

In the opinion of the court there is no doubt that in the M'Naghten rules 'wrong' means contrary to law and not 'wrong' according to the opinion of one man or of a number of people on the question whether a particular act might or might not be justified. In the present case, it could not be challenged that the appellant knew that what he was doing was contrary to law, and that he realized what punishment the law provided for murder. That was the opinion of both the doctors who gave evidence.

NOTES AND QUESTIONS
1. Presumably the court in *Windle* was attempting to narrow the meaning of the term 'wrong'. However, it might be argued that the decision could have the opposite effect. What if an insane individual appreciated that his act was morally wrong but, due to his mental illness, not that it was legally wrong?
2. Is the requirement that the insane defendant should not know that his act was legally wrong consistent with the general rule that 'ignorance of the law is no excuse'?

There is a second branch of *M'Naghten* relating to partial delusions. The relevant question is set out in the *M'Naghten* extract (above). It is doubtful whether anything is added to the 'core' test by this passage. A person under a delusion is presumably incapable of understanding the nature and quality of his act.

M'Naghten is concerned with cognitive disabilities. The defendant is unable, due to a defect of reason from disease of the mind, to comprehend what he is doing or that it is wrong. What, however, if the defendant is able to comprehend what he is doing, but is unable to stop himself from doing it?

R v Sodeman
[1936] 2 All ER 1138, Privy Council

The petitioner, who was a labourer, took a young girl for a ride on his bicycle, strangled her, tied her hands behind her back, stuffed some of her clothing into her mouth, and left her for dead. The cause of death was suffocation. The petitioner had committed three previous murders in very similar ways. The petitioner's defence was that he was insane at the time. At the trial two government prison doctors and a specialist in mental diseases gave evidence in support of that defence. No expert evidence on that issue was tendered by the Crown.

VISCOUNT HAILSHAM LC: . . . [I]t is suggested by the petitioner that the rules in *M'Naghten's* case (1843) 10 Cl & F 200 are no longer to be treated as an exhaustive statement of the law with regard to insanity, and that there is to be engrafted upon those rules another rule that where a man knows that he is doing what is wrong, none the less he may be held to be insane if he is caused to do the act by an irresistible impulse produced by disease. It is admitted by Mr Pritt that, so far as this country is concerned, the more recent cases, . . . excludes that addition to the law in *M'Naghten's* case, but it is argued that, since there have been earlier decisions which suggest that such a rule exists, this is a good opportunity for establishing the law beyond doubt. Their Lordships do not think that the argument is a sound one. If they are to take a different view of the law from that which prevailed [in recent cases] the effect will be that different standards of law will prevail in England and in the Dominions. The adoption of such a view obviously cannot alter the authorities laid down by the English Court of Criminal Appeal, and their Lordships do not think that the ground suggested is one for granting special leave to appeal in a criminal case. . . .

QUESTIONS

1. There seems to be strong judicial antipathy to the concept of an irresistible impulse. Is it because, as is sometimes said, there is no such thing as an irresistible impulse when there is a police officer at one's elbow? Or is it that the more an impulse increases in strength, the greater the legal sanction needed to counteract its effect?

2. Is the rejection of an irresistible impulse defence consistent with the principle of capacity?

Statistically the insanity defence was not often raised, at least not by defendants (it can be raised by the Crown if defendants place their mental state in issue. See *Bratty v Attorney-General for Northern Ireland* [1963] AC 386. See generally Mackay, 'Fact and fiction about the insanity defence' [1990] Crim LR 247). The reason could be found in the effect of a verdict of not guilty by reason of insanity. In the case of other defences, if the jury accepted the defence, the defendant was released, a free person. Not so in the case of a successful insanity defence. If the defendant's defence of insanity succeeded, and the jury returned a verdict of 'not guilty by reason of insanity', the defendant did not go free but was committed to a mental hospital, to remain at 'Her Majesty's Pleasure', which could be forever. Thus there was little incentive to plead insanity except when the charge was murder, where there existed the possibility of the death penalty. After the death penalty for murder was abolished, and there also became available the plea of diminished responsibility (see Chapter 5) which served to reduce the crime of murder to manslaughter, there was little to be gained by pleading insanity. So the defence lay dormant. At least until 1992.

   The Criminal Procedure (Insanity and Unfitness to Plead) Act 1991 attempted to address two troublesome aspects relating to the mentally ill offender. First was the problem of the accused who may have had a valid defence to the charges other than insanity but who was unable to obtain a trial because his mental state rendered him unfit to plead. Second was the issue of mandatory commitment following a verdict of 'not guilty by reason of insanity', which doubtless deterred many defendants from raising an insanity defence. The Act provides as follows:

Criminal Procedure (Insanity and Unfitness to Plead) Act 1991

2. Findings of unfitness to plead etc.

For section 4 of the Criminal Procedure (Insanity) Act 1964 ('the 1964 Act') there shall be substituted the following sections—

Finding of unfitness to plead

4.—(1) This section applies where on the trial of a person the question arises (at the instance of the defence or otherwise) whether the accused is under a disability, that is to say, under any disability such that apart from this Act it would constitute a bar to his being tried.

(2) If, having regard to the nature of the supposed disability, the court are of opinion that it is expedient to do so and in the interests of the accused, they may postpone consideration of the question of fitness to be tried until any time up to the opening of the case for the defence.

(3) If, before the question of fitness to be tried falls to be determined, the jury return a verdict of acquittal on the count or each of the counts on which the accused is being tried, that question shall not be determined.

(4) Subject to subsections (2) and (3) above, the question of fitness to be tried shall be determined as soon as it arises.

(5) The question of fitness to be tried shall be determined by a jury and—
- (a) where it falls to be determined on the arraignment of the accused and the trial proceeds, the accused shall be tried by a jury other than that which determined that question;
- (b) where it falls to be determined at any later time, it shall be determined by a separate jury or by the jury by whom the accused is being tried, as the court may direct.

(6) A jury shall not make a determination under subsection (5) above except on the written or oral evidence of two or more registered medical practitioners at least one of whom is duly approved.

3. Powers to deal with persons not guilty by reason of insanity or unfit to plead etc.

For section 5 of the 1964 Act there shall be substituted the following section—

Powers to deal with persons not guilty by reason of insanity or unfit to plead etc.

5.—(1) This section applies where—
- (a) a special verdict is returned that the accused is not guilty by reason of insanity; or
- (b) findings are recorded that the accused is under a disability and that he did the act or made the omission charged against him.

(2) Subject to subsection (3) below, the court shall either—
- (a) make an order that the accused be admitted, in accordance with the provisions of Schedule 1 to the Criminal Procedure (Insanity and Unfitness to Plead) Act 1991, to such hospital as may be specified by the Secretary of State; or
- (b) where they have the power to do so by virtue of section 5 of that Act, make in respect of the accused such one of the following orders as they think most suitable in all the circumstances of the case, namely—
  - (i) a guardianship order within the meaning of the Mental Health Act 1983;
  - (ii) a supervision and treatment order within the meaning of Schedule 2 to the said Act of 1991; and
  - (iii) an order for his absolute discharge.

(3) Paragraph (b) of subsection (2) above shall not apply where the offence to which the special verdict or findings relate is an offence the sentence for which is fixed by law.

The defence of insanity propounded in *M'Naghten* has changed little since its inception in 1843, despite major advances in the understanding and treatment of mental illness. It remains a legal rather than a medical test. The judicial extension of the defence to those who suffer from physical illnesses that render them prone to violent episodes may constitute a further departure from the original objective. Indeed, it seems to suggest that the courts have viewed the defence of insanity as a means whereby the law can impose a form of preventive detention on some dangerous individuals who cannot be convicted of a crime. Whether the 1991 Act will bring about a change in this misuse of the defence is unclear.

In any event, basic questions remain. What functions are served by the defence? To whom should the defence be available? Is insanity a medical condition or a legal excuse? Should the mentally ill offender be dealt with within the criminal justice system or within the mental health system? Over the years many of the alternatives to *M'Naghten* which have been proposed have sought to bring insanity closer to a medical model of mental illness. Consider the merits of the Draft Criminal Code's approach (based to a large extent on the recommendations of the Butler Committee (1975)):

Draft Criminal Code Bill 1989

34. In this Act—
'mental disorder' means—
  (a) severe mental illness; or
  (b) a state of arrested or incomplete development of mind; or
  (c) a state of automatism (not resulting only from intoxication) which is a feature of a disorder, whether organic or functional and whether continuing or recurring, that may cause a similar state on another occasion;
'return a mental disorder verdict' means—
  (a) in relation to trial on indictment, return a verdict that the defendant is not guilty on evidence of mental disorder; and
  (b) in relation to summary trial, dismiss the information on evidence of mental disorder;
'severe mental illness' means a mental illness which has one or more of the following characteristics—
  (a) lasting impairment of intellectual functions shown by failure of memory, orientation, comprehension and learning capacity;
  (b) lasting alteration of mood of such degree as to give rise to delusional appraisal of the defendant's situation, his past or his future, or that of others, or lack of any appraisal;
  (c) delusional beliefs, persecutory, jealous or grandiose;
  (d) abnormal perceptions associated with delusional misinterpretation of events;
  (e) thinking so disordered as to prevent reasonable appraisal of the defendant's situation or reasonable communication with others;
'severe mental handicap' means a state of arrested or incomplete development of mind which includes severe impairment of intelligence and social functioning.

35.—(1) A mental disorder verdict shall be returned if the defendant is proved to have committed an offence but it is proved on the balance of probabilities (whether by the prosecution or by the defendant) that he was at the time suffering from severe mental illness or severe mental handicap.

(2) Subsection (1) does not apply if the court or jury is satisfied beyond reasonable doubt that the offence was not attributable to the severe mental illness or severe mental handicap.

(3) A court or jury shall not, for the purposes of a verdict under subsection (1), find that the defendant was suffering from severe mental illness or severe mental handicap unless two medical practitioners approved for the purposes of section 12 of the Mental Health Act 1983 as having special experience in the diagnosis or treatment of mental disorder have given evidence that he was so suffering.

(4) Subsection (1), so far as it relates to severe mental handicap, does not apply to an offence under section 106(1), 107 or 108 (sexual relations with the mentally handicapped).

36. A mental disorder verdict shall be returned if—
    (a) the defendant is acquitted of an offence only because, by reason of evidence of mental disorder or a combination of mental disorder and intoxication, it is found that he acted or may have acted in a state of automatism, or without the fault required for the offence, or believing that an exempting circumstance existed; and
    (b) it is proved on the balance of probabilities (whether by the prosecution or by the defendant) that he was suffering from mental disorder at the time of the act.

37. A defendant may plead 'not guilty by reason of mental disorder'; and
    (a) if the court directs that the plea be entered the direction shall have the same effect as a mental disorder verdict; and
    (b) if the court does not so direct the defendant shall be treated as having pleaded not guilty.

38.—(1) Whether evidence is evidence of mental disorder or automatism is a question of law.

(2) The prosecution shall not adduce evidence of mental disorder, or contend that a mental disorder verdict should be returned, unless the defendant has given or adduced evidence that he acted without the fault required for the offence, or believing that an exempting circumstance existed, or in a state of automatism, or (on a charge of murder) when suffering from mental abnormality as defined in section 57(2).

(3) The court may give directions as to the stage of the proceedings at which the prosecution may adduce evidence of mental disorder.

39. Schedule 2 has effect with respect to the orders that may be made upon the return of a mental disorder verdict, to the conditions governing the making of those orders, to the effects of those orders and to related matters.

40. A defendant shall not, when a mental disorder verdict is returned in respect of an offence and while that verdict subsists, be found guilty of any other offence of which, but for this section, he might on the same occasion be found guilty—
    (a) on the indictment, count or information to which the verdict relates; or
    (b) on any other indictment, count or information founded on the same facts.

NOTES AND QUESTIONS

1. If the definition of insanity is to become more medically orientated, who should determine the defendant's sanity – a judge, a jury, or a panel of mental health experts? One possibility would be to hold a bifurcated trial – in the first stage a jury would decide whether the defendant committed the crime charged; and in the second, assuming a verdict of guilty in the first stage, a panel of mental health experts would determine whether the defendant was insane at the time of the crime. A second question would be whether the defendant is still insane, and, if so, what should be the appropriate disposition.

2. Another alternative (and perhaps the logical import of the suggestion in the preceding paragraph for a bifurcated trial) is to abolish the insanity defence altogether and hold that insanity only becomes relevant at the time of sentencing. A judge should be allowed to sentence a defendant (found 'guilty but insane' by a jury) to an institution in which he can receive appropriate treatment. The length of the sentence, however, would not be affected by the place of confinement. What are the merits of this approach?

3. Even if a defendant is found 'unfit to plead' questions will remain as to whether the defendant 'did the act charged', see *Attorney-General's Reference (No. 3 of 1998)* [1999] 3 WLR 1194.

4. If the insanity defence is to be retained and determined by the jury, perhaps a stripped-down, simplified version is needed. Consider the pros and cons of the formula proposed in 1953 by the Royal Commission on Capital Punishment:

> [A person is not responsible for his unlawful act if] at the time of the act the accused was suffering from disease of the mind (or mental deficiency) to such a degree that he ought not to be held responsible.

SECTION 3: **Automatism**

Not every affirmative act which on its face violates the law will result in criminal liability. The act has to be voluntary, i.e., an act of the will; or, stated perhaps more accurately, an act that one had, by the exercise of one's will, the power to refrain from doing. The justification for the voluntariness requirement is that an actor cannot be said to be responsible (in the moral sense of the term) for a truly involuntary act. Punishment is also pointless from a deterrence perspective, as involuntary acts cannot be deterred.

It may seem that characterising an act as involuntary is simply another way of saying that the defendant did not act with *mens rea*. In most instances the result of either line of analysis will be the same. However, in the case of strict liability crimes, where no *mens rea* need be proved and there is consequently no *mens rea* element which can be negated, only an involuntary act defence will be available to an accused.

A: Acts which are the product of an external force

There are two distinct types of involuntary act cases. One involves the situation where the defendant's act is the product of an external force. Say X pushes Y into Z, who falls into the path of an oncoming lorry. Y's acts are not voluntary, and she is not responsible for the injuries to Z. Indeed, if the push was deliberate, X may well be liable; Y is nothing more than X's innocent agent, even though her acts are the direct cause of the resulting harm.

The same basic principle may also apply where the defendant's acts, although not caused by an external force, are the product of external circumstances beyond the defendant's control. Is the following case an appropriate example?

Burns v *Bidder*

[1966] 3 All ER 29, Queen's Bench Division

The appellant was driving a motor car at a speed which was not high towards a pedestrian crossing. The road surface was good, although slightly wet. He passed the offside of a bus which had stopped at the crossing and which had been stationary there for several seconds. Several persons were using the crossing. The appellant failed to stop his car, at no time did he apply his hand-brake, and the car continued over the crossing and struck a pedestrian who was on the crossing some five or six feet from the centre of the road. The car came to a halt some distance beyond the crossing. Immediately afterwards the appellant complained that his footbrake had failed and, at the request of a police officer, took the car to a police station, where it was tested by an experienced traffic patrol officer who found that the footbrake worked correctly. On an information charging the appellant with unlawfully failing to accord precedence to a foot-passenger who was on the carriageway within the limits of an uncontrolled crossing, contrary to reg. 4 of the Pedestrian Crossings Regulations 1954, the stipendiary magistrate was not satisfied on a balance of probabilities that the brakes of the car had failed, nor was he satisfied that they had not failed and, as he considered that the offence was an absolute offence, he convicted the appellant.

JAMES J: . . . Counsel for the appellant contended that the learned stipendiary magistrate was wrong in his construction of that regulation as imposing an absolute obligation, and urges that to accord precedence involves a positive act such as 'a granting' or 'a bestowing' of something, and that, where the driver of a vehicle is precluded from doing a positive act, then he cannot be said to be failing to accord. Counsel for the appellant further points out that the magistrate was not satisfied that there was not a sudden failure of the brakes, and that there therefore remained a possibility that, due to a latent defect in the braking system, the appellant had been prevented through no fault of his own from according precedence to the pedestrian; this, he contends, being a regulation not imposing absolute obligations there was on that basis a complete defence to the information laid. . . . Some circumstances over which the driver had no reasonable or possible control brought about the collision. The basis is the same as that referred to by Nield J, in *Levy* v *Hockey* (1961) 105 SJ 157. Regulation 4 must be read 'subject to the principle of impossibility', as he put it in that case. In my judgment, the regulation does not impose an absolute duty come what may, and there is no breach of the obligation under the regulation in circumstances where the driver fails to afford precedence to a foot-passenger solely because his control of the vehicle is taken from him by the occurrence of an event which is outside his possible or reasonable control and in respect of which he is in no way at fault.

The cases of the driver suddenly stunned by a swarm of bees or suffering a sudden epileptiform disabling attack, or of a vehicle being propelled forward by reason of another vehicle hitting it from behind are illustrations of where no offence may be shown, because control over the vehicle is taken completely out of the hands of the driver, and his failure to accord precedence on that account would be no offence. Likewise, in my view, a sudden removal of control over the vehicle occasioned by a latent defect of which the driver did not know, and could not reasonably be expected to know, would render the resulting failure to accord precedence no offence, provided that he is in no way at fault himself. Beyond that limited sphere, however, the obligation of the driver under the regulations can properly be described, as it has been described, as an absolute one. . . .

B: Insanity v automatism

The second type of involuntary act is generally referred to as automatism. There are two subcategories of automatism cases. One involves the situation where the defendant is conscious, but his acts are the product of a spasm, reflex, or convulsion. For example, a doctor hits a patient in the knee with a rubber hammer to test the patient's reflexes. The patient's reflexes are extraordinary and his leg flies forward, striking the doctor's assistant. There is little doubt that, if charged with assault, the patient would have a defence based on the fact that his act was a reflex action and involuntary.

The second subcategory of automatism involves the situation where the defendant commits an act in an unconscious or semi-conscious state, or in a state of impaired consciousness. This type of automatism case has proved quite resistant to reasoned analysis. While there is agreement that the automatism negates an element of the crime, there is disagreement as to whether the element negated is the *actus reus* or the *mens rea*, or both.

When the automatism is due to a disease of the mind, the confusion seems to be compounded. Is the appropriate defence in such a case insanity or automatism? If insanity, the burden of proof rests on the defendant, who must establish insanity on the balance of probabilities. If the appropriate defence is automatism, the burden of negating automatism rests on the prosecution, because it is required to establish both *actus reus* and *mens rea* by proof beyond a reasonable doubt. Thus, regardless of whether automatism is seen as negating the *actus reus* or the *mens rea* of the offence, the burden of negating automatism is on the prosecution. The defendant does, however, bear the initial burden of introducing evidence (medical evidence will almost always be necessary) to show automatism, for until he does, the Crown is entitled to rely on the presumption that a defendant has the capacity to commit the crime.

Bratty v *Attorney-General for Northern Ireland*
[1961] 3 All ER 523, House of Lords

The accused killed a girl, with whom he was driving in his car on an errand. He took off her stocking and strangled her with it. He gave evidence that a 'blackness' came over him and that 'I didn't know what I was doing. I didn't realise anything.' He also said that previously he had had 'feelings of blackness' and headaches, and there was evidence of his odd behaviour at times, of his mental backwardness and his religious leanings. There was medical evidence that the accused might have been suffering from an attack of psychomotor epilepsy, which was a disease of the mind affecting the reason and which could cause ignorance of the nature and quality of acts done. No other pathological cause for the accused's acts, or a state of automatism on his part was assigned by medical evidence at the trial. The defences of automatism (i.e., unconscious involuntary action) and of insanity within the M'Naghten rules were raised at the trial. The trial judge refused to leave the defence of automatism to the jury, but left to them the defence of insanity, which the jury rejected. The accused was convicted of murder.

VISCOUNT KILMUIR LC: My Lords, this is an appeal from the Court of Criminal Appeal in Northern Ireland. . . . The court certified that the decision involved two points of law of general public importance, namely:

(i) Whether, his plea of insanity having been rejected by the jury, it was open to the accused to rely on a defence of automatism; and

(ii) If the answer to (i) be in the affirmative, whether, on the evidence, the defence of automatism should have been left to the jury.

. . . The Court of Criminal Appeal [agreed] that the learned judge was right in not leaving to the jury the defence of automatism in so far as it purported to be founded on a defect of reason from disease of the mind within the M'Naghten rules. In this I think that they were right. To establish the defence of insanity within the M'Naghten rules the accused must prove on the preponderance of probabilities first a defect of reason from a disease of the mind, and, secondly, as a consequence of such a defect, ignorance of the nature and quality (or the wrongfulness) of the acts. We have to consider a case in which it is sought to do so by medical evidence to the effect that the conduct of the accused might be compatible with psychomotor epilepsy, which is a disease of the mind affecting the reason, and that psychomotor epilepsy could cause ignorance of the nature and quality of the acts done, but in which the medical witness can assign no other cause for that ignorance. Where the possibility of an unconscious act depends on, and only on, the existence of a defect of reason from disease of the mind within the M'Naghten rules, a rejection by the jury of this defence of insanity necessarily implies that they reject the possibility.

The Court of Criminal Appeal also took the view that where the alleged automatism is based solely on a disease of the mind within the M'Naghten rules, the same burden of proof rests on the defence whether the 'plea' is given the name of insanity or automatism. I do not think that statement goes further than saying that when one relies on insanity as defined by the M'Naghten rules one cannot by a difference of nomenclature avoid the road so often and authoritatively laid down by the courts.

What I have said does not mean that, if a defence of insanity is raised unsuccessfully, there can never, in any conceivable circumstances, be room for an alternative defence based on automatism. For example, it may be alleged that the accused had a blow on the head after which he acted without being conscious of what he was doing or was a sleep-walker. There might be a divergence of view whether there was a defect of reason from disease of the mind (compare the curious position which arose in *R v Kemp* [1957] 1 QB 399). The jury might not accept the evidence of a defect of reason from disease of the mind, but at the same time accept the evidence that the prisoner did not know what he was doing. If the jury should take that view of the facts they would find him not guilty. But it should be noted that the defence would only have succeeded because the necessary foundation had been laid by positive evidence which, properly considered, was evidence of something other than a defect of reason from disease of the mind. In my opinion, this analysis of the two defences (insanity and automatism) shows that where the only cause alleged for the unconsciousness is a defect of reason from disease of the mind, and that cause is rejected by the jury, there can be no room for the alternative defence of automatism. . . It is necessary that a proper foundation be laid before a judge can leave 'automatism' to the jury. That foundation, in my view, is not forthcoming merely from unaccepted evidence of a defect of reason from disease of the mind. . . .

Nevertheless, one must not lose sight of the overriding principle, laid down by this House in *Woolmington's* case [1935] AC 462, that it is for the prosecution to prove every element of the offence charged. One of these elements is the accused's state of mind; normally the presumption of mental capacity is sufficient to prove that he acted consciously and voluntarily and the prosecution need go no further. But, if, after considering evidence properly left to them by the judge, the jury are left in real doubt whether or not the accused acted in a state of automatism, it seems to me that on principle they should acquit because the necessary mens rea – if indeed the actus reus – has not been proved beyond reasonable doubt. . . .

LORD DENNING: My Lords, in *Woolmington* v *Director of Public Prosecutions* [1935] AC 462 Viscount Sankey LC, said: 'When dealing with a murder case the Crown must prove (a) death as the result of a voluntary act of the accused and (b) malice of the accused.' The requirement that it should be a voluntary act is essential, not only in a murder case, but also in every criminal case. No act is punishable if it is done involuntarily: and an involuntary act in this context – some people nowadays prefer to speak of it as 'automatism' – means an act which is done by the muscles without any control by the mind such as a spasm, a reflex action or a convulsion; or an act done by a person who is not conscious of what he is doing such as an act done whilst suffering from concussion or whilst sleepwalking. . . . The term 'involuntary act' is, however, capable of wider connotations: and to prevent confusion it is to be observed that in the criminal law an act is not to be regarded as an involuntary act simply because the doer does not remember it. When a man is charged with dangerous driving, it is no defence for him to say 'I don't know what happened. I cannot remember a thing': see *Hill* v *Baxter* [1958] 1 All ER 193. Loss of memory afterwards is never a defence in itself, so long as he was conscious at the time; see *Russell* v *H. M. Advocate* [1946] SC (J) 37]; *R* v *Podola* [[1959] 3 All ER 418]. Nor is an act to be regarded as an involuntary act simply because the doer could not control his impulse to do it. . . .

My Lords, I think that Devlin J, was quite right in *R* v *Kemp* [1957] 1 QB 399 in putting the question of insanity to the jury, even though it had not been raised by the defence. When it is asserted that the accused did an involuntary act in a state of automatism, the defence necessarily puts in issue the state of mind of the accused man: and thereupon it is open to the prosecution to show what his true state of mind was. The old notion that only the defence can raise a defence of insanity is now gone. The prosecution are entitled to raise it and it is their duty to do so rather than allow a dangerous person to be at large. . . .

On the other point discussed by Devlin J, namely, what is a 'disease of the mind' within the M'Naghten rules, I would agree with him that this is a question for the judge. The major mental diseases, which the doctors call psychoses, such as schizophrenia, are clearly diseases of the mind. But in *R* v *Charlson* [1955] 1 WLR 317, Barry J, seems to have assumed that other diseases such as epilepsy or cerebral tumour are not diseases of the mind, even when they are such as to manifest themselves in violence. I do not agree with this. It seems to me that any mental disorder which has manifested itself in violence and is prone to recur is a disease of the mind. At any rate it is the sort of disease for which a person should be detained in hospital rather than be given an unqualified acquittal.

. . . [W]hilst the *ultimate* burden rests on the Crown of proving every element essential in the crime, nevertheless in order to prove that the act was a voluntary act, the Crown is entitled to rely on the *presumption* that every man has sufficient mental capacity to be responsible for his crimes: and that if the defence wish to displace that presumption they must give some evidence from which the contrary may reasonably be inferred. . . .

The presumption of mental capacity of which I have spoken is a provisional presumption only. It does not put the legal burden on the defence in the same way as the presumption of sanity does. It leaves the legal burden on the prosecution, but nevertheless, until it is displaced, it enables the prosecution to discharge the ultimate burden of proving that the act was voluntary. Not because the presumption is evidence itself, but because it takes the place of evidence. In order to displace the presumption of mental capacity, the defence must give sufficient evidence from which it may reasonably be inferred that the act was involuntary. The evidence of the man himself will rarely be sufficient unless it is supported by medical evidence which points to the cause of the mental incapacity. . . . When the only cause that is assigned for an involuntary act is drunkenness, then it is only necessary to leave drunkenness to the jury, with the consequential directions, and not to leave automatism at all. When the only cause that is assigned for it is a disease of the mind, then it is only necessary to leave insanity to the jury, and not automatism. When the cause assigned is concussion or sleepwalking, there should be some evidence from which it can reasonably be inferred before it should be left to the jury. If it is said to be due to concussion, there should be evidence of a severe blow shortly beforehand. If it is said to be sleepwalking, there should be some credible support for it. His mere assertion that he was asleep will not suffice. Once a proper foundation is thus laid for automatism, the matter becomes at large and must be left to the jury. . . .

This brings me to the root question in the present case: Was a proper foundation laid here for the defence of automatism apart from the plea of insanity? There was the evidence of the appellant himself that he could not remember anything because 'this blackness was over me'. He said 'I did not realise exactly what I was doing', and added afterwards 'I didn't know what I was doing. I didn't realise anything'. He said he had four or five times previously had 'feelings of blackness' and frequently headaches. There was evidence, too, of his odd behaviour at times, his mental backwardness and his religious leanings. Added to this there was the medical evidence. Dr Sax, who was called on his behalf, said there was a possibility that he was suffering from psychomotor epilepsy. It was, he said, practically the only possibility that occurred to him. Dr Walker, his general practitioner, said you could not leave the possibility out of account. Dr Robinson, a specialist, who gave evidence on behalf of the Crown, said he thought it was extremely unlikely that it was an epileptic attack, but one could not rule it out. All the doctors agreed that psychomotor epilepsy, if it exists, is a defect of reason due to disease of the mind: and the judge accepted this view. No other cause was canvassed.

In those circumstances, I am clearly of opinion that, if the act of the appellant was an involuntary act, as the defence suggested, the evidence attributed it solely to a disease of the mind and the only defence open was the defence of insanity. There was no evidence of automatism apart from insanity. There was, therefore, no need for the judge to put it to the jury. And when the jury rejected the defence of insanity, they rejected the only defence disclosed by the evidence. . . .

NOTES AND QUESTIONS

1. Is it appropriate to characterise epilepsy as a mental disorder? Is this a medical opinion? The view of the ordinary person? Or a definition adopted by the judges for legal purposes?
2. For an automatism claim to succeed, there must be a total loss of voluntary control; impaired or reduced control is not enough. See *Attorney-General's Reference (No. 2 of 1992)* (1993) 97 Cr App R 429.
3. Why should the defence of insanity trump the defence of automatism? Is it a matter of legal principle, or because judges do not want persons who cannot control their actions running around loose, which would be the case if they could successfully claim automatism? Until recently, a person acquitted by reason of insanity was automatically committed to a mental institution 'at Her Majesty's pleasure'. Thus, an accused found not guilty by reason of insanity would be locked away in a mental institution, and the community would be safe; while an accused who raised a successful automatism defence would be released back into the community. However, under the Criminal Procedure (Insanity and Unfitness to Plead) Act 1991, commitment no longer automatically follows from a verdict of not guilty by reason of insanity. The decision lies within the discretion of the judge. Still, however, the defendant who successfully pleads automatism goes free.

    When a defendant raises a defence of automatism, the prosecution is allowed to introduce evidence of insanity and to argue that the appropriate verdict should be not guilty by reason of insanity. Prior to the 1991 Act, the defendant who wished to raise a defence of automatism had to take the not inconsiderable risk that the prosecution would argue insanity, and that the jury would agree, with the result that the defendant would be confined to a mental institution, possibly for life. It is possible that some defendants made a strategic decision not to risk this eventuality and consequently not to raise a possible automatism defence. The 1991 Act to a large extent removes this deterrent.

The issues raised in *Bratty* were further explored in *R v Quick and Paddison*:

R v Quick, R v Paddison
[1973] QB 910, Court of Appeal

LAWTON LJ: In its broadest aspects these appeals raise the question what is meant by the phrase 'a defect of reason from disease of the mind' within the meaning of the M'Naghten Rules. More particularly the question is whether a person who commits a criminal act whilst under the effects of hypoglycaemia can raise a defence of automatism, as the appellants submitted was possible, or whether such a person must rely on a defence of insanity if he wishes to relieve himself of responsibility for his acts, as Bridge J ruled.

The appellants were both employed at Farleigh Mental Hospital, Flax Bourton, Somerset. Quick was a charge nurse, Paddison a state enrolled nurse. At the trial it was not disputed that, at about 4 p.m. on 27th December 1971, one Green, a paraplegic spastic patient, unable to walk, was sitting in Rosemount Ward at the hospital, watching television. Quick was on duty; Paddison had gone off duty at 2 p.m. but was still present in the ward. Half an hour later, Green had sustained two black eyes, a fractured nose, a split lip which required three stitches, and bruising of his arm and shoulders. There was undisputed medical evidence that these injuries could not have been self-inflicted.

The Crown's case was that Quick had inflicted the injuries on Green and that Paddison had been present aiding and abetting him, not by actual physical participation, but by encouragement. On arraignment Quick pleaded not guilty. At the close of the evidence, following a ruling by the judge as to the effect in law of the evidence relied on by Quick to support a defence of automatism, he pleaded guilty to count 2 of the indictment. The judge's ruling was to the effect that this evidence could only be relied on to support a defence of insanity.

. . . Quick said that he could not remember assaulting Green. He admitted that he had been drinking and that his drinks had included whisky and a quarter of a bottle of rum. He also said that he was, and had been since the age of seven, a diabetic and that that morning he had taken insulin as prescribed by his doctor. After taking the insulin he had had a very small breakfast and no lunch. Dr Cates said that on 12 or more occasions Quick had been admitted to hospital either unconscious or semiconscious due to hypoglycaemia, which is a condition brought about when there is more insulin in the bloodstream than the amount of sugar there can cope with. When this imbalance occurs, the insulin has much the same effect as an excess of alcohol in the human body. At the onset of the imbalance the higher functions of the mind are affected. As the effects of the imbalance become more marked, more and more mental functions are upset; and unless an antidote is given (and a lump of sugar is an effective one) the sufferer can relapse into coma. In the later stages of mental impairment a sufferer may become aggressive and violent without being able to control himself or without knowing at the time what he was doing or having any recollection afterwards of what he had done. . . .

At the trial and before this court it was accepted by the Crown that the evidence to which we have referred was enough to justify an issue being left to the jury whether Quick could be held responsible for what he had done to Green. If the jury were to accept the evidence relied on by Quick what should the verdict be? Quick's counsel submitted 'not guilty'; counsel for the Crown submitted that it should be 'not guilty by reason of insanity'. The judge ruled in favour of the Crown. As Quick did not want to put forward a defence of insanity, after consulting with his counsel, he pleaded guilty to count 2.

. . . In this case, if Quick's alleged condition could have been caused by hypoglycaemia and that condition, like psychomotor epilepsy, was a disease of the mind, then Bridge J's ruling was right. The question remains, however, whether a mental condition arising from hypoglycaemia does amount to a disease of the mind. . . .

. . . Quick was setting up a defence of insanity. He may have been at the material time in a condition of mental disorder manifesting itself in violence. Such manifestations had occurred before and might recur. The difficulty arises as soon as the question is asked whether he should be detained in a mental hospital? No mental hospital would admit a diabetic merely because he had a low blood sugar reaction; and common sense is affronted by the prospect of a diabetic being sent to such a hospital when in most cases the disordered mental condition can be rectified quickly by pushing a lump of sugar or a teaspoonful of glucose into the patient's mouth.

The 'affront to common sense' argument, however, has its own inherent weakness, as counsel for the Crown pointed out. If an accused is shown to have done a criminal act whilst suffering from a 'defect of reason from disease of the mind', it matters not 'whether the disease is curable or incurable . . . temporary or permanent' (see *R* v *Kemp* [1957] 1 QB 399, per Devlin J). If the condition is temporary, the Secretary of State may have a difficult problem of disposal; but what happens to those found not guilty by reason of insanity is not a matter for the courts.

In *Hill* v *Baxter* [1958] 1 All ER 193, Lord Goddard CJ did not equate unconsciousness due to a sudden illness, which must entail the malfunctioning of the mental processes of the sufferer, with disease of the mind, and in our judgment no one outside a court of law would . . . It seems to us that the law should not give the words 'defect of reason from disease of the mind' a meaning which would be regarded with incredulity outside a court . . .

In this quagmire of law seldom entered nowadays save by those in desperate need of some kind of a defence, *Bratty* v *Attorney-General for Northern Ireland* [1963] AC 386; [1961] 3 All ER 523 provides the only firm ground. Is there any discernible path? We think there is – judges should follow in a common sense way their sense of fairness. . . . In our judgement no help can be obtained by speculating (because that is what we would have to do) as to what the judges who answered the House of Lords' questions in 1843 meant by disease of the mind, still less what Sir Matthew Hale meant in the second half of the 17th century. A quick backward look at the state of medicine in 1843 will suffice to show how unreal it would be to apply the concepts of that age to the present time. Dr Simpson had not yet started his experiments with chloroform, the future Lord Lister was only 16 and laudanum was used and prescribed like aspirins are today. Our task had been to decide what the law means now by the words 'disease of the mind'. In our judgment the fundamental concept is of a malfunctioning of the mind caused by disease. A malfunctioning of the mind of transitory effect caused by the application to the body of some external factor such as violence, drugs, including anaesthetics, alcohol and hypnotic influences cannot fairly be said to be due to disease. Such malfunctioning, unlike an accused from criminal responsibility. A self-induced incapacity will not excuse . . . nor will one which could have been reasonably foreseen as a result of either doing, or omitting to do something, as, for example, taking alcohol against medical advice after using certain prescribed drugs, or failing to have regular meals whilst taking insulin. From to time to time difficult borderline cases are likely to arise. When they do, the test suggested by the New Zealand Court of Appeal . . . is likely to give the correct result, viz can this mental condition be fairly regarded as amounting to or producing a defect of reason from disease of the mind?

In this case Quick's alleged mental condition, if it ever existed, was not caused by his diabetes but by his use of the insulin prescribed by his doctor. Such malfunctioning of his mind as there was, was caused by an external factor and not by a bodily disorder in the nature of a disease which disturbed the working of his mind. It follows in our judgment that Quick was entitled to have his defence of automatism left to the jury and that Bridge J's ruling as to the effect of the medical evidence called by him was wrong. Had the defence of automatism been left to the jury, a number of questions of fact would have had to be answered. If he was in a confused mental condition, was it due to a hypoglycaemic episode or to too much alcohol? If the former, to what extent had he brought about his condition by not following his doctor's instructions about taking regular meals? Did he know that he was getting into a hypoglycaemic episode? If Yes, why did he not use the antidote of eating a lump of sugar as he had been advised to do? On the evidence which was before the jury Quick might have had difficulty in answering these questions in a manner which would have relieved him of responsibility for his acts. We cannot say, however, with the requisite degree of confidence, that the jury would have convicted him. It follows that his conviction must be quashed on the ground that the verdict was unsatisfactory.

Appeals allowed.

NOTES AND QUESTIONS
1. The Court of Appeal in *Quick* drew a distinction between those acts of a diabetic which may be attributable to insulin, an external source, and those which may be attributable to the diabetes, an internal source. What if a patient who is prescribed medication to control a mental illness suffers an adverse reaction from the medication which causes the patient to go out of control? Are acts done in this state attributable to the disease or to the medication? Are not the two inextricably linked?
2. What if the external source is psychological rather than physical? Compare *R v Rabey* (1978) 79 DLR 3d 435 (automatism defence rejected where defendant claimed his crime was committed while in a disassociative state brought on by his rejection by a girl with whom he was infatuated) with *R v T* [1990] Crim LR 256 (see p. 421) (automatism defence available where defendant was suffering from Post Traumatic Stress Disorder brought on as a result of having been raped).

In *Quick* there was evidence that the defendant, contrary to his doctor's instructions, may have been drinking alcohol and not eating food. If so, indicated the court, such evidence may have defeated his automatism claim. The issue of self-induced automatism was re-examined in *R v Bailey*:

R v Bailey
[1983] 1 WLR 760, Court of Appeal

GRIFFITHS LJ: At the Crown Court at Bolton on October 14, 1982, the appellant was convicted of wounding with intent to cause grievous bodily harm, contrary to section 18 of the Offences against the Person Act 1861 (24 & 25 Vict. c. 100). The jury were not required to give a verdict on an alternative count of unlawful wounding contrary to section 20 of that Act. He now appeals against this conviction.

The appellant is a diabetic and has been so for some 30 years. He requires to take insulin to control his condition. His defence at the trial was that he was acting in a state of automatism caused by hypoglycaemia.

In early January 1982, the woman with whom the appellant had been living for the previous two years left him and formed an association with the victim, Mr Harrison. At about 7 p.m. on January 20, 1982, the appellant, seeming upset, visited Mr Harrison at his home. They had a cup of tea and discussed the matter. After 10 or 15 minutes the appellant said that he felt unwell and asked Mr Harrison to make him some sugar and water, which the appellant drank. About 10 minutes later the appellant started to leave. He then said that he had lost his glove and that it might be down the side of the chair on which he had been sitting. Mr Harrison bent down to look and the appellant struck him on the back of the head with an iron bar, which was a case opener about 18† long. The appellant remained there holding the iron bar. Mr Harrison ran from the house. His wound required 10 stitches.

The Crown's case was that although it was theoretically possible, from a medical point of view, for there to have been a temporary loss of awareness due to hypoglycaemia, as the appellant claimed, this was not what had happened. On the contrary, it was contended that the appellant, upset and jealous about Mr Harrison's relationship with his girlfriend, had armed himself with the iron bar and gone to Mr Harrison's house with the intention of injuring him. . . .

When he gave evidence, the appellant, who was a man of good character, maintained he had no intention of harming Mr Harrison and he had acted in a state of automatism. He said that he had to take two doses of insulin a day and was under his general practitioner and a special clinic. He had arrived home at 5.30 p.m. and had his insulin and a cup of tea. At 7 p.m. he decided to go and see Harrison and his account of what took place accorded with that of Mr Harrison up to the point where he asked Mr Harrison to look for his glove. The next thing he could remember was standing with the bar in his hand. He saw that Mr Harrison was injured and he said: 'What the hell am I doing?' He then described how he went home and later to the public house where he was arrested.

The appellant's general practitioner gave evidence. He confirmed that the appellant was a diabetic and received insulin treatment, after which he had to take food within a short period. If he failed to do so it could produce symptoms of weakness, palpitations, tremor and sweating. He might develop more aggressive tendencies than normal and this could be accompanied by loss of memory. After describing what the appellant had said he had had to eat he said that the appellant had not had sufficient to counteract and balance the dose of insulin. So far as he was aware the appellant in 30 years had never developed a condition of coma due to hypoglycaemia. He said that the effect of taking sugar and water in Mr Harrison's house would be to help bring back the sugar level within five or ten minutes. When he was cross-examined he said he thought it unlikely that there could have been the sudden switch-off effect alleged by the appellant and he regarded the likelihood of such a thing happening as being remote if sugar and water had been taken five minutes before it happened.

It was therefore the appellant's case that the attack had taken place during a period of loss of consciousness occurring due to hypoglycaemia caused by his failure to take sufficient food following his last dose of insulin. Accordingly it was submitted that he had neither the specific intent to cause grievous bodily harm for the purpose of section 18 nor the appropriate mens rea or basic intent for the purpose of the section 20 offence.

But the recorder, in effect, told the jury that this defence was not available to the appellant. . . . The recorder appears to have derived this proposition, which he applied to both counts of the indictment, from *R* v *Quick* [1973] QB 910. . . .

But in that case, the offence, assault occasioning actual bodily harm, was an offence of basic intent. No specific intent was required. It is now quite clear that even if the incapacity of mind is self-induced by the voluntary taking of drugs or alcohol, the specific intent to kill or cause grievous bodily harm may be negatived: see *R* v *Majewski* [1977] AC 443. This being so, as it is conceded on behalf of the Crown, the direction to which we have referred cannot be correct so far as the offence under section 18 is concerned.

But it is also submitted that the direction is wrong or at least in too broad and general terms, so far as the section 20 offence is concerned. If . . . *R* v *Quick* correctly represents the law, then the direction given by the recorder was correct so far as the second count was concerned even though the appellant may have had no appreciation of the consequences of his failure to take food and even though such failure may not have been due to deliberate abstention but because of his generally distressed condition. In our judgment the passage from Lawton LJ's judgment was obiter and we are free to re-examine it.

Automatism resulting from intoxication as a result of a voluntary ingestion of alcohol or dangerous drugs does not negative the mens rea necessary for crimes of basic intent, because the conduct of the accused is reckless and recklessness is enough to constitute the necessary mens rea in assault cases where no specific intent forms part of the charge: see *R* v *Majewski* [1977] AC 443, 476 . . . But it seems to us that there may be material distinctions between a man who consumes alcohol or takes dangerous drugs and one who fails to take sufficient food after insulin to avert hypoglycaemia.

It is common knowledge that those who take alcohol to excess or certain sorts of drugs may become aggressive or do dangerous or unpredictable things, they may be able to foresee the risks of causing harm to others but nevertheless persist in their conduct. But the same cannot be said without more of a man who fails to take food after an insulin injection. If he does appreciate the risk that such a failure may lead to aggressive, unpredictable and uncontrollable conduct and he nevertheless deliberately runs the risk or otherwise disregards it, this will amount to recklessness. But we certainly do not think that it is common knowledge, even among diabetics, that such is a consequence of a failure to take food and there is no evidence that it was known to this appellant. Doubtless he knew that if he failed to take his insulin or proper food after it, he might lose consciousness, but as such he would only be a danger to himself unless he put himself in charge of some machine such as a motor car, which required his continued conscious control.

In our judgment, self-induced automatism, other than that due to intoxication from alcohol or drugs, may provide a defence to crimes of basic intent. The question in each case will be whether the prosecution have proved the necessary element of recklessness. In cases of assault, if the accused knows that his actions or inaction are likely to make him aggressive, unpredictable or uncontrolled with the result that he may cause some injury to others and he persists in the action or takes no remedial action when he knows it is required, it will be open to the jury to find that he was reckless. . . .

But we have to consider whether, notwithstanding these misdirections, there has been any miscarriage of justice and whether the jury properly directed could have failed to come to the same conclusion. As Lawton LJ said in *Quick's* case at p. 922, referring to the defence of automatism, it is a 'quagmire of law seldom entered nowadays save by those in desperate need of some kind of a defence . . .' This case is no exception. We think it very doubtful whether the appellant laid a sufficient basis for the defence to be considered by the jury at all. But even if he did we are in no doubt that the jury properly directed must have rejected it. Although an episode of sudden transient loss of consciousness or awareness was theoretically possible it was quite inconsistent with the graphic description that the appellant gave to the police both orally and in his written statement. There was abundant evidence that he had armed himself with the iron bar and gone to Mr Harrison house for the purpose of attacking him because he wanted to teach him a lesson and because he was in the way.

Moreover the doctor's evidence to which we have referred showed it was extremely unlikely that such an episode could follow some five minutes after taking sugar and water. For these reasons we are satisfied that no miscarriage of justice occurred and the appeal will be dismissed.

Appeal dismissed.

In the early cases the courts often cited the sleepwalker as the prototype example of the automaton. When the actual fact situation finally came before the courts, however, it turned out to be more complicated.

R v *Burgess*
[1991] 2 QB 92, Court of Appeal

LORD LANE CJ: On 20 July 1989 in the Crown Court at Bristol before Judge Sir Ian Lewis and a jury, the appellant was found not guilty by reason of insanity on a charge of wounding with intent. He was ordered to be admitted and detained in such hospital as the Secretary of State should direct. He now appeals against that verdict by certificate of the trial judge under section 12 of the Criminal Appeal Act 1968.

The appellant did not dispute the fact that in the early hours of 2 June 1988 he had attacked Katrina Curtis by hitting her on the head first with a bottle when she was asleep, then with a video recorder and finally grasping her round the throat. She suffered a gaping three centimetre laceration to her scalp requiring sutures.

His case was that he lacked the mens rea necessary to make him guilty of the offence, because he was 'sleep walking' when he attacked Miss Curtis. He was, it was alleged, suffering from 'non-insane' automatism and he called medical evidence, in particular from Dr d'Orban and Dr Eames to support that contention.

Where the defence of automatism is raised by a defendant, two questions fall to be decided by the judge before the defence can be left to the jury. The first is whether a proper evidential foundation for the defence of automatism has been laid. The second is whether the evidence shows the case to be one of insane automatism, that is to say, a case which falls within the M'Naghten Rules, or one of non-insane automatism.

The judge in the present case undertook that task and on the second question came to the conclusion that – assuming the appellant was not conscious at the time of what he was doing – on any view of the medical evidence so far as automatism was concerned, it amounted to evidence of insanity within the M'Naghten Rules and not merely to evidence of non-insane automatism. The sole ground of appeal is that that ruling was wrong.

There can be no doubt but that the appellant, on the basis of the jury's verdict, was labouring under such a defect of reason as not to know what he was doing when he wounded Miss Curtis. The question is whether that was from 'disease of the mind'. The first point that has to be understood is that the phrase is 'disease of the mind' and not 'disease of the brain'. . . .

The appellant plainly suffered from a defect of reason from some sort of failure (for lack of a better term) of the mind causing him to act as he did without conscious motivation. His mind was to some extent controlling his actions which were purposive rather than the result simply of muscular spasm, but without his being consciously aware of what he was doing. Can it be said that that 'failure' was a *disease* of the mind rather than a defect or failure of the mind not due to disease? That is the distinction, by no means always easy to draw, upon which this case depends, as others have depended in the past.

What help does one derive from the authorities as to the meaning of 'disease' in this context? Lord Denning in *Bratty* v *Attorney-General for Northern Ireland* [1963] AC 386, 412 said:

> Upon the other point discussed by Devlin J, namely, what is a 'disease of the mind' within the M'Naghten Rules, I would agree with him that this is a question for the judge. The major mental diseases, which the doctors call psychoses, such as schizophrenia, are clearly diseases of the mind. But in *Charlson's* case [1955] 1 WLR 317, Barry J seems to have assumed that other diseases such as epilepsy or cerebral tumour are not diseases of the mind, even when they are such as to manifest themselves in violence. I do not agree with this. It seems to me that any mental disorder which has manifested itself in violence and is prone to recur is a disease of the mind. At any rate it is the sort of disease for which a person should be detained in hospital rather than be given an unqualified acquittal.

It seems to us that if there is a danger of recurrence that may be an added reason for categorising the condition as a disease of the mind. On the other hand, the absence of the danger of recurrence is not a reason for saying that it cannot be a disease of the mind. Subject to that possible qualification, we respectfully adopt Lord Denning's suggested definition.

It seems to us that on [the] evidence the judge was right to conclude that this was an abnormality or disorder, albeit transitory, due to an internal factor, whether functional or organic, which had manifested itself in violence. It was a disorder or abnormality which might recur, though the possibility of it recurring in the form of serious violence was unlikely. Therefore since this was a legal problem to be decided on legal principles, it seems to us that on those principles the answer was as the judge found it to be. . . .

The judge was alive to the apparent incongruity of labelling this sort of disability as insanity. He drew attention, as we would also wish to do, to the passage of the speech of Lord Diplock in *R* v *Sullivan* [1984] AC 156, where he said, at p. 173:

it is natural to feel reluctant to attach the label of insanity to a sufferer from psychomotor epilepsy of the kind to which Mr Sullivan was subject, even though the expression in the context of a special verdict of 'not guilty by reason of insanity' is a technical one which includes a purely temporary and intermittent suspension of the mental faculties of reason, memory and understanding resulting from the occurrence of an epileptic fit. But the label is contained in the current statute, it has appeared in this statute's predecessors ever since 1800. It does not lie within the power of the courts to alter it. Only Parliament can do that. It has done so twice; it could do so once again.

This appeal must accordingly be dismissed.

Appeal dismissed.

NOTES AND QUESTIONS
1. Sleepwalkers seem to fall somewhere between a state of consciousness and unconsciousness. They are able to manoeuvre their way about, opening doors and walking down steps, for example, without injuring themselves. Yet they seem to have no conscious awareness or subsequent recollection of their actions. Is it appropriate (just?) to characterise the sleepwalker as insane? Why does the law do so?
2. What disposition should be made in the case of the sleepwalkers who commit serious violent crimes such as murder? Should they be sent to prison? To a mental institution? Or should they be allowed to return to the community?
3. Suppose that James begins to drive home from work in a state of extreme drowsiness. He subsequently falls asleep at the wheel and is involved in an accident. If charged with dangerous driving, should he be able to assert a defence of automatism? Is *Burgess* distinguishable? See *Hill v Baxter* [1958] 1 All ER 193. Sometimes the issue of automatism can be avoided by finding an antecedent act on which to premise criminal liability, such as the fact that defendant began driving knowing that he was sleepy. The decision to drive under such circumstances may itself be a reckless or dangerous act satisfying the *actus reus* (as well as the *mens rea*) elements of the crime.
4. There are some mental health experts who believe that what one does while sleepwalking reflects what one subconsciously wants to do but cannot bring oneself to do while in a conscious state. Assuming the validity of this hypothesis for the sake of argument, should it have any bearing on the sleepwalker's criminal liability?

10

Defences

SECTION 1: Introduction

There are several different types of defence that need to be considered. The first relates to capacity, which was examined in the previous chapter. Although perhaps not a defence within either of the two senses in which the term is used below (negating an element of the crime, or establishing a justification or an excuse for the crime's commission), a claim of incapacity is similar in some ways to these affirmative defences. The accused has the initial burden of introducing evidence to support the claim. If the claim succeeds, it will preclude a conviction, regardless of the crime charged.

A different type of defence that is often raised at trial seeks to negate an element of the crime charged, usually the *actus reus* or *mens rea*. Mistake and intoxication, to be discussed in this chapter, provide examples. It is questionable whether 'defence' is the appropriate term to be used in this context, for the defendant's argument is that a reasonable doubt exists as to an element of the offence.

A third category of defence does not relate to any particular element of the crime, but provides a basis for not imposing liability even though all of the elements of the crime have been established. Perhaps it is best to characterise these as *affirmative defences*. The defendant admits the elements of the crime charged but argues that there are other factors to consider. In effect the defendant says 'Yes, but . . .'. Duress, necessity, crime prevention, self-defence and defence of others are defences of this sort.

Whether a defence is an affirmative defence or one that negates an element of the crime can in theory have important ramifications as far as the burden of proof is concerned. The Crown must prove each and every element of a crime by proof beyond a reasonable doubt, and thus must bear the ultimate burden of persuading the jury as to the existence of *all* elements of the crime. A defendant will have the burden of going forward or introducing evidence as to a defence that negates an element, but once there is sufficient evidence to take the issue to the jury, the burden of persuading the jury that the element is not negated or, stated affirmatively, is proved, rests on the Crown by proof beyond a reasonable doubt. See *Woolmington* v *Director of Public Prosecutions* [1935] AC 462.

In theory, a jury's consideration of an affirmative defence will not take place until the jurors have satisfied themselves that the Crown has established each and every element of the crime by proof beyond a reasonable doubt. There is at this point no theoretical objection to shifting to the defendant the burden of persuasion as to a defence that would lift the defendant's conduct out of the realm of the criminal. In effect, the law would say to the defendant: 'The Crown has proved its case; now you show us why you should not be convicted.'

This theoretical analysis notwithstanding, for most affirmative defences, with the primary exception of insanity, the courts have placed the ultimate burden of negating the defence on the prosecution. The defendant, however, bears the initial burden of producing some evidence to establish the defence.

A somewhat different type of defence challenges the validity of the law under which the defendant is being prosecuted because it conflicts with European law which takes priority. This challenge needs to be distinguished from that which is now available under the Human Rights Act (discussed in Chapter 1) is enacted into law. The effect of the Act is to incorporate the provisions of the European Convention on Human Rights into domestic law, and thereby provide a defendant with a new basis for challenging a criminal statute. The claim is that the statute violates rights embodied in the Convention. This is in contrast to the supremacy of European Union law which is already well established. See European Communities Act 1972, s. 9(2).

SECTION 2: Defences which negate an element of the crime

A: Mistake

A mistake by a defendant may be relevant to criminal liability where it negates an element of the offence. For example, the mistake may prevent the defendant from forming the relevant *mens rea*, as when Jones mistakenly believes that the umbrella he is walking away with belongs to him when it belongs to Smith. Another situation in which a mistake may be relevant is where it causes the defendant to form a distorted view of the surrounding circumstances of the crime, as when the defendant believes he is being attacked, whereas he is in fact being lawfully arrested. In these circumstances the defendant may have made a mistake as to circumstances which would provide an excuse for his actions if the situation actually was as he believed it to be.

(i) *Mistake and* mens rea
Mistake, which may be of law or fact, most commonly serves to negate the *mens rea* element of the crime. Some mistakes are irrelevant, however.

R v Ellis, Street and Smith
(1987) 84 Cr App R 235, Court of Appeal

O'CONNOR LJ: . . . All three appellants accepted that they participated in importing large quantities of cannabis into this country concealed in secret compartments in motor cars. They were indicted in the ordinary form for being knowingly concerned in the fraudulent evasion of the prohibition on the importation of a controlled drug contrary to section 170(2) of the Customs and Excise Management Act 1979. The particulars of offence were that on the relevant dates they were in relation to a class B controlled drug, namely in the case of Ellis and Street 29.3 kilogrammes and in the case of Smith 24.85 kilogrammes of cannabis, 'knowingly concerned in the fraudulent evasion of the prohibition on importation imposed by section 3(1) of the Misuse of Drugs Act 1971.'

In both cases the defendants as they then were pleaded not guilty and at once asked for a ruling as to whether they had a defence in law if the facts were that they knew that they were participating in the importation of prohibited goods but believed that the goods were pornographic goods which they knew to be subject to a prohibition and which were in fact subject to a prohibition.

. . . '"[K]nowingly" in the section in question is concerned with knowing that a fraudulent evasion of a prohibition in respect of goods is taking place.' It seems to us that it cannot make any difference whether a particular defendant says: 'I don't know what the goods were; I only know they were prohibited' or a defendant says: 'I didn't know what the goods in fact were. I thought that they were some other prohibited goods' . . .

NOTES AND QUESTIONS
1. Another approach that the Crown might have taken in *Ellis, Street and Smith* would have been to charge the defendants with an attempt to import pornographic goods. Would such a charge more accurately have captured the true nature of the defendants' fault (assuming that their story was to be believed)?
2. Another example of an irrelevant mistake is where X kills Y, thinking the victim is Z, or while aiming at Z. The identity of the victim is legally irrelevant and, as has been previously discussed, the courts will 'transfer' X's intent to murder Z to his killing of Y. See Chapter 6.
3. If a defendant receives stolen video tapes, believing them to be boxes of soap powder, will he be guilty of handling stolen goods? See *R v McCullum* (1973) 57 Cr App R 645.

An ongoing controversy has been whether the mistake must be reasonable in order to constitute a defence.

R v Williams (Gladstone)
(1983) 78 Cr App R 276, Court of Appeal

LORD LANE CJ: The facts were somewhat unusual and were as follows. On the day in question the alleged victim, a man called Mason, saw a black youth seizing the handbag belonging to a woman who was shopping. He caught up with the youth and held him, he said with a view to taking him to a nearby police station, but the youth broke free from his grip. Mason caught the youth again and knocked him to the ground, and he then twisted one of the youth's arms behind his back in order to immobilise him and to enable him, Mason, so he said, once again to take the youth to a police station. The youth was struggling and calling for help at this time, and no one disputed that fact.

Upon the scene then came the appellant who had only seen the latter stages of this incident. According to Mason he told the appellant first of all that he was arresting the youth for mugging the lady and secondly, that he, Mason, was a police officer. That was not true. He was asked for his warrant card, which obviously was not forthcoming, and thereupon something of a struggle ensued between Mason on the one hand and the appellant and others on the other hand. In the course of these events Mason sustained injuries to his face, loosened teeth and bleeding gums.

The appellant put forward the following version of events. He said he was returning from work by bus, when he saw Mason dragging the youth along and striking him again and again. He was so concerned about the matter that he rapidly got off the bus and made his way to the scene and asked Mason what on earth he was doing. In short he said that he punched Mason because he thought if he did so he would save the youth from further beating and what he described as torture.

There was no doubt that none of these *dramatis personae* was known to each other beforehand.
. . .

One starts off with the meaning of the word 'assault.' 'Assault' in the context of this case, that is to say using the word as a convenient abbreviation for assault and battery, is an act by which the defendant, intentionally or recklessly, applies unlawful force to the complainant. There are circumstances in which force may be applied to another lawfully. Taking a few examples: first, where the victim consents, as in lawful sports, the application of force to another will, generally speaking, not be unlawful. Secondly, where the defendant is acting in self-defence: the exercise of any necessary and reasonable force to protect himself from unlawful violence is not unlawful. Thirdly, by virtue of section 3 of the Criminal Law Act 1967, a person may use such force as is reasonable in the circumstances in the prevention of crime or in effecting or assisting in the lawful arrest of an offender or suspected offender or persons unlawfully at large. In each of those cases the defendant will be guilty if the jury are sure that first of all he applied force to the person of another, and secondly that he had the necessary mental element to constitute guilt.

The mental element necessary to constitute guilt is the intent to apply unlawful force to the victim. We do not believe that the mental element can be substantiated by simply showing an intent to apply force and no more.

What then is the situation if the defendant is labouring under a mistake of fact as to the circumstances? What if he believes, but believes mistakenly, that the victim is consenting, or that it is necessary to defend himself, or that a crime is being committed which he intends to prevent? He must then be judged against the mistaken facts as he believes them to be. If judged against those facts or circumstances the prosecution fail to establish his guilt, then he is entitled to be acquitted.

The next question is, does it make any difference if the mistake of the defendant was one which, viewed objectively by a reasonable onlooker, was an unreasonable mistake? In other words should the jury be directed as follows: 'Even if the defendant may have genuinely believed that what he was doing to the victim was either with the victim's consent or in reasonable self-defence or to prevent the commission of crime, as the case may be, nevertheless if you, the jury, come to the conclusion that the mistaken belief was unreasonable, that is to say that the defendant as a reasonable man should have realised his mistake, then you should convict him.'

. . . The reasonableness or unreasonableness of the defendant's belief is material to the question of whether the belief was held by the defendant at all. If the belief was in fact held, its unreasonableness, so far as guilt or innocence is concerned, is neither here nor there. It is irrelevant. Were it otherwise, the defendant would be convicted because he was negligent in failing to recognise that the victim was not consenting or that a crime was not being committed and so on. In other words the jury should be directed first of all that the prosecution have the burden or duty of proving the unlawfulness of the defendant's actions; secondly, if the defendant may have been labouring under a mistake as to the facts, he must be judged according to his mistaken view of the facts; thirdly, that is so whether the mistake was, on an objective view, a reasonable mistake or not.

In a case of self-defence, where self-defence or the prevention of crime is concerned, if the jury came to the conclusion that the defendant believed, or may have believed, that he was being attacked or that a crime was being committed, and that force was necessary to protect himself or to prevent the crime, then the prosecution have not proved their case. If however the defendant's alleged belief was mistaken and if the mistake was an unreasonable one, that may be a powerful reason for coming to the conclusion that the belief was not honestly held and should be rejected.

Even if the jury come to the conclusion that the mistake was an unreasonable one, if the defendant may genuinely have been labouring under it, he is entitled to rely upon it.

B v DPP

[2000] 2 WLR 452, House of Lords

For facts and holding, see p. 338.

LORD NICHOLLS OF BIRKENHEAD: . . . In *Sweet v Parsley* [1970] AC 132 Lord Diplock referred, at p. 163, to a general principle of construction of statutes creating criminal offences, in similar terms:

> a general principle of construction of any enactment, which creates a criminal offence, [is] that, even where the words used to describe the prohibited conduct would not in any other context connote the necessity for any particular mental element, they are nevertheless to be read as subject to the implication that a necessary element in the offence is the absence of a belief, held honestly and upon reasonable grounds, in the existence of facts which, if true, would make the act innocent.

The 'reasonable belief' school of thought held unchallenged sway for many years. But over the last quarter of a century there have been several important cases where a defence of honest but mistaken belief was raised. In deciding these cases the courts have placed new, or renewed, emphasis on the subjective nature of the mental element in criminal offences. The courts have rejected the reasonable belief approach and preferred the honest belief approach. When *mens rea* is ousted by a mistaken belief, it is as well ousted by an unreasonable belief as by a reasonable belief. In the pithy phrase of Lawton LJ in *R v Kimber* [1983] 1 WLR 1118, 1122, it is the defendant's belief, not the grounds on which it is based, which goes to negative the intent. This approach is well encapsulated in a passage in the judgment of Lord Lane CJ in *R v Williams (Gladstone)* [1987] 3 All ER 411, 415:

> The reasonableness or unreasonableness of the defendant's belief is material to the question of whether the belief was held by the defendant at all. If the belief was in fact held, its unreasonableness, so far as guilt or innocence is concerned, is neither here nor there. It is irrelevant. Were it otherwise, the defendant would be convicted because he was negligent in failing to recognise that the victim was not consenting . . . and so on.

Considered as a matter of principle, the honest belief approach must be preferable. By definition the mental element in a crime is concerned with a subjective state of mind, such as intent or belief. To the extent that an overriding objective limit ('on reasonable grounds') is introduced, the subjective element is displaced. To that extent a person who lacks the necessary intent or belief may nevertheless commit the offence. When that occurs the defendant's 'fault' lies exclusively in falling short of an objective standard. His crime lies in his negligence. A statute may so provide expressly or by necessary implication. But this can have no place in a common law principle, of general application, which is concerned with the need for a mental element as an essential ingredient of a criminal offence.

The traditional formulation of the common law presumption, exemplified in Lord Diplock's famous exposition in *Sweet v Parsley*, cited above, is out of step with this recent line of authority, in so far as it envisages that a mistaken belief must be based on reasonable grounds. This seems to be a relic from the days before a defendant in a criminal case could give evidence in his own defence. It is not surprising that in those times juries judged a defendant's state of mind by the conduct to be expected of a reasonable person.

I turn to the recent authorities. The decision which heralded this development in criminal law was the decision of your Lordships' House in *R v Morgan* [1976] AC 182. This was a case of rape. By a bare majority the House held that where a defendant had sexual intercourse with a woman without her consent but believing she did consent, he was not guilty of rape even though he had no reasonable grounds for his belief. The intent to commit rape involves an intention to have intercourse without the woman's consent or with a reckless indifference to whether she consents or not. It would be inconsistent with this definition if an honest belief that she did consent led to an acquittal only when it was based on reasonable grounds. One of the minority, Lord Edmund-Davies, would have taken a different view had he felt free to do so. In *R v Kimber*, a case of indecent assault, the Court of Appeal applied the approach of the majority in *Morgan's* case. The guilty state of mind was the intent to use personal violence to a woman without her consent. If the defendant did not so intend, he was entitled to be found not guilty. If he did not so intend because he believed she was consenting, the prosecution will have failed to prove the charge, irrespective of the grounds for the defendant's belief. The court disapproved of the suggestion made in the earlier case of *R v Phekoo* [1981] 1 WLR 1117, 1127, that this House intended to confine the views expressed in *Morgan's* case to cases of rape.

This reasoning was taken a step further in *R v Williams (Gladstone)* [1987] 3 All ER 411. There the Court of Appeal, presided over by Lord Lane CJ, adopted the same approach in a case of assault occasioning actual bodily harm. The context was a defence that the defendant believed that the person whom he assaulted was unlawfully assaulting a third party. In *Beckford v The Queen* [1988] AC 130 a similar issue came before the Privy Council on an appeal from Jamaica in a case involving a defence of self-defence to a charge of murder. The Privy Council applied the decisions in *Morgan's* case and *Williams's* case. Lord Griffiths said, at p. 144:

> If then a genuine belief, albeit without reasonable grounds, is a defence to rape because it negatives the necessary intention, so also must a genuine belief in facts which if true would justify self-defence be a defence to a crime of personal violence because the belief negatives the intent to act unlawfully.

Lord Griffiths also observed, at a practical level, that where there are no reasonable grounds to hold a belief it will surely only be in exceptional circumstances that a jury will conclude that such a belief was or might have been held. Finally in this summary, in *Blackburn v Bowering* [1994] 1 WLR 1324, the Court of Appeal, presided over by Sir Thomas Bingham MR, applied the same approach to the exercise by the court of its contempt jurisdiction in respect of an alleged assault on officers of the court while in the execution of their duty.

The Crown advanced no suggestion to your Lordships that any of these recent cases was wrongly decided. This is not surprising, because the reasoning in these cases is compelling. Thus, the traditional formulation of the common law presumption must now be modified appropriately. Otherwise the formulation would not be an accurate reflection of the current state of the criminal law regarding mistakes of fact. Lord Diplock's dictum in *Sweet v Parsley* [1970] AC 132, 163, must in future be read as though the reference to reasonable grounds were omitted.

R v K

[2001] 3 All ER 897, House of Lords

For facts and holding see p. 327.

NOTES AND QUESTIONS

1. The argument in favour of retaining a requirement of reasonableness is that it forces an individual to think carefully before resorting to force. See A. Simester, 'Mistakes in Defence' (1992) 12 OJLS 295 and D. Elliot, 'Necessity, Duress and Self-defence' [1989] Crim LR 611. What is the relationship between this new 'subjectivist approach' and provocation, duress and self-defence?
2. The more reasonable the mistake, the more likely the defendant is to persuade the jury that the mistake was genuine. Consider:

Director of Public Prosecutions v Armstrong-Braun
[1999] Crim LR 416, Queen's Bench Division

The defendant wished to protect the habitat of a protected species, namely, Great Crested Newts which occupied a site for which planning permission had been granted. A licence had been granted pursuant to section 16 of the Wildlife and Countryside Act 1981 to disturb and take the newts in order to provide them with an alternative habitat. O, who was using a mechanical digger, was carrying out the organisational and practical measures needed to ensure compliance with the terms of the licence. When the defendant came onto the site, he took a wooden stake and tried to use it to jam the foot controls of the digger. He also struck the roll bar of the digger with the stake. O then became angry and chased the defendant, who struck him once with the stake on his arm. The defendant was charged with assault contrary to section 39 of the Criminal Justice Act 1998. The defendant contended that, if he had struck O, he had done so in the honest belief, however misguided, that O's continued use of the digger would be a crime, or that O would hurt him and it was on that basis that the force he had used was no more than he genuinely thought was the minimum necessary to stop the machine or to protect himself. The justices noted that the test of reasonableness was not entirely objective and that it would have some subjective element, but did not accept that the defendant's use of force was reasonable in the circumstances. They accordingly convicted the defendant. He appealed by way of case stated. He submitted that the question as to whether the degree of force was reasonably necessary was to be tested subjectively, provided that the defendant recognised that the community at large would also regard the degree of force as reasonably necessary.

Held, dismissing the appeal, the force used by a defendant accused of battery in self-defence was to be assessed in an objective sense as to whether it was reasonably necessary in the circumstances as the defendant subjectively believed them to be. There was no necessity for an additional test requiring a subjective approach to the question of proportionality of the response.

NOTE

The European Court of Human Rights has recognised that States have a duty to protect their citizens against unlawful attack. (See, for example, *A v UK*; for facts and findings, see p. 299.) The Court has also recognised that, before deadly force can be used in self-defence, the person using the force must honestly believe, for good reason, that the force is absolutely necessary. (See *McCann v UK* (1996) 21 EHRR 97; for facts and findings, see p. 514.) Taken together, do these cases suggest that the subjective test of mistake enunciated by the Court of Appeal in *Williams* might fail to adequately protect the rights of UK citizens as guaranteed by the European Convention on Human Rights?

(ii) *The relationship between mistake and other defences*
Where a mistake is made because of insanity or diminished responsibility, those defences will take precedence. The issue of reasonableness is subsumed by the determination of whether the defendant knew the nature and quality of his act, or whether his mental condition substantially impaired his responsibility for killing.

The greatest difficulty has been encountered where the defendant has made a drunken mistake as to facts which would have justified his actions if the facts had been as he believed them to be. Compare the following cases:

R v O'Grady

[1987] 3 WLR 321, Court of Appeal

The appellant, who was intoxicated, killed a man and stated to the police, 'If I had not hit him I would be dead myself.' He was tried on a count charging murder. The jury were directed that, if the appellant mistakenly believed he was under attack, he was entitled to defend himself but was not entitled to go beyond what was reasonable.

LORD LANE CJ: . . . How should the jury be invited to approach the problem? One starts with the decision of this court in *R v Williams (Gladstone)* (1983) 78 Cr App R 276, namely, that where the defendant might have been labouring under a mistake as to the facts he must be judged according to that mistaken view, whether the mistake was reasonable or not. It is then for the jury to decide whether the defendant's reaction to the threat, real or imaginary, was a reasonable one. The court was not in that case considering what the situation might be where the mistake was due to voluntary intoxication by alcohol or some other drug.

We have come to the conclusion that where the jury are satisfied that the defendant was mistaken in his belief that any force or the force which he in fact used was necessary to defend himself and are further satisfied that the mistake was caused by voluntarily induced intoxication, the defence must fail. We do not consider that any distinction should be drawn on this aspect of the matter between offences involving what is called specific intent, such as murder, and offences of so called basic intent, such as manslaughter. Quite apart from the problem of directing a jury in a case such as the present where manslaughter is an alternative verdict to murder, the question of mistake can and ought to be considered separately from the question of intent. A sober man who mistakenly believes he is in danger of immediate death at the hands of an attacker is entitled to be acquitted of both murder and manslaughter if his reaction in killing his supposed assailant was a reasonable one. What his intent may have been seems to us to be irrelevant to the problem of self-defence or no.

Jaggard v Dickinson

[1980] 3 All ER 716, Queen's Bench Division

MUSTILL J: . . . The facts set out in the case are short but striking. On the evening of 12th October 1978 the appellant had been drinking. At 10.45 pm she engaged a taxi to take her to 67 Carnach Green, South Ockendon, a house occupied by Mr R F Heyfron, a gentleman with whom she had a relationship such that, in the words of the magistrates, she had his consent at any time to treat his property as if it was her own. Alighting from the taxi, she entered the garden but was asked to leave by a Mrs Raven who was a stranger to her. Persisting, she broke the glass in the hallway of the house. She then went to the back door where she broke another window and gained entry to the house, damaging a net curtain in the process. At some time thereafter, in circumstances not described by the magistrates, it became clear that the house was not 67 Carnach Green but 35 Carnach Green, a house of identical outward appearance, occupied by Mrs Raven. The magistrates have found that the appellant did believe that she was breaking into the property of Mr Heyfron but that this mistake was induced by a state of self-induced intoxication.

. . . If the basis of the decision in *R v Majewski* [1976] 2 WLR 623 had been that drunkenness does not prevent a person from having an intent or being reckless, then there would be grounds for saying that it should equally be left out of account when deciding on his state of belief. But this is not in our view what *Majewski* decided. The House of Lords did not conclude that intoxication was irrelevant to the fact of the defendant's state of mind, but rather that, whatever might have been his actual state of mind, he should for reasons of policy be precluded from relying on any alteration in that state brought about by self-induced intoxication. The same considerations of policy apply to the intent or recklessness which is the mens rea of the offence created by s. 1(1) [Criminal Damage Act 1971] and that offence is accordingly regarded as one of basic intent (see *R v Stephenson* [1979] 1 QB 695). It is indeed essential that this should be so, for drink so often plays a part in offences of criminal damage, and to admit drunkenness as a potential means of escaping liability would provide much too ready a means of avoiding conviction. But these considerations do not apply to a case where Parliament has specifically required the court to consider the defendant's actual state of belief, not the state of belief which ought to have existed. This seems to us to show that the court is required by s. 5(3) to focus on the existence of the belief, not its intellectual soundness; and a belief can be just as much honestly held if it is induced by intoxication as if it stems from stupidity, forgetfulness or inattention.

It was, however, urged that we could not properly read s. 5(2) in isolation from s. 1(1), which forms the context of the words 'without lawful excuse' partially defined by s. 5(2). Once the words are put in context, so it is maintained, it can be seen that the law must treat drunkenness in the same way in relation to lawful excuse (and hence belief) as it does to intention and recklessness, for they are all part of the mens rea of the offence. To fragment the mens rea, so as to treat one part of it as affected by drunkenness in one way and the remainder as affected in a different way, would make the law impossibly complicated to enforce.

If it had been necessary to decide whether, for all purposes, the mens rea of an offence under s. 1(1) extends as far as an intent (or recklessness) as to the existence of a lawful excuse, I should have wished to consider the observations of James LJ, delivering the judgment of the Court of Appeal in *R v Smith* [1974] 1 All ER 632 at 636. I do not however find it necessary to reach a conclusion on this matter and will only say that I am not at present convinced that, when these observations are read in the context of the judgment as a whole, they have the meaning which the respondent has sought to put on them. In my view, however, the answer to the argument lies in the fact that any distinctions which have to be drawn as to the relevance of drunkenness to the two subsections arises from the scheme of the 1971 Act itself. No doubt the mens rea is in general indivisible, with no distinction being possible as regards the effect of drunkenness. But Parliament has specifically isolated one subjective element, in the shape of honest belief, and has given it separate treatment and its own special gloss in s. 5(3). This being so, there is nothing objectionable in giving it special treatment as regards drunkenness, in accordance with the natural meaning of its words.

In these circumstances, I would hold that the magistrates were in error when they decided that the defence furnished to the appellant by s. 5(2) was lost because she was drunk at the time. I would therefore allow the appeal.

R v Richardson and Irwin

[1999] Crim LR 494, Court of Appeal

The defendants and the complainant were university students. After drinking at the student union bar they went to a flat belonging to one of the defendants. There was some horseplay and the defendants lifted the complainant over the edge of the balcony and dropped him. He fell about 10ft or 12 ft and suffered injuries. The prosecution case was that the defendants had acted both unlawfully and maliciously in the sense that they each actually foresaw that dropping the complainant would or might cause harm and they nevertheless took the risk of doing so. The defendants' case was that the complainant had consented to the horseplay and that his fall was an accident. The defendants were convicted of inflicting grievous bodily harm contrary to section 20 of the Offences Against the Person Act 1861. They appealed against conviction on the grounds that the judge wrongly directed the jury that the intention of each defendant should be on the basis of a reasonable, (i.e. not under the influence of drink) man and not (as they were) under the influence of drink.

Held, allowing the appeals and quashing the convictions, that the judge should have directed the jury along the following lines, which were consistent with the standard Judicial Studies Board directions:

The complainant . . . suffered bodily harm because he slipped or was dropped . . . No question of self defence arises. To convict either defendant you must be sure: (1) that he alone or with the other defendant put [the complainant] into the position from which he slipped or was dropped; (2) that [the complainant] did not consent to being put there; (3) that he realised that [the complainant] did not consent; (4) that his actions in putting [the complainant] there were deliberate i.e. not accidental; (5) that when doing this either (a) he realised that [the complainant] might slip or be dropped and thus sustain some degree of bodily harm, albeit of a minor character, or (b) he would have realised that had he not been drinking. Questions (3) and (5)(a) are about the defendant's state of mind. When considering both you must take account of the evidence that the defendant's mind was affected by alcohol. In relation to question (3) you cannot convict if you find that the defendant did mistakenly believe or might have mistakenly believed that [the complainant] did consent. Take the evidence of his consumption of alcohol into account when considering this. Similarly in relation to question (5)(a) you cannot convict if you find that the defendant did not realise or might not have realised that [the complainant] might slip or be dropped and be injured. Here too you must take account of the evidence of the defendants' consumption of alcohol into account. In the same way the alcohol consumed by [the complainant] bears on question (2).

NOTES AND QUESTIONS

1. In *O'Grady*, Lord Lane CJ said that mistake and intent ought to be considered separately. Is this possible?
2. Derek, when drunk, shoots Percy and is charged with murder. Of what relevance is the fact that Derek mistakenly believes (a) that Percy was a bear, (b) that Percy was attacking him violently, (c) that Percy was an alien attacking him?
3. *O'Grady*, *Jaggard v Dickinson* and *Richardson and Irwin* involved mistakes due to intoxication, and the results may be affected by public policy considerations which arise in that context (and which are examined later in this chapter). They need to be reviewed after consideration of that topic.

(iii) *Ignorance of law*

There is a presumption that a citizen is aware of the requirements of the law. From this presumption flows the well-known (and generally correct) axiom that ignorance of the law is no excuse.

R v Lee (Dennis Percival)

[2001] 1 Cr App R 19, Court of Appeal

ROSE L.J. (Vice President). The question raised by this appeal is whether on a charge, under section 38 of the Offences against the Person Act 1861, of assault with intent to resist lawful apprehension for failing a roadside breathalyser test, it is a defence that the defendant honestly believed that he had not failed the test. Put another way, and more widely, does the *mens rea* for assault with intent to resist lawful apprehension include an absence of honest belief in the defendant that the arrest was lawful?

The relevant facts can be shortly stated. On September 24, 1999, the appellant was driving a motor car in Mace Lane, Ashford. He was stopped by police for a roadside safety check. His breath smelt of alcohol. He said he had only drunk a pint and a half. He was asked to provide a breath specimen. He did so in an alcolyser bag. It was common ground that the officers said the test was positive, in that the crystals had changed colour beyond the red line, but the appellant immediately, in subsequent interviews and in evidence, disputed this: he said there was a bubble in the crystals so that it was not clear that the line had been reached or crossed. According to the officers, after he had been told he was being arrested, the appellant punched both of them. The appellant admitted pushing one officer and punching the other. It is conceded on the appellant's behalf that there was evidence on which the jury could conclude that the officers were acting lawfully because the breath-alyser test provided possible reasonable grounds to suspect the commission of a drink-driving offence.

The judge directed the jury as to the elements of the offence in a manner about which complaint is made by Mr Patterson, on behalf of the appellant, in only one presently relevant respect. The judge stressed that the offence could only be committed if the apprehension were lawful and that it would be lawful if the person arresting reasonably believed an arrestable offence had been committed. Mr Patterson submits that if the appellant genuinely, albeit wrongly, believed his arrest were unlawful he could not have intended to resist lawful apprehension: the judge should therefore have gone further and directed the jury that they must be sure that the defendant had no honest belief that he had not failed the breathalyser test. That is not a submission which Mr Patterson made to the trial judge when these matters were being discussed in the absence of the jury: but that would not be fatal to this appeal if the submission is well-founded.

. . .

In our judgment, the relevant authorities can be summarised in this way.

(1) *Fennell* and Lord Diplock's speech in *Sweet v. Parsley* [1970] A.C. 132 at 163 are no longer authority for the proposition that, in order to afford a defence to offences involving *mens rea*, a defendant's belief as to facts must be reasonable, as well as genuine or honest. That approach, in relation to self-defence, was rejected in *Williams (Gladstone)* which was approved by the Privy Council in *Beckford* and by the House of Lords in *B*. And, in the light of *Morgan*, Lord Diplock's observations were expressly disapproved in *B* (see in particular, the speech of Lord Nicholls at 456B–457A and Lord Steyn at 470F).

(2) A genuine or honest mistake may afford a defence in relation to many criminal offences requiring *mens rea*, e.g. rape, if made as to the woman's consent (*Morgan*), indecent assault if made by a 15-year-old as to the girl's age (*B*) and offences of violence if made as to the nature of the victim's behaviour towards the defendant (*Beckford*) or another (*Williams (Gladstone)*).

(3) Such a mistake may afford a defence in relation to assault with intent to resist arrest (*Brightling* (transcript, January 15, 1991, page 13D-F)) or assaulting an officer in the execution of his duty. (*Blackburn v. Bowering* [1994] 1 W.L.R. 1324 at 1329A) if it relates to whether or not the victim is a police officer. In such a case, the defendant's mistake may be relevant to whether he intended to assault a police officer and to whether he was acting in reasonable self-defence.

(4) But, to afford such a defence, the mistake must be one of fact. In *Blackburn v. Bowering* at 1329C Sir Thomas Bingham, then Master of the Rolls, referred to *Fennell* and to 'the important qualification that the mistake must be one of fact (particularly as to the victim's capacity) and not a mistake of law as to the authority of a person acting in that capacity'. This approach accords with the passage in Smith and Hogan on which Mr Fowler relies, with the passages in *Archbold* and *Blackstone* on which Mr Patterson relies and also with Sir John Smith's comment on *Brightling*, once it is understood that by 'circumstances' in that comment he was referring to facts this construction is supported by the passage in Smith and Hogan on which Mr Patterson relies, where circumstances are equated with facts.

(5) In *Bentley* (1850) 4 Cox C.C. 408, Talfourd J. put the point at page 410 in a way which in our judgment is still good law:

'I think that, to support a charge of resisting a lawful apprehension, it is enough that the prisoner is lawfully apprehended, and it is his determination to resist it. If the apprehension is in point of fact lawful, we are not permitted to consider the question, whether or not he believed it to be so, because that would lead to infinite niceties of discrimination. The rule is not, that a man is always presumed to know the law, but that no man shall be excused for an unlawful act from his ignorance of the law. It was the prisoner's duty, whatever might be his consciousness of innocence, to go to the station-house and hear the precise accusation against him. He is not to erect a tribunal in his own mind to decide whether he was legally arrested or not. He was taken into custody by an officer of the law, and it was his duty to obey the law.'

Applying these principles to the present case, it is clear that, even had the appellant given evidence (which it appears he did not) that he resisted arrest because his interpretation of the alcolyser lead him honestly to believe his arrest was unlawful, this would not have afforded a defence. Such a belief would have been not about any facts relating to the identity or conduct of the police officers at the time of the attempted arrest but about the legal consequences of believed antecedent facts. The appellant's position is, in our judgment, indistinguishable from that of a person sought to be arrested on grounds of reasonable suspicion for any arrestable offence which he knows or believes he has not committed. If, in such circumstances, that person assaults an officer whom he knows is acting as a police officer, we have never known it to be suggested that belief in innocence could afford a defence to assault, either with intent to resist arrest or on an officer in the execution of his duty.

In our judgement, once the lawfulness of the proposed arrest is established, the *mens rea* necessary for a section 38 offence is an intention by the defendant to resist arrest, accompanied by knowledge that the person he assaults (who may or may not be a police officer) is a person who is seeking to arrest him. Whether or not an offence has actually been committed or is believed by the defendant not to have been committed is irrelevant.

We reach this conclusion without regret. Neither public order nor the clarity of the criminal law would be improved if juries were required to consider in relation to section 38 offences the impact of a defendant's belief as to the lawfulness of his arrest in cases where a lawful arrest is being properly attempted on reasonable grounds.

Accordingly this appeal is dismissed.

Appeal dismissed.

R v Bailey

(1800) Russ & Ry 1, Crown Cases Reserved

It was then insisted that the prisoner could not be found guilty of the offence with which he was charged, because the Act of the 39 Geo. III. c. 37, upon which (together with the statute relating to maliciously shooting (9 Geo. I. c. 22; Black Act) the prisoner was indicted at this Admiralty Sessions, and which Act of the 39 Geo. III. is entitled, 'An Act for amending certain defects in the law respecting offences committed on the high seas,' only received the royal assent on the 10th of May, 1799, and the fact charged in the indictment happened on the 27th of June, in the same year, when the prisoner could not know that any such Act existed (his ship, the 'Langley', being at that time upon the coast of Africa).

Lord Eldon told the jury that he was of opinion that he was, in strict law, guilty within the statutes, taken together, if the facts laid were proved, though he could not then know that the Act of the 39 Geo. III. c. 37 had passed, and that his ignorance of that fact could in no otherwise affect the case, than that it might be the means of recommending him to a merciful consideration elsewhere should he be found guilty.

NOTES AND QUESTIONS
1. Even if Bailey had access to the statute books, how likely is it that he would have checked the law? Is this a relevant enquiry? Does the true basis of the decision rest on the court's reluctance to create any exceptions to the general rule?

2. If a statutory instrument has not been published, ignorance may excuse. See Statutory Instruments Act 1946, s. 3(2).

When it is said that ignorance of the law is no excuse, the ignorance being referred to relates to the law which the accused is alleged to have violated. Ignorance as to some other law, usually a collateral civil law, may serve to negate *mens rea*.

R v Smith (David)
[1974] QB 354, Court of Appeal

JAMES LJ: . . . The question of law in this appeal arises in this way. In 1970 the appellant became the tenant of a ground-floor flat at 209, Freemason's Road, E.16. The letting included a conservatory. In the conservatory the appellant and his brother, who lived with him, installed some electric wiring for use with stereo equipment. Also, with the landlord's permission, they put up roofing material and asbestos wall panels and laid floor boards. There is no dispute that the roofing, wall panels and floor boards became part of the house and, in law, the property of the landlord. Then in 1972 the appellant gave notice to quit and asked the landlord to allow the appellant's brother to remain as tenant of the flat. On September 18, 1972, the landlord informed the appellant that his brother could not remain. On the next day the appellant damaged the roofing, wall panels and floorboards he had installed in order – according to the appellant and his brother – to gain access to and remove the wiring. The extent of the damage was £130. When interviewed by the police, the appellant said: 'Look, how can I be done for smashing my own property. I put the flooring and that in, so if I want to pull it down it's a matter for me.'

. . . Section 1 of the Criminal Damage Act 1971 reads:

(1) A person who without lawful excuse destroys or damages any property belonging to another intending to destroy or damage any such property or being reckless as to whether any such property would be destroyed or damaged, shall be guilty of an offence.

. . . Construing the language of section 1(1) we have no doubt that the actus reus is 'destroying or damaging any property belonging to another.' It is not possible to exclude the words 'belonging to another' which describes the 'property.' Applying the ordinary principles of mens rea, the intention and recklessness and the absence of lawful excuse required to constitute the offence have reference to property belonging to another. It follows that in our judgment no offence is committed under this section if a person destroys or causes damage to property belonging to another if he does so in the honest though mistaken belief that the property is his own, and provided that the belief is honestly held it is irrelevant to consider whether or not it is a justifiable belief.

Secretary of State for Trade and Industry v Hart
[1982] 1 WLR 481, Queen's Bench Division

The defendant, who was a director and secretary of one company and a director of another, audited the annual accounts for the companies for the year ending March 31, 1979. Informations were preferred against him alleging that he had acted as an auditor when he knew that he was disqualified from so acting by reason of the offices that he held within the companies, contrary to section 161(2) of the Companies Act 1948 and section 13 of the Companies Act 1976. The magistrate accepted that the defendant was unaware of the offence and dismissed the informations on the ground that knowledge of the disqualification was a necessary ingredient of an offence under section 13(5).

On appeal by the prosecutor:—

Held, dismissing the appeal, that, giving the words of section 13(5) and (6) their ordinary meaning, 'knowledge' in subsection (5) had to be construed as knowledge not only of the relevant facts that constituted the offence but that in consequence of those facts a director was disqualified under the subsection from auditing the companies' accounts; that, accordingly, since the defendant had no knowledge of the statutory provisions, he had been properly acquitted of the offence. . . .

QUESTIONS

1. The criminal law is constantly expanding, and there are now close to 10,000 different crimes. Few lawyers, let alone members of the public, are familiar with all of these laws, many of which are extremely technical. Given this reality, why is there a presumption that all persons are aware of the law? What functions are served by the rule that ignorance of the law is no excuse?

2. What if the defendant consults a solicitor who advises that a proposed course of action is not illegal? It turns out that the solicitor is mistaken and criminal charges are brought against the defendant. Should the good faith reliance on the advice of the solicitor be a defence? The courts have said not (see *Cooper* v *Simmons* (1862) 7 H and N 707). Why? What more can an ordinary citizen do (be expected to do)?

B: Intoxication

(i) *Rationale*

Intoxication, whether the result of alcohol, drugs or medication, can impair a person's judgment, perception and self-control. It can cause persons to commit crimes which they would never have considered committing while sober. In these situations, should the law take the intoxication into account? Should intoxication be a defence? Should it be a factor to be taken into account in sentencing?

Over the years the courts have manifested an ambivalent attitude to intoxication. On the one hand, they recognise that, as a matter of theory, there should be a valid defence available to the defendant whose drunken state prevents him from formulating the *mens rea* of the crime charged. In order to secure a conviction, a prosecutor must establish *mens rea* by proof beyond a reasonable doubt. The drunk defendant may well lack *mens rea*. The reason why he lacked *mens rea* should be irrelevant. On the other hand, reducing oneself to a drunken state is not the type of conduct that the legal system wants to be seen to be either condoning or encouraging. Drunkenness serves little socially useful purpose, and often leads to significant social harm.

(ii) *Voluntary intoxication*

The courts have distinguished between voluntary and involuntary intoxication. Voluntary intoxication is not *per se* a defence. It may, however, be relevant evidence as to whether the defendant had the requisite *mens rea* for the offence.

Director of Public Prosecutions v *Majewski*
[1977] AC 443, House of Lords

LORD ELWYN-JONES LC: . . . In view of the conclusion to which I have come that the appeal should be dismissed and of the questions of law which arise in the case, it is desirable that I should refer in some detail to the facts, which were largely undisputed. During the evening of February 19, 1973, the appellant and his friend, Leonard Stace, who had also taken drugs and drink, went to the Bull public house in Basildon. The appellant obtained a drink and sat down in the lounge bar at a table by the door. Stace became involved in a disturbance. Glasses were broken. The landlord asked Stace to leave and escorted him to the door. As he did so, Stace called to the appellant: 'He's putting me out.' The appellant got up and prevented the landlord from getting Stace out and abused him. The landlord told them both to go. They refused. The appellant butted the landlord in the face and bruised it, and punched a customer. The customers in the bar and the landlord forced the two out through the bar doors. They re-entered by forcing the outer door, a glass panel of which was broken by Stace. The appellant punched the landlord and pulled a piece of broken glass from the frame and started swinging it at the landlord and a customer, cutting the landlord slightly on his arm. The appellant then burst through the inner door of the bar with such force that he fell on the floor. The landlord held him there until the police arrived. The appellant was violent and abusive and spat in the landlord's face. When the police came, a fierce struggle took place to get him out. He shouted at the police: 'You pigs, I'll kill you all, you f. . . . pigs, you bastards,' P.C. Barkway said the appellant looked at him and kicked him deliberately.

P.C. Bird was kicked on the shins. During the struggle to get the appellant into the police car he said to P.C. Barrett: 'You bastard, I'll get you' and then kicked him.

The appellant was placed in the cells of Basildon police station. The next morning Police Inspector Dickinson heard banging and saw the appellant in his cell trying to remove a metal flap under the bed platform. The inspector asked him, what he was doing. According to the inspector he said: 'Come in here and I will stripe you with this. I'll break your neck.' The inspector and other officers entered the cell. Before he was restrained, he struck the inspector with the handcuffs on his wrists. Dr Mitchell arrived and gave him an injection.

Cross-examined as to the appellant's condition that evening the publican said he seemed to have gone berserk, his eyes were a bit glazed and protruding. A customer said he was 'glarey-eyed,' and went 'berserk' when the publican asked Stace to leave. He was screaming and shouting. A policeman said he was in a fearful temper.

The appellant gave evidence and said that on Saturday, February 17, 1973, he bought, not on prescription, about 40 Dexadrine tablets ('speeds') and early on Sunday morning consumed about half of them. That gave him plenty of energy until he 'started coming down.' He did not sleep throughout Sunday. On Monday evening at about 6 p.m. he acquired a bottle full of sodium nembutal tablets which he said were tranquillisers – 'downers,' 'barbs' and took about eight of them at about 6.30.

He and his friends then went to the Bull. He said he could remember nothing of what took place there save for a flash of recollection of Stace kicking a window. All he recollected of the police cell was asking the police to remove his handcuffs and then being injected.

In cross-examination he admitted he had been taking amphetamines and barbiturates, not on prescription, for two years, in large quantities. On occasions he drank barley wine or Scotch. He had sometimes 'gone paranoid.' This was the first time he had 'completely blanked out.'

Dr Bird called for the defence, said that the appellant had been treated for drug addiction since November 1971. There was no history in his case of psychiatric disorder or diagnosable mental illness, but the appellant had a personality disorder. Dr Bird said that barbiturates and alcohol are known to potentiate each other and to produce rapid intoxication and affect a person's awareness of what was going on . . ..

What then is the mental element required in our law to be established in assault? This question has been most helpfully answered in the speech of Lord Simon of Glaisdale in *R* v *Morgan* [1976] AC 182, 216:

> By 'crimes of basic intent' I mean those crimes whose definition expresses (or, more often, implies) a *mens rea* which does not go beyond the *actus reus*. The *actus reus* generally consists of an act and some consequence. The consequence may be very closely con-

nected with the act or more remotely connected with it: but with a crime of basic intent the *mens rea* does not extend beyond the act and its consequence, however, remote, as defined in the *actus reus*. I take assault as an example of a crime of basic intent where the consequence is very closely connected with the act. The *actus reus* of assault is an act which causes another person to apprehend immediate and unlawful violence. The *mens rea* corresponds exactly. The prosecution must prove that the accused foresaw that his act would probably cause another person to have apprehension of immediate and unlawful violence, or would possibly have that consequence, such being the purpose of the act, or that he was reckless as to whether or not his act caused such apprehension. This foresight (the term of art is 'intention') or recklessness is the *mens rea* in assault.

How does the fact of self-induced intoxication fit into that analysis? If a man consciously and deliberately takes alcohol and drugs not on medical prescription, but in order to escape from reality, to go 'on a trip', to become hallucinated, whatever the description may be and thereby disables himself from taking the care he might otherwise take and as a result by his subsequent actions causes injury to another – does our criminal law enable him to say that because he did not know what he was doing he lacked both intention and recklessness and accordingly is entitled to an acquittal?

. . . The authority which for the last half century has been relied upon in this context has been the speech of the Earl of Birkenhead LC in *Director of Public Prosecutions* v *Beard* [1920] AC 479, who stated, at p. 494:

> Under the law of England as it prevailed until early in the 19th century voluntary drunkenness was never an excuse for criminal misconduct; and indeed the classic authorities broadly assert that voluntary drunkenness must be considered rather an aggravation than a defence. This view was in terms based upon the principle that a man who by his own voluntary act debauches and destroys his will power shall be no better situated in regard to criminal acts than a sober man.

Lord Birkenhead LC made a historical survey of the way the common law from the 16th century on dealt with the effect of self-induced intoxication upon criminal responsibility. This indicates how, from 1819 on, the judges began to mitigate the severity of the attitude of the common law in such cases as murder and serious violent crime when the penalties of death or transportation applied or where there was likely to be sympathy for the accused, as in attempted suicide. Lord Birkenhead LC concluded, at p. 499, that (except in cases where insanity is pleaded) the decisions he cited

> establish that where a specific intent is an essential element in the offence, evidence of a state of drunkenness rendering the accused incapable of forming such an intent should be taken into consideration in order to determine whether he had in fact formed the intent necessary to constitute the particular crime. If he was so drunk that he was incapable of forming the intent required he could not be convicted of a crime which was committed only if the intent was proved. . . . In a charge of murder based upon intention to kill or to do grievous bodily harm, if the jury are satisfied that the accused was, by reason of his drunken condition, incapable of forming the intent to kill or to do grievous bodily harm . . . he cannot be convicted of murder. But nevertheless unlawful homicide has been committed by the accused, and consequently he is guilty of unlawful homicide without malice aforethought, and that is manslaughter: *per* Stephen J in *R* v *Doherty* (1887) 16 Cox CC 306, 307.

He concludes the passage:

> the law is plain beyond all question that in cases falling short of insanity a condition of drunkenness at the time of committing an offence causing death can only, when it is available at all, have the effect of reducing the crime from murder to manslaughter.

From this it seemed clear – and this is the interpretation which the judges have placed upon the decision during the ensuing half century – that it is only in the limited class of cases requiring proof of specific intent that drunkenness can exculpate. Otherwise in no case can it exempt completely from criminal liability.

. . .

I do not for my part regard that general principle as either unethical or contrary to the principles of natural justice. If a man of his own volition takes a substance which causes him to cast off the restraints of reason and conscience, no wrong is done to him by holding him answerable criminally for any injury he may do while in that condition. His course of conduct in reducing himself by drugs and drink to that condition in my view supplies the evidence of *mens rea*, of guilty mind certainly sufficient for crimes of basic intent. It is a reckless course of conduct and recklessness is enough to constitute the necessary *mens rea* in assault cases; see *R* v *Venna* [1975] 3 WLR 737 *per* James LJ at p. 743. The drunkenness is itself an intrinsic, an integral part of the crime, the other part being the evidence of the unlawful use of force against the victim. Together they add up to criminal recklessness. . . .

NOTES AND QUESTIONS

1. What is the difference between specific intent and basic intent? Is it possible to predict which crimes will be deemed to be ones of basic intent before an authoritative decision is actually handed down?
2. Why does the House of Lords distinguish between basic and specific intent? Is it because self-induced intoxication is itself a reckless act which will satisfy the recklessness requirement of a crime of basic intent? See also *R* v *Caldwell* [1982] AC 341 (p. 167). If self-induced intoxication is itself the *mens rea*, it cannot be the basis for arguing that the defendant lacked *mens rea*. Indeed, a defendant would be ill-advised to raise intoxication as a defence when charged with a crime of basic intent, for by doing so he in effect concedes *mens rea*.
3. In what sense is it accurate to say that the person who voluntarily becomes intoxicated is reckless? Most persons who get drunk simply wind up making fools of themselves, and eventually passing out. Is such an individual reckless in not foreseeing that he or she would become violent or dangerous, particularly if such a reaction had never occurred previously? Or is the court's point that a *reasonable person* would have appreciated before taking the first drink that there was a risk of becoming drunk and, that while drunk, engaging in antisocial activity of a criminal sort? If so, is the court saying that the recklessness in deciding to drink, which may occur long before the crime charged is committed, will satisfy the *mens rea* for that crime? Are there then not both 'concurrence' and 'transferred intent' issues buried within *Majewski*? Does the court adequately address these issues?
4. It may make more sense to explain the disallowance of a defence based on voluntary intoxication as simply a policy decision that persons who get drunk take the risk that the alcohol may impair their judgment, lead to a loss of self-control, and cause them to do something which they might not have done if sober; and if that happens, and if what they do would be a crime if *mens rea* could be proved, they will not be allowed to use their intoxication as a defence. Whatever social utility is gained from drinking is not sufficient for the law to excuse the antisocial criminal acts which may follow. If that is the reasoning, as several of their Lordships imply at various points in *Majewski* (and as Lord Mustill indicated in *R* v *Kingston*, below), then does the distinction between crimes of basic and specific intent make any sense? In the Draft Criminal Code Bill 1989, the distinction is abandoned.
5. Despite the fact that intoxication *may* serve as the basis for a defence to a crime of specific intent, a jury may conclude that, notwithstanding the defendant's intoxication, the defendant had the requisite *mens rea*. Moreover, even if the jury conclude that the defendant lacked specific intent because of intoxication, it does not mean that the defendant will escape

punishment altogether. If, for example, the defendant is acquitted of murder (a specific intent crime) he may still be found guilty of involuntary manslaughter (a basic intent crime).

6. The emphasis on 'subjectivism' that appears in *B v DPP* [2000] 2 WLR 452 (for facts and holding, see p. 338) seems to have led the courts to admit voluntary intoxication as a defence where it causes a mistake. See *Jaggard-Dickinson* and *R v Richardson and Irwin* (above). Are these cases reconcilable with *Majewski* and *O'Grady*?

(iii) *Involuntary intoxication*

If the rationale for imposing criminal liability on persons who *voluntarily* become intoxicated is in part that they are responsible for their predicament, the same cannot be said of the person who is *involuntarily* intoxicated. Nor can it be maintained that such a person assumed the risks associated with becoming drunk. Involuntary intoxication can occur when someone is given a drink containing alcohol or drugs but not told of that fact. Whether involuntary intoxication is a defence was addressed by the House of Lords in *Kingston*:

R v Kingston
[1994] 3 All ER 354, House of Lords

LORD MUSTILL: My Lords, this appeal concerns the effect on criminal liability of involuntary intoxication.

. . . The relevant facts are simple. The respondent was in dispute over business matters with a couple named Foreman, who employed Penn to obtain damaging information which they could use against the respondent, who is a homosexual with paedophiliac predilections. As part of this plan Penn invited the youth to his room. According to the evidence given by the youth at the trial he remembered nothing between the time when he was sitting on the bed and when he woke up, still in Penn's room, the following morning. It was the case for the prosecution, which the jury by their verdict on the second count must have accepted, that the boy fell asleep because Penn had secretly given him a soporific drug in a drink. On the same evening the respondent went to the room where the youth lay unconscious. He and Penn indulged in gross sexual acts with him. As part of the plan Penn made a recording of what was going on, and also took some photographs. Since an appeal against sentence is pending I will say nothing about these, although they obviously played an important part in the trial. Later, this material came into the hands of the police and charges were brought.

At the outset of the trial counsel for the respondent foreshadowed a defence on the lines that as part of the plan Penn had secretly administered drugs not only to the boy but also to the respondent. It was not said, and, in the light of the recordings and photographs, could not have been said, that the consequence was to make the respondent, like the boy, insensible; nevertheless his case was he had suffered effects which annulled the criminal liability which his acts would otherwise have involved. At rather short notice two questions were raised for decision:

    (i)   If the jury find that Mr Kingston assaulted [the youth] pursuant to an intent induced by the influence of drugs administered secretly to him by Penn, is it open to them to find him not guilty?

   (ii) If the jury find that at the time of the alleged offence Mr Kingston was intoxicated by drugs secretly administered to him by Kevin Penn, is it open to them to find that this intoxication made negative intent/ *mens rea* so as to find Mr Kingston not guilty?

. . . What the judge told the jury was:

For the purposes of this case an assault is an act by which a person intentionally applies, intentionally or recklessly applies, unlawful force to another. The degree of force does not matter, thus a touching is enough. An indecent assault is an assault accompanied by circumstances of indecency, on the part of the accused whose case you are considering, towards the victim, in this case [D]. Thus, so far as Mr Kingston is concerned on the first count, the Crown must prove that he intentionally – intentionally – assaulted [D]; that the assault or the circumstances accompanying, were capable of being considered by right-minded people as indecent (and having seen those photographs can you doubt that?) and that the defendant Kingston intended such indecency. Thus, ladies and gentlemen, Kingston's intention is of all importance for you may think the fact as to what happened is beyond dispute – but there I go into your province, you decide whether a fact of what happened is beyond dispute or not. In that connection you have the photographs and the tape. In deciding what Kingston's intent was at the time of the alleged offence – and I emphasise that: *intent at the time of the offence* – you can look at what he did and what he said at the time, and here you have the photographs of the one and the tape of the other. You look at his actions before, at the time and after the alleged offence. All these things may shed light on his intention at the critical moment. In deciding whether Kingston intended to commit this offence, you must take into account any findings that you may make that he was affected by drugs. If you think that because he was so affected by drugs he did not intend or may not have intended to commit an indecent assault upon [D], then you must acquit him; but if you are sure that despite the effect of any drugs that he might have been slipped – and it is for you to find whether he was drugged or not – this part of the case is proved, because a drugged intent is still an intent. So intention is crucial, intention at the time; and, of course, members of the jury, you will bear in mind there is a distinction between intention at the time and a lack of memory as to what happened after the time.

After this direction the jury by a majority returned a verdict of Guilty against the respondent on the first count, and the learned judge imposed a sentence of five years' imprisonment. The respondent appealed against conviction and sentence. The Court of Appeal, Criminal Division allowed the appeal and quashed the convictions (see [1993] 4 All ER 373).

In our judgment, the question can be answered by turning to first principles. The importance of ensuring, under a system of law, that members of the community are safeguarded in their persons and property is obvious and was firmly stated in *DPP v Majewski* [1976] 2 All ER 142 at 168 per Lord Edmund-Davies, for example. However, the purpose of the criminal law is to inhibit, by proscription and by penal sanction, antisocial acts which individuals may otherwise commit. Its unspoken premise is that people may have tendencies and impulses to do those things which are considered sufficiently objectionable to be forbidden. Having paedophiliac inclinations and desires is not proscribed; putting them into practice is. If the sole reason why the threshold between the two has been crossed is or may have been that the inhibition which the law requires has been removed by the clandestine act of a third party, the purposes of the criminal law are not served by nevertheless holding that the person performing the act is guilty of an offence. A man is not responsible for a condition produced 'by stratagem, or the fraud of another'. If therefore drink or a drug, surreptitiously administered, causes a person to lose his self-control and for that reason to form an intent which he would not otherwise have formed, it is consistent with the principle that the law should exculpate him because the operative fault is not his. The law permits a finding that the intent formed was not a criminal intent or, in other words, that the involuntary intoxication negatives the *mens rea*. As was pointed out in argument, there is some analogy to be found here in the rationale underlying the defence of duress. While it is not necessary for the decision of this case, it appears to us that, if the principle applies where the offence is one of basic intent, it should apply also where the offence is one of specific intent. We would add that there must be evidence capable of giving rise to the defence of involuntary intoxication before a judge is obliged to leave the issue to the jury. However, once there is an evidential foundation for the defence, the burden is upon the Crown to prove that the relevant intent was formed and that notwithstanding the evidence relied on by the defence it was a criminal intent. By answering the first of the questions put to him at the beginning of the trial in the negative, the learned judge may have inhibited a sufficient ventilation of this issue at a later stage. Further, by summing up as he did, the learned judge effectively withdrew the issue from the jury. In our judgment, that amounted to a material misdirection.

The court accordingly quashed the conviction.

In due course the prosecutor obtained from the Court of Appeal a certificate that a point of law of general public importance was involved in the decision to allow the appeal, namely:

(a) Whether, if it is proved that the necessary intent was present when the necessary act was done by him, a defendant has open to him a defence of involuntary intoxication;

(b) if so, on whom does the burden of proof lie?

The starting point is the verdict of guilty coupled with the judge's direction on the necessity for intent. This implies that the majority either (a) were sure that the respondent had not involuntarily taken a drug or drugs at all or (b) were sure that whatever drug he may have taken had not had such an effect on his mind that he did not intend to do what he did. We are therefore not concerned with what is picturesquely called automatism; nor was it suggested that the effect of the drug was to produce a condition of temporary insanity. What then was said to have been the induced mental condition on which the respondent relies? Inevitably, since the judge's ruling meant that whatever medical evidence there may have been was not developed we cannot be sure. Still, the general nature of the case is clear enough. In ordinary circumstances the respondent's paedophiliac tendencies would have been kept under control, even in the presence of the sleeping or unconscious boy on the bed. The ingestion of the drug (whatever it was) brought about a temporary change in the mentality or personality of the respondent which lowered his ability to resist temptation so far that his desires overrode his ability to control them. Thus we are concerned here with a case of disinhibition. The drug is not alleged to have created the desire to which the respondent gave way, but rather to have enabled it to be released. . . .

On these facts there are three grounds on which the respondent might be held free from criminal responsibility. First, that his immunity flows from general principles of the criminal law. Secondly, that this immunity is already established by a solid line of authority. Finally, that the court should, when faced with a new problem acknowledge the justice of the case and boldly create a new common law defence.

It is clear from the passage already quoted that the Court of Appeal adopted the first approach. The decision was explicitly founded on general principle. There can be no doubt what principle the court relied upon, for at the outset the court recorded the submission of counsel for the respondent that 'the law recognises that, exceptionally, an accused person may be entitled to be acquitted if there is a possibility that, although his act was intentional, the intent itself arose out of circumstances for which he bears no blame' . . .

My Lords, with every respect I must suggest that no such principle exists or, until the present case, had ever in modern times been thought to exist. Each offence consists of a prohibited act or omission coupled with whatever state of mind is called for by the statute or rule of the common law which creates the offence. In those offences which are not absolute the state of mind which the prosecution must prove to have underlain the act or omission – the 'mental element' – will in the majority of cases be such as to attract disapproval. The mental element will then be the mark of what may properly be called a 'guilty mind'. The professional burglar is guilty in a moral as well as a legal sense; he intends to break into the house to steal, and most would confidently assert that this is wrong. But this will not always be so. In respect of some offences the mind of the defendant, and still less his moral judgment, may not be engaged at all. In others, although a mental activity must be the motive power for the prohibited act or omission the activity may be of such a kind or degree that society at large would not criticise the defendant's conduct severely or even criticise it at all. Such cases are not uncommon. Yet to assume that contemporary moral judgments affect the criminality of the act, as distinct from the punishment appropriate to the crime once proved, is to be misled by the expression *'mens rea'*, the ambiguity of which has been the subject of complaint for more than a century. Certainly, the 'mens' of the defendant must usually be involved in the offence; but the epithet 'rea' refers to the criminality of the act in which the mind is engaged, not to its moral character.

. . .

Accordingly, so far as general principles of criminality are concerned I would reject the respondent's argument. His second ground is more narrow, namely that involuntary intoxication is already recognised as a defence by authority which the House ought to follow. . . . [I]t is impossible to consider the exceptional case of involuntary intoxication without placing it in the context of intoxication as a whole. This area of the law is controversial, as regards the content of the rules, their intellectual foundations, and their capacity to furnish a practical and just solution. Since the law was not explored in depth during the arguments and since it is relevant only as part of the background it is better not to say any more about it than is strictly necessary. Some consideration of the law laid down in *DPP v Majewski* [1976] 2 All ER 142 is however inevitable. As I understand the position it is still the law that in the exceptional case where intoxication causes insanity the M'Naghten rules apply: see *DPP v Beard* [1920] AC 479 at 501 and *A-G for Northern Ireland v Gallagher* [1961] 3 All ER 299. Short of this, it is no answer for the defendant to say that he would not have done what he did had he been sober, provided always that whatever element of intent is required by the offence is proved to have been present. As was said in *R v Sheehan, R v Moore* [1975] 2 All ER 960 at 964, 'a drunken intent is still an intent'. As to proof of intent, it appears that at least in some instances self-induced intoxication can be taken into account as part of the evidence from which the jury draws its conclusions; but that in others it cannot. I express the matter in this guarded way because it has not yet been decisively established whether for this purpose there is a line to be drawn between offences of 'specific' and of 'basic' intent. That in at least some cases a defendant cannot say that he was so drunk that he could not form the required intent is however clear enough. Why is this so? The answer must, I believe, be the same as that given in other common law jurisdictions: namely that such evidence is excluded as a matter of policy. As Mason J put the matter in *R v O'Connor* (1979) 146 CLR 64 at 110:

> the view is taken that the act charged is voluntary notwithstanding that it might not be ordinarily considered so by reason of the condition of the perpetrator, because his condition proceeds from a voluntary choice made by him. These cases therefore constitute an exception to the general rule of criminal responsibility.

There remains the question by what reasoning the House put this policy into effect. As I understand it two different rationalisations were adopted. First that the absence of the necessary consent is cured by treating the intentional drunkenness (or more accurately, since it is only in the minority of cases that the drinker sets out to make himself drunk, the intentional taking of drink without regard to its possible effects) as a substitute for the mental element ordinarily required by the offence. The intent is transferred from the taking of drink to the commission of the prohibited act. The second rationalisation is that the defendant cannot be heard to rely on the absence of the mental element when it is absent because of his own voluntary acts. Borrowing an expression from a far distant field it may be said that the defendant is estopped from relying on his self-induced incapacity.

Your Lordships are not required to decide how these two explanations stand up to attack, for they are not attacked here. The task is only to place them in the context of an intoxication which is not voluntary. Taking first the concept of transferred intent, if the intoxication was not the result of an act done with an informed will there is no intent which can be transferred to the prohibited act, so as to fill the gap in the offence. As regards the 'estoppel' there is no reason why the law should preclude the defendant from relying on a mental condition which he had not deliberately brought about. Thus, once the involuntary nature of the intoxication is added the two theories of *Majewski* fall away, and the position reverts to what it would have been if *Majewski* had not been decided, namely that the offence is not made out if the defendant was so intoxicated that he could not form an intent. Thus, where the intoxication is involuntary *Majewski* does not *subtract* the defence of absence of intent; but there is nothing in *Majewski* to suggest that where intent is proved involuntary intoxication *adds* a further defence.

To recognise a new defence of this type would be a bold step. The common law defences of duress and necessity (if it exists) and the limited common law defence of provocation are all very old. Since counsel for the appellant was not disposed to emphasise this aspect of the appeal the subject was not explored in argument, but I suspect that the recognition of a new general defence at common law has not happened in modern times. Nevertheless, the criminal law must not stand still, and if it is both practical and just to take this step, and if judicial decision rather than legislation is the proper medium, then the courts should not be deterred simply by the novelty of it. So one must turn to consider just what defence is now to be created. The judgment under appeal implies five characteristics.

(1) The defence applies to all offences, except perhaps to absolute offences. It therefore differs from other defences such as provocation and diminished responsibility.

(2) The defence is a complete answer to a criminal charge. If not rebutted it leads to an outright acquittal, and unlike provocation and diminished responsibility leaves no room for conviction and punishment for a lesser offence. The underlying assumption must be that the defendant is entirely free from culpability.

(3) It may be that the defence applies only where the intoxication is due to the wrongful act of another and therefore affords no excuse when, in circumstances of no greater culpability, the defendant has intoxicated himself by mistake (such as by short-sightedly taking the wrong drug). I say that this may be so, because it is not clear whether, since the doctrine was founded in part on the dictum of Park J, the 'fraud or stratagem of another' is an essential element, or whether this was taken as an example of a wider principle.

(4) The burden of disproving the defence is on the prosecution.

(5) The defence is subjective in nature. Whereas provocation and self-defence are judged by the reactions of the reasonable person in the situation of the defendant, here the only question is whether this particular defendant's inhibitions were overcome by the effect of the drug. The more susceptible the defendant to the kind of temptation presented, the easier the defence is to establish.

My Lords, since the existence or otherwise of the defence has been treated in argument at all stages as a matter of existing law the Court of Appeal had no occasion to consider the practical and theoretical implications of recognising this new defence at common law, and we do not have the benefit of its views. In their absence, I can only say that the defence appears to run into difficulties at every turn. In point of theory, it would be necessary to reconcile a defence of irresistible impulse derived from a combination of innate drives and external disinhibition with the rule that irresistible impulse of a solely internal origin (not necessarily any more the fault of the offender) does not in itself excuse although it may be a symptom of a disease of the mind: see *A-G for the State of South Australia* v *Brown* [1960] 1 All ER 734. Equally, the state of mind which founds the defence superficially resembles a state of diminished responsibility, whereas the effect in law is quite different. It may well be that the resemblance is misleading, but these and similar problems must be solved before the bounds of a new defence can be set.

On the practical side there are serious problems. Before the jury could form an opinion on whether the drug might have turned the scale witnesses would have to give a picture of the defendant's personality and susceptibilities, for without it the crucial effect of the drug could not be assessed; pharmacologists would be required to describe the potentially disinhibiting effect of a range of drugs whose identity would, if the present case is anything to go by, be unknown; psychologists and psychiatrists would express opinions, not on the matters of psychopathology familiar to those working within the framework of the Mental Health Acts but on altogether more elusive concepts. No doubt as time passed those concerned could work out techniques to deal with these questions. Much more significant would be the opportunities for a spurious defence. Even in the field of road traffic the 'spiked' drink as a special reason for not disqualifying from driving is a regular feature. Transferring this to the entire range of criminal offences is a disturbing prospect. The defendant would only have to assert, and support by the evidence of well-wishers, that he was not the sort of person to have done this kind of thing, and to suggest an occasion when by some means a drug might have been administered to him for the jury be sent straight to the question of a possible disinhibition. The judge would direct the jurors that if they felt any legitimate doubt on the matter – and by its nature the defence would be one which the prosecution would often have no means to rebut – they must acquit outright, all questions of intent, mental capacity and the like being at this stage irrelevant.

My Lords, the fact that a new doctrine may require adjustment of existing principles to accommodate it, and may require those involved in criminal trials to learn new techniques, is not of course a ground for refusing to adopt it, if that is what the interests of justice require. Here, however, justice makes no such demands, for the interplay between the wrong done to the victim, the individual characteristics and frailties of the defendant, and the pharmacological effects of whatever drug may be potentially involved can be far better recognised by a tailored choice from the continuum of sentences available to the judge than by the application of a single yea-or-nay jury decision. . . .

NOTES AND QUESTIONS

1. Kingston involved a situation where the defendant was unaware that drugs had been administered to him. What if the defendant is aware that he is taking drugs, but is unaware of the effect that the drugs will have? See *R v Allen* [1988] Crim LR 698.

2. Section 6(5) of the Public Order Act 1986 provides:

   . . . a person whose awareness is impaired by intoxication shall be taken to be aware of that of which he would be aware if not intoxicated, unless he shows either that his intoxication was not self-induced or that it was caused solely by the taking or administration of a substance in the course of medical treatment.

R v Hardie
[1984] 3 All ER 848, Court of Appeal

PARKER LJ: Shortly after 9.15 p.m. on 2 January 1982 fire broke out in a wardrobe in the bedroom of the ground-floor flat at 55 Bassingham Road, London SW 10. At that time there were in the flat the appellant, Mrs Jeanette Hardie, with whom the appellant had been living at the premises since May 1974 and who had changed her name to Hardie by deed poll in 1976, and her daughter Tonia. The upstairs flat was occupied by a Mrs Young.

Shortly before 2 January the appellant's relationship with Mrs Hardie had broken down and she had insisted that he must leave. He did not wish to do so, but on the morning of 2 January he packed a suitcase. At about lunchtime the appellant found two bottles of tablets in a cabinet. One contained valium which Mrs Hardie had had in 1974 and the other some tablets to assist urination.

The appellant's evidence in regard to this was that he had never taken valium before, that he took one at about 12 noon to calm him down, for he was in a distressed state, that it did not have much effect, that he and Mrs Hardie had then gone shopping, that he had taken two more in front of her and she had said, 'Take as many as you like, they are old stock and will do you no harm', that he had taken two more shortly afterwards, that he may have taken two of the other tablets also, and that shortly thereafter on return to the house he had fallen into a deep sleep and could thereafter remember only periods.

He was in fact collected from the flat by his mother and remained with her until returning to the flat again at 9.15 p.m. It was not disputed that he must have started the fire, for he was alone in the bedroom when it started. Having started it, he emerged, returned to the sitting room where were Mrs Hardie and Tonia and stayed there. Shortly afterwards Mrs Hardie heard sounds from the bedroom, went there and found smoke and flames coming from the wardrobe. There was evidence that before, at the time of and after the fire the appellant was exhibiting signs of intoxication and that such signs might have resulted from the taking of valium some hours earlier.

The defence was that the appellant was so affected by the valium that he could remember nothing about the fire and had not the necessary *mens rea* to constitute either of the offences charged. On the basis no doubt of *DPP* v *Majewski* [1976] 2 All ER 142 and *R* v *Caldwell* [1981] 1 All ER 961, [1982] AC 341, the judge directed the jury in effect that, as the valium was voluntarily self-administered, it was irrelevant as a defence and its effects could not negative *mens rea*. The first point taken on appeal was that this was a misdirection.

. . .

In the present instance the defence was that the valium was taken for the purpose of calming the nerves only, that it was old stock and that the appellant was told it would do him no harm. There was no evidence that it was known to the appellant or even generally known that the taking of valium in the quantity taken would be liable to render a person aggressive or incapable of appreciating risks to others or have other side effects such that its self-administration would itself have an element of recklessness. It is true that valium is a drug and it is true that it was taken deliberately and not taken on medical prescription, but the drug is, in our view, wholly different in kind from drugs which are liable to cause unpredictability or aggressiveness. It may well be that the taking of a sedative or soporific drug will, in certain circumstances, be no answer, for example in a case of reckless driving, but if the effect of a drug is merely soporific or sedative the taking of it, even in some excessive quantity, cannot in the ordinary way raise a *conclusive* presumption against the admission of proof of intoxication for the purpose of disproving *mens rea* in ordinary crimes, such as would be the case with alcoholic intoxication or incapacity or automatism resulting from the self-administration of dangerous drugs.

In the present case the jury should not, in our judgment, have been directed to disregard any incapacity which resulted or might have resulted from the taking of valium. They should have been directed that if they came to the conclusion that, as a result of the valium, the appellant was, at the time, unable to appreciate the risks to property and persons from his actions they should then consider whether the taking of the valium was itself reckless. We are unable to say what would have been the appropriate direction with regard to the elements of recklessness in this case for we have not seen all the relevant evidence, nor are we able to suggest a model direction, for circumstances will vary infinitely and model directions can sometimes lead to more rather than less confusion. It is sufficient to say that the direction that the effects of valium were necessarily irrelevant was wrong.

NOTES AND QUESTIONS
1. The Court of Appeal is not saying that Hardie should have been acquitted; only that the trial judge had erred in directing the jury that the effects of the valium were irrelevant. The jurors should have been directed that if they concluded that as a result of taking the valium the defendant could not have appreciated the risks to property from his action, they should then have considered whether the taking of the drug was itself a reckless act. Was it?
2. Compare *Hardie* with the case where a defendant is taking drugs pursuant to medical prescription, and the drugs have an unanticipated, violent side effect. Is this a stronger or a weaker case for allowing the defence? Would it matter if the defendant exceeded the proscribed dosage?

(iv) *'Dutch courage'*

What of the defendant who gets drunk in order to summon the courage to commit a crime?

Attorney-General for Northern Ireland v Gallagher

[1963] AC 349, House of Lords

LORD DENNING: My Lords, every direction which a judge gives to a jury in point of law must be considered against the background of facts which have been proved or admitted in the case. In this case the accused man did not give evidence himself. And the facts proved against him were:

He had a grievance against his wife. She had obtained a maintenance order against him and had been instrumental in getting him detained in a mental hospital.

He had made up his mind to kill his wife. He bought a knife for the purpose and a bottle of whisky – either to give himself Dutch courage to do the deed or to drown his conscience after it.

He did in fact carry out his intention. He killed his wife with the knife and drank much of the whisky before or after he killed her.

There were only two defences raised on his behalf: (1) Insanity; (2) Drunkenness. The Lord Chief Justice directed the jury that the *time* when they had to consider whether he was insane or not (within the M'Naughten Rules) was before he started on the bottle of whisky.' 'You should direct your attention,' he said to them, 'to the state of his mind before he opened the bottle of whisky.' If he was sane at that time, he could not make good the defence of insanity 'with the aid of that bottle of whisky.' Immediately after the jury retired, Mr Kelly took up this point of *time*. He suggested that it was inaccurate and inconsistent with the M'Naughten Rules. But the Lord Chief Justice adhered to his view. He declined to modify his charge to the jury on the matter. 'If I'm wrong,' he said, 'I can be put right.' It was on this view point of *time* that the Court of Criminal Appeal reversed him. His direction was, they said, 'inconsistent with the M'Naughten Rules,' which fix the crucial time as 'the time of the committing of the act,' that is, the time of the killing and not at an earlier time.

The question is whether the direction of the Lord Chief Justice as to the *time* was correct. At least that is how I read the question posed by the Court of Criminal Appeal. It is complicated by the fact that, according to the medical evidence, the accused man was a psychopath. That does not mean that he was insane. But it sharpens the point of the question. He had a disease of the mind. It was quiescent before he started on the whisky. So he was sane then. But the drink may have brought on an explosive outburst in the course of which he killed her. Can he rely on this self-induced defect of reason and put it forward as a defence of insanity?

My Lords, this case differs from all others in the books in that the accused man, whilst sane and sober, before he took to the drink, had already made up his mind to kill his wife. This seems to me to be far worse – and far more deserving of condemnation – than the case of a man who, before getting drunk, has no intention to kill, but afterwards in his cups, whilst drunk, kills another by an act which he would not dream of doing when sober. Yet by the law of England in this latter case his drunkenness is no defence even though it has distorted his reason and his will-power. So why should it be a defence in the present case? And is it made any better by saying that the man is a psychopath?

The answer to the question is, I think, that the case falls to be decided by the general principle of English law that, subject to very limited exceptions, drunkenness is no defence to a criminal charge, nor is a defect of reason produced by drunkenness. . . .

My Lords, I think the law on this point should take a clear stand. If a man, whilst sane and sober, forms an intention to kill and makes preparation for it, knowing it is a wrong thing to do, and then gets himself drunk so as to give himself Dutch courage to do the killing, and whilst drunk carries out his intention, he cannot rely on this self-induced drunkenness as a defence to a charge of murder, nor even as reducing it to manslaughter. He cannot say that he got himself into such a stupid state that he was incapable of an intent to kill. So also when he is a psychopath, he cannot by drinking rely on his self-induced defect of reason as a defence of insanity. The wickedness of his mind before he got drunk is enough to condemn him, coupled with the act which he intended to do and did do. A psychopath who goes out intending to kill, knowing it is wrong, and does kill, cannot escape the consequences by making himself drunk before doing it. That is, I believe, the direction which the Lord Chief Justice gave to the jury and which the Court of Criminal Appeal found to be wrong. I think it was right and for this reason I would allow the appeal.

NOTES AND QUESTIONS

1. The theoretical problem raised by *A-G for Northern Ireland* v *Gallagher* was one of concurrence between *actus reus* and *mens rea*. At the actual moment of committing the crime the defendant's self-induced drunkenness may have prevented him from having the specific intent to kill, even though he may have had this intent at some previous point in time. What counterarguments can the Crown raise?

2. The 'Dutch courage' cases may provide insight into why the law generally takes a harsh attitude to voluntary intoxication as a defence. Many criminals fortify themselves with drink before embarking on their criminal enterprises. In court this may translate into a defence of lack of *mens rea* based on intoxication. It is clearly not in society's interest to structure its legal rules to encourage such claims.

(v) *Intoxication and mistake*

We have seen previously in *DPP* v *Morgan* [1976] AC 182 and *R* v *Williams (Gladstone)* (1983) 78 Cr App R 276, that where a defendant proceeds under a mistake of fact which, were he correct, would negate an element of the crime, he is to be judged as if the mistaken version of the facts was the true version. What if, however, the defendant makes a mistake when drunk that he would not have made when sober? Should the drunkenness be taken into account? Compare the following cases:

Jaggard v *Dickinson*
[1980] 3 All ER 716, Queen's Bench Division
For the facts and holding, see p. 450.

R v *O'Grady*
[1987] 3 WLR 321, Court of Appeal
For the facts and holding, see p. 450.

R v *Richardson and Irwin*
[1999] Crim LR 494, Court of Appeal
For the facts and holding, see p. 451.

NOTES AND QUESTIONS

1. Are *Jaggard* v *Dickinson*, *Richardson and Irwin* and *O'Grady* reconcilable? Are *O'Grady* and *Richardson* reconcilable with *Majewski*?

2. What has happened to the concept of basic intent crimes?

3. In a Consultation Paper published in 1993, the Law Commission proposed a new offence of causing harm while intoxicated. In its final report, *Legislating the Criminal Code: Intoxication and Criminal Liability*, the Commission, influenced by considerable judicial opposition to its

proposals, changed its mind and recommended adherence to the law based on *Majewski* with some minor amendments. What considerations argued against the adoption of the original proposal? Is there any merit in allowing a verdict of 'guilty but intoxicated' or creating a separate offence of 'dangerous drunkenness'?

(vi) *Intoxication and insanity*

Prolonged use of alcohol or drugs can sometimes result in brain damage or severe mental impairment. In such cases, should the defendant's proper defence be intoxication or insanity?

R v Davis

(1881) 14 Cox CC 563, Newcastle Crown Court

> On the 14th day of January, 1881, the prisoner (who had been previously drinking heavily, but was then sober) made an attack upon his sister-in-law, Mrs Davis, threw her down, and attempted to cut her throat with a knife. Ordinarily he was a very mild, quiet, peaceable, well-behaved man, and on friendly terms with her. At the police station he said, 'The man in the moon told me to do it. I will have to commit murder, as I must be hanged.' He was examined by two medical men, who found him suffering from *delirium tremens*, resulting from over-indulgence in drink. According to their evidence he would know what he was doing, but his actions would not be under his control. In their judgment neither fear of punishment nor legal nor moral considerations would have deterred him – nothing short of actual physical restraint would have prevented him acting as he did. He was disordered in his senses, and would not be able to distinguish between moral right and wrong at the time he committed the act. Under proper care and treatment he recovered in a week, and was then perfectly sensible.
>
> For the defence it was submitted that he was of unsound mind at the time of the commission of the act, and was not responsible for his actions.

STEPHEN J to the jury: The prisoner at the bar is charged with having feloniously wounded his sister-in-law, Jane Davis, on the 14th day of January last with intent to murder her. You will have to consider whether he was in such a state of mind as to be thoroughly responsible for his actions. And with regard to that I must explain to you what is the kind or degree of insanity which relieves a man from responsibility. Nobody must suppose – and I hope no one will be led for one moment to suppose – that drunkenness is any kind of excuse for crime. If this man had been raging drunk, and had stabbed his sister-in-law and killed her, he would have stood at the bar guilty of murder beyond all doubt or question. But drunkenness is one thing and the diseases to which drunkenness leads are different things; and if a man by drunkenness brings on a state of disease which causes such a degree of madness, even for a time, which would have relieved him from responsibility if it had been caused in any other way, then he would not be criminally responsible. In my opinion, in such a case the man is a madman, and is to be treated as such, although his madness is only temporary. If you think he was so insane – that if his insanity had been produced by other causes he would not be responsible for his actions – then the mere fact that it was caused by drunkenness will not prevent it having the effect which otherwise it would have had, of excusing him from punishment. Drunkenness is no excuse, but *delirium tremens* caused by drunkenness may be an excuse if you think it produces such a state of mind as would otherwise relieve him from responsibility. . . .

NOTES AND QUESTIONS
1. Is *Davis* consistent with *DPP* v *Majewski* and its progeny? In the latter cases, the focus seems to be on the defendant's fault in becoming intoxicated and not on the effects of the intoxication; but in *Davis* the focus is clearly on the effects of the intoxication. Why should this be so?
2. Davis was approved by the House of Lords in *Attorney-General for Northern Ireland* v *Gallagher* (above) and in *Director of Public Prosecutions* v *Beard* [1920] AC 479.

SECTION 3: **Affirmative defences**

A: Duress, necessity and duress of circumstances

(i) *Rationale*

The defences of necessity, duress, and duress of circumstances are close relatives. All are affirmative defences in that they do not come into play until the prosecution have established all elements of the offence charged. The situation that the defences are concerned with is one in which the actor is faced with a choice of evils: either the defendant has to commit a crime or incur even more unpleasant consequences.

If someone held a knife to your throat and said: 'Your money or your life,' and you chose the former, nobody would be so crass as to assert that your relinquishment of your money was a truly voluntary act. But if that same somebody held a knife to your throat and said 'Help me rob the bank or I will kill you', and you chose to help rob the bank, can it be said that your participation in the bank robbery was voluntary? Again arguably not, but both of these examples involve a different kind of involuntariness than that which we examined in regard to *actus reus*. When we talked about an involuntary *actus reus*, we were concerned with situations where the defendant was physically unable to resist the doing of the act. In duress and necessity cases, the defendant is physically capable of not committing the crime. The defendant has a choice, but an unpalatable one. She or he can choose not to commit the crime, but in so doing may have to suffer an extremely unpleasant consequence.

Yet this distinction between the *physical* inability to resist doing a criminal act and the *normative* inability to resist doing that act accounts in no small measure for the hostility of judges to the defences of duress, necessity, and duress of circumstances. The judges are concerned that these defences will be invoked in circumstances where persons with a tougher moral fibre would not have given in to the pressures to commit the offence. The judges want to provide a disincentive in the form of a potential criminal sanction to encourage persons to resist giving in.

While the defences cannot be justified on either an involuntary act theory, or, for that matter, a theory that the defendant lacked mental capacity (for the defendant did have the ability to make a rational choice and arguably did make a rational choice), there are two arguments in their favour:

(a) No individual should be punished for doing something that the reasonable man or woman in the same situation would have done. If the reasonable person would not have resisted the pressure to commit the crime, then the unlucky soul who actually found himself in that predicament should not be held criminally liable either. The law should recognise that the deterrent value of criminal sanctions will have little effect on the person faced with loss of life or grievous harm.

(b) Public policy should encourage a defendant to choose the lesser and avoid the greater evil, even if that means that a crime has to be committed. If the harm which will result from compliance with the law is greater than the harm which will result from violation of the law, it would be a strange legal system which required the defendant to choose the greater evil.

Notice that the first rationale is based on pragmatism and is an argument of excuse; while the second rationale, which is based on utilitarian principles (crudely put, the greatest happiness for the greatest number), is an argument of justification.

The burden of introducing some evidence relating to duress, necessity or duress of circumstances rests on the defendant. Once that evidence is introduced, however, the burden shifts to the prosecution to negate the defence by proof beyond a reasonable doubt. In other words, the prosecution bears the ultimate burden of persuading the jury that the defence should not succeed.

(ii) *Necessity*
While the defence of duress is well established, there has always been some doubt as to whether a defence of necessity existed at law; and, if so, to what crimes it applied. The issue was first addressed in what is probably one of the most famous criminal cases of all time.

R v Dudley and Stephens
(1884) 14 QBD 273, Queen's Bench Division

At the trial of an indictment for murder it appeared, upon a special verdict, that the prisoners D and S, seamen, and the deceased, a boy between seventeen and eighteen, were cast away in a storm on the high seas, and compelled to put into an open boat; that the boat was drifting on the ocean, and was probably more than 1,000 miles from land; that on the eighteenth day, when they had been seven days without food and five without water, D proposed to S that lots should be cast who should be put to death to save the rest, and that they afterwards thought it would be better to kill the boy that their lives should be saved; that on the twentieth day D, with the assent of S, killed the boy, and both D and S fed on his flesh for four days; that at the time of the act there was no sail in sight nor any reasonable prospect of relief; that under these circumstances there appeared to the prisoners every probability that unless they then or very soon fed upon the boy, or one of themselves, they would die of starvation.

LORD COLERIDGE CJ: . . . From these facts, stated with the cold precision of a special verdict, it appears sufficiently that the prisoners were subject to terrible temptation, to sufferings which might break down the bodily power of the strongest man, and try the conscience of the best. Other details yet more harrowing, facts still more loathsome and appalling, were presented to the jury, and are to be found recorded in my learned Brother's notes. But nevertheless this is clear, that the prisoners put to death a weak and unoffending boy upon the chance of preserving their own lives by feeding, upon his flesh and blood after he was killed, and with the certainty of depriving, *him* of any possible chance of survival. The verdict finds in terms that 'if the men had not fed upon the body of the boy they would *probably* not have survived,' and that 'the boy being in a much weaker condition was *likely* to have died before them.' They might possibly have been picked up next day by a passing ship; they might possibly not have been picked up at all; in either case it is obvious that the killing of the boy would have been an unnecessary and profitless act. It is found by the verdict that the boy was incapable of resistance, and, in fact, made none; and it is not even suggested that his death was due to any violence on his part attempted against, or even so much as feared by, those who killed him. . . .

Now, except for the purpose of testing how far the conservation of a man's own life is in all cases and under all circumstances, an absolute, unqualified, and paramount duty, we exclude from our consideration all the incidents of war. We are dealing with a case of private homicide, not one imposed upon men in the service of their Sovereign and in the defence of their country. Now it is admitted that the deliberate killing of this unoffending and unresisting boy was clearly murder, unless the killing can be justified by some well-recognised excuse admitted by the law. It is further admitted that there was in this case no such excuse, unless the killing was justified by what has been called 'necessity.' But the temptation to the act which existed here was not what the law has ever called necessity. Nor is this to be regretted. Though law and morality are not the same, and many things may be immoral which are not necessarily illegal, yet the absolute divorce of law from morality would be of fatal consequence; and divorce would follow if the temptation to murder in this case were to be held by law an absolute defence of it. It is not so. To preserve one's life is generally speaking a duty, but it may be the plainest and the highest duty to sacrifice it. War is full of instances in which it is a man's duty not to live, but to die. The duty in case of shipwreck, of a captain to his crew, of the crew to the passengers, of soldiers to women and children, as in the noble case of the *Birkenhead*; these duties impose on men the moral necessity, not of the preservation, but of the sacrifice of their lives for others, from which in no country, least of all, it is to be hoped, in England, will men ever shrink, as indeed, they have not shrunk. It is not correct, therefore, to say that there is any absolute or unqualified necessity to preserve one's life.

. . . It is not needful to point out the awful danger of admitting the principle which has been contended for. Who is to be the judge of this sort of necessity? By what measure is the comparative value of lives to be measured? Is it to be strength, or intellect, or what? It is plain that the principle leaves to him who is to profit by it to determine the necessity which will justify him in deliberately taking another's life to save his own. In this case the youngest, the most unresisting, was chosen. Was it more necessary to kill him than one of the grown men? The answer must be 'No' –

> So spake the Fiend, and with necessity,
> The tyrant's plea, excused his delivish deeds.

It is not suggested that in this particular case the deeds were 'devilish,' but it is quite plain that such a principle once admitted might be made the legal cloak for unbridled passion and atrocious crime. There is no safe path for judges to tread but to ascertain the law to the best of their ability and to declare it according to their judgment; and if in any case the law appears to be too severe on individuals, to leave it to the Sovereign to exercise that prerogative of mercy which the Constitution has intrusted to the hands fittest to dispense it.

It must not be supposed that in refusing to admit temptation to be an excuse for crime it is forgotten how terrible the temptation was; how awful the suffering; how hard in such trials to keep the judgment straight and the conduct pure. We are often compelled to set up standards we cannot reach ourselves, and to lay down rules which we could not ourselves satisfy. But a man has no right to declare temptation to be an excuse, though he might himself have yielded to it, nor allow compassion for the criminal to change or weaken in any manner the legal definition of the crime. It is therefore our duty to declare that the prisoners' act in this case was wilful murder, that the facts as stated in the verdict are no legal justification of the homicide; and to say that in our unanimous opinion the prisoners are upon this special verdict guilty of murder.

NOTES AND QUESTIONS

1. The court in *Dudley and Stephens* said: 'We are often compelled to set up standards we cannot reach ourselves, and to lay down rules which we could not ourselves satisfy.' Do you agree? Can this statement be reconciled with the concept of *Caldwell* recklessness (see Chapter 4), which seeks to hold defendants to the standards of the reasonable person?

2. To what extent may the court in *Dudley and Stephens* have been influenced by the method of selecting the victim? Might the court have been more sympathetic if the victim had been chosen by lot, as occurred in the American counterpart to *Dudley and Stephens, United States v Holmes*, 26 F Cas 360 (No. 15,383) (CCED 1842)? If the randomness of the selection process in *Holmes* offends, is there a more rational method of choosing the victim?

3. Do numbers matter? Consider the following science fiction (?) scenario: A mad scientist has affixed a bomb to an innocent victim. If the bomb explodes, thousands will be killed or seriously injured. The bomb can be dismantled only by first killing the innocent person to whom it is attached. Would such a killing be justified?

4. Necessity, duress and duress of circumstances as well, are all-or-nothing defences. Unlike provocation or diminished responsibility, these defences will not serve to reduce the seriousness of a crime from, say, murder to manslaughter. Rather, if successful, they lead to an acquittal. However, even if the defence does not succeed, a court may take into account the defendant's dilemma in sentencing him. See *R v Emery (and Another)* (1993) 14 Cr App R (S) 394 (although the defendant's claim of duress was rejected, evidence that she was abused by the father of her child, to the point where she was helpless and unable to stop his assaults on the child, was received in mitigation of sentence). In *Dudley and Stephens*, the defendants, although convicted of murder, had their sentence commuted to six months' imprisonment. Usually, however, there can be no variance from the mandatory life sentence for murder.

Whether 'necessity' can justify the taking of an innocent life arose again in more recent times but, for some, in even more tragic and compelling circumstances.

Re A (Conjoined Twins: Medical Treatment)
[2001] 1 FLR 1, Court of Appeal

LORD JUSTICE WARD: In the past decade an increasing number of cases have come before the courts where the decision whether or not to permit or to refuse medical treatment can be a matter of life and death for the patient. I have been involved in a number of them. They are always anxious decisions to make but they are invariably eventually made with the conviction that there is only one right answer and that the court has given it.

In this case the right answer is not at all as easy to find. I freely confess to having found it truly difficult to decide – difficult because of the scale of the tragedy for the parents and the twins, difficult for the seemingly irreconcilable conflicts of moral and ethical values and difficult because the search for settled legal principle has been especially arduous and conducted under real pressure of time.

The problems we have faced have gripped the public interest and the case has received intense coverage in the media. Everyone seems to have a view of the proper outcome. I am very well aware of the inevitability that our answer will be applauded by some but that as many will be offended by it. Many will vociferously assert their own moral, ethical or religious values. Some will agree with

Justice Scalia who said in the Supreme Court of the United States of America in Cruzan v Director, Missouri Department of Health (1990) 110 S. Ct. 2841, 2859:–

> 'The point at which life becomes "worthless", and the point at which the means necessary to preserve it become "extraordinary" or "inappropriate", are neither set forth in the constitution nor known to the nine Justices of this Court any better than they are known to nine people picked at random from the Kansas City telephone directory.'

It is, however, important to stress the obvious. This court is a court of law, not of morals, and our task has been to find, and our duty is then to apply the relevant principles of law to the situation before us – a situation which is quite unique.

It truly is a unique case. In a nutshell the problem is this. Jodie and Mary are conjoined twins. They each have their own brain, heart and lungs and other vital organs and they each have arms and legs. They are joined at the lower abdomen. Whilst not underplaying the surgical complexities, they can be successfully separated. But the operation will kill the weaker twin, Mary. That is because her lungs and heart are too deficient to oxygenate and pump blood through her body. Had she been born a singleton, she would not have been viable and resuscitation would have been abandoned. She would have died shortly after her birth. She is alive only because a common artery enables her sister, who is stronger, to circulate life sustaining oxygenated blood for both of them. Separation would require the clamping and then the severing of that common artery. Within minutes of doing so Mary will die. Yet if the operation does not take place, both will die within three to six months, or perhaps a little longer, because Jodie's heart will eventually fail. The parents cannot bring themselves to consent to the operation. The twins are equal in their eyes and they cannot agree to kill one even to save the other. As devout Roman Catholics they sincerely believe that it is God's will that their children are afflicted as they are and they must be left in God's hands. The doctors are convinced they can carry out the operation so as to give Jodie a life which will be worthwhile. So the hospital sought a declaration that the operation may be lawfully carried out. Johnson J. granted it on 25th August 2000. The parents applied to us for permission to appeal against his order. We have given that permission and this is my judgment on their appeal.

. . .

3. The interface with the criminal law.

It should not need stating that the court cannot approve of a course of action which may be unlawful. The stark fact has to be faced in this case that to operate to separate the twins may be to murder Mary. It seems to me, however, that the question of what is in the best interests of the child is a discrete question from whether what is proposed to be done is unlawful. A patient in terminal decline, racked with pain which treatment may not be able fully to alleviate, may beg to die and it may be said – at least by some – that it is in his best interests that he should be allowed to do so, but that would not justify unlawfully killing him. In my judgment, although the nature of what is proposed to be done has a bearing on how one ascertains where the patient's best interests lie, the ascertainment of those interests is the first but a separate stage of the court's task. If the operation is in the best interests of a child patient, then the court can, as Stage 1 of the task which it has to undertake, give leave for the operation to be undertaken provided, and this will become Stage 2 of the court's task, it can be lawfully done.

. . .

1. Introduction.

It is obvious that the question whether or not this operation can be lawfully performed is crucial to the outcome of the appeal. What I confess I had not fully appreciated was how rooted in obscurity the answer to those difficulties was. Brooke L.J. was fully aware of all the intricacies and he set counsel a rigorous reading list to meet our concerns. I am, therefore, grateful to him for leading the way. In his judgment which I have read in draft, he so fully sets out the relevant material that

I am happy to adopt it and I need not add to this lengthy judgment by needless repetition. In the light of his full exposition of the law, I can state the gist of my reasons for agreeing with him quite shortly.

2. Is there some immunity for doctors?

Archbold 2000: Criminal Pleading Evidence & Practice, para. 19–38, states that:–

> 'Bona fide medical or surgical treatment is not "unlawful" and therefore death resulting therefrom does not amount to murder, even though death or serious injury is foreseen as a probable consequence. Nor does it amount to manslaughter, unless the person giving the treatment has been guilty of "gross negligence" '.

No authority is given for this sweeping statement. It is true that in Gillick Lord Scarman said at p. 190:–

> 'The bona fide exercise by a doctor of his clinical judgment must be a complete negation of the guilty mind which is an essential ingredient of the criminal offence of aiding and abetting the commission of unlawful sexual intercourse.'

Lord Mustill speaks of it in Bland. Yet hanging over Bland is the spectre of murder. To have crossed the Rubicon would have been to murder. I, therefore, approach the question of lawfulness of the proposed separation on the basis that, whatever immunity doctors do enjoy, they have no complete immunity. I have to be satisfied that in this case they will not be guilty of unlawfully killing Mary by active intervention – and perhaps of unlawfully killing Jodie by omitting to act in her interests if there is a duty upon them to do so.

. . .

7. Unlawfully.

7.1 *The search for settled principle*

The search for settled principle is difficult where the law is as uncertain in this area as Brooke L.J.'s masterly analysis has shown it to be. Doing the best I can, I have come to these conclusions.

7.2 *Necessity*

Necessity in the Dudley and Stephens sense arises where A. kills B. to save his own life. The threat to A.'s life is posed by the circumstances, rather than an act of threat by B. on A. in conventional self-defence terms.

7.3 *Duress*

Similar considerations apply to duress. There is, of course, a difference between them but as Lord Hailsham of St. Marylebone L.C. said in Reg. v Howe [1987] 1 A.C. 417, 427:–

> 'This, however, is, in my view a distinction without a relevant difference, since on this view duress is only that species of the genus of necessity which is caused by wrongful threat. I cannot see that there is any way in which a person of ordinary fortitude can be excused from one type of pressure on his will rather than the other.'

7.4 *The policy of the law*

The policy of the law is to prevent A. being judge in his own cause of the value of his life over B.'s life or his loved one C.'s life, and then being executioner as well. The policy of the law was expressed in similar terms in Hale's Pleas of the Crown (1736), Vol. 1, p. 51, and Blackstone, Commentaries on the Laws of England (1857 Ed.) Vol. 4, p. 28. Blackstone wrote that a man under duress 'ought rather to die himself than escape by the murder of an innocent'. The sanctity of life and the inherent equality of all life prevails. Several passages in Howe show this. Lord Hailsham said:–

> 'This brings me back to the question of principle. I begin by affirming that, while there can never be a direct correspondence between law and morality, an attempt to divorce the

two entirely is and has always proved to be, doomed to failure, and in the present case, the overriding objects of the criminal law must be to protect innocent lives and to set a standard of conduct which ordinary men and women are expected to observe if they are to avoid criminal responsibility': p. 428 E.

'Other considerations necessarily arise where the choice is between the threat of death or a fortiori of serious injury and deliberately taking an innocent life. In such a case a reasonable man might reflect that one innocent human life is at least as valuable as his own or that of his loved one. In such a case a man cannot claim he is choosing the lesser of two evils. Instead he is embracing the cognate but morally disreputable principle that the end justifies the means': p. 431 C.

'It may well be thought that the loss of a clear right to a defence justifying or excusing the deliberate taking of an innocent life in order to emphasise to all the sanctity of a human life is not an excessive price to pay in the light of these mechanisms': p. 431 F.

Lord MacKay of Clashfern was equally emphatic:–

'It seems to me plain that the reason that it was for so long stated by writers of authority that the defence of duress was not available in a charge of murder was because of the supreme importance that the law afforded to the protection of human life and that it seemed repugnant that the law should recognise in any individual in any circumstances, however extreme, the right to choose that one innocent person should be killed rather than another. In my opinion, that is the question which we still must face. Is it right that the law should confer this right in any circumstances, however extreme?'

The question posed by Lord MacKay is the crucial question to resolve in this case. To arrive at the right answer, it is in my view necessary to state two important features of this case.

7.5 A legal duty?

The first important feature is that the doctors cannot be denied a right of choice if they are under a duty to choose. They are under a duty to Mary not to operate because it will kill Mary, but they are under a duty to Jodie to operate because not to do so will kill her. It is important to stress that it makes no difference whether the killing is by act or by omission. That is a distinction without a difference: see Lord Lowry in Bland at p. 877. There are similar opinions in the other speeches. Lord Browne-Wilkinson said at p. 885 G:–

'Finally, the conclusion I have reached will appear to some to be almost irrational. How can it be lawful to allow a patient to die slowly, though painlessly, over a period of weeks from lack of food but unlawful to produce his immediate death by lethal injection, thereby saving his family from yet another ordeal to add to the tragedy that has already struck them? I find it difficult to find a moral answer to that question. But it is undoubtedly the law . . .'

. . .

7.7 Offending the sanctity of life principle

The second reason why the right of choice should be given to the doctors is that the proposed operation would not in any event offend the sanctity of life principle. That principle may be expressed in different ways but they all amount to the same thing. Some might say that it demands that each life is to be protected from unjust attack. Some might say as the joint statement by the Anglican and Roman Catholic bishops did in the aftermath of the Bland judgment that because human life is a gift from God to be preserved and cherished, the deliberate taking of human life is prohibited except in self-defence or the legitimate defence of others. The Archbishop defines it in terms that human life is sacred, that is inviolable, so that one should never aim to cause an innocent person's death by act or omission. I have added the emphases. The reality here – harsh as it is to state it, and unnatural as it is that it should be happening – is that Mary is killing Jodie. That is the effect of the incontrovertible medical evidence and it is common ground in the case. Mary uses Jodie's heart and lungs to receive and use Jodie's oxygenated blood. This will cause Jodie's heart to fail and cause Jodie's death as surely as a slow drip of poison. How can it be just that Jodie should be required to tolerate that state of affairs? One does not need to label Mary with the American terminology which would paint her to be 'an unjust aggressor', which I feel is wholly inappropriate language for the sad and helpless position in which Mary finds herself. I have no difficulty in agreeing that this unique happening cannot be said to be unlawful. But it does not have to be unlawful. The six year boy indiscriminately shooting all and sundry in the school playground is not acting unlawfully for he is too young for his acts to be so classified. But is he 'innocent' within the moral meaning of that word as used by the Archbishop? I am not qualified to answer that moral question because, despite an assertion – or was it an aspersion? – by a member of the Bar in a letter to The Times that we, the judges, are proclaiming some moral superiority in this case, I for my part would defer any opinion as to a child's innocence to the Archbishop for that is his territory. If I had to hazard a guess, I would venture the tentative view that the child is not morally innocent. What I am, however, competent to say is that in law killing that six year old boy in self-defence of others would be fully justified and the killing would not be unlawful. I can see no difference in essence between that resort to legitimate self-defence and the doctors coming to Jodie's defence and removing the threat of fatal harm to her presented by Mary's draining her life-blood. The availability of such a plea of quasi self-defence, modified to meet the quite exceptional circumstances nature has inflicted on the twins, makes intervention by the doctors lawful.

8. Conclusion.

For these reasons, very shortly expressed, I conclude that the operation which I would permit can be lawfully carried out.

LORD JUSTICE BROOKE: Although I am in full agreement with Ward LJ on the family law issues in this appeal, I have been constrained to prepare a judgment of my own because of the exceptionally difficult issues of criminal law which this appeal has raised. In this judgment I am happy to adopt the description of the facts of this case which Ward LJ has set out.

. . .

19. The Queen against Dudley and Stephens

This was the legal background against which the case of R v Dudley and Stephens (1884) 14 QBD 273 was set. In AWB Simpson's Cannibalism and the Common Law (1984) the author described how the three survivors of the yacht Mignonette were landed from a German sailing barge at Falmouth in September 1884, a year after Stephen's History of the Criminal Law of England was published. On the day they landed all three of them described the circumstances in which the fourth member of the crew, the ship's boy had been killed and eaten on their twentieth day of survival on the open sea without water or food (apart from two tins of turnips). As part of the historical back-ground of the case Mr Simpson describes in Chapter 5 of his book (gruesomely entitled 'The Customs of the Sea') a large number of similar instances in the nineteenth century of shipwrecks leading to cannibalism, some of which were described by Samuel Plimsoll in 1875 in a parliamentary debate.

The law report shows how a jury at the Devon and Cornwall Assizes had found the facts of the case in a special verdict. The case was then ordered to be argued in London before a court of five judges. In giving the judgment of the court Lord Coleridge CJ considered earlier writings (including the judgment of a circuit court in Pennsylvania in United States v Holmes 26 Fed Cas 360 (1842) about necessity being a possible justification for homicide before he concluded that the facts stated in the jury's verdict provided no legal justification for the homicide in the present case. His reasoning can be seen in two passages towards the end of his judgment (at pp 286–288):

'Now it is admitted that the deliberate killing of this unoffending and unresisting boy was clearly murder, unless the killing can be justified by some well-recognised excuse admitted by the law. It is further admitted that there was in this case no such excuse, unless the killing was justified by what has been called "necessity". But the temptation to the act which existed here was not what the law has ever called necessity. Nor is this to be regretted. Though law and morality are not the same, and many things may be immoral which are not necessarily illegal, yet the absolute divorce of law from morality would be of fatal consequence; and such divorce would follow if the temptation to murder in this case were to be held by law an absolute defence of it . . .'

'It is not needful to point out the awful danger of admitting the principle which has been contended for. Who is to be the judge of this sort of necessity? By what measure is the comparative value of lives to be measured? Is it to be strength, or intellect or what? It is plain that the principle leaves to him who is to profit by it to determine the necessity which will justify him in deliberately taking another's life to save his own. In this case the weakest, the youngest, the most unresisting, was chosen. Was it more necessary to kill him than one of the grown men? The answer must be "No"—

"So spake the Fiend, and with necessity,

The tyrant's plea, excused his devilish deeds."

It is not suggested that in this particular case the deeds were "devilish", but it is quite plain that such a principle once admitted might be made the legal cloak for unbridled passion and atrocious crime. There is no safe path for judges to tread but to ascertain the law to the best of their ability and to declare it according to their judgment: and if in any case the law appears to be too severe on individuals, to leave it to the Sovereign to exercise that prerogative of mercy which the Constitution has entrusted to the hands fittest to dispense it.'

Sir James Stephen was not a member of the court, although he authorised Lord Coleridge to say that the language he had used about necessity in his History of the Criminal Law of England was not meant to cover a case like this. Three years later, in his Digest of the Criminal Law (1887), Stephen attempted a description of the doctrine of necessity in these terms at pp 9–11:

'An act which would otherwise be a crime may in some cases be excused if the person accused can show that it was done only in order to avoid consequences which could not otherwise be avoided, and which, if they had followed, would have inflicted upon him or upon others whom he was bound to protect inevitable and irreparable evil, that no more was done than was reasonably necessary for that purpose, and that the evil inflicted by it was not disproportionate to the evil avoided.

The extent of this principle is unascertained. It does not extend to the case of shipwrecked sailors who kill a boy, one of their number, in order to eat his body.'

It is not necessary for present purposes to refer to the detail of the long footnote in which he commented, not always favourably, on the judgment of the court in R. v Dudley and Stephens.

That case has sometimes been taken as authority for the proposition that necessity can never under any circumstances provide a legal justification for murder. While it is true that a passage in the speech of Lord Hailsham in R v Howe [1987] 1 AC 417 at p 429C-D might be interpreted to this effect, in my judgment neither that passage nor a similar passage in Lord Mackay of Clashfern's speech at p 453 C-D displays any evidence that they had in mind a situation in which a court was invited to sanction a defence (or justification) of necessity on facts comparable to those with which we are confronted in the present case. I accept Miss Davies's submission that R. v Dudley and Stephens, endorsed though it was by the House of Lords in R. v Howe, is not conclusive of the matter.

. . .

Professor Williams addressed the issues with which we are confronted in this case. He began his treatment of the subject by saying that many people believed in the sanctity of life, and consequently believed that killing was absolutely wrong. It was for this reason, he said, that the defence of necessity, if allowed at all, was given very narrow scope in this area. He distinguished private defence from necessity (although the two overlapped) on the grounds that (unlike necessity) private defence involved no balancing of values, while on the other hand private defence operated only against aggressors (who, with rare exceptions, were wrongdoers) whereas the persons against whom action was taken by necessity might not be aggressors or wrongdoers. In this context, he mentioned R v Bourne [1939] 1 KB 687 (where Macnaghten J had suggested in his summing up that there might be a duty in certain circumstances to abort an unborn child to save the life of the mother), as an example of the defence of necessity, even though it was a case not of homicide but of feticide.

Professor Williams came to the heart of the matter at p 604:

'Might this defence apply where a parent has killed his grossly malformed infant?

Doubtless not. It may of course be argued that the value of such an infant's life, even to himself, is minimal or negative, and that if parents are obliged to rear him they may be disabled from having another and normal child. But it is not a case for applying the doctrine of necessity as usually understood. The child when born, unlike the fetus, is regarded as having absolute rights. Besides, there is no emergency.

The usual view is that necessity is no defence to a charge of murder. This, if accepted, is a non-utilitarian doctrine; but in the case of a serious emergency is it wholly acceptable? If you are roped to a climber who has fallen, and neither of you can rectify the situation, it may not be very glorious on your part to cut the rope, but is it wrong? Is it not socially desirable that one life, at least, should be saved? Again, if you are flying an aircraft and the engine dies on you, it would not be wrong, but would be praiseworthy, to choose to come down in a street (where you can see you will kill or injure a few pedestrians), rather than in a crowded sports stadium.

But in the case of cutting the rope you are only freeing yourself from someone who is, however involuntarily, dragging you to your death. And in the case of the aircraft you do not want to kill anyone; you simply minimise the slaughter that you are bound to do one way or the other. The question is whether you could deliberately kill someone for calculating reasons.

We do regard the right to life as almost a supreme value, and it is very unlikely that anyone would be held to be justified in killing for any purpose except the saving of other life, or perhaps the saving of great pain or distress. Our revulsion against a deliberate killing is so strong that we are loth to consider utilitarian reasons for it.

But a compelling case of justification of this kind is the action of a ship's captain in a wreck. He can determine who are to enter the first lifeboat; he can forbid overcrowding; and it makes no difference that those who are not allowed to enter the lifeboat will inevitably perish with the ship. The captain, in choosing who are to live, is not guilty of killing those who remain. He would not be guilty even though he kept some of the passengers back from the boat at revolver-point, and he would not be guilty even though he had to fire the revolver.'

Between 1985 and 1993 the Law Commission returned to the topic of necessity on three separate occasions. In 1985 it published a report prepared by three professors of criminal law, who included Professor John Smith, on The Codification of the Criminal Law (1985 Law Com No. 143). Their recommendation (at para 13.26) was in these terms:–

'Necessity is not a topic to which we can apply our normal procedure of restatement, for which the present law does not provide suitable material. We cannot ourselves conduct a law reform exercise and propose a general defence of necessity of our own devising. And, as indicated above, we cannot support the Law Commission's totally negative proposals. In these circumstances our main proposal is that necessity should remain a matter of common law. That is, to the extent that the defence is now recognised, it should be unaffected by the Criminal Code Act; and (probably more important, because the present status of the defence is so limited and uncertain) the courts should retain the power that they now have to develop or clarify the defence. Necessity, that is to say, would fall within the general saving for common law defences declared by clause 49. Our only specific necessity provision is clause 46, which admits a defence in circumstances so closely analogous to those of the duress defence that it might indeed be 'the apotheosis of absurdity' to admit the one and to deny the other. The kind of situation catered for by clause 46 has, indeed, sometimes been called "duress of circumstances".'

21. Necessity: modern academic writers

Those who prepared that report [a Law Commission Report] would have been familiar with a modern update of the 'two men on a plank' dilemma (which dates back to Cicero, de Officiis) and the 'two mountaineers on a rope' dilemma which was mentioned by Professor John Smith in his 1989 Hamlyn Lectures (published under the title 'Justification and Excuse on the Criminal Law'). At the coroner's inquest conducted in October 1987 into the Zeebrugge disaster, an army corporal gave evidence that he and dozens of other people were near the foot of a rope ladder. They were all in the water and in danger of drowning. Their route to safety, however, was blocked for at least ten minutes by a young man who was petrified by cold or fear (or both) and was unable to move up or down. Eventually the corporal gave instructions that the man should be pushed off the ladder, and he was never seen again. The corporal and many others were then able to climb up the ladder to safety.

In his third lecture, 'Necessity and Duress', Professor Smith evinced the belief at pp 77–78 that if such a case ever did come to court it would not be too difficult for a judge to distinguish R. v Dudley and Stephens. He gave two reasons for this belief. The first was that there was no question of choosing who had to die (the problem which Lord Coleridge had found unanswerable in R. v Dudley and Stephens at p 287) because the unfortunate young man on the ladder had chosen himself by his immobility there. The second was that unlike the ship's boy on the Mignonette, the young man, although in no way at fault, was preventing others from going where they had a right, and a most urgent need, to go, and was thereby unwittingly imperilling their lives.

I would add that the same considerations would apply if a pilotless aircraft, out of control and running out of fuel, was heading for a densely populated town. Those inside the aircraft were in any event 'destined to die'. There would be no question of human choice in selecting the candidates for death, and if their inevitable deaths were accelerated by the plane being brought down on waste ground, the lives of countless other innocent people in the town they were approaching would be saved.

It was an argument along these lines that led the rabbinical scholars involved in the 1977 case of conjoined twins to advise the worried parents that the sacrifice of one of their children in order to save the other could be morally justified. George J Annas, 'Siamese Twins: Killing One to Save the Other' (Hastings Center Report, April 1987 at p 27, described how they:

'. . . reportedly relied primarily on two analogies. In the first, two men jump from a burning aeroplane. The parachute of the second man does not open, and as he falls past the first man, he grabs his legs. If the parachute cannot support them both, is the first man morally justified in kicking the second man away to save himself? Yes, said the rabbis, since the man whose parachute didn't open was "designated for death".

The second analogy involves a caravan surrounded by bandits. The bandits demand a particular member of the caravan be turned over for execution; the rest will go free. Assuming that the named individual has been "designated for death", the rabbis concluded it was acceptable to surrender him to save everyone else. Accordingly, they concluded that if a twin A was "designated for death" and could not survive in any event, but twin B could, surgery that would kill twin A to help improve the chance of twin B was acceptable'.

Before I leave the treatment afforded to the topic of necessity by modern academic writers of great distinction (there is a valuable contemporary summary of the issues in the Ninth Edition of Smith and Hogan's Criminal Law (1999) at pp 245–252), I must mention the section entitled 'Justifications, Necessity and the Choice of Evils' in the Third Edition (1999) of 'Principles of Criminal Law' by Professor Andrew Ashworth. After referring to the facts of the Zeebrugge incident he said at pp 153–4.

'No English court has had to consider this situation, and it is clear that only the strongest prohibition on the taking of an innocent life would prevent a finding of justification here: in an urgent situation involving a decision between n lives and n + 1 lives, is there not a strong social interest in preserving the greater number of lives?

Any residual principle of this kind must be carefully circumscribed; it involves the sanctity of life, and therefore the highest value with which the criminal law is concerned. Although there is a provision in the Model Penal Code allowing for a defence of "lesser evil", it fails to restrict the application of the defence to cases of imminent threat, opening up the danger of citizens trying to justify all manner of conduct by reference to overall good effects. The moral issues are acute: "not just anything is permissible on the ground that it would yield a net saving of lives". Closely connected with this is the moral problem of "choosing one's victim", a problem which arises when, for example, a lifeboat is in danger of sinking, necessitating the throwing overboard of some passengers, or when two people have to kill and eat another if any of the three is to survive. To countenance a legal justification in such cases would be to regard the victim's rights as morally and politically less worthy than the rights of those protected by the action taken, which represents a clear violation of the principle of individual autonomy. Yet it is surely necessary to make some sacrifice, since the autonomy of everyone simply cannot be protected. A dire choice has to be made, and it must be made on a principle of welfare or community that requires the minimisation of overall harm. A fair procedure for resolving the problem – perhaps the drawing of lots – must be found. But here, as with self-defence and the "uplifted knife" cases, one should not obscure the clearer cases where there is no need to choose a victim: in the case of the young man on the rope-ladder, blocking the escape of several others, there was no doubt about the person who must be subjected to force, probably with fatal consequences.'

. . .

I have considered very carefully the policy reasons for the decision in R v Dudley and Stephens, supported as it was by the House of Lords in R v Howe. These are, in short, that there were two insuperable objections to the proposition that necessity might be available as a defence for the Mignonette sailors. The first objection was evident in the court's questions: Who is to be the judge of this sort of necessity? By what measure is the comparative value of lives to be measured? The second objection was that to permit such a defence would mark an absolute divorce of law from morality.

In my judgment, neither of these objections are dispositive of the present case. Mary is, sadly, self-designated for a very early death. Nobody can extend her life beyond a very short span. Because her heart, brain and lungs are for all practical purposes useless, nobody would have even tried to extend her life artificially if she had not, fortuitously, been deriving oxygenated blood from her sister's bloodstream.

It is true that there are those who believe most sincerely – and the Archbishop of Westminster is among them – that it would be an immoral act to save Jodie, if by saving Jodie one must end Mary's life before its brief allotted span is complete. For those who share this philosophy, the law, recently approved by Parliament, which permits abortion at any time up to the time of birth if the conditions set out in Section 1(1)(d) of the Abortion Act 1967 (as substituted) are satisfied, is equally repugnant. But there are also those who believe with equal sincerity that it would be immoral not to assist Jodie if there is a good prospect that she might live a happy and fulfilled life if this operation is performed. The court is not equipped to choose between these competing philosophies. All that a court can say is that it is not at all obvious that this is the sort of clear-cut case, marking an absolute divorce from law and morality, which was of such concern to Lord Coleridge and his fellow judges.

There are sound reasons for holding that the existence of an emergency in the normal sense of the word is not an essential prerequisite for the application of the doctrine of necessity. The principle is one of necessity, not emergency: see Lord Goff (in In re F at p 75D), the Law Commission in its recent report (Law Com No 218, paras 35.5 to 35.6), and Wilson J in Perka (at p 33).

There are also sound reasons for holding that the threat which constitutes the harm to be avoided does not have to be equated with 'unjust aggression', as Professor Glanville Williams has made clear in Section 26.3 of the 1983 edition of his book. None of the formulations of the doctrine of necessity which I have noted in this judgment make any such requirement: in this respect it is different from the doctrine of private defence.

If a sacrificial separation operation on conjoined twins were to be permitted in circumstances like these, there need be no room for the concern felt by Sir James Stephen that people would be too ready to avail themselves of exceptions to the law which they might suppose to apply to their cases (at the risk of other people's lives). Such an operation is, and is always likely to be, an exceptionally rare event, and because the medical literature shows that it is an operation to be avoided at all costs in the neonatal stage, there will be in practically every case the opportunity for the doctors to place the relevant facts before a court for approval (or otherwise) before the operation is attempted.

According to Sir James Stephen, there are three necessary requirements for the application of the doctrine of necessity:

(i)   the act is needed to avoid inevitable and irreparable evil;

(ii) no more should be done than is reasonably necessary for the purpose to be achieved;

(iii) the evil inflicted must not be disproportionate to the evil avoided.

Given that the principles of modern family law point irresistibly to the conclusion that the interests of Jodie must be preferred to the conflicting interests of Mary, I consider that all three of these requirements are satisfied in this case.

Finally, the doctrine of the sanctity of life respects the integrity of the human body. The proposed operation would give these children's bodies the integrity which nature denied them.

For these reasons I, too, would dismiss this appeal.

Appeal dismissed

NOTES AND QUESTIONS

1. *Re A* was a difficult case not only because of its unusual and tragic facts but also because it raised complicated questions of Medical Law, Family Law and Criminal Law. Further complicating the case were the fundamental moral and religious issues raised by the facts, and in respect to the latter the court received submissions from the Roman Catholic Archbishop of Westminster. As summarised by Lord Justice Walker:

   Those submission make five salient points based on Roman Catholic faith and morality. These are, first, that human life is sacred and inviolable. Secondly, a person's bodily integrity should not be invaded when that can confer no benefit. Thirdly, the duty to preserve one person's life cannot without grave injustice be effected by a lethal assault on another.

Fourthly, there is no duty on doctors to resort to extraordinary means in order to preserve life. Fifthly, the rights of parents should be overridden only where they are clearly 'contrary to what is strictly owing to their children'.

Did the Archbishop's submissions clarify, or confuse the resolution of the legal issues?

2. The parents of the twins refused to give their consent to the operation, believing that their children's fate should rest with God. Should their views count?

3. In Family Law, the paramount consideration is the child's best interest. Does this principle advance the analysis of the criminal law issues in the case? Were the interests of the twins in irreconcilable conflict? Was the Court ineluctably drawn into balancing the interests of one child against another?

4. Consider the dilemma faced by the doctors. They have a duty to preserve life and if they failed to operate Jody would die; if they operated, Mary would die. Legally, they could be liable for Jody's death as a result of their failure to operate, or Mary's death if they performed the operation. What were they to do?

5. Is there a difference between the *sanctity* of life and the *quality* of life that is relevant to the analysis of the necessity issue? Was Mary 'designated for death' in any event? Should this matter? The argument that the operation could not be justified by necessity is cogently presented in Michalowski (2002) 'Sanctity of life – are some lives more sacred than others?' 22 Legal Studies 377.

While the necessity defence can trace its origins to the common law, many contemporary statutes, such as the Control of Pollution Act 1974, specifically recognise a necessity defence. Other statutes are said to raise the defence by implication.

Criminal Damage Act 1971

1.—(1) person who without lawful excuse destroys or damages any property belonging to another intending to destroy or damage any such property or being reckless as to whether any such property would be destroyed or damaged shall be guilty of an offence.

The key phrase is 'without lawful excuse'. If one commits damage but in a situation of necessity, is the act with lawful excuse? An example might be a case where the defendant blows up a house for the purpose of diverting a rampaging river that is threatening to flood the town.

Is there, on the other hand, a more general defence of necessity.

R v *Bourne*
[1939] 1 KB 687, Central Criminal Court

The evidence called on behalf of the Crown proved that on 14 June 1938, the defendant performed an operation on the girl in question at St Mary's Hospital, and thereby procured her miscarriage. The following facts were also proved: On 27 April 1938, the girl, who was then under the age of 15, had been raped with great violence in circumstances which would have been most terrifying to any woman, let alone a child of fourteen, by a man who was in due course convicted of the crime. In consequence of the rape the girl became pregnant. Her case was brought to the attention of the defendant, who, after examination of the girl, performed the operation with the consent of her parents.

The defence put forward was that, in the circumstances of the case, the operation was not unlawful. The defendant was called as a witness on his own behalf and stated that, after he had made careful examination of the girl and had informed himself of all the relevant facts of the case, he had come to the conclusion that it was his duty to perform the operation. He had satisfied himself that the girl was in fact pregnant in consequence of the rape committed on her. He had also satisfied himself that she had not been infected with venereal disease; if he had found that she was so infected, he would not have performed the operation, since in that case there would have been a risk that the operation would cause a spread of the disease. Nor would he have performed the operation if he had found that the girl was either feeble-minded or had what he called a 'prostitute mind,' since in such cases pregnancy and child-birth would not be likely to affect a girl injuriously. He satisfied himself that she was a normal girl in every respect, though she was somewhat more mature than most girls of her age. In his opinion the continuance of the pregnancy would probably cause serious injury to the girl . . .

MACNAGHTEN J: . . . The charge against Mr Bourne is made under s. 58 of the Offences Against the Person Act, 1861, that he unlawfully procured the miscarriage of the girl who was the first witness in the case. . . .

Nine years ago Parliament passed an Act called the Infant Life (Preservation) Act, 1929 (19 & 20 Geo. 5, c. 34). Sect. 1, sub-s. 1, of that Act provides that

> any person who, with intent to destroy the life of a child capable of being born alive, by any wilful act causes a child to die before it has an existence independent of its mother, shall be guilty of felony, to wit, of child destruction, and shall be liable on conviction thereof on indictment to penal servitude for life: Provided that no person shall be found guilty of an offence under this section unless it is proved that the act which caused the death of the child was not done in good faith for the purpose only of preserving the life of the mother.

It is true, as Mr Oliver has said, that this enactment provides for the case where a child is killed by a wilful act at the time when it is being delivered in the ordinary course of nature; but in my view the proviso that it is necessary for the Crown to prove that the act was not done in good faith for the purpose only of preserving the life of the mother is in accordance with what has always been the common law of England with regard to the killing of an unborn child. No such proviso is in fact set out in s. 58 of the Offences Against the Person Act, 1861; but the words of that section are that any person who 'unlawfully' uses an instrument with intent to procure miscarriage shall be guilty of felony. In my opinion the word 'unlawfully' is not, in that section, a meaningless word. I think it imports the meaning expressed by the proviso in s. 1, sub-s. 1, of the Infant Life (Preservation) Act, 1929, and that s. 58 of the Offences Against the Person Act, 1861, must be read as if the words making it an offence to use an instrument with intent to procure a miscarriage were qualified by a similar proviso.

In this case, therefore, my direction to you in law is this – that the burden rests on the Crown to satisfy you beyond reasonable doubt that the defendant did not procure the miscarriage of the girl in good faith for the purpose only of preserving her life. If the Crown fails to satisfy you of that, the defendant is entitled by the law of this land to a verdict of acquittal. If, on the other hand, you are satisfied that what the defendant did was not done by him in good faith for the purpose only of preserving the life of the girl, it is your duty to find him guilty. It is said, and I think said rightly, that this is a case of great importance to the public and, more especially, to the medical profession; but you will observe that it has nothing to do with the ordinary case of procuring abortion to which I have already referred. In those cases the operation is performed by a person of no skill, with no medical qualifications, and there is no pretence that it is done for the preservation of the mother's life. Cases of that sort are in no way affected by the consideration of the question which is put before you to-day.

NOTES AND QUESTIONS
1. Does *Bourne* turn on the wording of the statute, or on the existence of an implied defence of necessity? See also *In Re F (Mental Patient: Sterilisation)* [1990] 2 AC 1; *R v Bournewood Community and Mental Health Trust ex parte L.* [1999] 1 AC 458.
2. Many crimes, such as assault and criminal damage, contain the word 'unlawful' in their definition, usually in respect to the *actus reus* of the crime. It might seem that the word 'unlawful' is otiose, since an *actus reus* is by definition unlawful. The argument that gives content to 'unlawful' is that the term should be interpreted to mean 'without excuse or justification'. But arguably this begs the question of what is a legally recognised excuse or justification. Does *Bourne* help answer this question?

(ii) *Duress*
Duress can be viewed as a sub-category of necessity but one where the pressure on the defendant to commit a crime comes from a natural person. X threatens Y with harm unless he commits the offence or, more typically perhaps, assist X in committing the offence. The issues can be broken down into five heads:

(a) the defendant must have reasonably believed in the facts alleged to amount to duress;

(b) his belief must be one which might be expected of a person of reasonable firmness;

(c) his belief must have amounted to good cause to fear death or serious bodily harm.

(d) whether the circumstances should be judged from the perspective of the defendant or that of an ordinary person of reasonable firmness:

(e) the relevance of alternative courses of action.

It might be observed that these same issues tend to preoccupy the courts in analysing clims of necessity and duress of circumstances.

The harm to be avoided must be death or serious bodily injury. A threat of exposure will not suffice (see *Singh* [1973] 1 All ER 122). However, the harm threatened need not necessarily be to the defendant. Often in duress cases the threat is not to the defendant but to a close family member. Should this matter? See *Ortiz* (1986) 83 Cr App R. 173.

It is often said that the harm threatened must be present and immediate. Doubt as to this requirement, however, has been raised:

R v Hudson and Taylor
[1971] 2 QB 202, Court of Appeal

LORD PARKER CJ: . . . These appellants were convicted of perjury at the Manchester Crown Court on May 18, 1970, and each was granted a conditional discharge. They now appeal against their convictions by leave of the single judge.

On April 6, 1969, a fight took place in a Salford public house between one Wright and one Mulligan with the result that Wright was charged with wounding Mulligan. Each of the present appellants gave statements to the police and they were the principal prosecution witnesses at Wright's trial. Elaine Taylor is 19, and Linda Hudson is 17.

Wright's trial took place on August 4, 1969, but when called to give evidence the appellants failed to identify Wright as Mulligan's assailant. Taylor said that she knew no one called Jimmy Wright, and Hudson said that the only Wright she knew was not the man in the dock. Wright was accordingly acquitted and, in due course, the appellants were charged with perjury. At their trial they admitted that the evidence which they had given was false but set up the defence of duress. The basis of the defence was that, shortly after the fight between Wright and Mulligan, Hudson had been approached by a group of men including one Farrell who had a reputation for violence and was warned that if she 'told on Wright in court' they would get her and cut her up. Hudson passed this warning to Taylor who said that she had also been warned by other girls to be careful or she would be hurt. The appellants said in evidence that, in consequence of these threats, they were frightened and decided to tell lies in court in order to avoid the consequences which might follow if they testified against Wright. This resolve was strengthened when they arrived at court for Wright's trial and saw that Farrell was in the gallery.

. . .

This appeal raises two main questions; first, as to the nature of the necessary threat and, in particular, whether it must be 'present and immediate'; secondly, as to the extent to which a right to plead duress may be lost if the accused has failed to take steps to remove the threat as, for example, by seeking police protection.

It is essential to the defence of duress that the threat shall be effective at the moment when the crime is committed. The threat must be a 'present' threat in the sense that it is effective to neutralise the will of the accused at that time. Hence an accused who joins a rebellion under the compulsion of threats cannot plead duress if he remains with the rebels after the threats have lost their effect and his own will has had a chance to re-assert itself: *R v M'Growther* (1746) Fost 13; *Attorney-General v Whelan* [1934] IR 518. Similarly a threat of future violence may be so remote as to be insufficient to overpower the will at that moment when the offence was committed, or the accused may have elected to commit the offence in order to rid himself of a threat hanging over him and not because he was driven to act by immediate and unavoidable pressure. In none of these cases is the defence of duress available because a person cannot justify the commission of a crime merely to secure his own peace of mind.

When, however, there is no opportunity for delaying tactics, and the person threatened must make up his mind whether he is to commit the criminal act or not, the existence at that moment of threats sufficient to destroy his will ought to provide him with a defence even though the threatened injury may not follow instantly, but after an interval. This principle is illustrated by *Subramaniam v Public Prosecutor* [1956] 1 WLR 965, when the appellant was charged in Malaya with unlawful possession of ammunition and was held by the Privy Council to have a defence of duress fit to go to the jury, on his plea that he had been compelled by terrorists to accept the ammunition and feared for his safety if the terrorists returned.

In the present case the threats of Farrell were likely to be no less compelling, because their execution could not be effected in the court room, if they could be carried out in the streets of Salford the same night. In so far, therefore, as the recorder ruled as a matter of law that the threats were not sufficiently present and immediate to support the defence of duress we think that he was in error. He should have left the jury to decide whether the threats had overborne the will of the appellants at the time when they gave the false evidence.

R v *Abdul-Husain and Others*
[1999] Crim LR 570, Court of Appeal

The appellants were all Shiite Muslims from Southern Iraq. All save Hoshan had offended against the laws or regulations of the Saddam Hussein regime, from which they were fugitives. In 1996 they were living in Sudan and feared return to Iraq, where they believed they would face death. Hoshan had a valid permit to reside in the United Kingdom and would have become entitled to a right of permanent settlement. He helped Iraqis to obtain false papers and to bribe officials and believed that, because of his involvement in helping others, he was at risk of detection and deportation to Iraq where he would probably be executed. The appellants made several unsuccessful attempts to leave Sudan using false passports. By the end of August 1996 they were all overstayers in Sudan and feared deportation to Iraq. They decided to hijack an aeroplane. Accordingly, they boarded a Sudanese airbus bound for Amman in Jordan. They were equipped with plastic knives and plastic mustard bottles filled with salt, modified with black tape and plasticine to look like hand grenades. Once the flight was in Egyptian airspace they gained control of the aircraft by threatening the crew with the imitation knives and grenades. The aeroplane eventually landed at Stansted airport 12 hours later. After negotiations lasting some eight hours the passengers and crew were released and the appellants surrendered. At their trial they admitted the charge of hijacking but contended that they had done so as a last resort to escape death, either of themselves or of their families, at the hands of the Iraqi authorities. The trial judge ruled that the defence of necessity or duress of circumstances should not be left to the jury because the threat was insufficiently close and immediate to give rise to a virtually spontaneous reaction to the physical risk arising. They were all convicted and appealed against conviction on the grounds that the judge erred in withdrawing the defence of duress from the jury's consideration.

Held, allowing the appeals, that the defence of duress was available in relation to hijacking aircraft, although the terror induced in innocent passengers would generally raise issues of proportionality; that imminent peril of death or serious injury to the defendant or his dependants had to operate on the mind of the defendant at the time he committed the act so as to overbear his will, but the execution of the threat need not be immediately in prospect; that the period of time which elapsed between the inception of the peril and the defendant's act was a relevant but not determinative factor; that all the circumstances of the peril, including the number, identity and status of those creating it, and the opportunities (if any) to avoid it were relevant, initially for the judge and, in appropriate cases, for the jury, when assessing whether the defendant's mind was affected so as to overbear his will; and that, accordingly, the judge interpreted the law too strictly in seeking a virtually spontaneous reaction. He should have asked himself, in accordance with *R v Martin* (1989) 88 Cr App R 345 whether there was evidence of such fear operating on the minds of the appellants at the time of the hijacking as to impel them to act as they did and whether, if so, there was evidence that the danger they feared objectively existed and that hijacking was a reasonable and proportionate response to it. Had he done so he must have concluded that there was evidence for the jury to consider and that they should have been permitted to do so.

Per curiam. For the fourth time in five years the Court of Appeal emphasised the urgent need for legislation to define the defence of duress with precision.

NOTES AND QUESTIONS
1. John Smith in his commentary in the Criminal Law Review ([1999] Crim LR 571) on *R v Abdul-Husain* asserts that the threat must be 'imminent' but need not be 'immediate'. What is the difference? How do the two concepts apply in *Hudson and Taylor*? In *Abdul-Husain*?
2. Mary is kidnapped. Her kidnappers give her parents one month to raise the ransom money and tell them that if the ransom is not paid, Mary will be killed. They inform Mary that they are serious. Two weeks before the ransom is due, while her kidnappers are in another room,

Mary finds a pair of scissors. She attacks her kidnappers with the scissors and kills them. Will her defence fail because no immediate harm was threatened?

3. A similar case to *Hudson and Taylor*, reaching a similar result, is *Lewis* (1993) 96 Cr App R 412 (discussed later in this chapter).

As we saw in respect to necessity, the most troublesome cases involve situations where the life of an innocent victim is in issue. Relying on the authority of *Dudley and Stephens*, courts commonly would state that a defendant who killed an innocent victim could not raise the defence of duress. The issue arose in more modern times in a series of cases beginning with *Director of Public Prosecutions for Northern Ireland* v *Lynch* [1975] AC 653. The defendant in *Lynch* was the driver on an IRA terrorist expedition in the course of which a police officer was killed. He was charged with aiding and abetting a murder. His defence was that he believed that he would be shot if he did not cooperate. In a three to two decision the House of Lords held that the defence of duress was available to one charged with aiding and abetting a murder. Two years later, however, in *Abbott* v *R* [1977] AC 755, the Lords, sitting as the Judicial Committee of the Privy Council, held that the defence of duress was not available to one charged as a principal to murder. There was an obvious tension between *Lynch* and *Abbott*, which the Lords had to resolve:

R v *Howe and Others*
[1987] 1 AC 417, House of Lords

LORD HAILSHAM OF ST MARYLEBONE: . . . *Count 1: murder of Elgar.* The first victim was a 17-year old youth called Elgar. He was offered a job as a driver by Murray. On the evening of 10 October 1983 all five men were driven by Murray up into the hills between Stockport and Buxton, eventually stopping at some public lavatories at a remote spot called Goytsclough. Murray at some stage told both appellants in effect that Elgar was a 'grass,' and that they were going to kill him. Bannister was threatened with violence if he did not give Elgar 'a bit of a battering.' From thenceforwards Elgar, who was naked, sobbing and begging for mercy, was tortured, compelled to undergo appalling sexual perversions and indignities, he was kicked and punched. Bannister and Howe were doing the kicking and punching. The coup de grace was executed by Bailey who strangled Elgar with a headlock. It is unnecessary to go into further details of the attack on Elgar which are positively nauseating. In brief the two appellants asserted that they had only acted as they did through fear of Murray, believing that they would be treated in the same way as Elgar had been treated if they did not comply with Murray's directions. The prosecution were content to assent to the proposition that death had been caused by Bailey strangling the victim, although the kicks and punches would have resulted in death moments later even in the absence of the strangulation. The body was hidden by the appellants and the other two men. On this basis the appellants were in the position of what would have earlier been principals in the second degree and duress was left to the jury as an issue on this count.

Count 2: murder of Pollitt. Very much the same course of conduct took place as with Elgar. On 11 October 1983 the men picked up Pollitt, a 19-year-old labourer, and took him to the same place where all four men kicked and punched the youth. Murray told Howe and Bannister to kill Pollitt, which they did by strangling him with Bannister's shoe lace. As the appellants were in the position of principals in the first degree, the judge did not leave duress to the jury on this count.

Count 3: conspiracy to murder Redfern. The third intended victim was a 21-year old man. The same procedure was followed, but Redfern suspected that something was afoot and managed with some skill to escape on his motorcycle from what would otherwise have inevitably been another horrible murder. The judge left the defence of duress to the jury on this charge of conspiracy to murder. The grounds of appeal, which are the same in respect of each of these appellants, are as follows. That the judge erred in directing the jury (1) in respect of count 2, that the defence of duress was not available to a principal in the first degree to the actual killing; (2) in respect of counts 1 and 3, that the test as to whether the appellants were acting under duress contains an 'objective' element; that is to say, if the prosecution prove that a reasonable man in the position of the defendant would not have felt himself forced to comply with the threats, the defence fails.

. . .

In general, I must say that I do not at all accept in relation to the defence of murder it is either good morals, good policy or good law to suggest, as did the majority in *Lynch* [1975] AC 653 and the minority in *Abbott* [1977] AC 755 that the ordinary man of reasonable fortitude is not to be supposed to be capable of heroism if he is asked to take an innocent life rather than sacrifice his own. Doubtless in actual practice many will succumb to temptation, as they did in *Dudley and Stephens*. But many will not, and I do not believe that as a 'concession to human frailty' the former should be exempt from liability to criminal sanctions if they do. I have known in my own lifetime of too many acts of heroism by ordinary human beings of no more than ordinary fortitude to regard a law as either 'just or humane' which withdraws the protection of the criminal law from the innocent victim and casts the cloak of its protection upon the coward and the poltroon in the name of a 'concession to human frailty.'

. . .

LORD GRIFFITHS: . . . [A]re there any present circumstances that should impel your Lordships to alter the law that has stood for so long and to extend the defence of duress to the actual killer? My Lords, I can think of none. It appears to me that all present indications point in the opposite direction. We face a rising tide of violence and terrorism against which the law must stand firm recognising that its highest duty is to protect the freedom and lives of those that live under it. The sanctity of human life lies at the root of this ideal and I would do nothing to undermine it, be it ever so slight.

   . . . If the defence is not available to the killer what justification can there be for extending it to others who have played their part in the murder. I can, of course, see that as a matter of commonsense one participant in a murder may be considered less morally at fault than another. The youth who hero-worships the gangleader and acts as lookout man whilst the gang enter a jeweller's that shop and kill the owner in order to steal is an obvious example. In the eyes of the law they are all guilty of murder, but justice will be served by requiring those who did the killing to serve a longer period in prison before being released on licence than the youth who acted as lookout. However, it is not difficult to give examples where more moral fault may be thought to attach to a participant in murder who was not the actual killer; I have already mentioned the example of a contract killing, when the murder would never have taken place if a contract had not been placed to take the life of the victim. Another example would be an intelligent man goading a weakminded individual into a killing he would not otherwise commit.

   It is therefore neither rational nor fair to make the defence dependent upon whether the accused is the actual killer or took some other part in the murder.

NOTES AND QUESTIONS
1. Is the decision in *Howe* based on legal principle or social policy? Should it be reconsidered in light of *Re A* [2001] 1 FLR 1, or is *Re A* distinguishable?
2. What if the defendant's efforts to kill prove unsuccessful, and the charge is attempted murder. Should duress be a defence? Given that an innocent life has not been taken, does the logic of *Abbott* apply? In *R v Gotts* [1992] 2 AC 412, the House of Lords held that duress could not serve as a defence to attempted murder.

3. The courts seem to take a fairly dogmatic approach when considering the nature of the harm avoided and the nature of the harm caused, tending to place absolute limitations on each of these elements. Is this in fact the correct approach, though? Arguably, when a defendant, through no fault of his own, is faced with a choice of evils, he should have a defence if he chooses the lesser of the evils. Why not balance the harm avoided against the harm caused, allowing the defence when the former is greater than the latter?

If the controlling question were to be whether the defendant chose the lesser of two evils, many of the limitations which have developed would be exposed as questionable. Why should the defence be available only when one is threatened with death or grievous bodily harm? Why should not, for example, a homeless derelict who seeks shelter from the cold in an unoccupied building have a defence of necessity to a charge of trespass? And why should not one be able to kill an innocent victim to save the lives of many innocent persons? In analysing case of duress, as well as cases of necessity and duress of circumstances, should the courts look at the situation objectively, through the eyes of a reasonable person, or subjectively, through the defendant's eyes?

R v Cairns
[1999] Crim LR 826, Court of Appeal

The appellant was returning home in his car late one evening when a young man, A, presented himself in front of the car and clambered on to the bonnet where he stayed spread-eagled with his face up against the windscreen. The appellant was frightened and thought the best course was to drive on. He did so for a significant distance, with A still on the bonnet, until he came to a speed hump in the road where he applied his brakes. A fell off the car and the appellant drove over him. A suffered a fracture to his spine which rendered him paraplegic. These events were observed by a group of young people who had been with A and, from the evidence they later gave at the trial, were endeavouring to stop A behaving in the way that he did. They followed the car shouting and gesturing. The appellant did not stop but when interviewed the next day by the police he made it plain that he had not stopped because he had felt threatened not only by A but also by the other young people chasing after the car. The appellant was charged with causing grievous bodily harm with intent and dangerous driving. His principal defence was that of duress of circumstances. The trial judge directed the jury that that defence was only available if the action taken by the accused was 'actually necessary to avoid the evil in question'. The appellant was acquitted of causing grievous bodily harm with intent but convicted of the lesser alternative of causing grievous bodily harm. He was also convicted of dangerous driving. He appealed against conviction on the grounds that the judge's direction to the jury was wrong.

Held, allowing the appeal, that, on the authority of *R v Martin* (1989) 88 Cr App R 345, what the jury had to be concerned with was the accused's perception of the threat with which he was confronted and to consider whether or not in relation to that perceived threat he acted reasonably and proportionately in responding as he did; that nowhere in the direction suggested in *Martin* did it appear that the threat perceived by the accused relying upon the defence had, in the event, to prove to be an actual or real threat; so that in directing the jury in the terms that he did the judge wrongly departed from the guidance given in *Martin* and subsequently affirmed in *R v Abdul-Hussain* [1999] Crim LR 570.

Should the defence of duress be available to a person who voluntarily, or recklessly, places himself in the predicament in which he must choose to commit a crime or suffer harm?

R v *Sharp*

[1987] QB 853, Court of Appeal

The appellant, who joined a gang of robbers, knew that they used firearms and he participated in a robbery during which the gang leader shot and killed the victim. The appellant was tried on a count charging murder. He submitted that the defence of duress was available to him since he had wished to pull out of the robbery but had participated in fear because a gun had been pointed at his head by the gang leader with a threat to blow it off if the appellant did not participate. The submission was rejected by the trial judge and the appellant was convicted of manslaughter.

LORD LANE CJ: . . . [Counsel] agrees that everything in this appeal depends upon whether the judge was correct or not in ruling that a defendant who has voluntarily joined a gang such as this cannot subsequently rely upon the defence of duress.

. . .

No one could question that if a person can avoid the effects of duress by escaping from the threats, without damage to himself, he must do so. In other words if there is a moment at which he is able to escape, so to speak, from the gun being held at his head by Hussey, or the equivalent of Hussey, he must do so. It seems to us to be part of the same argument, or at least to be so close to the same argument as to be practically indistinguishable from it, to say that a man must not voluntarily put himself in a position where he is likely to be subjected to such compulsion.

[I]n our judgment, where a person has voluntarily, and with knowledge of its nature, joined a criminal organisation or gang which he knew might bring pressure on him to commit an offence and was an active member when he was put under such pressure, he cannot avail himself of the defence of duress. . . .

QUESTION

Consider the following variant of *Sharp*. An advocacy group is formed whose objective is to get across its message through peaceful picketing. The picketing is ignored by both the public and the media. The leaders of the group decide to escalate their activities to include destruction of governmental property. At this point a minority of members seek to withdraw, but are threatened by the majority with violence if they do not participate. What result under *Sharp* if the minority reluctantly go along with the majority? See *R v Shepherd* (1988) 86 Cr App R 47.

Sharp was reconsidered in *R v Lewis*:

R v *Lewis*

(1993) 96 Cr App R 412, Court of Appeal

The appellant was convicted of robbery and sentenced to 12 years' imprisonment. Whilst serving his sentence he was savagely attacked in the prison yard by a co-prisoner, an accomplice in the robbery. At the trial of his attacker, the appellant refused to give evidence, stating through his solicitor that he would be willing to explain his refusal when he was on his own. Proceedings were brought against him for contempt of court; but the judge failed to give him the opportunity to explain his earlier refusal. However, the appellant's counsel made it clear to the judge that the appellant had feared reprisals if he gave evidence. He was found in contempt of court. On appeal against that finding.

BELDAM LJ: . . . In our judgment, once it was clear that the explanation given by the appellant for his unwillingness to give evidence was his fear of reprisal should he do so, the judge ought to have given the appellant the opportunity to give evidence. The judge would then have been in a position to decide whether the appellant was indeed in contempt because his refusal was free and voluntary, or whether it was the result of a well-founded fear of further attack, so real and compelling that he could not reasonably be expected to act otherwise.

The judge's failure to consider these questions was a sufficient ground for allowing the appeal. But Mr Richardson, for whose argument as *amicus* we are indebted, raised and argued the further question whether, in any event, the defence of duress was open to the appellant in the circumstances of this case. He emphasised the importance of ensuring that those who were prepared to use violence to achieve criminal ends should not be able to frustrate the course of justice. Thus, he argued, if a person embarked with others on violent crime, he ought not to be able to rely on the defence of duress if he has knowingly combined with violent men whom he could reasonably expect would be willing to use such violence to prevent their conviction.

He invited the Court to apply the reasoning in *R* v *Sharp* (1987) 85 Cr App R 207. In that case, at page 210, Lord Lane CJ said:

> No one could question that if a person can avoid the effects of duress by escaping from the threats, without damage to himself, he must do so. . . . It seems to us to be part of the same argument or at least to be so close to the same argument as to be practically indistinguishable from it, to say that a man must not voluntarily put himself in a position where he is likely to be subjected to such compulsion.

On the basis of these principles, he submits that where a person joins an enterprise of robbery knowing that he is associating with men prepared to use violence for criminal ends, it is readily foreseeable that similar violence might be used against him should he become a witness against his former confederates and, in such circumstances, the law should not, as a matter of policy, permit him to rely on a defence of duress if he should decline to give evidence or should commit perjury.

We acknowledge the force of Mr Richardson's submission. However, in the present case, the violence directed to the appellant, and the fear of further reprisal if he gave evidence against Cross, whilst it arose out of the appellant's participation with Cross in the robbery, was not so closely or immediately connected with his participation in the armed robbery that it could be said that he voluntarily exposed himself to the risk of the subsequent violence upon himself by agreeing to take part.

Moreover we do not read the case of *Sharp* as laying down so wide a general principle that any person who participates knowingly in an offence of violence cannot subsequently rely on a defence of duress where, for example, he has served his sentence for the offence and has abandoned a life of crime but is compelled by threats of violence to himself or his family from his former associates to play some part in a subsequent crime. This suggests to us that to deprive him of a defence of duress, the coercion must be closely and not remotely connected with the offence of violence in which he has joined. Lord Lane CJ expressed this connection by the qualification 'and was an active member when he was put under such pressure.'

There are two further qualifications which we think are significant. First, it is voluntary participation in, or association with persons known to be part of, a paramilitary or gangster-tyrant style of organisation which deprives a defendant of the defence. Whilst these are not intended as exhaustive definitions, they do nevertheless imply a question of degree. Secondly, it is this question of degree which led Mustill LJ to refer to members of such groups as being taken to anticipate what may happen to them. In short, to preclude a defendant from relying on the defence, there must be evidence which satisfies the court that the defendant knew or was aware that he was exposing himself to the risk of threats of death or serious harm if he did not participate with, or conform to, the wishes of his criminal associates.

In the present case, no such evidence was before the court. Accordingly, we allowed the appeal, set aside the judge's holding that the appellant was guilty of contempt and quashed the sentence of nine months' imprisonment.

NOTES AND QUESTIONS

1. Sharp was followed in *R* v *Heath* [2000] Crim LR 109 where the Court of Appeal held that the defence of duress was not open to someone who became indebted to a drug dealer even though he was not a member of any illegal gang or organisation. Would the same apply to gambling debts?
2. Assume that a defendant subjectively believes that in order to avoid threatened harm, it is necessary to commit a crime. Will the defendant lose the defence of duress or necessity if a reasonable person would have reached a different conclusion as to the need to commit the crime?

R v *Bowen*
[1996] 2 Cr App R 157, Court of Appeal

STUART-SMITH LJ: On August 2, 1995 in the Crown Court at Luton the appellant was convicted of five counts of obtaining services by deception. He was subsequently sentenced to 18 months' imprisonment, concurrent on each count. He now appeals against his convictions with leave of the single judge.

. . .

The appellant gave evidence; he accepted that he had obtained the goods on credit and had made few payments. He asserted that throughout the period he had acted under duress. He had been approached first by an acquaintance when buying a television for himself, and asked what was needed to obtain credit. Thereafter two men had accosted him in a public house, and he had been threatened by them that he and his family would be petrol-bombed if he did not obtain goods for them. On each occasion he was told what goods the men required. He was told that if he went to the police his family would be attacked. He said that he had not told the police this in interview because he was worried about the possible repercussions.

Two psychologists were called, Ms Kingswood for the appellant and Dr Gudjonsson for the Crown. . . .

Before the jury, Ms Kingswood said that the appellant had an I.Q. of 68 and a reading age of a child of six years and eight months. His level of ability was in the lowest 2 per cent of the population. She found him abnormally suggestible. She said he was unlikely to have appreciated the significance of the questions put to him. She felt he was a 'vulnerable' individual.

Dr Gudjonsson did not accept these conclusions. He thought the appellant might be faking a poor result; he thought that the appellant's I.Q. was higher than 68.

The classic statement of the law is to be found in the judgment of the Court of Appeal in *Graham* (1982) 74 Cr App R 235. At pp. 240, 241 and p. 299 respectively, Lord Lane CJ, giving the judgment of the Court, quoted a passage from the Law Commission Report No. 83 on Defences of General Application at paragraph 2.28, which includes this passage:

> Whether the words 'in his situation' comprehend more than the surrounding circumstances, and extend to the characteristics of the defendant himself, it is difficult to say, and for that reason we would not recommend without qualification the adoption of that solution. We think that there should be an objective element in the requirements of the defence so that in the final event it will be for the jury to determine whether the threat was one which the defendant in question could not reasonably have been expected to resist. This

will allow the jury to take into account the nature of the offence committed, its relationship to the threats which the defendant believed to exist, the threats themselves and the circumstances in which they were made and the personal characteristics of the defendant. The last consideration is, we feel, a most important one. Threats directed against the weak, immature or disabled person, may well be much more compelling than the same threats directed against a normal healthy person.

As a matter of public policy, it seems to us essential to limit the defence of duress by means of an objective criterion formulated in terms of reasonableness. Consistency of approach in defences to criminal liability is obviously desirable. Provocation and duress are analogous. In provocation the words or actions of one person break the self-control of another. In duress the words or actions of one person break the will of another. The law requires a defendant to have the self-control reasonably to be expected of the ordinary citizen in his situation. It should likewise require him to have the steadfastness reasonably to be expected of the ordinary citizen in his situation. So too with self-defence, in which the law permits the use of no more force than is reasonable in the circumstances. And, in general, if a mistake is to excuse what would otherwise be criminal, the mistake must be a reasonable one.

It follows that we accept Mr Sherrard's submission that the direction in this case was too favourable to the appellant. The Crown having conceded that the issue of duress was open to the appellant and was raised on the evidence, the correct approach on the facts of this case would have been as follows: (1) Was the defendant, or may he have been, impelled to act as did because, as a result of what he reasonably believed King had said or done, he had good cause to fear that if he did not so act King would kill him or (if this is to be added) cause him serious physical injury? (2) If so, have the prosecution made the jury sure that a sober person of reasonable firmness, sharing the characteristics of the defendant, would not have responded to whatever he reasonably believed King said or did by taking part in the killing? The fact that a defendant's will to resist has been eroded by the voluntary consumption of drink or both is not relevant to this test.

This formulation was approved by the House of Lords in *R v Howe* (1987) 85 Cr App R 32 (see *per* Lord Mackay of Clashfern at pp. 65, 66).

But the question remains, what are the relevant characteristics of the accused to which the jury should have regard in considering the second objective test? This question had given rise to considerable difficulty in recent cases. It seems clear that age and sex are, and physical health or disability may be, relevant characteristics. But beyond that it is not altogether easy to determine from the authorities what others may be relevant.

. . .

What principles are to be derived from [the] authorities? We think they are as follows:

(1) The mere fact that the accused is more pliable, vulnerable, timid or susceptible to threats than a normal person are not characteristics with which it is legitimate to invest the reasonable/ordinary person for the purpose of considering the objective test.

(2) The defendant may be in a category of persons who the jury may think less able to resist pressure than people not within that category. Obvious examples are age, where a young person may well not be so robust as a mature one; possibly sex, though many woman would doubtless consider they had as much moral courage to resist pressure as men; pregnancy, where there is added fear for the unborn child; serious physical disability, which may inhibit self protection; recognised mental illness or psychiatric condition, such as post traumatic stress disorder leading to learned helplessness.

(3) Characteristics which may be relevant in considering provocation, because they relate to the nature of the provocation, itself will not necessarily be relevant in cases of duress. Thus homosexual-

ity may be relevant to provocation if the provocative words or conduct are related to this charac-teristic; it cannot be relevant in duress, since there is no reason to think that homosexuals are less robust in resisting threats of the kind that are relevant in duress cases.

(4) Characteristics due to self-induced abuse, such as alcohol, drugs or glue-sniffing, cannot be relevant.

(5) Psychiatric evidence may be admissible to show that the accused is suffering from some mental illness, mental impairment or recognised psychiatric condition provided persons generally suffering from such condition may be more susceptible to pressure and threats and thus to assist the jury in deciding whether a reasonable person suffering from such a condition might have been impelled to act as the defendant did. It is not admissible simply to show that in the doctor's opinion an accused, who is not suffering from such illness or condition, is especially timid, suggestible or vulnerable to pressure and threats. Nor is medical opinion admissible to bolster or support the credibility of the accused.

(6) Where counsel wishes to submit that the acccused has some characteristic which falls within (2) above, this must be made plain to the judge. The question may arise in relation to the admissibility of medical evidence of the nature set out in (5). If so, the judge will have to rule at that stage. There may, however, be no medical evidence or, as in this case, medical evidence may have been introduced for some other purpose, e.g. to challenge the admissibility or weight of a confession. In such a case counsel must raise the question before speeches in the absence of the jury, so that the judge can rule whether the alleged characteristic is capable of being relevant. If he rules that it is, then he must leave it to the jury.

(7) In the absence of some direction from the judge as to what characteristics are capable of being regarded as relevant, we think that the direction approved in *Graham* without more will not be as helpful as it might be, since the jury may be tempted, especially if there is evidence, as there was in this case, relating to suggestibility and vulnerability, to think that these are relevant. In most cases it is probably only the age and sex of the accused that is capable of being relevant. If so, the judge should, as he did in this case, confine the characteristics in question to these.

How are these principles to be applied in this case? Miss Levitt accepts, rightly in our opinion, that the evidence that the appellant was abnormally suggestible and a vulnerable individual is irrelevant. But she submits that the fact that he had, or may have had, a low I.Q. of 68 is relevant since it might inhibit his ability to seek the protection of the police. We do not agree. We do not see how low I.Q., short of mental impairment or mental defectiveness, can be said to be a characteristic that makes those who have it less courageous and less able to withstand threats and pressure. Moreover, we do not think that any such submission as is now made, based solely on the appellant's low I.Q., was ever advanced at the trial. Furthermore, it is to be noted that in two places – at pp. 14C-D and 42D-G – the judge told the jury that if they thought the appellant passed the subjective test they should acquit him. We are quite satisfied that in the circumstances of this case the judge's direction was sufficient. He directed the jury to consider the only two relevant characteristics, namely age and sex. It would not have assisted them and might well have confused them, if he had added, without qualification, that the person of reasonable firmness was one who shared the characteristics of the appellant.

NOTES AND QUESTIONS

1. The Court accepts that mental and psychiatric illness may be a relevant characteristic, but concludes that low intelligence is not. Does not this distinction put too great a premium on whether a psychologist testifies that a defendant suffered from mental retardation or was just not very intelligent? Likewise, should it matter whether an expert witness testifies that a mother, who had been abused by the father of her child and thus was afraid to prevent him killing the child, suffered from excessive timidity or the medical condition of 'dependent helplessness'? See *R v Emery (and Another)* (1993) 14 Cr App R (S) 394, and generally see

A. Buchanan and G. Vigo 'Duress and Mental Abnormality' [1999] Crim LR 517 and K. Smith 'Duress and Steadfastness: In pursuit of the unintelligible' [1999] Crim LR 363.

2. As the defences of duress, necessity and duress of circumstances are commonly said to be concessions to human frailty, why should the defendant's vulnerability and timidity not be proper factors to be taken into account?

3. In *R v Flatt* [1996] Crim LR 576, the Court of Appeal held that drug addiction is not a relevant characteristic. Is this because drug addiction is self-induced, or because it does not affect the addict's ability to resist committing a crime?

Related to the issue of whether a reasonable person of ordinary firmness would have resisted committing a crime is the question of alternative courses of action. If a defendant has a legal means to avoid the threatened harm, must he take that avenue, even if it entails some risks?

R v Gill

[1963] 2 All ER 688, Court of Criminal Appeal

EDMUND DAVIES J: . . . The appellant was charged at Bedford County Sessions and convicted of (i) conspiring with James Lockett and other persons unknown to steal a lorry and its load, and (ii) with larceny pursuant to that conspiracy. Against those convictions he now appeals by leave of the full court. The appellant, who was employed as a lorry-driver by A. E. Meeks, Ltd., himself testified that he was approached by a group of men (of whom his co-accused Lockett was not one) who suggested that he should steal a valuable load from his employers and hand it over to them in return for a payment of £1,000, and that he agreed to do this. It was arranged that he would leave the loaded lorry in a car-park in Bristol, that during his absence it would be driven away, and that he would then falsely report to the police that it had been stolen without his knowledge. On this evidence, the learned deputy-chairman rightly told the jury that the conspiracy charge was clearly established on the appellant's own testimony, and (subject to two matters later to be mentioned) no question now arises as to the correctness of that direction or of the conviction on that count. According to the appellant, however, although the lorry and its load were in fact later stolen by his fellow-conspirators, this was done not pursuant to the conspiracy to which he had been a party, but wholly against his will. He testified that he repented of the conspiracy the day after he entered into it, and that, when 'Reg' (one of his fellow-conspirators) and three others arrived at his home by arrangement to collect him for the purpose of the theft being effected, he told them that he was not going through with it. They thereupon threatened physical violence both to him and to his wife, one of them flourishing a crowbar and another showing him a bottle of petrol, and, in great fear for the safety of his wife and himself, he obeyed their orders to accompany them to his employers' premises. They dropped him outside, he went into the yard and then, still in fear, collected his lorry and drove it to a point on the M.1 near St. Albans, where he was forced by threats to leave the lorry. It was then promptly driven away and has never since been recovered. When later seen by the police, however, the appellant signed two statements in which he confessed that he had been a party to the larceny and made no mention of having been subjected to duress.

. . .

The third and most interesting point taken relates only to the larceny count, it being submitted that the learned deputy-chairman wrongly directed the jury that it was for the appellant to establish that he was acting under duress. The account given by the appellant himself makes it very doubtful whether such a defence was strictly open to him, inasmuch as there was a time after the alleged threats when, having been left outside his employers' yard and having then entered it, he could presumably have raised the alarm and so wrecked the whole criminal enterprise. In *M'Growther's*

Case (1746) Fost 13, Lee LCJ, directed the jury that, to establish a plea of duress, the defendant must have resisted or fled from the wrongdoer if that were possible. Seemingly, the position under American law is the same, as appears from the statement in *Professor Rollin Perkins Criminal Law* that, 'The excuse (of compulsion) is not available to someone who had an obviously safe avenue of escape before committing the prohibited act.'

The issue of duress was, nevertheless, left to the jury in the present case, and that may well have been the prudent course. Having been left, did the burden rest on the Crown conclusively to destroy this defence, in the same way as it is required to destroy such other defences as provocation or self-defence? Or was the appellant required to establish it, on the balance of probabilities? . . . The Crown are not called on to anticipate such a defence and destroy it in advance. The accused, either by the cross-examination of the prosecution witnesses or by evidence called on his behalf, or by a combination of the two, must place before the court such material as makes duress a live issue fit and proper to be left to the jury. But, once he has succeeded in doing this, it is then for the Crown to destroy that defence in such a manner as to leave in the jury's minds no reasonable doubt that the accused cannot be absolved on the grounds of the alleged compulsion. . . .

R v Hudson and Taylor
[1971] 2 QB 202, Court of Appeal

For the facts, see p. 485.

LORD PARKER CJ: . . . Mr Franks, however contends that the recorder's ruling can be supported on another ground, namely, that the appellants should have taken steps to neutralise the threats by seeking police protection either when they came to court to give evidence, or beforehand. He submits on grounds of public policy that an accused should not be able to plead duress if he had the opportunity to ask for protection from the police before committing the offence and failed to do so. The argument does not distinguish cases in which the police would be able to provide effective protection, from those when they would not, and it would, in effect, restrict the defence of duress to cases where the person threatened had been kept in custody by the maker of the threats, or where the time interval between the making of the threats and the commission of the offence had made recourse to the police impossible. We recognise the need to keep the defence of duress within reasonable bounds but cannot accept so severe a restriction upon it. The duty, of the person threatened, to take steps to remove the threat does not seem to have arisen in an English case but, in a full review of the defence of duress in the Supreme Court of Victoria (*R v Hurley and Murray* [1967] VR 526), a condition of raising the defence was said to be that the accused 'had no means, with safety to himself, of preventing the execution of the threat.'

In the opinion of this court it is always open to the Crown to prove that the accused failed to avail himself of some opportunity which was reasonably open to him to render the threat ineffective, and that upon this being established the threat in question can no longer be relied upon by the defence. In deciding whether such an opportunity was reasonably open to the accused the jury should have regard to his age and circumstances, and to any risks to him which may be involved in the course of action relied upon. . . .

NOTES AND QUESTIONS
1. Are *Gill* and *Hudson and Taylor* reconcilable?
2. The alternative course of action most often suggested is for the defendant to notify the police. If one under duress fails to do so when presented with the opportunity, then the defence may be lost. The problem is that the police often will not intervene until a crime has been committed or is about to be committed. Nor is notification of the police seen as an attractive alternative when the person threatened is a close relative. Why? Should the courts treat this case differently?

3. How speedily must one notify the police in order not to lose one's defence? See *R. v Pommell* (1995) 2 CR App R 607 (for facts and holding, see p. 501).

(iii)

Discussing the defence of necessity, we noted that there was some question as to whether the defence actually existed. In many ways the issue has become moot. Beginning in the mid-1980s, the courts began to develop the independent defence of duress of circumstances. This differs from the traditional defence of duress in the following respect. In the protypical case of duress the defendant is ordered to commit a crime by a third party, who threatens him with death or serious injury if he does not comply. If there is no direct command to commit a crime, or indeed if the threatener does not specify the crime to be committed, a defence of duress will not succeed (see *R v Cole* [1994] Crim LR 582). In contrast, duress of circumstances is not dependent upon the defendant being ordered to commit a crime. As in necessity, the defendant commits the offence because of the pressure of outside circumstances. Unlike in necessity, however, the pressure comes not from natural events, but from a human source (or perhaps a combination of human and natural sources).

R v Martin
[1989] 1 All ER 652, Court of Appeal

SIMON BROWN LJ: . . .

The circumstances which the appellant desired to advance by way of defence of necessity were essentially these. His wife has suicidal tendencies. On a number of occasions before the day in question she had attempted to take her own life. On the day in question her son, the appellant's stepson, had overslept. He had done so to the extent that he was bound to be late for work and at risk of losing his job unless, so it was asserted, the appellant drove him to work. The appellant's wife was distraught. She was shouting, screaming, banging her head against a wall. More particularly, it is said she was threatening suicide unless the appellant drove the boy to work.

The defence had a statement from a doctor which expressed the opinion that 'in view of her mental condition it is likely that Mrs Martin would have attempted suicide if her husband did not drive her son to work'.

The appellant's case on the facts was that he genuinely, and he would suggest reasonably, believed that his wife would carry out that threat unless he did as she demanded. Despite his disqualification he therefore drove the boy. He was in fact apprehended by the police within about a quarter of a mile of the house.

Sceptically though one may regard that defence on the facts (and there were, we would observe, striking difficulties about the detailed evidence when it came finally to be given before the judge in mitigation), the sole question before this court is whether those facts, had the jury accepted they were or might be true, amounted in law to a defence. If they did, then the appellant was entitled to a trial of the issue before the jury. The jury would of course have had to be directed properly on the precise scope and nature of the defence, but the decision on the facts would have been for them. As it was, such a defence was pre-empted by the ruling. Should it have been?

In our judgment the answer is plainly not. The authorities are now clear. Their effect is perhaps most conveniently to be found in the judgment of this court in *R v Conway* [1988] 3 All ER 1025. The decision reviews earlier relevant authorities.

The principles may be summarised thus: first, English law does, in extreme circumstances, recognise a defence of necessity. Most commonly this defence arises as duress, that is pressure on the accused's will from the wrongful threats or violence of another. Equally however it can arise from other objective dangers threatening the accused or others. Arising thus it is conveniently called 'duress of circumstances'.

Second, the defence is available only if, from an objective standpoint, the accused can be said to be acting reasonably and proportionately in order to avoid a threat of death or serious injury.

Third, assuming the defence to be open to the accused on his account of the facts, the issue should be left to the jury, who should be directed to determine these two questions: first, was the accused, or may he have been, impelled to act as he did because as a result of what he reasonably believed to be the situation he had good cause to fear that otherwise death or serious physical injury would result; second, if so, would a sober person of reasonable firmness, sharing the characteristics of the accused, have responded to that situation by acting as the accused acted? If the answer to both those questions was Yes, then the jury would acquit; the defence of necessity would have been established.

That the defence is available in cases of reckless driving is established by *R v Conway* itself and indeed by an earlier decision of the court in *R v Willer* (1986) 83 Cr App R 225. *R v Conway* is authority also for the proposition that the scope of the defence is no wider for reckless driving than for other serious offences. As was pointed out in the judgment, 'reckless driving can kill' (see [1988] 3 All ER 1025 at 1029).

We see no material distinction between offences of reckless driving and driving whilst disqualified so far as the application and scope of this defence is concerned. Equally we can see no distinction in principle between various threats of death; it matters not whether the risk of death is by murder or by suicide or indeed by accident. One can illustrate the latter by considering a disqualified driver being driven by his wife, she suffering a heart attack in remote countryside and he needing instantly to get her to hospital.

It follows from this that the judge quite clearly did come to a wrong decision on the question of law, and the appellant should have been permitted to raise this defence for what it was worth before the jury.

It is in our judgment a great pity that that course was not taken. It is difficult to believe that any jury would have swallowed the improbable story which this appellant desired to advance. There was, it emerged when evidence was given in mitigation, in the house at the time a brother of the boy who was late for work, who was licensed to drive, and available to do so; the suggestion was that he would not take his brother because of 'a lot of aggravation in the house between them'. It is a further striking fact that when apprehended by the police this appellant was wholly silent as to why on this occasion he had felt constrained to drive. But those considerations, in our judgment, were essentially for the jury, and we have concluded, although not without hesitation, that it would be inappropriate here to apply the proviso to s. 2(1) of the 1968 Act.

In the result this appeal must be allowed and the conviction quashed.

NOTES AND QUESTIONS

1. Is *Martin* a case of necessity, ordinary duress (the wife's threat to kill herself if the defendant did not commit the crime) or duress of circumstances? Does it matter? In *R v Backshall* [1998] 1 WLR 1506 the Court of Appeal followed *Martin* and extended the defence to a charge of careless driving where the defendant was in fear because of a 'road rage' incident. But in *R v Rodger and Rose* [1998] 1 Cr App R 143 the court refused to extend it to prisoners who sought to justify escaping from prison by pleading the pressure caused by their suicidal tendencies.

2. The first of the duress of circumstances cases was *R v Willer* (1986) 83 Cr App R 225 (see below). It was followed in *R v Conway* [1988] 3 All ER 1925. Both involved charges of reckless driving.

R v Willer

[1987] RTR 22, Court of Appeal

WATKINS LJ: The appellant is 19 years of age. He is of excellent character. He appeals against his conviction for reckless driving.

What happened to bring him to conviction was that at about 9.30 p.m. on 24 April 1984 he and two school friends, Martin and Richard Jordan, were driving around the town of Hemel Hempstead in the appellant's Vauxhall Cavalier car. They heard a broadcast on the car's, what is known as, Citizen Band radio. From what they heard, the appellant was persuaded to drive to a shopping precinct at Leverstock Green. There they expected to meet another enthusiast of Citizen Band radio. At one stage of the journey the appellant had to drive up a very narrow turning off a road called Green Lane in order to keep his assignment with the other enthusiast mentioned. As he made his way up what is called Leaside, which is, as we see from the photographs, an alleyway, he was suddenly confronted with a gang of shouting and bawling youths, 20 to 30 strong. He heard one of them shouting: 'I'll kill you Willer' – and – 'I'll kill you Jordan'.

He stopped and tried to turn the car round. These youths surrounded him. They banged on the car. A youth called Smallpiece opened the rear door of the car and dived upon Richard Jordan who was sitting in the back of it. Martin Jordan, his brother, got out of the front seat to help. The appellant realised that the only conceivable way he could somehow escape from this formidable gang of youths, who were obviously bent upon doing further violence, was to mount the pavement on the right-hand side of Leaside and on the pavement to drive through a small gap into the front of the shopping precinct. That he did quite slowly, it was accepted, at about 10 mph.

Having gained the security, if that was what it could be called, of the front of the shopping precinct and moved somewhere in the vicinity of a car park which was there, he realised that he had lost one of his companions. So he turned the car round and drove very slowly, at five mph, back towards the gap and through it. He had to make a couple of turns in his search for his missing companion. All this time Smallpiece was in the back of the car fighting with Richard Jordan. With that going on the appellant drove to the local police station and reported the matter. For his pains he was prosecuted – a very surprising turn of events indeed.

He was charged with reckless driving. Very properly, so it seems to us, he chose trial by jury. He appeared at the Crown Court of St Albans on 16 April 1985. The trial was presided over by Mr Curwen, an assistant recorder. During the course of the trial an argument developed between the assistant recorder and counsel over the question whether or not the defence of necessity was available to the appellant. The assistant recorder ruled that it was not. . . .

. . . The appellant in fact said: 'I could do no other in the face of this hostility than to take the right turn as I did, to mount the pavement and to drive through the gap out of further harm's way – harm to person and harm to my property'. Thus the defence of duress, it seems to us, arose but was not pursued. What ought to have happened here, therefore, was that the assistant recorder on those facts should have directed that he would leave to the jury the question whether or not on the outward or the return journey, or both, the appellant was wholly driven by force of circumstances into doing what he did and did not drive the car otherwise than under that form of compulsion.

NOTES AND QUESTIONS

1. The defendant in *Willer* took it upon himself to violate the law because of his perceived fear that to do otherwise would have resulted in serious bodily harm. Should it matter whether his judgment was correct? Reasonable?

2. Is one justified in speeding on a deserted road in order not to be late for an important appointment? Does it matter how 'important' the appointment is? Why one is late?

What, if any, are the limitations on the defence of duress of circumstances?

Director of Public Prosecutions v Lorraine Tomkinson (2001)

[2001] EWHC Admin 182, DC (Latham LJ, Potts J) 16/2/2001

The Director of Public Prosecutions ('DPP') appealed by the way of case stated against a decision by magistrates to dismiss an information laid against the respondent ('D'), which alleged an offence of driving a motor vehicle having consumed excess alcohol contrary to s.5 *Road Traffic Act 1988*. D had been physically attacked by her husband in the marital home, who then left her alone, injured. Before leaving, D's husband destroyed the telephones in the house, warning her not to be at home when he returned. D did not know anyone in the area. Since she was frightened for her life a distance of 72 miles to her former home town. The magistrates accepted D's plea of necessity by way of duress of circumstances. The DPP submitted that: (i) there was no credible evidence to support the defence of duress; and (ii) had such evidence existed, it was no longer available by the time of D's arrest.

HELD: This case was distinguished from Director of Public Prosecutions v Bell (1992) RTR 334, where the defendant had escaped his terror of serious physical harm by driving, despite having been drinking all the evening. However, there was no evidence that he had driven further than necessary. In the present case, D had driven further than had been necessary to escape the danger she had sought to avoid. The facts of this case had more in common with those of Director of Public Prosecutions v Jones (1990) RTR 33, where the defendant drove further than was necessary and the Court of Appeal held that the defendant could not rely on the defence of duress. Therefore, the magistrates had not been correct in concluding that the defence of duress was available to D.

Appeal allowed.

R v Pommell

(1995) 2 Cr App R 607, Court of Appeal

KENNEDY LJ: . . . On October 27, 1993 the appellant appeared before the Crown Court at Woolwich charged on two indictments. The first indictment alleged in Count 1 that on June 4, 1993 he had, without authority, in his possession a firearm, namely a sub-machine gun, contrary to section 5(1)(a) of the Firearms Act 1968. The second count alleged that on the same date he had possession of 55 rounds of ammunition without a firearm certificate, contrary to section 1(1)(b) of the same Act. In the second indictment there was one count. It alleged that on the same date he had possession of counterfeit currency notes. To that second indictment he pleaded guilty, and no issue now arises in relation to it. However, so far as the first indictment is concerned, the trial judge indicated at the outset of the proceedings his view that the defence which it was proposed to advance would not amount to a defence in law. Having heard submissions he so ruled, and the appellant then, on re-arraignment, entered pleas of guilty to both counts. As to those counts he now appeals against conviction by leave of the full court.

. . . [T]he prosecution case was that at about 8 a.m. on June 4, 1993 police officers entered the appellant's home to execute a search warrant. He was found lying in bed with a loaded gun in his right hand. He was asked if the gun was his and he replied, 'I took it off a geezer who was going to do some people some damage with it'. In the same bedroom police officers found a brown holdall containing ammunition. The appellant was arrested and interviewed. When interviewed he was asked to explain his possession of the gun, and he said:

> Last night someone come round to see me, this guy by the name of Erroll, and he had it with him with the intention to go and shoot some people because they had killed his friend and he wanted to kill their girlfriends and relatives and kids, and I persuaded him, I took it off him and told him that it's not right to do that.

The appellant went on to say that Erroll had called between 12.30 a.m. and 1 a.m. and, after he left, the appellant took the gun upstairs and kept it from his girlfriend and took the bullets out of it. He appears to have achieved this by removing a loaded magazine containing 23 rounds. He then decided to wait until morning and decided to put the bullets back into it. To do this he must have inserted the loaded magazine back into the gun. He agreed that at the time of his arrest he was lying in bed with the gun against his leg because, he said, he did not want his girlfriend to see it. He said that he was going to hand the gun to his brother so that he could hand it to the police because his brother gets on with the police and had handed in guns in the past. For present purposes, it is unnecessary to look at the interview in any greater detail.

We turn now to the events of October 27, 1993. In the course of an *ex parte* application as to discovery, prosecuting counsel advised the judge that the defence was going to be that the defendant had the weapon in his possession, holding it for another, so that the defence might be described as a defence of necessity . . ..

That brings us to the central question of whether on the facts, as they emerged from the prosecution papers, the judge was entitled to conclude that as a matter of law the defence of necessity could not be established.

The two provisions of the Firearms Act 1968 with which we are concerned in this case, so far as they are material, read as follows:

Section 1 (1) . . . it is an offence for a person—. . .

(b) to have in his possession . . . any ammunition to which this section applies without holding a firearm certificate in force at the time, . . .

Section 5(1) A person commits an offence if, without the authority of the Defence Council, he has in his possession, . . .

(a) any firearm which is so designed or adapted that two or more missiles can be successively discharged without repeated pressure on the trigger, . . .

We accept that the provisions of the Firearms Act are intended to be strictly enforced. . . .

. . . There is an obvious attraction in the argument that if A finds B in possession of a gun which he is about to use to commit a crime, and if A is then able to persuade B to hand over the gun so that A may hand it to the police, A should not immediately upon taking possession of the gun become guilty of a criminal offence. . . .

The strength of the argument that a person ought to be permitted to breach the letter of the criminal law in order to prevent a greater evil befalling himself or others has long been recognised (see, for example, *Stephen's Digest of Criminal Law*), but it has, in English law, not given rise to a recognised general defence of necessity . . . As Dickson J said in the Supreme Court of Canada in *Perka et al v R* (1985) 13 DLR (4th) 1, at p. 14:

'. . . no system of positive law can recognise any principle which would entitle a person to violate the law because on his view the law conflicted with some higher social value'. The Criminal Code his specified a number of identifiable situations in which an actor is justified in committing what would otherwise be a criminal offence. To go beyond that and hold that ostensibly illegal acts can be validated on the basis of their expediency, would import an undue subjectivity into the criminal law. It would invite the courts to second-guess the legislature and to assess the relative merits of social policies underlying criminal prohibitions.

However, that does not really deal with the situation where someone commendably infringes a regulation in order to prevent another person from committing what everyone would accept as being a greater evil with a gun. In that situation it cannot be satisfactory to leave it to the prosecuting authority not to prosecute, or to individual courts to grant an absolute discharge. The authority may, as in the present case, prosecute because it is not satisfied that the defendant is telling the truth, and then, even if he is vindicated and given an absolute discharge, he is left with a criminal conviction which, for some purposes, would be recognised as such.

It was, as it seems to us, to meet this difficulty that the limited defence of duress of circumstances has been developed in English law in relation to road traffic offences. It was first recognised in *R v Willer* (1986) 83 Cr App R 225, where the accused drove onto a pavement and in and out of a shopping centre in order to escape a gang of youths seeking to attack him and his passenger. *Willer* was followed and applied in *R v Conway* (1989) 88 Cr App R 159, in which the Court of Appeal quashed a conviction on a charge of reckless driving. Having considered existing authorities, textbooks and the proposals of the Law Commission, the Court in that case said at p. 164:

> . . . it is still not clear whether there is a general defence of necessity or, if there is, what are the circumstances in which it is available.

In our judgment, that is still the position, but the Court in *Conway* went on to say that necessity can be a defence to a charge of reckless driving where the facts establish duress of circumstances, that is to say when the defendant is constrained to drive as he did to avoid death or serious bodily harm to himself or some other person.

Then came *Martin*, a decision to which we referred earlier in this judgment, and *DPP v Bell* [1992] RTR 335, where the defendant, whose alcohol level was over the prescribed limit, was pursued to his car and, fearing serious injury, drove some distance down the road. The Crown Court allowed his appeal on the basis of duress of circumstances, and an appeal by way of case stated was dismissed. The Divisional Court particularly noted the finding of fact that the appellant drove only some distance down the road and not, for example, all the way home, so that the defence of duress of circumstances continued to avail him. In *DPP v Jones* [1990] RTR 33, it was held that any defence of necessity available to a driver would cease to be available if he drove for a longer period than necessary. Commenting on the case of *Bell*, Professor Sir John Smith has written:

> All the cases so far have concerned road traffic offences but there are no grounds for supposing that the defence is limited to that kind of case. On the contrary, the defence, being closely related to the defence of duress by threats, appears to be general, applying to all crimes except murder, attempted murder and some forms of treason, . . .': see [1992] Crim LR 176.

We agree.

7. Conclusion

That leads to the conclusion that in the present case the defence was open to the appellant in respect of his acquisition of the gun. The jury would have to be directed to determine the two questions identified in the passage which we have cited from the judgment in *Martin*. That leaves the question as to his continued possession of the gun thereafter. In our judgment, the test laid down in *Martin* is not necessarily the appropriate test for determining whether a person continues to have a defence available to him. For example, a person takes a gun off another in the circumstances in which this appellant says he did and then locks it away in a safe with a view to safeguarding it while the police are informed. When the gun is in the safe, the test laid down in *Martin* may not be satisfied: there would then be no immediate fear of death or serious injury. In our judgment, a person who has taken possession of a gun in circumstances where he has the defence of duress by circumstances must 'desist from committing the crime as soon as he reasonably can' . . .

. . . Can it be said, in this case, that there was no evidence upon which a jury could have reached the conclusion that the appellant did desist, or may have desisted, as soon as he reasonably could? In answering this question, the jury would have to have regard to the delay that had occurred between, on the appellant's account, his acquisition of the gun and ammunition at 12.30 to 1 a.m., and the arrival of the police some hours later. The appellant has offered an explanation for that delay, but, as it seems to us, the defence of duress of circumstances could not avail him once a reasonable person in his position would have known that the duress, in this case the need to obtain and retain the firearm, had ceased. In the present case the judge said that the failure of the appellant to go immediately to the police 'robs him of a defence'. We accept that in some cases a delay, especially if unexplained, may be such as to make it clear that any duress must have ceased to operate, in which case the judge would be entitled to conclude that even on the defendant's own account of the facts, the defence was not open to him. There would then be no reason to leave the issue to the jury. However, the situation does not seem to us to have been sufficiently clear cut to make that an appropriate step in the present case. In the first place, the delay of a few hours overnight might not be regarded as being unduly long and, secondly, the defendant did offer an explanation for it, therefore, in our judgment, the proposed defence should have been left to the jury.

We have considered whether the reloading of the gun and the fact that the appellant had the gun in his bed deprived him of the defence. Must a person who has acquired a gun in circumstances in which he has the defence of duress of circumstances not only desist from committing the offence as soon as he reasonably can but, in the meanwhile, act in a reasonable manner with the gun? The answer is that if he does not do so, it will be difficult for the court to accept that he desisted from committing the offence as soon as he reasonably could. Therefore, in our judgment, the acts of reloading and putting the gun in the bed do not of themselves deprive him of the defence, but are matters which may be taken into account by the jury in deciding the issues to which we have already made reference.

B: Private defence and prevention of crime

As a practical matter, one who is forcefully attacked by another will instinctively resort to self-defensive actions. The law gives recognition to this reaction by allowing the defender in such circumstances a defence to criminal charges.

So too if one acts not from selfish but from altruistic motives and goes to the aid of another in trouble. Many believe that the law should encourage citizens to help one another. To deny a defence in this situation would be a positive discouragement. A further point is that the fact that the law is prepared to allow force in response to an attack may deter would-be attackers. Nonetheless, the law proceeds cautiously, not wanting to appear to give license to vigilantes.

Self-defence and defence of another are similar to duress, necessity and duress of circumstances in many respects. All are affirmative defences which do not come into play until the prosecution have established the elements of the crime. None of the defences is aimed at negating *mens rea* or any other element of the crime (although there are some theorists who argue that absence of excuse or justification is part of *actus reus*). All are all-or-nothing defences in the sense that they either succeed or fail, but do not serve as a basis for reducing the seriousness of the crime, as does provocation. The defendant pleading one of these defences, like the defendant pleading duress, necessity or duress of circumstances, has been caught in a choice of evils situation. Either the person must commit a crime, most often assault or homicide, or submit to a harm being inflicted upon himself or another.

Self-defence and defence of another are, on the other hand, distinguishable from duress, necessity and duress of circumstances in that they are deemed to justify the defendant's actions, not simply to excuse them. Partly for this reason some of the limitations which have evolved in respect of the former have not been extended to self-defence and defence of another. One can raise self-defence or defence of another as a defence to murder. Nor does one have to be defending against death or serious bodily harm to invoke these defences.

(i) *Crime prevention*

Force used in self-defence or defence of another is usually directed against an assailant who is attempting an unlawful attack. This suggests that these defences will often overlap with two others – prevention of crime and the making of a lawful arrest. Interestingly, while defence of another and self-defence have not been codified in statute, and continue to have their development shaped by common law principles, the common law rules regarding lawful arrest and crime prevention have been replaced by statute.

Criminal Law Act 1967

3.—(1) A person may use such force as is reasonable in the circumstances in the prevention of crime, or in effecting or assisting in the lawful arrest of offenders or suspected offenders or of persons unlawfully at large.

(2) Subsection (1) above shall replace the rules of the common law on the question when force used for a purpose mentioned in the subsection is justified by that purpose.

NOTES AND QUESTIONS
1. Which defence controls in those situations where the defendant uses force both in self-defence and to prevent the commission of a crime? Can a defendant plead both, or must the defendant choose? See *R* v *Cousins* [1982] QB 526.
2. In cases where the assailant has not in fact committed a crime, the defendant will be restricted to claiming self-defence or defence of another. This is not necessarily fatal, however, as these defences may be available even though the attack which the defendant sought to repel was not unlawful. See, *Williams (Gladstone)*, above.

(ii) *Elements of the defences*

The critical words in s. 3(1) of the Criminal Law Act 1967, and the core concepts around which revolve the defences of self-defence and defence of another, are force that is 'reasonable in the circumstances'. This is a question of fact for the jury.

Reasonable force may be used in self-defence, defence of another, crime prevention and lawful arrest. In *Re A* (Conjoined Twins: Medical Treatment) [2001] 1 FLR 1 (for facts and holding, see p. 473) Ward, LJ described Mary as an 'innocent' aggressor who threatened the life of her conjoined twin, Jodie. Is this an appropriate case for invoking the doctrine of defence of another? What does it mean to be an aggressor? Would causing Mary's death be 'reasonable force' *in the circumstances*? Who judges what constitutes reasonable force?

R v *Williams (Gladstone)*
(1983) 78 Cr App R 276, Court of Appeal

For facts and holding, see pp. 445.

R v Dadson
(1881) 3 Car & Kerr 148, Kent Assizes

A, a constable employed to guard a copse from which wood had been stolen, saw B come from it, who, on being called to stop, ran away, and A, having no other means of apprehending B fired at and wounded him. B had just before committed a felony in the copse, but A did not know it. A was convicted of having feloniously wounded B.

ERLE J: It appeared that the prisoner, being a constable, was employed to guard a copse from which wood had been stolen, and for this purpose carried a loaded gun. From this copse he saw the prosecutor come out, carrying wood, which he was stealing, and called him to stop. The prosecutor ran away, and the prisoner having no other means of bringing him to justice fired, and wounded him in the leg. These were the facts on which the prisoner acted, but it was alleged in addition that Waters was actually committing a felony, he having been before convicted repeatedly of stealing wood; but these convictions were unknown to the prisoner, nor was there any reason for supposing that he knew the difference between the rules of law relating to felony and those relating to less offences.

I told the jury that this shooting by the prisoner with intent to do grievous bodily harm amounted to the felony charged, unless from other facts there was a justification, and that neither the belief of the prisoner that it was his duty to fire if he could not otherwise apprehend the prosecutor, nor the alleged felony, it being unknown to him, constituted such justification.

The jury found the prisoner guilty of the felony.

QUESTIONS

1. Why should unknown circumstances of justification not be a defence? The *Dadson* rule has been heavily criticised in the literature. Nonetheless, it was affirmed in *Chapman* v *DPP* [1988] Crim LR 843.

2. Why should the law allow an accused a defence when he is incorrect in his assumptions about the need for force? Will this not encourage intervention without adequate investigation of the circumstances? In both *Dadson* and *Williams (Gladstone)*, the views of the reasonable person were seemingly disregarded. Why?

(iii) *The need to employ force (the necessity prong)*

If an attack is not threatened until some future time, can it be said that any force is necessary beforehand? The use of a preemptive strike is obviously more difficult to justify than force used during an actual attack. Indeed, it is often said that one who acts in self-defence or defence of another must be faced with an immediate or imminent threat of harm. But is an absolutist approach appropriate? Desirable? Consider the following case:

Devlin v Armstrong
[1971] NILR 13, Court of Appeal

After serious disturbances in the City of Londonderry the appellant was charged with and convicted of four offences of riotous behaviour and incitement to riotous behaviour in Londonderry on 13 August 1969, and she was sentenced to six months' imprisonment. The facts found by the resident magistrate showed that on different occasions on 13 August the appellant had exhorted a crowd of people who had been stoning the police to build a barricade to keep the police out of an area known as the Bogside, to man the barricades and to fight the police with petrol bombs, and that the appellant had herself thrown a stone towards the police. The defence was one of justification, it being submitted that the appellant did the acts complained of because she honestly and reason-ably believed that the police were about to behave unlawfully in assaulting people and damaging property in the Bogside, though it was not suggested that there had in fact been any unlawful conduct on the part of any of the police.

Held by the Court of Appeal that, if it be assumed that the appellant did honestly and reasonably believe that the police were about to behave unlawfully in the ways mentioned, such belief did not afford a defence to the charges against her in that: (i) it was one of the common purposes of the appellant and the persons incited to exclude the police from the Bogside by force; (ii) the danger which the appellant was alleged to have anticipated was not sufficiently specific or imminent to justify her actions; and since the police were at the time engaged in containing a riot in the course of their duty, the interventions of the appellant were too aggressive and premature to rank as justifiable efforts to prevent the prospective danger of the police getting out of hand and behaving unlawfully; (iii) the force used by the appellant, assuming it to have been in the exercise of a right of self-defence or of a statutory right to prevent crime, was so excessive as to be unwarrantable; (iv) as regards the charges of incitement, there was no evidence or finding to show that those who were exhorted by the appellant to riot were actuated by an honest and reasonable apprehension of unlawful violence on behalf of the police such as the appellant is assumed to have had. Her incitements were therefore directed to encourage others to do what for them was prima facie unlawful; (v) while it might be that in a case of extreme necessity where the forces of law are absent or have ceased to act as such, individuals could be justified in doing acts which would otherwise be unlawful, the right to do such acts could not justify action directed against a lawfully constituted constabulary while acting as such in the exercise of its proper functions; (vi) there was no sufficient relationship between the appellant and the people of the Bogside to justify her acting in their defence or exercising a right of self-defence on their behalf; (vii) the common law duty imposed on all citizens to help in the suppression of riots and assist the constabulary in so doing made it impossible for the appellant to justify her conduct in encouraging the rioters as she did.

NOTES AND QUESTIONS
1. In *Beckford* v *R* [1988] 1 AC 130, a case decided by the Privy Council, Lord Griffiths, speaking for their Lordships, said *obiter* (at p. 144): '[A] man about to be attacked does not have to wait for his assailant to strike the first blow or fire the first shot; circumstances may justify a pre-emptive strike.' How close should an attack have to be before one should be allowed to engage in a preemptive strike?
2. The argument against preemptive action is that when the attack is not threatened until the future, there is time to take other action, such as notifying the police. The police, however, may not be able to provide effective protection. Reconsider in this context *Hudson and Taylor*, above.
3. If a preemptive strike is permitted, does it follow that one can justify reasonable but illegal preparatory actions, such as arming oneself, in anticipation of the expected attack, if these preparatory actions would otherwise themselves be criminal? See *Attorney-General's Reference (No. 2 of 1983)* [1984] QB 456.

Another troublesome issue relating to the necessity prong is whether any force is necessary when one who is attacked can, by retreating, avoid the need for force. Should there be a duty to retreat, when retreat can be safely accomplished, before resort to force? Does the law make cowards of us all, or simply demand that we behave in a prudent manner?

R v Bird

[1985] 1 WLR 816, Court of Appeal

LORD LANE CJ: . . . On 24 January 1985 in the Crown Court at Chelmsford, the appellant, as she now is, this court having given her leave to appeal against conviction, was convicted after a re-trial of unlawful wounding under section 20 of the Offences against the Person Act 1861, and she was sentenced to nine months' youth custody.

The facts of the case are these. On 10 March 1984 the appellant, Debbie Bird, was celebrating her seventeenth birthday. There was a party at a house in Harlow. Unhappily it was at that party that the events occurred which ended with her being sent to youth custody. There was a guest at the party called Darren Marder, who was to be the victim of the events which occurred thereafter. He and the appellant had been friendly and had been going out together between about January and the middle of 1983. That close friendship had come to an end, but Marder arrived at the party with his new girl friend and, for reasons which it is not necessary to explore, an argument broke out. After a great deal of bad language and shouting, the appellant told Marder to leave, and leave he did. A little later he unwisely came back and a second argument took place together with a second exchange of obscenities between the two of them. What happened thereafter was the subject of dispute between the parties, though not so much dispute as often arises in these sudden events. The appellant poured a glassful of Pernod over Marder, and he retaliated by slapping her around the face. Further incidents of physical force took place between them. The appellant said that the time came when she was being held and held up against a wall, at which point she lunged at Marder with her hand, which was the hand, unhappily, which held the Pernod glass. The glass hit him in the face, broke, and his eye as a result was lost. It was a horrible event in the upshot, but of course she would not realise the extent to which she was going to cause injury to this young man.

The prosecution case was this, that Marder only slapped the appellant once and that was in order to calm her down, the commonly believed remedy for hysterics. The jury were accordingly invited to infer from that that she could not possibly have been acting in reasonable self-defence when she retaliated against that slap with a weapon as grave as a glass. Secondly, there was evidence of Marder, and also a Miss Bryant, who was his new girl friend, that so far from showing remorse after the event, the appellant said that she would do it again if the same situation arose. Thirdly, there was the evidence of Mrs Sharpe, who was the owner of the house where the party was taking place, who said that after the incident the appellant had admitted to her, Mrs Sharpe, that she had slashed Marder in the face with a glass after he had punched her.

The appellant herself was interviewed by the police. She said that it was only afterwards that she realised that a glass was in her hand, the hand with which she struck the appellant. The appellant gave evidence. She insisted that she had been acting in self-defence. She was being pushed. Marder had said to her that he would hit her if she did not shut up. He slapped her in the face, she was being held by him and thought the only thing for her to do was to strike back to defend herself. In the agony of the moment, so to speak, she did not realise that she was holding the glass. These are the comparatively simple facts of the case.

The grounds of appeal are these. First of all, the judge was in error in directing the jury that before the appellant could rely upon a plea of self-defence, it was necessary that she should have demonstrated by her action that she did not want to fight. That really is the essence of the appellant's case put forward by Mr Pavry to this court in what, if we may say so, was a most helpful argument.

The relevant passages in the summing up are these – first, towards the beginning of the direction to the jury:

> You cannot wrap up an attack in the cloak of self-defence and it is necessary that a person claiming to exercise a right of self-defence should demonstrate by her action that she does not want to fight. At one time it was thought that in order to demonstrate that, that the

person seeking to raise a question of self-defence had to retreat. That is not so any longer at all, but there is an obligation to see whether the person claiming to exercise the right of self-defence should have demonstrated that she does not want to fight at all.

Towards the end of the summing up the judge used these words:

> You will have to consider whether in the circumstances of this case self-defence has any application at all. Does it look to you that this lady, who was behaving in this fashion, had demonstrated that she did not want to fight, was the use of the glass with a hard blow which broke it, reasonable in the circumstances? All these are matters for you and not for me.

The court in *R* v *Julien* [1969] 1 WLR 839 was anxious to make it clear that there was no duty, despite earlier authorities to the contrary, actually to turn round or walk away from the scene. But reading the words which were used in that judgement, it now seems to us that they placed too great an obligation upon a defendant in circumstances such as those in the instant case, an obligation which is not reflected in the speeches in *Palmer* v *The Queen* [1971] AC 814.

The matter is dealt with accurately and helpfully in *Smith and Hogan Criminal Law*, 5th ed. (1983), p. 327:

> There were formerly technical rules about the duty to retreat before using force, or at least fatal force. This is now simply a factor to be taken into account in deciding whether it was necessary to use force, and whether the force was reasonable. If the only reasonable course is to retreat, then it would appear that to stand and fight must be to use unreasonable force. There is, however, no rule of law that a person attacked is bound to run away if he can but it has been said that – '. . . what is necessary is that he should demonstrate by his actions that he does not want to fight. He must demonstrate that he is prepared to temporise and disengage and perhaps to make some physical withdrawal.' [*R* v *Julien* [1969] 1 WLR 839, 842]. It is submitted that it goes too far to say that action of this kind is *necessary*. It is scarcely consistent with the rule that it is permissible to use force, not merely to counter an actual attack, but to ward off an attack honestly and reasonably believed to be imminent. A demonstration by [the defendant] at the time that he did not want to fight is, no doubt, the best evidence that he was acting reasonably and in good faith in self-defence; but it is no more than that. A person may in some circumstances so act without temporising, disengaging or withdrawing; and he should have a good defence.

We respectfully agree with that passage. If the defendant is proved to have been attacking or retaliating or revenging himself, then he was not truly acting in self-defence. Evidence that the defendant tried to retreat or tried to call off the fight may be a cast-iron method of casting doubt on the suggestion that he was the attacker or retaliator or the person trying to revenge himself. But it is not by any means the only method of doing that.

It seems to us therefore that in this case the judge – we hasten to add through no fault of his own – by using the word 'necessary' as he did in the passages in the summing up to which we have referred, put too high an obligation upon the appellant.

NOTES AND QUESTIONS

1. What are the pros and cons of a retreat rule?
2. Is part of the reluctance to impose a retreat rule the difficulty of making a defendant who is faced with an attack guess at his peril whether as a matter of law he has to retreat? Is it 'reasonable' to expect one who is attacked to make such a calculation? United States Supreme Court Justice Oliver Wendell Holmes poignantly observed: 'Detached reflection cannot be demanded in the face of an uplifted knife.'

3. Even if there is no formal duty to retreat, it behoves one contemplating using force in self-defence to make clear that he is willing to cease and desist, if for no other reason than to lay the groundwork for a subsequent defence. To the extent that the announcement of a willingness to desist is a relevant evidentiary consideration, then arguably its importance increases with the amount of force that is contemplated being used. If deadly force is contemplated, it is arguable that a fairly clear indication of willingness to desist should be made before resort to such force. Presumably a communication that one is prepared to desist is unnecessary, however, when it would clearly be useless; even more so when it would be dangerous to take the time to make such a communication.

4. Is an offer to retreat, as maintained by the court, in fact the best evidence that the defendant was acting in a reasonable manner? See *R v Shannon* (1980) 71 Cr App R 192.

(iv) *The amount of permissible force (the proportionality prong)*

Only reasonable force is permitted. But how does one measure reasonableness? The generally stated position is that the force used in defence must be proportional to the attack. If it exceeds that amount, it is unreasonable.

Palmer v R
[1971] AC 814, Privy Council

LORD MORRIS OF BORTH-Y-GEST: . . . In their Lordships' view the defence of self-defence is one which can be and will be readily understood by any jury. It is a straightforward conception. It involves no abstruse legal thought. It requires no set words by way of explanation. No formula need be employed in reference to it. Only common sense is needed for its understanding. It is both good law and good sense that a man who is attacked may defend himself. It is both good law and good sense that he may do, but may only do, what is reasonably necessary. But everything will depend upon the particular facts and circumstances. Of these a jury can decide. It may in some cases be only sensible and clearly possible to take some simple avoiding action. Some attacks may be serious and dangerous. Others may not be. If there is some relatively minor attack it would not be common sense to permit some action of retaliation which was wholly out of proportion to the necessities of the situation. If an attack is serious so that it puts someone in immediate peril then immediate defensive action may be necessary. If the moment is one of crisis for someone in imminent danger he may have to avert the danger by some instant reaction. If the attack is all over and no sort of peril remains then the employment of force may be by way of revenge or punishment or by way of paying off an old score or may be pure aggression. There may no longer be any link with a necessity of defence. Of all these matters the good sense of a jury will be the arbiter. There are no prescribed words which must be employed in or adopted in a summing up. All that is needed is a clear exposition, in relation to the particular facts of the case, of the conception of necessary self-defence. If there has been no attack then clearly there will have been no need for defence. If there has been attack so that defence is reasonably necessary it will be recognised that a person defending himself cannot weigh to a nicety the exact measure of his necessary defensive action. If a jury thought that in a moment of unexpected anguish a person attacked had only done what he honestly and instinctively thought was necessary that would be most potent evidence that only reasonable defensive action had been taken. A jury will be told that the defence of self-defence, where the evidence makes its raising possible, will only fail if the prosecution show beyond doubt that what the accused did was not by way of self-defence. But their Lordships consider that if the prosecution have shown that what was done was not done in self-defence then that issue is eliminated from the case. If the jury consider that an accused acted in self-defence or if the jury are in doubt as to this then they will acquit. The defence of self-defence either succeeds so as to result in an acquittal or it is disproved in which case as a defence it is rejected. . . .

NOTES AND QUESTIONS

1. Lord Morris states in *Palmer* that what an attacked individual 'honestly and instinctively thought was necessary . . . would be most potent evidence that only reasonable defensive action had been taken'. Lecturer believes that deadly force is necessary to prevent Student from stealing her notes, and kills Student. Is Lecturer's belief really the 'most potent evidence that only reasonable defensive action had been taken'?

2. A distinction is often drawn between the use of force and the threat to use force. One may be able to threaten to use more force than one in fact would be legally privileged to use. Why?

The question with the most far-reaching consequences is 'When may one use deadly force?'

Attorney-General for Northern Ireland's Reference (No. 1 of 1975)
[1976] 3 WLR 235, House of Lords

The accused was a soldier serving with the armed forces of the Crown. His unit was engaged in the suppression of terrorist activities in Northern Ireland. The accused was a member of an army patrol on foot in an area where terrorists were believed to be active. During the course of the patrol the accused saw the deceased, who was on his own, and ordered him to halt. The deceased ran off and thereupon the accused shot and killed him. The accused was charged with murder and was tried by a judge sitting alone under s. 2 of the Northern Ireland (Emergency Provisions) Act 1972. The accused was acquitted. The judge gave a judgment stating his reasons for finding the accused not guilty and set out his findings of fact in considerable detail. In particular the judge stated that he was not satisfied that it had been accused's intention to kill or seriously wound the deceased. Following the acquittal the Attorney-General, acting under s. 48A of the Criminal Appeal (Northern Ireland) 1968 and the Criminal Appeal (References of Points of Law) (Northern Ireland) Rules 1973, referred, inter alia, the following point of law to the Court of Criminal Appeal in Northern Ireland: 'Whether a soldier commits a crime when, in the circumstances set out in [the reference], he fires to kill or seriously wound an unarmed person because he honestly and reasonably believes that that person is a member of a proscribed organisation (in this case the Provisional IRA) who is seeking to run away, and the soldier's shot kills that person.' Paragraph 2 of the reference, in accordance with r. 3(1) of the 1973 rules, set out the 'facts of the case [which were] necessary for the proper consideration of the point of law'. Those facts, which were taken from the judgment of the trial judge, included expressions of opinion as to the likelihood of attack on the patrol and as to the accused's state of mind at the time when he fired the shot. The Court of Criminal Appeal gave its opinion on the point of law and, on the application of the Attorney-General, referred the point to the House of Lords under s. 48A(3) of the 1968 Act.

LORD DIPLOCK: . . . My Lords, to kill or seriously wound another person by shooting is prima facie unlawful. There may be circumstances, however, which render the act of shooting and any killing which results from it lawful; and an honest and reasonable belief by the accused in the existence of facts which if true would have rendered his act lawful is a defence to any charge based on the shooting. So for the purposes of the present reference one must ignore the fact that the deceased was an entirely innocent person and must deal with the case as if he were a member of the Provisional IRA and a potentially dangerous terrorist, as the accused honestly and reasonably believed him to be.

The facts to be assumed for the purposes of the reference are not capable in law of giving rise to a possible defence of 'self-defence'. The deceased was in fact, and appeared to the accused to be, unarmed. He was not attacking the accused; he was running away. So if the act of the accused in shooting the deceased was lawful it must have been on the ground that it was done in the performance of his duty to prevent crime or in the exercise of his right to stop and question the deceased under s. 16 or to arrest him under s. 12 of the Northern Ireland (Emergency Provisions) Act 1973.

There is little authority in English law concerning the rights and duties of a member of the armed forces of the Crown when acting in aid of the civil power; and what little authority there is relates almost entirely to the duties of soldiers when troops are called on to assist in controlling a riotous assembly. Where used for such temporary purposes it may not be inaccurate to describe the legal rights and duties of a soldier as being no more than those of an ordinary citizen in uniform. But such a description is in my view misleading in the circumstances in which the army is currently employed in aid of the civil power in Northern Ireland. In some parts of the province there has existed for some years now a state of armed and clandestinely organised insurrection against the lawful government of Her Majesty by persons seeking to gain political ends by violent means, that is by committing murder and other crimes of violence against persons and property. Due to the efforts of the army and police to suppress it the insurrection has been sporadic in its manifestations but, as events have repeatedly shown, if vigilance is relaxed the violence erupts again. In theory it may be the duty of every citizen when an arrestable offence is about to be committed in his presence to take whatever reasonable measures are available to him to prevent the commission of the crime; but the duty is one of imperfect obligation and does not place him under any obligation to do anything by which he would expose himself to risk of personal injury, nor is he under any duty to search for criminals or seek out crime. In contrast to this a soldier who is employed in aid of the civil power in Northern Ireland is under a duty, enforceable under military law, to search for criminals if so ordered by his superior officer and to risk his own life should this be necessary in preventing terrorist acts. For the performance of this duty he is armed with a firearm, a self-loading rifle, from which a bullet, if it hits the human body, is almost certain to cause serious injury if not death.

The use of force in the prevention of crime or in effecting the lawful arrest of suspected offenders is now regulated by s. 3 of the Criminal Law (Northern Ireland) Act 1967 as follows:

(1) A person may use such force as is reasonable in the circumstances in the prevention of crime, or in effecting or assisting in the lawful arrest of offenders or suspected offenders or of persons unlawfully at large.

(2) Subsection (1) shall replace the rules of the common law as to the matters dealt with by that subsection.

That section states the law applicable to the defence raised by the accused at the trial of his case.

In the instant reference the relevant purpose for which it is to be assumed that force was used by the accused is the prevention of crime. That is the purpose for which the power to stop and question is conferred on soldiers by s. 16 of the Northern Ireland (Emergency Provisions) Act 1973; and it has not been suggested that shooting to kill or seriously wound would be justified in attempting to effect the arrest under s. 12 of a person who, though he was suspected of belonging to a proscribed organisation (which constitutes an offence under s. 19), was not also believed on reasonable grounds to be likely to commit actual crimes of violence, if he succeeded in avoiding arrest.

What amount of force is 'reasonable in the circumstances' for the purpose of preventing crime is, in my view, always a question for the jury in a jury trial, never a 'point of law' for the judge.

The form in which the jury would have to ask themselves the question in a trial for an offence against the person in which this defence was raised by the accused, would be: are we satisfied that no reasonable man (a) with knowledge of such facts as were known to the accused or reasonably believed by him to exist (b) in the circumstances and time available to him for reflection (c) could be of opinion that the prevention of the risk of harm to which others might be exposed if the suspect were allowed to escape, justified exposing the suspect to the risk of harm to him that might result from the kind of force that the accused contemplated using?

To answer this the jury would have first to decide what were the facts that did exist and were known to the accused to do so and what were mistakenly believed by the accused to be facts. In respect of the latter the jury would have had to decide whether any reasonable man on the material available to the accused could have shared that belief. To select, as is done in para. 2(13) of the reference, two specific inferences of fact as to which it is said that the accused had no belief is merely to exclude them from the jury's consideration as being facts mistakenly believed by the accused to exist; but this does not preclude the jury from considering what inferences of fact a reasonable man would draw from the primary facts known to the accused.

The jury would have also to consider how the circumstances in which the accused had to make his decision whether or not to use force, and the shortness of the time available to him for reflection, might affect the judgment of a reasonable man. In the facts that are to be assumed for the purposes of the reference there is material on which a jury might take the view that the accused had reasonable grounds for apprehension of imminent danger to himself and other members of the patrol if the deceased were allowed to get away and join armed fellow members of the Provisional IRA who might be lurking in the neighbourhood, and that the time available to the accused to make up his mind what to do was so short that even a reasonable man could only act intuitively. This being so, the jury in approaching the final part of the question should remind themselves that the postulated balancing of risk against risk, harm against harm, by the reasonable man is not undertaken in the calm analytical atmosphere of the court room after counsel with the benefit of hindsight have expounded at length the reasons for and against the kind and degree of force that was used by the accused; but in the brief second or two which the accused had to decide whether to shoot or not and under all the stresses to which he was exposed.

In many cases where force is used in the prevention of crime or in effecting an arrest there is a choice as to the degree of force to use. On the facts that are to be assumed for the purposes of the reference the only options open to the accused were either to let the deceased escape or to shoot at him with a service rifle. A reasonable man would know that a bullet from a self-loading rifle if it hit a human being, at any rate at the range at which the accused fired, would be likely to kill him or to injure him seriously. So in one scale of the balance the harm to which the deceased would be exposed if the accused aimed to hit him was predictable and grave and the risk of its occurrence high. In the other scale of the balance it would be open to the jury to take the view that it would not be unreasonable to assess the kind of harm to be averted by preventing the deceased's escape was even graver – the killing or wounding of members of the patrol by terrorists in ambush, and the effect of this success by members of the Provisional IRA in encouraging the continuance of the armed insurrection and all the misery and destruction of life and property that terrorist activity in Northern Ireland has entailed. The jury would have to consider too what was the highest degree at which a reasonable man could have assessed the likelihood that such consequences might follow the escape of the deceased if the facts had been as the accused knew or believed them reasonably to be.

My Lords, the facts as they have been stated for the purpose of the reference are much less detailed than those that were proved at the trial of the accused before MacDermott J without a jury.

As stated they are so scanty and couched in such general terms (e.g. there was 'a real threat') that for my part I should not find it possible as a judge of fact to say that in the circumstances as stated the force used by the accused was not reasonable.

In the result I do not think that this House can give to the first question in the reference any more specific answer than that which was given by the majority of the Court of Criminal Appeal in Northern Ireland:

> Point (i) The facts and circumstances set out in the reference are sufficient to raise an issue for the tribunal of fact as to whether the Crown had established beyond reasonable doubt that the respondent's act of shooting constituted, in the circumstances, unreasonable force.

NOTES AND QUESTIONS

1. In respect of the necessity prong, and in light of the subsequent decision in *Williams (Gladstone)*, it would seem that the reasonableness of a belief in the need for force is no longer necessary so long as the defendant's belief was honest. Is *Attorney-General's Reference* to this extent modified or should a different rule apply when deadly force is contemplated?

2. In *Attorney-General's Reference*, was the defendant himself under threat of immediate attack? Was anybody? Was the threat, if it did exist, real or hypothetical? If the defendant believed that at some future point in time the escaped individual would expose another to harm, would that have been sufficient to justify the use of deadly force under Lord Diplock's test? Would it matter if that point in time was the following week? The following month? The following year? Ten years hence?

3. The burden of persuading the jury that deadly force was not reasonable in the circumstances rests on the prosecution. Once the defendant has introduced some relevant evidence, the prosecution must negate the claim by proof beyond a reasonable doubt.

The use of deadly force, and the State's responsibility for the decision to authorise the use of deadly force, have been examined by the European Court of Human Rights:

McCann v *United Kingdom*
(1996) 21 EHRR 97, European Court of Human Rights

Following intelligence information that the Provisional IRA were planning a terrorist attack on Gibraltar, SAS soldiers were sent to assist the Gibraltar authorities to arrest the IRA active service unit. The three suspects were subsequently shot and killed by members of the SAS. The applicants complained that the killings violated Article 2 of the Convention and claimed just satisfaction under Article 50.

In its report of 4 March 1994, the Commission made the following findings on questions of fact:

— that the suspects were effectively allowed to enter Gibraltar to be picked up by the surveillance operatives in place in strategic locations for that purpose;

— that there was no evidence to support the applicants' contention of a premeditated design to kill Mr McCann, Ms Farrell and Mr Savage;

— that there was no convincing support for any allegation that the soldiers shot Mr McCann and Ms Farrell when they were attempting to surrender or when they were lying on the ground. However the soldiers carried out the shooting from close proximity. The forensic evidence indicated a distance of as little as three feet in the case of Ms Farrell;

— Ms Farrell and Mr McCann were shot by Soldiers A and B at close range after the two suspects had made what appeared to the soldiers to be threatening movements. They were shot as they fell to the ground but not when they were lying on the ground; – it was probably either the sound of the police siren or the sound of the shooting of Mr McCann and Ms Farrell at the Shell garage, or indeed both, which caused Mr Savage to turn round to face the soldiers who were behind him. It was not likely that Soldiers C and D witnessed the shooting of Mr McCann and Ms Farrell before proceeding in pursuit of Savage;

— there was insufficient material to rebut the version of the shooting given by Soldiers C and D. Mr Savage was shot at close range until he hit the ground and probably in the instant as or after he hit the ground. This conclusion was supported by the pathologists' evidence at the subsequent inquest;

— Soldiers A to D opened fire with the purpose of preventing the threat of detonation of a car bomb in the centre of Gibraltar by suspects who were known to them to be terrorists with a history of previous involvement with explosives;

— a timer must in all probability have been mentioned at the Commissioner's operational briefing. For whatever reason, however, it was not a factor which was taken into account in the soldiers' view of the operation.

The Government submitted that the deprivations of life to which the applications relate was justified under Article 2(2)(a) as resulting from the use of force which was no more than absolutely necessary in defence of the people of Gibraltar from unlawful violence and the Court was invited to find that the facts disclosed no breach of Article 2 of the Convention in respect of any of the three deceased.

The applicants submitted that the Government have not shown beyond reasonable doubt that the planning and execution of the operation was in accordance with Article 2 H 2 of the Convention. Accordingly, the killings were not absolutely necessary within the meaning of this provision.

As to the law

I. Alleged violation of Article 2 of the Convention The applicants alleged that the killing of Mr McCann, Ms Farrell and Mr Savage by members of the security forces constituted a violation of Article 2 of the Convention which reads:

1. Everyone's right to life shall be protected by law. No one shall be deprived of his life intentionally save in the execution of a sentence of a court following his conviction of a crime for which this penalty is provided by law.

2. Deprivation of life shall not be regarded as inflicted in contravention of this Article when it results from the use of force which is no more than absolutely necessary:

(a) in defence of any person from unlawful violence;
(b) in order to effect a lawful arrest or to prevent the escape of person lawfully detained;
(c) in action lawfully taken for the purpose of quelling a riot or insurrection.

The Court considers that the exceptions delineated in paragraph 2 indicate that this provision extends to, but is not concerned exclusively with, intentional killing. As the Commission has pointed out, the text of Article 2, read as a whole, demonstrates that paragraph 2 does not primarily define instances where it is permitted intentionally to kill an individual, but describes the situations where it is permitted to 'use force' which may result, as an unintended outcome, in the deprivation of life. The use of force, however, must be no more than absolutely necessary for the achievement of one of the purposes set out in sub-paragraphs (a), (b) or (c) (see *Stewart* v *The United Kingdom* (appl. no. 10444/82), 10 July 1984, Decisions and Reports, volume 39, pp. 169–171).

In this respect the use of the term 'absolutely necessary' in Article 2(2) indicates that a stricter and more compelling test of necessity must be employed from that normally applicable when determining whether State action is 'necessary in a democratic society' under paragraph 2 of Articles 8 to 11 of the Convention. In particular, the force used must be strictly proportionate to the achievement of the aims set out in sub-paragraphs (2)(a), (b) and (c) of Article 2.

In keeping with the importance of this provision in a democratic society, the Court must, in making its assessment, subject deprivations of life to the most careful scrutiny, particularly where deliberate lethal force is used, taking into consideration not only the actions of the agents of the State who actually administer the force but also all the surrounding circumstances including such matters as the planning and control of the actions under examination.

In carrying out its examination under Article 2 of the Convention, the Court must bear in mind that the information that the United Kingdom authorities received that there would be a terrorist attack in Gibraltar presented them with a fundamental dilemma. On the one hand, they were required to have regard to their duty to protect the lives of the people in Gibraltar including their own military personnel and, on the other, to have minimum resort to the use of lethal force against those suspected of posing this threat in the light of the obligations flowing from both domestic and international law.

Several other factors must also be taken into consideration. In the first place, the authorities were confronted by an active service unit of the IRA composed of persons who had been convicted of bombing offences and a known explosives expert. The IRA, judged by its actions in the past, had demonstrated a disregard for human life, including that of its own members.

Secondly, the authorities had had prior warning of the impending terrorist action and thus had ample opportunity to plan their reaction and, in co-ordination with the local Gibraltar authorities, to take measures to foil the attack and arrest the suspects. Inevitably, however, the security authorities could not have been in possession of the full facts and were obliged to formulate their policies on the basis of incomplete hypotheses.

Against this background, in determining whether the force used was compatible with Article 2, the Court must carefully scrutinise, as noted above, not only whether the force used by the soldiers was strictly proportionate to the aim of protecting persons against unlawful violence but also whether the anti-terrorist operation was planned and controlled by the authorities so as to minimise, to the greatest extent possible, recourse to lethal force. The Court will consider each of these points in turn.

It is recalled that the soldiers who carried out the shooting (A, B, C and D) were informed by their superiors, in essence, that there was a car-bomb in place which could be detonated by any of the three suspects by means of a radio-control device which might have been concealed on their persons; that the device could be activated by pressing a button; that they would be likely to detonate the bomb if challenged, thereby causing heavy loss of life and serious injuries, and were also likely to be armed and to resist arrest.

As regards the shooting of Mr McCann and Ms Farrell, the Court recalls the Commission's finding that they were shot at close range after making what appeared to Soldiers A and B to be threatening movements with their hands as if they were going to detonate the bomb.

. . .

It was subsequently discovered that the suspects were unarmed, that they did not have a detonator device on their persons and that there was no bomb in the car.

All four soldiers admitted that they shot to kill. They considered that it was necessary to continue to fire at the suspects until they were rendered physically incapable of detonating a device. According to the pathologists' evidence Ms Farrell was hit by eight bullets, Mr McCann by five and Mr Savage by sixteen.

The Court accepts that the soldiers honestly believed, in the light of the information that they had been given, as set out above, that it was necessary to shoot the suspects in order to prevent them from detonating a bomb and causing serious loss of life. The actions which they took, in obedience to superior orders, were thus perceived by them as absolutely necessary in order to safeguard innocent lives.

It considers that the use of force by agents of the State in pursuit of one of the aims delineated in paragraph 2 of Article 2 of the Convention may be justified under this provision where it is based on an honest belief which is perceived, for good reasons, to be valid at the time but which subsequently turns out to be mistaken. To hold otherwise would be to impose an unrealistic burden on the State and its law enforcement personnel in the execution of their duty, perhaps to the detriment of their lives and those of others.

It follows that, having regard to the dilemma confronting the authorities in the circumstances of the case, the actions of the soldiers do not, in themselves, give rise to a violation of this provision.

The question arises, however, whether the anti-terrorist operation as a whole was controlled and organised in a manner which respected the requirements of Article 2 and whether the information and instructions given to the soldiers which, in effect, rendered inevitable the use of lethal force, took adequately into consideration the right to life of the three suspects.

. . .

The decision not to stop the three terrorists from entering Gibraltar is a relevant factor to take into account under this head.

The Court notes that at the briefing on 5 March attended by Soldiers A, B, C, and D it was considered likely that the attack would be by way of a large car-bomb. A number of key assessments were made. In particular, it was thought that the terrorists would not use a blocking car; that the bomb would be detonated by a radio-control device; that the detonation could be effected by the pressing of a button; that it was likely that the suspects would detonate the bomb if challenged; that they would be armed and would be likely to use their arms if confronted.

In the event, all of these crucial assumptions, apart from the terrorists' intentions to carry out an attack, turned out to be erroneous. Nevertheless, as has been demonstrated by the Government, on the basis of their experience in dealing with the IRA, they were all possible hypotheses in a situation where the true facts were unknown and where the authorities operated on the basis of limited intelligence information.

In fact, insufficient allowances appear to have been made for other assumptions. For example, since the bombing was not expected until 8 March when the changing of the guard ceremony was to take place, there was equally the possibility that the three terrorists were on a reconnaissance mission. While this was a factor which was briefly considered, it does not appear to have been regarded as a serious possibility.

In addition, at the briefings or after the suspects had been spotted, it might have been thought unlikely that they would have been prepared to explode the bomb, thereby killing many civilians, as Mr McCann and Ms Farrell strolled towards the border area since this would have increased the risk of detection and capture. It might also have been thought improbable that at that point they would have set up the transmitter in anticipation to enable them to detonate the supposed bomb immediately if confronted.

Moreover, even if allowances are made for the technological skills of the IRA, the description of the detonation device as a 'button job' without the qualifications subsequently described by the experts at the Inquest, of which the competent authorities must have been aware, over-simplifies the true nature of these devices.

It is further disquieting in this context that the assessment made by Soldier G, after a cursory external examination of the car, that there was a 'suspect car-bomb' was conveyed to the soldiers, according to their own testimony, as a definite identification that there was such a bomb. It is recalled that while Soldier G had experience in car-bombs, it transpired that he was not an expert in radio communications or explosives; and that his assessment that there was a suspect car bomb, based on his observation that the car aerial was out of place, was more in the nature of a report that a bomb could not be ruled out.

In the absence of sufficient allowances being made for alternative possibilities, and the definite reporting of the existence of a car-bomb which, according to the assessments that had been made, could be detonated at the press of a button, a series of working hypotheses were conveyed to Soldiers A, B, C and D as certainties, thereby making the use of lethal force almost unavoidable.

However, the failure to make provision for a margin of error must also be considered in combination with the training of the soldiers to continue shooting once they opened fire until the suspect was dead. As noted by the Coroner in his summing up to the jury at the Inquest, all four soldiers shot to kill the suspects. Soldier E testified that it had been discussed with the soldiers that there was an increased chance that they would have to shoot to kill since there would be less time where there was a 'button' device. Against this background, the authorities were bound by their obligation to respect the right to life of the suspects to exercise the greatest of care in evaluating the information at their disposal before transmitting it to soldiers whose use of firearms automatically involved shooting to kill.

Although detailed investigation at the Inquest into the training received by the soldiers was prevented by the public interest certificates which had been issued, it is not clear whether they had been trained or instructed to assess whether the use of firearms to wound their targets may have been warranted by the specific circumstances that confronted them at the moment of arrest.

Their reflex action in this vital respect lacks the degree of caution in the use of firearms to be expected from law enforcement personnel in a democratic society, even when dealing with dangerous terrorist suspects, and stands in marked contrast to the standard of care reflected in the instructions in the use of firearms by the police which had been drawn to their attention and which emphasised the legal responsibilities of the individual officer in the light of conditions prevailing at the moment of engagement.

This failure by the authorities also suggests a lack of appropriate care in the control and organisation of the arrest operation.

In sum, having regard to the decision not to prevent the suspects from travelling into Gibraltar, to the failure of the authorities to make sufficient allowances for the possibility that their intelligence assessments might, in some respects at least, be erroneous and to the automatic recourse to lethal force when the soldiers opened fire, the Court is not persuaded that the killing of the three terrorists constituted the use of force which was no more than absolutely necessary in defence of persons from unlawful violence within the meaning of Article 2(2)(a) of the Convention.

Accordingly, it finds that there has been a breach of Article 2 of the Convention.

NOTES AND QUESTIONS

1. The European Court of Human Rights notes that the suspects were not arrested at the time that they entered Gibraltar. Might limitations in the law of attempt (discussed in Chapter 11) have affected the decision not to arrest?
2. Is the test of when deadly force is permissible articulated by the European Court of Human Rights more or less stringent than that articulated by the House of Lords in *Attorney-General for Northern Ireland's Reference (No. 1 of 1975)*?
3. In *Andronicou and Constantinou v Cyprus* (1998) 25 EHRR 491, the European Court of Human Rights again had occasion to examine the use of deadly force by State authorities. C was being held hostage by A, who was known by police to be armed and unstable. In response to being shot at by A, the special police unit discharged several rounds of automatic fire. A was killed instantly; C was wounded and died shortly thereafter. While regretting the use of so much fire power, the Court nonetheless found that it did not exceed what was 'absolutely necessary' under the circumstances. What are the differences between *Andronicou* and *McCann*? Both cases were decided by the narrowest of margins (ten votes to nine in *McCann*; five votes to four in *Andronicou*), suggesting strong divisions within the Court.

In determining what constitutes reasonable force, should the answer turn on what the actor considers to be reasonable, or on what an ordinary person would consider reasonable?

R v *Owino*

[1996] 2 Cr App R 128, Court of Appeal

COLLINS J: On October 17, 1994 the appellant, a senior registrar in microbiology, appeared before the Crown Court at Wood Green on an indictment charging him with four offences of violence against his wife, Marie. The first alleged the causing of grievous bodily harm with intent; the other three, assault occasioning actual bodily harm . . .

It is clear that in relation to counts 3 and 4, self-defence was being raised, the appellant's case being that any bruising suffered by his wife for which he was responsible was caused only by reasonable force used in restraining her and in preventing her from assaulting him. In those circumstances it was obviously incumbent upon the learned judge to give a full and proper direction as to the elements of self-defence and also to draw the jury's attention to the distinction between provocation by words or by conduct, which would not, and threats or actual attack which could raise an issue of self-defence. If there is material which raises this issue, the burden is of course on the prosecution to prove that the violence used was excessive and was not used in self-defence.

Unfortunately, the learned judge did not refer to self-defence at all in his summing-up and the jury retired shortly after 1 p.m. without any such direction being given to them. It was perfectly plain that such a direction ought to have been given.

Then about an hour and a half after their retirement, the jury sent a note to the judge. It read as follows:

> Question on law:
> We have come to an impasse on the issue of the definition of assault. If a person reacts to being assaulted themselves by grabbing or pushing, is that assault? What might be regarded as unreasonable force, i.e. is lifting someone out of a room against their will (struggling) regarded as an assault? Also, one or two of us wish to take into account provocation, others of us do not believe we should do. Can you direct us, is it a question of fairness?

With the greatest of respect to the learned judge, if, as indeed was clear, the issue of self-defence had been raised on the evidence, he had a duty to put it to the jury and to direct the jury upon it. The fact, if it be a fact, that counsel had not specifically referred to self-defence in the course of their speeches was no reason for the learned judge not to deal with it in his summing-up.

. . . The essential elements of self-defence are clear enough. The jury have to decide whether a defendant honestly believed that the circumstances were such as required him to use force to defend himself from an attack or a threatened attack. In this respect a defendant must be judged in accordance with his honest belief, even though that belief may have been mistaken. But the jury must then decide whether the force used was reasonable in the circumstances as he believed them to be.

R v *Scarlett* (1994) 98 Cr App R 290 was a case where a landlord of a public house had been ejecting, and perfectly lawfully and properly ejecting, a drunken customer from his public house. The allegation was that he had used excessive force in the course of ejecting him so that the customer fell down the steps of the entrance to the pub and unfortunately hit his head and was killed. What Mr Mendelle relies upon in the case of *Scarlett* is a passage at pp. 295, 296 and p. 636 of the respective reports, where Beldam LJ, giving the judgment of the Court, said this:

> Where, as in the present case, an accused is justified in using some force and can only be guilty of an assault if the force used is excessive, the jury ought to be directed that he cannot be guilty of an assault unless the prosecution prove that he acted with the mental element necessary to constitute his action in assault, that is 'that the defendant intentionally or recklessly applied force to the person of another'. Further, they should be directed that the accused is not to be found guilty merely because he intentionally or recklessly

used force which they consider to have been excessive. They ought not to convict him unless they are satisfied that the degree of force used was plainly more than was called for by the circumstances as he believed them to be and, provided he believed the circumstances called for the degree of force used, he is not to be convicted even if his belief was unreasonable.

In this case the learned judge gave no direction to the jury that the prosecution, to establish an assault, had to prove that the appellant intentionally or recklessly applied excessive force in seeking to evict the deceased.

. . . [W]hat, in the context, the learned Lord Justice was really saying was, in our view, this: he was indicating that the elements of an assault involved the unlawful application of force. In the context of an issue of self-defence or reasonable restraint, which was what *Scarlett* was essentially about, then clearly a person would not be guilty of an assault unless the force used was excessive, and in judging whether the force used was excessive, the jury had to take account of the circumstances as he believed them to be. That is what is made clear in the first part of the sentence, which we will isolate and read again:

> They ought not to convict him unless they are satisfied that the degree of force used was plainly more than was called for by the circumstances as he believed them to be and, provided he believed the circumstances called for the degree of force used, he is not to be convicted even if his belief was unreasonable.

So far as the second half of the sentence is concerned, what we understand the learned Lord Justice to have been saying was that, in judging what he believed the circumstances to be, the jury are not to decide on the basis of what was objectively reasonable; and that even if he, the defendant, was unreasonable in his belief, if it was an honest belief and honestly held, that he is not to be judged by reference to the true circumstances. It is in that context that the learned Lord Justice talks about '[belief] that the circumstances called for the degree of force used', because clearly you cannot divorce completely the concept of degree of force and the concept of the circumstances as you believe them to be. In our judgment, that is effectively all that the learned Lord Justice was saying.

What he was not saying, in our view (and indeed if he had said it, it would be contrary to authority) was that the belief, however ill-founded, of the defendant that the degree of force he was using was reasonable, will enable him to do what he did. As Kay J, indicated in argument, if that argument was correct, then it would justify, for example, the shooting of someone who was merely threatening to throw a punch, on the basis that the defendant honestly believed, although unreasonably and mistakenly, that it was justifiable for him to use that degree of force. That clearly is not and cannot be, the law.

NOTES AND QUESTIONS

1. Is *Owino* consistent with *Williams (Gladstone)*? Why should the need for any force be judged from a subjective point of view while the appropriate amount of force is judged from an objective point of view?

2. If the defendant's force is deemed excessive, the claim of self-defence will fail. But should a flawed or imperfect claim of self-defence serve to reduce the seriousness of the defendant's crime? The House of Lords in *R v Clegg* [1995] 1 AC 482 expressed some sympathy for this position, but concluded that it was Parliament's responsibility to change the law. This is a debatable point, as self-defence is of common law origin and not codified in statute. In any event, Parliament has yet to reform the law.

PART IV

Inchoate Offences and Parties to Crime

11

Incitement, Conspiracy and Attempt

The offences of incitement, conspiracy and attempt are designed to permit law enforcement personnel to intervene at an early stage, before any actual harm has been done. These offences are commonly referred to as 'inchoate' crimes, the *Oxford English Dictionary* defining 'inchoate' as 'just begun, rudimentary, unformed'. The inchoate offences are committed when steps have been taken to commit a crime but the crime has not been carried through to its intended conclusion. When an inchoate offence is charged, it is not necessary for the prosecution to prove that actual social harm has occurred. Although the aim is to prevent harm, the prosecution must nonetheless provide evidence of the defendant's willingness to break the law. However, the intervention must not be too soon as evil thoughts alone do not constitute an offence.

R v Higgins
(1801) 2 East 5, King's Bench Division

LE BLANC J: It is contended that the offence charged in the second count, of which the defendant has been convicted, is no misdemeanor, because it amounts only to a bare wish or desire of the mind to do an illegal act. If that were so, I agree that it would not be indictable. But this is charge of an act done; namely, an actual solicitation of a servant to rob his master, and not merely a wish or desire that he should do so. A solicitation or inciting of another, by whatever means it is attempted, is an act done; and that such an act done with a criminal intent is punishable by indictment has been clearly established by the several cases referred to. . . .

SECTION 1: **Incitement**

There are some statutory forms of incitement. Examples include the following:

Offences Against the Person Act 1861

4. Conspiring or soliciting to commit murder
All persons who shall conspire, confederate, and agree to murder any person, whether he be a Subject of Her Majesty or not, and whether he be within the Queen's Dominions or not, and whosoever shall solicit, encourage, persuade, or endeavour to persuade, or shall propose to any

person, to murder any other person, whether he be a Subject of Her Majesty or not, and whether he be within the Queen's Dominions or not, shall be guilty of a misdemeanor, and being convicted thereof shall be liable, at the discretion of the court, to be kept in penal servitude for any term not more than ten and not less than three years, – or to be imprisoned for any term not exceeding two years, with or without hard labour.

Incitement to Disaffection Act 1934

1. If any person maliciously and advisedly endeavours to seduce any member of His Majesty's forces from his duty or allegiance to His Majesty, he shall be guilty of an offence under this Act.

Sexual Offences (Conspiracy and Incitement) Act 1996

This Act makes it an offence to conspire to commit, or to incite another person to commit, certain sexual acts against children abroad. It is directed towards the problem of 'child sex tourism', *i.e.* the activities of paedophiles who travel overseas in order to exploit children for sexual purposes. Statistics illustrating the disturbing extent of this problem were cited in Parliament: current assessments, for example, put the number of child prostitutes in Thailand at between 100,000–200,000, in the Philippines at 40,000–60,000 (two-thirds of whom are boys) and in Sri Lanka at 30,000. These children, many of whom are pathetically young, are at the mercy of 'sex tourists' from more developed nations, who are able to exploit them with effective impunity by acts that would be visited with the most serious consequences if done in their own countries. Moreover an industry has begun to grow up around this phenomenon, with tours being planned and publications produced specifically for the sex tourism market.

2. Incitement to commit certain sexual acts outside the United Kingdom
    (1) This section applies where—
        (a) any act done by a person in England and Wales would amount to the offence of incitement to commit a listed sexual offence but for the fact that what he had in view would not be an offence triable in England and Wales,
        (b) the whole or part of what he had in view was intended to take place in a country or territory outside the United Kingdom, and
        (c) what he had in view would involve the commission of an offence under the law in force in that country or territory.
    (2) Where this section applies—
        (a) what he had in view is to be treated as that listed sexual offence for the purposes of any charge of incitement brought in respect of that act, and
        (b) any such charge is accordingly triable in England and Wales.
    (3) Any act of incitement by means of a message (however communicated) is to be treated as done in England and Wales if the message is sent or received in England and Wales.

A: *Actus reus*

The *actus reus* of incitement usually consists of encouraging or persuading another to commit a crime. However, one can incite by threats and also by putting pressure on someone to commit the crime.

Race Relations Board v *Applin*
[1973] 1 QB 815, Court of Appeal

LORD DENNING MR: Mr and Mrs Watson have for 23 years fostered children in need of a temporary home. They do it from sincere and unselfish motives. They see it as a practical expression of their Christian faith. Normally they take four or five children at a time, but it may rise to seven on occasion. The children only stay for two or three weeks. Quite a number of the children are coloured. Just over half, about 60 per cent.

In January 1970 Mr and Mrs Watson moved to 61 Oakroyd Avenue, Potters Bar, Hertfordshire. There they hoped to extend their good work. At first some of the neighbours objected. They said that the house was under covenant to be used for residential purposes only. But those objections were overcome. Soon afterwards, however, objections were made on another score. An organisation calling itself the National Front complained that most of the children fostered by Mr and Mrs Watson were coloured children. The National Front acted through its branch organiser, Mr Applin, and its area organiser, Mr Taylor, the defendants. These two gentlemen brought pressure on Mr and Mrs Watson to get them to take white children only. These were some of the things they did: on August 5, 1971, Mr Applin sent a circular to the residents of Oakroyd Avenue. It referred to 'the enlargement of premises in Oakroyd Avenue for use as a foster home for largely non-British children.' It accused Mr and Mrs Watson of making 'malicious and disgraceful attacks' on their neighbours. It stated as a fact: 'that immigrant parents, because of their different standards and attitudes are quite prepared to let others take responsibility for their excess offspring.'

In a letter to Mr Watson of August 16, 1971, Mr Taylor said:

> In answer to your question asking me if I am urging you to tell the local authorities that you will only except (sic) white children. Yes I am, as stated in my letter: 'Charity should begin at home.' The number of immigrant parents who are only too ready to dump their unwanted children on to the local ratepayers is a national scandal. Every week one sees advertisements in local papers and in shop windows concerning immigrants who wish to foster out their children. In my opinion, if we the indigenous population did likewise, there would be hell to play.

On August 26, 1971, the National Front organised a public meeting at Potters Bar. Mr Applin read extracts from the circular. Mr Taylor said:

> While you have people such as Mr Watson who delight in putting immigrants' welfare before their own people's, this process of turning more and more of British towns and cities into coloured ghettoes will continue.

On February 9, 1972, the Race Relations Board issued proceedings in the county court claiming that the acts done by Mr Applin and Mr Taylor were unlawful and seeking an injunction.

It is not easy to apply the Act to the situation before us, but I will try and explain it. It is quite clear that Mr and Mrs Watson were acting perfectly lawfully. They were fostering children without making any difference between them on the ground of colour. Mr Applin and Mr Taylor were bringing pressure to bear on Mr and Mrs Watson to get them to take white children only, and not coloured ones. That pressure did not succeed. Mr and Mrs Watson have resisted it. They have continued to take white and coloured children without making any difference. They continue so to take them. But, the point is this: suppose the pressure had succeeded. Suppose that Mr and Mrs Watson had stipulated 'We will only take white children.' Would that conduct of Mr and Mrs Watson have been unlawful? If it would have been unlawful, then it was unlawful of Mr Applin and Mr Taylor to bring pressure to bear on Mr and Mrs Watson to do an unlawful act. This follows from section 12 of the Act of 1968, which says:

> Any person who deliberately aids, induces or incites another person to do an act which is unlawful by virtue of any provision of this Part of this Act shall be treated for the purposes of this Act as doing that act.

If therefore, Mr Applin and Mr Taylor 'incited' Mr and Mrs Watson to do an unlawful act, i.e., to take white children only, they are to be treated as themselves doing that act, even though the incitement did not succeed. Here I may mention a small point. Mr Vinelott suggested that to 'incite' means to urge or spur on by advice, encouragement, and persuasion, and not otherwise. I do not think the word is so limited, at any rate in this context. A person may 'incite' another to do an act by threatening or by pressure, as well as by persuasion. Mr Applin and Mr Taylor undoubtedly brought pressure to bear on Mr and Mrs Watson to take white children only, and thus 'incited' them to do so.

Notice that, as in *Race Relations Board* v *Applin*, a defendant may be guilty of incitement even though the person incited refuses to succumb to the incitement. The incitement need not be directed to anyone in particular, and may be implied.

R v *Most*
(1881) 7 QBD 244, Queen's Bench Division

> M was indicted under 24 & 25 Vict. c. 100, s. 4. The encouragement and endeavour to persuade to murder, proved at the trial, was the publication and circulation by him of an article, written in German in a newspaper published in that language in London, exulting in the recent murder of the Emperor of Russia, and commending it as an example to revolutionists throughout the world.

LORD COLERIDGE CJ: . . . We have to deal here with a publication proved by the evidence at the trial to have been written by the defendant, to have been printed by the defendant, that is, he ordered and paid for the printing of it, sold by the defendant, called by the defendant his article, and intended, as the jury have found, and most reasonably found, to be read by the twelve hundred or more persons who were the subscribers to, or the purchasers of, the *Freiheit* newspaper; and, further, one which the jury have found, and I am of opinion have quite rightly found, to be naturally and reasonably intended to incite and encourage, or to endeavour to persuade persons who should read that article to the murder either of the Emperor Alexander, or the Emperor William, or, in the alternative, the crowned and uncrowned heads of states, as it is expressed in one part of the article, from Constantinople to Washington. . . .

. . . An endeavour to persuade or an encouragement is none the less an endeavour to persuade or an encouragement, because the person who so encourages or endeavours to persuade does not in the particular act of encouragement or persuasion personally address the number of people, the one or more persons, whom the address which contains the encouragement or the endeavour to persuade reaches. The argument has been well put, that an orator who makes a speech to two thousand people, does not address it to any one individual amongst those two thousand; it is addressed to the number. It is endeavouring to persuade the whole number, or large portions of that number, and if a particular individual amongst that number addressed by the orator is persuaded, or listens to it and is encouraged, it is plain that the words of this statute are complied with; because according to well-known principles of law the person who addresses those words to a number of persons must be taken to address them to the persons who, he knows, hear them, who he knows will understand them in a particular way, do understand them in that particular way, and do act upon them. . . .

Invicta Plastics v *Clare*
[1976] RTR 251, Queen's Bench Division

The defendant company manufactured a device called 'Radatec', which emitted a high-pitched whine when within 800 yards of wireless telegraphy transmissions including those used for police radar speed traps. The company advertised the device in a motoring magazine, the advertisement reading: 'You ought to know more about Radatec. Ask at your accessory shop or write for name of nearest stockist to' the company; the advertisement also depicted a view of a road and a speed limit sign through a car windscreen with the device attached.

PARK J: . . . The first question which the justices had to decide was whether a person who used the Radatec in his motor car without a licence from the Secretary of State would be using apparatus for wireless telegraphy contrary to section 1 of the Act of 1949. On the evidence before them they decided that such a person would be committing such an offence. There is no submission to this court that the justices were wrong in coming to that conclusion. So, on the first summons, which concerned the company, the question was whether the company by the advertisement in the magazine incited its readers to commit an offence under the Act.

When summing up to the jury on a case of incitement, judges sometimes use such words as 'incitement involves the suggestion to commit the offence' or 'a proposal to commit the offence' or 'persuasion or inducement to commit the offence' which the defendant is alleged to have incited. But Lord Denning MR considered the meaning of 'incitement' in *Race Relations Board* v *Applin* [1973] QB 815, 825 G, where he said:

> Mr Vinelott suggested that to 'incite' means to urge or spur on by advice encouragement, and persuasion, and not otherwise. I do not think the word is so limited, at any rate in this context. A person may 'incite' another to do an act by threatening or by pressure, as well as persuasion.

Accordingly, the justices had to decide whether, in the context, the advertisement amounted to an incitement to the readers of the magazine to commit the offence.

It is submitted on behalf of the company that, before the offence of incitement could be committed by means of the advertisement, there had to be in it an incitement to use the device which was advertised; that, if not, any matter in the advertisement would not constitute incitement, as it would not be sufficiently proximate to the offence alleged to have been incited; and that, as the advertisement merely encouraged readers to find out more about the device, it did not amount to incitement in fact or in law.

I think that it is necessary to look at the advertisement as a whole. Approaching it in this way, I have come to the conclusion that the company did incite a breach of the Act by means of the advertisement. I think, therefore, that the justices were right to convict the company of this offence.

NOTES AND QUESTIONS
1. In *Invicta Plastics* what constituted the incitement? What crime was incited?
2. An incitement is normally not committed until the communication reaches the notice of those it is intended to reach. If the communication fails to reach the intended recipient, the defendant may be nonetheless guilty of an attempt to incite.

R v *Ransford*
(1874) 13 Cox CC 9, Court of Appeal

The prisoner was tried at the September Sessions of the Central Criminal Court, 1874, upon the following indictment:

First count. – That at the time of committing the offence hereinafter in this count mentioned, one William D'Arcy Gardiner O'Halloran was a youth of the age of fourteen years, and was a scholar in the school of Christ's Hospital, and was under the care, custody, and control of the Governors of Christ's Hospital, in the city of London, and was then being educated in the said school in the principles of religion, morality, and virtue, with the object that he might there-after, when beyond the care and control of the said Governors, enter into the society of his fellow men, and be received by them as a man of honourable, manly, and virtuous habits, and that Edward Ransford, being a person of wicked, immoral, and depraved mind and disposition, with intent to debauch the said William D'Arcy Gardiner O'Halloran, and to vitiate and corrupt his mind, on the 5th of September, 1874, unlawfully and wickedly did write and send, and cause and procure to be written and sent to the said William D'Arcy Gardiner O'Halloran, a certain lewd and indecent letter, in the words and figures following, that is to say:

Henderson's Oakley-square, 5th Sept. 1874.

Dear O'Halloran, – The fates have hitherto prevented us from meeting, owing to my engagements. On Wednesday next, all being well, I shall meet you positively in the South Transept of St Paul's. I shall be there between 2½ o'clock and 2¾: we can then settle where to go. How long can you stay out in the evening? Answer by return. – Yours truly, P. DELAR. HARRISON.

I shall only be here to-morrow, and therefore a post-office is my safest address.

(The conclusion of the letter is unfit for publication.)

. . .

Seventh count. – That the said Edward Ransford afterwards, to wit, on the same day and in the year aforesaid, unlawfully, wickedly, and indecently did write and send, and cause and procure to be written and sent to the said William D'Arcy Gardiner O'Halloran, a certain letter, to wit, the letter mentioned and set forth in the first count of this indictment, with intent thereby to move and incite the said William D'Arcy Gardiner O'Halloran to attempt and endeavour, feloniously and wickedly, to commit and perpetrate with him the said Edward Ransford, the detestable crime of buggery, and by the means aforesaid with unlawfully and wickedly attempt and endeavour to incite the said William D'Arcy Gardiner O'Halloran to attempt to commit and perpetrate with him the said Edward Ransford, the detestable, horrid, and abominable crime aforesaid.

KELLY CB: I am clearly of opinion, in point of law, that any attempt to commit a misdemeanor is itself a misdemeanor, and I am also of opinion that to incite or even solicit another person to commit a felony, or to do any act with intent to induce another person to commit such offence, is a misdemeanor. The seventh count charges a valid offence, for it alleges that the prisoner did write and send a certain letter with intent to solicit and incite the boy, as to which there might be some doubt, for the letter was not read by the boy, and the boy, therefore, might be said not to have been solicited. But the seventh count is free from any difficulty of that nature, as the charge therein is that the prisoner endeavoured to solicit and incite the boy to the commission of a certain offence. . . .

QUESTION

Given that a defendant will be guilty of incitement if the person incited in a letter declines to commit the crime (see *Race Relations Board* v *Applin* above), why should the defendant not also be guilty of incitement when the letter goes astray? Is the defendant any less culpable?

(i) *Success or failure?*

If the incitement has the desired effect and the person incited commits a crime, the incitor becomes an accessory to the crime (see Chapter 12), and both parties may be guilty of conspiracy. If the incitement fails the incitor remains liable for incitement.

(ii) *Where the act incited is not a crime*

Three situations can arise:

   (a) Where the act done by the person incited would not amount to a crime.

   (b) Where the person incited is entitled to a defence.

   (c) Where the person incited is a victim intended to be protected by the criminal offence in question.

R v *Whitehouse*
[1977] QB 868, Court of Appeal

SCARMAN LJ: . . . The indictment which the defendant faced in 1976 was an indictment charging him with incitement to commit incest, and the particulars of the offence charged were that he, on a date unknown between December 1, 1975, and February 10, 1976, unlawfully incited a girl then aged 15, who was to his and her knowledge his daughter, to have sexual intercourse with him. To that count he pleaded guilty, as also to a second count charging incitement to commit incest, but on a different occasion, and he pleaded guilty to that as well.

   When the court saw those two counts framed in the way I have just described, we queried whether it was an offence known to law and we doubted whether it was because a girl aged 15 is incapable of committing the crime of incest. Later in this judgment it will be necessary to look at the terms of section 11 of the Sexual Offences Act 1956 but that shortly is the effect of the section so far as material to the issue in this case.

   . . . It is of course accepted by the Crown that at common law the crime of incitement consists of inciting another person to commit a crime. When one looks at this indictment in the light of the particulars of the offence pleaded, one sees that it is charging the defendant, with inciting a girl to commit a crime which in fact by statute she is incapable of committing. If therefore the girl was incapable of committing the crime alleged, how can the defendant be guilty of the common law crime of incitement? The Crown accepts the logic of that position and does not seek in this court to rely on section 11 of the Act of 1956 or to suggest that this man could be guilty of inciting his daughter to commit incest, to use the old phrase, as a principal in the first degree. But the Crown says that it is open to them upon this indictment to submit that it covers the offence of inciting the girl to aid and abet the man to commit the crime of incest upon her. Section 10 of the Act of 1956 makes it an offence for a man to have sexual intercourse with a woman whom he knows to be his daughter, and the Crown says that upon this indictment it is possible to say that the defendant has committed an offence known to the law, the offence being that of inciting his daughter under the age of 16 to aid and abet him to have sexual intercourse with her.

There is no doubt of the general principle, namely, that a person, provided always he or she is of the age of criminal responsibility, can be guilty of aiding or abetting a crime even though it be a crime which he or she cannot commit as a principal in the first degree. There are two famous illustrations in the books of this principle. A woman can aid and abet a rape so as herself to be guilty of rape, and a boy at an age where he is presumed impotent can nevertheless aid and abet a rape. . . .

The important matters in our judgment are these. First this girl, aged 15, belongs to a class which is protected, but not punished, by sections 10 and 11 of the Sexual Offences Act 1956, and secondly the girl is alleged to be the victim of this notional crime. The whole question has an air of artificiality because nobody is suggesting either that the father has committed incest with her or that she has aided and abetted him to commit incest upon her. What is suggested is that the father has committed the crime of incitement because by his words and conduct he has incited her to do that which, of course, she never has done.

. . . Clearly the relevant provisions of the Sexual Offences Act 1956 are intended to protect women and girls. Most certainly, section 11 is intended to protect girls under the age of 16 from criminal liability, and the Act as a whole exists, in so far as it deals with women and girls exposed to sexual threat, to protect them. The very fact that girls under the age of 16 are protected from criminal liability for what would otherwise be incest demonstrates that this girl who is said to have been the subject of incitement was being incited to do something which, if she did it, could not be a crime by her.

. . .

We have therefore come to the conclusion, with regret, that the indictment does not disclose an offence known to the law because it cannot be a crime on the part of this girl aged 15 to have sexual intercourse with her father, though it is of course a crime, and a very serious crime, on the part of the father. There is here incitement to a course of conduct, but that course of conduct cannot be treated as a crime by the girl. Plainly a gap or lacuna in the protection of girls under the age of 16 is exposed by this decision. It is regrettable indeed that a man who importunes his daughter under the age of 16 to have sexual intercourse with him but does not go beyond incitement cannot be found guilty of a crime. . . .

NOTES AND QUESTIONS
1. *Whitehouse* was decided as it was because of a gap in the law. The defendant in *Whitehouse* would now be guilty of an offence under s. 54 of the Criminal Law Act 1977.
2. Generally, if the individual incited lacks the capacity to commit a crime, such as in the case of a child below the age of criminal responsibility, the defendant cannot be convicted of incitement. Why should this be so? If the child commits the *actus reus* of the crime, however, the defendant may be liable as a principal acting through an innocent agent.
3. A victim is not liable as an accessory where the crime was created to protect her vulnerability. See *R* v *Tyrrell* [1894] 1 QB 710. Does it follow that a defendant should be guilty of inciting such a victim to commit that crime?

B: *Mens rea*

The defendant must intend that the offence incited should be committed. But what exactly does this mean?

R v Shaw

[1994] Crim LR 365, Court of Appeal

S was charged with incitement to obtain property by deception. He was employed as an after-sales co-ordinator for a car leasing company. The incited person, K, was a senior maintenance controller employed by the same company who had to check invoices submitted by garages for work done on company vehicles and authorising payment of such garages. The Crown alleged that S dishonestly incited K dishonestly to obtain cheques from the company by falsely accepting bogus invoices, supplied by S, as real invoices for real work done by real garages. When S was arrested one such cheque had been issued. S's defence was that he set up the scheme not to make a profit for himself but to disclose to his employers how easily the company's security arrangements were circumvented; he had drawn certain deficiencies to the attention of a superior but nothing had been done. He hoped by perpetrating the scheme to gain esteem and perhaps promotion in the company. He did not tell K what his purpose was behind the scheme but would eventually have done so. After the jury had retired to consider their verdict they returned with a note asking whether they had to be satisfied only as to the statement of offence or also as to the particulars of the offence on the indictment: some of the jurors felt that particulars referring to S 'profiting from the scheme' were not satisfied because they believed it possible that S wished to demonstrate the insecurity of the company's system; to convict on the wording of the statement of offence in the indictment might be taken to include a finding of guilt in relation to the particulars which some jurors were not prepared to do. The judge restated to the jury (and gave them a written copy of) his direction on dishonesty, explaining that when S said he told K about his scheme intending K to take it as a dishonest scheme to obtain dishonest benefits he intended to obtain benefits by reason of the incited person's dishonesty. S appealed against conviction, submitting that the judge had misdirected the jury.

Held allowing the appeal, the jury were concerned with the proof of *mens rea* both of S and of K, since both had to be considered. (Blackstone, *Criminal Practice*, p. 75.) Moreover, the particulars of offence included the phrase 'with the intention of permanently depriving them thereof by deception' which must have caused the jury difficulty in this case. The judge in his reply did not deal with the difficulty they raised. He should instead have told the jury that the possible finding they mentioned in relation to the particulars of offence would lead to an acquittal; and he should have indicated that if they merely thought, rather than believed, it possible that S was concerned to demonstrate to the firm the insecurity of their system the verdict should be not guilty. The jury quickly returned a verdict of guilty after the judge had restated his direction to them. Although there was no criticism of the summing-up itself, the failure to deal properly with the jury's concern on the vital question in the case rendered the conviction unsafe.

NOTES AND QUESTIONS

1. Does the Court in *Shaw* confuse intent and motive? Does it matter why Shaw incited K to obtain property by deception? Does it matter whether Shaw had the *mens rea* for obtaining property by deception?

2. The Draft Criminal Code would provide:

   (1) A person is guilty of incitement to commit an offence or offences if
   (a) he incites another to do or cause to be done an act or acts which, if done, will involve the commission of the offence or offences by the other; and
   (b) he intends or believes that the other, if he acts as incited, shall or will do so with the fault required for the offence or offences.

   What would the result be in *Shaw* under this provision?

Is it necessary for a conviction for incitement that the person incited intended to commit a criminal offence?

R v Curr

[1968] 2 QB 944, Court of Appeal

FENTON ATKINSON J: . . . The facts shortly were these, that he was in fact a trafficker in family allowance books. His method was to approach some married woman who had a large family of children and lend her money on the security of her family allowance book. A woman would borrow from him, let us say, £6, and would sign three of the vouchers in her family allowance book to the value of, let us say, £9, and hand over the book to him as security. He then had a team of women agents whom he sent out to cash the vouchers, and he would pocket the proceeds in repayment of the loans and thereafter return the books. He admitted quite freely in evidence that he had done, as he put it, 40 to 80 books a week, and he said, in February, 1966, he had between three and five women agents assisting him in this matter, and when he was arrested he had about 80 family allowance books in his possession. He agreed quite frankly that he knew he was not legally entitled to receive these payments, and that it could be risky; in dealing with the husband of one of the women concerned he said: 'When you're doing business like this, you should keep your big mouth shut.' So it is quite plain that the dealings of this man were highly objectionable, and the assistant recorder who tried the case clearly had very strong views about it; on two occasions in his summing-up he spoke of preying on these women with large families, and he finished up his direction to the jury with words to this effect: 'If you are getting interest at 800 per cent per annum it is not bad, is it? That is what the prosecution say here, that the whole system was corrupt,' and the language there used was no whit too strong.

But the very nature of the case being bound to arouse strong prejudice in the mind of any right-thinking juror, for that reason it was all the more important to put the law on each count clearly to the jury, and to make sure that the defence was clearly put before them.

Section 9 is headed 'Penalty for obtaining or receiving payment wrongfully,' and provides:

> If any person − . . . (b) obtains or receives any such sum as on account of an allowance, either as in that person's own right or as on behalf of another, knowing that it was not properly payable, or not properly receivable by him or her; that person shall be liable on summary conviction to imprisonment for a term not exceeding three months or to a fine not exceeding fifty pounds or to both such imprisonment and such fine.

Mr Kershaw's argument was that if the woman agent in fact has no guilty knowledge, knowing perhaps nothing of the assignment, or supposing that the defendant was merely collecting for the use and benefit of the woman concerned, then she would be an innocent agent, and by using her services in that way the defendant would be committing the summary offence himself, but would not be inciting her to receive money knowing that it was not receivable by her. He contends that it was essential to prove, to support this charge, that the woman agent in question in this transaction affecting a Mrs Currie knew that the allowances were not properly receivable by her. Mr Hugill's answer to that submission was that the woman agent must be presumed to know the law, and if she knew the law, she must have known, he contends, that the allowance was not receivable by her. . . . in our view the defendant could only be guilty on count 3 if the woman solicited, that is, the woman agent sent to collect the allowance, knew that the action she was asked to carry out amounted to an offence. As has already been said, the defendant himself clearly knew that his conduct in the matter was illegal and contrary to section 9(b), but it was essential in our view for the jury to consider the knowledge, if any, of the woman agent. The assistant recorder dealt with this count by referring to soliciting as follows: 'Solicited means encouraged or incited another person to go and draw that money which should have been paid, you may think, to Mrs Currie.' He later dealt with ignorance of the law being no excuse. He went on to deal with statutory offences, section 4 of the Family Allowances Act, 1945, telling the jury in effect that, apart from the case of sickness, nobody else could legally receive these allowances, and then went on to consider the position of the defendant, asking the rhetorical question whether he could be heard to say with his knowledge of this matter and his trafficking in these books that it was not known to be wrong to employ an agent to go and collect the family allowances. But the assistant recorder never followed that with the question of the knowledge of the women agents, and in the whole of the summing-up dealing with this matter he proceeded on the assumption that either guilty knowledge in the woman agent was irrelevant, or, alternatively, that any woman agent must be taken to have known that she was committing an offence under section 9(b).

NOTES AND QUESTIONS
1. Was the defendant simply charged with the wrong crime (conspiracy) as opposed to being a principal to the substantive offence (the women being his innocent agents)?
2. Incitement may be committed even though the person incited is unmoved (see *Applin*, above). If so, why does the *mens rea* of the person incited matter? In *DPP* v *Armstrong (Andrew)* (1999) 96 (45) LSG 32 the defendant was accused of attempting to incite a police officer to supply him with pornographic pictures. The officer had access to such pictures but no intention of supplying them to the defendant. It was held that the defendant could be convicted despite the lack of *mens rea* of the officer. Where does this leave *Curr*? Is it still good law?

C: Impossibility

The law generally distinguishes between legal and factual impossibility. If the acts incited would not, if committed, constitute a crime, then the defendant is not guilty of incitement. This is a case of legal impossibility. Thus if A urges B to drive at 50 mph thinking that the speed limit on the road is 40 mph when it is in fact 70 mph, he is not guilty of incitement. Similarly, if a woman attempts to persuade a married man to commit adultery in the belief that adultery is a criminal offence (which it is not), she will not be guilty of incitement.

Factual impossibility is another matter. Here there is incitement to commit what is a crime but due to factual circumstances unknown to the incitor, the crime is incapable of being committed. As we shall see, by statute factual impossibility is not a defence to a charge of either attempt or conspiracy. However, in *R* v *Fitzmaurice* [1983] QB 1083, the Court of Appeal stated in *obiter* that if an offence was factually impossible, the defendant could not be liable for incitement. An example would be where A incites B to kill C who is already dead. Difficulties may arise where the incitement to kill C 'next Thursday' takes place on Monday when C is alive, but C dies on Wednesday – is the defendant guilty of incitement? Consider the following case:

R v *Shephard*
[1919] 2 KB 125, Court of Appeal

On 20 September, 1917, the appellant wrote to one Cicely Maria, Shephard, who was then about six weeks gone with child, a letter in which he said: 'When the kiddie is born you must lie on it in the night. Do not let it live.' The child was born alive on 31 May 1918. In March, 1919, the appellant was convicted at the Central Criminal Court on an indictment which charged him with having 'on September 20, 1917, solicited and endeavoured to persuade Cicely Maria

Shephard thereafter to murder a newly born child lately before then born of her body.' The indictment was framed under s. 4 of the Offences against the Person Act 1861.

BRAY J: . . . All that is essential to bring a case within the section is that there should be a person capable of being murdered at the time when the act of murder is to be committed. If there is such a person then in existence it is quite immaterial that that person was not in existence at the date of the incitement. . . .

NOTES AND QUESTIONS
1. Ivor incites Dan to steal a diamond ring, telling him that there will be an opportunity to take it in three days' time. Will Ivor be guilty of incitement in each of the following circumstances?
   (a) the ring belongs to Dan;
   (b) before Dan has an opportunity to take the ring the owner loses it down a well;
   (c) the owner of the ring gives it to Dan immediately after the incitement;
   (d) the opportunity to take the ring never arises.
2. In theory, is there any reason why the law in respect to factual impossibility in regard to incitement should be different than it is in respect to conspiracy and attempt? The Law Commission in its Draft Criminal Code would bring incitement into line with attempt and conspiracy. See Draft Criminal Code 1989, s. 50.

SECTION 2: Conspiracy

The laws of conspiracy are aimed at the special dangers posed by criminal groups. As in respect of incitement, there are statutes which address specific forms of conspiracy as well as a general offence of conspiracy:

Offences Against the Person Act 1861

4.   Conspiring or soliciting to commit murder

Sexual Offences (Conspiracy and Incitement) Act 1996

This act has been considered in the context of incitement (above p. 470). The following provisions extend the jurisdiction of the United Kingdom courts in the context of the offence of conspiracy.

1.   Conspiracy to commit certain sexual acts outside the United Kingdom
   (1) Where each of the following conditions is satisfied in the case of any agreement, Part I of the Criminal Law Act 1977 (conspiracy) has effect in relation to the agreement as it has effect in relation to an agreement falling within section 1(1) of that Act.
   (2) The first condition is that the pursuit of the agreed course of conduct would at some stage involve—
      (a) an act by one or more of the parties, or
      (b) the happening of some other event, intended to take place in a country or territory outside the United Kingdom.

(3) The second condition is that that act or other event constitutes an offence under the law in force in that country or territory.

(4) The third condition is that the agreement would fall within section 1(1) of that Act as an agreement relating to the commission of a listed sexual offence but for the fact that the offence would not be an offence triable in England and Wales if committed in accordance with the parties' intentions.

(5) The fourth condition is that—

(a) a party to the agreement, or a party's agent, did anything in England and Wales in relation to the agreement before its formation, or

(b) a party to the agreement became a party in England and Wales (by joining it either in person or through an agent), or

(c) a party to the agreement, or a party's agent, did or omitted anything in England and Wales in pursuance of the agreement.

(6) In the application of Part I of that Act to such an agreement, any reference to an offence is to be read as a reference to what would be the listed sexual offence in question but for the fact that it is not an offence triable in England and Wales.

At common law the general offence was defined as an agreement between two or more persons to do 'an unlawful act or a lawful act by unlawful means'. This included agreements to commit acts which would not of themselves be crimes. The usual justification for this was that a number of people engaged in a harmful enterprise was more menacing to society than one person. (*R* v *Mulcahy* (1868) LR 3 HL 306, *R* v *Kamara* [1974] AC 104.) More ambitious, sophisticated and complex crimes become possible, and the likelihood of successful execution increases as more minds and bodies lend themselves to the task at hand. Peer group pressure may also militate against abandonment of the criminal enterprise. (There is also the possibility, of course, that the more people who are involved, the greater the chance of a cock-up.) See generally I. Dennis, 'The rationale of criminal conspiracy' (1977) 93 LQR 785.

The law is now in a state of change. The goal of the Law Commission was to confine the offence of conspiracy to agreements to commit acts which would amount to a criminal offence if committed by a single individual. The current legislation does not fully achieve this aim and leaves some grey areas. Further reform awaits the outcome of a review of the law relating to fraud and indecency. The current relevant statutes are the Criminal Law Act 1977, as amended by the Criminal Attempts Act 1981, and the Criminal Justice Act 1987.

It is now an offence to agree:

(a) to commit any criminal offence triable within the jurisdiction, even an offence triable only summarily (it should be noted that jurisdictional rules will change with the passing of the Criminal Justice Act 1993);

(b) to defraud, whether or not the fraud amounts to a crime;

(c) to do an act which tends to corrupt public morals or outrage public decency, whether or not the act amounts to a crime.

Section 1 of the Criminal Law Act 1977 creates the offence of statutory conspiracy.

Criminal Law Act 1977

(as amended by the Criminal Attempts Act 1981)

1.—(1) Subject to the following provisions of this Part of this Act, if a person agrees with any other person or persons that a course of conduct shall be pursued which, if the agreement is carried out in accordance with their intentions, either—

(a) will necessarily amount to or involve the commission of any offence or offences by one or more of the parties to the agreement, or

(b) would do so but for the existence of facts which render the commission of the offence or any of the offences impossible,

he is guilty of conspiracy to commit the offence or offences in question.

Note

In *R* v *Ayres* [1984] AC 447, the House of Lords held that where the carrying out of the conspiracy would necessarily involve a crime, the indictment must allege a statutory conspiracy and not a common law conspiracy. This led to great difficulties, particularly where an offence of conspiracy to defraud was alleged. Defendants argued that the behaviour envisaged would amount to a crime so that the common law conspiracy indictment against them was improper. This rule has now been reversed in respect of conspiracy to defraud by the Criminal Justice Act 1987, s. 12:

Criminal Justice Act 1987

12.—(1) If—

(a) a person agrees with any other person or persons that a course of conduct shall be pursued; and

(b) that course of conduct will necessarily amount to or involve the commission of any offence or offences by one or more of the parties to the agreement if the agreement is carried out in accordance with their intentions, the fact that it will do so shall not preclude a charge of conspiracy to defraud being brought against any of them in respect of the agreement.

A: Common elements in statutory and common law conspiracies

(i) *Agreement*

The essence of conspiracy is an agreement. The agreement need never be put into effect. The offence is complete when the agreement is made but continues as long as the agreement subsists.

Director of Public Prosecutions v *Doot*

[1973] AC 807, House of Lords

The respondents, American citizens, formed a plan abroad to import cannabis into the United States by way of England. In pursuance of the plan, two vans with cannabis concealed in them were shipped from Morocco to Southampton. The cannabis in one of the vans was discovered at Southampton; the other van was traced to Liverpool, from where the vans were to have been shipped to America, and the cannabis in it was found. The respondents were charged with, *inter alia*, conspiracy to import dangerous drugs. At the trial, they contended that the court had no jurisdiction to try them on that count since the conspiracy had been entered into abroad. Lawson J overruled that submission, but the Court of Appeal quashed the respondents' convictions, holding that the offence of conspiracy was completed when the agreement was made.

On appeal by the Director of Public Prosecutions:—

LORD WILBERFORCE: . . . In my opinion, the key to a decision for or against the offence charged can be found in an answer to the question why the common law treats certain actions as crimes. And one answer must certainly be because the actions in question are a threat to the Queen's peace, or, as we would now perhaps say, to society. Judged by this test, there is every reason for, and none that I can see against, the prosecution. Conspiracies are intended to be carried into effect, and one reason why, in addition to individual prosecution of each participant, conspiracy charges are brought is because criminal action organised, and executed, in concert is more dangerous than an individual breach of the law. Why, then, refrain from prosecution where the relevant concert was, initially, formed outside the United Kingdom?

Often in conspiracy cases the implementing action is itself the only evidence of the conspiracy – this is the doctrine of overt acts. Could it be said, with any plausibility, that if the conclusion or a possible conclusion to be drawn from overt acts in England was that there was a conspiracy, entered into abroad, a charge of conspiracy would not lie? Surely not: yet, if it could, what difference should it make if the conspiracy is directly proved or is admitted to have been made abroad? The truth is that, in the normal case of a conspiracy carried out, or partly carried out, in this country, the location of the formation of the agreement is irrelevant: the attack upon the laws of this country is identical wherever the conspirators happened to meet; the 'conspiracy' is a complex, formed indeed, but not separately completed, at the first meeting of the plotters.

. . .

VISCOUNT DILHORNE: . . . The conclusion to which I have come after consideration of these authorities and of many others to which the House was referred but to which I do not think it is necessary to refer is that though the offence of conspiracy is complete when the agreement to do the unlawful act is made and it is not necessary for the prosecution to do more than prove the making of such an agreement, a conspiracy does not end with the making of the agreement. It continues so long as the parties to the agreement intend to carry it out. It may be joined by others, some may leave it. Proof of acts done by the accused in this country may suffice to prove that there was at the time of those acts a conspiracy in existence in this country to which they were parties and, if that is proved, then the charge of conspiracy is within the jurisdiction of the English courts, even though the initial agreement was made outside the jurisdiction.

NOTES AND QUESTIONS
1. Should the result in *DPP* v *Doot* be affected by whether or not the conspirators would be subject to prosecution in the country in which the conspiracy was formed? Might those who conspire to engage in illegal international trade be subject to prosecution in multiple jurisdictions? Is this fair?
2. Note the jurisdictional issue decided in *DPP* v *Doot*: a conspiracy formed outside of the jurisdiction can be prosecuted in the UK if the parties committed acts within the jurisdiction. In *Somchai Liangsiriprasert* v *United States* [1990] AC 607, the Privy Council went further and held that no overt act need be committed within the jurisdiction. See also *R* v *Sansom* [1991] 92 Cr App R 115. In *R* v *Naini (Jamshid Hashami)* [1999] 2 Cr App R 398 the Court of Appeal held that if the conspiracy was entered into in England and Wales but to do something in a

foreign country, there was no jurisdiction. If the conspiracy, whenever made, was to do something in England and Wales, even if no overt act was committed, there was jurisdiction in the courts of England and Wales.

3. Conspiracy is a continuing offence, and from time to time new members may join an existing conspiracy. They too become liable for conspiracy, although not for crimes committed prior to their joining. Thus it often becomes important to determine the period during which a defendant is a member of the conspiracy.

R v Scott

(1979) 68 Cr App R 164, Court of Appeal

GEOFFREY LANE LJ: . . . The prosecution put their case in two ways. They suggested that the appellant must have known from the beginning what Jensby and Donovan were up to; having acquired that knowledge she continued to help them, and was therefore proved to have conspired. Had the prosecution left the matter there, no difficulty would have arisen. There was a formidable body of evidence to support the argument; the appellant herself admitted that she knew that Jensby and Donovan were involved in a scheme which was illegal and added 'the only conclusion I could draw since Jan (Jensby) was in Kenya was that I suspected it was drugs. I suppose I closed my mind.'

However, the prosecution, in an endeavour to make assurance double sure, contended that the appellant's admitted knowledge acquired on February 28, 1976, even if that was the first time she had the guilty knowledge, was enough to prove her guilty of conspiracy, despite the fact that thereafter she did no overt act in pursuance of the illegal scheme. She admitted that if she had been asked after that date to help by paying in cheques received from Donovan, she would have done so, but it was plain that she had not been so asked, and that she had not informed either Jensby or Donovan whether or not she was willing to help.

The judge, in directing the jury on the second limb of the prosecution case, used the following words:

> If up to that point she had been an innocent party in doing what she did, she then ceased to be an innocent party [say the prosecution] and became a conspirator so as to render herself liable to conviction in respect of this offence. That is what it comes to, and you have to decide what was meant by it when it was said, if it was . . . that if the cheques had arrived she would have paid them in. Is that, members of the jury, from your point of view, evidence which convinces you that at that stage she was prepared to act in furtherance of her agreement? Is it evidence that the agreement which she was saying that she then had was, whether she liked it or not, to assist in the supplying of drugs by being a person who would, if the cheques had arrived, no doubt as a result of the supply and sale of drugs, she would have then paid them into such accounts as she had been asked to – and thereby assist in the workings of this conspiracy?

What the learned judge was doing there was to put forward to the jury the prosecution's proposition, namely, that even if she was not aware of the illegality of Jensby's activities until February 28, 1976, yet nevertheless she was guilty of conspiracy at that moment by reason of her secret and uncommunicated intention to deal in the way Jensby had requested with any cheques which might arrive from Donovan.

It may be that the jury came to the conclusion (not entirely disavowed by the prosecution) that the appellant was until February 28, 1976, unaware of the true nature of Jensby's activities. On that date she learnt for the first time for certain that he was smuggling drugs. She then determines that she would nevertheless continue to help him in what she then realised for the first time were illegal activities relating to the importation of cannabis. That determination she never communicated to anyone else. It was submitted for the respondent that this was sufficient to make her party to an agreement to assist in the supply of controlled drugs and therefore a conspirator. We do not think it was. It is evidence that she had secretly determined to assist Jensby in his importation and supply of cannabis, should the opportunity arise. It is evidence of what doubtless she would have done, given the chance. But an intent, should the occasion arise, to join in an illegal enterprise, an intent which is never communicated in any way whatsoever to any other person, remains only an intent and cannot at any rate in these circumstances amount to an indictable conspiracy.

The further suggestion put forward is equally untenable, namely that the appellant, by failing to notify Jensby or Donovan after February 28, 1976, that she was no longer prepared to help, notionally or constructively became a party to the illegal enterprise. An intention to enter into an agreement must, to become effective as an agreement, be communicated to the other party by some means or other. It is difficult to see how non-communication can amount to communication. The long and short of this matter is that after February 28 the appellant never went beyond the intention or wish to act illegally. However reprehensible that may be, it was not proof of the conspiracy alleged. To that extent the prosecution's second contention and the judge's direction based upon it were wrong.

. . .

NOTES AND QUESTIONS

1. At lunch Ian proposes to Elaine and Eleanor that they spray-paint the university's administrative building that evening at midnight. Neither responds one way or the other. At midnight Elaine, but not Eleanor, shows up outside the administration building, where Ian is waiting. Is there a conspiracy to commit criminal damage? Between whom? When was it formed? Did Eleanor need to inform either Ian or Elaine that she did not wish to participate in order to avoid liability?

2. If there is an agreement in principle but details remain to be ironed out, the parties can still be convicted of conspiracy.

(ii) *Agreement with whom?*

There must be another human conspirator, although he/she need not be identified (*R v Phillips* (1987) 86 Cr App R 18).

R v McDonnell
[1966] 1 QB 233, Queen's Bench Division

At all material times the defendant was a director and the sole person in each of two companies responsible for the acts of the company. He was charged on an indictment containing ten counts: two of the counts (one in respect of each company) charged him with conspiring with the company to defraud, one with conspiring with one of the companies to induce persons to acquire a right or interest in land, four counts charged him with fraudulent conversion of the property of the companies.

NIELD J: . . . [T]hese charges of conspiracy cannot be sustained, upon the footing that in the particular circumstances here, where the sole responsible person in the company is the defendant himself, it would not be right to say that there were two persons or two minds. If it were otherwise, I feel that it would offend against the basic concept of a conspiracy, namely, an agreement of two or more to do an unlawful act, and I think it would be artificial to take the view that the company, although it is clearly a separate legal entity, can be regarded here as a separate person or a separate mind, in view of the admitted fact that this defendant acts alone so far as these companies are concerned.

NOTES AND QUESTIONS

1. For purposes of the criminal law, a company is often treated as if it were a person (see Interpretation Act 1889). In *R v ICR Haulage Ltd* [1944] 1 All ER 691 it was held that a company could be guilty of conspiracy. Why, then, the holding in *McDonnell*? What more would a prosecutor need to show in order to secure a conviction?

2. There is a number of combinations of people whose agreement to commit a crime will not amount to a conspiracy if there are no other parties involved. Thus a husband and wife cannot conspire by themselves, although they can commit conspiracy with a third party. This rule may have made sense at common law, where husband and wife were treated as a unity; but in a modern age, where both husband and wife have separate, independent legal identities, is there any justification for preserving the rule relating to conspiracy? (See Criminal Law Act 1977, s. 2 (2); *Mawji v R* [1957] AC 126.)

3. Where the only other party to the conspiracy is a child under 10 or the intended victim of the offence (Criminal Law Act 1977, s. 2 (2)) there again can be no conspiracy. Why? The Draft Criminal Code Bill would remove these exemptions, leaving the various situations to be governed by general principles relating to conspiracy.

Although a person may be exempt from liability as a principal, the exemption may not necessarily extend to liability for conspiracy:

R v Burns (and others)

(1984) 79 Cr App R 173, Court of Appeal

By s. 56 of the Offences Against the Person Act 1861: 'Whosoever shall unlawfully . . . by force . . . take away . . . any child under the age of 14 years, with intent to deprive any parent . . . of the possession of such child . . . shall be . . . liable, at the discretion of the court, to imprisonment for any term not exceeding seven years . . . Provided that no person who shall have claimed any right to the possession of such child, or shall be the mother or shall have claimed to be the father of an illegitimate child, shall be liable to be prosecuted by virtue hereof on account of the getting possession of such child, or taking such child out of the possession of any person having lawful charge thereof.'

The appellant J B married a second time in 1975 and had two children. Between the births of those children he had another child by his second wife's sister who was also living with them. That child became a ward of court and J B divorced his second wife. The children were committed to the care of their mothers, both of whom had returned to their parents' home to live. J B was not allowed access to the children. He decided to seize the children and recruited the three applicants, R, J and S B, for that purpose. One night all four men drove to the house where the women and children were living, forced an entry and took the children, then aged between three and six and a half years, out of the house and into the waiting car. J B then took the children to accommodation he had prepared for them and the three applicants returned to their respective homes. All four men were charged with conspiracy to take the children and substantive counts, again against all four, of child stealing contrary to s. 56 of the Offences Against the Person Act 1861. When put to his election, prosecution counsel decided to proceed on the conspiracy count only against J B, and on the child stealing count only against the three applicants. All four were convicted. J B appealed against his conviction on the ground that the judge should not have exercised his discretion in a way that allowed him to be put in jeopardy of being convicted of conspiracy to commit an offence when he could not have been charged with the substantive offence (which he had in fact committed) because of the immunity from prosecution provided by s. 56 of the 1861 Act.

WATKINS LJ: . . . The dangers of permitting a father of children to collect a posse of men and suddenly to launch a seige of the home of his erstwhile wife, to break in and then snatch away sleeping children are surely self-evident. The criminal law does not in our view permit that sort of conduct. When a father who is exempt under section 56 behaves in that way, it is, in our judgment, not only lawful but right and just that the prosecution should be free to bring a charge of conspiracy against him.

NOTES AND QUESTIONS

The Court states that the dangers of a father's breaking into his wife's home and snatching the children are 'surely self-evident'. But equally surely, these dangers were self-evident to Parliament who granted the husband exemption from the substantive crime. Why should a court be able to evade this policy decision of the legislature and impose liability through the back door of conspiracy? Section 56 of the Offences Against the Person Act 1861 was repealed by the Child Abduction Act 1984. On the conspiracy point, see also *R v Whitchurch* (1890) 24 QBD 420.

Section 5(8) and (9) of the Criminal Law Act 1977 addresses the situation where some but not all of the conspirators are acquitted. Can the convictions of the others stand?

Criminal Law Act 1977

5.—(8) The fact that the person or persons who, so far as appears from the indictment on which any person has been convicted of conspiracy, were the only other parties to the agreement on which his conviction was based have been acquitted of conspiracy by reference to that agreement (whether after being tried with the person convicted or separately) shall not be a ground for quashing his conviction unless under all the circumstances of the case his conviction is inconsistent with the acquittal of the other person or persons in question.

(9) Any rule of law or practice inconsistent with the provisions of subsection (8) above is hereby abolished.

R v *Longman and Cribben*
(1980) 72 Cr App R 121, Court of Appeal

THE LORD CHIEF JUSTICE: The facts of the case were these. Longman was the proprietor of a garage and car-sales business. Cribben worked for him as a salesman. The prosecution allegation was that they had conspired to defraud an insurance company of £3,323 by making a false claim in respect of the theft of a car; that the purported purchase of the car by Longman from a man called Pentow and the purported sale by Longman to Cribben were shams; that the car was never stolen; that the whole pretended transaction was designed by the two men with a view to perpetrating a fraud on the insurance company.

The evidence adduced by the prosecution was mostly circumstantial evidence of suspicious or highly suspicious actions by the two men. Longman was seen by the police and throughout hotly denied all the allegations made against him. He asserted that the man Pentow had brought the car to his garage, it was apparently in good repair; he bought it and later sold it to Cribben in the ordinary course of business. He denied any fraud.

The case against Cribben was much stronger. In addition to the circumstantial evidence, he made what amounted to a full confession to the police, stating in terms that he had, in fact, conspired with Longman to defraud the insurance company and that the car had never been delivered to the garage at all and had certainly never been bought by him. In short, that confession, if the jury were satisfied as to its truth, was conclusive evidence against Cribben that he had conspired with Longman in the way that the prosecution alleged. Longman gave evidence at the trial. Cribben did not.

. . . [T]he situation has been changed by the provisions of the Criminal Law Act 1977, s. 5(8) and (9) . . .

In our judgment the effect of those two subsections is to . . . [abolish] the rule of common law that if two persons are accused of conspiring together and one is acquitted and the other convicted, the conviction must be quashed. They also mean that the trial judge is no longer obliged to direct juries that they must convict both conspirators or acquit both conspirators . . . .

We also respectfully adopt the conclusion reached by the Court in that case that the provisions of the Criminal Law Act 1977, s. 5 (8) and (9) do not mean that such a direction may never be given if the circumstances warrant it. When a trial judge is faced with the task of directing a jury in a case of this sort, where the charge is that A and B conspired together but with no one else to commit crime, he will, as in other cases involving two defendants, as a general rule have to tell the jury that they must consider the evidence against each defendant separately. Where the strength of the evidence against each is markedly different, usually (as in the instant case) because A has confessed and B has not, he should then go on to explain that because there is that difference in the evidence against each, the jury may come to the conclusion that the prosecution have proved beyond doubt against A that A conspired with B, but have not proved against B that any such conspiracy existed.

That may appear to be illogical, but it is the necessary result of the rules of evidence which are designed to ensure fairness. If, therefore, the jury are satisfied that A conspired with B but are not satisfied that there is adequate evidence of B's guilt, they should convict A and acquit B. We can see no reason why the jury should not understand such a direction.

Where at the close of the prosecution case the evidence against one of the defendants is such that it would be unsafe to ask any jury to convict, then it goes without saying that the judge should so rule, and the case can then continue against the other defendant.

There will, however, be cases where the evidence against A and B is of equal weight or nearly so. In such a case there may be a risk of inconsistent verdicts, and the judge should direct the jury that because of the similarity of the evidence against each, the only just result would be the same verdict in respect of each: that is to say, both guilty or both not guilty. He must be careful to add, however, that if they are unsure about the guilt of one, then both must be found not guilty.

Whether he gives such a direction will, of course, depend on the way the evidence has emerged. The test is this. Is the evidence such that a verdict of guilty in respect of A and not guilty in respect of B would be, to all intents and purposes, inexplicable and therefore inconsistent? If so, it would be an occasion for the 'both guilty or both not guilty' direction. If not, then the separate verdict direction is required.

B: Statutory conspiracy

The definition of the offence of conspiracy is contained in the Criminal Law Act 1977, s. 1(1) (see p. 536).

(i) *Agreement that a course of conduct shall be pursued*

At common law the prosecution had to prove that each conspirator intended the commission of the offence envisaged. Otherwise there would exist the possibility that a conspiracy could exist even though no conspirator actually intended an offence to be committed. The phrase 'course of conduct' within the statute is thus not limited to physical acts but includes intended consequences. The *mens rea* implicit in the requirement of an agreement is an intention that the offence will be committed, even if the offence itself may be committed with a lesser *mens rea* than intent. An example is a conspiracy to murder, which requires an intention to kill on the part of the conspirators. Murder itself can be committed by a defendant who intends only grievous bodily harm, but such an intent is not sufficient to establish a conspiracy to murder. Similarly, even though strict liability or negligence may suffice as to a circumstance of a crime, a conspiracy to commit the crime cannot be established without proof that the conspirators 'intend or know' that the relevant circumstance will exist at the time the offence is to take place. The courts, however, have not always been strictly logical in their approach.

R v *Anderson*

[1986] AC 27, House of Lords

LORD BRIDGE OF HARWICH: . . . In June 1981 the appellant and Ahmed Andaloussi were both in custody on remand in Lewes prison. Andaloussi was awaiting trial on charges of very serious drug offences and was rightly believed by the appellant to have large sums of money at his disposal. The appellant was on remand in connection with some entirely different matter. He spent one night in the same cell as Andaloussi. The appellant was then confidently expecting that in a short time he would be, as in the event he was, released on bail. During the night they spent together the appellant agreed with Andaloussi to participate in a scheme to effect Andaloussi's escape from prison. Other participants in the scheme were to be Ahmed Andaloussi's brother Mohammed and Mohammed Assou. They were to maintain contact with Ahmed in prison after the appellant's release. The appellant was to be paid £20,000 for his part in the escape scheme. It is not clear, nor is it significant for the purpose of any issue arising in the appeal, how far the details of the escape plan were worked out at the initial meeting in prison between the appellant and Ahmed Andaloussi. What is clear is that either at that meeting or after the appellant's release from prison and after one or more meetings between the appellant and Assou, it was agreed that the appellant would purchase and supply diamond wire, a cutting agent capable of cutting through metal bars, to be smuggled into the prison by Assou or Mohammed Andaloussi to enable Ahmed Andaloussi to escape from his cell. Further steps in the escape plan were to include the provision of rope and a ladder to enable Ahmed Andaloussi to climb on to the roof of an industrial building in the prison and thence over the main wall, transport to drive him away from the prison and safe accommodation where he could hide.

What happened in the event was that the appellant received from Assou a payment of £2,000 on account of the agreed fee of £20,000. Shortly after this the appellant was injured in a road accident and thereafter took no further step in pursuance of the escape plan. His admitted intention, however, was to acquire the diamond wire and give it to Assou. His further intention, according to the version of the facts which we must for present purposes accept, was then to insist that before he would proceed further he should be paid a further £10,000 on account, on receipt of which he would have left the country and gone to live in Spain, taking no further part in the scheme to effect Andaloussi's escape.

On those facts the submission for the appellant which was rejected both by the trial judge and the Court of Appeal was that the appellant lacked the mental element essential to sustain his conviction of a conspiracy to effect Andaloussi's escape, since he never intended that the escape plan, in which, according to what had been agreed, he was to play a major part, should be carried into effect nor, according to some of his statements to the police, which again we must for present purposes accept as indicating his true state of mind, did he believe that, in the circumstances, the plan to enable Andaloussi to escape could possibly succeed.

The Court of Appeal, having dismissed his appeal, certified that their decision involved a point of law of general public importance in terms which can conveniently be divided into two parts, since, in truth, there are two separate questions involved:

(1) Is a person who 'agrees' with two or more others, who themselves intend to pursue a course of conduct which will necessarily involve the commission of an offence, and who has a secret intention himself to participate in part only of that course of conduct, guilty himself of conspiracy to commit that offence under section 1(1) of the Criminal Law Act 1977?

(2) If not, is he liable to be indicted as a principal offender under section 8 of the Accessories and Abettors Act 1861?

. . . I am clearly driven by consideration of the diversity of roles which parties may agree to play in criminal conspiracies to reject any construction of the statutory language which would require the prosecution to prove an intention on the part of each conspirator that the criminal offence or offences which will necessarily be committed by one or more of the conspirators if the agreed course of conduct is fully carried out should in fact be committed. A simple example will illustrate the absurdity to which this construction would lead. The proprietor of a car hire firm agrees for a substantial payment to make available a hire car to a gang for use in a robbery and to make false entries in his books relating to the hiring to which he can point if the number of the car is traced back to him in connection with the robbery. Being fully aware of the circumstances of the robbery in which the car is proposed to be used he is plainly a party to the conspiracy to rob. Making his car available for use in the robbery is as much a part of the relevant agreed course of conduct as the robbery itself. Yet, once he has been paid, it will be a matter of complete indifference to him whether the robbery is in fact committed or not. In these days of highly organised crime the most serious statutory conspiracies will frequently involve an elaborate and complex agreed course of conduct in which many will consent to play necessary but subordinate roles, not involving them in any direct participation in the commission of the offence or offences at the centre of the conspiracy. Parliament cannot have intended that such parties should escape conviction of conspiracy on the basis that it cannot be proved against them that they intended that the relevant offence or offences should be committed.

There remains the important question whether a person who has agreed that a course of conduct will be pursued which, if pursued as agreed, will necessarily amount to or involve the commission of an offence is guilty of statutory conspiracy irrespective of his intention, and, if not, what is the *mens rea* of the offence. I have no hesitation in answering the first part of the question in the negative. There may be many situations in which perfectly respectable citizens, more particularly those concerned with law enforcement, may enter into agreements that a course of conduct shall be pursued which will involve commission of a crime without the least intention of playing any part in furtherance of the ostensibly agreed criminal objective, but rather with the purpose of exposing and frustrating the criminal purpose of the other parties to the agreement. To say this is in no way to encourage schemes by which police act, directly or through the agency of informers, as agents provocateurs for the purpose of entrapment. That is conduct of which the courts have always strongly disapproved. But it may sometimes happen, as most of us with experience in criminal trials well know, that a criminal enterprise is well advanced in the course of preparation when it comes to the notice either of the police or of some honest citizen in such circumstances that the only prospect of exposing and frustrating the criminals is that some innocent person should play the part of an intending collaborator in the course of criminal conduct proposed to be pursued. The mens rea implicit in the offence of statutory conspiracy must clearly be such as to recognise the innocence of such a person, notwithstanding that he will, in literal terms, be obliged to agree that a course of conduct be pursued involving the commission of an offence.

I have said already, but I repeat to emphasise its importance, that an essential ingredient in the crime of conspiring to commit a specific offence or offences under section 1(1) of the Act of 1977 is that the accused should agree that a course of conduct be pursued which he knows must involve the commission by one or more of the parties to the agreement of that offence or those offences. But, beyond the mere fact of agreement, the necessary mens rea of the crime is, in my opinion, established if, and only if, it is shown that the accused, when he entered into the agreement, intended to play some part in the agreed course of conduct in furtherance of the criminal purpose which the agreed course of conduct was intended to achieve. Nothing less will suffice; nothing more is required.

Applying this test to the facts which, for the purposes of the appeal, we must assume, the appellant, in agreeing that a course of conduct be pursued that would, if successful, necessarily involve the offence of effecting Andaloussi's escape from lawful custody, clearly intended, by providing diamond wire to be smuggled into the prison, to play a part in the agreed course of conduct in furtherance of that criminal objective. Neither the fact that he intended to play no further part in attempting to effect the escape, nor that he believed the escape to be impossible, would, if the jury had supposed they might be true, have afforded him any defence.

In the result, I would answer the first part of the certified question in the affirmative and dismiss the appeal. Your Lordships did not find it necessary to hear argument directed to the second part of the certified question and it must, therefore, be left unanswered.

NOTES AND QUESTIONS

1. Of what offence could Anderson have been convicted without distortion of the law of conspiracy? Could the examples given by Lord Bridge be adequately dealt with by charging aiding and abetting a conspiracy?
2. As a result of Lord Bridge's opinion, what is the position of the police officer who feigns agreement with persons already party to a conspiracy and, further, carries out minor acts towards completion of the offence? Is the officer guilty of conspiracy? See *Yip Chiu-Cheng* (below).
3. Anderson has been the object of much criticism, both judicial (see *Siracusa*, below) and academic (see, e.g., M. Allen, *Textbook on Criminal Law*, 5th ed. (1999), pp. 241–3).

R v *Siracusa (and others)*
(1990) 90 Cr App R 340, Court of Appeal

O'CONNOR LJ: . . . The case arises out of the operations of an organisation of smugglers engaged in moving massive quantities of heroin from Thailand and cannabis from Kashmir to Canada via England. The scheme was simple. The drugs were to be housed in secret compartments in selected items of locally produced furniture, which would be included in substantial shipments of furniture. The object of passing the consignments through England was to support the manifests to be presented to the Canadian customs declaring the country of origin of the goods as England.

. . .

The importation of controlled drugs into this country is prohibited by section 3(1)(a) of the Misuse of Drugs Act 1971. That section does not create any offence. The offence is created by section 170(2)(b) of the Customs and Excise Management Act 1979 which provides:

(2) . . . if any person is, in relation to any goods, in any way knowingly concerned in any fraudulent evasion or attempt at evasion: . . . (b) of any prohibition or restriction for the time being in force with respect to the goods under or by virtue of any enactment . . . he shall be guilty of an offence. . . .

At the relevant time, the effect of section 170(4) and Schedule 1 of the Act was that importation of drugs of Class A or Class B was punishable with up to 14 years' imprisonment.

In cases where controlled drugs are imported into this country and a substantive offence is charged as a contravention of section 170(2)(b), the particulars of the offence identify the drug and the class to which it belongs so that the appropriate penalty is not in doubt. Case law has established that although separate offences are created as a result of the different penalties authorised, the *mens rea* is the same. The prosecution must prove that the defendant knew that the goods were prohibited goods. They do not have to prove that he knew what the goods in fact were. Thus it is no defence for a man charged with importing a Class A drug to say he believed he was bringing in a Class C drug or indeed any other prohibited goods: *R* v *Hussain* (1969) 53 Cr App R 448; *R* v *Shivpuri* (1986) 83 Cr App R 178; *R* v *Ellis* (1987) 84 Cr App R 235.

The appellants contend that where conspiracy to contravene section 170(2)(b) is charged, the position is different so that in this case the prosecution had to prove against each defendant that he knew that the Kashmir operation involved cannabis and that the Thailand operation involved heroin. If this submission is well-founded, then it is said that the learned judge's direction on conspiracy is flawed and strength is added to the contentions of those appellants who submit that in respect of one, other or both counts, there was no case to go to the jury at the end of the prosecution case.

[In *R* v *Anderson* [1986] AC 27, Lord Bridge said: . . .]

> I have said already, but I repeat to emphasise its importance, that an essential ingredient in the crime of conspiring to commit a specific offence or offences under section 1(1) of the Act of 1977 is that the accused should agree that a course of conduct be pursued which he knows must involve the commission by one or more of the parties to the agreement of that offence or those offences. But, beyond the mere fact of agreement, the necessary *mens rea* of the crime is, in my opinion, established if, and only if, it is shown that the accused, when he entered into the agreement, intended to play some part in the agreed course of conduct in furtherance of the criminal purpose which the agreed course of conduct was intended to achieve. Nothing less will suffice; nothing more is required.

The last paragraph above cited must be read in the context of that case. We think it obvious that Lord Bridge cannot have been intending that the organiser of a crime who recruited others to carry it out would not himself be guilty of conspiracy unless it could be proved that he intended to play some active part himself thereafter. Lord Bridge had pointed out at p. 259 and p. 38 respectively that

> in these days of highly organised crime the most serious statutory conspiracies will frequently involve an elaborate and complex agreed course of conduct in which many will consent to play necessary but subordinate roles, not involving them in any direct participation in the commission of the offence or offences at the centre of the conspiracy.

The present case is a classic example of such a conspiracy. It is the hallmark of such crimes that the organisers try to remain in the background and more often than not are not apprehended. Secondly, the origins of all conspiracies are concealed and it is usually quite impossible to establish when or where the initial agreement was made, or when or where other conspirators were recruited. The very existence of the agreement can only be inferred from overt acts. Participation in a conspiracy is infinitely variable: it can be active or passive. If the majority shareholder and director of a company consents to the company being used for drug smuggling carried out in the company's name by a fellow director and minority shareholder, he is guilty of conspiracy. Consent, that is the agreement or adherence to the agreement, can be inferred if it is proved that he knew what was going on and the intention to participate in the furtherance of the criminal purpose is also established by his failure to stop the unlawful activity. Lord Bridge's *dictum* does not require anything more.

We return to the first sentence of this paragraph in Lord Bridge's speech. He starts by saying: 'I have said already, but I repeat to emphasise its importance. . . .' We have cited what he had already said when dealing with his clause 2. It is clear that he was not intending to say anything different. So when he goes on to say:

> an essential ingredient in the crime of conspiring to commit a specific offence or offences under section 1(1) of the Act of 1977 is that the accused should agree that a course of conduct be pursued which he knows must involve the commission by one or more of the parties to the agreement of that offence or those offences,

he plainly does not mean that the prosecution have to prove that persons who agree to import prohibited drugs into this country know that the offence which will be committed will be a contravention of section 170(2) of the Customs and Excise Act. He is not to be taken as saying that the prosecution must prove that the accused knew the name of the crime. We are satisfied that Lord Bridge was doing no more than applying the words of section 1 of the Criminal Law Act 1977, namely, that when the accused agreed to the course of conduct, he knew that it involved the commission of an offence.

The *mens rea* sufficient to support the commission of a substantive offence will not necessarily be sufficient to support a charge of conspiracy to commit that offence. An intent to cause grievous bodily harm is sufficient to support the charge of murder, but is not sufficient to support a charge of conspiracy to murder or of attempt to murder.

. . .

Yip Chiu-Cheung v *R*
[1994] 3 WLR 514, Privy Council

LORD GRIFFITHS: On 27 March 1991 the defendant was convicted of conspiracy to traffic in heroin and on 28 March sentenced to 15 years' imprisonment. His appeal was dismissed by the Court of Appeal of Hong Kong on 15 May 1992 and he now appeals from that decision.

The indictment charged the defendant as follows:

> *Statement of offence.* Conspiracy to traffic in a dangerous drug, contrary to common law and section 4 of the Dangerous Drugs Ordinance, c. 134.
>
> *Particulars of offence.* Yip Chiu-Cheung, between 19 August 1989 and 15 November 1989 in Thailand and Hong Kong, conspired with Philip Needham and another person unknown to traffic in a dangerous drug, namely salts of esters of morphine commonly known as heroin.

. . .

The prosecution case was based primarily on the evidence of Philip Needham who was an under-cover drug enforcement officer of the United States of America and named in the indictment as a co-conspirator. The other conspirator, referred to in the indictment as a person unknown, was introduced to Needham by the defendant under the name of Hom.

In outline Needham's evidence was that he had a series of meetings in Thailand with the defendant, at one of which Hom also took part, at which it was arranged that Needham would act as a courier to carry five kilos of heroin from Hong Kong to Australia, travelling by air.

The arrangement was that Needham would fly to Hong Kong on 22 October 1989 under the name of Larsen, where he would be met by the defendant. He would then stay at the Nathan Hotel in Kowloon for a few days and then fly on to Australia with five kilos of heroin supplied by the defendant. For this service he would be paid U.S.$16,000. In fact Needham did not fly to Hong Kong on 22 October because the flight was delayed and he missed the rescheduled flight. Needham said he had no way of contacting the defendant in Hong Kong and had been advised by the Hong Kong authorities that the Nathan Hotel would be a dangerous place for him to stay. Needham therefore proceeded no further with the plan, and did not go to Hong Kong.

The defendant raised a number of grounds of appeal before the Court of Appeal all of which failed, and only one of which is now pursued before the Board, which is that Needham, the drug enforcement officer, cannot in law be a co-conspirator because he lacked the necessary *mens rea* for the offence.

. . .

On the principal ground of appeal it was submitted that the trial judge and the Court of Appeal were wrong to hold that Needham, the undercover agent, could be a conspirator because he lacked the necessary *mens rea* or guilty mind required for the offence of conspiracy. It was urged upon their Lordships that no moral guilt attached to the undercover agent who was at all times acting courageously and with the best of motives in attempting to infiltrate and bring to justice a gang of criminal drug dealers. In these circumstances it was argued that it would be wrong to treat the agent as having any criminal intent, and reliance was placed upon a passage in the speech of Lord Bridge of Harwich in *R* v *Anderson (William Ronald)* [1986] AC 27, 38 – 39; but in that case Lord Bridge was dealing with a different situation from that which exists in the present case. There may be many cases in which undercover police officers or other law enforcement agents pretend to join a conspiracy in order to gain information about the plans of the criminals, with no intention of taking any part in the planned crime but rather with the intention of providing information that will frustrate it. It was to this situation that Lord Bridge was referring in *Reg* v *Anderson*. The crime of conspiracy requires an agreement between two or more persons to commit an unlawful act with the intention of carrying it out. It is the intention to carry out the crime that constitutes the necessary *mens rea* for the offence. As Lord Bridge pointed out, an undercover agent who has no intention of committing the crime lacks the necessary *mens rea* to be a conspirator.

The facts of the present case are quite different. Nobody can doubt that Needham was acting courageously and with the best of motives; he was trying to break a drug ring. But equally there can be no doubt that the method he chose and in which the police in Hong Kong acquiesced involved the commission of the criminal offence of trafficking in drugs by exporting heroin from Hong Kong without a licence. Needham intended to commit that offence by carrying the heroin through the customs and on to the aeroplane bound for Australia.

Neither the police, nor customs, nor any other member of the executive have any power to alter the terms of the Ordinance forbidding the export of heroin, and the fact that they may turn a blind eye when the heroin is exported does not prevent it from being a criminal offence.

. . .

Naturally, Needham never expected to be prosecuted if he carried out the plan as intended. But the fact that in such circumstances the authorities would not prosecute the undercover agent does not mean that he did not commit the crime albeit as part of a wider scheme to combat drug dealing.

NOTES AND QUESTIONS

1. Does *Yip Chiu-Cheung* v *R* provide a more satisfactory approach to the undercover officer than that suggested in *Anderson*? Would it make more sense to take a 'unilateral' view of agreement, whereby X may agree with Y even though Y need only give nominal consent, such that any hidden reservations on Y's part (e.g., stemming from the fact that he is working for the police) are irrelevant?

2. The Law Commission would require that at least two persons share an intent that the crime be committed in order for there to be a conspiracy.
3. A and B add alcohol to C's lemonade, intending him to drive with a higher alcohol level than permitted by law. What must the prosecution show before A and B can be convicted of a conspiracy to commit an offence? What if A but not B believed that the alcohol added was insufficient to cause C to be guilty of an offence?

(ii) *Necessarily involve a crime*

Under the Criminal Law Act 1977, s. 5, the agreement that a course of conduct shall be pursued must be such that if carried out in accordance with the conspirators' intention, it would amount to or involve the commission of an offence or offences by one or more parties to the agreement (or would have done so except for facts which made the commission of the offence impossible). Sometimes an agreement may involve a number of alternative courses of action which will be pursued by the conspirators depending on other events. If one course of action is criminal and the other not, is this an agreement to pursue a course of conduct which will necessarily involve a crime? Similarly, if two different crimes are envisaged, which crime have the defendants agreed to?

R v *Reed*
[1982] Crim LR 819, Court of Appeal

The fourth submission was that the summing up had not adequately conveyed the requirements of the Criminal Law Act 1977, s. 1 (1). These, it was said, clearly indicate that a course of conduct agreed upon must necessarily amount to or involve the commission of an offence if the agreement is carried out in accordance with the parties' intentions. The agreement on the relevant course of conduct must therefore not be capable of a successful conclusion without a crime being committed (*cf.* Smith and Hogan, *Criminal Law* (4th ed.), pp. 226–227). It was argued that the most that could be inferred about the nature of the agreement between L and R was that L would visit individuals and either give them faith healing, consolation and comfort while discouraging suicide or he would actively help them to commit suicide, depending on his assessment of the appropriate course of action. Such an agreement was capable of execution without the law being broken, and therefore should not have attracted the charge of conspiracy. It was argued that the jury should have at least been made aware of such a possible defence in the directions given.

The Court held against the applicant on this point. Donaldson LJ considered two examples:

In the first, A and B agree to drive from London to Edinburgh in a time which can be achieved without exceeding the speed limits, but only if the traffic which they encounter is exceptionally light. Their agreement will not necessarily involve the commission of any offence, even if it is carried out in accordance with their intentions, and they do arrive from London to Edinburgh within the agreed time. Accordingly the agreement does not constitute the offence of statutory conspiracy or indeed of any offence. In the second example, A and B agree to rob a bank, if when they arrive at the bank it seems safe to do so. Their agreement will necessarily involve the commission of the offence of robbery if it is carried out in accordance with their intentions. Accordingly, they are guilty of the statutory offence of conspiracy. The instant case is an example of the latter type of agreement. If circumstances had permitted and the agreement of R and L had been carried out in accordance with their intentions L would have aided, abetted, counselled, and procured a suicide. . . .

. . .

R v Jackson
[1985] Crim LR 442, Court of Appeal

The appellants were convicted of conspiracy to pervert the course of public justice. Their co-defendant, Whitlock, pleaded guilty to inciting a person to have a firearm with criminal intent. All four had discussed Whitlock's plan to have himself shot so as to provide mitigation in the event of being convicted of the burglary offence for which he was being tried. Before the end of that trial Whitlock was shot in the leg and was permanently disabled. The appellants had spent part of the evening in question with Whitlock but lied to the police about their whereabouts. They eventually admitted knowing of the plan. In their defence the appellants denied having any part in the plan and claimed not to have taken Whitlock seriously. The particulars of the offence, charged that the appellants made false statements as to their and Whitlock's whereabouts; that they concealed the identity of the person responsible for the shooting and that they concealed the fact that Whitlock had arranged to be shot to mislead his court of trial. The appellants appealed against conviction on the ground that no offence had been committed since it depended upon a contingency which might not have taken place – the conviction of Whitlock for burglary. Counsel relied upon examples cited in *Reed* (CACD: March 26, 1982) and submitted that the agreement did not 'necessarily' involve the commission of an offence.

Held, dismissing the appeals, planning was taking place for a contingency and if that contingency occurred the conspiracy would necessarily involve the commission of an offence. 'Necessarily' is not to be held to mean that there must inevitably be the carrying out of an offence, it means, if the agreement is carried out in accordance with the plan, there must be the commission of the offence referred to in the conspiracy count. . . .

NOTES AND QUESTIONS
1. In the driving example given in *Reed*, why did the court feel there was no conspiracy? Was there not an agreement to commit a crime in the event of heavy traffic being encountered?
2. What would be the result in the following situations?
   (a) An agreement to burgle a house, using violence if the occupier returns.
   (b) An agreement to steal a car unless police officers are patrolling the street.
   (c) An agreement to have intercourse with a woman whether or not she consents.
3. In *R v O'Hadhmaill* [1996] Crim LR 509, the defendant (a member of the IRA) was convicted of conspiracy to carry out explosions. The appeal involved an evidentiary point relating to the defendant's contention that he did not plan to cause explosions so long as the cease-fire then in force held. Both the trial court and the Court of Appeal proceeded on the assumption that this conditional intent was sufficient for conspiracy.

(iii) *Impossibility*
The difference between factual and legal impossibility was outlined in the section on incitement. The issue of impossibility in respect to conspiracy is now dealt with by s. 1(1)(b) of the Criminal Law Act 1977, which was inserted by the Criminal Attempts Act 1981, s. 5 (see above). Whatever ambiguity there may have been in the law before the Act, it is now clear that factual impossibility is not a defence.

C: Common law conspiracies

(i) *Conspiracy to defraud*
The common law offence of conspiracy to defraud was expressly preserved by s. 5(2) of the Criminal Law Act 1977, pending a review of the law relating to fraud

by the Law Commission which has yet to be completed. The overlap between conspiracy to defraud and statutory conspiracy is addressed by s. 12 of the Criminal Justice Act 1987:

Criminal Justice Act 1987

12.—(1) If—

(a) a person agrees with any other person or persons that a course of conduct shall be pursued; and

(b) that course of conduct will necessarily amount to or involve the commission of any offence or offences by one or more of the parties to the agreement if the agreement is carried out in accordance with their intentions,

the fact that it will do so shall not preclude a charge of conspiracy to defraud being brought against any of them in respect of the agreement.

NOTE AND QUESTION

The choice for the prosecutor of whether to charge statutory or common law conspiracy is governed by guidelines issued by the Director of Public Prosecutions under the Prosecution of Offences Act 1985, s. 10. Is this a satisfactory approach to the issue?

The common law crime of conspiracy to defraud will usually take one of three forms:

(a) Where loss is suffered.

(b) Where the victim is deceived into taking an economic risk.

(c) Where a public official is induced by deception to act contrary to his public duty.

(*a*) *Where loss is suffered.* Where actual loss is suffered by the victim, no deceit on the part of the defendant needs to be shown.

Scott v *Metropolitan Police Commissioner*
[1975] AC 819, House of Lords

VISCOUNT DILHORNE: . . . During the course of the opening of the case for the prosecution Mr Blom-Cooper, who represented the appellant, said that the appellant was prepared to admit, and the appellant did admit, the following facts, namely, that he

> Agreed with employees of cinema owners temporarily to abstract, without permission of such cinema owners, and in return for payments to such employees, cinematograph films, without the knowledge or consent of the owners of the copyright and/or of distribution rights in such films, for the purpose of making infringing copies and distributing the same of a commercial basis.

On these admitted facts Mr Blom-Cooper submitted the appellant could not be convicted on the first count. His contention that there could not be a conspiracy to defraud unless there was deceit was rejected by Judge Hines and the appellant then pleaded guilty to the first and seventh counts and was sentenced to two years' imprisonment on count one and one year's imprisonment on count two.

. . .

The Court of Appeal certified that a point of law of general public importance was involved in the decision to dismiss the appeal against conviction on count one, namely,

> Whether, on a charge of conspiracy to defraud, the Crown must establish an agreement to deprive the owners of their property by deception; or whether it is sufficient to prove an agreement to prejudice the rights of another or others without lawful justification and in circumstances of dishonesty.

. . .

In the course of the argument many cases were cited. It is not necessary to refer to all of them. Many were cases in which the conspiracy alleged was to defraud by deceit. Those cases do not establish that there can only be a conspiracy to defraud if deceit is involved and there are a number of cases where that was not the case.

. . .

One must not confuse the object of a conspiracy with the means by which it is intended to be carried out. In the light of the cases to which I have referred, I have come to the conclusion that Mr Blom-Cooper's main contention must be rejected. I have not the temerity to attempt an exhaustive definition of the meaning of 'defraud.'

As I have said, words take colour from the context in which they are used, but the words 'fraudulently' and 'defraud' must ordinarily have a very similar meaning. If, as I think, and as the Criminal Law Revision Committee appears to have thought, 'fraudulently' means 'dishonestly,' then 'to defraud' ordinarily means, in my opinion, to deprive a person dishonestly of something which is his or of something to which he is or would or might but for the perpetration of the fraud be entitled.

In *Welham* v *Director of Public Prosecutions* [1961] AC 103, 124 Lord Radcliffe referred to a special line of cases where the person deceived is a person holding public office or a public authority and where the person deceived was not caused any pecuniary or economic loss. Forgery whereby the deceit has been accomplished, had, he pointed out, been in a number of cases treated as having been done with intent to defraud despite the absence of pecuniary or economic loss.

In this case it is not necessary to decide that a conspiracy to defraud may exist even though its object was not to secure a financial advantage by inflicting an economic loss on the person at whom the conspiracy was directed. But for myself I see no reason why what was said by Lord Radcliffe in relation to forgery should not equally apply in relation to conspiracy to defraud.

In this case the accused bribed servants of the cinema owners to secure possession of films in order to copy them and in order to enable them to let the copies out on hire. By so doing Mr Blom-Cooper conceded they inflicted more than nominal damage to the goodwill of the owners of the copyright and distribution rights of the films. By so doing they secured for themselves profits which but for their actions might have been secured by those owners just as in *R* v *Button*, 3 Cox CC 229 the defendants obtained profits which might have been secured by their employer. In the circumstances it is, I think, clear that they inflicted pecuniary loss on those owners.

(b) Where the victim is deceived into taking an economic risk.

R v Allsop
(1976) 64 Cr App R 29, Court of Appeal

The appellant was a sub-broker for a hire-purchase company. His function as such was to introduce prospective purchasers of cars and to fill in application forms in respect of them. From time to time he put false particulars in the forms so as to induce the hire-purchase company to accept applications which they might otherwise have rejected. When doing this the appellant expected and believed that these transactions would be completed satisfactorily so that the hire-purchase company would profit from them. The appellant was charged with conspiracy to defraud.

SHAW LJ: This appeal raises a short but interesting question in relation to the nature of the intent requisite to constitute the offence of conspiracy to defraud. The argument advanced by Mr Mervyn Heald on behalf of the appellant is that such an intent involves as an essential element the objective of causing actual economic loss to the person alleged to have been defrauded so that it is not sufficient if that person's economic interests are merely threatened incidentally. Miss Goddard, for the Crown, asserts that no more is necessary than the intent to bring about a situation in which the economic interests of the person deceived are threatened or prejudiced, or are likely to be threatened or prejudiced, albeit that such threat or prejudice is undesired or incidental so far as the person responsible for the deceit is concerned.

. . .

It seemed to this Court that Mr Heald's argument traversed the shadowy region between intent and motive. Generally the primary objective of fraudsmen is to advantage themselves. The detriment that results to their victims is secondary to that purpose and incidental. It is 'intended' only in the sense that it is a contemplated outcome of the fraud that is perpetrated. If the deceit which is employed imperils the economic interest of the person deceived, this is sufficient to constitute fraud even though in the event no actual loss is suffered and notwithstanding that the deceiver did not desire to bring about an actual loss.

. . . 'Economic loss' may be ephemeral and not lasting, or potential and not actual; but even a threat of financial prejudice while it exists it may be measured in terms of money.

. . .

···In the present case, the part of the history which is common ground reveals that in this sense Prestige did suffer actual loss for they paid too much for cars worth less than their pretended value; and they relied upon the creditworthiness of hire-purchasers as measured by the deposit stated to have been paid when none had been paid.

It matters not that in the end the hire-purchasers concerned paid to Prestige what was due to them. In the interim that corporation suffered economic loss in consequence of the misrepresentation made by the appellant. Mr Heald argues that this is neither here nor there. The essential consideration so his argument ran is what the appellant intended at the outset; he averred that, it is not sufficient if the intention to put Prestige's interests at risk was merely incidental when the ultimate purpose was not to injure them. We do not agree. Interests which are imperilled are less valuable in terms of money than those same interests when they are secure and protected. Where a person intends by deceit to induce a course of conduct in another which puts that other's economic interests in jeopardy he is guilty of fraud even though he does not intend or desire that actual loss should ultimately be suffered by that other in this context.

(c) *Where a public official is induced by deception to act contrary to his public duty.*

Welham v *Director of Public Prosecutions*
[1961] AC 103, House of Lords

The appellant was tried on an indictment which included two counts which charged him with uttering forged documents, contrary to s. 6 of the Forgery Act 1913. The appellant, as sales manager of Motors (Brighton) Ltd, had witnessed forged hire-purchase agreements on the strength of which certain finance companies had advanced large sums of money to Motors (Brighton) Ltd. The appellant's defence was that he had believed that the agreements were brought into being to enable the finance companies to lend money which they could not ordinarily do because of credit restrictions, and because by their memorandum and articles of association they could not act as moneylenders. He claimed that the purpose of the hire-purchase agreements was to make it appear that the finance companies were advancing money in the way of their business as finance companies, and he accordingly contended that he had had no intention to defraud the finance companies but was merely uttering the documents to mislead the relevant authority who might inspect the records to see that the credit restrictions were being observed and whose duty it was to prevent their contravention. The jury were directed that this was a sufficient intention to defraud and the appellant was convicted. He appealed on the ground that his intention was merely an intention to deceive and not an intention to defraud, which involved causing some economic loss to the person deceived.

LORD DENNING: . . . Much valuable guidance is to be obtained from the dictum of Buckley J in the *Whittaker Wright* case, *In re London and Globe Finance Corporation* [1903] 1 Ch 728, but this has been criticised by modern scholars. It has even been hinted that it conceals within it the fallacy of the illegitimate antistrophe, which sounds, I must say, extremely serious. These scholars seem to think they have found the solution. 'To defraud,' they say, involves the idea of economic loss. I cannot agree with them on this. If a drug addict forges a doctor's prescription so as to enable him to get drugs from a chemist, he has, I should have thought, an intent to defraud, even though he intends to pay the chemist the full price and no one is a penny the worse off.

Seeing, therefore, that the words of the statute are of doubtful import, it is, I think, legitimate to turn for guidance to the previous state of the law before the Act. And here I would say at once that the phrase 'with intent to defraud' has been the standard usage of lawyers in defining forgery for over 160 years. In 1796 all the judges of England laid down the definition of forgery as 'the false making of a note or other instrument *with intent to defraud*' (see *R* v *Parkes and Brown* (1797) 2 Leach 775, 785); and ever since that time it has been held that the very essence of forgery is an *intent to defraud*, and it must be laid in the indictment (see East, Pleas of the Crown (1803), vol. 2, p. 988; Chitty, Criminal Law (1826), vol. 3, pp. 1039, 1042). I cannot help thinking that when Parliament in section 4(1) of the Act of 1913 used a phrase so hallowed by usage, it used it in the sense in which it had been used by generations of lawyers. It was never by them confined to the causing of economic loss. Let me prove this by taking some examples: Take the case where a man forges a reference as to character, intending to get employment by means of it. It is clear forgery: see *R* v *Sharman* (1854) 1 Dears CC 285; *R* v *Moah* (1858) 7 Cox CC 503, 504. But there may well be no economic loss intended. The man may intend, if he gets the job, to render full service in return for his wages. Or the post which he seeks may be unpaid, such as a justice of the peace. But he has the intent to defraud all the same.

Take next the case where a servant steals his master's money and afterwards forges a receipt or other document so as to cover up his defalcations. This, too, is forgery: see *R* v *Martin* (1836) 1 Mood CC 483. He does not intend to deprive his master of anything: for he has already done that. He may not even do it so as to keep his job, because he may be under notice. What he really intends to do is to cover up his tracks so that he should not be found out. But he has the intent to defraud none the less.

Then there are the cases concerned with the release of prisoners. If a man forges an order or letter to the sheriff or to the governor of a prison, intending thereby to secure the release of a prisoner, he is guilty of forgery at common law: see *Fawcett's* case (1793) 2 East PL 862 and *R* v *Harris* 1 Mood CC 393. There is no idea of economic loss here. He has no intent to deprive the gaoler of any money or valuable thing. But at common law he is held to have an intent to defraud. Mr Gardiner rather suggested that the reason for those decisions was that the documents were documents of a public nature. But I do not so read them. Even if they were public documents it was still essential that there should be an intent to defraud. Ever since *Ward's* case 2 LD Ryam 1461, 3 LD Ryam 358; 2 Str 787 in 1726 public and private documents were at common law on the same footing in this respect: see East's Pleas of the Crown, pp. 859–861. The forgery of any of them was a misdemeanour if done with intent to defraud, but not otherwise: see *R v Hodgson* Dedrs. B. 3, 8 by Jervis CJ.

There remains the case of *R v Toshack* 4 Cox CC 38, 41, which is to my mind decisive. Toshack, a seaman, forged a certificate of good conduct so as to be admitted to sit for an examination for his master's certificate. He had no intention to deprive the examiners or Trinity House of any money or valuable thing. The piece of paper, value one penny, was not mentioned in the counts on which he was convicted. But he was held guilty of forgery. Alderson B said: 'It does amount to a very serious offence if persons do forge certificates of this sort and are found to utter them for the purpose of deceiving the Trinity House.'

What is the common element in all these cases? It is, I think, best expressed in the definition given by East in his Pleas of the Crown, vol. 2, p. 852. He treats the subject, I think, better than any writer before or since:

> *To forge*, (a metaphorical expression borrowed from the occupation of the smith), means, properly speaking, no more than to *make* or *form*: but in our law it is always taken in an evil sense; and therefore Forgery at common law denotes a *false* making (which includes every alteration of or addition to a true instrument), a making malo animo, of any written instrument for the purpose of fraud and deceit. This definition results from all the authorities ancient and modern taken together.

That was written in 1803, but it has been always accepted as authoritative. It seems to me to provide the key to the cases decided since it was written, as well as those before. The important thing about this definition is that it is not limited to the idea of economic loss, nor to the idea of depriving someone of something of value. It extends generally to *the purpose of fraud and deceit*. Put shortly, 'with intent to defraud' means 'with intent to practise a fraud' on someone or other. It need not be anyone in particular. Someone in general will suffice. . . .

At this point it becomes possible to point the contrast in the statute between an 'intent to deceive' and an 'intent to defraud.' 'To deceive' here conveys the element of deceit, which induces a state of mind, without the element of fraud, which induces a course of action or inaction. Take the case of a private document. For instance, where a man fabricates a letter so as to puff himself up in the opinion of others. Bramwell B put the instance: 'If I were to produce a letter purporting to be from the Duke of Wellington inviting me to dine, and say, "See what a respectable person I am"': *R v Moah*. There would then be an intent to deceive but it would not be punishable at common law or under the statute, because then it would not be done with intent to defraud. Take next the case of a public document. For instance, a parish register. If a man should falsify it so as to make himself appear to be descended of noble family, for the sake of his own glorification, he would not be guilty of an intent to defraud and would therefore not be punishable at common law (see *R v Hodgson*), but he would have an intent to deceive and he would be punishable under the present statute, as indeed he was under its predecessors, such as the Forgery Act 1861, s. 36.

So much for the principal point under discussion. Mr Gerald Gardiner did make a further point. He said that the intent must be to defraud the particular person to whom the document is first presented or his agent, and that it was insufficient if he intended to defraud somebody else. This is not correct. It has long been ruled that it is no answer to a charge of forgery to say that there was no intent to defraud any particular person, because a general intent to defraud is sufficient to constitute the crime. So also it is no answer to say that there was no intent to defraud the recipient, if there was intent to defraud somebody else: see *R v Taylor* (1779) 1 Leach 214.

NOTES AND QUESTIONS

1. *Welham* v *DPP* was not a case concerning conspiracy to defraud but it seems to be generally accepted that the same principles are applicable.

2. Note that in the third category of conspiracy to defraud, the possibility or actuality of economic loss is irrelevant. Why should this be so?

(*d*) Mens rea. There must be dishonesty according to the test set out in *Ghosh* [1982] QB 1053. Although the *Ghosh* case dealt with the *mens rea* of theft, the test of dishonesty which it established has been applied in other contexts, including the present one. The test has two prongs:

(i) was the defendant dishonest as judged by the current standards of reasonable and honest people; and

(ii) did the defendant realise that his acts were contrary to that standard?

There has been confusion in the case law as to whether a defendant has the requisite intent for conspiracy to defraud where there is no intent to cause economic loss. This issue was addressed by the Privy Council in *Wai Yu-tsang* v *R*.

Wai Yu-tsang v *R*
[1991] 4 All ER 664, Privy Council

LORD GOFF OF CHIEVELEY: . . . The appellant was the chief accountant of the Hang Lung Bank (the bank). He was charged that, between 7 September and 13 November 1982, he conspired together with Cheng Eng-kuan, Lee Hoi-kwong and others to defraud the bank and its existing and potential shareholders, creditors and depositors, by dishonestly concealing in the accounts of the bank the dishonouring of US dollar cheques in the sum of $US124m, drawn on the account of Overseas Maritime Co. Ltd SA with Citibank International, Chicago, such cheques having been purchased by the bank. Of the other members of the alleged conspiracy, Cheng was the managing director of the bank and Lee was the general manager. Cheng fled the jurisdiction, as did another associate of his, John Mao. Lee originally stood trial with the appellant but, following preliminary argument on the admissibility of certain evidence, the Crown abandoned its case against him. In the result, the appellant stood trial alone.

The events giving rise to the charge against the appellant were as follows. For some years a cheque-kiting cycle, known as the Capri cycle, had been run by John Mao, using a number of companies as its principal vehicle. In May 1982, in order to bring the Capri cycle to an end, a new cheque-kiting cycle (known as the OMC cycle) was set up to create funds for Overseas Maritime Co. Ltd SA (OMC). The object was to transfer the funds into the Capri cycle so that the final cheques in circulation in that cycle could be met. The bank purchased cheques in US currency via a company called Southseas Finance Co. Ltd (SSF). The cheques, drawn on the OMC account, were purchased by the bank from SSF. The proceeds were credited to the account of SSF with the bank, and the cheques were cleared through the bank's foreign exchange with Chemical Bank. Those purchases required the approval of Cheng as the managing director of the bank. However, on 7 September 1982 a rumour started by a taxi-driver caused a run on the bank, and in consequence Cheng gave instructions that no further US dollar cheques or drafts were to be purchased. This had the effect that the second cheque-kiting cycle was brought to a premature end, and that cheques then in circulation could not be met. On 14 September Chemical Bank advised the bank that two or three of the OMC cheques had been returned, and on 18 September another seven. The total face value of those cheques (which had been purchased by the bank from SSF) was $US124m (the equivalent of $HK755m), an amount which exceeded the assets of the bank at that time.

There was no suggestion that the appellant was in any way involved in either of the two cheque-kiting cycles. It was however alleged that he conspired with Cheng and others to defraud the bank and its existing and potential shareholders, creditors and depositors, by dishonestly concealing in the bank's accounts the dishonouring of the US dollar cheques in the sum of $US124m which had been purchased by the bank. During the run on the bank, it had been supported by the Standard Chartered Bank, to which the appellant was under a duty to report, as he was to the Commissioner of Banking. He did not however report the dishonour of the cheques, nor did he cause the dishonour to be recorded in the bank's computerised ledgers. The details of the transactions were recorded only in private ledgers, called 'K' vouchers. Instead there were recorded in the bank's accounts entries purporting to show that the bank had drawn 16 US dollar drafts on Chemical Bank in amounts equivalent to the total amount of the dishonoured cheques, and had sold them to SSF, that short-term loans had been granted to two companies called Thring Trading Ltd (Thring) and Texas Finance Ltd (Texas), and that SSF had paid for the drafts with cheques drawn on its own account and on the accounts of Thring and Texas. The drafts were never presented for payment, although the accounts were debited with the amounts of the cheques. This gave the false picture of balances in the Chemical Bank account and in the SSF account which were approximately the same as they would have been if the dishonoured cheques had been recorded as debits in the SSF account and credits in the Chemical Bank account.

. . .

Before the Court of Appeal, a number of issues were raised by the appellant founded upon criticisms of the summing up of the learned judge. All of those criticisms were rejected by the Court of Appeal. Before their Lordships, however, the appellant's case was directed solely to the judge's direction on the mental element required for a conspiracy to defraud. The judge explained to the jury that the appellant must have been party to an agreement with one or more of the other named conspirators which had a common intention to defraud one or more of the persons or categories of persons named in the indictment. He explained that such an intention must involve dishonesty on the part of the conspirators, and continued as follows:

> It is fraud if it is proved that there was the dishonest taking of a risk which there was no right to take, which – to Mr Wai's knowledge at least – would cause detriment or prejudice to another, detriment or prejudice to the economic or proprietary rights of another. That detriment or prejudice to somebody else is very often incidental to the purpose of the fraudsman himself. The prime objective of fraudsmen is usually to gain some advantage for themselves, any detriment or prejudice to somebody else is often secondary to that objective but nonetheless is a contemplated or predictable outcome of what they do. If the interests of some other person – the economic or proprietary interests of some other person are imperilled, that is sufficient to constitute fraud even though no loss is actually suffered and even though the fraudsman himself did not desire to bring about any loss.

It is plain that that direction was founded upon the judgment of the Court of Appeal in *R* v *Allsop* (1976) 64 Cr App R 29. It was the contention of the appellant that the direction was erroneous in so far as it stated that, for this purpose, the imperilling of an economic interest or the threat of financial prejudice was sufficient to establish fraud, whatever the motive of the accused may have been; and that in so far as *Allsop's* case so decided, it was wrong and should not be followed.

[In *Scott* v *Metropolitan Police Commissioner* [1975] AC 819, Lord Diplock said:]

> . . . (2) Where the intended victim of a 'conspiracy to defraud' is a private individual the purpose of the conspirators must be to cause the victim economic loss by depriving him of some property or right, corporeal or incorporeal, to which he is or would or might become entitled . . . (3) Where the intended victim of a 'conspiracy to defraud' is a person performing public duties as distinct from a private individual it is sufficient if the purpose is to cause him to act contrary to his public duty . . .

With the greatest respect to Lord Diplock, their Lordships consider this categorisation to be too narrow. In their opinion, in agreement with the approach of Lord Radcliffe in *Welham's* case, the cases concerned with persons performing public duties are not to be regarded as a special category in the manner described by Lord Diplock, but rather as exemplifying the general principle that conspiracies to defraud are not restricted to cases of intention to cause the victim economic loss. On the contrary, they are to be understood in the broad sense described by Lord Radcliffe and Lord Denning in *Welham's* case – the view which Viscount Dilhorne favoured in *Scott's* case, as apparently did the other members of the Appellate Committee who agreed with him in that case (apart, it seems, from Lord Diplock).

. . . The question whether particular facts reveal a conspiracy to defraud depends upon what the conspirators have dishonestly agreed to do, and in particular whether they have agreed to practise a fraud on somebody. For this purpose it is enough for example that, as in *R v Allsop* and in the present case, the conspirators have dishonestly agreed to bring about a state of affairs which they realise will or may deceive the victim into so acting, or failing to act, that he will suffer economic loss or his economic interests will be put at risk. It is however important in such a case, as the Court of Appeal stressed in *Allsop's* case, to distinguish a conspirator's intention (or immediate purpose) dishonestly to bring about such a state of affairs from his motive (or underlying purpose). The latter may be benign to the extent that he does not wish the victim or potential victim to suffer harm; but the mere fact that it is benign will not of itself prevent the agreement from constituting a conspiracy to defraud. Of course, if the conspirators were not acting dishonestly, there will have been no conspiracy to defraud; and in any event their benign purpose (if it be such) is a matter which, if they prove to be guilty, can be taken into account at the stage of sentence.

NOTES AND QUESTIONS

1. What was the defendant's motive in *Wai Yu-tsang* v *R*? His intent? Does motive play a different role depending on which category of conspiracy to defraud is at issue? Or does the Privy Council reject the idea of categories completely?

2. If no intention to cause economic loss is required in the case of deceit of private persons, why is it not a crime to pretend to be of noble descent (see Denning in *Welham*)?

3. If a victim suffers no economic loss, there is no substantive offence. Is it inconsistent that there should be liabiity for conspiracy? The Law Commission has acknowledged the tension but has recommended preservation of the *status quo* pending a comprehensive review of dishonesty offences.

(ii) *Conspiracy to corrupt public morals or outrage public decency*
Section 5(3) of the Criminal Law Act 1977, specifically preserves the common law offence of conspiracy to corrupt public morals or outrage public decency.

Criminal Law Act 1977

5.—(1) Subject to the following provisions of this section, the offence of conspiracy at common law is hereby abolished.

(2) . . .

(3) Subsection (1) above shall not affect the offence of conspiracy at common law if and in so far as it may be committed by entering into an agreement to engage in conduct which—

    (a) tends to corrupt public morals or outrages public decency; but

    (b) would not amount to or involve the commission of an offence if carried out by a single person otherwise than in pursuance of an agreement.

NOTES AND QUESTIONS

1. Is it possible to know from a reading of the statute what behaviour will be caught by these offences? If not, how can people who desire to be law-abiding regulate their conduct to avoid prosecution?
2. The Law Commission has recommended the abolition of common law conspiracies to corrupt public morals or outrage public decency, but neither the courts nor Parliament have been willing to do so. Prosecutions, while infrequent, are not unknown.

Knuller v *Director of Public Prosecutions*
[1973] AC 435, House of Lords

The appellants were directors of a company which published a fortnightly magazine. On an inside page under a column headed 'Males' advertisements were inserted inviting readers to meet the advertisers for the purpose of homo-sexual practices. The appellants were convicted on counts of conspiracy to corrupt public morals and conspiracy to outrage public decency.

LORD SIMON OF GLAISDALE: . . . In my view, counsel for the appellants was right to concede that there is a common law offence of conspiring to outrage public decency.

(3) As for whether such an offence is applicable to books and newspapers, the argument based on section 2(4) of the Obscene Publications Act 1959 is concluded against the appellants by the construction put upon that subsection in *Shaw* v *Director of Public Prosecutions* [1962] AC 220. The passage I have cited from *Mirehouse* v *Rennell* (1833) 1 Cl & F 527, 546 indicates that the fact that the authorities show no example of the application of the rule of law in circumstances such as the instant does not mean that it is not applicable, provided that there are circumstances, however novel, which fall fairly within the rule. Counsel for the appellants could not suggest any demarcation in principle. To attempt delimitation would produce absurd anomalies. The newspaper placard would presumably fall within the offence: it would be odd if similar material on the exposed front page of the newspaper did not do so. A picture fly-posted in a small village would fall within the offence; but, on the argument for the appellants, not the same picture contained in a newspaper or book of mass circulation. Safeguards are to be found in the requirement of publicity for the offence to be established, and in the parliamentary undertaking to which my noble and learned friend, Lord Reid, has referred – this must be taken to apply to conspiracy to outrage public decency as much as to conspiracy to corrupt public morals.

(4) I turn, then, to the requirement of publicity. *R* v *Mayling* [1963] 2 QB 717 shows that the substantive offence (and therefore the conduct the subject of the conspiracy) must be committed in public, in the sense that the circumstances must be such that the alleged outrageously indecent matter could have been seen by more than one person, even though in fact no more than one did see it. If it is capable of being seen by one person only, no offence is committed.

It was at one time argued for the appellants that the matter must have been visible to two or more people simultaneously; and that an article in a newspaper did not fulfil this requirement. But this point was rightly abandoned, and I need not examine it further.

. . .

It was argued for the Crown that it was immaterial whether or not the alleged outrage to decency took place in public, provided that the sense of decency of the public or a substantial section of the public was outraged. But this seems to me to be contrary to many of the authorities which the Crown itself relied on to establish the generic offence. The authorities establish that the word 'public' has a different connotation in the respective offences of conspiracy to corrupt public morals and conduct calculated to, or conspiracy to, outrage public decency. In the first it refers to certain fundamental rules regarded as essential social control which yet lack the force of law:

when applicable to individuals, in other words, 'public' refers to persons in society. In the latter offences, however, 'public' refers to the place in which the offence is committed. This is borne out by the way the rule was framed by my noble and learned friend, Lord Reid, in *Shaw* v *Director of Public Prosecutions* [1962] AC 220 in the passage which I have just cited. It is also borne out by what is presumably the purpose of the legal rule – namely, that reasonable people may venture out in public without the risk of outrage to certain minimum accepted standards of decency.

On the other hand, I do not think that it would necessarily negative the offence that the act or exhibit is superficially hid from view, if the public is expressly or impliedly invited to penetrate the cover. Thus, the public touting for an outrageously indecent exhibition in private would not escape: see *R* v *Saunders* (1875) 1 QBD 15. Another obvious example is an outrageously indecent exhibit with a cover entitled 'Lift in order to see. . . .' This sort of instance could be applied to a book or newspaper; and I think that a jury should be invited to consider the matter in this way. The conduct must at least in some way be so projected as to have an impact in public: cf. *Smith* v *Hughes* [1960] 1 WLR 830.

(5) There are other features of the offence which should, in my view, be brought to the notice of the jury. It should be emphasised that 'outrage,' like 'corrupt,' is a very strong word. 'Outraging public decency' goes considerably beyond offending the susceptibilities of, or even shocking, reasonable people. Moreover the offence is, in my view, concerned with recognised minimum standards of decency, which are likely to vary from time to time. Finally, notwithstanding that 'public' in the offence is used in a locative sense, public decency must be viewed as a whole; and I think the jury should be invited, where appropriate, to remember that they live in a plural society, with a tradition of tolerance towards minorities, and that this atmosphere of toleration is itself part of public decency.

(6) The Court of Appeal said of the direction on count 2 that it might be that it was not wholly satisfactory. I would myself go further. I regard it as essential that the jury should be carefully directed, on the lines that I have ventured to suggest, on the proper approach to the meaning of 'decency' and 'outrage' and the element of publicity required to constitute the offence. The summing up was generally a careful and fair one, but I think it was defective in these regards; and I therefore do not think it would be safe to allow the conviction on count 2 to stand.

R v *Gibson and Another*

[1991] 1 All ER 439, Court of Appeal

For the facts and holding, see p. 68.

NOTES AND QUESTIONS
1. Is it possible to know from a reading of the cases what behaviour will be caught by these offences? If not, how can people who desire to be law-abiding regulate their conduct to avoid prosecution?
2. In *Knuller* v *DPP* the House of Lords stated that the courts had no residual discretion to create new criminal offences. Does this signal an awareness of the potential abuses inherent in common law crimes?
3. Are conspiracies to corrupt public morals or outrage public decency common law or statutory conspiracies?
4. The Criminal Law Act 1977, s. 5(3) stipulates that a charge of conspiracy will lie only where there would be an offence if carried out by a single person. While cases such as *Gibson* confirm the existence of a substantive offence of outraging public decency, it is still unclear whether there is behaviour outside the definition of the substantive offence which would not amount to an offence if done by one person, but which might amount to a common law conspiracy to outrage public decency if done by several. Nor is it clear

whether there is a substantive offence of corrupting public morals. The House of Lords did not determine the issue in *Shaw* v *DPP* although the Court of Appeal held that there was such a substantive offence. Even if there is such an offence, a similar uncertainty will arise as to the offence of outraging public decency. The fact that the ruling in *Ayres* (above, p. 536) still applies to these two conspiracies makes the distinction important, as does the different rules on impossibility (see below). The statute is unhelpful and the whole area ripe for reform.

If the offence charged is a common law conspiracy, impossibility remains a defence.

Director of Public Prosecutions v *Nock*
[1978] AC 979, House of Lords

LORD RUSSELL OF KILLOWEN: My Lords, I have had the advantage of reading in draft the speech in these consolidated appeals of my noble and learned friend, Lord Scarman. I agree with his conclusion that these appeals should be allowed and with the reasons to which he attributes that conclusion.

The important point to note is that the agreement that is said to have been an unlawful conspiracy was not an agreement in general terms to produce cocaine, but an agreement in specific terms to produce cocaine from a particular powder which in fact, however treated, would never yield cocaine. In order to see whether there is a criminal conspiracy it is necessary to consider the whole agreement. The specific limits of the agreement cannot be discarded, leaving a general agreement to produce cocaine, for that would be to find an agreement other than that which was made: and that is not a permissible approach to any agreement, conspiracy or other.

It is, I apprehend, clear on authority that neither appellant, discovered in the act of vainly and optimistically applying sulphuric acid (or any other treatment) to this particular powder, would be guilty of an attempt to produce cocaine. It would appear to me strange that the two should be guilty of a crime if together they bent over the same test tube, having agreed on the joint vain attempt. These appellants thought that they would succeed in their endeavour. But what if they had doubted success, and their agreement had been to 'try it'? That would be an agreement to attempt, and since the attempt would not be unlawful the agreement could not be a criminal conspiracy. But if the conclusion against which these appeals are made were correct, it would mean that those erroneously confident of success would be guilty of the crime of conspiracy, but not those who, unconvinced, agreed to try. The gullible would be guilty, the suspicious stainless. That could not be right.

D: Organised crime

While some conspiracies are formed for the purpose of committing a one-off offence, after which its members disband, others are in fact criminal organisations whose business consists of criminal activity. The latter are conspiracies in arguably their most virulent form. Their members are professional criminals. Among the offences typically committed by such criminal organisations or syndicates are drug trafficking, money laundering, extortion, and the trafficking in women and children. Crimes of violence, including murder for hire, are also not uncommon.

Complicating the problem of bringing these, often large, criminal organisations to justice is the fact that they often operate in more than one State. Questions of extradition, jurisdiction and conflicts of laws can arise. In response to these problems and to facilitate cooperation among member States, the European Union has promulgated the following Joint Action:

Joint Action of 21 December 1998 (98/733/JHA)

Adopted by the Council on the basis of Article K.3 of the Treaty on European Union, on making it a criminal offence to participate in a criminal organisation in the Member States of the European Union

Article 1

Within the meaning of this joint action, a criminal organisation shall mean a structured association, established over a period of time, of more than two persons, acting in concert with a view to committing offences which are punishable by deprivation of liberty or a detention order of a maximum of at least four years or a more serious penalty, whether such offences are an end in themselves or a means of obtaining material benefits and, where appropriate, of improperly influencing the operation of public authorities.

The offences referred to in the first subparagraph include those mentioned in Article 2 of the Europol Convention and in the Annex thereto and carrying a sentence at least equivalent to that provided for in the first subparagraph.

Article 2

1. To assist the fight against criminal organisations, each Member State shall undertake, in accordance with the procedure laid down in Article 6, to ensure that one or both of the types of conduct described below are punishable by effective, proportionate and dissuasive criminal penalties:

(a) conduct by any person who, with intent and with knowledge of either the aim and general criminal activity of the organisation or the intention of the organisation to commit the offences in question, actively takes part in:

— the organisation's criminal activities falling within Article 1, even where that person does not take part in the actual execution of the offences concerned and, subject to the general principles of the criminal law of the Member State concerned, even where the offences concerned are not actually committed,

— the organisation's other activities in the further knowledge that his participation will contribute to the achievement of the organisation's criminal activities falling within Article 1;

(b) conduct by any person consisting in an agreement with one or more persons that an activity should be pursued which, if carried out, would amount to the commission of offences falling within Article 1, even if that person does not take part in the actual execution of the activity.

2. Irrespective of whether they have elected to make the type of conduct referred to in paragraph 1(a) or (b) a criminal offence, Member States will afford one another the most comprehensive assistance possible in respect of the offences covered by this Article, as well as those offences covered by Article 3(4) of the Convention relating to extradition between the Member States of the European Union, drawn up by the Council on 27 September 1996.

Article 3

Each Member State shall ensure that legal persons may be held criminally or, failing that, otherwise liable for offences falling within Article 2(1) which are committed by that legal person, in accordance with procedures to be laid down in national law. Such liability of the legal person shall be without prejudice to the criminal liability of the natural persons who were the perpetrators of the offences or their accomplices. Each Member State shall ensure, in particular, that legal persons may be penalised in an effective, proportionate and dissuasive manner and that material and economic sanctions may be imposed on them.

Article 4

Each Member State shall ensure that the types of conduct referred to in Article 2(1)(a) or (b) which take place in its territory are subject to prosecution wherever in the territory of the Member States the organisation is based or pursues its criminal activities, or wherever the activity covered by the agreement referred to in Article 2(1)(b) takes place.

Where several Member States have jurisdiction in respect of acts of participation in a criminal organisation, they shall consult one another with a view to coordinating their action in order to prosecute effectively, taking account, in particular, of the location of the organisation's different components in the territory of the Member States concerned.

Article 5

1. In cases where the Convention relating to extradition between the Member States of the European Union, drawn up by the Council on 27 September 1996, applies, this joint action shall not affect in any manner whatsoever the obligations under the Convention or the interpretation thereof.

2. Nothing in this joint action shall prevent a Member State from making punishable conduct in relation to a criminal organisation which is of broader scope than that defined in Article 2(1).

NOTES AND QUESTIONS

1. Does the UK law of conspiracy meet the obligations created by the Joint Action? Does it go beyond the minimum requirements of Article 2?
2. Although the Joint Action purports to use mandatory language ('each Member State shall'), the precise status of Joint Actions within the European Union is somewhat a matter of dispute. The UK has taken the position that they are not necessarily legally binding, and the actual text of the Joint Action needs to be examined.

SECTION 3: Attempt

There may be little difference between the person who tries to commit a crime and fails (the would-be murderer whose gun misfires or whose aim is off) and his counterpart who is more successful in achieving his criminal objective. Both may be equally dangerous and in need of rehabilitation and restraint. Therein lies the rationale behind a crime of attempt.

Attempting to commit a crime is now a statutory offence defined by the Criminal Attempts Act 1981. The basic definition is contained in s. 1:

Criminal Attempts Act 1981

1.—(1) If, with intent to commit an offence to which this section applies, a person does an act which is more than merely preparatory to the commission of the offence, he is guilty of attempting to commit the offence.

(2) A person may be guilty of attempting to commit an offence to which this section applies even though the facts are such that the commission of the offence is impossible.

(3) In any case where—

(a) apart from this subsection a person's intention would not be regarded as having amounted to an intent to commit an offence; but

(b) if the facts of the case had been as he believed them to be, his intention would be so regarded, then, for the purposes of subsection (1) above, he shall be regarded as having had an intent to commit that offence.

(4) This section applies to any offence which, if it were completed, would be triable in England and Wales as an indictable offence, other than—

(a) conspiracy (at common law or under section 1 of the Criminal Law Act 1977 or any other enactment);

(b) aiding, abetting, counselling, procuring or suborning the commission of an offence;

(c) offences under section 4(1) (assisting offenders) or 5(1) (accepting or agreeing to accept consideration for not disclosing information about an arrestable offence) of the Criminal Law Act 1967.

NOTES AND QUESTIONS

1. Because the law of attempt has now been codified by Parliament, cases decided before the Act must be approached with considerable caution.

2. Under s. 1(4)(b) of the Act it is no longer an offence to attempt to aid and abet the commission of an offence. However, in some instances aiding and abetting is, by statute, itself an offence. Where this is so, there can be a conviction for attempting to commit the statutory crime. An example is assisting suicide contrary to the Suicide Act 1961, s. 2(1).

3. Under the Act, can there be an offence of attempting to commit a summary offence? An offence of attempting to commit an offence by omission to act? Attempted voluntary manslaughter?

Jurisdiction can sometimes pose a problem. When acts which arguably constitute an attempt occur outside the UK, can a prosecution be brought within the UK?

Director of Public Prosecutions v *Stonehouse*
[1977] 2 All ER 909, House of Lords

LORD DIPLOCK: My Lords, in 1974, the appellant, John Thomson Stonehouse ('the accused'), was a well-known public figure in this country. A member of Parliament and a Privy Councillor, he had held a number of ministerial posts in the government during the six years up to 1970. Thereafter he became active in business through a company, Export Promotion and Consultancy Services Ltd, which he controlled.

By the summer of 1974, however, his personal finances were in a disastrous state. He decided to fake his death by drowning and to start life afresh under a new identity with money dishonestly obtained and clandestinely transferred to his chosen country of refuge, Australia. He carried out this plan, but was discovered living in Australia under his false identity some five weeks after his pretended death by drowning. He was extradited and stood his trial at the Central Criminal Court on an indictment charging him with 16 complete offences of dishonesty and forgery and five offences of attempting to obtain property by deception (counts 17 to 21).

This House is not concerned in this appeal with any of the charges of complete offences. He was convicted on 13 of these. Your lordships are concerned with those five counts (17 to 21) which charged him with the inchoate crime of attempting to obtain property by deception. The intended victims of the deception charges were five different life insurance companies, which had issued to Mrs Stonehouse, the wife of the accused, policies amounting in all to £125,000 payable on her husband's death within five years.

The facts that gave rise to these charges can be stated briefly. Mrs Stonehouse was not a party to the accused's plan. She was intended to believe that he had died by drowning. The accused intended to transfer to Australia all the money that he could lay his hands on; so on his death being presumed, his estate would be insolvent. To provide for his wife, ostensibly his widow, after his disappearance, there were taken out between July and September 1974, in Mrs Stonehouse's name, the five policies of insurance to a total amount of £125,000 payable to her on the death of her husband within five years. Active steps in arranging for the issue of the policies to his wife were taken by the accused himself in England. On 20th November 1974 the accused faked his death by accidental drowning in the sea off Miami in Florida, USA, to which city he had gone with a business associate. Ostensibly for a business meeting. He had made an appointment for such a meeting later on that day and pending this had told his companion that he was going to the beach to have a swim. When he failed to keep the business appointment, enquiries were set on foot. His clothes, valuables and passport were found to be still in his hotel room and his bath robe was found in a bathing hut on the beach. Of the accused himself there was no trace. In fact he had left Miami secretly by air, wearing a new suit of clothes which he had secreted and equipped with a false passport to conceal his identity. He eventually reached Australia and remained there undetected until 24th December 1974.

As soon as his disappearance at Miami was discovered in the circumstances summarised above, the hue and cry was raised. The police were brought in and, as was inevitable, the circumstances of his disappearance hit the headlines in the press, and on television and radio, in England. What the accused had done ensured, as he intended, that the news of his death by drowning should be communicated in England to his wife, who he intended should claim the policy moneys, and to the insurance companies, who he intended should pay them over to her.

At his trial the accused was convicted on the five counts of attempting to obtain property by deception. He had discharged his counsel early in the proceedings and no point was taken at the trial that these offences were committed outside the territorial jurisdiction of the English court.

On his appeal to the Court of Appeal, Criminal Division, the accused was represented by counsel who took the territorial jurisdiction point and two other points of law. They were that the acts of the accused at Miami on 20th November 1974 were not sufficiently proximate to the complete offence of obtaining property by deception to be capable in law of constituting an attempt to commit that crime: or, in the alternative, that the question whether they were sufficiently proximate was one of fact for the jury and that the judge had wrongly treated it as one of law and withdrawn that question for them.

The appeal was dismissed, but the Court of Appeal certified that the following point of law of general public importance was involved in the decision to dismiss the appeal against conviction on counts 17 to 21:

> Whether the offence of attempting on 20th November 1974 to obtain property in England by deception, the final act alleged to constitute the offence of attempt having occurred outside the jurisdiction of the English courts is triable in an English court, all the remaining acts necessary to constitute the complete offence being intended to take place in England.

... I start by considering the territorial element in their jurisdiction to try the complete crime; for on this and on the corresponding offence under s. 32 of the Larceny Act 1916, which has been replaced by s. 15 of the Theft Act 1968, there is long-standing authority to the effect that in a result-crime the English courts have jurisdiction to try the offence if the described consequence of the conduct of the accused which is part of the definition of the crime took place in England.

This was called the 'terminatory theory' of jurisdiction by Professor Glanville Williams in an article, Venue and the Ambit of the Criminal Law where he contrasted it unfavourably with the 'initiatory theory' that the crime is committed where the offender is when he does the acts which constitute the essential physical element of the crime. The terminatory theory has been acted on as a ground of jurisdiction since it was first laid down in *R v Ellis* [1899] 1 QB 230, a case where the false representations were made in Scotland but the property was obtained in England. As I ventured to point out in *Treacy v Director of Public Prosecutions* [1971] AC 537, there is no reason in principle why the terminatory theory should have the effect of excluding the initiatory theory as an alternative ground of jurisdiction, though this was held to be so in *R v Harden* [[1962] 1 All ER 286]; but since in the instant case all the physical acts of the accused himself on which the prosecution rely were done in the United States, your Lordships are not concerned to consider whether *R v Harden* was rightly decided.

In those reported cases where the false representations have been made abroad but the property has been obtained in England, the property has been obtained by the offender himself and this has in fact involved some physical act in England by the offender or by someone else, not necessarily an accomplice but possibly an innocent agent or bailee accepting possession or control of the property on the offender's behalf. In the instant case if the crime which the accused was charged with attempting to commit had been completed he would have enabled another person, Mrs Stonehouse, to obtain the property, viz the policy moneys, for herself and no further act would have needed to be done in England by the accused himself or anyone acting on his behalf. Should this make any difference? In my opinion it does not. The basis of the jurisdiction under the terminatory theory is not that the accused has done some physical act in England, but that his physical acts, wherever they were done, have caused the obtaining of the property in England from the person to whom it belonged. Whether he has caused it to be obtained for himself through the instrumentality of an innocent agent, such as the Post Office, acting on his behalf, or has caused it to be obtained by an innocent third party cannot in my view make any difference to the jurisdiction of the English court to try the offence.

My Lords, if this be the principle on which the English courts would have had jurisdiction to try the complete offence which the accused was charged with attempting to commit, that principle is broad enough to cover also their jurisdiction to try the inchoate offence of attempting to commit it. The accused had done all the physical acts lying within his power that were needed to comply with the definition of a complete crime justiciable by an English court; and his state of mind at the time he did them also satisfied the definition of that crime. All that was left was for him not to be found out before the intended consequence could occur. Once it is appreciated that territorial jurisdiction over a 'result-crime' does not depend on acts done by the offender in England but on consequences which he causes to occur in England. I see no ground for holding that an attempt to commit a crime which, if the attempt succeeded, would be justiciable in England does not also fall within the jurisdiction of the English courts, not withstanding that the physical acts intended to produce the proscribed consequences in England were all of them done abroad.

NOTES AND QUESTIONS

1. The jurisdiction over attempts generally depends on the jurisdiction of the court over the substantive offence. For example, murder by a British citizen is indictable in England or Wales wherever commited. However, most offences require acts of the defendant to have

some effect within the jurisdiction. What effect would Stonehouse's actions have had in England and Wales?

2. Is Jones guilty of attempted murder:
    (a) when in England he sends a letter bomb to an enemy in France;
    (b) when in France he sends a letter bomb to an enemy in England?

A: *Mens rea*

It must be shown that the defendant intended to commit the offence, whether or not intention is the *mens rea* for the completed offence.

R v *Whybrow*
(1951) 35 Cr App R 141, Court of Appeal

LORD GODDARD: . . . The facts of the case, so far as it is necessary to state them, are these: the appellant was living on bad terms with his wife and it is shown that at the time he, a married man with a family, was carrying on a liaison with another young woman. That, of course, was put forward as the motive, and, indeed, it is the oldest motive in the world that is brought up in cases of murder or attempted murder of a wife. It was proved to exist and a letter was produced from the appellant to that young woman's father which could leave no doubt in anybody's mind that the appellant's affections had been transferred to that young woman.

The appellant had had some, but no very great, experience of electrical installations. He had been a labourer in the employ of the electrical department of the Southend Corporation Electricity Works and had no doubt, on occassions, gone round with electricians. He also had had a wireless apparatus and so forth in this house and probably had what may be described as an amateur's knowledge of electricity. On the night of the alleged crime the wife was taking a bath and the appellant was in an adjoining room. He said that he was in the lavatory, but he might equally well have been in the bedroom. The wife was heard to call out, and she complained of having received an electric shock while in the bath. The next day it came to light that an apparatus had been connected with the soap dish, the bath being a porcelain bath and either the soap dish itself or its support being made of metal. An apparatus was found connected with this soap dish which, if prepared intentionally, showed a deliberate, cold-blooded resolve to administer a shock of 230 volts of electricity to a woman in her bath. It is common knowledge, and the appellant admitted that he knew it, that to administer an electric shock to a person in a bath is the most dangerous thing that can be done in that way.

The case lasted two days and the learned Judge's summing-up, so far as the facts were concerned, was meticulouly careful and meticulously accurate, but unfortunately he did, in charging the jury, confuse in his mind for a moment the direction given to a jury in a case of murder with the direction given to a jury in a case of attempted murder. In murder the jury is told – and it has always been the law – that if a person wounds another or attacks another either intending to kill or intending to do grievous bodily harm, and the person attacked dies, that is murder, the reason being that the requisite malice aforethought, which is a term of art, is satisfied if the attacker intends to do grievous bodily harm. . . . But, if the charge is one of attempted murder, the intent becomes the principal ingredient of the crime. It may be said that the law, which is not always logical, is somewhat illogical in saying that, if one attacks a person intending to do grievous bodily harm and death results, that is murder, but that if one attacks a person and only intends to do grievous bodily harm, and death does not result, it is not attempted murder, but wounding with intent to do grievous bodily harm. It is not really illogical because, in that particular case, the intent is the essence of the crime while, where the death of another is caused, the necessity is to prove malice aforethought, which is supplied in law by proving intent to do grievous bodily harm.

R v O'Toole

[1987] Crim LR 759, Court of Appeal

On July 31, 1986 the appellant who was a regular customer of a public house in North London was 'barred' from that public house. At closing time, the appellant returned with a can of petrol and splashed it around a vestibule at the entrance of the public house. When he was taxed by the barmaid, he stated that he did not care whether she be burned alive. He had earlier been heard to say that he would smash the public house. When arrested, he told the police that if he did not smash the public house up that night he would do it the following night. In interview he said 'I'll burn the lot of them and you (the police) as well.' The defence case was that the applicant was drunk. He had the can of petrol with him because he was filling the petrol reservoir of his motor car. Whilst doing so he had heard a noise from the public house. He decided to speak with the landlord. Whilst trying to look through a window, he had accidentally spilled petrol into the vestibule.

The appellant was charged with two counts, the first alleging that he attempted to damage by fire the public house intending to damage the same or being reckless as to whether it would be damaged and intending to endanger the life of the barmaid. Count 2 alleged as follows:

> On 31st day of July 1986 without lawful excuse attempted to damage by fire the Star Public House, Charlbert Street NW8 belonging to another, intending to damage the said property or being reckless as to whether property would be damaged and being reckless as to whether the life of [the barmaid] would thereby be endangered.

The defendant was convicted by the jury of count 2. In summing up the case to the jury, the learned trial judge defined 'attempt' and 'intent' and 'reckless' in relation to the question of damaging property. The jury having retired to consider their verdicts, sent a note in which they said that they were unanimous in their decision that the defendant was 'not guilty of intent (on both counts)' and asking how significant was 'being reckless.'

The learned trial judge directed them that their note seemed to have disposed of count 1. In relation to count 2 he defined 'attempt' yet again saying that if they were not sure that the appellant intended to damage by fire at all then they should acquit. However he went on to say that if they were satisfied that he attempted to damage, then they must go on to consider whether he intended to damage the property or was reckless as to whether it be damaged by fire.

The Court of Appeal in allowing the appeal and quashing the conviction held that intent is an element inherent in the definition of attempt and is the same at least if not greater than the intent necessary to constitute the full offence. The learned trial judge was in error in relating back to the question of recklessness and intent to damage. There was no room for a reckless damage to property when the offence itself is an attempt because the attempt must have the necessary intent.

It was further held that the difficulty in this case arose from the Indictment. When the offence is an attempt under section 1(1) of the Criminal Attempts Act 1981 it is unnecessary and wrong to include the words 'or being reckless as to whether property would be damaged.' When the substantive offence is charged as opposed to an attempt, the words used are correct. It is only when an attempt to damage property is charged that the words 'being reckless as to whether such property would be damaged' are otiose and wrong.

NOTES

1. The requirement that the defendant must intend to commit the offence attempted implicitly requires that the defendant have any intent required for the underlying offence. Thus if a defendant is charged with attempted theft it must be proved that the defendant intended permanently to deprive the victim of her property.

2. The requirement that the defendant must intend to commit the offence also means that if the offence is defined in terms of result (e.g., murder), it must be proved that the defendant intended to bring about the proscribed result. What if, however, the defendant does not

desire the result but knows that it is virtually certain to follow from his acts? As we have seen previously such knowledge may satisfy the *mens rea* for murder; but will it be sufficient for attempted murder?

R v *Walker and Hayles*

(1990) 90 Cr App R 226, Court of Appeal

LLOYD LJ: On September 9, 1988, these two appellants, Walker and Hayles, were convicted of attempted murder at the Central Criminal Court before the recorder and a jury. They were sentenced to seven years' and five years' imprisonment respectively.

They now appeal against their convictions. The facts were that Walker's sister, Christine, was having an affair with a man called Royston John, the victim. A week or so before September 20, 1987, there had been a violent quarrel between Christine and John. Christine received two black eyes and a torn fingernail.

On the evening in question (September 20), the two appellants visited Christine's flat. The appellant Hayles was living with another of Walker's sisters. Christine's flat was on the third floor of a block of flats in Battersea Park Road. Royston John was there. He had a key to Christine's flat. He was asked to hand over the key to Christine. He refused. There was then a fight. John ran out onto the balcony, which lead towards the central staircase. The appellants followed him.

According to the prosecution case, the appellants caught him up, lifted him over the balcony, and dropped him horizontally to the ground. Somehow or he other survived, perhaps because he landed on some grass. In the course of the fight the appellants had banged the victim's head against the wall, saying that they were going to kill him. There were bloodstains found on the wall. One of the appellants produced a knife and threatened the victim's throat. Just before they threw the victim over the balcony, he said: 'You deserve to die. I am going to kill you. We don't like you.'

. . .

We turn to the main ground of appeal, namely the direction on intention. Since the charge was attempted murder, the prosecution had to prove an intention to kill. Intention to cause really serious harm would not have been enough. We were told that this is the first case in which this Court has had to consider the correct direction in a case of attempted murder since *R* v *Moloney* (1985) 81 Cr App R 93, *R* v *Hancock and Shankland* (1986) 82 Cr App R 264 and *R* v *Nedrick* (1986) 83 Cr App R 267.

We have already said that there could be no criticism of the initial direction at the start of the summing-up, and repeated at the conclusion. The recorder was right to keep it short. 'Trying to kill' was the expression he used as a paraphrase. That was easy for the jury to understand, and could not on any view of the law be regarded as too favourable to the prosecution. 'Trying to kill' is synonymous with purpose. It has never been suggested that a man does not intend what he is trying to achieve. The difficulty only arises when he brings about a result which he is not trying to achieve.

But when the jury returned, the recorder, as we have seen, went further. . . .

We can . . . understand why the recorder went further, since he had only just given a direction in simple terms, which was as clear as could be. Moreover the position is not quite the same in a case of attempted murder as it is in murder. In the great majority of murder cases, as the Court pointed out in *Nedrick* (*supra*), the defendant's desire goes hand in hand with his intention. If he desires serious harm, and death results from his action, he is guilty of murder. A simple direction suffices in such cases. The rare and exceptional case is where the defendant does not desire serious harm, or indeed any harm at all. But where a defendant is charged with attempted murder, he may well have desired serious harm, without desiring death. So the desire of serious harm does not provide the answer. It does not go hand in hand with the relevant intention, as it does in the great majority of murder cases, since in attempted murder the relevant intention must be an intention to kill.

Considerations such as these may have led the recorder to give the expanded direction in terms of foresight. But, as we have said, it would have been better if he had not done so. The mere fact that a jury calls for a further direction on intention does not of itself make it a rare and exceptional case requiring a foresight direction. In most cases they will only need to be reminded of the simple direction which they will already have been given, namely that the relevant intention is an intention to kill, and that nothing less will suffice.

[The recorder] may have confused the jury. He may have led them to equate the probability of death and the foresight of death with an intention to kill. That was the very error exposed in *R v Moloney* (*supra*) and *Nedrick* (1986) 83 Cr App R 267.

[But it] is important to note that the recorder said that the jury would be *entitled* to draw the inference: he was not saying that they must draw the inference. By the use of the word 'entitled,' he was making it sufficiently clear to the jury that the question whether they drew the inference or not was a question for them. This is borne out by the passage which immediately followed in which the recorder said that the jury would be entitled to bear in mind the speed of events on the one hand and the speed at which a man can make up his mind on the other.

So we reject the submission that the recorder was equating foresight with intent, or that he may have given that impression to the jury. He was perfectly properly saying that foresight was something from which the jury could infer intent. He was treating the question as part of the law of evidence, not as part of the substantive law of attempted murder.

Where a lesser *mens rea* is required in respect of the circumstances of the offence, is the lesser *mens rea* sufficient for an offence of attempt?

R v Khan
[1990] 2 All ER 783, Court of Appeal

RUSSELL LJ: These appeals raise the short but important point of whether the offence of attempted rape is committed when the defendant is reckless as to the woman's consent to sexual intercourse. The appellants submit that no such offence is known to the law.

Before examining the submissions, we deal briefly with the facts. On 24 June 1987 at the Central Criminal Court before his Honour Judge Rant QC and a jury the appellants Mohammed Iqbal Khan, Mahesh Dhokia, Jaswinder Singh Banga and Navaid Faiz were convicted of the attempted rape of a 16-year-old girl. The case for the Crown was that on 19 March 1986 the girl met and danced with the appellant Dhokia at a daytime discotheque in Uxbridge. Thereafter she accompanied Dhokia and four other youths in a motor car which was driven to an address in Waltham Road, Uxbridge, where the occupants of the car, who included Faiz and Khan as well as Dhokia, were joined by others, including Banga.

Inside the house Dhokia, without success, attempted to have sexual intercourse with the girl. He was followed by others. Three youths succeeded in having sexual intercourse; three others, the remaining appellants, attempted to have sexual intercourse but failed. The girl did not consent to any sexual activity in the house. After her ordeal, she left and travelled to a friend's house, where she made a complaint.

The judge dealt with the offence of rape as follows:

. . . [W]e have had regard to the observations of Mustill LJ giving the judgment of the Court of Appeal, Criminal Division in *R v Millard and Vernon* [1987] Crim LR 393. That was a case involving a charge of attempting to damage property the particulars of offence reading:

> Gary Mann Millard and Michael Elliot Vernon, on 11th May 1985, without lawful excuse, attempted to damage a wooden wall at the Leeds Road Football Stand belonging to Huddersfield Town Association Football Club, intending to damage the said wall or being reckless as to whether the said wall would be damaged.

Mustill LJ said (and we read from the transcript):

> The appellants' case is simple. They submit that in ordinary speech the essence of an attempt is a desire to bring about a particular result, coupled with steps towards that end. The essence of recklessness is either indifference to a known risk or (in some circumstances) failure to advert to an obvious risk. The two states of mind cannot co-exist. Section 1(1) of the Criminal Attempts Act 1981 expressly demands that a person shall have an intent to commit an offence if he is to be guilty of an attempt to commit that offence. The word 'intent' may, it is true, have a specialised meaning in some contexts. But even if this can properly be attributed to the word where it is used in s. 1(1) there is no warrant for reading it as embracing recklessness, nor for reading into it whatever lesser degree of *mens rea* will suffice for the particular substantive offence in question. For an attempt nothing but conscious volition will do. Accordingly, that part of the particulars of offence which referred to recklessness was meaningless, and the parts of the direction which involved a definition of recklessness, and an implied invitation to convict if the jury found the appellants to have acted recklessly, were misleading. There was thus, so it was contended, a risk that the jury convicted on the wrong basis and the verdict cannot safely be allowed to stand. At the conclusion of the argument it appeared to us that this argument was logically sound and that it was borne out by the authorities cited to us, especially *R v Whybrow* (1951) 35 Cr App R 141, *Cunliffe v Goodman* [1950] 1 All ER 720 at 724 and *R v Mohan* [1975] 2 All ER 193, and that it was not inconsistent with anything in *Hyam v DPP* [1974] 2 All ER 41. Our attention had, however, been drawn to a difference of opinion between commentators about the relationship between the *mens rea* in an attempt and the ingredients of the substantive offence, and we therefore reserved judgment so as to consider whether the question was not perhaps more difficult than it seemed. In the event we have come to the conclusion that there does exist a problem in this field, and that it is by no means easy to solve, but also that it need not be solved for the purpose of deciding the present appeal. In our judgment two different situations must be distinguished. The first exists where the substantive offence consists simply of the act which constitutes the actus reus (which for present purposes we shall call the 'result') coupled with some element of volition, which may or may not amount to a full intent. Here the only question is whether the 'intent' to bring about the result called for by s. 1(1) is to be watered down to such a degree, if any, as to make it correspond with the mens rea of the substantive offence. The second situation is more complicated. It exists where the substantive offence does not consist of one result and one mens rea, but rather involves not only the underlying intention to produce the result, but another state of mind directed to some circumstance or act which the prosecution must also establish in addition to providing the result. The problem may be illustrated by reference to the offence of attempted rape. As regards the substantive offence the 'result' takes the shape of sexual intercourse with a woman. But the offence is not established without proof of an additional circumstance (namely that the woman did not consent), and a state of mind relative to that circumstance (namely that the defendant knew she did not consent, or was reckless as to whether she consented). When one turns to the offence of attempted rape, one thing is obvious, that the result, namely the act of sexual intercourse, must be intended in the full sense. Also obvious is the fact that proof of an intention to have intercourse with a woman, together with an act towards that end, is not enough: the offence must involve proof of something about the woman's consent, and something about the defendant's state of mind in relation to that consent. The problem is to decide precisely what that something is. Must the prosecution prove not only that the defendant intended the act, but also that he intended it to be non-consensual? Or should the jury be directed to consider two different states of mind, intent as to the act and recklessness as to the

circumstances? Here the commentators differ: contrast Smith and Hogan *Criminal Law* (5th edn, 1983) p 255 ff with a note on the Act by Professor Griew in *Current Law Statutes 1981*.

We must now grapple with the very problem that Mustill LJ identifies in the last paragraph of the passage cited.

In our judgment an acceptable analysis of the offence of rape is as follows: (1) the intention of the offender is to have sexual intercourse with a woman; (2) the offence is committed if, but only if, the circumstances are that (a) the woman does not consent *and* (b) the defendant knows that she is not consenting or is reckless as to whether she consents.

Precisely the same analysis can be made of the offence of attempted rape: (1) the intention of the offender is to have sexual intercourse with a woman; (2) the offence is committed if, but only if, the circumstances are that (a) the woman does not consent *and* (b) the defendant knows that she is not consenting or is reckless as to whether she consents.

The only difference between the two offences is that in rape sexual intercourse takes place whereas in attempted rape it does not, although there has to be some act which is more than preparatory to sexual intercourse. Considered in that way, the intent of the defendant is precisely the same in rape and in attempted rape and the *mens rea* is identical, namely an intention to have intercourse plus a knowledge of or recklessness as to the woman's absence of consent. No question of attempting to achieve a reckless state of mind arises; the attempt relates to the physical activity; the mental state of the defendant is the same. A man does not recklessly have sexual intercourse, nor does he recklessly attempt it. Recklessness in rape and attempted rape arises not in relation to the physical act of the accused but only in his state of mind when engaged in the activity of having or attempting to have sexual intercourse.

If this is the true analysis, as we believe it is, the attempt does not require any different intention on the part of the accused from that for the full offence of rape. We believe this to be a desirable result which in the instant case did not require the jury to be burdened with different directions as to the accused's state of mind, dependent on whether the individual achieved or failed to achieve sexual intercourse.

We recognise, of course, that our reasoning cannot apply to all offences and all attempts. Where, for example as in causing death by reckless driving or reckless arson, no state of mind other than recklessness is involved in the offence, there can be no attempt to commit it.

In our judgment, however, the words 'with intent to commit an offence' to be found in s. 1 of the 1981 Act mean, when applied to rape, 'with intent to have sexual intercourse with a woman in circumstances where she does not consent and the defendant knows or could not care less about her absence of consent'. The only 'intent', giving that word its natural and ordinary meaning, of the rapist is to have sexual intercourse. He commits the offence because of the circumstances in which he manifests that intent, i.e. when the woman is not consenting and he either knows it or could not care less about the absence of consent.

Attorney-General's Reference (No. 3 of 1992)
[1994] 2 All ER 121, Court of Appeal

SCHIEMANN J: The court has heard a reference made under s. 36(1) of the Criminal Justice Act 1972. The point of law which has been referred to us was formulated as follows:

> Whether on a charge of attempted arson in the aggravated form contemplated by Section 1(2) of the Criminal Damage Act 1971, in addition to establishing a specific intent to cause damage by fire, it is sufficient to prove that the defendant was reckless as to whether life would thereby be endangered.

Summary of the relevant facts

The acquittals which have given rise to this reference had the following background according to the prosecution evidence. Following previous attacks upon their property the complainants maintained a night-time watch over their premises from a motor car (a Ford Granada). In the early hours of the morning the defendants came upon the scene in a vehicle. Inside this car (a Sierra) was a milk crate containing a number of petrol bombs, matches, a petrol can and some rags. As the Sierra approached the complainants (four inside their car and two persons on the pavement talking to them) a lighted petrol bomb was thrown towards them from the Sierra. The Crown's case was that it was thrown at the Granada and its occupants. The petrol bomb in fact passed over the top of the Granada and smashed against the garden wall of a house a pavement's width away from the car. The Sierra accelerated away but crashed, and the defendants were arrested.

At the trial count 1 of the indictment alleged attempted aggravated arson, specifying in the particulars of offence, inter alia, an intent to endanger life. Count 2 alleged attempted aggravated arson, specifying in the particulars of offence, inter alia, recklessness as to whether life would be endangered. At the conclusion of the Crown's case the learned judge ruled that there was no evidence upon which the jury could find the necessary intent to endanger life required in count 1, and accordingly directed the jury to return 'not guilty' verdicts in respect of that count. This reference is not concerned with that ruling, but with her directing an acquittal in relation to count 2. In essence her reasoning was that (1) there can be no conviction of an attempt to commit an offence unless the defendant intends to commit that offence; (2) the evidence could not support an allegation that the defendants intended by the destruction of the car to endanger the life of its occupants, or the bystanders; (3) it is impossible to intend to be reckless as to whether the life of another would be endangered by damage to property; and therefore (4) it is impossible in law to convict of an attempt to commit aggravated arson if all that can be proved is that the defendant intended to damage property being reckless as to whether the life of another would be endangered by such damage.

. . .

So far as the completed simple offence is concerned, the prosecution needs to prove (1) property belonging to another was damaged by the defendant and (2) the state of mind of the defendant was one of the following: (a) he intended to damage such property or (b) he was reckless as to whether any such property would be damaged.

In the case of the completed aggravated offence the prosecution needs to prove (1) the defendant in fact damaged property, whether belonging to himself or another; and (2) that the state of mind of the defendant was one of the following, (a) he intended to damage property, and intended by the damage to endanger the life of another or (b) he intended to damage property and was reckless as to whether the life of another would be thereby endangered or (c) he was reckless as to whether any property would be damaged and was reckless as to whether the life of another would be thereby endangered.

It is to be noted that the property referred to under (1) (to which we shall hereafter refer as 'the first-named property') is not necessarily the same property as that referred to in (2) (to which we shall refer as 'the second-named property'), although it normally will be. Thus a man who (1) owns a crane from which is suspended a heavy object and (2) cuts the rope (the first-named property) which holds the object with the result that (3) the object falls and hits the roof of a passing car (the second-named property) which roof (4) collapses killing the driver would be guilty if it could be shown that he damaged the rope, was reckless as to whether this would damage the car, and was reckless as to whether the life of the driver of the car would be endangered by the damage to the car.

All the foregoing is common ground. The problem which has given rise to this reference relates to an attempt to commit the aggravated offence in circumstances where the first-named property is the same as the second-named property – in the instant case a car. It amounts to this: whether, if the

state of mind of the defendant was that postulated in (2)(b) above, namely that he intended to damage property and was reckless as to whether the life of another would thereby be endangered, and whilst in that state of mind he did an act which was more than merely preparatory to the offence, he is guilty of attempting to commit that offence.
. . .

We turn . . . to the attempt to commit the aggravated offence. In the present case, what was missing to prevent a conviction for the completed offence was damage to the property referred to in the opening lines of s. 1(2) of the 1981 Act . . . Such damage is essential for the completed offence. If a defendant does not intend to cause such damage he cannot intend to commit the completed offence. At worst he is reckless as to whether the offence is committed. The law of attempt is concerned with those who are intending to commit crimes. If that intent cannot be shown, then there can be no conviction.

However, the crime here consisted of doing certain acts in a certain state of mind in circumstances where the first-named property and the second-named property were the same, in short where the danger to life arose from the damage to the property which the defendant intended to damage. The substantive crime is committed if the defendant damaged property in a state of mind where he was reckless as to whether the life of another would thereby be endangered. We see no reason why there should not be a conviction for attempt if the prosecution can show that he, in that state of mind, intended to damage the property by throwing a bomb at it. One analysis of this situation is to say that although the defendant was in an appropriate state of mind to render him guilty of the completed offence the prosecution had not proved the physical element of the completed offence, and therefore he is not guilty of the completed offence. If, on a charge of attempting to commit the offence, the prosecution can show not only the state of mind required for the completed offence but also that the defendant intended to supply the missing physical element of the completed offence, that suffices for a conviction. That can not be done merely by the prosecution showing him to be reckless. The defendant must intend to damage property, but there is no need for a graver mental state than is required for the full offence.

The learned trial judge in the present case, however, went further than this and held that not merely must the defendant intend to supply all that was missing from the completed offence – namely damage to the first-named property – but also that recklessness as to the consequences of such damage for the lives of others was not enough to secure a conviction for attempt, although it was sufficient for the completed offence. She held that before a defendant could be convicted of attempting to commit the offence it had to be shown that he intended that the lives of others should be endangered by the damage which he intended.

She gave no policy reasons for so holding, and there is no case which bound her so to hold. . . .

An attempt was made in argument to suggest that *R* v *Khan* was wrongly decided. No policy reasons were advanced for that view and we do not share it. The result is one which accords with common sense, and does no violence to the words of the statute.

What was missing in *R* v *Khan* was the act of sexual intercourse, without which the offence was not complete. What was missing in the present case was damage to the first-named property, without which the offence was not complete. The mental state of the defendant in each case contained everything which was required to render him guilty of the full offence. In order to succeed in a prosecution for attempt, it must be shown that the defendant intended to achieve that which was missing from the full offence. Unless that is shown the prosecution have not proved that the defendant intended to commit the offence. Thus in *R* v *Khan* the prosecution had to show an intention to have sexual intercourse, and the remaining state of mind required for the offence of rape. In the present case, the prosecution had to show an intention to damage the first-named property, and the remaining state of mind required for the offence of aggravated arson.

While the learned judge in the instant case opined that *R* v *Khan* was distinguishable she did not indicate any policy reasons for distinguishing it. We see none, and none have been submitted to us directly.

We now remind ourselves of the precise question posed by the reference:

> Whether on a charge of attempted arson in the aggravated form contemplated by Section 1(2) of the Criminal Damage Act 1971, in addition to establishing a specific intent to cause damage by fire, it is sufficient to prove that the defendant was reckless as to whether life would thereby be endangered.

We answer it in the affirmative. We add that, in circumstances where the first-named property is not the same as the second-named property, in addition to establishing a specific intent to cause damage by fire to the first-named property, it is sufficient to prove that the defendant was reckless as to whether any second-named property was damaged and reckless as to whether the life of another would be endangered by the damage to the second-named property.

NOTES AND QUESTIONS

1. Is the analogy with *Khan* persuasive? See Elliott, 'Endangering Life by Destroying or Damaging Property' [1997] Crim LR 382.
2. Is the allowance of proof of recklessness as to a circumstance of the crime consistent with the requirement of proof of intention as to the crime itself? Whether *Caldwell* or *Cunningham* recklessness will need to be proved will depend on what type of recklessness must be shown for the underlying offence.
3. If the defendant has a 'conditional intent', i.e., an intention to commit the offence only if certain factors are found to exist, will he or she be guilty of attempt if acts which are more than merely preparatory are committed but the conditions are then found not to exist? This question proved troublesome until the enactment of the Criminal Attempts Act 1981, which specifically excluded the defence of impossibility. Now if a defendant were charged with attempt to steal items from a handbag and it was shown that he had an intention to steal those items if they were in the bag, he would be guilty of attempting to steal the items even if the bag were empty. (See below, impossibility.)

B: *Actus reus*

The *actus reus* of attempt is set out in the Criminal Attempts Act 1981, s. 1(1), and consists of the doing of an act 'which is more than merely preparatory to the commission of the offence'. The judge may decide that the threshold requirement of an act beyond mere preparation has not been met and direct the jury to acquit; but in the converse case, where the judge reaches the conclusion that the threshold requirement is met, he must leave it to the jury to decide whether the defendant's acts were more than merely preparatory.

Criminal Attempts Act 1981

4.—(3) Where, in proceedings against a person for an offence under section 1 above, there is evidence sufficient in law to support a finding that he did an act falling within subsection (1) of that section, the question whether or not his act fell within that subsection is a question of fact.

The line between 'mere preparation' and attempt is often difficult to draw in practice.

R v *Gullefer*
[1987] Crim LR 195, Court of Appeal

The appellant was convicted of attempted theft. During a race at a greyhound racing stadium the appellant had climbed on to the track in front of the dogs and in an attempt to distract them had waved his arms. His efforts were only marginally successful and the stewards decided it was unnecessary to declare 'no race.' Had they done so the bookmakers would have had to repay the amount of his stake to any punter, but would not have been liable to pay any winnings to those punters who would have been successful had the race been valid. The appellant told the police he had attempted to stop the race because the dog on which he had staked £18 was losing. He had hoped for a 'no race' declaration and the recovery of his stake. The appellant's main ground of appeal was that the acts proved to have been carried out by the appellant were not 'sufficiently proximate to the completed offence of theft to be capable of comprising an attempt to commit theft.'

Held, allowing the appeal and quashing the conviction, the appellant was not guilty of attempted theft. The judge's task was to decide whether there was evidence on which a jury could reasonably conclude that the defendant had gone beyond mere preparation and had embarked on the actual commission of the offence. If not, the judge had to withdraw the case from the jury. If there was such evidence, it was then for the jury to decide whether the defendant did in fact go beyond mere preparation. That was how the judge had approached the case and he had ruled there was sufficient evidence. Counsel for the appellant submitted his ruling had been wrong. The Court's first task was to apply the words of the Criminal Attempts Act 1981, s. 1, to the facts. Was the appellant still in the stage of preparation to commit the substantive offence, or was there a basis of fact which would have entitled the jury to say that he had embarked on the theft itself? Might it properly be said that when he jumped onto the track he was trying to steal £18? In the view of the Court it could not be said that at that stage he was in the process of committing theft. What he was doing was jumping onto the track in an effort to distract the dogs, which in its turn, he hoped, would force the stewards to declare 'no race,' which would in its turn give him the opportunity to demand his £18 stake from the bookmaker. There was insufficient evidence that the appellant had, when he jumped on the track, gone beyond mere preparation.

R v *Jones*
[1990] 1 WLR 1057, Court of Appeal

TAYLOR LJ: . . . The appellant, a married man, started an affair with a woman named Lynn Gresley in 1985. She lived with him in Australia during 1986. In September 1987, back in England, she began a relationship with the victim, Michael Foreman. She continued, however, to see the appellant to whom she was still very attached. In November 1987 she decided to break off the relationship with the appellant, but he continued to write to her, begging her to come back to him.

On 12 January 1988 the appellant applied for a shotgun certificate, and three days later bought two guns in company with two companions. He bought two more guns a few days later on his own. On 23 January he shortened the barrel of one of them and test fired it twice the following day.

The appellant told a colleague at work that he would be away on Tuesday, 26 January. On 24 January he phoned Lynn Gresley in a distraught state. The next day he apologised, but she again refused his invitation to resume their relationship. The appellant then told his wife he had packed a bag as he was going to Spain to do some work on their chalet. On 26 January he left home dressed normally for work, saying he would telephone his wife as to whether he was leaving for Spain that evening.

That same morning, the victim, Michael Foreman, took his daughter to school by car as usual. After the child left the car, the appellant appeared, opened the door and jumped into the rear seat. He was wearing overalls, a crash helmet with the visor down, and was carrying a bag. He and the victim had never previously met. He introduced himself, said he wanted to sort things out and asked the victim to drive on. When they stopped on a grass verge, the appellant handed over a letter he had received from Lynn. Whilst the victim read it, the appellant took the sawn-off shotgun from the bag. It was loaded. He pointed it at the victim at a range of some 10 to 12 inches. He said, 'You are not going to like this' or similar words. The victim grabbed the end of the gun and pushed it sideways and upwards. There was a struggle during which the victim managed to throw the gun out of the window. As he tried to get out, he felt a cord over his head pulling him back. He managed to break free and run away, taking the gun with him. From a nearby garage he telephoned the police.

Meanwhile, the appellant drove off in the victim's car. He was arrested jogging away from it carrying his holdall. He said he had done nothing and only wanted to kill himself. His bag contained a hatchet, some cartridges and a length of cord. He also had a sharp kitchen knife which he threw away. In the appellant's car parked near the school was £1,500 sterling together with a quantity of French and Spanish money. The evidence showed that the safety catch of the shotgun had been in the on position. The victim was unclear as to whether the appellant's finger was ever on the trigger. When interviewed, the appellant declined to make any comment.

At the end of the prosecution case, after the above facts had been given in evidence, a submission was made to the judge that the charge of attempted murder should be withdrawn from the jury. It was argued that since the appellant would have had to perform at least three more acts before the full offence could have been completed, i.e., remove the safety catch, put his finger on the trigger and pull it, the evidence was insufficient to support the charge. There was a discussion as to the proper construction of section 1(1) of the Criminal Attempts Act 1981. After hearing full argument, the judge ruled against the submission and allowed the case to proceed on count 1. Thereafter, the appellant gave evidence. In the result, the jury convicted him unanimously of attempted murder. It follows that they found he intended to kill the victim.

The sole ground of appeal is that the judge erred in law in his construction of section 1(1) and ought to have withdrawn the case. . . .

Counsel's second proposition is that section 1(1) of the Act of 1981 has not resolved the question as to which is the appropriate test. Thirdly, he submits that the test deriving from *R* v *Eagleton* (1855) 6 Cox CC 559 should be adopted.

This amounts to an invitation to construe the statutory words by reference to previous conflicting case law. We believe this to be misconceived. The Act of 1981 is a codifying statute. It amends and sets out completely the law relating to attempts and conspiracies. In those circumstances the correct approach is to look first at the natural meaning of the statutory words, not to turn back to earlier case law and seek to fit some previous test to the words of the section. . . .

We do not accept Mr Farrer's contention that section 1(1) of the Act of 1981 in effect embodies the 'last act' test derived from *R* v *Eagleton* [(1855) 6 Cox CC 559]. Had Parliament intended to adopt that test, a quite different form of words could and would have been used.

It is of interest to note that the Act of 1981 followed a report from the Law Commission on Attempt, and Impossibility in Relation to Attempt, Conspiracy and Incitement (1980) (Law Com. No. 102). At paragraph 2.47 the report states:

> The definition of sufficient proximity must be wide enough to cover two varieties of cases; first, those in which a person has taken all the steps towards the commission of a crime which he believes to be necessary as far as he is concerned for that crime to result, such as firing a gun at another and missing. Normally such cases cause no difficulty. Secondly, however, the definition must cover those instances where a person has to take some further step to complete the crime, assuming that there is evidence of the necessary mental element on his part to commit it; for example, when the defendant has raised the gun to take aim at another but has not yet squeezed the trigger. We have reached the conclusion that, in regard to these cases, it is undesirable to recommend anything more complex than a rationalization of the present law.

In paragraph 2.48 the report states:

> The literal meaning of 'proximate' is 'nearest, next before or after (in place, order, time, connection of thought, causation etc.).' Thus, were this term part of a statutory description of the actus reus of attempt, it would clearly be capable of being interpreted to exclude all but the 'final act'; this would not be in accordance with the policy outlined above.

Clearly, the draftsman of section 1(1) must be taken to have been aware of the two lines of earlier authority and of the Law Commission's report. The words 'an act which is more than merely preparatory to the commission of the offence' would be inapt if they were intended to mean 'the last act which lay in his power towards the commission of the offence.'

[T]he question for the judge in the present case was whether there was evidence from which a reasonable jury, properly directed, could conclude that the appellant had done acts which were more than merely preparatory. Clearly his actions in obtaining the gun, in shortening it, in loading it, in putting on his disguise, and in going to the school could only be regarded as preparatory acts. But, in our judgment, once he had got into the car, taken out the loaded gun and pointed it at the victim with the intention of killing him, there was sufficient evidence for the consideration of the jury on the charge of attempted murder. It was a matter for them to decide whether they were sure those acts were more than merely preparatory. In our judgment, therefore, the judge was right to allow the case to go to the jury, and the appeal against conviction must be dismissed.

R v Geddes
[1996] Crim LR 894, Court of Appeal

The appellant was convicted of attempted false imprisonment contrary to section 1(1) of the Criminal Attempts Act 1981. He had been seen by a teacher in the boys' lavatory block of a school. He had no connection with the school and no right to be there. He had a rucksack with him. A woman police officer who was, by chance, on the premises saw him and shouted at him, but he left. In a cubicle in the lavatory block there was a cider can which had belonged to the appellant. His rucksack was later found in some bushes. Its contents included a large kitchen knife, some lengths of rope and a roll of masking tape. The appellant was arrested and identified by the teacher and some pupils. The prosecution alleged that the presence of the cider can showed that the appellant had been inside a lavatory cubicle, and that the contents of the rucksack could have been used to catch and restrain a boy entering the lavatory. The defence was that the prosecution case was based on speculation. At the start of the trial the Crown had intended to rely on the evidence of a local authority housing officer who had a series of conversations with the appellant in which he had revealed that he harboured designs against young boys and wished to kidnap a child for sexual purposes. The judge ruled that that evidence was inadmissible, and the trial continued with very limited evidence called for the prosecution, a series of written admissions as to the factual basis of the Crown case having been agreed by counsel on both sides. At the close of the prosecution case the defence submitted that there was insufficient evidence to leave to the jury to support the allegation that the appellant was guilty of attempted false imprisonment. The judge rejected that submission, and the appellant called no evidence. The appellant appealed on the ground that the evidence, almost entirely contained in the factual admissions made on his behalf, did not permit the jury to conclude that he had done any act which was more than merely preparatory to the commission of a crime.

Held, allowing the appeal, that the authorities showed that the line of demarcation between acts which were merely preparatory and acts which might amount to an attempt was not always clear or easy to recognise. There was no rule of thumb test, and there must always be an exercise of judgment based on the particular facts of the case. It was an accurate paraphrase of the statutory test to ask whether the available evidence, if accepted, could show that a defendant had done an act showed that he had actually tried to commit the offence in question, or whether he had only got ready or put himself in a position or equipped himself to do so. In the present case there was not much room for doubt about the appellant's intention, and the evidence was clearly capable of showing that he had made preparations, had equipped himself, had got ready, had put himself in a position to commit the offence charged. It was true that he had entered the school, but he had never had any contact or communication with, nor had confronted, any pupil at the school. The whole story was one which filled the court with the gravest unease, but on the facts of the case the court felt bound to conclude that the evidence was not sufficient in law to support a finding that the appellant had done an act which was more than merely preparatory to wrongfully imprisoning a person unknown.

NOTES AND QUESTIONS
1. What more would Gullefer have had to have done to be guilty of attempt? While it might not make sense to require proof that the defendant did 'the last act necessary', does the converse follow? Where the defendant has done the last act which he intended to do, is there any reason why he should not be guilty of attempt, assuming the other elements of the crime are satisfied? Is this an apt description of *Gullefer*?
2. The court in *Jones* says that the defendant's acts in obtaining the gun, shortening it, loading it, putting on his disguise and going to the school 'could only be regarded as preparatory acts'. How much closer to the commission of the crime did he have to come?
3. In *Geddes* the Court of Appeal states 'there was not much room for doubt about the appellant's intention'. If so, and given that the appellant did more than just fantasise about committing the crime, did he escape conviction because he was lucky enough to have been stopped before a victim happened to appear? See also *R v Nash* [1999] Crim LR 308, where a letter requesting a specimen of urine was held not to be proximate enough to amount to an attempt to procure an act of gross indecency.
4. Part of the purpose of having a crime of attempt is to protect society by allowing the conviction of those who have manifested their dangerousness. Do the above decisions achieve this end? The courts themselves seem to have doubts on the matter. Consider *R v Campbell* [1991] Crim LR 268, where the defendant's conviction for attempted robbery was reversed. Campbell had been arrested outside a post office carrying an imitation firearm and a threatening note, which the court classified as mere acts of preparation. Were the police in effect penalised for their good detective work? Would they have been better advised to wait until Campbell had proceeded further? Does the existing law encourage a dangerous degree of brinkmanship where the police must risk the commission of the crime (and its social harm) or else lose the prosecution? Might the police be liable in the civil courts in negligence to the victim if they fail to intervene in the face of clear indications that a crime is about to be committed? See *Osman v United Kingdom* [1999] 1 FLR 193 (European Court of Human Rights).
5. Although the decisions rarely mention it as a factor, might the judge be impressed by the possibility that where the last act in the defendant's criminal scheme has yet to be committed, he still has room to repent and abandon the project?

C: Impossibility

Criminal Attempts Act 1981

(2) A person may be guilty of attempting to commit an offence to which this section applies even though the facts are such that the commission of the offence is impossible.
(3) In any case where—
(a) apart from this subsection a person's intention would not be regarded as having amounted to an intent to commit an offence: but

(b) if the facts of the case had been as he believed them to be, his intention would be
so regarded,

then, for the purposes of subsection (1) above, he shall be regarded as having had an intent to
commit that offence.

Although the statute seems to make clear that factual impossibility is not a defence
to a charge of attempt, the House of Lords failed to accept this position in *Anderton*
v *Ryan* [1985] AC 560. However, that decision was subsequently overruled.

R v *Shivpuri*
[1987] AC 1, House of Lords

LORD BRIDGE OF HARWICH: . . . The facts plainly to be inferred from the evidence, interpreted
in the light of the jury's guilty verdicts, may be shortly summarised. The appellant, on a visit to India,
was approached by a man named Desai, who offered to pay him £1,000 if, on his return to England,
he would receive a suitcase which a courier would deliver to him containing packages of drugs which
the appellant was then to distribute according to instructions he would receive. The suitcase was
duly delivered to him in Cambridge. On 30 November 1982, acting on instructions, the appellant
went to Southall station to deliver a package of drugs to a third party. Outside the station he and the
man he had met by appointment were arrested. A package containing a powdered substance was
found in the appellant's shoulder bag. At the appellant's flat in Cambridge, he produced to customs
officers the suitcase from which the lining had been ripped out and the remaining packages of
the same powdered substance. In answer to questions by customs officers and in a long written
statement the appellant made what amounted to a full confession of having played his part, as
described, as recipient and distributor of illegally imported drugs. The appellant believed the drugs
to be either heroin or cannabis. In due course the powdered substance in the several packages was
scientifically analysed and found not to be a controlled drug but snuff or some similar harmless
vegetable matter.

. . .

[T]he first question to be asked is whether the appellant intended to commit the offences of being
knowingly concerned in dealing with and harbouring drugs of Class A or Class B with intent to evade
the prohibition on their importation. Translated into more homely language the question may be
rephrased, without in any way altering its legal significance, in the following terms: did the appellant
intend to receive and store (harbour) and in due course pass on to third parties (deal with) packages
of heroin or cannabis which he knew had been smuggled into England from India? The answer is
plainly yes, he did. Next, did he in relation to each offence, do an act which was more than merely
preparatory to the commission of the offence? The act relied on in relation to harbouring was the
receipt and retention of the packages found in the lining of the suitcase. The act relied on in relation
to dealing was the meeting at Southall station with the intended recipient of one of the packages. In
each case the act was clearly more than preparatory to the commission of the *intended* offence;
it was not and could not be more than merely preparatory to the commission of the *actual*
offence, because the facts were such that the commission of the actual offence was impossible.
Here then is the nub of the matter. Does the 'act which is more than merely preparatory to
the commission of the offence' in section 1(1) of the Act of 1981 (the actus reus of the statutory
offence of attempt) require any more than an act which is more than merely preparatory to the
commission of the offence which the defendant intended to commit? Section 1(2) must surely
indicate a negative answer; if it were otherwise, whenever the facts were such that the commission
of the actual offence was impossible, it would be impossible to prove an act more than merely
preparatory to the commission of that offence and subsections (1) and (2) would contradict each
other.

This very simple, perhaps over simple, analysis leads me to the provisional conclusion that the appellant was rightly convicted of the two offences of attempt with which he was charged. But can this conclusion stand with *Anderton v Ryan* [1985] AC 560? The appellant in that case was charged with an attempt to handle stolen goods. She bought a video recorder believing it to be stolen. On the facts as they were to be assumed it was not stolen. By a majority the House decided that she was entitled to be acquitted. I have re-examined the case with care. If I could extract from the speech of Lord Roskill or from my own speech a clear and coherent principle distinguishing those cases of attempting the impossible which amount to offences under the statute from those which do not. I should have to consider carefully on which side of the line the instant case fell. But I have to confess that I can find no such principle.

If we fell into error, it is clear that our concern was to avoid convictions in situations which most people, as a matter of common sense, would not regard as involving criminality. In this connection it is to be regretted that we did not take due note of paragraph 2.97 of the Law Commission's report (Criminal Law: Attempt, and Impossiblity in Relation to Attempt, Conspiracy and Incitement (1980) (Law Commission No. 102)) which preceded the enactment of the Act of 1981, which reads:

> If it is right in principle that an attempt should be chargeable even though the crime which it is sought to commit could not possibly be committed, we do not think that we should be deterred by the consideration that such a change in our law would also cover some extreme and exceptional cases in which a prosecution would be theoretically possible. An example would be where a person is offered goods at such a low price that he believes that they are stolen, when in fact they are not; if he actually purchases them, upon the principles which we have discussed he would be liable for an attempt to handle stolen goods. Another case which has been much debated is that raised in argument by Bramwell B. in *R v Collins* (1864) 9 Cox CC 497. If A takes his own umbrella, mistaking it for one belonging to B and intending to steal B's umbrella, is he guilty of attempted theft? Again, on the principles which we have discussed he would in theory be guilty, but in neither case would it be realistic to suppose that a complaint would be made or that a prosecution would ensue.

The prosecution in *Anderton v Ryan* itself falsified the Commission's prognosis in one of the 'extreme and exceptional cases.' It nevertheless probably holds good for other such cases, particularly that of the young man having sexual intercourse with a girl over 16, mistakenly believing her to be under that age, by which both Lord Roskill and I were much troubled.

However that may be, the distinction between acts which are 'objectively innocent' and those which are not is an essential element in the reasoning in *Anderton v Ryan* and the decision, unless it can be supported on some other ground, must stand or fall by the validity of this distinction. I am satisfied on further consideration that the concept of 'objective innocence' is incapable of sensible application in relation to the law of criminal attempts. The reason for this is that any attempt to commit an offence which involves 'an act which is more than merely preparatory to the commission of the offence' but for any reason fails, so that in the event no offence is committed, must ex hypothesi, from the point of view of the criminal law, be 'objectively innocent.' What turns what would otherwise, fromthe point of view of the criminal law, be an innocent act into a crime is the intent of the actor to commit an offence. I say 'from the point of view of the criminal law' because the law of tort must surely here be quite irrelevant. A puts his hand into B's pocket. Whether or not there is anything in the pocket capable of being stolen, if A intends to steal, his act is a criminal attempt; if he does not so intend, his act is innocent. Aplunges a knife into a bolster in a bed. To avoid the complication of an offence of criminal damage, assume it to be A's bolster. If A believes the bolster to be his enemy B and intends to kill him, his act is an attempt to murder B; if he knows the bolster is only a bolster, his act is innocent. These considerations lead me to the conclusion that the distinction sought to be drawn in *Anderton* v *Ryan* between innocent and guilty acts considered 'objectively' and independently of the state of mind of the actor cannot be sensibly maintained.

NOTES AND QUESTIONS

1. Factual impossibility might be thought of as the flip-side of mistake of fact. If the defendant's conduct would be legal if the facts were as he believed them to be, he may not be guilty of an offence. But if he would have committed a crime if the facts were as he thought them to be then, by the same token, he should be guilty of an offence. Or is this argument flawed?

2. Albert intends to rape Jill. Unknown to him, however, Jill secretly desires to have intercourse with him and would readily have consented if asked. Albert, however, never asked. Is Albert guilty of attempted rape?

3. Legal impossibility, where the offence the defendant intends to commit is not a crime, is a valid defence. Thus, if Ivor tries to break the speed limit by driving at 50 mph but the limit is 70 mph, he has committed no crime of attempt. Why should this be so, given this manifestation of his willingness to ignore the demands of the law?

D: Abandonment

What if, after the defendant has gone beyond the preparatory stage but before the substantive offence has been completed, the defendant changes his mind and abandons the criminal enterprise? Is he still guilty of attempt? At common law the answer was 'yes', and that answer does not seem to have changed.

R v Becerra

(1975) 62 Cr App R 212, Court of Appeal

For facts and holding, see p. 627.

NOTES AND QUESTIONS

1. Why should voluntary abandonment not be a defence? Is a defendant who abandons his crime dangerous or in need of rehabilitation? Does the answer depend on whether there was a genuine change of heart, or the discovery of circumstances which rendered the completion of the crime more difficult, such as the fact that the bank to be robbed was surrounded by armed guards? Is it possible for the law to discriminate in practice between these types of cases?

2. In *R* v *Mitchell (Frank)* [1999] Crim LR 496 the Court of Appeal held that communication of withdrawal was necessary in a case of premeditated violence but not where the violence was spontaneous.

3. Does the reluctance of the law to recognise abandonment as a defence provide a disincentive to abandonment of a criminal project? (Abandonment might, of course, be taken into account as a mitigating factor in sentencing.)

4. Similar policy issues arise in respect of a conspirator who attempts to withdraw from the conspiracy. Technically such withdrawal will be ineffective, for the crime of conspiracy is already complete. On a policy level, however, a case can be made to allow withdrawal as a defence to encourage conspirators to withdraw.

SECTION 4: **Double inchoates**

(i) There is an offence of attempting to incite.

(ii) There is some doubt whether there is an offence of incitement to attempt although such an offence appears in the Draft Criminal Code (clause 47).

(iii) There is an offence of conspiring to incite.

(iv) The Criminal Law Act 1977, s. 5(7), abolished the offence of incitement to conspire.

(v) Incitement to incite remains an offence.

R v Evans
[1986] Crim LR 470, Court of Appeal

The appellant was charged, *inter alia*, with incitement to solicit to murder, the particulars being that she unlawfully incited B to solicit, encourage, persuade, endeavour to persuade and propose to a person or persons unknown, to murder E. The appellant had visited B, a clairvoyant and practitioner in the art of tarot cards. B also had a local reputation as a witch. The appellant told B her husband (E) had put a black magic curse on her. She said to B 'In your business I am sure you can see someone who can put a contract out on him . . . I want him dead.' The appellant offered B £1,000 and gave a description of her husband and his habits and movements. B said she would contact someone but instead went to the police. Later B gave the appellant the telephone number of another astrologer. The appellant telephoned him and they agreed to meet. At that meeting two police officers turned up instead pretending to be 'hit men.' The appellant again gave details and said they could make it appear an accident. The appellant denied the accounts given by B and the officers. She was con-victed of incitement to solicit to murder and of soliciting to murder. She appealed against the conviction for incitement on the ground that the Criminal Law Act 1977, s. 5(7) had abolished incitement to conspire and, it was submitted, to incite to solicit murder was in the circumstances the same as to incite to conspire to commit murder. The offence was an attempt to avoid the provisions of section 5(7) and an offence not known to the law.

Held, dismissing the appeal that the validity of that argument depended on whether inciting X to solicit murder was necessarily the same as inciting X to conspire with someone to murder. Was there any distinction between inciting to murder and conspiracy to commit murder? Prima facie there was a distinction between incitement and conspiracy. A person could incite another by threats or pres-sure as well as by persuasion. And, if as suggested, practically every incitement was a conspiracy to commit the offence incited there would be no need to have an offence for incitement at all. In the present case the facts of the appellant's incitement of B were not actually to enter into an agreement with X or anyone for the commission of a crime. B was being urged to procure an assassin and was not being urged to enter into a conspiracy with anyone, although a conspiracy might have resulted. . . .

(vi) Incitement to aid, abet, counsel or procure an offence is not an offence.

R v Bodin and Bodin
[1979] Crim LR 176, Lincoln Crown Court

LB and DB, being annoyed with DB's former husband G, paid to a publican P £50 for P to arrange to have G beaten up. P did not do as arranged and therefore the money was taken back some months later. LB and DB were charged with incitement to assault, contrary to common law. The particulars of the offence alleged that LB and DB on a day unknown between June 1, 1977, and December 31, 1977, unlawfully incited P to assault G. On a submission of no case to answer, the defence argued that to incite X to procure Y to assault Z where X does not actually procure Y is not an offence.

GEOFFREY JONES J: . . . I have come to the conclusion, despite the lack of authority, that it is not a crime to incite someone to be an accessory before the fact to a crime. I think it is probable that the reason is quite simple. I think it is this: The procurer, the accessory before the fact commits no crime in the act of procurement. While he is procuring there is no crime he is a party to. Once it is committed there can be a procurement. What I am saying is this: unless the main crime is committed there can be no accessory before the fact. Indeed there is no crime of accessory before the fact until the crime is committed. The Act incited in the evidence is the procurement of a crime and not a crime. The assault is the crime and is not what on the evidence is being incited or procured; it is the procurement of the crime that has been committed.

(vii) There is no such offence as an attempt to conspire.
See the Criminal Attempts Act 1981, s. 1(4).

SECTION 5: **Other inchoate offences**

While it has become traditional to think of incitement, conspiracy, and attempt as comprising the totality of inchoate crimes, in fact there are many more offences which could be seen in a similar light. Inchoate crimes share the common theme of punishing criminal behaviour which serves as a prelude to other (usually more serious) criminal behaviour. Viewed in this light, it can be seen that assault, defined as causing another to apprehend the application of immediate, unlawful force, is often an inchoate form of battery, which is the actual application of unlawful force. So too traffic offences, ranging from speeding to driving dangerously, are aimed in part at preventing more serious harms. Similarly, crimes like the unlawful possession of firearms are designed to prevent crimes committed with firearms. This is not to say that the criminalisation of such conduct does not serve other, independent purposes, only that there is an inchoate dimension to all of these offences.

One advantage of focusing on inchoate forms of crime is that it removes the 'fortuity of consequences' (see Chapter 3, section 3c). Why should a defendant whose gun misfires be guilty of attempted murder, while another whose weapon proves more reliable is convicted of the substantive offence? In recognition of this point the maximum punishment for the inchoate offence is usually the same as or comparable to that for the completed crime. However, the actual sentence imposed in practice may well be less. The practical point is underscored in respect to homicide, where the imposition of a life sentence for murder, but not for attempted murder, is mandatory.

QUESTIONS

1. Should all crimes be written in inchoate form to avoid the 'fortuity of consequences' (see Chapter 3 section 3c)? What are the arguments for and against?

2. Should all inchoate crimes be abolished on the theory that society is not harmed until the crime is completed? What are the arguments for and against?

3. In respect to crimes written in inchoate form, does it make sense to allow a conviction for an attempt to commit such a crime? For example, should there be such an offence as attempted burglary? Is this pushing the point of criminality too far back in time?

12

Parties to Crime

Often more than one person is involved in the commission of a criminal offence. On a conceptual level, we can identify four general classes of individuals who might be so involved. First, there are those who solicit or encourage others to commit a crime. Such persons are guilty of the independent offence of incitement (discussed in Chapter 11), but they may also be liable as an accessory to the substantive crime committed by the person whom they incite. Secondly, there are those who actually commit the crime, whose acts and mental state render them liable for the substantive offence itself. These persons are known in law as principals. Thirdly, there are those who assist or in some other way help the principal to commit the crime. The term 'accessory' is used to refer to these individuals. Lastly, there are those who help the perpetrator to escape capture and prosecution after the crime has been committed. The last group of post-crime assisters are not generally treated within the law of complicity; that is, they are not liable for the substantive offence, but may be guilty of separate statutory offences (see Criminal Law Act 1967, s. 4). This is a recognition of the fact that their crime is more appropriately characterised as one of obstructing the course of justice, rather than one of furthering the substantive offence which has already occurred.

This chapter focuses on the law as it relates to principals and accessories. Which category an offender falls into is usually clear, but, in any event, is often not of legal significance. Accessories and Abettors Act 1861 s. 8, provides that one can be charged as an accessory and convicted as a principal, and vice versa. Further, accessories and perpetrators are subject to the same maximum penalty. There do remain, however, evidentiary distinctions which can affect liability: the *actus reus* and *mens rea* elements which must be proved may differ depending on whether one is charged as a principal or an accessory; and some defences may be available to an accessory that are not available to a principal. One can also be convicted as an accessory to a crime for which the principal himself cannot be convicted, as illustrated in the following case:

R v Austin and Others
[1981] 1 All ER 374, Court of Appeal

A husband, who was living apart from his wife, employed a firm of enquiry agents, of which W was a member, to find his wife and their three-year-old child.

After the firm had done so, the husband instructed W to recover the child, who was in the lawful possession of the wife. W enlisted the services of A, T and F, and the four of them lay in wait, with the husband, for the wife and child. The husband forcibly snatched the child from the wife and then he and the others made off. W, A, T and F were charged with, and convicted of, child stealing, contrary to s. 56 of the Offences against the Person Act 1861. They appealed, contending that although they had deliberately aided and abetted the husband, they were not guilty of the offence charged because the husband had not been acting 'unlawfully' within the meaning of s. 56 and had committed no offence, or, alternatively, even if he had been acting unlawfully, they were entitled to immunity from prosecution under the proviso to s. 56 since they were the agents of a 'person who . . . claimed [a] right to the possession of such child'.

WATKINS LJ: . . . At the close of the case for the Crown in the Crown Court at Winchester counsel for the appellants, to whom we are extremely indebted for his restrained, able and frank submissions to us, made a number of concessions on behalf of the appellants. He has repeated them to this court. They are: (1) that each of these appellants aided and abetted King in taking Lara away from the possession of her mother; and (2) that the child was taken by King by the use of force on the mother and on the child. It was also conceded that they all knew the child was in the lawful possession of the mother, since there was no order in this country which affected her right to that at the material time and the order of the American court could not affect it in any practical way. It was also admitted that they had the intention to deprive the mother of possession of the child.

Having regard to those admissions and the background of this affair, one looks at s. 56 of the 1861 Act which provides:

> Whosoever shall unlawfully . . . by force . . . take away . . . any child under the age of fourteen years, with intent to deprive any parent . . . of the possession of such child . . . shall be liable, at the discretion of the court . . . to be imprisoned: Provided, that no person who shall have claimed any right to the possession of such child, or shall be the mother or shall have claimed to be the father of an illegitimate child, shall be liable to be prosecuted by virtue hereof on account of the getting possession of such child . . .

It is submitted that there are two questions relevant to the issue of whether the appellants were rightly convicted: (1) did King commit an offence under s. 56, bearing in mind that he assaulted his wife and when taking the child away the child too, and (2) if King committed an offence under s. 56, does it follow that the appellants are also guilty of that offence? Furthermore, suppose King had been indicted and found not guilty by reason only of being able to take advantage of the proviso, could the appellants have escaped conviction in that way too?

. . .

Undoubtedly King could properly have claimed a right of possession to the child and so have gained the protection of the proviso. What would have been the effect of that? The effect would have been that, although he had committed the offence of child stealing, because he was the child's father and could claim a right to possession of the child he would not have been prosecuted. It is submitted on the appellants' behalf that the proviso also protects a class of persons wide enough to include those who aid a person such as the father of the child in gaining possession of his child by force. They become his agents for the purpose. Many persons have from time to time the temporary possession of a child as agents of parents. Why are they not protected to the same extent as parents when regaining possession as agents of parents?

In our view the only sensible construction of the proviso allows of its protection being granted to a small class of persons only, which includes the father and the mother of the child, whether the child be legitimate or illegitimate, or a guardian appointed by a testamentary document, or by an order conferring the status of guardianship, or a person to whom is granted an order conferring some form of care, control, custody or access. We can think of no other who could claim exemption from prosecution by reason of the proviso.

What of these appellants? They had no good reason for doing what they did. They had no right to assert, and no interest in, the possession of the child. They were the paid hirelings of King to aid him in the commission of a criminal offence, namely stealing a child, and with him they committed it as aiders and abettors. While King may shelter behind the proviso, there is no room there for them. Parliament in its wisdom undoubtedly decided that the mischiefs of matrimonial discord which are unhappily so widespread should not give rise to wholesale criminal prosecutions arising out of disputes about children, about who should have possession and control of them. That and that alone is the reason for the existence of the proviso to s. 56. Thus, as we have said, its application is confined to the select class of persons we have endeavoured to define.

It should be clearly understood that those such as these appellants who aid a father or a mother to take possession of a child from the other parent, and who do so by the use of force as aiders and abettors to it, commit the offence of child stealing, and that they are not immune from prosecution.

This was a wicked example of aiding and abetting the commission of the offence, child stealing. In the judgment of this court, the appellants are extremely fortunate that the trial judge treated them so mercifully by the sentences he imposed. This kind of activity must be condemned and those who are tempted to engage in it should be deterred from doing so.

Appeals dismissed.

NOTES AND QUESTIONS
1. Why is it that the defendants in *Austin* could be guilty of an offence for helping another person to do something which would not have been an offence if that other person had acted alone? Has the court created a crime where none was intended by Parliament?
2. Sometimes Parliament addresses the issue more directly. For example, although it is no longer criminal to commit suicide, it is an offence to be an accessory to a suicide. See Suicide Act 1961.
3. The courts have sometimes seemed to apply a 'derivative' theory of accessorial liability; that is, a theory that views the accessory's liability as deriving from that of the principal. The strict logic of this theory would lead one to the conclusion that there could not be a guilty accessory unless there was a guilty principal. However, there are numerous cases, many of which will be examined in this chapter, that suggest that the courts' adherence to this theory is not as rigorous as it is sometimes represented to be. Confronting the basic thesis head-on, however, why should an accessory's liability depend on whether the principal is either guilty of or can be convicted of (the two are not necessarily the same) an independent crime? Why should not the accessory be judged on the basis of his or her own acts, and the mental state with which those acts were performed?

SECTION 1: **Liability as a principal**

The person who acts with the requisite intent and whose acts cause the prohibited harm is in law deemed to be the principal. It is not necessary, however, that the principal personally commits the act which causes the harmful result. A principal may act through an 'innocent agent', as in the case where a person sends a letter bomb through the post – the principal is the sender of the letter and not the postal employee who delivers it. Sometimes the innocent agent is a person who, had he or she been charged with the substantive offence, would have had a defence such as infancy or insanity.

There can be more than one principal to a crime.

Mohan v *R*
[1967] 2 AC 187, Privy Council

The appellants, father and son, were convicted at Port of Spain Assizes of the murder of M., who received several wounds in an encounter with the appellants and died from his injuries. He had received, together with minor wounds, a very severe wound on the right leg and a very severe wound in the back. On the evidence there was a possibility that the death might have been caused solely by the leg wound, and the case was considered on that hypothesis.

LORD PEARSON: . . . The question . . . arises whether each of the appellants can be held responsible for the leg wound, when it may have been inflicted by the other of them. There is conflicting evidence as to which of them struck the blow on Mootoo's leg, the evidence for the prosecution tending to show that the appellant Deonath struck it and the evidence for the defence tending to show that the appellant Ramnath struck it. There is uncertainty on that point.

Also it cannot be inferred with any certainty from the evidence that the appellants had a pre-arranged plan for their attack on Mootoo.

It is, however, clear from the evidence for the defence, as well as from the evidence for the prosecution, that at the material time both the appellants were armed with cutlasses, both were attacking Mootoo, and both struck him. It is impossible on the facts of this case to contend that the fatal blow was outside the scope of the common intention. The two appellants were attacking the same man at the same time with similar weapons and with the common intention that he should suffer grievous bodily harm. Each of the appellants was present, and aiding and abetting the other of them in the wounding of Mootoo.

That is the feature which distinguishes this case from cases in which one of the accused was not present or not participating in the attack or not using any dangerous weapon, but may be held liable as a conspirator or an accessory before the fact or by virtue of a common design if it can be shown that he was party to a pre-arranged plan in pursuance of which the fatal blow was struck. In this case one of the appellants struck the fatal blow, and the other of them was present aiding and abetting him. In such a case the prosecution do not have to prove that the accused were acting in pursuance of a pre-arranged plan.

NOTES AND QUESTIONS
1. Why is the court in *Mohan* not more concerned with which of the defendants struck the fatal blow? With both defendants attacking the victim, was it little more than chance whose blow was fatal? The case would presumably have been analysed differently if one defendant had attacked the victim with his fists and the other with a knife, the victim dying from a knife wound – or would it?
2. In *R* v *Peters and Parfitt* [1995] Crim LR 501, the Court of Appeal held that in a similar situation to that in *Mohan*, 'the common purpose or intention had to be more than merely them both separately intending to do some harm to J'. In this case, both defendants had punched the victim, and one (although it was not clear which) had delivered a fatal kick. The Court of Appeal quashed the conviction for manslaughter because the trial judge had not

adequately directed the jury as to whether the defendants had acted pursuant to a 'common purpose'.

There is a somewhat similar situation which needs to be distinguished, where the two defendants cannot be shown to be acting in concert. Say that the leaders of the Conservative, Labour, and Liberal Democrat parties closet themselves in a locked room to settle their political differences. Only two walk out alive. The third has been strangled to death. Both of the survivors claim that the other was the strangler. If the prosecution are unable to prove which of the two survivors was the murderer, even though they know for certain it was one of them, there cannot be a criminal conviction in the absence of a showing, as in *Mohan*, of a joint enterprise or concert of action. It may seem strange that one of our two surviving politicians will be literally getting away with murder but the burden of proof is upon the prosecution to establish guilt beyond a reasonable doubt, and all we really have is a fifty-fifty probability that each of the potential defendants is guilty (assuming the evidence against each is equal). The philosophy embodied in the requirement of proof beyond reasonable doubt is that it is preferable that a guilty person go free, which is what will happen, than that an innocent person go to jail, which is what would happen if both were to be convicted.

R v Lane
(1986) 82 Cr App R 5, Court of Appeal

CROOM-JOHNSON LJ: . . . The medical evidence went no further than to prove that the injuries from which Sara died had been caused at some time between 12.30 and 8.30 p.m. During that time each of the appellants, as has been said, had been alone for some time with the child. When the Crown opened the case on count 1, manslaughter, it was said that the child's injuries had been caused by one or other or both of the appellants, but that it could not be established which of them had done so. Analysing it further, there was no evidence of the time when the blow was struck, who did it, or even who was present when it happened.
. . .
At the close of the prosecution case it was submitted on behalf of both appellants that there was no case to answer. The learned judge rejected that submission. Neither appellant gave evidence. They both appeal to this Court on the ground that the judge erred in law in rejecting their submission, that he erred in law in his directions to the jury, and that the convictions are unsafe and unsatisfactory. The appeal raises again the problem where the evidence available to the prosecution goes to prove that someone caused the injury to the baby but there is no admissible evidence implicating one defendant rather than the other.
What is the law? The starting-point is R v Abbott (1955) 39 Cr App R 141; [1955] 2 QB 497. The headnote in 39 Cr App R 141 reads:

> The appellant was indicted and tried with one W for forgery. By the close of the case for the prosecution the case against the appellant had collapsed and a submission was made on his behalf that there was no case to go to the jury. The judge, however, allowed the case against the appellant to proceed, because he took the view that the jury could not acquit both prisoners and that the co-prisoner's case which sought to throw the whole blame on the appellant might be prejudiced if the case against the appellant were withdrawn from the jury. The jury convicted both prisoners.
> Held, that, there being no evidence against the appellant at the close of the case for the

prosecution, it was the duty of the judge to withdraw the case against him from the jury and that the conviction of the appellant must be quashed.

The classic passage in the judgment of Lord Goddard CJ is at p. 148 and p. 503, *viz.*:

> I think what possibly led the learned judge to act as he did when he was of opinion that there was no evidence against this appellant was that he had got into his mind that the jury could not say in this particular case: 'We find a verdict of Not Guilty in the case of both, because we are not satisfied which was guilty, if one of them was.' With great respect to the learned judge, that is not the law. If two people are jointly indicted for the commission of a crime and the evidence does not point to one rather than the other, and there is no evidence that they were acting in concert, the jury ought to return a verdict of Not Guilty in the case of both because the prosecution have not proved the case. If, in those circumstances, it is left to the defendants to get out of the difficulty if they can, that would put the onus on the defendants to prove themselves not guilty. . . .

The evidence against each appellant, taken separately, at the end of the prosecution's case did not establish his or her presence at the time when the child was injured, whenever that was, or any participation. Neither had made any admission; both had denied taking part in any injury; both had told lies but lies which did not lead to the inference of that defendant's presence.

The conclusion therefore is that the learned judge ought to have ruled in favour of the appellants on their submission of no case to answer.

NOTES AND QUESTIONS

1. Could a conviction against both parents have been obtained on the theory that one was guilty for having inflicted the fatal blow and the other for failing to obtain medical assistance, there being a legal duty to do so because of the parent-child relationship? See *R v Russell and Russell* (1987) 85 Cr App R 388, below. See also *R v Forman and Ford* [1988] Crim LR 677.

2. In *R v Gianetto* [1996] Crim LR 722, the Court of Appeal held that in a case of the murder of the defendant's wife, the jury must find that the defendant either killed his wife himself, or at least encouraged another to kill her. It did not matter which. If the prosecution could not say which, the jury must agree that the defendant had the *mens rea* and caused the result. The law did not require the prosecution to specify the means.

3. One must distinguish the situation where the principal acts through an innocent agent from that where a defendant is vicariously liable for the acts of some other person. Vicarious liability usually arises in the context of an employer-employee relationship, the employer being held vicariously liable for the crimes of the employee who has acted within the scope or authority of his employment. Liability is most often imposed by statute (or a court's interpretation of a statute). The employer can be vicariously liable not only for acts which he did not authorise (if he did authorise the acts, he would be liable on normal principal/accessory principles), but even for acts which he may have expressly forbidden. One cannot, however, be vicariously liable as an accessory, for, as will be discussed, proof of *mens rea* is required for accessorial liability. See *Ferguson v Weaving* [1951] 1 All ER 412. Curiously, where an employer is vicariously liable for the acts of an employee, the courts have held that the employee can be liable as an accessory. See *Griffiths v Studebakers* [1924] 1 KB 102.

SECTION 2: **Liability as an accessory**

An accessory is one who aids, abets, counsels or procures the commission of a crime but who is not the principal. The controlling statute is the Accessories and Abettors Act 1861, as amended by the Criminal Law Act 1977:

Accessories and Abettors Act 1861

8. Whosoever shall aid, abet, counsel, or procure the commission of any indictable offence, whether the same be an offence at common law, or by virtue of any Act passed or to be passed, shall be liable to be tried, indicted, and punished as a principal offender.

NOTE
See also the Magistrates' Courts Act 1980, s. 44.

A: Elements of the offence

In order to convict a defendant as an accessory, the prosecution must prove that:

(a) an offence was committed;

(b) the defendant aided, abetted, counselled or procured the offence (the *actus reus*); and

(c) the defendant had the intent to further the commission of the offence or knew that his assistance would have this effect (the *mens rea*). This intent must be proven even though the offence aided may be one of strict liability.

(i) *An offence was committed*
The prosecution must prove that an offence (or at least the *actus reus* of an offence) has been committed.

Thornton v Mitchell
[1940] 1 All ER 339, King's Bench

Appeal by the conductor by way of case stated from a decision of a court of summary jurisdiction sitting at Rochdale, whereby the conductor of an omnibus was convicted of having aided and abetted the driver of the omnibus in driving without due care and attention and without using reasonable consideration for others using the road. The charges against the driver were dismissed. On the hearing of the information, the following facts were proved or admitted. On 18 March 1939, the omnibus arrived at a road junction where all the passengers disembarked. Before the omnibus reversed, the conductor looked out of the back to see if the road was clear. Then he rang the bell three times as a signal to the driver to reverse. At the time when he gave the signal, the conductor, following his usual practice, was standing on the platform at the back of the omnibus. The time was about 7.45 p.m., and the visibility was poor. After giving the signal, the conductor jumped off the omnibus, which was reversed slowly. Two persons who had just disembarked were knocked down by the back of the omnibus as it was reversing, and one of them received fatal injuries. The driver could not see any person immediately behind the omnibus while he was reversing, owing to the obstruction caused by the steps to the upper deck, and owing to the height of the window at the back, and he had, therefore, to rely upon the conductor's signal.

LORD HEWART LCJ: In my opinion, it is quite clear that this appeal must be allowed. . . . [t]his case is *a fortiori* upon *Morris* v *Tolman* [1923] 1 KB 166, to which our attention has been directed. I will read one sentence from the judgment of Avory J, at p. 171:

> . . . in order to convict, it would be necessary to show that the respondent was aiding the principal, but a person cannot aid another in doing something which that other has not done.

That, I think, is the very thing which these justices have decided that this bus conductor did. In one breath they say that the principal did nothing which he should not have done, and in the next breath they hold that the bus conductor aided and abetted the driver in doing something which had not been done or in not doing something which he ought to have done. I really think that, with all respect to the ingenuity of counsel for the respondent, the case is too plain for argument, and this appeal must be allowed and the conviction quashed.

NOTES AND QUESTIONS

1. Why, once the case against the driver was dismissed, should the conductor have escaped all liability? After all, harm did occur and arguably would not have were it not for his reckless conduct. Are there other possible bases on which to premise a case against the conductor? Should accessorial liability be dependent on principal liability?

2. Is *Thornton* v *Mitchell* reconcilable with *Austin* (p. 587)?

3. In *R* v *Loukes* [1996] Crim LR 341 and *R* v *Roberts and George* [1997] Crim LR 209, drivers of tipper trucks were acquitted of causing death by dangerous driving because the dangerous condition of their vehicles would not have been 'obvious to a competent and careful driver', part of the *actus reus* of the offence. In both cases the employers' convictions for procuring were quashed. Compare these cases with *R* v *Millward* [1994] Crim LR 527, where the defendant was aware that the hitch between tractor and trailer was defective but nonetheless allowed H to drive the tractor. When the hitch detached, someone was killed. The driver was acquitted of causing death by reckless driving, but Millward's conviction for procuring was upheld. Is this result consistent with *Loukes*? If not, which makes better sense?

One must be careful to distinguish between the case where no crime has occurred and the case where a crime has occurred but the principal cannot be convicted. *Austin* (above) provides an example where the principal is exempt from prosecution, but what if the principal has a defence?

R v *Bourne*
(1952) 36 Cr App R 125, Court of Appeal

The appellant was convicted at Worcestershire Assizes on 21 May 1952, on two counts of an indictment charging him with aiding and abetting his wife to commit buggery with a dog, and was sentenced by Hallett J to eight years' imprisonment. He was also convicted on two counts charging incitement to commit buggery, and on two counts charging indecent assault on his wife, and in respect of these he received concurrent sentences.

The indictment alleged an offence to have been committed on two separate occasions. The evidence showed that the appellant had on each occasion sexually excited the animal, and then caused his wife to submit to its having connection with her *per vaginam*. The wife stated in her evidence that she had been terrorised into submission and that the acts were entirely against her will. The judge left questions to the jury as follows: – (1) 'Did the prisoner on a day in or about the month of September 1949, in the county of Stafford cause his wife, Adelaide Bourne, to have carnal knowledge of a dog?' to which the jury replied: 'Yes.' (2) 'Are you satisfied that she did not consent to having such carnal knowledge?' to which the jury replied: 'Yes, we are satisfied she did not consent,' and he also left two similar questions with regard to the second offence, and the jury returned similar answers.

THE LORD CHIEF JUSTICE: The case against the appellant was that he was a principal in the second degree to the crime of buggery which was committed by his wife, because if a woman has connection with a dog, or allows a dog to have connection with her, that is the full offence of buggery. She may be able to show that she was forced to commit the offence. I will assume that the plea of duress could have been set up by her on the evidence, and in fact we have allowed Mr Green to argue this case on the footing that the wife would have been entitled to be acquitted on the ground of duress. The learned judge left no question to the jury on duress, but the jury have found that she did not consent. Assuming that she could have set up duress, what does that mean? It means that she admits that she has committed the crime but prays to be excused from punishment for the consequences of the crime by reason of the duress, and no doubt in those circumstances the law would allow a verdict of Not Guilty to be entered. . . .

There may be certain doctrines with regard to murder which do not apply to other cases, but I am willing to assume for the purpose of this case, and I think my brethren are too, that if this woman had been charged herself with committing the offence, she could have set up the plea of duress, not as showing that no offence had been committed, but as showing that she had no *mens rea* because her will was overborne by threats of imprisonment or violence so that she would be excused from punishment. But the offence of buggery whether with man or beast does not depend upon consent; it depends on the act, and if an act of buggery is committed, the felony is committed.

. . .

In the opinion of the court, there is no doubt that the appellant was properly indicted for being a principal in the second degree to the commission of the crime of buggery. That is all that it is necessary to show. The evidence was, and the jury by their verdict have shown they accepted it, that he caused his wife to have connection with a dog, and if he caused his wife to have connection with a dog he is guilty, whether you call him an aider and abettor or an accessory, as a principal in the second degree. For that reason, this appeal fails and is dismissed.

Appeal dismissed

NOTES AND QUESTIONS

1. Note the critical distinction between an affirmative defence and a defence which negates an element of the crime. Duress is an affirmative defence; if the defence were one that negated an element of the crime there would be no crime to which the defendant could have been an accessory. What if the wife in *Bourne* could not have been convicted because of insanity. Would the same result have been reached? Do Bourne's acts become any less reprehensible

because of the reason why his wife could not be convicted of the substantive offence (or is this the wrong question to be asking)?

2. While the requirement of an offence having been committed seems to be logically inherent in the definition of accessorial liability, the courts at times seem prepared to hold a defendant liable as an accessory as long as the principal has committed the *actus reus* of the offence, even if the alleged principal cannot be convicted of the offence because he did not have the requisite *mens rea*. In these situations, ironically, it is *the accessory* who has the requisite *mens rea* for the substantive offence.

R v *Cogan and Leak*

[1976] 1 QB 217, Court of Appeal

The defendant L took the defendant C back to his home and told his wife that C wanted to have sexual intercourse with her and that he was going to see that she did. L's wife was not willing to have intercourse with C but she was frightened of L who made her go to the bedroom where C had sexual intercourse with her. The wife was sobbing throughout the intercourse. She did not struggle with C but she did try to turn away from him. C was charged with rape and L was charged with 'being aider and abettor to' that rape: the particulars of the offence being that he 'at the same time and place did abet counsel and procure [C] to commit the said offence.' At the trial, C's defence was that he believed that L's wife had consented to the intercourse. In a written statement he made to the police, L, who did not give evidence at the trial, confessed that he had procured C to have sexual intercourse with his wife, that she had not consented to that intercourse and that he had intended her to be raped by C. The jury found both defendants guilty and returned a special verdict that C had believed the wife was consenting but that he had no reasonable grounds for such belief. Both defendants appealed against conviction and C's appeal was allowed.

LAWTON LJ: . . . At the trial Cogan gave evidence that he thought Mrs Leak had consented. The basis for his belief was what he had heard from her husband about her. The drink he had had seems to have been a reason, if not the only one, for mistaking her sobs and distress for consent.

The trial started on October 23, 1974. A few days before, namely, on October 14, press publicity had been given to the fact that the Court of Appeal in *R v Morgan* [1976] AC 182 had certified a point of law of general public importance as to whether in rape the defendant can properly be convicted notwithstanding that he in fact believed that the woman consented if such belief was not based on reasonable grounds and had given leave to appeal to the House of Lords. In the course of his summing up the trial judge stressed the need for the jury to be sure before convicting either of the defendants that the wife had not consented to sexual intercourse. He then went on to direct them in relation to Cogan's case in accordance with the decision of the Court of Appeal in *R v Morgan*. He prudently decided to ask the jury to make a finding as to whether any belief in consent which Cogan may have had was based upon reasonable grounds. The jury returned a verdict of guilty against Cogan thereby showing that they were sure the wife had not consented. They went on to say that Cogan had believed she was consenting but that he had had no reasonable grounds for such belief.

As to Leak he directed the jury that even if Cogan believed that the wife was consenting and had reasonable grounds for such a belief they would still be entitled to find Leak guilty as charged.

Cogan's appeal against conviction was based on the ground that the decision of the House of Lords in *R v Morgan* [1976] AC 182 applied. It did. There is nothing more to be said. It was for this reason that we allowed the appeal and quashed his conviction.

Leak's appeal against conviction was based on the proposition that he could not be found guilty of aiding and abetting Cogan to rape his wife if Cogan was acquitted of that offence as he was deemed in law to have been when his conviction was quashed.

. . . [O]ne fact is clear – the wife had been raped. Cogan had had sexual intercourse with her without her consent. The fact that Cogan was innocent of rape because he believed that she was consenting does not affect the position that she was raped.

Her ravishment had come about because Leak had wanted it to happen and had taken action to see that it did by persuading Cogan to use his body as the instrument for the necessary physical act. In the language of the law the act of sexual intercourse without the wife's consent was the *actus reus*: it had been procured by Leak who had the appropriate *mens rea*, namely, his intention that Cogan should have sexual intercourse with her without her consent. In our judgment it is irrelevant that the man whom Leak had procured to do the physical act himself did not intend to have sexual intercourse with the wife without her consent. Leak was using him as a means to procure a criminal purpose.

Before 1861 a case such as this, pleaded as it was in the indictment, might have presented a court with problems arising from the old distinctions between principals and accessories in felony. Most of the old law was swept away by section 8 of the Accessories and Abettors Act 1861 and what remained by section 1 of the Criminal Law Act 1967. The modern law allowed Leak to be tried and punished as a principal offender. In our judgment he could have been indicted as a principal offender. It would have been no defence for him to submit that if Cogan was an 'innocent' agent, he was necessarily in the old terminology of the law a principal in the first degree, which was a legal impossibility as a man cannot rape his own wife during cohabitation. The law no longer concerns itself with niceties of degrees in participation in crime; but even if it did Leak would still be guilty. The reason a man cannot by his own physical act rape his wife during cohabitation is because the law presumes consent from the marriage ceremony: see *Hale, Pleas of the Crown* (1778), vol. 1, p. 629. There is no such presumption when a man procures a drunken friend to do the physical act for him. Hale CJ put this case in one sentence, at p. 629:

> . . . tho in marriage she hath given up her body to her husband, she is not to be by him prostituted to another: see loc. cit.

Had Leak been indicted as a principal offender, the case against him would have been clear beyond argument. Should he be allowed to go free because he was charged with 'being aider and abettor to the same offence'? If we are right in our opinion that the wife had been raped (and no one outside a court of law would say that she had not been), then the particulars of offence accurately stated what Leak had done, namely, he had procured Cogan to commit the offence. This would suffice to uphold the conviction. We would prefer, however, to uphold it on a wider basis. In our judgment convictions should not be upset because of mere technicalities of pleading in an indictment. Leak knew what the case against him was and the facts in support of that case were proved. But for the fact that the jury thought that Cogan in his intoxicated condition might have mistaken the wife's sobs and distress for expressions of her consent, no question of any kind would have arisen about the form of pleading. By his written statement Leak virtually admitted what he had done. As Judge Chapman said in *R v Humphreys* [1965] 3 All ER 689, 692:

> It would be anomalous if a person who admitted to a substantial part in the perpetration of a misdemeanour as aider and abettor could not be convicted on his own admission merely because the person alleged to have been aided and abetted was not or could not be convicted.

In the circumstances of this case it would be more than anomalous: it would be an affront to justice and to the common sense of ordinary folk. It was for these reasons that we dismissed the appeal against conviction.

NOTES

1. The rule that the acquittal of the principal does not necessarily exonerate an accessory was affirmed in *R v Millward* [1994] Crim LR 527.
2. If an accessory can be convicted of a crime committed by a principal even though the principal himself cannot be convicted of the crime, it would seem to follow that an accessory can be convicted of a more serious crime than the principal. For example, Alicia informs Benjamin that his wife is having an affair with Chatsworth. In the heat of passion Benjamin kills Chatsworth, as Alicia intended. Benjamin will most probably have his crime reduced to manslaughter because of the provocation, but Alicia may be convicted as an accessory to murder. See *R v Howe* [1987] 1 AC 417.
3. Sometimes the alleged principal is acquitted for lack of evidence. In this situation the jury have not found that no offence has occurred, only that there was insufficient evidence to convict the person charged. Thus an accomplice might still be convicted of aiding and abetting. See, e.g., *R v Hughes* (1860) Bell CC 242.

(ii) *Actus reus*

In order to secure a conviction as an accessory, the prosecutor must show that the defendant either aided, abetted, counselled or procured the offence. In theory each of these terms describes conceptually distinct behaviour. 'Aid' means to help or assist, 'abet' involves instigation or encouragement, 'counsel' implies advising or urging, and 'procure' has been defined as 'causing to be committed'. The line between the categories is often blurred, however, and the Crown is permitted to list all of these acts in the same charge. This is in part no doubt to avoid the absurdity of a defendant, charged with aiding, arguing that he is not guilty because he procured the offence, and then on a subsequent charge of procuring that he really was guilty of abetting, and then on a charge of abetting. . . .

The range of activity which will render one liable as an accessory is as diverse as the human imagination. While aiding, abetting, and counselling are fairly straightforward concepts, this is not true of procuring.

Attorney-General's Reference (No. 1 of 1975)
[1975] QB 773, Court of Appeal

LORD WIDGERY CJ: This case comes before the court on a reference from the Attorney-General under s. 36 of the Criminal Justice Act 1972, and by his reference he asks the following question:

> Whether an accused who surreptitiously laced a friend's drinks with double measures of spirits when he knew that his friend would shortly be driving his car home, and in consequence his friend drove with an excess quantity of alcohol in his body and was convicted of the offence under the Road Traffic Act 1972, s. 6(1) is entitled to a ruling of no case to answer on being later charged as an aider and abetter, counsellor and procurer, on the ground that there was no shared intention between the two, that the accused did not by accompanying him or otherwise positively encourage the friend to drive, or on any other ground. . . .

The present question has no doubt arisen because in recent years there have been a number of instances where men charged with driving their motor cars with an excess quantity of alcohol in the blood have sought to excuse their conduct by saying that their drinks were 'laced', as the jargon has it; that is to say some strong spirit was put into an otherwise innocuous drink and as a result the driver consumed more alcohol than he had either intended to consume or had the desire to consume. The relevance of all that is not that it entitles the driver to an acquittal, because such driving is an absolute offence, but that it can be relied on as a special reason for not disqualifying the driver from driving. Hence no doubt the importance which has been attached in recent months to the possibility of this argument being raised in a normal charge of driving with excess alcohol.

The question requires us to say whether on the facts posed there is a case to answer, and needless to say in the trial from which this reference is derived the judge was of the opinion that there was no case to answer and so ruled. We have to say in effect whether he is right.

The language in the section which determines whether a 'secondary party', as he is sometimes called, is guilty of a criminal offence committed by another embraces the four words 'aid, abet, counsel or procure'. The origin of those words is to be found in s. 8 of the Accessories and Abettors Act 1861 which provides:

> Whosoever shall aid, abet, counsel, or procure the commission of any misdemeanor, whether the same be a misdemeanor at common law or by virtue of any Act passed or to be passed, shall be liable to be tried, indicted, and punished as a principal offender.

Thus, in the past, when the distinction was still drawn between felony and misdemeanor, it was sufficient to make a person guilty of a misdemeanor if he aided, abetted, counselled or procured the offence of another. When the difference between felonies and misdemeanors was abolished in 1967, s. 1 of the Criminal Law Act 1967 in effect provided that the same test should apply to make a secondary party guilty either of treason or felony.

Of course it is the fact that in the great majority of instances where a secondary party is sought to be convicted of an offence there has been a contact between the principal offender and the secondary party. Aiding and abetting almost inevitably involves a situation in which the secondary party and the main offender are together at some stage discussing the plans which they may be making in respect of the alleged offence, and are in contact so that each knows what is passing through the mind of the other.

In the same way it seems to us that a person who counsels the commission of a crime by another, almost inevitably comes to a moment when he is in contact with that other, when he is discussing the offence with that other and when, to use the words of the statute, he counsels the other to commit the offence.

The fact that so often the relationship between the secondary party and the principal will be such that there is a meeting of minds between them caused the trial judge in the case from which this reference is derived to think that this was really an essential feature of proving or establishing the guilt of the secondary party and, as we understand his judgment, he took the view that in the absence of some sort of meeting of minds, some sort of mental link between the secondary party and the principal, there could be no aiding, abetting or counselling of the offence within the meaning of the section.

So far as aiding, abetting and counselling is concerned we would go a long way with that conclusion. It may very well be, as I said a moment ago, difficult to think of a case of aiding, abetting or counselling when the parties have not met and have not discussed in some respects the terms of the offence which they have in mind. But we do not see why a similar principle should apply to procuring. We approach s. 8 of the 1861 Act on the basis that the words should be given their ordinary meaning, if possible. We approach the section on the basis also that if four words are employed here, 'aid, abet, counsel or procure', the probability is that there is a difference between each of those four words and the other three, because, if there were no such difference, then Parliament would be wasting time in using four words where two or three would do. Thus, in deciding whether that which is assumed to be done under our reference was a criminal offence we approach the section on the footing that each word must be given its ordinary meaning.

To procure means to produce by endeavour. You procure a thing by setting out to see that it happens and taking the appropriate steps to produce that happening. We think that there are plenty of instances in which a person may be said to procure the commission of a crime by another even though there is no sort of conspiracy between the two, even though there is no attempt at agreement or discussion as to the form which the offence should take. In our judgment the offence described in this reference is such a case.

If one looks back at the facts of the reference: the accused surreptitiously laced his friend's drink. This is an important element and, although we are not going to decide today anything other than the problem posed to us, it may well be that in similar cases where the lacing of the drink or the introduction of the extra alcohol is known to the driver quite different considerations may apply. We say that because where the driver has no knowledge of what is happening, in most instances he would have no means of preventing the offence from being committed. If the driver is unaware of what has happened, he will not be taking precautions. He will get into his car seat, switch on the ignition and drive home and, consequently, the conception of another procuring the commission of the offence by the driver is very much stronger where the driver is innocent of all knowledge of what is happening, as in the present case where the lacing of the drink was surreptitious.

The second thing which is important in the facts set out in our reference is that following and in consequence of the introduction of the extra alcohol, the friend drove with an excess quantity of alcohol in his blood. Causation here is important. You cannot procure an offence unless there is a causal link between what you do and the commission of the offence, and here we are told that in consequence of the addition of this alcohol the driver, when he drove home, drove with an excess quantity of alcohol in his body.

Giving the words their ordinary meaning in English, and asking oneself whether in those circumstances the offence has been procured, we are in no doubt that the answer is that it has. It has been procured because, unknown to the driver and without his collaboration, he has been put in a position in which in fact he has committed an offence which he never would have committed otherwise. We think that there was a case to answer and that the trial judge should have directed the jury that an offence is committed if it is shown beyond reasonable doubt that the accused knew that his friend was going to drive, and also knew that the ordinary and natural result of the additional alcohol added to the friend's drink would be to bring him above the recognised limit of 80 milligrammes per 100 millilitres of blood.

NOTES AND QUESTIONS

1. Consider the case of the social host who encourages his guests to imbibe of a punch liberally laced with alcohol. The guests know that the punch contains alcohol but not the percentage amount. Is the host liable as an accessory to drunk driving in the case of those guests who drive home? Under these circumstances what would be your legal advice to the host?

2. Under the approach of the court in *Attorney-General's Reference (No. 1 of 1975)* there need be no agreement between principal and accessory, the two do not ever have to have met, and the principal does not have to know of the accessory's assistance or existence. If there is an agreement, on the other hand, the two may also be guilty of conspiracy (see Chapter 11).

Can one become an accessory by omission, by doing nothing?

R v *Clarkson and Others*
[1971] 3 All ER 344, Courts-Martial Appeal Court

MEGAW LJ: . . . The relevant facts will be recited as briefly as possible. The victim of the offences was an 18 year old girl named Elke von Groen. On 9th May 1970 she, having recently come out of hospital where she had undergone an operation to her womb, went to a party at the barracks at Menden. At about midnight she left the party to go to see a soldier with whom she had in the past been familiar. She went to his room. He was not there but other soldiers were there. Eventually she went to another room, room 64, where the rapes occurred. There she was raped at least by Newton, by Holloway and by Marshall at one time or another between midnight and about 3.15 a.m. She was physically injured and her clothes were torn to shreds. To say that those who attacked her behaved like animals would be unjust to animals. At some time after the raping began and when she had been screaming and moaning, there were clustered outside the door of room 64 a number of men, including the three appellants, no doubt listening to what was going on inside. The only thing to be said in their favour is that they may have been in a drunken condition when their moral sense and sense of the requirements of human decency had left them. The door of room 64 opened and they, including the three appellants, in the words of a witness 'piled in' to the room. There is no doubt that they remained there for a considerable time and there is no doubt that during that time the unfortunate girl was raped. . . . there was no evidence on which the prosecution sought to rely that either the appellant Clarkson or the appellant Carroll had done any physical act or uttered any word which involved direct physical participation or verbal encouragement. There was no evidence that they had touched the girl, helped to hold her down, done anything to her, done anything to prevent others from assisting her or to prevent her from escaping, or from trying to ward off her attackers, or that they had said anything which gave encouragement to the others to commit crime or to participate in committing crime. Therefore, if there was here aiding and abetting by the appellants Clarkson or Carroll it could only have been on the basis of inferences to be drawn that by their very presence they, each of them separately as concerns himself, encouraged those who were commit- ting rape. Let it be accepted, and there was evidence to justify this assumption, that the presence of those two appellants in the room where the offence was taking place was not accidental in any sense and that it was not by chance, unconnected with the crime, that they were there. Let it be accepted that they entered the room when the crime was committed because of what they had heard, which indicated that a woman was being raped, and they remained there.

R v Coney (1882) 8 QBD 534 decided that non-accidental presence at the scene of the crime is not conclusive of aiding and abetting. The jury has to be told by the judge, or as in this case the court- martial has to be told by the judge-advocate, in clear terms what it is that has to be proved before they can convict of aiding and abetting; what it is of which the jury or the court-martial, as the case may be, must be sure as matters of inference before they can convict of aiding and abetting in such a case where the evidence adduced by the prosecution is limited to non-accidental presence. What has to be proved is stated by Hawkins J in a well-known passage in his judgment in *R v Coney* where he said:

> In my opinion, to constitute an aider and abettor some active steps must be taken by word, or action, with the intent to instigate the principal, or principals. Encouragement does not of necessity amount to aiding and abetting, it may be intentional or unintentional, a man may unwittingly encourage another in fact by his presence, by misinterpreted words, or gestures, or by his silence, or non-interference, or he may encourage intentionally by expressions, gestures, or actions intended to signify approval. In the latter case he aids and abets, in the former he does not. It is no criminal offence to stand by, a mere passive spectator of a crime, even of a murder. Non-interference to prevent a crime is not itself a crime. But the fact that a person was voluntarily and purposely present witnessing the commission of a crime, and offered no opposition to it, though he might reasonably be expected to prevent and had the power so to do, or at least to express his dissent, might under some circumstances, afford cogent evidence upon which a jury would be justified in finding that he wilfully encouraged and so aided and abetted. But it would be purely a question for the jury whether he did so or not.

. . .

It is not enough, then, that the presence of the accused has, in fact, given encouragement. It must be proved that the accused intended to give encouragement; that he *wilfully* encouraged. In a case such as the present, more than in many other cases where aiding and abetting is alleged, it was essential that that element should be stressed; for there was here at least the possibility that a drunken man with his self-discipline loosened by drink, being aware that a woman was being raped, might be attracted to the scene and might stay on the scene in the capacity of what is known as a voyeur; and, while his presence and the presence of others might in fact encourage the rapers or discourage the victim, he himself, enjoying the scene or at least standing by assenting, might not intend that his presence should offer encouragement to rapers and would-be rapers or discouragement to the victim; he might not realise that he was giving encouragement; so that, while encouragement there might be, it would not be a case in which, to use the words of Hawkins J, the accused person 'wilfully encouraged'.

NOTES AND QUESTIONS

1. What more would the defendants in *Clarkson* have had to have done to be deemed accessories? What if they had shouted encouragement to the rapists? Would (should) it matter whether the rapists heard their shouts? Whether they were spurred on by them?
2. Should the defendants in *Clarkson* have been liable for failing to summon the police? Should failure to report a crime itself be a crime, perhaps on the theory that one has a social responsibility and duty as a citizen to do so? At one point in English history, such an offence (misprision of felony) existed (see *Sykes* v *Director of Public Prosecutions* [1961] 3 All ER 33), but it was abolished by the Criminal Law Act 1967. Now it is only a crime to accept consideration for not disclosing an arrestable offence (Criminal Law Act 1967, s. 5(1)). Should the law have gone in the opposite direction? If assistance to a victim of a crime can be provided at no risk to the actor, why should such assistance not be legally required, and why should one not be criminally liable for failing to provide such assistance?
3. Assume that the spectators in *Clarkson* had made a mental resolve to prevent the interruption of the rape, without communicating this resolve to the rapists. Would this be sufficient to hold them liable as accessories, even if it should turn out that their assistance was not required? How does this hypothetical situation differ from that where a defendant has agreed to serve as lookout for a principal but no third parties intervene, and therefore no need arises for a warning to the principal? Can a principal draw support from an uncommunicated resolve to help, or is this the wrong question to be asking? Consider *Allan*:

R v *Allan and Others*
[1965] 1 QB 130, Court of Criminal Appeal

EDMUND DAVIES J: . . . [T]he judge [in effect] directed the jury that they were duty bound to convict an accused who was proved to have been present and witnessing an affray if it was also proved that he nursed an intention to join in if help was needed by the side he favoured and this notwithstanding that he did nothing by words or deeds to evince his intention and outwardly played the role of a purely passive spectator. It was said that, if that direction is right, where A and B behave themselves to all outward appearances in an exactly similar manner, but it be proved that A had the intention to participate if needs be, whereas B had no such intention, then A must be convicted of being a principal in the second degree to the affray, whereas B should be acquitted. To do that, it is objected, would be to convict A on his thoughts, even though they found no reflection in his actions. For the Crown, on the other hand, it is contended that the direction was unimpeachable, and that in the given circumstances a jury doing its duty would be bound to convict A of aiding and abetting in an affray even though he uttered no word of encouragement and acted throughout in exactly the same manner as all the other spectators of what was happening.

. . . [W]e have come to the conclusion that, in effect, the trial judge here dealt with facts which, at most, might provide some evidence of encouragement as amounting to conclusive proof of guilt.

The jury were in terms told that a man who chooses to remain at a fight, nursing the secret intention to help if the need arose, but doing nothing to evince that intention, *must* in law be held to be principal in the second degree and that, on these facts being proved, the jury would have no alternative but to convict him. In our judgment that was a misdirection. . . . In our judgment, before a jury can properly convict an accused person of being a principal in the second degree to an affray, they must be convinced by the evidence that, at the very least, he by some means or other encouraged the participants. To hold otherwise would be, in effect, as the appellants' counsel rightly expressed it, to convict a man on his thoughts, unaccompanied by any physical act other than the fact of his mere presence.

NOTES AND QUESTIONS
1. A is aware that B and C plan to kill D. A is also aware that E has sent a telegram warning D of the danger. A orders the telegraph operator not to deliver the warning, which directive is obeyed. Is A, whose actions are not known to B or C, an accessory to the murder of D? See *State ex rel Attorney-General* v *Tally*, 102 Ala 25, 15 So 722 (1894).

Compare *Clarkson* with *Wilcox* v *Jeffery*.

Wilcox v Jeffery
[1951] 1 All ER 464, King's Bench Division

LORD GODDARD CJ: This is a Case stated by the metropolitan magistrate at Bow Street Magistrate's Court before whom the appellant, Herbert William Wilcox, the proprietor of a periodical called 'Jazz Illustrated,' was charged on an information that 'on Dec. 11, 1949, he did unlawfully aid and abet one Coleman Hawkins in contravening art. 1(4) of the Aliens Order, 1920, by failing to comply with a condition attached to a grant of leave to land, to wit, that the said Coleman Hawkins should take no employment paid or unpaid while in the United Kingdom, contrary to art. 18(2) of the Aliens Order, 1920.' Under the Aliens Order, art. 1(1), it is provided that

> . . . an alien coming . . . by sea to a place in the United Kingdom – (a) shall not land in the United Kingdom without the leave of an immigration officer . . .'

It is provided by art. 1(4) that:

> An immigration officer, in accordance with general or special direction of the Secretary of State, may, by general order or notice or otherwise, attach such conditions as he may think fit to the grant of leave to land, and the Secretary of State may at any time vary such conditions in such manner as he thinks fit, and the alien shall comply with the conditions so attached or varied . . .

If the alien fails to comply, he is to be in the same position as if he has landed without permission, i.e., he commits an offence.

The case is concerned with the visit of a celebrated professor of the saxophone, a gentleman by the name of Hawkins who was a citizen of the United States. He came here at the invitation of two gentlemen of the name of Curtis and Hughes, connected with a jazz club which enlivens the neighbourhood of Willesden. They, apparently, had applied for permission for Mr Hawkins to land and it was refused, but, nevertheless, this professor of the saxophone arrived with four French musicians. When they came to the airport, among the people who were there to greet them was the appellant. He had not arranged their visit, but he knew they were coming and he was there to report the arrival of these important musicians for his magazine. So, evidently, he was regarding the visit of Mr Hawkins as a matter which would be of interest to himself and the magazine which he was editing and selling for profit. Messrs Curtis and Hughes arranged a concert at the Princes Theatre, London. The appellant attended that concert as a spectator. He paid for his ticket. Mr Hawkins went on the stage and delighted the audience by playing the saxophone. The appellant did not get up and protest in the name of the musicians of England that Mr Hawkins ought not to be here competing with them and taking the bread out of their mouths or the wind out of their instruments. It is not found that he actually applauded, but he was there having paid to go in, and, no doubt, enjoying the performance, and then, lo and behold, out comes his magazine with a most laudatory description, fully illustrated, of this concert. On those facts the magistrate has found that he aided and abetted.

. . .

There was not accidental presence in this case. The appellant paid to go to the concert and he went there because he wanted to report it. He must, therefore, be held to have been present, taking part, concurring, or encouraging, whichever word you like to use for expressing this conception. It was an illegal act on the part of Hawkins to play the saxophone or any other instrument at this concert. The appellant clearly knew that it was an unlawful act for him to play. He had gone there to hear him, and his presence and his payment to go there was an encouragement. He went there to make use of the performance, because he went there, as the magistrate finds was justified in finding, to get 'copy' for his newspaper. It might have been entirely different, as I say, if he had gone there and protested, saying: 'The musicians' union do not like you foreigners coming here and playing and you ought to get off the stage.' If he had booed, it might have been some evidence that he was not aiding and abetting. If he had gone as a member of a *claque* to try to drown the noise of the saxophone, he might very likely be found not guilty of aiding and abetting. In this case it seems clear that he was there, not only to approve and encourage what was done, but to take advantage of it by getting 'copy' for his paper. In those circumstances there was evidence on which the magistrate could find that the appellant aided and abetted, and for these reasons I am of opinion that the appeal fails.

NOTES AND QUESTIONS
1. Would the defendant have been liable if he had written an unfavourable review? What about the members of the audience – did they also commit an offence? Did it matter whether or not they protested? Whether or not they applauded? Whether or not they had paid admission to the concert? The key to answering these questions lies in determining what constituted the aiding and abetting and at what point in time this occurred.
2. What is the difference between *Wilcox v Jeffrey* and *Clarkson*? Is it the fact that in *Clarkson* the rape was already underway when the alleged aiding occurred, while in *Wilcox v Jeffrey* there would have been no crime if there had been no audience? Did the audience in *Wilcox v Jeffrey* provide more in the way of positive encouragement than the audience in *Clarkson*? See also *R v Coney* (1882) 8 QBD 534.
3. Must there be a causal relationship between the acts of the accessory and the offence of the principal? It is often the case that while the accessory's assistance facilitates the commission of the offence, the principal would have in any event committed it. Does it depend on the form that the accessory's participation takes? Smith and Hogan, *Criminal Law* (9th ed.) (1998) p. 128, suggest:
   (a) 'procuring' implies causation but not consensus;
   (b) 'abetting' and 'counselling' imply consensus but not causation;
   (c) 'aiding' requires actual assistance but neither consensus nor causation.

   See also H.L.A. Hart and H. Honore, *Causation and the Law* (2nd ed.) (1985, ch. XIII).

In the context of liability for inaction you should recall (see Chapter 3) that in some instances one has a legal duty to act and the failure to act can give rise to criminal liability. Often the liability takes the form of a conviction for being an accessory. The following cases are illustrative:

R v *Russell and Russell*

(1987) 85 Cr App R 388, Court of Appeal

The appellants A and M were registered drug addicts, in receipt of daily pre-scriptions of methadone, which they obtained in liquid form. They were living with their 15-month-old daughter. One day the child died from a massive over-dose of methadone. When interviewed separately by the police the appellants both denied giving methadone to the child save that they had on occasion dipped her dummy into the liquid methadone to placate her while she was teething. The appellants were charged with the child's manslaughter (count 1) and with cruelty to a person under 16, contrary to s. 1(1) of the Children and Young Persons Act 1933 (count 2). The evidence at their trial was that, as to count 1, the amount of the drug in the child's body was such that it could not have been ingested solely by the dipping of the dummy into the mixture. Forensic evidence was given on the likely effect upon a baby of the administration of methadone on a dummy. At the close of the prosecution case a submission of no case to answer on behalf of A was overruled by the trial judge. The jury convicted A and M on both counts, as to count 1, indicating that they did so on the basis of deliberate administration.

THE LORD CHIEF JUSTICE: . . . Generally speaking, parents of a child are in no different position from any other defendants jointly charged with a crime. To establish guilt against either, the Crown must prove at the least that that defendant aided, abetted, counselled or procured the commission of the crime by the other. The only difference in the position of parents, as opposed to others jointly indicted, is that one parent may have a duty to intervene in the ill-treatment of their child by the other where a stranger would have no such duty. . . .

Appeals against conviction dismissed.

Rubie v *Faulkner*

[1940] 1 KB 571, King's Bench Division

The appellant, while in a motor vehicle driven by the holder of a provisional licence (a 'learner-driver') who was driving under his supervision in accordance with reg. 16(3)(a) of the Motor Vehicles (Driving Licences) Regulations 1937, was in a position to see that the driver was about to overtake another vehicle by pulling considerably to the offside at a pronounced bend of the road, but he neither said nor did anything to prevent it. An accident having occurred and the driver having been convicted of driving without due care and attention:—

Held, that the appellant was rightly convicted of aiding and abetting the driver in the commission of the offence.

LORD HEWART CJ: . . . [T]he condition on which the holder of a provisional licence is allowed to drive a motor-vehicle on a highway is that he is under the supervision of an experienced driver. The very essence of the matter is that there should be a supervisor competent to supervise. The duty being clear on the face of the regulation, it was a pure question of fact for the justices to decide whether that duty had been performed.

It seems to me that it was open to the justices to find that the appellant, by his passive conduct in circumstances which required him to be active, if only by exclaiming: 'Keep in!', failed to discharge the duty which he had undertaken, and thus was guilty of the offence with which he was charged. In my opinion, therefore, this appeal should be dismissed.

HILBERY J: I agree. The regulation is framed to make some provision for the protection of the public against the dangers to which they are exposed through a car being driven on the road by a driver who is still a learner and therefore assumed to be not fully competent. It is, I can only suppose, because a learner-driver is assumed to be not fully competent that the regulation provides that a supervisor shall accompany him. This being so, the supervisor must be intended by the regulation to have the duty, by supervision, of making up as far as possible for the driver's incompetence. In other words, it is the supervisor's duty, when necessary, to do whatever can reasonably be expected to be done by a person supervising the acts of another to prevent that other from acting unskilfully or carelessly or in a manner likely to cause danger to others, and to this extent to participate in the driving.

In this case it was found that the supervisor could see the driver was about to do the unlawful act of which he was convicted and the magistrates found that the supervisor remained passive. There is no hint in the case that the supervisor in evidence ever asserted that he did anything. For him to refrain from doing anything when he could see that an unlawful act was about to be done, and his duty was to prevent an unlawful act if he could, was for him to aid and abet.

(iii) *Mens rea*

The *mens rea* of accessorial liability is an intent to do acts which the actor intends will assist the commission of the crime or which the actor knows will have this effect. Several points follow:

(a) It is not enough simply to do acts which have the effect of furthering the commission of the crime – they must be done with the intent to further the commission of the crime or with the knowledge that they will have this effect. If, for example, Donald were to help Penny to move premises, not knowing that Penny's possessions were stolen, Donald would not be guilty of aiding in the transportation of stolen goods, although his acts would have had this effect. Even more compelling is the case where a bystander shouts at a youth to discontinue his assault on an old man but the youth misinterprets the shouting as encouragement.

(b) It is the state of mind of the accessory and not that of the principal which is determinative of liability. As discussed previously, an accessory can be convicted of a more serious offence than the principal; the accessory who intentionally provides a gun to the excited husband who has just discovered his wife's adultery may be an accessory to murder even though the husband may only be guilty of manslaughter.

Can one, through recklessness, become an accessory?

Blakely and Sutton v *Director of Public Prosecutions*
[1991] Crim LR 764, Queen's Bench Division

T was an associate of B's. On the nights when he intended to stay with B, he would leave his car at the meeting place, but if he intended to go home, he would drink no more than two pints, thereafter drinking tonic water. On the night in question, he told B that he intended to go home to his wife. She discussed this with S, who suggested that if T had alcohol he might be unwilling to drive. Unknown to T, they added vodka to his tonic water. B intended to tell him later believing that he would not be prepared to drive. However, at closing time, T left before B had told him. He was arrested, and charged with a drink-driving offence. He advanced special reasons for not being disqualified. B and S testified with the result that T was given an absolute discharge. They were charged with 'aiding, abetting, counselling, procuring and commanding' T to drive when his blood-alcohol level exceeded that prescribed. It was contended that they did not intend T to drive; contrariwise, they intended that he should not drive. Following dismissal of their appeal to the Crown Court, they appealed by case stated, the questions being (i) whether the offence of procuring could be committed by someone who brought it about, not intending that the offence should be committed but reckless as to whether it be committed or not; (ii) if so, whether the meaning of recklessness in such a case was that given to it by Lord Diplock in *Lawrence* [1981] 2 WLR 524, 535.

Held, allowing the appeal, recklessness had two limbs: (a) pursuing a course of conduct and giving no thought to the possibility that it involved a risk when there was an obvious risk (inadvertent); (b) recognising that the conduct involved a risk but going on nevertheless to run it (advertent). Although the charge was framed compendiously only procuring was alleged, so only the *mens rea* of procuring the commission of an offence by another need be considered. The relevant issue was what must be proved to have been the state of the accused's mind in relation to the offence which the principal offender went on to commit? Counsel for the appellants submitted that the accused must not only have done his own act intentionally but must also have intended thereby to bring about the principal offence. Alternatively, he must have been aware that his intentional act might bring about the principal offence and have been prepared to do it nevertheless. Counsel for the DPP contended that an accused might be convicted of procuring an offence of strict liability if he intentionally did an act, or brought about a state of affairs, without which the offence would not have been committed and, at the time, he either intended that offence to occur or was reckless, in either of the *Caldwell* and *Lawrence* senses, as to whether the other essential acts or states constituting that offence would occur.

In *Carter v Richardson* [1974] RTR 314, the supervising driver was charged with aiding and abetting the learner driver's drink-driving offence. There was only one reference (317H) to recklessness which was not part of the *ratio*. Elsewhere in his judgment, Lord Widgery referred to the supervisor's knowledge or awareness, and there was nothing to suppose that, in approving the justices' opinion containing the word 'reckless,' he was thinking of anything other than advertent recklessness. In *A-G's Reference (No. 1)* [1975] 2 All ER 684, Lord Widgery said that to procure meant 'to produce by endeavour. You procure a thing by setting out to see that it happens and taking the appropriate steps to produce that happening.' That strongly suggested that the procurer must be shown to have intended to bring about the commission of the principal offence, and that mere awareness that it might result would not suffice. The language throughout the judgment was of knowledge of the offence the driver went on to commit: there was no hint that recklessness, let alone inadvertent recklessness, might suffice to convict the procurer.

There was no warrant for the suggestion that an accessory before the fact, whether aider and abettor, counsellor, commander or procurer, might be convicted on what might be called a less strict *mens rea* than would suffice to convict a principal in the second degree. Indeed, in *Ferguson v Weaving* [1951] 1 KB 814, it was suggested that something more might be required to convict one who 'counsels and procures.' That case would also appear to negate the submission for the DPP that it might be the case that the *mens rea* for procuring an absolute offence was less strict than that required of a person accused of procuring an offence which itself required *mens rea* (see also *Thomas v Lindop* [1950] 1 All ER 966). The conclusions on the question of the *mens rea* of an accessory before the fact were as follows. While it might now be the law that advertent recklessness to the consequences of his deliberate act of assistance might suffice to convict some, if not all, of those accused of being an accessory before the fact, it was clear that inadvertent recklessness did not. It must, at least, be shown that the accused contemplated that his act would or might bring about or assist the commission of the principal offence: he must have been prepared nevertheless to do his own act, and he must have done that act intentionally. Those requirements matched those needed to convict principals in the second degree, and they fitted well with the liability of the parties to a joint enterprise. In relation to those accused only of procuring and perhaps also those accused only of counselling and commanding, it might be, as Lord Goddard's judgment in *Ferguson v Weaving* would permit and as Lord Widgery's judgment in *A-G's Reference (No. 1 of 1975)* strongly suggested, that it was necessary to prove that the accused intended to bring about the principal offence. The present case did not require that to be decided. The stated question would be answered: (1) the use of the word 'recklessness' was best avoided when considering the *mens rea* of a person accused of procuring the commission of a substantive offence; (ii) in so far as the correct approach to that *mens rea* accorded with the concept of 'recklessness,' 'No.'

NOTES AND QUESTIONS

1. In *Blakely* the defendants did not wish the crime of drink driving to take place – indeed, they spiked the victim's drink in order to induce him not to drive. Would the result in the case have been the same if they did not care whether or not he drove?
2. Consider the Draft Criminal Code Bill and what effect it would have had on the result if it had been in force?

Draft Criminal Code Bill 1989

27.—1. A person is guilty of an offence as an accessory if—
  (a) he intentionally procures, assists or encourages the act which constitutes or results in the commission of the offence by the principal; and
  (b) he knows of, or (where recklessness suffices in the case of the principal) is reckless with respect to, any circumstance that is an element of the offence; and
  (c) he intends that the principal shall act, or is aware that he is or may be acting, or that he may act, with the fault (if any) required for the offence.
2. In determining whether a person is guilty of an offence as an accessory it is immaterial that the principal is unaware of that person's act of procurement or assistance.
3. If recklessness were to be deemed a sufficient *mens rea* to convict one of being an accessory, should *Caldwell* (objective) recklessness suffice, or should liability be limited to *Cunningham* (subjective) recklessness?
4. The accessory does not have to desire that the crime be committed – he may be ambivalent about it, or may prefer that it not to be committed. For example, if X sells a gun to Y, which Y tells X that she is going to use to kill her husband, X may be an accessory even though he does not care whether Y actually goes through with the killing. His sole motivation is to make a profit from the sale of the gun. The seller's liability rests on his providing assistance to the crime, knowing that the assistance will facilitate the commission of the crime. While the seriousness of murder may argue for the law to be structured so as to maximise prevention of its occurrence, should this analysis be extended to less serious crimes?

National Coal Board v *Gamble*
[1959] 1 QB 11, Queen's Bench Division

On 3 October 1957, M, the servant of a firm of hauliers, took his lorry to a colliery of the National Coal Board where it was filled with coal from a hopper and was then taken to a weighbridge, where the weighbridge operator H, who was employed by the board, weighed the lorry and its load and told M that the load was nearly 4 tons overweight. M., saying that he would risk taking the over-load, took the weighbridge ticket from H and left the colliery premises. He was subsequently stopped by the police and his firm were later convicted of contravening the Motor Vehicles (Construction and Use) Regulations 1955. It appeared that the hauliers were collecting the coal for carriage to a power station of an electricity authority, to whom the Coal Board were bound by contract to supply a bulk quantity of coal. The board were charged with aiding and abetting the firm in the commission of an offence.

DEVLIN J: . . . It was contended on behalf of the board that Haslam had no option after weighing but to issue the ticket for the amount then in the lorry. I think that this contention is unsound. In the circumstances of this case the loading must be taken as subject to adjustment; otherwise, if the contract were for a limited amount, the seller might make an over-delivery or an under-delivery which could not thereafter be rectified and the carrier might be contractually compelled to carry away a load in excess of that legally permitted. I think that the delivery of the coal was not completed until after the ascertained weight had been assented to and some act was done signifying assent and passing the property. The property passed when Haslam asked Mallender whether he intended to take the load and Mallender said he would risk it and when the mutual assent was, as it were, sealed by the delivery and acceptance of the weighbridge ticket. Haslam could therefore after he knew of the overload have refused to transfer the property in the coal.

. . . [A] man is presumed to intend the natural and probable consequences of his acts, and the consequence of supplying essential material is that assistance is given to the criminal. It is always open to the defendant, as in *R v Steane* [1947] KB 997, to give evidence of his real intention. But in this case the defence called no evidence. The prima facie presumption is therefore enough to justify the verdict, unless it is the law that some other mental element besides intent is necessary to the offence.

This is what Mr Thompson argues, and he describes the additional element as the purpose or motive of encouraging the crime. No doubt evidence of an interest in the crime or of an express purpose to assist it will greatly strengthen the case for the prosecution. But an indifference to the result of the crime does not of itself negative abetting. If one man deliberately sells to another a gun to be used for murdering a third, he may be indifferent about whether the third man lives or dies and interested only in the cash profit to be made out of the sale, but he can still be an aider and abettor. To hold otherwise would be to negative the rule that mens rea is a matter of intent only and does not depend on desire or motive.

. . . [T]he facts show an act of assent made by Haslam after knowledge of the proposed illegality and without which the property would not have passed. If some positive act to complete delivery is committed after knowledge of the illegality, the position in law must, I think, be just the same as if the knowledge had been obtained before the delivery had begun. Of course, it is quite likely that Haslam was confused about the legal position and thought that he was not entitled to withhold the weighbridge ticket. There is no mens rea if the defendant is shown to have a genuine belief in the existence of circumstances which, if true, would negative an intention to aid. . . . But this argument, which might have been the most cogent available to the defence, cannot now be relied upon, because Haslam was not called to give evidence about what he thought or believed. . . .

NOTES AND QUESTIONS

1. What constituted the *actus reus* of the crime? The *mens rea*? The defendants had little interest in whether the lorry driver proceeded with his overweight load. They stood to gain neither financially nor in any other way.

2. What would have been your legal advice to the weighbridge operator? Is the effect of the decision to create a private police force – must citizens prevent crimes from being committed or risk being deemed accessories? Or is *Gamble* distinguished by the fact that the weighbridge operator *knew* that with the ticket he provided the lorry driver would commit a crime? Where should the law draw the line of liability as we move away from 'knowledge' to some lesser state of awareness? What about criminal consequences which are foreseen to a high degree of probability? Foreseen as more probable than not? Foreseen as a possibility but not a probability? See also *Carter* v *Richardson* [1974] RTR 314.

3. Should the nature of the aid provided be relevant? What if the aid consists of an item of ordinary commerce, purchasable anywhere? Arlene walks into Brian's cutlery shop and asks for a knife sharp enough to kill a human being. Brian, having read *Gamble* and suspecting that the knife may be used for a criminal purpose, refuses to sell. Will not Arlene now simply purchase the knife at another store, being less indiscreet about her intentions? Such was not the case with the weighbridge ticket.

A not uncontroversial civil case, *Gillick* v *West Norfolk & Wisbech Area Health Authority* [1986] AC 112, raises questions about the continuing force of *Gamble*. The issue in the case was whether a doctor could give contraceptive advice to a female under the age of 16 without parental consent. Among the arguments raised by the girl's mother was that by giving such advice the doctor was aiding and abetting a criminal offence, it being illegal to have sexual intercourse with a girl under the age of 16. In a passage approved by the majority of the House of Lords, Woolf J addressed this argument:

Gillick v *West Norfolk and Wisbech Area Health Authority*
[1984] 1 QB 581, Queen's Bench Division

WOOLF J: . . . *Does the prescribing of contraceptives to a girl under 16 amount to criminal conduct on the part of a doctor?*

Section 28(1) of the Sexual Offences Act 1956 makes it

> an offence for a person to cause or encourage . . . the commission of unlawful sexual intercourse with . . . a girl under the age of 16 for whom he is responsible.

Subsection (3) provides:

> The persons who are to be treated for the purposes of this section as responsible for a girl are . . . (c) any other person who has the custody, charge or care of her.

Putting aside the question of whether or not the doctor's conduct could be said to amount to encouraging unlawful sexual intercourse, I cannot accept Mr Wright's submission that when a girl goes to a clinic for advice and/or treatment, she is in the ad hoc care of the doctor or the clinic. The words should not be narrowly construed but, in my view, they are inappropriate to cover a situation where a girl attends a clinic to seek help.

So far as the offence against section 6 of the Sexual Offences Act 1956, is concerned, I accept that a doctor who is misguided enough to provide a girl who is under the age of 16, or a man, with advice and assistance with regard to contraceptive measures with the intention thereby of encouraging them to have sexual intercourse, is an accessory before the fact to an offence contrary to section 6. I stress the words 'with the intention thereby of encouraging them to have sexual intercourse.' However, this, I assume, will not usually be the attitude of a doctor.

There will certainly be some cases, and I hope the majority of cases, where the doctor decides to give the advice and prescribe contraceptives despite the fact he was firmly against unlawful sexual intercourse taking place but felt, nevertheless, that he had to prescribe the contraceptives because, whether or not he did so, intercourse would in fact take place and the provision of contraceptives would, in his view, be in the best interests of the girl in protecting her from an unwanted pregnancy and the risk of a sexually transmitted disease. It is as to whether or not in such a situation the doctor is to be treated as being an accessory, that I have found the greatest difficulty in applying the law.

Mr Wright submits, and I accept that he is right in this submission, that it is necessary to distinguish between motive and intent. Even if your motives are unimpeachable, if you in fact assist in the commission of an offence, Mr Wright submits you are an accessory. He relies on the judgment of Devlin J in *National Coal Board* v *Gamble* [1959] 1 QB 11. In that case, Devlin J said, at p. 20:

> A person who supplies the instrument for a crime or anything essential to its commission aids in the commission of it; and if he does so knowingly and with intent to aid, he abets it as well and is therefore guilty of aiding and abetting. . . . Another way of putting the point is to say that aiding and abetting is a crime that requires proof of *mens rea*, that is to say, of intention to aid as well as of knowledge of the circumstances, and that proof of the intent involves proof of a positive act of assistance voluntarily done.

Devlin J's judgment in that case was considered by Lord Simon of Glaisdale in *Director of Public Prosecutions for Northern Ireland* v *Lynch* [1975] AC 653, 698–699:

> As regards the *actus reus*, 'aiding' and 'abetting' are, as *Smith and Hogan* notes (p. 93), synonymous. But the phrase is not a pleonasm; because 'abet' clearly imports mens rea, which 'aid' might not. As Devlin J said in *National Coal Board* v *Gamble* . . . – and he quotes the passage I have just quoted – The *actus reus* is the supplying of an instrument for a crime or anything essential for its commission. On Devlin J's analysis the *mens rea* does not go beyond this. The act of supply must be voluntary (in the sense I tried to define earlier in this speech), and it must be foreseen that the instrument or other object or service supplied will probably (or possibly and desiredly) be used for the commission of a crime. The definition of the crime does not in itself suggest any ulterior intent; and whether anything further in the way of mens rea was required was precisely the point at issue in *Gamble's* case. Slade J thought the very concept of aiding and abetting imported the concept of motive. But Lord Goddard CJ and Devlin J disagreed with this. So do I. Slade J thought that abetting involved assistance or encouragement, and that both implied motive. So far as assistance is concerned, this is clearly not so. One may lend assistance without any motive, or even with the motive of bringing about a result directly contrary to that in fact assisted by one's effort.

However, in applying those statements of the law, three matters have to be borne in mind. First of all, contraceptives do not in themselves directly assist in the commission of the crime of unlawful sexual intercourse. The analogy of providing the motor car for a burglary or providing poison to the murderer, relied on in argument, are not true comparisons. While if the man wears a sheath, there may be said to be a physical difference as to the quality of intercourse, the distinction that I am seeking to draw is clearer where the woman takes the pill or is fitted with an internal device, when the unlawful act will not be affected in any way. The only effect of the provision of the means of contraception is that in some cases it is likely to increase the likelihood of a crime being committed by reducing the inhibitions of the persons concerned to having sexual intercourse because of their fear of conception or the contraction of disease. I therefore see a distinction between the assistance or aiding referred to by Lord Simon of Glaisdale and Devlin J and the act of the doctor in prescribing contraceptives. I would regard the pill prescribed to the woman as not so much 'the instrument for a crime or anything essential to its commission' but a palliative against the consequences of the crime.

The second factor that has to be borne in mind is that the girl herself commits no offence under section 6 since the section is designed to protect her from herself: see *R* v *Tyrrell* [1894] 1 QB 710. This creates problems with regard to relying upon any encouragement by the doctor as making him the accessory to the offence where the girl alone attends the clinic. The well-known case, *R* v *Bourne* (1952) 36 Cr App R 125, has to be distinguished because there, the woman can be said to have committed the offence although she was not criminally responsible because of duress. The doctor, if he is to be an accessory where the woman alone consults him, will only be an accessory if it can be shown that he acted through the innocent agency of the woman, the situation dealt with in *R* v *Cooper* (1833) 5 C & P 535.

The final point that has to be borne in mind is that there will be situations where long-term contraceptive measures are taken to protect girls who, sadly, will strike up promiscuous relationships whatever the supervision of those who are responsible for their well-being, the sort of situation that Butler-Sloss J had to deal with in *In re P (A Minor)* (1981) 80 LGR 301. In such a situation the doctor will prescribe the measures to be taken purely as a safeguard against the risk that at some time in the future, the girl will form a casual relationship with a man when sexual intercourse will take place. In order to be an accessory, you normally have to know the material circumstances. In such a situation the doctor would know no more than that there was a risk of sexual intercourse taking place at an unidentified place with an unidentified man on an unidentified date – hardly the state of knowledge which is normally associated with an accessory before the fact.

Under this limb of the argument, the conclusion which I have therefore come to is, that while a doctor could, in following the guidance, so encourage unlawful sexual intercourse as to render this conduct criminal, in the majority of situations the probabilities are that a doctor will be able to follow the advice without rendering himself liable to criminal proceedings. Before leaving this limb of the argument, I should make it absolutely clear that the absence of consent of the parents makes no difference to the criminal responsibility of the doctor. If his conduct would be criminal without the parents' consent, it would be equally criminal with their consent.

NOTES AND QUESTIONS

1. Are *Gillick* and *National Coal Board* v *Gamble* reconcilable? For all intents and purposes, did not the doctor in *Gillick* know as surely as the weighbridge operator in *National Coal Board* v *Gamble* that the assistance which he provided would lead to the commission of a crime? At the very least, was not the doctor guilty of 'wilful blindness'?

2. In his opinion in the House of Lords, Lord Scarman spoke of cases where '[t]he bona fide exercise by a doctor of his clinical judgment must be a complete negation of the guilty mind which is an essential ingredient of the criminal offence of aiding and abetting the commission of unlawful sexual intercourse'. Why should this be so? Is Lord Scarman confusing motive and intent? What is the difference between such a case and that of the seller who supplies a gun to a buyer whom the seller knows will use it for an illegal purpose, but who is ambivalent about that purpose? Assuming its validity, should the principle espoused by Lord Scarman be limited to doctors? Consider the case of prison officials who distribute condoms to prisoners to prevent AIDS, knowing that this will encourage the offence of buggery.

B: Scope of liability

Sometimes one who provides aid knows that a crime will be committed but does not know what crime. Is the aider then liable for whatever crime is committed?

R v *Bainbridge*
[1960] 1 QB 129, Court of Criminal Appeal

On the night of 30 October 1958, the Stoke Newington branch of the Midland Bank was broken into by cutting the bars of a window, the doors of the strong room and of a safe inside the strong room. They were opened by means of oxygen cutting equipment and nearly £18,000 was stolen. The cutting equipment was left behind and it was later found that that cutting equipment so left behind by the thieves had been purchased by the appellant, Alan Bainbridge, some six weeks earlier. He appealed against his conviction of being accessory before the fact to office-breaking.

LORD PARKER CJ: . . . The case against him [the appellant] was that he had bought this cutting equipment on behalf of one or more of the thieves with the full knowledge that it was going to be used, if not against the Stoke Newington branch of the Midland Bank, at any rate for the purposes of breaking and entering premises.

The appellant's case, as given in his evidence, was this:

> True, I had bought this equipment from two different firms. I had gone there with a man called Shakeshaft to buy it for him. As a result of conversation which I had with him I was suspicious that he wanted it for something illegal, I thought it was for breaking up stolen goods which Shakeshaft had received, and as the result in those purchases I gave false names and addresses, but I had no knowledge that the equipment was going to be used for any such purpose as it was used.

. . .

Mr Simpson, who has argued this case very well, contends that . . . in order that a man should be convicted of being accessory before the fact, it must be shown that at the time he bought the equipment in a case such as this he knew that a particular crime was going to be committed, and by a particular crime Mr Simpson means that the premises in this case which were going to be broken into were known to the appellant and contemplated by him, and not only the premises in question but the date when the breaking was going to occur; in other words, that he must know that on a particular date the Stoke Newington branch of the Midland Bank is intended to be broken into.

The court fully appreciates that it is not enough that it should be shown that a man knows that some illegal venture is intended. To take this case, it would not be enough if he knew – he says he only suspected – that the equipment was going to be used to dispose of stolen property. That would not be enough. Equally, this court is quite satisfied that it is unnecessssry that knowledge of the particular crime which was in fact committed should be shown to his knowledge to have been intended, and by 'particular crime' I am using the words in the same way in which Mr Simpson used them, namely, on a particular date and particular premises.

It is not altogether easy to lay down a precise form of words which will cover every case that can be contemplated but, having considered the cases and the law this court is quite clear that the direction of Judge Aarvold in this case cannot be criticised.

Judge Aarvold in this case . . . makes it clear that there must be not merely suspicion but knowledge that a crime of the type in question was intended, and that the equipment was bought with that in view. In his reference to the felony of the type intended it was, as he stated, the felony of breaking and entering premises and the stealing of property from those premises. The court can see nothing wrong in that direction.

Director of Public Prosecutions for Northern Ireland v Maxwell
[1978] 3 All ER 1140, House of Lords

The appellant was a member of an illegal organisation in Northern Ireland which had been responsible for sectarian murders and bombings. On the night of 3 January 1976 the appellant was told by a member of the organisation to guide a car at night to a public house in a remote country area. The appellant knew that he was being sent on a terrorist attack but did not know what form it would take.

Driving his own car he led another car containing three or four men to the public house. When he arrived there the appellant drove slowly past and then drove home. The other car stopped opposite the public house, one of the occupants got out, ran across to the public house and threw a pipe bomb containing 5 lbs of explosive into the hallway. The attack failed due to action taken by the licensee's son. The appellant was charged with doing an act with intent to cause an explosion by a bomb, contrary to s. 3(a) of the Explosive Substances Act 1883 and with possession of a bomb contrary to s. 3(b) of that Act. The appellant was convicted of both offences as principal in the second degree (i.e. as an accomplice). He appealed contending that since he did not know what form the attack would take or of the presence of the bomb in the other car he could not properly be convicted of aiding and abetting in the commission of crimes of which he was ignorant. The Court of Criminal Appeal in Northern Ireland dismissed his appeal. The appellant appealed to the House of Lords.

VISCOUNT DILHORNE: . . . At the trial, counsel for the appellant submitted that there was no evidence that the appellant knew the nature of the job that was to be done or that he knew of the presence of the bomb in the Cortina and that he could not be convicted of aiding and abetting in the commission of crimes of which he was ignorant. In the course of a careful and thorough judgment this submission was rejected by MacDermott J. It was repeated before the Court of Criminal Appeal in Northern Ireland and rejected by them. They, however, certified that the following point of law of general public importance was involved, namely:

> If the crime committed by the principal, and actually assisted by the accused, was one of a number of offences, one of which the accused knew the principal would probably commit, is the guilty mind which must be proved against an accomplice thereby proved against the accused?

. . . When the appellant was told at Dunadry what he was required to do, he must have known that he was required to take part in UVF 'military' operation. He cannot have thought that at that time of the evening welfare was involved. MacDermott J inferred that the preparation for timing and route of the journey indicated that the job was to be an attack on the Crosskeys bar. Even if the appellant did not appreciate that, which is most unlikely, he must have known that the 'military' operation was to take place at or near the Crosskeys Inn. Knowing that, he led the way and so played an important part in the operation. Counsel for the appellant however contended that he could not properly be convicted unless he knew either as a moral certainty or possibly beyond reasonable doubt or arguably on a balance of probabilities that a bomb was to be placed in the bar (count 1) and that the Cortina was carrying it (count 2).

I do not agree. In *R v Bainbridge* [1959] 1 QB 129 Bainbridge was convicted of being an accessory before the fact to office breaking. A bank had been broken into and oxygen cutting equipment left there. It was found to have been bought by Bainbridge some six weeks earlier. On appeal it was contended that he should not have been convicted unless it was shown that when he bought the equipment he knew it was to be used for breaking into that bank. Lord Parker CJ, delivering the judgment of the Court of Criminal Appeal, while recognising that it was not enough to show that a man knows that some illegal venture is intended, said that it was unnecessary that 'knowledge of the particular crime which was in fact committed should be shown to his knowledge to have been intended'. He approved of the direction given by Judge Aarvold who had told the jury that it must be proved that Bainbridge knew the type of crime which was in fact committed was intended.

That case establishes that a person can be convicted of aiding and abetting the commission of an offence without his having knowledge of the actual crime intended. I do not think that any useful purpose will be served by considering whether the offences committed by the UVF can or cannot be regarded as the same type of crime. Liability of an aider and abettor should not depend on categorisation. The question to be decided appears to me to be what conduct on the part of those in the Cortina was the appellant aiding and abetting when he led them to the Crosskeys Inn. He knew that a 'military' operation was to take place. With his knowledge of the UVF's activities, he must have known that it would involve the use of a bomb or shooting or the use of incendiary devices. Knowing that he led them there and so he aided and abetted whichever of these forms the attack took. It took the form of placing a bomb. To my mind the conclusion is inescapable that he was rightly convicted on count 1.

I would dismiss the appeal.

LORD HAILSHAM OF ST MARYLEBONE: My Lords, in my opinion this appeal should be dismissed. The appellant was the owner and driver of the guide car in what subsequently turned out to be a terrorist attack by members of the criminal and illegal organisation known as the Ulster Volunteer Force ('UVF') on a public house owned by a Roman Catholic licensee at 40 Grange Road, Toomebridge, and known as the Crosskeys Inn. The attack was carried out on the night of 3rd January 1976 by the occupants of a Cortina car and took the form of throwing a pipe bomb containing about five pounds of explosive into the hallway of the public house. The attack failed because the son of the proprietor had the presence of mind to pull out the burning fuse and detonator and throw it outside the premises where the detonator exploded either because the fuse had reached the detonator or on contact with the ground. . . .

The only substantial matter to be discussed in the appeal is the degree of knowledge required before an accused can be found guilty of aiding, abetting, counselling or procuring. To what extent must the accused be proved to have particular knowledge of the crime in contemplation at the time of his participation and which was ultimately committed by its principal perpetrators? For myself I am content for this purpose to adopt the words of Lord Parker CJ in *R* v *Bainbridge* [1959] 1 QB 129 when, after saying that it is not easy to lay down a precise form of words which will cover every case, he observed that 'there must not be merely suspicion but knowledge that a crime of the type in question was intended', and the words of Lord Goddard CJ in *Johnson* v *Youden* [1950] 1 KB 544, endorsed by this House in *Churchill* v *Walton* [1967] 1 All ER 497 at 502–503, that 'Before a person can be convicted of aiding and abetting the commission of an offence he must at least know the essential matters which constitute that offence'. The only question in debate in the present appeal is whether the degree of knowledge possessed by the appellant was of the 'essential matters constituting' the offence in fact committed, or, to put what in the context of the instant case is exactly the same question in another form, whether the appellant knew that the offence in which he participated was 'a crime of the type' described in the charge.

For that purpose I turn to two passages in the findings of fact of the learned judge. The first is as follows:

> In my judgment, the facts of this case make it clear to me that the accused knew the men in the Cortina car were going to attack the inn and had the means of attacking the inn with them in their car. The accused may not, as he says, have known what form the attack was going to take, but in my judgment he knew the means of the attack, be they bomb, bullet or incendiary device, were present in that car.

In the second passage MacDermott J said:

> In my judgment, the accused knew that he was participating in an attack on the inn. He performed an important role in the execution of that attack. He knew that the attack was one which would involve the use of means which would result in danger to life or damage to property. In such circumstances, where an admitted terrorist participates actively in a terrorist attack, having knowledge of the type of attack intended, if not of the weapon chosen by his colleagues, he can in my view be properly charged with possession of the

weapon with which it is intended that life should be endangered or premises seriously damaged.

The learned judge also found, *inter alia* that the word 'job' (as used in the appellant's statements) is 'synonymous with military action which raises, having regard to the proven activities of the UVF, the irresistible inference [that] the attack would be one of violence in which people would be endangered or premises seriously damaged'.

R. v Gilmour *(Thomas Robert Garfield)*
[2000] 2 Cr App R 407, Court of Appeal

CARSWELL L.C.J.: On July 12, 1998 in the early hours of the morning a large petrol bomb was thrown through the living room window of a house in Carnany Park, Ballymoney, in which six people were in bed asleep. A fierce fire quickly developed, and thick smoke filled the house, following which flames burst out of the ground floor windows. The three adults in the house escaped, not without difficulty and injury, but three young boys, children of Christine Quinn, were trapped by the fire and died from the effects of carbon monoxide poisoning, notwithstanding strenuous efforts by fire officers to rescue them.

The appellant was charged with the murder of the three boys, the attempted murder of the three adults and arson of the dwelling house. On October 29, 1999, following a trial at Belfast Crown Court before McCollum L.J. sitting without a jury, he was convicted on the three charges of murder. On the charges of attempted murder of Christine Quinn and Christina Archibald the judge found the appellant not guilty of attempted murder but guilty of attempting to cause them grievous bodily harm, and on the charge of attempted murder of Raymond Frank Craig he found him not guilty of that charge but guilty of causing him grievous bodily harm. The count of arson was ordered to lie on the file. On the three counts of murder the judge sentenced the appellant to imprisonment for life and on each of the three other counts on which he returned a verdict he sentenced him to 12 years imprisonment, to run concurrently. The appellant appealed to this Court against conviction and sentence on a number of grounds. The issue on which the appeal turned was the intention to be attributed to the appellant and whether the judge's conclusion that he realised that the petrol bomb was to be used in order to cause grievous bodily harm to the persons in the house could be sustained.

. . .

Throwing petrol bombs at dwelling houses is regrettably common and always contains an element of potential danger to the occupants. It is right to say, however, that it has fortunately been only a rare consequence that occupants have been injured in such attacks, and the majority of them appear, so far as judicial notice can take us, to cause only minor fires. There is not in our view sufficient evidence to conclude that the appellant was aware that the petrol was contained in an unusually large bottle, which might be expected to cause a larger conflagration and result in greater danger to the occupants. On the evidence he realised at a late stage that a petrol bomb attack was about to take place, and his intention was formed in that short period before he co-operated in driving the principals away from the scene. It would be difficult to attribute to him with any degree of certainty an intention that the attack should result in more than a blaze which might do some damage, put the occupants in fear and intimidate them into moving from the house. The principals and the appellant did have a grudge against Colm Quinn, but there is not sufficient evidence to establish that they expected him to be sleeping in the house that night. Nor do we think that the talk that Colm Quinn was 'going to be used as a Guy Fawkes' is enough to establish beyond reasonable doubt that the appellant intended that those who were in occupation should suffer injuries in the fire. We therefore do not consider that the judge's finding that he appreciated that the principals intended to inflict grievous bodily harm can be supported as a safe conclusion of fact.

We conclude accordingly that the appellant's conviction for murder cannot be sustained. Nor can his conviction on counts 4, 5 and 6, each of which involves an intention to commit grievous bodily harm. The issue then is whether he can be found guilty of manslaughter on the first three counts, on the basis that if the principals had thrown the petrol bomb into the house without the intention of killing or inflicting grievous bodily harm on any person they would have properly been convicted of that offence. It was argued on behalf of the appellant that if he did not share the intention of the principals he should not be found guilty of either murder or manslaughter, in the same way as if the principals go outside the contemplated acts involved in the joint enterprise the accessory cannot be convicted of either offence: see our recent decision in *Crooks* [1999] N.I. 226, following the principles laid down in *R. v. Powell and English* [1998] 1 Cr.App.R. 261, [1999] A.C. 1.

The issue is discussed in Blackstone's *Criminal Practice*, 2000 ed., para. A5.5 at p. 75, in which the example is posed where the principal and accessory agree that the principal will post an incendiary device to the victim, the accessory contemplating only superficial injuries but the principal foreseeing and hoping that the injuries will be serious or fatal. The principal will be guilty of murder and the accessory will not. The editors conclude that the accessory should in such a case be convicted of manslaughter, because the act done by the principal is precisely what was envisaged.

In our opinion this is the correct principle to apply in the present case. The appellant foresaw that the principals would carry out the act of throwing a petrol bomb into the house, but did not realise that in so doing they intended to kill or do grievous bodily harm to the occupants. To establish that a person charged as an accessory to a crime of specific intent is guilty as an accessory it is necessary to prove that he realised the principal's intention: see *Hyde* (1991) 92 Cr.App.R. 131, 135, [1991] Q.B. 134, 139, *per* Lord Lane C.J., approved by Lord Hutton in *R. v. Powell and English* [1998] 1 Cr.App.R. 261, 283, [1999] A.C. 1, 27–28. The line of authority represented by such cases as *Anderson and Morris* (1966) 50 Cr.App.R. 216, [1966] 2 Q.B. 110, approved in *R. v. Powell and English*, deals with situations where the principal departs from the contemplated joint enterprise and perpetrates a more serious act of a different kind unforeseen by the accessory. In such cases it is established that the accessory is not liable at all for such unforeseen acts. It does not follow that the same result should follow where the principal carries out the very act contemplated by the accessory, though the latter does not realise that the principal intends a more serious consequence from the act.

We do not consider that we are obliged by authority to hold that the accessory in such a case must be acquitted of manslaughter as well as murder. The cases in which an accessory has been found not guilty both of murder and manslaughter all concern a departure by the principal from the *actus reus* contemplated by the accessory, not a difference between the parties in respect of the *mens rea* of each. In such cases the view has prevailed that it would be wrong to hold the accessory liable when the principal committed an act which the accessory did not contemplate or authorise. We do not, however, see any convincing policy reason why a person acting as an accessory to a principal who carries out the very deed contemplated by both should not be guilty of the degree of offence appropriate to the intent with which he so acted. It is of course conceivable, as is suggested in *Blackstone, loc. cit.*, that in some cases the nature of the principal's *mens rea* may change the nature of the act committed by him and take it outside the type of act contemplated by the accessory, but it does not seem to us that the existence of such a possibility affects the validity of the basic principle which we have propounded. A verdict of guilty of manslaughter on this basis was upheld by the Court of Appeal in *Stewart and Schofield* [1995] 1 Cr.App.R. 441, [1995] 3 All E.R. 159. The judgment has been strongly criticised by Sir John Smith in [1995] Crim.L.R. 296 and [1995] Crim.L.R. 422 and in Smith & Hogan, *Criminal Law*, 9th ed., 1999 p. 145. Even if there may be ground for criticism of some of the propositions enunciated in the Court's judgment, the principle accepted as its basis is in our view sustainable.

We accordingly allow the appeal, substitute a verdict of not guilty of murder but guilty of manslaughter on counts 1 to 3 and set aside the verdicts of guilty on counts 4 to 6.

Appeals allowed.

NOTES AND QUESTIONS

1. Are *Maxwell* and *Gilmour* sufficiently distinguishable to warrant different results? How so?
2. If a dealer sells a gun to a person who is widely reputed to be a hit man for the mob, is the dealer an accessory to every murder which the buyer commits with the gun?
3. Cecil enters Margaret's house with the intent to steal a painting, having gained access by using a key supplied by the gardener. The gardener knew that Cecil's intention was not honourable, but did not know what specific crime he contemplated. While in the house, Cecil decided to rape Margaret. Is the gardener liable for rape? Burglary? Consider in this regard Lord Scarman's observation in *Maxwell* that 'An accessory who leaves it to his principal to choose is liable, provided always the choice is made from the range of offences from which the accessory contemplates the choice will be made'.

(i) *The scope of 'joint enterprises'*

When one of the principles in a joint enterprise goes beyond the scope of the agreement, are the others liable for his or her crimes?

R v Powell and another, R v English
[1997] 4 All ER 545, House of Lords

LORD HUTTON: My Lords, the appeals before your Lordships' House relate to the liability of a participant in a joint criminal enterprise when another participant in that enterprise is guilty of a crime, the commission of which was not the purpose of the enterprise.

. . .

In the case of Powell and Daniels the purpose of the joint enterprise was to purchase drugs from a drug dealer. Three men, including the two appellants, Powell and Daniels, went to purchase drugs from a drug dealer, but having gone to his house for that purpose, the drug dealer was shot dead when he came to the door. The Crown was unable to prove which of the three men fired the gun which killed the drug dealer, but it was the Crown case that if the third man fired the gun, the two appellants were guilty of murder because they knew that the third man was armed with a gun and realised that he might use it to kill or cause really serious injury to the drug dealer.

In the course of summing up to the jury at the trial, the Recorder of London said:

> . . . if B or C realised, without agreeing to such conduct being used, that A may kill or intentionally inflict serious injury and they nevertheless continue to participate with A in the venture, that will amount to a sufficient mental element for B or C to be guilty of murder if A with the requisite intent kills in the course of the venture. In those circumstances B and C have lent themselves to the enterprise and by so doing have given assistance and encouragement to A in carrying out an enterprise which they realised may involve murder. These are general principles which must be applied to the facts of this case.

Powell and Daniels were convicted of murder and their appeals were rejected by the Court of Appeal, and the question certified for the opinion of your Lordships' House is:

> Is it sufficient to found a conviction for murder for a secondary party to a killing to have realised that the primary party might kill with intent to do so or must the secondary party have held such intention himself?

In the case of English the purpose of the joint enterprise in which he and another young man, Weddle, took part was to attack and cause injury with wooden posts to a police officer, Sergeant Forth, and in the course of the attack Weddle used a knife with which he stabbed Sergeant Forth to death.

It was a reasonable possibility that English had no knowledge that Weddle was carrying a knife, and on this basis the learned trial judge, Owen J, stated in his summing up to the jury:

If he did not know of the knife then you have to consider whether nevertheless he knew that there was a substantial risk that Weddle might cause some really serious injury with the wooden post which was used in the manner which you find it to have been used. So there is the question; 'Has the prosecution proved' – and this is an alternative, of course – 'that English joined in an unlawful attack on the sergeant realising at that time that there was a substantial risk that in that attack Weddle might kill or at least cause some really serious injury to the sergeant. If no, not guilty' . . .

The judge then, in effect, directed the jury that if they answered that question in the affirmative they should find English guilty of murder.

Weddle and English were convicted of murder and their appeals were rejected by the Court of Appeal. English now appeals to your Lordships' House and the two questions certified for the opinion of the House are as follows:

(i) Is it sufficient to found a conviction for murder for a secondary party to a killing to have realised that the primary party might kill with intent to do so or with intent to cause grievous bodily harm or must the secondary party have held such an intention himself?

(ii) Is it sufficient for murder that the secondary party intends or foresees that the primary party would or may act with intent to cause grievous bodily harm, if the lethal act carried out by the primary party is fundamentally different from the acts foreseen or intended by the secondary party?

The question certified in the appeals of Powell and Daniels and the first question certified in the appeal of English raise the issue whether foresight of a criminal act which was not the purpose of the joint enterprise (in the case of Powell and Daniels the use of a gun, and in the case of English the use of a knife) is sufficient to impose criminal liability for murder on the secondary party in the event that the jury find that the primary party used the weapon with intent to kill or cause really serious harm.

In the case of Powell and Daniels, the Crown case was that the two appellants knew that the third man was armed with a gun, and the Crown accepted that if the jury did not find this knowledge the appellants would not be guilty of murder. But in the case of English the Crown case was that, even if he did not know that Weddle had a knife, English foresaw that Weddle would cause really serious injury to the police officer, and that this foresight was sufficient to impose criminal liability upon him for the murder. Accordingly the second question arises in the case of English and that question is, in essence, whether the secondary party is guilty of murder if he foresaw that the other person taking part in the enterprise would use violence that would cause really serious injury, but did not foresee the use of the weapon that was used to carry out the killing.

My Lords, the first question gives rise, in my opinion, to two issues. The first issue is whether there is a principle established in the authorities that where there is a joint enterprise to commit a crime, foresight or contemplation by one party to the enterprise that another party to the enterprise may in the course of it commit another crime, is sufficient to impose criminal liability for that crime if committed by the other party even if the first party did not intend that criminal act to be carried out. (I shall consider in a later part of this judgment whether the foresight is of a possibility or of a probability.) The second issue is whether, if there be such an established principle, it can stand as good law in the light of the decisions of this House that foresight is not sufficient to constitute the *mens rea* for murder in the case of the person who actually causes the death and that guilt only arises if that person intends to kill or cause really serious injury.

My Lords, I consider that there is a strong line of authority that where two parties embark on a joint enterprise to commit a crime, and one party foresees that in the course of the enterprise the other party may carry out, with the requisite *mens rea*, an act constituting another crime, the former is liable for that crime if committed by the latter in the course of the enterprise. This was decided by the Court of Appeal, constituted by five judges, in *R v Smith (Wesley)* [1963] 3 All ER 597.

. . .

My Lords, I recognise that as a matter of logic there is force in the argument advanced on behalf of the appellants, and that on one view it is anomalous that if foreseeability of death or really serious harm is not sufficient to constitute *mens rea* for murder in the party who actually carries out the killing, it is sufficient to constitute *mens rea* in a secondary party. But the rules of the common law are not based solely on logic but relate to practical concerns and, in relation to crimes committed in the course of joint enterprises, to the need to give effective protection to the public against criminals operating in gangs. As Lord Salmon stated in *DPP* v *Majewski* [1976] 2 All ER 142 at 157, in rejecting criticism based on strict logic of a rule of the common law, 'this is the view that has been adopted by the common law of England, which is founded on common sense and experience rather than strict logic'.

In my opinion, there are practical considerations of weight and importance related to considerations of public policy which justify the principle stated in *Chan Wing-siu* v *R* and which prevail over considerations of strict logic. One consideration is that referred to by Lord Lane CJ in *R* v *Hyde* [1990] 3 All ER 892 at 896, where he cited with approval the observation of Professor Smith in his comment on *R* v *Wakely*:

> If B realises (without agreeing to such conduct being used) that A may kill or intentionally inflict serious injury, but nevertheless continues to participate with A in the venture, that will amount to a sufficient mental element for B to be guilty of murder if A, with the requisite intent, kills in the course of the venture. As Professor Smith points out, B has in those circumstances lent himself to the enterprise and by so doing he has given assistance and encouragement to A in carrying out an enterprise which B realises may involve murder.

A further consideration is that, unlike the principal party who carries out the killing with a deadly weapon, the secondary party will not be placed in the situation in which he suddenly has to decide whether to shoot or stab the third person with intent to kill or cause really serious harm. There is, in my opinion, an argument of considerable force that the secondary party who takes part in a criminal enterprise (for example the robbery of a bank) with foresight that a deadly weapon may be used, should not escape liability for murder because he, unlike the principal party, is not suddenly confronted by the security officer so that he has to decide whether to use the gun or knife or have the enterprise thwarted and face arrest. This point has been referred to in cases where the question has been discussed whether in order for criminal liability to attach the secondary party must foresee an act as more likely than not or whether it suffices if the secondary party foresees the act only as a possibility.

In *Chan Wing-siu* v *R* [1985] AC 168 at 172 counsel for the Crown submitted:

> Regard must be had to public policy considerations. Public policy requires that when a man lends himself to a criminal enterprise knowing it involves the possession of potentially murderous weapons which in fact are used by his partners with murderous intent, he should not escape the consequences to him of their conduct by reliance upon the nuances of prior assessment of the likelihood that such conduct will take place. In these circumstances an accomplice who knowingly takes the risk that such conduct might, or might well, take place in the course of that joint enterprise should bear the same responsibility for that conduct as those who use the weapons with the murderous intent.

Sir Robin Cooke stated ([1984] 3 All ER 877 at 882):

> What public policy requires was rightly identified in the submissions of the Crown. Where a man lends himself to a criminal enterprise knowing that potentially murderous weapons are to be carried, and in the event they are in fact used by his partner with an intent sufficient for murder, he should not escape the consequences by reliance on a nuance of prior assessment, only too likely to have been optimistic.

. . .

Therefore, for the reasons which I have given I would answer the certified question of law in the appeals of Powell and Daniels and the first certified question in the appeal of English by stating that (subject to the observations which I make in relation to the second certified question in the case of English) it is sufficient to found a conviction for murder for a secondary party to have realised that in the course of the joint enterprise the primary party might kill with intent to do so or with intent to cause grievous bodily harm. Accordingly, I would dismiss the appeals of Powell and Daniels.

The second certified question in the appeal of English arises because of the last sentence in the following passage in the trial judge's summing up to the jury to which I have previously referred:

> If he had the knife and English knew that Weddle had the knife, what would have been –
> must have been – in the mind of English, bearing in mind whatever condition you find that
> he was in as a result of drink? So you have to ask that question. If he did not know of the
> knife then you have to consider whether nevertheless he knew that there was a substantial
> risk that Weddle might cause some really serious injury with the wooden post which was
> used in the manner which you find it to have been used.

In *R v Hyde* [1990] 3 All ER 892 at 896 as already set out, Lord Lane CJ stated:

> If B realises (without agreeing to such conduct being used) that A may kill or intentionally
> inflict serious injury, but nevertheless continues to participate with A in the venture, that
> will amount to a sufficient mental element for B to be guilty of murder if A, with the
> requisite intent, kills in the course of the venture.

. . .

[If] the weapon used by the primary party is different to, but as dangerous as, the weapon which the secondary party contemplated he might use, the secondary party should not escape liability for murder because of the difference in the weapon, for example, if he foresaw that the primary party might use a gun to kill and the latter used a knife to kill, or vice versa. . . .

R v Uddin
[1998] 2 All ER 744, Court of Appeal

BELDAM LJ: The appellant appeals against his conviction for the murder of Mark Sharp.

At about 1750 hrs on the afternoon of Sunday, 27 August 1995, as Mr Mark Sharp was driving his motor car in Haverlock Road, Luton, he was forced to brake sharply when a black Nova motor car driven by Mr Abdul Shahid stopped suddenly in front of him. Displeased by the actions of the driver of the Nova car, Mark Sharp overtook, making a rude gesture as he did so. Shortly afterwards he parked his car in High Town Road near a launderette. The Nova car pulled up beside him and the four Asian occupants, Shahid the driver, Mr Jomir Miah, Mr Forid Miah and Mr Abdul Tahid, got out and confronted Sharp. An argument ensued and one of the four who had been travelling in the Nova car returned to the car to make a call on a mobile telephone. Shortly afterwards, two other Asians, Mr Rejan Uddin and Mr Abdul Abbadin, and possibly two others, joined the four occupants of the Nova car. They were obviously friends. The two new arrivals appeared to Mr Hughes, a witness, to be older and bigger than the original four. Sharp and the six Asians were all on the pavement and close to a wall. Mr Hughes turned to go back to his car and had hardly taken a step or two when hearing a noise he turned and saw that the six Asians were attacking Sharp. Three of them appeared to be using weapons made out of the bottom half of a snooker cue. He saw Sharp being hit around the head and generally all over the body. The three who did not have weapons were punching and kicking Sharp. As he was being hit around the head, Sharp fell to his knees but the attackers carried on until he fell down completely and was lying still. The six attackers then ran off to their car. The attack had lasted, he thought, 30 seconds. He saw no attempt by Sharp to strike at the attackers or deliver any blows. His impression was that all six attackers were taking part in the violence but he could not say which of them used weapons or which of them kicked or punched. Mr Tatham, who owned the launderette, also witnessed the attack. He had come from a shop about two doors away and noticed an argument with five or six young Asian males standing around a white man, who was swearing. The Asians then seemed calm and standing around. From just inside the launderette he saw them on the opposite side of the road and, out of the corner of his eye, he noticed a man to his left strike a blow at Sharp, who went down. As he went down all the others converged on him and as they did so he heard someone shout: 'Stab him!'

The blow with the knife was delivered by Abdul Tahid who apparently produced a flick-knife from his pocket as he joined in the attack. Apart from the shout of 'Stab him' heard by the witness Mr Tatham, there was no evidence that the other defendants knew that Abdul Tahid had a knife and all denied doing so.

We now come to the main grounds of appeal which were: (a) that the verdict in the appellant's case was inconsistent with the verdicts of manslaughter in the cases of the three co-defendants (Abdul Shahid, Jomir Miah, Forid Miah) who were acquitted of murder. The appellant was in no different position from those co-defendants. In each case there was no evidence that the defendant knew that a fourth defendant (Abdul Tahid) had a knife or would use it. A single stab wound to the head was the cause of death. (b) In dealing with joint enterprise the learned judge failed to direct the jury that as a secondary party to the killing, they had to be sure that the appellant foresaw the use of a knife as a possibility if he was to be found guilty of murder: *R v Powell, R v English* [1997] 4 All ER 545.

We think it convenient to deal with the second ground of appeal before considering whether the verdicts were inconsistent. As Lord Hutton made clear in his speech in *R v English* [1997] 4 All ER 545, if one party to a joint enterprise suddenly forms an intention to kill making use of a deadly weapon and, acting in a way which no party to the common design could suspect, kills using that deadly weapon the others taking part in the common enterprise are to be judged as secondary parties and are not guilty of murder unless the actions of the party causing death are of a type which they foresee but do not necessarily intend. But as he later explains ([1997] 4 All ER 545 at 566), if the weapon used by the primary party is different from, but as dangerous as, the weapon which the secondary party contemplated he might use, the secondary party should not escape liability for murder because of the difference in the weapon. For example, if he foresaw that the primary party might use a gun to kill and the latter used a knife to kill or vice versa. On the question of the degree of foresight required to impose liability, he agreed with the judgment of the Privy Council in *Chan Wing-siu v R* [1984] 3 All ER 87 that if a secondary party contemplated the act causing death as a possible incident of the joint venture, he is liable unless the risk was so remote that the jury take the view that the secondary party genuinely dismissed it as altogether negligible.

Such an analysis of the assessment of risk, whilst appropriate in the case of criminals who agree together in advance to commit an offence such as armed robbery, does not readily fit the spontaneous behaviour of a group of irrational individuals who jointly attack a common victim, each intending severally to inflict serious harm by any means at their disposal and giving no thought to the means by which the others will individually commit similar offences on the same person. In truth each in committing his individual offence assists and encourages the others in committing their individual offences. They are at the same time principals and secondary parties. Because it is often a matter of chance whether one or other of them inflicts a fatal injury, the law attributes responsibility for the acts done by one to all of them, unless one of the attackers completely departs from the concerted actions of the others and in so doing causes the victim's death. An example found in the observations of Lord Parker CJ in *R v Anderson and Morris* [1966] 2 All ER 644 at 648 is when one of the participants suddenly forms an intent to kill using a weapon in a way in which no other party could suspect.

In this example the party departing from the common enterprise has not only formed a different intent but has acted in a way which no other party could suspect. In short he has not merely brought about the death of the victim with a different intent but has used a weapon which the others did not know or suspect he had with him. The essential ingredients of his offence are different and the actions of the others coincided with, but did not contribute to or assist, the commission of his offence. The difficulty in applying these principles to a case such as the present led to the expression in the speeches of Lord Mustill and Lord Steyn in *R v Powell* [1997] 4 All ER 545 of the difficulties in the concepts of joint enterprise and accessory liability and their calls for urgent review of the law of homicide. Notwithstanding these difficulties, we think that the principles applicable to a case such as the present are as follows.

(i) Where several persons join to attack a victim in circumstances which show that they intend to inflict serious harm and as a result of the attack the victim sustains fatal injury, they are jointly liable for murder; but if such injury inflicted with that intent is shown to have been caused solely by the actions of one participant of a type entirely different from actions which the others foresaw as part of the attack, only that participant is guilty of murder.

(ii) In deciding whether the actions are of such a different type the use by that party of a weapon is a significant factor. If the character of the weapon, eg its propensity to cause death is different from any weapon used or contemplated by the others and if it is used with a specific intent to kill, the others are not responsible for the death unless it is proved that they knew or foresaw the likelihood of the use of such a weapon.

(iii) If some or all of the others are using weapons which could be regarded as equally likely to inflict fatal injury, the mere fact that a different weapon was used is immaterial.

(iv) If the jury conclude that the death of the victim was caused by the actions of one participant which can be said to be of a completely different type to those contemplated by the others, they are not to be regarded as parties to the death whether it amounts to murder or manslaughter. They may nevertheless be guilty of offences of wounding or inflicting grievous bodily harm with intent which they individually commit.

(v) If in the course of the concerted attack a weapon is produced by one of the participants and the others knowing that he has it in circumstances where he may use it in the course of the attack participate or continue to participate in the attack, they will be guilty of murder if the weapon is used to inflict a fatal wound.

(vi) In a case in which after a concerted attack it is proved that the victim died as a result of a wound with a lethal weapon, eg a stab wound, but the evidence does not establish which of the participants used the weapon, then if its use was foreseen by the participants in the attack they will all be guilty of murder notwithstanding that the particular participant who administered the fatal blow cannot be identified (see *R v Powell*). If, however, the circumstances do not show that the participants foresaw the use of a weapon of this type, none of them will be guilty of murder though they may individually have committed offences in the course of the attack.

(vii) The mere fact that by attacking the victim together each of them had the intention to inflict serious harm on the victim is insufficient to make them responsible for the death of the victim caused by the use of a lethal weapon used by one of the participants with the same or shared intention.

As we have said, in the present case there was no evidence upon which the jury could find that before the attack began the others involved knew that Abdul Tahid was carrying a flick-knife.

If the jury accepted the evidence of Mr Tatham who said that whilst in his laundrette on the opposite side of the road from the attack he heard the shout 'Stab him' as the attack began, they could as we have said have concluded that those of the defendants who then took part in the attack did so being aware, or at least foreseeing, that a knife might be used with intent to cause really serious harm. Whether those who having heard the shout attacked the deceased with shortened billiard cues as clubs themselves committed the offence of inflicting grievous bodily harm with intent or not, they would be guilty of murder as secondary parties.

The judge's direction clearly left it to the jury to say whether one of the accused had gone beyond the common purpose of the concerted attack and he told them that if one of the defendants had done an act which went beyond the agreed plan and they were not sure that the act was one which another defendant knew was a real possibility, the necessary common intention would not have been established. It was suggested that the jury may from this direction have concluded that if a particular defendant had an intention to do really serious harm the existence of that intention was sufficient to make that defendant guilty of murder even though the action of the party who had caused the death went outside the common purpose of the attack. We do not think that the judge's direction was susceptible of this interpretation but we do think that since *R v English* it is necessary for the jury to have their attention directed particularly to the nature of a weapon used in a concerted or combined attack and to knowledge or foresight of the use of such a weapon.

Whilst the jury were carefully directed to consider whether the actions of any of the accused went so outside the common purpose that they were not foreseen by the others, the jury's attention was not specifically focused on the use of the knife by Abdul Tahid and whether on the evidence they were sure that the others were aware that he might use it. There was evidence from which the jury could conclude that those of the accused who took part after the shout of 'Stab him' must have been aware that one of them had a knife and might use it with intent to do serious harm. Lord Hutton stressed the lethal nature of a knife as a weapon, it was for the jury to say whether its use in this attack was so different from the concerted actions of hitting the deceased with clubs and kicking him with the shod foot that Tahid's actions went beyond the common purpose.

It was also for the jury to say in each case whether those taking part were aware, whether from the shout or otherwise, that one of their number might use a knife.

We are further troubled by the distinction apparently drawn by the jury between the parts played by the three accused convicted of manslaughter and the part played by the appellant. If the actions of Tahid did in fact go outside the common purpose of the attack then those who took part aware that a knife might be used were guilty of murder as secondary parties; if they were not aware that a knife might be used they were entitled to be acquitted. (See the observations of Lord Hutton in *R v English*). If, however, the use of the knife did not go outside the common purpose of the attack which from the actions of those taking part was plainly to cause Sharp really serious harm, it is difficult to discern the basis for the verdict of manslaughter or the basis on which the participation of those accused was found by the jury to be different from the participation of the appellant. It is true that each of those accused convicted of manslaughter gave evidence that they did not know that any of their number had a knife and therefore that it might be used with intent to do serious harm but equally there was no evidence that before the attack began and the shout of 'Stab him', the appellant knew that Tahid had a knife. In the circumstances of this case we think that it would be unsafe to allow the conviction of the appellant for murder to stand. We think, however, that as there was evidence from which the jury directed in accordance with *R v English* [1997] 4 All ER 545 could have concluded that the appellant was guilty of murder that there should be a retrial.

NOTES AND QUESTIONS

1. A supplies B with a gun with which to kill C; B instead kills D. Is A liable as an accessory to D's death? Here the crime contemplated has not changed but the victim has. See *Saunders and Archer* (1573) 2 Plowden 473. Note that if B, shooting at C, had missed and hit D, it would be a case of transferred intent and neither B's nor A's liability would be affected. Should the result be different because B on his own initiative decided to kill D instead of C?

2. F supplies G with a gun to kill H but the gun malfunctions. Unwilling to be defeated, G strangles H to death. Is F liable? What aid or assistance has F supplied?

3. P and Q agree to rob V. P stands lookout while Q approaches V in a dark alley. Q not only robs

V, but kills him as well. This was not part of their plan, but P knew that Q always went armed. Would P be guilty as an accessory to murder? See *Lovesey* v *Pearson* [1970] 1 QB 352; *Davies* v *Director of Public Prosecutions* [1954] 1 All ER 507. Compare *R* v *Betty* (1963) 48 Cr App R 6. What if P did not know that Q was carrying a deadly weapon?

C: Defences

(i) *Protected individuals*

Where the law exists to protect a category of potential victims, it makes little sense to charge the victim as an accessory.

R v *Tyrrell*
[1894] 1 QB 710, Court for Crown Cases Reserved

The defendant, Jane Tyrrell, was on 15 September 1893, tried and convicted at the Central Criminal Court on an indictment charging her, in the first count, with having unlawfully aided and abetted, counselled, and procured the commission by one Thomas Ford of the misdemeanor of having unlawful carnal knowledge of her whilst she was between the ages of thirteen and sixteen, against the form of the statute, etc.; and, in the second count, with having falsely, wickedly, and unlawfully solicited and incited Thomas Ford to commit the same offence.

It was proved at the trial that the defendant did aid, abet, solicited and incited Thomas Ford to commit the misdemeanor made punishable by s. 5 of the Criminal Law Amendment Act 1885. The question for the opinion of the Court was, 'Whether it is an offence for a girl between the ages of thirteen and sixteen to aid and abet a male person in the commission of the misdemeanor of having unlawful carnal connection with her, or to solicit and incite a male person to commit that misdemeanor.'

LORD COLERIDGE CJ: The Criminal Law Amendment Act 1885, was passed for the purpose of protecting women and girls against themselves. At the time it was passed there was a discussion as to what point should be fixed as the age of consent. That discussion ended in a compromise, and the age of consent was fixed at sixteen. With the object of protecting women and girls against themselves the Act of Parliament has made illicit connection with a girl under that age unlawful; if a man wishes to have such illicit connection he must wait until the girl is sixteen, otherwise he breaks the law; but it is impossible to say that the Act, which is absolutely silent about aiding or abetting, or soliciting or inciting, can have intended that the girls for whose protection it was passed should be punishable under it for the offences committed upon themselves. I am of opinion that this conviction ought to be quashed.

MATHEW J: I am of the same opinion. I do not see how it would be possible to obtain convictions under the statute if the contention for the Crown were adopted, because nearly every section which deals with offences in respect of women and girls would create an offence in the woman or girl. Such a result cannot have been intended by the legislature. There is no trace in the statute of any intention to treat the woman or girl as criminal.

Conviction quashed.

QUESTIONS

1. Is the result in *Tyrrell* justified on the theoretical basis that, since the purpose of the statute was in part to protect emotionally immature girls from themselves, it would be perverse to punish them for that same immaturity; or the practical basis that it would be counterproductive to prosecute the victim, for it would discourage victims from reporting crimes?

2. Of what relevance is Parliamentary intent? Is it possible in *Tyrrell* to determine what Parliament intended?

3. What if another girl of the victim's age assisted Tyrrell by arranging the rendezvous – could she be convicted as an accessory? Is the decision of the court helpful in answering this question?

4. Does the reasoning of *Tyrrell* apply to:
    (a) the woman who voluntarily subjects herself to an illegal abortion;
    (b) the previously unmarried partner in a bigamous marriage?

Is the common thread in these cases the fact that two persons are inevitably necessary to the commission of the crime, but the relevant statute punishes only one? If so, then how does one explain the following decision?

Sayce v *Coupe*
[1953] 1 QB 1, Queen's Bench Division

Two informations were preferred by the appellant, George Sayce, an officer of the Customs and Excise, against the respondent, Wilson Coupe, the licensee of the Plough Inn, Manchester Street, Oldham, alleging (1) that on 4 December 1951, he knowingly kept uncustomed goods, namely, 3,580 American cigarettes, with intent to defraud His Majesty of the duty thereon contrary to s. 186 of the Customs Consolidation Act 1876, and (2) that on 24 November 1951, he did aid, abet, counsel and procure a person unknown to sell certain tobacco, to wit 5,600 cigarettes, otherwise than as a licensed manufacturer of or dealer in or retailer of tobacco selling tobacco in his entered premises or on premises wherein he carried on the business of a licensed dealer in or retailer of tobacco contrary to s. 13 of the Tobacco Act 1842, as amended by s. 8 of the Revenue Act 1867.

LORD GODDARD CJ: [In the first part of its opinion the court found that the respondent had committed the offence of keeping uncustomed goods with intent to defraud the Revenue of the duties thereon.]

The second summons charged the respondent with aiding and abetting Wood – it says a person unknown but it must have been Wood – to commit an offence under section 13 of the Tobacco Act, 1842, by buying the cigarettes from a person who to his knowledge was not a licensed dealer in tobacco, and it is quite clear that the offence charged in the second information was committed.

Mr Hinchliffe has argued that because the statute does not make it an offence to buy, but only makes it an offence to sell, we ought to hold that the offence of aiding and abetting the sale ought not to be preferred or could not be preferred. It is obvious that it can be preferred. The statute does not make it an offence to buy, but obviously, on ordinary general principles of criminal law, if in such a case a person knows the circumstances and knows, therefore, that an offence is being committed and takes part in, or facilitates the commission of the offence, he is guilty as a principal in the second degree, for it is impossible to say that a person who buys does not aid and abet a sale.

For these reasons the justices ought also to have convicted on the second information.

QUESTIONS

1. On what basis is *Sayce* v *Coupe* distinguishable from *Tyrrell*?

2. Is the decision in *Sayce* v *Coupe* consistent with Parliamentary intent? Presumably Parliament must have appreciated that in every sale there would be both a buyer and a seller, and, in making only the seller liable, made a conscious decision not to penalise the buyer.

3. A child is kidnapped. The parents, without informing the police, pay the ransom. Are they accessories to kidnapping?

(ii) *Withdrawal*

Is it the rule that once an accomplice, always an accomplice? A thief who steals another's property cannot escape liability if she has a subsequent change of heart and returns the stolen goods; the crime is already complete. Should the same be true in cases of an accessory?

R v *Becerra*
(1975) 62 Cr App R 212, Court of Appeal

> The appellant, B, broke into the house with two other men C and one G. Their intention was to steal from the householder. While in the house, the tenant of a flat on the first floor surprised them and B calling 'let's go' climbed out of a window followed by G and ran away. C, meanwhile, who had been handed a knife by B, stabbed and killed the tenant. B and C were charged, *inter alia*, with the tenant's murder, and at their trial the prosecution case was that B and C were acting in concert in pursuance of a common agreement to kill or inflict bodily harm should the need arise. B contended that he had withdrawn from the joint adventure before the attack on the tenant and, therefore, was not liable to be convicted of murder. The jury were directed that the words 'let's go' and the appellant B's departure through the window were insufficient to constitute a withdrawal. Both B and C were convicted of murder.

ROSKILL LJ: . . . The basic prosecution case against Becerra and Cooper was that they had entered into a common agreement to use such force as was necessary against anyone in the house to get the money or to avoid identification or arrest. It was urged that this common agreement included the use, if necessary, of the knife to inflict serious bodily injury, if not death, and it was alleged that Cooper, in furtherance of that common agreement, murdered Lewis with the knife in his left hand while he pinioned Lewis from behind with his right arm around Lewis's shoulder.

. . . It was argued . . . on behalf . . . of Becerra, that even if there were this common design, . . . whatever Cooper did immediately before and at the time of the killing of Lewis, Becerra had by then withdrawn from that common design and so should not be convicted of the murder of Lewis. . . .

It is necessary, before dealing with that argument in more detail, to say a word or two about the relevant law. It is a curious fact, considering the number of times in which this point arises where two or more people are charged with criminal offences, particularly murder or manslaughter, how relatively little authority there is in this country upon the point. But the principle is undoubtedly of long standing.

Perhaps it is best first stated in *R* v *Saunders and Archer* (1577) 2 Plowden 473 (in the eighteenth year of the first Queen Elizabeth) at p. 476, in a note by *Plowden*, thus:

> . . . for if I command one to kill J. S. and before the Fact done I go to him and tell him that I have repented, and expressly charge him not to kill J. S. and he afterwards kills him, there I shall not be Accessory to this Murder, because I have countermanded my first Command, which in all Reason shall discharge me, for the malicious Mind of the Accessory ought to continue to do ill until the Time of the Act done, or else he shall not be charged; but if he had killed J. S. before the Time of my Discharge or Countermand given, I should have been Accessory to the Death, notwithstanding my private Repentance.

The next case to which I may usefully refer is some 250 years later, but over 150 years ago: *R* v *Edmeads and Others* (1828) 3 C & P 390, where there is a ruling of Vaughan B at a trial at Berkshire Assizes, upon an indictment charging Edmeads and others with unlawfully shooting at game keepers. At the end of his ruling the learned Baron said on the question of common intent, at p. 392,

> that is rather a question for the jury; but still, on this evidence, it is quite clear what the common purpose was. They all draw up in lines, and point their guns at the game-keepers, and they are all giving their countenance and assistance to the one of them who actually fires the gun. If it could be shewn that either of them separated himself from the rest, and showed distinctly that he would have no hand in what they were doing, the objection would have much weight in it.

I can go forward over 100 years. Mr Owen (to whose juniors we are indebted for their research into the relevant Canadian and United States cases) referred us to several Canadian cases, to only one of which is it necessary to refer in detail, a decision of the Court of Appeal of British Columbia in *Whitehouse (alias Savage)* (1941) 1 WWR 112. I need not read the headnote. The Court of Appeal held that the trial judge concerned in that case, which was one of murder, had been guilty of misdirection in his direction to the jury on this question of 'withdrawal.' The matter is, if I may most respectfully say so, so well put in the leading judgment of Sloan J.A., that I read the whole of the passage at pp. 115 and 116:

> Can it be said on the facts of this case that a mere change of mental intention and a quitting of the scene of the crime just immediately prior to the striking of the fatal blow will absolve those who participate in the commission of the crime by overt acts up to that moment from all the consequences of its accomplishment by the one who strikes in ignorance of his companions' change of heart? I think not. After a crime has been committed and before a prior abandonment of the common enterprise may be found by a jury there must be, in my view, in the absence of exceptional circumstances, something more than a mere mental change of intention and physical change of place by those associates who wish to dissociate themselves from the consequences attendant upon their willing assistance up to the moment of the actual commission of that crime. I would not attempt to define too closely what must be done in criminal matters involving participation in a common unlawful purpose to break the chain of causation and responsibility. That must depend upon the circumstances of each case but it seems to me that one essential element ought to be established in a case of this kind: Where practicable and reasonable there must be timely communication of the intention to abandon the common purpose from those who wish to dissociate themselves from the contemplated crime to those who desire to continue in it. What is 'timely communication' must be determined by the facts of each case but where practicable and reasonable it ought to be such communication, verbal or otherwise, that will serve unequivocal notice upon the other party to the common unlawful cause that if he

proceeds upon it he does so without the further aid and assistance of those who withdraw. The unlawful purpose of him who continues alone is then his own and not one in common with those who are no longer parties to it nor liable to its full and final consequences.

The learned judge then went on to cite a passage from 1 Hale's *Pleas of the Crown* 618 and the passage from *Saunders and Archer* (*supra*) to which I have already referred.

In the view of each member of this Court, that passage, if we may respectfully say so, could not be improved upon and we venture to adopt it in its entirety as a correct statement of the law which is to be applied in this case.

. . .

We therefore turn back to consider the direction which the learned judge gave in the present case to the jury and what was the suggested evidence that Becerra had withdrawn from the common agreement. The suggested evidence is the use by Becerra of the words 'Come on let's go,' coupled, as I said a few moments ago, with his act in going out through the window. The evidence, as the judge pointed out, was that Cooper never heard that nor did the third man. But let it be supposed that that was said and the jury took the view that it was said.

On the facts of this case, in the circumstances then prevailing, the knife having already been used and being contemplated for further use when it was handed over by Becerra to Cooper for the purpose of avoiding (if necessary) by violent means the hazards of identification, if Becerra wanted to withdraw at that stage, he would have to 'countermand,' to use the word that is used in some of the cases or 'repent' to use another word so used, in some manner vastly different and vastly more effective than merely to say 'Come on, let's go' and go out through the window.

It is not necessary, on this application, to decide whether the point of time had arrived at which the only way in which he could effectively withdraw, so as to free himself from joint responsibility for any act Cooper thereafter did in furtherance of the common design, would be physically to intervene so as to stop Cooper attacking Lewis, as the judge suggested, by interposing his own body between them or somehow getting in between them or whether some other action might suffice. That does not arise for decision here. Nor is it necessary to decide whether or not the learned judge was right or wrong, on the facts of this case, in that passage which appears at the bottom of p. 206, which Mr Owen criticised: 'and at least take all reasonable steps to prevent the commission of the crime which he had agreed the others should commit.' It is enough for the purposes of deciding this application to say that under the law of this country as it stands, and on the facts (taking them at their highest in favour of Becerra), that which was urged as amounting to withdrawal from the common design was not capable of amounting to such withdrawal. Accordingly Becerra remains responsible, in the eyes of the law, for everything that Cooper did and continued to do after Becerra's disappearance through the window as much as if he had done them himself.

Cooper being unquestionably guilty of murder, Becerra is equally guilty of murder. Mr Owen's careful argument must therefore be rejected and the application by Becerra for leave to appeal against conviction fails.

NOTES AND QUESTIONS
1. As a matter of social policy, should the law allow a defence of withdrawal? What are the arguments for and against?
2. Should the reason for the withdrawal be relevant? Compare the case of the accessory who experiences a genuine change of heart because he appreciates the moral wrongfulness of his conduct with that of the accessory who experiences a change of mind because he encounters police at the scene of the crime.
3. What more would Beccara have had to have done for his defence to succeed? Does there come a point where it is too late to withdraw? Had Beccara reached that point? Consider the case where G provides information to burglars regarding the premises to be burgled, including the location of alarms and what must be done to neutralise them. Before the

burglary G has a change of heart, and announces that he no longer wishes to be involved. Is this sufficient to constitute a withdrawal? The rub is that by this point G is irrelevant as he has already provided all the help that the burglars need to succeed. See *Grundy* [1977] Crim LR 543.

4. If the law is to recognise a defence of withdrawal, what must an accessory do in order to be able to lay claim to it? Is it enough for the accessory to refrain from any further involvement in the criminal enterprise, or should he have to report the principal to the police or otherwise frustrate the accomplishment of the crime? The answer may depend on how far the criminal enterprise has progressed:

   (a) If all that the accessory has done is to encourage a crime, a verbal countermand of the former encouragement or instructions, or otherwise making clear that there has been a change of mind may be enough, but in *R v Rook* [1993] 1 WLR 1005 the Court of Appeal left this question open. Note, however, that the accessory may still be guilty of incitement.

   (b) If the crime is already well under way, then arguably the accessory should have to take steps, such as notifying the victim, or perhaps even the police, to prevent the crime's commission. However, in *R v Mitchell (Frank)* [1999] Crim LR 496 the Court of Appeal held that communication of withdrawal from a joint enterprise was necessary where the offence was one of premeditated violence but not where the violence was spontaneous. Is this ruling too favourable to the defendant?

5. Withdrawal, while it may affect one's liability as an accessory, will not affect one's liability for conspiracy or attempt (if the enterprise has gone beyond the stage of mere preparation). See Chapter 11.

(iii) *Entrapment*

What of the person who inveigles another into committing a crime for the purpose of seeing that other person arrested? A 'friend' tells you that there is a valuable painting inside a home and that the owners are away. The friend offers to stand guard while you enter the home and take the painting, if you will agree to split the proceeds of the sale with him. As soon as you are inside the home, however, the friend telephones the police, who arrive and arrest you. Under these circumstances, should you be entitled to a defence of entrapment?

R v Birtles
(1969) 53 Cr App R 469, Court of Appeal

The appellant pleaded guilty at West Riding Quarter Sessions in March 1969 to burglary and to carrying an imitation firearm with intent to commit burglary and was sentenced by the Chairman to consecutive terms of three years' and two years' imprisonment.

THE LORD CHIEF JUSTICE: . . . As I have said, no one will perhaps ever know the exact truth, but it certainly seems to this Court, doing the best that they can in the matter, that there is a real possibility here that the appellant was encouraged by the informer and indeed by the police officer concerned to carry out this raid on the post office. Whether or not he would have done it without that, again no one can say, but there is, as it seems to this Court, a real likelihood that he was encouraged to commit an offence which otherwise he would not have committed.

It is in those circumstances that this Court is asked to review this sentence. On that assumption, that he was so encouraged, the Court is quite satisfied that some reduction in sentence is required. Doing the best they can, bearing in mind not only this possible encouragement but at the same time the fact that the appellant had been minded to use a real firearm, this Court feels that the greatest reduction that they can make is to make these two sentences concurrent instead of consecutive, in other words, that the appellant in the circumstances shall serve three years' imprisonment.

Before leaving this case, the Court would like to say a word about the use which, as the cases coming before the Court reveal, is being made of informers. The Court of course recognises that, disagreeable as it may seem to some people, the police must be able in certain cases to make use of informers, and further – and this is really a corollary – that within certain limits such informers should be protected. At the same time, unless the use made of informers is kept within strict limits, grave injustice may result. In the first place, it is important that the Court of trial should not be misled. A good example of that occurred in the case of *R v Macro and Others*, again a raid on a sub-post office, which came before this Court on February 10 ([1969] Crim LR 205; *The Times*, February 11, 1969). There the charge was one of robbery with aggravation, with a man 'unknown.' In fact, the man 'unknown' was an informer who, together with the police, had warned the victim of what was going to take place, and had in fact gone through the pretence of tying up the victim while the police were concealed upon the premises. Now there the effect was that the appellant in that case pleaded Guilty to an offence which had never been committed. If the facts had been known, there could not have been a robbery at all, and accordingly it was for that reason that the Court substituted the only verdict apt on the facts which was open to it, namely, a verdict of larceny. There is, of course, no harm in not revealing the fact that there is an informer, but it is quite another thing to conceal facts which go to the quality of the offence.

Secondly, it is vitally important to ensure so far as possible that the informer does not create an offence, that is to say, incite others to commit an offence which those others would not otherwise have committed. It is one thing for the police to make use of information concerning an offence that is already laid on. In such a case the police are clearly entitled, indeed it is their duty, to mitigate the consequences of the proposed offence, for example, to protect the proposed victim, and to that end it may be perfectly proper for them to encourage the informer to take part in the offence or indeed for a police officer himself to do so. But it is quite another thing, and something of which this Court thoroughly disapproves, to use an informer to encourage another to commit an offence or indeed an offence of a more serious character, which he would not otherwise commit, still more so if the police themselves take part in carrying it out.

In the result, this appeal is allowed and the sentence reduced to one of three years.

Sentence reduced.

NOTES AND QUESTIONS
1. Should it matter whether the entrapper is a 'friend' or a police officer? Why? From the entrapped individual's perspective, is it not a matter of fortuity? See *R v Hardwicke* [2001] Crim LR 220 (entrapment by journalists).
2. The right to a fair trial under Article 6 of the European Convention on Human Rights may be implicated by the use of evidence obtained as a result of police entrapment. In *Teixeira de Castro v Portugal* (1999) 28 EHRR 101, the defendant had been induced by two undercover police officers to purchase illegal drugs on their behalf. The European Court of Human Rights found a violation of Article 6. The Court distinguished its prior decision in *Ludi v Switzerland* (1993) 15 EHRR 173, also involving a police officer posing as a purchaser of drugs, because the drugs deal was already under way.
3. Should it matter whether the entrapper plants the idea for the crime in the principal's head, or whether the principal conceives of the plan on his own, with the entrapper simply encouraging the principal to carry through with it? Where the police create, rather than simply encourage, the commission of the offence, is there a stronger case for allowing a defence? Why? What purpose is served by freeing a defendant who has demonstrated

a disposition to break the law when given the opportunity? Allen, *Textbook on Criminal Law*, 4th ed. (1997), pp. 206–7, suggests a distinction between:

(a) those who merely observe the crime but play no part in the instigation of the offence;
(b) those decoys who accede to the accused's suggestions and thereby help provide the opportunity for the commission of the offence;
(c) those decoys who expose the accused to temptation and thereby facilitate the commission of the offence; and
(d) those decoys who actively entice, encourage or persuade the accused to commit an offence which he would not otherwise commit.

Should the law attempt to discriminate between these categories? How so?

What of the entrapper? Is he guilty as an accessory?

R v Clarke
(1984) 80 Cr App R 344, Court of Appeal

MACPHERSON J: . . . On November 22, 1983, before Judge Gerber, Dennis Geoffrey Clarke was convicted by a jury of an offence of aiding and abetting burglary. He was absolutely discharged. He appeals against conviction by certificate of the trial judge who certified the case as fit for appeal on the ground that: 'I directed the jury with regard to count 2 as follows. The prosecution have to prove that: (a) Clarke knew the burglary was to be committed. (b) With that knowledge he volunteered and deliberately assisted Larch and Emery to carry it out. I further directed the jury that the fact that Clarke had prior to the date of the burglary given full information about it to a police officer was no defence to the charge set out in count 2.'

As we can see from the judgment upon counsels' submissions and the summing-up, the learned judge did in fact direct the jury to convict upon count 2 should they acquit (as they did) on count 1 of the indictment which the appellant faced . . .

Before the trial began it was known to all, because of what the appellant had said to the policeman who arrested him on June 3, 1984, that he, Clarke, would accept that he did indeed participate in the burglary. But he asserted that he took part solely in order to give information to a police sergeant named Eastwood with whom he had made contact, and with whom he had been involved since 1982 both as an accused man in another matter and as an informer. The appellant said that he had told Sergeant Eastwood about the proposed Muswell Hill burglary two or three weeks before it took place, and he said that not only had he kept Eastwood informed but that Eastwood knew that the appellant was going to take part in the burglary, and told the appellant to try to find out the full identity of Ross, the inside man. The appellant said that he had arranged a place for the storage of the stolen goods, but that this also was done so that he could tell Sergeant Eastwood where the goods were so that they would be recovered almost at once. The appellant was saying that he did not act 'in a criminal sense' (as the judge put it in his summing-up) but was involved solely to assist the police and to give Eastwood information. And he was saying that his intention was that the others should not get away with their crime, and that the stolen goods would be recovered so that their owner would not be deprived permanently of them.

. . . [T]he judge directed the jury to convict on count 2 even if they accepted the appellant's evidence that he was acting honestly and solely in order to betray his associates and ensure the recovery of the goods.

In the result the jury acquitted the appellant on count 1 [burglary] and convicted on count 2. The basis upon which the jury acquitted him on count 1 must have been that they were not sure that the appellant was acting dishonestly (because he intended to bring his confederates to justice), and/or that they were not sure that he intended permanently to deprive the owner of his goods.

Counsel for the Crown accepted in argument in this Court that it is a necessary consequence of his submissions that any person acting as the appellant did, whether he was a police officer or someone acting as an informer or on his behalf, is necessarily and in all circumstances guilty of aiding and abetting provided only that (a) the offence is complete (as of course the burglary was upon the instant facts) before steps are taken to bring those involved to justice, and (b) the accused aider and abettor in some way positively assisted in the carrying out of the offence, knowing all the circumstances . . ..

When a man says (as did the appellant) that he joined the team solely to betray the others involved and to defeat the long term retention by the team of the owner's goods, the question whether he did so and joined thus honestly into a 'laid on' offence or crime ought in our judgment to be at least a matter for the jury's decision in a case where it is appropriate for an aiding and abetting allegation or count to be considered at all.

Normally in an entrapment case the encouraging or entrapping policeman or informer will not have a defence, since they counsel or procure the commission of the offence by their encouragement. 'The fact that the counsellor and procurer is a policeman or police informer, although it may be of relevance in mitigation of penalty for the offence, cannot affect the guilt of the principal offender; both the physical element (*actus reus*) and the mental element (*mens rea*) of the offence with which he is charged are present in his case' (*R v Sang* (1979) 69 Cr App R 282, 286). Such cases, it should be noted, are properly cases of incitement or procurement to offend, and would properly be charged as such or as cases of counselling or procuring rather than aiding and abetting in any event.

The present case falls in our judgment within the compass of the *dicta* of Lord Parker CJ in the case of *R v Birtles* (1969) 53 Cr App R 469, 472–473. . . .

In using the expression 'it may be perfectly proper' the Lord Chief Justice was, in our judgment, contemplating that in such exceptional cases where an informer (and/or a policeman) took part in a 'laid on' case there should be no finding that it was unlawful so to do. It would indeed be a rare case in which the facts would allow such a defence and in which a jury would say that a man might have been thus acting lawfully. But that there are such cases and that the jury should decide whether or not a case is within that exceptional and rare category is in our judgment both right and just. The learned judge should (if this had been a case in which the count of aiding and abetting remained alive at all) at least have left the matter to the jury. . . .

Further, however, we are convinced that this was a case in which the alternative count should not have been added or finally pursued. As a matter of exact analysis the appellant could of course have been said to have aided and abetted the others involved, but in reality he was either a burglar and guilty as such as a primary offender or, in our judgment, he was to be acquitted. Doubtless the appellant Clarke was exceedingly fortunate to be acquitted on count 1 upon the evidence. . . . But the jury did acquit him, and it must have been upon the basis that his evidence may have been true. It would in our judgment be illogical that the appellant should be not guilty of count 1 (in which he accepted that he was fully involved but said that he acted honestly and lawfully within the confines of the Lord Chief Justice's statement in *Birtles'* case), but guilty upon count 2 of aiding and abetting. In our judgment he should be guilty or not guilty of count 1, the full offence, and should not have been made guilty by the artificial addition of count 2.

NOTES AND QUESTIONS

1. Does the entrapper have the *mens rea* of an accessory? On the one hand, the entrapper's objective is not to see a crime successfully committed but precisely the opposite. But in *Yip Chiu-Cheung* v *R* [1994] 3 WLR 514 (for facts and holding, see p. 547) the Privy Council held that the motive of a defendant who intended to traffick in heroin was irrelevant even where that motive was the detection of crime. On the other hand, the entrapper has encouraged or counselled, and in some cases aided, the commission of a crime that might not otherwise have taken place. Has the entrapper performed a public service, or is he a public nuisance?

2. Is the court in *Clarke* correct that it is illogical to acquit an entrapper of the substantive offence while convicting him of aiding and abetting? Do not the crimes require proof of different *mens rea*?

3. Should motive be relevant? What if the entrapper's motive is not to expose a would-be criminal but to gain private revenge? See *Wilson v People*, 103 Colo 441, 87 P 2d 5 (1939).

4. The Draft Criminal Code Bill 1989 would allow a defence for *agents provocateurs* who actually prevent the commission of a crime.

INDEX